Pugh's Dictionary of Acronyms and Abbreviations

Pugh's Dictionary of Acronyms and Abbreviations

Abbreviations in management, technology and information science

5th edition

Compiled by ERIC PUGH

LA

THE LIBRARY ASSOCIATION
LONDON

ALA

AMERICAN LIBRARY ASSOCIATION
CHICAGO

A Dictionary of Acronyms was first published in 1968 by
Clive Bingley Ltd, and then in a second, expanded edition in 1970.
Second Dictionary of Acronyms and Abbreviations was published in 1974.
Third Dictionary of Acronyms and Abbreviations was published in 1976.
A cumulation of the three dictionaries, with additional entries, was
published by Clive Bingley Ltd as Pugh's Dictionary of Acronyms
and Abbreviations in 1981.
This fifth edition (the second full edition) published in the United
Kingdom in 1987, by Library Association Publishing Ltd, 7 Ridgmount Street,
London WC1E 7AE, and in the United States by The American Library
Association, 50 East Huron Street, Chicago, Illinois 60611.
Typeset by SB Datagraphics Ltd, Colchester, Essex.
Printed and bound in the UK by Redwood Burn Ltd,
Trowbridge, Wiltshire.

British Library Cataloguing in Publication Data
Pugh, Eric
Pugh's dictionary of acronyms and
abbreviations: abbreviations in management,
technology and information science. ——5th ed.
1. Technology——Abbreviations
I. Title
601'.48 T8

ISBN (LA) 0-85365-537-5

Library of Congress Cataloging-in-Publication Data
Pugh, Eric.
Pugh's Dictionary of acronyms and abbreviations.

1. Technology——Acronyms. 2. Management——Acronyms.
3. Information science——Acronyms. I. Title.
T8.P79 1986 601.48 86-17352
ISBN (ALA) 0-8389-2044-6

Introduction

I began this work in 1965, but over the years my wife Joan has played an increasing part. In the process of integrating the earlier volumes, the checking for duplicates, the up-dating of entries plus the addition of over 3,000 new entries in this edition, she has played the major role.

We are pleased to acknowledge the support inherent in the interest shown by A J Walford, J C Andrews, the late S G Berriman, and the late D W King in the continuation of this work.

The following should be noted:

(a) The word 'program'—accepted as relative to computer software has not been used in that sense in this work. 'Programme' has been used to cover data processing and 'program' reserved to cover proceedings or projects undertaken by institutions etc, in the USA.

(b) Memberships of institutions such as 'A—Associate', 'AM—Associated member', 'F—Fellow' are not prefixed to any entry.

(c) It must be stressed that some of the acronyms and abbreviations listed are registered trade names and care should be taken in their use.

This volume is dedicated to all those whose task is to supply information to others and especially those colleagues, 'professional' and 'non-professional', with whom I have worked in public and special libraries over many years.

ERIC PUGH

Teddington, Middlesex
June 1986

A

A
Adrenalin
prefix to numbered:dated series of Aircraft Bolts Standards issued by BSI (letter is sometimes preceded by a number)

A&AEE
Aeroplane and Armament Experimental Establishment (MINTECH) (now MOD)

A-SCOOR
Air-Scooping Orbital Rocket

A/CASP
Air Conditioning Analytical Simulation Package

A/D
Altitude/Depth
Analogue/Digital

A/S
Aksjeselskap (share company)
Aktieselskap (share company)

AA
Acetic Anhydride
Acrylamide
Acupuncture Anaesthesia
Aerolineas Argentinas (Argentina)
Air-to-Air
Airborne Alert
Aluminum Association (USA)
Amino Acid
Anti-Aircraft
Antiproton Accumulator
Arachidonic Acid
Architectural Association
Ascorbic Acid
Atomic Absorption
Attack Assessment
Australian Academy of Science (Australia)
Automobile Association

AAA
American Academy of Allergy (USA)
American Academy of Pediatrics (USA) Anti-Actin Antibody
American Airship Association (USA)
American Anthropological Association (USA)
American Arbitration Association(USA)
American Automobile Association (USA)
Anti-Aircraft Artillery
Army Audit Agency (US Army)

AAAA
Army Aviation Association of America (USA)

AAAB
American Association of Architectural Bibliographers (USA)

AAAF
Association Aeronautique et Astronautique de France (France) (Aeronautic and Astronautic Association of France)

AAAI
American Association for Artificial Intelligence (USA)
Association of Australian Aerospace Industries (Australia)

AAAIA
All-India Automobile and Ancillary Industries Association (India)

AAAIP
Advanced Army Aircraft Instrumentation Program (US Army)

AAAM
American Association for Automotive Medicine (USA)

AAAS
American Association for the Advancement of Science (USA)

AAAS-HAC
American Association for the Advancement of Science, Herbicide Assessment Commission (USA)

AAASA
Association for the Advancement of Agricultural Sciences in Africa (Ethiopia)

AAAT
Anti-Aircraft Armoured Truck

AAB
American Association of Bioanalysts (USA)

AABB
American Association of Blood Banks (USA)

AABDFC
Association des Archivistes Bibliothecaires Documentalistes Francophones de la Caraibe (Haiti) (Association of French-speaking Archivists, Librarians and Documentalists in the Caribbean)

AABFS
Amphibious Assault Bulk Fuel System

AABG
American Association of Botanic Gardens (USA)

AABM
Association of American Battery Manufacturers (USA)

AABNCP
Advanced Airborne National Command Post (USAF)

AABP
Australian Association of Business Publications (A ustralia)

AABSHIL
Aircraft Anti-collision Beacon System High Intensity Light

AABW
Antarctic Bottom Water

AAC
Alaskan Air Command (USAF)
Arabian Automotive Company (Saudi Arabia)
Association of American Colleges (USA)
Average Annual Cost

AACA
Asian and Australasian Congress of Anaesthesiology

AACB
Aeronautics and Astronautics Coordinating Board (of DOD and NASA)

AACC
Airport Associations Co-ordinating Committee
Airport Associations Co-ordinating Council
American Association for Contamination Control (USA)
American Association of Clinical Chemists (USA)
American Associations of Cereal Chemists (USA)
American Automatic Control Council (USA)
Area Approach Control Centre

AACCH
American Association for Child Care in Hospital (USA)

AACE
American Association of Cost Engineers (USA)

AACG
American Association for Crystal Growth (USA)

AACIA
American Association for Clinical Immunology and Allergy (USA)

AACO
Advanced and Applied Concepts Office (US Army)
Arab Air Carriers Organization

AACOBS
Australian Advisory Council on Bibliographical Services (Australia)

AACOMS
Army Area Communications System (US Army) (now ATACS)

AACP
Advanced Airborne Command Post (USAF)
American Academy for Cerebral Palsy (USA)
American Academy of Child Psychiatry (USA)
American Association of Colleges of Pharmacy (USA)

AACR
American Association for Cancer Research (USA)
Anglo-American Cataloguing Rules

AACS
Advanced Automatic Compilation System
Airborne Astrographic Camera System

AACT
American Academy of Clinical Toxicology (USA)

AACU
American Association of Clinical Urologists (USA)

AACV
Assault Air Cushion Vehicle

AACVB
Asian Association of Convention and Visitor Bureaus

AAD
Administrative Applications Division (of ASQC (USA))
Army Automation Directorate (US Army)

AADB
Army Air Defense Board (US Army)

AADC
Advanced Avionic Digital Computer
All-Application Digital Computer

AADFI
Association of African Development Finance Institutions

AADM
Airport and Airspace Delay Model

AADP
American Association of Dental Publishers (USA)

AADS
Airspeed And Direction Sensor
American Association of Dental Schools (USA)

AAE
American Association of Engineers (USA)
prefix to dated-numbered series of reports issued by Department of Aeronautical and Astronautical Engineering, Illinois University (USA)

AAEA American Agricultural Economic Association (USA)
AAEC Australian Atomic Energy Commission (Australia)
AAEDC American Agricultural Economics Documentation Center (USA)
AAEE Aeroplane and Armament Experimental Establishment (MINTECH) (now MOD)
American Academy of Environmental Engineers (USA)
American Association of Electromyography and Electrodiagnosis (USA)
AAEER Aerophysics and Aerospace Engineering Research Report
AAEL American Association of Equipment Lessors (USA)
AAELSS Active Arm External Load Stabilization System
AAES Advanced Aircraft Electrical System
Association of American Engineering Societies (USA)
AAFCE Allied Air Forces Central Europe (of NATO)
AAFE Advanced Applications Flight Experiments (of NASA)
AAFE RADSCAT Advanced Applications Flight Experiment Radiometer-Scatterometer sensor
AAFFSS Advanced Aerial Fire Support System
AAFIF Automated Air Facility Information File (of DMAAC (USDOD))
AAFP American Academy of Family Physicians (USA)
AAFRA Association of African Airlines
AAFS American Academy of Forensic Sciences (USA)
AAFSS Advanced Aerial Fire Support System
AAG Association of American Geographers (USA)
AAGS American Association for Geodetic Surveying (USA)
AAH Advanced Armed OR Attack Helicopter
Advanced Attack Helicopter
Anti-Armour Helicopter
AAHPER American Association for Health, Physical Education and Recreation (USA)
AAHS American Aviation Historical Society (USA)
AAI Airlines Avionics Institute (USA)
American Association of Immunologists (USA)
AAII Association for the Advancement of Invention and Innovation (USA)
AAIMS An Analytical Information Management System
AAIN American Association of Industrial Nurses (USA)
AAL Absolute Assembly Language
Arctic Aeromedical Laboratory (USAF)
Association of Assistant Librarians
AALA American Automotive Leasing Association (USA)
AALAS American Association for Laboratory Animal Science (USA)
AALC Amphibious Assault Landing Craft
AALL American Association of Law Libraries (USA)
AALS Acoustic Artillery Location System
Association of American Library Schools (USA)
AAM Air-to-Air Missile
Arma Aerea de la Marina (Spain) (Naval Air Force)
AAMA American Apparel Manufacturers Association (USA)
Architectural Aluminum Manufacturers Association (USA)
Automotive Accessories Manufacturers of America (USA)
AAMC Association of American Medical Colleges (USA)
AAMCA Army Advanced Materiel concepts Agency (US Army)
AAMD American Association on Mental Deficiency (USA)
AAMESBICS American Association of MESBICS (USA)
AAMF Association Aeromedicale de France (France) (Aeromedical Association of France)
AAMI Association for the Advancement of Medical Instrumentation (USA)
AAMRDL Army Air Mobility Research and Development Laboratory (US Army)
AAMSI American Association for Medical Systems and Informatics (USA)
AAMVA American Association of Motor Vehicle Administrators (USA)
AAMW American Association of Medical Writers (USA)
AAN American Academy of Neurology (USA)
American Association of Neuropathologists (USA)
Aminoacetonitrile
AANCP Advanced Airborne National Command Post (USAF)
AANI Arkticheskii i Antarkticheskii Nauchno Issledovatel'skiy Institut (USSR) (Arctic and Antarctic Scientific Research Institute)
AAO Abastumanskaya Astrofizicheskaya Observatoriya (USSR) (Abastumani Astrophysical Observatory)
American Academy of Optometry (USA)
Authorized Acquisition Objective
AAOHN American Association of Occupational Health Nurses (USA)
AAOM American Academy of Occupational Medicine (USA)
AAOO American Academy of Opthalmology and Otolaryngology (USA)
AAOS American Academy of Orthopaedic Surgeons (USA)
AAP Ambient Absolute Pressure
American Academy of Pediatrics (USA)
American Academy of Psychoanalysis (USA)
American Association of Physicians (USA)
Analyst Assistance Programme
APOLLO Applications Programme
Association for the Advancement of Psychology
Association of American Publishers (USA)
Average Annual Precipitation
AAPA Advertising Agency Production Association
American Association of Port Authorities (USA)
Australian Asphalt Pavement Association (Australia)
AAPC Afro-American Purchasing Center (USA)
AAPG American Association of Petroleum Geologists (USA)
AAPM American Association of Physicists in Medicine (USA)
AAPMA Association of Australian Port and Marine Authorities (Australia)
AAPMR American Academy of Physical Medicine and Rehabilitation (USA)
AAPS Alternative Automotive Power Systems (a program of EPA (USA))
American Association of Plastic Surgeons (USA)
Automated Astronomic Positioning System
AAPSC American Association of Psychiatric Services for Children (USA)
AAPSD Alternative Automotive Power System Division (of EPA (USA))
AAPSP Advanced Automotive Power Systems Program (of NAPCA (USA))
AAPSS American Academy of Political and Social Science (USA)
AAPT American Association of Physics Teachers (USA)
Association of Asphalt Paving Technologists (USA)
AAPTS&R Australian Association for Predetermined Time Standards and Research (Australia)

AAR Air-to-Air Refuelling
Association of American Railroads (USA)
Average Annual Rainfall
prefix to numbered series of Aircraft Accident Reports issued by NTSB (USA)

AARB Advanced Aerial Refuelling Boom

AARF Australian Accounting Research Foundation (Australia)

AARL Aeronautical and Astronautical Laboratory (of Ohio State University (USA))

AARLS Arkansas Association of Registered Land Surveyors (USA)

AARRO Afro-Asian Rural Reconstruction Organization (India)

AARS Aerospace Rescue and Recovery Service (of Military Airlift Comman (USAF))

AART American Association for Respiratory Therapy (USA)

AARV Aerial Armoured Reconnaissance Vehicle

AAS Advanced Administrative System
Advanced Antenna System
American Antiquarian Society (USA)
American Astronautical Society (USA)
American Astronomical Society (USA)
Association for Academic Surgery (USA)
Atlantoaxial Subluxation
Atomic Absorption Spectrophotometry
Atomic Absorption Spectroscopy
Automatic Addressing System

AASA American Association of School Administrators (USA)
Architectural Association School of Architecture

AASC Aerospace Applications Studies Committee (of AGARD (NATO))
Australian Accounting Standards Committee (Australia) (of Institute of Chartered Accountants in Australia AND Australian Society of Accountants)

AASE Department of Aerophysics and Aerospace Engineering, Mississippi University (USA)

AASHO American Association of State Highway Officials (USA)

AASHTO American Association of State Highway and Transportation Officials (USA)

AASIR Advanced Atmospheric Sounder and Imaging Radiometer

AASL American Association of School Librarians (USA)

AASLH American Association for State and Local History (USA)

AASMA Advanced Avionic Systems for Multi-mission Application

AASMM Associated African States, Madagascar and Mauritius (now absorbed into Association of African, Caribbean and Pacific States)

AASRC American Association of Small Research Companies (USA)

AASS Advanced Airborne Surveillance Sensor

AAST American Association for the Surgery of Trauma (USA)

AASU Department of Aeronautics and Astronautics, University of Southampton

AAT Air Abrasive Trimming
Alanine Amino-transferase NTSB (USA)
Anglo-Australian Telescope (in New South Wales, Australia)
Association of Accounting Technicians
Average Annual Temperature

AATB Army Aviation Test Board (US Army)

AATCC American Association of Textile Chemists and Colorists (USA)

AATMS Advanced Air Traffic Management Systems

AATRAA Association Argentina de Tecnicos de Refrigeracion y Acondicionamiento de Aire (Argentina) (Refrigeration and Air-conditioning Technical Association)

AATRI Army Air Traffic Regulations and Identifications System (US Army)

AATS Committee on the Application of Aerospace Technology to Society (of AIAA (USA))

AATT American Association for Textile Technology (USA)

AAU American Association of Universities (USA)

AAUP American Association of University Professors (USA)
Association of American University Presses (USA)

AAUTA Australian Association of University Teachers of Accountancy (Australia)

AAV Adeno Associated Virus
Advanced Aerospace Vehicle (a program of USAF)
Airborne Assault Vehicle

AAVA Army Audio-Visual Agency (US Army)

AAVCS Anti-aircraft Artillery Visual Cueing Sensor

AAVS Aerospace Audio-Visual Service (USAF)

AAVSO American Association of Variable Star Observers (USA)

AAW Air-to-Air Warfare
Anti-Air Warfare
Anti-submarine Warfare and Anti-aircraft Warfare

AAWS Automatic Attack Warning System

AAWSA Addis Ababa Water and Sewerage Authority (Ethiopia)

AAZPA American Association of Zoological Parks and Aquariums (USA)

AB Aktiebolaget (Limited Company)
Automated Bibliography

ABA Abscisic Acid
American Bankers Association (USA)
American Blasting Association (USA)
American Booksellers Association (USA)
Arbejderbevaegelsens Bibliotek og Arkiv (Denmark) (Library and Archives of the Labour Movement)
Australian Booksellers Association (Australia)
Azobenzenearsonate

ABAA Antiquarian Booksellers Association of America (USA)

ABAC A Basic Coursewriter
Air Battle Analysis Center (USAF) (disbanded 1965)
Association of British Aviation Consultants
Association of Business and Administrative Computing

ABACR Acrylonitrile Butadiene Alternating Copolymer Rubber

ABACUS Air Battle Analysis Center Utility System
Architecture and Building Aids Computer Unit, Strathclyde (Strathclyde University)
Automatic, Block-schematic Advanced Control User-oriented System

ABAE Advisory Board of Accountancy Education

ABAG Association of Bay Area Governments (USA)

ABAR Advanced Battery Acquisition Radar
Alternate Battery Acquisition Radar

ABASS Assembly for Behavioral and Social Sciences (of National Research Council (USA))

ABBA American Brahman Breeders Association (USA)

ABBF Association of Bronze and Brass Founders

ABBM Automatic Baseband Monitor

ABBMM Association of British Brush Machinery Manufacturers

ABC Abridged Building Classification for Architects, Builders and Civil Engineers
Advanced BONUS Core
Advanced-Booking Charter
Advancing-Blade Concept
Africa Bibliographic Centre (Tanzania)
Airborne Control
Alarms By Carrier
Already Been Converted
America, Britain, Canada
Analysis Bar Charting
Anchored By Cassini
Antigen-Binding Capacity
Approach by Concept
Associated Builders and Contractors (USA)
Australian Broadcasting Commission (Australia)
Automatic Bar and Chucking
Automatic Bias Control
Automatic Brake Control
Automatic Brightness Control
Automation of Bibliography through Computerization

ABCA American Business Communication Association (USA)
American, British, Canadian, Australian
United States-United Kingdom-Canada-Australia

ABCA/UES ABCA – Unification of Engineering Standards

ABCC Association of British Chambers of Commerce
Atomic Bomb Casualty Commission (Japan) (reorganised in 1975 and became RERF)

ABCCC Airborne Battlefield Command and Control Centre
Airborne Command, Control and Communications

ABCFRC Auke Bay Coastal Fisheries Research Center (of NMFS (USA))

ABCIL Antibody Mediated Cell Dependent Immune Lympholysis

ABCM Association of British Chemical Manufacturers (now Chemical Industries Association)
Association of Building Component Manufacturers

ABCP Associacao Technica Brasileira de Celulose e Papel (Brazil) (Brazilian Technical Association for Pulp and Paper)

ABCS Automatic Base Communication Systems
Automatic Broadcast Control System

ABCU Association of BURROUGHS Computer Users

ABD Applied Ballistics Department (of Ordnance Board (MOD))
Association Belge de Documentation (Belgium) (Belgian Documentation Association)

ABDOSD Arbeitsgemeinschaft der Bibliotheken und Dokumentationsstellen der Osteuropa-, Sudosteuropa- und DDR-Forschung (Association of Libraries and Documentation Centres for the Study of Eastern Europe, South-eastern Europe and the German Democratic Republic)

ABDP Association of British Directory Publishers

ABDR Aircraft Battle Design Repair

ABE Arithmetic Building Element
Association of Business Executives

ABEM Association Belge pour l'Etude, l'Essais et l'Emploi des Materiaux (Belgium) (Belgian Association for the Study, Testing and Use of Materials)

ABES Air Breathing Engine System
Association for Broadcast Engineering Standards (USA)

ABET Accreditation Board for Engineering and Technology (USA)
Accreditation Board for Engineering and Technology (USA)

ABF Association des Bibliothecaires Francaise (France) (Association of French Librarians)

ABFL Auke Bay Fisheries Laboratory (of NMFS (NOAA) (USA))

ABFM Association of Business Forms Manufacturers (USA)

ABGSM Association of British Generating Set Manufacturers

ABHM Association of British Hardware Manufacturers

ABHP American Board of Health Physics (USA)

ABIFARMA Associacao Brasileira de Industria Farmaceutica (Brazilian Association of the Pharmaceutical Industry)

ABIH American Board of Industrial Hygiene (USA)

ABIIS Automated Blood Inventory Information System

ABIISE Agrupación de Bibliotecas para la Integración de la Información Socio-Económica (Perú) (Association of Libraries to Pool Social and Economic Information)

ABIR All-Band Intercept Receiver

ABIRD Aircraft Based Infra-Red Detector

ABIS APOLLO Bioenvironmental Information System

ABITA Association Belge des Ingenieurs et Techniciens de l'Aeronautique et de l'Astronautique (Belgium) (Belgian Association of Aeronautical and Astronautical Engineers and Technicians)

ABL Automated Biological Laboratory

ABLC Association of British Launderers and Cleaners

ABLE A Better Language Experiment
Acquisition Based on Consideration of Logistic Effects (a project of USAF)
Activity Balance Line Evaluation
Agricultural-Biological Literature Evaluation
Asymptotically Best Linear Estimate

ABLES Airborne Battlefield Light Equipment System

ABLISS Association of British Library and Information Science Schools

ABLP Air Bearing Lift Pad

ABLR American Burkitt Lymphoma Registry

ABLS Association of British Library Schools
ATLAS (CHEMICAL INDUSTRIES) Biomedical Literary System

ABLV Air-Breathing Launch Vehicle

ABM Air Battle Model
Anti-Ballistic Missle
Apogee Boost Motor
Associacao Brasileira de Metais (Brazil) (Brazilian Association for Metals)

ABMA American Boiler Manufacturers Association (USA)
American Brush Manufacturers Association (USA)
Army Ballistic Missile Agency (US Army)

ABMAC Association of British Manufacturers of Agricultural Chemicals (now British Agrochemicals Association)

ABMDA Advanced Ballistic Missile Defense Agency (US Army)
Army Ballistic Missile Defense Agency (US Army)

ABMEWS Anti-Ballistic Missile Early Warning System

ABMEX Association of British Mining Equipment Exporters

ABMIS Airborne Ballistic Missile System

ABMM Anti-Ballistic Missile Missile

ABMS American Board of Medical Specialities (USA)
Automated Breathing Metabolic Simulator

ABMT Autologous Bone-Marrow Transplantation

ABMTX Autologous Bone-Marrow Transplantation

ABN Amber Boron Nitride
Aseptic Bone Necrosis
Australian Bibliographic Network (Australia)

ABNT Associaco Brasiliera de Normas Tecnicas (Brazil) (Brazilian Technical Standards Association)

ABO Apparent Body Orientation
Aviator's Breathing Oxygen

ABOI Association of British Oceanological Industries (now Association of British Offshore Industries (of BMEC))

ABP Accounting Principles Board (of AICPA (USA))
American Business Press (USA) (association of specialized business publications publishers)
Androgen Binding Protein

ABPA Australian Book Publishers Association (Australia)

ABPC American Book Publishers Council (USA)
Association of British Pewter Craftsmen

ABPI Association of the British Pharmaceutical Industry

ABPIF British Printing Industries Federation

ABPM American Board of Preventive Medicine (USA)

ABR prefix to numbered series of Australian Navy Books of Reference

ABRACE Associacao Brasileira de Computadores Electronicos (Brazil) (Brazilian Association for the Use of Electronic Computers)

ABRACO Associacao Brasileira de Corrosao (Brazil) (Brazilian Corrosion Association)

ABRALOC Acoustic Beacon Ranging and Location

ABRAM Associacao Brasileira de Emprezas de Apoio Maritimo (Brazil) (Brazilian Association of Marine Components Manufacturers)

ABRC Advisory Board of the Research Councils

ABRES Advanced Ballistic Re-Entry System

ABRO Animal Breeding Research Organisation (of Agricultural Research Council)

ABRV Advanced Ballistic Re-entry Vehicle

AbS Analysis by Synthesis

ABS Acrylonitrile Butadiene Styrene
Adaptive Braking System
Alkyl Benzene Sulphonates
American Bureau of Shipping (USA)
Australian Bureau of Statistics (Australia)

ABSTECH American Bureau of Shipping Worldwide Technical Services (USA)

ABSTI Advisory Board on Scientific and Technical Information (Canada)

ABSW Association of British Science Writers

ABT Arbeitsstelle fur Bibliothekstechnik (Germany) (Study Centre for Library Technology)

ABTA Association of British Travel Agents

ABTAPL Association of British Theological and Philosophical Libraries

ABTICS Abstract and Book Title Index Card Service (now of the Metals Society)

ABTM Association of British Transport Museums

ABTOAD Air Blast Time-of-Arrival Detector

ABU Ahmadu Bello University (Nigeria)
Asia-Pacific Broadcasting Union (Headquarters in Japan)

ABW Air Base Wing (USAF)

ABWA American Business Women's Association (USA)

AC Acrylonitrile
Activated Charcoal
Adaptive Control
Amygdaloid Complex
Asphaltic Concrete
Automatic Control

ACA Acetylacetone
Advanced Combat Aircraft
Advisory Committee on Asbestos (of HSE)
Agile Combat Aircraft
Air Cushion Aircraft
American Cartographic Association (USA)
American Chain Association (USA)
American Chiropractors Association (USA)
American College of Apothecaries (USA)
American Cryptogram Association (USA)
American Crystallographic Association (USA)
Arms Control Association (USA)
Association of Canadian Archivists (Canada)
Association of Chartered Accountants
Association of Commuter Airlines (USA) (now part of National Air Transportation Conferences)
Association of Consulting Architects
Australasian Corrosion Association (Australia)
Australian Consumer Association (Australia)

ACAA Army Concepts Analysis Agency (US Army)

ACAAI Air Cargo Agents Association of India (India)

ACAAPS Advisory Committee on Advanced Automotive Power Systems (USA)

ACAB Air Conditioning Advisory Bureau (of the Electricity Council)

ACACE Advisory Council for Adult and Continuing Education

ACACT Associate Committee on Air-Cushion Technology (of NRC(Canada))

ACAD Atmospheric Containment Atmosphere Dilution

ACADI Association des Cadres Dirigeants de l'Industrie (France) (Association of Industrial Executives)

ACAE Australian Commission on Advanced Education (Australia)

ACAF Aero-Club Air France (France)

ACAM Augmented Content-Addressed Memory

ACAMPS Automated Communications And Message Processing System

Acap Advanced Composite Airframe Program (of US Army)

ACAP Aviation Consumer Action Project (USA)

ACARD Advisory Committee on Advanced Research and Development

ACARS ARINC (CORPORATION (USA)) Communications Addressing and Reporting System

ACAS Advisory, Conciliation and Arbitration Service
Agricultural Chemicals Approval Scheme (of MAFF)
Aircraft Collision Avoidance System

ACASS Association of Chartered Accountants Students Societies

ACASSI Association of Chartered Accountants Students Societies in Ireland

ACAST Advisory Committee on the Applications of Science and Technology (of UN)

ACB Antibody-Coated Bacteria
Assam Carbon Black
Association Canadienne des Bibliotheques (Canada) (Canadian Library Association)
Association of Clinical Biochemists
Societe des Ateliers et Chantiers de Bretagne (France)

ACBLF Association Canadienne de Bibliothecaires de Langue Francaise (Canada)

ACBS Accrediting Commission for Business Schools (USA)

ACC Active Clearance Control
Adaptive Control Constraint
Adjustable Chain Clutch
Administrative Committee on Co-ordination (of UN)
Amateur Computer Club
American College of Cardiology (USA)
Annual Capital Charge
Antarctic Circumpolar Current
Armament Control Computer
Army Communications Command (US Army)
Asian Coconut Community
Associated Cement Companies (India)
Association of County Councils
Australian Computer Conference
Average Correlation Coefficients

ACCA Air Charter Carriers Association
Associated Colleges of the Chicago Area (USA)
Association of Certified and Corporate Accountants

ACCAP Autocoder to COBOL Conversion-Aid Programme

ACCAT Advanced Command and Control Architecture Testbed

ACCC Advisory Committee to the Canada Centre for Inland Waters (Canada)

ACCCI American Coke and Coal Chemicals Institute (USA)

ACCEL Automated Circuit Card Etching Layout

ACCESS Access Characteristics Estimation System
Afloat Consumption, Cost and Effectiveness Surveillance System (USN)
AIR CANADA Cargo Enquiry and Service System
ALLIED CHEMICAL CORPORATION'S (USA) Energy Saving System
Architects Central Constructional Engineering Surveying Service (Greater London Council)

ACCESS Architects, Construction and Consulting Engineers, Specialists Service
ARGONNE (NATIONAL LABORATORY) Code Center Exchange and Storage System
Automatic Computer-Controlled Electronic Scanning System

ACCG American Committee for Crystal Growth (USA)

ACCHAN Allied Command Channel (of NATO)

ACCIS Automated Command and Control Information System (of NATO)

ACCLAIM Automated Circuit Card Lay-out And Implementation

ACCM Association of Competition Car Manufacturers

ACCMS Army Command and Control Management Structure (US Army)

ACCOMP Academic Computer Group (USA)

ACCORD Army Computer Capabilities On-line Repository and Disseminator (US Army)

ACCORDD informal association of Regional Dissemination Centers (of NASA (USA))

ACCP American College of Chest Physicians (USA)

ACCR Annual Cost of Capital Recovery

ACCRA Australian Chart and Code for Rural Accounting (Australia)

ACCS Airborne Command and Control Squadron (USAF)
Army Command and Control System (US Army)

ACCU Automatic Combustion Control Unmanned

ACCV Armoured Cavalry Cannon Vehicle

ACD Acid-Citrate-Dextrose
Acute Coronary Disease
Admiralty Chart Datum
American College of Dentists (USA)
Asymptotic Conical Dipole
Automatic Call Distribution

ACDA Arms Control and Disarmament Agency (USA)

ACDB Association du Catalogue Documentaire du Batiment (France) (Building Catalogue Association)

ACDDR International Centre for Diarrhoeal Diseases Research

ACDL Asynchronous Circuit Design Language

ACDP Advisory Committee on Dangerous Pathogens
Armament Control and Display Panel

ACDPI Association for a Competitive Data Processing Industry (USA)

ACDPS Automated Cartographic, Drafting and Photogrammetric System

ACDS Aircraft Control Display System
Automatic Counter-measures Dispensing System

ACE Air Cushion Equipment
Allied Command Europe (of NATO)
American Council on Education (USA)
Angiotensin-Converting-Enzyme
Animated Computer Education
Armoured Combat Earthmover
Association des Compagnies Aeriennes (Association of Air Companies) (Charter airline equivalent of IATA)
Association for Centrifuge Enrichment
Association for Cooperation in Engineering (USA)
Association of Consulting Engineers
Asynchronous Communication Element
Attitude Control Electronics
Audit, Control and Evaluation
Automated Computing Engine
Automated Cost Estimates
Automatic Clutter-Eliminator
Average Cumulative Error

ACE-S/C Acceptance Checkout Equipment-Spacecraft

ACEA Action Committee for European Aerospace
Association of Computing in Engineering and Architecture
Association of Cost and Executive Accountants

ACEAA Advisory Committee on Electrical Appliances and Accessories

ACEARTS Airborne Countermeasures Environment And Radar Target Simulator

ACEBD Airborne and Communications – Electronics Board (US Army)

ACEC Advisory Council on Energy Conservation
American Consulting Engineers Council (USA)
Association of Consulting Engineers of Canada (Canada)
Ateliers Constructions Electriques de Charleroi (BELGIUM)

ACEE Aircraft Energy Efficiency (a program of NASA (USA))

ACEFEL Arctic Construction and Frost Effects Laboratory (US Army) (merged into CRREL in 1961)

ACEI Association of Consulting Engineers of Ireland

ACEL Aerospace Crew Equipment Laboratory (of Naval Air Engineering Center, USN)

ACEMAN Acoustic Emission Analysis system

ACEMB Annual Conference on Engineering in Medicine and Biology

ACENZ Association of Consultant Engineers of New Zealand (New Zealand)

ACEP American College of Emergency Physicians (USA)

ACEQ Association of Consulting Engineers of Quebec (Canada)

ACER Australian Council for Educational Research (Australia)

ACers American Ceramic Society (USA)

ACERT Advisory Committee for the Education of Romany and other Travellers

ACES Advanced Concept Escape System
Australian Council for Educational Standards (Australia)

ACESA Arizona Council of Engineering and Scientific Associations (USA)

ACESS Akron Council of Engineering and Scientific Societies (USA)

ACETA Australasian Commercial and Economics Teachers Association

ACEVAL Air Combat Evaluation

ACEVAL/AIMVAL Air Combat Evaluation/Air Intercept Missile Evaluation

ACF Advanced Communication Function
Air Combat Fighter
Air Cushion Ferry
Australian Conservation Foundation (Australia)
Automatic Cop Feeder

ACFAS Association Canadienne Francais pour l'Avancement des Sciences (Canada) (French Canadian Association for the Advancement of Science)

ACFHE Association of Colleges for Further and Higher Education

ACFOD Asian Cultural Forum on Development (Thailand)

ACG Activated Charcoal Granules
American College of Gastroenterology (USA)

ACGIH American Conference of Government Industrial Hygienists (USA)

ACGM Advisory Committee on Genetic Manipulation

ACGR Associate Committee on Geotechnical Research (of NRC (Canada))

ACGS Aerospace Cartographic and Geodetic Service (USAF) (Disbanded 1972)

ACh Acetylcholine

ACH Acetone Cyanohydrin
Acetylcholinesterase
Alcohol Dehydrogenase
Automated Clearing House

ACHA American College of Hospital Administrators (USA)

ACHCEW Association of Community Health Councils in England and Wales

AChE Acetlycholinersterase

ACHEX Aerosol Characterization Experiment

ACHLIS Australian Clearing House for Library and Information Science (Australia)

AChR Acetylcholine Receptor

ACI Adjacent Channel Interference
Airborne Controlled Intercept
Alloy Casting Institute (a division of SFSA (USA))
American Concrete Institute (USA)
Automatic Car Identification ('Car' here is US word for Railway Carriage/Wagon)

ACIA Asynchronous Communications Interface Adapter

ACIC Aeronautical Chart and Information Center (USAF) (now Defense Mapping Agency Aerospace Center)

ACICAFE Association du Commerce et de l'Industrie du Cafe dans la C.E.E. (Association of the Coffee Trade and Industry in the European Economic Community)

ACID Acceleration, Cruising, Idling, Deceleration

ACIDS Aircraft Integrated Data System

ACIF Anti-Complement Immunofluoresence

ACIL American Council of Independent Laboratories (USA)

ACIM Axis-Crossing Interval Meter

ACIMGA Associazione Costruttori Italiani Macchine Grafiche e Affini (Italy) (Italian Association of Manufacturers of Machinery and Equipment for the Graphic Arts and Allied Trades)

ACIMIT Associazione Costruttori Italiani di Macchinario per l'Industria Tessile (Italy) (Italian Association of Machinery Manufacturers for the Textile Industry)

ACIMS Aircraft Component Intensive Management System (US Army)

ACIP Advisory Committee on Immunization Practices (of Center for Disease Control (USA))

ACIR Advisory Commission on Intergovernmental Relations (USA)
Automotive Crash Injury Research

ACIRL Australian Coal Industries Research Laboratories (Australia)

ACIS Arms Control Impact Statement

ACJMS Air Corporations Joint Medical Service (of BEA and BOAC)

ACL Allowable Cabin Load
Association for Computational Linguistics (USA)
Association of Cinema Laboratories (USA)
Atlas Computer Laboratory (of Science Research Council)
Audit Command Language
Avionics Cooling Loop

ACLAM American College of Laboratory Animal Medicine (USA)

ACLANT Allied Command Atlantic (of NATO)

ACLD Association for Children with Learning Disabilities (USA)

ACLG Air-Cushion Landing Gear

ACLICS Airborne Communications Location, Identification and Collection System

ACLM American College of Legal Medicine

ACLO Association of Cooperative Library Organizations

ACLOS Automatic Command to Line Of Sight

ACLS Air Cushion Landing System
Aircraft Carrier Landing System
All-weather Carrier Landing System
American Council of Learned Societies (USA)
Analog Concept Learning System
Automatic Carrier Landing System

ACLUM Advisory Committee on Legal Units of Measurement

ACM Advanced Composite Materials
Advanced Cruise Missile
Air Combat Manoeuvering
Air Cycle Machine
Anti-armour Cluster Munition
Associated Colleges of the Midwest (USA)
Association for Computing Machines (USA)
Association of Crane Makers (now part of Federation of Manufacturers of Construction Equipment and Cranes)
Associative Communications Multiplexer
Authorised Controlled Material

ACMA Advanced Civil/Military Aircraft
Asbestos Cements Manufacturers Association
Asphalt and Coated Macadam Association

ACMC Agricultural and Construction Machinery Council (of SAE (USA))
Association of Canadian Medical Colleges (Canada)

ACME Advanced Computer for Medical Research
Association of Consulting Management Engineers (USA)

ACMH Advisory Committee on Major Hazards

ACMI Air Combat Manoeuvring Instrumentation

ACMIS Automated Career Management and Information System (USDOD)

ACMR Air Combat Manoeuvring Range (USN)

ACMRR Advisory Council on Marine Resources Research (of IOC)

ACMS Advance Configuration Management System
Air Combat Manoeuvring Simulator
Application Control and Management System
Approved Coal Merchants Scheme
Australasian Conference on the Mechanics of Structures and Materials

ACMT Advanced Cruise Missile Technology

ACNA Aziende Colori Nazionali Addini (Italy)

ACNS Advisory Committee on Nuclear Safety (Israel)

ACO Adaptive Control Organization
Admiralty Compass Observatory

ACODAC Acoustic Data Capsule

ACODS Army Container-Oriented Distribution Systems (US Army)

ACOG American College of Obstetricians and Gynaecologists (USA)

ACOLAG Active Control Landing Gear Analysis

ACOMPLIS A Computerized London Information Service (of the Greater London Council)
ACOMR Advisory Committee on Oceanic Meteorological Research (of WMO (un))
ACONDA Activities Committee on New Directions for the ALA (American Library Association (USA))
ACOP Advisory Committee on Pilotage (of Dept of Trade)
ACOPI Asociacion Colombiana Popular de Industriales (Colombia)
ACOPS Advisory Committee on Oil Pollution of the Sea
ACORD Advisory Council on Research and Development for Fuel and Power (of Dept of Energy)
ACORDD Advisory Committee for the Research and Development Department (of the BL)
ACORN Associative Content Retrieval Network
Automatic Coder of Report Narrative
ACOS Advisory Committee on Safety (of IEC)
American College of Osteopathic Surgeons (USA)
ACOSH Appalachian Center for Occupational Safety and Hewalth (of NIOSH (USA))
ACOT Associate Committee on Tribology (of NRC (Canada))
ACOUSID Acoustic Seismic Intrusion Detector
ACOUSTINT Acoustical Intelligence
ACP Accomplishment/Cost Procedure
Acyl-Carrier Protein
Advisory Committee on Pesticides
African, Caribbean and Pacific states
Allied Communications Publication
American College of Psychiatrists (USA)
Association of Canadian Publishers (Canada)
ACPA Adaptive Controlled Phased Array
American Concrete Paving Association (USA)
Association of Computer Programers and Analysts (USA)
ACPDS Advisory Committee on Personal Dosimetry Services (NSF) (USA)
ACPL Zero-g Atmospheric Cloud Physics Laboratory (aboard the "Spacelab")
ACPM Advisory Committee for Programme Management (of EEC)
American College of Preventive Medicine (USA)
American Congress of Physical Medicine and Rehabilitation (USA)
ACPO Association of Chief Police Officers of England, Wales and Northern Ireland
ACPR Advanced Core Performance Reactor
Annular Core Pulse Reactor
ACPS Arab Company for Petroleum Services (of OAPEC)
Attitude-Control Propulsion System
ACQM Automatic Circuit Quality Monitoring
ACQS Association of Consultant Quantity Surveyors
ACR Active Cavity Radiometer
Advanced Converter Reactor
Aeroelastically Conformable Rotor
American College of Radiology (USA)
Antenna Coupling Regulator
Automatic Compression Regulator
Avalanche Controlled Rectifier
prefix to numbered series of conferences, etc. proceedings sponsored by Office of Naval Research (USN)
ACRA Association of Company Registration Agents
ACRE Advanced Chemical Rocket Engineering program (of NASA (USA) and USDOD)
Advanced Cryogenic Rocket Engineering
Air Cushion Relief Equipment
Automatic Call Recording Equipment
Automatic Climatological Recording Equipment
ACRH Argonne Cancer Research Hospital (of USAEC)
ACRI Air-Conditioning and Refrigeration Institute (USA)
ACRiLIS Australian Centre for Research in Library and Information Science (Riverina College of Advanced Education (Australia))
ACRL Association of College and Research Libraries (ALA) (USA)
ACRM Air Cushion Rig Mover
American Congress of Rehabilitation Medicine (USA)
ACRODABA Acronym Data Base
ACRS Advisory Committee on Reactor Safeguards (USA) (absorbed into Nuclear Regulatory Commission 1974 (USA))
Air Cushion Restraint System
ACRV Armoured Command and Reconnaissance Vehicle
ACS Accelerated Climatic Simulator
Adhesive Component System
Air Coating System
American Cancer Society (USA)
American Ceramic Society (USA)
American Chemical Society (USA)
American College of Surgeons (USA)
Assembly Control System
Association of Consultant Surveyors
Association of Consulting Scientists
Attitude Command System
Attitude Control System
Australian Computer Society (Australia)
Automatic Checkout System
Automatic Control System
Auxiliary Cooling System
Auxiliary Core Storage
ACS/DCI American Chemical Society/Division of Chemical Information (USA)
ACSA Aerocargo SA (Mexico)
Allied Communications Security Agency (of NATO)
Army Communications Systems Agency (US Army)
ACSAP Automated Cross Section Analysis Programme
ACSAS Advanced Conformal Submarine Acoustic Sensor
ACSE Association of Consulting Structural Engineers (Australia)
ACSF Artificial Cerebrospinal Fluid
ACSI American Ceramic Society, Incorporated (USA)
Assistant Chief of Staff for Intelligence (US Army)
ACSIL Admiralty Centre for Scientific Information and Liaison (later NSTIC now DRIC)
ACSIM Accelerated Constrained Simplex technique
ACSL Advanced Continuous Simulation Language
ACSM Advanced Conventional Stand-off Missile
American Congress on Surveying and Mapping (USA)
Assemblies, Components, Spare parts and Materials
ACSNI Advisory Committee on Safety of Nuclear Installations
ACSP Advanced Control Signal Processor
Advisory Council on Scientific Policy (now CSP)
ACSPIC ACS (APPLIED COMPUTING AND SOFTWARE) Production and Inventory Control
ACSR Aluminium Conductors, Steel-Reinforced
ACSS Accelerated Acetic Acid Salt Spray test
Automated Colour Separation System
ACST Advisory Council on Science and Technology (Australia)
ACSTI Advisory Committee for Scientific and Technical Information
ACSTIS Advanced Circular Scan Thermal Imaging System
ACSTT Advisory Committee on the Supply and Training of Teachers
ACSVD Advisory Committee on Safety in Vehicle Design (of ATAC (Australia))

ACSW Advanced Conventional Stand-off Weapon

ACT Active Control Technology
Activity Control Technique
Actuarial Programming Language
Adrenocorticotrophin
Advance Corporation Tax
Advanced Concept Train
Advanced Concept Tyre
Advisory Council on Technology
Aids to Corporate Thinking
Air Cushion OR Cushioned Transporter
Analogical Circuit Technique
Anti-Comet Tail
Association des Communicateurs Techniques (France) (Association of Technical Communicators)
Autocoder to COBOL Translator
Automated Contingency Translator
Automatic Coulometric Titration

ACTA Association de Coordination Technique Agricole (France) (Association for the Coordination of Agricultural Techniques)

ACTD Automatic Telephone Call Distribution

ACTDG Advisory Committee for the Transport of Dangerous Goods (Australia)

ACTES Annual Cycle Thermal Energy Storage

ACTH Adrenocorticotropic Hormone

ACTI Advisory Committee on Technology Innovation (of BOSTID (NAS) (usa))

ACTION Accepting Challenges of Today In Our New-world

ACTIS Auckland Commercial and Technical Information Service (New Zealand)

ACTIVE Advanced Computer Training In a Versatile Environment

ACTO Automatic Computing Transfer Oscillator

ACTOL Air Cushion Take-off and Landing

ACTP Advanced Computer Techniques Project (disbanded 1979)

ACTRAN Autocoder-to-COBOL Translation

ACTS Acoustic Control and Telemetry System
Advanced Communications Technology Satellite
Advisory Committee on Toxic Substances (of HSE)
Automatic COBOL Translation System

ACTSU Association of Computer Time-Sharing Users (USA)

ACTU Australian Council of Trade Unions (Australia)

ACTV Armored Cavalry TOW Vehicle

ACU Address Control Unit
Arithmetic and Control Unit
Asian Clearing Union (Bangladesh, India, Iran, Nepal, Pakistan and Sri Lanka)
Association of Commonwealth Universities
Automatic Calling Unit
Avionic Control Unit

ACUCAA Association of College, University, and Community Arts Administration (USA)

ACUG Association of Computer User Groups

ACUP Association of Canadian University Presses (Canada)

ACURIL Association of Caribbean University, Research and Institutional Libraries

ACUTA Association of College and University Telecommunications Administrators (USA)

ACUTE Accountants Computer Users Technical Exchange (USA)

ACV Air Cushion Vehicle
Analysis of Covariance

ACVA American Council of Voluntary Agencies (USA)

ACVP Advisory Committee on Vehicle Performance (of ATAC (Australia))

ACVWS Armoured Combat Vehicle Weapon System

AD Air Dried
American Academy of Dermatology (USA)
prefix to dated-numbered series of Airworthiness Directives issued by FAA (USA)
prefix to dated-numbered series of reports issued by Airdrop Engineering Laboratory (of NLABS (US Army)
prefix to numbered series of reports issued through Defense Documentation Center (USDOD) and usually sold by NTIS (USA) (now issued through DTIC (USDOD) or NTIS (USA) and its agents)

Ada A computer language named in honour of Lady Ada Augusta Byron who worked with Babbage on his mechanical computing engine

ADA Action Data Automation System
Adenosine Deaminase
Aeronautical Development Agency (India)
Agricultural Development Association
Air Defence Area
Air Defence Artillery
Air Defense Agency (USA)
Airborne Data Automation
Allgemeiner Deutscher automobile Club (Germany) (German Automobile Association)
Aluminium Development Association (now part of the Aluminium Federation)
American Dental Association (USA)
American Diabetes Association (USA)
American Dietetic Association (USA)
Automated Differential Agglutination
Automated Dispensing Analyzer
Automatic Data Acquisition

ADABAS Adaptable Data Base System

ADAC Automated Direct Analogue Computer

ADACS Automated Data Acquisition and Control System

ADAI Adenosine Deaminase Inhibitor

ADAL Action Data Automation Language

ADAM Adaptive Digital Avionics Module
Adaptive Dynamic Analysis and Maintenance
Advanced Data Access Method
Advanced Data Management
Advanced Direct-landing APOLLO Mission
Air Deflection And Modulation
Air Delivered Attack Marker
Area Denial Artillery Munition
Artillery-Delivered Anti-personnel Mine
Automatic Distance and Angle Measurement

ADAMHA Alcohol, Drug Abuse and Mental Health Administration (of DHSS (USA))

ADAP Airport Development Aid Program (of FAA (USA))

ADAPS Armament Delivery Analysis Programming System
Automated Design And Packaging Service

ADAPSO Association of Data Processing Service Organizations (USA)

ADAPT Adaption of Automatically Programmed Tools
ARPA (USDOD) Data-base Access and Presentation Terminal

ADAPTICOM Adaptive Communication

ADAPTS Air-Delivered Anti-Pollution Transfer System
Analogue/Digital/Analogue Process and Test System

ADAR Advanced Design Array Radar

ADARS Adaptive Antenna Receiver System

ADAS Agricultural Development and Advisory Service (of MAFF)
Airborne Dat Annotation System
Automatic Dialing Alarm System
Auxiliary Data Annotation Set

ADATE Automatic Digital Assembly Test Equipment

ADATS Air Defence Anti-Tank System

ADAU Auxiliary Data Acquisition Unit

ADAUA Association pour le Developpement Naturel d'une Architecture et d'un Urbanisme Africains (Upper Volta) (Association for the National Development of African Architecture and Town Planning)

ADAWS Action Data Automation and Weapon System

AdB Acceleration Decibel

ADB African Development Bank (Ivory Coast)
Arctic Drill Barge
Asian Development Bank (Philippines)

ADBI Agricultural Development Bank of Iran (Iran)

ADBS Association des Documentalistes et des Bibliothecaires Specialises (France)

ADC Aerospace Defense Command (USAF)
Agricultural Development Corporation (Korea)
Agricultural Development Corporation (Pakistan)
American Diabetes Association (USA)
Analogue-to-Digital Converter
Areas of Deeper Convection
Armament Development Center (US Army)
Association of District Councils
Association of Diving Contractors

ADCA Advanced Design Composite Aircraft
Aerospace Department Chairmens Association (USA)
Australian Department of Civil Aviation (Australia)

ADCC Antibody-Dependent Cell-mediated Cytotoxity

ADCCP Advanced Data Communication Control Procedures (of ANSI (USA))

ADCI American Die Casting Institute (USA)

ADCIS Association for the Development of Computer-based Instruction Systems (USA)
Association for the Development of Computer-based Instructional Systems (USA)

ADCJ Air Defence Communications Jammer

ADCO Abu Dhabi Oil Company

ADCOM Aerospace Defense Command (USAF)
Aerospace Defense Command (USAF)

ADCS Advanced Defence Communications Satellite
Air Data Computing Systems
Association of District Council Surveyors

ADCT Assisted-Draught Crossflow Tower
Association of District Council Treasurers

ADCU Association of Data Communications Users (USA)

ADD Activated Dough Development
Airstream Direction Detector
Ascent Descent Director
Automatic Document Distribution (a program of DTIC (USDOD))

ADDA Australian Database Development Association (Australia)

ADDAM Adaptive Dynamic Decision Aiding Methodology

ADDAS Airborne Digital Data Acquisition System

ADDDS Automatic Direct Distance Dialling System

ADDM Automated Drafting and Digitizing Machine

ADDS Advanced Data Display System
Advanced Deep Diving Submersible

ADDSRTS Automated Digitized Document Storage, Retrieval and Transmission System

ADE Automated Design Equipment
Automated Draughting Equipment
Automatic Data Entry

ADEA Army Development and Employment Agency (US Army)
Association Belge pour le Developpement pacifique de l'Energie Atomique (Belgium)

ADELA Atlantic Community Development Group for Latin America

ADEM Automatic Data Equalised Modem

ADEN Armament Development Enfield gas operated aircraft cannon ('Enfield' is taken from Small Arms Factory at Enfield, London)

ADEPA Association pour le Developpement de la Production Automatisee (France) (Association for the Development of Automated Production)

ADEPT A Display-Expedited Processing and Tutorial system
A Distinctly Empirical Prover of Theorems
Advanced Development Prototype

ADES Admiralty Distilling Experimental Station (MOD)
Automated Data Entry System

ADETIM Association pour le Developpment des Techniques des Industries Mecaniques (France) (Association for the Improvement of Mechanical Engineering Techniques)

ADF Airborne Direction Finder
Automatic Direction Finder

ADFAED Abu Dhabi Fund for Arab Economic Development

ADFSC Automatic Data Field Systems Command (US Army)

ADGE Air Defence Ground Environment

ADGLC Abu Dhabi Gas Liquefaction Company (Abu Dhabi) (partly Government owned)

ADGS Air Defence Gun System

ADGUIDES Admiralty Guides

ADH Alaska Department of Highways (USA)
Alcohol Dehydrogenase
Antidiuretic Hormone

ADI Acceptable Daily Intake
Alternating Direction Implicit
Alternating Direction Iterative
American Documentation Institute (USA) (now American Society for Information Science)
Attitude Direction Indicator
Attitude Director Indicator
Automatic Direction Indicator

ADICEP Association de Directeurs de Centres Europeens de Plastiques (Association of Directors of European Plastics Associations)
Association des Directeurs des Centres des Matières Plastiques (Association of Directors of Plastics Materials Centres)

ADIOS Analog Digital Input Output System

ADIP Automated Data Interchange Systems Panel (of ICAO)

ADIS A Data Interchange System
Association for Development of Instructional Systems (USA)
Attitude Director Indicator System
Automated Data Interchange Systems (a panel of ICAO)
Automatic Data Interchange System

ADIT Automatic Detection and Integrated Tracking

ADITES Asociacion de Investigacion de la Tecnicas del Subsuelo (Spain) (Research Association on Subsoil Technology)

ADIU Armament and Disarmament Information Unit (Sussex University)

ADIZ Air Defence Identification Zone

ADL Armament Datum Line
Automatic Data Link
Automatic Data Logger

ADLIPS Automatic Data Link Plotting System

ADLS Automatic Drag-Limiting System

ADM Activity Data Method
Adaptive Delta Modulation
Advanced Development Models
Aid in Decision Making
Air Defence Missile
Air-launched Decoy Missile
Atomic Demolition Munitions

ADMA Abu Dhabi Marine Areas (a company) (Abu Dhabi)
Aviation Distributors and Manufacturers Association (USA)
ADMARC Agricultural Development and Marketing Corporation (a government agency) (Malawi)
ADMIG Australian Drug and Medical Information Group (Australia)
ADMIRAL Advanced Mega Internet Research for Alvey (Alvey Directorate (DTI))
ADMIRE Automatic Diagnostic Maintenance Information Retrieval
ADMS Automatic Digital Message Switching
ADMSC Automatic Digital Message Switching Centers (of DOD)
ADN Adiponitrile
ADNOC Abu Dhabi National Oil Company (Abu Dhabi)
ADO Advanced Development Objectives
ADOC Air Defence Operations Centre
ADOIT Automatically Directed Outgoing Intertoll Trunk test circuit
ADOM Air Deployed Oceanographic Mooring
ADONIS Automatic Digital On-line Instrumentation System
ADOPT Approach to Distributed Processing Transaction
ADP Acoustic Data Processor
Adenosine Diphosphate
Aggregate Demand Potential
Ammonium Dihydrogen Phosphate
Association of Database Producers
Automatic Data Processing
ADPA American Defense Preparedness Association (USA)
ADPACS Automated Data Processing and Communications Service (of GSA (USA))
ADPC Abu Dhabi Petroleum Company (Abu Dhabi) (now ADCO)
ADPCM Adaptive Differntial Pulse Code Modulation
ADPD Angular Dependent Photoelectron Diffraction
ADPE Automatic Data Processing Equipme
ADPE/S Automatic Data Interchange System
Automatic Data Processing Equipment and Software
ADPESO Automatic Data Processing Equipment Selection Office (USN)
ADPL Association of Data Processing Librarians (USA)
ADPLAN Advancement Planning
ADPREP Automatic Data Processing Resource Estimating Procedures
ADPS Automatic Data Processing System
ADPU Association of Public Data Users (USA)
ADQC Almost Difference Quasiternary Code
ADR Accelerated Depreciation Range
Accident Data Recorder
Accord European Relative au Transport International des Marchandises Dangereuses par Route (European Agreement on the International Transport of Dangerous Goods by Road)
Association pour le Developpement de la Recherche (France) (Association for the Development of Research)
Automatical Digital Relay
ADRA Automatic Dynamic Response Analyser
ADRC Automatic Digital Relay Center (Of NORAD)
ADREP Accident/Incident Reporting system (of ICAO)
ADREPP Aircraft Accident Data Reporting Panel (of ICAO)
ADRES Aircraft Data Recording Evaluation System
Army Data Retrieval Engineering System (US Army)
ADRI Automatic Dead-Reckoning Instrument
ADRS Australian Design Rules
ADRS Analogue-to-Digital Data Recording System
ADS Accessory Drive System
Accurately Defined Systems
Activity Data Sheet
Advance Diving System
Advanced Debugging System
Advanced Dosimetry System
Aerial Delivery System
Aerodynamic Deceleration System
Air Data Subsystem
Air Data System
Aircraft Development Services (of FAA) (USA)
Atmospheric Diving Suit
ADSA Air Derived Separation Assurance
American Dairy Science Association (USA)
ADSAF Automated Data Systems with the Army in the Field (US Army)
ADSARM Advanced Defence Suppression Anti-Radiation Missile
ADSAS Air-Derived Separation Assurance System
ADSATIS Australian Defence Science and Technology Information
Automatic Data Interchange System Service (of Department of Supply and Department of the Army (Australia))
ADSCOM Advanced Ships Communications
ADSE Alternative Delivery Schedule Evaluator
ADSEL Address Selective
ADSG Alternative Delivery Schedule Generator
ADSIA Allied Data System Inter-operability Agency (NATO)
ADSID Air Delivered Acoustic Implant Seismic Intrusion Detector
Air-Delivered Seismic Intrusion Detector
ADSM Air Defence Suppression Missile
ADSOL Analysis of Dynamical Systems On-line
ADSP Advanced Digital Signal Processor
ADSPECS Admiralty Specifications
ADSS Australian Defence Scientific Service (of DSTO (Dept of Defence) (Australia))
ADSTAR Automatic Document Storage And Retrieval
ADSTEEL Automated Drafting System-Structural Steel Detailing
ADSW Advanced Defence Suppression Weapon
ADSYM Automobile De-fog/de-frost System Model
ADT Automatic Detection and Tracking
Autonomous Data Transfer
Average Daily Traffic
ADTA Augmented Target Docking Adaptor
ADTAM Air Delivered Target Activated Munitions
ADTC Armament Development and Test Center (USAF)
ADTEC ABMDA Data Processing Testbed and Evaluation Center (US Army)
ADTECH Advanced Decoy Technology
ADTS Automated Data and Telecommunications Service (of General Service Administration (USA))
Automatic Data Test System
ADTU Automatic Digital Test Unit
ADU Ammonium Diuranate
Auxiliary Display Unit
ADV Air-Defence Variant (of the MRCA Tornado')
Aleutian Disease Virus
Arbeitsgemeinschaft Deutscher Verkehrsflughafen (Germany)
ADVCAP Advanced Capabilities
ADVICE Analytical Determination of the Values of Information to Combat Effectiveness
ADVISER Airborne Dual-channel Variable Input Severe Environmental Recorder/Reproducers
ADVUL Air Defence Vulnerability
ADWS Automatic Digital Weather Switch

ADX Automatic Data Exchange
Automatic Digital Exchange

Ae prefix to numbered series of publications issued by the Aerodynamics Division of NPL

AE Acoustic Emission
Acousto-Electric
Aero-Electronic
Aerodermatitis Enteropathica
Aktiebolaget Atomenergi (Sweden)
Atomic Emission
Auroral Electrojet Magnetic Activity Index
prefix to numbered series of reports issued by Department of Aerospace Engineering, Cincinnati University (USA)
prefix to numbered-lettered series of reports issued by Department of Aeronautical Engineering, Indian Institute of Science (India)

AEA Advanced Engine, Aerospike
Agricultural Engineers Association
All-Electric Aircraft
Aluminium Extruders Association
American Electronics Association (USA)
American Engineering Association (USA)
Association of European Airlines
Atomic Energy Authority

AEAI Association of Engineers and Architects in Israel (Israel)

AEB Advanced Engine, Bell
American Egg Board (USA)
Associated Examing Board
Atomic Energy Board (South Africa)
Atomic Energy Bureau (of STA (Japan))

AEBIG ASLIB Economic and Business Information Group

AEC Alcohol Education Centre (at the Maudsley Hospital, London)
Association Europeene de Ceramique (European Ceramic Association)
Association des Enducteurs, Calandreurs et Fabricants de revetements de sols plastiques de la C.E.E. (Association of Coated Fabrics, Plastic Films and Plastic and Synthetic Floor Coverings (EEC)
Atomic Energy Commission (India)
Atomic Energy Commission (USA) (disbanded in 1974 and replaced by ERDA and Nuclear Regulatory Commission)
Atomic Energy Committee (New Zealand)

AECB Association for the Export of Canadian Books (Canada)
Atomic Energy Control Board (Canada) (renamed Nuclear Control Board (ofMOSST (Canada) in 1978)

AECC Associacion Espanola para el Control de la Calida (Spain) (Spanish Association for Quality Control)

AECE Automotive Electronics Conference and Exposition

AECL Atomic Energy of Canada Ltd (Canada)

AECM Active Electronic Counter-Measures

AECMA Association Européenne des Constructeurs de Matériel Aérospatiale (European Association of Manufacturers of Aerospace Material)

AECT Association for Educational Communications and Technology (USA)

AED Aerodynamic Equivalent Diameter
Association of Equipment Distributors (USA)
Automated Engineering Design
Automatic External Defibrillator
ALGOL Extended for Design

AEDC ARNOLD Engineering Development Center (USAF)

AEDCAP Automated Engineering Design Circuit Analysis Programme

AEDE Aircraft Economic Design Evaluation

AEDPS Automated Engineering Documentation Preparation System

AEDS Advanced Electric Distribution System
Association for Educational Data Systems (USA)
Atomic Energy Detection Systems

AEDU Admiralty Experimental Diving Unit (of AUWE (MOD))

AEE Abstract Evolution Equation
Airborne Evaluation Equipment
Association of Energy Engineers (USA)
Atomic Energy Establishment

AEEC Airline Electronic Engineering Committee (USA)
Airlines Electronics Engineering Council (USA)

AEED Association Europeene des Enseignants Dentaires (European Association of Teachers of Dentistry)

AEEE Army Equipment Engineering Establishment (Canada)

AEEF Association Europeenne des Exploitation Frigorifiques (European Association for Refrigeration Development)

AEEP Association of European Engineering Periodicals
prefix to series of reports issued by Department of Aerospace Engineering and Engineering Physics, Virginia University (USA)

AEESG Aircraft Engines Emissions Study Group (of ICAO) (now CAEE)

AEET Atomic Energy Establishment, Trombay (India)

AEEW Atomic Energy Establishment WINFRITH (of UKAE)

AEF Airborne Equipment Failure

AEFA Aviation Engineering Flight Activity (of AVRADCOM)

AEG Active Element Group
Allgemeine Elektricitats-Gesellschaft (Germany)
Association of Engineering Geologists (USA)

AEGIS An Existing General Information System
not an acronym or abbreviation – it is the name of a weapon system named after Zeus' mythological breastplate

AEHA Army Environmental Hygiene Agency (US Army)

AEI American Enterprise Institute for Public Policy Research (USA)
Americans for Energy Independence (USA) (a non-profit group)
Associazione Ellettrotecnica Italiana (Italy) (Italian Electronics Association)

AEIA Australian Electronics Industry Association (Australia)

AEIC Association of Edison Illuminating Companies (USA)

AEIE Association of Indian Engineering Industry (India)

AEIH Association Europeenne des Industries de l'Habillement (European Association of Clothing Manufacturers)

AEIMS Administrative Engineering Information Management System

AEIS Association of Electronic Industries in Singapore (Singapore)

AEJI Association of European Jute Industries

AEK Atomenergikommissionen (Denmark) (Atomic Energy Commission)

AEL Admiralty Engineering Laboratory (MOD) (now part of NGTE)

AELC Accident–Experience Learning Curve

AELU Mutual Atomic Energy Liability Underwriters (USA)

AEM Acoustic Emission Monitor OR Monitoring
Analytical Electron Microscope
Applications Explorers Missions (of NASA (USA))

AEMB Alliance for Engineering in Medicine and Biology (USA)

AEMIE Association Europeene de Medecine Interne d'Ensemble (European Association of Internal Medicine)
AEMP Association of European Management Publishers
AEMS American Engineering Model Society (USA)
AEN Affaiblissement Equivalent pour la Nettete (Articulation Reference Equivalent)
AENSB Association de l'Ecole Nationale Superieure de Bibliothecaires (France) (Association of the National College of Librarians)
AEO Acousto-Electric Oscillator
Association of Exhibition Organisers
AEOI Atomic Energy Organisation of Iran (Iran)
AEOS Astronomical, Earth and Ocean Sciences (a directorate of NSF (USA))
AEOSS Advanced Electro-Optical Sensor Simulation
AEP Averaged Evoked Potential
AEPA Aminoethylphosphonic Acid
AEPB Association pour l'Emploi des Plastiques dans le Batiment (France) (Association for the Use of Plastics in Building)
AEPS Advanced Extra-vehicular Protective System
Asociacion Espanola de Prevencion y Seguridad (Spain) (Spanish Association of Health and Safety)
AEQA Alabama Environmental Quality Association (USA)
AER Apical Ectodermal Ridge
AERA American Education Research Association (USA)
Association pour l'Etude et la Recherche Astronautique et cosmique (France) (Association for Astronautics and Cosmic Study and Research)
AERALL Association d'Études et de Recherches sur les Aéronefs Allégés (France)
AERCAB Aircrew Escape/Rescue System Capability
AERD Agricultural Engineering Research Division (of ARS (USDA))
AERDL Army Electronics Research and Development Laboratory (US Army)
AERE Atomic Energy Research Establishment
AERI Atomic Energy Research Institute (Korea)
AERIS Automatic Electronic Ranging Information System
AERO Air Education and Recreation Organization
Air Education and Research Organisation
prefix to dated/numbered series of reports issued by Department of Aeronautics, London University
prefix to reports issued by Aerodynamics Division of the National Physical Laboratory
AERODESA Aeronaves del Ecuador SA (Ecuador)
AEROS Aeronomy Satellite
AEROSOL Aero dynamic-solar
AEROSTAT Aeronautical Services Satellite
AERTEL Association Europeenne Rubans, Tresses, Tissus Elastiques (European Association for Ribbons, Braid, Elastic Textiles)
AES Abrasive Engineering Society (USA)
Aerospace Electrical Society (USA)
Aerospace Electronics Systems
Airways Engineering Society (USA)
Allyl Elthenesulphonate
American Electroencephalographic Society (USA)
American Electroplaters Society (USA)
Anti-eosinophil
APOLLO Extension System
Architectural Engineering System
Artificial Earth Satellite
Attenuation Efficiency Score
Audio Engineering Society
Auger Electron Spectroscopy
Auger Emission Spectroscopy
Automatic Extraction System
AESA Aerolineas el Salvador SA (Panama)
AESD Acoustic Environment Support Detachment (of the Office of Naval Research (USN))
AESE Association of Earth Science Editors (USA)
AESN Association of Export Subscription Newsagents
AESO Aircraft Environmental Support Office (of NEPSS (USN))
AESOP An Experimental Structure for On-line Planning
Artificial Earth Satellite Observation Program (USN)
Association for Energy Systems, Operations and Programming (USA)
Automated Engineering and Scientific Optimization Programme
AESS Aerospace and Electronics Systems Society (of IEEE (USA))
AeSSA Aeronautical Society of South Africa (South Africa)
AET Acoustic Emission Testing
Automatic Exchange Tester
AeTBD Aerobically Thioglycolate Broth Disk
AETE Aerospace Engineering Test Establishment (of the Canadian Armed Forces)
AETFAT Association pour l'Etude Taxonomique de la Flore d'Afrique Tropical (Germany) (Association for the Taxonomic Study of Tropical Africa Flora)
AETMS Airborne Electronic Terrain Map System
AEU Asia Electronics Union (Japan)
AEVS Automatic Electronic Voice Switch
AEW Admiralty Experiment Works (MOD) (merged into AMTE in 1977)
Airborne Early Warning
AEW&C Airborne Early Warning and Control
AEWB Army Electronic Warfare Board (US Army)
AEWC Alaska Eskimo Whaling Commission
AEWES Army Engineer Waterways Experiment Station (US Army)
AEWIS Army Electronic Warfare Information System (US Army)
AEWM Acoustic Emission Weld Monitor OR Monitoring
AEWS Advanced Earth Satellite Weapon System
AEWSPS Aircraft Electronic Warfare Self-Protection System
AF Air Foundation (USA)
Anti-fouling
Aspect Factor
Atomic Fluorescence
Atrial Fibrillation
Atrial Flutter and Fibrillation
Audio Frequency
AF-CCB Air Force Configuration Control Board (USAF)
AF-EOAR Air Force—European Office, Office of Aerospace Research (USAF)
AF-ES prefix to dated-numbered and lettered series of Environmental Surveys issued by USAF
AFA Abstract Family of Acceptors
Air Force Association (USA)
Army Finance Association (US Army)
AFAA Air Force Audit Agency (USAF)
AFAADS Advanced Forward Area Air Defence System
AFAC American Fisheries Advisory Committee (USA)
AFACO Association Française des Amateurs Constructeurs l'Ordinateurs (France) (French Association of Amateur Computer Builders)
AFAEP Association of Fashion, Advertising and Editorial Photographers
AFAFC Air Force Accounting and Finance Center (USAF)
AFAHA Association Française des Amateurs Horlogerie Ancienne (France)
AFAL Air Force Avionics Laboratory (USAF)

AFALD Air Force Acquisition Logistics Division (of AFLC (USAF))

AFAM Airfield Attack Munition
Automatic Frequency Assignment Model

AFAMIC Air Force Aerospace Materials Information Center (USAF)

AFAP Artillery Fired Atomic Projectile
Association Francaise pour l'Accroissement de la Productivitie (France) (French Association for Increased Productivit

AFAPL Air Force Aero Propulsion Laboratory (USAF)

AFAR African Asian Rift
Azores Fixed Acoustic Range (A research project of the Defence Research Group of NATO)

AFARL Air Force Aeronautical Research Laboratories (USAF)

AFARMADE Asociacion de Fabricantes de Armaments y Material de Defensa (Spain)

AFARV Armoured Forward Area Re-arm Vehicle

AFASE Association For Applied Solar Energy (USA)

AFATL Air Force Armament Laboratory (USAF)

AfB Arbeitsstelle fur das Bibliothekswesen (Germany) (Library Study Centre)

AFB Air Force Base
American Foundation for the Blind (USA)

AFBC Atmospheric (pressure) Fluidized Bed Combustion

AFBD Association of Futures Brokers and Dealers

AFBMA Anti-Friction Bearing Manufacturers Assocation (USA)

AFC Atomic Fuel Corporation (Japan)
Automatic Fare Collection
Automatic Field Control
Automatic Flight Control
Automatic Frequency Control
Average Fixed Cost

AFCA Association Francaise pour la Communaute Atlantique (France) (French Association for the Atlantic Community)
Atom Fluorescence for Chemical Analysis

AFCAC African Civil Aviation Commission

AFCC Air Force Communications Command (USAF)

AFCCS Air Force Command and Control System (USAF)

AFCEA Armed Forces Communications and Electronics Association (USA)

AFCEC Air Force Civil Engineering Center (USA) (now AFETO)

AFCENT Allied Forces Central Europe (of NATO)

AFCET Association Francaise pour la Cybernetique Economique et Technique (France) (French Association for Economic and Technical Cybernetics)

AFCFS Advanced Fighter Control Flight Simulator

AFCGIC Air Force Ceramics and Graphite Information Center (USAF)

AFCIQ Association Francaise pour le Controle Industriel de Qualite (France) (French Association for Industrial Quality Control)

AFCMA Aluminium Foil Container Manufacturers Association

AFCMD Air Force Contract Management Division (of AFSC)

AFCMR Armed Forces Central Medical Registry (School of Aerospace Medicine (USAF))

AFCORS Advanced Fire Control Radar System

AFCR American Federation of Clinical Research (USA)

AFCRL Air Force Cambridge Research Laboratories (USAF)

AFCRL-PSRP USAF Cambridge Research Laboratories–Physical Sciences Research Paper

AFCS Adaptive Flight Control System
Air Force Communications Service (USAF)
Automatic Flight Control System
Auxiliary Flight Control System

AFCSC Air Force Cryptologic Support Center (of ESC (USAF))

AFD Accelerated Freeze Drying
Amplitude Frequency Distribution
Appointed Factory Doctor

AFDA Abstract Family of Deterministic Acceptors

AFDAA Air Force Data Automation Agency (USAF)

AFDBS Association Francaise des Documentaires et des Bibliothecaires Specialises (France) (French Association of Documentalists and Special Librarians)

AFDC Artillery Fire Data Computer
Automatic Formation Drone Control

AFDEC Association of Franchised Distributors of Electronic Components

AFDH American Fund for Dental Health (USA)

AFDIN Association Française de Documentation et d'Information Nucleaires (France) (French Association of Nuclear Documentation and Information)

AFDL Abstract Family of Deterministic Languages

AFDMIC Air Force Defense Metals Information Center (USAF)

AFDS Advanced Flight Deck Simulator
Autopilot Flight Director System

AFDSC Air Force Data Services Center (USAF)

AFDSDC Air Force Data Systems Design Center (USAF)

AFEB Armed Forces Epidemiological Board (USA)

AFECI Association des Fabricants Europeens de Chauffebains et Chauffe-eau Instantanes au Gaz (Association of Manufacturers of Gas Water Heaters)

AFECOGAZ Association des Fabricants Européens d'Appareils de Contrôle pour le Gaz et l'Huile (European Association of Gas and Oil Control Manufacturers)

AFEI Americans for Energy Independence (USA)
Association Française pour l'Étiquetage d'Information (France) (French Association for Informative Labelling)

AFELIS Air Force Engineering and Logistics Information System (USAF)

AFEPIC Air Force Electronic Properties Information Center (USAF)

AFERNOD Association Francaise pour l'Etude et la Recherche des Nodules (France)

AFES Automatic Feature Extraction System

AFESA Air Force Engineering and Services Agency (USAF)

AFESC Air Force Engineering and Services Center (USAF)

AFESD Arab Fund for Economic and Social Development

AFETO Air Force Engineering Technology Office (USAF)

AFETR Air Force Eastern Test Range (USAF)

AFEWC Air Force Electronic Warfare Center (of ESC) (USAF)

AFF An Foras Forbartha (Eire) (Institute for Physical Planning and Construction Research)
Auditory-Flutter Fusion

AFFDL Air Force Flight Dynamics Laboratory (USAF)

AFFF Aqueous Film-Forming Foam

AFFRI Armed Forces Radiobiology Research Institute (USDOD)

AFFSCE Air Forces Flight Safety Committee Europe

AFFT Auditory-Flutter Fusion Threshold

AFFTC Air Force Flight Test Center (USAF)

AFG Association des Fabricants de Glucose (Association of Manufacturers of Glucose) (of the EEC)

AFGL	Air Force Geophysics Laboratory (USAF)
AFGWC	Air Force Global Weather Central (USAF)
AFHF	Air Force Historical Foundation (USA)
AFHRL	Air Force Human Resources Laboratory (USAF)
AFI	American Film Institute (USA) Audio Frequency Interference
AFI-RAN	Africa, India Ocean Region Air Navigation
AFIAS	Association Francaise d'Intelligence Artificielle et des Systemes de Simulation (France) (French Association of Artificial Intelligence and Simulation Systems)
AFICCS	Air Force Interim Command and Control System (USAF)
AFIP	Armed Forces Institute of Pathology (USDOD)
AFIPS	American Federation of Information Processing Societies (USA)
AFIS	Air Force Intelligence Service (USAF) Aircraft Fault Identification System
AFISA	Aero Fletes Internacionales SA (Panama)
AFISC	Air Force Inspection and Safety Center (USAF)
AFIT	Air Force Institute of Technology (USAF)
AFITAE	Association Francaise d'Ingenieurs et Techniciens de l'Aeronautique et de l'Espace (France) (French Association of Aeronautical and Space Engineers and Technicians (now part of AAAF)
AFJINTACCS	Air Force Program for Joint Interoperability of Tactical Command and Control Systems (USAF)
AfK	Arbeitgemeinschaft fuer Kommunikationsforschung (Germany) (Study Group for Communications Research)
AFL	Abstract Family of Languages
AFL-CIO	American Federation of Labor-Congress of Industrial Organizations (USA)
AFLC	Air Force Logistics Command (USAF)
AFLC-OA	Air Force Logistics Command – Operations Analysis Office (USAF)
AFLCON	AFLC Operations Network
AFLIR	Advanced Forward Looking Infra-Red
AFLL	Army Fuels and Lubricants Laboratory (US Army)
AFLMC	Air Force Logistics Management Center (USAF)
AFLNE	Association Francaise pour l'Industrie Nucleaire d'Equipment (France) (French Association for the Nuclear Equipment Industry)
AFLOSH	AUDDIT Fault Logic Simulation Hybrid
AFLRL	Army Fuels and Lubricants Research Laboratory (US Army)
AFLSC	Air Force Legal Services Center (USAF)
AFM	Air Force Manual (numbered series issued by USAF)
AFMA	Armed Forces Management Association (USA)
AFMAG	Air Force Management Analysis Group (USAF)
AFMCH	American Foundation for Maternal and Child Health (USA)
AFMD	Accounting and Financial Management Division (of GAO (USA))
AFMDC	Air Force Machinability Data Center (USAF) Air Force Missile Development Center (USAF)
AFMEA	Air Force Management Engineering Agency (USAF)
AFML	Air Force Materials Laboratory (USAF)
AFMMFO	Air Force Medical Materials Field Office (USAF)
AFMPC	Air Force Manpower and Personnel Center (USAF)
AFMPDC	Air Force Mechanical Properties Data Center (USAF)
AFMR	Antiferromagnetic Resonance
AFMS	Association of Fleet Maintenance Supervisors (USA)
AFMSC	Air Force Medical Services Center (USAF)
AFMTC	Air Force Missile Test Center (USAF)
AFNE	Americans for Nuclear Energy (USA)
AFNETF	Air Force Nuclear Engineering Test Facility (USAF)
AFNIL	Agence Francophone pour la Numérotation Internationale du Livre (France) (acts also for Belgium and Switzerland) (Agency for International Standard Book Numbering)
AFNORTH	Allied Forces Northern Europe (of NATO)
AFO	Advanced File Organization
AFOAR	Air Force Office of Aerospace Research (USAF)
AFOG	Asian Federation of Obstetrics and Gynaecology
AFOR	Association Francaise de Normalisation (France) (French Standards Association)
AFOS	Advanced Field Operating System Automation of Field Operations and Services (of National Weather Service (USA))
AFOSH	prefix to Air Force Occupational Safety and Health standards (USAF)
AFOSI	Air Force Office of Special Investigations (USAF)
AFOSP	Air Force Office of Security Policy (USAF)
AFOSR	Air Force Office of Scientific Research (USAF)
AFP	Abstract Family of Processors Air Force Pamphlet (numbered series issued by USAF) Alpha Foetoprotein Associative File Processor
AFP/SME	Association for Finishing Processes of the Society of Manufacturing Engineers (USA)
AFPA	American Fighter Pilots Association (USA) Association pour la Formation Professionnelle des Adultes (France) (Association for the Professional Training of Adults) Australian Fire Protection Association (Australia) Automatic Flow Process Analysis
AFPCS	Automatic Flight Path Control System
AFPDC	Air Force Publications Distribution Center (USAF)
AFPG	Abelian Finitely Presented Group
AFPRO	Air Force Plant Representative Office (USAF)
AFPTRC	Air Force Personnel and Training Research Center (USAF)
AfPU	African Postal Union
AFQT	Armed Forces Qualification Test (USDOD)
AFR	Abstract Family of Relations Air/Fuel Ratio
AFRA	Average Freight Rate Assessment
AFRAA	African Airlines Association (Kenya)
AFRAL	Association Francaise de Reglage Automatique (France) (French Association for Automatic Tuning)
AFRAM	Air Force Recoverable Assembly Management system (USAF)
AFRASEC	Afro-Asian Organisation for Economic Cooperation
AFRC	Agricultural and Food Research Council Area Frequency Response Characteristic Automatic Frequency Ratio Controller
AFRCC	Air Force Rescue Coordination Center (USAF)
AFREIC	Air Force Radiation Effects Information Center (USAF)
AFRES	Air Force Reserve (USAF)
AFRID	Automatic Fuze Radiograph Inspection Device
AFROSAI	African Organization of Supreme Audit Institutions
AFROTC	Air Force Reserve Officers Training Corps (USAF)
AFRPL	Air Force Rocket Propulsion Laboratory (USAF)
AFRRI	Armed Forces Radiobiology Research Institute (USDOD)
AFRTS	American Forces Radio and Television Service

AFS — Aeronautical Fixed Service
American Fertility Service (USA)
American Fisheries Society (USA)
American Foundrymens Society (USA)
Atomic Fluorescence Spectrometry
Atomic Fluorescence Spectroscopy

AFSAB — Air Force Science Advisory Board (USAF)

AFSATCOM — Air Force Satellite Communications System (USAF)

AFSC — Air Force Systems Command (USAF)
Automatic Frame Scan Control

AFSCF — Air Force Satellite Control Facility (USAF)

AFSCM — Air Force Systems Command Manual (series issued by USAF)

AFSCP — Air Force System Command Pamphlet (series issued by USAF)

AFSCR — Air Force Systems Command Regulation (series issued by USAF)

AFSIG — Air Force Surveys In Geophysics (USAF)

AFSINC — Air Force Service Information and News Center (USAF)

AFSOUTH — Allied Forces Southern Europe (of NATO)

AFSWC — Air Force Special Weapons Center (USAF)

AFT — Analysis of the Functions of Transportation

AFTA — Avionics Fault Tree Analyzer

AFTAC — Air Force Technical Applications Center (USAF)

AFTEC — Air Force Test and Evaluation Center (USAF)

AFTER — Air Force Thermionic Engineering and Research (a program at Stanford University (USA))

AFTI — Advanced Fighter Technology Integration (a project of USAF)

AFTN — Aeronautical Fixed Telecommunications Network

AFTO — Air Force Technical Order (USAF)

AFTP — Association Francaise de Techniciens du Petrole (France) (French Association of Petroleum Technicians)

AFTPRC — Air Force Thermophysical Properties Research Center (USAF)

AFV — Armoured Fighting Vehicle

AFVG — Anglo-French Variable Geometry aircraft

AFVOA — Aberdeen Fishing Vessel Owners Association

AFWL — Air Force Weapons Laboratory (USAF)

AFWTR — Air Force Western Test Range (USAF)

AG — Advisory Group
Aktiengesellschaft (Public Stock Company)
Alternate Gradient
Anti-Globulin

AGA — Abrasive Grain Association (USA)
Aerodrome, Air Routes and Ground Aids (a division of ICAO)
Air-to-Ground-to-Air
American Gas Association (USA)
Australian Gas Association (Australia)

AGACS — Automatic Ground-to-Air Communications System
Automatic Ground-to-Air Communications Systems

AGARD — Advisory Group for Aerospace Research and Development (of NATO)

AGARD-LS — AGARD (of NATO) Lecture Series

AGARDograph — prefix to numbered series of monographs issued by AGARD (of NATO)

AGASS — Automated Geomagnetic Airborne Survey System

AGATE — Accessibility to Gate Arrays through Technology and Engineering

AGAVE — Automatic Gimbled-Antenna Vectoring Equipment

AGC — Advanced Gas Centrifuge
Air Ground Chart
Associated General Contractors of America (USA)
Automatic Gain Control

AGCA — Automatic Ground-Controlled Approach

AGCAS — Association of Graduate Careers Advisory Services

AGCL — Automatic Ground-Controlled Landing

AGCT — Adenine-Guanine-Cytosine-Thymine

AGD — Agar Gel Diffusion
Axial Gear Differential

AGDT — Advisory Group on Data Transmission (of NEDO)

AGE — Aerospace Ground Equipment
Allyl Glycidyl Ether
Asian Geotechnical Engineering (an information centre of the Asian Institute of Technology (Thailand))

AGED — Advisory Group on Electron Devices (USDOD)

AGES — Air/Ground Engagement Simulation

AGET — Advisory Group on Electron Tubes (USDOD)

AGF — Arbeitsgemeinschaft Getreideforschung (Germany) (Grain Research Association)

AGHS — Australian Garden History Society (Australia)

AGHTM — Association Generale des Hygienistes et Techniciens Munipaux (General Association of Municipal Health and Technical Experts)

AGI — American Geological Institute (USA)

AGID — Association of Geoscientists for International Development

AGIFORS — Airlines Group of International Federation of Operations Research Societies

AGIL — Airborne General Illumination Light

AGILE — Analytic Geometry Interpretive Language
AUTONETICS General Information Learning Equipment

AGIPA — Adaptive Ground Implemented Phased Array

AGIPAC — AGIE (A.G. fur Industrielle Elektronic (Switzerland)) Interactive Programming and Calculations

AGIS — Acoustographic Imaging System
Association of Ground Investigation Specialists

AGISS — AGFA-GEVAERT Identification Security System

AGL — Above Ground Level
Aktionsgemeinschaft Luftfahrt (Germany) (Association for Promoting Aviation)
Automated Group Learning

AGLINET — Agricultural Libraries Information Network (of IAALD & FAO (un))

AGM — Air-to-Ground Missile
Auxiliary General Missile

AGMA — American Gear Manufacturers Association (USA)

AGMC — Aerospace Guidance and Metrology Center (USAF)

AGN — Active Galactic Nuclei
Acute Glomerulonephritis

AGNIS — Azimuth Guidance Nose-In Stand

AGO — Atmospheric Gas Oil

AGOR — Auxiliary General Oceanographic Research

AGP — Agar Gel Precipitation

AGPA — American Group Psychotherapy Association (USA)

AGPS — Australian Government Publishing Service (Australia)

AGPU — Aviation Ground Power Unit

AGR — Advanced Gas-cooled Graphite-moderated Reactor
Advanced Gas-cooled Reactor

AGRA — Association of Genealogists and Record Agents

AGRE — Atlantic Gas Research Exchange (of British Gas Corporation, American Gas Association and Gaz de France)

AGREE Advanced Ground Receiving Equipment Experiment (of NASA (USA) and Nippon Hoso Kyokai (Japan))
Advisory Group for Reliability of Electronic Equipment (USDOD and US Industry)

AGREP Permanent Inventory of Agricultural Research Projects (in the EEC)

AGRI/MECH prefix to numbered series issued by the Group of Experts on Mechanization of Agriculture (of ECE (UNO))

AGRICC Automatic Generation and Retrieval of Information on Chemical Components

AGRICOLA Agricultural On-Line Access (of National Agricultural Library (USA)

AGRIS International Information System for the Agricultural Sciences and Technology (of FAO (UN))

AgRISTARS Agricultural and Resources Inventory Survey through Aerospace Remote Sensing (USA)

AGRR Association Generale de Retraite par Repartition (France)

AGS Acoustic Guidance Sonar
Air Grease System
Aircraft General Standards (issued by SBAC)
Alternating-Gradient Synchroton

AGSD Advisory Group on Systems Definitions (of the Post Office and telecommunications industry)

AGT ADAGE Graphics Terminal
Advanced Gas Turbine
Advanced Ground Transport
Aircraft-derivative Gas Turbine

AGTELIS Automated Ground Transportable Emitter Location and Identification System

AGTV Active-Gated Television
Advanced Ground Transportation Vehicle

AGU American Geophysical Union (USA)

AGVG Anglo-German Variable Geometry aircraft

AGVS Automatic Guided Vehicles System

AGW Air-to-Ground Warfare

AGWN Additive Gaussian White Noise

AH Adenohypophysis
Armed Helicopter

AHA American Heart Association (USA)
American Hospital Association (USA)
American Humane Association
Area Health Authority

AHAB Attacking Hardened Air Bases

AHAM Association of Home Appliance Manufacturers (USA)

AHAMS Advanced Heavy Anti-tank Missile System
Advanced Heavy Assault Missile System

AHAS Acetohydroxy Acid Synthase

AHC Acute Haemorrhagic Conjunctivitis
Australian Heritage Commission (Australia)

AHD Audio High Density

AHEA American Home Economics Association (USA)

AHEAD Army Help for Education and Development (a project of the US Army)

AHEM Association of Hydraulic Equipment Manufacturers

AHF Antihaemophilic Factor

AHFITB Agricultural, Horticultural and Forestry Industry Training Board

AHFRAC Army Human Factors Research Advisory Committee (US Army)

AHG Anti-Haemophilic Globulin

AHH Aryl Hydrocarbon Hydroxylase

AHI Approach, Horizon Indicator

AHIL Association of Hospital and Institution Libraries (USA)

AHIRS Australian Health Information and Research Service (Australia)

AHIS Automated Hospital Information System

AHL Alcohol Induced Hyperlipidemia

AHMA American Hotel and Motel Association (USA)

AHME Association for Hospital Medical Education (USA)

AHMI Appalachian Hardwood Manufacturers, Inc (USA)

AHMSA Altos Hornos de México SA (Mexico)

AHONAS Association of Highway Officials of the North Atlantic States (USA)

AHP Association for Humanistic Psychology (USA)

AHPA Appalachian Helicopter Pilots Association

AHPL A Hardware Programming Language

AHR Acceptable Hazard Rate
Aqueous Homogeneous Reactor
Association for Health Records (USA)

AHRI ARMAUER HANSEN Research Institute (Ethiopia)

AHRS Attitude and Heading Reference System

AHRTAG Appropriate Health Resources and Techologies Group

AHS American Helicopter Society (USA)
Antiquarian Horological Society

AHSB Authority Health and Safety Branch (UKAEA) (now Authority Safety and Reliability Directorate)

AHSE Assembly, Handling and Shipping Equipment

AHSP Association for High Speed Photography

AHT Anchor Handling Tugs
Association of Highway Technicians

AHU Anti-Halation Undercoat

AHV Altos Hornos de Vizcaya (Spain)

AI Air-India (India)
Airborne Intercept OR Interception
Articulation Index
Artificial Insemination
Artificial Intelligence
Asphalt Institute (USA)
Attitude Indicator

AIA Abrasive Industries Association
Accident/Incident Analysis
Aerospace Industries Association (USA)
Asbestos Information Association (USA)
Association of International Accountants
Associazione Italiana delle Industrie Aerospaziali (Italy) (Italian Aerospace Industry Association)

AIAA American Institute of Aeronautics and Astronautics (USA)

AIAAM Advanced Intercept Air-to-Air Missile

AIAC Air Industries Association of Canada (Canada) (now Aerospace Industries Association of Canada)

AIAG Aluminium Industrie AG (Switzerland)

AIB Accidents Investigation Branch (of DTp)
Anti-Inflation Board (Canada)
Association des Industries de Belgique (Belgium)
Associazione Italiana Biblioteche (Italy) (Italian Library Association)
prefix to numbered series of Agriculture Information Bulletins issued by USDA (USA)

AIBA Agricultural Information Bank for Asia (a project of SEARCA (Philippines))

AIBC Architectural Institute of British Columbia (Canada)

AIBCM Association of Industrialised Building Component Manufacturers

AIBD Association of International Bond Dealers

AIBDA Asociacion Interamericana de Bibliotecarios y Documentalistas Agricolas (Inter-American Association of Agricultural Librarians and Documentalists)

AIBF Advanced Internally-Blown jet Flap

AIBN Azobisisobutyronitrile

AIBS American Institute of Biological Sciences (USA)

AIC
Academie Internationale de la Ceramique (Switzerland) (International Academy of Ceramics)
Agricultural Institute of Canada (Canada)
American Institute of Chemists (USA)
Asbestos Information Committee
Asociacion Interamerican de Contabilidad (Inter-American Association of Accountants)
Association Internationale Cybernetique (Belgium) (International Cybernetic Association)
Association Internationale de la Couleur (International Colour Association)
Associazione Italiana Cartografia (Italian Cartographic Association)
Automatic Iris Control
H. AKAIKE Information Criterion
prefix to numbered/dated series of Aeronautical Information Circulars issued by CAA

AIC/INT
Aerodynamic Influence Coefficients with Interference

AICA
Association Internationale pour le Calcul Analogique (International Association for Analogue Computing)
Associazione Italiana per il Calco Automatico (Italy) (Italian Association for Automatic Data Processing)

AICBM
Anti-Intercontinental Ballistic Missile

AICC
All-Indian Congress Committee (India)
Antibody-Induced Cell-mediated Cytoxicity

AICCF
Association Internationale des Congres des Chemins de Fer (International Railway Congress Association)

AICD
Accelerated Individual and Company Development

AICE
American Institute of Consulting Engineers (now part of ACEC (USA))

AICH
Automatic Integrated Container Handling

AIChE
American Institute of Chemical Engineers (USA)

AICMA
Association Internationale des Constructeurs de Matériel Aérospatial (now AECMA)

AICMR
Association Internationale des Constructeurs de Matériel Roulant (International Association of Rolling Stock Manufacturers (federated into UNIFE in 1976))

AICN
Asociacion de Inestigacion de la Construccion Naval (Spain) (Shipbuilding Research Association)

AICOBOO
All-India Confederation of Bank Officers Organisations (India)

AICPA
American Institute of Certified Public Accountants (USA)

AICQ
Associazione Italiana per il Controllo della Qualita (Italy) (Italian Association for Quality Control)

AICR
Association for International Cancer Research

AICRO
Association of Independent Contract Research Organisations

AICS
Advanced Interior Communication System
Air Intake Control System
Association of Independent Computer Specialists
Automated Industrial Control System
Automatic Inlet Control System

AICV
Armoured Infantry Combat Vehicle

AID
Adaptive Intelligent Dialogue
Aeronautical Inspection Directorate (MINTECH)
Agency for International Development (of State Department (USA))
Airborne Intelligent Display
Amphibious Inhaul Device
Analogue Interface Device
Area Imaging Device
Artificial Insemination by Donor
Associative Interactive Dictionary
Attached Inflatable Decelerator
Automated Industrial Drilling
Automatic Information Distribution
Automatic Interaction Detection

AIDA
Analysis of Interconnected Decision Areas
Association Internationale de la Distribution des Produits Alimentaires et des Produits de Grande Consommation
Associazione Italiana per le Documentatione (Italy) (Italian Documentation Association)
Australian Industries Development Association (Australia)
Automatic Intruder Detector Alarm

AIDAPS
Automatic Inspection, Diagnostic And Prognostic Systems

AIDAS
Advanced Instrumentation and Data Analysis System

AIDATS
Army In-flight Data Transmission System (US Army)

AIDC
Australian Industry Development Corporation (Australia)

AIDD
American Institute for Design and Drafting (USA)
Auckland Industrial Development Division (of DSIR (New Zealand))

AIDE
Automated Integrated Design and Engineering

AIDE/TPS
Advanced Interactive Data Entry/Transaction Processing System

AIDES
Automated Image Data Extraction System

AIDI
Associazione Italiana per la Documentazione e l'Informazione (Italy) (Italian Association for Documentation and Information)

AIDIS
Asocacion Inter-americana de Ingeniera Sanitaria (Inter-American Association of Sanitary Engineering)
Associazione Italiana di Ingeneria Sismica (Italy) (Italian Institute of Seismic Engineering)

AIDJEX
Arctic Ice Dynamics Joint Experiment (a project of Canada and USA)

AIDR
Association Internationale de Developpement Rural (Belgium) (International Association for Rural Development)

AIDS
Acoustic Intelligence Data System
Acquired Immune Deficiency Syndrome
Adaptive Intrusion Data System
Advanced Impact Drilling System
Advanced Interactive Display System
Advanced Interconnection Development System
Airborne Information Display System
Aircraft Integrated Data System
Aircraft Intrusion Detection System
All-purpose Interactive Debugging System
American Institute for Decision Sciences (USA)
Automated Information Dissemination System

AIDSCOM
Army Information Data Systems Command (US Army)

AIDUS
Automated Information Directory Update System
Automated Input and Document Update System

AIEA
Agence Internationale de l'Energie Atomique (International Atomic Energy Agency)

AIEC
Association of Iron Exporting Countries

AIECE
Association d'Instituts Europeens de Conjecture Economique (Association of European Institutions of Economic Forecasting)

AIEE
American Institute of Electrical Engineers (now IEEE) (USA)

AIEI
Association of Indian Engineering Industry (India)

AIENDF
Atomics International Evaluation Nuclear Data File

AIEP
Association Internationale des Usagers d'Embranchements Particuliers (International Association of Users of Private Branch Railway Sidings)

AIESEC — Association Internationale des Etudiants en Sciences Economiques et Commerciales (International Association of Students of Economic and Commercial Sciences)

AIF — Arbeitsgemeinschaft Industrieller Forschungsvereinigungen (Germany) (Association of Industrial Research Organisations)
Army Industrial Fund (US Army)
Atomic Industrial Forum (USA)

AIFST — Australian Institute of Food Science and Technology (Australia)

AIFTAA — Anglo–Irish Free Trade Area Agreement

AIFV — Armoured Infantry Fighting Vehicle

AIG — Architects in Industry Group
Association Internationale Geodesie (France) (International Association of Geodesy)
Augmented Inertial Guidance

AIGA — American Institute of Graphic Arts (USA)

AIGMF — All India Glass Manufacturers Federation (India)

AIHA — American Industrial Hygiene Association (USA)

AIHC — American Industrial Health Conference (USA)
American Industrial Health Council (USA)

AIIC — Association Internationale des Interpretes de Conference (France) (International Association of Conference Interpreters)

AIIE — American Institute of Industrial Engineers (USA) (became IIE in 1982)

AIIHPH — All India Institute of Hygiene and Public Health (India)

AIIM — Association for Information and Image Management (USA)

AIIMH — All India Institute of Mental Health (India)

AIIMS — All-India Institute of Medical Sciences

AIIP — Advanced Industrial Instrumentation Project (of MINTECH)

AIIPMR — All India Institute of Physical Medicine and Rehabilitation (India)

AIISUP — Association Internationale d'Information Universitaire et Professionnelle (International Association for Educational and Vocational Information)

AIL — American Institute of Laundering (USA)
Association of International Libraries

AIL-SST — American Industry and Labor for the Super-Sonic Transport (USA) (a committee)

AILAS — Automatic Instrument Landing Approach System

AILS — Advanced Integrated Landing System

AILSA — Aerospace Industrial Life Sciences Association (USA)

AILSS — Advanced Integrated Life Support System

AIM — Accuracy In Media (an organization) (USA)
Advanced in Medicine (a charitable trust)
Aerial Intercept Missile
Aerothermodynamic Integration Model
Aerotriangulation by observation of Independent Models
Air Intercept Missile
American institute for Microminiaturization (USA)
Asian Institute of Management (Philippines)
Association des Ingénieurs Électriciens sortis de l'Institut Èlectrotechnique Montefiore (Belgium)
Association pour les Applications de l'Informatique a la Medecine (France) (Association for the Application of Data Processing to Medicine)
Associazione Italiani di Metallurgia (Italy) (Italian Association of Metallurgy)
Atlantic International Marketing Association (USA)
Australian Institute of Management (Australia)
Australian Institute of Metals (Australia)
Automated Inventory Management
Avalanche Induced Migration

AIM-TWX — Abridged INDEX MEDICUS via the Teletypewriters Exchange Network (of NLM (USA))

AIMA — All-India Management Association (India)

AIMAV — Association Internationale pour la Recherche et la Diffusion des Méthodes Audio-Visuelles et Structuroglobales

AIMC — Association of Internal Management Consultants (USA)

AIME — American Institute of Mining, Metallurgical and Petroleum Engineers (USA)
AUTODIN Interface in a Multiprogramming Environment

AIMES — Automated Inventory Management Evaluation System

AIMEX — Symposium and Exhibition of Advanced Industrial Measurement and Control

AIMF — Australasian Institute of Metal Finishing (Australia)

AIMIC — Association of Insurance Managers in Industry and Commerce (now AIRMIC)

AIMILO — Army/Industrial Material Information Liaison Offices (USA)

AIMIS — Advanced Integrated Modular Instrumentation System

AIMLS — Australian Institute of Medical Laboratory Scientists (Australia)

AIMMPE — American Institute of Mining, Metallurgical and Petroleum Engineers (USA)

AIMO — All-India Manufacturers Organisation (India)
Association of Industrial Medical Offices

AIMP — Anchored Interplanetary Monitoring Platform

AIMS — Air Traffic Control Radar System, Identification Friend or Foe, Military Identification System
Air traffic control/Identity friend or foe/Mark II Military classified Systems
Airborne Integrated Maintenance System
Airport Income Management System
Altitude Identification and Military System
American Institute of Merchant Shipping (USA)
ARBAT (CONSULTANTS) Interactive Multi-user System
Arlington Inventory Management System
Association for Improvements in the Maternity Services
AUERBACH Information Management System
Australian Institute of Marine Science (Australia)
Automated Industrial Management System

AIMVAL — Air Intercept Missile Evaluation (a joint program of USN and USAF)

AIN — American Institute of Nutrition (USA)
Australian Institute of Navigation (Australia)

AINA — American Institute of Nautical Archaeology (USA)
Arctic Institute of North America (USA)

AINDT — Australian Institute for Non-Destructive Testing (Australia)

AINE — Asociacion de Ingenerios Navales de Espana (Spain) (Spanish Association of Naval Engineers)

AINS — Area-Inertial Navigation System

AINSE — Australian Institute of Nuclear Science and Engineering (Australia)

AIO — Action Information Organization
Arecibo Ionospheric Observatory (Puerto Rico)

AIOD — Automatic Identification of Outward Dialing
Automatic Identified Outward Dialing

AIOP — Association Internationale d'Oceanographie Physique (International Association of Physical Oceanography)

AIOPI Association of Information Officers in the Pharmaceutical Industry

AIOTT Action Information Organisation and Tactical Trainer

AIP Aldosterone-Induced Protein
American Institute of Physics (USA)
American Institute of Planners (USA)
Anti-Inflammatory Protein
Association Internationale de Photobiologie (International Photobiology Association)
Associazione Italiana Prefabbricazione per l'Edilizia Industrializzata (Italy) (Italian Association for Prefabrication in Industrialised Building)
Australian Institute of Petroleum (Australia)
Automated Imagery Processing

AIPA Accident Initiation and Progression Analysis (a project sponsored by ERDA (USA))
Associazione Italiana Planificazione Aziendale (Italy)
Australian Independent Publishers Association (Australia)

AIPC Agar Immersion, Plating and Contact
Association Internationale des Palais de Congress (International Association of Congress Centres)
AssociationInternationale des Ponts et Charpentes (International Association for Bridge and Structural Engineering)

AIPCEE Association des Industries du Poisson de la C.E.E. (Association of the Fish Industries of the European Economic Community)

AIPE American Institute of Plant Engineers (USA)

AIPH Association Internationale des Producteurs de l'Horticulture (International Association of Horticultural Producers)

AIPMA All-India Plastics Manufacturers Association (India)

AIPND Associazione Italiana Prova Non Distruttiva (Italy) (Italian Non-destructive Testing Association)

AIPS Australian Institute of Political Science (Australia)

AIPU Associative Information Processing Unit

AIR Acoustic Intercept Receiver
Aerospace Information Report (series issued by SAE)
Air Inflatable Retarder
Air Injection Reactor
Air Intercept Rocket
Airborne Interceptor Rocket
Airworthiness (a committee of ICAO)
All-India Radio (India)
American Institute for Research in the Behavioral Sciences (USA)
Asociacion Interamericana de Radiodifusion (USA) (Inter-American Broadcasting Association)
prefix to numbered series of standards issued by DTCA (France)

AIR/MMH Acoustic Intercept Receiver/Multimode Hydrophone system

AIRAC Aeronautical Information Regulation and Control
Australian Ionising Radiation Advisory Council (Australia)

AIRAPT Association International pour l'Advancement de la Recherche et de la Technologie aux Haute Pressions (International Association for the Advancement of Research and Technology of High Pressures)

AIRC Airworthiness Committee (of ICAO)
Associazione Italiana per la Ricera sul Cancro (Italy) (Italian Association for Cancer Research)

AIRCAT Automated Integrated Radar Control for Air Traffic

AIRCO Air-line Industrial Relations Conference (USA)

AIRCOM Air Force Communications System (USAF)

AIRD Asian Institute for Rural Development (India)

AIRDIS Australian Industrial Research and Development Incentives Scheme (Australia)

AIREA American Institute of Real Estate Appraisers (USA)

AIRES Advanced Imagery Requirements Exploitation System

AIRG Australian Industrial Research Group (Australia)

AIRIA All India Rubber Industries Association (India)

AIRIEL Italian Association for Research in the Application of Elastomers (Italy)

AIRLOC Air Lines of Communication

AIRLORD Airline Load Optimisation, Recording and Display

AIRMAP Air Monitoring, Analysis and Prediction

AIRMEC Association Internationale pour la Recherche Medicale et les Echanges Culturels (France) (International Association for Medical Research and Intellectual Exchanges)

AIRMIC Association of Insurance and Risk Managers in Industry and Commerce

AIRO Associazione Italiana di Ricerca Operativa (Italy) (Italian Association for Operational Research)

AIROF Anodic Iridium Oxide Film

AIRPAP Air Pressure Analysis Programme

AIRS Advanced Inertial Reference Sphere
African (EAST AFRICAN AIRWAYS) International Reservation System
Airborne Integrated Reconnaissance System
Airport Information Retrieval System
Alliance of Information and Referral Services (USA)
Automatic Image Retrieval System

AIRScoop Air-Scooping vehicle

AIRSOUTH Allied Air Forces Southern Europe (NATO)

AIRSS ABRES Instrumentation Range Safety System

AIRTRANS Intra-Airport Transportation System

AIS Abbreviated Injury Scale
Adaptive Information Selector
Advanced Isotope Separation
Air System Interrogator
American Interplanetary Society (USA) (later American Rocket Society)
Answer in Sentence
Association Internationale de la Savonnerie et de la Detergence (Belgium) (International Association of Soap and Detergents Manufacturers)
Automated Information System
Automatic Intercept System
Avionics Intermediate Shop

AISB Society for the Study of Artificial Intelligence and the Simulation of the Brain)

AISC American Institute of Steel Construction (USA)
Association of Independent Software Companies (USA)
Australian Institute of Steel Construction (Australia)

AISE Association of Iron and Steel Engineers (USA)
Average Integral Square Error

AISG Accountants International Study Group (of the three chartered institutes of the United Kingdom, the Canadian Institute of Chartered Accountants, and the AICPA (USA))

AISI American Iron and Steel Institute (USA)

AISLE An Inter-Society Liaison Committee on the Environment (USA)

AISM Association Internationale de Signalisation Maritime (International Association of Marine Signalling)

AISR Army Institute of Surgical Research (US Army)

AIST	Agency of Industrial Science and Technology (of MITI (Japan))
	Automatic Informational Station
AIT	Acoustic Impact Technique OR Test
	Advanced Individual Training
	Advanced Information Technology
	Alliance Internationale de Tourisme (Switzerland) (International Alliance for Tourism)
	Asian Institute of Technology (Thailand)
	Asociacion de Investigacion del Transporte (Spain) (Transport Research Association)
	Auto-Ignition Temperature
AITC	American Institute of Timber Construction (USA)
	Association Internationale des Traducteurs de Conference (Switzerland) (International Association of Conference Translators)
AITFA	Association des Ingenieurs et Techniciens Francaise des Aeroglisseurs (France) (Association of French Air Cushion Vehicle Engineers and Technicians)
AITPCI	Association des Ingenieurs, Techniciens et Professionnels du Controle Industrielle (France) (Association of Engineers, Technicians and Training Officers of Industrial Control)
AITUC	All-India Trades Union Congress (India)
AIU	Advanced Instrumentation Unit (of NPL)
	Association Internationale des Universites (International Association of Universities)
AIUFFAS	Association Internationale des Utilisateurs de Files de Fibres Artificielles et Synthétiques (France) (International Association of Users of Artificial and Synthetic Yarn)
AIUM	American Institute of Ultrasound in Medicine (USA)
AIV	AMETS Instrumentation Vehicle
AIVF	Association des Ingenieurs des Villes de France (France) (Municipal Engineers Association of France)
AIW	Auroral Infrasonic Wave
	Auroral Intrasonic Wave
AJ	Anti-Jam
	Antijamming
AJIS	Automated Jail Information System (County of Los Angeles (USA))
AJM	Abrasive Jet Machining
AJPC	Accountants Joint Parliamentary Committee
AJRT	Adaptive Jam-Resistant Tranceiver
AKEB	Aktiengesellschaft fur Kernenergie Beteiligungen (Switzerland)
AKES	Automatic Kinetic Enzyme System
AKEW	Arbeitsgemeinschaft Kernkraftwerk der Elektrizitatswirtschaft (Austria)
AKF	Amtskommunernes og Kommunernes Forskningsinstitut (Denmark) (Regional and Local Authorities Research Institute)
	Australian Kidney Foundation (Association)
AKIE	Arbeitskries Industrial Engineering (Germany)
AKK	Atomkraft Konsortiet Krangede (Sweden)
AKM	Apogee Kick Motor
AKWIC	Author and Key Word In Context
AL	Action Learning
	Aeronomy Laboratory (of ESSA (USA)) (now of NOAA (USA))
	Assembler Language
Al-Li	Aluminium-Lithium
ALA	American Library Association (USA)
	American Logistics Association (USA)
	Aminolevulinic Acid
	Austral Lineas Aereas (Argentina)
ALA-COA	American Library Association Committee on Accreditation (USA)
ALA-ISAD	American Library Association's Information Science and Automation Division (USA)
ALAC	Artificial Limb and Appliance Centre
ALAD	Aminolevulinic Acid Dehydratase
ALADIN	Algebraic Automated Digital Iterative Network calculation
ALAF	Asociacion Latinoamericana da Ferrocarriles (Argentina) (Latin-American Railways Asociation
ALAHUA	Associacion Latino Americana para la Promocion de l'Habitat, la Arquitectura y el Urbanismo (Ecuador) (Latin American Association for the Promotion of the Habitat, Architecture and Town Planning)
ALAINEE	Asociacion Latinoamericana de la Industria Electrica y Electronica (Latin-American Electrical and Electronic Association)
ALAIRS	Advanced Low Altitude Infra-Red Reconnaissance Sensor
ALALC	Asociacion Latinoamericana de Libre Comercio (Latin-America Free trad Association)
ALAM	Association of Lightweight Aggregate Manufacturers
	Atlas LISP Algebraic Manipulator
ALAP	Associative Linear Array Processor
ALARA	As Low As is Reasonably Achievable (occupational radiation exposure)
ALARM	A Logistics Analysis and Ranking Model
	Air-Launched Anti-Radiation Missile
	Alerting Long Range Airborne Radar for MTI (Moving Target Indicator)
	Automatic Light Aircraft Readiness Monitor
ALARR	Air-Launched Air-Recoverable Rocket
ALAS	Automated Literature Alerting System
ALAT	Aviation Legere de l'Armee de Terre (France) (Light Aviation Wing of the French Army)
ALAW	Advanced Light Anti-tank Weapon
ALB	Airborne Laser Bathymeter
	Arbeitsgemeinschaft Landwirtschaftliches Bauwesen (Germany) (Working Committee on Farm Buildings)
	Assembly Line Balancing
ALBANY	Adjustment of Large Blocks with ANY number of photos, points and images, using ANY photogrammetric measuring instrument and on ANY computer
ALBI	Air-Launched Ballistic Interceptor
ALBM	Air-Launched Ballistic Missile
ALBO	Automatic Line Build-Out
ALBSU	Adult Literacy and Basic Skills Unit (Of the National Institute of Adult Education)
ALC	Adaptive Logic Circuit
	Amoeba-less Life Cycle
	Armament Logistics Command (US Army)
ALCA	American Leather Chemists Association (USA)
ALCAPP	Automative List Classification And Profile Production
ALCARS	Airborne Launch Control and Recovery System
ALCASA	Aluminio del Caroni SA (Venezuela)
ALCATEL	Societe Alsacienne de Constructions Atomiques, de Telecommuncations et d'Electronique (France)
ALCC	Airborne Launch Control Centre
	Association of London Computer Clubs
ALCH	Approach-Light Contact Height
ALCL	Association of London Chief Librarians
ALCM	Air-Launched Cruise Missile
ALCOR	ARPA – LINCOLN (LABORATORY (of MIT (USA)) Coherent Observable Radar
	ARPA (USA) (Laboratory of MIT (USA)) C-band Observable Radar
	ARPA-LINCOLN Coherent Observable Radar
ALCS	Airborne Launch Control System
	Airborne Launch Control System
	Authors Lending and Copyright Society Ltd

ALCU Agricultural Librarians in Colleges and Universities

ALD Advanced Laser Designator
Advanced Logic Design

ALDCS Active Lift Distribution Control System

ALDEP Automated Layout Design Programme

ALDP Automatic Language Data Processing

ALDS Analysis of Large Data Sets

ALE Automatic Line Equalization
Aviazione Leggera Esercito (Italy) (Army Air Corps)
Avionics Logistics Effects

ALEA Airborne Law Enforcement Association (USA)

ALEBCI Asociacion Latinoamericana de Escuelas de Bibliotecologia y Ciencias de la Informacion (Mexico) (Latin American Association of Schools of Librarianship and Information Science)

ALEC Analysis of Linear Electronic Circuits

ALECS Automated Law Enforcement Communications System (USA)
AFWL LOS ALAMOS EMP (Electromagnetic Pulse) Calibration and Simulation (a facility of the USAF)

ALECSO Arab League Educational, Cultural and Scientific Organization (Tunis)

ALEGEO Latin American Association of Editors in the Earth Sciences

ALEM Association of Loading Equipment Manufacturers

ALEMAS Agrupacion Nacional de Alquitrones, Emulsiones, Asfaltos Impermeabilizantes (Spain)

ALERT Alcohol Level Evaluation Roadside Test
All Africa Leprosy Rehabilitation and Training Centre (Ethiopia)
All-Africa Leprosy and Rehabilitation Training Centre (Ethiopia)
Automated Law Enforcement Reporting Technique

ALERTS Airborne Laser Equipment Real-Time Surveillance

ALF Approach Light Facility
Automatic Letter Facer

ALFA Automatic Line Fault Analysis

ALFC Automatic Load-Frequency Control

ALFGL Automatic Low Frequency Gain Limiting

ALFT Aviation Légère de la Force Terreste (Belgium) (Army Air Force)

ALG Antilymphocyte Globulin

ALGaAS Aluminium Gallium-Arsenide-Silicon

ALGEC Algorithmic Language for Economics Calculations

ALGES Association of Local Government Engineers and Surveyors

ALGOL Algorithmic Language

ALGS Approach and Landing Guidance System
Association of London Graduates and Students (of Institution of Civil Engineers)

ALH Advanced Light Helicopter

ALI Air-Launched Interceptor
Annual Limit of Intake

ALIA Association of Lecturers in Accountancy

ALIC Australian Libraries and Information Council (Australia)

ALICS Assembly Language by INFORMATION CONTROL SYSTEMS, INC.

ALIMD Association of Life Insurance Medical Directors (USA)

ALIRATS Airborne Laser Illuminator, Ranging and Tracking System

ALIRT Adaptive Long Range Infra-Red Tracker

ALISE Association for Library and Information Science Education (USA)

ALIT Advanced Technology Light Twin (a project of NASA (USA))
Automatic Line Insulation Test

ALKEM Alpha Chemie und Metallurgie (Germany)

ALL Acute Lymphoblastic Leukaemia
Airborne Laser Laboratory

ALLA Allied Long Lines Agency (of NATO)

ALLC Association of Literary and Linguistic Computing

ALLD Airborne Locator Laser Designator

ALLP Adaptive Lattice Linear Prediction

ALM Airfield Landing Mat
Atelier de Fabrication du Mans (France (of GIAT))

ALMC Army Logistic Management Center (US Army)

ALMIDS Army Logistics Management Integrated Data System (US Army)

ALMS Air-Lift Management System (USAF)
Aircraft Landing Measurement System
Analytic Language Manipulation System
Automated Logic Mapping System

ALMSA Automated Logistics Management Systems Agency (US Army)

ALMV Air Launched Miniature Vehicle

ALO Albuquerque Operations Office (of USAEC)

ALOC Air Line of Communication

ALOFT Airborne Light/Optical Fiber Technology (a program of the USN)

ALOHA Additive Links On-line Hawaii Area System (of Hawaii University)

ALOIT Association of Library Officers-in-Training (Australia)

ALOR Advanced Lunar Orbital Rendezvous

ALORS Advanced Large Object Recovery System

ALOSH Appalachian Laboratory for Occupational Safety and Health (of NIOSH (USA))

ALOTS Airborne Lightweight Optical Tracking System

ALP Alternative Launch Point
Arithmetic and Logic Processor
Articulated Loading Platform
AUTOCODE List Processing

ALPAC Automatic Language Processing Advisory Committee (of NAS)

ALPC Army Logistics Policy Council (US Army)

ALPHA Army Materiel Command Logistics Program – Hardcore Automated (US Army)
Automatic Lector Position Handwriting machine
Automatic Literature Processing, Handling and Analysis

ALPS Advanced Liquid Propulsion System
Assembly Line Planning System
Automated Letter Preparation System
Automatic Landing and Positioning System

ALPSP Association of Learned and Professional Society Publishers

ALQAS Aircraft Landing Quality Assessment Scheme

ALR Arbeitsgruppe fur Luft-und Raunfahrt (Aerospace Task Force) (a group of Swiss Scientists)
Artillery Locating Radar

ALRA Adult Literacy Resource Agency (of the National Institute of Adult Education) (disbanded 1978)

ALRC Anti-Locust Research Centre (now merged into Centre for Overseas Pest Research of the Overseas Development Administration of the Foreign and Commonwealth Office)

ALRI Airborne Long Range Input

ALS Advanced Logistics System (of AFLC (USAF))
Amyotrophic Lateral Sclerosis
Antilymphocytic Serum
Approach-Light System
Associative List Searcher
Automated Library System
Azimuth Laying Set
ALSA Annular Lens Soft Aperture
ALSAM Air-Launched Surface Attack Missile
ALSATEX Societe Alsacienne d'Etude et d'Exploitation (France)
ALSBM Air Launched Small Ballistic Missile
ALSC Advanced Logistics Systems Center (USAF)
Aluminium Linear Shaped Charge
Association for Library Services to Children (USA)
Automatic Level and Slope Control
ALSE APOLLO Lunar Sounder Experiment
Aviation Life Support Equipment
ALSEP APOLLO Lunar Surface Experiment Package
ALSER Axle-Load Survey Recorder
ALSPES Automated Laser Seeker Performance Evaluation System
ALSRC APOLLO Lunar Sample Return Container
ALSS Advanced Location Strike System
Airborne Location and Strike System
ALT Accelerated-Life Testing
Airborne Laser Tracker system
Approach and Landing Test (of the Space Shuttle)
Average Logistic Time
ALTA American Land Title Association (USA)
American Library Trustees Association (USA)
Association of Local Transport Airlines (USA)
ALTAIR ARPA Long-range Tracking and Instrumentation Radar
ALTAPE Automatic Line Tracing and Processing Equipment
ALTDS Army Laser Target Designator System (US Army)
ALTEL Artillery-Launched Television system
ALTEX Automatic Laboratory Techniques Exhibition
ALTS Automated Library Technical Services
ALTTC Advanced Level Telecommunications Training Centre (India)
ALU Adult Literacy Unit (within the National Institute of Adult Education)
Advanced Logical Utility
Arithmetic and Logic Unit
ALUPA Association Luxembourgeoise pour l'Utilisation Pacifique de l'Energie Atomique (Luxembourg) (Luxembourg Association for the Peaceful Uses of Atomic Energy)
ALV Air Launched Vehicle
Avian Leukosis Virus
ALVAO Association des Langues Vivantes pour l'Afrique Occidentale (Nigeria) (West African Modern Languages Association)
ALVRJ Air-launched, Low-Volume, Ramjet-powered
ALWIN Algorithmic Wiswesser Notation
ALWT Advanced Light-Weight Torpedo
AM Airlock Module
Alveolar Macrophages
Amplitude Modulation
Arbeitsgemeinschaft Magnetismus (Germany) (Study Group on Magnetism)
prefix to dated/numbered series on Aviation Medicine issued by the Office of Aviation Medicine (Federal Aviation Administration (USA))
prefix to numbered series issued by Applied Mechanics Division, California University (USA)
AM-MEMO prefix to numbered series of Memoranda issued by Aviation Medicine Branch, Department of Civil Aviation (Australia)
AM/MDA Airlock Module and Multiple Docking Adapter
AMA Adhesives Manufacturers Association
Aerospace Medical Association (USA)
Air Materiel Area (USAF) (now known as Air Logistics Center)
American Management Association (USA)
American Maritime Association (USA)
American Medical Association (USA)
Association of Metropolitan Authorities
Australian Medical Association (Australia)
Automatic Message Accounting
Automobile Manufacturers Association (USA)
AMA-MTR Automatic Message Accounting-Magnetic Tape Recording
AMAC Aircraft Monitoring and Control
AMACON a division of American Management Association
AMACUS Automated Microfilm Aperture Card Updating System
AMAD Activity Median Aerodynamic Diameters
Aircraft Mounted Accessory Drive
Airframe Mounted Accessory Drive
Airframe Mounted Auxiliary Drive system
AMAIS Agricultural Materials Analysis Information Service (of the Laboratory of the Government Chemist)
AMAP Aerospace Medical Association of the Philippines
AMAPI Association of Medical Advisers in the Pharmaceutical Industry
AMARC Army Materiel Acquisition Review Committee (US Army)
AMARS AUTONETICS Modular Airborne Radar Systems
AMARV Advanced Manoeuvring Re-entry Vehicle
AMAS Advanced Midcourse Active System
Astrometric Multiplexing Area Scanner
AMAVU Advanced Modular Audio Visual Unit
AMBIT Algebraic Manipulation By Identity Translation
AMC Acceptable Means of Compliance (series issued by ICAO)
Air Materiel Command (USAF) (reverted to original title in 1984)
Alkyd Moulding Compounds
American Mining Congress (USA)
American Movers Conference (USA)
Army Materiel Command (US Army) (became DARCOM in 1976)
Association of Municipal Corporations
Auto-Manual Centre
AMCA Advanced Materiel Concepts Agency (US Army)
Air Movement and Control Association (USA)
Air Moving and Conditioning Association (USA)
Architectural Metal Craftsmens Association
AMCAP Advanced Microwave Circuit Analysis Programme
AMCAWS Advanced Medium-Calibre Aircraft Weapon System
AMCCOM Armament Munitions and Chemical Command (US Army)
AMCEE Association for Media-based Continuing Education for Engineers (USA)
AMCL Advanced Material Concepts Laboratory (US Army)
AMCM Advanced Mine-Countermeasures
Airborne Mine Counter Measures
AMCO International Conference on Atomic Masses and Fundamental Constants
AMCOS ALDERMASTON Mechanized Cataloguing and Ordering System (of AWRE (MOD))
AMCP prefix to numbered series of Army Material Command Pamphlets (US Army)
AMCPSCC Army Materiel Command Packaging, Storage and Containerization Center (US Army)
AMCR Army Material Command Regulations (US Army)

AMCS Airborne Missile Control System
prefix to numbered series of reports issued by Division of Applied Mathematics and Computer Science, University of Virginia (USA)

AMD Aerospace Material Document – numbered/ lettered series of Specifications issued by SAE
Aerospace Medical Division (USAF)
Avions Marcel Dassault (France)
prefix to numbered series of Amendments to Standards already issued by BSI
prefix to numbered series on Atomic Molecular Data issued by ASTM (USA)

AMDA Advanced Manoeuvring Demonstration Aircraft
Airline Medical Directors Association

AMDEA Association of Manufacturers of Domestic Electrical Appliances

AMDEL Australian Mineral Development Laboratories (Australia)

AMDF Absolute Magnitude Difference Function

AMDI Acoustic Miss Distance Indicator

AMDRS Automatic Mobile Director and Reporting System

AMDS Arctic Mobile Drilling Structure

AME Acoustic-magneto-electric
Angle Measuring Equipment
Automatic Microfiche Editor
Automatic Monitoring Equipment
Aviation Medical Examiner

AMEAMS Adaptive Multibeam Experiment for Aeronautical and Maritime Services

AMECAP Mexican Personnel Training Association (Mexico)

AMEDA Automatic Microscope Electronic Data Accumulator

AMEDDPAS Army Medical Department Property Accounting System (US Army)

AMEDS Army Medical Service (US Army)
Automated Measurement Evaluator and Director System

AMEE Admiralty Marine Engineering Establishment (MOD)

AMEME Association of Mining, Electrical and Mechanical Engineers

AMES Air Medical Evacuation System
Automated Medical Examination System
Automatic Message Entry System

AMESA Ateliers Mecaniques et Electrotechniques SA (Switzerland)

AMETA Army Management Engineering Training Agency (US Army)

AMETS Artillery Meteorological System

AMF ACE Mobile Force (of NATO)

AMFIS Automatic Microfilm Information System

AMFR Advanced Muti-Function Radar

AMH Anti-Mullerian Hormone
Automated Materials Handling
Automated Medical History

AMHS American Material Handling Society (USA)

AMHT Automated Multi-phase Health Testing

AMHTS Automated Multiphasic Health Testing and Services

AMI Active Microwave Instrument
Advanced Manned Interceptor
Advanced Material Information – series issued by SAE (USA)
Aeronautica Militare Italiana (Italy) (Military Air Force)
Alternate Mark Inversion
Association for Multi-Image (USA)
Association of Medical Illustrators
Average Mutual Information

AMIC Aerospace Materials Information Center (operated by University of Dayton Research in conjunction with AFML (USAF))
Asian Mass Communications Research and Information Centre (Singapore)
Australian Microcomputer Industry Clearinghouse (Australia)
Australian Mining Industrial Council (Australia)

AMICEE Asociacion Mexicana de Ingenieros en Communicaciones Electricas y Electronica (Mexico) (Mexican Association of Electrical and Electronic Communication Engineers)

AMICOM Army Missile Command (US Army)

AMICS Aircraft Maintenance Irregularity Control System

AMIEV Association Médicale Internationale pour l'Étude des Conditions de Vie et de Santé (International Medical Association for the Study of Living Conditions and Health)

AMIF Automated Map Information File (of Defense Mapping Agency Aerospace Center (USDOD))

AMIL A Microprogramming Language

AMINA Association Mondiale des Inventeurs (Belgium) (World Federation of Inventors)

AMIO Arab Military Industrialisation Organisation

AMIRA Australian Mineral Industry Research Association (Australia)

AMIS Airport Management Information System
Aspirin Myocardial Infarction Study (by NHLBI (USA))
Automated Management Information System
Automated Mask Inspection System

AMK Anti-Misting Kerosene

AML Acute Myelogenous Leukaemia
Admiralty Materials Laboratory (MOD) (became ARE in 1984)
Aeronautical Materials Laboratory
Algebraic Manipulation Language
Amplitude Modulated Link

AMLC Aerospace Medical Laboratory (Clinical) (USAF)

AMLEC ADMIRALTY MATERIALS LABORATORY Eddy Current detector

AMM Advanced Manufacturing Methods (a research project sponsored by IITRI (USA))
Alternative Method of Management
Anti-Missile Missile

AMMA Australian Margarine Manufacturers Association (Australia)

AMME Automated Multi-Media Exchange

AMMINET Automated Mortgage Management Information Network

AMMIS Aircraft Maintenance Management Information System

AMML Automated Microbian Metabolism Laboratory

AMMO Alliance of Manufacturing and Management Organisations

AMMRC Army Materials and Mechanics Research Center (US Army)

AMMRL Aircraft Maintenance Material Readiness List (USN)

AMMRPV Advanced Multi-Mission R

AMMS Automated Multi-Media Switch

AMMSS Automatic Message and Mail Sorting Systems

AMMT Automated Multi-Media Terminal

AMNH American Museum of Natural History (USA)

AMNIP Adaptive Man-machine Non-arithmetical Information Processing

AMO Air Mass Zero
Alternant Molecular Orbit

AMOP Association of Mail Order Publishers

AMOS ARPA Maui (Hawaii) Optical Site (USDOD)
Acoustic Meteorological Oceanographic Survey
Adjustable Multi-class Organizing System
Anti-reflection coated Metal Oxide Semiconductor
Automatic Meteorological Observing Station
Automatic Meteorological Observing System
Army Map Service (US Army) (now part of TOPOCOM)
Automated Maintenance System
Automatic Meteorological System
prefix to series of numbered/lettered series of reports issued by Department of Aerospace and Mechanical Sciences, Princeton University (USA)

AMOSS Adaptive Mission-Oriented Software System

AMP Acetaldehyde Monoperacetate
Active Medium Propagation
Adenosine Monophosphate
Advanced Manned Penetrator aircraft
Aerospace Medical Panel (of AGARD (NATO))
Airborne Maintenance Processor

AMPA Adaptive Multi-beam Phased Array
Advanced Maritime Patrol Aircraft
American Medical Publishers Association (USA)

AMPB Advanced Multi-mission Patrol Boat

AMPL A Macro Programming Language

AMPLO Administrators of Medium-sized Public Libraries in Ontario (Canada)

AMPP Advanced Microprogrammable Processor

AMPRS Automated Military Construction Progress Reporting System (of Corps of Engineers, US Army)

AMPS Advanced Mobile Phone Service

AMPS Assembly Manufacturing Payroll System
Association of Motorists Protection Services
Atmospheric, Magnetospheric and Plasmas-in-Space
Automatic Message Processing System

AMPSS Advanced Manned Penetrating Strategic System

AMPTC Arab Maritime Petroleum Transport Company (jointly owned by a number of Arab oil exporting companies)

AMPTE Active Magnetospheric Particle Tracer Explorer

AMQUA American Quaternary Association (USA)

AMR Advanced Modular Radar
Automatic Map Reader
Automatic Message Routing

AMRA Army Materials Research Agency (US Army)

AMRAAM Advanced Medium-Range Air-to-Air Missile

AMRAD ARPA (USDOD) Measurements Radar

AMRC Abadina Media Resource Centre (Nigeria)

AMRF African Medical and Research Foundation
Automated Manufacturing Research Facility (of NBS (USA))

AMRG Air Management Research Group (of OECD)

AMRIID Army Medical Research Institute of Infectious Diseases (US Army)

AMRL Aerospace Medical Research Laboratory (USAF)
Applied Mechanics Research Laboratory (University of Texas (USA))

AMRRDC Army Manpower Resources Research and Development Center (US Army) (now ARI (US Army))

AMRV Advanced Manoeuvrable Re-entry Vehicle
Astronaut Manoeuvring Research Vehicle
Atmospheric Manoeuvring Re-entry Vehicle

AMS Acoustic Measuring System
Acute Mountain Sickness
Administrative Management Society (USA)
Advanced Metallic Structures (a project of USAF)
Advanced Monopulse Seeker
Aeronautical Material Specification (series issued by SAE)
Aerospace Material Specification (numbered/lettered series issued by SAE(USA))
Agricultural Marketing Service (of USDA)
American Mathematical Society (USA)
American Meteorological Society (USA)
Anisotropy of Magnetic Susceptibility
Anti-reflection Metal Semiconductor
Applied Mathematics Series (issued by NBS)

AMSA Advanced Manned Strategic Aircraft
Aeronaves de Mexico S.A. (Mexico)
American Metal Stamping Association (USA)

AMSAA Army Material Systems Analysis Agency (US Army)
Army Materiel Systems Analysis Activity (US Army)

AMSAC Advanced Multi-Stage Axial-flow Compresor (a program of NASA (usa))

AMSAM Anti-Missile Surface-to-Air Missile

AMSAT Radio Amateur Satellite Corporation (headquarters in USA)

AMSAT-UK United Kingdom branch of AMSAT

AMSC Advanced Military Spaceflight Capability
Army Mathematics Steering Committee (US Army)

AMSEC Analytical Method for System Evaluation and Control

AMSIC Army Missile Command (US Army)

AMSO Association of Market-Survey Organisations

AMSOC American Miscellaneous Society (USA)

AMSOG Army Molecular Sieve Oxygen Generator (US Army)

AMSR Automated Microform Storage and Retrieval

AMSS Advanced Meteorological Sounding System

AMSSEE Area Museums Service for South-Eastern England

AMST Advanced Medium STOL Transport

AMSTAC Australian Marine Sciences and Technologies Advisory Committee (Australia)

AMSUS Association of Military Surgeons in the United States (USA)

AMT Advanced Manufacturing Technique or Technology
Audio-frequency Magneto-tellurics
Automated Microfiche Terminal

AMTA Antenna Measurement Techniques Association (USA)
Arab Maritime Transport Academy (Egypt)

AMTC Advanced Manufacturing Technology Committee (of DTI)

AMTCL Association for Machine Translation and Computational Linguistics (USA) (now Association for Computational Linguistics)

AMTD Automatic Magnetic Tape Dissemination (a program of DTIC and NTIS (USA))

AMTDA Agricultural Machinery and Tractor Dealers Association

AMTE Admiralty Marine Technology Establishment (MOD)

AMTEG Australian Metal Trades Export Group (Australia)

AMTEX Air Mass Transportation Experiment

AMTF Aerobic-Media Trickling Filter

AMTI Airborne Moving Target Indicator
Area Moving Target Indicator
Automatic Moving Target Indicator

AMTICP Asociacion Mexicana de Tecnicos de las Industrias de la Celulosa y del Papel (Mexican Technical Association of the Pulp and Paper Industries)

AMTRAK formal title is National Railroad Passenger Corporation (USA) (a quasi-governmental agency)

AMTRAN Automatic Mathematical Translator

AMTT Automated Mixed Traffic Transit

AMU Aligarh Muslim University (India)
American Malacological Union (USA)
Associated Midwestern Universities (USA)
Astronaut Manoeuvring Unit
Atomic Mass Unit

AMUT Arya-Mehr University of Technology (IRAN)

AMUX Avionics Multiplex System

AMV Area of Mutual Visibility
Avian Myeloblastosis Virus

AMVCB Australian Motor Vehicle Certification Board (of Dept. of Transport (Australia))

AMVER Atlantic Merchant Vessel Report
Automated Merchant Vessel Report system (of the United States Coast Guard)

AMWA American Medical Writers Association (USA)

AMX Atelier de Construction d'Issy-les-Moulineaux (France)

AMZ Association Mondiale de Zootechnie (Italy) (World Association for Animal Production)

AN Acetonitrile
Aeronautical Note (numbered series issued by NAE (Canada))

AN SSR Akademiya Nauk SSR (Academy of Sciences of the USSR)

ANA All Nippon Airways (Japan)
American Nurses Association (USA)
Anti-nuclear Antibodies
Article Numbering Association
Association of National Advertisers (USA)
Automated Naval Architecture
Automatic Number Analysis

ANA II Nuclear Asco II (Spain)

ANAAS Australian and New Zealand Association for the Advancement of Science

ANABA Asociacion Nacional de Bibliotecarios, Archiveros y Aequelogos (Spain) (National Association of Librarians, Archivists and Archaeologists)

ANACOM Analogue Computer

ANACONDA Analytical Control and Data

ANAHL Australian National Animal Health Laboratory (of CSIRO (Australia))

ANAIP Agrupacion National Autonoma de Idustriales de Plasticos (Spain) (National Approvals Board for Plastics)

ANALIT Analysis of Automatic Line Insulation Tests

ANAP Airport Noise Abatement Plan

ANARE Australian National Antarctic Research Expedition

ANB Ambient Noise Buoy

AnBD Anaerobic Broth Disk

ANBFM Adaptive Narrow-Band Frequency Modulation Modem

ANC Air Navigation Conference (of ICAO)

ANCA Allied Naval Communications Agency (of NATO)

ANCAHA Association Nationale des Collectionneurs et Amateurs d'Horologerie Ancienne (France) (National Association of Collectors and Lovers of Antique Clocks and Watches)

ANCAR Australian National Committee for Antarctic Research (of Australian Academy of Sciences)

ANCB Association Nationale des Comptables de Belgique (Belgium) (National Association of Accountants of Belgium)

ANCC Associazione Nazionale per il Controllo della Combustione (Italy) (National Association for the Inspection of Combustion Equipment)

ANCE Associazione Nazionale Costruttori Elili (Italy) (National Association of Building Constructors)

ANCET Analytical Nuclear Casualty Estimation Technique

ANCHOR Alpha-Numeric Character Generator

ANCI Asociacion Nacional de Construcciones Industrializadas (Spain) (National Association of Industrialised Building)
Associazione Nazionale Calzaturifici Italiani (Italy) (Italian National Association of Footwear Manufacturers)

ANCIF Automated Nautical Chart Index File (of USDOD)

ANCIRS Automated News Clipping, Indexing, and Retrieval System

AnCO An Chomhairle Oiluna (Eire) (Industrial Training Authority)

ANCOLD Australian National Committee on Large Dams (Australia)

ANCOVA Analysis of Covariance

ANCS American Numerical Control Society (USA)
Association Nationale des Clubs Scientifiques (France) (National Association of Scientific Clubs)

AnTBD Anaerobically Thioglycolate Broth Disk

AND Alpha-Numeric Display

ANDAS Automatic Navigation and Data Acquisition System

ANDCP Association Nationale des Directeurs et Chefs due Personnel (France) (National Association of Personnel Managers)

ANDECE Agrupacion Nacional de Derivados del Cemento (Spain)

ANDES Aerolineas Nacionales del Ecuador SA (Ecuador)

ANDI Asociacion Nacional de Industriales (Colombia) (National Association of Industrialists)

ANDIMA Agrupacion Nacional Sindical de Industrias de Materiales Aislantes (Spain)

ANDIN Associazione Nazionale di Ingeneria Nucleare (Italy) (National Association of Nuclear Engineering)

ANDMS Advanced Network Design and Management System

ANDRA Agence Nationale pour la Gestion des Dechets Radioactifs (France) (National Agency for the Management of Radioactive Waste)
Agence Nationale pour la gestion des Dechets Radioactifs (France) (National Agency for the Management of Radioactive Waste)

ANDS Automated Newspaper Delivery System

ANDVT Advanced Narrow-band Digital Voice Terminal

ANEDA Association Nationale d'Etudes pour la Documentation Automatique (France) (National Association of Automatic Documentation Studies)

ANEHOP Agrupacion Nacional Espanola de Fabricantes de Hormigon Preparado (Spain) (Spanish National Group of Manufacturers of Ready Mixed Concrete)

ANEP Airport Noise Evaluation Process

ANEZA Association National des Enterprises du Zaire (Zaire) (National Association of Companies in Zaire)

ANF Anti-nuclear Factor
Atlantic Nuclear Force

ANFAC Asociacion Espanola de Fabricantes de Automoviles, Camiones, Tractores y sus Motors (Spain) (Spanish Association of Vehicle Manufacturers)

ANFI Automatic Noise Figure Indicator

ANFIA Associazione Nazionale fra Industrie Automobilistiche (Italy) (National Association for the Automobile Industry)

ANFIMA Associazione Nazionale fra i Fabbricanti Imballaggi Metalici ed Affini (Italy) (National Association for the Manufactuire of Metal Containers and Allied Industries)

ANFO Ammonium Nitrate and Fuel Oil

ANG Air National Guard (USA)
ANGLFN Angle Function
ANGTS Alaska Natural Gas Transportation System (USA)
ANGUS A Navigable General Purpose Underwater Surveyor
ANHSSO Association of National Health Service Supplies Officers
ANHUL Australian National Humanities Libraries (Australia)
ANI Australian Naval Institute (Australia)
Automatic Number Identification
ANIE Associazione Nazionale Industrie Elettrotechniche ed Elettroniche (Italy) (National Association for the Electrotechnical and Electronics Industry)
ANIM Association of Nuclear Instrument Manufacturers (USA)
ANIMA Associazione Nazionale Industria Meccanica Varia ed Affine (Italy) (National Association of Mechanical Engineering and Allied Industries)
ANIP Army–Navy Instrumentation Program (USDOD)
ANIPLA Associazione Nazionale Italiana per l'Automazione (Italy) (Italian National Association for Automation)
ANIRC Annual National Information Retrieval Colloquium (USA)
ANISA Anglo Naval e Industrial SA (Spain)
ANIT Agence Nationale pour l'Information Touristique (France) (National Agency for Tourist Information)
ANKOR AUTONETICS KALMAN Optimum Reset
ANL Argonne National Laboratory (of USAEC) (now of DOE (USA))
National Library of Australia (Australia)
ANLL Acute Non-Lymphocytic Leukaemia
ANLP Alpha-Numeric Logic Package
ANMC American National Metric Council (of ANSI (USA))
ANMCC Advanced National Military Command and Control
Alternate Military Command Center (USDOD)
Alternate National Military Command Center (for USA)
ANMI Air Navigation Multiple Indicator
ANMRC Australian Numerical Meterology Research Centre (Australia)
ANNAF Joint Army/Navy/NASA/Air Force (USA)
ANO Air Navigation Order (series issued by CAA)
ANOM Analysis of Means
ANOVA Analysis of Variance
ANP Aircraft Nuclear Propulsion
Arbeitsgemeinschaft Nuklear Prozesswarme (Germany)
ANPA American Newspaper Publishers Association (USA)
ANPA/RI American Newspaper Publishers Association/Research Institute (USA)
ANPP Army Nuclear Power Program (US Army)
ANPRM prefix to dated-numbered series of Advanced Notices of Proposed Rule Making issued by FAA (USA)
ANPUEU Association Nationale des Proprietaires et Usagers d'Embranchements Particuliers (France) (National Association of Owners and Users of Private Branch Railway Sidings)
ANQUE Associación Nacional de Qûmicos de España (Spain) (National Chemical Association)
ANR Australian National Railways (Australia)
ANRAO Australian National Radio Astronomy Observatory (Australia)
ANRPC Association of Natural Rubber Producing Countries (Malaysia)
ANRT Association Nationale de la Recherche Technique (France) (National Association of Technical Research)
ANS American Nuclear Society (USA)
Astronomical Netherlands Satellite
prefix to lettered/numbered series of Standards issued by ANSI (USA)
ANSI American National Standards Institute (USA)
ANSIM Analogue Simulator
ANSLICS Aberdeen and North of Scotland Library and Information Co-operative Service
ANSOL Australian National Social Sciences Library (Australia)
ANSPI Agrupacion Nacional Sindical de Pinturas (Spain)
ANSR Add-on Non-Stop Reliability
ANSSMFE Australian National Society of Soil Mechanics and Foundation Engineering (Australia)
ANSSR Aerodynamically Neutral Spin Stabilized Rocket
ANSTEL Australian National Scientific and Technological Library (Australia)
ANSWER Algorithm for Non-Synchronized Waveform Error Reduction
ANT Assessment of New Techniques (a scheme operated by the Wiring Regulations Committee of IEE)
Autonomous Navigation Technology
ANTAC Air Navigation and Tactical Control
ANTARES Antenna Tracking Altitude, Azimuth and Range by Electronic Scan
ANTC Australian National Television Council (Australia)
ANTE Adjoint Neutron Transport Equation
ANTEC Annual Technical Conference
ANTEL Administracion Nacional de Telecomunicaciones (El Salvador) (National Telecommunications Administration)
ANTELCO Administracion Nacional de Telecommunicaciones (Paraguay) (National Telecommunications Administration)
Administracion Nacional de Telecomunicaciones (Peru) (National Telecommunications Administration)
Administracion National de Telecomunicaciones (Paraguay) (National Administration of Telecommunications)
ANTS Airborne Night Television System
ANU Australian National University (Australia)
ANU-P Australian National University, Research School of Physical Sciences (Australia)
ANV Advanced Naval Vehicle
ANVA Australian Nuclear Veterans Association (Australia)
ANVAR Agence Nationale pour la Valorization de la Recherche (France) (National Agency for the Evaluation of Research)
ANVCE Advanced Naval Vehicles Concepts Evaluation (a project of USN)
ANVIS Aviation Night Vision Imaging System
ANWES Association of Naval Weapon Engineers and Scientists (USA)
ANZ Air New Zealand (New Zealand)
ANZAAS Australian and New Zealand Association for the Advancement of Science
ANZCAN Australia, New Zealand and Canada
ANZCP Australian and New Zealand College of Psychiatrists (Australia)
ANZECS Australia-New Zealand-Europe Container Service (an international consortium)
ANZUS Australia, New Zealand, United States
ANZWONA Australian and New Zealand Web Offset Newspaper Association (now PANPA)

AO Acousto-optic
Announcement of Opportunity (NASA (USA))
Argon-Oxygen

AOA Aerodrome Owners Association
American Optometric Association(USA)
American Ordnance Association (USA)
American Orthopsychiatric Association (USA)
Angle of Arrival of radio signals
Ascending Order Arrangement

AOAA Amino-oxy-acetic acid

AOAC Association of Official Agricultural Chemists (title changed in 1965 to Association of Official Analytical Chemists (USA))

AOAP Army Oil Analysis Program (US Army)

AOB Atmospheric Observation Bell

AOBD Acousto-Optic Beam Deflector

AOC Air Operation Centrals
Association of Old Crows (USA)
Attitude and Orbit Control

AOCI Airport Operators Council International

AOCM Advanced Optical Counter-Measures

AOCR Advanced Optical Character Reader
Advanced Optical Character Recognition

AOCS American Oil Chemists Society (USA)

AOD Argon-Oxygen Decarburization
Auriculo-Osteodysplasia

AODC Association of Offshore Diving Contractors

AOEL Advanced Ocean Engineering Laboratory (Scripps Institution of Oceanography) (USA)

AOGA Alaska Oil and Gas Association (USA)

AOH Acid Open Hearth

AOHC American Occupational Health Conference

AOI Acousto-Optical Imaging

AOINST numbered series issued by Administrative Office, Department of the Navy (USN)

AOIP Association Ouvriers Instruments Precision (France) (Association of Precision Instrument Operatives)

AOIPS Atmospheric and Oceanographic Information Processing System (of NASA (USA))

AOL Admirality Oil Laboratory (MOD) (now part of NGTE)
Airborne Oceanographic Lidar
Atlantic Oceanographic Laboratories (of ESSA (USA)) (now of NOAA)
Atlantic Oceanographic Laboratory (of Bedford Institute of Oceanography (Canada))

AOM Acoustic-Optic Modulator
Argon-Oxygen Melted

AOMA American Occupational Medical Association (USA)
Arab Organization for the Manufacture of Armaments

AOML Atlantic Oceanographic and Meteorological Laboratories (of ERL (noaa) (usa))

AOML/FD Acousto-Optic Mode-Locker/Frequency Doubles

AONB Areas of Outstanding Natural Beauty

AOO American Oceanic Organisation (USA)

AOOSY Automatic Orbital Operations System for Satellites and Space Probes

AOP Association of Optical Practitioners

AOPA Aircraft Owners and Pilots Association

AOPU Asian-Oceanic Postal Union (Philippines)

AOQ Average Outgoing Quality

AOQC Australian Organisation for Quality Control (Australia)

AOQL Average Outgoing Quality Limit

AOQS Acousto-Optic Q-Switch

AOR Auxiliary Oiler Replenishment

AORB Aviation Operational Research Branch (of CAA)

AORE Army Operational Research Establishment (now DOAE)

AORG Army Operational Research Group (now DOAE)

AORS Army Operations Research Symposium (US Army)

AOS Advanced Operating System
American Opthalmological Society (USA)
Amphibious Objective Studies

AOSO Advanced Orbiting Solar Observatory

AOSP Automatic Operating and Scheduling Programme

AOSS Airborne Oil Surveillance System

AOSTRA Alberta Oil Sands Technology and Research Authority (Canada)

AOT Alignment Optical Telescope

AOTC Associated Offices Technical Committee (of several insurance companies)

AOTT Automatic Outgoing Trunk Test

AOU Apparent Oxygen Utilisation

AOV Analysis Of Variance

AP Air Pollution (numbered series by US Public Health Service)
Air Publication (numbered series issuedby Ministry of Defence (Air Force Department))
Ammonium Perchlorate
Anomalous Propagation
Antennas and Propagation
Anti-Personnel
Applied Physics (numbered series issued by Applied Physics Division, National Physical Laboratory)
Armour Piercing
Association of Professions (USA)
Associative Processor
Audio Processing
prefix to numbered series of publications issued by Air Programs Office (of EPA (USA))
prefix to numbered series of reports on Atmospheric Physics issued by School of Physics and Astronomy, Minnesota University (USA)

AP(SE) Armour Piercing (Special Effects)

AP-HC Armour Piercing Hard Core

APA American Pharmaceutical Association (USA)
American Photoplatemakers Association (USA)
American Physicists Association (USA)
American Plywood Association (USA)
American Polygraph Association (USA)
American Psychological Association (USA)
Anthracite Producers Association (South Africa)
Asociacion para la Prevencion de Accidentes (Spain) (Association for the Prevention of Accidents)
Association for the Prevention of Addiction
Association of Professional Architects (replaced by ACA)

APAA Automotive Parts and Accessories Association (USA)

APAC Asphalt-Plastic-Asphalt-Chip

APACE Advanced Planning And Central Executive
ALDERMASTON Project for the Application of Computers to Engineering

APACHE Accelerator for Physics and Chemistry of Heavy Elements
Analogue Programming And Checking
Application Package for Chemical Engineers
Aviation Performance Assessment in a Chemical Environment

APACS Airborne Position and Attitude Camera System

APADAS Automated Phase and Amplitude Data Acquisition System (USN)

APAE Association of Public Address Engineers (became ASCE in 1977)

APAIS Australian Public Affairs Information Service (of the National Library of Australia)

APAM Anti-Personnel/Anti-Material cluster weapon

APAREL A Parse-Request Language
APAS Adaptable-Programmable Assembly System
APAT Auxiliary Propelled Anti-Tank Gun
APAU Accident Prevention Advisory Unit (of HSE)
APB Accounting Principles Board (of AICPA (USA))
Acute Pernicious Beriberi
Air Portable Bridge
Antiphase Boundary
APBE Anti-Phase Boundary Energy
APC Accounting Principles Committee (South Africa)
Adaptive Predictive Coding
Agricultural Productivity Commission (Philippines)
Agricultural Prices Commission (India)
American Power Conference (USA)
Approach Power Compensator
Area Positive Control
Armour Piercing, Capped
Armoured Personnel Carrier
Auditing Practices Committee (of CCAB)
Australian Postal Commission (Australia)
Auto-Plot Controller
Automatic Peripheral Control
Automatic Phase Control
Automatic Potential Control
Automatic Pressure Controller
APCA Air Pollution Control Association (Canada)
Air Pollution Control Association (USA)
APCBC Armour Piercing, Capped, Ballistic Cap
APCC Association of Professional Computer Consultants
APCL Atmospheric Physics and Chemistry Laboratory (of NOAA (USA))
APCM Adaptive Pulse Code Modulator
Authorized Protective Connecting Module
APCO Air Pollution Control Office (of EPA (USA)) (now Air Programs Office)
Associated Public-safety Communications Officers (USA)
APCOM International Symposium on the Application of Computer Methods in the Mineral Industry
International Symposium on the Application of Computers in the Mining Industry
APCP Aquatic Plants Control Program (of Athens College (USA))
APCR Armour Piercing, Composite Rigid
APCS Approach Power Compensator System
Associative Processor Computer System
Attitude and Pointing Control System
APD Amplitude Probability Distribution
Approach Progress Display
Avalanche Photo-Diode
APDC Ammonioum Pyrrolidene Dithiocarbamate
APDL Algorithmic Processor Description Language
APDM Associative Push Down Memory
APDS Armour Piercing Discarding Sabot
APE Automatic Photomapping Equipment
APEA Association of Professional Engineers, Australia (Australia)
Australian Petroleum Exploration Association (Australia)
APEBC Association of Professional Engineers of British Columbia (Canada)
APEDE Asociacion Panamena de Ejecutivos de Empresas (Panama) (Panamanian Association of Management)
APEE Association for Pediatric Education in Europe
APEGGA Association of Professional Engineers, Geologists, and Geophysicists of Alberta (Canada)
APEO Association of Professional Engineers of Ontario (Canada)
APER Association of Publishers Educational Representatives
APES Association of Professional Engineers of Saskatchewan (Canada)
APET Application Programme Evaluator Tool
APETT Association of Professional Engineers of Trinidad and Tobago
APEX Advanced Purchase Excursion
Assembler and Process Executive
Automatic Precision Elemental X-ray
APF Association of Paper Finishers (of BPBIF)
Atomic Packing Factor
APFA American Production Finishers Association (USA)
APFC Asia-Pacific Forestry Commission
APFD Auto-Pilot and Flight Director
APFR Automatic Programmable Film Reader
APFSD Armour-Piercing, Fin-Stabilized, Discarding Sabot
APFSDS Armour Piercing, Fin Stabilised, Discarding Sabot
APG A Power for Good (an action group to support nuclear power)
Aberdeen Proving Ground (of US Army)
Application Programme Generator
Azimuth Pulse Generator
APGC Air Proving Ground Center (USAF)
APHA American Printing History Association (USA)
American Public Health Association (USA)
Australian Pneumatic and Hydraulic Association (Australia)
APHB American Printing House for the Blind (USA)
APHE Armour-Piercing High Explosive
APHI Association of Public Health Inspectors
APHIS Animal and Plant Health Inspection Service (of USDA)
API Air Position Indicator
American Paper Institute (USA)
American Petroleum Institute (USA)
Armour Piercing Incendiary
Association of Physicians of India
Automated Pronunciation Instructor
API-T Armour Piercing Incendiary-Tracer
APIC APOLLO Parts Information Centre (NASA)
APICS American Production and Inventory Control Society (USA)
APIDC Andhra Pradesh Industrial Development Corporation (India) (government owned)
APIN Association for Programmed Instruction in the Netherlands
APIS Apogee-Perigee Injection System
APIT Association of Psychiatrists in Training
APITCO Andhra Pradesh Industrial and Technical Consultancy Organisation (a subsidiary of IDBI (India))
APL A Programming Language
Aero Propulsion Laboratory (USAF)
Allowance Parts List
Aluminium-Polythene Laminate
Applications Programming Language
Applied Physics Laboratory (of Johns Hopkins University (USA))
Applied Physics Laboratory (of University of Chicago (USA))
Association for Programmed Learning
Association of Photographic Laboratories
Associative Programming Language
APL/JHU-TPR Applied Physics Laboratory, Johns Hopkins University – Transportation Programs Report
APLA Atlantic Provinces Library Association (Canada)
APLE Airportable Lifting Equipment
Association of Public Lighting Engineers
APLET Association for Programmed Learning and Educational Technology
APLG Akron Polymer Lecture Group (USA)

APLIC Association of Population/Family Planning Libraries and Information Centers (USA)

APLL Analog Phased-Locked Loop
Automatic Phased-Locked Loop

APM Academy of Psychosomatic Medicine (USA)
Air Power Museum (USA)
Aminprophos Methyl
Automatic Plugging Meter

APMC Andhra Pradesh Mining Corporation (India) (government owned)
Automatic Permanent Magnetic-field Compensator

APME Advisory Panel on Management Education (BIM and CBI)
Association of Plastics Manufacturers in Europe

APMI American Powder Metallurgy Institute (USA)
Area Precipitation Measurement Indicator

APML Acute Promyelocytic Leukaemia

APMS Advanced Power Management System
Automatic Performance Management System

APO Air Programs Office (of EPA (USA))
Asian Productivity Organization (Headquarters are in Japan)
Australian Post Office (Australia) (split into Australian Postal Commission AND Australian Telecommunications Commission in 1975)

APOA Arctic Petroleum Operators Association (Canada)
Australian Purchasing Officers Association (Australia)

APOE Aerial Port of Embarkation

APOL Aerospace Program-Oriented Language

APOLLO Article Procurement with On-line Local Ordering

APP Advance Procurement Plan
Aggregate Production Planning
Air Pollution Potential
Ammonium Polyphosphate
Associative Parallel Processor

APPA American Public Power Administration (USA)
Artificial Pilot Phased Array
Asbestos Pipe Producers Association
Association des Pilotes et Propriétaires d'Aéronefs (France) (Association of Private Aircraft Owners)
Association pour la Prevention de la Pollution Atmospherique (France) (Association for the Prevention of Atmospheric Pollution)

APPARAT Archive Preservation Programme And Retrieval by Automated Techniques

APPC Advance Procurement Planning council (USDOD)

APPES American Institute of Chemical Engineers Physical Properties Estimation System

APPI Advanced Planning Procurement Information

APPITA Technical Association of the Australian and New Zealand Pulp and Paper Industry

APPLE Analogue Phased Processing Loop Equipment
ARIANE (artificial satellite) Passenger Payload Experiment
Associative Processor Programming Language

APPS Analytical Photogrammetric Positioning System

APQI Associacao Portuguesa para a Qualide Industrial (Portugal) (Portuguese Association for Quality Control)

APR Air Profile Recording
Airborne Profile Recorder
Annual Percentage Rate
Association of Petroleum Re-Refiners (USA)
Automatic Power Reserve

APRA Air Public Relations Association
Australian Plastics Research Association (Australia)

APRAC Air Pollution Research Advisory Committee (of CRC and EPA (USA))

APRAGAZ Association des Propriétaires de Récipients à Gaz Comprimés (Belgium)

APRC Army Personnel Research Committee (of Medical Research Council)

APRCG Asia-Pacific Railway Co-operation Group

APRD Army Pulse Radiation Directorate (US Army)

APRE Army Personnel Research Establishment (MOD)

APRF Army Pulse Radiation Facility (US Army)

APRG Air Pollution Research Group (NPL (CSIR)) (South Africa)

APRICOT Automatic Printed Circuit Board Routing with Intermediate Control of the Tracking

APRIL Aquaplaning Risk Indicator for Landings
Automatically Programmed Remote Indication Logging

APRIS ALCOA (Aluminium Company of America) Picturephone Remote Information System

APRO Aerial Phenomena Research Organisation (USA)
Army Personnel Research Office (now BESRL) (US Army)
Army Procurement Research Office (US Army)

APROBA Association Professionelle pour l'Accroissement de la Productive dans l'Industrie du Batiment (France) (Association for Increasing Productivity in the Building Industry)

APROC Adaptive Statistical Processor

APRS Association of Professional Recording Studies
Automatic Position Reference System

APRST Averaged Probability Ratio Sequential Test

APRT Adenine Phosphoribosyltransferase

APRU Applied Psychology Research Unit (Medical Research Council)

APS Aircraft Position Sensor
Allotment-of-Probability Shares
Alphanumeric Photocomposer System
American Physical Society (USA)
American Physiological Society (USA)
American Phytopathological Society (USA)
American Proctologic Society (USA)
American Psychosomatic Society (USA)
Appearance Potential Spectroscopy
Ascent Propulsion System
Assembly Programming System
Association of Police Surgeons
Atropine-like Psycho-chemical Substance
Australian Photogrammetric Society (Australia)
Australian Psychological Society (Australia)
Automatic Patching System
Autotext Publication System
Auxiliary Power System
Auxiliary Propulsion System

APSA Aerolineas Peruanas S.A. (Peru)
African Purchasing and Supply Association
American Political Science Association (USA)
Ammunition Procurement and Supply Agency (US Army)
Association for the Psychiatric Study of Adolescents

APSE Ada Programming Support Environment
Armour Piercing, Secondary Effect
Automatic Programming and Scaling of Equations

APSFC Andhra Pradesh State Financial Corporation (India)

APSO Asian Physical Society

APSSIDC Andhra Pradesh Small Scale Industrial Development Corporation (India)

APST Association of Professional Scientists and Technologists

APSTC Andhra Pradesh State Road Transport Corporation (India) (Govt owned)

APSTRAT Aptitude Strategies

APT	Advanced Passenger Train
	Advanced Pilot Training
	Airborne Pointer and Tracker
	Armour Piercing Tracer
	Association of Photographic Technicians (now Technicians Section of Institute of Incorporated Photographers)
	Automatic Picture Transmission
	Automatic Position Telemetering
	Automatically Programmed Tooling
	Automatically Programmed Tools
APTA	American Physical Therapy Association (USA)
	American Public Transit Association (USA)
	Asian Pineapple Traders Association
APTD	prefix to numbered series issued by Air Programs Office (of EPA (USA))
APTE	Automatic Production Test Equipment
APTI	Automatic Print Transfer Instrument
APTIC	Air Pollution Technical Information Center (of EPA (USA))
APTIS	All-Purpose Ticket Issuing System
APTS	Association for the Prevention of Theft in Shops
APTT	Activated Partial Thromboplastin Time
APU	After Power Unit
	Applied Psychology Unit (of Medical Research Council)
	Assessment of Performance Unit (of DES)
	Auxiliary Power Unit
APUD	Amine Precursor Uptake and Decarboxylation
APV	Automatic Patching Verification
APVDC	Association of Parents of Vaccine-Damaged Children
APW	Augmented Plane Wave
APWA	American Public Works Association (USA)
APWR	Advanced Pressurized Water Reactor
APX	L'Atelier de Construction de Puteaux (of Groupement Industriel des Armements Terrestres (France))
AQAD	Aeronautical Quality Assurance Directorate (MOD (PE))
AQAP	prefix to series of Allied Quality Assurance Publications issued by NATO
AQC	Air Quality Control
AQCR	Air Quality Control Regions (USA)
AQD	Aeronautical Quality Directorate (MOD)
AQL	Acceptable Quality Level
AR	Advisory Report
	Anti-Reflective
	Aspect Ratio
	Autoregressive
ARA	Aerial Rocket Artillery
	Airborne Radar Approach
	Aircraft Rescue Association
	Aircraft Research Association
	Amateur Rocket Association (USA)
	Amateurs Radio Algeriens (Algeria) (Amateur Radio Society of Algeria)
	American Rheumatism Association (USA)
	Area Redevelopment Administration (USA)
	Armada Republica Argentina (Republica of Argentina Navy)
	Association of River Authorities
	Attitude Reference Assembly
ARAAV	Armoured Reconnaissance Airborne Assault Vehicle
	Armoured Reconnaissance Airborne Assault Vehicle
ARABSAT	Arab Satellite Communications Organisation (headquarters in Saudi Arabia)
ARAC	Aerospace Research Applications Center (cooperative unit of NASA, Indiana University, and industry (USA))
	Array Reduction Analysis Circuit
ARAD	Association des Radio Amateurs de Djibouti (Association of Radio Amateurs of Djibouti)
ARADCOM	United States Army Air Defense Command
ARADMAC	Army Aeronautical Depot Maintenance Center (US Army)
ARAE	Advanced Radio Astronomy Explorer
ARAEN	Appareil de Reference pour la determination de l'Affaiblissement Equivalent pour la Nettete (Reference Apparatus for the Determination of AEN)
ARAL	Automatic Record Analysis Language
ARAMIS	Automation Robotics and Machine Intelligence System
ARANZ	Archives and Records Association of New Zealand (New Zealand)
ARAPT	ATLANTIC RESEARCH Automatic Position Telemetering
ARAS	Ascending Reticular Activating System
ARB	Air Registration Board (replaced by the Airworthiness Requirements Board of the CAA in 1972)
ARBA	American Road Builders Association (USA)
ARBED	Acieries Reunies de Burbach-EichDudelange (Luxembourg)
ARBICA	Arab Regional Branch of the International Council on Archives
ARBITS	Army Base Information Transfer System (US Army)
ARBRL	Army Ballistics Research Laboratory (US Army)
ARBS	Angle Rate Bombing System
	Angular Rate Bombing System
ARC	Accounting Research Committee (Canada)
	Acoustic Research Centre (of DARPA (USA))
	Action Resource Centre (a registered charity that organises community projects)
	Adaptive Residual Coding
	Addiction Research Center (of NIMH (USA))
	Aerial Reconnaissance Camera
	Aeronautical Research Committee (of CSIR (India))
	Aeronautical Research Council (MOD (PE))
	Agricultural Refinance Corporation (India)
	Agricultural Research Council (now AFRC)
	Alberta Research Council (Canada)
	Altitude Rate Command
	Ames Research Center (of NASA (USA))
	Amplitude Ratio Characteristic
	Arthritis and Rheumatism Council
	Attached Resource Computer
	Augmentation Research Center (of Stanford Research Institute (USA))
	Automatic Revenue Collection
ARCA	Asbestos Removal Contractors Association
ARCADE	Automatic Radar Control and Data Equipment
ARCAIC	Archives and Record Cataloguing and Indexing by Computer
ARCAS	All-purpose Rocket Carrier for Atmospheric Soundings
	Automatic Radar Chain Acquisition System
ARCCM	Automatic Remote Controlled Continuous Miner
ARCHI	Asociacion de Radiodifusoras de Chile (Chile)
ARCI	Addiction Research Center Inventory (of National Institute of Drug Abuse (USA))
ARCIS	AGRICULTURAL RESEARCH COUNCIL Computerized Information System
ARCM	Agricultural Research Council of Malawi (Malawi)
ARCO	ALITALIA Reservation and Communication System
	Automatic Reservation and Communication
ARCOM	Arctic Communications
ARCP	Aerodrome Reference Code Panel (of ICAO)
ARCRL	Agricultural Research Council Radiobiological Laboratory

ARCS Airborne Advanced Reconfigurable Computer System
Automated Reproduction and Collating System
Automated Revenue Collection System
Automated Ring Code System
Automatic Recognition of Continuous Speech

ARCSL prefix to numbered series of reports issued by Armament Research and Development Command, Chemical Systems Laboratory (US Army)

ARCUK Architects Registration Council of the United Kingdom

ARD Adenovirus Respiratory Disease
Advanced Rescue System
Agricultural Research Service (USDA)
American Radium Society (USA)
Arbeitsgemeinschaft der Oeffentlich Rechlichen Rundfunkanstalten der Bundesrepublik Deutschland (Germany)
Astrophysics Research Division (of the Appleton Laboratory)

ARDC Aberdeen Research and Development Center (of APG (US Army))
Agricultural Refinance and Development Corporation (India)
Air Research and Development Command (USAF)

ARDCS Association of Rural District Council Surveyors

ARDE Armament Research and Development Establishment (India)
Armament Research and Development Establishment (now RARDE)

ARDF Airborne Radio Direction Finding

ARDI Analysis, Requirements Determination, Design and Development, and Implementation and Evaluation

ARDIS Army Research and Development Information System (US Army)

ARDISO Army Research and Development Information Systems Office (USArmy)

ARDMA Auto-Refresh Direct Memory Access

ARDS Adult Respiratory Distress Syndrome
Advance Remote Display System

ARDU Aircraft Research and Development Unit (Australia)
Analytical Research and Development Unit (of AERE (UKAEA))

ARE Admiralty Research Establishment (MOD)
Association for Recurrent Education
Asymptotic Relative Efficiency
Atelier de construction de Roanne (of Groupement Industriel des Armements Terrestres (France))

AREA American Railway Engineering Association (USA)
American Recreational Equipment Association (USA)
Association of Records Executives and Administrators (USA)

AREC Amateur Radio Emergency Corps (USA)

ARELEM Arithmetic Element

ARELS Association of Recognized English Language Schools

ARENBD Armor and Engineer Board (US Army)

ARENTO Arab Republic of Egypt National Telecommunications Organization (Egypt)

ARENTS Advanced Research Environmental Test Satellite

AREPS Advanced Reconnaissance Electrically Propelled Spacecraft

ARES Advanced Research Electro-magnetic Simulator
Advanced Rocket Engine/Storable

ARETO Arab Republic of Egypt Telecommunications Organization (Egypt)

ARETS Armour Remoted Target System

ARF Acute Renal Failure
Apparel Research Foundation (USA)
Auto-regressive Random Field

ARFA Allied Radio Frequency Agency (of NATO)

ARG Akron Rubber Group (USA)

ARGADS Army Radar/Gun Air Defense System (US Army)

ARGC Australian Research Grants Committee (Australia)

ARGE Arbeitsgemeinschaft Meerestechnik (Germany) (an ocean engineering consortium)
European Federation of Associations of Lock and Builders Hardware Manufacturers

ARGMAT ARGYRIS Matrix Code

ARGS Advanced Raster-Graphics System
Anti-Radar Guidance Sensor
Anti-Radiation Guidance Sensor

ARH Advanced Reconnaissance Helicopter

ARH/IR Anti-Radiation Homing/Infra-Red

ARHS Australian Railway Historical Society (Australia)

ARI Air-conditioning and Refrigeration Institute (USA)
Animal Research Institute (Ghana)
Army Research Institute for the Behavioral and Social Sciences (US Army)
Automated Readability Index

ARIA Advanced Range Instrumentation Aircraft
APOLLO Range Instrumented Aircraft

ARIAL Automatic Radar Identification Analysis and Alarm

ARIEM Army Research Institute of Environmental Medicine (US Army)

ARIES Astronomical Radio Interferometric Earth Surveying
Automated Reliability Interactive Estimation System

ARIMA Autoregressive Integrated Moving Average

ARIP Automatic Rocket Impact Predictor

ARIS Activity Reporting Information System
Advanced Range Instrumentation Ship
Audio Response Interface System
Automated Reactor Inspection System

ARKISYST International Information System for Architecture (a project of UNESCO)

ARL Admiralty Research Laboratory (MOD) (merged into AMTE in 1977)
Aeronautical Research Laboratories (of Department of Supply (Australia))
Aeronautical and Astronautical Research Laboratory, Ohio State University (USA)
Aerospace Research Laboratories (USAF)
Air Resources Laboratory (of ESSA (USA)) (now of ERL (NOAA))
Applied Research Laboratories, Texas University (USA)
Applied Research Laboratory (Pennsylvania State University (USA))
Association of Research Libraries (USA)
Atlantic Regional Laboratory (of NRC (Canada))
Australian Radiation Laboratory (Australia)
Average Run Length

ARLB Automatic Radio Location Beacon

ARLIS Arctic Research Laboratory Ice Station
Art Libraries Society

ARLIS/NA Art Libraries Society of North America

ARM Accelerated Relaxation Method
AMPEX Replacement Memory
Anhysteretic Remanent Magnetisation
Anisotropic Remanent Magnetism
Anti-Radar Missile
Anti-Radiation Missile
Association of Recreation Managers

ARMA American Records Management Association (USA)
Association of Records Managers and Administrators (USA)
Australian Rubber Manufacturers Association (Australia)
Auto-Regressive Moving Average
ARMACS Aviation Resources Management And Control System (USN)
ARMADA Aircraft Reliability, Maintainability, Availability Design Analysis
ARMAN Artificial Methods Analyst
ARMCOM Armament Command (US Army)
ARMCOMSAT Arab Communications Satellite System
ARME Automatic Reseau Measuring Equipment
ARMIS Agricultural Research Management Information System
ARMM Automatic Reliability Mathematical Model
ARMMS Automated Reliability and Maintainability Measurement System
Automatically Reconfigurable Modular Multiprocessor System
ARMOP Army Mortar Program (US Army)
ARMPC Atlanta Region Metropolitan Planning Commission (USA)
ARMS Aerial Radiological Measuring Survey
Amateur Radio Mobile Society
Applications of Remote Manipulators in Space
Army Master Data File Reader Microfilm System (US Army)
Association of Researchers in Medical Science
Atmospheric Roving Manipulator System
preface to numbered series on Aerial Radiological Measuring System issued by Atomic Energy Commission (USA)
ARMSCOR Armaments Development and Production Corporation (South Africa)
ARMSPAN ARGONNE (NATIONAL LABORATORY (USAEC)) Multi-channel Stored Program Analyzer
ARN Atmospheric Radio Noise
ARNG Army National Guard (US Army)
ARNMD Association for Research in Nervous and Mental Disease (USA)
ARO Army Research Office (US Army)
ARO-D Army Research Office – Durham (US Army) (now Army Research Office)
AROA Air Taxi Operators Association
AROD Airborne Radar Orbital Determination
Airborne Range and Orbit Determination
AROM Alterable Read-Only Memory
ARP Account Reconciliation Package
Advanced Re-Entry Programme
Aeronautical Recommended Practice (series issued by SAE)
Aerospace Recommended Practice (series issued by SAE)
Age Replacement Policy
Airborne Radar Platform
Analogous Random Process
Anti-Radiation Projectile
ARGONNE (NATIONAL LABORATORY) Reactor Physics (USAEC)
Assimilation Regulatory Protein
Attack Reference Point
ARPA Advanced Research Projects Agency (USDOD)
Area Radar Prediction Analysis
ARPAC Agricultural Research Policy Advisory Committee (of ARS (USDA))
ARPANET ARPA (USDOD) Computer Network
ARPCCA Association for Regional Parks and Countryside Commissions of Australia (Australia)
ARPCFT Automated Reiter Protein Complement-Fixation Test
ARPEFS Angle-Resolved Photoemission Extended Fine Structure
ARPEGE Air Pollution Episode Game
ARPEL Asistencia Reciproca Petrolera Estatal Latinoamericana
ARPES Angle-Resolved Photoelectron Spectroscopy
ARPL A Retrieval Process Language
ARPPIS African Regional Postgraduate Programme in Insect Science (of ICIPE)
ARPS Advanced Radar Processing System
Advanced Real-time Processing System
Aerospace Research Pilot School (USAF)
Arab Physical Society (Lebanon)
Association of Railway Preservation Societies
Australian Radiation Protection Society (Australia)
Australian Royal Photographic Society (Australia)
ARQ Automatic Repeat Request
Automatic Repeat Request
ARR Accountants' Report Rules 1975
Airborne Reference Radar
ARRA Amateur Radio Retailers Association
ARRADCOM Armament Research And Development Command (US Army) (merged into AMCCOM in 1983)
ARRB Australian Road Research Board (Australia)
ARRCOM Army Armament Readiness Command (US Army) (merged into AMCCOM in 1983)
ARRDO Australian Railway Research and Development Organisation (Australia)
ARRES Automatic Radar Reconnaissance Exploitation System
ARRL American Radio Relay League (USA)
ARRS Aerospace Rescue and Recovery Service (USAF)
Aircraft Refueling and Rearming System
ARRV Armoured Regain and Recovery Vehicle
ARS (Horse) Antirabies Serum
Absolute Radiation Scale
Acoustic Rate Sensor
Active Radar Seeker
Agricultural Research Service (USA)
Air Refuelling Squadron (USAF)
American Rocket Society (USA) (later merged with Institute of Aerospace Sciences)
Atelier de construction de Rennes (of Groupement Industriel des Armaments Terrestres (France))
Atmosphere Revitalization System
Automatic Route Setting
ARSA Airport Radar Service Area
ARSAP Army Small Arms Program (US Army)
ARSI Amateur Radio Society of India (India)
ARSP Aerospace Research Support Program (USAF)
ARSPA Aerial Reconnaissance and Surveillance Penetration Analysis
ARSR Air Route Surveillance Radar
ARSSM Active-Radar Sea-Skimming Martel missile
ARST All-Reflecting Schmidt Telescope
ARSTEC Adaptive Random Search Technique
ARSV Armoured Reconnaissance Scout Vehicle
ART Advanced Reactor Technology
Airborne Radiation Thermometer
Algebraic Reconstruction Technique
Animated Reconstruction of Telemetry
Applied Research and Technology
Arithmetic Reconstruction Technique
Automated Reagin Test
Automated Request Transmission
ARTAC Advanced Reconnaissance and Target Acquisition Capability
ARTADS Army Tactical Data Systems (US Army)
ARTCC Air Route Traffic Control Centre

ARTCS Advanced Radar Traffic Control System
ARTE Admiralty Reactor Test Establishment (MOD) (now Royal Naval Nuclear Propulsion Test and Training Establishment)
ARTEMIS Administrative Real Time Express Mortgage and Investment System
ARTI Acoustic Ray Trace Indicator
Advanced Rotorcraft Technology Integration
Arab Regional Telecommunication Institute (Saudi Arabia)
ARTINS Army Terrain Information System (US Army)
ARTISS Agricultural Real Time Imaging Satellite System
ARTL Army Research and Technology Laboratories (US Army)
ARTOC Army Tactical Operations Central
ARTRAC Advanced Range Testing, Reporting and Control
ARTS Advanced Radar Traffic-control System
Audio Response Time-shared System
Automated Radar Terminal System
Automated Radar Tracking System
ARTT Automatic Rubber Tensile Tester
ARTTel Automated Request Transmission by Telephone
ARU Architecture Research Unit (University of Edinburgh)
Astrophysics Research Unit (of Science Research Council)
Attitude Reference Unit
Audio Response Unit
Auxiliary Read-out Unit
ARUPS Angle-Resolved Ultraviolet Photoemission Spectroscopy
ARV Advanced Aerial Armed Reconnaissance Vehicle
Armoured Recovery Vehicle
ARVAC Association of Researchers in Voluntary Action and Community Involvement
ARW Aeroelastic Research Wing
Air Refuelling Wing (USAF)
AS Aeronautical Specification
Aerospace industry Standard (numbered series issued by SAE (USA))
Airports Service (of FAA (USA))
Amorphous Semiconductor
Artificial Satellite
Auger Spectroscopy
prefix to Aerospace Standards issued by SAE (USA)
prefix to Standards issued by SAA
prefix to dated-numbered series of reports issued by Division of Aeronautical Sciences, University of California (USA)
AS&C Aerospace Surveillance and Control
AS&TS The Associated Scientific and Technical Societies (South Africa)
AS/R Automatic Storage and Retrieval
AS/RS Automated Storage/Retrieval System
ASA Accoustical Society of America (USA)
Acetylsalicylic Acid
Advanced System Avionics
Advertising Standards Authority
Aluminium Stockholders Association
American Society of Agronomy (USA
American Society of Anesthesiologists (USA)
American Society of Appraisers (USA)
American Sociological Association (USA)
American Soybean Association (USA)
American Standards Association (later USASI)
American Statistical Association (USA)
American Subcontractors Association (USA)
American Surgical Association (USA)
Anti-Static Additive
Army Security Agency (US Army)
Australian Society of Accountants (Ausatralia)
Australian Society of Authors (Australia)
Automatic Separation System
Automatic Spectrum Analyzer
ASAB Association for the Study of Animal Behaviour
ASAC Asian Standards Advisory Committee
ASAE Advanced School of Automobile Engineering
American Society for Aerospace Education (USA)
American Society of Agricultural Engineers (USA)
American Society of Association Executives (USA)
ASAIHL Association of Southeast Asian Institutes of Higher Learning
ASALM Advanced Strategic Air-Launched Multi-mission Missile
ASAM American Society for Abrasive Methods (USA)
ASAP Aircraft Synthesis Analysis Programme
Alcohol Safety Action Program (of NHTSA (USA))
Antennas-Scatterers Analysis Programme
Army Scientific Advisory Panel (US Army) (succeeded by ASB in 1978)
As Soon As Possible (software for data processing)
Automated Statistical Analysis Programme
Automatic Spooling with Asynchronous Processing
ASAR Advanced Surface-to-Air Ramjet
ASARC Army Systems Acquisition Review Council (US Army)
ASARS Advanced Strategic Airborne Radar System
Advanced Synthetic Aperture Radar System
ASAS ATKINS (COMPUTING SERVICES LTD) Stress Analysis System
ASAS/SEWS All Sources Analysis System/SIGINT Electronic War Subsystem
ASAT Anti-Satellite Technology
Anti-Satellite weapon
Arbeitsgemeinschaft fur Satellitentragersysteme (Germany)
ASATT Advanced Small Axial Turbine Technology
ASB Apostilb
Army Science Board (US Army)
Association of Shell Boilermakers
Asymtomatic Bacteriuria
ASBAPP American Standards Association (later USASI)
Assessment of Sea Based Air Platform Project (of USN)
ASBC American Society of Biological Chemists (USA)
American Standard Building Code
ASBCA Armed Services Board of Contract Appeal (USA)
ASBD Advanced Sea-Based Deterrent
ASBE American Society of Body Engineers (USA)
ASBI Advisory Service for the Building Industry
ASBM Air-to-Surface Ballistic Missile
ASBPA American Shore and Beach Preservation Association (USA)
ASBU Arab States Broadcasting Union
ASC Accounting Standards Committee (of ICAEW, ICAS, ICAI, ACA, ICMA and CIPFA)
Adaptive Speed Control
Adhesive and Sealant Council (USA)
Advanced Science Computer
Advanced Scientific Computer
Advanced Simulation Center (US Army)
American Society for Cybernetics (USA)
American Society of Cinematographers (USA)
American Society of Consulting Arborists (USA)
American Society of Cytology (USA)
Anglian Standing Conference
Associative Structure Computer
Automatic System Controller
ASCA Association for Scientific Cooperation in Asia
Automatic Science Citation Alerting
ASCATS APOLLO Simulation Checkout and Training

ASCC Aeronautical Services Communications Centre
Air Standardization Coördinating Committee (of NATO)
American Society of Concrete Constructors (USA)
Australian Society of Cosmetic Chemists (Australia)
Automatic Sequence Controlled Calculator

ASCD Association for Supervision and Curriculum Development (USA)

ASCE American Society of Civil Engineers (USA)
Association of Sound and Communication Engineers

ASCEND Advanced System for Communications and Education in National Development

ASCH American Society of Clinical Hypnosis (USA)

ASCHIMICI Italian Chemical Manufacturers Association (Italy)

ASCI Administrative Staff College of India (India)
American Society for Clinical Investigation (USA)

ASCII American Standard Code for Information Interchange

ASCIS Australian Schools Cataloguing Information Service (Australia)

ASCL Advanced Sonobuoy Communications Link
Advanced System Concepts Laboratory (US Army)

ASCLA Association of Specialised and Co-operative Library Agencies

ASCM Anti-Ship Cruise Missile
Association of Ships Compositions Manufacturers (now part of PMAGB)

ASCMS American Society of Contemporary Medicine and Surgery (USA)

ASCN American Society for Clinical Nutrition (USA)

ASCNEB Association des Stagiares du College National des Experts Compatables de Belgique (Belgium) (Association of Accountancy Students of Belgium)

ASCO American Society on Contemporary Opthamology (USA)
Automatic Sustainer Cut-Off

ASCOBIC African Standing Conference on Bibliographic Control

ASCOG Association of South Central Oklahoma Governments (USA)

ASCOLBI Asociacion Colombiana de Bibliotecarios (Colombia) (Library Association of Colombia)

ASCOM Arvi Satellite Communication Project (India)
Association of Telecommunication Services

ASCON Automated Switched Communications Network

ASCOP A Statistical Computing Procedure

ASCOPE ASEAN Council on Petroleum

ASCOT Atmospheric Studies in Complex Terrain

ASCP American Society of Clinical Pathologists (USA)

ASCS Agricultural Stabilization and Conservation Service (USDA)

ASCS-AP ASCS (USDA)–Aerial Photography Specification

ASCU Association of Small Computer Users (USA)

ASCVD Atherosclerotic Cardiovascular Disease

ASD Acceleration Spectral Density
Adult Services Division (of American Library Association (USA))
Aeronautical (now Aerospace) Systems Division (USAF)

ASDA Accelerate-Stop Distance Available

ASDAR Aircraft-to-Satellite Data Relay system

ASDB Asian Development Bank (of ECAFE) (Philippines)

ASDC Aeronomy and Space Data Center (of NOAA (USA)) (now part of National Geophysical and Solar Terrestrial Data Center)

ASDE Airport Surface Detection Equipment

ASDF Air Self Defence Force (Japan)

ASDI Automatic Selective Dissemination of Information

ASDIC Anti-Submarine Detection and Identification Committee
Association of Information and Dissemination Centers (USA)

ASDIRS Army Study Documentation and Information Retrieval System (US Army)

ASDM Association of Steel Drum Manufacturers

ASDR Avionic Systems Demonstrator Rig

ASE Active Seismic Experiment
Aircraft Stabilization Equipment
Aircraft Survivability Equipment
Amplified Spontaneous Emission
Amplified Stimulated Emission
Anisotropic Stress Effect
Anomolous Skin Effect
Association Suisse des Electriciens (Switzerland)
Association for Science Education
Association of Senior Engineers (USA)
Automatic Stabilization Equipment

ASEA Allmanna Svenska Elektriska Aktiebolaget (Sweden)
Arizona State Electronics Association (USA)

ASEAN Association of South East Asian Nations (Philippines, Indonesia, Thailand, Singapore, Malaysia)

ASEANIP ASEAN Institute of Physics

ASEB Aeronautics and Space Engineering Board (of National Academy of Engineering (USA))
Assam State Electricity Board (India)

ASECNA Agence pour la Securite de la Navigation Aerienne en Afrique et a Madagascar (Agency for Air Traffic Control in Africa and to Madagascar)

ASED Aviation and Surface Effects Department (of NSRDC (USN))

ASEE American Society for Engineering Education (USA)

ASEE/COED American Society for Engineering Education, Computers in Education Division (USA)

ASEFCA Asociacion Sindical Espanola de Fabricantes de Coias y Adhesives (Spain)

ASEIB Asociacion de Egresados de la Escuela Interamericana de Bibliotecologia (Colombia) (Association of Graduates of the Inter-American School of Librarianship)

ASELT Association Europeenne pour l'Echange de la Litterature Technique dans le domaine de la siderurgie (European Association for the Exchange of Technical Literature in the Field of Ferrous Metallurgy)

ASEM American Society of Engineering Management (USA)
Anti-Surface Euromissile consortium

ASEP American Society for Experimental Pathology (USA)
American Society of Electroplated Plastics (USA)

ASESA Armed Services Electro-Standards Agency (USDOD)

ASESB Armed Services Explosives Safety Board (US DOD))

ASET Aeronautical Satellite Earth Terminal
Author System for Education and Training

ASETA Asociacion de Empresas Estatales de Telecomunicaciones del Acuerdo Subregional Andino (Association of State Telecommunication Undertakings of the Andean Sub-regional Agreement)
Association Suisse pour l'Équipement de l'Agriculture (Switzerland) (Swiss Association for Agricultural Technology)

ASEW Airborne and Surface Early Warning

ASF Advanced Simulation Facility (Missile Command (US Army))
Alternative Salient Futures
Antistreptolysin Factor
ASFA American Science Film Association (USA)
ASFIR Active Swept Frequency Interferometer Rader
ASFIS Aquatic Sciences and Fisheries Information System (of FAO (UN) and IOC (Intergovernmental Oceanographic Commission) (UNESCO)
ASFIT Anisotropic Source Flux Iteration Technique
ASFTS Airborne Systems Functional Test Stand
ASG Advanced Study Group
Aeronautical Standards Group
ASGE American Society for Gastrointestinal Endoscopy (USA)
ASGLS Advanced Space-Ground Link Sub-system
ASGW Air-to-Surface Guided Weapon
ASH Action on Smoking and Health
Advanced Scout Helicopter
Aerial Scout Helicopter
American Society of Hematology (USA)
ASHA American Social Health Association (USA)
American Speech and Hearing Association (USA)
Association for the Application of Science to Human Affairs (India)
ASHAY Aeronomic South Hemisphere and Antarctic Year
ASHBEAMS American Society of Hospital Based Emergency Air Medical Services (USA)
ASHE American Society of Hospital Engineering (USA)
ASHP American Society of Hospital Pharmacists (USA)
ASHRACE American Society of Heating, Refrigerating and Air-Conditioning Engineers (USA)
ASHRAE American Society of Heating, Refrigerating and Air-conditioning Engineers (USA)
ASHS American Society for Horticultural Science (USA)
ASI Advanced Study Institute (conferences held by NATO)
Air Speed Indicator
American Society of Indexers (USA)
Asian Statistical Institute (Japan)
Astronomy Society of India (India)
United States of America Standards Institute (now ANSI (USA))
ASIA Association Suisse de l'Industrie de l'Aviation (Switzerland)
ASIAC Aerospace Structures Information and Analysis Center (USAF)
ASIC Application Specific Integrated Circuit
Association Scientifique Internationale du Cafe (International Scientific Association of Coffee)
Avionics Subsystems Interface Contractor
ASIDES ABERDEEN (UNIVERSITY) Studies In Defence Economics
ASIDIC Association of Scientific Information Dissemination Centers (USA) (changed title in 1975 to Association of Information and Dissemination Centers)
ASIDP American Society of Information and Data Processing (USA)
ASII American Science Information Institute (USA)
ASIL Associazione Italiana di Studio del Lavoro (Italy) (Italian Work Study Association)
Asymptotic Stability In the Large
ASIM American Society of Internal Medicine (USA)
Arbeitsgemeinschaft fuer Simulation (Germany)
ASIN Agricultural Services Information Network (of National Agricultural Library (USA))
ASINEL (Electrical Industry Research Association)
Asociacion de Investigacion Industrial Electrica (Spain)
ASIO Australian Security Intelligence Organisation (Australia)
ASIP Aircraft Structural Integrity Program (USAF)
ASIPLA Associacion de Industrias Plasticas (Chile) (Association of the Plastics Industry)
ASIRC Aquatic Sciences Information Retrieval Center (of University of Rhode Island, USA)
ASIS Abort Sensing and Instrumentation System
American Society for Information Science (USA)
AOKI (CONSTRUCTION COMPANY (Japan)) Shadow Investigation System
ASISES American Section of the International Solar Energy Society (USA)
ASIT Adaptable Surface Interface Terminal
ASIWPCA Association of State and Interstate Water Pollution Control Administrators (USA)
ASJA American Society of Journalists and Authors (USA)
ASK Amplitude-Shift Keying
ASKA Automatic System for Kinematic Analysis
ASKS Automatic Station Keeping System
ASL American Sign Language (for the deaf)
Antenna Systems Laboratory (University of New Hampshire (USA))
Atmospheric Sciences Laboratory (US Army)
ASLA American Society of Landscape Architects (USA)
Association of State Library Agencies (USA)
Australian School Library Association (Australia)
ASLAB Atomic Safety and Licensing Appeal Board (USA)
ASLB Atomic Safety and Licensing Board (USA) (absorbed into the Nuclear Regulatory Commission in 1974)
ASLE American Society of Lubrication Engineers (USA)
ASLG American Studies Library Group (administered by Bodleian Library, Oxford)
Aviation Signal Light Gun
Aslib a registered name sometimes expanded as Association of Special Libraries and Information Bureaux (became Aslib (The Association for Information Management) in 1983)
ASMA Aerospace Medical Association (USA)
ASLO American Society of Limnology and Oceanography (USA)
ASLP Association of Special Libraries of the Philippines
ASM Advanced Surface-to-air Missile
Air-to-Surface Missile
American Society for Metals (USA)
American Society for Microbiology (USA)
American Society of Mammalogists (USA)
Association for Systems Management (USA)
Asynchronous Sequential Machine
ASMA Aerospace Medical Association (USA)
Alaska State Medical Association (USA)
ASMC Association of Stores and Materials Controllers
ASMD Anti-Ship Missile Defence
ASMD/EW Anti-Ship Missile Defence/Electronic Warfare
ASME American Society of Mechanical Engineers (USA)
Association for the Study of Medical Education
ASMI Aerodrome or Airfield or Airport Surface Movement Indicator
Airfield Surface Movement Indication
ASMMA American Supply and Machinery Manufacturers Association (USA)
ASMO Arab Organisation for Standardisation and Metrology
ASMP Aerospace Medical Panel (of AGARD (NATO))
American Society of Magazine Photographers (USA)
ASMR Advanced Short-to-Medium Range
ASMS Advanced Surface Missile System
American Society for Mass Spectrometry (USA)
Anti-Ship Missile Defence
Asian Society for Manpower Development
Atmosphere Sensing and Maintenance System

ASMT American Society of Medical Technologists (USA)
Anti-Ship Missile Target
ASN Average Sample Number
ASNAP Automatic Steerable Null Antenna Processor
ASNE American Society of Naval Engineers (USA)
ASNT American Society for Nondestructive Testing (USA)
ASO Airborne Science Office (Ames Research Center (of NASA (USA))
American Society for Oceanography (USA) (merged into Marine Technology Service)
Anisotropic Spin-Orbit
Antistreptolysin O
Aviation Supply Office (USN)
ASOAP Army Spectrometric Oil Analysis Program (US Army) (now AOAP)
ASOC Air Support Operations Center (USAF)
ASODDS ASWEPS Submarine Oceanographic Digital Data System
ASOS American Society of Oral Surgeon (USA)
Association Suisse d'Organisation Scientifique (Switzerland) (Swiss Association for Scientific Management)
ASOSAI Asian Organization of Supreme Audit Institutions
ASOVAC Asociacion Venezolana para el Avance de la Ciencia (Venezuela) (Venezuelan Association for the Advancement of Science)
ASOVII Asociacion Venezolana de Ingenieros Industrales (Venezuela) (Association of Industrial Engineers)
ASP Accelerated Surface Post
Acoustic Signal Processor
Activated Sludge Process
Aerospace Plane
All Altitude Spin Projectile
American Selling Price
American Society for Photobiology (USA)
American Society of Photogrammetry (USA) (became ASPRS in 1984)
Analysis of Synthetic Programmes
APOLLO Simple Penetrometer
Army Strategic Plan (US Army)
Association–Storing Processor
Association Suisse du Pneu (Switzerland) (Association of the Swiss Tyre Industry)
Associative Structures Package
Astronomical Society of the Pacific (USA)
Asymmetric Multiprocessing System
Attached Support Processor
Automatic Synthesis Programme
numbered series on Advice on Standards for Protection issued by NRPB and published by HMSO
ASPA Alloy Steel Producers Association (India)
American Society for Personnel Administration (USA)
Association of South Pacific Airlines
Automatic Systems Pressure Alarms
ASPAC Asian and Pacific Council (Headquarters in Thailand)
ASPAN Association Suisse pour le Plan d'Amenagement National (Switzerland) (Swiss Association for the National Development Plan)
ASPB Assault Support Patrol Boat
ASPE Alabama Society of Professional Engineers (USA)
American Society of Plumbing Engineers (USA)
ASPEA Association Suisse pour l'Energie Atomique (Switzerland) (Swiss Association for Atomic Energy)
ASPEC Association pour la Prévention et l'Étude de la Contamination (France) (Association for the Prevention and Study of Contamination)
ASPECT Acoustic Short-Pulse Echo-Classification Techniques
Automatic Speckle Cancellation Techniques
ASPEN Asian Physics Education Network (Malaysia)
ASPET American Society for Pharmacology and Experimental Therapeutics (USA)
ASPEX Automated Surface Perspectives
ASPF Australian Society of Perfumers and Flavourists (Australia)
ASPI Advanced Propulsion Subsystem Integration
ASPJ Advanced OR Airborne Self-Protection Jammer
ASPM Armed Services Procurement Manual (USDOD)
ASPO American Society of Planning Officials (USA)
American Society of Plumbing Officials (USA)
ASPP American Society of Plant Physiologists (USA)
ASPQ Association Suisse pour la Promotion de la Qualite (Switzerland) (Association for Quality Improvement)
ASPR Armed Services Procurement Regulations (USDOD) (now DAR)
ASPRS American Society of Photogrammetry and Remote Sensing (USA)
American Society of Plastic and Reconstructive Surgery (USA)
ASPS Aerospace Physiologists Society (USA)
Annular Suspension and Pointing System
ASPT American Society of Plant Taxonomists (USA)
ASQ Deutsche Arbeitsgemeinschaft fur Statistische Qualitatskontrolle (Germany) (German Society for Statistical Quality Control) (now Deutsche Gesellschaft fur Qualitat (German Society for Quality))
ASQC American Society for Quality Control (USA)
ASR ADMIRALTY Standard Range
Air-Sea Rescue
Airborne Surveillance Radar
Airport Surveillance Radar
Analogue Shift Register
Astronomy Space and Radio Board (of SERC)
Automatic Send-Receive
Auxiliary Submarine Rescue ship
ASRA Applied Science and Research Applications (a directorate of NSF (USA)
ASRAAM Advanced Short-Range Air-to-Air Missile
ASRADI Adaptive Surface Signal Recognition And Direction Indicator
ASRAPS Acoustic Sensor Range Prediction System
ASRC Atmospheric Sciences Research Center (of SUNY (USA))
ASRCT Applied Scientific Research Corporation of Thailand (Thailand)
ASRD Authority Safety and Reliability Directorate (of UKAEA)
ASRDI Aerospace Safety Research and Data Institute (of NASA (USA))
ASRE American Society of Regrigeration Engineers (now ASHRAE)
ASRL Aeroelastic and Structures Research Laboratory (of Massachusetts Institute of Technology) (USA)
Average Sample Run Length
ASRM American Society of Range Management (USA)
Antenna System Readiness Monitor
ASRO Astronomical Roentgen Observatory Satellite
ASROC Anti-Submarine Rocket
ASRS Automatic Seat Reservation System
Automatic Storage and Retrieval System
Aviation Safety Reporting System (of NASA (USA))
ASRV Armoured Scout Reconnaissance Vehicle
ASRWPM Association of Semi-Rotary Wing Pump Manufacturers
ASRY Arab Shipbuilding and Repair Yard (at Bahrain; financed by OAPEC)

ASS Admiralty Standard Stockless anchor
American Statistical Society (USA)
Atelier de chargement de Salbris (of Groupement Industriel des Armements Terrestres (France))

ASSASSIN Agricultural System for Storage And Subsequent Selection of Information

ASSBRA Association Belge des Brasseries (Belgium) (Belgian Association of Breweries)

ASSC Accounting Standard Steering Committee (became ASC in 1975 with membership of ICAEW, ICAS, ICAI, ACA, ICMA and CIPFA)
Automatic Support Systems Symposium

ASSCHIMICI Associazione Nazionale Industria Chimica (Italy) (National Chemical Industry Association)

ASSE American Society of Safety Engineers (USA)
American Society of Sanitary Engineers (USA)

ASSEA Association of Surgeons of South East Asia

ASSESS Airborne Science/Shuttle Experiment System Simulation
Airborne Science/Spacelab Experiments Simulation System
Analytical Studies of Surface Effects of Submerged Submarines

ASSET Advanced Systems Synthesis and Evaluation Technique
Aerothermodynamic-aerothermoelastic Structural Systems Environmental Test
Aircraft Support and Service Equipment Tug
Automated System for Security Entries and Transactions

ASSH American Society for Surgery of the Hand (USA)

ASSI AB Statens Skogsindustrier (Sweden)

ASSIFONTE Association de l'Industrie de la Fonte de Fromage (of EEC) (Association of the Processed Cheese Industry)

ASSIG ASLIB Social Sciences Information Group

ASSIST Award Scheme for Science, Industry and School-Teaching (of Science Research Council)

ASSM Anti-Ship Supersonic Missile
Anti-Surface Ship Missile

ASSOCHAM Associated Chambers of Commerce and Industry (India)

ASSOCOM Association of Chambers of Commerce (South Africa)

ASSOFOND Associazione Nazionale delle Fonderie (Italy) (National Association of Foundries)

ASSOGOMMA Associazione Nazionale fra le Industrie della Gomma (Italy) (National Association of the Rubber Industry)

ASSOPOMAC Association des Obteneurs de la Pomme de Terre des Pays de la C.E.E. (Association of Potato Growers of the Countries of the European Economic Community)

ASSORT Automatic System for Selection Of Receiver and Transmitter

ASSP Acoustics, Speech and Signal Processing

ASSR Airborne Sea and Swell Recorder

ASSRS Adaptive Step Size Random Search

ASSS Automatic Spectrum Surveillance System

ASST Action-Speed Tactical Trainer
Anti-Ship Surveillance and Targeting
Automatic System Self-Test
Azienda di Stato per i Servizi Telefonici (Italy) (State Telephone Service Undertaking)

ASSUC American Society of Sanitary Engineers (US Countries of the European Economic Community)
Association des Organizations Professionelles du Commerce des Sucres pour les Pays de la C.E.E. (Association of the Sugar Industry for the

ASSW Anti-Strategic Submarine Warfare

AST Advanced Simulation Technology
Advanced Supersonic Technology
Air Service Training (an aviation school at Perth Aerodrome, Scotland)
Apparent Sidereal Time
Apparent Solar Time
Automatic Scan Tracking

ASTA Adaptive Search and Track Array
Aerial Surveillance and Target Acquisition
American Seed Trade Association (USA)
American Society of Travel Agents (USA)
Association of Short-Circuit Testing Authorities
Automatic System Trouble Analysis
Aviation Systems Test Activity (US Army)

ASTAC Assembly Science and Technology Advisory Council (of California Assembly General Research Committee (USA))

ASTANO Astilleros y Talleres del Noroeste (Spain)

ASTAP Advanced Statistical Analysis Programme

ASTC Airport Surface Traffic Control

ASTD American Society for Training and Development (USA)

ASTE Association pour le developpement des Sciences et Techniques de l'Environnement (France) (Association for the Development of Environmental Sciences and Techniques)

ASTEC Australian Science and Technology Council (Australia)

ASTEO Association Scientifique et Technique pour l'Exploitation des Oceans (France) (Scientific and Technical Association for the Exploitation of the Oceans)

ASTF Aeropropulsion System Test Facility (USAF)

ASTHO Association of State and Territorial Health Officials (USA)

ASTI Anti-Submarine Training Indicator
Automated System for Transport Intelligence

ASTIA Armed Services Technical Information Agency (later DDC, now DTIC (USDOD))

ASTM American Society for Testing and Materials (USA)

ASTME American Society of Tool and Manufacturing Engineers (USA) (now Society of Manufacturing Engineers)

ASTNO Anti-Submarine Torpedo
Astilleros Telleres del Noroeste (Spain)

ASTOVL Advanced Short Take-Off and Vertical Landing

ASTP Aging and Surveillance Test Programme
APOLLO-SOYUZ Test Programme

ASTRA Advanced Structural Analyzer
Advanced System for Radiological Assessment
Applications of Space Techniques Relating to Aviation (panel of ICAO)
Applied Space Technology—Regional Advancement
Astronomical Space Telescope Research Assembly
Astronomical and Space Techniques for Research on the Atmosphere (a project at the University of Washington (USA))
Automatic Scheduling and Time-dependent Resource Allocation
Automatic Scheduling with Time-integrated Resource Allocation
cell for the Application of Science and Technology to Rural Areas (of IIS (India))

ASTRAC ARIZONA Statistical Repetitive Analog Computer

ASTRAIL Analogue Schematic Translator to Algebraic Language
Assurance and Stabilization Trends for Reliability by Analysis of Lots

ASTRAL Automatic System of Telecommunications and Reservations for AER LINGUS (Eire)

ASTRAP Application of Space Techniques Relating to Aviation Panel (of ICAO)

ASTRE Airport Surface Traffic Radar Equipment
ASTRO Advanced Spacecraft Truck/Trainer/Transport Reusable Orbiter
America's Sound Transportation Review Organisation (USA)
Astrophysical satellite
ASTROS Automated Shell Theory for Rotating Structures
ASTS Air to Surface Transport System
Association Suisse pour la Technique du Soudage (Switzerland) (Swiss Association for the technique of Welding)
Association of Scientific and Technical Societies (South Africa)
ASTT Action–Speed Tactical Trainer
Action Speed Tactical Teacher
ASTUTE Association of System 2000 Users for Technical Exchange
ASU Arizona State University (USA)
ASUPT Advanced Simulation OR Simulator Undergraduate Pilot Training
ASUTS American Society of Ultrasound Technical Specialists (USA)
ASUW Anti-Surface Warfare
ASV Air-to-Surface Vessel
Anodic Stripping Voltammetry
Ardal og Sundal Verk (Norway)
Avian Sarcoma Virus
ASVAB Armed Services Vocational Aptitude Battery (USDOD)
ASVILMET Associazione Italiana per lo Sviluppo degli Studi Sperimentali sulla Lavorazione dei Metalli (Italy) (Italian Association for the Promotion of Metalworking Research)
ASVIP American Standard Vocabulary for Information Processing
ASW Acoustic Surface-Wave
Anti-Submarine Warfare
Artificial Seawater
ASW-SOW Anti-Submarine Warfare Stand-Off Weapon
ASWAC Anti-Submarine Warfare Advisory Committee (of NSIA (USA))
ASWBLP Armed Services Whole Blood Processing Laboratory (USDOD)
ASWCCS Anti-Submarine Warfare Command and Control System
ASWCR Airborne Surveillance Warning and Control Radar
ASWE Admiralty Surface Weapons Establishment (MOD) (became ARE (MOD) in 1984)
ASWEPS Anti-Submarine Warfare Environmental Prediction Service (USN)
ASWF Arithmetic Series Weight Function
ASWOT Anti-Submarine Warfare Opposed Transit
ASWS Automatic Surface Weathern System
ASZ American Society of Zoologists (USA)
ASZD American Society for Zero Defects (USA)
AT Anomalous Transmission
Appropriate Technology
Ataxia Telangiectasia
Atomic Time
Autotransformer
AT/AV Anti-Tank/Anti-Vehicle
AT/GW Anti-Tank Guided Weapon
ATA Advanced Test Accelerator
Air Transport Association
Air Transport Association of America (USA)
Alimentary Toxic Aleukia
American Transit Association (USA) (merged into APTA, 1974)
American Translators Association (USA)
American Trucking Association (USA)
Anti-Tubulin Antibody
Atlantic Treaty Association
Atmospheres Absolute
Automatic Threat Alert
ATAADS Anti-Tank Assault, Air-Defence System
ATABE Automatic Target Assignment Battery Evaluation
ATAC Active Thermo-Atmosphere Combustion
Air Transport Association of Canada (Canada)
Air-To-Air Combat
Army Tank-Automotive Command (USA Army)
Auburn (Alabama (USA)) Technical Assistance Center
Australian Transport Advisory Council (Australia)
ATACC Advanced Technology Axial Centrifugal Compressor
Airborne Tactical Air Control Capability
ATACO Air Tactical Control Operator
ATACS Advanced Tactical Air Combat Simulation
Advanced Tactical Air Command and Control System
Army Tactical Communications System (US Army)
ATAF Allied Tactical Air Force (NATO)
ATAFCS Airborne Target Acquisition and Fire Control System
ATAR Air-to-Air Recovery
Airborne Tracking, Acquisition and Recognitio
Anti-Tank Aircraft Rocket
Association des Transporteurs Aeriens Regionaux (France) (Association of Regional Air Carriers)
ATARS Air Traffic Advisory Resolution System
Anti-Terrain Avoidance Radar System
Automated Traffic Avoidance and Resolution System
Automated Travel Agents Reservation Systems
ATAS Automated Telephone Answering System
ATAWS Autonomous Tactical All-Weather Strike aircraft
ATB Acetyle Tetrabromide
Advanced Technology Bomber
Agricultural Training Board
Ampere-turn Balance Detector
ATBM Anti-Tactical Ballistic Missile
ATC Adaptive Transform Coding
Adiabatic Toroidal Compressor
Advanced Technology Components
Advanced Thermodynamic Cycle
Agence Transcongolaise des Communications (Congo)
Air Traffic Conference of America (USA)
Air Traffic Control
Air Training Command (USAF)
Alaska Transportation Commission
Alloy-Tin Couple
Approved Type Certificate
Armoured Troop Carrier (a vessel)
Australian Telecommunications Commission (Australia)
Automated Technical Control
Automatic Tool Charger
Automatic Train Control
Average Total Cost
ATCA Advanced Tanker/Cargo Aircraft
Air Traffic Control Association (USA)
Allied Tactical Communications Agency (NATO)
Australian Tuberculosis and Chest Association (Australia)
ATCAC Air Traffic Control Advisory Committee (USA)
ATCAP Army Telecommunications Automation Program (US Army)
Automatic Thyristor Circuit Analysis Programme
ATCAS Air Traffic Control Automated System
ATCase Aspartate Transcarbamylase
ATCC American Type Culture Collection (USA)

ATCD Automatic Telephone Call Distribution
ATCEU Air Traffic Control Evaluation Unit
ATCP Antarctic Treaty Consultative Parties
Asociacion Mexicana de Tecnicos de las industrias de la Celulosa y del Papel (Mexico) (Mexican Association for the Technology of the Wood Pulp and Paper Industry)
ATCRBS Air Traffic Control Radar Beacon System
ATCS Air Traffic Control Board (of MoD and Dept of Industry)
ATCU Air Transportable Communication Unit
ATD Aerospace Technology Division (of Library of Congress, USA) (now disbanded)
Armoured Tank Destroyer
Articulotrochanteric Distance
Audio-Tactile Display (for enabling blind people to use electronic calculators)
ATDA Army Training Device Agency (US Army)
Augmented Target Docking Adaptor
Australian Telecommunications Development Association (Australia)
ATDD Average Total Diametrical Displacement
ATDE Advanced Technology Demonstrator Engine
ATDL Air Resources Atmospheric Turbulence and Diffusion Laboratory (of NOAA (USA))
ATDM Asynchronous Time-Division Multiplexing
ATDS Airborne Tactical Data System
ATDSIA Allied Tactical Data Systems Inter-operability Agency (NATO)
ATE Advanced Technology Engine
Atelier de fabrication de Toulouse (of Groupement Industriel des Armements Terrestres (France))
Automatic Test Equipment
ATEA Army Transportation Engineering Agency (US Army)
Automatic Test Equipment Association (USA)
ATEC Air Transport Electronics Council
Automated Technical Control
Automated Test Equipment Complex
Aviation Technician Education Council (USA)
ATECI Asociacion Tecnica Espanola de la Construccion Industrialialzada (Spain) (Spanish Technical Association of Industrialised and Prefabricated Building)
ATEE Association for Teacher Education in Europe
ATEG Asociatión Téecnica Española de Galvanización (Spain) (Spanish Technical Association of Galvanising)
ATEGG Advanced Turbine Engine Gas Generator (a project of the USAF)
ATEMIS Automatic Traffic Engineering and Management Information System
ATEN Association Technique pour l'Énergie Nucléaire (France) (Nuclear Energy Technology Association) (disbanded in 1975)
ATEP Asociacion Tecnica Espanola del Pretensado (Spain)
ATERB Australian Telecommunications and Electronics Research Board (of CSIRO (Australia))
ATES Air Transportable Earth Station
ATESA Aero Taxis Ecutorianas SA (Ecuador)
ATET Advanced Technology Experimental Transport
ATEV Approximate Theoretical Error Variance
ATEWS Advanced Tactical Electronic Warfare System
ATEX Atlantic Tradewind Experiment (by Germany, United Kingdom and USA)
ATF Acoustic Test Facility (NAL) (India)
Amorphous Thin Film
Automatic Transmission Fluid
ATFA Advanced Techniques in Failure Analysis symposium
Association of Technicians in Financing and Accounting
ATFAS Association of Teachers of Foundry and Allied Subjects
ATFB Alcohol, Tobacco, Firearms Bureau (of the Department of the Treasury (USA))
ATFC Automatic Traffic-Flow Control
ATFE Advanced Thermal Control Flight Experiment
ATG Adaptive Threshold Gate
Alternative Technology Group (of the Open University)
Automatic Test Generation
ATGM Anti-Tank Guided Missile
ATGW Anti-Tank Guided Weapon
ATH Automatic Attitude Hold
Autonomous Terminal Homing
ATI Aero Trasporti Italiani (Italy)
Association of Technical Institutions (changed to ACFHE in 1970)
Australian Textile Institute (Australia)
Automotive Tyre Industry (India) (a manufacturers association)
Average Total Inspection
ATIC Australian Tin Information Centre (Australia) (of the Tin Research Institute)
ATICELA Associazione Tecnica Italiana per la Cellulosa e la Carta (Italy) (Italian Technical Association for Wood Pulp and Paper)
ATICPA Asociacion de Tecnicos de la Industria Papelera e Celulosa Argentina (Argentina) (Technical Association for the Paper and Wool Pulp Industry)
ATIEL Association Technique de l'Industrie Européenne de Lubrifiants (Technical Association of European Lubricant Manufacturers)
ATIFAS Associazione Tessiture Italiano Artificiali e Sintetiche (Italy) (Italian Association for Weaving Artificial and Synthetic Fabrics)
ATIGS Advanced Tactical Inertial Guidance System
ATII Advanced Techniques for Imagery Interpretation
ATIM Asociacion de Investagacion Tecnica de las Industrias de la Madera y Corcho (Spain) (Technical Research Association of the Wood and Cork Industries)
ATIP Association Technique de l'Industrie Papetiere (France) (Technical Association of the Paper Industry)
ATIRA Ahmedabad Textile Industry's Research Association (India)
ATIS Automatic Terminal Information Service
Automatic Transmitter Identification System
ATITA Air Transport Industry Training Association
ATJS Advanced Tactical Jamming System
Airborne Tactical Jamming System
ATK Available Tonne-Kilometre
ATL Adult T-cell Leukaemia
Analogue-Threshold Logic
Appliance Testing Laboratories (of the Electricity Council)
Applications Terminal Language
Applied Technology Laboratory (of AVRADCOM)
Automated or Automatic Tape Library
ATLA American Theological Library Association (USA)
AtlantMIRO Atlantic Nauchno-Issledovatelskiy Institut Rybnogo i Okeanografii (USSR) (Atlantic Scientific Research Institute for Fisheries and Oceanography)
ATLAS Abbreviated Test Language for All Systems
Abbreviated Test Language for Avionics Systems
Advanced Tactical Lightweight Air Superiority radar
Advanced Target Location And Strike

Anti-Tank Laser Assisted System
Automatic Tape Lay-up System
group of European Airlines (Air France, Iberia, Lufthansa, Alitalia, and Sebena) Sebena)

ATLB Air Transport Licensing Board (absorbed into CAA, 1972)

ATLD Air-Transportable Loading Dock

ATLIS Army Technical Libraries and Information Systems (US Army)
Army Technical Library Improvement Studies (US Army) (now TISAP)
Automatic-Tracking Laser Illumination System

ATLIT Advanced Technology Light Twin airplane

ATLS Air Transport LORAN C System

ATM Advanced Technology Mining
Air Traffic Management
APOLLO Telescope Mount
Association of Teachers of Management
Association of Teachers of Mathematics
Asynchronous Time Multiplexing
Asynchronous Traction Motor
Atmospheric Structure Advisory Committee (of ESRO)
Atmospheric Structure and Meterology
Automated Teller Machine
Automatic Teller Machine

ATMA Alabama Textile Manufacturers Association (USA)
American Textile Machinery Association (USA)
American Textile Manufacturers Association (USA)

ATMAC Advanced Technology Microelectronic Array Computer
Air Traffic Management Automated Centers (US Army)

ATME Aluminium Tube Multi-Effect

ATME-I American Textile Machinery Exhibition – International (USA)

ATMI American Textile Manufacturers Institute (USA)

ATMP Air Target Materials Program (US DOD)

ATMR Advanced Technology Medium-Range

ATMS Advanced Text Management System
Automatic Transmission Measuring System

ATMSS Automatic Telegraph Message Switching System

ATN Aid-to-Navigation buoys

ATNAV Acoustic Transponder Navigation

ATO Automatic Train Operation

ATOL Assisted Take-Off and Landing

ATOLL Acceptance, Test, or Launch Language

ATOLS Automatic Testing On-Line System

ATOMIC Automated Train Operation by Minicomputer

ATOMS Automated Technical Order Maintenance Sequences

ATP Adenosine Triphosphate
Advanced Turboprop
Array-Transform Processor
prefix to numbered-dated series of publications on Agricultural Trade Policy issued by FAS (USDA)

ATPC Association of Tin Producing Countries

ATPM Association of Teachers of Preventive Medicine (USA)

ATR ADMIRALTY Test Rating
Advanced Test Reactor
Advanced Thermal Reactor
Air-Turbo-Rocket
Attenuated Total Reflection
Auto-Thermal Reformer
Automatic Target Recognizer

ATRAC Angle Tracking Computer

ATRAN Automatic Terrain Recognition And Navigation

ATRD Automatic Target Recognition Device

ATRF Animal Tumor Research Facility (Rochester University (USA))
Australian Transport Research Forum

ATRID Automatic Terrain Recognition and Identification Device

ATRIF Air Transportation Research International Forum

ATRL Anti-Tank Rocket Launcher

ATROI After-Tax Return-on-Investment

ATS Acoustic Target Sensor
Administrative Terminal System
Advanced Technological Satellite
Air Traffic Service (FAA (USA))
Air Traffic System
Air-to-Surface
Alkali-Treated Straw
American Tentative Society (USA)
American Thoracic Society (USA)
Analytic Trouble Shooting
Anti-Thymocyte Serum
Applications Technology Satellite
Atelier de construction de Tarbes (of Groupement Industriel des Armaments Terrestres (France))
Atomiteknillinen Seura-Atomtekniska Sallskapet (Finland) (Nuclear Society)
Automated Telemetry System
Automated Test System
Automatic Tally and Sort
Automatic Train Stopping
Automatic Trim System
Auxiliary Tug Service
Avionics Test System

ATS/JEA Automated Test System/Jet Engine Accessories

ATSD Airborne Traffic and Situation Display

ATSIT Automatic Techniques for the Selection and Identification of Targets

ATSJEA Automatic Test System for Jet Engine Accessories

ATSM Advanced Tactical Stand-off Missile

ATSO Association of Transportation Security Officers (USA)

ATSR Along-Track Scanning Radiometer

ATSS Augmented Target-Screening Subsystem
Automatic Telegraph – Sub System
Automatic Test Support Systems

ATSSS Air Transportable Sonar Surveillance System

ATSTM-LIB Office of Administration and Technical Services – Libraries Branch (of NOAA (USA))

ATSU Association of Time-Sharing Users (USA)

ATT Advanced Technology Transport
Avalanche Transit-Time

ATTC American Towing Tank Conference

ATTI Arizona Transportation and Traffic Institute (USA)

ATTITB Air Transport and Travel Industry Training Board (disbanded in 1982)

ATTO Avalanche Transit-Time Oscillator

ATTR Advanced Threat Reactive receiver

ATTRA Automatic Tracking Telemetry Receiving Antenna

ATTS Asymptotic Temporary Threshold Shift

ATU Arab Telecommunication Union

ATUG Australian Telecommunications Users Group (Australia)

ATuS Antitumour Serum

ATV Abwassertechnische Vereinigung (Germany) (Sewage Technical Research Association)
Akademiet for de Tekniske Videnskaber (Denmark) (Academy of Technical Sciences)
All-Terrain Vehicle
Automatic Ticket Vendor

ATVS Advanced Television Seeker

ATWL Acoustic Travelling Wave Lens

ATWS	Anticipated Transients Without Scram Automatic Telephone Weather Service (of the Post Office Corporation) Automatic Track While Scan
AU	Air University (USAF) Astronomical Unit Auburn University (USA) prefix to numbered series of Automobile Standards issued by BSI
AUA	Argonne Universities Association (USA)
AUC	Airline Users Committee (of CAA) (renamed Air Transport Users Committee in 1978)
AUCANUKUS	Australia, Canada, United Kingdom, United States
AUCAS	Association of University Clinical Academic Staff
AUCC	Association of Universities and Colleges of Canada (Canada)
AUCET	Association of University Chemical Education Tutors
AUD	Asynchronous Unit Delay
AUDACIOUS	Automatic Direct Access to Information with the On-line UDC System
AUDDIT	Automatic Dynamic Digital Test System
AUDREY	Audio Reply
AUIPD	Air University Institute for Professional Development (USAF)
AUL	Above Upper Limit
AUM	Animal Unit Month
AUMA	Ausstellungs-und Messe-Asschub de Deutschen Wirtschaft (Germany) (German Council of Trade Fairs and Exhibitions)
AUNTIE	Automatic Unit for National Taxation and Insurance
AUPELF	Association des Universites Partiellement ou Entierement de Lange Francaise (Association of Partially or Wholly French Language Universities)
AURA	Association of Universities for Research in Astronomy (USA)
AURI	Angkatan Udari Republik Indonesia (Indonesia) (Military Air Force)
AUS	prefix to numbered series of Austenitic Cast Irons
AUSA	Association of the United States Army (USA)
AUSEX	Aircraft Undersea Sound Experiment (of DARPA and later US Navy)
AUSIMM	Australian Institute of Mining and Metallurgy (Australia)
AUSINET	Resource Sharing Networks in Australia (National Library of Australia)
AUSREP	Australian Ship Reporting System
AUSSAT	Australian National Satellite System
AUSTACCS	Australian Tactical Command and Control System (Australian Army)
AUSTPAC	Australian Packet-switching network
AUSTRIATOM	Österreichische Interessengemeinschaft für Nukleartechnik (Austria) (Austrian Nuclear Industry Group)
AUT	Advanced User Terminal Assembly Under Test Automated Unit Test
AUTA	Association of University Teachers of Accounting
AUTE	Association of University Teachers of Economics
AUTEC	Atlantic Undersea Test and Evaluation Center (US Navy)
AUTO CARTO	International Symposium on Computer-Assisted Cartography
AUTO-TRIP	Automatic Transportation Research Investigation Programme
AUTOCOM	Automated Combustor design code
AUTODIN	Automatic Digital Network (of USDOD)
AUTODOC	Automated Documentation
AUTOGRADE	Automatic Pattern Grading
AUTOMAST	Automatic Mathematical Analysis and Symbolic Translation
AUTOMAT	Automatic Methods And Times
AUTOMEX	Automatic Message Exchange
AUTONET	Automatic Network Display Programme
AUTOPOL	Automatic Programming Of Lathes
AUTOPROS	Automated Process Planning System
AutoSACE	Automatic Shorebased Acceptance Checkout Equipment
AUTOSATE	Automated Data Systems Analysis Technique
AUTOSCAN	Automatic Satellite/Computer Aid to Navigation
AUTOSCRIPT	Automated System for Composing, Revising, Illustrating and Phototypesetting
AUTOSEVOCOM	Automatic Secure Voice Communications
AUTOSPOT	Automatic System for Positioning Tools
AUTOSTATIS	Automatic Statewide Auto Theft Inquiry (California, USA)
AUTOSTRAD	Automated System for Transportation Data (USDOD)
AUTOVON	Automatic Voice Network
AUTRAN	Automatic Translation Automatic Utility Translator
AUTRANAV	Automated Transponder Navigation system
AUUA	American Univac Users Association (USA)
AUVMIS	Administrative Use Vehicle Management Information System (US Army)
AUW	All-Up-Weight
AUWE	Admiralty Underwater Weapons Establishment (became ARE (MOD) in 1984)
AUXCP	Auxiliary Airborne Command Post
AUXINI	Empresa Auxiliar de la Industria (Spain)
AUXRC	Auxiliary Recording Control Circuit
AV	Analysis of Variance Audio-Visual
AV-MF	Aviatsiya Voennomorskovo Flota (USSR) (Naval Air Force)
AVA	Aerodynamische Versuchanstalt (Germany) (Aerodynamics Experimental Station) Aerovais del Valle (Costa Rica) Automatic Voice Alarm
AVAB	Automatic Vending Association of Britain
AVACOM-ETARP	Availability Computation – Element Transient and Asymptotic Repair Process
AVADS	Autotrack Vulcan Air Defence System
AVAP	Airport Vicinity Air Pollution model
AVARD	Association of Voluntary Agencies for Rural Development (India)
AVASI	Abbreviated Visual Approach Slope Indicator
AVATI	Asphalt Vinyl and Asbestos Tile Institute (USA)
AVBL	Armoured Vehicle Bridge Launcher
AVC	Automatic Volume Control Average Variable Cost
Avcat	Aviation High-flash Turbine Fuel
AVCC	Average Carbonaceous Chondrites
AVCOM	Aviation Materiel Command (US Army) (now Army Aviation Systems Command)
AVCS	Advanced Vidicon Camera System
AVD	Aeronautical Vehicles Division (of NASA) Axial Velocity-Density
AVDS	Articulated Vehicle Dynamic Simulator
AVE	Associacion Venezolana de Ejecutivos (Venezuela) (Venezuelan Association of Managers) Atmospheric Variability Experiment
AVEC	Amplitude Vibration Exciter Control
AVEM	Association of Vacuum Equipment Manufacturers (USA)
AVENSA	Aerovias Venzolanas SA (Vemezuela)
AVERE	European Electric Road Vehicle Association

AVF All-Volunteer Force
Azimuthally Varying Field
AVGAS Aviation Gasoline
AVH Acute Variceal Haemorrhage
Alexander von Humboldt-Stiftung (Germany) (Alexander von Humboldt Foundation)
AVHRR Advanced Very High Resolution Radiometer
AVI Adjustable Voltage Inverter
Automatic Vehicle Identification
AVIACO Aviacion y Comercia (Spain)
AVIANCA Aerovias Nacionales de Colombia (Colombia)
AVID Audio Visual Instructional Division (of ISRO (India))
AVIG Antivaccinial Immunoglobulin
AVIOS American Voice Input/Output Society (USA)
AVISNET Avionics Integrated Support Networks
AVIT Audio-Visual Integrated Trainer
AVL Automatic Vehicle Location
AVLABS Aviation Laboratories (US Army)
AVLB Armoured Vehicle Launched Bridge
AVLIS Atomic Vapour Laser Isotope Separation
AVLOC Airborne Visible Laser Optical Communications
AVLS Automatic Vehicle Location System
AVM Atelier de Vitrification de Marcoule (France)
Automatic Vehicle Monitoring
AVMA American Veterinary Medical Association (USA)
AVMF Aviatsiya Voenno-Morskava Flota (USSR) (Naval Air Force)
AVMUX Avionic Multiplex
AVOCON Automated Vocabulary Control
AVOID Airfield Vehicle Obstacle Indication Device
Avionic Observation of Intruder Danger
AVOS Acoustic Valve Operating System
AVP Anti-Viral Protein
Arginine Vasopressin
Avionics Panel (of AGARD (NATO))
Office of Aviation Policy (of FAA (USA))
AVPAS Audiovisual and Presentation Advisory Service
AVR Arbeitsgemeinschaft Versuchreaktor (Germany)
Automatic Volume Recognition
AVRADA Army Aviation Research and Development Activity (of AVRADCOM)
AVRADCOM Aviation Research and Development Command (US Army) (became part of AVSCOM in 1983)
AVRI Animal Virus Research Institute (of AFRC)
AVRS Audio Video Recording System
Audio/Visual Recording System
AVS Aerospace Vehicle Simulation
American Vacuum Society (USA)
AVSAIL Avionics Systems Analysis and Integration Laboratory (USAF)
AVSC Assets Valuation Standards Committee (of RICS)
AVSCOM Army Aviation Systems Command (US Army) (disbanded 1977)
Aviation Systems Command (US Army) (formed 1983)
AVST Automated Visual Sensitivity Tester
AVT Added Value Tax
All-Volatile Treatment
Arginine Vasotocin
AVTA Automatic Vocal Transaction Analysis
Avtag Aviation Wide-cut Turbine Fuel
AVTR Airborne Video Tape Recorder
Avtur Aviation Turbine Fuel
AW Augmentor Wing
AWA Aluminium Window Association
Anglian Water Authority
Anomalous Winter Absorption
Antique Wireless Association (USA)
AWACS Airborne Warning and Control Squadron (USAF)
Airborne Warning and Control System
AWACTS Airborne Warning and Control Training Squadron (USAF)
AWACW Airborne Warning and Control Wing (USAF)
AWADS Adverse Weather Aerial Delivery System
All-Weather Aerial Delivery System
AWANS Aviation Weather and Notice to Airmen System
AWAR Area Weighted Average Resolution
AWARE Advance Warning Equipment
AWARS Airborne Weather and Reconnaissance System
All-Weather Airborne Reconnaissance System
AWAS Airborne Wind-shear Alert Sensor
AWAVS Aviation Wide-Angle Visual System
AWC Air War College (USAF)
Australian Wool Corporation (Australia)
AWCD All-Weather Chassis Dynamometer
AWCLS All-Weather Carrier Landing System
AWCS Air Weapons Control System
Airborne Weapons Control System
AWDATS Artillery Weapon Data Transmission System
AWDREY Atomic Weapon Detection, Recognition and Yield
AWEA American Wind Energy Association (USA)
AWES Association of Western Europe Shipbuilders
AWG Astronomy Working Group (of ESA)
AWGC Australian Woolgrowers and Graziers Council (Australia)
AWGN Additive White Gaussian Noise
AWI American Watchmakers Institute (USA)
Architectural Woodwork Institute (USA)
AWIS All-Weather Identification Sensor
Association for Women in Science (USA)
AWJSRA Augmentor Wing Jet STOL Research Aircraft
AWL All-Weather Landing
AWLS All-Weather Landing System
AWMPF Australian Wool and Meat Producers Federation (Australia)
AWN Automated Weather Network (USAF)
AWOP All-Weather Operations Panel (of ICAO)
AWPA American Wood Preservers Association (USA)
Australian Women Pilots Association
AWPB American Wood Preservers Bureau (USA)
AWPI American Wood Preservers Institute (USA)
AWRA American Water Resources Association (USA)
Australian Welding Research Association (Australia)
AWRC Australian Water Resources Council (Australia)
AWRE Atomic Weapons Research Establishment (UKAEA) (transferred from UKAEA to MOD, 1973)
AWRS Airborne Weather Reconnaissance System
AWS Air Weather Service (USAF)
American Welding Society (USA)
Automatic Warning System
AWSG Army Work Study Group (MOD) (now Army Management Service Group (Work Study))
AWSO All-Weather Surface Observations (aboard a space shuttle)
AWSS Altitude Warning Signal System
AWT Actual Work Time
AWTMS All-Weather Topographic Mapping System
AWTR Advanced Waste Treatment Processes
AWTSS All-Weather Tactical Strike System
AWV Association of the German Photographic Industry (Germany)
Ausschus fur Wirtschafliche Verwaltung (Germany (Committee for Efficiency in Administration)
AWWA American Water Works Association (USA)
AWWF All-Weather Wood Foundations

AWWS Automated Want/Warrant System (Los Angeles Police Department (USA))
AWWV Abeitsgemeinschaft der Wasserwirtschafsverbaende (Germany) (Water Utilisation Research Association)
AX Attack Experimental
AXAF Advanced X-ray Astrophysics Facility (of NASA (USA))
AXBT Airborne Expendable Bathythermograph
AXLE Axiomatic Language
AXM Acetocycloheximide
AYRS Amateur Yacht Research Society
AZAS Adjustable Zero Adjustable Span
AZBN Azobisisobutyronitrile
AZHD-EPD Arizona Highway Department, Environment Planning Division (USA)
AZTAC ALCOA Impedence Test for Anodic Coatings
AZTRAN Azimuth from Transit

B

B-CAS Beacon-based Collision Avoidance System
BA Beta Anneal
Booksellers Association of Great Britain and Ireland
British Airways
British Association for the Advancement of Science
Butyl Acrylate
BA-SIS Bibliographic Author of Subject Interactive Research
BA-SIS-H BA – SIS – History
BA-SIS-P BA – SIS – Political Science, Public Administration, Urban Studies, and International Relations
BA-SIS-S BA – SIS – Sociology
BAA British Acetylene Association (merged into BCGA, 1971)
British Agrochemicals Association
British Airports Authority
British Anodising Association
British Association of Accountants and Auditors
BAAA British Association of Accountants and Auditors
BAAG British Aerospace Aircraft Group
BAAL British Association for Applied Linguistics
BAAPCD Bay Area (San Francisco (USA)) Air Pollution Control District
BAAR British Acupuncture Association and Register
BAAS British Association for American Studies
British Association for the Advancement of Science
BAB British Airways Board
BABA British Anaerobic and Biomass Association
BABO Boolean Approach for Bivalent Optimization
BABS Blind Approach Beacon System
British Association for Brazing and Soldering
BABT British Approvals Board for Telecommunications
BABW Beratender Ausschuss fur Bildungs-und Wissenschaftspolitik (Germany) (Advisory Commission for Education and Science Policy)
BAC Background Analysis Center (University of Michigan, USA)
Blood Alcohol Concentration
British Atlantic Committee (of the Atlantic Treaty Association)
BACA British Acupuncture Association
BACAN British Association for the Control of Aircraft Noise
BACAT Barge Aboard Catamaran
BACCHUS BRITISH AIRCRAFT CORPORATION Commercial Habitat Under the Sea
BACCI Beton Arme, Constructions Civiles et Industrielles (France)
BACE Basic Aircraft Check-out Equipment
BACEA British Airport Construction and Equipment Association
BACER Biological And Climatic Effects Research (a program of EPA (USA))
BACH Backscatler/Absorption Chamber
BACIE British Association for Commercial and Industrial Education
BACIS British Association of CIRP Industrial Sponsors
BACMM British Association of Clothing Machinery Manufacturers
BACo BASEEFA Advisory Council
BACS Bankers Automated Clearing Services
British Association for Chemical Specialties
BACT Best Available Control Technology
BACVSR British Air Cushion Vehicle Safety Requirements
BAD British Association of Dermatologists
Buck-A-Day (production cost-cutting program in USA)
BADADUQ Banque de Données à Accès Direct de l'Université du Québec (Canada) (On-line Bank of Quebec University)
BADGE Base Air Defence Ground Environment
BAe British Aerospace Corporation (government owned – formed in 1977)
BAE Bureau of Agricultural Economics (Australia)
BAeA British Aerobatic Association
BAEC British Agricultural Export Council
British Amateur Electronics Club
BAED British Airways European Division
BAEE British Army Equipment Exhibition
BAFA British Accounting and Finance Association
BAFM British Association of Friends of Museums
BAFRA British Aluminium Foil Rollers Association
BAFS British Academy of Forensic Sciences
BAGDA British Advertising Gift Distributors Association
BAGS Bullpup Automatic Guidance System
BAH British Airways Helicopters (a part of British Airways)
BAHO British Association of Helicopter Operators
BAHPA British Agricultural and Horticultural Plastics Association
BAI Bank Administration Institute (USA)
BAIE British Association of Industrial Editors
BAIR British Airports Information Retrieval
BAIT Bacterial Automated Identification Technique
BAK Barrier Arresting Kit
Bundesassistenkonferenz (Germany) (Federal University Assistants Conference)
BAL Basic Assembler Language
Blood Alcohol Level
BALARE Buoyancy Actuated Launch and Retrieval Elevator
BALCO Bharat Aluminium Corporation (India) (government owned)
BALI British Association of Landscape Industries
BALLAD Ballistic LORAN Assist Device
BALLOTS Bibliographic Automation of Large Library Operations using Time Sharing (now RLIN)
BALM Block And List Manipulator
BALPA Balance of Payments
BALTHUM Balloon Temperature and Humidity
BALUN Balance to Unbalanced
BAM Basic Access Method
Bundesanstalt fur Materialprufung (Germany) (Federal Institute for Materials Testing)

BAMA British Aerosol Manufacturers Association

BAMAC British Automobile Manufacturers Association in Canada

BAMBI Bayesian Analysis Modified By Inspection

BAMIRAC Ballistic Missile Radiation Analysis Center (University of Michigan) (USA)

BAMM British Association of Manipulative Medicine

BAMP Basic Analysis and Mapping Programme

BAMTM British Association of Machine Tool Merchants

BANS Bright Alphanumeric Sub-system
British Association of Numismatic Societies

BANSDOC Bangladesh National Scientific and Technical Documentation Centre (Bangladesh)

BANZ Booksellers Association of New Zealand

BAO British Association of Orthodontists
British Association of Otolaryngologists

BAOD British Airways Overseas Division

BaP Benz(a)pyrene

BAP Basic Assembly Programme

BAPC British Aircraft Preservation Council

BAPE Balloon Atmospheric Propagation Experiment

BAPEX British Association of Paper Exporters

BAPM&R British Association of Physical Medicine and Rheumatology (now British Association for Rheumatology and Rehabilitation)

BAPN Beta-amino Propionitrile

BAPP British Association for Perinatal Paediatrics

BAPS Beam And Plate System
British Association of Paediatric Surgeons

BAPTA Bearing And Power Transfer Assembly

BAR Base-band Radar
Browning Automatic Rifle

BARB Broadcasters Audience Research Board (of the BBC, IBA and advertising industry)

BARBI Baseband Radar Bag Initiator

BARC Bay Area Reference Center (administered by California State Library (USA))
Bhabha Atomic Research Centre (India)
Business Assistance and Resource Center (University of New Mexico (USA))

BARCIS British Airport Rapid Control and Indication Systems

BARCS Battlefield Area Reconnaissance System

BARITT Barrier-Injection and Transit-Time

BARON Business/Accounts Reporting Operating Network

BARR British Association for Rheumatology and Rehabilitation

BARS Bangladesh Amateur Radio Society (Bangladesh)
Baseband Radar Sensor Technology
Behaviourally Anchored Rating Scale
BELL (TELEPHONE LABORATORIES) Audit Relate System

BARTD Bay Area Rapid Transit District (San Francisco) (USA)

BARTG British Amateur Radio Teleprinter Group

BARUK Board of Airline Representatives in the United Kingdom

BARV Beach Armoured Recovery Vehicle

BAS Battlefield Automated System
BELL (TELEPHONE LABORATORIES) Audit System
Boresight Adjustment System
British Acoustical Society (in 1974 merged into the Institute of Acoustics)
Building Advisory Service (of NFBTE)
Bureau of Aviation Safety (of National Transportation Safety Board (USA))

BASAM British Association of Grain, Seed Feed and Agricultural Merchants

BASAR Breathing Apparatus Self-Contained Compressed Air Search and Rescue

BASC British Aerial Standards Council

BASE Bank-Americard Service Exchange (USA)
Basic Army Strategic Estimate (US Army)
Brokerage Accounting System Elements
Business Assessment Study and Evaluation

BASEC British Approvals Service for Electric Cables

BASEEFA British Approvals Service for Electrical Equipment in Flammable Atmospheres (became part of RLSD (HSE) in 1975)

BASF Badische Anilin und Soda-Fabrik (Germany)

BASIC Basic Aviation Sub-system Integration Concept
Beginner's All-purpose Symbolic Instruction Code
Biological Abstracts Subjects In Context

BASIC/PTS BASIC Paper Tape System

BASICS British Association of Immediate Care Schemes

BASIL BARCLAYS (BANK) Advanced Staff Information Language

BASIS Bank Automated Service Information System
BATELLE (MEMORIAL INSTITUTE (USA)) Automated Search Information System for the Seventies

BASJE Bolivian Air Shower Joint Experiment

BASMM British Association of Sewing Machine Manufacturers (became BACMM in 1977)

BASOPS Base Operating Information System (US Army)

BASP Biomedical Analogue Signal Processor
British Association for Social Psychiatry

BASRA British Amateur Scientific Research Association

BASRM British Association of Synthetic Rubber Manufacturers

BASS Basic Analogue Simulation System
KAILASH M. BAFNA Stacker Simulator

BASYC Benefit Assessment for System Change

BASYS Building Aid System

BAT Battalion Anti-Tank
Best Available Technology
Bureau of Apprenticeship and Training (Department of Labor (USA))
Bureau of Apprenticeship and Training (USA)

BATC British Amateur Television Club
British Arabian Technical Co-operation (a Government agency)

BATEA Best Available Technology Economically Achievable

BATES Battlefield Artillery Target Engagement System

BATHY Bathythermograph

BATS Ballistic Aerial Target System

BATSC Bay Area Transportation Study Commission (USA)

BATSS Battlefield Targeting Support System

BAU Bangladesh Agricultural University (Bangladesh)

Bau-BG Bau-Berufsgenossenschaft (Germany) (State Insurance Organisation for Building)

BAUA British Aircraft Users Association

BAUS British Association of Urological Surgeons

BAVIP British Association of Viewdata Information Providers

BAW Bulk Accoustic Wave

BAWA British Academy of Western Acupuncture

BAWS Basic Acoustic Warfare System

BAYS British Association Young Scientists (of British Association for the Advancement of Science)

BBA British Beekeepers Association
British Board of Agrément
British Brazing Association

BBAC British Balloon and Airship Club
Bus-to-Bus Access Circuit

BBB Blood-Brain Barrier

BBBS Bang-Bang-Bang Surfaces

BBC Black Body Cavity
British Broadcasting Corporation
Bromobenzylcyanide

BBD Bucket Brigade Device

BBEA Brewery and Bottling Engineers Association (now merged with PPA)

BBIRA British Baking Industries Research Association (merged into FMBRA in 1967)

BBLL Blackbody Limited Line

BBMA British Brush Manufacturers Association
Building Board Manufacturers Association

BBMRA British Brush Manufacturers Research Association

BBOL Building Block Oriented Language

BBP Benyl Butyl Phthalate

BBSI British Boot and Shoe Institution

BBSLG British Business Schools Librarians Group

BBSP Balloon-Borne Solar Pointer

BC Ballistic Coefficient
Bathyconductograph
Bottom Contour
Broadcasting

BC-ECOR British Committee for ECOR

BCA Barium Chloranilate
Bilderberg Continuum Atmosphere

BCAA Branched-chain Amino Acids
British Commuter Airlines Association

BCAAC Brant County Antique Arms Collectors Association (Canada)
British Columbia Arms Collectors Association (Canada)

BCAB British Computer Association for the Blind

BCAR British Civil Airworthiness Requirement

BCAS Beacon Collision Avoidance System
Beacon-based Collision Avoidance System
British Compressed Air Society

BCASC British Civil Aviation Standing Conference

BCAVM British Catalogue of Audiovisual Materials (of the British Library)

BCB British Consultants Bureau

BCC Bharat Coking Coal Ltd (India) (Government owned)
Block Check Character
British Chilean Council
British Colour Council
British Cryogenics Council

BCCA Beer Can Collectors of America (USA)

BCCD Bulk-channel Charge-Coupled Device
Buried-Channel Charge-Coupled Device

BCCF British Cast Concrete Federation

BCCL Bharat Coking Coal Limited (India) (government owned)

BCCS British Carpet Classification Scheme (now operated by BCMA)

BCD Binary Coded Decimal
Burst Cartridge Detection

BCDP Bubble Chamber Data Processing

BCEAO Banque Centrale des Etats de l'Afrique de l'Ouest (Central Bank of the West African States)

BCECA British Chemical Engineering Contractors Association

BCEI British Colour Education Institute (of British Colour Council) FMBRA in 1967) Environment Planning Division)

BCEMA British Combustion Equipment Manufacturers Association

BCEOM Bureau Central d'Etudes pour les Equipements d'Outre-Mer (France) (Central Study Bureau for Overseas Equipment)

BCeramRA British Ceramic Research Association

BCF Bromochlorodifluoromethane
Building Construction Forum
Bulked Continuous Filament
Bureau of Commercial Fisheries (of NOAA (USA)) (now NMFS)

BCFA British Contract Furnishing Association

BCG Bacillus Calmette Guerin
Ballistocardiograph

BCGA British Compressed Gases Association

BCGLO British Commonwealth Geographical Liaison Office

BCH Bose-Chaudhui-Hocquenenghem code

BCHAC British Columbia Historical Arms Collectors (Canada)

BCIA Bounded Carry Inspection Adder

BCIPPA British Cast Iron Pressure Pipe Association

BCIRA British Cast Iron Research Association

BCIS Building Cost Information Service (of RICS)

BCISC British Chemical Industrial Safety Council (of CIA) (replaced in 1975 by CISHEC (of CIA))

BCITA British Carpet Industry Technical Association (disbanded 1976)

BCL Base-Coupled Logic
Biological Computer Laboratory (Illinois University, USA)

BCM Benzilylcholine Mustard
Beyond Capability of Maintenance
Budget Correcting Mechanism (of EEC)

BCMA British Capacitor Manufacturers Association (a federated member of BEAMA)
British Carpet Manufacturers Association
British Council of Maintenance Associations

BCME Bis(Chloromethyl) Ether

BCMEA Bureau Commun du Machinisme et de l'Equipment Agricole (France)

BCMN Bureau Central de Mesures Nucleaires (Belgium) (Central Office for Nuclear Measures)

BCN Biomedical Communication Network

BCOA Bituminous Coal Operators Association (USA)

BCP Byte Control Protocol

BCPA British Concrete Pumping Association
British Copyright Protection Association
British Council of Productivity Associations

BCPL Basic Combined Programming Language

BCPMA British Chemical Plant Manufacturers Association (now merged with TIPA)

BCPMMA British Ceramic Plant and Machinery Manufacturers Association

BCPS Beam – Candle-Power – Seconds

BCPV Bovine Cutaneous Papilloma Virus

BCR Bituminous Coal Research, Inc (USA)
British Columbia Railway (Canada)

BCRA British Carbonisation Research Association
British Cave Research Association
British Ceramic Research Association
British Coke Research Association

BCRC British Columbia Research Council (Canada)

BCRD British Council for the Rehabilitation of the Disabled (merged into RADAR in 1977)

BCRS Bar-Code Reader/Sorter

BCRU British Committee on Radiological Units (now BCRUM)

BCRUM British Committee on Radiation Units and Measurements

BCS B.A. Bilby, A.H. Cottrell and K.H. Swinden model of a crack with yielding
Basic Court System
Battery Computer System
Bounded Cellular Space
British Calibration Service (of DTI)
British Cartographic Society
British Chemical Standard
British Computer Society

BCSA British Constructional Steelwork Association

BCSAA British Computer Society ALGOL Association

BCSIR Bangladesh Council for Scientific and Industrial Research (Bangladesh)
BCSLA British Columbia School Librarians Association (Canada)
BCSOC Binary Convolutional Self-Orthogonal Code
BCSP Board of Certified Safety Professionals (USA)
BCT Building Centre Trust
BCTC British Ceramic Tile Council
BCU Ballistics Computer Unit
BCUA Business Computers Users Association
BCURA British Coal Utilisation Research Association (disbanded 1971)
BCV Barge-Carrying Vessel
BCWMA British Clock and Watch Manufacturers Association
BD Borna Disease
Butadiene
BDA Battle Damage Assessment
Bomb Damage Assessment
Brick Development Association
British Dental Association
British Diabetic Association
British Dietetic Association
Bund Deutscher Architekten (Germany) (Federation of German Architects)
BDAE Boston Diagnostic Aphasia Examination
BDAM Basic Direct Access Method
BDC Binary-Differential Counter
Book Development Council (of the Publishers Association)
Building Data Council (Sweden)
Bureau International de Documentation des Chemins de Fer (France) (International Bureau of Railway Documentation)
Bureau of Domestic Commerce (of Department of Commerce (USA))
BDDRG British Deep-Drawing Research Group
BDDT Bench Detergency Dispersancy Test
BDEAC Banque de Developpement des Etats de l'Afrique Centrale (Bank for Development of Central Africa States)
BDF Backwards Differentiation Formulas
Box-car Doppler Filter
BDHI Bearing, Distance and Heading Indicator
BDI Base-Diffusion Isolation
Bearing Deviation Indication
Bundesverband der Deutschen Industrie (Germany) (Federal Association of German Industry)
BDIAC Battelle Defender Information Analysis Center (BMI)
BDL Building Description Language
BDLI Bundesverband der Deutschen Luft- und Raumfahrtindustrie (Germany) (Federal Association of German Aerospace Industry)
BDM Bomber Defence Missile
BDMA Benzl Dimethyl Amine
British Defence Manufacturers Association
BDMMA British Direct Mail Marketing Association
BDMS BURROUGHS (CORPORATION) Data Management System
BDO Butanediol
BDP J.F. BENDER's Decomposition Principle
BDPA British Disposable Products Association
BDR Battle Design Repair
BDS British Deer Society
Building Design Systems
BDSA British Drilling and Sawing Association
Business and Defense Services Administration (of Dept of Commerce (USA)) (now Bureau of Domestic Commerce)
BDSM Base Depot Stockage Model
BDU Battle Dress Uniform
BDWTT BATELLE Drop Weight Tear Test
BE Beryllium
BEA Basic Electric Arc
Blue Etch-Anodize OR Anodizing
British Epilepsy Association
British European Airways (now BEAD of British Airways)
Bureau of Economic Analysis (USA)
BURROUGHS Extended ALGOL
BEAB British Electrical Approvals Board for Domestic Appliances (now British Electrotechnical Approvals Board for Household Appliances)
BEAC Banque des Etats de l'Afrique Centrale (Bank of Central African States)
BEACON BRITISH EUROPEAN AIRWAYS Computerized Office Network
BEAIRA British Electrical and Allied Industries Research Association
BEAM Bidders Early Alert Message (a service of the National Small Business Association (USA))
Building Equipment, Accessories and Materials programme (of DOI, Canada)
BEAMA British Electrical and Allied Manufacturers Association now split into:—
a) Association of Manufacturers Allied to the Electrical and Electronics Industry
b) Power Generation Association
c) Rotating Electrical Machines Association
d) BEAMA Transmission and Distribution Association
e) Electrical and Electronic Insulation Association
f) Control and Automation Manufacturers Association
g) Electrical Installation Equipment Manufacturers Association
h) Welding Manufacturers Association
i) Process Heating Plant Manufacturers Association
j) British Capacitor Manufacturers Association
BEAMOS Beam-Addressable Metal Oxide Semiconductor
BEAMS Base Engineer Automated Management System (USAF)
BEAST BROOKINGS (INSTITUTE (USA)) Economics And Statistical Translator
BEB British Export Board
BEBC Big European Bubble chamber (of CERN)
BEC Board for Engineering Cooperation (USA) (governing body of the Association for Cooperation in Engineering)
Boron Electron Centre
British Electrotechnical Committee
Building Employers Confederation
Business Education Council (became part of BTEC in 1983)
BECA Beam Calibrator
BECAMP Ballistic Environmental Characterization and Measurements Program (US Army)
BECCR British Empire Cancer Campaign for Research (now Cancer Research Campaign)
BECSM British Electric Conduit Systems Manufacturers (now British Electrical Systems Association)
BECTIS BELL COLLEGE (OF TECHNOLOGY) (Scotland) Technology Information Service
BECTO British Electric Cable Testing Organisation
BED Bridge-Element Delay
Bureau of Energy Development (Philippines)
BEE Business Efficiency Exhibition
BEEF Beef Energy and Economic evaluator for Farms
Business and Engineering Enriched FORTRAN
BEEG Binary Error-Erasure Channel
BEEP Building Energy Estimating Programme

BEHA British Export Houses Association
BEI British Electricity International Ltd (the overseas consultancy arm of CEGB, Electricity Council, and distribution boards)
BEIR Advisors Committee on the Biological Effects of Ionizing Radiations (of NAS/NRC (USA))
BEIS British Egg Information Service
BEL Bharat Electronics Limited (India) (government owned)
BELGOSPACE Association Belge Interprofessional des Activities Spatiales (Belgium)
BELINDIS Belgian Information and Dissemination Service (of the Ministry of Economic Affairs) (Belgium)
BELLREL BELL (TELEPHONE) LABORATORIES Library Real-time Loan
BELVAC Societe Belge de Vacuologie et de Vacuotechnique (Belgium) (Belgian Society for Vacuum Science and Technology)
BEMA Bristol and West of England Engineering Manufacturers Association
Business Equipment Manufacturers Association (USA)
Business Equipment Manufacturers Association (USA) (now CBEMA)
BEMAC British Export Marketing Advisory Committee
BEMS Bakery Equipment Manufacturers Society (merged with PPA)
BEN Bureau d'Etudes Nucleaires (Belgium) (Nuclear Studies Bureau)
BENELUX Belgium, the Netherlands, Luxembourg
BENS Bounded Error Navigation System
BeO Beryllium Oxides
BEO Bureau d'Etudes Oceanographiques (France) (Oceanography Research Bureau)
BEPC British Electrical Power Convention
BEPI Bureau d'Etudes et de Participations Industrielles (Morocco) (Industrial Development Bureau)
BEPO British Experimental Pile Operation
BER Bit Error Rate
Board for Engineers Registration (of the Engineering Council)
BERSAFE BERKELEY (NUCLEAR LABORATORIES (CEGB)) Stress Analysis Finite Elements
BERU Building Economics Research Unit (of University College, London)
BES Biological Engineering Society
BESA British Electrical Systems Association
BESO British Executive Service Overseas (sponsored by CBI, DTI, and The Institute of Directors)
BESRL Behavioral Science Research Laboratory (now Behavior and Systems Research Laboratory of ARI (US Army))
BEST Ballastable Earthmoving Sectionalized Tractor
Basic Executive Scheduler and Timekeeper
Battery Energy Storage Test facility (sponsored by DOE (USA) and others)
Business EDP System Technique
BET Balanced-Emitter Transistor
Best Estimate of Trajectory
BRUNAUER (STEPHEN), EMMETT (PAUL) and TELLER (EDWARD) procedure for determining the specific area of particulates
BETA Basic English for Testing Applications
Battlefield Exploitation and Targeting Acquisition system
Business Equipment Trade Association
BETECH International Conference on Boundary Element Technology
BEU Bulk Encryption Unit
BEUC Bureau Europeen des Unions Consommateurs (Bureau of European Consumer Organisations)
BEV Bovine Enterovirus
BF Beam-Foil
BFA Balloon Federation of America (USA)
British Franchise Association
BFAP Binary Fault Analysis Programme
BfB Bundesanstalt fur Bodenforschung (Germany) (became BGR in 1975)
BFC Braking Force Coefficient
BFDC Banana and Fruit Development Corporation (India)
BFEC British Food Export Council
BFI Battlefield Interdiction
Beam-Forming Interfact
Beat-Frequency Interferometer
British Film Institute
BFIA British Flower Industry Association
BFIC Binary Fault Isolation Chart
BFICC British Facsimile Industry Compatibility Committee (of CCITT)
BFL Betonforskningslaboratoriet (Sweden) (Concrete Research Laboratory)
BFM Basic Flight Module
British Furniture Manufacturers Federated Association
BFME British Furniture Manufacturers Export Club
BFMF British Footwear Manufacturers Federation
BFMIRA British Food Manufacturing Industries Research Association
BFMP British Federation of Master Printers (now British Printing Industries Federation)
BFN Beam-Forming Network
BFO Beat Frequency Oscillator
BFPDDA Binary Floating Point Digital Differential Analyzer
BFPR Binary Floating Point Resistor
BFPSA British Fire Protection Systems Association
BFR Statens Rad for Byggnadsforskning (Sweden) (National Council for Building Research)
BFRP Boron Fibre Reinforced Plastics
BFS Bundesastalt fur Flugsicherung (Germany) (Air-Traffic Control Authority)
BFSA British Fire Services Association
British Fulbright Scholars Association
BFSVEA British Fishing and Small Vessel Equipment Association (now BSSEA)
BFT Bulk Function Transfer
BGA British Gliding Association
Business Graduates Association
BGC British Gas Corporation
BGFS British Ground Freezing Society
BGIRA British Glass Industry Research Association
BGLA British Growers Look Ahead (a conference and exhibition)
BGMA British Gear Manufacturers Association
BGN Board on Geographic Names (of US Department of the Interior)
BGR Bundesanstalt fur Geowissenschaften und Rohstoffe-Tatigkeitsbericht (Germany) (Federal Institute for Geosciences and Natural Resources)
BGRG British Geomorphological Research Group (now Geomorphological Study Group of the Institute of British Geographers)
BGRR BROOKHAVEN'S Graphite Research Reactor (BNL)
BGRV Boost Glide Re-entry Vehicle
BGS British Geological Survey
British Geotechnical Society
BGSDA Brilliant Green Sulphadiazine-Deoxycholate Agar
BGSM Biennial General Scientific Meeting
BGSU Bowling Green State University (USA)
BGTA Birmingham Group Training Association
BGW Battlefield Guided Weapon
BGWF British Granite and Whinstone Federation

BH Buried Heterostructure
BHA Butylated Hydroxyanisole
BHAB British Helicopter Advisory Board
BHC Benzine Hexachloride
BHCSA British Hospitals Contributory Schemes Association
BHEC British Health-care Export Council
BHEL Bharat Heavy Electricals Limited (India) (government owned)
BHF Bureau of Health Facilities (of HRA (USA))
BHGMF British Hang Glider Manufacturers Federation
BHI British Horological Institute
BHMA British Hard Metal Association
British Herbal Medical Association
British Holistic Medical Association
BHME Bureau of Health Manpower Education (of NIH (USA))
BHN Brinell Hardness Number
BHP Biological Hazard Potential
BHRA British Hydromechanics Research Association
BHS British Horse Society
BHSL Basic Hytran Simulation Language
BHT Butylated Hydroxytoluene
BHU Banaras Hindu University (India)
BHW Boiling Heavy Water
BHWR Boiling Heavy Water Reactor
BIA Binding Industries of America (of PIA (USA))
Boating Industry Association (USA)
British Insurance Association
BIAA Beijing Institute of Aeronautics and Astronautics (China)
British Industrial Advertising Association
BIAC Bio-Instrumentation Advisory Council (of AIBS)
Business and Industry Advisory Committee (of OECD)
BIALL British and Irish Association of Law Librarians
BIAS Battlefield Illuminator Airborne System
Broadcast Industry Automation System
Buoy Integrated Antenna Submarine
BIB Balanced Incomplete Block
Berliner Institut fur Betriebsfuhrung (Germany) (Berlin Business Management Institute)
Bibliography
Brunel Institute for Bio-engineering
BIBA British Insurance Brokers Association
BIBDES Bibliographic Data Entry System
BIBM Bureau International du Beton Manufacture (International Bureau of the Precast Concrete Industry)
BIBO Bounded-Input Bounded-Output
BIBRA British Industrial Biological Research Association
BIC Beam-Induced Current
Biodeterioration Information Centre (University of Aston in Birmingham)
British Importers Confederation
Bureau International des Containers (International Bureau of Containers)
Bureau of International Commerce (of Dept. of Commerce, USA)
BIC-CID Bureau of International Commerce, Commercial Intelligence Division (USA)
BICEMA British Internal Combustion Engine Manufacturers Association
BICEPS Basic Industrial Control Engineering Programming System
Bonus Initiative Commodity Export Programs (USA)
BICERA British Internal Combustion Engine Research Association
BICERI British Internal Combustion Engine Research Institute
BICS BURROUGHS Inventory Control System
BICSI Building Industry Consulting Service International (USA)
BICTA British Investment Casters Technical Association
BIDAP Bibliographic Data Processing Programme
BIDC Barbados Industrial Development Corporation (Barbados)
BIDS Bangladesh Institute of Development Studies (Bangladesh)
BENDIX Integrated Data System
BIDU Bio-medical Instrumentation Development Unit (Toronto University (Canada))
BIE Boundary-Integral Equation
BIF Banded Iron Formation
BIFA British Industrial Film Association (now part of BISFA)
BIFF Battlefield Identification Friend or Foe
BIFN Banque Internationale pour le Financement de l'Énergie Nucléaire
BIFOA Betriebswirtschafliches Institut fur Organisation und Automation (Germany)
BIFORE Binary Fourier Representation
BIG Biological Isolation Garment
BIGA Bundesamt fur Industrie, Gewerbe und Arbeit (Switzerland)
BIGFET Bipolar Insulated-Gate Field-Effect Transistor
BIGS Booster Inertial Guidance System
BIH Bureau International de l'Heure
BIIT Blood Incubation OR Inoculation Infectivity Test
BILA BATTELLE (MEMORIAL) INSTITUTE Learning Automation
BILBO Built-in Logic Block Observer
BILD Board of Industrial Leadership and Development (Ontario, Canada)
BILG Building Industry Libraries Group
BIM An Bord Iascaigh Mhara (Eire) (Sea Fisheries Board)
Blade Inspection Method
British Institute of Management
BIMA British Industrial Marketing Association
British Interlining Manufacturers Association
BIMACS Blood Bank Information and Management Control System
BIMCAN British Industrial Measuring and Control Apparatus Manufacturers Association
BIMCO Baltic and International Maritime Conference
BIML Bureau International de Metrologie Legale (of (OIML) (International Bureau of Legal Metrology)
BIMRAB BuWeps-Industry Material Reliability Advisory Board (USN)
BIMSOC British Institute of Management Secretariat for Overseas Countries
BINA Bureau International des Normes de l'Automobile (International Bureau of Automobile Standards)
BINDT British Institute of Non-Destructive Testing
BINGO Business International Non-Governmental Organisation
BINS BARCLAYS (BANK) Integrated Network System
BIOD BELL (LABORATORIES) (USA) Integrated Optical Device
BIOMASS Biological Investigation of Marine Antarctic Systems and Stocks (a project managed by ICSU)
BIOMOD Biological Modelling
BIOS Biological Investigations of Space
British Intelligence Objectives Sub-committee
BIOSIS Bio-Sciences Information Service of Biological Abstracts (USA)
BIOSS Brunel Institute of Organisation and Social Studies (Brunel University)

BIOTRAP Regional Centre for Tropical Biology (Indonesia) (of ASEAN)

BIP Balanced In Plane
Balloon Interrogation Package
Binary Image Processor
Bitumen Product

BIPAR Bureau International des Producteurs d'Assurances et Reassurances (International Bureau of Insurance and Re-Insurance Intermediaries)

BIPAVER International Federation of National Association of Tyre Specialists and Retreaders

BIPE Bureau d'Information et de Previsions Economiques (France) (Bureau for Information and Economic Forecasting)

BIPM Bureau International des Poids et Mesures (International Bureau of Weights and Measures) (France)

BIPS British Integrated Programme Suite

BIR British Institute of Radiology
Bureau International de la Recuperation (International Bureau for Secondary Materials)

BIRDIE Battery Integration and Radar Display Equipment

BIRMO British Infra-Red Manufacturers Organization

BIRPI Bureaux Internationaux Reunis pour la Protection de la Propriete Intellectuelle (United International Bureaux for the Protection of Intellectual Property) (now WIPO)

BIRS Basic Indexing and Retrieval System
British Institute of Recorded Sound

BIRT Bird Impact Resistant Transparency (windscreen)

BIS Bank for International Settlements (Switzerland)
Biological Information Service (of the Institute of Biology AND the British Library)
British Interplanetary Society
Bureau of Information Science
Bureau of Labor Statistics (USA)
Business Information Systems

BISA British Internation Studies Association

BISAD Business Information Systems Analysis and Design

BISAM Basic Indexed Sequential Access Method

BISCUS Business Information System/Customer Service

BISF British Iron and Steel Federation

BISFA British Industrial and Scientific Film Association
Bureau International pour la Standardisation des Fibres Artificielles (Switzerland) (International Bureau for the Standardisation of Synthetic Fibres)

BISG Book Industry Study Group (USA)

BISITS British Industrial and Scientific International Translations Service (now of the Institute of Metals)

BISPA British Independent Steel Producers Association

BISRA British Iron and Steel Research Association (now the Corporate Laboratories of the British Steel Corporation)

BISRA-PE prefix to series of reports issued by the Plant Engineering Department of BISRA

BISS Base and Installation Security System (an organization of ESD (USAF))
Bioisolator Suit Systems

BISTAR Bistatic Thinned Array Radar

BISYNC Binary Synchronous Communication

BIT Bench Integration Test
Binary digit
Birla Institute of Technology (India)
Board of Internal Trade (Tanzania)
Built-In-Test

BITA British Industrial Truck Association

BITCO Bihar Industrial and Technical Consultancy Organisation (India) (a subsidiary of Industrial Development Bank of India)

BITE Benthic Inflatable Toolstore Enclosure
Built-In Test Equipment

BITM Birla Industrial and Technological Museum (India)

BITO British Institution of Training Officers

BJA British Jewellers Association

BJCG British Joint Corrosion Group (disbanded 1974)
British Junior Chambers of Commerce

BJT Bi-polar Junction Transistor

BJTRA British Jute Trade Research Association

BKB Braunschweigische Kohlen-Bergwerke (Germany)

BKD Bilateral Kinaesthetic Differences

BKSTS British Kinematograph Sound and Television Society

BKW Bernische Kraftwerke (Switzerland)

BL The British Library

BLAC British Light Aviation Centre

BLADE Binary Level Access DIRK Editor

BLADES BELL (TELEPHONE) LABORATORIES Automatic Design System

BLAISE BRITISH LIBRARY Automated Information Service

BLARD Boat Launching and Recovery Device

BLAST Building Loads Analysis and System Thermodynamics
Building Thermal Loads Analysis and System Simulation Technique

BLATS Built-up Low-cost Advanced Titanium Structures

BLC Boundary Layer Control
British Lighting Council (disbanded 1968)

BLCMP Birmingham Libraries Co-operative Mechanisation Project (now a commercial company–BLCMP Library Services Ltd.)

BLDSC British Library Document Supply Centre

BLEACH Babel Language Editing And Checking

BLEAP Bought Ledger and Expenditure Analysis Package

BLEND Birmingham and Loughborough Electronic Network Development

BLET Bureau of Libraries and Educational Technology (USOE) (now Bureau of Libraries and Learning Resources)

BLEU Belgo-Luxemburg Economic Union
Blind Landing Experimental Unit (of RAE) (now RAE Flight Systems Division 2)

BLEVE Boiling Liquid-Expanding Vapour Explosion

BLF Ballast Lumen Factor

BLHA British Linen Hire Association

BLHS Ballistic Laser Holographic System

BLIC Beam-Lead Individual Carrier

BLIP (now ERDA) BROOKHAVEN (NATIONAL LABORATORY) (USAEC) LINAC Isotope Producer
Background Limited Infrared Photoconductor
Background-Limited Infra-red Photography
Big Look Improvement Program (USN)
Boundary Layer Instrument Package

BLISS Basic List-oriented Information Structures System

BLL Below Lower Limit

BLLD British Library Lending Division of the British Library (the division formed by merging the National Central Library and National Lending Library for Science and Technology in 1973) (now British Library Document Supply Centre)

BLLR Bureau of Libraries and Learning Resources (USOE)

BLM Basic Language Machine
Bilayer Lipid Membrane
Bimolecular Lipid Membrane
Bureau of Land Management (US Dept of the Interior)

BLOC BOOTH LIBRARY On-line Circulation system (Eastern Illinois University (USA))

BLOCS BUCKNELL (UNIVERSITY) (USA) On-Line Circulation System

BLODI-G Block Diagram Graphics

BLODIB Block Diagram Compiler B

BLOS Beyond-Line-Of-Sight

BLOWS British Library of Wildlife Sounds (of British Institute of Recorded Sound)

BLPES British Library of Political and Economic Science (of London School of Economics and Political Science)

BLRA British Launderers Research Association

BLRD British Library Reference Division (of the British Library)

BLRDR prefix to numbered series of reports issued by the British Library Research and Development Department

BLS Bilinear System
Bureau of Labor Statistics (USDL)

BLSGMA British Lampblown Scientific Glassware Manufacturers Association

BLSJ Beam-Lead Sealed-Junction

BLTC Bottom Loading Transfer Cask

BLUE Best Linear Unbiased Estimate

BLWA British Laboratory Ware Association

BM Bench Mark
British Museum
Bromine-Methanol
Bureau of Mines (Department of the Interior (USA))

BM/C^3 Battle Management/Command, Control and Communications

BMA Bahrain Monetary Agency (Bahrain)
British Medical Association

BMAA British Medical Acupuncture Association
British Microlight Aircraft Association

BMAT Beginning of Morning Astronomical Twilight

BMB Barium Metaborate

BMBW Bundesministerium fur Bildung und Wissenschaft (Germany) (Federal Ministry for Education and Science)

BMC Book Marketing Council
Botswana Meat Commission (Botswana)
Bulk Moulding Compound

BMCC British Metal Castings Council

BMCI BUREAU OF MINES (USA) Correlation Index

BMCS Bureau of Motor Carrier Safety (of FHWA (USA))

BMD Ballistic Missile Defence

BMDATC Ballistic Missile Defense Advanced Technology Center (US Army)

BMDC Bihar Mineral Development Corporation (India) (government owned)
Biomedicinska Dokumentationscentralen (Sweden) (Biomedical Data Centre)

BMDCA Ballistic Misile Defense Communications Agency (USACC)

BMDDP Bureau of Medical Devices and Diagnostic Products (of FDA (USA))

BMDF British Management Data Foundation

BMDSCOM Ballistic Missile Defense System Command (US Army)

BME Bio-Medical Engineering
Bundesverband Materialwirtschaft und Einkauf (Germany) (National Association of Materials Management and Purchasing)

BMEC British Marine Equipment Council

BMEG British Microfilm Export Group (of BETA)
Building Materials Export Group

BMEWS Ballistic Missile Early Warning System

BMF Bimodal Filter

BMFSA British Metal Finishing Suppliers Association

BMFT Bundesministerium fur Forschung und Technologie (Germany) (Federal Ministry for Research and Technology)

BMI Battelle Memorial Institute (USA)
Bismaleimide
Book Manufacturers Institute (USA)
Bundesministerium des Innern (Federal Interior Ministry) (Germany)

BMIC Bureau of Mines Information Circular (series issued by BOM)

BMILS Bottom-Mounted Impact Location System

BML Basic Machine Language
British Museum Library (now part of The British Library)
Bundesministerium für Ernahrung, Landwirtschaft und Forsten (Germany) (Federal Ministry of Food, Agriculture and Forestry)

BMLA British Maritime Law Association

BMLD Binaural Masking Level Difference

BMM Basic Multi-Minutes

BMMFF British Man-Made Fibres Federation

BMMG British Microcomputer Manufacturers Group

BMO Ballistic Missile Office (of USAF Systems Command)
Bonding Molecular Orbitals

BMOM Base Maintenance and Operational Model

BMP National Council of Building Material Producers

BMPA British Medical Pilots Association

BMPE British Manufacturers of Petroleum Equipment

BMPR Bimonthly Progress Report

BMR Basal Metabolic Rate
Bearingless Main Rotor
BROOKHAVEN'S Medical Reactor (BNL)
Bureau of Mineral Resources (Australia)
Bureau of Mineral Resources, Geology and Geophysics (Australia)

BMRA Basic Multi-Role Avionics

BMRC Bureau of Meteorology Research Centre (Australia)

BMRDA Bombay Metropolitan Region Development Authority (India)

BMS Balanced Magnetic Switch
Ballistic Missile Ship
Breathing Metabolic Simulator

BMSA British Metals Sinterings Association

BMSP British Modal Speaking Position

BMT Basic Motion times
Bone Marrow Transplant or Transplantation
British Maritime Technology (Limited company formed April 1985 from BSRA and NMI Ltd, formerly National Maritime Institute)

BMTA British Mining Tools Association

BMTEC British Management Training Export Council

BMTFA British Malleable Tube Fittings Association

BMTP Bureau of Mines Technical Paper (series issued by BOM)

BMV Basic Minute Values

BMWF Bundesministerium fur Wissenschaftliche Forschung (Germany) (Federal Ministry of Scientific Research)

BN Belgonucleaire (Belgium)

BNA Beta-naphthylamine
Biblioteca Nacional de Angola (Angola) (National Library of Angola)
Bureau des Normes de l'Automobile (France) (Bureau of Automobile Standards)
Bureau of National Affairs (USA)

BNAE Bureau de Normalisation de l'Aeronautique et de l'Espace (France) (Aeronautical and Aerospace Standards Bureau)

BNASEES British National Association for Soviet and East European Studies

BNB British National Bibliography

BNBC British National Book Centre (of the National Central Library)

BNBRF British National Bibliography Research Fund

BNCCI Bengal National Chamber of Commerce and Industry (India)

BNCE British National Committee for Electroheat

BNCIEA British National Committee for International Engineering Affairs

BNCM British National Committee on Materials

BNCOE British National Committee on Ocean Engineering (became BC-ECOR in 1978)

BNCOR British National Committee for Oceanographic Research (of The Royal Society)

BNCS British Numerical Control Society

BNCSR British National Committee on Space Research
British Nuclear Design and Construction Ltf (absorbed into NNC in 1975)
Bulk Negative Differential Conductivity

BNDC British Nuclear Design and Construction Ltd (absorbed into NNC in 1975)

BNDD Bureau of Narcotics and Dangerous Drugs (Department of Justice (USA))

BNEA British Naval Equipment Association (of BMEC)

BNEC British National Export Council (now BOTB)

BNES British Nuclear Energy Society

BNF Backus-Naur-Form
British Nuclear Forum
British Nuclear Fuels Limited (a State Corporation)

BNFC British National Film Catalogue (now part of BISFA)

BNFL British Nuclear Fuels Limited (a State Corporation)

BNFMRA British Non-Ferrous Metals Research Association (became British Non-Ferrous Metals Technology Centre in 1973)

BNGS Bomb-Navigation Guidance System

BNIG Boron Nitride Image Guide

BNIST Bureau National de l'Information Scientifique et Technique (France) (National Bureau of Scientific and Technological Information) (superseded by MIDISIT in 1979)

BNL Berkeley Nuclear Laboratories (of CEGB)
British Nuclear Laboratories (of CEGB)
Brookhaven National Laboratory (USAEC) (now of DOE) (USA))

BNM Bureau National de Metrologie (France) (National Metrology Bureau)

BNMA British Non-wovens Manufacturers Association

BNOA British Naturopathic and Osteopathic Association

BNOC British National Oil Corporation

BNP Banque Nationale de Paris (France)

BNQ Bibliotheque Nationale du Quebec (Canada) (National Library of Quebec)

BNS Bombing-Navigation System

BNTC Bircham Newton Training Centre (of the CITB)

BNX British Nuclear Export Executive

BOA British Optical Association

BOAC British Overseas Airways Corporation (now British Airways Overseas Division) (of British Airways)

BOADICEA BRITISH OVERSEAS AIRWAYS Digital Information Computer for Electronic Automation

BOAL Basic Organization of Associated Labour

BOB Bureau of Biologics (FDA (USA))
Bureau of Biologics (USA)
Bureau of the Budget (USA) (now Office of Management and Budget)

BOBMA British Oil Burner Manufacturers Association (now BCEMA)

BOBS Beacon Only Bombing System

BOC Block-Oriented Computer

BOCA Building Officials Conference of America (USA) (now Building Officials and Code Administrators International)

BOCES Board of Cooperative Educational Services (of New York State (USA))

BOCI Business Organization Climate Index

BOCS BENDIX Optimum Configuration Satellite
Bisynchronous Oriented Communications System

BOD Biochemical Oxygen Demand
Biological Oxygen Demand

BODS British Oceanographic Data Service (now of the Institute of Oceanographic Services)

BODY British Organ Donor Society

BOE (The) Bank of England

BOE Barrels of Oil Equivalent

BOEA British Offshore Equipment Association (of BMEC) (now part of ABOI)

BOFADS Business Office Forms Administration Data System

BOHC Boron-Oxygen Hole Centre

BOHS British Occupational Hygiene Society

BOI Board of Investments (Philippines)

BOID Basic Oxygen Furnace

BOLD Bibliographic On-Line Display
Bibliographic On-line Library Display

BOLDS BURROUGHS Optical Lens Docking System

BOLOVAC Bolometric Voltage and Current

BOM Bureau of Mines (Department of the Interior (USA))

BOMA Building Owners and Managers

BOMEX Barbados Oceanographic and Meteorological Experiment (of NOAA) (usa)

BOMP Bill Of Material Processor

BOMROC Bombardment Rocket

BOMS Base Operations Maintenance Simulator

BONUS Boiling Nuclear Superheater

BOP Basic Oxygen Process
Bend-Over Point
Blow-Out Preventer
Building Optimization Programmes

BOPP Biaxially Oriented Polypropylene

BOR Bureau of Operating Rights (of CAB (USA))

BORAM Block Oriented Random Access Memories

BORD Book Order and Record Document

BORIS Book Ordering, Registering and Inventory System
Breathe On Recirculation Ignition System

BORO Bulk-Oil-Roll-on/Roll-off ship

BOS Basic Oxygen Steel

BOSP Bioastronautics Orbital Space Program (USAF)

BOSR prefix to series of Reports issued by Bureau of Safety (of CAB (USA))

BOSS Biased Optimal Steering Selector
BRE (BUILDING RESEARCH ESTABLISHMENT) On-line Search System
Broad Ocean Scoring System
Business Oriented Software System
International Conference on the behaviour of Off-Shore Structures

BOSS-WEDGE Bomb Orbital Strategic System-Weapon Development Glide Entry

BOSTCO Boston (USA) Standardized Components

BOSTI Buffalo Organization for Social and Technological Innovation (USA)

BOSTID Board on Science and Technology for International Development (of National Academy of Sciences (USA))

BOT Board of Trade (disbanded 1970)
Bulk Oil Temperature

BOTAC Board of Trade Advisory Committee
British Overseas Trade Advisory Council (a channel of communication between BOTB and industry and commerce)

BOTB British Overseas Trade Board

BOTEX British Office for Training Exchange (of BACIE)

BOTGI British Overseas Trade Group for Israel

BOTH Bombing Over-the-Horizon

BOTOSS Bottom Topography Survey System (of NAVOCEANO (USN))

BOU British Ornithologists Union

BP Basic Protein
British Patent

BP&BMA British Paper and Board Makers Association (now BPBIF)

BPA Back Pain Association
Biological Photographic Association (USA)
Bisphenol
British Paediatric Association
British Parachute Association
British Parking Association
British Photographic Association
Bush Pilots Airways (Australia)
Byggproduktion AB (Sweden)

BPAM Basic Partitional Access Method

BPANZ Book Publishers Association of New Zealand (in February 1977 Book Publishers Representatives Association and the New Zealand Book Publishers Association amalgamated to form BPANZ)

BPAS British Pregnancy Advisory Service (a non-profit registered charitable trust)

BPATSS Bias Power And Temperature Step Stress

BPBA British Paper Box Association

BPBF British Paper Bag Federation

BPBIF British Paper and Board Industry Federation

BPBIRA British Paper and Board Industry Research Association (now PIRA)

BPBMA British Paper and Board Makers Association (now BPBIF)

BPC Blast-furnace Portland Cement
British Pharmaceutical Codex
British Productivity Council

BPCA British Pest Control Association

BPCF British Concrete Federation

BPCI Bulk Packaging and Containerization Institute (USA)

BPD Bombrini Parodi-Delfino (Italy)

BPDA Bibliographic Pattern Discovery Algorithm

BPDC Book and Periodical Development Council (Canada)

BPDMS Basic Point-Defence Missile System

BPEG British Photographic Export Group

BPF Bandpass Filter Equipment
Blade-Passing Frequency
Bottom Pressure Fluctuation
British Plastics Federation
British Property Federation

BPH Benign Prostatic Hypertrophy

BPI British Phonographic Industry

BPIA British Photographic Importers Association

BPICA Bureau Permanent International des Constructeurs d'Automobiles (Permanent International Agency of Motor Manufacturers)

BPICS British Production and Inventory Control Society

BPKT Basic Programming Knowledge Test
Building Regulations Advisory Committee (of DOE)

BPL Betapropiolactone
Business Planning Language

BPM Batch Processing Monitor
Beam Path Multiplier (now British Photographic Association)
British Printing Machinery Association
British Pump Manufacturers Association

BPMA British Photographic Manufacturers Association (became BPA in 1977)

BPME Branching Process with Markovian Environments

BPMMA British Paper Machinery Makers Association

BPNET British Petroleum Network

BPO Benzoyl Peroxide
British Post Office

BPOC British Post Office Corporation (State owned)

BPP Boundary Phase Plasticity

BPPMA British Power Press Manufacturers Association (now MMMA)

BPR Bonded Particle Rolling
Bureau of Public Roads (USA)
By-Pass Ratio

BPRA British Pattern Recognition Association

BPRE Branching Process with Random Environments

BPRS Brief Psychiatric Rating Scale

BPS Balanced Pressure system
Benchmark Portability System
British Psychological Society
Bureau of Product Safety (of FDA (USA)) (now Consumer Product Safety Commission)

BPSK Bi-Phase Phase Shift Key modulation

BPT Best Practicable Technology
Bound Plasma Tryptophan
Break Pressure Tank

BPTI Bovine Pancreatic Trypsin Inhibitor

BPU British Powerboating Union

BPWR Burnable Poison Water Reactor

BQA Benzoquinone Acetic Acid
British Quality Association

BQSF British Quarrying and Slag Federation

BR Bacteriorhodopsin
Boil Resistant
British Rail
prefix of numbered series of Books of Reference issued by MOD (Navy Department)
prefix to numbered series issued by British Railways Board

BRA Bee Research Association
Brewing Research Association
British Refrigeration Association
British Robot Association

BRAB Building Research Advisory Board (of NAS/NRC (USA))

BRAC Basic Rest-Activity Cycle

BRACA British Refrigeration and Air Conditioning Association

BRACAN submarine telephone cable between Brazil and the Canary Islands
BRAD BROOKHAVEN NATIONAL LABORATORY (USAEC) (now ERDA) Raster Display
BRAGS Bioelectrical Repair and Growth Society (Japan)
BRAILLE Balanced Resource Allocation Information for Logical Lucid Evaluation
BRAMS(A) Beacon Range Altitude Monitor System (Airborne)
BRANDY Boron Recovery and Electrodialysis
BRASTACS Bradford Scientific, Technical and Commercial Service
BRAZO Spanish word for Arm—used as a name for an Air-to-Air Anti-radiation missile guidance concept by the USN and USAF
BRB Ballistic Recoverable Booster
British Railways Board
BRBC Burro Red Blood Cell
BRBMA Ball and Roller Bearing Manufacturers Association
BRC Biological Records Centre (of the Nature Conservancy)
Bituminous Roofing Council
BRCMA British Radio Cabinet Makers Association
BRD Binary Rate Divider
Building Research Division (of National Bureau of Standards (USA)
BRDC Belvoir Research and Development Center (US Army)
BRDT Bayesian Reliability Demonstration Test
Bayesian Reliability Demonstration Tests
BrdU Bromodeoxyuridine
BRE Building Research Establishment (of DOE)
BRECSU Building Research Energy Conservation Support Unit
BREIG British Railway Industry Export Group
BREL British Rail Engineering Limited (state owned)
BREMA British Radio Equipment Manufacturers Association (renamed in 1980 as British Radio and Electronic Equipment Manufacturers Association but retain abbreviation)
BREPAIR Bolted Repair
BRGM Bureau de Recherches Geologiques et Minieres (France) (Bureau of Geological and Mining Research)
BRH British Rail Hovercraft
Bureau of Radiological Health (of FDA (USA))
BRH/DEP Bureau of Radiological Health, Division of Electronics Products (of FDA (USA))
BRH/DER Bureau of Radiological Health, Division of Environmental Radiation (of FDA (USA))
BRH/DMRE Bureau of Radiological Health, Division of Medical Radiation Exposure (of FDA (USA))
BRH/NERHL Bureau of Radiological Health, North Eastern Radiological Health Laboratory (of FDA (USA))
BRH/ORO Bureau of Radiological Health, Office of Regional Operations (of FDA (USA))
BRH/SERHL Bureau of Radiological Health, South-Eastern Radiological Health Laboratory, (of FDA (USA))
BRH/SWRHL Bureau of Radiological Health, South-Western Radiological Health Laboratory (of FDA (USA))
BRI Building Research Institute (Japan)
BRIC British Reclamation Industries Confederation
BRICS Bureau of Research Information Control System (of USOE)
BRIGHTPAD BRITISH RAIL Interactive Graphical Aid To Production And Design
BRIMEC British Mechanical Engineering Confederation
BRINDEX British Independent Oil Exploration Companies Association
BRISC Buffered Remote Interactive Search Console
BRISCC British Iron and Steel Consumers Council
BRIT British Indigenous Technology Group
BRITE Basic Research in Industrial Technologies in Europe (EEC)
Bright Radar Indicator Tower Equipment
BRITSHIPS British Shipbuilding Integrated Production System
BRL Ballistics Research Laboratories (US Army)
BRLESC BALLISTIC RESEARCH LABORATORIES Electronic Scientific Computer (US Army)
BRLT Basic Reference Lottery Ticket
BRM Binary Rate Multiplier
BRMA British Rubber Manufacturers Association
BRMC Business Research Management Center (USAF)
BRMCA British Ready Mixed Concrete Association
BROM Bipolar Read-Only Memory
BRP Block Replacement Policy
BRPA British Radiological Protection Association
BRPM Bureau de Recherches et de Participations Minieres (Morocco) (Mining Research and Development Bureau)
BRRI Building and Road Research Institute (Ghana)
BRS Building Research Station (now part of the Building Research Establishment (DOE))
BRT Belgische Radio en Televisie (Belgium) (Flemish Language network)
BRTA British Road Tar Association
BRU Broadcasting Research Unit (of BBC, IBA and BFI)
BRUCE Buffer Register Under Computer Edict
BRUFMA British Rigid Urethane Foam Manufacturers Association
BRUTE BRITISH RAILWAYS Universal Trolley
BRVMA British Radio Valve Manufacturers Association
BS Back-scattering Spectrometry
Bathymetric Swath Survey System
Biochemical Society
Biological Society (USA)
Brillouin Scattering
D. BLOOM'S Syndrome
prefix to numbered series of British Standards issued by BSI
BSA Bearing Specialists Association (USA)
Boundary-Spanning Activity
Bovine Serum Albumin
British Society of Audiology
Building Societies Association
Bund Schweizer Architekten (Switzerland) (Federation of Swiss Architects)
BSAB Byggandets Samordning AB (Sweden) (Building Co-ordination Centre)
BSAC British Sub-Aqua Club
BSALS British Society for Agricultural Labour Science
BSAM Basic Sequential Access Method
BSANZ Bibliographical Society of Australia and New Zealand
BSAP British Society of Animal Production
BSAS Battlefield Surveillance Airship System
BSBB Baryon Symmetric Big Bang
BSBG Bibbebschiffahrts – Berufsgenossenschaft (Germany) (Inland Waterways Authority)
BSBI Botanical Society of the British Isles
BSC Binary Symmetric Channel
Binary Synchronous Communications
Biological Stain Commission (USA)
British Safety Council
British Society of Cinematographers
British Society of Commerce
BSCA Binary Synchronous Communication Adapter
BSCC British Society for Clinical Cytology
British Steelmakers Creep Committee
British-Swedish Chamber of Commerce

BSCE Bird Strike Committee Europe
BSCL Biological Standards Control Laboratory (of Medical Research Council)
BSCP Biological Sciences Communications Project (George Washington University (USA))
Bovine Spinal Cord Protein
British Standard Code of Practice (series issued by BSI)
BSCRA British Steel Castings Research Association (now part of Steel Castings Research and Trade Association)
BSCS Binary Synchronous Communication System
BSD Bibliographic Services Division (of the British Library)
British Society of Dowsers
BSDA British Spinners and Doublers Association
BSE Bahrain Society of Engineers (Bahrain)
Medium-Scale Broadcasting Satellite for Experimental Purpose
BSES Building Services Engineering Society (now BCF)
BSF Bandstop Filter
Blade Slap Factor
British Shipping Federation (merged into GCBS in 1975)
Bulk Shield Facility (of AFNETF)
BSFC Bihar State Finance Corporation (India)
Brake Specific Fuel Consumption
BSG Boro-Silicate Glass
BSI British Standards Institution
BSIA British Security Industry Association
BSID Battlefield System Integration Directorate (of DARCOM (US Army))
BSIRA British Scientific Instrument Research Association (now known as the SIRA Institute)
BSIS Biomedical Sciences Instrumentation Symposium
BSISA British Standards Institution Standards Associates
BSL Basic Switching Surge Insulation Level
Bokaro Steel Limited (India) (government owned)
BSLSS "Buddy" Secondary Life Support System
BSMMA British Sugar Machinery Manufacturers Association
BSMV Barley Stripe Mosaic Virus
BSN Barium Sodium Niobate
BSNDT British Society for Non-Destructive Testing
BSNM British Society of Nutritional Medicine
BSO Benzene-soluble Organics
Broad System of Ordering
Business Statistics Office (a branch of the Government Statistical Service)
BSOEA British Stationery and Office Equipment Association
BSP Binomial Sampling Plan
BSPA British Sports Photographers Association
BSPL Behavioral Science Programming Language
BSPMA British Sewage Plant Manufacturers Association
BSQI Basic Schedule of Quantified Items
BSR Bacteria Survival Ratio
BSRA British Ship Research Association (became part of BMT in 1985)
BSRC British Sporting Rifle Club
BSRD Behavioural Sciences Research Division (of the Civil Service Department)
BSS Balanced Salt Solution
Biological and Social Sciences (a directorate of NSF (USA))
British Standards Society
prefix to numbered Building Science Series issued by Building Research Division, National Bureau of Standards (USA)
BSSC Bit Synchronizer/Signal Conditioner
British Shooting Sports Council
Building Seismic Safety Council (USA)
BSSEA British Special Ship Equipment Association (of BMEC)
BSSM British Society for Strain Measurement
BSSRS British Society for Social Responsibility in Science
BST Baker-Schmidt Telescope
Blast Saturation Temperature
British Summer Time
Bulk Supply Tariff
BSTAR Battlefield Surveillance Target Acquisition Radar
BSTM Biaxial Shock Test Machine
BSTR Batch, Stirred-Tank Reactor
BT Bandwidth-Time
Bathythermograph
Benzotriazole
Beozotriazole
Body Temperature
British Telecom (Government owned then privatised in 1984)
Butanthiol
BTA Benzotriazole
British Thoracic Association
British Tourist Authority
British Transport Advertising (a branch of the British Railways Board and National Bus Company)
BTAD Benzophenone Tetracarboxylic Acid Dianhydride
BTAM Basic Telecommunications Access Method
BTANZ British Trade Association of New Zealand (New Zealand)
BTB Bus Tie Breaker
BTBMF British Tin Box Manufacturers Federation (now MPMA)
BTBS British Talking Book Service for the Blind (administered by RNIB)
BTC Benzotrichloride
British Technical Council for the Motor and Petroleum Industries
British Technical Council of the Motor and Petroleum Industries
British Textile Confederation
British Transport Commission
BTCMPI British Technical Council of the Motor and Petroleum Industries
BTDB British Transport Docks Board
BTE Battery Terminal Equipment
Bureau of Transport Economics (Australia)
BTEA British Textile Employers Association
BTEC Business and Technician Education Council
BTF Binary Transversal filter
BTG British Technology Group (of NEB and NRDC)
BTH Beyond The Horizon
BTI Board of Trade and Industries (South Africa)
Bridged Tap Isolator
BTIA British Tar Industry Association
BTL Board Test Language
BTLV Biological Threshold Limit Value
BTM Bromotrifluoromethane
BTMA British Toy Manufacturers Association
British Typewriter Manufacturers Association
Busy Tone Multiple-Access
BTN Brussels Tariff Nomenclature
BTO British Trust for Ornithology
BTPS Body Temperature, Pressure, and Saturation
BTR Behind the Tape Reader
Blood Transfusion Reactions
BTRA Bombay Textile Research Association (India)
BTRL British Telecom Research Laboratories
BTSA British Tensional Strapping Association

BTSD Basic Training for Skill Development
BTSS Basic Time Sharing System
BTT Bank-to-Turn Type
BTTA British Thoracic and Tuberculosis Association
BTTP British Towing Tank Panel
BTU British Thermal Unit
BTV Basic Transportation Vehicle
Buoyancy Transport Vehicle
BTx Batrachotoxin
BTX Bathythermometer-Expendable
Benzene, Toluene, and Xylenes
Botulinum Toxin
BTZ Benzotriazole
Bureau Technique Zborowski (France)
BU Binding Unit
BuAer Bureau of Aeronautics (USN) (later BuWeps)
BUAV British Union for the Abolition of Vivisection
BUBGRO Bubble Growth
BUCCS Bath University Comparative Catalogue Study (now CCR)
BUDR Bromodeoxyuridine
BUDS Building Utility Design System
BUDSU British Urban Services Development Unit (of DOE) (disbanded 1978)
BUDWSR BROWN UNIVERSITY (USA) Display for Working Set Reference
BUE Built-Up-Edge
BUET Bangladesh University of Engineering and Technology (Bangladesh)
BUFC British Universities Film Council (now BUFVC)
BUFORA British Unidentified Flying Objects Research Association
BUFVC British Universities Film and Video Council
BUG Basic Update Generator
BUGS BROWN UNIVERSITY (USA) Graphic System
BUIC Back-Up Interceptor Control
BUILD Base for Uniform Language Definition
BUIST Beijing University of Iron and Steel Technology (China)
Bull Bulletin
BuMed Bureau of Medicine and Surgery (USN) (now NAVMEDCOM)
BuMINES Bureau of Mines (Department of the Interior (USA))
BUN Blood Urea Nitrogen
BuOrd Bureau of Ordnance (USN) (later BuWeps)
BuPers Bureau of Naval Personnel (USN) (now NAVMILPERSCOM)
BURD Biplane Ultra-light Research Device
BuRec Bureau of Reclamation (Department of the Interior (USA)
BURISA British Urban and Regional Information Systems Association
BURN British Unemployment Resource Network
BuSandA Bureau of Supply and Accounts (USN)
BuShips Bureau of Ships (USN) (now NSSC)
BUSS Balloon-borne Ultraviolet Stellar Spectograph
Balloon-borne Ultraviolet Stellar Spectrometer
BUTEC British Underwater Test and Evaluation Centre (MOD)
BUV Backscatter Ultra-Violet
BUVS Backscatter Ultra-Violet Spectrometer
BuWeps Bureau of Naval Weapons (USN) (now split into NAVSEA and NAVAIR)
BV Beslocten Venootschap (private limited company)
Bureau Veritas (international register for the classification of ships and aircraft)
BVA British Radio Valve Manufacturers Association (ceased to operate in 1973) (member companies became direct members of the Electronic Components Board)
British Veterinary Association
British Videogram Association
BVD Beacon Video digitizer
BVDT Brief Vestibular Disorientation Test
BVH Biventricular Hypertrophy
BVM Bureau of Veterinary Medicine (of FDA (USA))
BVMA British Valve Manufacturers Association
BVR Beyond-Visual-Range
BVRLA British Vehicle Rental and Leasing Association
BVS Buoyant Venus Station
BW Biological Warfare
BWA British Waterworks Association
BWB British Waterways Board (of DOE)
Bundestamt für Wehrtechnik und Beschaffung (Germany) (Federal Office for Military Technology and Procurement)
BWCMA British Wood Chipboard Manufacturers Association
BWD Basic Work Data
Biological Warfare Defence
BWEA British Wind Energy Association
British Wind Engineering Association
BWETPA British Water and Effluent Treatment Plant Association
BWF British Woodworking Federation
BWFAB Bangladesh Wireless and Frequency Allocation Board (Bangladesh)
BWIR Black and White Infra-Red
BWMA British Woodwork Manufacturers Association
BWMB British Wool Marketing Board (became BMDF in 1979)
BWO Backward Wave Oscillator
BWPA Backward-Wave Power Amplifier
British Waste Paper Association
British Women Pilots Association
British Wood Preserving Association
British Wood Pulp Association
BWR Boiling Light-water Cooled and Moderated Reactor
Boiling Water Reactor
BWRA British Welding Research Association (now part of The Welding Institute)
BWSTMA British Welded Steel Tube Manufacturers Association
BWTA British Wood Turners Association
BWYV Beet Western Yellow Virus
BYGGDOK Institatek for Byggdokumentation (Sweden) (Institute of Building Documentation)
BZ Benzene
Benzodiazepines

C

C Computer
prefix to numbered series of Command Papers issued between 1870-1899
prefix to numbered: dated series of Aircraft Ground Service Connections issued by BSI
C&CA Cement and Concrete Association
C&GS Office of Charting and Geodetic Services (of NOS (NOAA))
C&MS Consumer and Marketing Service (USDA) (title changed to Agricultural Marketing Service in 1972)

C&MS-SRA — C&MS – Service and Regulatory Announcement (USDA)
C&SC — Cleaners and Solvents Council (USA)
C-ARMS — Commercial-Accounts Receivable Management System
C-B-S — Contact Bend Stretch
C-DTE — Character-mode Data Terminal Equipment
C-LAW — Close Combat Laser Assault Weapon
C-MU — Carnegie-Mellon University (USA)
C-SIT — Committee on Social Implications of Technology (of IEEE (USA))
C-V-P — Cost-Volume-Profit
C/COS — Computer-Controlled Operating System
C/I — Carrier to Interference ratio
C/MOS — Complementary Metal Oxide Semiconductor
C/OM — Clothing and Organic Materials Laboratory (of Natick Laboratories (US Army)
C/PLSEL — Clothing and Personal Life Support Equipment Laboratory (of Natick Laboratories (US Army)
C/SCSC — Cost/Schedule Control System Criteria (of USDOD)
Cost/Schedule Control Systems Criteria
C/STOL — Controlled STOL
C0B — Commission des Opérations en Bourse (France) (Stock Exchange Commission)
C2 — Command and Control
C3 — Command, Control and Communication
C3I — Communications, Command, Control and Intelligence
C3D — Cascade Charge Coupled Device
C3EM — Curriculum Committee for Computer Education for Management (of ACM (USA))
C3RAM — Continuously Charge-Coupled Random Access Memory
C4 — Command and Control, Communications and Computers
CA — Catecholamine
Cellulose Acetate
Cholamines
Common Antigen
Complex Angle
Consumers Association
Corpus Allatum
Criticality Analysis
Crotonaldehyde
prefix to numbered series of Civil Aviation publications issued by Civil Aviation Authority (previously issued by Board of Trade and later by DTI)
Ca-ATPase — Calcium-dependent Adenosine Triphophatase
Ca-DTPA — Chelating agent Diethylenetriaminepentaacetic acid
CA-HY-BD — California State, Division of Highways, Bridge Department (USA)
CA(Aust) — Institute of Chartered Accountants in Australia (Australia)
CAA — Canadian Authors Association (Canada)
Cement Admixtures Association
Central African Airways Corporation
Civil Aeronautics Administration (Taiwan)
Civil Affairs Agency (USACDA)
Civil Aviation Authority
Collision Avoidance Aids
Commonwealth Association of Architects
Community Action Agency (USA)
Concepts Analysis Agency (US Army)
Conformal-Array Antenna
CAAA — Commuter Airline Association of America (USA)
CAAC — Civil Aviation Administration of China (China)
CAAD — Computer-Aided Architectural Design
CAADRP — Civil Aircraft Airworthiness Data Recording Programme (project of CAA, MOD and DOI)
CAAIS — Computer Assisted Action Information System
CAALE — Centro Addrestzamento Aviazione Leggera dell-'Esercito (Italy) (Army Light Aviation Training Centre)
CAAM — Conventional Airfield Attack Missile
CAARC — Commonwealth Advisory Aeronautical Research Council
CAAS — Ceylon Association for the Advancement of Science (Ceylon)
Computer-Aided Approach Sequencing
CAAT — Campaign Against Arms Trade
CAB — Captive Air Bubble
Cellulose Acetate Butyrate
Citizen Advice Bureau
Civil Aeronautics Board (USA) (disbanded 1984)
Commonwealth Agricultural Bureaux
Computer Aided Building
Corrosion Advice Bureau (of BISRA) (now part of the British Steel Corporation)
Critical Air Blast
Current Awareness Bibliography
CABAS — City and Borough Architects Society
Computerized Automated Blood Analysis System
CABD — Computer-Aided Building Design
CABEI — Central American Bank for Economic Integration
CABIN — Campaign Against Building Industry Nationalisation
CABLE — Cardington Atmospheric Boundary Layer Experiment
Collaborative Atmospheric Boundary Layer Experiment
Computer Assisted BAY AREA (San Francisco (USA)) Law Enforcement
CABO — Council of American Building Officials (USA)
CABOS — Carbon Absorption Bio-oxidation System
CaBP — Calcium Binding Protein
CABRA — Copper and Brass Research Association (USA)
CABS — Computer Aided Batch Scheduling
Computer Augmented Block System
Computerised Annotated Bibliography System
CABSII — Computer Automated Block System Two Station Separation
CABT — Cesium Atomic Beam Tube
CABWA — Copper and Brass Warehouse Association (USA)
CAC — Calcium Aluminate Cement
Carbon-Arc Cutting
Central Arbitration Committee (of ACAS)
Clean Air Council (disbanded 1979)
Codex Alimentarius Commission (of FAO (UN))
Commonwealth Association of Architects
Computer Acceleration Control
CAC/RS — prefix to numbered-dated series of Recommended International Standards issued by the Codex Alimentarius Commission (FAO(UN))
CACA — Canadian Agricultural Chemicals Association (Canada)
Computer Aided Circuit Analysis
CACAC — Civil Aircraft Control Advisory Committee
CACAS — Civil Aviation Council of Arab States
CACC — Council for the Accreditation of Correspondence Colleges
CACCI — Committee on the Application of Computers in the Construction Industry
Confederation of Asian Chambers of Commerce and Industry
CACD — Computer-Aided Circuit Design
CACDA — Combined Arms Combat Development Activity (US Army)
CACGP — Commission on Atmospheric Chemistry and Global Pollution
CACHE — Computer Aids for Chemical Engineering Education (of Committee of the National Academy of Engineering (USA))

CACI Caribbean Aero Clubs International (USA)
Chicago Association of Commerce and Industry (USA)

CACL Canadian Association of Childrens Librarians (Canada)

CACM Central American Common Market

CACODS Commonwealth Advisory Committee on Defence Science (Australia)

CACP Cartridge-Actuated Compaction Press

CACS Comprehensive Airport Communications System
Core Auxiliary Cooling System

CACSD Computer Aided Control System Design

CACTIS Computer Assistant to a Community Telephone Information Service

CACTOS Computation And Trade-Off Study

CACTQ Citizens Advisory Committee on Transportation Quality (USA)

CACUL Canadian Association of College and University Libraries (Canada)

CACWS Core Auxiliary Cooling Water System

CAD Cartridge Activated Device
Cartridge Actuated Device
Certification and Assessment Department (of BSI)
Circulatory Assist Device
Civil Aviation Department (India)
Computer Aided Design
Computer Aided Design and Test
Computer Aided Detection
Computer Aided Dispatching
Coronary Artery Disease
International Conference and Exhibition on Computers in Engineering and Building Design

CAD-E Computer-Aided Design and Engineering

CADA Computer Assisted Distribution and Assignment

CADACS Computer-Aided Design and Construction System

CADAM Computer-graphics Augmented Design and Manufacturing

CADANCE Computer Aided Design and Numerical Control Effort

CADAPSO Canadian Association of Data Processing Service Organisations (Canada)

CADAR Computer-Aided Design, Analysis and Reliability

CADAS Computerized Automatic Data Acquisition System

CADAVRS Computer-Assisted Dial Access Video Retrieval System

CADC Central Air Data Computer
Computer Aided Design Centre (became private company–CAD Centre Ltd in 1983)
Computer Automated Diameter Control

CADC/CC Central Air Data Computer/Central Computer

CADCOM Computer-Aided Design for Communications

CADD Computer Aided Design-Drafting

CADE Computer Aided Design Engineering
Computer Aided Design Evaluation
Computer Assisted Data Evaluation

CADENS CONUS Air Defense Engagement Simulation

CADEP Computer Assisted Description of Patterns

CADET City Air Defense Evaluation Tool (a computer model used by the US Army)
Computer-Aided Design Experimental Translator

CADF Cathode-ray tube Automatic Direction Finding

CADFISS Computation And Data Flow Integrated Sub-Systems

CADIC Computer Aided Design of Integrated Circuits

CADICS Computer Aided Design of Industrial Cabling Systems

CADIG Coventry and District Information Group

CADLIC Computer-Aided Design of Linear Integrated Circuits

CADM Clustered Airfield Defeat Munition

CADMAT Computer Aided Design Manufacture and Testing
Computer System for Management and Analysis of Large Accumulations of Data

CADNIP CAMBRIDGE Atmospheric Density Numerical Integration Programme

CADO Central Air Documents Office (USAF) (now disbanded)

CADOCR Computer-Aided Design of Optical Character Recognition

CADOPCART Computer Aided Design of Printed Circuit Artwork

CADPIN Customs Automated Data Processing Intelligence Network (Bureau of Customs (USA))

CADPL Communications/Automatic Data Processing Laboratory (of ECOM (US Army))

CADRE Center for Aerospace Doctrine Research and Education (of Air University (USAF))
Current Awareness and Document Retrieval for Engineers

CADS Computer Aided Design System
Containerized Ammunition Distribution System (US Army)
Content Addressable File Store
Conversational Analyzer and Drafting System

CADSAT Computer Aided Design and Specification Analysis Tool

CADSYS Computer-Aided Design System

CADTES Computer Aided Design and Test

CAE Compagnie Europeene d'Automatisme Electronique (France)
Computer Aided Engineering
Computer-Assisted Electrocardiography
Cost Analysis Cost Estimating

CAEDM Community/Airport Economic Development Model

CAEE Committee on Aircraft Engine Emissions (of ICAO)

CAEGAM Commission for Agricultural Meteorology (of WMO (UN))

CAEJ Communante des Associations d'Editeurs de Journaux (Community of Associations of Newspaper Publishers (of the EEC))

CAEM Cargo Airline Evaluation Model
Companhia Auxiliar de Empresos de Mineraca (Brazil)

CAEND Centro Argentino de Ensayos no Destructivos de Materiales (Argentine) (Centre for Non-Destructive Testing of Materials)

CAEPE Centre d'Assemblage et d'Essais des Propulseurs et des Engins (France) (Launchers and Missiles Assembly and Testing Centre)

CAES Canadian Agricultural Economics Society (Canada)
Center for Advanced Engineering Study (Massachusetts Institute of Technology (USA)
Centre for Advanced Engineering Studies (Southampton University)
Compressed Air Energy Storage

CAET Corrective Action Evaluation Team

CAF Canadian Armed Forces (Canada)
Cardiac Assessment Factor
Charities Aid Foundation

CAFB Chemically Active Fluidised Bed

CAFC Computed Automatic Frequency Control

CAFE Computer-Aided Film Editor
Corporate Average Fuel Economy

CAFEA-ICC Commission on Asian and Far Eastern Affairs–International Chamber of Commerce

CAFEOEREM Civil Aviation Form (numbered series issued by Civil Aviation Dept., BOT)

CAFF Computer Aided Fault Finding

CAFI Commercial Advisory Foundation in Indonesia (Indonesia)
CAFIG Circuit Analyzer-Fault Isolation Generator
CAFL Compagnie des Ateliers et Forges de la Loire (France)
CAFMS Computer Assisted Force Management System (of USAF)
CAFOD Catholic Fund for Overseas Development
CAFS Cartridge-Actuated Flame System
Content Addressed File System
Content Addressed Film System
CAFU Civil Aviation Flying Unit (of DTI)
CAG Canadian Association of Geographers (Canada)
Centre for Applied Geology (Saudi Arabia)
Cooperative Automation Group
CAGAC Civil Aviation General Administration of China (China)
CAGC Continuous-Access Guided Communication
CAGD Computer-Aided Geometric Design
CAGE Computerised Aerospace Ground Equipment
CAGI Compressed Air and Gas Institute (USA)
CAGR Commercial Advanced Gas-cooled Reactor
CAH Chronic Active Hepatitis
CAHA Connecticut Aeronautical Historical Association (USA)
CAHE Core Auxiliary Heat Exchanger
CAHOF Canadian Aviation Hall of Fame (Canada)
CAHS Canadian Aviation Historical Society (Canada)
CAI Computer Aided Instruction
Computer-Administered Instruction
Concrete Association of India (India)
Confederation of Aerial Industries
Container Aid International (Belgium)
CAI-TM prefix to numbered series of Technical Memoranda issued by Florida State University, Computer Assisted Instruction Center (USA)
CAI-TR prefix to numbered series of Technical Reports issued by Florida State University, Computer Assisted Instruction Center (USA)
CAIC Cities-Aerospace Industry Coalition (USA)
Computer Assisted Indexing and Classification
CAIN Cataloguing and Indexing System (of National Agricultural Library (USA)) (now AGRICOLA)
CAINIPS Computer-Assisted Instruction for the National Military Command System Information Processing System
CAINS Carrier Aircraft Inertial Navigation System
Computer Aided Instruction System
CAINT Computer Assisted Interrogation
CAIR Counter-measures Airborne Infra-Red
CAIRS Central Automated Inventory and Referral System (of USDOD) (replaced by ACMIS)
Computer Assisted Information Retrieval System
CAIS Canadian Association for Information Science (Canada)
Central Abstracting and Indexing Service (of the American Petroleum Institute)
Computer Aided Insurance System
CAJE Consolidated Anti-Jam Equipment
CAKE Computer Assisted Keyboard Evaluator
CAL Canadian Arsenals Limited (Canada (a Crown Corporation))
Commonwealth Acoustic Laboratories (Australia)
Computer Assisted Learning
Continuous Annealing Line
Conversational Algebraic Language
Cornell Aeronautical Laboratory (USA) (changed name to Calspan Corporation and became a for-profit organisation in 1972)
CAL-OSHA California Occupational Safety and Health Administration (USA)
CALA Computer Aided Loads Analysis
CALAS Canadian Association for Laboratory Animal Science (Canada)
Computer-Assisted Language Analysis System
CALB Computer Aided Line Balancing
CALC Cargo Acceptance and Load Control
CALCHEM Computer Assisted Learning in Chemistry (project of NDPCAL)
CALD Computer Assisted Logic Design
CALDIS Calderdale Information Service for Business and Industry
CALIBRE Cassette Library for the Blind and Handicapped
CALL Canadian Association of Law Libraries (Canada)
Computer-Aided Loft Lines
Computerized Ambulance Location Logic
Current Awareness–Library Literature
CALM Campaign Against the Lorry Menace
Catenary Anchor Leg Mooring
Collected Algorithms for Learning Machines
Computer-Aided Layout of Masks
Computer-Assisted Library Mechanization
Continuously Advancing Longwall Mining
Crane Attachment Lorry Mounted
CALMS Credit and Load Management System
CALP Computer Analysis of Library Postcards (of library buildings)
CALPHAD Calculation of Phase Diagrams (an international working group on thermo-chemistry)
CALROC Calibration Rocket
CALRS Centralized Automated Loop Reporting System
CALS Committee for Ammunition Logistics Support (US Army)
Connecticut Association of Land Surveyors (USA)
CALTECH California Institute of Technology (USA)
CALUS Centre for Advanced Land Use Studies (College of Estate Management) (University of Reading)
CAM Calculated Access Method
Cartographic Automatic Mapping
Cellulose Acetate Membrane
Cement-Aggregate Mixture
Center for the Application of Mathematics (Lehigh University (USA))
Character Address Module
Chorioallantoic Membrane
Committee for Analytical Methods
Communications Access Manager
Computer Assessment of Media
Computer-Aided Manufacturing
Content Addressed Memory
Continuous Air Monitor
Crassulacean Acid Metabolism
Cybernetic Anthropomorphous Machine
CAMA Centralised Automatic Message Accounting
Civil Aviation Medical Association (USA)
Computer Aided Mathematical Analysis
Control and Automation Manufacturers Association
CAMAC Computer Aided Measurement And Control
Computer Aided Monitoring And Control
Computer Automated Measurement and Control
CAMAL CAMBRIDGE (UNIVERSITY) Algebra System
CAMBS Command Active Multi-Beam Sonobuoy
CAMC Canadian Association of Management Consultants (Canada)
CAMDS Chemical Agent Munitions Dispersal System
CAMECEC Carpentreria Metalica y Cerrajania de la Construccion (Spain)
Computer Aided Machine Loading
Computer-Aided Layout of Masks
CAMELOT Computerization And Mechanization of Local Office Tasks
CAMEN Centro Applicazioni Militari Energia Nucleare (Italy)

CAMERA Co-operating Agency Method for Event Reporting and Analysis
CAMESA Canadian Military Electronics Standards Agency
CAMET Centre for Advancement of Mathematical Education in Technology (Loughborough University)
CAMFAX Civil Aviation Meteorological Facsimile network
CAMI Civil Aeromedical Institute (of FAA (USA))
CAMMS Computer-Assisted Map Manoeuvre System
CAMOL Computer Assisted Management Of Learning
CAMOS Computer Aided Mapping of Sonar
Computer-aided Abrasive Machining Oscillation Studies
CAMP Co-operative African Microform Project (administered by Center for Research Libraries, Chicago (USA))
Compiler for Automatic Machine Programming
Computer Aided Maintenance Project (of the British Post Office)
Computer Aided Mask Preparation
Computer Assisted Manual Preparation
Computer Assisted Movie Production
Computer-Assisted Menu Planning
Continuous Air Monitoring Project (of NAPCA (USA))
Controls And Monitoring Processor
Craft Attitude Monitoring Package
CAMP-PDE Cyclic Adenosine Monophosphate Phosphodiesterase
CAMPRAD Computer Assisted Message Preparation Relay And Distribution
CAMPS Centralised Automated Military Pay System (US Army)
Computer Aided Mission Planning System
Computer Assisted Message Processing System
CAMPUS Computerized Analytical Methods in Planning University System
CAMR Canadian Association for the Mentally Retarded (Canada)
Centre for Applied Microbiology and Research (of PHLS)
Computer Assisted Micrographic Retrieval
CAMRA Campaign for Real Ale (an organisation)
CAMS Chinese Academy of Medical Sciences (China)
Coast Anti-Missile System
Coastal Anti-Missile System
Computer-Controlled Container Automatic Marking System
Control of Aircraft Maintenance and Servicing
Crew and Administrative Management System
Cybernetic Anthropomorphous Machine System
CAMSPEK Chemical Analysis by Microwave Spectroscopy
CAN Cascade Activity Numbering
Centro Administrativo Nacional (Colombi
Committee on Aircraft Noise (of ICAO)
Her Majesty's Custom's Assigned Number
CAN/OLE Canadian On-Line Enquiry (of CISTI (Canada))
CAN/SDI Canadian Selective Dissemination of Information (of CISTI (Canada))
CAN/TAP Canadian Technical Awareness Programme (of CISTI (Canada))
CANBER submarine telephone cable between Canada and Bermuda
CANCAM Canadian Congress of Applied Mechanics
CANCASS Canadian Command Active Sonobuoy System
CANCEE Canadian National Committee for Earthquake Engineering (of NRC (Canada))
CANCER Computer Analysis of Nonlinear Circuits Excluding Radiation
CANDE Culvert Analysis and Design
CANDO Computer Analysis of Networks with Design Orientation
CANDOFD Computer Analysis of Networks with Design Orientation in the Frequency Domain
CANDU Canadian Deuterium Uranium
CANE Chemical Applications of Nuclear Explosions
Computer-Aided Navigation Equipment
CANEWS Canadian Electronic Warfare System
CANFARM Canadian Farm Management Data System
CANFUT Canadian Future Study Group (Canada)
CANINE Computer Analysis of Networks via Inversion of Network Equations
CANMET prefix to dated-numbered series of reports issued by Canada Centre for Mineral and Energy Technology
CANP Civil Air Notification Procedure
Civil Aircraft Notification Procedure
CANSIM Canadian Socio-Economic Information Mannagement System
CANTAP Canadian Technical Awareness Programme (a service of CISTI (Canada))
CANTAT submarine telephone cable between Scotland and Canada
CANTOT Computer Analysis of Troubles on Trunk Circuits
CANTRAN Cancel in Transmissio
CANTV Compania Anonima Nacional Telefonos de Venezuela (Venezuela)
CANWEC Canadian National Committee of the World Energy Conference (Canada)
CAO Committee on Atmosphere and Oceans (of seven US Government agencies)
Computer Applications Office (of Library of Congress (USA))
CAOCS Carrier Aircraft Operational Compatibility System
CAOCS-MOD2 Carrier Aircraft Operational Compatibility System–Model 2
CAOG Central Association of Obstetricians and Gynecologists (USA)
CAORE Canadian Army Operational Research Establishment
CAORF Computer-Aided Operations Research Facility (of the Merchant Marine Academy (USA))
CAOS Computer-Augmented Oscilloscope System
CAP Canadian Association of Physicists (Canada)
Catabolite Activator Protein
Centre Aeroporte de Toulouse (of DTAT (France))
Chloro-aluminium Phthalocyanine
Civil Air Patrol (USA)
Civil Air Publications (numbered series issued by Civil Aviation Authority) (previously issued by the Board of Trade and later by DTI)
College of American Pathologists (USA)
Combat Air Patrol
Common Agricultural Policy (of EEC)
Commonwealth Association of Planners
Communications Analysis Package
Community Action Program (USA)
Computer Aided Planning
Computer Aided Programming
Computer Assisted Placement
Configuration Analysis Programme
Control Anticipation Parameter
Cover, Artillery Protection (for IKE TOW missile crew)
Crew Assignment Programme
Cryotron Associative Processor
CAPA Canadian Association of Purchasing Agents (Canada)
Central Airborne Performance Analyser
Confederation of Asian and Pacific Accountants
Corrosion and Protection Association (became the Corrosion Science Division of the Institution of Corrosion and Technology in 1975)
CAPABLE Controls And Panel Arrangement By Logical Evaluation

CAPAC Cathodic Protection by Automatically Controlled Impressed Current
Composers, Authors and Publishers Association of Canada (Canada)

CAPAL Computer and Photographic Assisted Learning

CAPARS Computer Aided Placement And Routing System

CAPB Compression-Annealed Pyrolytic Boron nitride

CAPC Computer Aided Production Control

CAPCIS Corrosion and Protection Centre, Industrial Services unit (of Dept of Industry and UMIST)

CAPCOM Capsule Communications

CAPD Continuous Ambulatory Peritoneal Dialysis

CAPDAC Computer-Aided Piping Design And Construction

CAPE Computer Aided Planning and Estimating
Computer Aided Process Engineering
Computerized Accommodated Percentage Evaluation
Conduction Analysis Programme using Eigenvalues
Consortium for the Advancement of Physics Education (Kansas-Missouri region of the USA)

CAPER Combined Active/Passive Emitter Rangings
Component Assessment Program and Engineering Review (of US Army)
Computer Aided Pattern Evaluation and Recognition
Computer Aided Perspective
Cost of Attaining Personnel Requirements

CAPERTSIM Computer Assisted Programme Evaluation Review Technique Simulation

CAPES Controlled Alternating Parachute Exit System

CAPEXIL Chemicals and Allied Products Export Promotion Council (India)

CAPFCE Comité Administrador del Programa Federal de Construción de Escuelas (Mexico) (Administrative committee of the Federal Programme for the Building of Educational Institutes)

CAPG Compression-Annealed Pyrolytic Graphite

CAPICS Computer Aided Processing of Industrial Cabling Systems

CAPITAL Computer Assisted Placing In The Areas of London (a project of the Employment Services Agency)

CAPITB Chemical and Allied Products Industry Training Board
Clothing and Allied Products Industry Training Board

CAPL Canadian Association of Public Librarians (Canada)

CAPLIN Computer Assisted Physics Laboratory Instruction (a project of Indiana University (USA))

CAPM Capital Asset Pricing Model
Computer Aided Production Management

CAPMS Central Agency for Public Mobilisation and Statistics (Egypt)

CAPO Computer-Aided Platforms Operation

CAPOSS Capacity Planning and Operation Sequencing System

CAPP Computer Aided Part Planning
Computer Aided Process Planning

CAPPS Computer Aided Project Planning System

CAPRE Commissao de Co-ordenacao das Atividades de Processamento Electronico (Brazil) (Coordinating Commission for Electronic Processing Activities)

CAPRI Centre d'Application et de Promotion des Rayonnements Ionisants (of Commissariat a l'Energie Atomique (France))
Computer Aided Personal Reference Index
Computerized Administration of Patent Documents Reclassified According to the INTERNATIONAL PATENT CLASSIFICATION
Computerized Advance Personnel Requirements and Inventory
Computerized Analysis for Programming Investments

CAPRIS Combat Active and Passive Radar and Identification System

CAPS Casette Programming System
Civil Aviation Purchasing Service (of ICAO)
Co-operative Awards in Pure Science (of the Science Research Council)
Coastal Aerial Photo-laser Survey
COLLINS (RADIO) Adaptive Processing System
Combat Air Patrol Support aircraft
Computer Aided Project Study
Computer-Aided Planning System
Computer-Aided Problem Solving
Computer-based Aid to Aircraft Project Studies
Costs and Productivity Scheme (of the Road Haulage Association)
COURTAULD'S All Purpose Simulator

CAPSR Cost Account Performance Status Report

CAPT Clearinghouse for Applied Performance Testing (North-west Regional Educational Laboratory, Portland (USA))

CAPTAC Conference des Administrations des Postes et Telecommunications de l'Afrique Centrale (Conference of Posts and Telecommunications Administrations of Central Africa)

CAPTOR Encapsulated Torpedo

CAQA Computer-Aided Quality Assurance

CAR Ceskomoravsky Avaz Radioamatero (Czechoslovakia) (Czech-Moravian Union of Radio Amateurs)
Change Agent Research
Cloudtop Altitude Radiometer
Cockpit Assessment of Reach
Computer Aided Retrieval

CARA Circular Active Reflector Antenna
Combat Air Rescue Aircraft

CARAD Computer Aided Reliability And Design

CARB California (USA) Air Resources Board

CARBINE Computer Automated Real-time Betting Information Network

CARBS Computer-Aided Rationalised Building System

CARC Chemical-Agent-Resistant Coating
Commercial Aircraft Requirements Committee

CARD Civil Aeronautics Research and Development Policy Study (of DOT and NASA (USA))
Compact Automatic Retrieval Device OR Display
Computer Augmented Road Design
Continuous Automatic Remote Display

CARDA Computer Aided Reliability Data Analysis
CONUS (USA) Airborne Reconnaissance for Damage Assessment

CARDAN Centre d'Analyses et de Recherche Documentaires pour l'Afrique Noire (France) (Documentary Analysis and Research Centre for Black Africa)

CARDE Canadian Armament Research and Development Establishment (of DRB)

CARDIAC Cardboard Illustrative Aid to Computation

CARDIS Cargo Data Interchange System

CARDS Card Automated Reproduction and Distribution System (of the Library of Congress (USA))
Computer Aided Recording of Distribution Systems
Computer Aided Reliability Data System
Computer-Assisted Radar Display System

CARE Computer-Aided Reliability Estimation
Continuous Aircraft Reliability Evaluation

CARE-SOM Coordinated Accident Rescue Endeavour–State of Mississippi (a state project on highway emergency medical services) (USA)

CARES Certification Authority for Reinforcing Steels
Computation And Research Evaluation System

CARETS Central Atlantic Regional Ecolological Test Site (a project of the Geological Survey and NASA (USA))

CARF Canadian Amateur Radio Federation (Canada)

CARIAC Cardboard Illustrative Aid to Computation

CARICOM The Caribbean Community

CARIFTA Caribbean Free Trade Area

CARIRI Caribbean Industrial Research Institute (Trinidad)
Change Agent Research)ssed Currentout of Masks
Current Agricultrual Research Information System (a project of FAO (UN))

CARISED Caribbean Surveying Education

CARL Canadian Academic Research Libraries (Canada) (became Canadian Association of Research Libraries in 1976)
Code Analysis Recording by Letters
Combustion Aerodynamics Research Laboratory (Sheffield University)

CARML County and Regional Municipality Librarians (an association of librarians in Ontario (Canada))

CARMRAND Civilian Application of the Results of Military Research and Development

CAROL a shipping consortium formed by Hapag-Loyd AG (Germany), Harrison Line (UK), KNSM (Holland) and CGM (France)

CAROT Centralized Automatic Reporting On Trunks

CARP Comprehensive Aerial Rainfall Programme
Computed Air Release Point

CARPA Caribbean Psychiatric Association

CARPS Calculus Rate Problem Solver

CARS Central Agricultural Research Station (Somalia)
Central America Research Station (of Center for Disease Control) (of PHS (USA))
Coherent Anti-Stokes Raman Scattering
Coherent Anti-Stokes Raman Spectroscopy
Community Antenna Relay Service (USA)
Computer Aided Routing System
Computer Audit Retrieval System
Computer-Assisted Reliability Statistics
Computerized Automotive Replacement Scheduling

CARSO Carnegie Southern Observatory (Chile) (financed by the Carnegie Institution of Washington (USA))

CART Cargo Automation Research Team (of IATA)
Collision Avoidance Radar Trainer
Command, Arming, Recording and Timing
Containerized Automated Rail-Highway Transportation
Continuous Air Resistance Tester

CARTA Contouring Analysis Random Triangular Algorithm

CARTE Centre for Agrarian Research and Training and Education (India)

CARTG Canadian Amateur Radio Teletype Group (Canada)

CARTONEX Conference for the Carton and Case Making Industry

CARTS Computer Automated Reserved Track System

CAS Calibrated Air Speed
Canadian Anaesthetists Society (Canada)
Canadian Cooperative Applications Satellite (cooperation between Canadian Department of Communications and NASA (USA))
Center for Acoustical Studies (North Carolina State University (USA))
Centre for Administrative Studies (of The Civil Service Department)
Centre for Agricultural Strategy (Reading University)
Chemical Abstracts Service (American Chemical Society)
China Association for Standardization (China)
Chinese Academy of Sciences (China)
Circuits And Systems
Close Air Support
Collision Avoidance System
Commission for Atmospheric Sciences (of WMO (UN))
Committee on Atmospheric Sciences (of IUGG)
Computer Accounting System
Computer Algebra Systems
Computer Arts Society
Conciliation and Arbitration Service (name changed in 1975 to ACAS)
Contract Administration Services (USDOD)
Controlled Air Space
Cooperative Applications Satellite (co-operation between France and the USA)
County Architects Society
Current Awareness Service

CAS-C Cooperative Applications Satellite C (co-operation between Canada and NASA (USA))

CAS/CPA Computer Accounting System/Computer Performance Analysis

CAS/PWI Collission Avoidance System/Pilot Warning Indicator

CASA Centre for Advanced Study of Astronomy (Osmania University) (Pakistan)
Computer and Automated Systems Association (of Society of Manufacturing Engineers (USA))
Construcciones Aeronauticas S.A. (Spain)
Cooperative Applications Satellite (co-operation between France and NASA (USA))

CASAA Combined Arms Studies and Analysis Activity (US Army)

CASAN Clean Air Society of Australia and New Zealand (Australia)

CASAO Chartered Accountants Students Association of Ontario (Canada)

CASAPS COMPUTER APPLIED SYSTEMS (USA) Accounts Payable System

CASARA Civil Air Search and Rescue Association (Canada)

CASBAR Collision Avoidance System using Baseband Reflectrometry

CASC China Aviation Supplies Corporation (China)
Computer-Assisted Cartography

CASCADE Centralized Administrative Systems Control and Design
Computer Aided Scantling Determination
Computer Aided System for Circuit Analysis and Design
Content And Source of Cataloguing Data for local use

CASCAID Careers Advisory Service Computerised Aid

CASCOMP Comprehensive Airship Sizing and Computer Programme

CASD Computer Aided System Design

CASDAC Computer-Aided Ship Design And Construction

CASDOS Computer Aided Structural Detailing of Ships

CASE Centre for Advanced Studies in Environment (of the Architectural Association)
Commision d'Aeronautique Sportive Internationale (of FAI) (International Aeronautical Sports Commission)
Committee on Academic Science and Engineering (of FCST (USA))

	Committee on the Atlantic Salmon Emergency
	Computer Aided Systems Engineering
	Computer Application-Specific Enabling standards
	Computer-Aided Systems Evaluation
	Concept Attainment Simulation Experiment
	Consumer Association of Singapore (Singapore)
	Cooperative Awards in Science and Engineering (of SERC)
	Coordinated Aerospace Supplier Evaluation (name now changed to Coordinated Agency for Supplier Evaluation) (an organization of aerospace industrial concerns in USA)
	Counselling Assistance to Small Enterprises (of the Dept of Industry, Trade and Commerce (Canada))
CASEC	Committee of Associations of Specialist Engineering Contractors
CASEVAC	Casualty Evacuation
CASF	Composite Air Strike Force
CASH	Charge Amplified Sample and Hold
	Commercial Applications Systems from HOSKYNS
	Computer Aided Stock Holdings
	Computer Aided System Hardware
CASI	Canadian Aeronautics and Space Institute (Canada)
CASIMS	Calibrated Airborne Special Infrared Measurement System
CASING	Cross-linking by Activated Species of Inert Gases
CASLE	Commonwealth Association of Surveying and Land Economy
	Commonwealth Association of Surveying and Land Engineering
CASLIS	Canadian Association of Special Libraries and Information Services (Canada)
CASM	Close Air Support Missile
CASO	Computer Assisted System Operation
CASOE	Computer Accounting System for Office Expenditure
CASOFF	Control And Surveillance Of Friendly Forces
CASP	Computer Assisted Search Planning
CASPAR	CAMBRIDGE Analog Simulator for Predicting Atomic Reactions
	Cushion Aerodynamic System Parametric Assessment Research (a programme of NRC (Canada))
	Cushion Air System Parametric Assessment Rig
CASPER	CLARKSON'S Automatic System for Passenger and Agent Reservations
CASPERS	Computer-Automated Speech Perception System
CASS	Chartered Accountant Students Society
	Combat Area Surveillance System
	Commanded Active Sonobuoy System
	Computer Automatic Scheduling System
	Computerized Algorithmic Satellite Scheduler
	Copper Accelerated Acetic Acid Salt Spray
	Crab-Angle Sensing System
CASSA	Continental Army Command Automated Systems Support Agency (US Army)
CASSIS	Communications And Social Science Information Service
CAST	Capillary Action Shaping Technique
	Centre d'Actualisation Scientifique et Technique (France)
	CFSTI Announcements in Science and Technology
	Chinese Academy of Space Technology (China)
	Computer Applications and Systems Technology
	Computer Assisted Scanning Techniques
	Computer-Aided Structural Technology
CASTARAB	Conference of Ministers in Arab States responsible for the Application of Science and Technology to Development
CASTASIA	Conference on the Application of Science and Technology to the development of Asia
CASTLE	Computer Assisted System for Theater Level Engineering (US Army)
CASTOR	Corps Airborne Stand-Off Radar
CASW	Counter Anti-Submarine Warface
CASWS	Close Air Support Weapon System
CAS^3	Combined Arms and Services Staff School (US Army)
CAT	Cable Avoiding Tool
	Capillary Agglutination Test
	Carbon Adsorber Tube
	Centre for Alternative Technology
	Choline Acetyltransferase
	Clear Air Turbulence
	COBOL Automatic Translator
	College of Advanced Technology
	Computer Aided Teaching
	Computer Aided Training
	Computer Assisted Teleconferencing
	Computer of Average Transients
	Computer-Aided Technology
	Computer-Aided Translation
	Computer-Aided Tree
	Computer-Aided Typesetting
	Computer-Automated Tester
	Computerized Axial Tomography
	Consolidated Atomic Time
	Controlled Attenuator Timer
	Crack Arrest Temperature
	Credit Authorization Telephones
	Credit Authorization Terminal
CATA	Canadian Air Transportation Administration (Canada)
CATALYST	Computer Assisted Teaching And Learning System
CATB	Combat Arms Training Board (US Army)
CATC	Circular-Arc-Toothed Cylindrical
	College of Air Traffic Control
	Commonwealth Air Transport Council
	Computer Assisted Test Construction
CATCC	Canadian Association of Textile Colourists and Chemists (Canada)
CATCC-DAIR	Carrier (warship) Air Traffic Control Centre—Direct Altitude Identity Readout
CATCH	Centre for the Analysis of Technical Change
	Character Allocated Transfer Channel
CATE	Computer Assisted Traffic Engineering
	Computer Controlled Automatic Test Equipment
	CONVAIR Automatic Test Equipment
CATED	Centre d'Assistance Technique et de Documentation du Batiment et des Travaux Publique (France) (Centre for Technical Assistance and Documentation for Building and Public Works)
CATER	Centro Andino de Tecnologia Rural (Ecuador) (Andean Centre for Rural Technology)
CATGEN	Computer Aided Test Generator
CATIB	Civil Air Transport Industry Training Board
CATIE	Centro Agronomico Tropical de Investigacion y Ensenanza (Costa Rica) (Tropical Agricultural Research and Training Centre)
CATIES	Common Aperture Technique for an Imaging Electro-optical Sensor
CATIS	Computer Aided Tactical Information System
CATLAS	Centralized Automatic Trouble Locating and Analysis System
CATNIP	Computer Assisted Technique for Numerical Index Preparation
CATO	Civil Air Traffic Operations
CATPASS	Computer-Aided Telephony Performance Assessment
CATR	Compact Antenna Test Ranges
CATRA	Cutlery and Allied Trades Research Association
CATRALA	Car and Truck Renting and Leasing Association (USA)

CATS Centralised Automatic Test System
Centre for Advanced Television Studies
Chicago Area Transport
Computer Aided Time Standards
Computer Aided Trouble-shooting

CATSS Cataloguing Support System (of Library Automation Systems Division, University of Toronto (Canada))

CATT Ceramic Audio Tone Transducer
Controlled Avalanche Transit-Time

CATTS Combat Arms Tactical Training Simulator
Combined Arms Tactical Training Simulator OR System
Computer-Aided Training in Troubleshooting

CATV Cable Telecommunications and Video
Cable Television
Community Antenna Television

CATVA Computer Assisted Total Value Assessment

CATVCMA Cable Television Cable Makers Association

CAUDAR Computer Assisted Unit Data Acquisition/Reduction

CAUSE College and University Systems Exchange (USA)
Computer Assisted Underwriting System at EQUITABLE (Life Assurance Society (USA))

CAUT Canadian Association of University Teachers (Canada)

CAV Construction Assistance Vehicle

CAVAL Cooperative Action by Victorian Academic Libraries (Victoria, Australia)

CAVAP Concave Assignment Problem

CAVE Consolidated Aquanauts Vital Equipment

CAVEA Connecticut Audio-Visual Education Association (USA)

CAVEAT Code and Visual Entry Authorisation Technique

CAVORT Coherent Acceleration and Velocity Observance in Real Time

CAVU Ceiling and Visibility Unlimited

CAW Carbon-Arc Welding
Channel Address Word
Close Assault Weapon
Common Aerial Working
Computer Aided Writing

CAWC Central Advisory Water Committee

CAWI Continuous Alcohol and Water Injection (standby power system for aircraft)

CAWS Cannon Artillery Weapons System
Central Aural Warning System
Communications Afloat Work Study (USN)

CAWSPS Computer-Aided Weapons Stowage Planning System (a project of NAEC (USN))

CAX Community Automatic Exchange

CAZRI Central Arid Zone Research Institute (India)

CB Certification Body (of CEE)
Chlorobromomethane
Citizen's Band

CBA Canadian Booksellers Association (Canada)
Christian Booksellers Association (USA)
Citizen's Band Association
Concrete Block Association
Cost-Benefit Analysis
Council for British Archaeology

CBAE Commonwealth Board of Architectural Education

CBAS City and Borough Architects Society

CBAT Central Bureau for Astronomical Telegrams (of the International Astronomical Union)

CBB Centre Belge du Bois (Belgium) (Belgian Timber Research Centre)

CBBI Cast Bronze Bearing Institute (USA)

CBC Canadian Broadcasting Corporation (Canada)
Cannabichromene
Compact Bipartite Committee (of National Apex Body (India))
Computer Based Conferencing
Coordinated Building Communication

CBCC Canada–British Columbia Consultative Board (Canada)

CBCT Customer Bank Communication Terminal

CBD Cannabidiol
Cash Before Delivery

CBDS Carcinogenesis Bioassay Data System

CBE Chemical, Biological and Environmental
Council of Biology Editors (USA)

CBEC Canadian Book Exchange Centre (Canada)

CBEL Current Balance Earth Leakage

CBEMA Canadian Business Equipment Manufacturers Association (Canada)
Computer and Business Equipment Manufacturers Association (USA)
Computer and Business Equipment Manufacturers Association (USA)

CBEUS Center for Business Economics and Urban Studies (Lehigh University (USA))

CBF Cerebral Blood Flow

CBFM Constant Bandwidth Frequency Modulation

CBI Chesapeake Bay Institute (Johns Hopkins University (USA))
Computer-Based Instruction
Confederation of British Industry

CBIS Computer-Based Information System
Computer-Based Instructional System

CBL Cannabicyclol
Chesapeake Biological Laboratories (University of Maryland (USA))

CBLS Carrier Bombs Light Store

CBM Centre Scientifique et Technique de la Brasserie, de la Malterie et des industries connexes (Belgium) (Scientific and Technical Centre for the Brewing, Malting and Related Industries)
Chemical Biological Munitions
Confidence Building Measure

CBMA Canadian Business Manufacturers Association (Canada)

CBMIS Computer-Based Management Information System
Council of British Manufacturers of Petroleum Equipment

CBMPE Council of British Manufacturers of Petroleum Equipment (name now changed to Council of British Manufacturers and Contractors serving the Petroleum and Process Industries)

CBMS Computer Based Message Service
Conference Board of the Mathematical Sciences (USA)

CBN Cannabinol
Cubic Boron Nitride

CBNM Central Bureau for Nuclear Measurements (of EURATOM)

CBNS Chemical Business News Service (of UKCIS)

CBO Compensation by Objectives
Congressional Budget Office (USA)

CBOSS Count, Back Order, and Sample Select

CBP CHORLEYWOOD Bread Process
County Business Patterns (series issued by Census Bureau, Dept of Commerce, USA)

CBPC Canadian Book Publishers Council (Canada)

CBPDC Canadian Book and Periodical Development Council (Canada)

CBPQ Corporation de Bibliothecaires Professionnels du Quebec (Canada) (Quebec Guild of Professional Librarians)

CBR California Bearing Ratio
Centralina Biblioteka Rolnicza (Poland) (Central Agricultural Library)
Centre for Business Research (Manchester Business School, University of Manchester)
Chemical, Biological, Radiological
Cloud Base Recorder

CBRA Chemical Biological Radiological Agency (USACDC)

CBRI Central Building Research Institute (India)

CBRM Charger-Battery-Regulator Modul

CBS Canadian Biochemical Society (Canada)
Centraal Bureau voor de Statistiek (Netherlands) (Central Statistical Bureau)
City Business (of British Telecom)
Columbia Broadcasting System (USA)
Commission for Basic Systems (of WMO (UN))

CBSC China Broadcasting Satellite Corporation (China)

CBT Center for Building Technology (of NBS (USA))
Centre Belge de Traductions (Belgium) (Belgian Translations Centre)
Clean Ballast Tank
Computer-Based Training

CBTS Cyclohexylbenzothiazyl Sulphenamide

CBTU Connecticut Board of Title Underwriters (USA)

CBU Clustered Bomb Unit

CBURC Computer Board for Universities and Research Councils

CBW Chemical and Biological Warfare
Chemical and Biological Weapons

CC Charge-Coupled
Chemurgic Council (USA)
Closure-Covering
Colon Classification
Computerized Conferencing
Constant Current
Control Computer
Corpus Cardiacum
Cushion Craft

CC&SS Central Computer and Sequencing

CC-DLTS Constant Capacitance Deep Level Transient Spectroscopy

CC-RAM Charge-Coupled Random Access Memory

CCA Canadian Construction Association (Canada)
Cannonical Correlation Analysis
Cement and Concrete Association
Central Computer Agency (of the Civil Service Department) (became CCTA in 1980)
Centre for Computing and Automation (of Imperial College of Science and Technology)
Chemical Coaters Association (USA)
Chick Cell Agglutination
Copper-Chrome-Arsenic
Current Cost Accounting
Customer Cost Analysis

CCAB Consultative Committee of Accountancy Bodies

CCABC Cancer Control Agency of British Columbia (Canada)

CCAE Canberra College of Advanced Education (Australia)

CCAF Community College of the Air Force (USAF)

CCAIA California Council of the American Institute of Architects (USA)

CCAID Charge-Coupled Area Imaging Device

CCAM Canadian Congress of Applied Mechanics

CCAP Conversational Circuit Analysis Programme
Culture Centre of Algae and Protozoa (of the Natural Environment Research Council)

CCB Command Communications Boat
Configuration Control Board

CCBS Center for Computer-based Behavioral Studies (California University (USA))

CCBV Compound Correlated Bivariate Poisson

CCC Classified Catalogue Code (of RANGANATHAN)
Commidity Credit Corporation (Dept. of Agriculture (USA))
Control Core Cell
Copyright Clearance Center (USA) (of the Association of American Publishers Technical, Scientific, Medical Division (USA))
Council for Cultural Co-operation (of the Council of Europe)
Customs Co-operation Council (68 countries are members)

CCCI Copenhagen (Denmark) Conference on Computer Impact

CCCO Committee on Climatic Changes and the Ocean (of IOC and SCOR)

CCCR Co-ordinating Committee for Cancer Research (of Joint Cancer Research Campaign, Imperial Cancer Research Fund and Medical Research Council)

CCD Calcite Compensation Depth
Carbonate Compensation Depth
Central Council for the Disabled (merged into RADAR in 1977)
Charged-Coupled Device
Circumscribing Circle Diameter
Conference of the Committee on Disarmament
Continuous Counter-current Decantation
Copolymer Composition Distribution

CCDA Commercial Chemical Development Association (USA)
Commission de Coordination de la Documentation Administrative (France) (Administrative Documentation Co-ordination Committee)

CCDS Command, Control and Detection System

CCE Carbon-Chloroform Extract
Commercial Construction Equipment
Council of Construction Employers (USA)

CCEB Combined Communications Electronics Boards

CCEER Center for Civil Engineering Earthquake Research (Nevada University (USA))

CCEHAEN Comision Chilena de Energia Nuclear (Chile) (Chilean Nuclear Energy Commission)

CCEI Composite Cost Effectiveness Index

CCEL Commission for Climatology (of WMO (UN))

CCEN Comision Chilena de Energia Nuclear (Chile) (Chilean Nuclear Energy Commission)

CCEP Coordinating Committee for Earthquake Prediction (Japan)

CCERO Centre d'Etudes de Recherche Operationelle (Belgium) (Operational Research Study Centre)

CCESP Coordinating Committee of Engineering Society Presidents (USA)

CCETSW Central Council for Education and Training in Social Work

CCF Carbonaceous Chondrite Fission
Common Communications Format (of UNESCO)
Commutated Capacitor Filter
Complex Coherence Function
Compressed Citation File
Conglutinating Complement Fixation
Crown Competition Factor

CCFF Critical Colour Flicker Frequency

CCFL Counter Current Flow Limiting

CCFM Council of Canadian Film Makers (Canada)
Cryogenic Continuous-Film Memory

CCG Canadian Coast Guard (Canada)

CCGT Closed-cycle Gas Turbine

CCH Computerized Criminal History (of NCIC (FBI) (USA))

CCHAP Circulation Coupled Hover Analysis Program

CCHMS Central Committee for Hospital Medical Services (of British Medical Association)

CCI Chambre de Commerce Internationale (International Chamber of Commerce)
Cotton Corporation of India (India)
Cotton Council International
CCIA Computer and Communications Industry Association (USA)
CCIE Countercurrent Immunoelectrophoresis
CCIG Cold Cathode Ion Gauge
CCIIW Canadian Council of the International Institute of Welding (Canada)
CCIP Continuously Computed Impact Point
CCIR Comite Consultatif International des Radiocommunications (of ITU) (International Telecommunications Consultative Committee)
CCIRID Charge-Coupled Infra-Red Information Device
CCIRRS Container and Chassis Identification Reporting and Recording System (USDOD)
CCIS Command Control Information System
Common Channel Inter-office Signalling
Computer-Controlled Inter-connect System
CCITT Comite Consultatif International Telegraphique et Telephonique (of ITU) (International Telegraph and Telephone Consultative Committee)
CCIW Canada Centre for Inland Waters (Canada)
CCK Cholecystokinin
CCL Coating and Chemical Laboratory (US Army)
Colour Centre Laser
Commodity Control List (USA)
Common Command Language
CCLC City Company Law Committee (of the Bank of England)
CCLN Committee for Computerized Library Networks (USA)
Council for Computerized Library Networks (USA)
CCLO Coordinating Council of Library Organizations (USA)
CCM Counter-Countermeasures
Cuban Cane Molasses
CCMA Canadian Council of Management Association (Canada)
Certified Color Manufacturers Association (USA)
Contract Cleaning and Maintenance Association
CCMD Continuous Current Monitoring Device
CCMIS Commodity Command Management Information System (US Army)
CCMM Complete Correlation Matrix Memory
CCMMI Council of Commonwealth Mining and Metallurgical Institutions
CCMS Committee of the Challenges of Modern Society (of North Atlantic Council (NATO))
Computer Centre Management System
CCMT Computer Controlled Machine Tool
CCMV Cowpea Chlorotic Mottle Virus
CCN Cloud Condensation Nuclei
Common-Carrier Network
Companhia Comercio e Navegacao (Brazil)
Copper Concentric Neutral
CCNA Canadian Community Newspapers Association (Canada)
CCNDT Canadian Council for Non-Destructive Technology (Canada)
CCNG Computer Communications Networks Group (University of Waterloo (Canada))
CCNR Canadian Coalition for Nuclear Responsibility (Canada)
Consultative Committee for Nuclear Research (of the Council of Europe)
Current-Controlled Negative Resistance
CCNSC Cancer Chemotherapy National Service Center (USA)
CCNY City College of New York (USA)
CCO Coconut Oil
Curent-Controlled Oscillator
CCOH Corrosive Contaminants, Oxygen and Humidity
CCOM Chicago College of Osteopathic Medicine (USA)
CCOP Committee for Co-Ordination of Joint Prospecting for Mineral Resources in Asian Offshore Areas (of ECAFE)
CCOP/SOPAC Committee for Co-ordination of Joint Prospecting for Mineral Resources in South Pacific Offshore Areas (of ECAFE)
CCOR Continuously Computed Optimum Release
CCOU Construction Central Operations Unit (of Health and Safety Executive)
CCP Chance-Constrained Programming
Computer Controlled Polisher
Conditional Command Processor
CCPA Cemented Carbide Producers Association (USA)
Consultative Committee of Plantation Associations (India)
Court of Customs and Patent Appeals (USA)
CCPC Communications Computer Programming Center (of AFCS (USAF))
CCPDS Command Centre Processing Display System
CCPE Canadian Council of Professional Engineers (Canada)
CCPI Coordinating Committee for Project Information (within the construction industry)
CCPIT China Council for the Promotion of International Trade (China)
CCPMO Consultative Council of Professional Management Organisations
CCPS Consultative Committee for Postal Studies (of UPU)
CCPWP Comparative Construction Performance Working Party (of industry, trade unions, Dept of Industry and NEDO)
CCR Centre for Catalogue Research (Bath University)
Circulation Control Rotor
Coastal Confluence region
COCKERELL (SIR CHRISTOPHER) Contouring Rafts
Coherent Crystal Radiation
Computer-Controlled Retrieval
Counter-Current Regeneration
CCRESPAC Current Cancer Research Project Analysis Center (USA)
CCRI Comite Consultatif de Recherche en Informatique (France) (Advisory Committee for Data Processing)
CCRL Cement and Concrete Reference Laboratory (of ASTM and NBS (usa))
CCRM Center for Chinese Research Materials (of the Association of Research Libraries (USA))
CCRMP Canadian Certified Reference Materials Project
CCROS Card Capacity Read Only Storage
CCRP Continuously Computed Release Point
CCRS Canada Centre for Remote Sensing (Canada)
CCRST Comite Consultatif de la Recherche Scientifique et Technique (France) (Consultative Committee for Scientific and Technical Research)
CCRT Cathodochromic Cathode Ray Tube
CCS Call Contact System
Canadian Ceramic Society (Canada)
Center for Cybernetic Studies (Texas University (USA))
Cold Crank Simulator
Common Channel Signaling
Conformal Countermeasures System
Controlled Combustion System
Countryside Commission for Scotland
Coupled-Cavity Structure
Critical Crevice Solution
CCSA Common-Controlled Switching Arrangement
Customer Controlled Switching Arrangement

CCSEM Computer-Controlled Scanning Electron Micrsocope
CCSL Compatible OR Comparative Current Sinking Logic
CCSOC Character-error Correcting Convolutional Self-Orthogonal Code
CCSS Commodity Command Standard System (US Army)
Conversational Computer Statistical System
CCST Center for Computer Sciences and Technology (of NBS (USA))
CCT Centre-Cracked Tension
Comite Consultatif de Thermometrie (Consultative Committee on Thermometry)
Comite de Coordination des Telecommunications (France)
Common Customs Tariff (of EEC)
Computer Compatible Tape
Continuous Cooling Transformation
Correlated Colour Temperature
Creosote Coal Tar
CCTA Canadian Cable Television Association (Canada)
Central Computer and Telecommunications Agency (now part of the Trasury)
CCTE Compound Cycle Turbofan Engine
CCTI Composite Can and Tube Institute (USA)
CCTR CULHAM (LABORATORY) Conceptual Tokamak Reactor
CCTS Canaveral Council of Technical Societies (USA)
CCTSC China Computer Technical Service Corporation (China)
CCTU Comite de Coordination des Telecommunications (of CNET (FRANCE)) (Committee for the Coordination of Telecommunications)
CCTV Closed Circuit Television
Closed-circuit Cable Television
CCTV/LSD Closed-Circuit Television/Large-Screen Display
CCTWT Coupled Cavity Travelling Wave Tube
CCU Central Capabilities Unit (of the Cabinet Office)
Central Computer Unit (of NPL (DTI))
CCUAP Computer Cable Upkeep Administrative Programme
CCURR Canadian Council on Urban and Regional Research (Canada)
CCV Control Configured Vehicle
CCVS COBOL Compiler Validation System
CCW Counter Clockwise
CD Capacitor Discharge
Certificate of Deposit
Circular Dichroism
Common Digitizer
Compact Disc
Contracting Definition
Crohn's Disease
CD5 Constant Dose Range
Critical Design Review
CDA Canadian Dental Association (Canada)
Canadian Department of Agriculture (Canada)
Ciliary Dyskinesia Activity
Co-operative Development Agency
Command and Data Acquisition
Compania Dominicana de Aviacion (Dominican Republic)
Computer Dealers Association
Conference of Defence Associations (Canada)
Continuous-Descent Approach
Controlled Droplet Application
Cool Dehumidified Air
Copper Development Association
Copper Development Association (USA)
Core Disruptive Accident
CDAP Community Development Action Plan
CDAPSO Canadian Data Processing Service Organisation (Canada)
CDB Cast Double Base
Consolidated Data Base
CDBA Clearance Diving Breathing Apparatus
CDBD Chemical Data Base Directory (of NLM (USA))
CDC Canada Development Corporation (Canada) (government sponsored)
Canadian Dairy Commission (Canada)
Cathodic Dichromate
Center for Disease Control (of PHS (HEW) (USA))
Centro de Documentacao Cientifica (Portugal) (Scientific Documentation Centre)
Chenodeoxycholic acid
Comb-line Directional Coupler
Combat Development Command (US Army)
Commonwealth Development Corporation
Compagnie des Compteurs (France)
Computer Display Channel
Cryogenic Data Center (of NBS (USA))
CDCA Chenodeoxycholic Acid
CDCEC Combat Developments Command Experimentation Center (US Army)
CDCED Combat Developments Command Experimentation Command (US Army)
CDCF Continuous Dress Creep Feed
CDCIA Combat Developments Command Infantry Agency (US Army)
CDCINTA Combat Developments Command Intelligence Agency (US Army)
CDCR Center for Documentation and Communication Research (of Western Reserve University, USA)
CDCS Centralised Digital Control System
CDDC Comision de Documentation Cientifica (Argentina) (Science Documentation Centre)
CDE Chemical Defence Establishment (MOD)
Conference on Confidence and Security Building Measures and Disarmament in Europe
CDEC Central Data Conversion Equipment
Combat Developments Experimentation Command (US Army)
CDEE Canadian Defence Education Establishment (of DRB (Canada))
Chemical Defence Experimental Establishment (MOD (now CDE))
CDES COMPUTEK (COMPUTEK INCORPORATED (USA)) Data Entry System
CDF California Department of Forestry (USA)
Confined Detonating Fuse
Contiguous-Disk File
Critical Demulsification Temperature
Cumulative Density Function
Cumulative Distributive Function
CDFR Commercial Demonstration Fast Reactor
CDG Chromatography Discussion Group
CDHS Comprehensive Data Handling System
CDI Center for Defense Information (USA) (independent research and educational agency)
Centre de Diffusion de l'Innovation (of ANVAR (France)) (Information Centre on Innovation)
Collector Diffusion Isolation
Compass Direction Indicator
Course Deviation Indicator
CDIC Carbon Dioxide Information Center (of DOE (USA))
CDICP Centrul de Documentare al Industriel Chimice si Petroliere (Romania) (Documentation Centre for the Chemical and Oil Industries)
CDICS Centralised Dealer Inventory Control System
CDIUPA Centre de Documentation des Industries Utilisatrices de Produits Agricoles (France) (Documentation Centre of Industries using Agricultural Products)

CDL Call Description Language
Central Dockyard Laboratory (MOD)
Centrala Drift Ledningen (Sweden) (Central (Power) Operating Board)
Command Definition Language
Computer Description Language
Computer Design Language

CDM Centrul de Documentare Medicala (Romania) (Medical Documentation Centre)
Code-Division Multiplexing

CDMA Code Division Multiple Access

CDMLS Commutated Doppler Microwave Landing System

CDMS Commercial Data Management System

CDNA Complementary DNA

CDP Central Data Processing
Certification Council for the Certificate in Data Processing (of ICCP (USA))
Charged-Drop Precipitator
Committee of Directors of Polytechnics
Common Depth Point
Continuous Distending Pressure
Contract Definition Procedure
Crustal Dynamics Project (of NOAA (USA))
prefix to numbered/single capital letter series of publications issued by the Civil Engineering Division of the Ministry of Works and Development (New Zealand)

CDPIRS Crash Data Position Indicator Recorder Subsystem

CDPS Computing and Data Processing Society (Canada)

CDR Crystal Diffusion Reflection

CDRA Canadian Drilling Research Association (Canada)
Committee of Directors of Research Associations

CDRB Canadian Defence Research Board (Canada)

CDRD Carbon Dioxide Research Division (of DOE (USA))

CDRI Central Drug Research Institute (India)

CDROM Computer Disc Read-Only Memory

CDRS Control and Data Retrieval System for remotely piloted vehicle concepts

CDS Case Data System
Central Department of Statistics (of the Ministry of Finance and National Economy (Saudi Arabia))
Central Dynamic Store
Centrul de Documentare Stiintifica (Rumania) (Scientific Documentation Centre)
Charged-Droplet Scrubber
Compatible Discrete
Comprehensive Display System
Computerized Documentation Service (of UNESCO)
Construction Differential Subsidy
Control Display System

CDSC Communicable Disease Surveillance Centre (of the PHLS)

CDSO Commonwealth Defence Science Organisation

CDSS Customer Digital Switching System

CDST Centre de Documentation Scientifique et Technique (of CNRS (France)) (Science and Technology Documentation Centre)

CDSU Computer and Data Systems Unit (of the Central Statistical Office)

CDT Cyclododecatriene

CDTA Cyclohexanediaminetetraacetic acid

CDTF Community Development Trust Fund (Tanzania)

CDTPA Calcium Diethylene-Triamine-Pentaacetic Acid

CDU Capacitor Discharge Unit
Control and Display Unit

CDVTPR Centre de Documentation du Verre Textile et des Plastiques Renforces (France) (Documentation Centre of Glass Fibre and Reinforced Plastics)

CDW Charge Density Wave

CE California Encephalitis
Carbon Equivalent
Compacted Earth
Composition Exploding
Critical Examination
prefix to lettered/numbered/dated series of reports issued by Control Engineering Department of BISRA

CE(PV) Ministry of Technology Committee of Enquiry on Pressure Vessels

CEA Canadian Electrical Association (Canada)
Carcino-Embryonic Antigen
Carcinoembryonic Antigen
Centre Est Aeronautique (France)
Centres d'Etudes Architecturales (Belgium) (Architecture Research Centre)
Combustion Engineering Association
Comité Européen des Assurances (European Committee for Security)
Commissariat a l'Energie Atomique (Belgium) (Atomic Energy Commission)
Commissariat a l'Energie Atomique (France) (Atomic Energy Commission)
Commodity Exchange Authority (of USDA)
Communications-Electronics Agency (USACDC)
Compania Ecutoriana de Aviacion (Ecuador)
Confederation Europeene de l'Agriculture (European Confederation of Agriculture)
Consejo Estatal de Azucar (Dominican Republic) (State Sugar Council)
Cost-Effectiveness Analysis
Council of Economic Advisors (USA)

CEAB Construction Exports Advisory Board (disbanded 1978)

CEAC Committee for European Airspace Co-ordination (of NATO)

CEADI Coloured Electronic Attitude and Direction Indicator

CEAELACOFI California (USA) Cooperative Oceanic Fisheries Investigations

CEAF Comite European des Associations de Fonderie (European Committee of Foundry Associations)

CEAM Centre d'Experences Aeriennes Militaires de Mont-de-Marsan (France)
Centre d'Experiences Aerienne Militaire (France) (Military Aircraft Test Centre)

CEAO Communaute Economique et Douaniere de l'Afrique de l'Ouest (Economic and Customs Community of West Africa)

CEARC Computer Education and Applied Research Centre

CEAS College of Engineering and Applied Sciences (Pennsylvania University (USA))

CEAT Centre d'Etudes Aerodynamiques et Thermiques (France)
Centre des Essais Aeronautiques de Toulouse (France)

CEB Central Electricity Board (Mauritius)
Combined Effects Bomblet
Comite Electrotechnique Belge (Belgium) (Belgian Electrotechnical Committee)
Comite Europeen du Beton (European Committee for Concrete)

CEBEC Certification mark of CEB (Belgium)

CEBEDAIR Centre Belge d'Etudes et de Documentation de l'Air (Belgium) (Belgi Centre for the Study and Documentation of Air)

CEBEDEAU Centre Belge d'Etude et de Documentation des Eaux (Belgium) (Belgian Water Study and Documentation Centre)

CEBELCOR Centre Belge d'Etude de la Corrosion (Belgium) (Belgian Corrosion Study Centre)

CEBLS Council of EEC Builders of Large Ships

CEBTP Centre Experimental de Recherches et d'Etudes du Batiment et des Travaux Publics (France) (Test Centre of Building and Public Works Research and Studies)

CEBWEWNA Centre Belge de Recherches Navales (Belgium) (Belgian Marine Research Centre)

CEC Cation Exchange Capacity
Centicycle
Ceramic Educational Council (USA)
Cholesteryl Erucyl Carbonate
Circular Exhaust Cloud
Clothing Export Council of Great Britain
Co-ordinating European Council for the Development of Performance Tests for Lubricants and Engine Fuels
Commonwealth Engineering Conference
Compound Elliptic Concentrator
Consejo Economico Centroamericana (of CACM) (Central American Economic Council)
Consulting Engineers Council (USA) (now part of ACEC)
Council for Exceptional Children (USA)

CEC-F Consulting Engineers Council of Florida (USA)

CEC/MINN Consulting Engineers Council of Minnesota (USA)

CEC/NYS Consulting Engineers Council of New York State (USA)

CEC/PA Consulting Engineers Council of Pennsylvania (USA)

CECA Communaute Europeenne du Charbon et de l'Acier (European Coal and Steel Community)

CECC California Educational Computer Consortium (USA)
CENEL Electronic Components Committee
Consulting Engineers Council of Colorado (USA)

CECE Centre d'Etude et d'Exploitation des Calculateurs Electroniques (Belgium) (Centre for the Study and Use of Electronic Computers)
Committee for European Construction Equipment

CECED Conseil Europeen de la Construction Electro-Domestique (European Council for the Manufacture of Domestic Electrical Equipment)

CECEP Corps of Engineers (US Army), Colorado Citizens Coordinating Committee on Environmental Planning

CECIMO Comité Européen de Coopération des Industries de la Machine-Outil (European Committee for Coöperation of Machine Tool Industries)

CECIOS Conseil Europeene de la Comite International de l'Organisation Scientifique (European Council of the International Committee of Scientific Management)

CECLA Comite Especial Coordinator Latinoamericano (Special Co-ordination Commission of Latin America)

CECM Commission pour l'Etude de la Construction Metallique (Belgium) (Commission for the Study of Metal Building)

CECO Consulting Engineers Council of Oregon (USA)

CECOL Civil Engineering College (of the CITB)

CECOMAF Comite Europeen des Constructeurs de Materiel Frigorifique (European Committee of Manufacturers of Refrigeration Equipment)

CECRI Central Electro-Chemical Research Institute (India)

CECS Civil Engineering Careers Service (of the structural and civil engineering institutions)
Civil Engineering Computing System
Closed Environmental Control System

CECT Comite Europeen de la Chaudronnerie et de la Tolerie (European Committee for Boilermaking and Metal Work)

CECU Consulting Engineers Council of Utah (USA)

CECUA Conference of European Computer User Associations

CED Capacitance Electronic Disc
Carbon–Equivalent–Difference
Committee for Economic Development (USA) (non-profit and educational organisation)
Communications-Electronics Doctrine
Community and Economic Development Division (of GAO (USA))
Competitive Engineering Definitions
Computer Entry Device
Continuing Engineering Development
prefix to numbered series of Command Papers issued between 1900–1918

CEDA Canadian Electrical Distributors Association (Canada)
Committee for Economic Development of Australia (Australia)
Communications Equipment Distributors Association (USA)

CEDAC Computer Energy Distribution and Automated Control
Computerized Energy Distribution And Control

CEDAR Computer-aided Environmental Design Analysis and Realisation

CEDATEE Cadmium Telluride

CEDB Central Engineering and Design Bureau (India)

CEDDA Center for Experimental Design and Data Analysis (of NOAA (usa))

CEDEP Centre Europeen d'Education Permanente (France)

CEDIC Centro Espanola de Informacion de Cobre (Spain) (Spanish Centre for Information on Copper)
Committee on Environmental Planning Army)lfof Masks Comite Europeen des Ingenieurs-Co

CEDIF Compagnie Europeene pour le Developpement Industriel et Financier (Belgium)

CEDIGAZ Centre International d'Information sue le Gaz Naturel et tous Hydrocarbures Gazeux (International Information Centre on Natural Gas and Gaseous Hydrocarbons)

CEDIMOM Centre European pour le Developpement Industriel et la Mise en valeur de l'Outre-Mer

CEDO Centre for Educational Development Overseas

CEDOC Centre Belge de Documentation et d'information de la Construction (Belgium) (Belgian Documentation and Information Centre for Building)

CEDOCOS Centre de Documentation sur les Combustibles Solides (Belgium) (Documentation Centre on Solid Fuels)

CEDPA California Educational Data Processing Association (USA)

CEDR Conference on Electron Device Research

CEDRIC Centre d'Etudes, de Documentation et de Recherches pour l'Industrie du Chaufage, du Conditionnement d'Air et des Branches Connexes (Belgium) (Centre for Research Studies and Documentation on Heating and Air Conditioning)
Customs and Excise Departmental Reference and Information Computer

CEE Commission Internationale de Reglementation en veu de l'Approbation de l'Equipement Electrique (International Commission on Rules for the Approval of Electrical Equipment)
Council for Environmental Education (Reading University)

CEEANAWP Central North American Water Project

CEEFAX See-the-Facts

CEEIA Communications Electronics Engineering Installation Agency (US Army)

CEEIA-WH CEEIA (US Army)–Western Hemisphere

CEEMA Centro de Enseñanza y Experimentación de Maquinaria Agrícola (Argentina) (Training and Research Centre of Agricultural Machinery)

CEEMAC Certification of Electrical Equipment for Mining Advisory Council (of HSC)

CEEMAT Centre d'Études et d'Expérimentation du Machinisme Agricole Tropicale (France) (Study and Experimentation centre of Tropical Agricultural Machinery)

CEEP Centre European de l'Entreprise Publique (European Centre of Public Sector Organizations) (of EEC)

CEER Center for Energy and Environment Research (Puerto Rico)

CEERI Central Electronics Engineering Research Institute (India)

CEF Centrifugal–Electrostatic–Focused
Chick Embryo Fibroblasts

CEFACEF Comite Europeen des Fabricants d'Appareils de Chauffage en Fonte

CEFB Centre d'Etudes des Fontes de Batiment (France) (Research Centre for Cast Iron in Building)

CEFIC Conseil Europeen des Federations de l'Industrie Chimique (European Council of Chemical Manufacturers Federations)

CEFRACOR Centre Francais de la Corrosion (France) (French Corrosion Centre)

CEG Centre d'Etudes de Gramat (of DTAT (France))

CEGB Central Electricity Geneating Board

CEGTS Controlled Environment Gravity Tube System

CEH Conférence Européenne des Horaires et des Services directs (European Conference of Timetables and Direct Services)

CEI Centre d'Études Industrielles (Switzerland) (Center for Education in International Management)
Comitato Electtrotecnico Italiano (Italy) (Italian Electrotechnical Committee)
Commission Electrotechnique International (International Electrotechnical Commission)
Comte Espanol de Iluminacion (Spain)
Configuration End Item
Contract End Item
Cost Effectiveness Index
Council of Engineering Institutions (disbanded 1983)

CEIF Council of European Industrial Federations

CEIR Comite Europeen de l'Industrie de la Robinetterie (European Committee for the Brass-founding and Finishing Industry)

CEL Carbon-Equivalent, Liquidus
Central Electronics Limited (India) (government owned)
Centre d'Essais des Landes (France) (Test Centre for Weapons, Missiles and Launchers)
Compagnie d'Energetique Lineaire (France)
Conversational Extensible Language
Corporate Engineering Laboratory (of the British Steel Corporation)

CELA Centro de Estudios Latinoamericanos (Panama)
Committee for Exports to Latin America (of BNEC) (amalgamated into CELAC, 1971) Sector Organizations) (of EEC)NITTEE ON ENVIRONMENTAL PLANNING Army)l

CELAC Committee for Exports to Latin America and the Caribbean (of BNEC)

CELADE Centro Latinoamericano de Demografía (Chile) (Latin-America Centre of Demography)

CELAR Centre d'Electronique de l'Armament (of DGA France)) (Electronics System Command of the French Air Force)

CELC Commonwealth Education Liaison Committee

CELDS Computer-aided Environmental Legislation Data System (of CERL (US Army))

CELME Centro Sperimentale Lavorazione Metalli (Italy) (Research Institute for Metalworking)

CELNUCO Comite European de Liaison des Negociants et Utilisateurs de Combustibles (European Liaison Committee of Merchants and Users of Fuels)

CELOS Centrum voor Landbouwkundig Onderzoek in Suriname (Surinam) (Centre for Agricultural Research in Surinam)

CELPA Centro Espacial de Lanzamientos para la Prospeccion Atmosferica (Argentine)

CELPLO Chief Executives of Large Public Libraries in Ontario (Canada)

CELS Continuing Education for Library Staffs in the South-west (a project of the Southwestern Library Association (USA))

CELSS Closed Ecology Life-Support System

CELTE Constructeurs Européens de Locomotives Thermiques et Électriques (European Association of Manufacturers of Thermal and Electric Locomotives (Federated into UNIFE in 1976)

CELTIC Cell Transport Integral Calculation

CEM Centre d'Essais de la Mediterranee (of DRME) (France) (now of DEn)
Channel Electron Multiplier
Communications–Electronics–Meteorology
Compagnie Electro-Mecanique (France)
Conventional Electron Microscope
Cost and Effectiveness Method

CEMA Canadian Electrical Manufacturers Association (Canada)
Catering Equipment Manufacturers Association
Centre d'Etudes Marine Avances (France) (now merged with COCEAN)
Channel Electron Multiplier Array
Comite Europeen des Groupements de Constructeurs du Machinisme Agricole (European Committee of Associations of Manufacturers of Agricultural Machinery)
Conveyor Equipment Manufacturers Association (USA)
Council for Economic Mutual Assistance SEE UNDER COMECON

CEMAC Committee of European Associations of Manufacturers of Active Electronic Components (now merged into CEMEC)

CEMAG Centre d'Étude de la Mécanisation en Agriculture (Belgium) (Centre for the Study of Mechanisation in Agriculture)

CEMAST Control of Engineering Material, Acquisition, Storage and Transport

CEMBUREAU Cement Statistical and Technical Organization (France)

CEMC Canadian Engineering Manpower Council (Canada)

CEMEC Committee of European Associations of Manufacturers of Electronic Components

CEMEL Clothing, Equipment and Materials Engineering Laboratory (US Army)

CEMI Conseil European pour la Marketing Industriel (European Council for Industrial Marketing)

CEMIS Client-Employee Management Information System

CEMP Centre d'Etude des Matieres Plastiques (France) (Research Centre for Plastics)

CEMS Centre d'Etude de la Meteorologie Spatiale (France) (Centre for Space Meteorology Studies)

CEMU Centro Sperimentale per le Macchine Utensili (Italy) (Research Institute for Machine Tools)

CEMUL Centro de Mecanica e Materiais de Universidade Tecnica de Lisbon (Portugal) (Mechanics and Materials Centre of the Technical University of Lisbon)

CEN Centre d'Etude de l'Energie Nucleaire (Belgium) (Nuclear Research Centre)
Comite Europeen de Normalisation (France) (European Committee for Standardisation)

CEN-CEA Centre d'Etudes Nucleaires de Cadarache (of CEA) (France) (Cadarache Nuclear Research Centre)

CEN-FAR Centre d'Etudes Nucleaires de fontenany-Aux-Roses (of CEA) (France) (Fontenany-Aux-Roses Nuclear Research Centre)

CEN-G Centre d'Etudes Nucleaires de Grenoble (of CEA) (France) (Grenoble Nuclear Research Centre)

CEN-S Centre d'Etudes Nucleaires de Saclay (of CEA) (France) (Saclay Nuclear Research Centre)

CENA Centre d'Experimentation de la Navigation Aerienne (France) (Air Navigation Experimental Centre)

CENATRA Centre National d'Assistance Technique et Recherche Applique (Belgium) (National Centre for Technical Assistance and Applied Research)

CENCER Certification Body of CEN (Comité Européen de Normalisation)

CENCOMS Center for Communications Sciences (of Comm/ADP (US Army))

CENDHRRA Centre for the Development of Human Resources in Rural Asia (Philippines)

CENEL Comite Europeen de Coordination des Normes Electrotechniques (European Committee for the Co-ordination of Electrotechnical Standards)

CENELEC European Organization for Electrotechnical Standardisation

CENET Centro Nacional de Electronica y Telecommunicaciones (Chile) (National Centre for Electronics and Telecommunications)

CENFAM Centro Nazionale di Fisica dell Atmospera e Meteorologia (Italy) (National Centre of Physics of the Atmosphere and Meteorology)

CENID Centro Nacional de Informacion y Documentacion (Chile) (National Centre for Information and Documentati

CENIM Centro Encional de Investigaciones Metalurgicas (Spain) (of Ciudad University)
Centro Nacional de Investigaciones Metalúrgicas (Spain) (National Centre for Metallurgical Research)

CENIP Centro Nacional de Productividad (Peru) (National Centre for Productivity)

CENL Community Equivalent Noise Level

CENOP Cenogoic Palaeoceanography

CENPHA Centro Nacional de Pesquisas Habitacionais (Brazil) (National Housing Research Council)

CENSA Committee of European National Shipowners Associations (now includes Japan)
Construccion de Elementos Normalizados S.A. (Spain)
Council of European and Japanese National Shipowners Association

CENSEI Center for Systems Engineering and Integration (US Army)

CENTA Committee for Establishing a National Testing Authority

CENTACS Center for Tactical Computer Sciences (of Comm/ADP (US Army))

CENTAG Central Army Group (of AFCENT (NATO))
Standard issued by CENTO

CENTEC Gesellschaft fur Centrifugentechnik (Germany) (a company— shareholders are the United Kingdom, Federal Republic of Germany and the Netherlands)

CENTEXBEL Centre Scientifique et Technique de l'Industrie Textile Belge (Belgium) (Scientific and Technical Centre for the Belgian Textile Industry)

CENTI Centre pour le Traitement de l'Informatique (France)

CENTO Central Treaty Organisation

CENTROMIN Empresa Minera del Centro del Perú (Peru) (government controlled)

CENUSA Centrales Nucleaires SA (Spain)

CEO Comprehensive Electronics Office
Consulting Engineers of Ontario (Canada) (an association)

CEOC Colloque Europeen des Organismes de Controle (a group of independent European inspecting organizations)

CEP Centre d'Essais des Propulseurs (France) (Aerospace Engines Test Centre)
Centre d'Etudes des Matieres Plastiques (Belgium) (Research Centre for Plastics Materials)
Chain Elongation Proteins
Circular Error Probability
Co-operative Engineering Program (a branch of SAE (USA))
Complementary Even Parity
Concentrated Employment Program (USA)
Confederation Europeene d'Etudes Phystosanitaires (France) (European Confederation for Plant Protection Research)
Council on Economic Priorities
Counter Electrophoresis
Cylinder Escape Probability

CEPA Civil Engineering Program (ADP) ASSOCIATION (USA))

CEPAC Conféderation Européenne de l'Industrie des Pâtes, Papiers et Cartons (European Confederation of the Paper and Card-board Industries)

CEPACC Chemical Education Planning and Coordinating Committee (of American Chemical Society (USA))

CEPACS Customs Entry Processing And Cargo System

CEPAL Comision Economica para America Latina (of UNO) (Economic Commission for Latin America)

CEPAR Curing, Extrusion, Plasticity and Recovery

CEPC Committee of the Engineering Professors Conference

CEPCEO Association of the Coal Producers of the European Community

CEPE Central Experimental and Proving Establishment (Royal Canadian Air Force)
Chain-Extended Polyethylene
Compagnie d'Electronique et de Piezo-Electricite (France)

CEPEC Committee of European Associations of Manufacturers of Passive Electronic Components (now merged into CEMEC)

CEPER Centre d'Etudes et de Perfectionnement (of ANDCP (France))

CEPEX Controlled Ecosystem Pollution Experiment
Controlled Ecosystem Pollution Experiment (a joint project of American, British and Canadian scientists)

CEPM Centre d'Exploitation Postal Metropolitain (France) (French Postal Department)

CEPR Centre d'Essais de Propulseus (DCAé) (France)

CEPRIG Centre de Perfectionnement pour la Recherche Industrielle et sa Gestion (France) (Centre for Improving Industrial Research and its Management)

CEPS Central Europe Pipeline System
Cornish Engines Preservation Society (now absorbed into The Trevithick Society)

CEPT Conference Europeenne des Administrations des Postes et des Telecommunications (European Conference on Postal and Telecommunications Administration)

CEQ Council on Environmental Quality (of the Executive Office of the President (USA)

CER Civil Engineering Report
Conditioned Emotional Response
Cost Estimating Relationship
Cross-linking Electron Resist
prefix to dated-numbered-lettered series of reports issued by Colorado State University, Department of Civil Engineering (USA)

CERA Civil Engineering Research Association (now CIRIA)

CERAFER Centre National d'Etudes Techniques et de Recherches Technologiques pour l'Agriculture, l'Equipement Rural et les Forets (France) (National Centre for Technical Studies and Technological Research for Agriculture, Rural Equipment and Forests)

CERBOM Centre d'Etudes et de Recherches de Biologie et d'Oceanographie Medicale (France) (Study and Research Centre for Medical Biology and Oceanography)

CERC Coastal Engineering Research Center (US Army)
Computer Entry and Read-out Control

CERCA Compagnie pour l'Etude et la Realisation de Combustibles Atomiques (France)

CERCHAR Centre d'Etudes et Recherche des Charbonnages de France (France) (Study and Research Centre of the French National Coal Industry)

CERCI Compagnie d'Etudes et de Realisations de Cybernetique Industrielle (France)

CERCOL Centre de Recherches Scientifiques et Techniques des Conserves de Legumes et des Industries Connexes (Belgium) (Scientific and Technical Research Centre for the Vegetable Canning and Allied Industries)

CERCOM Communications and Electronics Materiel Readiness Command (US Army)

CERE Centre d'Etudes et de Recherches de Environnement (Belgium) (Centre for Environmental Study and Research)
Computer Entry and Read-out Equipment

CERED Centre de Recherches d'Etudes Deniographiques (Morocco) (Research Centre for Demographic Studies)

CERES Centre d'Essais et de Recherches d'Engins Speciaux (France) (Centre for Test and Research of Missiles)
Computer Enhanced Radio Emission Surveillance System
Cross-polarization Evaluation Radio Echo System

CERF Centre d'Etudes et de Recherches en Fonderies (Belgium) (Foundries Study and Research Centre)
Civil Engineering Research Facility (of UNM (USA))

CERI Centre d'Etudes et de Recherches en Informatique (Algeria) (Data Processing Study and Research Centre)
Centre d'Études sur la Recherche et l'Innovation (France) (a non-profit association)
Centre for Educational Research and Innovation (of OECD)
Clean Energy Research Institute (University of Miami (USA))
Colorado Energy Research Institute (USA)

CERIB Centre d'Etudes et de Recherches de l'Industrie du Beton (France) (Study and Research Centre of the Concrete Industry)

CERL Central Electricity Research Laboratories (of CEGB)
Computer-based Education Research Laboratory (University of Illinois (USA)) Oceanography)ncele Sof Masks

CERMA Centre d'Etudes et de Recherches de Medicine Aerospatiale (France) (Aerospace Medicine Study and Research Centre)

CERMET Ceramic-Metal

CERMO Centre d'Etudes et de Recherches de la Machine-Outil (France) (Machine Tool Research and Study Centre)

CERN Organisation Europeene pour la Recherche Nucleaire (European Organisation for Nuclear Research) (formerly Centre Europeen de Recherches Nucleaires')

CERP Centre Europeen des Relations Publiques (European Centre of Public Relations)

CERPHOS Centre d'Etudes et de Recherches des Phosphates Mineraux (France) (Study and Research Centre on Mineral Phosphates)

CERS Carrier Evaluation and Reporting System (of MTMC (USDOD))

CERT Centre d'Etudes et de Recherches de Toulouse (France) (Aerospace Research Centre)
Combined Environment Reliability Testing (a program of USAF)
Constant Extension Rate Test
Council for Education, Recruitment and Training for the Hotel Industry (Eire)

CERTICO Committee on Certification (of ISO)

CERTS Centred'Etudes et Recherches en Technologie Spatiale (France) (Aerospace Technology Study and Research Centre)

CERTSM Centre d'Etudes et de Recherches Techniques Sous-Marines (France) (Underwater Techniques Studies and Research Centre)

CERVA Consortium Europeen de Realisation et de Vente d'Avions

CES Centre for Environmental Studies
Cleveland Engineering Society (USA)
Committee of European Shipowners (merged with CENSA in 1974)
Conference of European Statisticians (of UN)
Constant Elasticity of Substitution
prefix to numbered series of Corporate Engineering Standards issued by British Steel Corporation
prefix to numbered series of reports issued by Department of Civil Engineering, West Virginia University (USA)

CESA Central Ecuatoriana de Servicios Agricolas (Ecuador) (Centre for Agricultural Services)

CESAO Centre d'Etudes Economiques et Sociales d'Afrique Occidentale (Upper Volta) (Centre for West African Economic and Social Studies)

CESAR CERN Electron Storage and Accumulation Ring

CESD Composite External Symbol Dictionary

CESE Council for Environmental Science and Engineering (of CEI and CSTI)

CESEMI Computer Evaluation of Scanning Electron Microscope Images

CESI Centre d'Etudes Superieures Industrielles (France) (Centre for Advanced Industrial Studies)
Centre for Economic and Social Information (of ECOSOC (UN))
Computer Education Society of Ireland (Eire)

CESL Civil Engineering Systems Laboratory (University of Illinois (USA))

CESM Continuous Electro-Slag Melting

CESME Centro de Servicios Metalurgicos (Chile) (Central Metallurgical Industrial and Domestic Equipment Testing Centre)

CESMM Civil Engineering Standard Method of Measurement (of ICE and FCEF)

CESO Council of Engineers and Scientists Organisations (USA)

CESP Centrais Electricas de Sao Paulo SA (Brazil) (State Electric Power Enterprise)
Correlation Echo Sound Processor

CESR Centre d'Etudes Spatiales des Rayonnements (France) (Space Radiation Study Centre)

CESSAM Conversion Equipment System, Surface-to-Air Missiles

CESSE Council of Engineering and Scientific Society Executives (USA)

CESSS Council of Engineering and Scientific Society Secretaries (Canada and USA)

CEST Compacted Earth Sodium Treated

CESTI Centre d'Etudes des Sciences et Techniques de l'Information (Dakar) (Mass Communication Institute)

CET Combat Engineer Tractor
Common External Tariff (of EEC)
Corrected Effective Temperature
Council for Educational Technology for the United Kingdom
Critical Emulsification Temperature

CETA Centro des Estudos Technicos de Automocion (Spain) (Centre for Technical Studies on Automation)
Conference of Engineering Trade Associations
Corrosion Evaluation and Test Area (a project of NASA (USA))

CETAMA Commission d'Establissement des Methodes d'Analyse (France)

CETCA Comite Especifico Tarifario Centro-Americano

CETEHOR Centre Technique de l'Industrie Horlogere (France) (Clock and Watch Industry Technical Centre)

CETEPA Centre Interprofessionnel Technique d'Etudes de la Pollution Atmospherique (France)

CETEX Centro Tecnologico de Exercito (Brazil) (Military Technology Centre)

CETF Clothing and Equipment Test Facility (of US Army Infantry Board)

CETHEDEC Centre d'Etudes Theorique de la Detection et des Communications (France) (Detection and Communication Theory Research Centre)

CETI Committee for Energy Thrift in Industry (of DOI)
Communication with Extra-Terrestrial Intelligence
Cooperative d'Entreprises de Transport Internationaux (Switzerland)

CETIA Control, Electronics, Telecommunications, Instrument Automation
International Control, Electronics, Telecommunications, Instruments, Automation Exhibition

CETIE Centre Technique Internationale de l'Embouteillage (France) (International Technical Centre of Bottling)

CETIEF Centre Technique des Industries de l'Estampage de la Forge (France) (Drop Forging and Forging Industries Technical Centre)

CETIH Centre d'Etude Technique des Industries de l'Habillement (France) (Technical Research Centre for the Clothing Industries)

CETIL Committee of Experts for the Transfer of Information between Community Languages (of the Commission of the European Communities)

CETIM Centre Technique des Industries Mecaniques (France) (Mechanical Industries Technical Centre)

CETIUS Centre de Traitement de l'Information Scientifique (of EURATOM) (Scientific Information Processing Centre)

CETME Centro de Estudios Tecnicos de Materieles Especiales (Spain)

CETOP Comite Europeene des Transmissions Oelohydrauliques et Pneumatiques (European Oil-Hydraulic and Pneumatic Committee)

CETS Conference Europeene des Telecommunications Spatiales
Conference on European Telecommunications Satellites

CETT Centro de Entreamiento para Tecnicos en Telecomunicaciones (Venezuela) (Training Centre for Telecommunications Technicians)
Compagnie Europeenne de Teletransmissions (France)

CETUC Centro de Estudos en Telecomunicacoes da Universidade Catolica (Brazil) (Centre for Studies in Telecommunications of the Catholic University)

CETUS Computerised Exploration and Technical Underwater Surveyor

CEUSA Committee for Exports to the United States of America (of BOTB)

CEV Carbon Equivalent Value
Centre d'Essais en Vol (France) (Flight Test Centre)

CEWI Combat Electronic Warfare Intelligence

CEWT Central England Winter Temperature

CEX Civil Effects

CEZUS Compagnie Europeenne du Zirconium Ugine-Sandvik (France)

CF Characteristic Frequencies
Complement Fixation
Context Free
Conversion Facility
Corrosion Fatigue
Cortico-Fugal
Cystic Fibrosis

CF2 Central Flow Control Facility (of FAA (USA))

CFA Canadian Forestry Association (Canada)
Cash Flow Accounting
Complete Freund's Adjuvant
Complex Field Amplitude
Component Flow Analysis
Comunaute Financiere Africaine (African Financial Community)
Consumer Federation of America (USA)
Contract Flooring Association
Council of Ironfoundry Associations
Cross-Field Amplifier

CFADC Canadian Forces Air Defence Command (Canada)

CFAE Council for Financial Aid to Education (USA)

CFAM Commission for Aeronautical Meteorology (of WMO)

CFANS Canadian Forces Air Navigation School (Canada)

CFAR Constant False Alarm Rate

CFB Circulating Fluidised Bed

CFBS Canadian Federation of Biological Societies (Canada)

CFC Capillary Filtration Coefficient
Carbon Fibre Cement Composite
Chlorfluorocarbon
Consolidated Freight Classification
CRANFIELD (INSTITUTE OF TECHNOLOGY) Fluidics Conference

CFCF Central Flow Control Facility (of FAA (USA))

CFCGR Corrosion-Fatigue Crack Growth Rate

CFCP Corrosion Fatigue Crack Propagation

CFD Computational Fluid Dynamics

CFE CATERPILLAR (COMPANY OF AMERICA) Fundamental English
Chlorotrifluoroethylene
Commision Federal de Electricidad (Mexico) (Federal Electrical Commission)
Compagnie Belge de Chemins de Fer et d'Entreprises (Belgium)
Confederation Fiscale Europèene (European Tax Confederation)
Contractor Furnished Equipment (USA)
Controlled Flash Evaporation

CFEM Compagnie Francaise d'Entreprises Metalliques (France)

CFF Chemins der Fer Federaux (Switzerland) (Swiss Federal Railways)
Critical Flicker Frequency
Critical Fusion Frequency

CFFT Critical Flicker Fusion Threshold

CFI Central Fuel Injection

CFIA Commonwealth Forestry Institute (Oxford University)
Corporacion de Fomento Industrial (Dominican Republic) (Industrial Development Corporation)
Council of the Forest Industries of British Columbia (Canada)
Cavity Foam Insulation Association
Component Failure Impact Analysis

CFIAM Canadian Forces Institute of Aviation Medicine

CFIEM Canadian Armed Forces Institute of Environmental Medicine (Canada)

CFIT Committee for Industrial Technology (of DTI) (now of Dept of Industry)
Controlled Flight Into Terrain accident

CFL Calibrated Focal Length
Central Film Library (of the Central Office of Information) (now officially known as CFL Vision)
Context-Free Language

CFLOS Cloud-Free Line-Of-Sight

CFLP Central Fire Liaison Panel (of British Insurance Association, Fire Protection Association, Confederation of British Industry and Chief Fire Officers Association)

CFM Cerebral Function Monitor
Chlorofluoromethane
Collision-Force Method
Cubit Feet per Minute

CFMA Conflict Free Multiple Access

CFMI Cystic Fibrosis Mucociliary Inhibitor

CFMS Chained File Management System

CFMU Compagnie Francaise des Minerais d'Uranium (France)

CFO Central Forecasting Office (of the Meteorological Office)
Consolidated Functions Ordinary

CFP Common Fisheries Policy (of the EEC)
Compagnie Francaise des Petroles (France)
Cystic Fibrosis Protein
prefix to numbered series of Canadian Forces Publications issued by Dept. of National Defence, Canada

CFPA Conference of Fire Protection Associations

CFPG Context-Free Programmed Grammar

CFPMO Canadian Forces Project Management Office (Canada)

CFPRA Campden Food Preservation Research Association

CFPSG Context Free Phrase Structure Grammar

CFR Caile Ferate Romane (Romania) (State Railways)
Center for Future Research (University of California (USA))
Civil Fast Reactor
Co-ordinating Fuel Research
Commercial Fast-breeder Reactor
Crash, Fire, Rescue service

CFRG Carbon Fibre Reinforced Glass

CFRGC Carbon Fibre Reinforced Glass-Ceramic

CFRI Central Fuel Research Institute (India)

CFRP Carbon Fibre Reinforced Plastic
Carbon Fibre Reinforced Polymers

CFS Central Frequency Sounding
Combined File Search
prefix to numbered series of publications issued by Commercial Fisheries Bureau (of Dept. of the Interior (USA))

CFSG Cometary Feasibility Study Group (of ESRO)

CFSPL Canadian Forces Special Project Laboratory (of DREV (Canada))

CFSS Combined File Search System

CFST Context-Free Syntactical Translator

CFSTI Clearinghouse for Federal Scientific and Technical Information (now NTIS (Department of Commerce (USA))

CFT Charge-Flow Transistor
Compagnie Francaise de Television (France)
Complement-Fixation Test

CFTC Commodity Futures Trading Commission (USA)

CFTH Compagnie Francaise Thomson-Houston (France)

CFTRI Central Food Technological Research Institute (India)

CFTS Computerized Flight Test System

CFTT Controlled Flight Toward Terrain

CFU Coefficient of Fuel Utilisation

CFUC Colony Forming Units in Culture

CFUR Carrier Fire Unit Repair

CFUS Colony-Forming Units in Spleen

CFV Cavalry Fighting Vehicle
Conventional Friend Virus

CG Centre of Gravity
Coast Guard (of DOT (USA))
Compacted-Graphite

CGA Canadian Gas Association (Canada)
Clean GULF (OF MEXICO) Associates
Coal Gasifier Atmosphere
Compagnie Generale d'Automatisme (France)
Compressed Gas Association (USA)

CGAA Computer Graphic Aerodynamic Analysis

CGBR Central Government Borrowing Requirement

CGC Caenorhabditis Genetics Center (Missouri University (USA))

CGCRI Central Glass and Ceramic Research Institute (India)

CGCT Compagnie Generale de Constructions Telephoniques (France)

CGE Compagnie Generale d'Electricite (France)

CGER Centre de Gestion et d'Économie Rurale (France) (Centre of Rural Management and Economy)
CGG Compagnie Generale de Geophysique (France)
CGH Computer-Generated Hologram
CGI Commissione Geodetica Italiana (Italy) (Italian Geodetic Commission)
Computer-Generated Image
Computer-Generated Imagery
Cruise Guide Indicator
CGIAR Consultative Group on International Agricultural Research (of the World Bank, UN Development Programme and FAO (UN))
CGIT Compressed-Gas-Insulated Tube
Compressed Gas-Insulated Transmission
CGL Chronic Granulocytic Leukaemia
Corrected Geomagnetic Latitude
CGLI City and Guilds of London Institute
CGLO Commonwealth Geological Liaison Office
CGMP Cyclic Guanosine Monophosphate
CGMPTB Ceramic, Glass and Mineral Products Training Board
CGMS Co-ordination on Geostationary Meteorological Satellites
CGMW Commission for the Geological Map of the World
CGOU Coast Guard Oceanographic Unit (US Coast Guard)
CGPL Conversational Graphical Programming Language
CGPM Conference Generale des Poids et Mesures (General Conference on Weights and Measures)
CGPS Canadian Government Purchasing Service (Canada)
CGR/DC Coast Guard Research and Development Center (USCG (USA))
CGRA Canadian Good Roads Association (Canada)
CGRI Central Glass and Ceramic Research Institute (India)
CGRS Central Government Recommended Standard (CCTA)
CGS Canadian Geotechnical Society (Canada)
Crew Gunnery Simulator
Cyclic Group Signal
CGSA Computer Graphics Structural Analysis
CGSB Canadian Government Specifications Board
CGSI Computer Generated Synthesized Imagery
CGT Capital Gains Tax
Compagnie Generale Transatlantique (France)
Corrected Geomagnetic Time
CGU Canadian Geophysical Union (Canada)
CGVH Computer-Generate Volume Hologram
CH Chloral Hydrate
CHA Canadian Hospital Association (Canada)
Concentric Hemispherical Analyser
Coupled-Hard-Axis
CHABA Committee on Hearing, Bioacoustics and Biomechanics (of NAS/NRS (USA))
CHAD Code to Handle Angular Data
CHAG Compact High-performance Aerial Gun
CHAIS Consumer Hazards Analytical Information Service (of Laboratory of the Government Chemist)
CHALMAN CHALMERS (UNIVERSITY OF TECHNOLOGY (SWEDEN)) L-band Maritime Antenna
CHAM Combustion, Heat and Mass transfer
CHAMP Character Manipulation Procedures
Community Health Air Monitoring Program (of EPA (USA))
CRANFIELD (INSTITUTE OF TECHNOLOGY) Hybrid Automatic Maintenance Programme
CHAMPUS Civilian Health And Medical Program of the Uniformed Services (USA)
CHAMPVA Civilian Health and Medical Program of the Veterans Administration (USA)
CHAP Computer Charring Ablation Programme
Controlled Helium Atmosphere Plant
CHAPS Chance-constrained Programming System
Clearing House Automated Payments System
Clearing Houses Automated Payments System
CHARM Checking, Accounting and Reporting for Member firms (of the London Stock Exchange)
CHAT Cheap Access Terminal
Crisis Home Alerting Technique
CHAUD Chemical Audit and Distribution
CHC Community Health Councils
CHD Coronary Heart Disease
CHDB Compatible High Density Bipolar
CHDL Computer Hardware Description Language
CHE Cholinesterase
CHEC Channel Evaluation and Call
Commonwealth Human Ecology Council
CHEM Containerized Hospital Emergency Mobile
CHEMFET Chemically-sensitive Field-Effect Transistor
CHEMLINE Chemical Dictionary On-Line (of NLM (USA))
CHEMRAWN Chemical Research Applied to World Needs (a project of IUPAC)
CHEMSAFE Chemical Industry System for Assistance in Freight Emergencies
CHEMTREC Chemical Transportation Emergency Center (of Manufacturing Chemists Association (USA))
CHESF Centrais Hidroelectricas Sao Francisco (Brazil)
CHESS Chemical Engineering Simulation System
Community Health and Environmental Surveillance System (a program of EPA (USA))
Cornell High Energy Synchroton Source (Cornell University (USA))
CHETA Chemical Thermodynamics and Energy Hazard Appraisal
CHEW Overhead Earth Wire
CHEY Commission for Hydrometeorology (of WMO)
CHF Crimean Haemorrhagic Fever
Critical Heat Flux
CHG Chlorhexidine Glucomate
CHI Community Health Initiative
Computer Human Interaction
CHIA Canadian Hovercraft Industries Association (Canada)
CHIC Complex Hybrid Integrated Circuit
CHILD Cognitive Hybrid Intelligent Learning Device
Computer Having Intelligent Learning and Development
CHILL CCITT High Level Language
CHINA Chronic Infectious Neuropathic Agents
CHIPS Calculator Help In Processing Signals
Clearing House Interbank Payment System
CHIRP Confidential Human Factors Incident Report
CHIRU Community Health Initiatives Resource Unit (of DHSS and NCVO)
CHITO Container Handling In Terminal Operations
CHLA Canadian Health Libraries Association (Canada)
CHM Chemical Machining
CHMOS Complementary High-Performance Metal Oxide Semiconductor
CHORD-S Computer Handling Of Reactor Data-Safety
CHP Combined Heat and Power generation
Council of Housing Producers (USA)
CHPAE Critical Human Performance And Evaluation
CHPG Combined Heat and Power Group (of DOE)
CHR Coherent Heterodyne Receiver
CHRAC Construction and Housing Research Advisory Council

CHRIS Chemical Hazards Response Information Systems (of the US Coast Guard)
Cloud Height Remote Indicating System

CHRT Co-ordinated Human Resource Technology

CHS Canadian Hydrographic Service (Canada)
Collimated Holes Structure

CHSL Cleveland (Ohio) Health Sciences Library (USA)

CHSS Co-operative Health Statistics System

CHT Catadioptric-Herschelian Telescope
Collection, Holding, and Transfer

CHU Centigrade Heat Unit

CHUM Aeronautical Chart Updating Manual (of USDOD)

CI Chemical Inspectorate (MOD) (later Quality Assurance Directorate (Materials), now Materials Quality Assurance Directorate)
Chromatid Interchange
Combustion Institute (USA)
Configuration Inspection
Current-awareness Information

CIA Catering Institute of Australia (Australia)
Central Intelligence Agency (USA)
Chemical Industries Association
Clumping Inducing Agent
Commission Internationale d'Aerostation (of FAI) (International Ballooning Commission)
Compagnia Industriale Aerospaziale (Italy) (an industrial consortium)
Computer Industry Association (USA) (NOW CCIA)

CIABC Centre d'Instruction de l'Arme Blinde Cavaleries (France) (Armoured Cavalry Training Centre) (of the French Army)

CIACA Commission Internationale d'Aeronefs de Construction Amateur (of FAI) (International Commission of Amateur Built Aircraft)

CIAG CAMAC Industry Applications Group (USA)
Commission Internationale d'Aviation Generale (of FAI) (International General Aviation Commission)
Construction Industry Advisory Council

CIAI Conference Internationale des Associations d'Ingenieurs (International Federation of Engineering Associations)

CIAJ Communication Industries Association of Japan

CIAM Commission Internationale d'Aeromodelisme (of FAI) (International Aeromodelling Commission)
Congres Internationaux d'Architecture Moderne (International Congresses for Modern Architecture)

CIAME Commission Interministerielle pour les Appareils de Mesures Electriques et Electroniques (France)

CIANE Comite Interminsterielle d'Action pour la Nature et l'Environment (France) (Inter Ministerial Action Committee for Nature and the Environment)

CIANS Collegium Internationale Activas Nervosae Superioris (International Colloquy of Higher Nervous Functions) (of the World Psychiatric Association)

CIAP Centre d'Information de l'Aviation Privee (France)
Climatic Impact Assessment Program (of Department of Transportation (USA))

CIArb Chartered Institute of Arbitrators

CIASA Compania Internacional Aerea S.A. (Ecuador)

CIASTR Commission Internationale d'Astronautique (of FAI) (International Astronautics Commission)

CIAT Centro Internacional de Agricultura Tropical (Colombia) (International Centre of Tropical Agriculture)

CIATO Centre International d'Alcoologie/Toxixomanies (International Centre of Alcohol/Drug Addiction)

CIB Centralised Intercept Bureau
Classification Internationale des Brevets (International Classification of Patents)
Conseil International du Batiment pour la recherche, l'etude et la documentation (International Council for Building Research, Studies and Documentation) (Netherlands)
Convective Instability Base

CIBC Confédération Internationale de la Boucherie et de la Charcuterie (Switzerland) (International Federation of Meat Traders Association)

CIBE Confederation Internationale des Betteraviers Europeens (International Confederation of European Sugar Beet Growers)

CIBLE Critical Inspection of Bearings for Life Extension

CIBS Chartered Institution of Building Services

CIC Centre d'Information de la Couler (France) (Colour Information Centre)
Chemical Institute of Canada
Cloud In Cell
Committee on Institutional Cooperation (of a number of Universities in the USA)
Custom Integrated Circuit

CIC-MHE College–Industry Committee on Material Handling Education (USA)

CICA Canadian Institute of Chartered Accountants (Canada)
Centro de Investigaciones Ciencias Agronómicas (Argentina) (Scientific Agriculture Research Centre)
Confederation Internationale du Credit Agricole (International Confederation for Agricultural Credit)
Confederation of International Contractors Associations (France)
Construction Industry Computing Association

CICAF Compagnie Industrielle des Combustibles Atomiques Frittes (France)

CICAR Co-operative Investigations of the Caribbean and Adjacent Regions (of IOC (UNESCO)

CICAS Computer Integrated Command and Attack Systems

CICC Construction Industry Council of California (USA)

CICG Centre International de Conferences de Geneve (Switzerland) (International Conference Centre of Geneva)

CICH Centro de Informacion Cientifica y Humanistica (of UNAM (Mexico) (Centre for Information on Science and the Humanities)
Comité International de la Culture du Houblon (Hop Growers International Committee)

CICI Confederation of Information Communication Industries

CICIND International Congress on Industrial Chimneys

CICL Centre for Industrial Consultancy and Liaison (Edinburgh University)

CICP Committee to Investigate Copyright Problems (USA)

CICPND Comitato Italiano di Coordinamento par le Prova Non-Distruttiva (Italy) (Italian Committee for the Co-ordination of Non-destructive Testing)

CICRIS Co-operative Industrial and Commercial Reference and Information Service
West London Commercial and Technical Library Service (formerly 'Co-operative Industrial and Commercial Reference and Information Service')

CICS Committee for Index Cards for Standards
Customer Information Control System

CICS/VS Customer Information Control System/Vertical Storage

CICSA Centro Informacion y Computo SA (Colombia)

CID	Centre for Information and Documentation (EURATOM) Centro de Informacion de Archivos (Spain) Centro de Investigacion Documentaria (Argentina) (Centre for Documentation Research) Charge-Injection Device Collision-Induced Dissociation Combined Immunodeficiency Disease Component Identification Number Controlled Impact Demonstration
CIDA	Canadian International Development Agency (Canada) Centre International de Developpement d'Aluminium (International Centre fro the Development of Aluminium) Comite Interamericano de Desarrollo Agricola (Inter-American Committee for Agricultural Development)
CIDADEC	Confederation Internationale des Associations d'Experts et de Conseils (International Confederation of Associations of Experts and Consultants)
CIDB	Centre d'Information et de Documentation du Batiment (France) (Building Information and Documentation Centre)
CIDBEQ	Centre d'Informatique Documentaire pour les Bibliothèques d'Enseignement du Québec (Canada)
CIDE	Centro Informativo de la Edificacion (Spain) (Information Centre on Building)
CIDEC	Conseil International pour le Developpement du Cuivre (International Council for the Development of Copper) (Switzerland) Conseil International pour le Developpement du Cuivre (International Council for the Development of Copper) (Switzerland) (now dissolved)
CIDECT	Comité International pour le Développement et l'Étude de la Construction Tubulaire (International Committee for the Development and Study of Tubular Construction)
CIDEP	Chemically Induced Dynamic Electron Polarization
CIDESA	Centre International de Documentation Economique et Sociale Africaine (Belgium) (International Centre for African Economic and Social Documentation)
CIDET	Centro de Investigacion y Desarrollo de Telecomunicaciones (Mexico)
CIDHEC	Centre Intergouvernemental de Documentation sur l'Habitat et l'Environnement (Intergovernmental Centre for Documentation on Dwellings and the Environment)
CIDNP	Chemically Induced Dynamic Nuclear Polarization
CIDS	Chemical Information and Data System (US Army)
CIDST	Committee for Information and Documentation on Science and Technology (of the European Communities)
CIE	China Institute of Electronics (China) Commission Internationale de l'Eclairage (International Commission on Illumination) Computer Interrupt Equipment Control by Importance and Exception Coras Iompair Eireann (Eire) (Public Transport Authority) Counter-immuno electrophoresis
CIEA	Commission Internationale de l'Enseignement Aeronautique et Spatial (of FAI) (International Aviation and Space Education Commission)
CIEADH	Council of Industrial Engineering Academic Department Heads (USA)
CIEC	Centre International des Engrais Chimiques (International Centre for Chemical Fertilizers) Conference on International Economic Cooperation
CIEI	Center for International Environment Information (USA)
CIEN	Comisao Interamericana de Energia Nucleaire (OAS) Commision Interamericana de Energia Nuclear (OAS) Commission Interamericaine d'Energie Nucleaire (OAS)
CIEP	Counter Immunoelectrophoresis
CIES	Consejo Interamericana Economico y Social (Inter-American Economic and Social Council)
CIESM	Commission Internatinale pour l'Exploration Scientifique de la Mediterranee (International Commission for the Scientific Exploration of the Mediterranean Sea) (Monaco)
CIETA	Calcutta Import and Export Trade Association (India)
CIF	Canadian Institute of Forestry (Canada) Central Information File Centre Inter-Enterprises de Formation et d'Etudes Superieures Industrelles (France) Construction Industry Federation Construction Industry Foundation (USA) Cork Industry Federation Cost, Insurance and Freight
CIFA	Committee for Inland Fisheries of Africa (of FAO (UN))
CIFAS	Consortium Industriel Franco-Allemand pour le satellite SYMPHONIE
CIFC	Centre for Inter-Firm Comparison
CIFFOP	Centre Interuniversitaire de Formation a la Fonction Personnel (France)
CIFRI	Central Inland Fisheries Research Institute (India)
CIFRR	Common Instrument Flight Rules Room
CIFT	Central Institute of Fisheries Technology (India)
CIG	Centre d'Information Generale (Belgium) Cold-Insoluble Globulin Comite International de Geophysique (International Geophysics Committee) Commission Internationale de Giraviation (of FAI) (International Helicopter Commission) Coordinate Indexing Group (of Aslib)
CIGB	Commission Internationale des Grands Barrrages de la Conference Mondiale de l'Energie (International Commission of Large Dams of the World Power Conference)
CIGE	Centro de Instrucao de Guerra Electronica (Brazil) (Electronic Warfare Training Centre (of the Brazilian Army))
CIGFET	Complementary Insulated-Gate Field-Effect Transistor
CIGGT	Canadian Institute of Guided Ground Transport (Canada)
CIGR	Commission Internationale du Genie Rural (International Commission of Rural Engineering)
CIGRE	Conference Internationale des Grands Reseaux Electriques (International Conference on High Tension Electric Systems) Conference Internationale des Grands Reseaux Electriques (International Conference on High Tension Systems)
CIGS	Cataloguing and Indexing Group in Scotland
CIGTF	Central Inertial Guidance Test Facility (of AFMDC)
CIHM	Commission International d'Histoire Maritime (International Commission of Maritime History)

CII Centre for Industrial Innovation (University of Strathclyde)
Centre for Innovation in Industry
Chartered Insurance Institute
Collective Investment Institution
Compagnie Internationale pour l'Informatique (France)

CIIA Canadian Institute of International Affairs (Canada)

CIIN CAD/CAM Integrated Information Network

CIINTE Centralny Institut Informacji Naukow-Techniczznei i Ekonomiczney (Poland) (Central Institute for Scientific, Technical and Economic Information)

CIIT Chemical Industry Institute of Toxicology (USA)

CIL Chief Inspectorate of Electronics (Ministry of Defence (India))
Coal India Ltd (India) (government owned)
Computer Interpreter Language

CILA Casualty Insurance Logistics Automated

CILAS Compagnie Industrielle des Lasers (France)

CILE Call Information Logging Equipment

CILES Central Information Library and Editorial Section (of CSIRO (Australia))

CILG CIRIA Information Liaison Group
Construction Industry Information Liaison Group

CILOP Conversion In Lieu Of Procurement

CILSS Comité Inter-Etats pour la lutte contre la sécheresse au Sahel (Permanent Inter-State Committee on Drought Control in the Sahel)

CIM Canadian Institute of Mining and Metallurgy (Canada)
Co-operative Investigations in the Mediterranean (of IOC (UNESCO))
Commission on Industry and Manpower (disbanded 1970)
Computer Integrated Manufacturing
Computer-Input Microfilm
Continuous Image Microfilm
Convention Internationale sur le Transport de Marchandises par Chemins de Fer (International Convention Concerning the Carriage of Goods by Rail)

CIMA Construction Industry Manufacturers Association (USA)

CIMAC Congres International des Machines a Combustion (International Congress on Combustion Engines)

CIMAF Centro de Cooperacao dos Industriais de Maquinas-Ferramentas (Portugal) (Cooperative Centre for Machine Tool Manufacturers)

CIMAH Control of Industrial Major Accident Hazards

CIMAO Société Ciments de l'Afrique de l'Ouest (a company owned by Togo, the Ivory Coast and Ghana)

CIMAS Cooperative Institute for Marine and Atmospheric Studies (jointly sponsored by NOAA and Miami University (USA))

CIMB Construction Industry Manpower Board

CIMC Colombian Internal Medical Congress

CIMCLG Construction Industry Metric Change Liaison Group

CIME Centro de Investigacion de Metodos y Tecnicas para Pequenas y Medianas Empresas (Argentina) (Centre for Investigating the Organisation and Methods of Small and Medium-Sized Businesses)
Council of Industry for Management Education

CIMEC Comite des Industries de la Mesure Electrique et Electronique de la Communaute (Committee for the Electrical and Electronic Instrument Engineering Industries of the EEC)

CIMED Centro de Investigaciones in Metodos Estadisticos para Demogratia (Colombia)

CIMES Concours International du Meilleur Enregistrement Sonore (Annual International Sound Recording Contest)

CIMG Construction Industry Marketing Group

CIML Comite International de Metrologie Legale (of OIML) (INTERNATIONAL Committee of Legal Metrology)

CIMM Canadian Institute of Mining and Metallurgy (Canada)
Centro de Investigacion Minera y Metalurgica (Chile) (Research Centre for Minerals and Metallurgy)

CIMMYT Centro Internacional de Mejoramiento de Maíz y Trigo (International Maize and Wheat Improvement Centre) (Mexico)

CIMO Commission for Instruments and Methods of Observation (of WMO (UN))
Confederation of Importers and Marketing Organizations (EEC)

CiMOS CINCINNATI MILACRON (LTD) Operating System

CIMP Commission Internationale Medico-Physiologique (of FAI) (International Medico-Physiological Commission)

CIMPLE Card Image Manipulator for Large Entities

CIMPO Central Indian Medicinal Plants Organization (India)

CIMRST Comite Interministeriel de la Recherche Scientifique et Technique (France)

CIMS Co-ordination and Interference Management System
Computer Installation Management System
Computer Integrated Manufacturing System
Countermeasures Internal Management System

CIMTC Construction and Industrial Machinery Technical Committee (of SAE (USA))

CIMTEC International Meeting on Modern Ceramics Technologies

CIMTECH Centre for Information Media and Technology

CINAP CINCINNATI Numerical Automatic Programming

CINCCHAN Commander-in-Chief Allied Command Channel (of NATO)

CINCNORTH Commander-in-Chief Allied Forces Northern Europe (of NATO)

CINCSOUTH Commander-in-Chief Allied Forces Southern Europe (of (NATO)

CINCUKAIR Commander-in-Chief United Kingdom Air Force (of NATO)

CINDA CHRYSLER Improved Numerical Differencing Analyzer
Computer Index of Neutron Data

CINDAS Center for Information and Numerical Data Analysis and Synthesis (Purdue University (USA))

CINE Council on International Non-theatrical Events

CINECA Co-operative Investigations of the northern part of the Eastern Central Atlantic (of IOC (UNESCO)

CINF Commission Intersyndicale de l'Instrumentation et de le Mesure Nucleaire Francaise (France) (French Nuclear Instrumentation and Measurement Group)

CINFAC Counterinsurgency Information Analysis Center (American University, USA)
Cultural Information Analysis Center (of CRESS (USA))

CINP Collegium Internationale Neuro-Psychopharmacologicum

CINS CENTO Institute of Nuclear Science

CINTAC Communications Internal Tactical

CINTEL Computer Interface to Televisiðn

CIOA Centro Italiano Assidatori Anodici (Italy) (Italian Centre of Aluminium Anodizers)

CIoB Chartered Institute of Building

CIOMR Confédération Interalliée des Officiers Médicaux de Réserve (of NATO) (Inter-Allied Confederation of Reserve Medical Officers)

CIOMS Council for International Organisations of Medical Sciences

CIOS Combined Intelligence Objectives Sub-Committee
Conseil International pour l'Organisation Scientifique (International Council for Scientific Management) (Now known as the World Council of Management)

CIOSTA Comite International d'Organisation Scientifique du Travail en Agriculture (International Committee for Scientific Management in Agricultural Work)

CIOT Centro Internacional de Operacion Telegrafica (Argentine) (International Operations Centre for Telegraphy)

CIP Canadian Institute of Planners (Canada)
Cataloguing In Publication
Centro Internacional de la Papa (Peru) (International Potato (Research) Centre)
Cold Isostatic Pressing
Compensator Improvement Programme
Complex Information Processing
Council of Iron Producers (dissolved 1972)
Current Injection Probe

CIPA Canadian Industrial Preparedness Association (Canada)
Chartered Institute of Patent Agents
Comitato Interministeriale per l'Ambiente (Italy) (Inter-Ministerial Committee for the Environment)
Comité Internationale de Photogrammétrie Archtectural (International Committee for Architectural Photogrammetry)

CIPAC Collaborative International Pesticides Analytical Council

CIPASH Committee on International Programs in Atmospheric Sciences and Hydrology (of NAS/NRC)

CIPE Comitato Inter-ministeriale per la Programmazione Economica (Italy) (Inter-Departmental Committee for Economic Planning)

CIPEC Conseil Intergovernmental des Pays Exportateurs du Cuivre (France) (Intergovernmental Council of Copper Exporting Countries)

CIPFA Chartered Institute of Public Finance and Accountancy

CIPI Comité Interministéreil de Politique Industrielle (France) (Inter-Ministerial Committee on Industrial Policy)

CIPM Council for International Progress in Management (USA)

CIPOM Committee on Computers, Information Processing and Office Machines (of CSA (Canada))

CIPPRS Canadian Image Processing and Pattern Recognition Society

CIPR Continuous In-Flight Performance Recorder

CIPRA Cast Iron Pipe Research Association
Clothing Industry Productivity Resources Agency
Commission Internationale pour la Protection des Régions Alpines (International Commission for the Protection of Alpine Regions)

CIPS Canadian Information Processing Society (Canada)

CIR Canada India Reactor
Chlorinated Rubber
Colour Infra-Red film
Commission on Industrial Relations
Controlled Intact Re-entry
Cooled Infrared Radiometer
Cost Information Report
Council of Industrial Relations

CIRA Centro Italiano Radiatori Alluminio (Italy) (Italian Aluminium Radiators Manufacturers Association)
Commission Internationale pour la Reglementation des Ascenseurs et Monte-charges (International Commission for the Regulations concerning Elevators, Escalators and Lifts)
Conference of Industrial Research Associations

CIRA1965 COSPAR International Reference Atmosphere of 1965

CIRC Centralized Information Reference and Control
Circulation Input Recording Centre system

CIRCA Computerized Information Retrieval and Current Awareness

CIRCAL Circuit Analysis

CIRCE Computerised Issue of Results and Certificates for Entries (of CGLI)

CIRCUS Circuit Simulator

CIRED International Conference on Electricity Distribution

CIRFS Comite International de la Rayonne et des Fibres Synthetiques (France) (International Rayon and Synthetic Fibres Committee)

CIRGAME Command Information Requirements Game

CIRIA Construction Industry Research and Information Association

CIRIEC Centre Internationale de Recherches et d'Information sur l'Economie Collective (International Centre of Research and Information on Public and Cooperative Economy)

CIRIS Completely Integrated Reference Instrumentation System

CIRIT Comité Interprofessionel de Renovation de l'Industrie Textile (France) (Inter-professional Committee for the Restructuring of the Textile Industry)

CIRK COMPUTING TECHNOLOGY CENTER (UNION CARBIDE CORPORATION (USA)) Information Retrieval from Keywords

CIRM Celestial Infra-Red Mapper
Centro Internazionale Radio-Medico (International Radio-Medical Centre)
Comite International Radio-Maritime (International Maritime Radio Committee)

CIRMF International Centre of Biomedical Research in Franceville (Gabon)

CIRNA Compagnie pour l'Ingenierie des Reacteurs au sodium (France)

CIRP College International pour l'etude Scientifique des Techniques de Production Mechanique (France) (International Institution for Production Engineering Research)
International Conference on Infrared Physics

CIRSEA Compagnia Italiana Ricerche Sviluppo Equipaggiamenti Aerospaziali (Italy)

CIRT Canadian Institute of Surveying (Canada)
Conference on Industrial Robot Technology

CIS Canadian Institute of Surveying (Canada)
Cataloguing In Source
Center for Information Services (of University of Akron (USA))
Center for the Information Sciences (of Lehigh University (USA))
Central Information Service (of LRCC (University of London))
Central Information Service (University of London)
Centre International d'Information de Securite et d'Hygiene due Travail (International Occupational Safety and Health Information Centre)

Chartered Institute of Secretaries (now Institute of Chartered Secretaries and Administrators)
Chemical Information System (of NIH and EPA (USA))
Coal Industry Society
Control Indicator Set
Cue Indexing System
Current Information Selection
Custom Integrated System

CIS&P Canadian Institute of Surveying and Photogrammetry (Canada)

CISA Canadian Industrial Safety Association (Canada)
Centro Italiano Studi Aziendali (Italy) (Italian Centre for Business Studies)

CISAC Confederation Internationale des Societes d'Auteurs et Compositeurs

CISAVIA Civil Service Aviation Association

CISC Canadian Institute of Steel Construction (Canada)
Compound Induction Step Control
Construction Industry Stabilization Committee (USA)

CISCO Inter-Society Cooperation Committee (of ASIS (USA))
The Civil Service Catering Organization

CISDEN Centro Italiano di Studi di Diritto dell'Energia Nucleare (Italy) (Italian Centre for the Study of Nuclear Energy Law)

CISE Centro Informazioni Studi Esperienze (of ENEL (Italy))
Council of the Institution of Structural Engineers

CISHEC Chemical Industry Safety and Health Council (of CIA)

CISI Command Inspection System Inspection (of AFISC (USAF))
Compagnie Internationale de Service et Informatique (France)

CISIC California (USA) Information Systems Implementation Committee

CISILI Crash Injury Scale Intermediate Level Investigation

CISIR Ceylon Institute of Scientific and Industrial Research (Ceylon is now Sri Lanka)

CISL Confederation Internationale des Syndicats Libres (International Confederation of Free Trade Unions)

CISO Comité International des Sciences Onomastiques (International Committee of Onomastic Sciences)

CISPI Cast Iron Soil Pipe Institute (USA)

CISPR Comite International Special des Perturbations Radioelectriques (Special International Committee on Radio Interference)
Comite International Special des Perturbations Radioelectriques Fuerzas Armadas Argentina) (Armed Forces Scientific and Technical Research Institute)

CISR Center for Information Systems Research (of Alfred P. Sloan School of Management, MIT (USA))
Center for International Systems Research (State Dept, USA)

CISRC Computer and Information Science Research Center (Ohio State University (USA))

CISRI Central Iron and Steel Research Institute (China)

CISS Conference on Information Sciences and Systems

CISSY Campaign to Impede Sex Stereotyping in the Young (a women's group)

CISTI Canada Institute for Scientific and Technical Information (of National Research Council (Canada))

CISTIP Committee on International Scientific and Technical Information Programs (of Commission on International Relations (NAS/NRC (USA))

CIT California Institute of Technology (USA)
Carnegie Institute of Technology (USA) (now Carnegie-Mellon University)
Central Institute of Technology (New Zealand)
Charcoal Inhalation Tester
Chartered Institute of Transport
Comite International de Television (International Television Committee)
Comite International des Transports par chemins de fer (International Railway Transport Committee)
Compagnie Industrielle des Telecommunications (France)
Convective Instability Top
Crack Initiation Temperature

CITA Commercial Industrial Type Activities

CITAV Centro Informacion Tecnica de Aplicaciones de Vidrio (Spain) (Technical Information Centre on the Use of Glass)

CITB Construction Industry Training Board

CITC Construction Industry Training Centre

CITCE Comite International de Thermodynamique et de Cinetique Electro-Chimiques (International Committee of Electro-Chemical Thermodynamics and Kinetics) (now known as International Society of Electrochemistry (Switzerland))

CITE Compression–Ignition–and Turbine Engine
Contractors Independent Technical Effort
Current Information Tapes for Engineers

CITEC Compagnie pour l'Information et les Techniques Electroniques de Controle (France)
Contractor Independent Technical effort

CITEFA Instituto de Investigaciones Cientificas y Tecnicas de las

CITEL Conferencia Interamericana de Telecomunicaciones (Inter-American Telecommunications Conference (of OAS))

CITEN Comite International de la Teinture et du Nettoyage (International Committee for Dyeing and Cleaning)

CITEPA Centre Interprofessional Technique d'Etudes de la Pollution Atmospherique (France)

CITES Convention on International Trade in Endangered Species of Wild Fauna and Flora (signed in Washington USA in 1973)
Current Intelligence Traffic Exploitation System

CITG Coal Industry Tripartite Group (of the Dept of Energy, National Coal Board and coal miners' unions)

CITRA Compagnie Industrielle de Travaux (France)

CITRAC Central Integrated Traffic Control

CITS Central Integrated Test System
Commission Internationale Technique du Sucrerie (International Commission of sugar Technology)

CITS-MUX Central Integrated Test System Multiplex

CITTA Confederation Internationale des Fabricants de Tapis et de Tissus pour Ameublement (International Confederation of Manufacturers of Cloth and Woven Material for Furnishings)

CIU Computer Interface Unit

CIUMR Commission Internationale des Unites et Mesures Radiologiques (Internal Commission of Radiological Units and Measures)

CIV Convention Internationale sur le Transport des Voyageurs et des Bagages par Chemins de Fer (International Convention concerning the Carriage of Passengers and Luggage by Rail)
Corona Inception Voltage

CIVA Commission Internationale de Voltige Aerienne (of FAI) (International Aerobatics Commission)

CIVD Cold-Induced Vasodilation

CIVL	Commission Internationale de Vol Libre (of FAI) (International Commission of Free Flight)
CIVM	Collision-Imparted Velocity Method
CIVRES	Congres International des Techniques du Vide en Recherche Spatiale (International Congress for Vacuum Techniques in Space Research)
CIVV	Commission Internationale Vol a Voile (International Commission for Gliding)
CIWS	Close-In Weapon System
CJIS	California (USA) Criminal Justice Information System
CK	Creatine Kinase
CKD	Completely Knocked-Down
CKIC	Chemical Kinetics Information Center (of National Bureau of Standards (USA))
CKMTA	Cape Kennedy Missile Test Annex (of NASA) (renamed Cape Canaveral)
CL	Cathodoluminescence Chemiluminescence Compiler Language Cutter Location
CLA	California Library Association (USA) Canadian Library Association (Canada) Cargo Landing Adaptability Catholic Library Association (USA) Centre Line Average CHANDLEY (G.D.)–LAMB (J.N.)–Air Commonwealth Library Association (Jamaica) Communication Link Analyzer Community Land Act (repealed 1979) Computer Law Association (USA) Copyright Licensing Agency Country Landowners Association
CLACSO	Consejo Latinoamericano de Ciencies Sociales (Argentina) (Latin-American Social Sciences Council)
CLAD	Cover Layer Automated Design
CLADES	Centre Latino-Americain pour la Documentation Economique et Sociale (Latin-America Centre for Economic and Social Documentation)
CLAF	Centro Latinoamericano de Fisica (Brazil) (Latin American Centre for Physics) Centro Latinoamericano de Fisica (Brazil) (Latin American Centre for Physics)
CLAFIC	Class Featuring Information Compression
CLAH	Container Lift Adapter-Helicopter
CLAIM	Centre for Library and Information Management (Loughborough University)
CLAIMS	Class Codes, Assignee, Index, Method, Search (of the Patent Office (USA))
CLAIRA	Chalk Lime and Allied Industries Research Association (now WHRA)
CLAM	Chemical Low-Altitude Missile CONTROL DATA CORPORATION LISP Algebraic Manipulator
CLAMP	Chemical Low Altitude Missile Puny Closed Loop Aeronautical Management Program (of USN Aviation Supply Office) Computer Listing and Analysis of Maintenance Programmes
CLANN	College Libraries Activities Network in New South Wales (Australia)
CLAO	Consejo Latino Americano de Oceanografia (Uruguay) (Latin–American Council on Oceanography)
CLAQ	Centro Latinoamericano de Quimica (Latin American Centre for Chemistry)
CLARA	CORNELL Learning and Recognizing Automaton
CLARC	Consejo Latino-Americano de Radiacon Cosmica (Bolivia) (Latin–American Council on Cosmic Radiation)
CLAS	Clinical Laboratory Automated System
CLASB	Citizens League Against the Sonic Boom (USA)
CLASP	Circuit Layout, Automated Scheduling and Production Closed Line Assembly for Single Particles Closed-Loop Adaptive Single Parameter Coded Label Additional Security and Protection system Computer Laboratory Systems Project (of the Royal School of Mines) Consortium of Local Authorities Special Programme Cylindrical Laser Plasma
CLASS	California Library Authority for Systems and Services (USA) CANBERRA (INDUSTRIES) (USA) Laboratories Automation Software System Capacity Loading and Scheduling System Cargo Logistics Airlift System Study (by government and industry in USA)) Carrier Landing Aid Stabilization System Close Air Support System Closed Loop Accounting for Stores Sales Computer-based Laboratory for Automated School Systems Container-Lighters Aboard Ship system
CLASSIC	Class-room Interactive Computer Custom Logic and Array Simulation Systems for Integrated Circuits
CLAUDIUS	COOPERS & LYBRAND (ASSOCIATES) Accounting and Distributive Inventory System
CLAW	Consortium of Local Authorities in Wales
CLAWSA	Cities of London and Westminster Society of Architects
CLB	Continuous Line Bucket
CLBRP	Cannon Launched Beam Rider Projectile
CLC	Cholesteric Liquid Crystal Cost of Living Council (USA) Course Line Computer Current Leading Components
CLCB	Committee of London Clearing Bank
CLCCD	Clearinghouse and Laboratory for Census Data (of Center for Research Libraries (USA))
CLCCS	CAMMELL LAIRD Cable Control System
CLCR	Controlled Letter Contract Reduction
CLD	Central Library and Documentation branch (of ILO) Coincidence–Ledge–Dislocation Compression Load Deflection Crystal Lattice Dislocation Current-Limiting Device
CLDATA	Cutter Location Data
CLEA	Conference on Laser Engineering and Applications (of OSA and IEEE (USA)) Council of Local Education Authorities
CLEAN	Comprehensive Lake Ecosystem Analyzer
CLEANS	Clinical Laboratory Evaluation and Assessment of Noxious Substances (a program of EPA (USA))
CLEAR	Campaign for Lead Free Air Closed Loop Evaluation And Reporting County Law Enforcement Applied Regionally (Hamilton County, USA)
CLEAT	Computer Language for Engineers and Technologists
CLED	Cysteine Lactose Electrolyte-Deficient
CLEM	Closed Loop Ex-vessel Machine Composite for the Lunar Excursion Module
CLENE	Continuing Library Education Network and Exchange (of National Commission on Libraries and Information Science (USA))
CLEO	Clear Language for Expressing Orders
CLEOPATRA	Comprehensive Language for Elegant Operating system And Translator design
CLEOS	Conference on Laser and Electro-optical Systems

CLEPA Comite de Liaison de la Construction d'Equipements et de Pieces d'Automobiles (of EEC) (Liaison Committee of the Manufacture of Automobile Fittings and Parts)

CLETS California (USA) Law Enforcement Telecommunications System

CLF Capacitive Loss Factor

CLFM Coherent Linear Frequency Modulator

CLGP Cannon-Launched Laser-Guided Projectile

CLGS Compressed Limit Gauging Sampling

CLI Calling–Line–Identity

CLIA Collective Linear Ion Accelerator

CLIC Command Language for Interrogating Computers
Computer Layout of Integrated Circuits

CLICS Computer-Linked Information for Container Shipping

CLIM Cellular Logic-In-Memory

CLIMAP Climate Long-range Investigation, Mapping and Prediction study

CLIMATE Computer and Language Independent Modules for Automatic Test Equipment

CLIP Cellular Logic Image Processor
Closed Loop Incremental Positioner
Computer Layout Installation Planner

CLIPER Climatology and Persistence

CLIPR Computer Laboratory for Instruction in Psychological Research (University of Colorado (USA))

CLIRA Closed Loop In-Reactor Assembly

CLIS Clearinghouse for Library and Information Sciences (of ERIC (USOE))

CLISP Conversational LISP

CLL Chronic Lymphocytic Leukaemia

CLLR International Symposium on Computing in Literary and Linguistic Research

CLM Commutatorless Motor
Crane-Load Moment-indicator
Culham Laboratory (of UKAEA)

CLM-PDN prefix to numbered/dated series of Program (adp) Documentation Notes issued by Culham Laboratory (UKAEA)

CLMS Company Lightweight Mortar (artillery) System

CLN Cellulose Nitrate

CLO Campylobacter-Like Organism

CLOAX Corrugated–Laminated Coaxial

CLODS Computerized Logic-Oriented Design System

CLOG Computer Logic Graphics

CLOOGE Continuous Log of On Going Events

CLOR Centraine Laboratorium Ochrony Radiologiczenj (Poland)

CLOS Command to Line Of Sight
Controlled Line of Sight

CLP China Light and Power Company Ltd (Hong Kong)
Contact Lens Practitioners

CLR Co-ordinating Lubricants Research
Combined Line and Recording
Constant Load Rupture
Council on Library Resources (USA)

CLRB Canada Labour Relations Board (Canada)

CLRI Central Leather Research Institute (India)

CLRU Cambridge Language Research Unit

CLS Characteristic Loss Spectroscopy
Commercial Loan System
Comparative Systems Laboratory (Western Reserve University (USA))
Computerised Literature Search
Constrained Least Squares
County Library Service (New Zealand)

CLSA California Land Surveyors Association (USA)

CLSD CULHAM (LABORATORY) Language for System Development

CLT Communications Line Terminals

CLTA Canadian Library Trustees Association (Canada)

CLUE Computer Language Utility Extension

CLUMIS Cadastral and Land-Use Mapping Information System

CLUSAN Cluster Analysis

CLUSTER Central London Land Use System and Employment Register

CLV Ceiling Limit Value
CHANDLEY (G.D.)–LAMB (J.N.)–Vacuum

CLW College of Librarianship, Wales
Council for a Livable World (USA)

CLYDE Computer-graphics Language for Your Design Equations

CM Central Meridian
Clothing and Organic Materials Division (of Natick Laboratories (US Army)
Configuration Management
Corrective Maintenance

CM/CCM Countermeasures/Counter Countermeasures

CMA Canadian Manufacturers Association (Canada)
Canadian Medical Association (Canada)
Canadian Museums Association (Canada)
Cement Manufacturers Association (India)
Coal Mines Authority Ltd (India) (government owned)
Colonic Mucoprotein Antigen
Commonwealth Medical Association
Compania Mexicana de Aviacion (Mexico)
Composite Medium Amplifier
Computerized Management Account
Contractors Mutual Association (USA)
Cylindrical Mirror Analyser

CMAA Crane Manufacturers Association of America (USA)

CMAAO Confederation of Medical Associations in Asia and Oceania (headquarters in Manila)

CMAC Cerebellar Model Articulation Control system

CMAE Contingency Movement After-Effect

CMAI Clothing Manufacturers Association of India (India)

CMAL Coal Mines Authority Ltd (India) (government owned)

CMAP Charge Materials Allocation Processor

CMARS Cable Monitoring and Rating System

CMAS Circular Map Accuracy Standard
Confédération Mondiale des Activités Subaquatiques (France) (World Confederation of Underwater Activities)

CMB Composite Minimum Brightness
Composite Modified Double-Base
Consortium for Method Building
Corrective Maintenance Burden

CMBES Canadian Medical and Biological Engineering Society (Canada)

CMBI Citrus Marketing Board of Israel (Israel)

CMC California (USA) Advisory Commission on Marine and Coastal Resources
CANTON Matic Carding
Carboxymethyl Cellulose
Cell-Mediated Cytolysis
Cell-Mediated Cytotoxicity
Code for Magnetic Characters
Comparison Measuring Circuit
Computer Maintenance Corporation (India) (govt owned)
Conservation Monitoring Centre (of IUCN)
Critical Micellar Concentration
Critical Micelle Concentration

CMCA Cruise Missile Carrier Aircraft

CMCLT Current Mode Complementary Transistor Logic

CMCR Continuous Melting, Casting and Rolling

CMCSA Canadian Manufacturers of Chemical Specialties Association (Canada)

cmd prefix to numbered series of Command Papers issued between 1919–1955/6

CMD Cartridge Module Drive
Central Marine Depot (of the British Post Office)
Contract Management Division (of USAFSC)
Conventional Munition Disposal
Count Median Diameter

CMDS Chaff/flare Countermeasures Dispenser System

CME Compania Maritima de Exportaciones (Spain)

CMEA Council for Mutual Economic Assistance (headquarters in USSR)

CMERI Central Mechanical Engineering Research Institute (India)

CMES Center for Marine and Environmental Studies (Lehigh University (USA))

CMF Cast Metal Federation
Cement Makers Federation
Coherent Memory Filter
Common Mode Failure
Constant Magnetic Field
Cytoplasmic Metabolic Factor

CMFRI Central Marine Fisheries Research Institute (India)

CMG Commission on Marine Geology (of IUGS)
Control Moment Gyro

CMI Cell-Mediated Immunity
Christian Michelsen's Institute (Norway)
Comite Maritime International (Belgium) (International Maritime Committee)
Commonwealth Mycological Institute
Computer Mediated Interaction
Computer-Managed Instruction
CORNELL Medical Index Questionnaire

CMIC Controlled Monitor Interface Calibrator

CMIR Carnegie-Mellon Institute of Research (of Carnegie-Mellon University (USA))

CMIS Common Manufacturing Information System
Computer-oriented Management Information System

CML Chronic Myeloid Leukaemia
Current-Mode Logic

CMLA Canadian Maritime Law Association (Canada)

CMM Commission for Maritime Meteorology (of WMO)
Computerized Modular Monitoring
Coordinate Measuring Machine

CMMA Concrete Mixer Manufacturers Association
Crane Manufacturers Association of America (USA)

CMMC Commonwealth Mining and Metallurgical Congress

CMME Chloromethyl Methyl Ether

CMMI Commonwealth Mining and Metallurgical Institutions

CMMP Commodity Management Master Plan

CMN Cerium Magnesium Nitrate
Cerous Magnesium Nitrate
Constructions Mecaniques de Normandie (France)

cmnd Command Paper (numbered series authorised by Parliament and published by HMSO)

CMOS Complementary Metal Oxide Semiconductor
Complementary-symmetry Metal Oxide Semiconductor

CMOS-SOS Complementary Metal Oxide Semiconductor Silicon-on-Sapphire

CMP Canadian Mineral Processors (Canada)
COBOL Macro Processor
Concrete Mixing and Placing
Corrugated Metal Pipe

CMPC Compañia Manufacturera de Papeles y Cartones (Chile)

CMPNAN Cytidine Monophosphate-N-Acetylneuraminic acid

CMR Center for Materials Research (Stanford University (USA))
Code Matrix Reader
Committee on Manpower Resources
Common-Mode Rejection
Continuous Maximum Rating

CMRA Canadian Maritime Rescue Auxiliary
Chemical Marketing Research Association (USA)

CMRB Chemicals and Minerals Requirements Board (of DOI)

CMREF Committee on Research, Education and Facilities (of NCMRED (USA))

CMRR Common Mode Rejection Ratio

CMRS Central Mining Research Station (India)

CMS Cement-Modified Soil
Chemical Metallizing System
Christian Medical Society (USA)
Circuit Maintenance System
College of Marine Studies (Delaware University (USA))
Common Mounting System
Compensated Meatball Stabilization
Compiler Monitor System
Computer Management System
Condition Monitoring System
Construction Management System
Conversational Monitor System
Council on Material Science (of DOE (USA))

CMSC Catalina Marine Science Center (of USC (USA))

CMSCI Council of Mechanical, Speciality Contracting Industries (USA)

CMSR Central Management Staff Record
Continuous-Moment Sum Rules

CMT Cadmium Mercury Telluride
California Mastitis Test
Committee on Marine Technology (replaced by MTRB in 1972)
Computer Mediated Teleconferencing
Computer-Managed Training
Construction Materials Testing
Coupled Mode Theory

CMTC Coventry Management Training Centre (of Coventry & District Engineering Employers Association)

CMTI Central Machine Tool Institute (India)

CMTM Capsule Mechanical Training Model

CMTOS Cassette Magnetic Tape Operating System

CMTP Canadian Manpower Training Programme (of DMI (Canada))

CMTT Commission Mixte CCIR/CCITT pour les Transmissions Televisuelles et Sonores

CMV Cytomegalovirus

CMVPCB California Motor Vehicle Pollution Control Board (USA)

CMVSS Canadian Motor Vehicle Safety Standard

CMVTSS Canadian Motor Vehicle Tyre Safety Standard

CN Carbon-Nitrogen
Centre-Notch tension
Cetane Number
Chloroacetetophenone
Cholesteryl Nonanoate
Chromosome Number
Coordination Number

CNA Canadian Nuclear Association (Canada)
Center for Naval Analyses (USN)
Chemical Notation Association (USA)
Committee for Nautical Archaeology
Cosmic Noise Absorption

CNA(UK) Chemical Notation Association « United Kingdom Branch

CNAA Council for National Academic Awards

CNAD — Conference of National Armaments Directors (of NATO)

CNADS — Conference of National Armaments Directors (of NATO)

CNAE — Comissao Nacional de Actividades Espaciais (Brazil) (National Committee for Space Activities)

CNAM — Conservatoire National des Arts et Metiers de Paris (France)

CNAS — Chemical Nomenclature Advisory Service (of the Laboratory of the Government Chemist)

CNB — Chloroacetophenone in Benzene and Carbon Tetrachloride

CNBOS — Comite National Belge de l'Organisation Scientifique (Belgium) (Belgian National Committee for Scientific Management)

CNbr — Cyanogen Bromide

CNC — Chantiers Navals de La Ciotat (France)
Chloroacetophenone in Chloroform
Computer Numerically-Controlled
Computerized Numerical Control

CNC/IAPS — Canadian National Committee for the International Association on the Properties of Steam (Canada)

CNCIEC — China National Chemicals Import and Export Corporation (China)

CNCT — Consejo Nacional de Ciencia y Tecnologia (Mexico) (National Council of Science and Technology)

CND — Campaign for Nuclear Disarmament
Comité National de Documentation (France) (National Committee for Co-ordinating Government Information)

CNDF — Complex-valued Non-linear Discriminant Function

CNDO — Complete Neglect of Differential Overlap

CNDST — Centre National de Documentation Scientifique et Technique (Belgium) (National Centre for Scientific and Technical Documentation)

CNE — Combined Neutral and Earth
Communication, Navigation and Identification
Composite Noise Index
Confederacao Nacional da Industria (Brazil) (National Confederation of Industry)
Consolidated National Intervenors (USA) (an environmental conservation group)

CNEA — Comision Nacional de Energia Atomica (Argentina) (National Atomic Energy Commission)

CNEC — Chilean Nuclear Energy Commission (Chile)
Comision Nacional de Energia Nuclear (Chile) (National Atomic Energy Commission)

CNEEMA — Centre National d'Etudes et d'Experimentation de Machinisme Agricole (France) (National Design and Experimental Centre for Agricultural Machinery)

CNEIA — Comite National d'Expansion pour l'Industrie Aeronautique (France) (National Committee for the Expansion of the Aeronautical Industry)

CNEL — Community Noise Equivalent Level
Community Noise Exposure Level
Cutaneous Non-epidermotropic Lymphomas

CNEN — Comision Nacional de Energia Nuclear (Mexico) (National Atomic Energy Commission)
Comissao Nacional de Energia Nuclear (Brazil) (National Atomic Energy Commission)
Comitato Nazionale per l'Energia Nucleare (Italy) (National Atomic Energy Authority) (now ENEA)
Conseil National de l'Energie Nucleaire (Luxembourg) (National Council for Atomic Energy)

CNEP — Cable Network Engineering Programme

CNERA — Centre National d'Etudes et de Recherches Aeronautiques (Belgium) (National Centre for Aeronautical Studies and Research)

CNES — Centre National d'Etudes Spatiales (France) (National Centre for Space Studies)

CNET — Centre National d'Etudes des Telecommunications (France) (National Centre of Telecommunication Studies)

CNEUPEN — Commission Nationale pour l'Etude de l'Utilisation Pacifique de l'Energie Nucleaire (Belgium) (National Commission for Research and Use of Nuclear Energy for Peaceful purposes)

CNEWS — Consolidated Navy Electronic Warfare School (USA)

CNEXO — Centre National d'Exploitation des Oceans (France) (National Centre for Oceanographic Research)

CNFRA — Centre National Francais de la Recherches Antarctiques (France) (French National Centre for Antarctic Research)

CNFRE — Comite Nation Francaise de Recherches dans l'Espace (France)

CNFRO — Comite National Francaise de Recherche Oceanique (France) (National Committee for Oceanographic Research)

CNG — Compressed Natural Gas

CNGA — California Natural Gas Association (USA)

CNIAR — Central National al Industrei Aeronautice Romane (Romania) (National Centre of the Romanian Aircraft Industry)

CNIB — Canadian National Institute for the Blind

CNIC — Centre National de l'Information Chimique (France) (National Centre of Chemical Information)

CNIE — Comision Nacional de Investigaciones Especiales (Argentine) (National Commission for Space Research)

CNIF — Conseil National des Ingénieurs Français (France) (National Council of French Engineers)

CNIM — Constructions Navales et Industrielles de la Mediterranee (France)

CNIPA — Committee of National Institutes of Patents Agents

CNIS — (English) Channel Navigation Information Service (of H.M. Coastguard)

CNK — Cellular Natural Killing
Common Noun Keywords

CNL — Corrected Noise Level

CNLA — Council of National Library Associations (USA)

CNMR — Carbon-13 Nuclear Magnetic Resonance search system (of NIH and EPA (USA))

CNOF — Comite National de l'Organisation Francaise (France) (French National Committee for Management)

CNOOC — China National Offshore Oil Corporation (China)

CNOS — Comitato Nazionale per l'Organizzazione Scientifica (Italy) (National Committee for Scientific Administration)

CNP — Card Network Planning
Comitato Nazionale per la Producttivita (Italy) (National Council for Productivity)
Communications, Navigation and Positioning

CNPF — Conseil National du Patronat Francais (France) (French National Council of Employers)

CNPIO — Comissao Nacional Portuguesa para Investigacao Oceanografico (Portugal) (Portuguese National Committee for Oceanographic Research)

CNR — Canadian National Railways
Carboxy Nitroso Rubber
Carrier-to-Noise Ratio
Composite Noise Rating
Consiglio Nazionale delle Ricerche (Italy) (National Research Council)

CNRA — Centre National de Recherches Agronomiques (France) (National Rural Economy Research Centre)

CNRC — Centro Nacional de Radiacion Cosmica (Argentine) (National Cosmic Radiation Centre)

CNRE — Centre National de Recherches de l'Espace (Belgium) (National Centre for Space Research)

CNRM — Centre National de Recherches Metallurgiques (Belgium) (National Metallurgical Research Centre)

CNRS — Centre National de la Recherche Scientifique (France) (National Scientific Research Centre)

CNRST — Centre National de la Recherche Scientifique et Technologique (Upper Volta) (National Centre for Scientific and Technological Research)

CNS — Central Nervous System
Chloroacetophenone and Chloropicrin in Chloroform
Communications Network Simulator

CNSEE — Convention of National Societies of Electrical Engineers of Western Europe

CNSG — Consolidated Nuclear Steam Generator

CNSL — Cashew Nut Shell Liquid

CNSS — Consolidated Nuclear Steam System

CNSTAT — Committee of National Statistics (of NAS-NRC (USA))

CNT — Canadian National Telecommunications (Canada) (govt. owned enterprise)

CNTIC — China National Technical Import Corporation (China)

CNV — Contingent Negative Variation

CO — Coconut Oil
College of Osteopaths

CO-ASIS — Central Ohio Chapter of ASIS (USA)

COA — College of Aeronautics (now Cranfield Institute of Technology)
Committee on Accreditation (of the American Library Association (USA))

COACH — Canadian Organization for the Advancement of Computers in Health (Canada)

COADS — Command and Administrative Data System (USDOD)

COAL — Committee on Arid Lands (of AAAS (USA))

COALCOM — Coal, Coke, Oil and Megawatts

COAMP — Computer Analysis of Maintenance Policies

COAP — California (USA) Comprehensive Ocean Area Plan
Combat Optimization and Analysis Programme
Cyclophosphamide, Vincristine, Cytarabine, Prednisolone

COAS — Crew Optical Alignment Sight

COAT — Coherent Optical Adaptive Technique
Combination Of All Technologies

COAX — COBOL Abbreviation Expander

COB — Centre Oceanologique de Bretagne (France)
Commission des Opérations en Bourse (France) (Stock Exchange Commission)

COBAE — Commissao Brasiliera de Ativdades Espaciais (Brazil) (Brazilian Commission for Space Activities)

COBE — Cosmic Background Explorer

COBELDA — Compagnie Belge d'Electronic et d'Automation (Belgium)

COBELPA — Association des Fabricants de Pates, Papiers et Cartons de Belgique (Belgium) (Belgian Association of Pulp, Paper and Carton Manufacturers)

COBESTCO — Computer Based Estimating Technique for Contractors

COBET — Common Basic Electronics Training (US Army)

COBET SITE — COBET Student Instructional and Testing Environment (US Army)

COBI — Council on Biological Information

COBILITY — COBOL Utility

COBLOC — Codap Language Block-Oriented Compiler

COBLOS — Computer Based Loans System (of AERE)

COBOL — Common Business Oriented Language

COBRA — Computadores a Sistemas Brasilerios SA (Brazil)
Computadores Brasileirs (Brazil)
Computer Oriented Bearing Response Analysis
Curved Orthotropic Bridge Analysis

COBSI — Council on Biological Sciences Information (of FASEB (USA))

COC — Cholesteryl Oleyl Carbonate
Combat Operations Center (of NORAD)

COCAAHOS — Committee on Classical Articles and History of Statistics (USA)

COCB — Crossed Olivocochlear Bundle

COCEAN — Compagnie d'Etudes et d'Exploitation des Techniques Oceans (France)

COCEMA — Comite des Constructeurs Europeens de Material Alimentaire (Committee of European Manufacturers of Foodstuffs)

COCERAL — Federation of Trade Associations for Grain and Feeding-Stuffs (of EEC)

COCESNA — Corporacion Centroamericana de Servicios de Navegacion Aerea (of CACM) (Honduras) (Central American Air Navigation Service Corporation)

COCHASE — Code for Coupled Channel Shrödinger Equations

COCI — United Kingdom Consortium on Chemical Information

COCOAS — CONARC Class One Automated System (US Army)
Coordinating Committee (of NATO)

COCOM — Consultative Group–Coordinating Committee (comprising Japan and the NATO countries except Iceland)

COCOR — Commission de Coordination pour la Nomenclature des Produits Sidérurgiques (of ECSC) (Commission for Co-ordinating the Naming of Metallurgical Products)

COCOSEER — Coordinating Committee for Slavic and East European Library Services

COCS — Container Operating Control System

COCT — Copper Oxidation Corrosion Test

COD — Carrier-Onboard Delivery
Carrier-Onboard Delivery aircraft
Chemical Oxygen Demand
Constrained Optimal Design
Crack Opening Displacement
Cyclo-octadiene

CODA — Crack Opening Displacement Application

CODAC — Computer Design of Armoured Cables

CODAG — Combined Diesel And Gas

CODAP — Client-Oriented Data Acquisition Programme
Comprehensive Occupational Data Analysis Programme

CODAS — Council of Departments of Accounting Studies
Customer Oriented Data System

CODASYL — Conference on Data Systems and Languages

CODATA — Committee on Data for Science and Technology (of ICSU)

CODC — Canadian Oceanographic Data Centre (Canada)

CODE — Controlled Object Deck Exploitation

CODEC Coder-Decoder
Coding-Decoding Device

CODED Computer Oriented Design of Electronic Devices

CODEM Coded Modulator-Demodulator
Computerized Design from Engineering Models

CODENE Comite pour la Desarmement Nucleaire en France (France) (Committee for Nuclear Disarmament in France)

CODEST Committee for European Development of Science and Technology (of EEC)

CODEVTEL Course Development in the field of Telecommunications (a project of ITU, UNDP and others)

CODEX Compiler of Differentiable Expressions

CODICAF Conseil des Directeurs des Compagnies Aeriennes en France (France)

CODIFAC Comite de Developpement d'Industrie de la Chaussure et des Articles Chaussants (France) (Committee for the Development of the Footwear Industry)

CODIL Context Dependent Information Language

CODILS Commodity Oriented Digital Input Label System

CODIMPA Compagnie Francaise Industrielle et Miniere du Pacifique (France)

CODM Committee on Dynamic Measurement (of American Petroleum Institute (USA))

CODOG Combined Diesel Or Gas

CODOT Classification of Occupations and Directory of Occupational Titles (of Department of Employment)

CODP prefix to numbered series of reports issued by Cranfield Institute of Technology, Department of Aircraft Design

CODS COMPUTERON (CORPORATION (USA)) Office Diskette Software

CODSIA Council of Defense and Space Industry Associations (USA)

COE Cross-Over Electrophoresis
Crude Oil Equivalent
prefix to numbered series of reports issued by the Coastal and Ocean Engineering Division, Texas A and M University (USA)

COEA Cost and Operational Efectiveness Analysis

COEC Comite Central d'Oceanographie et d'Etudes des Cotes (France) (Central Committee of Oceanography and Coastal Studies)

COED Char Oil Energy Development
Composition and Editing Display

COEES Central Office Equipment Estimation System

COEMIS Corps of Engineers Management Information Systems (US Army Corps of Engineers)

CoEnCo Committee for Environmental Conservation

COESA Committee on Extension to the Standard Atmosphere (USA)

COFACE Export Credit Guarantee Department (France)

COFACTS Cost Factoring System

COFAD Computerized Facilities Design

COFAG Comite des Fabricants d'Acide Glutamique (Committee of Manufacturers of Glutamic Acid) (of the EEC)

COFFTI Contracting Operator Fast Fourier Transform Identification

COFI Committee on Fisheries (of FAO)
Council of Forest Industries of British Columbia (Canada)

COFIPS Central Ohio Federation of Information Processing Societies (USA)

COFIRS COBOL from INTERNATIONAL BUSINESS MACHINES RPG Specifications

COFPAES Committee on Federal Procurement of Architect-Engineer Services (USA)

COFRENA Comite Francaise de l'Equipement Naval (France) (French Marine Equipment Committee) (an association)

COFREND Comité Français pour l'Étude des Essais Non Destructifs (France) (French Committee for the Study of Non-Destructive Testing)

COFT Conduct of (Weapon) Fire Trainer

COG Metropolitan Washington Council of Governments (USA)

COGAG Combined Gas And Gas

COGAP Computer Graphics Arrangement Programme

COGD Circular Outlet Gas Duct

COGEMA Compagnie Générale des Matières Nucleaires (France) (a subsidiary of CEA)

COGENE Committee on Genetic Experimentation (of ICSU)

COGENT Compiler and Generalised Translator

COGEODOC Commission on Geologic Documentation (of IUGS)

COGLA Canadian Oil and Gas Lands Administration (Canada)

COGLAD COAST GUARD (USA) Assistance Device

COGM Committee on Natural Gas Fluids Measurement (of American Petroleum Institute (USA))

COGMA Concrete Garage Manufacturers Association

COGO Coordinated Geometry

COGOG Combined Gas Or Gas

COGP Commission on Government Procurement (USA)

COGS Combat Oriented General Support
Continuous Orbital Guidance Sensor

COHART Costs of Hard Rock Tunnelling

COHb Carboxyhaemoglobin

COHO Coherent Oscillator

COI Central Office of Information
Crack Opening Interferometry
Cube per Order Index

COIC Canadian Oceanographic Identification Centre (Canada)
Careers and Occupational Information Centre (of Employment Services Agency)

COID Council of Industrial Design (became the Design Council in 1972)

COIE Committee on Invisible Exports

COIL COMPAS (Computer Acquisition System) On-line Interactive Language

COIN COBOL Indexing and Maintenance Package
Counter-Insurgency

COINS Committee on Improvement of National Statistics (of IASI)
Computer and Information Sciences
Coordinated Inventory Control System
Counter-Insurgency
International Symposium on Computer and Information Service
prefix to dated-series of reports on Computer and Information Science issued by Massachusetts University (USA)

COIPM Comité International Permanent pour la Recherche sur la Préservation des Matériaux en Milieu Marin (of OECD) (Permanent International Committee for Research on Corrosion in a Marine Environment)

COIS Committee on International Standardization (of ASTM (USA))

COL Computerized Office Layout

COLA Co-operation in Library Automation (a project of LASER)
Cost of Living Adjustment
Cost of Living Allowance
Cost of Living Award

COLCIENCIAS Fondo Colombiano de Investigaciones Científicas y Proyectos Especiales Francisco José de Caldas' (Colombia)

COLD Chronic Obstructive Lung Disease
COLED Combat Loss and Expenditure Data
COLIDAR Coherent Light Detecting And Ranging
COLING International Conference on Computational Linguistics
COLIPA Comité de liaison des Syndicates Européens de l'Industrie de la Parfumerie et des Cosmétiques (of the EEC) (Liaison Committee of European Groups of the Perfumery and Cosmetics Industry)
COLMIS Collection Management Information System (solid waste collection)
COLRAD College on Research and Development (of TIMS (USA))
COLSS Core Operating Limit Supervisory System
COLT Council on Library Technology (USA)
COLTS Contrast Optical Laser Tracking System
COM Coal-Oil Mixtures
Commission on Ore Microscopy (of International Mineralogical Association)
Computer Output Microfilm
Computer Output Microfilmer
Computer Output Microfilming
Computer Output Microform
Computer Output to Microfilm
COMA Committee on Medical Aspects of Food Policy
COMAAFCE Commander Allied Air Forces Central Europe (of NATO)
COMAC Continuous Multiple Access Collator
COMAD Computer Methods for Automatic Diagnosis
COMAIRBALTAP Commander Allied Air Forces Baltic Approaches (of NATO)
COMANSEC Computation and Analysis Section (of Defence Research Board, Canada)
COMAP Conversational Macro Package
COMAR Committee on Man and Radiation (of IEEE (USA))
COMARAIRMED Commander Maritime Air Forces Mediterranean (of NATO)
COMAT Committee on Materials (USA) (an inter-agency committee)
Computer-Assisted Training
COMBAT Cost Oriented Models Built to Analyze Trade-offs
COMBIMAN Computerized Biomechanical Man-model
COMBO Computation of Miss Between Orbits
COMCAN Common Cause Analysis
COMCON IEEE Computer Society International Conference
COMCORDET Standing Committee for Coordination of Research, Development, Evaluation and Training (of Rural Electrification Corporation (India))
COMDAC Component Design Augmented by Computer
COMECON Council for Mutual Economic Cooperation and Assistance (comprising Poland, Czechoslovakia, Hungary, Romania, East Germany, Mongolia, Cuba, Bulgaria, and USSR) (administrative headquarters in USSR)
COMED Combined Map and Electronic Display
COMEDS Continental (USA) Meteorological Data system (USAF)
COMEINDORS Composite Mechanised Information and Documentation Retrieval System
COMEPA Comite European de Liaison du Commerce de Gros des Papiers et Cartons (European Liaison Committee of Wholesalers of Paper and Cardboard)
COMER College of Mineral and Energy Resources (West Virginia University (USA))
COMES Comite de l'Energie Solaire (France) (Committee for Solar Energy)
COMESA Committee on Meteorological Effect of Stratospherical Aircraft
COMET Committee for Middle East Trade (of BOTB)
Controllability, Observability and Maintenance Engineering Technique
METEROLOGICAL OFFICE Computer
COMEX Compagnie Maritime d'Expertises (France)
COMEXO Comite d'Exploitation des Oceans (France)
COMFET Conductivity-Modulated Field Effect Transistor
COMFOR International Computer Forum and Exposition
COMFORT Compulogic FORTRAN Tidy
COMGEOM Combinatorial Geometry
COMIBOL Corporacion Minera de Bolivia (Bolivia) (State Mining Corporation)
COMIC Colorant Mixture Computer
COMICORD Association des Industries de Corderie-Ficellerie de la CEE (merged into EUROCORD in 1975)
COMICS Computer-Oriented Managed Inventory Control System
COMINT Communications Intelligence
COMIS Command Management Information System
Committee Meeting Information System (of House of Representatives (USA))
COMIT Computing System MASSACHUSETTS INSTITUTE OF TECHNOLOGY (USA)
COMITEXTIL Co-ordinating Committee of the European Textile Industries (of EEC)
COMJAM Communications Jamming
COMLA Commonwealth Library Association
COMLO Compass Locator
COMLOSA Committee of Liner Operators–South America
comm/ADP Communications/Automatic Data Processing Laboratory (of ECOM (US Army))
COMMANDS Computer Operated Marketing, Mailing and News Distribution System (of Building Research Establishment (DOE))
COMMEN Compiler Oriented for Multiprogramming and Multiprocessing Environments
COMMEND Computer-aided Mechanical Engineering Design
COMMODORE Command Modular Operation Room Equipment
COMMS Central Office Maintenance Management System
COMNAVSOUTH Commander, Allied Naval Forces Southern Europe (of NATO)
COMP Computer-Oriented Microwaves Practices
Council on Municipal Management (USA)
COMPAC Commonwealth Pacific Cable (submarine telephone cable connecting Canada, Hawaii, Fiji, New Zealand, and Australia)
Computer Output Microfilm Package
COMPACE Control of Material Planning Activities
COMPACS Computer Output Microforms Program And Concept Study (of US Army)
COMPACT Computer Oriented Modular Planning and Control
Computer Predicting and Automatic Course Tracking
Computer-Operated Micro-Programme Automatic Commissioning Technique
COMPARE Computer Oriented Method of Programme Analysis, Review and Evaluation
Computerized Peformance and Analysis Response Evaluator
Console for Optical Measurement and Precise Analysis of Radiation from Electronics
COMPAS Committee of Organisations for Materials Management, Purchasing and Supply
Committee on Physics and Society (of American Institute of Physics (USA))
Computer Acquisition System
COMPASS Computer Assisted Classification and Assignment System
Computer Optimal Media Planning And Selection System
Computer Oriented Method of Patterns Analysis for Switching Systems

	Computerized Movement Planning And Status System
	Cooperative Observational and Modeling Project for the Analysis of Severe Storms
	Council of Mapping, Photogrammetry and Surveying Societies (USA) (Co-ordinating body of ACA, AAGS, ASPRS and NSPS)
COMPCON	IEEE (USA) Computer Society International Conference
COMPEC	Computer Peripherals, Small Computer and Systems Exhibition and Conference
COMPENDEX	Computerized Engineering Index
COMPETA	Computer and Peripherals Equipment Trade Association
COMPLEX	Committee on Planetary and Lunar Exploration (of NAS (USA))
COMPROS	collective name for the European Community's national bodies for the Simplification of International Trade Procedures
COMPSAC	International Computer Software and Applications Conference
COMPSAP	Computerized Static Automatic Restoring Equipment for Power System
COMPSO	Computer Software and Peripherals Shows and Conferences (USA)
COMPSTAT	Conference on Computational Statistics
COMPSY	Computer Support in Military Psychiatry (US Army)
COMPUMAG	Conference on Computations of Magnetic Fields
COMRAC	Combat Radius Capability
COMRADE	Computer Aided Design Environment
COMRATE	Committee on Mineral Resources and the Environment (of NRC (usa))
COMS	Computer-based Operations Management System
COMSAC	Computerized Measurements for Safeguards and Accountability
COMSAT	Committee on the Survey of Materials Science and Engineering (of National Academy of Sciences (USA))
	Communications Satellite
	Communications Satellite corporation (USA) (management services contractor for INTELSAT)
COMSATS	Control Organisation Methods And Techniques Study
comSEC	Communications Security
COMSEC	Telecommunications Security
COMSEQIN	Component Sequencing and Insertion
COMSER	Commission on Marine Science and Engineering Research (of UN)
COMSL	Communications System Simulation Language
COMSOAL	Computer Method of Sequencing Operations for Assembly Lines
COMSS	Coastal/Oceans Monitoring Satellite System
COMSUP	Communications Supervisor
COMT	Catechol-O-Methyltransferase
COMTEC/RAT	Comision Tecnica de la Red Andina Telecomunicaciones (Technical Commission for the Andean Telecommunication Network)
COMTECH	Computer Micrographics Technology
COMTEL	Comision Nacional de Telecommunications (Chile) (National Telecommunications Commission)
COMTELCA	Comision Tecnica de las Telecomunications de Centroamericana (of CEMA) (Nicaragua) (Technical Commission for Telecommunications in Central America)
COMTRAC	Computer Aided Traffic Control
COMURHEX	Societe pour la Conversion de l'Uranium en Metal et en Hexafluorure (France)
COMVE	Committee on Motor Vehicle Emissions (of ATAC (Australia))
CONACS	Contractors Accounting System
CONACYT	Consejo Nacional de Ciencia y Tecnologia (Mexico) (National Council for Science and Technology)
CONAD	Continental Air Defense Command (US DOD) (inactivated 1975)
CONADE	Consejo Nacional de Desarrollo (Argentina) (National Development Council)
CONAES	Committee on Nuclear and Alternative Energy Systems (of National Research Council (USA))
CONAG	Combined Nuclear Steam And Gas
CONAPT	Concrete Articulated Production Tower
CONARC	Continental Army Command (US Army)
CONART	Consejo Nacional de Radiodifusion y Television (Argentina) (National Radio Broadcasting and Television Council)
CONASTIL	Compania Colombiana de Astilleros Ltda. (Colombia)
CONASUPO	Compania Nacional de Subsistencias Populares (Mexico) (State Grain Purchasing and Sales Agency)
CONBAT	Converted Battalion Anti-Tank
CONCANACO	Confederacion de Camaras Nacionales de Comercio (Mexico) (Confederation of National Chambers of Commerce)
CONCAP	Conversational Circuit Analysis Programme
CONCAT	Conventional Catamaran
CONCAWE	Conservation of Clean Air and Water (a Western European Study Group set up by some oil companies)
CONCEPT	Computation Online of Networks of Chemical Engineering Processes
CONCERT	Consultative Group on Certification (of CEN (France))
CONCEX	Conselho Nacional de Comercio Exterior (Brazil) (National Council for External Trade)
CONCORD	Conference Coordinator (a computer programme)
CONDECA	Council of Central American Defense
CONDEEP	Concrete Deepwater Structure
CONDOC	Consortium to Develop an Online Catalog (USA)
CONDRILL	Concrete Drilling Semi-submersible
CONDUIT	Consortium for the Dissemination of Computer-based Curricular Materials (consists of over 300 colleges and universities in the USA)
CONESCAL	Centro Regional Construcciones Escolares para America Latina (Mexico) (Regional Centre for School Building in Latin America)
CONEX	Container Express
CONF	Conference
CONFICS	COBRA (Huey Cobra Helicopter) Night Fire Control System
CONFORM	Constrained Force Model
	Continuous Forms Manufacturers Association of South Africa
	Conversational Form Format Generator
CONICIT	Consejo Nacional de Investigaciones Cientificas y Tecnologicas (Venezuela) (National Council for Scientific and Technological Research)
CONICYT	Comision Nacional de Investigacion Cientifica y Tecnologica (Chile) (National Commission for Scientific and Technical Research)
CONIDA	Comisión Nacional de Investigación y Desarrollo Aeroespacial (Peru) (National Commission for Aerospace Research and Development)
CONIE	Comision Nacional de Investigacion del Espacio (Spain) (National Commission for Space Research)
CONIT	Connector for Network Information Transfer
CONOG	Combined Nuclear Steam Or Gas
CONPASP	Construction Project Alternative Selection Programme

CONRAD Contour Radar Data
Conversational On-line Real-time Algorithm Definition

CONREDS Contingency Readiness System

CONREP Connected Replenishment

CONSAL Conference of South-east Asian Librarians

CONSAS Conference of South African Surveyors

CONSER Consolidation of Serial data bases (a project of Council on Library Resources (USA))
Conversion of Serials

CONSIDER Conselho Nacional da Industria Siderurgica (Brazil) (National Council of the Steel Industry)

CONSORT Conversation System with On-line Remote Terminals

CONSTRADO Constructional Steel Research and Development Organization (of the British Steel Corporation)

CONSTRONIC Conference on Mechanical Aspects of Electronic Design

CONSUB Continental Shelf Submersible

CONSUEL Comite National pour la Securite des Usagers de l'Electricite (France) (National Committee for the Safety of Users of Electricity)

CONSUL Control Sub-routine Language

CONTACCT CONUS (USA) Tactical Communications Team Conference (USA)

CONTAD Concealed Target Detection

CONTEL Conselho Nacional de Telecomunicacoes (Brazil) (National Telecommunications Council)

CONTRAC Conversational Transient Radiation Analysis Programme

CONTREQS Contingency Transportation Requirements System

CONTU National Commission on New Technological Uses of Copyrighted Works (USA)

CONUS Continental United States (USA)

COO Chicago Operations Office (of USAEC)

COOLS Concealed Original Optical Locating System

COP Calculator-Oriented Processor
Coefficient of Performance
Commissie Opvoering Productivitiet (Netherlands) (Productivity Centre)
Compact Periscope
Control-Oriented Processor
Customer Order Processing

COPA Comite des Organisations Professionnelles Agricoles de la CEE (Committee of the Agricultural Industry Associations of the European Economic Community)
Compania Panemena de Aviacion (Panama)

COPAC Committee on Pollution Abatement and Control (National Research Council (USA))

COPAFS Council of Professional Associations on Federal Statistics (USA)

COPAG Collision Prevention Advisory Group (of US Government and Industry)

COPANT Commission Pan-Americana de Normas Tecnicas (Pan-American Commission for Technical Standards)

COPCO Committee on Consumer Policy (of ISO)

COPD Chronic Obstructive Pulmonary Disease

COPE CAMA (Centralised Automatic Message Accounting) Operator Position Exercise
Choice of Probability/Effect
Cognitive Policy Evaluation
Common Pattern Origin Evolver
Compagnie Orientale des Pétroles d'Egypte (Egypt) (partly government owned)
Conference on Protective Equipment

COPEBRAS Companhia Petroquimica Brasilieira (Brazil)

COPEP Commission Permanente de l'Electronique au Commissariat general du Plan (France)
Committee on Public Engineering Policy (of National Academy of Engineering, USA)

COPES Computer Oriented Purchasing and Engineering System

COPI Computer-Oriented Programmed Instruction

COPICS Communications Oriented Production Information and Control System
Copyright Office Publication and Interactive Cataloging System (of the Library of Congress (USA))

COPILOT Cost Oriented Production and Inventory Loading Operations Technique Works (USA)

COPM Committee on Petroleum Measurement (of the American Petroleum Institute (USA))

COPMEC Comite des Petites et Moyens Entreprises Commerciales (Committee of Small and Medium Commercial Enterprises) (of the EEC)

COPOL Council of Polytechnic Librarians

COPOLCO Committee on Consumer Policy (of ISO)

COPQ Committee on Overseas Qualifications (Australia)

COPR Centre for Overseas Pest Research (of ODM) (now TDRI (of ODA))

COPRAI Comissao de Produtividade da Associaco Industrial Portuguesa (Portugal) (Productivity Committee of the Portuguese Industrial Association)

COPS Computer-Oriented Police System (New York State (USA))
Computerized Optimization Procedure for Stabilators
Controller Oriented Processor Series
Conversational Problem Solver
Costing Out Policy Systems

COPSS Committee of Presidents of Statistical Societies (USA)

COPT Circumoval Precipitin Test

COPTEC Controller Overload Prediction Technique

COPUOS Committee on the Peaceful Uses of Outer Space (of the UN)

COQ Cost-of-Quality

COR Coherent-On-Receive
Curiosity-Oriented Research

CORA Code for One-dimensional Reactor Analysis

CORADCOM Communications Research and Development Command (US Army)

CORAL Class Oriented Ring Associative Language
Coherent Optical Radar Laboratory (USAF)
Computer On-line Real-time Applications Language

CORAPRAN COBELDA Radar Automatic Preflight Analyser

CORAPRO Controle-Radioprotection (Belgium)

CORAT Christian Organisations Research and Advisory Trust

CORC Co-operative Octane Requirement Committee
Co-ordinated Programme on the Radiation Chemistry of Food and Food Components
CORNELL Computing language

CORD Computer Reinforced Design
Computer with On-line Remote Devices
Coordination (computer programme)

CORDA Computerised Reservations System ROYAL DUTCH AIRLINES

CORDE Corporacion Dominicana Empresas Estatalas (Dominican Republic) (State Aerospace Corporation)

CORE Common Operational Research Equipment (to be carried in "Spacelab")
International Centre of Operations Research and Econometrics

CORECI Compagnie de Regulation et de Controle Industriel (France)

COREDIF Compagnie de Realisation d'Usines de Diffusion Gazeuse (France)
CORELAP Computerized Relationship Layout Planning
COREN Combustibili per Reattori Nucleari (Italy)
Council of Registered Engineers in Nigeria (Nigeria)
COREPER Comité des Représentants Permanents (Committee of Permanent Representatives) (of the EEC)
CORESTA Centre de Cooperation pour les Recherches Scientifiques relatives au Tabac (France) (Co-operative Centre for Scientific Research on Tobacco)
CORFO Corporacion de Fomento de la Produccion (Chile) (Production Development Corporation)
CORG Combat Operations Research Group
CORGI Confederation for Registration of Gas Installers
CORM Council for Optical Radiation Measurements (USA)
CORMAR Coral Reef Management and Research (a group at the University of Hawaii)
CORODIM Correlation of the Recognition of Degradation with Intelligibility Measurements
CORPORAL Corporate Resource and Allocation
CORPOSANA Corporacion de Obras Sanitarias (Paraguay) (Water and Sewage Service Corporation)
CORRIM Committee on Renewable Resources for Industrial Materials (of NAS/NRC (USA))
CORS Canadian Operational Research Society (Canada)
CORSA Cosmic Radiaton Satellite
CORSPERS Committee on Remote Sensing Programs for Earth Surveys (of NAS/NRC (USA))
CORTEX Communications Orientated Real-Time Executive
CORTEZ COBOL Oriented Real Time Environment
CORTS Conversion of Range Telemetry System
COS Canadian Otolaryngological Society (Canada)
Carbonyl Sulphide
Central Operations System
Clinical Orthopedic Society (USA)
Committee on Standards (of ASTM (USA))
Communications Oriented System
Contaminated Oil Settlings
Cosmic Rays and Trapped Radiation Committee (of ESRO)
COS/MOS Complementary Symmetry Metal Oxide Semiconductor
COSA Cost of Sales Adjustment
Council of Sections and Affiliates (of Land Survey Division, ACSM (USA))
COSA NOSTRA Computer Oriented System And Newly Organised Storage-to-Retrieval Apparatus
COSAG Combination of Steam And Gas
COSAM Co-Site Analysis Model
COBOL Shared Access Method
COSAMC Commission for Special Applications of Meteorology and Climatology (of WMO (UN))
Commission for Special Applications of Meteorology and Climatology
COSAR Compression Scanning Array Radar
COSATI Committee on Scientific And Technical Information (of FCST)
COSBA Computer Services and Bureau Association (merged into Computer Services Association, 1975)
COSEBI Corporación de Servicios Bibliotecarios (Puerto Rico)
COSEC CULHAM (Laboratory) On-line Single Experimental Console
COSEM Compagnie Generale des Semi-Conducteurs (France)
COSEMCO Comite des Semences du Marche Commun (Seed Committee of the Common Market (European Economic Community))
COSEPUP Committee on Science, Engineering and Public Policy (of NAS (USA))
COSERS Computer Science and Engineering Research Study (a project sponsored by NSF (USA))
COSFAD Computerized Safety and Facility Design
COSH Control Ordered Sonar Hardware
COSI Committee on Scientific Information (USA)
COSINE Committee on Computer Science in Electrical Engineering Education (of Association for Computing Machinery, USA)
Computer Sciences in Electrical Engineering (committee of the Commission on Education of the National Academy of Engineering (USA))
COSIP College Science Improvement Program (of National Science Foundation, USA)
COSIRA Council for Small Industries in Rural Areas
COSIT Computing Services Industry Training Council
COSM Committee on Static Measurement (of the American Petroleum Institute (USA)
COSMA Computer Services for Motor-freight Activities
COSMAT Committee on the Survey of Materials Science and Engineering (of the Nationaxl Academy of Sciences (USA))
COSMEP Committee of Small Magazine/Press Editors & Publishers (USA)
COSMIC Coherent Optical System of Modular Imaging Collectors
Computer Software Management and Information Center (University of Georgia, USA)
Computer Systems for Management Information and Control
COSMIS Computer System for Medical Information Services
COSMO Communications Simulation Model
COSMOS a consortium embracing Aerospatial (France), Marconi Space and Defence Systems Ltd (UK), ETCA (Belgium), Siemens (Germany), Selenia (Italy), MATRA (France), MBB (Germany)
a European Industrial Consortium (consisting of ETCA (Belgium), GEC-Marconi (UK), MBB (Germany) and SNIAS (France))
Centralization of Supply Management Operations System (US Army)
Coastal Survey Marine Observation System
Commercial Systems using Modular Software
Complementary Symmetry Metal Oxide Semiconductor
Comprehensive Option Stiffness Method of Structural Analysis
Computer Optimization and Simulation Modeling for Operating Supermarkets
Computer Orientated System for Manufacturing Order Synthesis
Consortium of Selected Manufacturers Open System
COURTAULD'S Own System for Matrix Operations
COSPAR Committee on Space Research (France) (of the International Council of Scientific Unions)
COSPUP Committee on Science and Public Policy (of National Academy of Sciences, USA)
COSRIMS Committee on Research in the Mathematical Sciences (of National Academy of Sciences, USA)
COSRO Conical Scan Read Only
COSSA Containerized Shipment and Storage of Ammunition
Council of Social Science Associations (USA)
CSIRO Office for Space Science and Applications (Australia)
COSSACK Computer Systems Suppliers Advisory Committee (of BETA)

COSSECC Connecticut Surban and Shoreline Educational Computer Center (USA)

COST Committee for Overseas Science and Technology (of the Royal Society)
Committee on Science and Technology (India)
Continental Offshore Stratigraphic Test
Cooperation Europeenne dans le domaine de la recherche Scientifique et Technique (Foundation to Sponsor European Cooperation in Science and Technology)

COSTAR Combat Service Support to the Army (US Army)
Computer Stored Ambulatory Record
Conversational On-line Storage And Retrieval

COSTED Committee on Science and Technology in the Developing Countries (India) (of ICSU)

COSTER Cost Optimizing System To Evaluate Reliability

COSTI Centre for Scientific and Technological Information (of NCRD (Israel)

COSTIC Comite Scientifique et Technique de l'Industrie du Chauffage, de la ventilation et du conditionnement d'air (France) (Heating, Ventilating and Air Conditioning Scientific and Technical Committee)

COSTPRO Canadian Organization for the Simplification of Trade Procedures (Canada)

COT Centrum voor Oppervlaketechnologie (Netherlands) (Centre for Surface Treatment Technology)
Committee on Terminology (of ASTM (USA))
Computer-Output-Typesetting
Cyclo-octatetraene
Cyclooctatetraenyl

COTAM Commandement du Transport Aerien Militaire (France) (Air Transport Command of the French Air Force)

COTANCE Confederation des Associations Nationales des Tanneurs et Megissiers de la CEE (Confederation of Tanners Association of the EEC)

COTAR Correlation Tracking And Ranging

COTAT Correlation Tracking And Triangulation

COTAWS Collision, Obstacle, Terrain and Warning Systems

COTC Canadian Overseas Telecommunications Corporation (Canada)

COTCO Committee on Technical Committee Operations (of ASTM (USA))

COTI Central Officials Training Institute (Korea)
Coordinator Operational Technical Investigations (Canadian Army)

COTMS Computer-Operated Transmission Measuring Set (USA)

COTRAMA Sosiete Civile Cooperative d'Etudes des Transports et de Manutention (France)

COTRAN Code-Transformation

COTRANS Coordinated Transfer Application System (of the Association of American Medical Colleges (USA))

COTS Container Off-loading and Transfer System
Customer Order Tracking System

COTTI Commission du Traitement et de la Transmission de l'Information (France) (Commission for Data Handling and Transmission)

COTTU Committee on Technology Transfer and Utilization (of National Academy of Engineering (USA))

COURT Cost Optimization Utilizing Reference Techniques

COV Counter Obstacle Vehicle

COVENIN Comision Venzolana de Normas Industriales (Venezuela) (Industrial Standards Commission)

COVINCA Corporación Venezolana de la Industria Naval CA (Venezuela) (government owned corporation)

COVOS Groupe d'Etudes sur les Consequences des Vols Stratospheriques (France) (Study Group on the Effects of Stratospheric Flight)

COW Centrum voor Onderzoek Waterkeringen (Netherlands) (Centre for Water Defence) (e.g. dykes)
Chlorinated Organics in Wastewater analyzer
Cold War game
Crude Oil Washing

COWAR Committee on Water Resources (of ICSU)

COZI Communications Operation Zone Indicator

CP Chronic Pancreatitis
Circuit-to-Pin ratio
Companhia dos Caminhos de Ferro Portugueses (Portugal)
Conference Paper
Conference Proceedings
Constant Potential
Contractile Pulse
Coproporphyrin
Corporate Planning
Creatine Phosphate
Critical Path
Current Paper
prefix to numbered series of Codes of Practice issued by BSI

CP/M Control Programmes for Microcomputers

CPA Canadian Petroleum Association (Canada)
Canadian Pharmaceutical Association (Canada)
Canadian Psychological Association (Canada)
Chesapeake Physics Association (USA)
Chicago Publishers Association (USA)
Chipboard Promotion Association
Closest Point of Approach
Clyde Port Authority
Coherent Potential Approximation
Combat Pilots Association (USA)
Commonwealth Pharmaceutical Association
Commonwealth Postal Administration
Commonwealth Preference Area
Compensated Pulse Alternator
Concrete Pipe Association of Great Britain
Construction Plant Association
Consumer Protection Agency (USA)
Contractors Plant Association
Critical Path Analysis

CPAA Current Physics Advance Abstracts (of American Institute of Physics (USA))

CPAB Computer Programmer Aptitude Battery

CPAC Centre for Protection Against Corrosion (of the Fulmer Research Institute)
Corrosion Prevention Advisory Centre

CPACS Comprehensive Payroll Accounting System

CPAF Chlorpropamide-Alcohol Flushing
Cost-plus-Award Fee

CPAG Collision Prevention Advisory Group (USA)

CPAI Canvas Products Association International (USA)

CPAM Committee of Purchasers of Aircraft Material (consortium of 15 European airlines)

CPAR Co-operative Pollution Abatement Research (a programme of the Environment Dept (Canada))

CPARS Compact Programmed Airline Reservation System

CPB Centraal Planbureau (Netherlands) (Central Planning Bureau)
Corporation for Public Broadcasting (USA)
Critical Path Bar chart
Current Physics Bibliographies (of American Institute of Physics (USA))

CPBW Charged Particle Beam Weapons

CPC Card Programmed Calculator
Ceramic Printed Circuit
Ceylon Petroleum Company (Sri Lanka) (government owned)

Coated Powdered Cathode
Collimated Proportional Counter
Community Patent Convention (MORE PROPERLY Convention for the European Patent for the Common Market)
Compound Parabolic Concentrator
Computerized Production Control
Controlled-Pore Ceramic
Corrosion Preventive Compound

CPCH Controllable Pitch propellor

CPCI Canadian Prestressed Concrete Institute (Canada)

CPCRI Central Plantation Crops Research Institute (India)

CPCS Cabin Pressure Control System

CPD Citrate-Phosphate-Dextrose
Contact Potential Difference
Continuing Professional Development

CPDA Clay Pipe Development Association
Council for Periodical Distributors Association (USA)

CPDL Canadian Patents and Developments Limited (Canada)

CPDM Centre for Physical Distribution Management
Chebychev Polynomial Discriminant Method

CPDS Carboxypyridine Disulphide
Computerized Preliminary Design System

CPE Centre de Prospective et d'Evaluation (France) (Feasibility and Evaluation Centre)
Chlorinated Polyethylene
Conductive Polyethylene
Continuing Professional Education
Contractor Performance Evaluation
Council on Physics in Education (USA)
Cytopathic Effect
Cytopathogenic Effects

CPEA Chemically Pure Ethylamine
Colorado Professional Electronic Association (USA)
Confederation of Professional and Executive Associations
Cooperative Program for Educational Administration (USA)

CPEHS Consumer Protection and Environmental Health Service (of Public Health Service (HEW) (USA))

CPEM Conference on Precision Electromagnetic Measurements (USA)

CPES Consumer Products Efficiency Standards (of DOE (USA))

CPEUG Computer Performance Evaluation Users Group (USA)

CPFA Cyclopropenoid Fatty Acid

CPFF Cost Plus Fixed Fee

CPFRC Central Pacific Fisheries Research Center (of NMFS (USA))

CPG Clock-Pulse Generator
Controlled-Pore Glass

CPH Computer Polarization Holography

CPHA Canadian Public Health Association (Canada)
Commission on Professional and Hospital Activities (USA) (not-profit, non-governmental research and education center)

CPHERI Central Public Health Engineering Research Institute (India)

CPHL Central Public Health Laboratory (of PHLS)

CPI Cathodic Protection Index
Closed Pore Insulation
Coherent Processing Interval
Computing Power Index
Confederation of Photographic Industries (British)
Consumer Price Index (USA)
Coronary Prognostic Index
Corrugated Plate Inteceptor
Council of the Printing Industries of Canada (Canada)

CPIA Chemical Propulsion Information Agency (USA)

CPIC Canadian Police Information Centre (Canada) (nation-wide automated police information service)
Coastal Patrol and Interdiction Craft

CPICC Consumer Product Information Coordinating Center (of General Services Administration (USA))

CPIF Cost–Plus–Incentive Fee

CPILS Correlation Protected Instrument Landing System
Correlation Protection Integrated Landing System

CPIS Computerised Personnel Information System

CPK Creatinine Phosphokinase

CPL Chemistry and Physics Laboratory (of EPA (USA))
Classification Packaging and Labelling
Commonwealth Parliamentary Library (Australia)
Computer Programme Library (of NEA (OECD))

CPLEE Charged Particle Lunar Environment Experiment (part of ASLEP)

CPLIA Contracting Plasterers and Lathers International Association (USA)

CPM (Punched) Cards Processed per Minute
College of Petroleum and Minerals (Saudi Arabia)
Computer Performance Monitor
Continuous Performance Measure
Continuous Processing Machine
Contract Planning Model
Critical Path Method
Current Physics Microform (of American Institute of Physics (USA))

CPMA Computer Peripheral Manufacturers Association (USA) (now ACDPI)

CPMS Computer Plotting Matrix System
Constant Position Mounting System

CPODA Contention Priority Oriented Demand Assignment

CPP Civilian Personnel Pamphlet (numbered series issued by US Army)
Computer Position Profile
Computer Printout Processing
Concrete Paver Project
Controllable Pitch Propeller
Curie Point Pyrolysis
Current Purchasing Power

CPPA Canadian Periodical Publishers Association (Canada)
Canadian Pulp and Paper Association (Canada)
Cementitious Packaged Products Association
Coal Preparation Plant Association

CPPG Construction Programme Policy Group (of NJCC)

CPR Cardio-Pulmonary Resusatation
Center for Population Research (of NICHD (NIH) (USA))
Committee on Polar Research (of NAS/NRC)
Continuing Property Record
Cost Performance Report

CPRI Cold Pressor Recovery Index

CPRL Charged Particle Research Laboratory (Illinois University (USA))

CPRM Companhia de Pesquisas de Recursos Minerais (Brazil) (Mineral Resources Research Group of the Ministry of Mines and Energy)

CPRS Central Policy Review Staff (of the Cabinet Office)

CPS Capacitance Proximity Sensor
CERN Proton Synchroton
Complete Packet Sequence
Contingency Planning System

Contour Plotting System
Conversational Programming System
COOLEY Programming System (Cooley Electronics Laboratory, Michigan University (USA))
Crankshaft Position Sensor
Creative Problem-Solving
Critical Path Scheduling

CPSA Clay Pigeon Shooting Association
Commonwealth Preference Standstill Area
Current Physics Selected Articles (of American Institute of Physics (USA))

CPSase Carbamyl Phosphate Synthetase

CPSC Consumer Product Safety Commission (USA)

CPSK Coherent Phased-Shift Keyed

CPSR COSSOR Precision Secondary Radar

CPST Capacitive Position Sensing Transducer

CPSU California Polytechnic State University (USA)

CPT Canadian Pacific Telecommunications (Canada) (privately owned enterprise)
Center for Particle Theory (University of Texas (USA))
Cockpit Procedures Trainer
Continuous Peformance Test
Contralateral Pyramidal Tract
Current Physical Titles (of the American Institute of Physics (USA))
Current Pulse Technique

CPTB Clay Products Technical Bureau of Great Britain

CPTS Council of Professional Technological Societies

CPU Central Packaging Unit (of MINTECH)
Central Processing Unit
Collective Protection Unit

CPUC California Public Utilities Commission (USA)

CPV Concrete Pressure Vehicle
Cytoplasmic Polyhedrosis Virus

CPVC Chlorinated Polyvinyl Chloride

CPWD Central Public Works Department (India)

CPWM Clock Pulse Width Modulation

CPX Charged Pigment Xerography
Command Post Exercise

CQA Computer-aided Question Answering
Office of Quality Assurance (of the Social Security Administration (USA))

CQMS Circuit Quality Monitoring System

CR Cellular Radio
Chemical Report
Chloroprene
Compression Ratio
Conference Report
Consultant Report
Contract Report
Contractor Report
Control Relay
Convertible Report
Counter Rotation

CRA California Redwood Association (USA)
Cargo Reinsurance Association
Chemical Recovery Association
Composite Research Aircraft
Computer Retailers Association

CRAAM (Universidade Mackenzie (Brazil)) (Radio Astronomy and Astrophysics Centre)
Centro de Radio-Astronomia e Astrofisica

CRAB Cement River Assault Boat

CRABS Close Range Analytical Bundle System

CRAC Careers Research and Advisory Centre
Construction Research Advisory Council (now Construction and Housing Research Advisory Council)

CRAD Chief Research and Development Branch (of DND (Canada))
Committee for Research into Apparatus for the Disabled enterprise)

CRAE Committee for the Reform of Animal Experimentation

CRAF Civil Reserve Air Fleet (USAF)

CRAFT Computerized Relative Allocation of Facilities Technique

CRAM Card Random Access Memory
Centre de Recherche sur les Atomes et les Molecules (Universite Laval (Canada)) (Research Centre on Atoms and Molecules)
Computerized Reliability Analysis Method
Conditional Relaxation Analysis Method
CONRAIL (CONSOLIDATED RAIL CORPORATION (USA)) Analysis Method
Critical Resource Allocation Method

CRAMD Cosmic Ray Anti-Matter Detector

CRAME Compania Radio Eerea Maritima Espanola (Spain)

CRAMM Coupon Reading And Marking Machine

CRAMP Comprehending Reflex development, Attitude formation, Memorising, Procedural learing

CRAS Composite Radar Absorbing Structures

CRBRP Clinch River Breeder Reactor Plant (USA)

CRC Cancer Research Campaign
Carbon Reinforced Cement
Center for Naval Analyses Research Contribution (USN)
Centre d'Études et de Recherches des Chefs d'Entreprises (France)
Centre de Recherches techniques et scientifiques industries de la tannerie, de la chaussure, de la pantoufle et des autres industries transformatrices du Cuir (Belgium) (Technical and Scientific Research Centre for the Tannery, Shoe, Slipper, and other Leather-Working Industries)
Clinical Research Centre (of MRC)
Co-ordinating Research Council (sponsored by SAE and American Petroleum Institute (USA))
Communications Research Centre (Department of Communications (Canada))
Communications Research Centre (of the Federal Communications Department (Canada))
Cotton Research Corporation
Cumulative Results Criterion
Cyclic Redundancy Character
Cyclic Redundancy Check
Cyclic Redundancy Code

CRC-APRAC Coordinating Research Council–Air Pollution Research Advisory Committee (USA)

CRCC Cyclic Redundancy Check Character

CRCP Continuously Reinforced Concrete Pavement enterprise)

CRD Committee In Energy Research and Development (of IEA (OECD))
Communications Research Division (of Institute for Defense Analyses (USA))
Computer Read-out Device

CRDF Cathode Ray Direction Finder

CRDL Chemical Research and Development Laboratories (US Army)

CRDM Control-Rod Device Mechanism

CRDME Committee for Research into Dental Materials and Equipment

CRDS Certified Reliability Data Shell

CRDSD Current Research and Development in Scientific Documentation (numbered series issued by National Science Foundation, USA)

CRDT Cone Roller Toroidal Drive

CRE Commercial Relations and Exporters (a division of the Dept of Trade)
Cone Research Establishment (of the National Coal Board)
Controlled Thermonuclear Research (formerly of USAEC, now a division of ERDA (USA))
Conversion of Refuse to Energy

CREAM Contention for Resources Evaluation and Analysis Model

CREATE Computational Resources for Engineering and Simulation, Training and Education

CREATION Crew Allocation

CREDD Customer Requested Earlier Due Date

CREDIT Cost Reduction Early Decision Information Techniques

CREDOC Centre de Recherche et de Documentation sur la Consommation (France) (Research and Documentation Centre on Consumer Affairs)

CREEP Container, Restrainer, Environment, Energy absorption, Post-crash failures (factors affecting survival in an air crash)

CREG Controlled Reluctance Eddy Current Generator

CREO Centre de Recherches et d'Etudes Oceanographiques (France) (Centre of Oceanographic Research and Studies)

CRES Center for Research in Engineering Science (University of Kansas (USA))
Constant Ratio Elasticity of Substitution
Corrosion Resistant

CRESA Combat Reporting System (USAF)
Cuarzo Radioelectrico Espanol SA (Spain) enterprise)

CRESS Center for Research in Social Systems (of the American Institutes for Research (USA))
Centre for Research in Experimental Space Science (York University, Toronto, Canada)
Combined Re-entry Effort in Small Systems
Computerised Reader Enquiry Service System

CREST Committee on Reactor Safety Technology (of NEA (OECD)) (became CSNI in 1973)
Crew Escape Technologies
Scientific and Technological Research Committee (of EEC)

CREST-IT Scientific and Technological Research Committee–Informatics Training Group (of EEC)

CRESTS COURTAULD's Rapid Extract, Sort and Tabulate System

CRETE Common Range of Electrical Test Equipment

CRF Capital Recovery Factor
Chronic Renal Failure
Composite Rear Fuselage
Contrast Rendering Factor
Corticotrophin Releasing Factor

CRFB Centre de Recherches du Fer-Blanc (France) (Tinplate Research Centre)

CRFI Custom Roll Forming Institute (USA)

CRFS Copper Reverbatory Furnace Slag
Crash-Resistant Fuel System

CRG Catalytic-Rich Gas
Centre de Recherches de Gorsem (Belgium) (Gorsem Research Centre)
Classification Research Group

CRH Critical Relative Humidity

CRHA Canadian Retail Hardware Association (Canada)

CRHL Collaborative Radiological Health Laboratory (USA) (Colorado State University)

CRI Caribbean Research Institute (University of the Virgin Islands)
Cement Research Institute of India (India)
Coconut Research Institute (Sri Lanka)
Comite de Recherche en Informatique (France) (Research Committee on Data Processing)
Crops Research Institute (Ghana)
Cure Rate Integrator

CRIC Centre de Recherches de l'Industrie Belge de la Ceramique (Belgium) (Belgian Ceramic Industry Research Centre)
Centre de Recherches Industrielles sur Contrats (France) (Industrial Research Centre on Contracts)

CRIEPI Central Research Institute of the Electrical Power Industry (Japan)

CRIF Centre de Recherches et techniques de l'Industrie Fabrications metalliques (Belgium) (Scientific and Technical Research Centre for the Metals Manufacturing Industry)

CRILA Credit Insurance Logistics Automated

CRIMP Computer Report on Importance

CRIN Cocoa Research Institute of Nigeria (Nigeria)

CRINC Center for Research Incorporated (University of Kansas (USA))

CRIPE Centre de Recherches et techniques pour l'Industrie des Produits Explosifs (Belgium) (Scientific and Technical Research Centre for the Explosives Industry)

CRIQ Centre de Recherche Industrielle du Québec (Canada) (Quebec Industrial Research Centre)

CRIS Centro de Recuperacio i d'Investigacions Submarines (Spain) (Undersea Recovery and Investigations Centre)
Command Retrieval Information System
Comprehensive Research Injury Scale
Current Research Information System

CRISP Comprehnsive RNSTS Inventory System Project
Control-Restrictive Instructions for Structured Programming
Controlled Regenerated Inhibited Solvent Process

CRISTAL Contracts Regarding an Interim Supplement to Tanker Liability for Oil Pollution

CRITICOM Critical Intelligence Communications

CRJE Conversational Remote Job Entry

CRJP Center for Research on Judgement and Policy (University of Colorado (USA))

CRL Center for Research Libraries (USA)
Centre for Research in Librarianship (Toronto University (Canada))
Council on Library Resources (USA)

CRLLB Center for Research on Language and Language Behavior (of University of Michigan, USA)

CRLS Coastguard Radio Liaison Station

CRLT Center for Research on Learning and Teaching (Michigan University (USA))

CRLUIS California Regional Land Use Information System

CRM Centre de Recherches Mathématiques (Université de Montréal (Canada)) (Centre of Mathematical Research)
Centre de Recherches Métallurgiques (Belgium) (Metallurgy Research Centre)
Chemical Remanent Magnetization
Committee on Medical Research and Public Health (of EEC)
Computer Resources Management
Control and Reproducibility Monitor

CRME Centre Regional de Mouvements d'Energie (France)

CRMS Close Range Missile System

CRN Cardiac-Recurrent Nerve

CRNL Chalk River Nuclear Laboratories (of AECL) (Canada)

CRO Cathode Ray Oscilloscope
Cave Rescue Organization of Great Britain
Centro di Riferimento Oncologico (Italy) (Centre for the Study of Tumours)
Companies Registration Office

CRODISS Computer Recording Of Defects In Sewerage Systems

CROF Controllerate Royal Ordnance Factories (MOD)

CROM Capacitative Read Only Memory
Control and Ready-Only memory

CROS Computerized Reliability Optimization System

CROSS Computer Rearrangement Of Subject Specialities

CROSSA — Centre Régional Opérationnel de Surveillance et de Sauvétage pour l'Atlantique (France) (Regional Operational Centre for Atlantic Search and Rescue)

CROSSBOW — Computerised Retrieval of Organic Structures Based On Wiswesser

CROSSMA — Centre Régional Opérationnel de Surveillance et de Sauvétage pour la Manche (France) (Regional Operational Centre for the English Channel Search and Rescue)

CRP — Centre de Recherche Physique (France) (Physics Research Centre)
Collaborative Reference Program (of NBS (USA) and TAPPI (USA))
Combined Refining Process
Components Reliability Programme
Constant Rate of Penetration
Controllable Reversible Pitch
Counter-Rotating Platform

CRPE — Centre de Recherches en Physique de l'Environnement terrestre et solaire (France) (Centre for Physical Research on the Terrestrial and Solar Environment)

CRPL — Central Radio Propagation Laboratory (USA) (now Institute for Telecommunication Sciences and Aeronomy (of NOAA (USA))

CRR — Carrier Removal Rate
Centre de Recherches Routieres (Belgium) (Road Research Centre)
Churchill Research Range (of NCR (Canada))
Constant Ratio Rule

CRREL — Cold Regions Research and Engineering Laboratory (US Army)

CRRERIS — Commonwealth Regional Renewable Energy Energy Resources Information System

CRRI — Central Road Research Institute (India)

CRRL — Canadian Radio Relay League (Canada)

CRS — Coast Radio Stations (of the British Post Office)
Congenital Rubella Syndrome
Congressional Research Service (of the Library of Congress (USA))
Controlled Radial Steering

CRSA — China Radio Sports Association (China)
Concrete Reinforcement Steel Association

CRSC — Center for Research in Scientific Communication (Johns Hopkins University (USA))

CRSE — prefix to numbered/lettered series of monographs on Cold Regions Science and Engineering issued by CRREL (US Army)

CRSI — Concrete Reinforcing Steel Institute (USA)

CRSIM — Centre de Recherches Scientifiques, Industrielles et Maritimes (France) (Scientific, Industrial and Maritime Research Centre)

CRSR — Center for Radiophysics and Space Research (Cornell University (USA))

CRSS — Canada Remote Sensing Society (Canada)
Critical Resolved Shear Stress

CRSSA — Centre de Recherches du Service de Sante des Armees (France) (Army Medical Service Research Centre)

CRSSI — Council for the Rationalisation of the Shipbuilding and Shipping Industries (Japan)

CRT — Cathode Ray Terminal
Cathode Ray Tube
Choice Reaction Time
Combat Readiness Training
Computer Remote Terminal

CRTC — Canadian Radio and Television Commission (Canada)
Cold Regions Test Center (US Army)

CRTF — Create Test Files

CRTPB — Canadian Radio Technical Planning Board (Canada)

CRU — Centre de Recherche d'Urbanisme (France) (Urban Planning Research Centre)
Compass Re-transmission Unit
Control and Reporting Unit

CRUESI — Research Centre for the Utilization of Saline Water Irrigation (Tunisia)

CRUS — Centre for Research on User Studies (Sheffield University)

CRUSK — Center for Research on Utilisation of Scientific Knowledge (of ISR (Michigan University (USA))

CRUZEIRO — Servicos Aereos do Sul SA (Brazil)

CRWR — Center for Research in Water Resources (Texas University (USA))

CS — Center for Cybernetic Studies (University of Texas (USA))
Commercial Standard (numbered series issued by NBS, USA)
Computer Science
Computer Simulation
Conditioned Stimulus
Crystallographic Shear
Ortho-chlorobenzliden-malonitrile (a gas named after its inventors—Dr. B. B. Carson and Dr. R. W. Stoughton)
prefix to numbered series issued by Central States Forest Experiment Station (Forest Service, USDA)
prefix to numbered series of Recommended Practices for Cast Steel Shot issued by SAE (USA)
prefix to numbered series of reports issued by the Department of Computer Science, Stanford University (USA)
The Chemical Society
The Concrete Society

CS/T — Combined Station/Tower

CS3 — Combat Service Support System (US Army)

CSA — Canadian Standards Association (Canada)
Cell-Surface Antigen
Central Surgical Association (USA)
Ceskoslovenske Aerolinie (Czechoslovakia)
Colony-Stimulating Activity
Computer Science Association (Canada)
Computer Services Association
Cryogenic Society of America (USA)
Cysteine Sulphinic Acid

CSAC — Consumer Standards Advisory Committee (of BSI)
Contemporary Scientific Archives Centre

CSAD — Capsule System Advanced Development

CSAE — Canadian Society of Agricultural Engineering (Canada)

CSAM — Conseil Superieur de l'Aviation Marchande (France) (Air Transport Advisory Board)

CSAR — Communication Satellite Advanced Research

CSAV — Ceskoslovenske Akademe Ved (Czechoslovak Academy of Science)

CSAWS — Cairngorm (Scotland) Summit Automatic Weather Station

CSB — Carrier and Side Band

CSC — ACM (USA) Computer Science Conference
Centrifugal Shot Casting
Commonwealth Science Council
Commonwealth Scientific Committee
Computer Science Center (University of Maryland (USA))
Computer Search Center (of IITRI (USA))

CSC/PRC — Committee for Scholarly Communication with the People's Republic of China (USA) (co-sponsored by NAS, SSRC and ACLS)

CSCAN — Carrier System for Controller Approach of Naval Aircraft

CSCC — Cumulative Sum Control Chart

CSCE Canadian Society for Chemical Engineering (Canada)
Canadian Society for Civil Engineering (Canada)
Conference on Security and Cooperation in Europe

CSCFE Civil Service Council for Further Education

CSChE Canadian Society for Chemical Engineering (Canada)

CSCPRC Committee on Scholarly Communication with the People's Republic of China (of National Research Council (USA))

CSCR Center for Surface and Coatings Research (Lehigh University (USA))

CSCS Cost-Schedule Control System

CSCSB California State College San Bernardino (USA)

CSD Ceskolovenske Statne Drahy (Czechoslovakia) (Czechoslovak State Railway)
Chemical Spray Deposition
Closed System Delivery
Computerized Standard Data
Constant Speed Drive
Construction Systems Division (of CERL (US Army))
Control Surveys Division (of ACSM (USA))
Controlled-Slip Differentials
Crack Surface Displacement
The Civil Service Department (now Management and Personnel Office (of the Cabinet Office))

CSDE Central Servicing Development Establishment (Royal Air Force)

CSDS Constant Speed Drive/Starter

CSDT Continuous Space-Discrete Time

CSE Central Studies Establishment (of Australian Defence Scientific Service)
Communication Satellite for Experimental purposes
Computers, Systems and Electronics Division (of the Dept of Industry)
Containment Systems Experiment

CSEA California State (USA) Electronics Association

CSEE Canadian Society for Electrical Engineering (Canada)
Compagnie des Signaux et d'Enterprises Electriques (France)

CSEI Concentrated Solar Energy Imitator

CSELT Centro Studi e Laboratori Telecommunicazioni (Italy) (Telecommunications Research Centre and Laboratory)

CSER Committee on Solar Electromagnetic Radiation

CSERB Computers, Systems and Electronics Requirements Board (of the Dept of Industry) (now EARB)

CSF Canadian Standard Freeness
Cerebrospinal Fluid
Colony Stimulating Factor
Compagnie Generale de Telegraphie sans Fil (France)
Completely Symmetric Function
Configuration State Function
Critical Success Factor

CSFA Canadian Science Film Association (Canada)

CSFB Channel State Feedback

CSG Consolidated Steam Generator
Constructive Solid Geometry
Consultative Shipping Group
Context-Sensitive Grammar
Council of State Governments (USA)

CSH Centralised Hydraulic System
Conventional Spin Hamiltonian

CSI Computer Society of India (India)
Computer Synthesized Imagery
Construction Specifications Institute (USA)
Construction Surveyors Institute
Council for the Securities Industry

CSIA Center for Science and International Affairs (of Harvard University (USA))

CSIC Consejo Superior de Investigaciones Cientificas (Spain) (Higher Council for Scientific Research)

CSICC Canadian Steel Industries Construction Council (Canada)

CSIE Center for the Study of Information and Education (Syracuse University (USA))

CSII Centre for the Study of Industrial Innovation
Continuous Subcutaneous Insulin Infusion

CSIO Cavity-Stablized IMPATT Oscillator
Central Scientific Instruments Organisation (India)

CSIP Combat Systems Improvement Program (of USN)

CSIR Council for Scientific and Industrial Research (Ghana)
Council for Scientific and Industrial Research (South Africa)
Council of Scientific and Industrial Research (India)

CSIRO Commonwealth Scientific and Industrial Research Organisation (Australia)

CSIS Center for Strategic and International Studies (Georgetown University (USA))
Containment Spray Injection System

CSIT Committee on Social Implications of Technology (of IEEE (USA))

CSJ Chemical Society of Japan (Japan)

CSK Co-operative Study of the Kuroshio and adjacent region (of IOC (UNESCO))

CSL Chemical Systems Laboratory (US Army)
Circle of State Librarians
Coincidence Site Lattice
Communication Sciences Laboratory (of Florida University (USA))
Comparative Systems Laboratory (Western Reserve University (USA))
Computer Systems Laboratory (of NIH (HEW) (USA))
Context-Sensitive Language
Control and Simulation Language
Current Switch Logic

CSLA Canadian School Library Association (Canada)

CSLC Coherent Side Lobe Cancellation

CSLP Center for Short-Lived Phenomena (USA) (previously of the Smithsonian Institute now an independent non-profit corporation)

CSM Camborne School of Mines
Cement-Sand-Molasses
Centro Sperimentale Metallurgico (Italy) (Metallurgy Research Centre)
Cerebrospinal Meningitis
Chopped Strand Mat
Close Support Missile
Colorado School of Mines (USA)
Command and Service Module
Commission for Synoptic Meteorology (of WMO (UN))
Committee on Safety of Medicines
Computer System Manual
Corn-Soya Milk

CSMA Carrier Sense Multiple Access
Chemical Specialities Manufacturers Association (USA)
Communications Systems Management Association (USA)

CSMA/CD Carrier Sense Multiple Access with Collision Detection

CSMCRI Central Salt and Marine Chemicals Research Institute (India)

CSME Canadian Society for Mechanical Engineers (Canada)

CSMI Commission for Small and Medium Industries (Philippines)

CSMMFRA Cotton, Silk and Man-Made Fibres Research Association

CSMP Continuous System Modelling Programme
Current Ship's Maintenance Project

CSMRS Central Soil Mechanics Research Station (India)

CSMS Computerized Specification Management System

CSN Canadian Switched Network (Canada)
Companhia Siderurgica Nacional (Brazil)
prefix to numbered series of Standards issued by Urad pro Normalizaci a Mereni (Office for Standards and Measurements) (Czechoslovakia)

CSNDT Canadian Society for Non-Destructive Testing (Canada)

CSNET Computer Science Research Network (of National Science Foundation (USA)

CSNI Committee on the Safety of Nuclear Installations (of NEA)

CSNTA Committee on Societal Needs and Technology Assessment (of Federation of Materials Societies (USA))

CSO Central Seismological Observatory (India)
Central Statistical Office (Ethiopia)
Central Statistical Organization (India)
Central Statistics Office (Iraq)
Colour Separation Overlay
The Central Statistical Office

CSOC Consolidated Space Operations Center (USAF)

CSOCR Code Sort Optical Character Recognition

CSOD Crack Surface Opening Displacement

CSP Cell-Surface Protein
Channeled-Substrate-Planar
Chartered Society of Physiotherapy
Chlorosulphonated Polyethylene
Circum-Sporozoite
Coherent Signal Processor
Commercial Sub-routine Package
Continuous Sampling Plan
Continuous Seismic Profiling
Controlled Surface Porosity
Council for Scientific Policy (disbanded 1972) (replaced by Advisory Board of the Research Councils)
Count Strength Product

CSPC Cost and Schedule Planning and Control

CSPE Chlorosulphonated Polyethylene

CSPG Canadian Society of Petroleum Geologists (Canada)

CSPI Center for Science in the Public Interest (USA)

CSPP Committee on Science and Public Policy (of AAAS (USA))

CSPRT Compound Sequential Probability Ratio Test

CSQ Central Site Queueing

CSQC Ceylon Society for Quality Control (Ceylon is now called Sri Lanka)

CSR Center for Space Research (Massachusetts Institute of Technology (USA))
Chemically Stimulated Rubber

CSRA Committee of Secretaries of Research Associations

CSRE Committee for Social Responsibility in Engineering (USA)

CSRL Computer Science Research Laboratory (University of Arizona (USA))

CSROEPM Communication, System, Results, Objectives, Exception, Participation, Motivation

CSRS Central Sericulture Research Station (India)
Constant-switch-pace Symmetric Random Signals
Cooperative State Research Service (of USDA)

CSS Central Statistical Office (Ethiopia)
Cockpit Systems Simulator
Combat Service Support
Computer Systems Simulator
Cordless Switchboard System
Council for Science and Society
Cryogenics Storage System

CSSA Crop Science Society of America (USA)

CSSB Compatible Single-Sideband

CSSCG Container Systems Standardization/Coordination Group (USDOD)

CSSD Chemically Sensitive Semiconductor Device

CSSDA Council of Social Science Data Archives (USA)

CSSE Conference of State Sanitary Engineers (USA)
Control Systems Science and Engineering Department (University of Washington (USA))

CSSEC Computer Systems Support and Evaluation Command (US Army)

CSSI Coriolis (Cross-coupled angular acceleration) Sickness Susceptibility Index

CSSL Continuous System Simulation Language
Cyclical Stress Sensitivity Limit

CSSM Central Site Simulation Model

CSSP Centre for Studies in Social Policy (merged into PSI in 1978)
Continuous System Simulation Programme
Council of Scientific Society Presidents (USA)

CSSRA Canadian Shipbuilding and Ship Repairing Association (Canada)

CSSS Canadian Soil Science Society (Canada)

CST Capillary Suction Times
Concentration Stress Test
Consolidated Schedule Technique
Critical Solution Temperature
Cumulative Sum Techniques

CSTA Combat Systems Test Activity (US Army)

CSTB Centre Scientifique et Technique du Batiment (France) (Building Science and Technology Centre)
Computer Science and Technology Board (of National Research Council (USA))

CSTC Centre Scientique et Technique de la Construction (Belgium) (Scientific and Technical Research Centre for the Construction Industry)

CSTD Committee on Science and Technology for Development (the secretariat for UNCSTD)

CSTI Council of Science and Technology Institutions

CSTMP Carotid Sinus Transmural Pressure

CSTP Committee for Scientific and Technical Personnel (of OECD) (of OECD) (disbanded 1970)
Committee for Scientific and Technological Policy (of OECD)

CSTR Continuous, Stirred-Tank Reactor

CSTS Central Statistical Office (Ethiopia)
Computer Sciences Teleprocessing System

CSU California State University (USA)
Central Services Unit for University and Polytechnic Careers and Appointments Services
Circuit Switching Unit
Cleveland State University (USA)
Colorado State University (USA)

CSU-ATSP Colorado State University, Department of Atmospheric Science (USA)

CSUF California State University, Fresno (USA)

CSUK Chamber of Shipping of the United Kingdom (merged into GCBS in 1975)

CSVTS Ceskolovenska Vedecko-Technika Spolecnost (Czechoslovakia) (Czechoslovakia Scientific and Technical Society)

CSW Cleveland School of Welding (USA)
Concentrated Sea Water

CSWIP Certification Scheme for Weldment Inspection Personnel (administered by the Welding Institute)

CSWS Crew-Served Weapon Night Vision Sight

CS² Coaxial Subscriber System

CT Circuit Theory
Community Technology
Compact Tension
Computed Tomography
Cryco-Thyroid

CT/Cosba Cape Town Computer Services and Bureaux Association (South Africa)

CTA California Trucking Association (USA)
Cellulose Triacetate
Cement-Treated Aggregate
Centro Tecnico Aeroespacial (Brazil) (Aerospace Technical Centre)
Chain Testers Association of Great Britain
Collision Threat Assessment
Committee on Thrombolytic Agents (of the National Heart Institute (USA))
Computerized Travel Aid (for the blind)
Conurbation Transport Authority
Cystine Trypticase Agar

CTAB Cetyltrimethylammonium Bromide
Commerce Technical Advisory Board (of Dept of Commerce (USA))

CTAF Comite des Transporteurs Aeriens Francais (France) (French Air Transport Association)

CTAP Cleveland (Ohio (USA)) Transport Action Program

CTAR Comite des Transporteurs Aeriens Regionaux (France) (Committee of Regional Air Carriers)

CTAS Centre Technique des Applications de Soudage (of SAF (France)) (Technical Centre of Welding Applications)

CTAT Computerized Transverse Axial Tomography

CTB Cement-Treated Base
Centre Technique de Bois (France) (Wood Research Centre)
Companhia Telefonica Brasileira (Brazil)
Comprehensive Test Ban (negotiations between Great Britain, USA & USSR)
Concentrator Terminal Buffer

CTBN Carboxyl Terminated Butadiene-acrylonitrile

CTBT Comprehensive Test Ban Treaty

CTC Canadian Transport Commission (Canada)
Carbon Tetrachloride
Central Training Council (of Department of Employment)
Centralised Traffic Control
Charge Transfer Complex
Chirp Transform Correlator
Chlorotetracycline
Compact Transpiration Cooling
Continuously Transposed Conductor

CTCA Canadian Telecommunications Carriers Association (Canada)
Channel to Channel Adapter

CTCC Central Transport Consultative Committee

CTCM Computer Timing and Costing Model

CTCS Component Time Control System

CTCSS Code Tone Call Selective Signalling
Continuous Tone Coded Squelch System

CTD Certificate of Tax Deposit
Charge-Transfer Device
Conductivity–Temperature–Depth

CTDH Command and Telemetry Data Handling

CTDS Continuous-Time-Discrete-Space

CTE Charge-Transfer Efficiency
Coefficient of Thermal Expansion
Computer Telex Exchange

CTEB Council of Technical Examining Bodies

CTEE Chlorotrifluor Ethylene

CTEIS California Total Educational Information System (USA)

CTEM Conventional Transmission Electron Microscope

CTF Chlorine Trifluoride
Coal Tar Fuel
Controlled Thermonuclear Fusion
Controlled-Temperature Furnace

CTFA Cosmetic, Toiletry and Fragrance Association (USA)

CTFC Central Time and Frequency Control

CTFM Continuous-Transmission Frequency-Modulated

CTFOIC Cabinet Task Force on Oil Import Control (USA)

CTFT Centre Technique Forestier Tropical (France) (Tropical Forest Technical Centre)

CTH Chalmers Tekniska Hogskola (Sweden) (Chalmers University of Technology)
Cure To Handling

CTI Calculo y Tratamiento de la Informacion (Spain)
Central Tyre Inflation
Charge Transfer Inefficiency
Coaxial Transceiver Interface
Comparative Tracking Index
Cooling Tower Institute (USA)

CTIAC Concrete Technology Information analysis Center (US Army)

CTICM Centre Technique Industriel de la Construction Metallique (France) (Industrial Technical Centre for Metal Construction)

CTIF Centre Techniques des Industries de la Fonderie (France) (Foundry Industries Technical Centre)

CTIO Cerro Tolo Interamerican Observatory (Chile) (operated by the Association of Universities for Research in Astronomy under contract with NSF (USA))

CTL Cincinnati Testing Laboratories (USA)
Compass Test Language
Compiler Target Language
Complementary Transitor Logic
Constant Time Loci
Cytolysis
Cytotoxic T Lymphocyte

CTM Capacity Ton-Mile
Clotrimazole
Composite-Tape-Memory

CTMA Commercial Truck Maintenance Association (USA)

CTN Cellulose Trinitrate

CTNA Catholic Telecommunication Network of America (USA)

CTNE Compania Telefonica Nacional de Espana (Spain) (National Telephone Company of Spain)

CTNSS Centre for Thai National Standard Specifications (Thailand)

CTO Charge Transforming Operator
Commonwealth Telecommunications Organisation
Culham Translations Office (of UKAEA)

CTOL Conventional Take-Off and Landing

CTP Charge Transforming Parameter
Ctyidine Triphosphate

CTPARU Canadian Forces Personnel Applied Research Unit (Canada)

CTPB Carboxyl-Terminated Polybutadiene Binder

CTPIB Carboxy-Terminated Polyisobutylene

CTPV Coal Tar Pitch Volatiles

CTR Chemical Transfer Reaction
Comision de Telecomunicaciones Rurales (Mexico)
Controllable Twist Rotor
Controlled Thermonuclear Reactor
Controlled Thermonuclear Research

CTRA Coal Tar Research Association

CTRL Cotton Technological Research Laboratory (India)
CTRS Computerized Test-result Reporting System
CTS Cab Tyred Sheathed
Center for Theoretical Studies (Miami University (USA))
Centre for Transport Studies (Cranfield Institute of Technology)
Commercial Transaction System
Committee on Teaching of Science (of ICSU)
Communications Technology Satellite
Controlled Thermal Severity
CTSIBV Centre Technique et Scientifique de l'Industrie Belge du Verre (Belgium) (Belgian Glass Industry Technical and Scientific Centre)
CTSRL Communications Theory and Systems Research Laboratory (University of Texas (USA))
CTSS Compatible Time Shared System
CTT Capital Transfer Tax
Computerized Transaxial Tomography
CTV Cable Television
CTVS Cockpit Television Sensor
Cockpit Television System
CU Colorado University (USA)
Columbia University (USA)
Consumers Union (USA)
CU-CSD Cornell University, Department of Computer Science (USA)
CUA Canadian Urological Surgeons
Circuit Unit Assembly
CUAG Computer Users Associations Group
CUBANA Empresa Consolidada Cubana de Aviacion (Cuba) (State Air Line)
CUBE Cooperative Users of BURROUGHS Equipment (USA)
CUBI Catalogo Unico delle Bibliogteche Italiane (Italy) (Italian Libraries Union Catalogue)
CUBITH Coordinated Use of Building Industrial Technology for Hospitals
CUC Coal Utilisation Council
CUCS Computation-Universal Cellular Space
CUCV Commercial Utility and Cargo Vehicle
CUDAS Computer Ultrasonic Data Analysis System
CUDN Common User Data Network
CUDOS Continuously Updated Dynamic Optimizing Systems
CUE Chemical Underwater Explosive
Coastal Upwelling Experiment
Component Utilization Effectiveness
Computer Updating Equipment
Configuration Utilization Evaluation
Correction–Update–Extension
CUE/DSO Configuration Usage Evaluator/Data Set Optimizer
Controllable Twist Rotor
CUEA Coastal Upwelling Ecosystem Analysis (a project of IDOE)
CUED Cambridge University Engineering Department
CUEP Central Unit on Environmental Pollution (of DOE)
CUERL Columbia University Electronics Research Laboratories (USA)
CUES Computer Utilities for Education Systems
CUFT Center for the Utilization of Federal Technology (of NTIS (USA))
CUG Closed User Group
CUHK Chinese University of Hong Kong (Hong Kong)
CUJT Complimentary Uni-Junction Transistor
CULDATA Comprehensive Unified Land Data
CULPRIT Cull and Print
CULT Chinese University Language Translator (a project at Hong Kong University)
CUM LAUDE Computerized Understanding of Morphology-Language Acquisition Under Development in Education
CUMA Canadian Urethane Manufacturers Association (Canada)
CUMARC Cumulated Machine-Readable Cataloguing
CUML Cambridge University Mathematical Laboratory
CUMM Council of Underground Mining Machinery Manufacturers
CUMREC College and University Machine Records Conference (USA)
CUMSAD Current Meter Speed And Detection
CUNY City University of New York (USA)
CUPE Cranfield Unit for Precision Engineering (Cranfield Institute of Technology)
CUPID Commercial Users Programme for Index Data
Commercial Users Programme to Index Data
Conversational Utility Programme for Information Display
Create, Update, Interrogate and Display
CUPM Committee on the Undergraduate Program in Mathematics (of the Mathematical Association of America)
CUR Commissie voor Uitvoering van Research (Netherlands) (Committee for Performing Research)
CURAC Coal Utilization Research Advisory Committee (Australia)
CURB Campaign on the Use and Restriction of Barbiturates (an organisation)
CURE Computer Users Replacement Equipment (a non-profit organisation based at Charles Keene College of Further Education, Leicester)
Control of Unwanted Radiated Energy
CURS Centre for Urban and Regional Studies (Birmingham University)
Centre Universitaire de la Recherche Scientifique (Morocco) (University Centre for Scientific Research)
CURTS Common User Radio Transmission Sounding
Common User Radio Transmission System
CURV Cable-controlled Underwater Research Vehicle
CUSC Computers in the Undergraduate Science Curriculum (a project of University College, London)
CUSIP Committee on Uniform Security Identification Procedures (of the American Bankers Association (USA))
CUSP Central Unit for Scientific Photography (of RAE)
CUSR Central United States Registry (of DOD (USA))
CUSRPG Canada-United States Regional Planning Group (of NATO)
CUSUM Cumulative Sum
CUT Chartered Union of Taxpayers
CUTS Computer Users Tape System
Computer Utilized Turning System
CUV Current Use Value
CUW Committee on Undersea Warfare (USDOD)
CV Calorific Value
Constant Viscosity
Constant Voltage
Continuous Vulcanization
Curriculum Vitae
CVA Calendar Variations Analysis
Canonical Variates Analysis
Current Value Accounting
CVC Current-Voltage Characteristic
CVCC Compound Vortex and Controlled Combustion
Compound, Vortex Controlled Combustion
CVCHP Cascade Variable Conductance Heat Pipe
CVCM Collected Volatile Condensable Material
CVCP Committee of Vice-Chancellors and Principals of the Universities of the United Kingdom

CVD Capacitive Voltage Divider
Carbon Vacuum Deoxidized
Chemical Vapour Deposition
Co-ordination of Valve Development (MOD)
Constancy of Visual Direction
Coupled Vibration-Dissociation
Current-Voltage Diagram

CVDT Constant Volume Drop Time

CVDV Coupled Vibration-Dissociation-Vibration

CVF Circular Variable Filter

CVFR Controlled Visual Flight Rules

CVFS Circular Variable-Filter Spectrometer

CVG Continuously Variable Gearbox

CVL Centruum voor Lastechniek (Netherlands) (now part of NIL)

CVMA Canadian Veterinary Medical Association (Canada)

CVN Charpy V-notch

CVP Central Venous Pressure
Cost-Volume-Profit

CVR Cockpit Voice Recorder
Continuous Video Recorder
Crystal Video Receiver
Current-Viewing Resistor

CVR(T) Combat Vehicle Reconnaissance (Tracked)

CVR(T)(APC) Combat Vehicle Reconnaissance (Tracked) (Armoured Personnel Carrier)

CVR(T)(GW) Combat Vehicle Reconnaisance (Tracked) (Guided Weapon carrier)

CVR(T)(REC) Combat Vehicle Reconnaissance (Tracked) (Recovery)

CVR(W) Combat Vehicle Reconnaissance (Wheeled)

CVRD Companhia Vale do Rio Doce (Brazil) (Government controlled)

CVRTC Cardiovascular Research and Training Center (University of Alabama (USA))
Commercial Vehicle and Road Transport Club

CVS Combat Vehicle Simulator
Computer-controlled Vehicle System (for traffic control)
Constant Volume Sampling

CVSD Continuous Variable Slope Delta
Continuously Variable Slope Delta modulation

CVSF Conduction Velocity of Slower Fibres

CVT Concept Verification Testing
Constant-Voltage Transformer
Constantly Variable Transmission
Continuously Variable Transmission
Continuously Variable Transmission

CVTR Carolinas-Virginia Tube Reactor
Charcoal Viral Transport

CW Carrier OR Composite OR Continuous Wave
Chemical Warfare
Clockwise
Cold Welding
Constant Weight
Continuous Weld

CWA Cooling Water Association

CWAC Central Water Advisory Committee

CWAR Continuous Wave Acquisition Radar

CWAS Contractor Weighted Average Share

CWB Canadian Welding Bureau (Canada)

CWC Cloud Water Content

CWD Clerical Work Data

CWDI Canadian Welding Development Institute (Canada)

CWFS Crashworthy Fuel Systems

CWHC Composite Wall Hollow Cathode

CWIC Compiler for Writing and Implementing Compilers

CWIP Clerical Work Improvement Programme

CWIT Colour-Word Interference Test
Concordance Words In Titles

CWM Cell Wall Material
Clerical Work Measurement

CWP Coalworkers' Pneumoconiosis

CWPC Central Water and Power Commission (India)

CWPRS Central Water and Power Research Station (India)

CWPS Council on Wages and Price Stabilization (of the Executive Office of the President (USA))

CWPU Central Water Planning Unit (of DOE)

CWR Continuous-Welded Rail

CWRA Canadian Water Resources Association (Canada)

CWRU Case Western Reserve University (USA)

CWS Canadian Welding Society (Canada)
Collision Warning System
Compiler Writing System
Continuous Seismic Wave
Control Wheel Steering
Cooperative Wage Study

CWSA Contract Work Study Association

CWVM Compiler Writer's Virtual Machine

CWW Cruciform Wing Weapon

CWWPS Cornish Water Wheels Preservation Society (now merged into the Trevithick Society)

CXT Common External Tariff (of EEC)

CYBERSOFT International Symposium on Cybernetics and Software

CYDAC Cytophotometric Data Conversion

CYRUS Computerized Yale (University) Retrieval and Updating System

CYTA Cyprus Telecommunications Authority (Cyprus)

CZAR CROWN ZELLERBACH (CORPORATION (USA)) Access Routine

CZT Chirp–Z–Transform
Chirp-Z-Transform

C^2 Counter-Counter Measures

C^2MUG Command Control Microelectronics Users Group (of US Army Communication-Electronics Command)

C^3 Cleaved Coupled Cavity

C^3CM Command, Control and Communications Counter-Measures

C^4IS Command, Control, Communications and Computer and Intelligence System

D

D & I Drawn and Ironed

D & T Detection and Tracking

D(I)C Defence (Industrial) Committee (Australia)

D-ECL Dielectrically-isolated Emitter Coupled Logic

D-MESFET Depletion-mode Metal Semiconductor Field-Effect Transistor

D/NCIG Day/Night (Approach) Computer Image Generator

DA Dalniya Aviatsiya (USSR) (the Long Range Aviation—a group of the Soviet Air Force)
Demand Assigned
Diphenylchloroarsine
Dopamine

DAA Data Access Arrangement
Desalanine-desasparagine
Diacetone Acrylamide
Diacetone Alcohol

DAACA Department of the Army Allocation Committee, Ammunition (US Army) (became CALS in 1975)

DAAD Deutscher Akademischer Austauschdienst (Germany) (German Academic Exchange Service)

DAAFAR Defensa Anti Aerea y Fuerza Aerea Revolucionaria (Cuba) (Anti-Aircraft Defence and Revolutionary Air Force)

DAAS Defence Automatic Addressing System (of DLA USDOD))
Department of Defence (USA) Automatic Addressing System

DABS Discrete Address Beacon System
Dynamic Air-Blast Simulator

DABS-IPC Discrete Address Beacon System with Intermittent Positive Control

DABXT Deep Airborne Expendable Bathythermograph

DAC Data Analysis and Control
Defense Acquisition Circulars (USDOD)
Deputate for Avionics Control (of AFSC(USAF))
Design Augmented by Computer
Development Assistance Committee (of OECD)
Diamond Anvil Cell
Didode-Assisted Commutation
Digital to Analogue Converter

DACA Diphenylaminochloroarsine

DACC Data and Computation Center (University of Wisconsin (USA))

DACE Data Acquisition and Control Executive

DACI Direct Adjacent Channel Interference

DACOM Double Average Comparison

DACOR Data Correction

DACOWITS Defense Advisory Committee on Women in the Services (USA)
Defense Advisory Committee on Women in the Services (USA)

DACS Data and Analysis Center for Software (USDOD)
Directorate of Aerospace Combat Systems (of Canadian Armed Forces)

DACT Directorate of Administrative and Computer Training (Dept of Defence (Australia))
Dissimilar Air Combat Training

DAD Dial-a-Design (computer based design service of Ferranti & Systemshare Ltd.)
Differential Amplitude Discriminator
Drum And Display

DADC Digital Air Data Computer

DADEC Design And Demonstration Electronic Computer

DADEE Dynamic Analog Differential Equation Equalizer

DADIOS Direct Analogue to Digital Input-Output System

DADM Deductively Augmented Data Management

DADP Dialkyl Dithiophosphate

DADPTC Defence ADP Training Centre (MOD)

DADS Data Acquisition and Display System
Digital Air Data System

DAE Department of Atomic Energy (India)

DAEC Danish Atomic Energy Commission (Denmark) (replaced by Danish Energy Agency in 1976)

DAEDAC Drug Abuse Epidemiology Data Center (Texas Christian University (USA))

DAEM Digital Acoustic Emission Monitor

DAES Direct Access Education System

DAF Dansk Arbejdsgiverforening (Denmark) (Danish Employers Confederation)
Delayed Auditory Feedback
Dissolved Air Flotation
Dynamic Axial Fatigue
van Doorne's Automobiel-fabriek (Holland)

DAFC Digital Automatic Frequency Control

DAFDTA Dipole Antenna with Feed-points Displaced Transverse to its Axis

DAFM Discard-At-Failure Maintenance

DAFS Department of Agriculture and Fisheries for Scotland

DAG Dysprosium Aluminium Garnet

DAGAS Dangerous Goods Advisory Service (of Laboratory of the Government Chemist)

DAGK Deutschen Arbeitsgemeinschaft Kybernetic (Germany) (German Study Group on Cybernetics)

DAGM Deutsche Arbeitgemeinschaft fuer Mustererkennung (Germany) (German Pattern Recognition Society)

DAI Deutscher Architekten und Ingenieurverband (Germany) (German Architecture and Engineering Society)
Direct Access Information
Doubly Auto-Ionizing

DAIGC Direct Aqueous Injection Gas Chromatography

DAIR Direct Altitude and Identity Readout
Driver Air, Information, and Routing

DAIRI Dissertation Abstracts International Retrospective Index

DAIS Defence Automatic Integrated Switching system
Digital Avionics Information System
Direct Access Intelligence Systems

DAISY Decision Aiding Information System
Displacement Automated Integrated Systems
Domestic Appliances Information System

DAK Dansk Atomreaktor Konsortium (Denmark)
Deutsche Atomkommission Geschaftsfuhrung (of BMWF) (German Atomic Energy Advisory Commission)

DAL Downed Aircraft Locator

DALE Digital Anemograph Logging Equipment

DALG D—Algorithm

DALR Dry-Adiabatic Lapse Rate

DALS Diver Auditory Localization System

DAM Data Addressed Memory
Diagnostic Acceptability Measure

DAMA Demand Assignment Multiple Access

DAME Digital Automatic Measuring Equipment
Director Area Mechanical Estimating

DAMID Discounting Analysis Model for Investment Decisions

DAMN Dynamic Analysis of Mechanical Networks

DAMOS Data Moving System

DAMPS Data Acquisition Multi-programming System

DAMUSC Direct Access, Multi-User, Synchrocyclotron Computer

DAMUT Ducted Air Medium Underground Transmission

DAN Diaminonaphthalene

DANAC DECCA Area Navigation Airborne Computer

DANATOM Selskabet for Atomenergiens Industrielle Udnyttelse (Denmark) (Association for the Industrial Development of Atomic Energy)

DANDE Dome Analysis and Design

DANE Departamento Administrativo Nacional de Estadistica (Colombia) (National Statistical Department)

DANI Department of Agriculture Northern Ireland

DANPRO Danish Committee on Trade Procedures (Denmark)

DANTES Defense Activity for Non-Traditional Education Support (an off-duty general education plan of USDOD)

DANTS Day and Night Television System

DAO Directory of Amateur Observers

DAP Deformation Alignment Phase
Derived Attainable Performance
Diallyl Phthalate
Diaminopimelic Acid
Distributed Array Processor

DAPA Diaminopimelic Acid

DAPCA Development And Production Costs for Aircraft

DAPHNE DIDO and PLUTO Handmaiden for Nuclear Experiments

DAPI Diamidino-phenylindole
DAPP Data Acquisition and Processing Program (of USAF) (name changed to DMSP, Dec 1973)
DAPR Digital Automatic Pattern Recognition
DAPS Direct Access Programming System
DAR Delayed Auto-Reclose
Directorate of Atomic Research (of DRB (Canada))
Division of Applied Research (of RANN (NSF) (USA))
DARA Deutsche Arbeitsgemeinschaft fur Rechenanlagen (Germany) (German Computer Association)
DARC Deutscher Amateur-Radio-Club (Germany)
Direct Access Radar Channel
DARCOM Army Materiel Development and Readiness Command (US Army) (reverted to AMC in 1984)
DARE Differential Analyzer Replacement
Document Abstract Retrieval Equipment
Documentation Automated Retrieval Equipment
Doppler Automatic Reduction Equipment
UNESCO Computerized Data Retrieval System for the Social and Human Sciences
DARES Data Analysis and Reduction System
DARIAS Digico Automated Radio-Immunoassay Analytical System
DARLI Digital Angular Readout by Laser Interferometry
DARME Directorate of Armament Engineering (of Canadian Armed Forces)
DARMS Digital Alternate Representation of Music Scores
DARPA Defense Advanced Research Projects Agency (USDOD)
DARS Data Acquisition Reduction System
Defense Acquisition Regulations (USDOD)
Digital Adaptive Recording System
Digital Attitude Reference System
DART Daily Automatic Rescheduling Technique
DATAGRAPHIX Automated Retrieval Techniques
Decomposed Ammonia Radioisotope Thruster
Demand Actuated Road Transit
Deployable Automatic Relay Terminal
Design Automation Routing Tool
Detection, Action and Response Technique
Digital Automatic Readout Tracker
Direct Airline Reservations Ticketing
Directional Automatic Realignment of Trajectory
Disappearing Automatic Retaliatory Target
Dual Axis Rate Transducer
Dynamic Acoustic Response Trigger
DAS Data Acquisition System
Data Analysis System
Data Automation System
Design Analysis System
Detector Angular Subtense
Digital Analogue Simulator
Directorate of Aerodrome Standards (of CAA)
District Auditors Society
DME-based Azimuth System
Dynamically Alterable System
DAS/CM Directory Assistance Systems/Computer and Microfilm
DASA Defense Atomic Support Agency (USDOD) (formerly Armed Forces Special Weapons Project now Defense Nuclear Agency)
DASC Double Aperture Speckle Camera
DASD Direct Access Storage Device
DASE Differential Absorption and Scattering technique
DASH Differential Air-Speed Hold
Drone Anti-Submarine Helicopter
Dynamic ALGOL String Handling
DASHER Dynamic Analysis of Shells of Revolution
DASI Diffusion of Arsenic in Silicon
DASIAC Defense Atomic Support Agency Information and Analysis Center (USDOD)
DASP Discrete Analogue Signal Processing
DASS Defined Antigen Substrate Sphere
Demand Assignment Signalling and Switching
Direct Access Signalling System
DASSC Double-Aperture Speckle Shearing Camera
DAST Design Architecture, Software and Testing (a committee of USAF)
Digital Aircraft System Trainer
Division of Applied Science and Technology (of FWPCA (USA))
Drones for Aerodynamic and Structural Testing
DASYS Data System Environment Simulator
DAT Data Abstract Tape
Designation-Acquisition-Track
Desk-top Analysis Tool
DATAB Dataspecialisten AB (Sweden)
DATACON Systems/Data Processing Conference
DATAN Data Analysis
DATAR Delegation General a l'Amenagement du Territoire et a l'Action Regional (France) (Government Regional Planning Agency)
Digital Auto Transducer and Recorder
DATAS Data in Associative Storage
DATE Dial Access Technical Education (telephone information service of IEEE (USA))
DATEC Differential and Alignment Unit and Total Error Corrector
DATEL Data Telecommunication
DAtF Deutsche Atomforum (Germany) (German Atomic Forum)
DATGEN Data Generator Utility Routines
DATICO Digital Automatic Tape Intelligence Check-out
DME-based Azimuth System
DATOM Data Aids for Training, Operations, and Maintenance
DATS Despun Antenna Test Satellite
Developing Area Transportation System
DATUM Dokumentation—und Ausbildungszentrum fur Theorie und Methode der Regional forschung (Germany) (Documentation and Education Centre for the Theory and Method of Regional Research)
DAU Data Adaptor Unit
DAV Data-Above-Voice
DAVC Delayed Automatic Volume Control
DAVI Dynamic Anti-resonant Vibration Isolator
Dynamic Antiresonant Vibration Isolator
DAW Deutscher Arbeitskreis Wasserforschung (Germany) (German Water Research Association)
DAWID Device for Automatic Word Identification
DAWN Drug Abuse Warning Network (of Drug Enforcement Administration (USA))
DAWNS Design of Aircraft Wing Structures
DB Decibel
Deutsche Budesbahn (Germany) (German Federal Railway)
DBA Deutsche Bauakademie (Germany) (German Building Academy)
DBAM Data Base Access Method
DBAS Delmarva Business Advisory Service (University of Delaware (USA))
DBAWG Database Administration Working Group (of British Computer Society and CODASYL Data Description Language Committee)
DBBD Dibromopolybutadiene
DBBOL Digital Building Block Oriented Language
DBBTZ Dibutylaminomethyl Benzotriazole
DBCATA Disposable Barrel Cartridge, Area Target Ammunition
DBCP Dibromochloropropane
DBCS Deterministic Bounded Cellular Space

DBDA	Database Design Aid
DBDL	Data Base Definition Language
DBE	Design Basis Earthquake
DBF	Digital Beam-Forming
DBH	Development Big Hydrofoil
DBHS	DATA Base Handling System
DBI	Deutsche Bibliotheksinstitut (Germany) (German Libraries Institute)
DBK	Deutsche Bibliothekskonferenz (Germany) (German Libraries Conference)
DBL	Data Base Language
DBM	Data Buffer Module
DBMIST	Direction des Bibliotheques, des Musees et de l'Information Scientifique et Technique (France) (Directorate of Libraries, Museums and Scientific and Technical Information)
DBMS	Data Base Management System
	Data Based Management System
DBN	DE BEERS Boron Nitride
	Dibutylnitrosamine
DBNS	Digital Bombing and Navigation System
DBOMP	Data Base Organization and Management Processor
DBOS	Disc-Based Operating System
DBP	Dibutylphthalate
DBR	Deutscher Bildungsrat (Germany) (German Education Council)
	Directorate of Biosciences Research (of DRB (Canada))
	Division of Building Research (of National Research Council, Canada)
DBS	Dibenzylsulphide
	Direct Broadcast Satellite
	Direct Broadcasting via Satellite
	Division of Biological Standards (of MRC)
	Division of Biologics Standards (of FDA (USA)) (now Bureau of Biologics)
	Dominion Bureau of Statistics (Canada)
	Doppler Beam-Sharpening
DBSO	Dibenzylsulphoxide
DBSS	Dutch BENELUX Simulation Society
DBST	Double Bituminous Surface Treatment
DBTDL	Dibutylin Dilaurate
DBTG	Data Base Task Group (of CODASYL)
DBTT	Ductile to Brittle Transition Temperature
DBTU	Dibutyl Thiourea
DBV	Deutscher Betoverein (Germany) (German Concrete Association)
	Deutscher Bibliotheksverband (Germany) (German Library Association)
DC	Antomet-Directional Control–Antomatic Meterological Compensation
	Danube Commission (Hungary)
	Data Classifier
	Dimensional Co-ordination
	Diphenylcyanoarsine
	prefix to numbered series of Dimensional Co-ordination Bulletins issues by MPBW
	prefix—preceded by date/number—of Draft Standards available for Public Comment issued by BSI
DCA	Defense Communications Agency (USDOD)
	Deoxycholate-Citrate Agar
	Department of Civil Aviation (Australia)
	Diagnostic Communication Ability
	Dichloracetylene
	Directorate of Civil Aviation (Jordan)
	Dynamic Channel Allocation
DCAA	Defense Contract Audit Agency (USDOD)
DCAE	Direction des Constructions Aeronautiques (of DGA (France))
DCAS	Defense Contract Administration Service (USDOD)

DCASA	Dyers and Colourists Association of South Africa
DCASEF	Defense Communications Agency System Engineering Facility (USDOD)
DCASR	Defense Contract Administrative Service Region (USDOD)
DCB	Decimal Currency Board (Australia)
	Double Cantilever Beam
DCBA	Damage Control Breathing Apparatus
DCBRE	Defence Chemical, Biological and Radiation Establishment (of DRB, Canada)
DCBRL	Defence Chemical, Biological, and Radiation Laboratories (of DRB) (now DCBRE)
DCC	Deck Compression Chamber
	Dicyclohexyl-carbodiimide
	Direct Contact Condensation
DCCA	Design Change Cost Analysis
DCCC	Domestic Coal Consumers Council
DCCG	Digital Check Character Generator
DCCRP	Domestic Council Committee on the Right of Privacy (USA)
DCCS	Distributed Command and Control System
DCD	Digital Correlation Detector
DCDB	Digital Cartographic Data Base
DCDFM	Dichlorodifluoromethane
DCDM	Digitally Controlled Delta Modulation
DCDMA	Diamond Core Drill Manufacturers Association (USA)
DCDS	Digital Control Design System
DCE	Data Circuit-terminating Equipment
	Dichloroethane
	Differential Compound Engine
	Domestic Credit Expansion
DCEO	Defense Communications Engineering Office (of Defense Communications Agency (USDOD))
DCF	Discounted Cash Flow
DCFP	Dynamic Cross-Field Photomultiplier
DCGFF	Diode-Coupled Gata Flip-Flop
DCGM	Decorticated Groundnut Meal
DCHN	Dicylohexylammonium Nitrite
DCHX	Direct Contact Heat Exchanger
DCI	Dispersive Corrosion Inhibitor
DCIC	Defense Ceramic Information Center (Battelle Memorial Institute (USA)) (now part of Metals and Ceramics Information Center)
DCIEM	Defence and Civil Institute of Environmental Medicine (of CRAD (DND)) (Canada)
DCIO	Direct Channel Interface Option
DCL	Defence Contractors List (of MOD)
	Direct Communications Link (a two satellites system connecting Washington and Moscow)
	Division of Chemical Literature of the American Chemical Society (USA)
DCLA	District of Columbia (USA) Library Association
DCLC	Drift Cyclotron Loss Cone
DCM	Defensive Counter Manoeuvring
	Dichloromethane
	Diversified Composite Materials
DCMA	Dry Color Manufacturers Association (USA)
DCMD	Descending Contralateral Movement Detector
DCMX	Dichloro-meta-xylenol
DCN	Direction des Constructions Navales (France) (Board of Naval Construction)
DCOA	Direct Current Operational Amplifier
DCOL	Direct Control Oriented Language
DCP	Defense Concept Plan (USDOD)
	Development Concept Paper
	Development Cost Plan
	Dicalcium Phosphate
	Digestible Crude Protein
	Digital Cursor Positioner
	Dry Chemical Powder

DCPA	Defense Civil Preparedness Agency (USDOD) Dicyclopentenyl Acrylate
DCPD	Dicyclopentadiene
DCPL	Distributed Control Programming Language
DCPM	Decision Critical Path Method
DCPSK	Differentially-Coherent Phase-Shift-Keyed
DCPU	Data Communication Protocol Unit (of Dept of Industry)
DCR	Digital Coded Radar Dried Coffee Residue Dual Cycle Rifle
DCRF	Die Casting Research Foundation (of the American Die Casting Institute (USA))
DCRP	Direct Current Reverse Polarity
DCRT	Division of Computer Research and Technology (of NIH (HEW) (USA))
DCS	Damage Control Suit Data Control System Decompression Sickness Defence Communications System Dichlorosilane Digital Command System Directa Centrala je Statistics (Romania) (Central Statistics Office) Distributed Computer System Distributed Computing System prefix to numbered series of technical reports issued by Department of Computer Science, Rutgers—the State University, New Brunswick (USA)
DCSC	Defense Construction Supply Center (USDOD)
DCSM	Deterministic Complete Sequential Machine
DCSP	Defense Communications Satellite Program (USDOD) (formerly IDCSP) Direct Current, Straight Polarity
DCSRDA	Deputy Chief of Staff Research, Development and Acquisition (US Army)
DCT	Detection, Classification and Targeting Digital Communications Terminal Disaster Control Team Discrete Cosine Transform
DCTL	Direct Coupled Transistor Logic
DCTM	Directional Control Test Missile
DCVD	Directorate Co-ordinated Valve Development (MOD)
DCWCS	Direction Control and Warning Communications System
DC^3I	Distributed Command, Control, Communications and Intelligence
DD	Definite Decoding prefix to numbered series of Drafts for Development issued by BSI
DDA	Delhi Development Authority (India) Diemaking and Diecutting Association (USA) Digital Differential Analyzer Dynamics Differential Analyzer
DDAM	Dynamic Design-Analysis Method
DDAS	Digital Data Acquisition System
DDB	Double-Declining Balance
DDC	Data Display Controller Deck Decompression Chamber Defense Documentation Center (USDOD) (now DTIC (USDOD)) Dewey Decimal Classification Diagnostic Display Console Direct Digital Control Dual Data Collection
DDCMP	Digital Data Communications Message Protocol
DDD	Detailed Data Display Direct Distance Dialling
DDDIC	Department of Defense Disease and Injury Code (USDOD)
DDF	Data Description Facility Design Disclosure Format
DDG	Deutsche Datel GmbH (Germany)
DDI	Depth Deviation Indicator Digital Display Indicator Direct Dialling-In
DDL	Data Definition Language Data Description Language Differential Distribution Laws Digital Data Link Digital system Design Language
DDLC	Data Description Languages Committee (of CODASYL)
DDM	Data Demand Module Difference-in-Depth-of-Modulation
DDMS	Department for the Design of Machine Systems (Cranfield Institute of Technology)
DDN	DREAM Design Notation
DDNP	Diazodinitrophenol
DDP	Department of Defence Production (Canada) Dispersed and Distributed Data Processing Distributed Data Processing
DDR	Decision-Directed Receiver Double-Drift-Region
DDR&E	Directorate of Defense Research and Engineering (USDOD)
DDS	Deep-Diving System Deployable Defence System Development Documentation System Digital Dynamics Simulator Discrete Depth Sampler Doped Deposited Silica
DDT	Deflagration to Detonation Transition Department of Development and Technology (of ESTEC) Dichlorodiphenyltrichlorethane Dynamic Debugging Technique
DDT&E	Design, Development, Test and Evaluation
DDTA	Derivative Differential Thermal Analysis
DDVP	Dimethyldichlorovinyl Phosphate
DDVR	Displayed Data Video Recorder
DE	Department of Employment Destroyer Escort Deterministic Equivalent Diatomaceous Earth
DE-H	Destroyer Escort Hydrofoil
DEA	Dairy Engineers Association (merged with PPA) Department of Economic Affairs (disbanded 1969) Department of External Affairs (Canada) Diethanolamine Diethylamine Drug Enforcement Administration (of Dept of Justice (USA))
DEACON	Direct English Access and Control
DEAE	Diethylaminoethyl
DEB	Digital European Backbone program (of Defense Communications Agency (USA))
DEBA	Dynamically-loaded Engineering Bearing Analysis
DECA	Digital Electronic Countermeasures Analyser
DECARP	Desert Encroachment Control And Rehabilitation Programme (India)
DECCO	Defense Commercial Communications Office (of Defense Communications Agency (DOD))
DECHEMA	Deutsche Gesellschaft für Chemisches Apparatewesen (Germany) (German Society for Chemical Apparatus)
DECIEM	Defence and Civil Institute of Environmental Medicine (of DRB (Canada))
DECL	Diode-Emitter Coupled Logic
DECM	Deception Electronic Counter-Measures

DECONSULT Deutsche Eisenbahn Consulting (Germany)

DECUS DIGITAL EQUIPMENT Computer Users Society (USA)

DEDAAS Digital Electrophysiological Data Acquisition and Analysis System

DEDUCOM Deductive Communicator

DEE Diethoxyethylene
Diethyl Ether
Digital Events Evaluator
Digited Evaluation Equipment

DEEB Development and Economy in Educational Building

DEEC Digital Electronic Engine Control

DEEP Data Exception Error Protection
Describe Each Element in the Procedure

DEEPSEAT Deep-Sea System for Evaluating Acoustic Transducers

DEES Dynamic Electromagnetic Environment Simulator
Dynamic Electronic Environment Simulator

DEF Diethyl Fumarate
Duck Embryo Fibroblasts
prefix to numbered series of Defence Specifications issued by the Ministry of Defence and published by HMSO

DEF(AUST) prefix to numbered series of Australian Defence Specifications and Standards issued by Defence (Industrial) Committee, Dept. of Defence (Australia)

DEFCON Defence Contract (MOD)

DEFI Digital Electronic Fuel Injection

DEFSATCOM Defence Satellite Communication System

DEFT Direct Electronic Fourier Transforms

DEFUNCT Desirability Function

DEG Diethylene Glycol

DEGS Diethylene Glycol Succinate

DEH Deepwater Escort Hydrofoil
Direct Electrical Heating

DEHA Diethylhydroxylamine

DEI Direction de l'Electronique et de l'Informatique (France)

DEIMOS Development and Investigation of a Military Orbital System

DEIS DOD (USDOD) Worldwide Energy Information System

DEK Data -och Elektronikkomitten (Sweden) (Commission on Computers and Electronics)
Deutsche Elektrotechnische Kommission (Germany) (German Electrotechnical Commission)

DEKRA West German Motor Vehicle Standards Institution

DEL Direct Exchange Line

DELDIS Delay Equalizer Selection

DELFIC Department of Defense Land Fallout Interpretive Code (USDOD)

DELIMITER Definitive Limit Evaluator

DELS Direct Electrical Linkage System

DELTA Daily Electronic Lane Tole Audit
Decision box, Event box, Logic box, Time arrow and Activity box

DELTIC Delay Line Time Compressor

DEM Dynode Electron Multiplier

DEMA Data Entry Management Association (USA)

DEMATEL Decision-Making and Trial Evaluation Laboratory (Battelle (Geneva))

DEMD Digital Engine Monitor Display

DEMKO Dansk Elektrische Materialkontrol (Denmark) (Danish Board for the Approval of Electrical Equipment)

DEMON Decision Mopping via Optimum Go-No Networks
Diminishing Error Method for Optimization of Networks

DEMOS DENDENKOSHA Multi-access On-line System
Directorate of Estate Management Overseas (of PSA (DOE))

DEMP Diethylmethylphosphate
Dispersed Electro-Magnetic Pulse

DEMPT Diethylmethylphosphorothionate

DEMS Defensively Equipped Merchant Ship

DEMUR Double Electron Muon Resonance

DEMVPI Department of Engineering Mechanics, Virginia Polytechnic Institute (USA)

DEn Department of Energy
Direction des Engins (DGA) (France)

DEN Diethylnitrosamine

DENACAL Departamento Nacional de Acueductos y Alacantarillados (Nicaragua)

DENTEL Departmento Nacional de Telecomunicacoes (Brazil) (National Department of Telecommunications)

DEP Deflection Error Probable
Department of Employment and Productivity (formerly Ministry of Labour) (now Department of Employment)
Di-isopropyl Ethylphosphate

DEPCT Diethyl Phosphorochloridothionate

DEPI Differential Equations Pseudo-code Interpreter

DEPICT Defense Electronics Products Integrated Control Technique

DEPLOC Depot-Location

DEPMIS Depot Management Information System (US Army)

DEQMAR Determining Economic Quantities of Maintenance Resources

DER Division of Environmental Radiation (Bureau of Radiological Health (USA))

DERE Dounreay Experimental Reactor Establishment (of UKAEA)

DERL Defence Electronics Research Laboratory (India)

DERT Division Électronique, Radioélectricité et Télécommunications (of SEE (France))

DERV Diesel Engine Road Vehicle

DES Data Encryption Standard
Department of Education and Science
Design and Evaluation System
Diethylstilboestrol
Draft Environmental Statement
Dynamic Environment Simulator
Federal Information Processing Data Encryption Standard (of NBS (USA))

DESC Defense Electronics Supply Center (DSA (USDOD))

DESCNET Data Network on Environmentally Significant Chemicals

DESIDOC Defence Scientific Information and Documentation Centre (India)

DESU Delhi Electric Supply Undertaking (India)

DESY Deutsches Elektronen Synchtronon (Germany)

DETA Diethylenediamine
Diethylenetriamine

DETC Defence Engineering Terminology Committee

DETE Distributed Electronic Telephone Exchange

DETG Defense Energy Task Group (USDOD)

DETS Diesel Engine Tuning System

DETU Diethyl Thiourea

DEU Data Exchange Unit

DEUA Diesel Engineers and Users Association

DEUCE Digital Electronic Universal Computing Engine

DEULA Deutsche Lehranstaeten für Agrartechnik (Germany) (German Farm Machinery Schools)

DEUS Dual Energy Use Systems

DEV Duck Embryo Vaccine

DEVCO Committee for Standardization in the Developing Countries (of ISO)

DEVIL Direct Evaluation of Index Language

DEVSIS Development of Sciences Information System (a project of IDRC, ILO, OECD, UNDP, and UNESCO)

DEVT Data-Entry Virtual Terminal

DEW Deutsche Edelstahlwerke (Germany)
Distant Early Warning

DEWIZ Distant Early Warning Identification Zone

DEXAN Digital Experimental Airborne Navigator

DF Decontamination Factor
Deuterium Fluoride
Direction Finding
Dissipation Factor

DFA Desferrioxamine

DFAA Dissolved Free Amino Acids

DFAM Derived File Access Method

DFB Deciduous Fruit Board (South Africa)
Distributed Feedback laser
Distribution Fuse Board

DFBW Digital Fly-By-Wire

DFC Dairy Farmers of Canada (Canada)
Data Flow Control
Digital Frequency Control

DFCS Digital Flight Control System

DFDAU Digital Flight Data Acquisition Unit

DFDC Defence Force Development Committee (Dept of Defence (Australia))

DFDP Distribution-Free Doppler Processor

DFDR Digital Flight Data Recorder

DFET Drift Field Effect Transistor

DFG Deutsche Forschungsgemeinschaft (German Research Association)

DFGA Distributed Floating Gate Amplifier

DFH Developmental Fast Hydrofoil

DFI Direct Flame Impingement

DFIK Dansk Forening for Industriel Kvalitetskontrol (Denmark) (Danish Society for Industrial Quality Control)

DFISA Dairy and Food Industries Supply Association (USA)

DFL Deutsche Forschungsanstalt fur Luftfahrt (Germany) (German Aeronautical Research Institute)
Display Formatting Language

DFLD Distribution Free Logic Design

DFOA Desferrioxamine

DFOLS Depth of Flash Optical Landing System

DFP Defluorinated Phosphate
Diisopropylflurophosphate

DFR Decreasing Failure Rate
Delayed Free Recall
DOUNREAY Fast Reactor (closed down 1977)

DFRA Drop Forging Research Association

DFRC Dryden Flight Research Center (of NASA (USA))

DFS Direct Function Search
Dispersive Fourier Spectroscopy

DFSC Defence Force Structure Committee (Dept of Defence (Australia))
Defense Fuel Supply Center (of Defense Supply Agency (USDOD))

DFSM Deterministic Finite-State Machine

DFT Digital Facility Terminal
Discrete Fourier Transform

DFTI Distance From Threshold Indicator

DFTS Dispersive Fourier Transform Spectroscopy

DFVLR Deutsche Forschungs- und Versuchsanstalt fur Luft- und Raumfahrt (Germany) (German Aerospace Research and Testing Institute)

DFW Diffusion Welding

DFWES Direct Fire Weapons Effect Simulator

DG Degaussing
Diesel Generator
prefix to numbered series of Defence Guides issued by the Ministry of Defence

DGA Delegation Generale pour l'Armement (France)
Dense Grade Aggregate
Diglycolamine

DGAC Direction Generation de l'Aviation Civile (France)

DGaO Deutsche Gesellschaft fur angewandte Optik (Germany) (German Society for Applied Optics)

DGAS Double Glazing Advisory Service (of IGA)

DGB Deutsche Gewerskschaftsbund (Germany) (German Trade Union Confederation)

DGC Diamond Grain Configuration

DGCMA Defense and Government Contracts Management Association (USA)

DGD Deutsche Gesellschaft fur Dokumentation (Germany) (Germany Society for Documentation)
Digalactosyl Diglyceride

DGE Division of Geothermal Energy (of DOE (USA))

DGEBA Diglycidyl Ether of Bisphenol A

DGF Deutsche Gesellschaft fur Flugwissenschaften (Germany) (German Society for Aeronautical Sciences)

DGFP Deutsche Gesellschaft fuer Personalfuhrung (Germany) (German Society for Personnel Management)

DGG Deutsche Gesellschaft fur Galvanotechnik (Germany) (German Society for Electroplating)
Deutsche Glastechnische Gesellschaft (Germany) (German Society for Glass Technology)

DGI Direction Generale des Impots (France)
Disseminated Gonococcal Infection

DGK Deutsche Geodatisch Kommission (Germany) (German Geodetic Commission)
Deutsche Gessellschaft fuer Kybernetik (Germany) (German Cybernetics Society)

DGLR Deutsche Gesellschaft fur Luft-und Raumfahrt (Germany) (German Society for Aeronautics and Space)

DGLRM Deutsche Gesellschaft fur Luft-und Raumfahrtmedizin (Germany) (German Society for Aeromedical Science)

DGM Digital Group Multiplexers

DGMR Directorate of Petroleum and Mineral Resources (Saudi Arabia)

DGMW Double Gimballed Momentum Wheel

DGN Deutsche Gessellschaft fuer Nuclearmedizin (Germany) (German Nuclear Medicine Society)

DGON Deutsche Gessellschaft fuer Ortung-und Navigation (Germany) (German Society for Radiolocation and Navigation)

DGOR Deutsche Gesellschaft fur Operations Research (Germany) (German Society for Operational Research)

DGP Dangerous Goods Panel (of ICAO)

DGRST Delegation Generale a la Recherche Scientifique et Technique (France) (Government Scientific and Technical Research Agency)

DGSO Director-General of Safety (Operations) (of CAA)

DGTD Directorate General of Technical Development (India)

DGU Display Generator Unit

DGVS Doppler Ground Velocity System

DGZfP — Deutsche Gesellschaft fur Zerstorungsfreie Pruvfverfahren (Germany) (German Society for Non-destructive Testing)

DH — Design Handbook
District Heating
Double Heterostructure

DHA — Dehydroepiandrosterone
District Health Authority
District Heating Association

DHAA — Dehydro-Ascorbic Acid

DHAP — Dihydroxyacetone Phosphate

DHC — Dihydrochalcone

DHE — Dihydroergotamine

DHFDH — Dihydrofolate Dehydrogenase

DHHS — Department of Health and Human Services (USA)

DHIA — Dairy Herd Improvement Associations (USA)

DHLLP — Digalactosyl Diglyceride
Direct-High-Level Language Processor

DHN — Diretoria de Hidrografia e Navegacão (Brazilian Navy) (Directorate of Hydrography and Navigation)

DHO — Dihydrogen Oxide

DHOase — Dihydroorotase

DHRS — Data Handling Recording System

DHS — Data Handling System
Dual Hardness Steel

DHSS — Department of Health and Social Security

DHSV — Down-Hole Safety Valve

DHT — Dihydro-Testerone
Discrete Hilbert Transform

DHX — Dump Heat Exchanger

DI — Delegation a l'Informatique (France) (Central Office for Data Processing)
Desert Institute (Egypt)

DIA — Defense Intelligence Agency (USDOD)

DIAC — Distributed Intelligence Acquisition and Control

DIAL — Databank Inquiry Answering Link
Differential Absorption LIDAR

DIALATOR — Diagnostic Logic Simulator

DIALOG — Direction for Army Logistics (US Army)

DIALS — DENDENKOSHA Immediate Arithmetic and Library Calculation System
Digital Integrated Automatic Landing System

DIAM — Data Independent Accessing Model
Data Independent Architecture Model

DIANE — Direct Information Access Network for Europe

DIAS — Dublin Institute for Advanced Studies (Eire)

DIC — Digital Incremental Computer
Digital Integrating Computer
Disseminated Intravascular Coagulation
Disseminated Intravascular Coagulopathy

DICA — Direction des Carburants (of the Ministere de l'Industrie et de la Recherche (France)) (Directorate of the Gas, Oil and Hydrocarbon Processing Industries)

DICAP — Digital Circuit Analysis Programme

DICASS — Directional Command Activated Sonobuoy System

DICB — Demolition Industry Conciliation Board

DICE — Digital Intercontinental Conversion Equipment
Digital Interface Countermeasures Equipment
Digitally Implemented Communications Experiment
Digitally Inter-laced Countermeasures Equipment

DICEF — Digital Communications Experimental Facility (USAF)

DICORS — Diver Communication Research System

DICTA — District Council Technical Association

DICUP — Dicumyl Peroxide

DID — Data Item Description (series issued by USDOD)
Drainage and Irrigation Department (Malaysia)

DIDA — Differential In-Depth Analysis

DIDDF — Dual Input Discrete Describing Function

DIDENT — Distortion Identity

DIDF — Dual Input Describing Function

DIDO — Device Independent Disk Open

DIDS — Defense Integrated Data System (of DLA (USDOD))
Digital Information Display System DLSC (USDOD) Integrated Data System

DIECAST — Display Interaction Enhancing Computer Aided Shape Technique

DIEN — Diethyltriamine

DIES — Dipole Environment for SGEMP

DIF — Deutsches Institut fur Forderung des Industriellen Fuhrungsnachwuchses (Germany) (German Institute for Industrial Management Development)
Drug Information Fulltext (data file of ASHP (USA))

DIFAR — Directional-Frequency Analysis and Ranging

DIFFTRAP — Digital Fast Fourier Transform Processor

DIFM — Digital Instantaneous Frequency Measurement

DIFMOS — Dual Injection Floating-gate Metal Oxide Semiconductor

DIG — Doppler-Inertial Gyrocompass

DIGITAC — Digital Tactical Aircraft Control

DIGS — Digital Inertial Guidance System

DIHE — Dorset Institute of Higher Education

DIHEST — Directly Induced High Explosive Simulation Technique

DIL — Digital Integrated Logic
Doppler Inertial LORAN

DILS — Doppler Inertial LORAN System
Doppler Instrument Landing System

DIM — Differential Interference Microscopy
Display Image Manipulation

DIMA — Direct Imaging Mass Analysis
Direct Imaging Mass Analyzer

DIMACE — Digital Monitor and Control Equipment

DIMATE — Depot Installed Maintenance Automatic Test Equipment

DIMDI — Deutsches Institute fur Medizinische Dokumentation und Information (Germany) (German Institute for Medical Documentation and Information)

DIME — Disc Management Environment

DIMELEC — Direction des Industries Mecaniques, Electriques et Electroniques (France)

DIMES — Defense Integrated Management Engineering System (US Army)
Development of Improved Management Engineering Systems (USDOD)
Digalactosyl Diglyceride
Digital Image Manipulation and Enhancement System

DIMOS — Double Implanted MOS

DIMP — Defence Industry and Materiel Policy Division (Dept of Defence (Australia))
Diisopropyl Methyl Phosphonate

DIMPLE — Deuterium Moderated Pile Low Energy

DIMS — Data Information and Manufacturing System
Distributed Intelligence Micro-computer Systems

DIMUS — Digital Multi-beam Steering System Sonar

DIN — Deutsche Industrie-Norm (German Industrial Standard)
Deutsches Institut für Normung (Germany) (German Standards Institute)

DINA — Diesel Nacional (Mexico)
Direct Noise Amplification

DINAP — Digital Filter Analysis Programme

DINP — Diisononyl Phthalate

DIOA Differential Input Operational Amplifier

DIODE Digital Input/Output Display Equipment

DIOS Distributed Input/Output System

DIP Defence Industry Productivity Programme (of Department of Industry, Trade and Commerce) (Canada)
Dual-in-line Package
Ductile Iron Pipe
Dynamic Inclined Plane

DIPA Diamond Industrial Products Association
Ductile Iron Pipe Association

DIPE Diisopropyl Ether

DIPEC Defense Industrial Plant Equipment Center (USDOD)

DIPS DENDENKOSHA Information Processing System
Digital Information Processing System

DIQAP Defence Industries Quality Assurance Panel (of MOD and Industry)

DIR Defect Introduction Rate
Defence Industrial Research Programme (of Defence Research Board (Canada))
Digital Instrumentation Radar
Draft ISO Recommendation

DIRAC Direct Access

DIRK Dosemeter Issue and Record Keeping

DIRSO Defense Industrial Resources Support Office (USDOD)

DIS Defense Investigative Service (of USDOD)
Dialectic Information System
Digalactosyl Diglycerideafta
Digital Integration System
Distributed Intelligence System
Ductile Iron Society (USA)
prefix to numbered series of Draft International Standards (issued by ISO)

DISA Diffraction Size Frequency Analyser

DISAC Digital Simulator and Computer

DISC Differential-Scatter
Direct-Injected Stratified Charge
Distribution Stock Control System
Domestic International Sales Corporation (of Domestic and International Business Administration (Dept of Commerce (USA))

DISCLOSE DUNCHURCH INDUSTRIAL STAFF TRAINING COLLEGE Learn Ourselves Exercise

DISCO Defense Industrial Security Clearance Office (USDOD)

DISCOID Direct Scan Operating with Integrating Delays

DISCOLA Digital Integrated Solid-state Controller for Low-cost Automation

DISCOM Digital Selective Communications

DISCON Defence Integrated Secure Communications Network

DISCOP Digital Simulation of Continuous Processes

DISCOS Disturbance Compensation System

DISCUS Data-Line Concentration System
Disposal and Collection User Simulation
Distributed Source Conducting-medium Underground-system Simulator

DISE Digital Systems Education (a project of University of Pittsburgh Department of Electrical Engineering (USA))

DISFP Disc Indexed Sequential File Management Package

DISH Differential Integrating Samp and Hold

DISID Disposable Seismic Intrusion Detector

DISLAN Display Language

DISM Defense-Institute of Security Management (USDOD)

DISPOSAL Developing Improved Sizing Procedures Over Sanitary Area Landfills

DISS Directorate of Information Systems and Settlement (of the Stock Exchange)

DISSPLA Display Integrated Software System and Plotting Language

DISTRIPRESS Association for the Promotion of the International Circulation of the Press

DIT Dual Input Transponder

DITA Design-In Test Points and Alarms

DITACS Digital Tactical System

DITB Distributive Industry Training Board

DITC Department of Industry, Trade and Commerce (Canada)

DITE Divertor Injection Tokamak Experiment (of Culham Laboratory) (UKAEA)

DITRAN Diagnostic FORTRAN

DIV Data In Voice

DIVA Digital Inquiry—Voice Answer

DIVADS Divisional Air Defence System

DIVEMA Divinyl Ethermaleic Anhydride

DIVIC Digital Variable Increment Computer

DIW Deutsches Institut für Wirtschaftforschung (Germany) (German Institute for Economic Research)

DJI Dow-Jones Index (USA)

DJNR Dow-Jones News Retrieval (USA)

DKfo Deutsche Kommission fur Ozeanographie (Germany) (German Commission for Oceanography)

DKG Deutsche Kautschuk Gesellschaft (Germany) (German Rubber Association)

DKGA Diketogulonic Acid

DKI Deutsches Kunstoff Institut (Germany) (German Plastics Institute)

DKS Dansk Kartografisk Selskab (Denmark) (Cartographic Society of Denmark)

DL Daresbury Laboratory (of Science Research Council)
Derived Limit
Diode Logic
prefix to numbered-lettered series of Defence Lists issued by the Ministry of Defence and published by HMSO

DLA Defense Logistics Agency (USDOD)
Distributed Lumped Active
Documentation, Libraries and Archives Directorate (of UNESCO)

DLC Data Link Control
Direct Lift Control

DLCB Drifting Limited OR Low Capability Buoy

DLCN Distributed Loop Computer Network

DLCO-EA Desert Locust Control Organization for Eastern Africa (Ethiopia)

DLCS Data-Line Concentration System

DLD Dark Line Defect
Digital Light Deflector

DLDBS Distributed Loop Data Base System

DLDV Differential Laser Doppler Velocimeter

DLE Digital Local Exchange

DLFET Depletion-mode Load Field Effect Transistor

DLG Deutsche Landwirtschafts Gesellschaft (Germany) (German Agricultural Society)
Dynamic Lead Guidance

DLH Deutsche Lufthansa (Germany)

DLI Department of Labour and Industry (Australia)

DLIFLC Defense Language Institute Foreign Language Center (USDOD)

DLIMP Descriptive Language for Implementing Macro-Processors

DLIR Depot Level Inspection and Repair
Downward Looking Infra-Red

DLL Delay Lock Loop
Dial Long Line
DLM Depolarized Light Mixing
DLMA Decorative Lighting Manufacturers and Distributors Association
DLMS Digital Land-Mass System
DLOGS Division Logistics System (US Army)
DLOR Downward Light Output Ratio
DLP Digital Laser Printer
Division of Library Programs (USOE)
Double-Level Polysilicon
Dynamic Limit Programming
DLPC Dilauroylphosphatidylcholine
DLR Deutsche Versuchsanstalt fur Luft-und Raumfahrt (Germany) (German Aeronautics and Space Laboratory)
DLRV Dual-mode Lunar Roving Vehicle
DLS Data Librarian System
Difference Limen Shift
Dital Logic Simulator
DME-based Landing System
DLSC Defense Logistics Services Center (USDOD)
DLSIE Defense Logistics Studies Information Exchange (US Army)
DLT Depletion-Layer Transitor
Development Land Tax
Direct Linear Transformation
DLTDP Dilaurylthio-di-propionate
DLTS Deep Level Transient-capacitance Spectroscopy
DLW Diesel Locomotive Works (India)
DM Arsenical Adamsite
Data Manager
Delta Modulation
Design Manual
Design Memorandum
Diphenylaminochloroarsine
prefix to numbered series of reports issued by Division of Mechanical Engineering (of NRC (Canada))
DMA Defence Manufacturers Association
Defense Mapping Agency (USDOD)
Delegation Ministerielle pour l'Armament (France) (of the Ministry of the Armed Forces)
Dimethylamine
Direct Memory Access
Division of Military Application (of ERDA (USA)) (formerly of USAEC)
Dominion Marine Association (Canada)
DMAA Dimethylacetamide
Direct Mail Advertising Association (USA)
DMAAC Defense Mapping Agency Aerospace Center (of DMA (USDOD))
DMAB Dimethylamine Borane
DMAC Dimethylacetamide
Direct Memory Access Channel
Diving Medical Advisory Committee (of AODC)
DMACS Descriptive Macro Code Generation System
DMAHC Defense Mapping Agency Hydrographic Center (of DMA (USDOD))
DMAHTC Defense Mapping Agency Hydrographic/Topographic Center (USDOD)
DMAP Dimethylaminophenol
DMAPA Dimethylaminopropylamine
DMAPN Dimethylaminoproionitrile
DMAPP Dimethylallyl Pyrophosphate
DMat prefix to series of reports issued by MOD(PE) Directorate of Materials
DMATC Defense Mapping Agency Topographic Center (of DMA (USDOD))
DMB Double Mouldboard ploughing
DMBA Dimethylbenzanthracene
DMBC Direct Material Balance Control
DMC Direct Manufacturing Cost
Dough Moulding Compound
DMD Digital Message Device
Dimethylmetadioxane
Double Meridian Distance
Duchenne Muscular Dystrophy
DMDEL Dimethyldiethyl Lead
DME Distance Measuring Equipment
Division of Mechanical Engineering (of NCR (Canada))
Dynamic-Mission Equivalent
DMED Digital Message Entry Device
DMET Distance Measuring Equipment TACAN
Distance Measuring Equipment with respect to Time
DMETU Dimethyl Thiourea
DMF Digital Matched Filter
Dimethyl Formamide
DMFA Dimethylformamide
DMFE Division of Magnetic Fusion Energy (of ERDA (USA))
DMI Department of Manpower and Immigration (Canada)
Department of Manufacturing Industry (Australia)
Division of Manpower Intelligence (of Health Manpower Education Bureau (HEW) (USA))
DMIC Defense Metals Information Center (Battelle Memorial Institute (USA)) (now part of Metals and Ceramics Information Center)
DMIS Distribution/transportation Management Information System
DMJTC Differential Multi-Junction Thermal Converter
DML Data Macro Language
Data Manipulation Language
Database Manipulation Language
Dimyristoyl Lecithin
DMLS Doppler Microwave Landing System
DMM Defense Market Measures system (USDOD)
Digital Multi-Meter
DMMP Dimethyl Methylphosphonate
DMN Dimethylnitrosamine
DMO Demetallized Oil
DMOD Displacement Measuring Optical Device
DMOS Double-diffused Metal Oxide Semiconductor
DMOST Double-diffused Metal Oxide Semiconductor Technology
DMP Digital Microprocessor
Diisopropyl Methylphosphate
Dimethylphosphate
DMPA Dimyristoylphosphatidic Acid
DMPCT Dimethyl Phosphorochloridothionate
DMPE Dimethoxphenylethylamine
DMPP Display and Multi-Purpose Processor
DMR Data Management Routines
Dynamic-Mechanical Response
DMRC Defence Maintenance and Repair Committee (MOD)
DMRE Division of Medical Radiation Exposure (of Bureau of Radiological Health (USA))
DMRL Decreasing Mean Residual Life
Defence Metallurgical Research Laboratory (India)
DMRP Dredged Material Research Program (of the Corps of Engineers, US Army)
DMS Data Management System
Defense Mapping School (of DMA (USDOD))
Dense Media Separation
Digital Measuring System

Dimethyl Sulphide
Direct Moulded Sole
Documentation of Molecular Spectroscopy
Dual Manoeuvring Simulator

DMSC Defence Materiel Standardization Committee (of MOD)
DMSDS Direct Mail Shelter Development System
DMSL Descriptive Macro Simulation Language
DMSO Dimethyl Sulphoxide
DMSP Defense Meteorological Satellite Program (of USAF)
DMSPC Defence Materiel Standardization Policy Committee (MOD)
DMSR Division of Management Survey and Review (of NIH (HEW) (USA))
DMSSO Defense Materiel Specifications and Standards Office (USDOD)
DMT Deep Mobile Target
Dimension-Motion Times
Dimethyl Terephthalate
Dimethyltryptamine
DMTG Data Manipulation Task Group (of CODASYL)
DMTI Digital Moving Target Indicator
DMTR DOUNREAY Materials Testing Reactor
DMTS Department of Mines and Technical Surveys (Canada)
Dynamic Multi-Tasking System
DMU Data Management Unit
Diesel-Multiple-Unit
Dual Manoeuvring Unit
DMV Dual-Mode Vehicle
DMVS Dynamic Manned Vehicle Simulator
DMX Data Multiplexer
DMZ Demilitarised Zone
DNA Defense Nuclear Agency (USDOD)
Deoxy-ribonuclei Acid
Deutscher Normenasschuss (Germany) (German Standards Institute) (name changed in 1975 to Deutsches Institut für Normung)
Direccion Nacional del Antartico (Argentina) (National Administration for the Antarctic)
Direction de la Navigation Aerienne (France) (Civil Aviation Administration)
DNAA Delayed Neutron Activation Analysis
DNAC Division of Numerical Analysis and Computing (of the National Physical Laboratory)
DNAM Division of Numerical and Applied Mathematics (of the National Physical Laboratory)
DNAP Deoxyribonucleoprotein
DNB Departure from Nucleate Boiling
DNBR Departure from Nucleate Boiling Ratio
DNC Delayed-Neutron Counting
Direct Numerical Control
DNCP Dirección Nacional de Construcciones Portuarias y Vías Navegables (Argentina) (National Directorate of Harbour Construction and Shipping Routes)
DND Department of National Defence (Canada)
DNDE Department of National Development and Energy (Australia) (became DRE in 1983)
DNEF Departamento Nacional de Estradas de Ferro (Brazil) (National Department of Railways)
DNER Departamento Nacional de Estradas de Rodagem (Brazil) (National Department of Highways)
DNF Disjunctive Normal Form
DNI Dana Normalisasi Indonesia (Indonesia) (Standards Institute)
DNIC Data Network Identification Code
Diffuse Noxious Inhibitory Controls
DNJ Det Norske Justervesen (Norway) (Norwegian Bureau of Weights and Measures)
Drone Noise Jammer
DNMS Division of Nuclear Materials Safeguards (of USAEC)
DNN Det Norske Nitridaktieselskap (Norway)
DNOC Dinitro-ortho-cresol
DNP Deoxyribonucleoprotein
Dinitrophenol
Dinitrophenyl
DNPL Daresbury Nuclear Physics Laboratory (of Science Research Council) (now the Daresbury Laboratory)
DNPM Departamento Nacional de Producao Mineral (Brazil) (National Department for Mineral Production)
DNPT Dinitrosopentamethylene Tetramine
DNR Department of National Revenue (Canada)
Deutscher Naturschutzring (Germany) (German Nature Conservation Organisation)
DNS Department for National Savings
DNSS Defence Navigation Satellite System
Doppler Navigation Satellite System
DNT Dinitrotoluene
DnV Det norske Veritas (Norwegian Ship Classification Society)
DNVT Digital Non-secure Voice Telephone
DO Dissolved Oxygen
DOA Department of Agriculture (USA)
Direction Of Arrival
Dominant Obstacle Allowance
DOAE Defence Operational Analysis Establishment (MOD)
DOAMS Distant Object Attitude Measurement System
DOAS Diesel Odour Analysis System
DOB Depth of Burst
Diesel Oil Bentonite
DOBETA Domestic Oil Burning Equipment Testing Association
DOC Delay Opening Chaff
Deoxycholate
Department of Commerce (USA)
Department of Communications (Canada)
Design Office Consortium
Developmental Optical Correlator
Direct Operating Costs
Dissolved Organic Carbon
DOCA Deoxycorticosterone Acetate
DOCB Deep Ocean Cable Burial system
DOCEX Document Exploitation
DOCS Distribution Operation Control System
DOCTOR Dictionary Operation and Control for Thesaurus Organisation
DOCUS Display-Orientated Computer Usage System
DOD Department of Defense (USA)
DODAC Department of Defense (USA) Ammunition Code
DODCI Department of Defense Computer Institute (of NDU (USA))
DODDAC Department of Defense Damage Assessment Center (USA)
DODGE Department of Defense Gravity Experiment (USA)
DODIS Distribution of Oceanographic Data at Isentropic Levels
DODISS Department of Defense Index of Specifications and Standards (USDOD)
DODS Definitive Orbit Determination System
DOE Department of Electronics (India)
Department of Energy (USA)
Department of the Environment
DOE/EIA Department of Energy/Energy Information Administration (USA)
DOE/TIC Department of Energy/Technical Information Center (USA)
DOES Direct Order Entry System

DOETS Dual Objects Electronic Tracking System
DOFIC Domain Originated Functional Integrated Circuit
DOFL Diamond Ordnance Fuze Laboratories (now HDL) (US Army)
DOI Department of Industry (Canada)
Department of Industry (DTI since 1983)
Descent Orbit Insertion
DOKZENTBW Dokumentationszentrum dem Bundeswehr (Germany) (Federal Armed Forces Documentation Centre)
DOL Department of Labor (USA)
Dioleoyl Lecithin
DOLAN Design Office Language
DOLARS Disk On-line Accounts Receivable System
DOM Design-Out Maintenance
Digital Ohmmeter
Dissolved Organic Matter
Dissolved Oxygen Monitor
DOMA Deep Ocean Minerals Association (Japan)
DOMAINS Deep Ocean Manned Instrumented Station
DOMES Deep Ocean Mining Experimental Study (of NOAA (USA))
DOMEX Display Oriented Macro Expander
DOMICS Direct Computation of Minimal Cut Sets
DOMINA Distribution-Oriented Management Information Analyser
DOMMDA Drawing Office Material Manufacturers and Dealers Association
DOMSATCOM Domestic Satellite Communications system
DON Dimensionality Of Nations
Distribution Octane Number
DONA Dynamic Organizational Network Analysis
DOOM Deep Ocean Optical Measurement
DOORS Defence Oriented On-line Retrieval System (of DRIC (MOD))
DOP Desoctapeptide
Dioctyl-Phthalate
DOPE DISAC Object Programme Encoder
DOPIC Documentation of Programme In Core
DOPLOC Doppler Phase Lock
DOQ Dynamic Order Quantity
DOR Digital Optical Recording
DORA Directorate of Operational Research and Analysis (of CAA)
DORACE Design Organization, Record, Analyse, Charge, Estimate
DORAN Doppler Ranging
DORC Defence Operational Requirements Committee (Dept of Defence (Australia))
DORDeC Domestic Refrigeration Development Committee
DORE Defence Operational Research Establishment (of DRB, Canada)
DORF Diamond Ordnance Radiation Facility (of HDL (US Army))
DORIS Deck Operated Remote Inspection Submersible
Designer's On-line Real-time Interactive Secretary
DORLS Directors of Ontario Regional Library Systems (Canada)
Directors of Regional Library Systems (of Ontario Canada))
DOS Di-Octyl Sebacate
Directorate of Overseas Surveys (of ODM)
Disk Operating System
DOSM Desialyated Ovine Submaxillary Mucin
DOSP Deep Oxean Sediment Probe
DOSS Deep Ocean Search System
DOSV Deep Ocean Survey Vehicle
DOT Deep Ocean Technology
Deep Ocean Transponder
Department of Trade (DTI since 1983)
Department of Transport (Canada)
Department of Transport (formed 1976 out of part of DOE)
Department of Transportation (USA)
Designating Optical Tracker
Displacement Oriented Transducer
Domain Tip
DOT-HS prefix to numbered series of Multidisciplinary Accident Investigations issued by Department of Transportation National Highway Traffic Safety Administration (USA)
DOT-TSC Department of Transportation, Transportation Systems Center (USA)
DOTG Di-o-tolyl-guanidine
DOTIPOS Deep Ocean Test Instrument Placement and Observation System
DOTRAM Domain Tip Randon Access Memory
DOTS Deviations Of Temperature and Salinity
DOV Data-over-Voice
Discrete Operational Vehicle
DOVACK Differential, Oral, Visual, Aural, Computerised Kinaesthetic
DOVAP Doppler Velocity And Position
DOWB Deep Operating Work Boat
DP Diphosgene
Durable Press
Dynamic Programming
DPA Diphenylamine
Direction de Piles Atomiques (of CEN (France)) (Directorate of Atomic Piles)
Distributed Processing Algorithm
Diversion Path Analysis
Domestic Policy Association (USA)
DPAG Dangerous Pathogens Advisory Group
DPAYZ Spatial Property Analyzer
DPB Department of Printed Books (of BLRD)
DPC Data Protection Committee
Defence Planning Committee (of NATO)
Defence Procurement Circulars (USDOD)
Digital Planimetric Compiler
Documentation Processing Office (of OSTI (DES))
DPCA Displaced Phase Centre Antenna
DPCC Double Potential Step Chronocoulometry
DPCM Differential Pulse Code Modulation
DPCP Department of Prices and Consumer Protection
DPD Dicyclopentadiene Dioxide
Diethyl Paraphenylene Diamine
DPDA Deterministic Pushdown Automata
DPDS Defense Property Disposal Service (of DSA (USDOD))
DPE Data Processing Equipment
Deuterated Polyethylene
DPEP Dexophylloerythroetioporphyrin
DPET Directoria de Pesquisas e Ensino Tecnico (Brazil) (Directorate of Research and Technical Education of the Brazilian Army)
DPEWS Design-to-Price Electronic Warfare System or Suite
DPF Dense Plasma Focus
DPG Diphosphoglycerate
Dugway Proving Ground (of TECOM (US Army))
DPH Diamond Pyramid Hardness
Diphenylhydantoin
DPI Domestic Product of Industry
DPL Dipalmitoyl Lecithin
DPLE Digital Principal Local Exchange
DPLL Digital Phase Locked Loop

DPM — Data Processing Model
Digital Panel Meter
Digital Plotter Map
Directional Policy Matrix
Disruptive Pattern Material

DPMA — Data Processing Management Association (merged into IDPM in 1978)

DPN — Dipropylnitrosamine

DPNR — Deproteinized Rubber

DPO — Digital-Processing Oscilloscope
Diphenyl Oxide

DPP — Diphenylol Propane

DPPC — Dipalmitoylphosphatidylcholine

DPPE — Dimerized Phenyl Propargyl Ether

DPPH — Diphenylpicrylhydrazyl

DPR — Dial Pulse Receiver
Direct Particle Rolling

DPRS — Dynamic Preferential Runway System

DPS — Descent Propulsion System
Design Problem Solver
Deterministic Pattern Search
Diagnostic Problem-Solving
Dial Pulse Sender
Differential Phase Shift
Disc Programming System
Distributed Processing Support
Distributed-Parameter System

DPSA — Data Processing Suppliers Association (now Input/Output Systems Association)
Data Processing Supplies Association (USA)
Deep-Penetration Strike Aircraft

DPSK — Differential Phase-Shift Keying

DPSO — Data Processing Systems Office (of Picatinny Arsenal (USDOD))

DPT — Depletion Perturbation Theory

DPTTC — Drilling and Production Technology Training Centre (of PITB)

DPVM — Demand-Page Virtual Memory

DPW — Department of Public Works (Canada)
Dried Poultry Waste

DQAB — Defence Quality Assurance Board (MOD)

DQABE — Defence Quality Assurance Board Executive (MOD)

DQE — Detective Quantum Efficiency

DR — Danmarks Radio (Denmark)
Data Report
Dead Reckoning
Deutsche Reischbahn (Germany) (German State Railway)
Direct Ratio
Double-Reduced
prefix to numbered series of reports issued by Atmospheric Sciences Laboratory of ECOM (US Army)
prefix to numbered series of reports issued by the Defence Research Board (Canada)

DR and O — Depot Repair and Overhaul

DR/V — Deep Research Vehicle

DRADS — Degradation of Radar Defence System

DRAE — Defence Research Analysis Establishment (Department of National Defence (Canada))

DRAI — Dead Reckoning Analogue Indicator

DRAM — Dynamic Random Access Memory

DRAMA — Digital Radio and Multiplex Acquisition

DRAW — Direct Read After Write

DRB — Defence Research Board (Canada) (now CRAD (DND))

DRBC — Delaware River Basin Commission (USA)

DRC — Damage Risk Criterion
Dielectric Relaxation Current
Digital Radar Code
Disaster Research Center (Ohio State University (USA))

DRCC — Data-Referencing and Conditioning Centre (of ESOC (ESA))

DRCM — Differential Reinforced Clostridial Medium

DRCS — Defence Research Centre Salisbury (of DSTO (Australia))

DRD — Draw and Re-Draw tin can manufacture

DRDO — Defence Research and Development Organization (India)

DRE — Department of Resources and Energy (Australia)

DREA — Defence Research Establishment Atlantic (of DRB, Canada) (now of CRAD (DND))

DREAC — Drum Experimental Automatic Computer

DREAM — Design Realization, Evaluation And Modelling
Digital Recording And Measurement

DRED — Directed Rocket Engine Development

DREO — Defence Research Establishment, Ottawa (of DRB (Canada)) (now of CRAD (DND))

DREP — Defence Research Establishment Pacific (of DRB, Canada) (now of CRAD (DND))

DREPS — Digital ortho Rectification of Planimetric System

DRES — Defence Research Establishment Suffield (of DRB, Canada) (now of CRAD (DND))

DRESS — DENDENKOSHA Real-time Sales and Inventory Management System

DRET — Defence Research Establishment Toronto (of DRB, Canada) (now of CRAD (DND))
Direction des Recherches Etudes et Techniques (France)

DREV — Defence Research Establishment, Valcartier (of DRB (Canada)) (now of CRAD (DND))

DRF — Deafness Research Foundation (USA)
Dual Role Fighter

DRG — Defence Research Group (of NATO)
Detroit Rubber Group (USA)
Dorsal Root Ganglia

DRI — Denver River Institute (University of Denver) (USA)
Direct Read-out Infra-red
Directorate of Research and Information (of MPBW)
Dynamic Response Index

DRI-UP — Decent Respectable Individuals—United for Progress (USA) (a society)

DRIC — Defence Research Information Centre (MOD (PE))

DRIFT — Diagnostic Retrievable Information For Teachers
Diversity Receiving Instrumentation For Telemetry

DRIMS — DELTA Redundant Inertial Measurement System

DRIP — Digital Ray and Intensity Projector

DRIR — Direct Read-out Infra-Red
Direct Read-out Infrared Radiometer

DRIS — Defense Retail Interservice Support (USDOD)

DRL — Data Retrieval Language
Direct Ranging LORAN

DRL(M) — Defence Research Laboratory (Materials) (India)

DRLMS — Digital Radar Land Mass Simulator
Digital Radar Land-Mass Simulation

DRM — Detrital Remanent Magnetization
Digital Ratiometer

DRME — Direction des Recherches et Moyens d'Essais (France) (Defence Agency for the Coordination of Research and Testing)
Direction des Recherches et Moyens d'Essais (now DRET (France))

DRML — Defence Research Medical Laboratories (of DRB) (now DRET)

DRMP Division of Regional Medical Programs (of NIH (USA))
DRO Destructive Readout
Digital Read-Out
Disablement Resettlement Officer
Doubly Resonant Oscillator
DROD Delayed Readout Detector
DROLS Defense RDTE On-Line System (of DTIC (USDOD))
DROM Decoder Read Only Memory
DRP Deutsches Reichs Patent (German State Patent)
Distribution Resource Planning
DRPA Delaware River Port Authority (USA)
DRPG Detroit Rubber and Plastics Group (USA) (became Detroit Rubber Group in 1975)
DRR Discounted Rate of Return
Division of Research Resources (of NIH (USA))
DRS Data Relay Satellite
Digital Radar Simulator
DRSS Data Relay Satellite System
DRT Dead Reckoning Tracer
Diagnostic Rhyme Test
DRTC Documentation Research and Training Centre (India)
DRTE Defence Research Telecommunications Establishment (of DRB) (now Communications Research Centre) (Department of Communications) (Canada)
DRTL Diode Resistor Transistor Logic
DRUA DATA RECOGNITION Users Association
DRUGR Drug Registry programme
DRVID Difference Range Versus Integrated Doppler
DRVS Doppler Radar Velocity Sensor
DS Dansk Standardiseringsraad (Denmark) (Danish Standards Institute)
Decomposition Sintering
Directional Solidification casting process
DS/V Deep Submergence Vehicle
DSA Defence Supply Agency (USDOD) (became Defense Logistics Agency in 1977)
Defense Supply Association (USA) (now American Logistics Association)
Dial Service Assistance
Dielectric Stimulated Arcing
Diffusion Self-Aligned
Dimensionally Stable Anode
Direct Ranging LORAN
Door and Shutter Association
Double-Submerged Arc
Down Sensor Assembly
Dynamic Shear Adhesion
DSAA Defense Security Assistance Agency (USDOD)
DSAC Defence Scientific Advisory Council (MOD)
Defense Security Assistance Council (USDOD)
DSAH prefix to numbered series of Defense Supply Agency Handbooks issued by USDOD
DSAI Digital Solar-Aspect Indicator
DSAM prefix to numbered series of Defense Supply Agency Manuals issued by USDOD
DSAP Data System Automation Program (of USAF)
DSARC Defense Systems Acquisition Review Council (USDOD)
DSB Danske Statsbaner (Denmark) (Danish State Railways)
Defense Science Board (USA)
Double Side-Band
DSBSC Double Sideband Suppressed Carrier
DSC Differential Scanning Calorimeter
Differential Scanning Calorimetry
Dynamically Self-Checked
DSCG Disodium Cromoglycate
DSCl Durable Sprayed Cladding
DSCS Defense Satellite Communications System (USDOD)
DSD Data-Scanner Distributor
DSDC Defence Source Definition Committee (Dept of Defence (Australia))
DSDP Deep Sea Drilling Project (of National Science Foundation (USA))
DSDT Deformographic Storage Display Tube
Discrete-Space Discrete-Time
DSE Data Switching Exchange
Defence Scientific Establishment (New Zealand)
Direct Sequence Encoding
Directionally Solidified Eutectic
DSEA Defense Security Assistance Agency (USA)
DSEP Defense Science and Engineering Program (USAF)
DSF Dansk Skibsteknisk Forkningsinstitut (Denmark) (Danish Ship Research Institute)
DSFAAS Domestic Solid Fuel Appliances Approval Scheme
DSFC Direct Side Force Control
DSFT Detection Scheme with Fixed Thresholds
Discrete Sliding Fourier Transform
DSG Digital Signal Generator
DSI Dairy Science International (USA)
Digital Speed Interpolation
Division of Science Information (of National Science Foundation (USA))
DSIATP Defense Sensor Interpretation and Application Training Program (USAF)
DSID Disposable Seismic Intrusion Detector
DSIF Deep Space Instrumentation Facility (of NASA)
DSIP Domestic Science Information Program (of Office of Science Information (NSF) (USA))
DSIR Department of Scientific and Industrial Research (disbanded 1965) (United Kingdom)
Department of Scientific and Industrial Research (New Zealand)
DSIS Defence Scientific Information Services (of DRB (Canada))
DSISI Double-Sided Inter-Symbol Interference
DSL Deep Scattering Layer
Defence Science Laboratory (India)
Defence Standards Laboratory (Australia) (became MRL of DSTO in 1974)
Digital Simulation Language
DSLC Defense Logistics Services Center (USDOD)
DSLIM Double-Sided Linear Induction Motor
DSLT Detection Scheme with Learning of Thresholds
DSM Dense-Staining Material
Dried Skim Milk
Dynamic Scattering Mode
Dynamic Stiffness Modulus
DSMS Defense Systems Management School (USDOD)
DSMTI Discrete Signal Moving Target Indicator
DSN Decisive Sample Number
Deep Space Network
Descriptive Supplement Number
Distributed Sensor Network
DSNS Division of Space Nuclear Systems (USAEC)
Doppler Sonar Navigation System
DSO Data Set Optimiser
Deck Stowage Only
DSP Digital Signal Processing
Direct System Platemaker
DSPA Desert Sportsman Pilots Association (USA)
DSR Depolymerized Scrap Rubber
Discriminating Selector Repeator
DSRK Deutsche Schiffs-Revision und Klassifikation
dsRNA Double-stranded Ribonucleic Acid
DSRS Distal Splenorenal Shunt

DSRV	Deep Submergence Rescue Vehicle OR Vessel Deep Submergence Rescue Vessel
DSS	Decision Support System Deep Seismic Sounding Department of Supply and Services (Canada) Distribution Scheduling System Distribution System Simulator
DSSM	Digital Signal Sinusoidal Modulation Dynamic Sequencing and Segmentation Model
DSSP	Deep Submergence Systems Project (USN)
DSSPO	Deep Submergence Systems Project Office (USN)
DSSPTO	Deep Submergence Systems Project Technical Office (USN)
DSSRG	Deep Submergence Systems Research Group (USN)
DSSS	Deep Space Surveillance Satellite
DSSV	Deep Submergence Search Vehicle
DST	Discrete Sine Transform
DSTAR	Direct Sea-To-Air Refuelling
DSTL	Digital-Summation Threshold-Logic
DSTO	Defence Sciences and Technology Organization (Dept of Defence (Australia))
DSTR	Dynamic Systems Test Rig
DSTV	Deutscher Stahlbau-Verband (Germany) (German Steel Construction Association) Digital Subscriber Voice Terminal
DSU/GSU	Direct Support Unit and General Support Unit Computer System (US Army)
DSUCR	Doppler-Shifted Ultrasonic Cyclotron Resonance
DSV	Deep Submergence Vehicle
DSW	Direct-Step-On-Wafer
DT	Delta Technique Deuterium-Tritium Diagnostic Technique Double Torsion Dynamic Tear Test
DTA	Differential Thermal Analysis Direccao de Exploracao dos Transportes Aereos (Mozambique) Dominion Traffic Association (Canada) Dynamic Test Article
DTAS	Data Transmission And Switching System Digital Transmission And Switching
DTASI	Digital Time Assignment Speech Interpolation
DTAT	Direction Technique des Armements Terrestres (France) (Technical Board of Land Armaments, of the Ministry of the Army)
DTB	Danmarks Tekniske Bibliotek (Denmark)
DTBC	Digital Time Base Correctors
DTC	Design To Cost Desk Top Computer
DTCA	Direction Technique des Constructions Aeronautiques (France) (Technical Board of Aeronautical Construction, of the Ministry of the Army)
DTCN	Direction Technique des Constructions Navales (France) (Technical Board of Naval Construction, of the Ministry of the Army) (now DCN)
DTD	prefix to numbered series of Specifications issued by MINTECH, later by DTI and Ministry of Aviation Supply, and now by MOD(PE) (published by HMSO)
DTDMA	Distributed Time Division Multiple Access
DTDS	Digital Television Display System
DTE	Data Ten to Eleven Data Terminal Equipment Data Terminating Equipment Detective Quantum Efficiency Direction Technique des Engins (France) (Technical Board for Missiles, of the Ministry of the Army) Dynamic Tear Energy
DTFA	Digital Transfer Function Analyzer
DTG	Derivative Thermogravimetry
DTGS	Deuterated Triglycine Sulphate
DTI	Department of Trade and Industry (formed in 1970 by the amalgamation of the Board of Trade and part of the Ministry of Technology) Department of Trade and Industry (split into Department of Trade (DOT) and Department of Industry (DOI) in 1974) (reconstituted 1983)
DTIC	Defense Technical Information Center (USDOD)
DTIE	Division of Technical Information Extension (of USAEC)
DTL	Diode Transistor Logic
DTLCC	Design-to-Life Cycle Cost
DTM	Development Test Model Digital Talk-out Module Digital Terrain Matrice Digital Terrain Model Director of Telecommunication Management (Office of Economic Preparedness (USA))
DTMB	David Taylor Model Basin (USN) (now part of Naval Ship Research and Development Center)
DTMF	Dual Tone Multi-Frequency
DTNSRDC	DAVID W TAYLOR Naval Ship Research and Development Center (USN)
DTO	Dansk Teknisk Oplysningstjeneste (Denmark) (Danish Technical Information Service)
DTOL	Digital Test Oriented Language
DTOT	Design Technical Operational Test Development Test, Operational Test
DTp	Department of Transport
DTP	Diptheria Tetanus Pertussis Directory Tape Processor
DTPA	Diethylenetriamine Penta-acetic Acid
DTPEWS	Design-to-Price Electronic Warfare System
DTPL	Domain Tip Propagation Logic
DTR	Damage Tolerance Rating Diffusion Transfer Reversal
DTRS	Data Transmission and Routing System
DTS	Dense Tar Surfacing Diagnostic Test Sequence
DTSS	DARTMOUTH (COLLEGE) (USA) Time-Sharing System
DTT	Dithiothreitol
DTUL	Deflection Temperature Under Load
DTUOC	Digital Tire Uniformity Optimizer Computer
DTUPC	Design-to-Unit Production Cost
DTV	Diver Transport Vehicle
DTWX	Dial Teletypewriter Exchange Service
DUA	Digitronics Users Association (USA)
DUAL	Dynamic Universal Assembly Language
DUALabs	National Data Use and Access Laboratories (USA)
DUBS	Durham University Business School
DUCE	Denied-Usage Channel Evaluator
DUCK	prefix to numbered series of reports issued by Drexel University Combustion Kinetics Laboratory (USA)
DUCS	Deep Underground Communication System
DUL	Design Ultimate Load
DUM	Dorsal Unpaired Median
DUMAND	Deep Underseas Muon and Neutrine Detector (the name adopted by a group of physicists, oceanographers and oceanographic engineers in the USA)
DUMETi	Dorsal Unpaired Median Extensor-Tibiae
DUMS	Deep Unmanned Submersibles
DUN	Depth Under Notch
DUNC	Deep Underwater Nuclear Counter
DUNMIRE	DUNDEE UNIVERSITY Numerical Methods Information Retrieval Experiment
DUSTSONDE	Balloon-borne Particle Counter
DUT	Device Under Test

DUTE Digital Diagnostic Unit Under Test
Digital Universal Test Equipment
DUV Damaging Ultraviolet
Data-under-Voice
DUVD Direct Ultrasonic Visualization of Defects
DUX Data Utility Complex
DVA Design Verification Article
Dynamic Visual Acuity
DVARS Doppler Velocity Altimeter Radar Set
DVB Deutscher Buchereiverband (Germany) (The German Association of Libraries)
Disability Veiling Brightness
Divinylbenzene
DVCCS Differential Voltage Controlled Current Source
DVCSB Delaware Valley Consumer Sounding Board (USA)
DVEO Department of Defense Value Engineering Services (USDOD)
DVG Deutsche Volkswirtschaftliche Gesellschaft (Germany) (German Economics Association)
DVGW Deutscher Verein vor Gas-und Wasserfachmannern (Germany) (German Society of Gas and Water Experts)
DVI Dust Veil Index
DVL Deutsche Versuchsanstalt fuer Luftfahrt (Germany) (German Aviation Experimental Centre)
DVLC The Driver and Vehicle Licensing Centre (of DOE)
DVM Deutscher Verband fuer Material-pruefung (Germany) (German Association for Materials Testing)
Digital Voltmeter
Double Vacuum Melting
DVNIGMI Dal'nevostochnyy Nauchno-Issledovatel'skiy Gidrometeorologicheski (USSR) (Far Eastern Scientific Research Hydro-meteorological Institute)
DVOR Doppler VHF Omni-Range
DVOSi Divinyloxydimethylsilane
DVP Discounted Present Value
DVS Deutscher Verband fuer Schweisstechnik (Germany) (German Welding Technology Association)
DVST Direct View Storage Tube
DVT Deep Vein Thrombosis
Deep Venous Thrombosis
Dynamic Velocity Taper
DVTWV Deutscher Verband Technisch-Wissenschaftlicher Verbands (Germany) (German Association of Technological Societies)
DVW Deutscher Verein fuer Vermessungswesen (Germany) (German Association for Surveying)
DVWG Deutche Verkehrswissen-Schaftliche Gesellschaft (Germany) (German Transportation Society)
DW Drop-Weight
DWBA Distorted-Wave Born Approximation
DWF Dry Weather Flow
DWI Drawn and Wall Ironed tin can
Driving While Impaired (by alcohol and/or drugs)
DWICA Deep Water Isotopic Current Analyzer
DWIM Do-What-I-Mean
DWL Derived Working Level
DWMI Diamond Wheel Manufacturers Institute (USA)
DWP Dyna Whirlpool Process
DWQRC Drinking Water Quality Research Center (of FIU (USA))
DWR Divided Winding-Rotor
DWS Disaster Warning Satellite
DWSMC Defense Weapons Systems Management Center (USDOD)
DWSS Disaster Warning Satellite System
DWT Deutsche Gesellschaft für Wehrtechnik (Germany) (German Society for Defence Technology)
DWTT Drop-Weight Tear Test
DX Destroyer Experimental
DXC Data Exchange Control
DYANA Dynamic Analyzer
DYDE Dynamic Debugger
DYMAC Dynamic Materials Control
DYNAMIT Dynamic Allocation of Manufacturing Inventory and Time
DYNAMO Dynamic Allocation Model
Dynamo Modeller
DYNAMO-S Dynamic Modeller-Simulator
DYNASAR Dynamic Systems Analyzer
DYNET Dynamic Network Planning Technique
DYNFET Dynamic Four Phase Non-overlapping Clock Field Effect Transistor
DYNSYS Dynamics Systems Simulator
DYSAC Digitally Simulated Analogue Computer
DYSTAC Dynamic Storage Analogue Computer
DYSTAL Dynamic Storage Allocation
DZ Dissociated Zircon
DZW Deutsche Dokumentations Zentrale Wasser (Germany) (German Water Documentation Office)
D^2B Digital Data Base

E

E prefix to numbered-dated series of standards on Electronic Components issued by BSI
E-D Expose-and-then-Develop
E-JFET Enhancement-mode Junction Field-Effect Transistor
E-O Electro-Optic
E/A Ethylene/Acrylic elastomer
EA Edgewood Arsenal (US Army) (became CSL in 1977)
Electro-Absorbtion
Energy Analysis
Engineer Agency (USACDC)
Environment Assessment
Environmental Agency (Japan)
Ethyacrylate
Ethylamine
Extrinsic Alveolitis
EAA East African Airways (ceased operations in 1977)
Electrical Aerosol Analyzer
Electrical Appliance Association
Electronics Association of Australia (Australia)
Essential Amino Acids
Ethylene Acrylic Acid
Experimental Aircraft Association (USA)
Extrinsic Allergic Alveolitis
EAAA European Association of Advertising Agencies (Switzerland)
EAAC East African Airways Corporation (Kenya) (disbanded 1977)
EAAFRO East African Agriculture and Forestry Research Organisation (Kenya)
EAAP Engineering Activity Board (of SAE (USA))
European Association for Animal Production
EAB Educational Activities Board (of IEEE (USA))
EABRD Electrically Actuated Band Release Device
EAC East African Community
Effective Attenuation Coefficient
Electro-Agricultural Centre (of the Electricity Council)

EACA Epsilon Aminocaproic Acid
EACC Error Adaptive Control Computer
EACEM European Association of Consumer Electronic Manufacturers (of the EEC)
EACHS East African Cargo Handling Services Ltd
EACN European Air Chemistry Network
EACR European Association for Cancer Research
EACRP European-American Committee on Reactor Physics
EACSO East Africa Common Services Organization (Kenya)
EADI Electronic Attitude Direction Indicator
Extrapolated Alternating Direction Implicit
EAE Ethylene/Acrylic Elastomer
Experimental Allergic Encephalomyelitis
Experimental Autoimmune Encephalomyelitis
EAEC European Airlines Electronic Committee
EAEE European Association for Earthquake Engineering
EAEG European Association of Exploration Geophysicists
EAEM European Airlines Electronics Meeting
EAES European Atomic Energy Society
EAESP Escola de Administracao de Empresas de Sao Paula (Brazil) (Sao Paula School of Business Administration)
EAET East African External Telecommunications Company
EAF Electron Arc Furnace
EAFFRO East African Freshwater Fisheries Research Organisation (Uganda)
EAFIT Escuela y Finanzas e Instituto Technologico (Colombia) (Management School)
EAG Electro-Antennogram
EAGE Electrical Aerospace Ground Equipment
EAGGF European Agricultural Guidance and Guarantee Fund (of EEC)
EAHC East African Harbours Corporation
EAHY European Architectural Heritage Year
EAIMR East African Institute for Medical Research (Tanzania)
EAIRO East African Industrial Research Organization (Kenya)
EALA East African Library Association (dissolved 1973)
EALM Electron-beam Addressed Light Modulator
EALRC East African Leprosy Research Centre (Uganda)
EALS East African Literature Service (Headquarters in East African Agriculture and Forestry Research Organization (Kenya))
EAM Electronic Accounting Machine
Emergency Action Method
EAMAC Ecole Africaine de la Meteorologie et de l'Aviation Civile (Niger) (African Meteorological and Civil Aviation School)
EAMC European Airlines Montparnasse Committee
EAMD East African Meteorological Department (Kenya)
EAMFRO East African Marine Fisheries Research Organization (Tanzania)
EAMG Experimental Autoimmune Myasthemia Gravis
EAMRC East African Medical Research Council (Tanzania)
EAMTC European Association of Management Training Centres (now European Foundations for Management Development)
EAMTMTS Eastern Area Military Traffic Management and Terminal Service (US Army)
EAMVBD East African Institute of Malaria and Vector-Borne Diseases (Tanzania)
EAN Europian Article Numbering
Experimental Allergic Neuritis
EANDC European Sewage and Refuse Engineering Symposium
European-American Nuclear Data Committee
Extensive Air Shower
EANDRO Electrically Alterable NDRO
EANPG European Air Navigation Planning Group (ICAO)
EANRRC East African Natural Resources Research Council (Kenya)
EANS European Article Numbering System
EAP Electroabsorption Avalanche Photodiode
English for Academic Purposes
Environmental Analysis and Planning
EAPCO East African Pesticides Control Organization
EAPFS Extended Appearance Potential Fine Structure
EAPM European Association for Personnel Management
EAPR European Association for Potato Research
EAPT East African Posts and Telecommunications Corporation
EAR East African Railways
Electronic Array Radar
Electronically-Agile Radar
Electronically-steered Agile Radar
Employee Attitude Research
Energy Absorbing Resin
European Association of Radiology
Experimental Array Radar
EARB Electronics and Aviation Requirements Board
European Airlines Research Bureau (now Association of European Airlines)
EARC East African Railways Corporation (disbanded 1977)
Extraordinary Administrative Radio Conference (of ITU)
EARDHE European Association for Research and Development in Higher Education
EARI Engineer Agency for Resources Inventories (US Army Corp of Engineers)
EARL Electronically Accessible Russian Lexicon
Extended Algorithmic "R" Languages
EARN European Academic and Research Network
European Academic Research Network
EAROM Electrically Alterable Read-Only Memory
EAROPH Eastern Regional Organization for Planning and Housing (India)
EARP Equipment Anti-Riot Projector
EARS Egypt Amateur Radio Society (Egypt)
Electro-Acoustic Rating System
Electronic Airborne Reaction System
Electronically Agile Radar System
Emergency Airborne Reaction System
Epilepsy Abstracts Retrieval System
EARSeL European Association of Remote Sensing Laboratories
EAS Directorate for Engineering and Applied Science (of National Science Foundation (USA))
Electronique Aero-Spatiale (France)
Energy Audit Scheme (of DOI)
Equivalent Airspeed
European Accident Statement
EASA East African School of Aviation (Kenya)
Electrical Apparatus Service Association (USA)
Engineers Association of South Africa (South Africa)
EASCON Electronics and Aerospace Systems Convention and Exposition (IEEE (USA))
EASE Electronic Airborne Systems Evaluator
Escape And Survival Equipment
EASEP Early APOLLO Scientific Experiments Package
EASHP European Association of Senior Hospital Physicians
EASIT European Association for Software Access and Information Transfer

EASL Engineering Analysis and Simulation Language
Experimental Assembly Sterilization Laboratory
EASP prefix to numbered series of Edgewood Arsenal (US Army) Special Publications
EASS Engine Automatic Stop and Start System
EASSG European Accountancy Students Study Group
EASTCON Electronics and Aerospace Systems Technical Convention (USA)
EASTEC Eastern Testing Exposition/Conference (of ASNDT (USA))
EASTT Experimental Army Satellite Tactical Terminals (US Army)
EASY Emulation Aid System
Engine Analyzer System
Exchange Assembly System
EAT Electronic Angle Tracking
Employment Appeal Tribunal
EATC Ehrlich Ascites Tumor Cell
Electronic Automatic Temperature Controller
EATCS European Association for Theoretical Computer Science
EATIC East African Tuberculosis Investigation Centre (Kenya)
EATRO East African Trypanosomiasis Research Organisation (Uganda)
EATS Extended Area Tracking System
EAU Extended Arithmetic Unit
EAVE Experimental Autonomous Vehicle
EAVRI East African Virus Research Institute (Uganda)
EAVRO East African Veterinary Research Organization (Kenya)
EAW Electrical Association for Women
Equivalent Average Words
EAX Electronic Automatic Exchange
EB Electron Beam
Environmental Buoy
Estradiol Benzoate
EBAA Eye Bank Association of America (USA)
EBAM Electron Beam Access Method
Electron-Beam-Accessed Memory
Electron-Beam-Addressed Memory
EBAS Electron Beam Activated Switch
EBBS European Brain and Behaviour Society
EBCDIC Extended Binary Coded Decimal Interchange Code (of USASI)
EBCM Extended Boundary Condition Method
EBCS European Barge Carrier System
EBES Electron Beam Exposure System
EBESSA Societe Reunis d'Energie du Bassin de l'Escaut SA (Belgium)
EBF Externally Blown Flap
EBI Electron Drift Instability
EBIAT Earnings Before Interest and after Taxes
EBIC Electron Beam Induced Conductivity
Electron Beam Induced Current
EBIG Electron Beam Inert Gas
EBIOC Electron Beam Induced Oxide Charging
EBIP European Biotechnology Information Project (of EEC)
EBIR Electron Bombardment Induced Response
EBIRD Electron Beam Ionization of Semiconductor Devices
EBIT Earnings Before Interest and Taxes
EBIV Electron Beam Induce Voltage
EBL Electron Beam Lithography
Exterior Ballistics Laboratory (US Army)
EBM Electron Beam Machining
EBMF Electron Beam Microfabricator
EBMLM Electron Beam Membrane Light Modulator
EBNA Epstein-Barr Nuclear Antigen
EBNF Extended Backus-Naur-Form
EBOR Experimental Beryllium Oxide Reactor
EBP Estradiol Binding Protein
Etching Back Process
EBQ Economic Batch Quantity
EBR Electron Beam Preproducer
Electron Beam Recorder
Electron Beam Recording
Electron Beam Remelting
Experimental Breeder Reactor
EBS Electron Beam Semiconductor
Electron Bombarded Semiconductor
Electron Bombarded Silicon
Emergency Broadcast System (USA)
EBSA Estuaries and Brackish Water Science Association
EBSC European Bird Strike Committee
EBU European Broadcasting Union
EBV Epstein-Barr Virus
Epstein-Barr Virus
EBVCA Epstein-Barr Virus Capsid Antigen
EBW Electron Beam Welding
Exploding Bridgewire
EBWR Experimental Boiling Water Reactor
EC (The) Engineering Council
Eddy Current
Electrical Conductivity
Electrochromic
Electrolytic Corrosion
Electronic Calculator
Electronic Computer
European Communities (consisting of ECSC, EEC, EURATOM)
EC&D Electronic Cover and Deception
EC/LSS Environmental Control/Life Support System
ECA Economic Commission for Africa (of UNO)
Electrical Contractors Association
Electronic Control Amplifier
European Combat Aircraft
European Confederation of Agriculture
Export Control Administration (of USCOMM)
ECAC Electromagnetic Compatibility Analysis Center (USDOD)
European Civil Aviation Conference
ECAFE Economic Commission for Asia and the Far East (of UN) (became ESCAP in 1974)
ECAM Extended Communications Access Method
ECAP Electronic Circuit Analysis Programme
ECARBICA East and Central African Regional Branch of the International Council on Archives
ECAS Energy Conversion Alternatives Study (by ERDA, NSF and NASA (USA))
ECATS Expandable Computerized Automatic Test System
ECB Efferent Cochlear Bundle
Electrically Controlled Bi-refringence
Electronic Components Board (merged in ECIF in 1977)
Environmental Conservation Board (of the Graphic Communications Industries (USA))
ECC Electro-chemochromic
Electrochemical Concentration Cell
Electrodeposited Composite Coating
Electronic Calibration Center (of NBS Radio Standards Laboratory) (USA)
Equipment Configuration Control
ECCI Experimental Consultative Conference of Industrialists (of NATO)
ECCM Electronic Counter-Countermeasures
ECCP Engineering Concepts Curriculum Project (USA)
ECCS Emergency Core Cooling Supply
Emergency Core Cooling System
European Convention for Construction Steelwork

ECCSL Emitter-Coupled Current Steering Logic
ECCTIS Educational Counselling and Credit Transfer Information Service
ECD Electrochromic Display
ECDG Electrochemical Discharge Grinding
ECDIN European Chemical Data and Information Network (of EURATOM)
ECDM Electrochemical and Electrical Discharge Machining
ECE Economic Commission for Europe (of UN)
Engineering Capacity Exchange
External Combustion Engine
prefix to numbered series of European Standards
ECE/HBP Economic Commission for Europe Committee on Housing, Building and Planning
ECEL European Council for Environmental Law
ECEPS Electronic Converter Electric Power Supply
ECETOC European Chemical Industry Ecology and Toxicology Centre (secretariat in Brussels, Belgium)
ECF Electro-Chemical Forming
Electro-Conductive Film
ECFA Engineering Consulting Firms Association (Japan)
European Committee for Future Accelerators
European Committee for Future Activities
ECFMG Educational Council for Foreign Medical Graduates (USA)
ECFRPC East Central Florida Regional Planning Council (USA)
ECG Electrocardiogram
Electrochemical Grinding
ECGC Export Credit and Guarantee Corporation (India)
ECGD Export Credits Guarantee Department
ECH Electrochemical Honing
Electron Cyclotron Heating
Epichlorohydrin
ECHM Earth Coverage Horizon Measurement
ECHO Electronic Computing Health Oriented (a conference held in USA)
Enteric Cytopathic Human Orphan
Enteric Cytopathogenic Human Orphan
European Community Host Organisation
Evolution of Competing Hierarchical Organisation
ECI Energy Component Improvement (a program of NASA (USA))
European Co-operation in Informatics (a partnership of European computer societies)
Export Consignment Identifying number
ECIC Export Credit Insurance Cooperation (Singapore)
ECIF Electronic Components Industry Federation
ECIL Electronics Corporation of India Limited (India) (government owned)
ECIP European Cooperation in Information Processing (an organisation)
ECIRC European Computer Industry Research Centre
ECIS Engineering Careers Information Service (sponsored by EITB, EEF and Confederation of Shipbuilding and Engineering Unions)
ECL Electrogenerated Chemiluminescence
Electronics Components Laboratory
Emitter-Coupled Logic
ECLA Economic Commission for Latin America (of UN)
ECLAT European Computer Lessors and Trading Association
ECLATEL Empresa Commercial Latinoamericana de Telecommunicaciones (Latin America Commercial Telecommunications Enterprise)
ECLIM European Conference on Laser Interaction with Matter and Laser Thermonuclear Fusion
ECLSS Environmental Control and Life Support System
ECM Electrochemical Machining
Electronic Countermeasures
Equivalence Class Mask
European Conference of Mixing
Extended Core Memory
ECM&MR European College of Marketing and Marketing Research
ECMA European Carton Makers Association
European Computer Manufacturers Association
ECMB European Conference on Molecular Biology
ECMBR European Committee for Milk/Butterfat Recording
ECMC Electric Cable Makers Confederation
ECMR Effective Common Mode Rejection
Electronic Control of the Mixture Ratio
ECMRA European Chemical Marketing Research Association
ECMRWF European Centre for Medium Range Weather Forecasts
ECMSA Electronics Command Meteorological Support Agency (US Army)
ECMT European Conference of Ministers of Transport (of OECD)
ECMU Extended Core Memory Unit
ECMWF European Centre for Medium-range Weather Forecasting
ECN Energieonderzoek Centrum Nederland (Netherlands Energy Research Foundation) (Netherlands)
ECNL Equivalent-Continuous Noise Level
ECNP Environmental Coalition on Nuclear Power (a Philadelphia (USA) environmental group)
ECOC European Conference on Optical Communication
ECODU European CONTROL DATA Users Association
ECoG Electrocorticograph
ECOLE Evaluation by Computer of the Learning Environment
ECOM Electronic Computer-Originated Mail
Electronics Command (US Army) (split into ERADCOM, CORADCOM and CERCOM in 1977)
ECOMA European Computer Measurement Association
ECONOMAN Effective Control of Manpower
ECOPC Experimental Changes of Practice Committees (of the British Post Office)
ECOPETROL Empresa Colombiana de Petroles (Colombia) (State oil company)
ECOR Engineering Committee on Ocean Resources (of CEI and the Royal Society)
Engineering Committee on Ocean Resources (of IOC (UNESCO))
ECORS Eastern Counties Operational Research Society
ECOSA European Conference on Optical Systems and Applications
ECOSEC European Cooperation Space Environment Committee
ECOSOC Economic and Social Council (of UN)
ECOWAS Economic Community of West African States
ECP Electronic Channelling Pattern
Engineering Change Proposal
Exchange Control Programme
ECPA Etablissement Cinematographique et Photographique des Armees (France)
Evangelical Christian Publishers Association (USA)
ECPD Engineers Council for Professional Development (USA) (now ABET)
ECPE External Combustion Piston Engine
ECPNL Equivalent Continuous Perceived Noise Level
ECPP Electromagnetic Containerless Processing Payload
ECPS Effective-Candle-Power-Seconds

ECQAC — Electronics Components Quality Assessment Committee (of CENEL)

ECR — Electrical Contact Resistance
Electronic Cash Register
Endogenous Circadian Rhythm
Error Cause Removal

ECRC — Electricity Council Research Centre

ECRH — Electron Cyclotron Resonance Heating

ECRI — Emergency Care Research Institute (USA)

ECRIM — Engineering, Construction, and Related Industries Manpower National Committee (of TSA)

ECRO — European Chemoreception Research Organization

ECS — Electro-Convulsive Shock
Electrochemical Society (USA)
Electronic Combat Squadron (USAF)
Embedded Computer System
Enable Control System
Energy Conversion System
Environmental Control System
Etched Circuits Society (USA)
European Communication Satellite
European Components Service (of Dept of Industry)
Executive Compensation Service (of Management Centre Europe)
Experimental Communications Satellite
Extended Character Set

ECSA — European Computing Services Association
Exchange Carriers Standards Association (USA)

ECSC — European Coal and Steel Community

ECSL — Extended Control and Simulation Language

ECSS — Electrical Command and Stability System
European Communication Satellite System
Extendable Computer System Simulator

ECSSID — European Co-operation in Social Science Information and Documentation

ECST — Electronic Control of Spark Timing

ECSTACY — Electronic Control for Switching and Telemetering Automobile Systems

ECT — Electroconvulsive Therapy
Emission Computed Tomography

ECTA — Everyman's Contingency Table Analyser

ECTC — East Coast Telecommunications Center (of STRATCOM)

ECTD — Emission Control Technology Division (of EPA (USA))

ECU — Electronic Control Unit
Energy Conservation Unit (of Dept of Energy)
Environmental Control Unit
European Currency Unit (of the EEC)
Experimental Cartography Unit (of Natural Environment Research Council)

ECUBE — Energy Conservation Using Better Engineering

ECUTORIANA — Compania Ecuatoriana de Aviacion (Ecuador)

ECV — Extracellular Virus

ECWA — Economic Commission for Western Asia (of UN)

EC^{2}M — Electronic Countercountermeasures

ED — Electro-Dialysis
Electrodeposition
Electron Device
Esaki Diode
Estate Duty (replaced by Capital Transfer Tax)
Ethyldichlorarsine
numbered series of Exposure Drafts issued by Accounting Standards Steering Committee
prefix to numbered series of documents issued by ERIC (of USOE)
prefix to numbered series of reports issued by Engineering Division, Army Engineer Reactors Group (US Army)

EdA — Ejercito del Aire (Spain) (Military Air Force) Committee (of TSA)

EDA — Economic Development Administration (of Department of Commerce (USA))
Electrical Development Advisory Division (of the Electricity Council)
Electrical Development Association
Electron-Donor Acceptor
Electronic Design Automation
Ethylene Diamine
European Demolition Association
European Disposables Association (Belgium) now EDANA (Belgium)
External Data Aiding

EDA-OER — Economic Development Administration, Office of Economic Research (Department of Commerce (USA))

EDAC — Engineering Design Advisory Committee (of the Design Council)

EDACT — Engineering Drawings to Automatic Control Tapes

EDAMA — European Domestic Appliance Manufacturers Association

EDANA — European Disposables and Non-Wovens Association (Belgium)

EDATS — Extra-Deep Armed Team Sweep

EDAX — Energy Dispersive Analysis X-ray

EDB — Engineering Data Bank (of GIDEP (USA))
Ethylene dibromide
European Development Board (Singapore)
Export Data Branch (of DTI)
Extruded Double Base

EDBS — Educational Data Base System

EDC — Economic Development Committee
Education and training of Chemists
Electronic Digital Computer
Energy Distribution Curve
Error Detection and Correction
Ethylene Dichloride
European Documentation Centres (of the European Communities)
Event Driven Component
Export Development Corporation (Canada) (a Federal Crown Corporation)

EdCAAD — EDINBURGH (UNIVERSITY) Computer-Aided Architectural Design

EDCC — Environmental Dispute Coordination Commission (Japan)

EDCCI — Economic Development Committee for the Chemical Industry

EDCL — Electric-Discharge Convection Laser

EDCS — Electronic Control System

EDD — Electronic Data Display

EDE — Electronic Defence Evaluator
Emitter Dip Effect

EDEW — Enhanced Distance Early Warning

EDF — Elecricite de France (France)
Environmental Defense Fund (USA)
European Development Fund (of EEC)

EDG — Electrical Discharge Grinding

EDGN — Ethylene Glycol Dinitrate

EDI — Electronic Data Interchange

EDIAC — Electronic Display of Indexing Association and Content

EDICT — Engineering Document Information Collection Technique

EDINET — Education Instruction Network

EDIS — Engineering Data Information System

EDIT — Engineering Design Intelligent Terminal
Examining, Diagnosis, Identification and Training

EDITEAST — South-East Asia Association of Science Editors

EDITERRA — European Association of Earth-Science Editors

EDL Electric Discharge Laser
Electrodynamic Levitation
Electrostatic Deflecting Lens
Embedded Design Language
Equipment Development Laboratory (of Weather Bureau (USA))

EDM Electrical Discharge Machine
Electrodischarge Machining
Electromagnetic Distance Measuring
Electronic Distance Measuring
Engineering Development Model

EDMF Extended Data Management Facility

EDMI Electronic Distance Measurement Instrument

EDML Electric Discharge Mixing Laser

EDNA Emergency Department Nurses Association (USA)

EDO Ethylene Dichloride

EDOS Extended Disk Operating System

EDOS/RJE Extended Disc Operating System with Remote Job Entry facilities

EDP Electronic Data Processing
Experimental Data Processor

EDPAA Electronic Data Processing Auditors Association (USA)

EDPD Energy-Dependent Photoelectron Diffraction

EDPE Electronic Data Processing Equipment

EDPS Electronic Data Processing System

EDR Environmental Deterioration Rating
Experimenterende Danske Radiomatorer (Denmark) (Danish Amateur Radio Society)

EDRA Environmental Design Research Association (USA)

EDRC Economic and Development Review Committee (of OECD)

EDRF Experienced Demand Replacement Factors

EDRS Engineering Data Retrieval System
ERIC Document Reproduction Service (USOE)
Expanded Data Reporting System

EDS Electronic Data Switching
Electronic Document Storage
Emergency Detection System
Energy Dispersive Spectrometer
Environmental Data Service (formerly of ESSA now of NOAA (USA))
Exchangeable Disk Store

EDSAC Electronic Delay Storage Automatic Calculator
Electronic Discrete Sequential

EDSAT Educational Satellite
Educational Television Satellite

EDSIM Event-based Discrete Simulation

EDSTM Environmental Data Service Technical Memoranda (formerly of ESSA now NOAA (USA))

EDT Division of Energy Demonstrations and Technology (of the TVA (USA))
Electrodeless Discharge Tube
Engineering Design Test

EDTA Ethylenediamine Tetra-acetic Acid
European Dialysis and Transplation Association

EDTAC Economic Development and Technical Assistance Center (of State University of New York (USA))

EDTC European Diving Technology Committee

EDTV Extended Definition Television

EDU Electronic Display Unit
European Democratic Union
Experimental Diving Unit

EDUCOM Interuniversity Communications Council (USA)

EDV Electro-Dynamic Venturi
Equivalent Daylight Visibility

EDVAC Electronic Discrete Variable Automatic Computer (OR Calculator)

EDX Energy Dispersive X-ray analysis
Energy Dispersive X-ray detector

EDXA Energy Dispersive X-ray Analysis

EDXRA Energy-Dispersive X-Ray Analysis

EDXRF Energy Dispersive X-Ray Fluorescence

EE Electrical Engineering
Exoelectron
Exoelectron Emission
Exponential Equation

EE-PROM Electrically Erasable Programmable Read-Only Memory

EEA Educational Equipment Association
Electronic Engineering Association
Essential Elements of Analysis
Experimental Aircraft Association (USA)
Explosive Embedment Anchor

EEAT End of Evening Astronomical Twilight

EEB Eastern Electricity Board
European Environmental Bureau (of the EEC)

EEC Electronic Engine Control
Electronic Experimental Centre
EUROCONTROL Experimental Centre (France)
European Economic Community

EECA European Electronic Component Manufacturers Association

EECGS Emergency Evaporative Coolant Garment System

EECL Emitter-Emitter Coupled Logic

EECMB Electrical Equipment Certification Management Board (of HSE)

EED Elastic Energy Density
Electro-Explosive Device

EEDC Electronics Economic Development Committee (of the National Economic Development Council)

EEE Eastern Equine Encephalitis
Electrical, Electronic and Electro-mechanical
Electromagnetic Environment Experiment (aboard the 'Spacelab')
Exoelectron Emission

EEF Encircled Energy Function
Engineering Employers Federation

EEG Electro-encephalograph

EEI Environmental Equipment Institute (USA)

EEIA Electrical and Electronic Insulation Association (part of BEAMA)

EEL Emergency Exposure Limit
Environmental Effects Laboratory (of WES (US Army))

EELS Electron Energy Loss Spectroscopy
Electronic Emitter Location System

EEM Eigenmode Expansion Method
Electronic Equipment Monitoring
Emission Electron Miscroscope

EEMAC Electrical and Electronic Manufacturers Association of Canada (Canada)

EEMIS Energy Emergency Management Information System

EEMJEB Electrical and Electronic Manufacturers Joint Education Board

EEMS European Environment Mutagen Society

EEMTIC Electrical and Electronic Measurement and Test Instrument Conference

EEO Energy Efficiency Office (DEn)
European Electro-Optics Conference and Exhibition

EEOA European Electro-Optics Association

EEOC Equal Employment Opportunity Commission (USA)

EEP Engineering Experimental Phase buoy

EEPA Electromagnetic Energy Policy Alliance (USA)

EEPAC Eastern Electronics Packaging Conference (USA)

EEPC Engineering Export Promotion Council (India)

EEPROM Electrically Erasable Programmable Read-Only Memory

EEQ Empresa Electrica Quito (Ecuador)
EER Energy-Efficiency Ratio
Explosive Echo Ranging
prefix to numbered series of reports issued by Ohio University, Department of Electrical Engineering (USA)
EERA Electrical and Electronic Retailers Association (merged with RTRA in 1974)
EERC Earthquake Engineering Research Center (California University (USA))
EERI Earthquake Engineering Research Institute (USA)
EERJ External Expansion Ramjet
EERL Explosive Excavation Research Laboratory (US Army)
EERM Establissement d'Etudes et de Recherches Meteorologiques (France) (Meteorological Study and Research Establishment)
EERO Explosive Excavation Research Office (of AEWES (US Army))
EEROM Electrically Erasable Read-Only Memory
EERRHV Emergency Escape Ramps for Runaway Heavy Vehicles
EES Electro-magnetic Environment Simulator
Energy Efficiency System
Engineering Experiment Station (Ohio State University (USA))
School of Electrical Engineering (of Georgia Institute of Technology (USA))
EESD Electromechanical and Environmental Systems Division (of CERL (US Army))
EEUA Engineering Equipment Users Association
EEVC European Experimental Vehicle Committee (secretariat provided by TRRC)
EEZ Economically Exclusive Zone
Exclusive Economic Zone
EF Electrofloatation
Engineering Foundation (USA)
EFA Empresa Ferrocarriles Argentinos (Argentine) (Argentine State Railways)
Epilepsy Foundation of America (USA)
Essential Fatty Acids
European Fighter Aircraft (a project of the UK, France, Germany, Italy and Spain)
EFAB Establishment d'Etudes et de Fabrications d'Armaments de Bourges (of Groupement Industriel des Armements Terrestres (France))
EFAPIT Euromarket Federation of Animal Protein Importers and Traders (of the EEC)
EFB Electrofluidized Bed
EFC Equivalent Full Charges
Etched Flexible Circuitry
European Federation of Corrosion
EFCE European Federation of Chemical Engineers
EFCIS Societe pour l'Etude et la Fabrication de Circuits Integres Speciaux (France)
EFCS Electrical Flight-Control System
Engineer Functional Component System (US Army)
European Federation of Cytological Societies
EFD Electro-Fluid-Dynamic
EFDARS Expandable Flight Data Acquisition and Recording System
EFDAS Epsylon Flight Data Acquisition System
EFE Early Fuel Evaporation
EFF European Furniture Federation
EFFF Electrical Field-Flow Fractionation
EFG Edge-defined, Film-fed Growth
Electric-Field-Gradient
EFI Electronic Fuel Injection
Elektrisitetsforsyningens Forskningsinstitutt (Norway) (Electricity Supply Research Institute)
Enrico Fermi Institute (University of Chicago (USA))
Erevanskii Fizcheskii Institut (USSR)
EFIBCA European Flexible Intermediate Bulk Container Association
EFIE Electric Field Integral Equation
EFIM Ente Partecipazione e Finanziamento Industria Manifatturiera (Italy) (Public Authority for Financing Industry)
EFINS Enrico Fermi Institute for Nuclear Studies (of Chicago University (USA))
EFIRA Electric-Field-Induced Infra-Red Absorption
EFIS Electronic Flight Instrument System
EFL Effective Focal Length
Emitter Function Logic
Explosion and Flame Laboratory (of the HSE)
EFLA Education Film Library Association (USA)
EFLC Engineers Foreign Language Circle
EFM Electronic Fuel Management
EFMA European Financial Marketing Association
EFMD European Foundation for Management Development
EFNMS European Federation of National Maintenance Societies
EFOP Economic Feasibility of Projects and Investments
EfP Electronics for Peace
EFP Endoneurial Fluid Pressure
European Federation of Purchasing
EFPB Employers Federation of Papermakers and Boardmakers (now part of British Paper and Board Industry Federation)
EFPD Effect Full-Power Days
EFPH Effective Full Power Hours
EFPS European Federation of Productivity Services
EFPW European Federation for the Protection of Waters
EFS Electronic Frequency Selection
Equivalent Standard Fillet
EFSUMB European Federation of Societies for Ultrasound in Medicine and Biology
EFT Earliest Finish Time
Electronic Financial Transaction
Electronic Funds Transfer
Embedded Figure Test
EFTA European Flexographic Technical Association
European Free Trade Association
EFTO Encrypt For Transmission Only
EFTPOS Electronic Funds Transfer at Point of Sale
EFTS Electronic Funds Transfer System
EFV Equilibrium Flash Vaporization
EFVA Educational Foundation for Visual Aids
EGA Edge Gradient Analysis
Effluent Gas Analysis
Evolved Gas Analysis
EGAM Ente di Gestione Aziende Minerarie (Italy) (Govt controlled) (disbanded 1977)
EGAS European Group on Atomic Spectroscopy
EGAT Electricity Generating Authority of Thailand (Thailand)
EGC Economic Growth Center (Yale University (USA))
EGCA Engineering and Grading Contractors Association (USA)
EGCI Export Group for the Construction Industry
EGCL Electro-generated Chemiluminescence
EGCM European Group for Co-operation in Management
EGD Electrogasdynamics
EGDA Ethylene Glycol Dimethacrylate

EGDN Ethylene Glycol Dinitrate
EGF Epidermal Growth Factor
EGGA European General Galvanizers Association
EGL External Granular Layer
EGME Ethylene Glycol Monomethyl Ether
EGO Eccentric Orbiting Geophysical Observatory
EGOT Erythrocyte Glutamic-Oxaloacetic Transaminase
EGOTI Egyptian General Organization for Trade and Industry (Egypt)
EGP Ethno-, geo-, polycentric
EGPA Egyptian General Petroleum Authority (Egypt)
EGPC Egyptian General Petroleum Corporation (Egypt) (replaced in 1976 by EGPA)
EGR Exhaust Gas Re-circulation
Exhaust Gas Re-cycle
EGT Exhaust Gas Temperature
EH prefix to numbered series of Guidance Notes on Environmental Hygiene issued by HSE and published by HMSO
EHA Enkephalin-Hydrolysing Activity
European Helicopter Association
EHAA Epidemic Hepatitis Associated Antigen
EHC Electrohydraulic Control
European Hotel Corporation (an association of BEA, BOAC, Alitalia, Swissair, Lufthansa and five banks)
EHD Elastohydrodynamic
Electrohydrodimerization
Electrohydrodynamic
EHDI Electronic Horizontal Director Indicator
EHF Experimental Husbandry Farm (or MAFF)
Extra OR Extremely High Frequency
EHL Elastohydrodynamic Lubrication
Environmental Health Laboratory (USAF)
EHM Engine Health Monitoring
EHMO Extended Huckel Molecular Orbital
EHOC European Helicopter Operators Committee (a Group of European Companies)
EHOG European Host Operators Group
EHP Extrinsic Hyperpolarizing Potential
EHPM Electro-Hydraulic Pulse Motor
EHS Environmental Health Service (of PHS (USA))
Experiment Horticulture Station (of MAFF)
EHSD Electronic Horizontal Situation Display
EHSI Electronic Horizontal Situation Indicator
EHT Electrothermal Hydrazine Thruster
EHV Electric Heart Vector
Extra High Voltage
EI Electrical Insulation
Electron Impact
Embrittlement Index
EIA Electronic Industries Association (USA)
Energy Information Administration (of DOE (USA))
Engineering Industries Association
Environmental Impact Analysis
Environmental Impact Assessment
Enzyme Immunoassay
EIA-J Electronics Industry Association of Japan (Japan)
EIAC Electronic Industries Association of Canada (Canada) (merged into EEMAC, 1976)
Ergonomics Information Analysis Centre (University of Birmingham)
EIAJ Engineering Industries Association of Japan (Japan)
EIB Economisch Instituut voor de Bouwnijverheid (Netherlands) (Building Industry Economic Institute)
Escuela Interamencana de Bibliotecologia (Colombia) (Interamerican Library School (at University of Antioquia))
European Investment Bank (of EEC)
EIC Energy Information Center (University of New Mexico (USA))
Engineering Institute of Canada
Equipment Identification Code
EICAS Engine Indication and Crew Alerting System
EICB Extra-Intracranial Bypass
EICF European Investment Casters Federation (Netherlands)
EICON Electronic Index Console
EICPC Electronic Industries Component Policy Council
EID Electrical Inspection Directorate (MINTECH) (now EQD)
Electron Impact Desorption
Electron-induced Ion Desorption
EIE Electronic Information Exchange
EIEC English Industrial Estates Corporation
EIED Electrically Initiated Explosive Device
EIEMA Electrical Installation Equipment Manufacturers Association
EIFAC European Inland Fisheries Advisory Commission (of FAO)
EIFLG Engineering Institutions' Foreign Language Group
EIFOV Effective Instantaneous Field-Of-View
EIII Association of the European Independent Informatics Industry
EIILC Electrical Installation Industry Liaison Committee
EIL Electrical Insulating Liquids
Electron Injection Laser
Engineers India Limited (India) (government owned technical consultancy agency)
EIM Effective Index Method
Excitability Inducing Material
EIMMA East India Metal Merchants Association (India)
EIMO Electronic Interface Management Office (of USN)
EIN Education Information Network (of EDUCOM)
European Informatics Network
EIO Extended Interactive Oscillator
EIP Educational Investing and Planning Programme
EIPA European Information Providers Association
EIPC European Institute of Printed Circuits
EIR Eidgenossisches Institut fur Reaktorforschung (Switzerland) (Federal Institute for Reactor Research)
EIRA Ente Italiano Rilievi Aerofotogrammetrici (Italy) (National Authority for Survey by Aerial Photogrammetry)
EIRMA European Industrial Research Management Association
EIRP Effective Isotropically Radiated Power
Equivalent Isotropic Radiated Power
EIS Economic Information System
Electron Impact Spectroscopy
Electronic Inquiry System
Environmental Impact Statement
Environmental Information System
Epidemiological Investigation Service (of CDC (PHS) (HEW) (USA))
Export Intelligence Service (of BOTB)
Extended Instruction Set
EISCAT European Incoherent Scatter Organisation
European Ionospheric Scatter (a project of an association of six European countries)
EISN Experimental Integrated Switched Network
EISSWA Experimental Information Service in two Social Welfare Agencies
EIT Electronic Information Technology
Environmental Interaction Theory of Personality
European Institute for Trans-National Studies in Group and Organizational Development
EITB Engineering Industry Training Board

EIWLS Extended Iterative Weighted Least Squares
EIZ Engineering Institute of Zambia (Zambia)
EJC Engineers Joint Council (USA)
EJCC Eastern Joint Computer Conference (USA)
EJCSC European Joint Committee of Scientific Cooperation (of the Council of Europe)
EJOTF Earth-Jupiter Orbiter Transfer Flight
EJP Excitatory Junctional Potential
EL Electro-Luminescence
Electronics Laboratory
ELA Equipment Leasing Association
ELAB Elektronikklaboratoriet (of NTH (Norway))
ELADS Early Launch Display System
ELAG European Library Automation Group
ELAMP Exchange Line Multiplexer Analysis Programme
ELAS Elasticity (a group of computer programmes)
ELB Electronic Lean Burn
Emergency Locator Beacon
ELB-A Emergency Location Beacon-Aircraft
ELBIN East London Business Information Network
ELC Environmental Liaison Centre (Kenya)
Extra Low-Carbon
ELCA Electronic Linear Circuit Analysis programme
ELCB Earth-Leakage Circuit Breaker
ELCD Evaporative Loss Control Device
ELCP Code of Practice Committee for Electrical Engineering (of BSI)
ELCU Electrical Control Unit
ELD Economic Load Dispatching
Electrolytic Display
ELDC European Lead Development Committee
ELDEMA Electronic Detection Machine
ELDO European Launcher Development Organisation (merged into ESA in 1975)
ELEC European League for Economic Cooperation
ELECSYS Integrated Electronic Engineering System
Electro-RAM Electro-mechanical Redundant Actuator Mechanism
ELEED Elastic Low Energy Electron Diffraction
ELEP European Federation of Anti-Leprosy Associations (name changed to ILEP in 1975)
ELEVAR Elevated Acquisition Radar
ELF Electronic Location Finder
Essence et Lubrifiants Francais (France)
Extensible Language Facility
Extremely Low Frequency
ELFA Electric Light Fittings Association
ELG Electrolytic Grinding
ELGO European Launcher for Geostationary Orbit
ELI Environmental Law Institute (USA)
Extra-Low Interstitial
ELIC Electric Lamp Industry Council
ELINT Electro-magnetic Intelligence
Electronic Intelligence
ELIP Electrostatic Latent Image Photography
ELIPS Electron Image Projection System
ELIRT Environmental Laboratories Information Retrieval Technique
ELISA Electronic Intelligence Search and Analysis
Enzyme-Linked Immunosorbent Assay
ELLIS European Legal Literature Information Service
ELM Extended Local Memory
ELMA Empressa Lineas Maritimas Argentinas (Argentina) (state owned shipping company)
ELMIA European Agricultural and Industrial Fair
ELMO Engineering and Logistics Management Office (of MERDC (US Army))
Engineering and Logistics Management Office (US Army)
Engineering Lunar Model Obstacle
ELMS Earth Limb Measurement Satellite
Elastic Loop Mobility System
Engineering Lunar Model Surface
Experimental Library Management System
ELMSIM Engine Life Management Simulation Model
ELOC Elastomeric-Oriented Copolyesters
ELOISE European Large Orbiting Instrumentation for Solar Experiments
ELOS Extended-Line-Of-Sight
ELPEX International Electronic Production Equipment Exhibition
ELR Engineering Laboratory Report
Environmental Report (a numbered series issued by many authorities in the USA—to identify the specific body originating the report it is often necessary to know also the EIS (Environmental Impact Statement) Number)
ELRAC Electronic Reconnaissance Accessory system
ELRAFT Efficient Logic Reduction Analysis of Fault Trees
ELRAT Electrical Ram Air Turbine
ELRO Electronics Logistics Research Office (US Army)
ELS Economic Lot Size
Emitter Location System
Energy Loss Spectroscopy
ELSA Electronic Lobe Switching Antenna
Emergency Life Support Apparatus
Experimental System for Simulation and Animation
ELSAG Elettronica San Giorgio (Italy)
ELSBM Exposed Location Single Buoy Mooring
ELSE (European Life Science Editors) is the acronym adopted by the European Association of Editors of Biological Periodicals
ELSEC Electronics Security
ELSI Esso Lubrication Service to Industry
Extra Large Scale Integrated
ELSIE Electronic Location of Status Indicating Equipment
Electronic Signalling and Indicating Equipment
Electronic Speech Information Equipment
Emergency Life-Saving Instant Exit
ELSP Economic Lot Scheduling Problem
ELSS Extravehicular Life Support System
ELSSE Electronic Sky Screen Equipment
ELT Emergency Locator Transmitter
ELV Expendable Launch Vehicle
Extra-Low Voltage
EM Electro-Modulation
Electromagnetic
Electronic Mail
Emergency Maintenance
Engineering Manual
Engineering Memorandum
Extensible Machine
EM & M Electronic Memories and Magnetics
EMA Egyptian Medical Association (Egypt)
Electro-Mechanical Actuator
Electromagnetic Accelerometer
Electron Microprobe Analysis
Employment Management Association (USA)
Engine Manufacturers Association (USA)
European Marketing Association
Excavator Makers Association
Extended Mercury Autocode
EMAA European Mastic Asphalt Association

EMAC Ecole Africaine de la Meteorologie et de l'Aviation Civile (of ASECNA) (East African School of Meteorology and Civil Aviation (Republic of Niger)
Educational Media Association of Canada (Canada)

EMACC Energy Materials Coordinating Committee (of DOE (USA))

EMAG Electron Microscopy and Analysis Group (of the Institute of Physics)

EMAS EDINBURGH (UNIVERSITY) Multi-Access System
Employment Medical Advisory Service (of Dept of Employment) (now of Health and Safety Executive)

EMAT Electromagnetic Acoustic Transducer Testing

EMATS Emergency Mission Automatic Transmission Service

EMATT Expendable Mobile Anti-submarine warfare Training Target

EMB Electron Beam Microanalysis
English Beet Molasses

EMBC European Molecular Biology Conference

EMBET Error Model Best Estimate of Trajectory

EMBL European Molecular Biology Laboratory (Germany)

EMBO European Molecular Biology Organization

EMBRAER Empresa Brasileira de Aeronautica (Brazil) (National Society for Aeronautical Construction)

EMBRAPA Empresa Basileiro de Pesquisa Agropecuaria (Brazil) (Brazilian Agricultural Information Institution)

EMBRATEL Empresa Brasileira de Telecomunicacoes (Brazil) (State owned company for inter-state and international telecommunication services)

EMC Electro-Magnetic Compatibility
Electromagnetically Compatible
Encephalomyocarditis
Energy Management and Control
Engineering Manpower Commission (of Engineers Joint Council (USA))
Enterprise Miniere et Chimique (France) (govt owned)
European Muon Collaboration

EMC-FOM Electro-Magnetic Compatibility Figure of Merit

EMCDAS Electro-Magnetic Compatibility Data Acquisition System

EMCF European Monetary Co-operation Fund (of EEC)

EMCON Emission Control
European Congress on Electron Microscopy

EMCOPS Electromagnetic Compatibility Operational System

EMCS Energy Monitoring and Control System

EMCSR European Meeting on Cybernetics and Systems Research

EMD Eidgenossische Militar-department (Switzerland) (Federal Defence Department)
Electromagnetic Motion Detector
Electronique Marcel Dassault (France)
Energy and Minerals Division (of GAO (USA))
Equivalent Martin Day
Extractive Metallurgy Division (of the Metallurgical Society of AIME)

EMDA Emergency Distance Available

EMDG Euromissile Dynamics Group (a consortium of Aerospatiale (France) MBB (Germany) and British Aerospace (UK))

EMDI Energy Management Display Indicator

EME Electromagnetic Effectiveness
Electromagnetic Emission
Electromagnetically Equivalent

EMEC Electronic Maintenance Engineering Center (US Army)

EMER Electromagnetic Molecular Electronic Resonance

EMETF Electromagnet Environmental Test Facility (US Army)

EMEU East Midland Educational Union

EMF Electromotive Force
European Meeting on Ferroelectrics

EMG Electromyogram
Electromyograph

EMI Electromagnetic Inference

EMIC Electronic Materials Information Centre (of RRE)

EMID Electro-Magnetic Intrusion Detector

EMIS Ecosytem of Machines Information System
Effluent Management Information System
Electronic Materials Information Service (of INSPEC)
Engineering Maintenance Information System
International Electromagnetic Isotope Separators Conference

EMISEC Emission Security

EMIT Electromagnetic Induction Tweeter
Enzyme Multiplied Immunassay Technique

EMKO Ethyl Michler's Ketone Oxime

EML Earthquake Mechanisms Laboratory (of ESSA (USA)) (later of NOAA, then transferred in 1973 to USGS)
Electromagnetic Launcher
Engineering Mechanics Laboratory (of NBSA)
Environmental Measurements Laboratory (DOE) (USA)
Equal Matrix Languages

EMM Earth, Moon and Mars
Electromagnetic Measurement
Electron Mirror Microscope

EMMA Electron Microscope-Microprobe Analyser
Electron Microscopy and Microanalysis
Electronic Mask Making Apparatus
Electronic Mathematic Model-Analogue
Engineering Mock-up and Manufacturing Aid
Equalized Maintenance, Maximum Availability
Eye Movement Measuring Apparatus

EMMIS Electronics Maintenance Management Information System

EMMS Electronic Mail and Message System

EMMSA Envelope Makers and Manufacturing Stationers Association

EMMSE Educational Modules for Materials Science and Engineering (a project of NSF (USA) administered by Pennsylvania State University)

EMO Emergency Measures Organisation (Canada)

EMORG East Midland Operational Research Group

EMOS Earth's Mean Orbital Speed
European Meteorological Satellite

EMP Electromagnetic Pulse
Ethylmercury Phosphate

EMPA Eidgenossiche Materialsprufungs und Versuchsanstalt (Switzerland) (Federal Materials Testing and Experiment Station)
Electron Microprobe Analysis
European Maritime Pilots Association

EMPAC Conference on Electricity for Materials Processing and Conservation

EMPASS Electromagnetic Performance of Aircraft and Ships System (a project of the USN)

EMPC Educational Media Producers Council (of the National Audio-Visual Association (USA))

EMPHASIS Evaluation Management using Past History Analysis for Scientific Inventory Simulation

EMPIRE Early Manned Planetary-Interplanetary Roundtrip Expedition
Electro-Magnetic Performance Information Research
Electro-Magnetic Phenomena Interference Repository

EMPRA Emergency Multiple Person Rescue Apparatus

EMPREMAR Empresa Maritima del Estado (Chile)

EMPRESS Electromagnetic Pulse Radiation Environment Simulator for Ships

EMQ Economic Manufacturing Quantity

EMR Department of Energy, Mines and Resources (Canada)
Electromagnetic Radiation
Electromagnetic Riveting

EMRA Extra Mural Research Agreement (between Dept of Industry and research bodies)

EMRB Engineering Materials Requirements Board (of DOI)

EMRC European Medical Research Councils (of ESF)

EMRIC Educational Media Research Information Center (USA)

EMRL Engineering Materials Research Laboratory (Brown University (USA))
Engineering Mechanics Research Laboratory (Texas University, USA)

EMRO Eastern Mediterranean Regional Office (of WHO (UN))

EMRS Export Marketing Research Scheme (of BOTB)

EMRU Electro-Magnetic Release Unit

EMS Early MARC Search (Library of Congress (USA))
Electromagnetic Susceptibility
Electromagnetic Suspension system
Electromotive Surface
Electronic Mail System
Electronic Message System
Emergency Medical Service
Energy Management System
Ente Minerario Siciliano (Sicily)
European Monetary System (of EEC)
Expected Mean Squares
prefix to numbered series of reports issued by the Environmental and Medical Sciences Division of AERE (UKAEA)

EMSA Electron Microscope Surface Area
Electron Microscopy Society of America (USA)

EMSC Electrical Manufacturers Standards Council (of NEMA, USA)

EMSL Environmental Monitoring and Surveillance Laboratory (of EPA (USA))

EMSU Epidemiology and Medical Statistics Unit (of the HSE)
European Medium and Small Business Union

EMT Electromechanical Transmission
Expanded Mobility Truck

EMTE European Machine Tool Exhibition

EMTG Electron Microscope Techniques Group (of BISRA)

EMTM Electron Microscope Technique Meeting

EMTN European Meteorological Telecommunications Network

EMU Economic and Monetary Union (being formed in stages by the European Communities)
Electrical-Multiple-Unit
Electronic Materials Unit (of RRE)
Extravehicular Mobility Unit

EMUS Electronic Multiplexing System
Engine Usage Monitoring System

EMUX Electronic Multiplexing

EMV Electro-Magnetic Vulnerability
Expected Monetary Value
Expected Monetary Values

EMVJ Etched Multiple Vertical Junction

EMXRF Electron-microprobe X-Ray Fluorescence

EN Emergency Number (prefix to numbered types of Steel)
Endemic Nephropathy
prefix to numbered series of Europaische Norm (European Standard accepted by CEN)

ENA Ecole Nationale d'Administration (France) (National School of Management)
Extractable Nuclear Antigen

ENAC Ecole Nationale de l'Aviation Civile (France) (National School of Civil Aviation)

ENAF Empresa Nacional de Fundiciones (Bolivia) (State Smelting Enterprise)

ENAMI Empresa Nacional de Mineria (Chile)

ENAP Empresa Nacional de Petroleo (Chile) (National Petroleum Authority)
Escuele Nacional de Administracion Publica (El Salvador) (National School of Public Administration)

ENASA Empresa Nacional de Autocamiones SA (Spain)

ENB Ethylidenenorborene

ENCC Ente Nazionale Cellulosa e Carta (Italy)

ENCI Empresa Nacional de Comercialización de Insumos (Peru)

ENCOE British National Committee on Ocean Engineering

ENCORD Interdepartmental Committee On Energy Research and Development

ENCORE Enlarged Compact by Respond

ENCOTEL Empresa Nacional de Correos y Telegrafos (Argentina)

END External Negative Differential

ENDC Eighteen Nation Committee on Disarmament (later Conference of the Committee on Disarmament)

ENDESA Empresa Nacional de Electricidad SA (Chile) (National Electricity Authority)

ENDEX Environmental Data Index (of EDS (NOAA) (USA))

ENDF Evaluated Nuclear Data File

ENDOR Electron Nuclear Double Resonance

ENDS EURATOM Nuclear Documentation System

ENEA Comitato Nazionale per la Ricerca e per lo Sviluppo dell'Energia Nucleare e delle Energie Alternative (Italy) (National Committee for Research and Development Nuclear and Alternative Energies)
European Nuclear Energy Agency (of OECD) (now NEA) (and includes Japan)

ENEE Empresa Nacional de Energia Electrica (Honduras)

ENEL Ente Nazional per l'Energia Elettrica (Italy) (State Electricity Authority)
Ente Nazionale Energia Elettri (Italy) (State National Electricity Board)

ENERGAS Empresa Nacional de Gas (Spain) (National Gas Enterprise)

ENEWS Effectiveness of Navy Electronic Warfare System

ENFORM ENGINEERING NUMERIES (CORPORATION (USA)) Information Management System

ENG Electronic News Gathering
Electronystagmogram

ENHER Empresa Hidroelectrica del Ribagorzana SA (Spain)
Empresa Nacionale Hidroelectrica del Ribagorzana (Spain)

ENI Ente Nazionale Idrocarburi (Italy) (National Hydrocarbons Authority)

ENIAC Electronic Numerical Integrator And Calculator

ENIKMAsh Eksperimental'nyy Nauchno Issledovatel'skiy Institut Kuznechno pressovogo Mashinostroyeniya (USSR) (Experimental Scientific Research Institute of Forging-Pressing-Machine Construction)

ENIMS Eksperimental'nyy Nauchno Issledovatel'skiy Institut Metallorezhushchikh Stankov (USSR) (Experimental Scientific Research Institute for Machine Tools)

ENIPP Eksperimental'nyy i Nauchno Issledovatel'skiy Institut Podshipnikovoy Promyshlennosti (USSR) (Experimental and Scientific Research Institute of the Bearing Institute)

ENMG Electroneuromyographic

ENMOD Convention on the Prohibition of Military or any other Hostile Use of Environmental Modification Techniques (of UN)

ENO Comite Hellenique de Normalisation (Greece) (Standards Organisation)

ENPI Ente Nazionale per la Prevenzione degli Infortuni (Italy) (National Authority for Accident Prevention)

ENPOCON Environmental Pollution Control

ENR Emissora Nacional de Radiodifusao (Portugal)
Equivalent Noise Resistance

ENRI Electronic Navigation Research Institute (Japan)

ENS European Nuclear Society

ENSA Equipos Nucleares SA (Spain)

ENSAE Ecole Nationale Superieure de l'Aeronautique et de l'Espace (France) (National College for Aeronautics and Aerospace)

ENSAIS Ecole Nationale Superieure des Arts et Industrie de Strasbourg (France)

ENSB Ecole Nationale Superieure de Bibliothecaires (France) (National College of Librarianship)

ENSEC European Nuclear Steelmaking Club

ENSIDESA Empresa Nacional Siderurgica SA (Spain)

ENSIP Turbine Engine Structural Integrity Program (of USAF)

ENST Ecole Nationale Superieure des Telecommunications (France) (National Higher College of Telecommunications)

ENSTA Ecole Nationale Superieure de Techniques Avancees (France) (National College of Advanced Techniques)

ENT Ear, Nose and Throat
Empresa Nacional de Telecomunicaciones (Argentine) (National Telecommunications Authority)
Equivalent Noise Temperature

ENTAC Engine-Teleguide-Anti-Char

ENTEC Esfahan Nuclear Technology Centre (of AEOI (Iran))

ENTEL Empresa Nacional de Telecomunicaciones (Argentina) (National Telecommunications Authority)
Empresa Nacional de Telecomunicaciones (Bolivia) (National Telecommunications Authority)
Empresa Nacional de Telecomunicaciones (Chile) (National Telecommunications Authority)
Empresa Nacional de Telecomunicaciones (Ecuador) (National Telecommunications Authority)
Empresa Nacional de Telecomunicaciones (Peru) (National Telecommunications Authority)
Escuela Nacional de Telecomunicaciones (Mexico)

ENU Ethylnitrosourea

ENUSA Empresa Nacional del Uranio SA (Spain)

ENVITEC International Exhibition for Environmental Protection and Environmental Technique
International Fair and Congress on Engineering in Environmental Protection

ENVP Expected Net Present Value

EO Electro-Optic
Ethylene Oxide

EOAR European Office of Aerospace Research (USAF)

EOARD Equal Opportunities Commission
European Office of Aerospace Research and Development (USAF)

EOB Electronic Order of Battle

EOC Elementary Operated Control
Equal Opportunities Commission

EOCCD European Organisation for the Control of Circulatory Diseases

EOCM Electro-Optical Countermeasures

EOD Explosive Ordnance Disposal

EODAP Earth and Ocean Dynamic Applications Program (of NASA (USA))

EODD Electro-Optic Digital Deflector

EODET Early Orbit Determination

EOFC Electro-Optical Fire Control

EOG Electro-oculogram
Electro-oculograph

EOGB Electro-Optical Glide Bomb
Electro-Optical Guided Bomb

EOI Electro-Optical Imaging

EOIS Electro-Optical Imaging System

EOL Expression-Oriented Language

EOM Electro-Optic Modulator

EOP English for Occupational Purposes
Executive Office of the President (USA)

EOQ Economic Order Quantity

EOQC European Organisation for Quality Control (Netherlands)

EOR Enhanced Oil Recovery
Explosive Ordnance Reconnaissance

EORA Explosive Ordnance Reconnaissance Agents

EORTC European Organization for Research on Treatment of Cancer

EOS Earth Observation Satellite
Earth to Orbit Shuttle
Egyptian Organization for Standardization (United Arab Republic)
Electro-Optical Systems
Electronic Office System
Enhanced Operating System
Equation Of State
European Orthodontic Society
Societe Anonyme Energie de l'Ouest Suisse (Switzerland)

EOSS Earth Orbital Space Station
Electro-Optical Sensor System
Electro-Optical Simulation System
Engineering Operational Sequencing System

EOT Electric Overhead Travelling crane

EOW Electro-Optical Warfare
Engine-Over-the-Wing
Engineer Order Wire

EP Easy Projection
Environmental Protection
Equine Piroplasmosis
Expanded Polystyrene
Extreme Pressure

EP/PB Electroplated/Pressure Bonded

EPA Economic Planning Agency (Japan)
Eicosapentaenoic Acid
Electron Probe Analyzer
Environmental Protection Agency (USA)

EPABX Electronic Private Automatic Branch Exchange

EPAM Elementary Perceiver and Memorizer

EPARCS Enhanced Perimeter Acquisition Radar Characterization System

EPASA Electron Probe Analysis Society of America (USA)

EPBX Electronic Private Branch Exchange

EPC Economic Policy Committee (of OECD)
Edge Punched Card
Educational Publishers Council (of the Publishers Association)
Electrically Pulsed Chamber
Engine-Performance Computer

	Engineering Professors' Conference
	European Patent Convention (*more properly* Convention on the Grant of European Patents)
	Experiment Pointing and Control
EPCA	Energy Policy and Conservation Act, 1975 (USA) (amended in NECPA, 1978)
	European Petrochemical Association
EPCCOM	Environmental Protection Co-ordinating Committee (Saudi Arabia)
EPCOT	Experimental Prototype Community of Tomorrow
EPD	Etch Pitch Density
EPDC	Electric Power Development Corporation (Japan) (a semi-governmental organisation)
EPDM	Ethylene-Polylene-Diene Monomer
EPERA	Extractor Parachute Emergency Release Assembly
EPF	European Packaging Federation (Netherlands)
EPFL	Ecole Polytechnique Federale de Lausanne (Switzerland)
EPGA	Emergency Petroleum and Gas Administration (USA)
EPhMRA	European Pharmaceutical Marketing Research Association
EPI	Electronic Position Indicator
	Engineering Projects (India) Limited (India) (government owned)
	EYSENCK (H J EYSENCK and S B G EYSENCK) Personality Inventory
EPIC	Earth-Pointing Instrument Carrier
	Educational Policy Information Centre (a project of NFER)
	Electron-Positron Intersecting Complex
	Electronic Photochromic Integrating Cathode ray tube
	Electronic Properties Information Center (USAF) (now under Purdue University (USA))
	Electronically Processed Inter-unit Cabling
	Employment of Personnel In Computing
	Engineering and Production Information Control
	Engineers Public Information Council (USA)
	Epitaxial Passivated Integrated Circuit
	Evidence Photographers International Council (USA)
	Exchange Price Information Computer
	Exchange Price Information Computer (of the London Stock Exchange)
	Extended Programme for Individual Compensation
EPICS	Energetic Pion Channel and Spectrometer
	Engine Production and Information Control System
EPID	Electrophoretic Image Display
	Electrophoretic Information Display
EPIL	Engineering Projects (India) Ltd (India)
EPIRB	Emergency Position-Indicating Radio Beacon
EPIT	Equipment Procurement and Installation Team
EPL	Economic Policy and Licensing (a branch of the Civil Aviation Authority)
	Electrophotoluminescence
	Emitter Position Location
EPLA	East Pakistan Library Association (Pakistan)
EPLAF	European Planning Federation
EPLD	Electrically Programmable Logic Device
EPLO	Electronic Plotting
EPM	Electric Pulse Motor
	Electro Print Marking
	Electron Probe Microanalysis
	Electrophoretic Mobility
	Empirical Pseudopotential Method
EPMA	Electron Photomicroscopic Analysis
	Electron Probe Micro-Analysis
	Electron Probe Microanalyzer
EPMS	Engine Performance Monitoring System
EPN	Ethyl p-nitrophenyl thionbenzene phosphonate
EPNdB	Effective Perceived Noise Decibels
EPNL	Effective Perceived Noise Level
EPO	Energy Policy Office (USA) (abolished 1974)
	European Patent Office (Germany)
EPOA	East Coast (of Canada) Petroleum Operators Association
EPOC	Earthquake Prediction Observation Centre (of ERI (Japan))
	Eastern Pacific Ocean Conference
EPOCS	Effectual Planning for Operation of Container System
EPOS	Electronic Point of Sale
EPOSS	Environmental Protection Oil Sands Systems
EPP	Electromagnetic wave Propagation Panel (of AGARD (NATO))
	Erythropoietic Protoporphyria
	European Pallet Pool
EPPMA	Expanded Polystyrene Product Manufacturers Association
EPPMP	European Power Press Manufacturers Panel
EPPO	European and Mediterranean Plant Protection Organisation
EPPS	Edwards Personal Preference Schedule
EPR	Electron Paramagnetic Resonance
	Engine Pressure Ratio
	Enriched Pulverised Refuse
	Ethylene and Propylene Rubber
	Exhaust Pressure Ratio
	Eye-Point-of-Regard
EPRF	Exhausted Publications Reference File (of USGPO)
EPRI	Electric Power Research Institute (USA)
EPRL	Environmental Physics Research Laboratories (of CSIRO (Australia)
EPROI	Expected Project Return On Investment
EPROM	Eraseable Programmable Read Only Memory
EPS	Earnings Per Share
	Econometric Programme System
	Electric Propulsion System
	Electron Proton Spectrometer
	European Physical Society
	Expandable Polystyrene
EPSCoR	Experimental Program to Stimulate Competitive Research (of NSF (USA))
EPSEL	Electric Power Systems Engineering Laboratory (Massachusetts Institute of Technology (USA))
EPSMA	European Association for Manufacturers of Self-Adhesive Materials
EPSOC	Earth Physics Satellite Observation Campaign (initiated by the Smithsonian Astrophysical Observatory)
EPSP	Excitatory Post-Synaptic Potential
EPSS	Experimental Packet Switched Service (of the British Post Office)
EPT	Electronic Perspective Transformation system
	Electrostatic Printing Tube
	Ethylene Propylene Terpolymer
EPTA	Expanded Programme of Technical Assistance (of UN)
EPTEL	Empresa Publica de Telecomunicacoes (Angola)
EPTISA	Estudios y Proyectos Tecnicos Industriales SA (Spain)
EPU	Electronics Processor Unit
	Epidermal Proliferative Unit
EPUL	Ecole Polytechnique de l'Universite de Lausanne (Switzerland) (Institute of Technology of the University of Lausanne)
EPW	Earth-Penetrating Warhead
EPWAPDA	East Pakistan Water and Power Development Authority (Pakistan)

EPXMA Electron Probe X-ray Microanalyzer
EPZ Electron Polar Zone
EQAS Energy Quick Advice Service (of Dept of Energy)
EQD Electrical Quality Assurance Directorate (of MOD) (now Electrical Quality Assurance Centre)
EQI Environmental Quality Index
EQO Environmental Quality Objective
EQQ Electric Quadrupole-Quadrupole
EQUALANT Equatorial Atlantic
EQUATE Electronic Quality Assurance Test Equipment
EQUIP Equipment Usage Information Programme
ER Electro-reflectance
Electro-Rheology
Electronic Reconnaissance
Endoplasmic Reticulum
Enhanced Radiation
Established Reliability
prefix to numbered series of Economic Regulations issued by the Civil Aeronautics Board (USA)
ERA Earthquake Risk Analysis
Electric Response Audiometry
Electrical Research Association (now a commercial service company and not a research body)
Electrical Research Association Ltd (changed title to ERA Technology Ltd in 1979)
Electron Ring Accelerator
Electronics Representatives Association (USA)
European Regional Airlines Organization
European Rotogravure Association (Germany)
Evaporative Rate Analysis
ERADCOM Electronics Research And Development Command (US Army)
Electronics Research And Development Command (US Army)
ERAM Extended Range Anti-armour Mine
ERAP Earth Resources Aircraft Program (USA)
Entreprise de Recherches Petrolieres (France)
Exchange Feeder Route Analysis Programme
ERAPS Expendable Reliable Acoustic Path Sonobuoy
ERASE Electromagnetic Radiation Source Elimination
Electronic Radiation Source Eliminator
ERAU Embry-Riddle Aeronautical University (USA)
ERB Earth Radiation Budget
Economic Requirement Batching
Engineers Registration Board (of the Council of Engineering Institutions)
ERBM Extended Range Ballistic Missile
ERBOS Earth Radiation Budget Observation Satellite
ERC Electronics Research Center (of NASA)
Electronics Research Center (University of Texas at Austin (USA))
Engineering and Research Center (of Bureau of Reclamation (USA))
Engineering Research Center (Arizona State University (USA))
Environmental Resources Center (Georgia Institute of Technology (USA))
Equatorial Ring Current
ERCB Energy Resources Conservation Board (Alberta, Canada)
ERCC Edinburgh Regional Computing Centre (of the Universities of Edinburgh, Glasgow, Strathclyde, and government research institutes located close to Edinburgh)
ERCO European Chemoreception Research Organisation
ERCP Endoscopic Retrograde Cholangrography and Pancreatography
ERCR Electronic Retina Computing Reader
ERCS Emergency Rocket Communications System (USAF)
ERD Emergency Return Device
Equivalent Residual Dose
ERDA Electronics Research and Development Activity (US Army)
Energy Research and Development Administration (USA) (merged into DOE in 1977)
ERDA-RDD ERDA Division of Reactor Development and Demonstration (USA)
ERDE Electronics and Radar Development Establishment (India)
Explosives Research and Development Establishment (MINTECH) (now MOD (PE) (now PERME)
ERDET Error Detection
ERDfender EXPLOSIVES RESEARCH AND DEVELOPMENT ESTABLISHMENT Ear Defender Headset
ERDIP Experimental Research and Development Incentives Program (of NSF (USA))
ERDL Engineer Research and Development Laboratory (became MERDC (US Army) in 1962))
Explosives Research and Development Laboratory (India)
EREP Earth Resources Experiment Package
ERF Epoxy Resins Formulators Division (of SPI, USA)
Established Risk Factor
ERFA Conference on Economics of Route Air Navigation Facilities and Airports
ERFB Extended Range Full Bore
ERG Electroretinogram
Energy Research Group (of the Open University)
Enrichment Reprocessing Group (Japan)
ERGA Evolution of Regulations Global Approval (A EEC Group)
ERGO Electric Power Generator Offshore
ERGOM European Research Group on Management
ERGS En-Route Guidance System
Experimental Route Guidance System
ERHPC Extra Rapid Hardening PORTLAND (ASSOCIATED PORTLAND CEMENT Manufacturers Ltd) Cement
ERI Earthquake Research Institute (Tokyo University (Japan))
Engineering Research Institute (Iowa State University (USA))
Engineering Research Institute (Massachusetts University (USA))
ERIA Estudios y Realizaciones en Informatic a Aplicada (Spain)
ERIC Educational Resources Information Center (USOE)
Energy Rate Input Controller
ERIC/AE ERIC Clearinghouse on Adult Education (Syracuse University (USA))
ERIC/chESS ERIC Clearinghouse for Social Studies (University of Colorado and Social Science Education Consortium (USA))
ERIC/CIR ERIC Clearinghouse on Information Resources (Stanford University (USA))
ERIC/CLIS ERIC Clearinghouse on Library and Information Science (of American Society for Information Science (USA)) (Merged with ERIC Clearinghouse on Educational Media and Technology in 1974 to form ERIC/IR (USA))
ERIC/CRESS ERIC Clearinghouse on Rural Education and Small Schools (New Mexico State University (USA))
ERIC/CRIER ERIC Clearinghouse on Retrieval of Information and Evaluation on Reading (Indiana University (USA))
ERIC/EM ERIC Clearinghouse on Educational Media and Technology (merged with ERIC/CLIS in 1974 to form ERIC/IR (USA))
ERIC/IR ERIC Clearinghouse on Information Resources (Stanford University (USA))
ERIM Environmental Research Institute of Michigan (USA)
ERIME Economic Research Institute for the Middle East (Tokyo, Japan)

ERIPLAN European Research Institute forBqRegional and Urban Planning

ERIR Extended-Range Instrumentation Radar

ERISTAR Earth Resources Information Storage, Transformation, Analysis and Retrieval (of Auburn University (USA))

ERIW European Research Institute for Welding

ERL Electronics Research Laboratory (Australia)
Electronics Research Laboratory (University of California (USA))
Emergency Reference Level
Environmental Research Laboratory (Arizona University (USA))
ESSA Research Laboratories (USA) (now Environmental Research Laboratories (of NOAA (USA))

ERLS Economic Release Lot-Sizes

ERLTM Environmental Research Laboratories Technical Memorandum (of NOAA (USA))
ESSA Research Laboratories Technical Memorandum

ERLUA Environmental Research Laboratory, University of Arizona (USA)

ERM Earth Re-entry Module

ERMA Extended-Red Multi-Alkali

ERMAC Electromagnetic Radiation Management Advisory Council (USA)

ERMISS Explosion Resistant Multi-Influence Sweep System for mines (NATO)

ERMS Electrical Resistivity Measuring System

ERN Effective Radiation Node

eRNA Engram Ribonucleic Acid

ERNIC Earnings Related National Insurance Contribution

ERNIE Electronic Random Number Indicating Equipment

ERNO Entwicklungsring Nord (Germany) (Northern Development Centre)

EROP Extensions and Restrictions of Operators

EROPA Eastern Regional Organization for Public Administration (Philippines)

EROS Earth Resources Observation Satellite
Earth Resources Observations Systems (a program of USGS (USA))
Eliminate Range Zero System
Engine Repair and Overhaul Squadron (of the RAF)
Environment and Radar Operation Simulator
Experimental Reflection Orbital Shot

EROWS Expendable Remote-Operating Weather Station

ERP Economic Review Period
Effective Radiated Power
Electronic Radiated Power
Electronic Road Pricing
Endoscopic Retrograde Pancreatography
Environmental Research Paper

ERPLD Extended-Range Phased-Locked Demodulator

ERR Explosive Echo-Ranging

ERRDF Earth Resources Research Data Facility (of NASA (USA))

ERRL Emergency Reference Level

ERS Earth Resources Satellite
Economic Research Service (USDA)
Engineering Research Station (of the Gas Council which became the British Gas Corporation in 1973)
Environmental Research Satellite
Ergonomics Research Society
Experiment Research Society (USA)
Extremal Regulation System

ERSA Extended Range Strike Aircraft
Extended-Range Strategic Aircraft

ERSATS Earth Resource Survey Satellites

ERSOS Earth Resources Survey Operational Satellite

ERSP Earth Resources Survey Program (USA)

ERSPRC Earth Resources Survey Program Review Committee (of NASA (USA))

ERSR Equipment Reliability Status Report

ERSS Earth Resources Survey Satellite

ERSTC Ergonomics Research Society Training Committee

ERSU Energy Research Support Unit (of Science Research Council)

ERT Electrical Resistance Thermometer

ERTE Edinburgh Remote Terminal Emulator

ERTS Earth Resources Technology Satellite (now known as Landsat)
ELIWT Receiver Test System

ERUPT Elementary Reliability Unit Parameter Technique

ERV Electronic Repair Vehicle
Expiratory Reserve Volume
Extract-Release Volume

ERW Electric Resistance Welding
Enhanced-Radiation Weapon

ES Earth Sciences Laboratory (of Natick Laboratories (US Army))
Electrical Sounding
Electrochemical Society (USA)
Environmental Survey
Ergonomics Society
Experiment OR Experimental Station
prefix to numbered-dated series of Emergency Standards issed by ASTM (USA)
prefix to numbered/dated series of reports issued by Environment Sub-committee of RNPRC(MRC)

ESA Department of Economic and Social Affairs (of UN)
Ecological Society of America (USA)
Electrically Small Antenna
Employment Services Agency (of the Manpower Services Commission)
Employment Standards Administration (of Department of Labor (USA))
Energy Systems Analysis
Entomological Society of America (USA)
Environmental Services Agency (USDOD)
European Space Agency
European Space Agency (Austria became associate member 1979)
Excited-State Absorption

ESAA Electricity Supply Association of Australia (Australia)

ESAC Economics and Social Affairs Committee (of BIM)
Environmental Systems Applications Center (Indiana University (USA))

ESACT European Society for Animal Cell Technology

ESAEI Electric Supply Authority Engineers Institute (New Zealand)

ESAIRA Electronically Scanned Airborne Intercept Radar Antenna

ESAN Escuela de Administración de Negocios para Graduados (Peru) (Graduate School of Business Administration)

ESANET European Space Agency Information Network

ESAR Electronically Steerable Array Radar
Employment Service Automatic Reporting system

ESARDA European Safeguards Research and Development Association (Italy)

ESARS Earth Surveillance and Rendezvous Simulator
Employment Security Automated Reporting System

ESAS Electronically Steerable Antenna System

ESASI European Society of Air Safety Investigators

ESAT Environmentally Sound and Appropriate Technology

ESB Electrical Simulation of the Brain
Electrical Standards Board (of USASI)
Electricity Supply Board (Eire)

ESBP European Society of Biochemical Pharmacology

ESC Economic and Social Committee (of EEC)
Electronic Security Command (USAF)
Electronic Systems Committee (of SAE (USA))
Elongation-Sensitive Cell
Energy Strategy Commission (Japan)
Engineering Society of Cincinnati (USA)
Enrichment Survey Committee (Japan) (disbanded 1975)
Entomological Society of Canada
Equipment Serviceability Criteria
Equivalent Safety Model
Erythropoietin-sensitive Stem Cells
European Space Conference (absorbed into ESA in 1975)
Evanescent Space Charge
Extended Core Storage

ESCA East Scotland College of Agriculture
Electron Spectroscopy for Chemical Analysis

ESCAP Economic and Social Commission for Asia and the Pacific (of UN)

ESCAWT European Steering Committee for APT Workshop Technology

ESCC Electrical Standards Coordinating Committee (MOD)

ESCES Experimental Satellite Communication Earth Station (of ISRO (India))

ESCI European Society for Clinical Investigation

ESCOE Engineering Societies Commission on Energy Inc. (USA) (non-profit corporation established by AICHE, AIME, ASME, ASCE and IEEE)

ESCOM Electricity Supply Commission (South Africa)

ESCOW Engineering and Scientific Committee on Water (New Zealand)

ESCP École Supérieure de Commerce de Paris (France) (Paris College of Commerce)

ESCS Emergency Satellite Communication System

ESCSP European Society of Corporate and Strategic Planners (Belgium)

ESD Electro-Static Discharge
Electron Simulated Desorption
Electronic Systems Division (USAFSC)
Electronics Systems Division (of ISRO (India))
Electrostatic Sensitive Device
Export Services Division (of DTI)

ESDAC European Space Data Centre (of ESRO) (now Department of Information Handling of ESOC (ESA)) Information Handling of ESOC (ESRO))

ESDERC European Semiconductor Device Research Conference

ESDIAD Electron Stimulated Desorption Ion Angular Distribution

ESDL ELECTRO TECHNICAL LABORATORY (Japan) System Description Language

ESDP Evolutionary System for Data Processing

ESDR European Society for Dermatological Research

ESDU Engineering Sciences Data Unit (of Royal Aeronautical Society)

ESE Ecole Superieure d'Electricite (France)
Electrical Support Equipment

ESF Electrostatic Air Filter
European Science Foundation
European Social Fund (of the EEC)
Extended Spooling Facility

ESFI Epitaxial Silicon Films on Insulators

ESFK Electrostatically Focused Klystron Amplifier

ESFP Environment-Sensitive Fracture Processes

ESG Electrically Suspended Gyroscope
Electronik-System-Gesellschaft (Germany)
Electrosplanchnography
Electrostatic Gyro

ESGM Electrostatically Supported Gyro Monitor

ESGM/SINS Electrostatically Supported Gyro Monitor/Ships Inertial Navigation System

ESH Equivalent Standard Hours

ESI Engineering and Scientific Interpreter
Equivalent Spherical Illumination

ESIC Ecological Sciences Information Center (of ORNL (USA))
Environmental Science Information Center (of EDS (NOAA) (USA))

ESIP Engineering Societies International Publications Committee

ESIS European Shielding Information Service

ESITB Electricity Supply Industry Training Board (now ESITC)

ESITC Electricity Supply Industry Training Committee

ESK Epitesugyi Szabvanyositasi Kospont (Hungary) (Building Standardization Centre)

ESL Earth Science Laboratories (of ESSA (now NOAA) (USA))
Earth Science Laboratory (of Utah University Research Institute (USA))
Earth Sciences Laboratory (of USAETL)
Electronic Systems Laboratory (of Massachusetts Institute of Technology (USA))
Electroscience Laboratory (of Ohio State University (USA))
Expected Significance Level

ESLAB European Space (Research) Laboratory (of ESRO) (now Department of Space Science of ESTEC (ESA))

ESLO European Satellite Launching Organisation Language

ESLS Energy Savings Loan Scheme (administered by Dept of Energy)

ESM Education Simulation Model (of UNESCO)
Effectiveness Simulation Model
Elastomeric Shield Material
Electronic Signal Monitoring
Electronic Support Measures

ESMA Electrical Sign Manufacturers Association
Engraved Stationery Manufacturers Association (USA)
Essential Manning

ESMALUX Societe d'Electricite de Sambre-et-Meuse, des Ardennes et du Luxembourg (Belgium)

ESMC Eastern Space and Missile Center (USAF)

ESMOC European Solar Meeting Organizing Committee

ESMR Electrically Scanning Microwave Radiometer

ESN European Scientific Notes (numbered series published monthly by ONRL (USN))

ESNA Electrical Survey-Net Adjuster
European Society of Nuclear Methods in Agriculture

ESNE Engineering Societies of New England (USA)

ESO Electronics Supply Office (USN)
European Southern Observatory (Chile) (administered by six European States)

ESOC European Space Operations Centre (of ESA)

ESOMAR European Society for Opinion and Market Research (Belgium)

ESONE European Standards of Nuclear Electronics (of EURATOM)

ESOP Employee Stock Ownership Plan

ESOR Electronically Scanned Optical Receiver

ESOT Employee Stock Ownership Trust

ESP Echeloned Series Processor
Economy Systems Plates
Electro-Sensitive Paper
Electro-Sonic Profiler
Electro-Static Precipitation
Electromagnetic Surface Profiler
Electronic Systems Planning
Electrostatic Precipitator
Engineering Society of Pennsylvania (USA)
English for Specific Purposes
Eosinophil Stimulation Promoter
Extended Segment Processing
Extra Sensory Perception
Extra-Sensory Phenomena

ESPA Electronically Steered Phased Array

ESPD Export Services and Promotions Division (of (DTI))

ESPI Electronic Speckle-Pattern Interferometer

ESPRI Education Service of the Plastics and Rubber Institute (operated from Loughborough College of Education)

ESPRIT European Strategic Programme for Research and Development in Information Technologies

ESQ Environmental Symptoms Questionnaire

ESQA English Slate Quarries Association

ESR Electro-Slag Refining
Electron Spin Resonance
Electronic Slide-Rule
Electronic Surface Recorder
Electroslag Remelting
Equivalent Series Resistance
Erythrocyte Sedimentation Rate

ESRANGE European Space (Sounding-Rocket Launching) Range (transferred to the control of Sweden in 1972 but retains name)

ESRC Economic and Social Research Council
European Science Research Council

ESRD End-Stage Renal Disease

ESRIN European Space Research Institute (now of ESA)

ESRM Electroslag Remelting

ESRO European Space Research Organisation (incorporated within ESA in 1975)

ESRS Electronic Scanning Radar System
European Synchrotron Radiation Source

ESRT Electroslag Refining Technology (division of BISRA)

ESRU Environmental Sciences Research Unit (Cranfield Institute of Technology)

ESS Electronic Switching System
Emplaced Scientific Station
Engineered Safeguard Systems
Expendible Sound Source

ESS ADF Electronic Switching System Arranged with Data Features

ESSA Environmental Science Services Administration (Department of Commerce (USA)) (merged into NOAA in 1970)
Environmental Survey Satellite

ESSCIRC European Solid-State-Circuits Conference

ESSDERC European Solid State Device Research Conference

ESSEC École Supérieure des Sciences Économiques et Commerciales (France) (College of Economic and Commercial Sciences)

ESSEX Effects of Sub-Surface Explosions (a project of the US Army)

ESSG Engineer Strategic Studies Group (US Army)

ESSLR Eye-Safe Simulated Laser Rangefinder

ESSS External Stores Support System

ESSWACS Electronic Solid-State Wide-Angle Camera System

EST Earliest Start Time
Elastic Surface Transformation
Electrolytic Sewage Treatment
Electronic Support and Training

ESTA Earth Sciences Technologies Association (USA)
Electronically Synchronised Transmission Assembly
Electronically-Scanned TACAN Antenna

ESTEC European Space Research and Technology Centre (formerly of ESRO, now part of ESA since 1975)

ESTL Electronic Systems Test Laboratory (of NASA(USA))
European Space Tribology Laboratory (of ESRO) (now of ESA)

ESTP Electronic Satellite Tracking Programme (of International Association of Geodesy)

ESTRACK European Space Satellite Tracking and Telemetry Network (of ESRO) (now Department of Satellite Data Acquisition of ESOC (now of ESA))

ESTS Electronic System Test Set

ESU Electronic Sequencing Unit
English Speaking Union
Environmental Simulation Unit

ESUS Electronically-agile Solid-state Universal Surveillance

ESV Earth-Satellite Vehicle
Epstein-Barr Virus
Experimental Safety Vehicle

ESWL Equivalent Single Wheel Load
Extracorporeal Shock-Wave Lithotripter

ESWS Earth Satellite Weapon System

ET Effective Temperature
Emerging Technology
Engineering Test
Ephemeris Time
Ethanthiol
Evapo-transpiration
Exponential Time

ET & DL Electronics Technology and Devices Laboratory (of ERADCOM (US Army))

ETA Educational Television Association

ETA/MDUSAS ENGINEERING TECHNOLOGY ANALYSTS, INC. Mobile Drilling Unit Structural Analysis System

ETA/NAME ENGINEERING TECHNOLOGY ANALYST, INC. Naval Architecture Marine Engineering computer programme

ETAADS Engine Technical And Administrative Data System

ETAC Environmental Technical Applications Center (USAF)

ETAD Ecological and Toxicological Association of the Dyestuffs Manufacturing Industry

ETAS Escort Towed Array System
Etablissement d'Experiences Techniques d'Angers (of DTAT (France))

ETASS Escort Towed Array Sonar System

ETB Electronic Test Block

ETBE European Tick-Borne Encephalitis

ETBS Etablissement d'Experiences Techniques de Bourges (of DTAT (France))

ETC Earth Terrain Camera
Effluent Treatment Cell
Energy Thrift Committee (of DOI)
Equal-Time Commutator
European Trade Committee (of BOTB)
European Translations Centre
Extended Text Compositor
Extendible Compiler
Extra Terrestrial Civilization

ETCA Etudes Techniques et Constructions Aerospatiales (Belgium)

ETCR Equivalent Effective Temperature Corrected for Radiation

ETD Electronic Tactical Display

Extension Trunk Dialling

ETEC Energy Technology Engineering Center (DOE) (USA)

ETEMA Engineering Teaching Equipment Manufacturers Association

ETFA European Technological Forecasting Association

ETH Eidgenossiche Technische Hochschule (Switzerland) (Federal Institute of Technology)
Extra-Terrestrial Hypothesis

ETHPA Epoxytetrahydrophthalic anhydride

ETI Education and Training Institute (of ASQC (USA))

ETIA European Tape Industry Association

ETIC English-Teaching Information Centre (of the British Council)
Environmental Teratology Information Center (of ORNL (USA))

ETIMR Electric Target Intermediate Markmanship Range

ETIP Experimental Technology Incentives Program (of NSF and NBS (USA))

ETK Epitesugyi Tajekoztatasi Kozpont (Hungary) (Information Centre for Building)

ETL Electro Technical Laboratory (Japan) (now General Electronic Research Laboratory)
Electrolytic Tinning Line
Emergency Locator Transmitter
Emergency Tolerance Limit
Engineer Topographic Laboratories (US Army)

ETM Elemental Time Monitor

ETMA English Timber Merchants Association

ETNA Electrolevel-Theodolite Naval Alignment system

ETNS Electronic Train Number System

ETO Ethylene Oxide

ETOC Expected Total Operating Cost

ETP Effluent Treatment Plant

ETPI Eastern Telecommunications Philippines Inc. (Philippines)

ETPM Societe Entrepose pour les Travaux Petroliers Maritimes (France)

ETPS Empire Test Pilots School

ETR Eastern Test Range (USAF)
Effective Thyroxine Ratio
Engineering Test Reactor

ETRAC Educational Television and Radio Association of Canada (Canada)

ETRB Electrical Technology Requirements Board (of DOI)

ETRTO European Technical Rim and Tyre Organisation
European Tyre and Rim Technical Organisation

ETS Educational Time-sharing System
Electronic Tandem Switching
Electronic Translator System
Engine Test Stand
Engineering Test Satellite
European Tetratology Society (Sweden)

ETSC Electrically-excited Thermally Stimulated Current
Engineering Terotechnology Steering Committee (of IEE, IMECHE, IPRODE, ICMA and BCMA)

ETSMA European Tyre Stud Manufacturers Association

ETSS Electronic Telecommunications Switching System

ETST Engineering Test-Service Test

ETSU East Tennessee State University (USA)
East Texas State University (USA)
Energy Technology Support Unit (of Dept of Energy)

ETT Evasive Target Tank (armoured fighting vehicle)
Expected Test Time
Explosion Tear Test

ETTA Eastern Townships Textile Association (Canada)

ETTDC Electronics Trade and Technology Development Corporation (India) (government owned)

ETTF European Tanker Task Force (of SAC (USAF))

ETTIC Education and Training Technology International Convention

ETU Ethylene Thiourea

ETUC European Trade Union Confederation

ETV Educational Television
Elevating Transfer Vehicle

ETW European Transonic Wind-tunnel

EU prefix to Euronorms which are Standards issued by the European Coal and Steel Community

EUA European Unit of Account (of EEC)

EUBS European Undersea Biomedical Society

EUC End-User Certificate
End-User Computing

EUCEPA European for Cellulose and Paper Association

EUCLID Easily Used Computer Language for Illustrations and Drawings

EUCOFF European Conference on Flammability and Fire Retardants

EUCON Energy Utilization and Conversation Exhibition and Conference

EUD European Union of Dentists

EUDISED European Documentation and Information System for Education (of the Council of Europe)

EUFODA European Food Distributors Association

EUGROPA Union des Distributeurs de Papiers et Cartons de la CEE (Union of Distributors of Paper and Cardboard of the European Economic Community)

EuIG Europium Iron Garnet

EUL Edinburgh University Library

EULEP European Late Effects Project Group

EUM-AFTN European Mediterranean Aeronautical Fixed Telecommunications Network

EUMABOIS European Committee of Woodworking Machinery Manufacturers

EUMAPRINT European Committee of Associations of Printing and Paper Converting Machinery Manufacturers

EUMETSAT European Meterological Satellite System

EUMOTIV European Association for the Study of Economic, Commercial and Industrial Motivation (Belgium)

EUPA European Union for the Protection of Animals (disbanded 1977)

EUPE European Union for Packaging and the Environment (of the EEC)

EUPSA European Union of Paediatric Surgical Associations

EUR prefix to numbered-lettered series of reports issued by EURATOM

EURAS European Anodisers Association

EURATOM European Atomic Energy Community

EUREL Convention of National Societies of Electrical Engineers of Western Europe

EUREMAIL Conference de l'Industrie Europeene Productrice d'Articles Emailles (Conference of the European Industry for the Production of Enamelled Goods)

EUREX Enriched Uranium Extraction

EURIM European Conference on Research into the Management of Information Systems and Libraries

EURIMA European Insulation Manufacturers Association

EURIPA Eurpean Information Providers Association

EURO Association of European Operational Research Societies
European Congress on Operational Research

EUROAVIA Association of European Aeronautical and Astronautical Students

EUROBIT European Association of Manufacturers of Office Machines and Data Processing Equipment

EUROCAE European Organisation for Civil Aviation Electronics (France)
EUROCEAN European Oceanographic Association (Monaco)
EUROCHEMIC European Organisation for the Chemical Processing of Irradiated Fuels (of OECD)
EUROCOM Eurogroup sub-group on Battlefield Communications
EUROCOMP European Computing Congress
EUROCON European Conference on Electrotechnics
EUROCONTROL European Organisation for the Safety of Air Navigation
EUROCOOP European Community of Co-operative Societies
EUROCOR European Congress on Metallic Corrosion
EUROCORD Fédération des Industries de Corderie-Ficellerie de l'Europe Occidental (France) (Federation of Western Europe Rope and Twine Industries)
EUROCOTON Comite des Industries du Coton et des Fibres Connexes de la CEE (Committee of the Cotton Industries of the European Economic Community)
EURODIDAC European Association of Manufacturers and Distributors of Education Materials
EURODOC Joint Documentation Service of ESRO, EUROSPACE and the European Organisation for the Development and Construction of Space Vehicle Launchers
EUROFER Association of European Steel Producers
EUROFEU European Committee of the Manufacturers of Fire Engines and Apparatus
EUROFINAS European Federation of Finance Houses Association (Belgium)
EUROFUEL Societe Europeene de Fabrication de Combustibles a Base d'Eranium pour Reacteurs a Eau Legere (France)
EUROGROPA Union des Distributeurs de Papiers et Cartons (European Union of Paper, Board and Packaging Wholesalers)
EUROMEAS Conference on Precise Electrical Measurement
EUROMECH European Mechanics Colloquia
EUROMICRO European Association for Microprocessing and Microprogramming
European Association of Microprocessor Users
EUROMPAP European Committee of Machinery Manufacturers for the Plastics and Rubber Industries
EURONAD Eurogroup Committee of National Armaments Directors
EURONET European Information Network for Science and Technology
EURONORM Standard issued by European Coal and Steel Community
EUROPEC European Offshore Petroleum Conference and Exhibition
EUROPHOT European Council of Professional Photographers (Belgium)
EUROPREFAB European Organization for the Promotion of Prefabrication and other Industrialized Building
EUROPUMP European Committee of Pump Manufacturers
EURORAD European Committee of Radiator Constructors
EUROSAC European Federation of Manufacturers of Multiwall Paper Sacks (France)
EUROSATELLITE a consortium comprising Aerospatial (France) MBB (Germany) and ETCA (Belgium)
EUROSEC Committee of four major European Offshore organizations (Association of British Oceanic Industries, Groupement Interprofessionnel pour l'Exploration des Oceans (France), Industriel Raad voor de Oceanologie (Holland) and Wirtschaftsvereinigung Industrielle Meerestechnik (Germany)
EUROSPACE European Industrial Space Research Group
EUROSTAT Statistical Office of the European Communities
EUROSTEST European Association of Testing Institutions
EUROSTRUCT-PRESS European Association of Publishers in the Field of Building and Design
EUROTEST European Association of Testing Institutions (association of European companies involved in the non-destructive testing of steel) (administered from Belgium)
EUROVENT European Committee of Ventilating Equipment Manufacturers
EUSAFEC Eastern United States Agricultural and Food Export Council (USA)
EUSAMA European Shock Absorber Manufacturers Association
EUSE European UNIVAC Scientific Exchange
EUSEC Conference of Engineering Societies of Western Europe and the USA (dissolved 1971)
EUSIDIC European Association of Scientific Information Dissemination Centres
EUSIREF Network for European Scientific Information Referral
EUT Equipment Under Test
EUUG European Unix User Group
EUV Energetic Ultra-Violet
Expected Utility Value
Extreme Ultra-Violet
EUVE Extreme Ultra-Violet Explorer
EUVSH Equivalent Ultra-Violet Solar Hours
EV Efficient Vulcanising
Efficient Vulcanization
Electric Vehicle
prefix to SAE (USA) numbered series of Austenitic Exhaust Valve Steels
EVA Electric Vehicle Association of Great Britain
Electronic Velocity Analyser
Ethylene Vinyl Acetate
Extravehicular Activity
EVAF Europaische Vereinigung Industrieller Marksforscher (European Association for Industrial Marketing Research)
EVAL Earth Viewing Applications Laboratory
Ethyl Vinyl Alcohol
EVATMI European Vinyl Asbestos Tile Manufacturers Institute
EVC Electric Vehicle Council (USA)
Eurovision Control Centre (of EBU)
EVDG Electric Vehicle Development Group
EVG Electrically-supported Vacuum Gyro
EVICT Evaluation of Intelligence Collection Tasks
EVIST Ethics and Values Implications of Science and Technology
EVKI Europaische Vereinigung der Keramik-Industrie (European Federation of the Electro-Ceramic Industry)
EVM Electronic Voltmeter
Engine Vibration Monitoring
EVOM Electronic Voltohmmeter
EVOP Evolutionary Operation
EVPI Expected Value of Perfect Information
EVR Electronic Video Recording and Reproduction
EVS Electro-optical Viewing System
Electro-optical Visual Sensor
Electronic Voice Switching System
Energie-Versorgung Schwaben (Germany)
Expected Value Saved
EVSA Electronically Variable Shock Absorber
EVT Equiviscous Temperature
EVVA Extra Vehicular Visor Assembly
EW Early Warning
Electronic Warfare
Electroslag Welding
Ether-Water

EWAC Effluent and Water Advisory Committee (of the Water Research Association)
Electronic Warfare Anechoic Chamber
EWACS Electronic Wide Angle Camera System
EWB Elektrizitätswerk der Stadt Bern (Switzerland)
EWE Extrapolated Water Elevation
EWEC Electromagnet Wave Energy Conversion
EWF Electrical Wholesalers Federation
EWGAE European Working Group on Acoustic Emission
EWI English Winter Index
EWL Electronic Warfare Laboratory (of ECOM (US Army))
EWMA Exponentially Weighted Moving Average
EWMIS Electronic Warfare Management Information System
EWOSE Electronic Warfare Operational Support Establishment (RAF)
EWP Exploding Wire Phenomena
EWPCA European Water Pollution Control Association
EWR Early Warning Radar
Entwicklungsring Sud (Germany)
EWRC European Weed Research Council
EWRS European Weed Research Society
EWS Electronic Warfare System
Engineering Writing and Speech
Experienced Worker's Standard
EWSF European Work Study Federation (now European Federation of Productivity Services)
EWSG Electronic Warfare Scenario Generator
EWSL Equivalent Single Wheel Load
EWSM Electronic Warfare Support Measures
EWSS Electronic Warfare Support System
EWU Eastern Washington University (USA)
EWZ Elektrizitätswerk der Stadt Zurich (Switzerland)
EX prefix to numbered series of "Exchange" Steels
EXACT International Exchange of Authenticated Electronic Component Performance Tests Data
EXAFS Extended X-ray Absorption Fine Structure
Extended X-ray Absorption Fine-structure Spectroscopy
EXAM Experimental Aerospace Multiprocessor
EXAMETNET Experimental Inter-American Meteorological Sounding Rocket Research Network
EXAPT Extended subsets of APT (Automatically Programmed Tools)
EXCO Executive Committee (of ISO (Switzerland))
EXDAMS Extendable Debugging And Monitoring System
EXELFS Extended X-ray-Edge Energy-Loss Fine Structure
EXFOR International Neutron Data Exchange System
EXIAC Explosives Information and Analysis Center (US Army)
EXJAM Expendable Jammer
EXO European X-ray Observatory (later known as ASRO)
EXOS Exospheric Satellite
EXOSAT European X-ray Observatory Satellite (previously known as HELOS)
EXRAY Expendable Relay
Expendable Remote Array
EXSM Excessive Soil Moisture
EXTELCOMS East African Telecommunications Company (Kenya)
EXTERRA Extraterrestrial Research Agency (US Army)
EXTRADOP Extended-range DOVAP
EXUV Extreme Ultraviolet and x-ray survey satellite
EXW Explosion Welding
EZP Elliptical Zone Plate
EZPERT Easy PERT (Programme Evaluation and Review Technique)
E^2PROM Electrically Erasable Programmable Read-Only Memory
E^3 Energy Efficient Engine (a program of NASA (USA)

F

F prefix to numbered series of Factory Forms issued by H.M. Factory Inspectorate, Dept. of Employment
prefix to numbered: dated series of Fabric Standards issued by BSI (letter is sometimes preceded by a number)
F/O Fibre Optics
FA Factory Automation
Ferrocarriles Argentinos (Argentina) (Argentina Railways)
Fluorescent Antibody
Formaldehyde
Frankford Arsenal (US Army) (closed 1977)
Frontoviya Aviatsiya (USSR) (the Frontal Aviation–a group of the Soviet Air Force)
Furfuryl Alcohol
FAA Faculty of Accountants and Auditors
Federal Aviation Administration (of DOT) (USA)
Fuerza Aerea Argentina (Argentina) (Military Air Force)
FAA-ADS Federal Aviation Administration Aircraft Development Service (of DOT (USA))
FAA-AM Federal Aviation Administration, Office of Aviation Medicine (of DOT (USA))
FAA-AV Federal Aviation Administration, Office of Aviation Policy and Plans (of DOT (USA))
FAA-AWS Federal Aviation Administration—Office of Airworthiness (USA)
FAA-EE Federal Aviation Administration—Office of Environment and Energy (USA)
FAA-EM Federal Aviation Administration, Office of Systems Engineering Management (of DOT (USA))
FAA-FS Federal Aviation Administration, Flight Standards Service (of DOT (USA))
FAA-MS Federal Aviation Administration, Office of Management Services (of DOT (USA))
FAA-NA Federal Aviation Administration, National Aviation Facilities Experimental Center (of DOT (USA))
FAA-NO Federal Aviation Administration, Office of Noise Abatement (of DOT (USA))
FAADS Forward Area Air Defence System
Forward Area Anti-aircraft Defence System
FAALS Field Artillery Acoustic Locating System
FAAP Federal Aid Airport Program (USA)
FAAQS Federal Ambient Air Quality Standards (USA)
FAAR Forward Area Alerting Radar
FAAS Furnace Atomic Absorption Spectrophotometry
FAB Flour Advisory Board
Flux-Asbestos Backing
Fuerza Aerea Boliviana (Bolivia) (Military Air Force)
Fuerza Aerea Brasileira (Brazil) (Military Air Force)
FABMDS Field Army Ballistic Missile Defence System
FABMIS Forward Area Ballistic Missile Intercept System
FABRIMETAL Federation des Entreprises de l'Industrie des Fabrications Metalliques (Belgium)

FAC — Fast Attack Craft
Food Additives and Contaminants Committee (of MAFF)
Forward Air Control
Fuerza Aerea de Chile (Chile) (Military Air Force)

FAC/SCAR — Forward Air Control/Self-Contained Airborne Reconnaissance

FACC — Food Additives and Contaminants Committee

FACCM — Fast Access Charge-Coupled Memory

FACE — Field Alterable Control Element
Field Artillery Computer Equipment
Florida Area Cumulus Experiment (of the National Hurricane and Experimental Meteorology Laboratory (NOAA (USA))

FACEJ — Forges et Ateliers de Construction Electrique de Jeumont (France)

FACEL — Feature Analysis Comparison and Evaluation Library

FACES — FORTRAN-Automatic Code Evaluation System

FACET — FABER (OSCAR FABER AND PARTNERS) Cost Estimating Technique
Fluid Amplifier Control Engine Test

FACI — First Article Configuration Inspection

FACMTA — Federal Advisory Council on Medical Training Aids (USA)

FACS — Federation des Amis des Chemins de Fer Secondaires (France) (Federation of the Friends of Light Railways)
Federation of American Controlled Shipping (USA)
Feedback and Analysis of Control Statistics
Financial Accounting and Control System
Fine Attitude Control System
Fluorescence-Activated Cell Sorter
Formal Aspects of Computing Science (a group of BCS)

FACSI — Fast Access Coded Small Images

FACSS — Federation of Analytical Chemistry and Spectroscopy Societies (USA)

FACT — Facility for Automation, Control and Test
Federation Against Copyright Theft
Fleet Analysis and Cost Trends
Flexible Automatic Circuit Tester
FORD (MOTOR COMPANY) Anodized Aluminum Corrosion Test
Fully Automated Cataloguing Technique

FACT-AID — FACT (Flexible Automatic Circuit Tester) Automatic Interconnection Device

FACT-LIFT — FACT (Flexible Automatic Circuit Tester) Low Insertion Force Technique

FACT-QUIC — FACT (Flexible Automatic Circuit Tester) Quick Universal Interface Connector

FACTAN — Factor Analysis

FACTS — Facsimile Transmission
Federation of Australian Commercial Television Stations (Australia)
Field Army Calibration Team Support (US Army)
Financial Accounting and Control Techniques for Supply (USDOD)
FLIR Augmented COBRA TOW Sight
FLIR-Augmented COBRA/TOW System

FAD — Flavin Adenine Dinucleotide
Fracture Analysis Diagram
Fuel Advisory Departure (an investigation by FAA (USA) and airlines)
Fuerza Aerea Dominicana (Dominican Republic) (Military Air Force)

FADAC — Field Artillery Digital Automatic Computer

FADAP — Fleet ASW Data Analysis Program (USN)

FADEC — Full Authority Digital Engine Control

FADES — Fuselage Automated Design

FADPUG — Federal ADP Users Group (USA)

FADS — Fixed Asset Depreciation System
Flexible Air Data System

FAE — Federation of Arab Engineers (Egypt)
Figural After-Effect
Fuel-Air Explosive
Fuerza Aérea Ecuatoriana (Ecuador) (Military Air Force)

FAeB — Force Aerienne Belge (Belgium) (Military Air Force)

FAEB — Fuerza Aerea Boliviano (Bolivia) (military air force)

FAeC — Force Aerienne Congolaise (Congo) (Kinshasa) (Military Air Force)

FAEC — Full Authority Electronic Control

FAeG — Fuerza Area Guatemalteca (Guatemala) (Military Air Force)

FAEP — Federation of Associations of Periodical Publishers (of the EEC)

FAESHED — Fuel Air Explosive System, Helicopter Delivered

FAF — Final Approach Fix

FAFR — Fatal Accident Frequency Rates

FAG — Flughafen Frankfurt AG (Germany)

FAGC — Fast Automatic Gain Control

FAGR — Floating Arm Graphic Recorder

FAGS — Federation of Astronomical and Geophysical Services (of IAPO)

FAH — Fuerza Aerea Hondurena (Honduras) (military air force)

FAHQMT — Fully-Automatic High Quality Machine Translation

FAI — Federation Aeronautique Internationale (International Aeronautical Federation)
Fertilizer Association of India (India)

FAIC — Federation of Australian Investment Clubs (Australia)

FAID — Food and Allied Industries Division (of ASQC (USA))

FAIR — Failure Analysis Information Retrieval
Fast Access Information Retrieval
Fast Access to Insurance Requirements
Fly-Along Infra-Red

FAIRS — Failure Report Sorting and Analysis
FAIRCHILD (CAMERA AND INSTRUMENT CORPORATION) Automatic Intercept and Response System
FEDERAL AVIATION ADMINISTRATION (USA) Information Retrieval System

FAK — Freight-All-Kinds

FAL — Facilitation Division (of ICAO)

FAM — Fast Auxiliary Memory
Fuerza Aerea Mexicana (Mexico) (Military Air Force)

FAMA — Fluorescent Antibody to Membrane Antigen test

FAMC — Foreign Area Materials Center (of New York State Education Dept.)

FAME — Fatty Acid Methyl Esters
Final Approach Monitoring Equipment
Financial, Accounting Marketing Exercise

FAMECE — Family of Military Engineer Construction Equipment (US Army)

FAMEM — Federation of Associations of Mining Equipment Manufacturers

FAMHEM — Federation of Associations of Materials Handling Equipment Manufacturers

FAMIS — Financial And Management Information System

FAMOS — Fleet Air Meteorological Observation Satellite (USN)
Floating-gate Avalanche-injection Metal Oxide Semiconductor

FAMOUS — French-American Mid-Ocean Underseas Study (of the Mid-Atlantic Ridge)

FAMS — Forecasting And Modelling System

FAMSNUB Frequencies And Mode Shapes of Non-Uniform Beams

FAN Free Amino Nitrogen

FANT Forces Armees Nationales Tchadiennes (Chad) (Chad National Defence Forces)

FANTAC Fighter Analysis Tactical Air Combat

FAO Food and Agricultural Organization (of UN) (Italy)

FAOE Federation of African Organisations of Engineers

FAOUSA Finance and Accounts Office, United States Army

FAP Failure Analysis Programme
Fluorapatite
Forschungsausschuss fur Planungsfragen (Switzerland) (Research Committee on Planning)
Fuerza Aerea del Paraguay (Paraguay) (Military Air Force)
Fuerza Aerea del Paraguay Paraguay) (Military Air Force)
Fuerza Aerea del Peru (Peru) (Military Air Force)
Fuerza Aerea Panamera (Panama) (Military Air Force)

FAPEL Fabrieken van Aktieve en Passieve Electronische Bouwelementen in Nederland (Netherlands)

FAPIG First Atomic Power Industry Group (Japan)

FAPMATC Fully Automated Pilot Monitored, Air Traffic Control

FAPRS Federal Assistance Programs Retrieval System (of USDA (USA))

FAPS Committee on the Future of the American Physical Society (of the Society (USA))
Financial Analysis and Planning System

FAQ Fair Average Quality

FAR False-Alarm Rate
Filament Atom Reservoir
Fixed Acoustic Range
Flight Aptitude Rating
Fuerza Aerea Revolucionaria (Cuba) (Military Air Force)
prefix to numbered series of Federal Aviation Regulations issued by FAA (USA)
The Foundation for Australian Resources (New South Wales Institute of Technology, (Australia))

FARA Formula Air Racing Association

FARADA Failure Rate Data

FARE Forward Area Refuelling Equipment

FARET Fast Reactor Test

FARFUL Feeder Analysis Routine For Unbalanced Load

FARP Fully Automatic Radar Plotter

FARRP Forward Area Refuelling and Rearming Point

FARS Failure Analysis Report Summary

FAS European Federation of Associations of Industrial Safety and Medical Officers
Faculty of Architects and Surveyors (now incorporating the Institute of Registered Architects)
Fast Announcement Service (of NTIS (USA)) (now Trade Announcement Service)
Federation des Architectes Suisses (Switzerland) (Federation of Swiss Architects)
Federation of American Scientists (USA)
Feel Augmentation System
Financial Analysis System
Foetal Alcohol Syndrome
Forces Aeriennes Strategiques (France)
Foreign Agriculture Service (USDA)
Foreign Area Studies (of The American University (USA))
Fuerza Aérea Salvadorena (Salvador) (Military Air Force)

FASA Final Approach Spacing for ARTS

FASB Financial Accounting Standards Board (USA) (Successor to AICPA)

FASCAM Family of Scatterable Mines

FASCIA Fixed Asset System Control Information and Accounting

FASDA Fast Analogue Scanner for Data Acquisition

FASE Federation of Acoustical Societies of Europe
Fundamentally Analyzable Simplified English

FASEB Federation of American Societies for Experimental Biology

FASEX Fastening and Mechanised Assembly Conference and Exhibition

FASFID Fédération des Associations et Sociétés Françaises d'Ingénieurs Diplômés (France) (Federation of French Associations and Societies of Chartered Engineers)

FASII Federation of Associations of Small Industries in India (India)

FASOR Forward Area Sonar Research

FASS Federation of Associations of Specialists and Subcontractors
Fore and Aft Scanner System

FASST Forum for the Advancement of Students in Science and Technology (USA)
Friends of Aerospace Supporting Science and Technology

FAST Facility for Accelerated Service Testing (of TTC Dept of Transportation (USA))
Factor Analysis System
Fan and Supersonic Turbine
Fast Automatic Shuttle Transfer
Federation Against Software Theft
Federazione delle Associazone Scientifiche e Techniche (Italy) (Federation of Scientific and Technical Associations)
Feed And Speed Technology
Fence Against Satellite Threats
Field Asymmetry Sensing Technique
File Analysis and Selection Technique
Fixed Abrasive Slicing Technique
Fleet-sizing Analysis and Sensitivity Technique
FLUOR Analytical Scheduling Technique
Forecasting and Assessment in Science and Technology (a programme of EEC)
Forecasting, Assessment and methodology in the field of Science and Technology
Formulae for Assessing the Specification of Trains
FORTRAN Analysis System
Freight Automated System (of USDOD)
Frequency Agile Search and Track Seeker
Friction Assessment Screening Test
Fuel and Sensor, Tactical
Fully Automated Switching Teletype
Fully Automatic SACE Translator
Function Analysis System Technique

FAST-VAL Forward Air Strike Evaluation

FASTAR Frequency Angle Scanning Tracking and Ranging

FASTNeT Fully Automated Switched Telecommunications Network

FAT Fluorescent Antibody Technique

FATAL Fit Anything To Anything you Like

FATAR Fast Analysis of Tape and Recovery

FATCAT Film and Television Correlation Assessment Technique
Frequency And Time Circuit Analysis Technique

FATE Formulating Analytical and Technical Estimate
Fuzing, Arming, Test and Evaluation

FATIMA Fatigue Indicating Meter Attachment

FATIPEC Federation d'Associations de Techniciens des Industries des Peintures, Vernis, Emaux et Encres d'Imprimerie de l'Europe Continentale (European Federation of Paint and Printing Ink Technologists)

FATME Fabbrica Apparecchiature Telefoniche e Materiale Elettrico (Italy)

FATOLA Flexible Aircraft Take-Off and Landing Analysis

FATS Fast Analysis of Tape Surfaces
FATT Forward Area Tactical Teletype
Forward Area Tactical Typewriter
Fracture Appearance Transition Temperature
FAU Florida Atlantic University (USA)
Fuerza Aerea Uruguaya (Uruguay) (Military Air Force)
FAUL Five Associated University Libraries (in Western New York (USA))
FAUSST French-Anglo-USA Talks on Supersonic Transport Operations
FAV Fast Attack Vehicle
Fuerzas Aereas Venezolanas (Venezuela) (Military Air Force)
FAWAC Farm Animals Welfare Advisory Committee
FAX Facsimile
Fuel-Air Explosion
FBA Farm Buildings Association
Federation of British Audio
Fluorescent Brightening Agent
Freshwater Biological Association
FBB Functional Building Block
FBC Fluidized-Bed Combustion
FBCM Federation of British Carpet Manufacturers (merged into BCMA in 1976)
FBCMA Fibre Bonded Carpet Manufacturers Association
FBCR Fluidized-Bed Control Rod
FBCS Foreground/Background Operating System
FBE Feeder Branch Edit
FBFC Franco-Belge de Fabrication de Combustible (Belgium)
FBFM Frequency Feedback Frequency Modulation
FBH Fluidized Bed Hydrogenator OR Hydrogenation
FBHX Fluid Bed Heat Exchanger
FBI Federation of British Industries (now CBI)
FBIS Foreign Broadcast Information Service (of CIA (USA))
FBM Fleet Ballistic Missile
FBO Fixed Base Operator
FBP Final Boiling Point
FBR Fast Breeder Reactor
Fast Burst Reactor
Full Boiling-Range fuel
FBRAM Federation of British Rubber and Allied Manufacturers
FBRF Full Boiling-Range Fuel
FBS Fixed-Base Simulator
Foetal Bovine Serum
FBW Fly By Wire
FC Fluorocarbon
Forestry Commission
Frozen-in Conductivity
Fuel Cell
FCA Flying Chiropractors Association (USA)
Frequency Control And Analysis
Functional Configuration Audit
FCAI Federal Chamber of Automotive Industries (Australia)
FCAP Flight Controls Analysis Programme
FCAS Frequency Coded Armament System
FCAW Flux Cored Arc Welding
FCC Face Centred Cubic
Federal Communications Commission (USA)
Flat Conductor Cable
Fluid Catalytic Cracking
FCCI Federal Clean Car Incentive program (USA)
FCCMS & SR Federal Coordinating Committee for Meteorological Services and Supporting Research (USA)
FCCR Fatigue Crack Growth Rate
FCCSET Federal Coordinating Council for Science, Engineering and Technology (USA)
FCCTS Federal COBOL Compiler Testing Service (of NBS and DOD (USA))
FCCU Fluid Catalytic Cracking Unit
FCCV Future Close Combat Vehicle
FCD Failure-Correction Decoding
FCDA Federal Capital Development Authority (Nigeria)
FCE Flight Control Electronics System
FCEC Federation of Civil Engineering Contractors
FCES Flight Control Electronics System
FCET Federation of Civil Engineering Contractors
FCF Free Cash Flow
FCG Fatigue Crack Growth
FCGR Fatigue Crack Growth Rate
FCH Fourier Colour Hologram
FCI Federated Chamber of Industries (South Africa)
Fertiliser Corporation of India (India)
Finance Corporation for Industry (of Finance for Industry)
Fluid Control Institute (USA)
Food Corporation of India (India)
Fuel-Coolant Interaction
FCIA Foreign Credit Insurance Association (USA)
FCIC Fiber and Composites Information Center (Battelle-Columbus Laboratories (USA))
FCIM Farm, Construction and Industrial Machinery
FCIN Fast Carry-propagation Iterative Network
FCL Freon Coolant Loop
Full Container Load
FCM prefix to dated-numbered series issued by Federal Coordinator for Meteorological Services and Supporting Research (of NOAA (USA))
FCMI Federation of Coated Macadam Industries
FCMU Foot-Controlled Manoeuvring Unit
FCP Fatigue Crack Propagation
FORD Combustion Process
Free Conducting Particle
Functional Communication Profile
FCR Fast Ceramic-Fuelled Reactor
FCRAM File Create And Maintenance
Flat Conductor Cable
FCRAO Five Colleges Radio Astronomy Observatory (Massachusetts University and four neighbouring colleges–Amherst, Mount Holyoke, Hampshire and Smith (USA))
FCRC Federal Contract Research Centers (USA)
FCRIM Freight Committee of the Rubber Industry of Malaysia
FCS (Gun) Fire Control System
Facsimile Communication System
Farmer Cooperative Service (USDA)
Federation of Concrete Specialists
Financial Control System
Floor-Ceiling Sandwich
Fluorescence Correlation Spectroscopy
Foetal Calf Serum
FCST Federal Council for Science and Technology (USA) (replaced by FCCSET in 1976)
FCT Field Controlled Thyristor
Flux-Corrected Transport
FCTC Federal Compiler Testing Center (USA)
FCW Flux Cored Welding Wire
FD Feedback Decoding
Free-Dried
FDA Flying Dentists Association (USA)
Food and Drug Administration (USA)
Force Development and Analysis Division (Ministry of Defence (Australia))
Form-dimethylamide
FDAA Federal Disaster Assistance Administration (USA)
FDAR Federal Department of Agricultural Research (Nigeria)

FDAU Flight Data Acquisition Unit

FDC Furniture Development Council

FDCC Facility Design and Construction Center (of USCG)

FDE Finite Differential Equation
Functional Differential Equation

FDEP Flight Data Entry and Print-out

FDES Fonds de Développement Économique et Social (France) (Economic and Social Development Funds)

FDEU Field Drainage Experimental Unit

FDFR Federal Department of Forestry Research (Nigeria)

FDI Fault Detection Isolation
Federation Dentaire Internationale (International Dental Federation)

FDL prefix to numbered series of Fish Disease Leaflets issued by Department of the Interior, USA

FDLS Fast Deployment Logistics Ship

FDM Frequency Division Multiplex
Fundamental Design Method

FDMA Frequency Division Multiple Access

FDNB Fluorodinitrobenzene

FDNR Frequency Dependent Negative Resistor
Frequency-Dependent Negative Resistance

FDO Frequency-Domain Oscilloscope

FDOS Floppy Disk Operating System

FDP Falling Dilute-Phase
Fast Digital Processor
Fibrinogen Degradation Products
Fluid Dynamics Panel (of AGARD (NATO))

FDPB Fatigue Decreased Proficiency Boundary

FDR Fast Dump/Restore
Flight Data Recorder
Frequency Domain Reflectometry

FDRAKE First Dynamic Response and Kinematics Experiment (in the Antarctic) (off ISOS (IDOE))

FDS Fence Disturbance Sensor
File Description System
Forschungszentrum des Deutschen Schiffbaus (Germany) (Shipbuilding Industry Research Organization)
FORTRAN Deductive System
Frame Difference Signal

FDTE Force Development Testing and Experimentation

FDTI Food, Drink and Tobacco Industry Training Board

FDVR Federal Department of Veterinary Research (Nigeria)

FDX Full-Duplex

FE Finite Element
Further Education

FE/PC Ferroelectric/Photoconductive

FEA Federal Energy Administration (USA) (absorbed into DOE in 1977)
Federal Executive Association (USA)
Federation Europeenne des Association Aerosols (European Federation of Aerosols Assocations)
Federation of European Aerosol Associations (Switzerland)

FEABL Finite Element Analysis Basic Library

FEACO Federation Europeene des Associations de Conseils en Organisation (European Federation of Management Consultants Associations)

FEAICSMT Federation Europeene des Associations d'Ingenieurs et Chefs de Services de Securite et des Medecins du Travail (European Federation of Associations of Engineers and Heads of Industrial Safety and Medical Services)

FEAMIS Foreign Exchange Accounting and Management Information System

FEANI Federation Europeenne d'Associations Nationales d'Ingenieurs (European Federation of National Associations of Engineers) (France)

FEASIBLE Finite Element Analysis Sensibly Implemented By Least Effort

FEAT Frequency of Every Allowable Term

FEB Functional Electronic Block

FEBA Forward Edge of Battle Area

FEBELBOIS Federation Belge des Industriels du Bois (Belgium) (Belgian Federation of the Timber Industry)

FEBELTEX Federation de l'Industrie Textile Belge (Belgium) (Federation of the Belgian Textile Industry)

FEBRAS Federation Belge de Recherches et d'Activitees Subaquatiques (Belgium)

FEBS Federation of European Biochemical Societies

FEC Fall Electronics Conference (IEEE (USA))
Forward Error Control
Forward Error Correction

FECA Facilities Engineering and Construction Agency (of HEW (USA))

FECAICA Federacion de Camaras y Associaciones Industriales de Centroamerica (Honduras) (of CACM) (Federation of Industrial Chambers and Associations of Central America)

FECAP Feeder Equipment Capacity

FECDBA Foreign Exchange and Currency Deposit Brokers Association

FECHIMIE Federation des Industries Chimiques de Belgique (Belgium) (Federation of the Belgian Chemical Industries)

FECO Fringes of Equal Chromatic Order

FECONS Field Engineer Control System

FECS Federation of European Chemical Societies

FECSA Fuerzas Electricas de Cataluna SA (Spain)
Fuerzas Electricas de Cataluna SA (Spain)

FEDAI Foreign Exchange Dealers Association of India (India)

FEDALT Feeder Alteration

FEDAP Feeder Data Assembly Programme

FEDAS Federation of European Delegation Associations of Scientific Equipment Manufacturers, Importers, and Dealers in the Laboratory, Industrial and Medical Fields

FEDB Failure Experience Data Bank (of GIDEP (USA))

FEDC Federation of Engineering Design Consultants

FEDES European Flexible Packagings Industry Association

FEDETAB Federation Belgo-Luxembourgeoise des Industries du Tabac (Belgium-Luxembourg Federation of Tobacco Industries)

FEDIS Front-End Design-Information System

FEDSIM Federal Computer Performance Evaluation and Simulation Center (of General Services Administration (USA))

FEEDBAC Foreign Exchange, Eurodollar and Branch Accounting

FEEM Field-Electron Emission Microscopy

FEF Fast Extrusion Furnace
Federation Europeenne de la Manutention (European Federation of Materials Handling)
Field-Effect Modified
Finite Element Method
Flat/Exponential Filter
Foundry Educational Foundation (USA)
Fundamental Electrical Standards
Fuze/Munitions Environment Characterization Symposium
prefix to numbered series of leaflets Fixed Equipment of the Farm issued by MAFF

FEFA Feeder Fault Analysis
Future European Fighter Aircraft

FEFANA Federation Europeenne des Fabricants d'Adjuvants pour la Nutrition Animale (European Federation of Manufacturers of Additional Ingredients for Animal Foodstuff)
FEFC Far Eastern Freight Conference
FEFCEB Federation Europeene des Fabricants de Caisses et Emballages en Bois (European Federation of Manufacturers of Timber Crates and Packing Cases)
FEFCO Federation Europeene des Fabricants de Carton Ondule (European Federation of Corrugated Container Manufacturers) (France)
FEFET Ferro-Electric Field Effect Transistor
FEFI Flight Engineers Fault Isolation
FEFP Fuel Element Failure Propagation
FEG Flug-Elektronik-Gesellschaft (Germany)
FEGUA Ferrocarriles de Guatemala (Guatemala) (State Railways)
FEHO Federation of European Helicopter Operators
FEI Financial Executives Institute (USA)
Fluidic Explosive Initiator
FEIBA Factor VIII Inhibitor Bypassing Activity
FEIC Federation Europeenne de l'Industrie du Contreplaque (European Federation of the Plywood Industry)
FEICRO Federation of European Industrial Co-operative Research Organizations (of EEC)
FEIS Final Environmental Impact Statement
FEJOB Finite Element Journal Bearing Analysis
FEL Food Engineering Laboratory (US Army)
Free Electron Laser
Fritz Engineering Laboratory (of Lehigh University (USA))
FELABAN Federacion Latinoamericana de Bancos (Colombia) (Latin-America Banking Federation)
FELCRA Federal Land Consolidation and Rehabilitation Authority (Malaysia)
FELDA Federal Land Development Authority (Malaysia)
FELIF Feeder Length In Feet
FELOS Feeder Load Search
FELT Fluid Encapsulated Launch Technique
FEM Fabrica de Metalicas (Brazil) (a subsidiary of CSN (Brazil)
FEMA Federal Emergency Management Agency (USA)
Fire Equipment Manufacturers Association (USA)
Flavor and Extract Manufacturers Association (USA)
Foundry Equipment Manufacturers Association (USA)
FEMECA Failure/Error Mode, Effect and Criticality Analysis
FEMEF Feeder Meter Flow
FEMS Federation of European Microbiological Societies
FEN Frequency Emphasing Network
FENOSA Fuerzas Electricas del Noroeste SA (Spain)
FEO Federal Energy Office (USA) (replaced by Federal Energy Administration in 1974)
FEP Film Epoxypolyamide
Fluorinated Ethylene-Propylene
Free Erythrocyte Protoporphyrin
Front-End Processor
FEPAP Federation of European Producers of Abrasives
FEPASA Ferrovia Paulista SA (Brazil)
FEPE Federation Européenne de la Publicité Extérieure (European Federation of Outdoor Advertising)
FEPEM Federation of European Petroleum Equipment Manufacturers
FEPF Federation Europeenne des Industries de Porcelain et de Faience de Table et d'Ornementation (European Federation of the Porcelain and Pottery Industries)
FEPS Far-Encounter Planet Sensor
FER Federation of Engine Remanufacturers
FERC Federal Energy Regulatory Commission (USA)
FERD Fuel Element Rupture Detector
FERFA Federation of Epoxy Resin Formulators and Applicators
FEROPA Federation Europeenne des Syndicats de Panneaux de Fibres (European Federation of Manufacturers Associations of Fibre Panels)
FES Final Environmental Statement
Final Environmental Survey
Flame Emission Spectroscopy
Fluidic Environmental Sensor
FRIEDRICH EBERT Stiftung (Germany) (Friedrich Ebert Foundation)
FESPA Federation of European Screen Printers Associations
FESS Finite Element Solution System
Flywheel Energy-Storage System
FeSV Feline Sarcoma Virus
FET Field Effect Transistor
FETA Fire Extinguishing Trades Association
FETC Field-Effect-Transistor-Capacitor
FETE FORTRAN Execution Time Estimator
FEU Further Education Unit (of DES)
FEUGRES Fédération Européenne des Fabricants de Tuyaux en Gré (European Federation of Manufacturers of Salt Glazed Pipes)
FeV Feline Leukaemia Virus
FEV Forced Expiratory Volume
FEVE Ferrocarriles de Via Estrecha (Spain) (State Narrow Gauge Railway Organisation)
FEWSG Fleet Electronic Warfare Support Group (USN)
FEXT Far-End Cross Talk
FF Flash-Filament
Frequency Feedback
FFA Flug- und Fahrzeugwerke Altenrhein (Switzerland)
Flygetniska Forsoksanstalten (Sweden) (Aeronautical Research Institute)
Free Fatty Acid
FFAG Fixed-Field Alternating-Gradient
FFAR Folding Fin Aircraft Rocket
Forward Firing Aerial Rocket
FFB Frequency Feedback
FFC Feed-Forward Control
Food Freezer Committee
FFCC Forward-Facing Crew Cockpit
FFDA Flying Funeral Directors of America (USA)
FFF Field-Flow Fractionation
FFG Forcing Function Generator
FFH Fast Frequency Hopping
FFHT Fast Fourier-Hadamard Transform
FFI Finance for Industry (of Bank of England and major clearing banks)
FFITP Federation Francaise d'Instituts Techniques du Petrole (France) (French Federation of Petroleum Technical Institutes)
FFMC Faceted Fixed Mirror Concentrator
FFMED Fixed Format Message Entry Device
FFO Furnace Fuel Oil
FFP Ferromagnetic Fine Particles
Firm Fixed Price
FFPLO Frequency Feedback Phase-Locked Oscillator
FFPS Flora and Fauna Preservation Society
FFR Flux Fraction Ratio
FFRDC Federally Funded Research and Development Center (USA)
FFS Formatted File System
FFSR Feed-Forward Signal Regeneration

FFT Fast Fourier Transform
Fixed Time Test
FFTF Fast Flux Test Facility (of USAEC)
FFTJS Frequency-Tracking Jitter Suppressor
FFTP Fast Fourier Transform Processor
FFTRI Fruit and Fruit Technology Research Institute (South Africa)
FFV Foersvarets Fabriksverk (Sweden)
Forenade Fabricksverken (Sweden) (government owned)
FFVMA Fire Fighting Vehicle Manufacturers Association
FFVV Federation Francaise de Vol a Voile (France) (French Federation of Gliding)
FFW Failure-Free Warranty
FGA Flat Glass Association
Floating-Gate Amplifier
FGAA Federal Government Accountants Association (USA)
FGAF Fraunhofer-Gessellschaft zur Forderung der Angewandten Forschung (Germany) (Fraunhofer Society for the Promotion of Applied Research)
FGB Fast Gun Boat
FGC Flight Guidance and Control
FGCB Fast Gas Cooled Reactor
FGCSP Fifth Generation Computer Systems Project (Japan)
FGD Flue Gas Desulphurisation
FGF Fibroblast Growth Factor
FGGE First GARP Global Experiment
FGIS Federal Grain Inspection Service (of USDA)
FGL Fixed-Gain Loop
FGMC Federal Government Micrographies Council (USA)
FGMDSS Future Global Maritime Distress and Safety System
FGMSD Financial and General Management Studies Division (of GAO (USA))
FGORC Flower Gardens Ocean Research Center (of Marine Biomedical Institute (University of Texas) (USA))
FGRAAL FORTRAN-extended Graph Algorithmic Language
FGS Fine Guidance Sensor
FGV Field-Gradient Voltage
FGW Forschunsgellschaft fur den Wohnungsbau (Austria) (Housing Research Association)
FH Frequency Hopping
FHA Familial Hypercholesterolaemia Association
Federal Housing Administration (USA)
Finance Houses Association
FHC FICOLL-HYPAQUE Centrifugation
FHE Fast Hydrofoil Escort
Forms Handling Equipment
FhF Fraunhofer-Gesellschaft zur Forderung der angewandten Forschung (Germany) (Fraunhofer Society for the Advancement of Applied Research)
FHF Fulminant Hepatic Failure
FHLBB Federal Home Loan Bank Board (USA)
FHMA Frequency Hopping Multiple-Access
FHom Faculty of Homeopathy
FHT Fast Hadamard Transform
Finite Hilbert Transform
FHW Flexible Working Hours
FHWA Federal Highway Administration (of Department of Transportation (USA))
FHWA-AK FHWA—Alaska Division (USA)
FHWA-ALA FHWA—Alabama Division (USA)
FHWA-ARK FHWA—Arkanas Division (USA)
FHWA-AS FHWA—American Samoa Division (USA)
FHWA-AZ FHWA—Arizona Division (USA)
FHWA-CA FHWA—California Division (USA)
FHWA-COLO FHWA—Colorado Division (USA)
FHWA-CONN FHWA—Connecticut Division (USA)
FHWA-DE FHWA—Delaware Division (USA)
FHWA-GA FHWA—Georgia Division (USA)
FHWA-HI FHWA—Hawaii Division (USA)
FHWA-IA FHWA—Iowa Division (USA)
FHWA-ILL FHWA—Illinois Division (USA)
FHWA-IND FHWA—Indiana Division (USA)
FHWA-KANS FHWA—Kansas Division (USA)
FHWA-KY FHWA—Kentucky Division (USA)
FHWA-LA FHWA—Louisiana Division (USA)
FHWA-MD FHWA—Maryland Division (USA)
FHWA-MICH FHWA—Michigan Division (USA)
FHWA-MN FHWA—Minnesota Division (USA)
FHWA-MO FHWA—Missouri Division (USA)
FHWA-MONT FHWA—Montana Division (USA)
FHWA-NC FHWA—North Carolina Division (USA)
FHWA-ND FHWA—North Dakota Division (USA)
FHWA-NEB FHWA—Nebraska Division (USA)
FHWA-NH FHWA—New Hampshire Division (USA)
FHWA-NJ FHWA—New Jersey Division (USA)
FHWA-NM FHWA—New Mexico Division (USA)
FHWA-NYS FHWA—New York State Division (USA)
FHWA-OHIO FHWA—Ohio Division (USA)
FHWA-OK FHWA—Oklahoma Division (USA)
FHWA-OR FHWA—Oregon District (USA)
FHWA-PA FHWA—Pennsylvania Division (USA)
FHWA-RI FHWA—Rhode Island Division (USA)
FHWA-SC FHWA—South Carolina Division (USA)
FHWA-SD FHWA—South Dakota Division (USA)
FHWA-TEX FHWA—Texas Division (USA)
FHWA-TN FHWA—Tennessee Division (USA)
FHWA-UT FHWA—Utah Division (USA)
FHWA-VA FHWA—Virginia Division (USA)
FHWA-VT FHWA—Vermont Division (USA)
FHWA-WA FHWA—Washington Division (USA)
FHWA-WIS FHWA—Wisconsin Division (USA)
FHWA-WV FHWA—West Virginia Division (USA)
FHWA-WYO FHWA—Wyoming Division (USA)
FI Field Ionization
FI-MS Field Ionization Mass Spectrometry
FI-X Fighter-Interceptor-Experimental
FIA Factory Insurance Association (USA)
Faridabad Industries Association (India)
Federation Internationale de l'Automobile (International Automobile Federation)
Flame Ionization Analysis
Fluorescent Indicator Adsorption
Forging Industry Association (USA)
FREUND's Incomplete Adjuvant
FIABCI International Real Estate Federation
FIAC Flight Information Advisory Committee (USA)
FIAF Fédération Internationale des Archives du Film (Belgium) (International Federation of Film Archives)
FIAMS Flinders Institute for Atmospheric and Marine Sciences (Flinders University of South Australia)
FIANE Fonds d'Intervention et d'Action pour la Nature et l'Environnement (France) (Environmental Action Fund) (administered by CIANE)
Fonds d'Intervention et l'Action pour la Nature et l'Environnement (France) (Action Fund for Nature and the Environment)
FIAP Federation Internationale de l'Art Photographique (Switzerland) (International Federation of Photographic Art)

FIAR	Fabbrica Italiana Apparechi Radio (Italy)
FIAS	Formation Internationale Aeronautique et Spatiale (France)
FIAT	Fabbrica Italiana Automobili Torini (Italy) Federation Internationale des Archives du Television (International Federation of Television Archives) Field Information Agency, Technical (USA) Fonds d'Intervention d'Amenagement du Territoire (France) (Development Fund)
FIATA	Federation Internationale des Associations de Transitaires et Assimiles (International Federation of Forwarding Agents Associations) (Switzerland) Assimiles (International Federation of Forwarding Agents Associations)
FIB	Focused Ion Beam
FIBC	Flexible Intermediate Bulk Container
FIBCA	Flexible Intermediate Bulk Container Association
FIBTP	Federation Internationale du Batiment et des Travaux Publics (International Federation of Building and Public Works)
FIC	Fast Ion Conduction Film Integrated Circuit Flame Ionization Detection Free-Induction Decay
FICCI	Federation of Indian Chambers of Commerce and Industry (India)
FICM	Fluidic Industrial Control Module
FICO	Flight Information and Control of Operations
FICS	Factory Information Control System Forecasting and Inventory Control System
FID	Federation Internationale de la Documentation (International Documentation Federation) Flame Ionization Detector Floating Input Distortion Forecasts-In-Depth
FID-RRS	Federation Internationale de la Documentation Research Referral Service
FID/CAO	Fédération Internationale de la Documentation Commission for Asia and Oceania
FID/CCC	FID Central Classification Committee (for the development of the UDC)
FID/CLA	FID Regional Commission for Latin America
FID/CR	FID Committee on Classification Research
FID/DC	FID Committee on Developing Countries
FID/DT	FID Committee on the Terminology of Information and Documentation
FID/ET	FID Committee on Education and Training
FID/II	FID Committee on Information for Industry
FID/LD	FID Committee on Linguistics in Documentation
FID/RI	FID Committee on Research on the Theoretical Basis of Information
FID/TMO	FID Committee on Theory, Methods and Operations of Information Systems and Networks
FIDA	Federal Industrial Development Authority (Malaysia)
FIDAC	Film Input to Digital Automatic Computer
FIDASE	Falkland Islands and Dependencies Aerial Survey Expedition
FIDC	Fishery Industry Development Council (Philippines)
FIDE	Federation de l'Industrie Dentaire en Europe (France) (Federation of the Dental Industry in Europe)
FIDIC	Federation Internationale des Ingenieurs Conseil (International Federation of Consulting Engineers) (Netherlands)
FIDO	Fog Investigation and Dispersal Operation Forklift Independent Distributors Organisation
FIDOR	Fibre Building Board Development Organisation
FIDUROP	Fédération des Fabricants de Ficelles et Cordages de l'Europe Occidentale (merged into EUROCORD in 1975)
FIE	Fluoride Ion Electrode
FIEJ	Federation Internationale des Editeurs de Journaux et Publications (International Federation of Editors of Journal and Publications)
FIELD	First Integrated Experiment for Lunar Development
FIEN	Forum Italiano dell Energia Nucleaire (Italy) (Italian Nuclear Forum)
FIEO	Federation of Indian Export Organisations (India)
FIER	Foundation for Intrumentation Education and Research (of Instrument Society of America)
FIET	Facultad de Ingenieria Electronica y Telecommunicaciones (Columbia) (School of Electronic and Telecommunications Engineering)
FIF	Formaldehyde-Induced Fluorescence
FIFI	Flexible Ideal Format for Information
FIFL	Federal Interagency Field Libraries (USA)
FIFO	First In First Out
FIFRA	Federal Insecticide, Fungicide and Rodenticide Act (USA)
FIG	Federation Internationale des Geometres (International Federation of Surveyors) (Germany)
FIGAZ	Federation de l'Industrie du Gaz (Belgium) (Gas Industry Federation)
FIGED	Federation Internationale des Grande Entreprises de Distribution (International Federation of Large Distribution Undertakings)
FIGLU	Formiminoglutamic acid
FIGO	Federation Internationale de Gynecologie et d'Obstetrique (Switzerland) (International Federation of Gynaecology and Obstetrics)
FIIG	Federal Item Identification Guide (of USDOD)
FIIRO	Federal Institute of Industrial Research Oshodi (Nigeria)
FIJPA	Federation Internationale des Journalistes Professionels de l'Aeronautique (International Federation of Writers on Aeronautics)
FILA	Federation of Indian Library Associations (India)
FILD	Fumeless In-Line Degassing
FILES	FAMECE (US Army) Integrated Logistics Evaluation Simulator
FILRAP	Formal Integrate Long Range Planning
FILS	FUJITSU (LTD) (Japan) Image Library System
FILTAN	Passive Filter Analysis
FILTECH	International Filtration and Separation Exhibition and Conference
FIM	Field Intensity Meter Field Ion Microscope Field Ion Microscopy Flame Ionisation Method Fédération Internationale Motocycliste
FIMA	Future International Medium Airlifter
FIML	Full-Information Maximum-Likelihood
FIMS	Financial Information Management System FIRESTONE (TIRE AND RUBBER COMPANY (USA)) Inventory Management System Functionally Identification Maintenance System
FIMTM	Federation des Industries Mecaniques et Transformatrices des Metaux (France) (Federation of Metal Processing Industries)
FINABEL	France, Italy, Netherlands, Allemagne, Belgium, Luxembourg (Army Chiefs of Staff Joint Committee)
FINAT	International Federation of Manufacturers and Converters of Pressure-Sensitive and Heatseal Materials on Paper and other Base Materials (Netherlands)
FINCO	Finance Committee (of ISO)

FIND — Facsimile Information Network Development
File Interrogation of NINETEEN-HUNDRED Data
Flight Information Display
Forecasting Institutional Needs for DARTMOUTH (Dartmouth College (USA))
prefix to numbered series of Fiche Index for Nuclear Dockets issued by USAEC

FINDER — Fingerprint-Reader

FINPRO — Finnish Committee on Trade Procedures (Finland)

FIO — Foreign Intelligence Office (of DARCOM (US Army))

FIP — Federation Internationale de la Precontrainte (International Federation of Prestressing)
Federation Internationale Pharmaceutique (Netherlands) (International Pharmaceutical Federation)
Federation of Indian Publishers (India)
Formed-In-Place

FIPA — Federation Internationale des Producteurs Agricoles (International Federation of Agricultural Producers)

FIPACE — Fédération Internationale des Producteurs Autoconsommateurs Industriels d'Electricité

FIPAGO — Fédération Internationale des Fabricants de Papiers Gommes (Netherlands) (International Federation of Manufacturers of Gummed Paper)

FIPP — Federation Internationale de la Presse Periodique (International Federation of the Periodical Press)

FIPS — Federal Information Processing Standards (issued by NBS (USA))
Flight-Inspection Positioning System

FIPS-PUB — prefix to numbered series of publications issued by NBS (USA) Office of Information Processing Standards

FIR — Far Infra-Red
Finite Duration Impulse Response
Flight Information Region

FIRA — Federal Investment Review Agency (Canada)
Furniture Industry Research Association

FIRAC — Federation Internationale des Radio Amateurs Cheminots (International Federation of Railroad Radio Amateurs)

FIRE — FAIRCHILD Integrated Real-time Executive

FIREMEN — Fire Resistant Materials Engineering

FireRO — Joint Fire Research Organisation

FIRES-T — Fire Response of Structures-Thermal (a computer Programme)

FIRL — Faceted Information Retrieval for Linguistics
Franklin Institute Research Laboratories (USA)

FIRM — Financial Information for Resource Management

FIRMI/FI — Fault Isolation Reporting Method/Fault Isolation

FIRO — Fundamental Interpersonal Relations Orientation

FIRP — Foreign Inward Remittance Payment Scheme (of the Reserve Bank of India)

FIRS — Far Infra-Red Spectra

FIRST — Fabrication of Inflatable Re-entry Structures for Test
Fast Interactive Retrieval System
Federal Information Research Science and Technology network (of COSATI) (USA)
Fire Information Retrieval System Techniques
Fleurs Interferometric Radio Synthesis Telescope (University of Sydney (Australia))
Futures Information Retrieval System (of the Library of Congress (USA))

FIRTA — Far Infra-Red Technical Area
Fishing Industry Research Trust Account

FIRTI — Far Infrared Target Indicator

FIRTO — Fire Insurers Research and Testing Organisation

FIS — Federation Internationale du Commerce des Semences (Netherlands) (International Federation of the Seed Trade)
Foam-In Salvage

FISAR — Fleet Information Storage and Retrieval (USN)

FISC — Flight Instrument Signal Converter
Fédération Internationale des Chasseurs du Son

FISHROD — Fiche Information Selectively Held and Retrieved On Demand

FISITA — Federation Internationale des Societies d'Ingenieurs et de Techniciens de l'Automobile (International Federation of Automobile Engineering Societies)

FIST — Fault Isolation by Semi-automatic Techniques
Field Intelligence Signal Terminal

FIT — Fault-Isolation Test
Federal Income Tax (USA)
Federation International des Traducteurs (International Federation of Translators)
Flexible Interface Technique
Floating Input Transistor
Florida Institute of Technology (USA)
Functional Industrial Training

FITAC — Federacion Interamericano de Touring y Automovil Clubes (Argentina) (Inter-American Federation of Touring and Automobile Clubs)
Film Industry Training and Apprenticeship Council

FITAP — Federation Internationale des Transports Aeriens Prives (International Federation of Independent Air Transport)

FITC — Fluorescein Isothiocynate
Foundry Industry Training Committee

FITCE — Federation des Ingenieurs des Telecommunications de Communaute Europeenne (Belgium) (Federation of Telecommunications Engineers of the European Community)

FITPRO — Czechoslovak Committee for the Facilitation of International Trade Procedures

FIU — Federation of Information Users (USA)
Florida International University (USA)

FIV — Federation de l'Industrie du Verre (Belgium) (Federation of the Glass Industry)

FJA — Functional Job Analysis

FJCC — Fall Joint Computer Conference (USA)

FJSRL — Frank J. Seiler Research Laboratory (USAF Academy)

FL — Fan Lift
Fight Level
Food Laboratory (of Natick Laboratories (US Army))
Foot Lambert
Fraunhofer Lines

FLA — Fiji Library Association (Fiji)

FLACTO — Frequency Locked Automatic Computing Transfer Oscillator

FLAD — Fluorescence-Activated Display

FLAG — FORTRAN Load And Go

FLAGS — Far-North Liquids and Associated Gas System

FLAIR — Fleet Location And Information Reporting (for police patrol cars)

FLAMES — Fabrication Labour and Material Estimating Service

FLAMR — Forward Looking Advanced Multimode Radar

FLANG — Flowchart Language

FLAP — FLORES Assembly Programme

FLAPS — Flexibility Analysis of Piping Systems

FLARE — Flight Anomaly Reporting
Florida Aquanaut Research Expedition (of NOAA (USA))

FLASH — Flash Lights And Send Help

FLAT — FORTRAN Language Augmentation Tool

FLC Federal Laboratory Consortium
Federal Library Committee (USA)
FLD Flux Lattice Dislocation
Fraunhofer Line Discriminator
FLECHT Full Length Emergency Cooling Heat Transfer
FLEE Fast Linkage Editor
FLEM Flyby-Landing Excursion Mode
FLEWEAFAC Fleet Weather Facility (USN)
FLEXAR Flexible, Adaptive Radar
FLEXEM Flexible Energy Management
FLEXIMIS Flexible Management Information System
FLIC Film Library Information Council (USA)
Flaw Locating and Imaging Computer
FLIM Fast Library Management
FLIMBAL Floated Inertial Measurement Ball
FLIP Film Library Instantaneous Presentation
Flight Information Publications (of USDOD)
Flight Launched Infrared Probe
Floated Instrument Platform
Floated Lightweight Inertial Platform
Floating Instrument Platform
Floating Laboratory Instrument Platform
Formal List Processor
Free-form Language for Image Processing
FLIR Forward Look Infrared
Forward Looking Infra-red Receiver
FLIRT FORTRAN Logical Information Retrieval Technique
FLITE Federal Legal Information Through Electronics (USDOD)
FLL Frequency Locked Looped
FLLS Focused Laser Lithographic System
FLO First Lunar Observatory
FLOAT Floating Offshore Attended Terminal
FLOCON Floating Container
FLOLS FRESNEL Lens Optical Landing System
FLOOD Fleet Observation of Oceanographic Data (USN)
FLOPAC Flight Operations Advisory Committee (of IATA)
FLOPP Floating Power Platform
FLOX Liquid Fluorine and Liquid Oxygen
FLP Facility Location Planner
FLR Forward Looking Radar
FLRA Federal Labor Relations Authority (USA)
FLS Forward Look Sonar
Fundacion La Salle de Ciencias Naturales (Venezuela)
FLSA Fair Labor Standards Act (USA)
FLSC Flexible Linear-Shaped Charge
FLT Flight Line Tester
FLTSATCOM Fleet Satellite Communication System (USN)
FLV Friend Leukaemia Virus
FLVD Fine Line Velocity Discriminator
FLYBAR Flying By Auditory Reference
FM Facilities Management
Feeder Monitor
Field Manual
File Maintenance
Fish Meal
Fracture Mechanics
Franklin and Marshall College (USA)
Frequency Modulation
Fuel Modifier
FMA Fabrica Militar de Aviones (Argentina) (Military Aircraft Factory) (State owned)
Fabricating Machinery Association (USA)
Farm Management Association (absorbed into BIM in 1978)
Ferrocenylmethyl Acrylate
Fire Marshals Association of North America (USA)
Fonds Monétaire Andin (Andean Monetary Fund)
Food Machinery Association (now merged with TIPA)
Fundamental Mode Asynchronous
FMANA Fire Marshals Association of North America (USA)
FMB Fast Missile Boat
Federation of Master Builders
FMBRA Flour Milling and Baking Research Association
FMBT Future Main Battle Tank
FMC Federal Maritime Commission (USA)
Fixed Mirror Concentrator
Fleet Maintenance Council (USA)
Flight Management Computer
Florida Metric Council
Foward Motion Compensation
FMCE Federation of Manufacturers of Construction Equipment (now part of Federation of Manufacturers of Construction Equipment and Cranes)
FMCEC Federation of Manufacturers of Construction Equipment and Cranes
FMCS Federal Mediation and Conciliation Service (USA)
Flight Management Computer System
FMCW Frequency Modulated Intermittent/Continuous Wave
FMD Foot and Mouth Disease
FMDV Foot and Mouth Disease Virus
FME Foundation for Management Education
FMEA Failure Mode and Effects Analysis
FMECA Failure Mode, Effects and Criticality Analysis
FMF Familial Mediterranean Fever
Flow Microfluorometry
Food Manufacturers Federation
FMFB Frequency-Modulation Feedback
FMFF Frequency Modulation Feed Forward
FMFM prefix of numbered series of Fleet Marine Force Manuals issued by US Marine Corps
FMFS Full Mission Fighter (aircraft) Simulator
FMG Foundry Marketing Group
FMH Falling Mass Hazard
FmHA Farmers Home Administration (of USDA)
FMI Financial Management Initiative
Functional Management Inspection system (of AFISC (USAF))
FMIC Frequency Monitoring and Interference Control
FMICW Frequency Modulated Intermittent/Continuous Wave
FMLP Field Mirror Landing Practice
FMLS Full-Matrix Least Squares
FMMA Ferrocenylmethyl Methacrylate
FMN Flavin Mononucleotide (State owned)
FMP Flight Mechanics Panel (of AGARD (NATO))
FMPS Functional Mathematical Programming System
FMR Fasting Metabolic Rate
Ferromagnetic Resonance
Field Maintenance Reliability
FMS Federation of Materials Societies (USA) (comprising ASNT, ASM, IEEE, ACS, SME, ACerS, NACE and AIChE)
Flexible Manufacturing System
Flexible Measuring System
Flight Management System
Foreign Military Sales (program of USDOD)
Frequency Monitoring System
Frequency-Multiplexed Subcarrier
FMSAEG Fleet Missile Systems Analysis and Evaluation Group (USN)
FMT Field Modulation Technique
FMTM Friction Materials Test Machine
FMU Freight Multiple Unit

FMV Foersvarets Materielverk (Sweden) (Defence Material Administration)
FMVSS Federal Motor Vehicle Safety Standards (USA)
FMW Fast Magnetosonic Wave
FN Fabrique Nationale Herstal (Belgium)
FNAF Federal Nigerian Air Force (Nigeria)
FNAL Fermi National Accelerator Laboratory (USA)
FNAP FORTRAN Network-Analysis Programme
FNET Fuzzy Network
FNI Electro-Naval et Industriel (Belgium)
Ente Nazionale Idrocarburi (Italy)
FNIC Food and Nutrition Information and Educational Materials Centre (of National Agricultural Library (USA))
FNIE Federation Nationale des Industries Electroniques (France) (Electronic Industries National Federation)
FNKe Fachnormenausschus Radiologie (Germany) (Radiology Standards Committee)
FNKE Fachnormenausschuss Kerntechnik (Germany) (Nuclear Technology Standards Committee)
FNOC Fleet Numerical Oceanography Center (USN)
FNP Floating Nuclear Power Plant
FNS Food and Nutrition Service (of USDA)
Functional Neuromuscular Stimulation
FNT FERMAT Number Transform
FNWC Fleet Numerical Weather Central (USN)
FNWF Fleet Numerical Weather Facility (USN)
FO Fibre Optics
FOA Forsvarets Forskningsanstalt (Sweden) (National Defence Research Institute)
FOAMS Forecasting, Order Administration and Master Scheduling
FOB Faculty of Building
FOB Free On Board
FOBS Fractional Orbiting Bombardment System
FOBW Frequencies of Occurrence of Binary Words
FOC Fire Offices Committee (of some of the fire insurance companies in Great Britain)
Flag of Convenience
FOCAL Formula Calculator
Formulating On-line Calculations in Algebraic Language
FOCAP Fiber Optic Cost Analysis Program (of USAF)
FOCAS Fibre Optic Cabling and Switching
Fibre Optic Communications for Aerospace Systems
FORD (MOTOR COMPANY) Operating Cost Analysis System
FOCCPAC Fleet Operations Control Center, Pacific Fleet (USN)
FOCIA Fibre Optics Coupled Image Amplifier
FOCIS Fiber Optic Communication Information Society (USA)
Financial On-line Central Information System
FOCMA Feline Oncornavirus-associated Cell Membrane Antigen
FOCON Fibre Cone Optics
FOCS Freight Operation Control System
FOCUS FACom Oriented Coordinative Utility System
Forum of CONTROL DATA Users (USA)
FOD Foreign Object Damage
FODAAP Fleet Operational Data Acquisition and Analysis Program (USN)
FOE Friends of the Earth (a society concerned with ecological and environmental problems)
FOEP Frog Otolith Experiment Package
FOF Field Observing Facility (of National Center for Atmospheric Research (USA))
FOFA Follow on Force Attack
FOG Fats, Oil and Grease
FOG-M Fibre Optic Guided Missile
FOGRA Forschungsgesellschaft fur Druck- und Reproduktionstecknik (Germany) (Research Society for the Printing and Graphic Arts Industry)
FOI Fleet Operational Investigation (USN)
Follow-On Interceptor
FOIA Freedom Of Information Act (USA)
FOIL File-Oriented Interpretive Language
FOIR Field of Interest Register
FOL Fuel, Oil and Lubricants
FOLAN Fibre-Optic Local Area Network
FOLIOS (The) Foreign Office (London) Integrated Office System
FOLPEN-BSD Foliage Penetration Battlefield Surveillance Device
FOM Figure Of Merit
Stichting voor Fundamenteel Onderzoek der Materie (Netherlands) (Society for Fundamental Research of Matter)
FONASBA Federation of National Associations of Ship Brokers and Agents
Federation of National Associations of Shipbrokers and Agents
FOOB Firing-Out-Of-Battery
FOOS Fail-Operational-Fail-Operational-Fail-Safe
FOP Forward Operating Pad
FOPERPIC Association for the Development of Further Professional Training in the Foundry and Related Industries (France)
FOPS Falling Object Protective Structure
File Oriented Programming System
Forecast Operating System
FOPSA Federation of Productivity Services Association
FOPT Fibre-Optics Photon Transfer
FORACS Fleet Operational Readiness Accuracy Check Site (USN)
Fleet Operational Readiness And Calibration Systems (of NATO)
FORATOM Forum Atomique Europeen (France) (European Atomic Forum)
FORBLOC FORTRAN-compiled Block-oriented simulation programme
FORD Floating Ocean Research Development station
FORDS Floating Ocean Research and Development Station
FOREM File Organization and Evaluation Modelling
FOREST Freedom Organisation for the Right to Enjoy the Smoking of Tobacco
FORIMS FORTRAN Oriented Information Management System
FORMAC Formula Manipulation Compiler
FORMAL Formula Manipulation Language
FORMAT FORTRAN Matrix Abstraction Techniques
FORMS Federation of Rocky Mountain States (USA)
File Organization Modelling System
FORPRIDECOM Forest Products Research and Industries Development Commission(Philippines)
FORSCOM Forces Command (US Army)
FORTRA Federation of Radio and Television Retailers Association
FORTRAN Formula Translation
FORTSIM FORTRAN Simulation
FORWARD Feedback Of Repair, Workshop And Reliability Data
FOS Fuel-Oxygen Scrap
FOSDIC Film Optical Sensing Device for Input to Computers
FOSIL FOCAL (Formulating On-line Calculations in Algebraic Language) Simulator Language

FOSMA Function-Oriented Symbolic Macromodelling Algorithm
FOSPLAN Formal Space Planning Language
FOSS Family of Systems Studies
FOT Faint Object Telescope
FOT & E Follow-on Operational Test and Evaluation
FOV Field of View
FOW Forge Welding
FP Fluorescent Particle
Fluorescent Penetrant
FPA Federal Preparedness Agency (of GSA (USA))
Fire Protection Association
Flexible Premium Annuity system
Flight Path Accelerometer
Flying Physicians Association (USA)
Focal Plane Array
Formacion Professional Acelerada (Spain) (Centre for the Accelerated Training of Craftsmen)
Fused Polyethylene Aluminium
FPB Fast Patrol Boat
FPBAI Federation of Publishers and Booksellers Association in India (India)
FPC Fast Patrol Boat
Federal Power Commission (USA) (now FERC)
Federation of Painting Contractors
Food Protein Concentrate
FPCC Flight/Propulsion Control Coupling
FPCD Federal Personnel and Compensation Division (of GAO (USA))
FPCEA Fibreboard Packaging Case Employers Association
FPCMA Fibreboard Packing Case Manufacturers Association
FPD Field-Plated Diode
Flame Photometric Detector
Flush Plate Dipole
FPDA Finnish Plywood Development Association
FPEC Four-Pile Extended Cantilever platform
FPF Fluoroprotein Foam
FPGA Field-Programmable Gate Array
FPH Fish Protein Hydrolysate
FPHS Fall-out Protection in Homes
FPI Fabry-Perot Interferometer
Federal Procurement Institute (of USDOD)
Fixed Price Incentive
FPIS Fixed Price Incentive with Successive Targets
FPL Forest Products Laboratory (of Forest Service (USDA))
FPLA Fair Packaging and Labelling Act (USA)
Field Programmable Logic Array
FPLE Field Programmable Logic Element
FPLS Field-Programmable Logic Sequencer
FPM Functional Planning Matrices system
prefix to numbered series of Federal Personnel Manuals issued by the Civil Service Commission (USA)
FPMIS Federal Personnel Management Information System (of Civil Service Commission (USA))
FPMR Federal Property Management Regulation (USA)
FPN Fixed Pattern Noise
Fixed Pattern NoiseMalators
FPP Fixed-Pitch Propeller
FPPS Flight Plan Processing System
FPR Federal Procurement Regulations (USA)
Flat Plate Radiometer
Fluorescence Photobleaching Recovery
FPRC Flying Personnel Research Committee (of Royal Air Force Institute of Aviation Medicine)
FPRI Fire Protection Research International (USA)
Forest Products Research Institute (Ghana)
FPRL Forest Products Research Laboratory (now the Princes Risborough Laboratory (of the Building Research Establishment (DOE))
FPRS Fabry-Perot Recycling Spectrometer
Forest Products Research Society (USA)
FPS Fauna Preservation Society
Federation of Piling Specialists
Financial Planning Simulator
Financial Planning System
Fine Particle Society (USCA)
Fixed Pattern Signal
Floating Point Systems
Fluid Power Society (USA)
Focus Projection and Scanning
FPSV Fixed Platform Supply Vessel
FPT Free Plasma Trytophan
Functional Programme Translator
FPTS Forward Propagation Tropospheric Scatter
FPV Fishery Patrol Vessel
Fowl Plague Virus
FQO Federated Quarry Owners of Great Britain
FQR Formal Qualification Review
FR Faculty of Radiologists
Final Report
FR-RSR Fortele Aeriene ale Republicii Populare Romania (Romania) (Air Force of the Romanian People's Republic)
FRA Federal Railroad Administration (Department of Transportation (USA))
FRACA Failure Reporting, Analysis and Corrective Action
FRACAS Filter Response Analysis for Continuously Accelerating Spacecraft
FRAH Fluid Regenerative Air Heater
FRALINE Fast Reaction Automatic Lightweight Inertial North-seeking Equipment
FRAM Failure Rate Assessment Machine
Fusible Random Access Memory
FRAMATEG Framatone Entreprise Générale (France)
FRAMATOME Societe Franco-Americaine de Constructions Atomiques (France)
FRAME Fund for the Replacement of Animals in Medical Experiments
FRAN Framed Structure Analysis
FRANK Frequency Regulation and Network Keying
FRANTIC Formal Reliability Analysis including Normal Testing, Inspection and Checking
FRAT Facilities Relative Allocation Technique
Free Radical Assay Technique
FRATE Formulae for Routes and Technical Equipment
FRB Fisheries Research Board (of the Department of Fisheries and Forestry (Canada))
FRC Fast Reaction Concept
Federal Radiation Council (USA)
Fibre Reinforced Composite
File Research Council
Fisheries Research Centre (MAF) (New Zealand)
Flight Research Center (of NASA)
Functional Residue Capacity
FRCAB Felt Roofing Contractors Advisory Board
FRCTF Fast Reactor Core Test Facility (USAEC)
FRD Foundation for Research Development (of CSIR South Africa))
FRE Fischer Rat Embryo
FREAVY Frequency Availability
FRED Fast Random Enquiry Display
Fast Reading Electronic Digitizer
Fast-Rate Electrodeposition
FREDDY Family Robot for Entertainment Discussion and Education, the Retrieval of Information and the Collation of Knowledge

FREI Forest Research and Education Institute (Sudan)
Research-Engineering Interaction
Reusable External Insulation

FRELIS Frequency Lists

FRESCANAR Frequency Scaning Fixed Array Radar

FRESCO Frequency Stability Code

FRESH Foil Research Ship Hydrofoil

FREWCAP Flexible Reworkable Chip Attachment Process

FRF Fire-Resistant Fuel

FRHB Federation of Registered House Builders

FRI Fisheries Research Institute (Washington University (USA))
Food Research Institute (of Agricultural Research Council)
Fulmer Research Institute (of Institute of Physics)

FRL Free-Recall Learning

FRM Field Reverse Mirror

FRME Frequency Response Measuring Equipment

FRMV Free Running Multivibrator

FRN Full Range Naptha

FROG Free Rocket Over Ground for tactical use (USSR)

FRP Failure Replacement Policy
Fast Retinal Potential
Fibre Reinforced Plastic

FRRC Fast Reaction Rescue Craft

FRS Festiniog Railway Society
Financial Results Simulator
Fire Research Station (merged into the Building Research Establishment, 1972 (of DOE))

FRSM Ferro-Resonance Servo Motor

FRSS Financial Results Simulator System

FRTC Fast Reactor Training Centre (UKAEA)

FRTP Fibreglass Reinforced Thermoplastic

FRTRA Federation of Radio and Television Retailers Association

FRTV Forward Repair and Test Vehicle

FRUCOM Federation Europeene des Importateurs de Fruits Secs, Conserves, Epices et Miel (European Federation of Importers of Dried Fruits, Preserves, Spices and Honey)

FRUSA Flexible Rolled-Up Solar Array

FRW Friction Welding

FRWI Framingham Relative Weight Index

FS Ferrovie dello Stato-Italia (Italian State Railways)
Fiber Society (USA)
Furnace Sensitize

FS5 Firing Squad Synchronization, Simulation and Solution System

FSA Finite State Automation

FSAA Flight Simulator for Advanced Aircraft

FSAS Fluidic Stability Augmentation System

FSB Floating Supply Base

FSC Federal Science Council (USA)
Fire Service College
Food Standards Committee (of MAFF)

FSCM Federal Supply Code for Manufacturer (USA)
Federal Supply Code for Manufacturers (USA)

FSCT Federation of Societies for Coatings Technology (USA)

FSD Fisher Significant Difference
Flying Spot Digitizer

FSDA Frequency Spectral Density Analysis

FSDO Flight Standards District Office (of FAA) (USA)

FSEA Full Shear Energy Absorption

FSEC Federal Software Exchange Centre (of GSA (USA) and NTIS (USA))

FSED Full Scale Engineering Development

FSF Fully Submerged Foil hydrofoil craft

FSG First Stage Graphitization

FSGTR-NC prefix to numbered series of Forest Service General Technical Reports of the North Central Forest Experiment Center (USA)

FSH Follicle Stimulating Hormone
prefix to numbered series of pamphlets issued by MAFF

FSII Fuel System Icing Inhibitor

FSK Frequency Shift Keying

FSL Food Science Laboratory (US Army)
Formal Semantic Language
Frequency-Selective Limiter

FSM Finite-State Machine

FSMS Flight Structural Monitoring System

FSPE Federation of Societies of Professional Engineers (South Africa)

FSPLS Florida Society of Professional Land Surveyors (USA)
Florida Society of Professional Land Surveyors (USA)

FSPS Federation of Sailing and Powerboat Schools
FERRANTI Sonobuoy Processing System

FSPT Federation of Societies for Paint Technology (USA)

FSQS Food Safety and Quality Service (of USDA)

FSR Feedback Shift Register
Free Spectral Range
Frequency Set-on Receiver

FSRB prefix to Forest Service Research Bulletins issued by the Forest Products Laboratory (USDA)

FSRN prefix to Forest Service Research Notes (issued by Forest Products Laboratory (USDA))

FSRP prefix to Forest Service Research Papers (issued by Forest Products Laboratory (USDA))

FSRS Frequency Set-on Receiving System

FSS Federal Supply Service (of GSA (USA))
Fixed Satellite Service
Flight Service Station
Flying Spot Scanner
Fossil Stromgen Sphere
Frequency-Selective Surface

FSST Flying Scot Scanner Tube

FSSU Federated Superannuation System for Universities

FST Flexible Switch Technology
Functional Simulator and Translator

FSTC Federal Software Testing Center (OIT (USA))
Foreign Science and Technology Center (US Army)

FSTS Fire Service Training School (DTI)

FSTT Floating Shuttle Tape Transport

FSTV Fast-Scan Television

FSU Florida State University (USA)

FSUC Federal Statistics Users Conference (USA)

FSV Feline Sarcoma Virus
Ferry Supply Vehicle

FT Ferroresonant Transformer
Fourier Transformation
Frequency and Time

FT-ICR Fourier Transform Ion Cyclotron Resonance

FT-IR Fourier-Transform-Infra-Red
International Fourier Transform Infra-Red Conference

FT/OPAS Funds-In-Trust Operational Assistance Scheme (of ITU (UN))

FTA Fault Tree Analysis Analysis
Flexographic Technical Association (USA)
Fluorescent Treponemal Antibody
Forced Transportation Arc
Freight Transport Association

FTA-ABS Fluorescent Treponemal Antibody Absorption

FTAS Division of Fluid Thermal and Aerospace Sciences (Case Western Reserve University (US))

FTB Fast Torpedo Boat

FTC Fair Trade Commission (Japan)
Fast Time Constant
Federal Trade Commission (USA)
Flight Test Centre
Float Trend Chart
FTCS International Symposium on Fault-Tolerant Computing
FTD Field Terminated Diode
Foreign Technology Division (of USAFSC)
FTDAS Flight Test Data Acquisition System
FTE Fracture Transition Elastic
FTESA Foundry Trades Equipment and Supplies Association
FTFET Four-Terminal Field-Effect Transitor
FTH Fourier Transform Hologram
FTI Financial Times Index
Fixed Time Interval
Free Thyroxine Index
FTIO Foreign Technical Intelligence Office (US Army)
FTIR Frustrated Total Internal Reflection
FTITB Furniture and Timber Industry Training Board
FTL (Military Electronics Laboratory)
Fast Transient Loader
Flight Transportation Laboratory (Massachusetts Institute of Technology (USA))
Forsvarets Teletekniska Laboratorium (Sweden)
FTLO Fast Tuned Local Oscillator
FTM Flight Test Manual
Full Travel Membrane
FTMA Federation of Textile Manufacturers Associations
FTMP Fault-Tolerant Multi-Processor
FTMT Final Thermal Mechanical Treatment
FTP File-Transfer Protocol
File-Transfer Protocolicaionscle Stimulating Hormone NoiseMalat
FTR Filestore Transfer Routine
Formation Temperature Ratio
Frustrated Total Reflectance
FTS Federal Telecommunications System (USA)
Flexible Test Station
Fourier Transform Spectrometry
FTSC Fault Tolerant Spaceborne Computer
FUB Fondazione Ugo Bordoni (Italy)
FUBAR FANGMEYER'S Utility, a Basic Algorithm for Revision
FUdR Fluorodeoxyuridine
FUDR Failure and Usage Data Report
FUE Federated Union of Employers (Eire)
FUFO Fly Under, Fly Out
Full Fusing Option bomb
FURNAS Central Electrica de Furnas (Brazil)
FURST FORTRAN Unit Record Simulation Technique
FUS Far Ultraviolet Spectrometer
FORTRAN Utility System
FUSE Federation for Unified Science Education (USA)
FV Fusing Voltage
FVC Forced Vital Capacity
FVCS FORTRAN Compiler Validation Suite
FVPRA Fruit and Vegetable Preservation Research Association
FVR Feline Viral Rhinotracheitis
FVRDE Fighting Vehicles Research and Development Establishment (MOD) (merged into MVEE, 1970)
FVS Fighting Vehicle System
FVT Flash Vacuum Thermolysis
FVTT Fishing Vessel Transmit Terminal
FW Filament Wound
Flash Welding
Fresh Water
FWA Fluorescent Whitening Agent
FWAG Farming and Wildlife Advisory Group
FWC Filament-Wound Cylinder
FWD Front Wheel Drive
FWEP Federal Wind Energy Program (USA)
FWG Forschungsanstalt fur Wasserchall und Geophysik (of BWB (Germany))
FWGPM Federal Working Group on Pest Management (USA)
FWH Flexible Working Hours
FWHM Full Width at Half Maximum
Full-Wave Half Modulation
FWID Federation of Wholesale and Industrial Distributors
FWO Federation of Wholesale Organisations (now FWID)
FWP Filament Wound Plastics
FWPCA Federal Water Pollution Control Act 1972 (USA)
Federal Water Pollution Control Administration (Department of the Interior (USA)) (later FWQA)
FWQA Federal Water Quality Administration (now Water Quality Office (of EPA (USA))
FWRM Federal of Wire Rope Manufacturers of Great Britain
FWS Filter Wedge Spectrometer
Fish and Wildlife Service (Department of the Interior) (USA)
FWT Fast Walsh Transform
Flexible Working Time
FWWMR Flame, Water, Weather and Mildew Resistant
FY Fiscal Year
FYDP Five-Year Defense Program (USDOD)
FZGB Federation of Zoological Gardens of Great Britain and Ireland
FZP Fresnel Zone Plate

G

G prefix to numbered: dated series of Electrical Equipment and Indicating Instruments standards issued by BSI (letter is sometimes preceded by a number)
G&FTEA Glazed and Floor Tile Export Association
G&FTHA Glazed and Floor Tile Home Trade Association
G/MFCS Gun/Missile Fire Control System
GA Gemmological Association
Gibberellic Acid
Group Atmosphere
GAAA Groupement Atomique Alsacienne Atlantique (France)
GAAC Graphic Arts Advertisers Council (USA)
GAADV Graphic Arts Association of the Delaware Valley (USA)
GaAlAs Gallium Aluminium Arsenide
GAAP Generally Accepted Accounting Principles
GaAs Gallium Arsenide
GaAsP Gallium Arsenide Phosphide
GAASS Government Agency Arbitrage and Swap System
GAATS GANDER (CANADA) Automatic Air Traffic System
GABA Gamma-Aminobutyric Acid
GAC Geological Association of Canada
Government Advisory Committee on International Book and Library Programs (USA)
GACIAC Guidance and Control Information and Analysis Center (of US Army Missile R & D Command)
GAD Glutamic Acid Decarboxylase
Graphic Active Device
GADO General Aviation District Office (of FAA(USA))

GADPET Graphic Data Presentation and Edit
GAEC Ghana Atomic Energy Commission (Ghana)
Greek Atomic Energy Commission (Greece)
GAELIC GRUMMAN AEROSPACE (CORPORATION) (USA) Language for Instructional Checkout
GAESD Graphic Arts Equipment and Supply Dealers (of Printing Industries of America (USA))
GAF Gesellschaft fur Aeroslforschung (Germany) (Society for Aerosol Research)
Government Aircraft Factories (of Department of Supply (Australia))
GAG Ground-to-Air-to-Ground
GAI Guild of Architectural Iremongers
GAIA Graphic Arts Industries Association (Canada)
GAIAL Groupement pour l'Amenagement et l'Exploitation des Infrastructures Aeroportuaires Locales (France)
GAIF General Assembly of Internation Federations (Switzerland)
GALAXY General Automatic Luminosity And X-Y measuring engine
GALCIT Guggenheim Aeronautical Laboratory of California Institute of Technology (USA)
GALF Groupement des Acousticiens de Langue Francaise (France)
GALM GAINS (R.S.) and LEE (C.Y.) Memory
GALS Generalized Assembly Line Simulator
Geographic Adjustment by Least Squares
GALT Gut Associated Lymphoid Tissue
GAMA Gas Appliance Manufacturers Association (USA)
General Aviation Manufacturers Association (USA)
GAMAS GULF (GENERAL ATOMIC INC.) Atomic Materials Assay System
GAMBICA Group of Associations of Manufacturers of British Instrumentation, Control and Automation (comprising BIMCAM, CAMA and SIMA)
GAMI Groupement pour l'Avancement de la Mecanique Industrielle (France)
GAMIS Graphic Arts Marketing and Information Service (of PIA) (USA))
GAMLOGS Gamma-ray Logs
GAMM Gesellschaft fur Angewandte Mathematik und Mechanik (Germany) (Association for Applied Mathematics and Mechanics)
GAMMA Graphically Aided Mathematical Machine
GAMP Global Atmospheric Program (of NASA and NCAR (USA))
GAMS Groupement pour l'Avancement des Methodes Physiques d'Analyse
GAMTA General Aviation Manufacturers and Traders Association
GAN Gaseous Nitrogen
Generalized Activity Network
Generating Activity Networks
Gyro-compass Automatic Navigation
GANDER Guidance And Navigation Development and Evaluation Routine
GAO General Accounting Office (USA)
Glavnaya Astronomicheskaya Observatoriya (USSR) (Main Astronomical Observatory)
GaP Gallium Phosphide
GAP General Assembly Programme
Graphical Automatic Programming
GAPE General Aviation Pilot Education
Graphic Acids to Packaging Equipment
GAPM Generalized Access Path Model
GAPSS Graphical Analysis Procedures for System Simulation
GARB Garment and Allied Industries Requirements Board (of DOI)
Guided Anti-Radiation Bomb
GARC Graphic Arts Research Center (Rochester Institute of Technology (USA))
GAREX Ground Aviation Radio Exchange
GARP Global Atmosphere Research Programme (of WMO and ICSU)
GARS Gibraltar Amateur Radio Society (Gibraltar)
Gyrocompassing Attitude Reference System
GARTEUR Group for Aeronautical Research and Technology in Europe
GAS General Adaption Syndrome
Granular Activated Carbon
Group Apprenticeship Scheme
Group Autonomous Specialised Working Party (of CCITT)
GASCO General Aviation Safety Committee
GASH Guanidinium Aluminium Sulphate Hexahydrate
GASNTI Gosudarstevennayasistema Nauchno-Tekncheskoi Informatsii (USSR) (State Scientific and Technical Information System)
GASP Gamma Ray Spectrum Analysis
General Activity Simulation Programme
Global Air Sampling Program (of NASA (USA))
Graphic Applications Subroutine Package
GASPT Generalized Axially Symmetrical Potential Theory
GASS Geomagnetic Airborne Survey System
GASSS Gas Steady State
GAST Greenwich Apparent Sidereal Time
GASUS Gas Unsteady State
GAT General Aviation Trainer
GEORGETOWN Automatic Translation
Greenwich Apparent Time
Ground-to-Air Transmitter
GATAC General Assessment Tridimensional Analogue Computer
GATB General Aptitude Test Battery (of USES)
GATC Graphic Arts Technical Committee (of ASQC (USA))
GATE GARP Atlantic Tropical Experiment (of WMO and ICSU)
Girls and Technician Engineering (EITB scheme)
Group to Advance Total Energy (of American Gas Association (USA))
GATF Graphic Arts Technical Foundation (USA)
GATL Group Aerien de Transport et de Liaison (Ivory) (air force carrying out military and civilian operations)
GATNIP Graphic Approach to Numerical Information Processing
GATT Gate Assisted Turn-off Thyristor
General Agreement on Tariffs and Trade (of UN) (administrative office in Switzerland)
GATTIS Georgia Institute of Technology (USA) Technical Information Service
GATTS General Area Time-based Train Simulator
GAVA Guild of Aviation Artists
GAVRS Gyrocompassing Attitude and Velocity Reference System
GAWR Gross Axle Weight Rating
GBD Grain Boundary Dislocation
GBH Graphiste-Benzalkonium-Heparin
GBIL Gosudarstvennaya Biblioteka SSR Imeni V I Lenina (USSR) (Lenin State Library)
GBR Grain-Boundary Reaction
GBRA Gas Breeder Reactor Association
GBRP General Bending Response Programme
GBS General Business System
Grain-Boundary Sliding
GBT Generalized Burst Trapping
Global Ballistic Transport
GBTC Generalized Burst Trapping Codes

GBU Guided Bomb Unit
GC Gas Chromatography
Gas Council (became British Gas Corporation in 1973)
GC-MS Gas Chromatograph linked with a Mass Spectrometer
GC-SICM Gas Chromatography-Single Ion Current Monitoring
GCA Glycosphingolipid Sorbent Assay
Graphic Communications Association (USA)
Ground Control Approach
Ground-Controlled Aircraft
Group Capacity Assessment
GCB General Circuit Breaker
GCBS General Council of British Shipping
GCC General Contracting Company (Saudi Arabia)
Gulf Co-operation Council (Gulf States)
GCCA Graphic Communications Computer Association (of PIA (USA))
GCDG Gas Chromatography Discussion Group (of the Institute of Petroleum)
GCEP Governing Council for Environmental Programmes (of the UN)
GCES Generalized Constant Elasticity of Substitution
GCFBR Gas Cooled Fast Breeder Reactor
GCFI Gulf and Caribbean Fisheries Institute (USA)
GCFR Gas Cooled Fast Reactor
GCFRC Gulf Coastal Fisheries Research Center (of NMFS (USA))
GCFRE Gas Cooled Fast Reactor Experiment
GCG Geological Curators Group (of the Museums Association)
GCHQ Government Communications Headquarters (of Foreign and Commonwealth Office)
GCI Ground Control Interceptor
GCL General Control Language
Ground-Controlled Landing
GCLWD Gulf (of Mexico) Coast Low Water Datum
GCM Gaussian Cosine Modulation
General Circulation Model
GCMA Government Contract Management Association of America (USA)
GCMI Glass Container Manufacturers Institute (USA)
GCMRU Genetic Control of Mosquitoes Research Unit (of ICMR (India))
GCMS Gas Chromatograph Mass Spectrometer
Gas Chromatography and Mass Spectroscopy
GCNR Gas Core Nuclear Rocket
GCOS General Comprehensive Operating Supervisor
GCP Guidance and Control Panel (of AGARD (NATO))
GCR Galactic Cosmic Radiation
Gas-cooled Graphite-moderated Reactor
General Component Refere
Group Coded Recording
GCRI Glass House Crops Research Institute (of Agricultural Research Council)
GCS Gate Controlled Switch
GCSC Guidance Control and Sequencing Computer
GCSPC Graphic Communications Specials Projects Section (of the Printing Industries of America (USA)
GCUGA Grounded Current Unity-Gain Amplifier
GCV Gross Calorific Value
GDA Gas Distribution Administration (Iraq)
GDAC Goldfields Dust Abatement Committee (Australia)
GDAS Geokinetic Data Acquisition System
GDBMS Generalized Data Base Management Systems
GDC Generalised Dynamic Charge
Gesellschaft Deutscher Chemiker (Germany) (Society of German Chemists)
GDCh Gesellschaft Deutscher Chemiker (Germany) (Society of German Chemists)
GDD Growing Degree Day
GDF Gaz de France (France)
GDGS Goal-Directed Group Support
GDIFS Gray and Ductile Ironfounders Society (USA)
GdIG Gadolinium Iron Garnet
GDL Gas-Dynamic Laser
GDM Gravitational Dipole Moment
GDMB Gesellschaft Deutscher Metallhutten-und Bergleute (Germany) (Society of German Metallurgical and Mining Engineers)
GDMS Generalized Data Management Systems
GDO Gunn Diode Oscillator
GDOP Geometric Dilution of Precision
GDP Glow Discharge Polymer
Gross Domestic Product
GDPA General Dental Practitioners Association
GDPS Global Data Processing System (of WWW (WMO))
GDS Graphical Display System
GDX Gated-Diode Crosspoint
GE Geoscience Electronics
GEA Garage Equipment Association (absorbed into SMMT in 1976)
Graph Extended ALGOL
GEANS Gimbaled ESG (Electrostatic Gyro) Aircraft Navigation System
Gimballed Electrostatic Aircraft Navigation System
GeAs(Cs) Gallium-Arsenide (Cesium)
GEBCO General Bathymetric Chart of the Oceans
GEBECOMA Groupement Belge des Constructeurs de Materiel Aerospatial (Belgium)
GECCMSEF Group to Establish Criteria for Certifying Munitions Systems to Electro-magnetic Fields (of USAEC and USDOD)
GECOS GENERAL ELECTRIC Comprehensive Operating Supervisory System
GECS Graphite-Epoxy Composite Structure
GEDRT Group European d'Echange d'Experience sur la Direction de la Recherche Textile (European Group for the Exchange of Information on Textile Research)
GEEC General Egyptian Electricity Corporation (Egypt)
GEEDA Groundnut Extractions Export Development Association (India)
GEEIA Ground Electronics Engineering Installation Agency (USAF) (merged into AFCS, 1971)
GEESE GENERAL ELECTRIC Electronic Systems Evaluator
GEFACS Groupement des Fabricants d'Appareils Sanitaires en Ceramique de la CEE (Group of Manufacturers of Ceramic Sanitary Ware of the European Economic Community)
GEFAP Groupement European des Associations Nationales de Fabricants de Pesticides (European Group of National Associations of Manufacturers of Pesticides)
GEIS Generic Environmental Impact Statement
GEISHA Geodetic Inertial Survey and Horizontal Alignment
Gun Electron Injection for Semiconductor Hybrid Amplification
GEK Geomagnetic Electrokinetograph
GELC Groupe des Editeurs de Livres de la CEE
GELIS-H Ground Emitter Location Identification System - High
GELTSPAP Group of Experts on Long-Term Scientific Policy and Planning (of IOC (UNESCO))

GEM General Epitaxial Monolith
General Expression Manipulation
General Matrix Manipulation
Generalized Effectiveness Method
Graphite Electrode Contouring Machine
Ground Effect Machine
Ground Elevation Meter
Guidance Evaluation Missile
GEMCOS Generalized Message Control System
GEMCS General Engineering and Management Computation System
GEMM Generalized Electronic Maintenance Model
GEMS Gamma Ray Environmental Mapping Spectrometer
GENERAL ELECTRIC Manufacturing Simulator
Generalized Evaluation Model Simulator
Global Environmental Monitoring System
GOODYEAR (AEROSPACE CORPORATION) Electronic Mapping System
GEMSIP GEMINI Stability Improvement Programme
GEMSS Ground Emplaced Mine Scattering System
GENA Ground Environment and Navigational Aid
GENDA General Data Analysis and Simulation
GENEMA Groupement d'Exportation des Navires et Engins de Mer en Acier (France)
GENESES General Network Service System
GENESYS General Engineering System for Structures
Graduate Engineering Education System (USA)
GENIRAS General Information Retrieval and Application System
GENISYS Generalised Information System
GENSTAT General Statistical programme
GENTRAS General Training System
GEO Gas and Electric Operations
Geosynchrous Earth Orbit
GEODSS Ground-based Electro-Optical Deep Space Surveillance
GEOMED Geometric Editor
GEON Gyro Erected Optical Navigation
GEOPS Geodetic Estimates from Orbital Perturbations of Satellites
GEOREF World Geographic Reference System
GEORGE General Organisational Environment
GEOS Geodetic Earth Orbiting Satellite
Geodynamics Experimental Ocean Satellite
GEOSAR Geosynchronous Synthetic Aperture Radar
GEOSCAN Geographic Scanning
GEOSECS Geochemical Ocean Sections Study (a project of NSF (USA) for IDOE)
GEOSS Integrated Geophysical Survey System (of NAVOCEANO)
GEPAC GENERAL ELECTRIC Programmeable Automatic Comparator
GEPEXS GENERAL ELECTRIC Parts Explosion System
GEPI Gestion e Partecipazioni Industriali (Italy) (a government holding company)
GEPOC Gesellschaft für Polymerchemie (Germany)
GEPS Groupe d'Etudes des Proteines de Soja (France) (Research Group on Oleaginous Proteins)
GERCOS Groupement d'Etudes et de Realizations des Compresseurs Speciaux (France)
GERD Gross National Expenditure on Research and Development
GEREC Groupement pour l'Etude et la Realisation d'Ensembles Controle-Commande (France)
GERS Groupe d'Etudes et de Recherches Sous-marines (France)
GERSD GULF (OIL COMPANY), Eastern Hempishere Operations, Refining, Supply and Distribution
GERSIS GENERAL ELECTRIC Range Safety Instrumentation System
GERT Graphical Evaluation and Review Technique
GERTS GENERAL ELECTRIC Remote Terminal System
GES Government Economic Service (of H M Treasury)
GESA Gas y Electricida SA (Spain)
Gas y Electricidad de Mallorca SA (government owned)
GESAMP Joint Group of Experts on the Scientific Aspects of Marine Pollution (of UNESCO, FAO, IMCO, WMO, WHO, and IAEA)
GeSe Germanium Selenide
GESM Group for Educational Services in Museums (of the Museums Association)
GESMA Groupe d'Études Sous-Marines de l'Atlantique (of the French Navy)
GESMO Generic Environment Statement on Mixed Oxide fuel (of the Nuclear Regulatory Commission (USA))
GESPL Generalised Edit System Programming Language
GESS Generator Exhaust Signature Suppression
GET Gross Error Test
Ground Elapsed Time
GETA General Equipment Test Activity (US Army)
GETCAP Generalized and Transmission-line Capacitance matrix
GETD General Equipment Testing Directorate (of TECOM)
GeTe Germanium Telluride
GETOL Ground Effect Take-Off and Landing
GETR GENERAL ELECTRIC (COMPANY) (USA) Test Reactor
GETT Group of European Manufacturers for the Advancement of Turbine Technology (a consortium of French and German companies)
GEU Genetic Evaluation and Utilization
GEW Ground Effect Wing
GEX Gas Exchange Experiment (aboard the VIKING spacecraft)
GF prefix to numbered series of Governmental Finances issued by Dept of Commerce, USA
GFA Group Feed-back Analysis
GFAA Graphite Furnace Atomic Absorption
GFAAS Graphite Furnace Atomic Absorption Spectrophotometry
GFAE Government (USA) Furnished Avionics Equipment
GFC Gel Filtration Chromatography
GFCG Government Fluidics Coordination Group (USA)
GFCI Ground Fault Circuit Interrupter
GFCM General Fisheries Council for the Mediterranean
GFCS Gas-Filter Correlation Spectrometer
Gun Fire Control System
GFDL Geophysical Fluid Dynamics Laboratory (of NOAA (USA))
GFE Government Furnished Equipment (USA)
GFEC Graphite-Fibre Epoxy-Composite
GFERC Grand Forks Energy Research Center (of ERDA (USA))
GFFSA German Federal Flight Security Agency
GFI Glas Forsknings Institutet (Sweden) (Glass Research Institute)
Groupement Francais d'Informatique (France)
GfK Gesellschaft fur Kernforschung (Germany) (Atomic Energy Research Association)
GFM Government (USA) Furnished Material
GFP Ground Fault Protector
GFR Gap Filler Radar
GFRP Glass Fibre Reinforced Plastic
GFS General Financial System
GFT Generalized Fast Transform
Graphical Firing Table

Gfw — Gesellschaft fur Weltraumforschung (Germany) (Society for Space Research)
GFW — Glass Filament Wound
GG — Gravity Gradient
GGD — General Government Division (of GAO (USA))
Generalized Gamma Distribution
GGE — General Graphical Editing
GGF — Glass and Glazing Federation
Ground Gained Forward
GGG — Gadolinium Galium Garnet
GGI — Gosudarstvennyy Girdrologicheskiy Institut (USSR) (State Hydrological Institute)
GGO — Glavnayo Geofizicheskaya Observatoriya (USSR) (Main Geophysical Observatory)
GGRA — Gelatine and Glue Research Association (now merged into BFMIRA)
GGS — Gravity Gradient Satellite
Ground Gained Sideways
Gyro Gunsight
GGTS — Gravity Gradient Test Satellite
GGU — Gor'kovskiy Gosudarstvennyy Universitet (USSR)
GH — Growth Hormone
GHA — Greenwich Hour Angle
GHAQ — General High Altitude Questionnaire
GHOST — Global Horizontal Sounding Technique
Graphical Output System
GHR — Gross Heat Rate
GHRH — Growth Hormone Releasing Hormone
GHS — Garden History Society
GHSP — Great High Schools Program (USA)
GHT — Gesellschaft fur Hochtemperatur-Reaktor-Technik (Germany)
GI — Geodesic Isotensoid
Gesellschaft für Informatik (Germany) (Society for Data Processing)
Government Initiated
GIAN — Gruppo Italiano Arricchimento Uranio (Italy) (Italian Uranium Enrichment Group)
GIAT — Groupement d'Industries Atomiques (France)
Groupement Industriel des Armements Terrestres (France)
GIC — General Impedance Converter
GIDC — Gujarat Industrial Development Corporation (India)
GIDEP — Government-Industry Data Exchange program (USA)
GIEC — Guangzhou Institute of Energy Conversion (China)
GIFAS — Groupement des Industries Françaises Aéronautiques et Spatiales (France) (French Aerospace Industry Association)
GIFI — General Information File Interrogation
GIFTI — Gor'kovskiy Nauchno Issledovatel'skiy Fiziko-Teknicheskiy Institut (USSR) (Gor'kiy Physical-Technical Scientific Research Institute)
GIFTS — Graphics-oriented Interactive Finite element Time-sharing System
GIGO — Garbage In, Garbage Out
GIGS — GEMINI Inertial Guidance System
GIHC — Ghana Industrial Holding Corporation (Ghana)
GIIN — Groupe Intersyndical de i'Industrie Nucleaire (France)
Groupe Intersyndicale de l'Industrie Nucleaire (France) (Inter-Association Nuclear Industry Group)
GIIP — Groupement Internationale de l'Industries Pharmaceutique des Pays de la CEE (International Group of the Pharmaceutical Industries of the European Economic Community)
GIIVT — Gor'kovskiy Institut Inzhenerov Vodnogo Transporta (USSR) (Gor'kiy Water Transportation Engineers Institute)
GIKI — Gosudarstvennyy Isseldovatel'skiy Keramicheskiy Institut (USSR) (State Ceramics Research Institute)
GILEP — Groupement Interprofessionel de Logistique et d'Equipements Petroliers (France)
GILT — General Internal Logic Test
GIM — Generalized Information Management
GIMIC — Guard Ring Implanted Monolithic Integrated Circuit
GIMPA — Ghana Institute of Management and Public Administration (Ghana)
GIMRADA — Geodesy Intelligence and Mapping Research and Development Agency (US Army) (now USAETL)
GIMS — Geographic-based Information Management System
GINA — Gas Industries Network Analyser
Graphical Input for Network Analysis
Graphical Interactive NMR Analysis
GINI F — GINO FORTRAN IV
GINO — Graphical Input Output
GINO-F — GINO FORTRAN IV
GIPEC — Groupe d'Etudes International pour l'utilization de Profils Creux dans la Construction (Switzerland) (International Study Group on the Use of Hollow Sections in Construction)
GIPME — Global Investigation of Pollution in the Marine Environment (a project of the IOC (UNESCO))
GIPSSY — Generalised Interactive Programme for the Simulation of Systems
GIPSY — General Information Processing System
Geographic Incremental Plotting System
GIPSYS — Graphic Input and Plotting System
GIRCFF — Government/Industry Research Committee on Flammable Fabrics (USA)
GIRI — Government Industrial Research Institute (Japan)
GIRL — Generalized Information Retrieval Language
GIRLS — Generalised Information Retrieval and Listing System
GIRO — not an acronym–it is derived from the Greek "gyros" meaning "to revolve"
GIS — Generalized Information System
Geoscience Information Society (USA)
Grazing Incidence Spectrometer
GISP — General Information System for Planning
Greenland Ice Sheet Program (of USA, Denmark, and Switzerland)
GIT — Georgia Institute of Technology (USA)
GITIS — prefix to dated/numbered series of reports issued by Georgia Institute of Technology School of Information Sciences (USA)
GKIAE — Gosudarstvennyy Komitet po Ispolzovaniyu Atomnoi Energi (USSR) (State Committee for the Utilization of Atomic Energy)
GKN — Gemeenschappelijke Kernenergiecentrale Nederland (Netherlands)
GKSS — Gesellschaft fur Kernenergieverwertung in Schiffbau und Schiffahrt (Germany) (Research Association for the Utilization of Atomic Energy in Ship Construction and Ship Propulsion)
GKV — Gesamtverband Kunststoffverarbeitende Industrie (Germany)
GKWW — Gesprachskrels Wissenschaft und Wirtschaft (Germany) (Science and Industry Discussion Committee)
GL/FICS — General Ledger/Financial Information and Control System
GLAADS — Gun Low Altitude Air Defence System

GLAD — GALS LESA-A-A AGILE Dialogue
Grenade Launcher Attachment Development
GLADS — Long-range Gun Low-altitude Air Defence System
GLASS — Germanium-Lithium Argon Scanning System
GLBC — Great Lakes Basin Commission (USA)
GLBSA — Greater London Building Surveyors Association
GLC — G-induced Loss of Consciousness
Gas-Liquid Chromatography
Greater London Council
GLCM — Ground-Launched Cruise Missile
GLDC — Great Lakes Data Center (of EDS (NOAA) (USA))
GLDS — Ground Laser Designator Station
GLEAM — Graphic Layout and Engineering Aid Method
GLEAP — Game Learning Players
GLEEP — Graphite Low Energy Experimental Pile
GLERL — Great Lakes Environmental Research Laboratory (of ERL (NOAA) (usa))
GLFC — Graphite Lunar module Fuel Cask
Great Lakes Fisheries Commission (USA)
GLIAS — Greater London Industrial Archaeology Society
GLIM — General Light Inter-reflection Model
GLLD — Ground Laser Locator Designator
GLM — Generalized Lagrange Multipliers
GLOBECOM — Global Communications System (USAF)
GLODIS — General Language-Operated Decision Implementation System
GLOL — GOLAY Logic Language
GLOMEX — Global Meteorological Experiment
GLOPAC — Gyroscopic Lower Power Attitude Controller
GLOPR — GOLAY Logic Processor
GLORIA — Geological Long Range Inclined ASDIC
GLOTRAC — Global Tracking network
GLOW — Gross Lift-Off Weight
GLP — General Letter Package
Generalized Lattice-Point
Good Laboratory Practice
GLR — Generalized Likelihood Ratio
GLS — General Lighting Service lamp
Generalised Least Squares
Graduate Library School (Denver University (USA))
Graduate Library School (Illinois University (USA))
Graduate Library School (Indiana University (USA))
Graduate Library School (Rutgers University (USA))
GLSE — Generalized Least Squares Estimation
GLU — Global Land Use
GLULAM — Glued Laminated wood
GLV — GEMINI Launch Vehicle
GMA — Gas Metal-Arc
GMAG — Genetic Manipulation Advisory Group (now ACGM)
GMAW — Gas Metal-Arc Welding
GMB — Glass Microballoon
GMBF — Gesellschaft für Molekularbiologische Forschung (Germany) (Society for Molecular Biology Research)
GMbH — Gesellschaft mit beschrankter Haftung (Limited Company)
GMC — General Medical Council
GMCC — Geophysical Monitoring for Climatic Change (a program of the Air Resources Laboratories (ERL) (NOAA) (USA))
GMD — Gesellschaft fur Mathematik und Datenverarbeitung (Germany) (Research Corporation for Mathematics and Data Processing)
GMDH — Group Method of Data Handling
GMDS — Gesellschaft fuer Medizinische Dokumentation Information und Statistik (Germany) (Society for Medical Documentation, Information and Statistics)
GMEI — Gulf of Mexico Estuarine Inventory
GMF — Glass Manufacturers Federation
GMLS — Guided Missile Launching System
GMO — Galolinium Molybdate
Glyceryl Monooleate
GMP — Good Manufacturing Practice
GMPA — Gas-Metal-Plasma-Arc
GMS — General Maintenance System
Geostationary Meteorological Satellite
Glyceryl Monostearate
GMSC — General Medical Services Committee (of the BMA)
GMSI — Generalized Multigroup System of calculations using the IBM 7030 (STRETCH) computer
GMT — Geometric Mean Titre
Greenwich Mean Time
GMTI — Ground Moving-Target Indicator
GMTO — Gas Meter Testing Office (of DTI)
GMTS — Gidrometeorologicheskyy Nauchno Issledovatelskiy Tsenter (USSR) (Scientific Research Center for Hydrometeorology)
GMWC — Graphite Moderated, Water Cooled
GN — Groundnut meal
GNATS — Generalized Numerical Analysis of Thermal Systems
GNaV — Graphic Area Navigation
GNC — Global Navigation Chart
Graphical Numerical Control
Gross Neutron Counter
GND — Gallium arsenic, Negative resistance, light-emitting Diode
GNERD — Gross National Expenditure on Research and Development
GNI — Generation of New Ideas
Grid Node Interface
GNMA — Government National Mortgage Association (USA)
GNP — Geonuclear Nobel Paso (France)
Graphic Nesting Programme
Gross National Product
GNR — Gaseous Nuclear Rocket
GnRH — Gonadotrophin Releasing Hormone
GNT — Gesellschaft für Nuklear-transporte (Germany)
GnV — Gesellschaft fur Nukleare Verfahrenstechnik (Germany)
GOAL — Ground Operations Aerospace Language
GOALS — Geometrical Optical Analysis of Lens Systems
GOB — Guided Optical Beam
GOBAC — Gold-plating Bath Analyzer and Controller
GOC — Graphics Operation Controller
Grosseinkaufsgesellschaft Osterreichischer Cunsumvereine (Austria)
GOCA — Groupement des Organismes de Controle Automobiles (Belgium) (Association of Automobile Inspection Organisations)
GOCC — GATE Operations Control Centre (Dakar)
GOCI — General Operator-Computer Interaction
GOCO — Government-owned Contractor-operated production plant
GOD — Guidance and Orbit Determination for Solar Electric Propulsion
GODAS — Graphically Oriented Design and Analysis System
GODE — Gulf Organization for Development of Egypt
GODORT — Government Documents Round Table (of the American Library Association (USA))
GOE — Ground Operating Equipment

GOES Geostationary Operational Environmental Satellite
GOFAR Global Ocean Floor Analysis and Research project (of NAVOCEANO)
GOGEGA Comite Generale de la Cooperation Agricole de la CEE (General Committee of Agricultural Cooperation of the European Economic Community)
GOI Gosudarstvennyy Opticheskiy (USSR) (State Optical Institute)
GOIN Gosudarstvennyy Okeanograficheskiy Institute (USSR) (State Oceanographic Institute)
GOLD Geometric On-Line Definition
GLASGOW (UNIVERSITY) On-Line Desk project
GOLD STAR Generalized Organization of Large Data-bases; a Set-Theoretic Approach to Relations
GOMAC Government Microcircuit Applications Conference (USA)
GOR Gained Output Ratio
Gas Oil Ratio
General Operations Requirement
GORID Ground Optical Recorder for Intercept Determination
GORSP Government Officials Responsible for Standardization Policies (a body of the Economic Commission for Europe (of UN
GOS Global Observing System (of WWW (WMO))
Graphical Output Scheme
GOSH Guild of Software Houses
GOSS Ground Operational Support System
GOSS+D GEORGE Operating System Support and Development
GOSSIP Generalized Organizational System Summarizer and Information Processor
GOST Gosudarstvennyy Obshchesoguznyy Standart (USSR) (State All-Union Standard)
GOT Glutamic Oxaloacetic Transaminase
GOX Gas Oxygen
Gaseous Oxygen
GP Growth in total Profit
GPA Gas Processors Association (USA)
Graphical PERT Analogue
GPAP General Purpose Associative Processor
GPATS General Purpose Automatic Test System
GPBTO General Purpose Barbed Tape Obstacle
GPC GEl Permeation Chromatography
Glass-Polymer Composite
Glycerylphosphorylcholine
Groupements de Producteurs de Ciment (Belgium)
GPCP Generalized Process Control Programming
GPCSA General Practice Computer Suppliers Association
GPDA Gypsum Plaster-board Development Association
GPDC General Purpose Digital Computer
GPDL Graphical Picture Drawing Language
GPDS General Purpose Display System
GPES Ground Proximity Extraction System
GPI Glide Path Indicator
Glucosephospate Isomerase
Ground Position Indicator
GPIB General Purpose Instrument OR Interface Bus
GPIS GEMINI Problem Investigation Status
GPL General Purpose Programming Language
Geograpic Position Locator
Graphic Programming Language
GPL/1 Graph Programming Language One
GPLA General Price Level Accounting
General Price-Level Adjusted
GPLS General Purpose Logic Simulator
GPMA Grocery Products Manufacturers Association (Canada)
GPMG General Purpose Machine Gun
GPMH Good Practices in Mental Health (a project of NHS)
GPMP Group on Parts, Materials and Packaging (of IEEE) (USA)
GPMS General Purpose Multiplex System
GPO General Post Office
Government Printing Office (USA)
GPP Graphic Part Programmer
GPRSS General Purpose Remote Sensor System
GPS General Problem Solver
Global Positioning System
GPSA Gas Processors Suppliers Association (USA)
GPSCS General Purpose Satellite Communications System
GPSDIC General Purpose Scientific Document Image Code
GPSDW General Purpose Scientific Document Writer
GPSS General Purpose System Simulation
General Purpose Systems Simulator
Global Positioning Satellite System
GPT Gas Power Transfer
Glutamic-Pyruvic Transaminase
Guild of Professional Translators (USA)
GPWS Ground-Proximity Warning System
GPYS General Purpose Yard Simulator
GQA Grain Quality Analyzer
GRA Gesellschaft fur Rechnergesteuerte Analagen (Germany)
GRA&I Government Reports Announcement and Index (published by NTIS (USA))
GRACE Graphic Arts Composing Equipment
GRAD General Recursive Algebra and Differentiation
GRAF Graphic Addition to FORTRAN
GRAFLAN Graphic Language
GRAID Graphical Aid
GRAIL Graphic Input Language
GRAMPA General Analytical Model for Proces Analysis
Ground Resonance Automatic Multi-Point Apparatus
GRAMS Ground Recording And Monitoring System
GRAN Global Rescue Alarm Network
GRAPE Gamma-Ray Attenuation Porosity Evaluator
GRAPHDEN Graphic Data entry
GRAPHIDI Graphical Interpretive Display System
GRAPHSYS Graphics Software System
GRAPL Graphics Programming Language
GRARE Ground Receiving and Ranging Equipment
GRAS Generally Recognised As Safe
GRASER Gamma Ray Laser
GRASP General Risk Analysis Simulation Programme
Generalized Retrieval and Storage Programme
Generation of Random Access Site Plans
Graphic Service Programme
GRASS Gas Release and Swelling Subroutine
Generalized Research Analysis Statistical System
GRB Geophysical Research Board (of National Research Council, USA)
GRBS Groupe de Recherche en Biologie Spatiale (France) (Space Biology Research Group)
GRC Geothermal Resource Council (USA)
Glass-fibre Reinforced Cement
Glass-fibre Reinforced Concrete
Glass-Reinforced Composite
Global Reference Code
GRCDA Government Refuse Collection and Disposal Association (USA)
GRD Gruppe fur Rustungsdienst (Switzerland) (Defence Procurement Agency of the Federal Defence Department)

GRDR Groupe de Recherche et de Realisations pour le Developpement Rural dans la Tiers Monde (France) (Research and Development Group for Rural Development in the Third World)

GRDSR Geographically Referenced Data Storage and Retrieval

GREAT Graphics Research with ELLERBE ARCHITECTS (USA) Technology

GRED Generalized Random Extract Device

GREMAS Generic Retrieval by Magnetic-tape Storage

GREMEX GODDARD Research Engineering Management Exercise (Goddard Space Flight Center, NASA)

GREMLIN Greater Manchester Local government Information Network

GRFM General Radio-Frequency Meter

GRG Generalised Reduced Gradient
Gravimetric Rain-Gauge

GRGS Groupe de Recherche de Geodesie Spatiale (France) (Space Geodesy Research Group)

GRH Gas Recycle Hydrogenator OR Hydrogenation

GRI Gas Research Institute (USA) (at the Institute of Gas Technology)
Gravure Research Institute (USA)
Groupe des Recherches Ionospheriques (France)

GRID Graphical Intermediate Data Format
National Geothermal Information Resource (sponsored by ERDA and located at University of California's Lawrence Berkeley Laboratory (USA)

GRIN Graded Refractive Index
Graded-Index
Gradient-Index
Graphical Interaction

GRIND Graphical Interpretive Display

GRIPS Gaming, Random Interfacing and Problem Structuring

GRIST Grazing-Incidence Solar Telescope

GRITS Geothermal Resource Interactive Temporal Simulation

GRO Gamma Ray Observatory (of NASA (USA))

GRP Gaussian Random Process
Glass Reinforced Plastic
Glass-fibre Reinforced Polyester
Graphical Rational Pattern
Group Repetition Period

GRPA Groupe des Rapporteurs pour la Pollution de l'Air (of Economic Commission for Europe)

GRPP Glass Reinforced Polypropylene

GRS Gamma Ray Spectrometer
General Retrieval System
Gesellschaft fuer Reaktorsicherheit (Society for Nuclear Reactor Safety) (Germany)

GRSCSW Graduate Research Center of the Southwest (USA)

GRSM Group for Regional Studies in Museums (of the Museums Association)

GRSU Geography Remote Sensing Unit (California University (USA))

GRT General Reactor Technology
Gross Registered Ton

GRTP Glass-fibre Reinforced Thermoplastics

GS Glaciological Society

GS/OPER prefix to numbered/dated/lettered series of reports issued by the General Steels Division of the British Steel Corporation

GSA General Services Administration (USA)
Genetics Society of America (USA)
Geological Society of America (USA)

GSAGR General Short Arc Geodetic Reduction

GSBCA General Services Board of Contract Appeals (USA)

GSC Gas-Solid Chromatography
Genetics Society of Canada (Canada)
Geological Survey of Canada (of Department of Energy, Mines and Resources (Canada)
Group Switching Centre

GSCA General and Speciality Contractors Association (USA)

GSCCMF Gujarat State Co-operative Cotton Marketing Federation (India)

GSD Genetically Significant Dose
Geometric Standard Deviation

GSDF Ground Self-Defence Force (Japan)

GSDT Generalized Syntax Directed Translation

GSE Geometric Standard Error
Ground-based Support Equipment

GSEL Ground Support Equipment Laboratory (of MICOM)

GSF Gesellschaft fur Strahlen- und Umweltforschung (Germany) (Radiation and Environmental Research Corporation)

GSFC GODDARD (ROBERT HUTCHINGS GODDARD) Space Flight Center (of NASA (USA))
Gujarat State Fertiliser Company (India)
Gujarat State Financial Corporation (Ind

GSGG Gadolinium Scandium Gallium Garnet

GSH Gesellschaft fur Schwerionenforschung (Germany) (Heavy Ion Research Corporation)

GSHPX Gluthathione Peroxidase

GSI Geological Survey of India (India)
Gesellschaft fur Schwerionenforschung (Germany)

GSIA Graduate School of Industrial Administration (of Carnegie-Mellon University (USA))

GSIC Gujarat Small Industries Corporation (India)

GSIS Group for Standardization of Information Services (USA)

GSL Geographic Sciences Laboratory (of USAETL)
Geophysical Sciences Laboratory (New York University (USA))

GSLIS Graduate School of Library and Information Sciences (Pittsburgh University (USA))

GSLP Center for Short-Lived Phenomena (of Smithsonian Institution (USA))

GSM/SM prefix to dated-numbered series of reports issued by Air Force Institute of Technology (USAF)

GSN Groupement des Soufflantes Nucleaires (France)

GSP Generalised System of Tariff Preferences

GSPI Gosudarstvennyy Soyuznyy Proyektnyy Institut (USSR) (State All-Union Planning Institute)

GSPRT Generalized Sequential Probability Ratio Test

GSR Galvanic Skin Resistance
Galvanic Skin Response
Ground Surveillance Radar

GSRI Global Solar Radiation Index

GSRS General Support Rocket System

GSS Galvanometer Scanning System
Geostationary Satellite
Gonad-Stimulating Substance
Graphic Service System

GSSC Georgia Schoolhouse Systems Council (USA)

GSSW Gas-Shielded Stud Welding

GST General Systems Theory
Ground Sensor Terminal

GSTP Generalised System of Tariff Preferences

GSU Governors State University (USA)

GSV GRUMMAN Submersible Vehicle

GT Group Technology

GT-HTGR Gas Turbine High Temperature Gas-cooled Reactor

GTA Gas–Tungsten Arc
Gravure Technical Association (USA)
Gun Trade Association
GTAC Ground-To-Air Cycles
GTACS Ground Target Attack Control System
GTAW Gas Tungsten-Arc Welding
GTC General Trading Company (Saudi Arabia)
Government Training Centre
GTD Geometrical Theory of Diffraction
Graphic Tablet Display
GTDA Groupement pour le development de la Teledection Aerospatiale (France) (of CNES, IGN, IFP and others)
GTE Gunner Tracking Evaluator
GTED Gas-Turbine Engine-Driven
GTG Gold-Thioglucose
GTIS Gloucestershire Technical Information Service
GTMA Gauge and Tool Makers Association
Georgia Textile Manufacturers Association (USA)
GTMS Graphic Text Management System
GTMTC Galvothermomagnetic Transport Coefficient
GTO Gate Turn-Off
GTOL Graphic Take-Off Language
GTP Guanosine Triphosphate
GTRE Gas Turbine Research Establishment (India)
GTS Geostationary Technology Satellite
Global Telecommunication System (of WWW (WMO))
GTSC Ground Testing and Simulation Committee (of AIAA (USA))
GTT Glucose Tolerance Test
Group Time Technique
GTZ Gesellschaft fur Technische Zusammenarbeit (Germany) (Agency for Technical Cooperation)
GUATEL Empresa Guatemalateca de Telecomunicaciones (Guatemala) (Telecommunications Agency of Guatemala)
GUB Generalized Upper Boundary
GUERAP General Unwanted Energy Rejection Analysis Programme
GUGK Glavnoje Upravlenije Geodesii i Kartografii (USSR) (Administrative Agency for Geodesy and Cartography)
GUGMS Glavnoje Upravlenije Gidrometeorologicheskoi Sluzhby (USSR) (Administrative Agency for the Hydrometeorological Service)
Glavnoje Upravlenije Gidrometeorologicheskoi Sluzhby (USSR) (Administrative Agency of the Hydrometeorological Service)
GUHA General Unary Hypotheses Automaton
GUI Genitourinary Infection
GUIDAR Guided Intrusion Detection And Ranging
GUIDE Guidance for Users of Integrated Data Equipment
GULP General Utility Language Processor
GUMR Groupment des Utilisateurs de Materiaux Refractaires (Group of Refractory Material Users)
GUPCO Gulf of Suez Petroleum Company
GURC Gulf Universities Research Consortium (USA)
GUS Gesellschaft fur Umweltsmulation (Germany) (Society for the Environment)
GUSTO Guidance Using Stable Tuning Oscillations
GUTS Grand Unified Theories
GUTS GERTS User's Terminal System
GV Germinal Vesicle
Granulosis Virus
GVB Gelatine Veronal Buffer
GVH Graft Versus Host
GVHD Graft Versus Host Disease
GVHR Graft Versus Host Reaction
GVM Generating Volt Meter
GVMDS Ground Vehicle Mine Dispensing System
GVO Gross Value of Output
GVRT General Vehicular Research Tool
GVT Gravity Vacuum Tube
Gravity-Vacuum Transit
GVUGA Grounded Voltage Unity-Gain Amplifier
GW Gigawatts
Guided Weapon
GWDB Ground-Water Development Bureau (Taiwan (China))
GWE Global Weather Experiment (of WMO and ICSU)
GWEN Ground Wave Energy Network
GWF Gesellschaft fur Werkzeugmaschinenbau und Fertigungstechnik (Switzerland)
GWh Gigawatt hour
GWHT Generalized WALSH-HADAMARD Transform
GWI Grinding Wheel Institute (USA)
GWK Gesellschaft zur Wiederaufarbeitung von Kernbrennstoffen (Germany)
GWPS prefix to publications issued by George Washington University (USA) on the Program of Policy Studies in Science and Technology
GWS Grid Wire Sensor
GWU George Washington University (USA)
GYFM General Yielding Fracture Mechanics
GYMPI Gyromagnetic Polarizing Interferometer
GZC Gas-size Exclusion Chromatography
GZG Gutegemeinschaft Zinngerat (Germany) (Pewter Quality Association)

H

H-SAT Heavy Satellite
HA Haemagglutination
Haemagglutinin
Hazard Analysis
Human Adaptability
Hydraulic Association
HAA Height Above Airport
Helicopter Association of America (USA)
Hepatitis Associated Antigen
Hospital Activity Analysis
Human Asset Accounting
HAAW Heavy Anti-tank Assault Weapon
HAB Heavy Assault Bridge
HABITAT United Nations World Conference on Human Settlements
HAC Herbicide Assessment Committee (of AAAS (USA))
High Alumina Cement
House Appropriations Committee (of United States Congress)
Hydrogen-Assisted Cracking
HACBSS Homestead and Community Broadcast Satellite Service (Australia)
HACC High Alumina Cement Concrete
HACLS HARPOON (missile) Aircraft Command and Launch Sub-system
HACS Hazard Assessment Computer System
HAD Haemadsorption
Head Acceleration Device
High Altitude Density rocket
HAD-N Haemadsorption-Neutralization
HADIOS HONEYWELL Analogous-Digital Input-Output Sub-system
HADIS Hadamard Imaging Spectrometer
Huddersfield and District Information Service

HADS Hypersonic Air Data Sensor
HAEC High Altitude Economic Carrier
HAECO Hong Kong Aircraft Engineering Company (Hong Kong)
HAES High Altitude Effects Simulation (a program sponsored by Defense Nuclear Agency (USDOD))
HAF Helicopter Association of Florida (USA)
Hellenic Air Force (Greece)
High Abrasion Furnace
High Altitude Fluorescence
HAFOE High Air Flow with Oxygen Enrichment
HAHST High Altitude, High Speed Target
HAI Haemagglutination Inhibition
Hellenic Aerospace Industries (Greece)
HAISAM Hashed Index Sequential Access Method
HAISS High Altitude Infra-red Sensor System
HAL Health Affairs Library (East Carolina University (USA))
Hindustan Aeronautics Limited (India) (Government owned)
HALDIS Halifax and District Information Service
HALE High Altitude Long Endurance
High Altitude, Long Endurance remotely piloted vehicle
HALO High Altitude Large Optics (a program of DARPA (USDOD))
High Altitude, Low Opening parachuting
HALS Hydrographic Airborne Laser Sounder
HAM Hardware Associative Memory
Holandsche Aanneming Maatschappij (Netherlands)
HAMOTS High Accuracy, Multiple Objects Tracking System
HAMT Human Aided Machine Translation
HANBA Hollow Anistropic Beam Analysis
HANDS High Altitude Nuclear Detection Studies
HANE Hereditary Angioneurotic Edema
High Altitude Nuclear Effects
High-Altitude Nuclear Explosion
HANES Health and Nutrition Examination Survey (of National Center for Health Statistics (USA))
HAOSS High Altitude Orbital Space Station
HAP Histamine Acid Phosphate
Hydroxyapatite
Hydroxylammonium Perchlorate
HAPDAR Hard Point Demonstration Array Radar
HAPDEC Hard-Point Decoy
HAPP High Altitude Pollution Program (of FAA (USA))
HAPPI Height And Plan Position Indicator
HARAC High Altitude Resonance Absorption Calculation
HARCO Hybolic Area Coverage
HARDS High Altitude Radiation Detection System
HARES High Altitude Radiation Environment Study (by FAA, USAF, USN and NASA (USA))
HARIS High Altitude Radiation Instrument System
HARL Human Attention Research Laboratory (UILU) (USA)
HARLS Horse Antiserum to Rabbit Lymphocytes
HARM High-speed Anti Radar Missile
High-speed Anti-Radiation Missile
High-velocity Anti-Radiation Missile
Hyper-velocity Anti-Radiation Missile
HARP Heater Above Reheat Point
Helicopter Airworthiness Review Panel (of ARB)
High Altitude Relay Point
High Altitude Research Project (OR Probe)
HARS Heading-Attitude Reference System
HARSAP Harbor Survey Assistance Program (of USN)
HART Hypervelocity Anti-aircraft Rocket Tactical
HARTRAN HARWELL ATLAS FORTRAN
HARV High Altitude Research Vehicle
HARVEST Highly Active Residues Vitrification Engineering Study (a project of UKAEA)
HARWAS Horizontal-Axis Rotating-wing Aeronautical System
HAS Hardened Aircraft Shelter
Hellenic Astronautical Society (Greece)
High Altitude Simulation
Hospital Advisory Service for England and Wales
Hydrographic Automated System
HASAWA Health and Safety at Work Act, 1974
HASINS High Accuracy Submersible Inertial Navigation System
HASJPL H. Allen Smith Jet Propulsion Laboratory (California Institute of Technology (USA))
HASL Health and Safety Laboratory (USAEC)
Hertfordshire Association of Special Libraries
HASP High Altitude Sampling Programme
High-Altitude Space Platform
Houston Automatic Spooling Programme
HASP/RJE Houston Automatic Spooling Priority with Remote Job Entry
HASPA High-Altitude Superpressure Powered Aerostat
HASS Home Accident Surveillance System (of DTI)
HAST High Altitude Supersonic Target
HASTE Have Auger Sensor Test and Evaluation
Helicopter Ambulance Service To Emergencies
HAT Height Above Touchdown
High Altitude Temperature
High Altitude Testing rocket
Hypoxanthine-aminopterin-thymidine
HATOFF Highest Astronomical Tide Of the Foreseeable Future
HATOL Horizontal Attitude Take-Off and Landing
HATOM Highest Astronomical Tide Of the Month
HATOY Highest Astronomical Tide of the Year
HATR High-temperature Attenuated Total Reflectance
HATRA Hosiery and Allied Trades Research Association
HATRACK Hurricane and Typhoon Tracking
HATRICS Hampshire Technical Research Industrial Commercial Service
HATS Helicopter Advanced Tactical System
Huntsville Association of Technical Societies (USA)
Hybrid Automatic Test System
HAU Haryana Agricultural University (India)
HAW Heavy Anti-tank Assault Weapon
HAWK Homing All-the-Way Killer missile
HAWT Horizontal Axis Wind Turbine
HAWTADS Helicopter Adverse Weather Target Acquisition and Destruction System
HAYSTAQ Have You Stored Answers to Questions?
HAZ Heat Affected Zone
HB symbol used to denote Brinell Hardness
HbA Haemoglobin Adult
HBAb Hepatitis B Antibody
HBAg Hepatitis B Antigen
HBC High Breaking Capacity
HBD Hydroxbutyric Dehydrogenase
HbF Haemoglobin Foetal
HBF House Builders Federation
HBO Hyperbaric Oxygen
HBP Committee of Housing, Building and Planning (of the Economic Commission for Europe)
Highway Bridge Parapet
HBP/SEM Committee of Housing, Building and Planning Seminar
HBP/WP Committee of Housing, Building and Planning Working Party
HBR High Burst Rate
HBS High-Beta Stellarator

HBsAb Hepatitis B Surface Antibody
HBsAg Hepatitis B Surface Antigen
HBSS Hanks Balanced Salt Solution
HBTX High Beta Toroidal Experiment
HBV Hepatitis B Virus
HBWR HALDEN Boiling Heavy Water Reactor
HC Historical Cost
Hydrocarbon
prefix to numbered: dated series of Aerospace Standards issued by BSI
HCB Hexachlorobenzene
High Capability Buoy
HCC Housing Consultative Council
HCD High Current Density
Hollow Cathode Discharge
HCE Hexachloroethane
Hollow-Cathode Effect
HCF Haemolytic Complement Fixation
Hardened Compacted Fibres
High Cycle Fatigue
HCFA Health Care Financing Administration (DHHS) (USA)
HCG Human Chorionic Gonadotrophin
HCGB Helicopter Club of Great Britain
Hover Club of Great Britain
HCHP Harvard Community Health Plan (U SA)
HCI Human-Computer Interaction
HCITB Hotel and Catering Industry Training Board
HCL Hindustan Copper Limited (India) (Government owned)
HCM Health Care Management
HCMM Heat Capacity Mapping Mission (of NASA)
HCMOS High-performance Complementary Metal Oxide Semiconductor
HCO Hydrogenated Coconut Oil
HCP Hardened Cement Paste
Hexachlorophane
Hexagonal Closed Packed
Hybrid Combustion Process
prefix to numbered series of House of Commons Papers (published by HMSO)
HCR High Charge Retention
HCS Hard Clad Silica
Helicopter Computer System
Human Chorionic Somatomammotropin
Hydrological Communications Satellite
HCSA Hospitals Consultants and Specialists Association
HCSS Hospital Computer Sharing System
HCSTR Homogeneous Continued Stirred Tank Reactor
HCUA HONEYWELL Computer Users Association
HD Haul-Dump
Hodgkin's Disease
prefix to numbered series of Harmonization Documents issued by CENELEC
HDA Hexamethylene Diamine
Hydrodealkylation
HDAS Hydrographic Data Acquisition System
HDB High Density Bipolar
HDC Harry Diamond Center (of ERADCOM (US Army)
HDCS Human Diploid Cell Strain
HDCV Human Diploid Cell Vaccine
HDD Head Down Display
Housing Development Directorate (of DOE)
HDDR High Density Digital Recording
HDF Highly Dispersive Filter
HDFPA High-Density Focal Plane Array
HDHC High-Density Hydrocarbon
HDHQ Hostility and Direction of Hostility Questionnaire
HDL Hardware Description Language
Harry Diamond Laboratories (US Army)
High Density Lipoproteins
Hydrologic Data Laboratory (of Agricultural Research Service (USDA))
HDLC High Level Data Link Control Procedures (of ISO (Switzerland))
HDMR High Density Moderated Reactor
High Density Multi-track Recording
hDNA Histone DNA
HDOS Health Disc Operating System
HDP Hydrazine Diperchlorate
HDPE High Density Polyethylene
HDR Health Data Recorder
HDRBG Heissdampfreaktor Betriebsgesellschaft (Germany)
HDST High Density Shock Tube
HDT Heat Distortion Temperature
HDTV High-Definition Television
HDW Hydrodynamic Welding
HDX Half-Duplex
HE High Explosive
High-Education
Hydrogen Embrittlement
HEA High Efficiency Anti-reflection
HEAC Higher Education Accommodation Consortium
HEAD Helium-Atom Diffraction
HEADS-UP Health Care Delivery Simulator for Urban Population
HEAE Hyperacute Experimental Autoimmune Encephalomyelitis
HEAFS High-Explosive Anti-tank Fin-Stabilised
HEALS HONEYWELL Error Analysis and Logging System
HEAO High Energy Astronomy Observatory
HEAP High Explosive Armour Piercing
HEAPS High Energy Alpha-Proton Spectrometer
HEART Hawaii Environmental Area Rapid Transport system
HEAT High Enthalpy Arc Tunnel
High-Explosive Anti-Tank
HEBA Home Extension Building Association
HEBAH Heat Engine/Battery Hybrid
HEC Health Education Council
Heavy Engineering Corporation (India) (Government owned)
Hidroelectrica de Catalue SA (Spain)
Hydrogen Embrittlement Cracking
HECAD Human Engineering Computer Aided Design
HECB Highways Engineering Computing Branch (of DOE)
HECTOR Heated Experimental Carbon Thermal Oscillator Reactor
HED Horizontal Electric Dipole
HEDP High Explosive Dual Purpose
HEED High Energy Electron Diffraction
HEEM Hardsite Engagement Effectiveness Model
HEF High Energy Fuel
HEI Heat Exchange Institute (USA)
High Energy Ignition
High Explosive Incendiary
High-energy Electronic Ignition
Holographic Exposure Index
HEI-T High Explosive Incendiary Tracer
HEIAC Hydraulic Engineering Information Analysis Center (US Army)
HEIAS Human Engineering Information and Analysis Service (of Tufts University (USA))
HEIT High Explosive Incendiary with Tracer

HEL High Energy Laser
Hugoniot Elastic Limit
Human Embryo Lung
Human Engineering Laboratories (US Army)
Hydraulic Engineering Laboratory (California University (USA))
HELAC Helix Linear Accelerator
HELAPS High Efficiency Linear Amplification by Parametric Synthesis
HELAST HUMAN ENGINEERING LABORATORY (US Army) Armor System Tests
HELBAT HUMAN ENGINEERING LABORATORY (US Army) Battalion Artillery Tests
HelCIS Helicopter Command Instrumentation System
HELEN Hydrogenous Exponential Liquid Experiment
HELHAT Human Engineering Laboratory (US Army) Helicopter Armament Tests
HELIP HAWK (missile) Electronic Limited Improvement Programme (of NATO)
HELIST HUMAN ENGINEERING LABORATORY (US Army) Infantry System Tests
HELIVALS Helicopter In-flight Validation System
HELLFIRE Heliborne Laser Fire and Forget missile system
Helicopter Launched, Fire and Forget missile
HELLIS Health Literature Library and Information Services (of WHO (UN))
HELM Heavy Lift Monitoring System
HELMS Helicopter Multifunction System
HELNAVS Helicopter Navigation System
HELO Heavy Lift Operability
HELORS Hellenic Operational Research Society (Greece)
HELOS Highly Eccentric Lunar Occultation Satellite
HELOSID Helicopter Delivered Seismic Detector
HELP Health Evaluation through Logical Processing
Heat Escape Lessening Posture
Heuristic Etching-pattern Layout Programme
High Energy Landing Problem
High Energy Level Pneumatic automobile bumpers
Highly Extendible Language Processor
HITACHI (COMPANY (Japan)) Effective Library for Programming
Hybrid Electronic Layout Programme
Hybrid Electronic Light-weight Packaging
HELPIS Higher Education Learning Programmes Information Service (of Council for Educational Technology) (now of BUFVC)
HELRATS High Energy Laser Radar Acquisition and Tracking System
HELTA High-Energy Laser Technology Assessment
HELTAD Helicopter Tank Destroyer
HEM Heat Exchanger Method
Hybrid Electro-Magnetic
HEMA Health Education Media Association (USA)
Hydroxethyl Methacrylate
HEMAC Hybrid Electro-Magnetic Antenna Coupler
HEMEL Hexamethylmelamine
HEMIS Health Education Materials Information Service (Dundee University)
HEMLAW Helicopter Mounted Laser Weapon
HEMLOC Heliborne Emitter Location-Countermeasures
HEMP High-altitude Electro-Magnetic Pulse
HENILAS Helicopter Night Landing System
HENRE High Energy Neutron Reaction Experiment
HEO High Earth Orbit
HEOS High Excentricity Orbit Satellite
HEP High Energy Physics
High Explosive, Plastic
High-Explosive Penetrating
HEPA High-Efficiency, Particulate Air
HEPAP High Energy Physics Advisory Panel (of Dept of Energy (USA))
HEPC Hydro-Electric Power Commission (Canada)
HEPCAT Helicopter Pilot Control And Training
HEPL High Energy Physics Laboratory (Stanford University, USA)
High-Energy-Pulse Laser
HEPS High-Energy-Proton Spectrometer
HER High Energy Rotor
Human Error Rate
Hydrogen Evolution Reaction
HERA High Explosive Rocket Assisted
HERALD Highly Enriched Reactor ALDERMASTON
HERC Hazard Evaluation and Risk Control
Humber Estuarial Research Committee (of Hydraulics Research Station and British Transport Docks Board)
HERCULES Helicopter Remote Classification and Localization System
HERF High Energy Rate Forming
HERMES Heavy Element and Radioactive Material Electromagnetic Separator
Helicopter Energy and Rotor Management System
HERO Hazards of Electromagnetic Radiation to Ordnance
Hot Experimental Reactor of O (ie 'Zero') power
HERPES High Energy Recovery Pressure and Enthalpy Sensor
HERSO High Erucic Acid Rapeseed Oil
HERTIS Hertfordshire Technical Information Service
High-Energy Real-Time Inspections System
HES Hydroxyethyl Starch
HESC International Congress of Scientists on the Human Environment
HeSCA Health Sciences Communications Association (USA)
HESH High Explosive Squash Head
HEST High Explosive Simulation Technique
HET Heavy Equipment Transporter
HETP High Equivalent to a Theoretical Plate
HEU High Enriched Uranium
HEVAC Heating, Ventilating and Air Conditioning Manufacturers Association
HEW Hamburgische Electricitats-Werke (Germany)
Health, Education and Welfare Department (USA) (now DHHS (USA))
HEWC Highly Enriched Waste Concentrates
HF Hydrogen Fluoride
HFAK Hollow Fibre Artificial Kidney
HFBR High Flux Beam Reactor
HFC Hard-Faced Composite
High Fructose Corn
HFD High Field Domain
HFDA High Fidelity Dealers Association
HFDF High Frequency Direction Finder
High Frequency Distribution Frame
HFE Human Factors Engineering
Human Factors in Electronics
HFEF Hot Fuel Examination Facility (of Argonne National Laboratory (USA))
HFEF/N Hot Fuel Examination Facility/North (of Argonne National Laboratories (USA))
HFF Horizontal Falling Film
HFG Heavy Free Gas
HFHP Hybrid Flood Routing Protocol
HFI Hydraulic Fluid Index
HFID Hydrogen Flame Ionisation Detection
HFIH High-Frequency Induction Heating
HFIM High Frequency Instruments and Measurements

HFIR High Flux Isotope Reactor
HFM Horizontal Flexible Mandrel
HFMD Hand-Foot-and-Mouth Disease
HFO High Frequency Oscillator
HFPAC High Frequency Powder Air Conveyor
HFRO Hill Farming Research Organisation
HFRT High-Frequency Resonance Technique
HFS Human Factors Society (USA)
Hyper-Fine Structure
Hypothetical Future Samples
HFSSC High Frequency Swept Spectrum Communications
HFT prefix to dated-numbered series of reports issued by the Human Factors in Technology Research Group, California University (USA)
HFWB High Frequency Wire Broadcasting
HGA High Gain Antenna
Homogentisic Acid
HGAS High Gain Antenna System
HGCA Home Grown Cereals Authority
HGDFS High Gain Direction Finding System
HGEEA Huntsville General Electric Engineers Association (USA)
HGH Human Growth Hormone
HGMS Helicopter Gravity Measuring System
High-Gradient Magnetic Separator
HGPRT Hypoxanthine-Guanine Phosphoribosyltransferase
HGR Hot Gas Re-injection
HGRT Hypoxanthine Guanine Phosphoribosyl Transferase
HGS Hydrologic Growing Season
HGSITVC Hot Gas Secondary Injection Thrust Vector Control
HGTAC Home Grown Timber Advisory Committee
HGW Heat Generating (nuclear) Waste
HHCC Higher Harmonic Circulation Control rotor
HHE Health Hazard Evaluation
HHHMU Hydrazine Hand-Held Manoeuvring Unit
HHMU Hand Held Manoeuvring Unit
HHPC High Harmonic Pitch Control
HHT High-temperature Helium Turbine
HHTV Hand-Held Thermal Viewer
HI Haemagglutinin Inhibition
Hudson Institute (USA)
Hydraulic Institute (USA)
HI-FMECA HITACHI (LTD) (Japan)–Failure Mode Effect and Criticality Analysis
Hi-OVIS Highly interactive Optical Visual Information System
HI-PI High Performance Intercept
HIA Hazard Integration Analysis
Hompolar Inductor Alternator
Housing Industry Association (Australia)
HIAA Hydroxyindoleacetic Acid
HIAS High Incidence Auto-Stabiliser
HIB Heavy Ion Beam
HIBEX High-G Boost Experiment
HIC Hot-Isostatic Compaction
Hybrid Integrated Circuit
HICASS HITACHI (ZOSEN) Computer-Aided Shipbuilding System
HICAT High Altitude Clear Air Turbulence
HICLASS Hierarchical Classification
HICSS Hawaii International Conference on System Sciences
HID High-Intensity Discharge
HIDEA High Desert Engineering Association (USA)
HIDECS Hierarchical Decomposition of Systems
HIDM High Information Delta Modulation
HIE Heat Input Equivalent
HIF Heavy Ion Fusion
HIFAR High Flux Australian Reactor (AAEC (Australia))
HIFRENSA Hispano-Francesa de Energia Nuclear SA (Spain)
HIG Hawaii Institute of Geophysics
HIL High-Intensity Lighting
HILA Health (and accident) Insurance Logistics Automated
HILAB Heavy Ion Laboratory
HILAC Heavy Ion Linear Accelerator
HILAP High Latitude Particles
HILIS High Light Intensity System
HILS High Intensity Lightweight Searchlight
HILT High Level Transaction
HIMAG High Mobility and Agility
HiMAT Highly Manoeuvrable Aircraft Technology (a project of NASA (USA))
HINDALCO Hindustan Aluminium Corporation (India)
HiNiL High Noise Immunity Logic
HIOMT Hydroxyindole-O-Methyl Transferase
HIP Hierachical Information Processor
Host Interface Processor
Hot Isostatic Pressing OR Pressure
Hot Isostatically Pressed
Hydraulic Institute (USA)
Hyperbolic Integer Programming
HIPAAS High Performance Advanced Attack System
HIPAC Heavy Ion Plasma Accelerator
HIPAR High Power Acquisition Radar
HIPEG High Performance External Gun
HIPERFLIR High-Performance Forward-Looking Infra-Red
HIPEX Harmonic Identification Pitch Extraction
HIPH High Institute of Public Health (Alexandria University (Egypt)
HIPO Hierarchical Input-Process-Output
HIPS High Impact Polystyrene
High Integrity Protective Systems
HIR prefix to numbered series of Hydrospace Information Reports issued by SAE (USA)
HIRA Handheld Infrared Alarm
HIRAD HITACHI Re-Adhesion Device
HIRD High Information Rate Display for aircraft cockpits
HIRL High Intensity Runway Lighting
HIRS Holographic Information Retrieval System
HIRT High Reynolds Number Tunnel (USAF)
HIRUP High Intensity Radiation Utilization Project (of BARC (India))
HIS Hood Inflation System
Hospital Information System
HISS Helicopter Icing Spray System
Holographic Ice Surveying System
HISSE Houston (University) Integrated Spatial/Spectral Estimator
HISSG Hospital Information Systems Sharing Group (USA)
HIT Homing Intercept Technology
HITAHR Hawaii Institute of Tropical Agriculture and Human Resources (Hawaii University)
HITI High Integrity Trip Initiators
HITP-SEAP High-Ignition-Temperature Propellants, Self Extinguishing at Atmospheric Pressure
HITS Hydro-acoustic Impact Timing System
HIVE High Integrity Voting Equipment
HIVIP HITACHI Visual Image Processing Robot
HIVOS High Vacuum Orbital Simulation
HKG Hochtemperatur Kernkraftwerk (Germany)
HKIE Hong Kong Institution of Engineers (Hong Kong)

HKMA Hong Kong Management Association (Hong Kong)

HLA Halifax Library Association (Canada)
Hawaii Library Association (USA)
Heavy-Lift Airship
Histoplasmin Latex Agglutination
Human Lencocyte Antigen

HLB Hydrophilic-lipophilic Balance

HLCADS High-Level Container Airdrop Sy

HLCC Home Laundering Consultative Council
Home Laundering Consultative Council

HLE High-Low-junction Emitter

HLFT Holographic Lens-less Fourier Transform

HLG Hybrid Lens Guide
Ministry of Housing and Local Government

HLH Heavy Lift Helicopter

HLH/ATC Heavy Lift Helicopter Advanced Technology Component

HLHS Heavy-Lift Helicopter System (US Army)

HLI Human Leukocyte Interferon

HLL High-Level Language

HLLV Heavy-Lift Launch Vehicle

HLLW High-Level Liquid Waste

HLM Habitations a Loyer Modere (France) (Moderate Rent Housing Organization)

HLP High-Level Protocol
Hyperlipoproteinaemia

HLRC High Latitude Rocket Campaign (a cooperative study by 7 laboratories in the UK)

HLS Heavy Liquid Separation
High Level Scheduler

HLSI Hybrid Large Scale Integrated

HLSUA (Europe) HONEYWELL Large Systems Users Association in Europe

HLV Herpes-Like Virus

HLW High-Level Waste

HM High Modulus
Hovermarine

HMA Hardware Manufacturers Association

HMAC Hazardous Materials Advisory Council (USA)

HMBP Heavy Machine Building Plant (India)

HMC Historical Manuscripts Commission

HMD Helmet-Mounted Display
Hexamethylenediamine
Hyaline Membrane Disease

HMDA Hexamethylene Diamine

HMDE Hanging Mercury Drop Electrode

HMDS Hexamethylene Disiloxane

HME Hull, Mechanical, and Electrical

HMEA Hazard Mode and Effects Analysis

HMFI Her Majesty's Factory Inspectorate (formerly of the Department of Employment, now of the Health and Safety Executive)

HMG Human Menopausal Gonadotrophin

HMGCC Her Majesty's Government Communications Centre

HMI Hahn-Meitner-Institute fur Kernforschung (Germany) (Hahn-Meitner Institute for Nuclear Research)
Hazardous Materials Incident
Heavy Maintenance Interval

HMM Heavy Meromyosin

HMME Hydroquinone Monomethyl Ether

HMMS C. HOLT, F. MODIGLIAN, J. MULT and H. SIMON mathematical model

HMNAO Her Majesty's Nautical Almanac Office

HMO Health Maintenance Organization (organization here means the state of being organized and not the name of a body)
Health Maintenance Organization (USA)

HMOS Health Maintenance Organization Service (of HEW (USA))
High-Performance MOS

HMP Hexametaphosphate
Hexamethyl-phosphoramide

HMPA Hexamethyl Phosphoramide

HMR Humidity Mixing Ratio

HMS Heavy Media Separation
Helmet Mounted Symbolic display
Hexose Monophosphate Shunt
Hull Monitoring System
Hybrids of High Modulus

HMSA Head-Mounted Sonic Aid

HMSD Helmet-Mounted Sight and Display

HMSO Her Majesty's Stationery Office

HMSS Helmet-Mounted Sighted System
Hospital Management Systems Society (USA)

HMT Hexamethylene Tetramine
Hindustan Machine Tools Limited (India) (Government owned)

HMTA Hexamethylenetetramine

HMTA-I Hexamethylenetetramine Hydroiodide

HMTT High Mobility Tactical Truck

HMW High Molecular Weight

HMX Cyclotetramethylenetetranitramine

HNB Hexanitrobenzene
Hexanitrobiphenyl

HNDICS Hellenic National Defence Integrated Communication System

HNDT Holographic Non-Destructive Testing

HNE Hexanitroethane

HNF Hydrazine Nitroform

HNIG Human Normal Immunoglobulin

HNIL High Noise Immunity Logic

HNR Handwritten Numerical Recognition

hnRA Heterogenous RNA

HnRNA Heterogeneous nuclear Ribonucleic Acid

HNS Hyperbolic Navigation System

HNV prefix to numbered series of High Alloy Intake Valve Material issued by SAE (USA)

HNVS Helicopter Night Vision System

HOB Horizontal Oscillating Barrel

HOBO Homing Bomb

HOBOS Homing Bombing System

HOC Heterodyne Optical Correlation
Hindustan Organic Chemicals (India) (government owned)

HOCUS Hand Or Computer Universal Simulator

HODRAL HOKUSHIN Data Reduction Algorithm Language

HOE Holographic Optical Element

HOEI Hover-One-Engine-Inoperative

HOGS Homing Optical Guidance System

HOJ Home-On Jamming

HOL High Order Language

HOLMES Home Office Large Major Enquiry System

HOMO Highest Occupied Molecular Orbital

HONDUTEL Empresa Hondurena de Telecomunicaciones (Honduras)

HOP High Oxygen Pressure

HOPBEG British Hotel and Public Building Equipment Group

HOPE Hazard-free Operation against Potential Emergencies (name of a symposium held by JSME (Japan) in 1976)
Health-Oriented Physician Education
Holistic Preference Evaluation

HOPES High Oxygen Pulping Enclosed System

HOPS (Air Pilot) Helmet Optical Position Sensor System
Highway Optimization Programme System

HORACE H_2O Reactor ALDERMASTON Critical Experiment

HORATIO Human Operator Response Analyser and Timer for Infrequent Occurrences
HORD Hydrogen-Oxygen Recombination Device
HORV Hydraulic and Optical Repair Vehicle
HOS High Order Software
Human Operator Simulator
HOSPACT Hospital Patient Accounting
HOSS Halo-Orbit Space Station
HOST Hardened Optical Sensor Testbed
HOT Holographic-One-Two
HOT-DAM Higher Order Tree Dual Approximation Method
HOTAS Hands On Throttle And Stick
HOTOL Horizontal Take-Off and Landing
HOV High Occupancy Vehicle
HOVVAC Hovering Vehicle Versatile Automatic Control
HOWLS Hostile Weapon Locating System
HP High Pressure
High Protein
Hydrazine Perchlorate
Hydroxyproline
Hygroscopicity Potential
Hyperbolic-Paraboloid
HPA Hexahydrophthallic Anhydride
High-Power Amplifier
Horn-Parabola Antenna
Hospital Physicists Association
HPAS High Power Airborne System
HPBW Half Power Beam-width
HPC Hindustan Paper Corporation (India) (govt. owned)
Hydroxpropylcellulose
HPCL Hindustan Petroleum Corporation Limited (India)
HPCM Hybrid Pulse Code Modulation
HPD Hard Point Defence
Hearing Protection Device
High Performance Diesel
Horizontally-Polarized Dipole
HOUGH-POWELL Device
HPDO High Performance Diesel Oil
HPEL Horn Point Environmental Laboratories (Maryland University (USA))
HPF Highest Priority First
Hot Pressed Ferrite
HPFH Heredilary Persistence of Foetal Haemoglobin
HPG Homopolar Generator
HPHF Hereditary Persistence of Foetal Haemoglobin
HPHW High Pressure Hot Water
HPI High Probability of Intercept
Hydrocarbon Processing Industry
HPIR High Probability of Intercept Receiver
HPL High-Level Programming Language
Human Placental Lactogen
HPLC High Performance Liquid Chromatography
High Pressure Liquid Chromatography
HPLL High Pressure Life Laboratory
Hybrid Phase-Locked Loop
HPM Health Physics and Medical Division (of AERE)
HPMA Hardwood Plywood Manufacturers Association (USA)
Heat Pump Manufacturers Association
HPMC Hydroxypropyl Methylcellulose
HPMIDC Himachul Pradesh Mineral and Industrial Development Corporation (India) (govt. owned)
HPMM Horizontal Planar Motion Mechanism
HPMV High Pressure Mercury Vapour
HPNS High Pressure Nervous Syndrome
HPP Homogeneous Poisson Process
HPPLC High-performance Preparative Liquid Chromatography
HPPM High Performance Propulsion Module
HPPO High Pressure Partial Oxidation
HPR High Penetration Resistant
Holding Period Return
Hot Particle Rolling
Human Performance Reliability
HPRT High Power Recovery Turbine
Hypoxanthine Phosphotibosyltransferase
HPS Hazardous Polluting Substances
Head Position Sensing
Health Physics Soc
Horizontal Pull Slipmeter
HPSEB Himachal Pradesh State Electricity Board (India)
HPSI High Pressure Safety Ignition
HPSN Hot Pressed Silicon Nitride
HPTA High Pressure Technology Association
Hire Purchase Trade Association
HPTF Hydraulic and Power Transmission Fluid
HQIR Hydro-Quebec Institute of Research (Canada)
HR Halorhodopsin
High Resilient
House of Representatives (USA)
prefix to numbered: dated series of Heat Resisting Wrought Alloys standards issued by BSI
HRA Health Resources Administration (USA)
High-speed Research Aircraft
Hypersonic Research Airplane
HRB Highways Research Board (USA) (now Transportation Research Board)
Hochtemperatur-Reaktorbau (Germany)
HRC High Rupturing Capacity
Rockwell "C" Hardness
HRCC Humanities Research Council of Canada (Canada)
HRD Conference on Current Theory and Practice in Human Resource Development
High Roughage Diet
Human Resources Development
Human Resources Division (of GAO (USA))
HRDI Human Resources Development Institute (USA)
HRDP Hypothetical Reference Digital Path
HRE Hypersonic Ramjet Engine
Hypersonic Research Engine
HREELS High Resolution Electron-Energy Loss Spectroscopy
HRELS High Resolution Energy Loss Spectroscopy
HREM High Resolution Electron Microscope
HRFAX High Resolution Facsimile
HRG Hemispherical Resonating Gyro
Hydrocarbon Research Group (of the Institute of Petroleum)
HRGS High Resolution Gamma Spectrometry
HRIG Human Antirabics Immunoglobulin
HRIR High Resolution Infrared Radiometer
HRIRS High Resolution Infra-red Radiation Sounder
HRIS Highway Research Information Service (of US HRB and AASHO)
Human Resource Information System
HRLEL High-Radiation-Level Examination Laboratory (of ORNL (USAEC))
HRM Human Resources Management
HRMR Human Readable Machine Readable
HRMS Human Resources Management System
HRP Horizontal Radiation Pattern
Horse-radish Peroxidase
Human Resources Planning
HRPT High Resolution Picture Transmission
HRR Heart Rate Reserve
HRRL High-Repetition-Rate Laser
HRRM High Range-Resolution Monopulse

HRS High Resolution Spectrometer
Human Resource System
Hydraulics Research Station (formerly of MINTECH subsequently transferred to DOE)

HRSCMR High-Resolution Surface-Composition Mapping Radiometer

HRSI High-temperature Re-usable Surface Insulation

HRT Heavy Rail Transit
Hormone Replacement Therapy

HRTEM High Resolution Transmission Electron Microscopy

HRTS High Resolution Telescope Spectograph

HRU Hydrologic Research Unit (of Natural Environment Research Council)

HRV Hyperbaric Rescue Vessel

HRW Hard Red Winter Wheat

HS Hereditary Spherocytosis
Holographic Stereogram
prefix to numbered series of reports issued by School of Hygiene and Public Health (Johns Hopkins University (USA))

HSA Hollandse Signaalapparaten (Netherlands)
Human Serum Albumin

HSAS Hard Stability Augmentation System

HSB Hochleistungs-schnellban Studiengesellschaft (Germany)

HSBR High Speed Bombing Radar

HSC Health and Safety Commission
Health Service Command (US Army)
High Sulphur Content
Hydrogen Stress Cracking

HSCI High Silicon Chromium Iron

HSCL Hindustan Steel Construction Limited (India) (Government owned)

HSCR High-Strength Cold-Rolled

HSD High Speed Diesel oil
High Speed Displacement
Hollow Spherical Dipole
Horizontal Situation Display

HSDA High Speed Data Acquisition

HSDD Half Second Delay Detonator

HSDT High Speed Diesel Train
Hypersonic Small Disturbance Theory

HSE Health and Safety Executive (of the Health and Safety Commission)
Heat-Stable Esterase

HSE(M) Health and Safety Executive Mining Approvals and Certification Service

HSEB Haryana State Electricity Board (India)

HSF Heat Stimulated Flow

HSF-ACTH Hypothalmic Secretory Factor for Adreno-Corticotropic Hormone

HSFG High Strength Friction Grip

HSFV High Speed Freight Vehicle

HSG High-Speed Grinding

HSGT High Speed Ground Transport

HSI Heat Stress Index
High Silicon Iron
Horizontal Situation Indicator

HSI/CDI Horizontal Situation Indicator/Course Deviation Indicator

HSL Health and Safety Laboratories (of Health and Safety Executive)
Hytran Simulation Language

HSLA High-Strength Low-Alloy

HSM Hard Structures Munition
Harmonic Subcarrier Method
High Speed Memory

HSMHA Health Services and Mental Health Administration (of PHS (USA))

HSORS High Seas Oil-Recovery System

HSP High Speed Printer

HSQB Health Standards and Quality Bureau (of DHHS (USA))

HSR High Speed Rail
High Speed Reader

HSRC Health Sciences Resource Centre (of CISTI (Canada))
Highway Safety Research Center (University of North Carolina (USA))

HSRD prefix to series of dated: numbered reports issued by National Center for Health Services Research and Development (of HEW (USA))

HSRI Highway Safety Research Institute (Michigan University (US

HSRU Health Services Research Unit (Kent University)

HSS High Speed Steel
High-strength Stainless Steel
History of Science Society (USA)
Hydrological Sensing Satellite

HSSR Hydrogeochemical and Stream Sediment Reconnaissance

HSST Heavy Section Steel Technology program (of USAEC)
High Speed Surface Transport

HST High Speed Train
Hubble Space Telescope (of NASA (USA))
Hypersonic Transport

HSTRU Hydraulic System Test and Repair Unit

HSTV-L High Survivability Test Vehicle–Lightweight

HSU Hartridge Smoke Units

HSUR Half Symmetric Unstable Resonator

HSURIA Half Symmetric Unstable Resonator with Internal Axicon
Half Symmetric Unstable Resonator with Intracavity Axicon

HSV Herpes Simplex Virus
Highly Selective Vagotomy

HT Heavy Terminal
High Tensile
HILBERT Transform

HTA Heterogeneity Arrangement
Horticultural Trades Association
Hypophysiotropic Area

HTAH High Temperature Air Heater

HTC Heat Transfer Coefficient
High Temperature Contact

HTCT High Temperature Chemical Technology (a project of UKAEA)

HTD High Torque Drive

HTE High-Temperature Electrolysis

HTES High Technology Ejection Seat

HTFS Heat Transfer and Fluid Flow Service (of UKAEA)

HTGCR High Temperature Gas Cooled Reactor

HTGR High Temperature Gas-cooled Reactor
High-temperature Gas-cooled Graphite-moderated Reactor

HTI High Temperature Isotropic
Highly Dense Isotropic

HTL Hearing Threshold Level
Heat Transfer Laboratory (of Minnesota University (USA))
High Threshold Logic

HTLS High-Torque, Low-Speed

HTLTR High Temperature Lattice Test Reactor

HTLV Human T-cell Leukaemia/lymphoma Virus

HTM Hypothesis Testing Model
prefix to numbered series of Health Technical Memoranda issued by DHSS and published by HMSO

HTMAEW Home Timber Merchants Association of England and Wales

HTO High Temperature Oxidation
Hydrous Titanium Oxide
HTOL Horizontal-Take-Off and Landing
HTOT High-Temperature Operating-Test
HTOVL Horizontal Take-Off Vertical Landing
HTP High Temperature Pyrolysis
High Test Peroxide
High-Temperature Phase
HTPB Hydroxyl Terminated Polybutadiene
HTPIB Hydroxy Terminated Polyisobutylene
HTR High-Temperature Reactor
HTRB High-Temperature Reverse-Bias
HTS Hadamard Transform Spectrometer
High Temperature Gas-cooled Reactor System
High Tensile Strength
High-Temperature Storage
Hyper-Thin Septum
HTSI Human Thyroid-Stimulating Immunoglobulin
HTSL High Temperature Sodium Loop
HTSR High Temperature Steam Reformer
High Tensile Safety Repair
HTSS HAMILTON Test Simulation System
HTST High-Temperature-Short Time
HTT Heat Treatment Temperature
HTTA Highway Traffic Technicians Association
HTTB High Technology Test Bed
HTTT High-Temperature Turbine Technology (a program of DOE (USA))
HTU Heat Transfer Unit
HTV High Temperature and Velocity
HTW High Temperature Water
HTX Histrionicotoxin
HU Hydroxyurea
HUCR Highest Useful Compression Ratio
HUD Department of Housing and Urban Development (USA)
Head-Up Display
Hull Technical Interloan Scheme
HUD-HPMC Department of Housing and Urban Development, Assistant Secretary for Housing Production and Mortgage Credit (USA)
HUDWAC Head-Up Display Weapon Aiming Computer
HUDWAS Head-up Display Weapon Aiming System
HUF Highway Users Federation for Safety and Mobility (USA)
HULDA Hull Design and Analysis
HULTIS Humberside Libraries Technical Inter-loan Scheme
HUMINT Human Intelligence
HumRRO Human Resources Research Organization (USA)
HURRAN Hurricane Analogue
HUSAT Human Sciences and Advanced Technology (a research group at Loughborough University)
HUSM Hamamatsu University School of Medicine (Japan)
HUSTLE Helium Underwater Speech Translating Equipment
HUTCH Humidity-Temperature Charts
HUW HARWELL (ATOMIC ENERGY RESEARCH ESTABLISHMENT) User's Workshop
HV Hochschulverband (Germany) (Association of University Teachers)
HVA Homovanillic Acid
HVAC Heating, Ventilating, Air-Conditioning
High Voltage Alternating Current
HVAP Hyper-Velocity, Armour Piercing
HVAR High-Velocity Airborne Rocket
HVB Heptyl Viologen Bromide
HVC High Velocity Cloud
HVCA Heating and Ventilating Contractors Association
HVCS High-Vacuum Calibration System
HVDB Heptyl Viologen Dibromide
HVDC High Voltage Direct Current
HVEM High Vacuum Electron Microscope
High Voltage Electron Microscope
High Voltage Electron Microscopy
HVGL High Velocity Grenade Launcher
HVGO Heavy Vacuum Gas Oil
HVHD High-Voltage-Hold-Down
HVHMD Holographic Visor Helmet Mounted Display
HVI High Viscosity Index
HVIRS Hull Vibration Information Retrieval System
HVJ Haemagglutinating Virus of Japan
HVL Half-Value Layer
HVM High Velocity Metallworking
Hyper-Velocity Missile
HVO Hawaii Volcano Observatory (of Geological Survey (USA))
HVOSM Highway Vehicle–Object Simulation Model
HVRA Heating and Ventilating Research Association (became Building Services Research and Information Association in 1975)
HVRAP Hyper-Velocity Rocket-Assisted Projectile
HVRN Highly Reliable Vowel Nuclei
HVS Human Visual System
HVSF High Velocity Sheet Forming
HVTO Hyperabruct Varactor Tuned Oscillator
HVTS High Volume Time Sharing
HWC Hot Waste Concentrates
HWCTR Heavy Water Components Test Reactor
HWGCR Heavy-Water-moderated, Gas-Cooled Reactor
HWHH Half-Width at Half-Height
HWLS Hostile Weapon Locating System
HWLWR Heavy-Water-moderated, Boiling Light-Water-cooled Reactor
HWM Hot-Water-cure Mortar
HWMD Hazardous Waste Management Division (of EPA (USA))
HWO Hot Water Oxidizer
HWOCR Heavy Water Organic Cooled Reactor
HWS Harassment Weapons System
Hazardous Waste Service (of UKAEA)
HWTA Houston World Trade Association (USA)
HWWA Hamburgisches Welt- Wirtschafts Archiv (Germany) (Hamburg World Business Archives)
HX Hydrogen Exchange
HXBT Helicopter Expendable Bathythermograph
HXIS Hand X-ray Imaging Spectrometer
HXRBS Hand X-Ray Burst Spectrometer
HY-BALL Hydraulic Ball
HyA Hydro- og Aerodynamisk Laboratorium (Denmark) (Hydrodynamics and Aerodynamics Laboratory)
HYBALL Hybrid Analog Logical Language
HYBLOC Hybrid computer Block-oriented Compiler
HYCPP High Yield Catalyst Polypropylene
HYCSOS Hydrogen Conversion and Storage System
HYDAS Hydrographic Data Acquisition System
HYDRA Hydrographic Digital Positioning and Depth Recording System
HYDROLANT Hydrographic Warning—Atlantic (originated by NOO (USN))
HYDROPAC Hydrographic Warning—Pacific (originated by NOO (Honolulu Branch) (USN))
HYFES Hypersonic Flight Environmental Simulator
HYPAR Hysterectomy Produced and Artificially Reared
HYPERDOP Hyperbolic Doppler
HYPSES Hydrographic Precision Scanning Echo Sounder
HYPTV Hypersonic Test Vehicle

HySAS Hydrofluic Stability Augmentation System
HYSTAD Hydrofoil Stabilization Device
HYSTU Hydrofoil Special Trials Unit (USN)
HYSURCH Hydrographic Surveying and Charting
HYSWAS Hydrofoil Small Waterplane Area Ship
HYTRESS High Test Recorder and Simulator System
HYVE Hydrogen Ventilated Enclosure
HZL Hindustan Zinc Limited (India) (Government owned)
HZP Hyperbolic Zone Plate

I

I&O Individual and Organization performance
I&R Information and Referral
I-ATTC Inter-American Tropical Tuna Commission
I-CAS Independent Collision-Avoidance System
I-CNI Integrated Communications-Navigation-Identification
I-MLS Interim Microwave Landing System
I/CNI Integrated Communications, Navigation and Identification
I/O Input/Output
IA Indian Airlines (India)
Indolamine
Institute of Actuaries
Inter-Arytenoid
Interciencia Association
IA-ECOSOC Inter-American Economic and Social Council (of OAS)
IAA Indoleacetic Acid
Institute of Automobile Assessors
Instituto Antartico Argentino (Argentina) (Argentine Antarctic Institute)
International Academy of Astronautics (of IAF)
International Advertising Association
International Association of Allergology (USA)
IAAAM International Association for Aquatic Animal Medicine
IAAB Inter-American Association of Broadcasters
IAAC Inter-American Accounting Conference
International Agricultural Aviation Centre (Netherlands)
IAAI International Airports Authority of India (India)
IAALD International Association of Agriculture Librarians and Documentalists
IAAP International Association of Applied Psychology
IAAPEA International Association Against Painful Experiments on Animals
IAAS Incorporated Association of Architects and Surveyors
Institute of Advanced Architectural Studies (University of York)
International Association of Agricultural Students
IAB ICSU Abstracting Board
Industrial Advisers to the Blind
Industry Advisory Board (of IEA (OECD))
International Association of Book-keepers
IABA International Association of Aircraft Brokers and Agents
IABG International Association of Botanic Gardens
IABO International Association of Biological Oceanography (of IUBS)
IABS International Association of Biological Standardization
IABSE International Association for Bridge and Structural Engineering
IAC Industrial Applications Centers (of NASA (USA))
Industries Assistance Commission (Australia)
Industry Advisory Committee (of the Health and Safety Commission)
Industry Advisory Council (of USDOD and Industry)
Information Analysis Centre
Institute of Company Accountants (merged into the Society of Company and Commercial Accountants in 1974)
International Agricultural Centre (Netherlands)
International Association for Cybernetics
IACA International Air Carrier Association
International Air Charter Association (Switzerland)
International Association of Consulting Actuaries
IACB Inter-Agency Coordination Board (of the UN)
International Association of Convention Bureaus
IACBDT International Advisory Committee on Bibliography, Documentation and Technology (of UNESCO)
IACC Indo-American Chamber of Commerce
IACES International Air Cushion Engineering Society
IACHEI International Association of Consultants in Higher Education Institutions
IACIA Incorporated Association of Cost and Industrial Accountants (merged into the Society of Company and Commercial Accountants in 1974)
IACME International Association of Crafts and Small and Medium-sized Enterprises
IACODLA International Advisory Committee on Documentation, Libraries and Archives (of UNESCO) (Superseded in 1976)
IACP Indian Association of Clinical Psychologists (India)
International Association of Chiefs of Police
International Association of Computer Programmers (USA)
Investment Advisory Centre of Pakistan (Pakistan)
IACPAP International Association for Child Psychiatry and Allied Professions
IACQ Instituto Argentino de Control de la Calidad (Argentina) (Institute for Quality Control)
IACS Indian Association for the Cultivation of Science (India)
Inertial Attitude Control System
Integrated Armament Control System
Integrated Avionics Communications System
Integrated Avionics Control System
International Annealed Copper Standard
International Association of Classification Societies
IAD Integrated Automatic Documentation
IADB Inter-American Defense Board (of OAS)
Inter-American Development Bank
IADC Inter-American Defense College (USA)
International Association of Drilling Contractors (USA)
IADIC Integrating Analog-to-Digital Converter
IADIWU International Association for the Development of International and World Universities
IADO Iran Agriculture Development Organization (Iran)
IADR International Association for Dental Research
IADS International Association of Dental Students
IAE Institute Atomnoi Energii (USSR) (Atomic Energy Institute)
Institute for the Advancement of Engineering (USA)
Institute of Automotive Engineers
Integral Absolute Error
IAEA International Atomic Energy Agency (Austria) (of UN)
Iraqi Atomic Energy Authority (Iraq)

IAEC International Association of Environmental Coordinators
Israel Atomic Energy Commission (Israel)
IAECOSOC Inter-American Economic and Social Council (of OAS)
IAEE International Association of Earthquake Engineering Enterprises
International Association of Energy Economists
IAEG International Association of Engineering Geology
IAEI International Association of Electrical Inspectors
IAES Interim Aquanaut Equipment System
IAESTE International Association for the Exchange of Students for Technical Experience
IAF Image Analysis Facility digital computer
Immobilizing Accelerating Factor
Indian Air Force (India)
Initial Approach Fix
International Astronautical Federation
IAFC International Association of Fire Chiefs
IAFF International Association of Fire Fighters
IAFS International Association of Forensic Sciences
IAG Institut fuer Angewandte Geodaesie (Germany) (Institute for Applied Geodesy)
Institute of Applied Geology (Saudi Arabia)
International Administrative Data Processing Group (of IFIP)
International Association of Geodesy
IAGA International Association of Geomagnetism and Aeronomy (USA)
IAGC Instantaneous Automatic Gain Control
International Association of Geochemistry and Cosmochemistry
IAGEBS International Association of Gerontology (European Biological Section)
IAGLO International Association of Governmental Labour Officials
IAGLP International Association of Great Lakes Ports (representing 16 United States and 5 Canadian ports)
IAGOD International Association for the Genesis of Ore Deposits
IAGP International Antarctic Glaciological Project (of Australia, France, USA and USSR)
IAgrE Institution of Agricultural Engineers
IAGS Inter-American Geodetic Survey (Defense Mapping Agency (USDOD))
Inter-American Geodetic Survey (US Army)
IAGUSP Instituto de Astronomía e Geofisica da Universidade de São Paulo (Brazil) (Sao Paulo University Institute of Astronomy and Geophysics)
IAH Immune Adherence Haemagglutination
IAHCSM International Association of Hospital Central Service Management
IAHR International Association for Hydraulic Research
IAHS International Association of Hydrological Sciences (Hungary)
IAI Ion Acoustic Instability Enterprises
Israel Aircraft Industries (Israel)
IAIABC International Association of Industrial Accident Boards and Commissions
IAIAS Inter-American Institute of Agricultural Sciences (of OAS)
IAIE Inter-American Institute of Ecology
IAII Inter-American Indian Institute (of Organisation of American States)
IAIMS Integrated Academic Information Management Systems
IAIN International Association of Institutes of Navigation
IAIR International Association of Industrial Radiation (France)
IAIS Industrial Aerodynamics Information Service (of British Hydromechanics Research Association)
IAL Indian Airlines (India)
International Association of Laryngetomees
International Association of Limnology
International Association of Theoretical and Applied Limnology
Investment Analysis Langua
IALA International Association of Lighthouse Authorities
IALL International Association of Law Libraries
IALP International Association of Logopedics and Phoniatrics (Spain)
IALS International Association of Legal Science (Belgium)
IAM Image Analyzing Microscope
Institute of Administrative Management
Institute of Advanced Motorists
Institute of Aviation Medicine
Interactive Algebraic Manipulation
IAM/TMD Institute of Administrative Management/Telecommunications Managers Division
IAMA Institut za Altane Masine i Alate (Yugoslavia) (Institute for Machine Tools and Tooling)
IAMAM International Association of Museums of Arms and Military History
IAMAP International Association of Meteorology and Atmospheric Physics (Canada) (of IUGG)
IAMC Institute for Advancement of Medical Communication (USA)
IAMCR International Association for Mass Communication Research (Switzerland)
IAMFE International Association on Mechanization of Field Experiments (Norway)
IAMFES International Association of Milk, Food and Environmental Sanitarians (USA) Enterprises
IAMG International Association for Mathematical Geology
IAML International Association of Music Librarians
IAMLANZ International Association of Music Librarians, Australia/New Zealand Branch
IAMM&D Institute for Advanced Materials, Mechanics and Design (US Army)
IAMRC International Antarctic Meteorological Research Centre
IAMS Institute for Archaeo-Metallurgical Studies
International Association of Microbiological Societies (Canada)
IAMTCT Institute of Advanced Machine Tool and Control Technology
IAN Instituto de Asuntos Nucleaires (Colombia)
IANEC Inter-American Nuclear Energy Commission (USA (of OAS)
IAOL International Association of Orientalist Librarians (Hawaii)
IAOPA International Council of Aircraft Owner and Pilot Associations
IAP Institute of Animal Physiology (of the Agricultural Research Council)
International Academy of Pathology
International Academy of Proctology
IAP-VO STRANY ISTREBITEL'NAYA AVIATSIYA P-VO STRANY (USSR) (Air Force of Anti-Aircraft Defence of the Homeland)
IAPA Industrial Accident Prevention Association (Canada)
Inter-American Press Association
IAPB International Agency for the Prevention of Blindness
IAPC International Association for Pollution Control
IAPCO International Association of Private Container Owners

International Association of Professional Congress Organizers (Belgium)
IAPG Interagency Advanced Power Group (USA)
Item Analysis Programme, General
IAPH International Association of Ports and Harbours
IAPHA International Association of Port and Harbour Authorities
IAPI Industrial Air Pollution Inspectorate
IAPIP International Association for the Protection of Industrial Property
IAPO International Association of Physical Oceanography
IAPP International Association for the Plant Physiology (Switzerland)
IAPR International Association for Pattern Recognition
IAPS International Affiliation of Planning Societies
Sanitarians Enterprises
International Association for the Properties of Steam (USA)
Ion Auxiliary Propulsion System
IAPSO International Association of the Physical Sciences of the Oceans (of IUGG)
IAPW International Association of Personnel Women
IAQ International Association for Quality (now International Academy for Quality)
IAQC International Association for Quality Circles (USA)
IAQR Indian Association for Quality and Reliability (India)
IAR Institut fur Angewandte Reaktorphysik (Germany) (Institute for Applied Reactor Physics)
Institute for Agricultural Research and Special Services (Ahmadu Bello University (Nigeria))
Instructive Address Register
IARB Italian Aviation Research Branch of Air-Britain
IARC International Agency for Research on Cancer (France) (of WHO (UN))
International Amateur Radio Club
IARD Information Analysis and Retrieval Division (of American Institute of Physics)
IARI Indian Agricultural Research Institute (India)
IARIGAI International Association of Research Institutes for the Graphic Arts Industry
IARIW International Association for Research on Income and Wealth
IArm Inspectorate of Armaments (MOD) (now QAD (Weapons))
IARP Indian Association for Radiation Protection (India)
IARS Institute of Agricultural Research Statistics (India)
IARU International Amateur Radio Union
IAS Immediate Access Store
Indicated Air Speed
Inelastic Atom Scattering
Institute of Accounting Staff
Institute of Advanced Studies (US Army)
Institute of Aerospace Science (USA) (now AIAA)
Institute of Aerospace-Sciences (USA)
Integrated Analytical System for global range planning
Integrated Antenna System
Interactive Application System
International Association of Sedimentology
Invariant-Azimuth States
Isolated Antenna System Sanitarians Enterprises
prefix to numbered series of International Accounting Standards issued by IASC (of ICCAP)
IASA Insurance Accounting and Statistical Association (USA)
International Air Safety Association
International Association of Sound Archives
IASC International Accounting Standards Committee (of ICCAP)
International Association for Statistical Computing
International Association of Seed Crushers
IASE Inter-American Association of Sanitary Engineering
IASG Inflation Accounting Steering Group
IASH International Association of Scientific Hydrology
IASI Inter-American Statistical Institute (of OAS)
IASL Illinois Association of School Librarians (USA)
International Association for the Study of the Liver (Belgium)
International Association of School Librarianship
IASLIC Indian Association of Special Libraries and Information Centres (India)
IASM Istituto per l'Assistenza allo Sviluppo del Mezzogiorno (Italy) (Institute for Assistance in the Development of Southern Italy)
IASP International Association of Scholarly Publishers
IASPEI International Association of Seismology and Physics of the Earth's Interior (USA)
IASPM International Association of Scientific Paper Makers
IASPS International Association for Statistics in Physical Sciences
IASS Incorporated Association of Architects and Surveyors
Institute of Advanced Architectural Studies
International Association for Shell Structures
International Association of Survey Statisticians
International Aviation Snow Symposium
IASSIST International Association for Social Science Information Service and Technology
IASSMD International Association for the Scientific Study of Mental Deficiency
IASTED International Association of Science and Technology for Development
IASY International Active Sun Years
IAT Institut Avtomatiki Telemekhaniki (USSR) (Automation and Remote Control Institute)
Enterprises
Institute for Applied Technology (of NBS) (disbanded 1978)
Institute of Animal Technicians
International Atomic Time
Iodine-Azide Test
IATA Instituto de Agroquimica y Tecnologia de Alimentos (Spain) (Institute of Agricultural Chemistry and Food Technology)
International Air Transport Association
IATAE International Accounting and Traffic Analysis Equipment
IATE Intermediate-level Automatic Test Equipment
IATFIS Inter-Agency Task Force on Information Systems
IATLIS Indian Association of Teachers of Library Science (India)
IATM International Association of Transport Museums
IATP International Airlines Technical Pool
IATTC Inter-American Tropical Tuna Commission
IATUL International Association of Technical University Libraries
IAU Industrial Applications Unit (of RRE)
Interface Adaptor Unit
International Association of Universities (France)
International Association of Volcanology and Chemistry of the Earth's Interior
International Astronomical Union (of ICSU)
IAVCEI International Association of Volcanology and Chemistry of the Earth's Interior (Italy)
IAVD International Association for Vehicle Design
IAVRS International Audiovisual Resource Service (sponsored by UNESCO)

IAVSD	International Association for Vehicle System Dynamics
IAWA	International Association of Wood Anatomists (USA)
IAWPR	International Association on Water Pollution Research
IB	Industrialized Building Isobutylene
IBA	Independent Broadcasting Authority Indian Banks Association (India) International Bauxite Association Isobutyl Alcohol Israel Broadcasting Authority (Israel)
IBAA	Independent Bankers Association of America (USA)
IBALS	Interactive Balancing through Simulation
IBAM	Institute of Business Administration and Management (Japan)
IBAR	Interafrican Bureau for Animal Resources (of OAU)
IBAS	International Business Assistance Service (Department of EnterprisesIpyosy Commerce (USA))
IBB	Invest in Britain Bureau (of DOI)
IBBD	Ionstituto Brasileiro de Bibliografia e Documentacao (Brazil) (Brazilian Institute of Bibliography and Documentation) (now IBICT)
IBBY	International Board on Books for Young People
IBC	Institute of Building Control Intermediate Bulk Container International Broadcasting Convention
IBCC	International Building Classification Committee International Bureau of Chambers of Commerce International Business Contact Club
IBCFA	Injected Beam Cross-Field Amplifier
IBCO	Institution of Building Control Officers
IBCS	Integrated Battlefield Control System
IBCS/TRICAP	Integrated Battlefield Communications Systems/Triple Capability–Armoured, Infantry and Air Cavalry
IBD	Inflammatory Bowel Disease
IBDA	Indirect Bomb Damage Assessment
IBDU	Isobutylidene diurea
IBE	Institute Belge de l'Emballage (Belgium) (Belgian Packaging Institute) International Bureau for Epilepsy International Bureau of Education (of UNESCO) Inventory By Exception
IBEC	Indo-British Economic Committee
IBEDATA	prefix to dated: numbered series issued by IBE (of UNESCO)
IBERLANT	Iberian Atlantic Command (of NATO)
IBES	Integration Building and Equipment Scheduling
IBETA	Irish Business Equipment Trade Association
IBF	Institute of British Foundrymen Internally Blown Flap International Booksellers Federation
IBFAN	International Baby Food Action Network
IBFD	International Bureau of Fiscal Documentation
IBFI	International Business Forms Industries (of Printing Industries of America (USA))
IBG	Institue of British Geographers Internationales Buro fur Gebirgsmechanik (International Bureau for Rock Mechanics)
IBHP	Institute Belge des Hautes Pressions (Belgium) (Belgian Institute for High Pressures)
IBI	Inter-governmental Bureau for Information (of UNESCO) International Broadcast Institute (Italy)
IBI-ICC	IBI-International Computation Centre (of UNESCO)
IBICT	Instituto Brasileiro de Informacao Cientifica e Technologica (Brazil) (Brazilian Institute of Scientific and Technological Information)
IBID	International Bibliographical Description
IBIE	International Brewing Industries Exposition
IBIS	Infrared Background-limiting Imaging Seeker Integrated Building Industry System Intense Bunched Ion Source Intranet Business Information System
IBK	Institut für Bauen mit Kunststoffen (Germany) (Institute for Building with Plastics)
IBKC	Infectious Bovine Keratoconjunctivitis
IBM	Indian Bureau of Mines (India) Instytut Budownictwa Mieszkaniowego (Poland) (Institute of House Building)
IBMS	Institute of Basic Medical Sciences
IBMX	Isobutylmethylxanthine
IBN	Institut Belge de Normalisation (Belgium) (Belgian Standards Institute)
IBNR	Incurred But Not Reported
IBOLS	Integrated Business-Oriented Language Support
IBP	Initial Boiling Point International Biological Programme (of ICSU)
IBP/CT	International Biological Programme Conservation of Terrestrial Biological Communities
IBPA	International Business Press Associates
IBPGR	International Board for Plant Genetic Resources (of CGIAR)
IBR	Infectious Bovine Rhinotracheitis Integral Boiling Reactor
IBRA	Institut Belge de Regulation et d'Automatisme (Belgium) (Belgian Institute for Control and Automation)
IBRD	International Bank for Reconstruction and Development (USA) (of UN)
IBRO	Inter-Bank Research Organisation International Brain Research Organisation (France)
IBS	Institut Belge de la Soudure (Belgium) (Belgian Institute of Welding) Institute for Basic Standards (of NBS) (disbanded 1978) Ionospheric Beacon Satellite
IBSA	Independent Battery Specialists Association
IBSAC	Industrialized Building Systems and Components
IBSAT	Indexing By Statistical Analysis Techniques
IBSCA	Ion Beam Spectrochemical Analysis
IBSFC	International Baltic Sea Fishery Commission
IBSR	Individual Battle Shooting Range
IBT	Incompatible Blood Transfusion Integrated Business Terminal Ion-Implantation Base Transistor Technology
IBTTA	International Bridge and Tunnel-Turnpike Association (USA)
IBVL	Institut voor Bewaring van Landbowprodukten (Netherlands) (Institute for Storage and Processing of Agricultural Produce)
IBW	Impulse Bandwith
IBWC	International Boundary and Water Commission (USA)
IBWC-PRB	International Boundary and Water Commission, Planning and Reports Branch (USA)
IBWM	International Bureau of Weights and Measures
IC	Immunocytochemistry Industrialized Country Information Circular Inspiratory Capacity Integrated Circuit Intermittent Claudication Internal Combustion Ion Chromatography
ICA	Ignition Control Additive

	Index of Competitive Ability
	Information Centre for Aeronautics (NAL) (India)
	Institute of Chartered Accountants in England and Wales
	Inter-Governmental Council for Automatic Data Processing
	International Cartographic Association
	International Chiropractors Association (USA)
	International Communications Association
	International Congress on Acoustics
	International Cooperative Alliance
	International Council for ADP in Government Administration
	International Council on Archives
ICAA	International Civil Airports Association (France)
	International Council on Alcohol and Addictions (Switzerland)
ICAD	Integrated Control And Display
	Inter-American Committee for Agricultural Development
ICADE	Interactive Computer-Aided Design Evaluation
ICADS	INTERDATA Computer Aided Drafting System
ICAES	International Congress of Anthropological and Ethnological Sciences
ICAEW	Institute of Chartered Accountants in England and Wales
ICAF	Industrial College of the Armed Forces (USA)
	International Committee on Aeronautical Fatigue
ICAFI	International Commission of Agricultural and Food Industries
ICAI	Institute of Chartered Accountants in Ireland
	International Commission for Agricultural Industries
ICAITI	Instituto Centroamericano de Investigacion y Technologia Industrial (Central American Research Institute for Industrial Technology) (Guatemala)
ICAM	Institute of Corn and Agricultural Merchants
	Integrated Communications Access Method
	Integrated Computer-Aided Manufacturing
ICAMC	International Conference on Automation of Mines and Collieries
ICAN	International Committee of Air Navigation
ICAO	International Civil Aviation Organisation (Canada) (of UN)
ICAP	Instituto Centroamericano de Administracion Publica (Costa Rica) (Central American Institute of Public Administration)
	International Committee of Architectural Photogrammetry (of ICOMOS and ISP)
	International Congress of Applied Psychology
ICAPR	Inter-departmental Committee on Air Pollution Research
ICAPS	Integrated (Aircraft) Carrier Acoustic Prediction System
	Integrated Carrier Anti-submarine-warfare Prediction System
	Integrated Command Acoustic Prediction System
ICAR	Indian Council of Agricultural Research (India)
ICARDA	International Centre for Agricultural Research in Dry Areas
ICARE	Instituto Chileno de Administracion Racional de Empresas (Chile) (chilean Institute of Management)
ICARVS	Interplanetary Craft for Advanced Research in the Vicinity of the Sun
ICAS	Institute of Chartered Accountants of Scotland
	Inter-departmental Committee for Atmospheric Sciences (of Federal Council for Science and Technology (USA))
	International Conference on Atomic Spectroscopy
	International Council of the Aeronautical Sciences
ICASSP	International Conference on Acoustics, Speech and Signal Processing
ICAT	International Convention of Amateurs in Television
ICATS	Intermediate Capacity Automated Telecommunications System (of AFCS (USAF))
ICAW	International Conference on Automation in Warehousing
ICB	International Congress of Biochemistry
	International Container Bureau
ICBA	International Community of Booksellers Associations (Australia)
ICBAM	Interpersonal Communication Behaviour Analysis Method
ICBL	International Conference on the Biology of Lipids
ICBM	Inter-Continental Ballistic Missile
ICBO	International Conference of Building Officials (USA) (now part of CABO)
ICBP	International Committee for Bird Protection
	International Council for Bird Preservation
ICC	Information Center Complex (Oak Ridge National Laboratory (USA))
	International Association for Cereal Chemistry
	International Chamber of Commerce (France)
	International Computation Centre (Italy)
	International Conference on Communications
	International Coordinating Committee for the Presentation of Science and the Development of Out-of-School Scientific Activities (Belgium)
	Interstate Commerce Commission (USA)
	Inverted Common Collector
ICCA	Independent Computer Consultants Association (USA)
	International Computer Chess Association
	International Conference on Computer Applications in Developing Countries
	International Corrugated Case Association
ICCAD	International Centre for Computer Aided Design
ICCAIA	International Coordinating Council of Aerospace Industries Associations
ICCAP	International Co-ordination Committee for the Accountancy Profession (succeeded by the International Federation of Accountants in 1977)
ICCAS	International Conference on Computer Applications in the Automation of Shipyard Operation and Ship Design
ICCAT	International Commission for the Conservation of Atlantic Tunas (of FAO)
ICCC	IEEE (USA) Conference on Computer Communications
	Imperial College Computing Centre
	International Conference on Co-ordination Chemistry
	International Conference on Computer Communication
	International Congress on Construction Communications
	International Council for Computer Communication
ICCDP	Integrated Circuit Communications Data Processor
ICCE	International Council for Correspondence Education
ICCG	International Conference on Crystal Growth
ICCH	International Commodities Clearing House
	International Conference on Computers and the Humanities
ICCLA	International Centre for Coordination of Legal Assistance (Switzerland)
ICCM	Inadequate Core Cooling Monitors
	International Conference on Composite Materials

ICCME Intersociety Council on Continuing Medical Education (USA)

ICCO International Carpet Classification Organization (Belgium)

ICCP Impressed Current Cathodic Protection
Information, Computers and Communications Policy (a working party of OECD)
Institute for Certification of Computer Professionals (USA)
International Conference on Cataloguing Principles

ICCS International Committee of Contamination Control Societies

ICD Immune Complex Disease
Initiative Communications Deception
Interface Control Document
International Classification of Diseases (of WHO)
Ion Controlled Diode
Isocitric Dehydrogenase

ICD-O International Classification of Diseases for Oncology (of WHO(UN))

ICDA International Classification of Diseases Adapted for Use in the United States
International Coalition for Development Action

ICDB Integrated Corporated Data Base

ICDC Indian Cotton Development Council (India)

ICDDR International Centre for Diarrhoeal Diseasesn Research

ICDDR,B International Centre for Diarrhoeal Diseases, Bangladesh (Bangladesh)

ICDH Isocitrate Dehydrogenase

ICDLI International Committee for the Decorative Laminate Industry (of the EEC and Scandinavia)

ICDO International Civil Defence Organisation
International Civil Defense Organization (Switzerland)

ICDRG International Contact Dermatitis Research Group

ICDT Institutual Central de Documentare Tehnica (Rumania) (Central Institute for Technical Documentation)

ICE In-Car Entertainment
In-Circuit Emulation or Emulator
Initial Cooling Experiment
Institute of Consumer Ergonomics
Institution of Civil Engineers
Instituto Costarricense de Electricidad (Costa Rica) (Institute of Electricity)
Integrated Cooling for Electronics
Interference Cancellation Equipment
Internal Combustion Engine
International (Halley's) Comet Explorer (of NASA (USA))
Inventory Control Effectiveness (US Army)
IOMTR Committee for Europe

ICEA Insulated Cable Engineers Association (USA)
International Consumer Electronics Association

ICEC International Cryogenic Engineering Conference

ICECAP Infrared Chemistry Experiments—Coordinated Auroral Program (part of HAES program sponsored by the Defense Nuclear Agency (USDOD))

ICECS Integrated Closed-loop Environmental Control System

ICED Inter-professional Commission on Environmental Design (USA)

ICEE Iranian Conference on Electrical Engineering (Iran)

ICEF International Conferences on Environmental Future

ICEL Industry Committee for Emergency Lighting
Instituto Colombiano de Energia Electrica (Colombia) (an agency of the Ministry of Public Works)
International Council of Environmental Law (Germany)

ICELA International Computer Exposition for Latin America

ICEM Intergovernmental Committee for European Migration (Switzerland)
International Council for Educational Media

ICEMES International Cooperation on Marine Engineering Systems

ICEP Intra-Corporate Entrepreneurial Programme

ICES Integrated Civil Engineering System
International Conference of Engineering Societies
International Council for the Exploration of the Sea

ICESA International Conference on Environmental Sensing and Assessment

ICET Institute for the Certification of Engineering Technicians (USA)

ICETEX Instituto Colombiano da Especializacion Tecnica en el Exterior (Colombia) (Colombian Institute for Advanced Training Abroad)

ICETK International Committee of Electrochemical Thermodynamics and Kinetics (now International Society of Electrochemistry)

ICETRAN Integrated Civil Engineering System FORTRAM

ICETT Industrial Council for Educational and Training Technology
Industrial Council for Training and Technology

ICEUM International Conference on Energy Use Management

ICF Inertial Confinement Fusion
International Congress on Fracture
International Cultural Foundation

ICFA International Committee for the Future of Accelerators (of ICSU)

ICFC Industrial and Commercial Finance Corporation (merged into FFI1973)

ICFET Inhomogeneous Channel Field-Effect Transistor

ICFG International Cold Forging Group

ICFM In-Core Fuel Management
Inlet Cubic Feet per Minute

ICFR Inter-departmental Committee on Futures Research (of Ministry of State for Science and Technology (Canada))

ICFS International Conference on Fluid Sealing

ICFTU International Confederation of Free Trade Unions

ICG Inter-Union Commission on Geodynamics (France) (of ICSU)
Interactive Computer Graphics
International Commission on Glass

ICGA Imperial Continental Gas Association (British public utility holding Company)

ICH Institute of Child Health

ICHCA International Cargo Handling Co-ordination Association

IChemE Institution of Chemical Engineers

ICHS Interafrican Committee for Hydraulic Studies

ICHSPP International Congress on High Speed Photography and Photonics

ICHT International Committee on Haemostasis and Thrombosis

ICHTSP International Conference on the Hydraulic Transport of Solids in Pipes

ICI Interagency Committee on Intermodal Cargo (of DOT, CAB, FMC, and ICC (USA))
International Copyright Information Centre (of UNESCO)
Investment Casting Institute (USA)

ICIASF International Congress on Instrumentation in Aerospace Simulation Facilities

ICIC International Copyright Information Centre (of UNESCO)
ICICI Industrial Credit and Investment Corporation of India (India)
ICID International Commission on Irrigation and Drainage
ICIE International Centre for Industry and the Environment
ICIPE International Centre of Insect Physiology and Ecology (Kenya)
ICIREPAT Paris Union Committee for International Cooperation in Information Retrieval among Patent Offices
ICIS International Conference on Ion Sources
ICISS Impact Collision Ion-Scattering Spectroscopy
ICITA International Co-operative Investigations of the Tropical Atlantic (of UNESCO)
ICLA International Commission on Laboratory Animals
ICLARM International Center for Living Aquatic Resources Management (Philippines)
ICLC International Congress on Lightweight Concrete
ICLCUA ICL Computer Users Association
ICLG International and Comparative Librarianship Group (of the Library Association)
ICLM Induced Course Load Matrix
ICLRN Interagency Council on Library Resources for Nursing (USA)
ICM Improved Capability Missile
Improved Conventional Munitions
Institute for Complementary Medicine
Institute for Composite Materials (USA)
Institute of Credit Management
Institution for Computermation Management (USA)
International Conference on the Mechanical Behaviour of Metals
ICM/MIRV Intercontinental Missile/Multiple Independently-guided Re-entry Vehicle
ICMA Industrial Capacitor Manufacturers Association (merged into BCMA in 1978)
Institut de Ceretari pentree Mecanizarea (Romania) (Mechanisation of Agriculture Research Institute)
Institute of Cost and Management Accountants
International Circulation Managers Association
International City Management Association (USA)
ICMBE International Conference on Medical and Biological Engineering
ICMC International Conference on Metallurgical Coatings
International Congress on Metallic Corrosion
ICMCST International Conference on Microelectronics, Circuits and System Theory
ICMEE Institution of Certificated Mechanical and Electrical Engineers (South Africa)
ICMES International Conference on Marine Engineering Systems
ICMF Indian Cotton Mills Federation (India)
ICMH International Commission on Military History
ICMI International Commission of Mathematical Instruction (of
ICMIS Integrated Computerized Management Information System
ICMM Incomplete Correlation Matrix Memory
ICMMA Industrial Cleaning Machine Manufacturers Association (now federated in BEAMA)
ICMMP International Committee on Military Medicine and Pharmacy
ICMOD International Conference on Management of Data
ICMP Interagency Committee on Metric Policy (of DOC (USA))
International Conference on Medical Physics
ICMPH International Centre of Medical and Psychological Hypnosis (Italy)
ICMR Indian Council for Medical Research (India)
ICMRT International Center for Medical Research and Training (of NIH (USA))
ICMS Inbucon Corporate Modelling System
Integrated Circuit and Message Switch
Interdepartmental Committee for Meteorological Services (USA)
ICMSE Interagency Committee on Marine Science and Engineering (USA)
ICMSF International Commission on Microbiological Specifications for Foods
ICMW Inherent Corrective Maintenance Workload
ICN International Council of Nurses (Switzerland)
ICNAF International Commission for the Northwest Atlantic Fisheries
ICNB International Committee of Nomenclature of Bacteria (now International Committee on Systematic Bacteriology (of IAMS))
ICNDT International Committee for Non-Destructive Testing
ICNIA Integrated Communications, Navigation and Identification Avionics
ICNND Interdepartmental Committee of Nutrition for National Defense (USA)
ICNT International Conference on Non-destructive Testing
ICNV International Committee for the Nomenclature of Viruses
ICO Inter-agency Committee on Oceanography (now Interagency Committee on Marine Research Facilities and Education) (USA)
International Coffee Organisation
International Commission for Optics
International Congress of Orientalists (South Africa)
ICOD International Centre for Ocean Development (Canada)
ICOGRADA International Council of Graphic Design Associations (Netherlands)
ICOLD International Congress on Large Dams
ICOM International Council for Museums
ICOMIA International Council of Marine Industry Associations
ICOMOS International Council of Monuments and Sites (France)
ICON Interactive Creation of NASTRAN
ICONS Information Center on Nuclear Standards (of ANS (USA))
ICONTEC Instituto Colombiano de Normas Tecnicas (Colombia) (Standards Institute)
ICOO Iraqi Company for Oil Operations (Iraq)
ICOR Incremental Capital Output Ratios
Interagency Commission on Ocean Resources (USA)
Intergovernmental Conference on Oceanic Research (UNESCO)
ICorrST Institution of Corrosion Science and Technology
ICorrT Institution of Corrosion Technology (amalgamated with CAPA in 1975 to form ICST)
ICOT Institute of Coastal Oceanography and Tides
Institute of New Generation Computer Technology (of MITI (Japan))
ICP Inductively Coupled Plasma
Industry Cooperation Programme (of FAO (UN))
International Center of Photography (USA)
International Classification of Patents (of the Council of Europe)

	International Congress of Pharmacology
	International Institute of Cellular and Molecular Pathology (Belgium)
	Intra-Cranial Pressure
	Investment Corporation of Pakistan (Pakistan)
ICP-OES	Inductively Coupled Plasma-Optical Emission Spectrometry
ICPCI	International Conference on the Performance of Computer Installations
ICPDS	Interactive Continuous Process Dynamic Simulation
ICPE	Internal Combustion Piston Engine
ICPEAC	International Conference on the Physics of Electronic and Atomic Collisions
ICPIG	International Conference on Phenomena in Ionised Gases
ICPL	International Committee of Passenger Lines
ICPM	International Commission on Polar Meteorology
	International Congress of Physical Medicine
ICPO	International Criminal Police Organization (also known as INTERPOL)
ICPP	Idaho Chemical Processing Plant (USAEC)
	Interactive Computer Presentation panel (an international research and development program between the USA and the Federal Republic of Germany)
	International Conference on the Internal and External Protection of Pipes
ICPR	Inter-university consortium for Political Research (USA)
	International Conference on Production Research
	Ion Cyclotron Resonance
ICPS	International Conference on the Properties of Steam
	International Congress of Photographic Science
ICQC	International Conference on Quality Control
ICR	Institute of Cancer Research
	Institution for Creation Research (of the Christian Heritage College (USA))
	Interactive Conflict Resolution
ICRA	International Centre for Research in Accounting (Lancaster University)
ICRAF	International Council for Research in Agroforestry (Kenya)
ICRC	International Committee of the Red Cross (Switzerland)
ICRCL	Interdepartmental Committee on the Redevelopment of Contaminated Land
ICRDB	International Cancer Research Data Bank (of NCI (USA))
ICRF	Imperial Cancer Research Fund
ICRH	Institute for Computer Research in the Humanities (of New York University, USA)
ICRISAT	International Crops Research Institute for the Semi-Arid Tropics (India)
ICRL	Injury Control Research Laboratory (of Community Environmental Management Bureau (HEW (USA))
ICRM	International Committee for Radionuclide Metrology (headquarters at LMRI (France))
ICRMS	Integrated Computer-Reactor Monitoring System
ICRO	International Cell Research Organization
ICRP	International Commission on Radiological Protection
ICRPG	Interagency Chemical Rocket Propulsion Group (USA)
ICRU	International Commission on Radiological Units (now International Commission on Radiation Units and Measurements) (USA)
ICRUM	International Commission on Radiation Units and Measurements (USA)
ICS	Information Control System
	Institute of Computer Science
	Integrated Composite Spinning
	Integrated Conning System
	International Chamber of Shipping
	International College of Surgeons
	International Computing Symposium
	International Continence Society
	Intra-cranial Stimulation
	Intracranial Self-stimulation
	Ionization Current Source
ICSA	Institute of Chartered Secretaries and Administrators
ICSB	International Committee on Systematic Bacteriology (of IAMS)
ICSC	Inter-ocean Canal Study Commission (USA)
	Interim Communications Satellite Commission (the Board of Governors of INTELSAT)
	International Civil Service Commission (of UN)
ICSDV	Ice-Cutter Semi-submersible Drilling Vessel
ICSEAF	International Commission for the South East Atlantic Fisheries (Spain)
ICSEMS	International Commission for the Scientific Exploration of the Mediterranean Sea
ICSH	Interstitial Cell Stimulating Hormone
ICSHB	International Committee for Standardization in Human Biology (Belgium)
ICSI	International Commission of Snow and Ice (of IASH)
	International Conference on Scientific Information
ICSID	International Centre for Settlement of Investment Disputes (USA)
	International Council of Societies of Industrial Design (Belgium)
ICSL	Interactive Continuous Simulation Language
ICSOBA	International Congress on Bauxite-Alumina-Aluminium
ICSP	Interagency Committee on Standards Policy (USA)
ICSPRO	Inter-Secretariat Committee on Scientific Programmes Related to Oceanography (of IOC (UNESCO))
ICSSD	International Committee for Social Sciences Documentation
ICSSR	Indian Council for Social Science Research (India)
ICST	Imperial College of Science and Technology
	Institute for Computer Sciences and Technology (of NBS (USA))
	Institution of Corrosion Science and Technology
ICSU	International Council of Scientific Unions (Italy)
ICSU/AB	ICSU Abstracting Board
ICT	Institution of Corrosion Technology (amalgamated with CAPA in 1975 to form ICST)
	Insulating Core Transformer
	International Council of Tanners
ICTA	International Confederation for Thermal Analysis
	International Conference on Thermal Analysis
ICTAF	Interdisciplinary Centre for Technological Analysis and Forecasting (Tel-Aviv University (Israel))
ICTAM	International Congress of Theoretical and Applied Mechanics
ICTB	International Customs Tariffs Bureau
ICTED	International Co-operation in the field of Transport Economics Documentation (of ECMT (OECD))
ICTF	International Coca Trades Federation
	International Conference on Thin Films
ICTME	International Conference on Tribo-Terotechnology and Maintenance Engineering
ICTP	International Centre for Theoretical Physics (Italy) (of IAEA and UNESCO)
ICTS	Integrated Computerised Test Set

	International Centre for Transportation Studies (Italy)
	International Congress on Transplantation
ICTU	Irish Congress of Trade Unions (Eire)
ICU	Interface Control Unit
ICUMSA	International Commission for Uniform Methods of Sugar Analysis
ICUS	International Conference on the Unity of the Sciences
ICV	Infantry Combat Vehicle
	Intracellular Virus
ICVA	International Council of Voluntary Agencies
ICVAN	International Committee on Veterinary Anatomical Nomenclature
ICVD	Isotopic Chemical Vapour Deposition
ICW	Institute of Clerks of Works
	Interrupted Continuous Wave
ICWA	Institute of Cost and Works Accountants (now Institute of Cost and Management Accountants)
	International Coil Winding Association
	Israel Centre for Waterworks Appliances (Israel)
ICWAI	Institute of Cost and Works Accountants of India (India)
ICWAR	Improved Continuous Wave Acquisition Radar
ICWES	International Conference of Women Engineers and Scientists
ICWM	International Committee of Weights and Measures
ICWP	Interstate Conference on Water Problems (USA)
ICY	International Co-operation Year
ICZ	Intertropical Convergence Zone
ICZN	International Commission on Zoological Nomenclature
ID	Industrial Dynamics
	Inside Diameter
	Intermediate Description
	International Division (of GAO (USA))
IDA	Iminodiacetic Acid
	Industrial Development Authority (Eire)
	Inpatient Data Administration
	Institute for Defense Analysis (USA)
	Integrated Digital Access
	Integrated Digital Avionics
	Intermediate Dialect of ATLAS (Abbreviated Test Language for Avionics Systems)
	International Development Association (USA) (of UN)
	Ionospheric Dispersion Analysis
	Iron Deficiency Anaemia
IDAAN	Instituto de Acueductos y Alcantarillados Nacionales (Panama) (Institute of National Aqueducts and Underground Sewers)
IDAB	Industrial Advisory Board
IDAC	Istituto di Acustica (of CNR (Italy)) (Institute of Acoustics)
IDADS	Information Displays Automatic Drafting System
IDAF	International Defence and Aid Fund
IDAMI	Istituto di Documentazione della Associazione Mecanica Italiana (Italy) (Documentation Institute of the Italian Mechanical Association)
IDAPS	Image Data Processing System
IDAS	Industrial Data Acquisition System
IDAST	Interpolated Data and Speech Transmission
IDATE	Institut pour le Developpment et l'Amenagement des Telecommunications et de l'Economie (France) (Institute for the Development and Harnessing of Telecommunications and the Economy)
IDB	Industrial Development Bank (Ireland)
	Inter-American Development Bank (Great Britain became a member in July 1976)
IDBI	Industrial Development Bank of India (India)
IDBRA	International Drivers Behaviour Research Association
IDBT	Industrial Development Bank of Turkey
IDC	Image Dissector Camera
	Imperial Defence College (now RCDS)
	Industrial Development Certificate
	Industrial Development Corporation (South Africa)
	Information Dissemination Committee (of S-CS (IEEE) (USA))
	Insulation Displacement Connector
	Inter-departmental Committee on Publicity for Engineering and Technology (of government departments, the CBI, industry and the nationalised industries)
	International Documentation in Chemistry
	Internationale Dokumentationsgesellschaft fuer Chemie (Germany) (International Documentation Society for Chemistry)
	Iterated Deferred Corrections
IDCA	Industrial Design Council of Australia
	International Development Cooperation Agency (USA)
IDCHEC	Intergovernmental Documentation Centre on Housing and Environment (France)
IDCI	Intradiplochromatid Interchange
IDCMA	Independent Data Communications Manufacturers Association (USA)
IDCOL	Industrial Development Corporation of Orissa Ltd (India)
IDCOOP	Industry Committee for the Development of Offsets to Offshore Procurement (Australia)
IDCS	Image Dissector Camera System
IDD	Insulin-Dependent Diabetes
	Integrated Data Dictionary
	International Direct Dialling
IDDD	International Direct Distance Dialing
IDDE	Instituto para el Desarrollo de la Direccion de Emprasa (Uruguay) (Institute for the Promotion of Scientific Management)
IDDM	Insulin-Dependent Diabetes Mellitus
IDDRG	International Deep-Drawing Research Group
IDE	Industrial Development Executive (of DTI)
	Instituto para Directores de Empresa (Mexico) (Institute for Business Managers)
	Israel Desalination Engineering Ltd. (Israel)
IDEA	Inductive Data Exploration and Analysis
	Information Display Evolution and Advances
	Instituto para el Desarrollo de Ejecutives en la Argentina (Argentina) (Institute for the Development of Managers)
	Integrated Digital Electric Aircraft
	Integrated Digital Electronic Automatic
	Interactive Data Entry/Access
	Interactive Differential Equation Algorithm
IDEAL	Integrated Design Engineering and Logistics
IDEALS	Ideal Design of Effective And Logical Systems
IDEAS	Integrated Design and Analysis System
	Integrated Design and Engineering Automated System
IDECS	Image Discrimination, Enhancement, Combination, Sampling
IDEEA	Information and Data Exchange Experimental Activities (US Army)
IDEL	Instantaneous Drilling Evaluation Log
IDEN	Interactive Data Entry Network
IDEP	Interservice Data Exchange Program (USDOD)
IDEX	Initial Defence Experiment
IDF	International Dairy Federation
	International Dental Federation
	International Diabetes Federation
IDFM	Induced Directional Frequency Modulation

IDFSS Infantry Direct-Fire Simulator System

IDFT Inverse Discrete Fourier Transform

IDG Immunodiffusion in Gel
Integrated Drive-Generator

IDGSS Integrated Digital Grid Switching System

IDH Isocitrate Dehydrogenase

IDHE Institute of Domestic Heating Engineers

IDHEC Institut Des Hautes Etudes Cinematographiques (France) (Institute for Advanced Studies in Cinematography)

IDHS Intelligence Data Handling System

IDI Improved Data Interchange
Institut de Developpement Industriel (France) (Industrial Development Institute)

IDICT Instituto de Documentacion e Informacion Cientifica y Tecnica (Cuba) (Scientific and Technical Documentation and Information Institute)

IDIIOM INFORMATION DISPLAYS INCORPORATED Input–Output Machine

IDIS Institut fur Dokumentation und Information uber Sozialmedizin und offentliches Gesundheitwesen (Germany) (Institute for Documentation and Information on Social Medicine and Public Health)
Intrusion Detection and Identification System

IDM Institute of Defence Management (India)
International Data Management (India) ("a workers' sector company") (a company formed to take over from INTERNATIONAL BUSINESS Machines in 1978)
Ion Drift Meter

IDMA Indian Drug Manufacturers Association (India)

IDMH Input Destination Message Handler

IDML Internal Data Manipulation Language

IDMS Integrated Database Management System

IDN Integrated (Switching and transmission) Digital Network

IDNE Inertial-Doppler Navigation Equipment

IDOC Inner Diameter of Outer Conductor

IDOE International Decade of Ocean Exploration (of IOC (UNESCO))

IDORT Instituto de Organizacao Racional do Trabalho (Brazil) (Institute of Management)

IDP Institute of Data Processing (merged in IDPM 1978)
Integrated Data Processing
Internal Design Pressure

IDPL Indian Drugs and Pharmaceuticals Limited (India) (Government owned)

IDPM Institute of Data Processing Management (formed April 1978 absorbing DPMA and IDP)

IDR Integrated Dry Route

IDRC International Development Research Centre (Canada)

IDRES Institute for the Development of Riverine and Estuarine Systems (Franklin Institute Research Laboratories (USA))

IDRO Industrial Development and Renovation Organization (Iran)

IDS Image Dissector Scanner
Institute of Development Studies
Integrated Data Store
Interdiction OR Interdictor Strike
Interim Decay Storage
International Dendrology Society

IDSA Institute for Defence Studies and Analysis (India)

IDSC International Demographic Statistics Center (of Population Division, Census Bureau, Department of Commerce (USA))

IDSCS Initial Defense Satellite Communications System (formerly Initial Defense Communications Satellite Program) (USDOD)

IDSS Integral Direct Station Selection

IDT Institut fur Datenverarbeitung (of Kernsforschungszentrum Karlsruhe (Germany))
Inter-Digital Transducer
Interactive Display Terminal
Isodensitracer

IDTS Improved Doppler Tracking System
Instrumentation Data Transmission System

IDU Idoxuridine
Independent Distinct Units
Industrial Development Unit

IDVM Integrating Digital Voltmeter

IDW Institut fur Dokumentationwesen (Germany) (Institute for Documentation Projects)

IDWR Interim Design and Workmanship Rules (issued by DOE)

IE Institution of Engineers (India)
Integral Electronics
Intensive Electrification

IE(Aust) Institution of Engineers, Australia

IE(I) Institution of Engineers (India)

IEA Indian Engineering Association (India)
Institut Elektrosvarki (USSR) (Electric Welding Institute)
Institute of Economic Affairs
Institute of Environmental Sciences (USA)
Instituto de Energia Atomica (Brazil) (Atomic Energy Institute)
Instruments, Electronics, Automation exhibition
Integral Error Squared
International Energy Agency (of OECD)
International Ergonomics Association
Intrinsic Electric Strength

IEAB Internacia Esperanto-Asocio de Bibliotekistoj (International Association for Esperanto Speaking Librarians)

IEAust Institution of Engineers, Australia

IEBM Interplay of Engineering with Biology and Medicine (a committee of the National Academy of Engineering (USA))

IEC Information Exchange Centre (of CISTI (Canada))
Integrated Electronics Components
International Electrotechnical Commission
Israel Electric Corporation (Israel) (Government controlled)

IECCA Inter-Establishment Committee for Computer Applications (of MOD (PE))

IECE Institute of Electronics and Communication Engineers (Japan)

IECEC Inter-society Energy Conversion Engineering Conference (of ASME, IEEE, and AICHE (USA))

IECEJ Institute of Electronics and Communication Engineers of Japan (Japan)

IECI Industrial Electronics and Control Instrumentation

IECIC International Engineering and Construction Industries Council (USA)

IECMS In-flight Engine Conditioning Monitoring System

IECPS International Electronic Packaging Symposium

IECQA International Electrotechnical Commission Quality Assessment

IED Improvised Explosive Device
Individual Effective Dose
Institution of Engineering Designers
Integrated Environmental Design

IEDD Improvised Explosive Device Disposal

IEDM International Electron Devices Meeting

IEDS Integrated Engineering Design Service

IEE Institution of Electrical Engineers

IEEE Institute of Electrical and Electronics Engineers (USA)

IEEE-PES IEEE (USA) Power Engineering Society

IEEF Ion-Exchange-Evaporation-Filter

IEEFI	Institut Europeen pour l'Etude de Fibres Industrielles (European Institute for the Study of Industrial Fibres)
IEEJ	Institute of Electrical Engineers of Japan (Japan)
IEETE	Institution of Electrical and Electronics Technician Engineers
IEF	Integral Equation Formulation
	International Environment Forum (USA) (sponsored by CIEI (USA))
	Isoelectric Focusing
IEG	Information Exchange Group
	Internal Engine Generagor
IEI	Institute of Electrical Inspectors (Australia)
	Institution of Engineering Inspection (now Institute of Quality Assurance)
	Institution of Engineers of Ireland
IEIA	Installation Environmental Impact Assessment
	Integrated Educational Information System
IEIC	Iowa Educational Information Center (University of Iowa, USA)
IEJE	Institut Economique et Juridique de l'Energie (France) (Energy Economic and Legal Institute)
IEM	Institut Elektromekhaniki (USSR) (Institute of Electromechanics)
	Ion-Exchange Membranes
IEMA	Indian Electrical Manufacturers Association (USA)
IEMATS	Improved Emergency Message Automatic Transmission System (of AUTODIN)
IEMP	Internal Electromagnetic Pulse
IEN	Institut d'Etudes Nucleaires (Algeria) (Institute of Nuclear Studies)
	Istituto Elettrotecnico Nazionale (Italy) (National Electrotechnical Institute)
IENS	Indian and Eastern Newspaper Society (India)
IEOP	Immunoelectroosmophoresis
IEOR	Department of Industrial Engineering and Operations Research (Southern Methodist University (USA))
IEP	International Education Project (of the American Council on Education (USA))
	Isoelectric Point
IEPG	Independent European Programme Group
	Independent European Programme Group (of the WEU)
IER	Institutes for Environmental Research (of ESSA)
IERE	Institution of Electronic and Radio Engineers
IERF	Industrial Educational and Research Foundation
IES	Illuminating Engineering Society (amalgamated with CIBS 1977)
	Illuminating Engineering Society (USA)
	Invariant-Ellipticity States
	Inverted Echo Sounder
IESA	Illuminating Engineering Society of Australia (Australia)
	Indiana Electronic Service Association (USA)
	Instituto de Estudios de Administracion (Venezuela) (Institute for Advanced Management Studies)
IESC	International Executive Service Corps (USA)
IESE	Instituto de Estudios Superiores de la Empresa (Spain) (Institute for Advanced Management Studies)
IESL	Institution of Engineers Sri Lanka (Sri Lanka)
IESS	Institution of Engineers and Shipbuilders in Scotland
	Instituto Ecuatoriano de Seguridad Social Ecudor) (Ecuadorian Institute of Social Security)
IESUA	Institut de l'Energie Solaire de l'Université d'Alger (Algeria) (Institute of Solar Energy of the University of Algiers)
IET	Institute of Educational Technology
IETCC	Instituto Eduardo Torroja de la Construccion y del Cemento (Spain)
IETEL	Instituto Ecuatoriano de Telecomunicaciones (Ecuador) (Telecommunications Administration of Ecuador)
IETS	Industrial Energy Thrift Scheme (of DOI)
	Inelastic Electron Tunneling Spectroscopy
IEVD	Integrated Electronic Vertical Display
IEWS	International Electronic Warfare System
IEX	Institute of Export
IExpE	Institute of Explosive Engineers
IF	Immunofluorescence
	Information Feedback
	Institute of Fuel
IFA	In-Flight Alignment
	Indirect Fluorescent Antibody
	Institut Fiziki Atmosfery (USSR) (Atmospheric Physics Institute)
	Institutt For Atomenergi (Norway) (Atomic Energy Institute)
	Instrumented Fuel Assembly
	Integrated File Adaptor
	Interface Adapter
	International Federation of Airworthiness
	International Fighter Aircraft
	International Fiscal Association
	Inverse-Function Amplifier
	Israel Futorologist Association (Israel)
	Istituto di Fisica dell Atmosfera (Italy) (Institute of Atmospheric Physics)
IFAA	International Flight Attendants Association
IFAC	International Federation for Automatic Control
	International Federation of Accountants
	International Industrial Finishing and Anti-Corrosion Exhibition
IFAC/IFIP SOCOCO	IFAC/IFIP Symposium on Software for Computer Control
IFACPRP	IFAC Conference on Instrumentation and Automation in the Paper, Rubber and Plastics Industries
IFAD	International Fund for Agricultural Development
IFAI	International Fire Administration Institute (State University of New York (USA))
IFAM	Information Systems for Associative Memories
IFAN	International Federation for the Application of Standards
IFAP	International Federation of Agricultural Producers
	Istituto Formazione Addestramento Professionale (of IRA (Italy) (Administration Training Institute)
IFAPT	Compagnie Internationale d'Informatique APT (Automatically Programmed Tools)
IFAS	International Federation for the Application of Standards
IFAT	Indirect Fluorescent Antibody Technique
	Indirect Fluorescent Antibody Test
	Indirect Immunofluorescence Test
IFATCA	International Federation of Air Traffic Controllers Associations
IFATCC	International Federation of Associations of Textile Chemists and Colourists (Switzerland)
IFATE	International Federation of Aerospace Technology and Engineering
	International Federation of Airworthiness Technology and Engineering (now International Federation of Airworthiness)
IFAWPCA	International Federation of Asian and Western Pacific Contractors Associations
IFB	Invitation For Bid
IFC	Industrial Finance Corporation (India)
	Institut Français du Caoutchouc (France) (French Rubber Institute)

Instrument Flight Center (USAF)
Inter-Firm Comparison
International Finance Corporation (USA) (of UN)
International Formulation Committee (OF International Conference on the Properties of Steam)
International Foundry Congress

IFCAS Integrated Flight Control and Augmentation System

IFCATI International Federation of Cotton and Allied Textile Industries

IFCB International Federation for Cell Biology

IFCC International Federation of Clinical Chemistry

IFCE Institut Francaise des Combustibles et de l'Energie (France) (French Institute of Fuels and Energy)

IFCI Industrial Finance Corporation of India (India)

IFCS Improved (Artillery) Fire Control System
In-Flight Checkout System
Integrated Fire Control System

IFD Internal Friction Damping

IFDO International Federation of Data Organizations

IFE Institution of Fire Engineers
Instituto de Fomento Economico (Panama) (Institute for Economic Development)

IFEBS Integrated Foreign Exchange and Banking System

IFEG Information for Energy Group

IFEMS International Federation of Electron Microscopes Societies

IFF Identification Friend or Foe
Institute For the Future (USA)
Institute of Freight Forwarders
International Flying Farmers (an association-membership mainly from USA, Canada and Mexico)

IFFCO Indian Farmers Fertiliser Co-operative Ltd (India) (partly government owned)

IFFJP International Federation of Fruit Juice Producers

IFFN Identification, Friend, Foe, Neutral

IFFSH Instrument Formation Flight System for Helicopter

IFFT Inverse Fast Fourier Transform

IFGO International Federation of Gynaecology and Obstetrics

IFHE International Federation of Hospital Engineering

IFHP International Federation for Housing and Planning

IFHPM International Federation of Hydraulic Platform Manufacturers

IFHTM International Federation for the Heat Treatment of Materials

IFI Industrial Fasteners Institute (USA)
Instituto de Fomento Industrial (Colombia) (govt. owned)

IFIA International Fence Industry Association (USA)

IFIAS International Federation of Institutes for Advanced Studies (Sweden)

IFIE Instituto Forestal de Investigaciones y Experiencias (Spain) (Institute for Forestry Research and Development)

IFIP International Federation for Information Processing (Switzerland)
International Food Irradiation Project (of ENEA, IAEA and FAO)

IFireE Institution of Fire Engineers

IFIS Infra-red Flight Inspection System
International Food Information Service

IFKh Institut Fizicheskoy Khimii (USSR) (Physical Chemistry Institute)

IFL Integer Function Language

IFLA International Federation of Landscape Architects
International Federation of Library Associations (renamed International Federation of Library Associations and Institutions in 1976)
International Finance and Leasing Association

IFM Instantaneous Frequency Measurement
Institut Fiziki Metallov (USSR) (Physics of Metals Institute)

IFMA International Federation of Margarine Associations
International Foodservice Manufacturers Association (USA)

IFMBE International Federation for Medical and Biological Engineering

IFME International Federation of Medical Electronics (now International Federation for Medical and Biological Engineering)
International Federation of Municipal Engineers

IFMI Irish Federation of Marine Industries (Eire)

IFMIS Integrated Facilities Management Information System (US Army)

IFN Institut Français de Navigation (France) (French Institute of Navigation)

IFORS International Federation of Operational Research Societies

IFOV Instantaneous Field-Of-View

IFP Institut Francaise du Petrole (France) (French Institute of Petroleum)
International Federation of Purchasing

IFPA Information Film Producers of America (USA)

IFPM In-Flight Performance Monitor

IFPMA International Federation of Pharmaceutical Manufacturers Association (Switzerland)

IFPMM International Federation of Purchasing and Materials Management

IFPRI International Food Policy Research Institute (USA)

IFPS Interactive Financial Planning System
International Fluid Power Symposium

IFPWA International Federation of Public Warehousing Associations

IFR Immediate Free Recall
Increasing Failure Rate
Institute of Fisheries Research (University of North Carolina, USA)
Instrument Flight Rules
prefix to numbered series of Imported Food Regulations issued by MAFF

IFRA Inca-Fiej Research Association (Germany)
Increasing Failure Rate Average

IFRB International Frequency Registration Board (of ITU)

IFRC International Fusion Research Council
International Futures Research Conference

IFRF International Flame Research Foundation

IFRI Inland Fisheries Research Institute (Sudan)

IFROLS Integrated FRESNEL Rainbow Optical Landing System

IFS Institute of Fiscal Studies
Institute of Fundamental Studies (Sri Lanka)
Instrumentation Field Station (of USPHS)
Integrated Facilities system (US Army)
Internal Focus Sensor
International Federation of Surveyors
International Foundation for Science (Sweden)
Iron Fortified common Salt
prefix to numbered series of Instrument Fact Sheets issued by NOIC (of NOAA (USA))

IFSCC International Federation of Societies of Cosmetic Chemists

IFSEA International Food Service Executives Association (USA)

IFSI Istituto di Fisica dello Spazio Interplanetario (Italy) (Institute of Interplanetary Space Physics)

IFSMA International Federation of Ship Master Associations
IFSS International Flight Service Station
IFSSEC International Fire, Security and Safety Exhibition and Conference
IFSTD Islamic Foundation for Science, Technology and Development (headquarters in Jeddah)
IFT Indirect Fluorescent Antibody Test
Institute of Food Technologists (USA)
Interfacial Tension
Isolation Functional Testing
IFTC International Federation of Thermalism and Climatism
International Film and Television Council (Italy)
IFTDO International Federation of Training and Development Organisations
IFTF International Fur Traders Federation
IFToMM International Federation for the Theory of Machines and Mechanisms
IFV Infantry Fighting Vehicle
IFVME Inspectorate of Fighting Vehicles and Mechanical Equipment (MOD) (now QUAD (FVE))
IFYGL International Field Year of the Great Lakes (a joint USA and Canada project, 1972)
IFZ Institut Fiziki Zemli (USSR) (Institute of Physics of the Earth)
IG Instructor's Guide
Iris Guide
IGA Insulation Glazing Association
International General Aviation
International Glaucoma Association
International Grenfell Association
IGAAS Integrated Ground/Airborne Avionics System
IGAEA International Graphic Arts Education Association (USA)
IGAT Iranian Gas Truck Pipeline (of National Iranian Oil Company) (between Iran and USSR)
IGBS International Gas Bearings Symposium
IGC Institute for Graphic Communication (USA)
Intergranular Corrosion
International Geological Congress
International Geophysical Committee
IGCA Industrial Gas Cleaning Association
International Garden Centres Association
IGCP International Geological Correlation Programme (of IUGS and UNESCO)
IGD Institut Gornogo Dela (USSR) (Institute of Mining)
Institute of Grocery Distribution
IGDS Iodine Generating and Dispensing System
IGE Institution of Gas Engineers
IGEMS Interactive Generalised Modeling System
IGER Institut National de Gestion et d'Économie Rurale (France) (National Institute of Rural Management and Economy)
IGES Initial Graphics Exchange Specification
IGF Insulin-like Growth Factor
IGFET Insulated Gate Field Effect Transistor
IGFVP Interservice Group for Flight Vehicle Power (USA) (now IAPG)
IgG Immunoglobulin G
IGGCI International Geological/Geophysical Cruise Inventory (of World Data Center-A (USA))
IGGT Institute for Guided Ground Transport (Canada)
IGH Interessengemeinschaft fuer Halonversuche (Switzerland) (Community of Interests in Halon Experiments)
IGI Institut Goryuchikh Iskopayemykh (USSR) (Institute of Mineral Fuels)
IGK Ingenieurgemeinschaft Kernverfahrenstechnik (Germany)
IGLD International Great Lakes Datum
IgM Immunoglobulin M
IGM Instituto Geografico Militar (Paraquay)
Istituto Geografico Militare (Italy) (Military Geography Institute)
IGN Institut Geographique National (France) (National Geographic Institute)
Instituto Geografico Nacional (Guatemala) (National Geographic Institute)
IGO International Governmental Organisation
IGOR Intercept Ground Optical Recorder
IGOSS Integrated Global Ocean Station System (of IOC (UNESCO))
IGP Inverted Groundplane
IGPAI Inspeccao-Geral dos Produtes Agricolas e Industriais (Portugal) (Inspectorate of Agricultural Products and Manufactured Goods)
IGPP Institute of Geophysics and Planetary Physics (of SIO)
IGR Insect Growth Regulator
IGRF International Geomagnetic Reference Field
IGS Inert Gas System
Inertial Guidance System
Institute of Geological Sciences (became British Geological Surveys in 1984)
Institute of Geological Studies (of Natural Environment Research Council)
Institute of Governmental Studies (of University of California (USA))
Integrated Graphics System
Intercapillary Glomerulosclerosis
IGSCC Inter-Granular Stress Corrosion Cracking
IGSN International Gravity Standardisation Net
IGSN71 International Gravity Standardization Net 1971
IGT Institute of Gas Technology (USA)
IGTDS Interactive Graphic Transit Design System
IGTechE Institution of General Technician Engineers
IGTS Interactive Graphic Transit Simulator
IGU International Gas Union
International Geographical Union (USA) (of ICSU)
IGV Infantile Gastroenteritis Virus
Inlet Guide Vane
IGWES Inert Gas Wire Enamel Stripper
IGY International Geophysical Year
IH Industrialized Housing
IHA Indirect Haemagglutination test
Institute of Hospital Administrators
IHADSS Integrated Helmet And Display Sighting System
IHAS Integrated Helicopter Avionics System
IHAT Indirect Haemagglutination Test
IHB International Hydrographic Bureau (of IHO (Monaco))
IHBTD Incompatible Haemolytic Blood Transfusion Disease
IHC Interstate Highway Capability
IHCS Integrated Helicopter Control System
IHD International Hydrological Decade
International Hydrological Decade (of UNESCO)
Ischaemic Heart Disease
IHDGA Indian Hot Dip Galvanizers Association (India)
IHE Insensitive High Explosive
Institution of Highway Engineers (now IHT)
IHEA International Health Evaluation Association
IHETS Indiana (USA) Higher Education Telecommunication System
IHF Industrial Hygiene Foundation of America (USA)
Institute of High Fidelity (USA)
International Hospital Federation
IHI Ishkawajima Harima Heavy Industries (Japan)
IHM Institute of Housing Managers
IHO International Hydrographic Organisation (Monaco)

IHospE Institute of Hospital Engineering
IHP Isostatic Hot Pressing
IHPC International Pacific Halibut Commission (a Canadian and USA agency at the University of Washington (USA)
IHR Infra-red Heterodyne Radiometer
IHS Indian Health Service (of HEW (USA))
Industrial Health and Safety Committee (of British Plastics Federation)
Integrated Heat Sink
Interactive Home Systems
IHSR Improved High Speed Rail
IHSS Integrated Hydrographic Survey System
IHT Institute of Highways and Transportation
IHTS Integrated Hybrid Transistor Switch
IHTU Interservice Hovercraft Trials Unit (MOD) (now IHU)
IHU Instantaneous Unit Hydrograph
Inter-Service Hovercraft Unit (MOD)
IHVE Institution of Heating and Ventilating Engineers (became CIBS in 1976)
IHW International Halley (Halley's comet) Watch
IHX Intermediate Heat Exchanger
II Image Intensification
Ion Implantation
IIA Inflationary Impact Assessment
Information Industries Association (USA)
Institute of Internal Auditors (headquarters in USA)
IIAC Industrial Injuries Advisory Council
IIAF Iranian Imperial Air Force (Iran)
IIAS Inter-American Institute of Agricultural Sciences
International Institute of Administrative Sciences
International Institute of Administrative Services
IIASA International Institute for Applied Systems Analysis (Austria)
IIB Institut International des Brevets (Netherlands) (International Patents Institute) (absorbed into EPO 1977)
International Investment Bank (of COMECON)
IIC Indian Investment Centre (India)
Innovation Information Center (George Washington University (USA))
International Institute for Conservation of Historic and Artistic Works
International Institute for Cotton
International Institute of Communications
Isotopes Information Center (ORNL (USAEC))
Istituto Internazionale delle Comunicazioni (Italy)
IICA Institute of Instrumentation and Control, Australia (Australia)
Instituto Interamericano de Ciencias Agricolas (Costa Rica) (Inter-American Institute of Agricultural Science)
IIChemE Indian Institute of Chemical Engineers (India)
IICL Institute of International Container Lessors
IIE Institute of Industrial Engineers (USA)
IIEC Inter-Industry Emission Control program (USA)
IIED International Institute for Environment and Development
IIEM Indian Institute of Experimental Medicine (India)
IIEP International Institute for Educational Planning (of UNESCO)
IIEQ Illinois Institute for Environmental Quality (USA)
IIF Institut International du Froid (International Institute of Refrigeration)
IIFET International Institute of Fisheries Economics and Trade
IIFT Indian Institute of Foreign Trade (India)
IIHR Iowa University Institute of Hydraulic Research (USA)
IIHS Insurance Institute for Highway Safety (USA)
IIIC International Irrigation Information Centre (Israel)
IIIE Indian Institute of Industrial Engineers (India)
IIL Integrated Injection Logic
IILS International Institute for Labour Studies (of ILO)
IIMA Indian Institute of Management (India)
IIMT International Institute for the Management of Technology (Italy)
IIN Istituto Italiano di Navigazione (Italy) (Italian Institute of Navigation)
IInfSc Institute of Information Scientists
IINTE Instytut Informacji Naukowej, Technicznej i Ekonomicznej (Poland) (Institute for Scientific, Technical and Economic Information)
IIOE International Indian Ocean Expedition
IIP Indian Institute of Packaging (India)
Indian Institute of Petroleum (India)
Institute of Incorporated Photographers
Israel Institute of Petroleum (Israel)
Israel Institute of Productivity (Israel)
Istituto Italiano del Plastici (Italy) (Italian Institute for Plastic Materials)
IIPA Indian Institute of Public Administration (India)
IIPACS Integrated Information Presentation and Control System
IIPE India Institute of Production Engineers (India)
IIPF International Institute of Public Finance
IIR Imaging Infra-Red
Infinite Duration Impulse Response
International Institute of Refrigeration
Isobutylene-isoprene Rubber
IIRA Integrated Inertial Reference Assembly
International Industrial Relations Association
IIRB Institut International de Recherches Betteravieres (Belgium) (International Institute for Sugar Beet Research)
IIRMS INDUSTRIAL INFORMATION'S (Industrial Information Inc. (USA)) Record Management System
IIRS Institute for Industrial Research and Standards (Eire)
IIS Indian Institute of Science (India)
Indonesian Institute of Sciences (Indonesia)
Institut International de la Soudure (International Institute of Welding)
Institute of Industrial Supervisors (later Institute of Supervisory Managers)
Institute of Information Scientists
Integral Information System
Investment Income Surcharge
Istituto Italiano della Saldatura (Italy) (Italian Welding Institute)
IISCO Indian Iron and Steel Company (India) (Government owned)
IISI International Iron and Steel Institute (Belgium)
IISL International Institute of Space Law (France)
IISN Institut Interuniversitaire des Sciences Nucleaires (Belgium) (Inter-University Institute of Nuclear Sciences)
IISO Institution of Industrial Safety Officers
IISRP International Institute of Synthetic Rubber Producers
IISS International Institute for Strategic Studies
IISWM Institute of Iron and Steel Wire Manufacturers
IIT Illinois Institute of Technology (USA)
Indian Institute of Technology (India)
Institute of Information Technology (Japan)
IITA International Institute of Tropical Agriculture (Nigeria)
IITC Insurance Industry Training Council
IITRAN ILLINOIS INSTITUTE OF TECHNOLOGY Translator

IITRI — Illinois Institute of Technology Research Institute (USA)
IIW — Indian Institute of Welders (India); International Institute of Welding
IJCAI — International Joint conference on Artificial Intelligence
IJIRA — Indian Jute Industry's Research Association (India)
IJMA — Indian Jute Mills Association (India)
IJP — Idiopathic Juvenile Periodontitis
IJS-R — prefix to numbered series of reports issued by Nuklearni Institut Jozef Stefan (Yugoslavia)
IK — Institut Kristallografii (USSR) (Institute of Crystallography)
IKAT — Interactive Keyboard And Terminal
IKBS — Intelligent Knowledge Based System
IKE — Institut fuer Kernenergetik und Energiesystem (Institute for Nuclear Energy and Energy Systems) (Stuttgart University)
IKh — Institut Khimii (USSR) (Institute of Chemistry)
IKhF — Institut Khimicheskoi Fiziki (USSR) (Institute of Chemical Physics)
IKO — Institut voor Kernphysisch Ondersoek (Netherlands) (Institute for Nuclear Physics Research)
IKRD — Inverse Kinetics Rod Drop
IKV — Institut fuer Kunststoffverarbeitung (Germany) (Institute for Plastics Manufacture)
IL — Interpretive Language
ILA — All India Library Association (India); Idaho Library Association (USA); Illinois Library Association (USA); Injection Locked Amplifier; Institute of Landscape Architects (now the Landscape Institute); Insurance Logistics Automated; International Law Association
ILAAS — Integrated Light Attack Avionic System
ILAB — International League of Antiquarian Booksellers
ILAC — International Laboratory Accreditation Council
ILACIF — Latin America Institute of Auditing Sciences
ILACS — Integrated Library Administration and Cataloguing System
ILAF — Identical Location of Accelerometer and Force
ILAFA — Instituto Latinoamericano del Fierro y el Acero (Latin-American Iron and Steel Institute)
ILAMA — International Life-saving Appliance Manufacturers Association
ILAMS — Infra-red Laser Atmospheric Monitoring System
ILAP — Instituto Latinoamericano del Plastico (Latin-American Institute of Plastics)
ILAR — Institute of Laboratory Animal Resources (USA)
ILAS — Inter-related Logic Accumulating Scanner
ILB — Import Licensing Branch (Board of Trade); In-shore Life Boat
ILC — Institute of Land Combat (USArmy); International Labelling Centre (of the Consumer Council)
ILCA — International Livestock Centre for Africa (Kenya)
ILCE — Instituto Latinoamericano de la Comunicacion Educativa (Latin-America Institute of Education Communication)
ILCEP — Inter-laboratory Committee on Editing and Publishing (USA)
ILCMC — International Loss Control Management College (USA)
ILCS — Institute of Land Combat Studies (US Army)
ILD — Indentation Load Deflection; Initial Lung Deposit; Injection Laser Diode; Integrating Light Detector
ILDA — Inter Laboratory Data Acceptance
ILEA — Inner London Education Authority
ILEC — Institut de Liaisons d'Etudes des Industries de Consommation (France)
ILEED — Inelastic Low Energy Electron Diffraction
ILEP — International Federation of Anti-Leprosy Associations
ILERA — International League of Esperantist Radio Amateurs
ILF — Inductive Loss Factor
ILIR — In-House Laboratories Independent Research
ILIS — Innovation-Link Investment Scheme (of DTI)
ILL — Institut Laue-Langevin (France) (funded jointly by France, Germany and the United Kingdom)
ILLGB — Low-Level Laser-Guided Bomb
ILLINET — Illinois Library and Information Network (USA)
ILLIP — ILLINOIS (UNIVERSITY (USA)) Integer programming code
ILLODIE-AIF — ILLINOIS (UNIVERSITY (USA)) Logical Design by Implicit Enumeration using the All-interconnection Inequality Formulation
ILLS — Integrated Life Support System; Inter-Laminar Shear Stress
IllumES — Illuminating Engineering Society
ILM — Independent Landing Monitor; Insulin-Like Material
ILMAC — International congress and Exhibition of Laboratory Measurement and Automation Techniques in Chemistry
ILN — International Logistic Negotiations (USDOD)
ILO — Industrial Liaison Officer; Injection Locked Oscillator; International Labour Office (of the International Labour Organization); International Labour Organization (Switzerland) (of UN)
ILPAC — Independent Learning Project for Advanced Chemistry
ILR — Institute of Library Research (University of California (USA)); Instituut voor Landbowteechniek en Rationalisatie (Netherlands) (Institute for Agricultural Techniques and Planning)
ILRAD — International Laboratory for Research on Animal Disease (Kenya)
ILRC — International Laser Radar Conference
ILRI — International Institute for Land Reclamation and Improvement (Netherlands)
ILRV — Integral Launch and Re-entry Vehicle
ILS — Ideal Liquidus Structures; Industrial Law Society; Industrial Liaison Scheme (of MINTECH and later DTI) (disbanded 1973); Instrument Landing System; Integrated Library System; Integrated Logistics Support; International Latitude Service
ILSAM — International Language for Servicing And Maintenance
ILSDM — Improved Light-Scattering Dust Monitor
ILSI — International Life Sciences Institute (USA)
ILSS — Inter-Laminar Shear Strength
ILST — Iterative Least Squares Technique
ILT — Interferometric Landmark Tracker
ILTFS — Injection Laser Terrain Following System
ILTMS — International Leased Telegraph Message Switching (of the British Post Office)
ILTS — Institute of Low Temperature Science (Japan)
ILU — Illinois University (USA); Institute of London Underwriters
ILW — Intermediate-Level Wastes
ILZIC — Indian Lead Zinc Information Centre (India)

ILZRO International Lead Zinc Research Organisation (USA)

IM Infectious Mononucleosis
Information Management
Institute of Marketing and Sales Management
Institutet for Metalforskning (Sweden) (Institute for Metals Research)
Institution of Metallurgists
Instrument Myopia
Instrumentation and Measurement
Inter-Modulation
Intramuscular

IM-S Instrumentation and Measurement Society (of IEEE (USA))

IM/FM Intensity Modulated/Frequency Modulated

IMA Indian Medical Association (India)
Indonesian Mining Association (Indonesia)
Industrial Medical Association (USA) (became AOMA in 1974)
Institute of Mathematics and its Applications
International Management Association
International Mineralogical Association
International Mohair Association
Ion Microprobe Analyzer
Irish Medical Association (Eire)

IMAC Illinois State Library (USA) Microfilm Automated Catalog
Integrated Microwave Amplifier Converter
International Management Advisory Council (of the British Institute of Management)

IMACE Association des Industries Margarinieres des pays de la CEE (Association of Margarine Manufacturing Industries of the Countries of the European Economic Community)

IMACS International Association for Mathematics and Computers in Simulation

IMAD Integrated Multi-sensor Airborne Survey

IMAGE Innovative Management and Administration of Group Insurance at EQUITABLE (LIFE ASSURANCE SOCIETY (USA))
Institut de Mathematiques de Grenoble (France) (Grenoble Institute of Mathematics)
Intruder Monitoring And Guidance Equipment

IMAJ International Management Association of Japan (Japan)

IMAM Instituto Mexicano de Administracion (Mexico) (Mexican Institute of Management)

IMarE Institute of Marine Engineers

IMAS Industrial Management Assistance Survey
International Marine and Shipping Conference

IMash Institut Mashinovedeniya (USSR) (Institute of Machine Science)

IMAT Intermodal Automated Transfer

IMBI Institute of Medical and Biological Illustration

IMBLMS Integrated Medical and Behavioral Laboratory Measurement System (a program of NASA (USA))

IMBM Institute of Municipal Building Management

IMC Image Motion Compensation
Institute of Management Consultants
Institute of Measurement and Control
Instrument Meteorological Conditions
Integrated Maintenance Concept
International Micrographic Conference

IMCAS Interactive Man/Computer Augmentation Systems

IMCE International Meeting of Cataloguing Experts

IMCO Improved Combustion
Intergovernmental Maritime Consultative Organization (of UN) (now IMO)

IMCS Intelligent Motion Control System

IMCYC Instituto Mexicano del Cemento y del Concreto (Mexico) (Mexican Institute for Cement and Concrete)

IMD Incremental Multiple Development
Independent Module Development
Indian Meteorological Department (India)
Institut fuer Maschinelle Dokumentation (Austria) (Institute of Mechanical Documentation)
Institute for Marine Dynamics (Canada)

IMDG International Maritime Dangerous Goods Code (of IMO)

IMDSO Intelligence Materiel Development Support Office (of ECOM (US Army))

IME Industria Macchine Elettroniche (Italy)
Institute of Mining Engineers
Institution of Military Engineers (India)
Institution of Municipal Engineers (incorporated into Institution of Civil Engineers in 1984)
International Magnetospheric Explorer

IMEA Institut d'etudes Metallurgiques et Electroniques Appliquees (Switzerland) (Institute of Studies in Applied Metallurgy and Electronics)

IMEC Information Management Exhibition and Conference

IMechE Institution of Mechanical Engineers

IMEDE Institut pour l'Etude des Methodes de Direction de l'Entreprise (Switzerland) (Institute for the Study of Business Management)

IMEKO International Measurement Congress (now International Measurement Confederation)

IMEP Indicated Mean Effective Pressure

IMER Institute for Marine Environmental Research (of NERC)
Instytut Mechanizacji i Elektrypikacji Rolnictwa (Poland) (Institute for Mechanization and Electrification of Agriculture)

IMet InstitutMekhaniki (USSR) (Institute of Mechanics)

IMET Institut Metallurgii (USSR) (Institute of Metallurgy)
Institute of Metals
International Military Education and Training (a program of USDOD)

IMF Institut de Mecanique des Fluides (France) (Institute of Fluid Mechanics)
Institute of Metal Finishing
Internation Meeting on Ferroelectricity
International Monetary fund (USA) (of UN)

IMFI Industrial Mineral Fiber Institute (USA)

IMFRAD Integrated Multiple Frequency Radar

IMG Inertial Measurement Group
International Modular Group (of CIB)

IMH Institute of Materials Handling

IMHE Institutional Management in Higher Education (a programme of OECD)

IMI Improved Manned Interceptor
Industria Macchine Idrauliche (Italy)
Institute of the Motor Industry
Interim Manned Interceptor
International Management Institute (Switzerland)
Irish Management Institute (Eire)
Israel Military Industries (of Ministry of Defence (Israel))

IMIA International Medical Informatics Association

IMIC Interval Modulation Information Coding

IMID Infrared Miniaturized Intrusion Detector

IMIF International Maritime Industry Forum

IMinE Institution of Mining Engineers

IMINOCO Iranian Marine International Oil Company (Iran) (partly government owned)

IMIS Institute of Medical Illustrators in Scotland
Integrated Management Information System
International Marketing Information Service (of Bureau of International Commerce (USA))

IML Intermediary Musical Language
Intermediate Machine Language

IMLA International Maritime Lecturers Association

IMLS Institute of Medical Laboratory Sciences

IMLSS Integrated Manoeuvring and Life Support System
IMLT Institute of Medical Laboratory Technology
IMM Institute of Mathematical Sciences (New York University (USA))
Institute of Mining and Metallurgy
Integrated Maintenance Management
Isotherm Migration Method
IMMA Ion Microprobe Mass Analysis OR Analyzer
IMMAC Inventory Management and Material Control
IMMAPI International Meeting of Medical Advisers in the Pharmaceutical Industry
IMMD Intensity-Maximizing Multidither
IMMR Institute for Mining and Minerals Research (University of Kentucky) (USA)
IMMS International Material Management Society (USA)
Ion Microprobe Mass Spectrometer
IMO Industrial Medical Officer
International Maritime Organisation (of UN)
International Meteorological Organization
IMOG Inter-Agency Mechanical Operations Group (of USAEC)
IMORL Infrared Mobile Optical Radiation Laboratory (a unit of the Naval Research Laboratory (USN))
IMOS Federal Interagency Task Force on Inadvertent Modification of the Stratosphere (USA)
Ion-implanted Metal Oxide Semiconductor
IMOX Implanted Micro-Oxide
IMP ICL Micromation Pack
Improved Manufacturing Procedures computer programme
Industry Market Potential
Injection into Microwave Plasma
Instrumental Match Prediction
Integrated Macro Package
Integrated Manufacturing Planning
Inter-industry Management Programme
Interactive Machine-language Programming
Interface Message Processor
Interplanetary Monitoring Platform
Intrinsic Multiprocessing
Inventory Management Package
IMPA International Marine Purchasing Association
International Maritime Pilots Association
International Masters Printers Association
IMPAC Information for Management Planning Analysis and Coordination
IMPACT Improved Management of Procurement and Contracting Techniques (US Army)
Information Management for Planning And Control at TAMESIDE
Instructional Model Prototypes Attainable in Computerised Training
Integrated Management Planning and Control Techniques
Integrated Microform Parts Cataloguing system
Intensive Matched Probation and After-Care Treatment
Inventory Management Programme And Control Technique
IMPATT Impact Avalanche and Transit Time
Impact Ionization Avalanche Transit Time
IMPAV Inter-urban Microwave-Powered Air-cushion Vehicle
IMPC International Mineral Processing Congress
International Municipal Parking Congress
Istituto di Arte Mineraria (Italy) (Institute of Mining Engineering)
IMPEL Insurance Management Performance Evaluation, Life
IMPHOS Institut Mondial du Phosphate (France) (World Phosphate Rock Institute)
IMPI International Microwave Power Institute
IMPICS Integrated Manufacturing Programme Information and Control System
IMPOS Interactive Multi-Programming Operating System
IMPRESS Inter-disciplinary Machine Processing for Research and Education in the Social Sciences
IMPRINT Imbricated Programme for Information Transfer
IMPS Integrated Magnetic Propulsion and Suspension
Integrated Master Programming and Scheduling System
Interface Message Processors
IMQ Istituto Italiano del Marchio de Qualità (Italy) (Italian Institution for Quality Branding)
IMR Improved Military Rifle
Institute for Materials Research (of NBS) (disbanded 1978)
Institute for Medical Research (Malaysia)
Institute of Marine Resources (California University (USA))
Institute of Metal Research (China)
IMRA Industrial Marketing Research Association
International Market Research Association
IMRADS Information Management Retrieval And Dissemination System
IMRS International Response System
IMRU Industrial Materials Research Unit (London University)
Library Management Research Unit (Loughborough University) (became Centre for Library and Information Management in 1977)
IMS Division of Inorganic and Metallic Structure (of the National Physical Laboratory)
Index Management System
Industrial Management Society (USA)
Industrial Mathematics Society (USA)
Inertial Measuring Set
Information Management System
Institute for Molecular Science (China)
Institute of Man and Science (USA)
Institute of Management Services
Institute of Manpower Studies (Sussex University)
Institute of Marine Science (University of Miami)
Institute of Mathematical Statistics (Michigan State University (USA))
Instruction Management System
Integrated Manufacturing System
International Magnetospheric Study
Ion Mobility Spectrometer
IMS/SSC International Magnetospheric Study/Satellite Situation Committee (of NASA (USA))
IMS/VS Information Management System/Virtual Storage
IMSCO Initial Maritime Satellite Consortium (six United States and two British oil companies and tanker operators)
IMSE Integrated Mean Square Error
IMSL International Mathematical and Statistical Library (software)
IMSO Institute of Municipal Safety Officers
IMSS Institute for Mathematical Studies in the Social Sciences (USA)
IMSSOC INSTITUTE OF MANPOWER STUDIES System of Occupational Classification
IMSUT Institute of Medical Science, University of Tokyo (Japan)
IMT Independent Model Triangulation
IMTA Indiana Motor Truck Association (USA)
Institute of Municipal Treasurers and Accountants (now Chartered Institute of Public Finance and Accountancy)
Institute of Municipal Treasurers and Accountants (South Africa)
IMTEC International Manpower Training for Educational Change (a branch of CERI (OECD))

IMTMA Indian Machine Tool Manufacturers Association (India)
IMTRAN Implicit Transport
IMU Inertial Measuring Unit
International Mathematical Union (of ICSU)
IMunE Institution of Municipal Engineers (incorporated into Institution of Civil Engineers in 1984)
IMW International Map of the World on the Millionth Scale
IMWIC International Maize and Wheat Improvement Centre (Mexico)
IMWoodT Institute of Machine Woodworking Technology
IMX Inquiry Message Exchange
IN Inertial Navigation
Institute of Navigation (USA))
IN2P3 Institute National de Physique Nucleaire et de Physique des Particules (France) (National Institute of Nuclear and Particle Physics)
INA Industrija Nafte (Yugoslavia) (State Oil Agency)
Institut National Agronomique (France) (National Agronomy Institute)
Institut National de l'Audiovisuel (France) (National Audiovisual Institute)
Institute of Nautical Archaeology (USA)
INAA Instrumental Neutron Activation Analysis
INAC Instituto Nazionale per le Applicazioni del Calco (Italy) (National Institute for Computer Applications)
INACAP Instituto Nacional de Capacitacion Profesional (Chile) (National Institute of Professional Training)
INACH Instituto Antartico Chileno (Chile) (Antarctic Institute of Chile)
INACOL Institut National pour l'Amelioration des Conserves des Legumes (Belgium) (National Institute for the Improvement of Vegetable Preserves)
INAD Instituto Nacional de Administracion para el Desarrollo (Guatemala)
INANTIC Instituto Nacional de Normas Tecnicas Industriales y Certificacion (Peru) (Standards Institute)
INAOE Instituto Nacional de Astrofisica, Optica y Electronica (Mexico)
INAP Inverse Nyquist Analysis Programme
INAPA Instituto Nacional de Aquas Potables y Alcantarillados (Dominica) (National Institute of Public Water Supply and Sewage)
INAR Institute of Northern Agricultural Research (USA)
INAS Inertial Navigation and Attack Systems
INAT Institut National d'Assistance Technique (Belgium) (National Institute of Technical Assistance)
INC Institut National de la Consommation (France) (National Institute on Consumer Affairs)
Instituto Nacional de Canalizaciones (Venezuela) (National Institute of Dredging)
INCA Innovation through Creative Analysis
Intelligence Communications Architecture (USDOD)
Inventory Control and Analysis
Inventory Control and Associated Disciplines
INCAE Instituto Centroamericano de Administracion de Empresas (Nicaragua) (Central American Institute of Business Management)
INCAP Institute of Nutrition for Central America and Panama (Guatemala)
Instituto de Nutricion de Centroamerica y Panama (Guatemala) (Institute of Nutrition of Central America and Panama)
INCAS Integrated Navigation and Collision Avoidance System
INCATEL Instituto de Telecomunicaciones de America Central (El Salvador)
INCB International Narcotics Control Board (of UN)
INCE Institute of Noise Control Engineering (USA)
Instituto Nacional para la Calidad de la Edificacion (Spain) (National Institute for Quality in Construction)
INCEF Institutul de Cercetari Forestiere (Romania) (Institute of Forestry Research)
INCIRS International Communication Information Retrieval System (Florida University (USA))
INCITE Instructional Notation for Computer-controlled Inspection and Test Equipment
INCO International Chamber of Commerce
INCOLDA Instituto Colombiano de Administracion (Colombia) (Colombian Institute of Management)
InCoLSA Indiana Cooperative Library Services Authority (USA)
INCOP Industria Costruzioni Oper Pubbliche (Italy)
INCOR Indian National Committee on Oceanic Research (India)
Intergovernmental Conference on Oceanographic Research
Israeli National Committee for Oceanographic Research (Israel)
INCORA Instituto Colombiano de la Reforma Agraria (Colombia) (Colombian Institute of Agrarian Reform)
INCOS Integrated Control System
INCOSAI International Congress of Supreme Audit Institutions
INCOSPAR Indian National Committee for Space Research (India)
INCPEN Industry Committee for Packaging and the Environment
INCRA International Copper Research Association (USA)
INCRAPLAN Integrated Crew and Aircraft Planning
INCUM Indiana Computer Users Meeting (USA)
IND Investigational New Drug (permits issued by FDA (USA))
INDA Instituto Nacional de Desenvolvimento Agrario (Brazil) (National Institute of Agrarian Development)
International Non-wovens and Disposables Association
INDAC Industrial Data Acquisition and Control
INDAL Indian Aluminium Company Limited (India)
INDC International Nuclear Data Committee (of IAEA)
INDECO Industrial Development Corporation (Zambia)
INDEP Industrias Nacionais de Defesa (Portugal) (National Defence Industries)
INDERENA Instituto Nacionais de los Recursos Naturales Renovables y del Ambiente (Colombia) (National Institute of Renewable Natural Resources and the Environment)
INDEX Inter-NASA Data Exchange
INDI International Neutron Dosimetry Intercomparison (a project of ICRUM)
INDIS Industrial Information System (of UNIDO)
INDITECNOR Instituto Nacional de Investigaciones Tecnologicas y Normalizacion (Chile) (National Institute for Technical Research and Standardisation)
INDO Intermediate Neglect of Differential Overlap
INDOC Information–Documentation and Communication
INDOR Internuclear Double Resonance
INDPRO Indian Committee for Simplifications of External Trade Documents (India)
INDSCAL Individual Differences Scaling
INDT Institute for Non-Destructive Testing (Milwaukee School of Engineering (USA))

INE Institution of Nuclear Engineers
INEA International Electronics Association (Germany)
INEC European Institute of Ecology and Cancer (Belgium)
INECEL Instituto Ecuatoriano de Electrificación (Ecuador) (Insitute of Electrification)
INEL Idaho National Engineering Laboratory (of Nuclear Regulatory Commission (USA))
International Exhibition of Industrial Electronics
INERHI Instituto Ecuatoriano de Recursos Hidrualicos (Ecuador) (Institute of Water Resources)
INF Intermediate-range Nuclear Forces (missiles) (disarmament discussions between USA and USSR-November 1981 to November 1983)
INFANT Iroquois Night Fighter And Night Tracker
INFCE International Nuclear Fuel Cycle Evaluation (a study by IAEA)
INFCO Working Group on Scientific and Technical Information on Standardization (of ISO)
INFIRS Inverted File Information Retrieval System (of UKCIS)
INFLO Integrated Flight Optimization system
INFN Istituto Nazionale di Fisica Nucleare (Italy) (National Institute of Nuclear Physics)
INFO Information Network For Operations
International Information Management Exposition and Conference
INFOL Information Oriented Language
INFOR Information Network and File Organization
INFORM Information for Minnesota (a service provided by a consortium of five libraries in Minnesota (USA))
International Reference Organization in Forensic Medicine and Sciences (USA)
INFORMAC Immediate Information For Merchant And Customer
INFORMAP Information Necessary for Optimum Resource Management and Protection
INFORMS Information Organisation Reporting and Management System
INFOTERM International Information Centre for Terminology (Austrian Standards Institute (Austria))
INFOTERRA International Referral System for Sources of Environmental Information (of the United Nations Environment Programme)
INFREMER Institut Francais de Recherche pour l'Exploitation de la Mer (France)
INFROSS Information Requirements Of the Social Sciences
ING Intense Neutron Generator
INGA Interactive Graphic Analysis
INGO International Non-Governmental Organisation
INGYO International Non-Governmental Youth Organization
INH Instituto Nacional de Hidrocarburos (Spain) (National Institute of Hydrocarbons)
Isonicotinic Acid Hydrazide
INHIGEO International Committee on the History of the Geological Sciences
INI Instituto Nacional de Industria (Spain) (National Institute of Industry)
Istituto Nazionale dell'Informazione (Italy) (National Institute of Information)
INIA Instituto Nacional de Investigaciones Agrarias (Spain) (National Institute for Agrarian Research)
INIBON Institut Nacnoj Informacii i Fundamental'naja Biblioteka po Obscestvennym Naukam (USSR) (INSTITUTE OF SCIENTIFIC INFORMATION AND MAIN LIBRARY OF THE SOCIAL SCIENCES)
INICHAR Institut National de l'Industrie Charbonniere (Belgium) (National Institute of the Coal Industry)
INICTEL Instituto Nacional de Investigacion y Capacitacion de Telecommunciaciones (Peru)
INID Institut National de Informare si Documentare (Romania) (National Institute of Information and Documentation)
INIDCYA Institute for the Intellectual Development of Children and Young Adults (Iran)
INIEX Institut National des Industries Extractives (Belgium)
INII Institutu Nacional de Investigacao Industrial (Portugal) (National Institute for Industrial Research)
INIS International Nuclear Information System (of IAEA)
INKhP Institut Neftekhimicheskikh Protsessov (USSR) (Institute of Petrochemical Processes)
INL Institut National du Logement (Belgium) (National Institute of Dwellings)
INLA International Nuclear Law Association (Belgium)
INLAW Infantry Laser Weapon
INLOGOV Institute of Local Government Studies
INLP Integer Non-Linear Programming
INM Institute of Naval Medicine (MOD)
Instituto Nacional de Meteorologia (Spain)
INMARSAT International Maritime Satellite Organization (of IMCO)
INMAS Institute of Nuclear Medicine and Allied Sciences (India)
INMM Institute of Nuclear Materials Management (USA)
INN Instituto Nacional de Normalización (Chile) (National Standards Institute)
International Nonproprietary Names (for pharmaceutical substances) (of WHO)
INNOTECH Regional Centre for Educational Innovation and Technology (Philippines) (of ASEAN)
INOC Iraq National Oil Company (Iraq) (government owned)
INORCOL Instituto de Normas Colombiana (Colombia) (Standards Institute)
INOSHAC Indian Ocean and Southern Hemisphere Analysis Centre
InP Indium Phosphide
INP Inert Nitrogen Protection
Instituto Nacional de Prevision (Spain) (government procurement agency)
INPADOC International Patent Documentation Centre (Austria)
INPC Irish National Productivity Committee (Eire)
INPE Instituto Nacional de Pesquisas Espaciais (Brazil) (National Institute for Space Research)
INPFC International North Pacific Fisheries Commission
INPI Institut National de la Propriété Industrielle (France) (National Institute of Industrial Patents)
INPLAY Random Access Microfilm Information Retrieval Display System
INPUT Induced Pulse Transient
research division of ADAPSO (USA)
INQUA International Association for Quaternary Research (USA)
INRA Institut National de la Recherche Agronomique (France) (National Institute for Agronomical Research)
Instituto Nacional de la Reforma Agraria (Cuba) (National Institute for Agrarian Reform)
INRAT Institut National de la Recherche Agronomique de Tunisie (Tunisia) (National Research Institute of Agronomy)
INRCA Istituto Nazionale di Ricovero e Cura Anziani (Italy)

INRF Institut National de Recherches Forestieres (Tunisia) (National Institute of Forestry Research)

INRIA Institut National de Recherche en Informatique et en Automatique (France) (National Institute for Research in Data Processing and Automation)

INRS Institut National de Recherche et de Securite pour la prevention des accidents du travail et des maladies professionelles (France) (National Institute for Occupational Safety and Health)
Institut National de recherche Scientifique (Rwanda) (National Institute of Scientific Research)

INRT Instituto Nacional de Racionalizacion del Trabajo (Spain) (National Institute for Business Management)

INS Immigration and Naturalization Service (of the Department of Justice (USA))
Inertial Navigation System
Institute for Nuclear Study (Tokyo University (Japan))
Institute of Naval Studies (of Center for Naval Analyses (USN))
Institute of Nuclear Sciences (of DSIR (New Zealand))
Integrated Network Simulation
Inter-Nation Simulation
Ion-Neutralization Spectroscopy

INSA Indian National Science Academy (India)
Institut National des Sciences Appliquees (France) (National Institute of Applied Sciences)
International Shipowners Association

INSAC International Systems And Computers (a subsidiary of the National Enterprise Board)

INSAT Indian National Satellite

INSCOM Intelligence and Security Command (US Army)

INSDOC Indian National Scientific Documentation Centre (India)

INSEAD Institut Europeen d'Administration des Affaires (France) (European Business Management Institute)

INSEAN Instituto per Studi ed Esperenze di Architettura Navale (Italy) (National Institute for Naval Architecture Research and Testing)

INSEE Institut National de la Statistique et des Etudes Economique (France) (National Institute for Statistics and Economics Studies)

INSERM Institut National de la Sante et de la Recherche Medicale (France) (National Institute of Health and Medical Research)

INSET In-Service Training

INSFOPAL Instituto Nacional de Fomento Municipal (Colombia)

INSIGHT Instructional Systems Investigation Graphic Tool
Interactive System for Investigation by Graphics of Hydrological Trends

INSITE Institutional Space Inventory Technique System
INTER (CORPORATION) (USA) Software Index and Technology Exchange

INSJ Institute for Nuclear Study, Tokyo University (Japan)

INSONA Indian Society of Naturalists (India)

INSORA Instituto de Organizacion y Administracion (Chile)

INSPEC Information Service for the Physics and Engineering Communities (of IEE)
Information Services in Physics, Electro-technology, Computers and Control (of IEE)

INSPECT Infra-red System for Printed Circuit Testing
Integrated Nationwide System for Processing Entries from Customs Terminals (Australia)

INSPEX Engineering Inspection and Quality Control Conference and Exhibition

INSTA Inter-Nordic Standard

INSTAAR Institute of Arctic and Alpine Research (Colorado University (USA))

INSTAB Information Service on Toxicity And Biodegradability (of WPRL (DOE))

INSTARS Information Storage And Retrieval Systems

InstF Institute of Fuel

InstGasE Institution of Gas Engineers

InstHE Institution of Highway Engineers (now IHT)

INSTIN Institut National des Sciences et Techniques Nucleaires (France) (National Institute of Nuclear Sciences and Technology)

InstM Institute of Marketing and Sales Management

InstMC Institute of Measurement and Control

InstMP Institute of Management in Printing

INSTN Institut National des Sciences et Techniques Nucleaires (France) (National Institute of Nuclear Science and Technology)

INSTOP Institut National Scientifique et Technique d'Oceanographie et de Peche (Tunisia) (National Scientific and Technical Institute of Oceanography and Fisheries)

InstP Institutè of Physics

InstPet Institute of Petroleum

InstPhys Institute of Physics

InstPS Institute of Public Supplies

INSTPS Institute of Purchasing and Supply

InstR Institute of Refrigeration

InstSCE Institute of Sound and Communications Engineers

InstT Institute of Transport

InstTA Institute of Transport Administration

InstW Institute of Welding

InstWPC Institute of Water Pollution Control

INSURV Board of Inspection and Survey (USN)

INT Division of International Programs (of NSF (USA))
Instituto Nacional de Tecnologia (Brazil) (National Institute of Technology)
Interior
Isaac Newton Telescope
prefix to series issued by the Intermountain Forest and Range Station (of the Forest Service, USDA)

INTA Instituto Nacional de Technología Agropecuaria (Argentina) (National Institute of Agriculture and Farmstock Technology)
Instituto Nacional de Tecnica Aerospacial (Spain) (National Institute of Aerospace Technology)
Istitution de Nutricion y Tecnologia de Alimentos (University of Chile) (Institute of Nutrition and Food Technology)

INTAAS Integrated Aircraft Armament System

INTABS International Terminal Accounting and Banking Service

INTACS Integrated Tactical Communications System

INTACT Inter-modal Air Cargo Test (a joint project of the US government and Industry)

INTAL Instituto para la Integracion de America Latina (Argentina) (Institute for Latin America Integration)

INTAMEL International Association of Metropolitan City Libraries

INTAPUC International Association of Public Cleansing

INTASAFCON International Tanker Safety Conference

INTASS INTEL Assembler

INTEC International Naval Technology Expo and Conference

INTECH Instituto Technologica (Chile) (Technical Institute)

INTECNOR Instituto Nacional de Tecnologia y Normalizacion (Paraguay) (National Institute of Technology and Standardization)
INTECOL International Association for Ecology
INTECOM International Council for Technical Communication
INTEL Instituto Nacional de Telecomunicaciones (Panama)
INTELCAM Société es Télécommunications Internationales du Cameroun (Cameroun)
INTELEC International Telecommunications Energy Conference
INTELSAT International Telecommunications Satellite Consortium
INTER- NOISE International Conference on Noise Control Engineering
INTER-EXPERT International Association of Experts
INTER/MICRO International Conference on Microscopy
INTERAN International Conference on the Analysis of Geological Materials
INTERBRANT Union Intercommunale des Centrales Electriques du Brabant (Belgium)
INTERCO International Code of Signals
INTERCOM Societe Intercommunale Belge de Gaz et Electricite (Belgium)
INTERCOMSA Intercontinental de Communicaciones per Satellite SA (Panama)
INTERCON International Convention and Exposition (of IEEE (USA))
INTERFACE Internationally Recognized Format for Automatic Commercial Exchange (of SITPRO)
INTERFAST International Industrial Fastener Engineering Exhibition and Conference
INTERGALVA International Galvanizing Conference
INTERGU International Copyright Society
INTERKAMA International Congress and Exhibition for Instrumentation and Automation
International Congress for Measurement and Automation
INTERLAINE Comite des Industries Lainieres (Committee for the Wool Industries) (of the EEC)
INTERMAG International Magnetics Conference (of IEEE (USA))
INTERNEPCON International Electronics Production Conference
INTERNET Interactive Network Analysis
International Congress on Project Planning by Network Analysis
INTEROCEAN International Conference and Exhibition for Marine Technology
INTERPIPE International Pipeline Technology Convention
INTERPLAS International Plastics Exhibition and Conference
INTERPOL SEE ICPO
INTERSPACE Interactive System for Pattern Analysis, Classification, and Enhancement
INTERTANKO International Association of Independent Tanker Owners
INTESCA Internacional de Ingenieria y Estudios Tecnicos SA (Spain)
INTEX Integer Extraction
INTHERM International Oil and Gas Firing Trade Fair
INTI Industrial and Technological Information
Instituto Nacional de Tecnologia Industrial (Argentina) (National Institute of Industrial Technology)
INTIB Industrial and Technological Information Bank (of UNIDO)
INTIME Interactive Textual Information Management Experiment
INTIPS Intelligence Information Processing System
INTLOC Interdiction of Lines of Communication
INTOP International Operations Simulation
INTOSAI International Organization of Supreme Audit Institutions
INTP Institut National des Telecommunications et des Postes (Madagascar) (National Institute of Telecommunications and Posts)
INTRACONS In-Transit Control System
INTRALAB Information Transfer Laboratory (of GSFC (NASA) (USA))
INTREX Information Transfer Experiments
INTUC Indian National Trade Union Congress (India)
INTUG International Telecommunications Users Group (Netherlands)
INU Inertial Navigation Unit
Istituto Nazionale di Urbanistica (Italy) (National Institute of Town Planning)
INUA Istituto Nazionale di Ultracustica (Italy) (National Institute of Ultrasonics)
INucE Institution of Nuclear Engineers
INV Institut National du Verre (Belgium) (National Institute of Glass)
INVL Invariant Magnetic Latitude
INW Institut fuer Nachrichtentechnik und Wellennausbreitung (Graz University (Austria))
INWATE Integrating Waveguide Technology
INWATS Inward Wide Area Telecommunication Service
IO Image Orthicon
IOA Indian Optometric Association (India)
Institute of Acoustics
International Omega Association (USA)
IOAHPR International Organisation for the Advancement of High Pressure Research (now International Association for the Advancement of High Pressure Research and Development)
IOB Institute of Building
Insurance Ombudsman Bureau
IOBC Indian Ocean Biological Centre (of IOC (India))
International Organization for Biological Control of Noxious Animals and Plants
IOC Indian Oil Corporation (India)
Indirect Operating Costs
Initial Operational Capacity
Integrated Optical Circuit
Intergovernmental Oceanographic Commission (of UNESCO)
IOCC International Optical Computer Conference
Interstate Oil Compact Commission (USA)
IOCS Input/Output Control System
IOCU International Organisation of Consumers Unions (Netherlands)
IOD Institute of Directors
Integrated Optical Density
IODE IOC (UNESCO) Working Committee on International Oceanographic Data Exchange
IODSTR Input and Output Driven Selt-Timing Repeater
IOE Institute of Offshore Engineering (Heriot-Watt University)
International Organisation of Employers (Switzerland)
IOF International Oceanographic Foundation
IOFC Indian Ocean Fisheries Commission (of FAO)
IOH Idiopathic Orthostatic Hypotension
IOHC Institute for Occupational Hazard Control (of New York University and AIIE (USA))
IOI International Ocean Institute (Malta)
International Ozone Institute (U
IOIC Integrated Operational Intelligence Center (USN)
IOL Institute Of Librarians (India)
IOLC Integrated Optical Logic Circuit
IOLR India Office Library and Records (BLRD)
IOM Institute of Marketing and Sales Management

	Institute of Medicine (of National Academy of Sciences (USA)
	Institute of Metals (merged into the Metals Society in 1974, re-formed by merger of Metals Society and Institution of Metallurgists, 1985)
	Institute of Office Management (now the Institute of Administrative Management)
IOMA	International Oxygen Manufacturers Association (USA)
IOMB	Instytut Organizacji i Mechanizacji Budownictwa (Poland) (Institute for the Organisation and Mechanisation of Building)
IOMP	International Organization for Medical Physics
IOMTR	International Office for Motor Trades and Repairs (Netherlands)
ION	Institute of Navigation (USA)
	Ionosphere and Aural Phenomena Advisory committee (of ESRO)
	Isthmo-Optic Nucleus
IONKh	Institut Obshchey i Neorganicheskoy Khimii (USSR) (Institute of General and Inorganic Chemistry)
IONS	Integrated Operational NUDET System
IOOC	International Conference on Integrated Optics and Optical Fibre Communication
	International Olive Oil Council
IOP	Input/Output Processor
	Institute of Packaging
	Institute of Physics
	Institute of Printing
	Instytut Obroki Plastycznej (Poland) (Materials Forming Institute)
	International Organization of Palaeobotany
IOPEC	International Oil Pollution Exhibition and Conference
	Iranian Oil Exploration and Production Company (Iran)
IOPL	Internal Optical Path Length
IOPM	Instytut Organizacjo Przemysiu Maszcynowego (Poland) (Institute for the Organisation of Mechanical Engineering)
IOPO	Internal Optical Parametric Oscillator
IOPPEC	International Oil Pollution Prevention Exhibition and Conference
IOR	Institute for Operational Research
IOR-TOCC	Technical and Operational Control Centre in the Indian Ocean Region (of INTELSAT management)
IORS	Inflatable Occupant Restraint Systems
	Operations Research Society of Ireland
IOS	Institute of Oceanographic Sciences (of Natural Environment Research Council)
	Instytut Obrobki Skrawanien (Poland) (Metal Cutting Institute)
	Iraqi Organisation for Standarization (Iraq)
IOSA	Integrated Optic Spectrum Analyzer
	Irish Offshore Services Association (Eire)
IOSH	Institution of Occupational Safety and Health
IOSN	Indian Ocean Standard Net
IOSYS	Input/Output System
IOT&E	Initial Operational Test and Evaluation
IOTA	Institute of Transport Administration
IOTA	Institute of Theoretical Astronomy
IOTT	Institute of Operating Theatre Technicians
IOTTSG	International Oil Tanker Terminal Safety Group
IOU	Industrial Operations Unit (of MINTECH)
IOUBC	Institute of Oceanography, University of British Columbia (Canada)
IOVST	International Organisation for Vacuum Science and Technology
IOX	Input-Output Executive
IP	Immunoperoxidase
	Impedance Probe
	Index of Preprogramming
	Induced Polarization
	Information Processor
	Information Provider
	Initial Phase
	Institut Poluprovodnikov (USSR) (Institute of Semiconductors)
	Institute of Petroleum
	Instrumentation Paper
	Integer Programming
	Ionization Potential
	Ionized Particle
IPA	Immunoperoxidase
	Independent Publishers Association (Canada) (became ACP in 1976)
	Industrial Participation Association
	Information Processing Association (Israel)
	Insolvency Practitioners Association
	Institute for Production and Automation
	Institute of Practitioners in Advertising
	Institute of Public Administration (Eire)
	Institute of Public Affairs (Australia)
	Institutional Patent Agreement (USA)
	International Paediatric Association (France)
	International Phonetic Alphabet
	International Phonetic Association
	International Psycho-analytical Association
	International Publishers Association
	Isopropyl Alcohol
IPAA	Independent Petroleum Association of America Research Council)
IPAC	Independent Petroleum Association of Canada (Canada)
	Iran Pan-American Oil Company (Iran) (partly government owned)
	Isopropyl Acetate
IPACK	International Packaging Material Suppliers Association
IPACS	Integrated Power/Attitude Control System
	Interactive Pattern Analysis and Classification System
IPAD	Integrated Programmes for Aerospace-vehicle Design
IPADE	Instituto Panamericano de Alta Direccion de Empresa (Mexico) (Panamerican Institute for Business Management)
IPAE	Instituto Peruano de Administracion de Empresas (Peru) (Peruvian Institute of Business Management)
	Isopropyl Aminoethanol
IPAG	Information, Planning and Analysis Group (of the Electronics Commission (India))
IPAI	International Primary Aluminum Institute (USA)
IPALS	Integrated Pathology Audio-visual Learning System
IPANY	Industrial Photographers Association of New York (USA
IPAP	Interactive Parameter Analysis Programme
IPAPS	Institute for Pure and Applied Physical Sciences (of California University (USA))
IPAR	Improved Pulse Acquisition Radar
IPARS	International Programmed Airlines Reservation System
IPART	Institute of Photographic Apparatus Repair Technicians
IPAT	European Conference on Ion Plating and Allied Techniques
	International Conference on Ion Plating and Allied Techniques
IPB	Inventions Promotion Board (India) (merged into NRDC in 1973)
IPBA	India, Pakistan, and Bangladesh Association
IPC	Impurity Photoconductivity

Information Processing Code
Institute for Interconnecting and Packaging Electronic Circuits (USA)
Institute of Paper Chemistry (USA)
Institute of Printed Circuits (USA)
Instituto de Plasticos y Caucho (Spain) (Institute of Plastics and Rubber)
Integrated Pest Control
Intermittent Positive Control
International Patents Classification (of the Council of Europe)
International Photographic Council (USA)

IPC-ASA Intermittent Positive Control–Automatic Separation

IPCA International Passengers Consumer Association (disbanded in 1974)

IPCC Inter-Departmental Packaging Co-ordinating Committee (of MOD, MINTECH, BIS)

IPCEA Insulated Power Cable Engineers Association (USA)
Insulated Power Cable Engineers Association (USA) (now ICEA (USA))

IPCL Indian Petro-Chemicals Corporation (India)

IPCR Institute of Physical and Chemical Research (Japan)

IPCS Image Photon Counting System
Integrated Propulsion Control System

IPD Improved Point Defence
Instituto de Pesquisas e Desenvolvimento (of CTA (Brazil) (Institute for Research and Development)
Isophorone Diamine

IPD/AC Institut Panafricain pour le Developpement, Afrique Centrale (Cameroun) (Pan-African Institute for Development, Central Africa)

IPD/TAS Improved Point Defence/Target Acquisition

IPDA International Periodical Distributors Association (USA)

IPDF Intensity Probability Density Function

IPDMS Improved Point Defence Missile System

IPDSMS Improved Point-Defence Surface Missile System

IPE Asociacion de Investigacion Tecnia de la Industria Papelera Espanola (Spain) (Technical Research Association of the Spanish Paper Industry)
Industrial Plant Equipment
Institution of Plant Engineers
Instituto Portugues da Embalagen (Portugal) (Portuguese Institute of Packaging)
Intelligent Programme Editor

IPEACS Instituto de Pesquisa Agropecuaria do Centrul Sul (Brazil) (South Centre Research Institute in Agriculture and Farmstock)

IPEN Instituto de Pesquisas Energeticas et Nucleares (Brazil) (Institute of Nuclear Energy Research)
Pan-American Naval Engineering Institute

IPF Institut Francaise du Petrole, des Carburants et Lubrifiants (France) (French Institute of Petrol, Motor Fuels and Lubricants)

IPFC Indo-Pacific Fisheries Council (Thailand) (of FAO)

IPFEO Institut des Producteurs de Ferro-alliages d'Europe Occidentale (Institute of Producers of Iron Alloys of Western Europe)

IPFM Integral Pulse Frequency Modulation

IPG In-circuit Programme Generator
Independent Publishers Guild
Information Policy Group (of OECD)

IPGEN Intersection Point Generator

IPHC International Pacific Halibut Commission (USA)

IPHE Institut fur Plasmaphysik (Germany) (Institute for Plasma Physics)
Institution of Public Health Engineers
Interpulse Period
Isopentenyl Pyrophosphate

IPI Identified Prior-to-Intercept
Industrial Production Index
Infinite Position Indicator
International Petroleum Institute
International Press Institute (Switzerland)

IPIA Induced Psycho-Intellectual Activity

IPICOL Industrial Promotion and Investment Corporation of Orissa Ltd. (India)

IPICS Initial Production and Information Control System

IPIECA International Petroleum Industry Environmental Conservation Association

IPIN Integrated Photogrammetric Instrument Network

IPIP Implantable Programmable Infusion Pump

IPIRA Indian Plywood Industries Research Association (India)

IPIS Instrument Pilot Instructor School (USAF)

IPKIR Institut Povysheniya Kvalifikkatsii Informatsionnykh Rabotnikov (USSR) (Institute for the Advancement of Qualifications of Information Workers)

IPL Image Processing Laboratory (California Institute of Technology (USA))
Improved Position Locator
Information Processing Language
Initial Programme Load

IPlantE Institution of Plant Engineers

IPLCA International Pipeline Contractors Association

IPLO Institute of Professional Librarians of Ontario (Canada)

IPM Institut de Physique Meteorologique (Senegal) (Institute of Physical Meteorology)
Institute of Personnel Management
Institute of Printing Management
Institute Pasteur du Maroc (Morocco) (Pasteur Institute of Morocco)
Integrated Manufacturing Planning
Integrated Pest Management
Interference Prediction Model
Inventory Policy Model

IPMA In-plant Printing Management Association (USA)
International Personnel Management Association (USA)

IPMS International Plastic Modellers Society
International Polar Motion Service
Isopropylmethane Sulphonate

IPN Institut de Physique Nucleaire (France) Institute of Nuclear Physics)
Inter-penetrating Polymeric Network

IPO Instituut voor Perceptie Onderzoek (Netherlands) (Institute for Perception Research)
International Projects Office (of NATO)

IPOD International Phase of Ocean Drilling (of JOIDES)

IPOEE Institution of Post Office Electrical Engineers

IPP Imaging Photopolarimeter
Impact Point Prediction
Institute of Plasma Physics (Nagoya University (Japan))

IPPA Irish Professional Photographers Association (Eire)

IPPB Intermittent Positive-Pressure Breathing

IPPF International Planned Parenthood Federation

IPPJ Institute of Plasma Physics, Japan

IPPMA In-Plant Printing Management Association (USA)

IPPNW International Physicians for the Prevention of Nuclear War (USA))

IPPR Intermittent Positive Pressure Respiration

IPPS Institute of Physics and the Physical Society (now the Institute of Physics)

IPPTA Indian Pulp and Paper Technical Association (India)

IPPV Intermittent Positive-Pressure Ventilation
IPR Institute for Plasma Research (of Stanford University (USA))
Instituto de Pesquisas Rodoviarias (Brazil) (Institute of Highway Research)
IPRA International Peace Research Association (Norway)
International Public Relation Association
IPRC Information Privacy Research Center (Purdue University (USA))
IPREIG Institute Professionnel de Recherches et d'Etudes des Industries Graphiques (France) (Professional Research Institute for the Printing Industry)
IPRI International Plant Research Institute (USA)
IPRO International Pallet Recycling Organisation
IProdE Institute of Production Engineers
IPRT Industrial Platinum Resistance Thermometer
IPS Improved Plow Steel
Inertial Positioning Systems
Institute of Polymer Science (Akron University (USA))
Institute of Purchasing and Supply
Interactive Planning System
Interactive Programming System
International Pyrheliometric Scale
IPSA International Professional Security Association
IPSC Instytut Przemyslu Skla i Ceramiki (Poland) (Glass and Ceramics Industries Institute)
IPSE Integrated Project Support Environment
IPSFC International Pacific Salmon Fisheries Commission (Canada)
IPSG Investment Policy Study Group (USDOD)
IPSJ Information Processing Society of Japan (Japan)
IPSM Institute of Purchasing and Supply Management (Australia)
IPSO Initiating Production by Sales Order
IPSP Inhibitory Post-Synaptic Potential
IPSS International Packet Switched Service
IPSSB Information Processing Systems Standards Board (of USASI)
IPST International Practical Scale of Temperature
IPT Individual Perception Threshold
IPTC International Press Telecommunication Committee
IPTG Isopropyl Thiogalactoside
IPTH Immunoreactive Parathyroid Hormone
IPTS International Practical Temperature Scale
IPU Integrating Processor Unit
IPWR Integrated Pressurized Water Reactor
IPWSOM Institute of Practitioners in Work Study, Organisation and Methods (became Institute of Management Services 1978)
IQ Information Quick
Institute of Quarrying
Intelligence Quotient
IQA Institute of Quality Assurance
IQC International Quality Centre (of EOQC)
IQCA Irish Quality Control Association (Eire)
IQEC International Quantum Electronics Conference
IQI Image Quality Indicator
IQMH Input Queue Message Handler
IQRP Interactive Query and Report Processor
IQS Institute of Quantity Surveyors
IQSY International Quiet Sun Year
IR Industrial Relations
Informal Report
Information Retrieval
Infrared
Infrared Radiation
Inland Revenue
Institut fur Raumfahrttecknik (Institute for Space Technology) (of Technical University, Berlin (Germany))
Insulation Resistance
Interagency Report
Intermediate Resonance
Israel Railways (Israel)
IR&D Independent Research and Development
IR-NDT Infra-Red Non-Destructive Testing
IR/UV-LS Infra-Red/Ultraviolet Line Scanner
IRA Inertial Reference Assembly
Information Retrieval using APL (ie A Programming Language)
Intermediate Range Aircraft
International Reading Association (USA)
International Registration Authority (of cultivated plant names)
International Rubber Association
Investment-Return Assumption
IRABA Institut de Recherche Appliquee du Beton Arme (France) (Applied Research Institute for Reinforced Concrete)
IRABOIS Institut de Recherche Appliquee du Bois (France) (Applied Research Institute for Wood)
IRAC Integrated Random Access Channel
Interdepartment Radio Advisory Committee (USA) (of OTP)
IRAD Independent Research And Development
Institute for Research on Animal Diseases (of the Agricultural Research Council)
IRADES Istituto Ricerche Applicate Documentazione e Studi (Italy)
IRAM Institut de Recherche Appliquee du Metal (France) (Institute for Applies Research Metal)
Instituto Argentino de Racionalizacion de Materiales (Argentina) (Standards Institute)
IRAN Inspection and Repair As Necessary
IRANDOC Iranian Documentation Centre (Iran)
IRANOR Industrial Research Assistance Programme (of NRC (Canada))
Instituto Nacional de Racionalización y Normalización (Spain) (National Institute of Standardization)
Interagency Radiological Assistance Plan (USA)
IRAR Infra-Red Airborne Radar
Integrator Register Address Register
IRAS Infra-Red Astronomical Satellite
Infra-Red Measuring Astronomical Satellite
Interdiction Reconnaissance Attack System
IRATE Inertial Range Atmospheric Turbulence Entrainment
Interactive Retrieval And Text Editor
Interim Remote Air Terminal Equipment
IRAWS Infra-Red Attack Weapons System
IRB Industry Reference Black
Infra-Red Binoculars
IRBM Intermediate Range Ballistic Missile
IRBT Intelligent Remote Batch Terminal
IRC Indian Roads Congress (India)
Industrial Reorganisation Corporation (disbanded 1970)
Institute of Naval Studies Research Contribution (of CNA (USN))
Integrator Register Counter
International Reference Centre (of WHO)
International Rubber Conference
IRCA International Railway Congress Association
IRCAM Institute for Research and Coordination into Acoustics and Music (France)
IRCCD Infra-Red Charge-Coupled Device
IRCCS Intrusion-Resistant Communications Cable System

IRCHA Institut National de Recherche Chimique Appliquee (France) (National Institute of Applied Chemistry Research)

IRCI Industrial Reconstruction Corporation of India Ltd (India)

IRCM Infra-Red Counter-Measures

IRCOL Institute for Information Retrieval and Computational Linguistics (of Bar Ilam University (Israel))

IRCR Integrator Register Control Register

IRCS International Research Communications System

IRCT Institut de Recherches du Coton et des Textiles Exotiques (France) (Cotton and Tropical Textiles Institute)

IRDC Industrial Research and Development Center (Virginia University (USA))

IRDE Instruments Research and Development Establishment (India)

IRDIA Industrial Research and Development Incentives Act (administered by Department of Industry, Trade and Commerce (Canada))
Industrial Research and Development Investment Assistance (of Department of Industry (Canada))

IRDM Illuminated Runway Distance Marker

IRDS Idiopathic Respiratory Distress Syndrome

IRDU Infra-Red Detection Unit

IRE Indian Rare Earths Limited (of Department of Atomic Energy (India))
Institut Radiotekhniki i Elektroniki (USSR) (Institute of Radio and Electronic Engineering)
Institute of Radio Engineers (now IEEE) (USA)

IREDA International Radio and Electrical Distributors Association

IREE Institution of Radio and Electronics Engineers (Australia)

IRENE Indicating Random Electronic Numbering Equipment (of Central Bank of the Philippines) (serves the same purpose as ERNIE in the United Kingdom)

IREPS Integrated Refractive Effects Prediction System

IREQ Institute of Research Quebec (Canada) (of Quebec Hydro-Electric Commission)

IRF Institute de Recherche Fondamentale (of CEA (France))
Instrument Reliability Factors
International Road Federation
Interrogation Repetition Frequency

IRFAA International Rescue and First Aid Association

IRFIS Inertial Referenced Flight Inspection System
International Research Forum in Information Science
Istituto Regionale per il Finanziamento alle Industrie in Sicilia (Italy) (Regional Institute for the Financing of Industry in Sicily)

IRFNA Inhibited Red Fuming Nitric Acid

IRG International Research Group on Wear of Engineering Materials
Interrelationship Graph

IRGA Infra-Red Gas-Analyser

IRGMA Information Retrieval Group of the Museums Association

IRGOM International Research Group on Management (headquarters in the University of Rochester (USA))

IRH Inductive Recording Head

IRHD International Rubber Hardness Degrees

IRHE Instituto de Recursos Hydraulicos y Electrificacion (Panama)

IRHO Institut de Recherches des Huiles et Oleagineaux (France) (Oils and Oil Seeds Research Institute)

IRI Immunoreactive Insulin
Industrial Research Institute (USA)
Institute for Rural Industrialization (India)
Institution of the Rubber Industry (amalgamated into PRI in 1975)
Instituto per la Ricostruzione Industriale (Italy) (Industrial Reconstruction Institute)
Interuniversitair Reactor Instituut (Netherlands)

IRIA Indian Rubber Industries Association (India)
Infra-Red Information And Analysis Center (ERIM (USA))
Institute Recherche d'Information et d'Automatique (France) (Research Institute of Data Processing and Automation)

IRIBS Inclination Removal Ionospheric Beacon Satellite

IRIE Infra-Red Interference Envelope

IRIG Inertial Reference Integrating Gyro system
Inter-Range Instrumentation Group (USDOD)

IRIS Industrial Relations Information System
Infra-Red Imaging Seeker (previously called IRISH)
Infra-Red Intruder System
Infrared Information Symposia (USA)
Infrared Interferometer Spectrometer
Integrated Reconnaissance Intelligence System
International Radiation Investigation Satellite

IRISH Infra-Red Image Seeker Head

IRL Index Retrieval Language
Interactive Root Locus
Ionosphere Research Laboratory (Pennsylvania State University (USA))

IRLA Independent Research Library Association (USA)

IRLC Illinois Regional Library Council (USA)

IRLCS International Red Locust Control Service (Zambia)

IRLED Infra-Red Light Emitting Diode

IRLS Infra-Red Line Scanner
Infra-Red Linescan System
Interrogation, Recording of Location Subsystem

IRLWR Institute for Research on Land and Water Resources (Pennsylvania State University (USA))

IRM Information Resources Management
Inspection, Repair and Maintenance
Interim Research Memorandum
Intermediate Range Monitor
Isothermal Remanent Magnetisation

IRMA Immunoradiometric Assay
Information Revision and Manuscript Assembly
Infra-Red Milk Analyser
Interactive Real-time Music Assembler
International Rehabilitation Medicine Association
Inverted Roof Membrane Assembly

IRMMH Institute of Research into Mental and Multiple Handicap

IRMR Infra-Red Micro-Radiometry

IRMRA Indian Rubber Manufacturers Research Association

IRNDT Infra-Red Non-Destructive Testing

IRNE Institutul de Reactori Nucleari Energetici (Romania)

IRO Industrial Relations Officer
Industriele Raad voor de Oceanologie (of TNO (Netherlands)) (Industrial Council for Oceanology)
International Relations Office (of the American Library Association)

IROD Instantaneous Read-Out Detector

IROM Industria Raffinazione Oli Minerali (Italy)

IROPCO Iranian Offshore Petroleum Company (Iran) (partly government owned)

IROR Improved Range Only Radar

IROS Increased Reliability of Operational Systems

IRP Image Retaining Panel
International Reference Preparation (medical preparations approved by WHO Expert Committee on Biological Standardization)

IRPA Institut Radioveshchatel'nogo Priyema i Akustiki (USSR) (Radio Reception and Acoustics Research Institute)
International Radiation Protection Association

IRPTC International Register of Potentially Toxic Chemicals

IRQC Infra-Red Quantum Counter

IRR Integral Rocket-Ramjet
Internal Rate of Return
Israel Research Reactor

IRR/SSM Integral Rocket-Ramjet Surface-to-Surface Missile

IRR/TTM Integral Rocket-Ramjet/Torpedo Tube Missile

IRRD International Road Research Documentation (of OECD)

IRRDB International Rubber Research and Development Board

IRRI International Rice Research Institute (Philippines)

IRRL Information Retrieval Research Laboratory (Illinois University (USA))

IRRP Improved Rearming Rates Project (USN)

IRRPOS Interdisciplinary Research Relevant to the Problems of Our Society (a project of NSF (USA))

IRRU Industrial Relations Research Unit (University of Warwick)

IRS Indian Register of Shipping (India)
Inertial Reference System
Information Retrieval Service (of ESA)
Information Retrieval System
Institut fur Reaktorsicherheit (Germany) (Institute for Reactor Safety)
Internal Revenue Service (of Treasury Dept) (USA)
Internal-Reflection Spectroscopy
International Referral System (of the UN Environment Programme)
Isotope Removal System

IRSA Industrial Radiographic Service Association (USA) (now NDTMA)

IRSAC Institut pour la Recherche Scientifique en Afrique Centrale (Congo) (Institute for Scientific Research in Central Africa)

IRSE Institution of Railway Signal Engineers
International Reactor Safety Evaluation

IRSG International Rubber Study Group

IRSH Infra-Red Spectral Hygrometer

IRSIA Institut pour l'encouragement de la Recherche Scientifique dans l'Industrie et l'Agriculture (Belgium) (Institute for the encouragement of Industrial and Agricultural Scientific Research)

IRSID Institut de Recherches de la Siderurgie Francaise (France) (Research Institute of the French Iron and Steel Industry)

IRSLL Image Recording System, Low Light

IRSS Infra-Red Simulation System

IRST Infra-Red Search and Track

IRSTDS Infra-Red Surveillance and Target Designation System

IRSTS Infra-Red Search and Tracking system

IRT Infra-Red Temperature
Institut de Recherche des Transports (France) (Transport Research Institute)
Institut fur Rundfunktechnik (Germany) (Institute for Radio Engineering)
Institute for Rapid Transit (USA) (merged into APTA in 1974)
Institute of Reprographic Technology
Inter-Response Time
Isotope Ratio Tracer

IRTDA Indian Roads and Transport Development Association (India)

IRTE Institute of Road Transport Engineers

IRTM Infra-Red Thermal Mapper

IRTS Infra-Red Temperature Sounder
Irish Radio Transmitters Society (Eire)

IRTTD Infra-Red Transmission Through the Diffusion

IRU Inertial Reference Unit
Institute de Recherche d'Urbanisme (France) (Urban Planning Research Institute)

IRUS Infantry Rifle Unit Study (US Army)

IRVAT Infra-Red Video Automatic Tracking

IRWR Infra-Red Warning Receiver

IS Information Science
Information System
Iowa State University of Science and Technology (USA)
prefix to Standards issued by Indian Standards Institute
The Industrial Society

IS&R Information Storage and Retrieval

IS(PE)MA Industrial Safety (Protective Equipment) Manufacturers Association Spectroscopy

ISA Information Systems Association
Instruction-Set Architecture
Instrument Society of America
International Safety Academy (USA)
International Searching Authorities (of the Patents Co-operation Treaty)
International Silk Association
International Society of Acupuncture
International Sociological Association
International Standard Atmosphere
Office of the Assistant Secretary of Defense (International Security Affairs (USDOD))

ISAA Institute of Shops Acts Administration
Institute of South African Architects (South Africa)
Israel Society for Aeronautics and Astronautics (Israel)

ISABE International Society on Air Breathing Engines

ISAD Information Science and Automation Division (of the American Library Association (USA)) (now LITA (USA))

ISADC Interim Standard Airborne Digital Computer

ISAE Indian Society of Agricultural Engineers (India)

ISAF Industria Siciliana Acido Forforico (Sicily)
Intermediate Super-Abrasion Furnace

ISAG Industry Supply Advisory Group (of IEA (OECD))

ISAGA International Simulation And Gaming Association

ISAGE International Symposium on Antarctic Glaciological Exploration

ISAGEX International Satellite Geodesy Experiments (sponsored by COSPAR)

ISAH International Symposium on Acoustical Holography

ISAHM International Society for Animal and Human Mycology

ISAL Information Service Access Line

ISAM Indexed Sequential Acces Method

ISAP Interactive Survey Analysis Package

ISAR Information Storage and Retrieval
Inter-Seamount Acoustic Range

ISAS Illinois State Academy of Science (USA)
Institute of Space and Aeronautical Science (India)
Institute of Space and Aeronautical Science (Tokyo University) (Japan)
Institute of Space and Atmospheric Studies (University of Saskatchewan (Canada))
Isotopic Source Assay System

ISASI International Society of Air Safety Investigators

ISATA International Symposium on Automotive Technology and Automation

ISAust Institute of Surveyors, Australia (Australia)

ISAV Institute of Sound and Vibration Research (Southampton University)

ISAVVT International Symposium on the Aerodynamics and Ventilation of Vehicle Tunnels

ISB Independent Sideband
International Society of Biometeorology

ISBA Incorporated Society of British Advertisers

ISBB International Society of Bioclimatology and Biometeorology

ISBD International Standard Bibliographic Description

ISBD(M) International Standard Bibliographic Description for Monographic Publications

ISBD(NBM) International Standard Bibliographic Description for Non-Book Materials

ISBD(S) International Standard Bibliograhic Description for Serials

ISBN International Standard Book Number

ISC Institut Scientifique Cherifien (Morocco) (National Scientific Institute)
Instruction Staticizing Control
International Seismological Centre
International Sericulture Commission
International Society of Cardiology
International Society of Chemotherapy
International Sugar Council

ISCA International Standards Steering Committee for Consumer Affairs (of ISO (Switzerland))

ISCAN Inertialess Steerable Communication Antenna

ISCAS International Symposium on Circuits and Systems

ISCC Inter-Society Color Council (USA)
Interdepartmental Sub-committee for Component Co-ordination
Iron and Steel Consumer Council

ISCHME International Society for Computational Methods in Engineering

ISCO International Standard Classification of Occupations (of the International Labour Office)

ISCOL International Systems Corporation of Lancaster (University of Lancaster

ISCOR Iron and Steel Corporation (South Africa)

ISCRE International Symposium on Chemical Reaction Engineering

ISCS International Symposium on Cooling Systems

ISCT Institute of Science Technology

ISCTR International Scientific Committee for Trypanosomiasis Research

ISD Induction System Deposit
Instructional System Development
International Subscriber Dialling

ISDC Industrial Studies and Development Centre (Saudi Arabia)

ISDG Information Science Discussion Group

ISDN Integrated Services Digital Network

ISDOS Information System Design and Optimization System

ISDP Ice Shelf Drilling Projects

ISDR Institut Superieur du l'Developpement Rural (Zaire) (Higher Institute for Rural Development)

ISDS Instruction Set Design System
International Serials Data System (of the UNISIST programme)

ISDS/IC International Centre of the International Serials Data System (of UNESCO)

ISDT International Symposium on Dredging Technology

ISE India Society of Engineers (India)
Institute of Space Engineering (University of Saskatchewan (Canada))
Institution of Sales Engineers
Institution of Structural Engineers
Integral of the Squared Error
International Society of Electrochemistry
International Society of Endocrinology (USA)

ISEAS Institute of South-East Asian Studies (Singapore)

ISEC International Solvent Extraction Conference

ISEE International Sun Earth Explorer

ISEF International Science and Engineering Fair (USA) (designed to popularize science in high schools and administered by Science Service, a non-profit organization)

ISEK International Society of Electrophysiological Kinesiology

ISEP Institut Superieur d'Electronique de Paris (France)
International Standard Equipment Practice

ISEPS International Sun–Earth Physics Satellite

ISES International Ship Electric Service Association
International Society of Explosives Specialists
International Solar Energy Society (Australia)

ISF International Shipping Federation
Intersection of the Shift Fringes

ISFA International Scientific Film Association

ISFC Indicated Specific Fuel Consumption

ISFET Ion-Sensitive Field Effect Transistor

ISFMS Index Sequential File Management System

ISG Immune Serum Globulin
Inland Shipping Group (of the Inland Waterways Association)
Interfacial Surface Generator

ISGP International Society of General Practice (Germany)

ISGSH International Study Group for Steroid Hormones

ISHC Intersociety Safety and Health Committee (of the foundry industry) (USA))

ISHCP Institute for Strategic Health-Care Planning (USA)

ISHM International Society for Hybrid Microelectronics

ISHS International Society for Horticultural Science

ISI In-Service Inspection
Indian Standards Institution (India)
Information Sciences Institute (of University of Southern California (USA))
Information Sciences Institute (Southern California University (USA))
Institute for Scientific Information (USA)
Instrument Systems Installation
Inter-Symbol Interference
International Statistical Institute (Netherlands)
Iron and Steel Institute (merged into The Metals Society in 1974)
Israel Standards Institute (Israel)

ISIB Institute for the Study of Intellectual Behavior (of University of Colorado (USA))

ISIC International Standard Industrial Classification of all Economic Activities (of UN)

ISIG Institute of Standards and Industrial Research (Ghana)

ISIJU Indian Statistical Institute and Jadaipur University (a computer developed by the two institutions)

ISIMEP International Symposium on Identification and Measurement of Environmental Pollutants

ISIO Institute for the Study of International Organisation (University of Sussex)

ISIP Iron and Steel Industry Profiles (of the Iron and Steel Institute)

ISIR International Society for Invertebrate Reproduction
International Symposium on Industrial Robots

ISIRI Institute of Standards and Industrial Research of Iran (Iran)

ISIS IATA Statistical Information System
Information Science Institute and Society (USA)
Instant Sales Indicator System
Integral Spar Inspection System
Integrated Scientific Information Service (of the International Labour Office) (Switzerland)
Integrated Set of Information Systems
Integrated Ship Instrumentation System
International Satellites for Ionospheric Studies
International Science Information Service (USA)
International Species Inventory System (at the Minnesota Zoological Garden and sponsored by the American Association of Zoological Parks and Aquariums)

ISIT Intensifier Silicon Intensifier Target

ISJCT International Symposium on Jet Cutting Technology

ISL Information Search Language
Initial Seizure Load
Integrated Schottky Logic
Interactive Simulation Language
International Society of Lymphology

ISLIC Israel Society of Special Libraries and Information Centres (Israel)

ISLS Improved Side-Lobe Suppression
Interrogation-path Side Lobe Suppression

ISLWG International Shipping Legislation Working Group (of UNCTAD)

ISM Independent Subcarrier Method
Industrial, Scientific and Medical
Institute of Sanitation Management (USA)
Institute of Sports Medicine
Institute of Supervisory Management
Interactive Siting Method
Interim Surface Missile
Interpretive Structural Modeling
Interstellar Matter
Interstellar Medium

ISMA Indian Sugar Mills Association (India)
International Superphosphate Manufacturers Association

ISMaC Industrial Safety Management Centre (Glasgow College of Technology)

ISMAP Instrumentation System Margin Analysis Programme

ISMCM Institut Superieur des Materiaux et de la Construction Mecanique (France) (Advanced Institute of Materials and Construction Mechanics)

ISME Institute of Sheet Metal Engineering
International Symposium on Marine Engineering

ISMEC Information Service in Mechanical Engineering (of IMechE and IEE) (acquired in 1975 by a division of Data Courier, Inc. (USA))

ISMES Instituto Sperimentale Modelli e Structure (Italy) (Models and Structures Experimental Institute)

ISMG International Scientific Management Group (of GARP Atlantic Tropical Experiment)

ISMH Input Source Message Handler

ISMLS Interim-Standard Microwave Landing System

ISMM International Society for Mini- and Microcomputers (USA)

ISMS Inherently Safe Mining Systems

ISN International Society for Neurochemistry
International Society of Nephrology

ISNQR International Symposium of Nuclear Quadruple Resonance Spectroscopy

ISO Information–Structure–Oriented
International Organization for Standardization (Switzerland)
International Sugar Organisation

ISO/REMCO International Organization for Standardization Reference Materials Committee

ISOA Improved State-of-the-Art

ISOC Individual System/Organisation Cost
International Shipping and Offshore Oil Conference

ISOCARP International Society of City and Regional Planners

ISOCC Input System for Operator Connected Calls

ISODARCO International School on Disarmament and Research on Conflicts (Italy)

ISODATA Iterative Self Organizing Data Analysis Technique A

ISODOC International Centre for Standards in Information and Documentation (of ISO)

ISON Isolation Network

ISONET INTERNATIONAL ORGANIZATION FOR STANDARDIZATION Information Network (ISO (Switzerland))

ISOO International Symposium on Ophthalmological Optics

ISOPEDAC Integrated System Of Pipework Estimating, Detailing And Control

ISORID International Information System on Research in Documentation (a project of UNESCO)

ISOS International Southern Ocean Studies (a component of IDOE)

ISP Image Storage Panel
Instant-Set Polymer
Institute of Sales Promotion
Instruction Set Processor
Instruction Set Processor
International Society for Photogrammetry

ISPA International Society for the Protection of Animals
International Software Products Association (France)

ISPCA Irish Society for the Prevention of Cruelty to Animals (Eire)

ISPCC International Ship Painting and Corrosion Conference

ISPE Institutul de Studii si Proiectari Energetice (Romania) (Institute for Power Studies and Designs)

ISPEC Interagency Scientific Products Evaluation Committee (administered by GSA (USA))

ISPEMA Industrial Safety (Personal Equipment) Manufacturers Association
Industrial Safety (Protective Equipment) Manufacturers Association

ISPF Integral Skinned Polyurethane Foam

ISPICE Interactive Simulated Programme with Integrated Circuit Emphasis

ISPL Incremental System Programming Language

ISPLS Indiana Society of Professional Land Surveyors (USA)

ISPN International Standard Program(me) Number

ISPO International Society for Prosthetics and Orthotics
International Statistical Programs Office (Dept of Commerce, USA)

ISPOG International Society of Psychosomatic Obstetrics and Gynaecology

ISPP Illinois State Physics Project (USA)

ISPPM Institut Scientifique et Technique des Peches Maritimes (France) (Sea Fishing Scientific and Technical Institute)

ISPT Division of Intergovernmental Science and Public Technology (of RANN (NSF) (USA))

ISQA Israel Society for Quality Assurance (Israel)

ISR Information Storage and Retrieval
Institute for Social Research (University of Michigan (USA))

Institute of Surgical Research (US Army)
Intersecting Storage Ring

ISRAIN Institut Superieur de Recherche Appliquee pour les Industries Nucleaires (Belgium) (Advanced Institute of Applied Research for the Nuclear Industries)

ISRCDVS International Society for Research on Civilisation Diseases and Vital Substances

ISRD Information Storage, Retrieval and Dissemination

ISRI Israel Shipping Research Institute (Israel)

ISRM International Society for Rock Mechanics

ISRO Indian Space Research Organisation (India)

ISRO-MIT (INSAT) Indian Space Research Organisation and Massachusetts Institute of Technology (USA) Studies on the Indian National Satellite project

ISRRT International Society of Radiographers and Radiological Technicians

ISRSA International Synthetic Rubber Safety Association

ISS Ideal Solidus Structures
Inertial Sensor System
Integrated Ship System (a project of the Maritime Administration (USA))
Integrated Support System
International Switching Symposium
Intra-list Stimulus Similarity
Ion Scattering Spectrometry
Ion Scattering Spectroscopy
Ion Source Spectrometry
Ionosphere Sounding Satellite
Istituto Superiore di Sanita (Italy) (Advanced Institute of Health)
Office of the Information Systems Specialists (Library of Congress (USA))

ISSA International Ship Suppliers Association
International Social Security Association
International Strategic Studies Association

ISSC Interdisciplinary Surface Science Conference
International Ship Structures Congress

ISSCC International Solid-State Circuits Conference (IEEE (USA))

ISSCT International Society of Sugar Cane Technology

ISSI Institute for Small-Scale Industries (University of the Philippines)

ISSLS International Symposium on Subscriber Loops and Services

ISSM Incompletely Specified Sequential Machine
Interim Surface-to-Surface Missile

ISSMFE International Society for Soil Mechanics and Foundation Engineering

ISSMIS Integrated Support Services Management Information System (US Army)

ISSMS Integrated Support Services Management System (US Army)

ISSN International Standard Serial Number (devised by ISO (Switzerland))

ISSOL International Society for the Study of the Origin of Life

ISSP Institute of Solid State Physics (of University of Tokyo (Japan))
Irish Society for Surveying and Photogrammetry (Eire)

ISSR International Symposium on Roofs and Roofing

ISSS Inherent Secondary Shutdown System
International Society of Soil Science

ISSSM Imaging Seeker Surface-to-Surface Missile

IST Information Sciences Technology
Institute for Science and Technology (University of Michigan (USA))
Institute of Science Technology
Integrated Switching and Transmission
Integrated System Transformer
Interim STOL Transport
International Skelton Tables
Intraspecific Antigenic Typing

ISTA Industrial Science and Technolgoy Agency (of MITI (Japan)
International Seed Testing Association
International Society for Technology Assessment

ISTAM Israel Society for Theoretical and Applied Mechanics (Israel)

ISTAT International Society of Transport Aircraft Traders (USA)
Istituto Centrale di Statistici (Italy) (Central Institute of Statistics)

ISTC Indo-Swiss Training Centre (India)
Institute of Scientific and Technical Communicators
International Steam Tables Conference (later ICPS)

ISTCL International Scientific and Technical Committee on Laundering

ISTE International Society for Tropical Ecology

ISTH International Society on Thrombosis and Haemostasis

ISTIC Institute of Scientific and Technical Information of China (China)

ISTPM Institut Scientifique et Technique des Peches Maritimes (France) (Sea Fisheries Scientific and Technical Institute)

ISTRAN/PL IHI (ISHIKAWAJIMA-HARIMA HEAVY INDUSTRIES COMPANY) (Japan) Structure Analysis/Plate Structure, Linear Analysis

IStructE Institution of Structural Engineers

ISTS International Symposium on Space Technology and Science

ISTVS International Society for Terrain-Vehicle Systems

ISU Inertial Sensing Unit
International Salavage Union
International Society of Urology
International Stereoscopic Union
Iowa State University (USA)

ISU-ERI Iowa State University, Engineering Research Institute (USA)

ISU/CCL Iowa State University, Cyclone Computer Laboratory (USA)

ISV Iron-Solution Value

ISVA Incorporated Society of Valuers and Auctioneers

ISVESTA Individual Survival Vest for Aircrew

ISVR Institute of Sound and Vibration Research (Southampton University)

ISWIM If you See What I Mean

ISWM Institute of Solid Waste Management

ISWRRI Iowa State Water Resources Research Institute (USA)

ISWS Illinois State Water Survey (USA)

IT Information Technology
Information Theory
Intermediate Technology
The Industrial Tribunal

ITA Independent Television Authority (now Independent Broadcasting Authority)
Industrial Transport Association (now merged with the Chartered Institute of Transport)
Industry and Trade Administration (of Dept. of Commerce (USA))
Institut du Transport Aerien (Institute of Air Transport) (France)
Institut Teoreticheskoy Astronomii (USSR) (Institute of Theoretical Astronomy)
International Tape Association (USA)
International Thermographers Association (of Printing Industries Association of America (USA)
International Tin Agreement (an organisation)
International Tunnelling Association

	International Typographic Association
ITAC	Industrial Training Atlantic Convention
	Intelligence and Threat Analysis Center (US Army)
ITACS	Integrated Tactical Air Control System
ITAE	Integral of Time Absolute Value of Error
ITAI	Institution of Technical Authors and Illustrators (now part of ISTC)
ITAI(Aust)	Institute of Technical Authors and Illustrators of Australia (Australia)
ITAL	Instituut voor Toepassing van Atoomenergie in de Landbouw (Netherlands) (Institute for the Application of Nuclear Energy to Agriculture)
ITALSIEL	Societa Italiana Sistemi Informativ Elettronica (Italy)
ITALTEL	Societa Italiana Telecomunicazioni (Italy)
ITAM	International Conference on Alpine Meteorology
ITAP	Information Technology Advisory Panel (of the Cabinet Office)
ITAR	International Traffic in Arms Regulations, 1976 (USA)
ITAV	Individual Tactical Air Vehicle
ITB	Industrial Training Board
	Instytut Techniki Budowlanej (Poland) (Institute of Building Research)
	Insurance Technical Bureau
	Integrated Tug/Barge
ITBTP	Institut Technique du Batiment et des Travaux Publics (France) (Building and Public Works Technical Institute)
ITC	Instytut Techniki Cieplnej (Poland) (Institute of Heating)
	Intelligent Tape Controller
	International Tea Council
	International Teletraffic Conference
	International Teletraffic Congress
	International Thyroid Conference
	International Tin Council
	International Trade Centre (of UNCTAD/GATT)
	International Training Centre for Aerial Survey (now International Institute for Aerial Survey and Earth Sciences (Netherlands))
	Ionic Thermoconductivity
	Ionic Thermocurrent
ITCA	Independent Television Companies Association
	Inter-American Technical Council of Archives
	International Typographic Composition Association (USA)
ITCC	International Technical Cooperation Centre (of the Association of Engineers and Architects (Israel))
ITCF	Institut Technique des Cereales et des Fourrages (of ACTA (France)) (Technical Institute for Cereals and Fodder)
ITCM	Integrated Tactical Counter-Measures
ITCS	Integrated Target Command System
ITCU	International Technological Collaboration Unit (of the Dept of Trade)
ITCZ	Inter-Tropical Convergence Zone
ITD	Instytut Technologii Drewna (Poland) (Timber Technology Institute)
ITDG	Intermediate Technology Development Group (Reading University)
ITDM	Intelligent Time Division Multiplexer
ITDS	Integrated Technical Data System
ITDT	Integrated Technical Documentation and Training
ITE	Institute of Television Engineers (Japan)
	Institute of Terrestrial Ecology (of the Natural Environment Research Council)
	Institute of Traffic Engineers (USA)
	Institution of Telecommunication Engineers (India)
	Intercity Transport Effectiveness
ITEB	Institut Technique d'Elevage Bovin (of ACTA (France)) (Technical Institute for Cattle Rearing)
ITEC	Information Technology Centres (of MSC and DTI)
	Instituto Tecnologico de Electronica y Communicaciones (Colombia) (Technical Institute of Electronics and Communications)
	International Total Energy Congress
ITED	Integrated Trajectory Error Display
ITEDC	Information Technology Economic Development Committee
ITEF	Institut Teoreticheskoy i Eksperimental'noy Fiziki (USSR) (Institute of Theoretical and Experimental Physics)
ITEG	Isotope-powered Thermoelectric Generator
ITEM	Integrated Test and Maintenance
ITESC	International Tanker Equipment Standing Committee
ITEWS	Integrated Tactical Electronic Warfare System
	Interim Tactical Electronic Warfare System
ITEX	Industrial Training Exhibition and Symposium
ITF	Institut Textile de France (France) (Textile Insitute of France)
	Interactive Terminal Facility
ITFS	Instructional Television Fixed Service
ITGA	Isothermogravimetric Analysis
ITI	Iceberg Transport International Ltd (Saudi Arabia)
	Indian Telephone Industries (India)
	Inter-Trial Interval
ITIC	International Tsunami Information Centre (Honolulu)
ITIPI	Interim Tactical Information Processing and Interpretation
ITIRC	IBM (INTERNATIONAL BUSINESS MACHINES) Technical Information Retrieval Center
ITIS	Intermediate Technology Industrial Services (a unit of ODM)
ITL	Integrate–Transfer–Launch
	Isothermal Luminescence
	Isotoptekniska Laboratoriet (Sweden) (Isotopes Techniques Laboratory)
ITLC	Instant Thin Layer Chromatography
ITM	Inch Trim Moment
	Institute of Tropical Meteorology (India)
	Instituto di Tecnologia Meccanica (Italy) (Institute of Mechanical Technology)
ITMC	International Transmission Maintenance Centre
ITMIS	Integrated Transportation Management Information System (US Army)
ITMT	Intermediate Thermal Mechanical Treatment
ITNA	Independent Television News Association (USA)
ITO	Indium/Tin Oxide
	Institute of Training Officers
ITOS	Improved TIROS Operational Satellite
ITP	Immune Thrombocytopenia
	Institute of Theoretical Physics (Stanford University (USA))
ITPA	Independent Telephone Pioneer Association (USA)
ITPAIS	Image Technology Patent Information System
ITPL	Long Term Procedural Language
ITPP	Institute of Technical Publicity and Publications (now part of ISTC)
ITPR	Infrared Temperature Profile Radiometer
ITPRL	Individual Training and Performance Research Laboratory (of ARI (US Army)
ITPS	Income Tax Payers Society
	Internal Tele-Processing System
ITR	Incore Thermionic Reactor
ITRAC	INTERDATA Transaction Controller

ITRC Industrial Toxicology Research Centre (India)
International Tin Research Council

ITRDC Inland Transport Research and Development Council (now the Planning and Transport Research Advisory Council)

ITRI Industrial Technology and Research Institute (Taiwan)
International Tin Research Institute

ITRU Industrial Training Research Unit (University College, London)

ITS Import Tabulation System (of ITC (UN))
Industrial Training Service (sponsored by the Department of Employment and the CTC)
Insertion OR Interval Test Signal
Institute for Telecommunication Sciences (of ESSA (USA))
Institute for Telecommunication Service (of Office of Telecommunications (USA))
Integrated Trajectory System

ITSA Independent Tank Storage Association
Information Technology Skills Agency (of CBI)
Institute for Telecommunication Sciences and Aeronomy (of ESSA) (formerly CRPL of NBS) (USA)

ITSC International Telephone Service Centres
International Tyre Specialists Congress

ITSE Integral of Time Squared Error

ITSU Information Technology Standards Unit (of DTI)

ITT Institute of Textile Technology (USA)
Instituut voor Tuinbowtechneik (Netherlands) (Institute of Agricultural Engineering)
Inter-stage Turbine Temperature
Internal Turbine Temperature

ITTC International Towing Tank Conference

ITTE Institute of Transportation and Traffic Engineering (University of California (USA))

ITU International Telecommunication Union (Switzerland) (of UN)

ITUSA Information Technology Users Standards Association

ITV Improved Tow Vehicle
Instructional Television

ITVA International Industrial Television Association (USA)

ITX Information Transfer Exchange

IUA International Union of Architects

IUAA International Union of Amateur Astronomers

IUAES International Union of Anthropological and Ethnological Sciences

IUAI International Union of Aviation Insurers

IUAPPA International Union of Air Pollution Prevention Associations

IUAT International Union Against Tuberculosis (France)

IUB International Union of Biochemistry (of ICSU)

IUBS International Union of Biological Sciences (of ICSU)

IUBSSA International Union of Building Societies and Savings Associations

IUBTP Inter-University Biology Teaching Project

IUC International University Contact for Management Education

IUCAF Inter-Union Commission for Allocation of Frequencies for Radio Astronomy and Space Science (of ICSU)

IUCN International Union for the Conservation of Nature and Natural Resources (Switzerland)

IUCr International Union of Crystallography (of ICSU)

IUCRM Inter-Union Commission on Radio Meteorology (of ICSU)

IUCS Inter-Union Commission on Spectroscopy (of ICSU)

IUCSTP Inter-Union Commission on Solar Terrestrial Physics (of ICSU)

IUE International Ultraviolet Explorer (a project of ESA, NASA, and the Science Research Council)
International Union for Electroheat

IUED Institut Universitaire d'Etudes du Developpement (Switzerland)

IUFRO International Union of Forest Research Organisations

IUGG International Union of Geodesy and Geophysics (of ICSU)

IUGG/CAS IUGG Committee on Atmospheric Sciences

IUGS International Union of Geological Sciences (of ICSU)

IUHE International Union for Health Education

IUHPS International Union for the History and Philosophy of Science
International Union for the History and Philosophy of Science (of ICSU)

IUIEC Inter-University Institute of Engineering Control

IUIS International Union of Immunological Societies

IULA International Union of Local Authorities

IULCS International Union of Leather Chemists Societies

IUMI International Union of Maritime Insurance

IUMP International Upper Mantle Project (project concluded December, 1970)

IUNS International Union of Nutritional Sciences (of ICSU)

IUOTO International Union of Official Travel Organizations

IUPAB International Union of Pure and Applied Biophysics (of ICSU)

IUPAC International Union of Pure and Applied Chemistry (of ICSU)

IUPAP International Union of Pure and Applied Physics (of ICSU)

IUPHAR International Union of Pharmacology

IUPPS International Union of Prohistoric and Prehistoric Sciences

IUPRAI Indian Unit for Pattern Recognition and Artificial Intelligence (India)

IUPS International Union of Physiological Sciences (of ICSU)

IUPUI Indiana University–Purdue University of Indianapolis (USA)

IUR International Union of Railways

IUREP International Uranium Resources Evaluation Project (of NEA (OECD) and IAEA)

IUS Inertial Upper Stage
Interim Upper Stage

IUSSP International Union for the Scientific Study of Population (Belgium)

IUTAM International Union of Theoretical and Applied Mechanics (of ICSU)

IUVSTA International Union for Vacuum Science Techniques and Applications

IUWDS International Ursigrams and World Days Service (URSI)

IV Interactive Video
Intravenous

IV&V Independent Verification and Validation

IVA Ingenjors Vetenskaps Akademeins (Sweden) (Academy of Engineering Societies)
Intra-Vehicular Activity

IVAML Instrumental Variable–Approximate Maximum Likelihood

IVBS Industriele Vereniging tot Bevordering van de Stralingsveiligheid (Netherlands) (Industrial Association to promote Security from Radiation)

IVC — Inspiratory Vital Capacity
International Vacuum Congress
IVCS — Interior Voice Communications System
IVD — Inductive Voltage Divider
Ion Vapour Deposition
IVDS — Independent Variable Depth Sonar
IVE — Institute of Vitreous Enamellers
IVF — In-Vitro Fertilisation
Instutet for Verkstadsteknisk Forskning (Sweden) (Institute for Production Engineering Research)
IVHM — In-Vessel Handling Machine
IVIC — Instituto Venezolano de Investigaciones Cienticas (Venezuela) (Venezuelan Institute of Scientific Research)
IVITA — Instituto Veterinario de Investigaciones Tropicales y de Altura (Peru) (Veterinary Institute for Tropical Climates and High Altitude Research)
IVL — Institutet for Vatten -och Luftvardoforskning (Sweden) (Institute for Water and Air Pollution Research)
IVMU — Inertial Velocity Measurement Unit
IVO — Imatran Voima Oy (Finland) (State Electricity Authority) (of ICSU)
IVP — Instituto Venezolano de Petroquimica (Venezuela) (State Petrochemical enterprise)
Intravenous Pyelogram
IVR — Instrumented Visual Range
IVS — Instituto Venezolano de los Seguros Sociales (Venezuela) (Venezuelan Institute of the Social Security Services)
Integrated Versaplot Software
IVSI — Instantaneous Vertical Speed Indicator
IVSN — Initial Voice Switched Network
IVT — Infinitely Variable Transmission
Intake Valve Throttling
Internationale Vereinigung der Textileinkaufsverbande (Germany) (International Association of Textile Purchasing Societies)
IVU — Intravenous Urogram
IW — Induction Welding
IWA — Inland Waterways Association
IWAHMA — Industrial Warm Air Heater Manufacturers Association
IWBS — Integral Weight and Balance System
IWC — International Whaling Commission
International Wheat Council
IWCC — International Wrought Copper Council
IWCS — Integrated Wideband Communications System
International Wire and Cable Symposium
IWE — Institution of Water Engineers
Interpolated Water Elevation
IWES — Institution of Water Engineers and Scientists
IWFNA — Inhibited White Fuming Nitric Acid
IWGNSRD — International Working Group on Nuclear Structure and Reaction Data
IWHS — Institute of Works and Highways Superintendents
IWL — Insensible Water Loss
IWLS — Iterative Weighted Least Squares
IWM — Imperial War Museum
Institution of Works Managers
IWMA — Institute of Weights and Measures Administration
IWOSC — International Working Group on Soil-less Culture
IWP — Indicative World Plan for Agricultural Development (of FAO(UN))
Inverse Wulff Plot
IWPA — International Word Processing Association
IWPC — Institute of Water Pollution Control
IWPPA — Independent Waste Paper Processors Association
IWR — Institute for Water Resources (US Army)
Institute of Water Resources (University of Alaska (USA))
IWRA — International Water Resources Association (USA)
IWRC — Independent Wire Rope Core
IWS — Industrial Welfare Society (now The Industrial Society)
Institute of Work Study (incorporated into IWSP)
International Wool Secretariat
IWSA — International Water Supply Association
IWSc — Institute of Wood Science
IWSOE — International Weddell Sea Oceanographic Expedition
IWSOM — Institute of Practitioners in Work Study, Organisation and Methods
IWSP — Institute of Work Study Practitioners (merged with The Organisation and Methods Society in 1975 to form the Institute of Practitioners in Work Study, Organisation and Methods)
IWTO — International Wool Textile Organisation
IWTRL — Industrial Waste Treatment Research Laboratory (of EPA (USA))
IWTS — Integrated, Worldwide, Topographic System
IYL — International Youth Library (Germany)
IYRU — International Yacht Racing Union
IZD — Implanted Zener Diode
IZP — Linear Zone Plate
I^2C — Inter-Integrated Circuit
I^2L — Integrated Injection Logic
I^2R — Imaging Infrared

J

J — Journal
J-SIIDS — Joint-Services (USDOD) Interior Intruder Detection System
JA — Journal Article
JAAT — Joint Air Attack Team (US Army/Air Force)
JAC — Joint Airworthiness Committee
JACA — Japan Air Cleaning Association (Japan)
JACC — Joint Automatic Control Conference (of AAC (USA))
JACC/CP — Joint Airborne Communications Center/Command Post (USDOD)
JACKPOT — Joint Airborne Communications Command Post (USDOD)
JACLAP — Joint Advisory Committee on Local Authority Purchasing (merged into LAMSAC in 1978)
JADPU — Joint Automatic Data Processing Unit (of the Home Office and London Metropolitan Police)
JAEC — Japan Atomic Energy Commission (Japan)
Joint Atomic Energy Committee (of United States Congress)
JAEIP — Japan Atomic Energy Insurance Pool (Japan)
JAERI — Japan Atomic Energy Research Institute (Japan)
JAES — Japan Atomic Energy Society (Japan)
JAFC — Japan Atomic Fuel Corporation (Japan)
JAFNA — Joint USAF/NASA
JAGUAR-V — Jamming Guarded Radio–VHF
JAICI — Japan Association for International Chemical Information (Japan)
JAIF — Japan Atomic Industrial Forum (Japan)
JAIMS — Japan-America Institute of Management Science (Hawaii)
JAIS — Japan Aircraft Industry Society (Japan)
JAL — Japan Air Lines (Japan)
JALFOS — JAPAN AIR LINES Flight Operations System

JALMACS Japan Air Lines Maintenance Administration and Control System
JAM Joint Analysed Make-up (computer controlled attachment to standard hydraulic tongs)
JAMA Japan Automobile Manufacturers Association (Japan)
JAMC Japan Aircraft Manufacturing Corporation (Japan)
JAMDA Japan Machinery Development Association (Japan)
JAMINTEL Jamaica International Telecommunications Limited (Jamaica)
JAMPACK Jamming Package
JAMRI Japan Maritime Research Institute (Japan)
JAMSAT Japan Radio Amateur Satellite Corporation
JAMSTEC Japan Marine Science and Technology Centre (Japan)
JAMTS Japan Association of Motor Trade and Service (Japan)
JANAIR Joint Army Navy Aircraft Instrument Research (USDOD)
JANET Joint Academic Network
JANNAF Joint Army-Navy-NASA-Air Force (USA)
JANS Joint Army–Navy Specification (USDOD)
JAPATIC Japan Patent Information Centre (Japan)
JAPCo Japan Atomic Power Company (Japan)
JAPEX Japan Petroleum Exploration Company (Japan)
JAPIA Japan Auto Parts Industries Association (Japan)
JAPIC
JAR Job Appraisal Review
JARE Japanese Antarctic Research Expedition
JARL Japan Amateur Radio League (Japan)
JARRP Japan Association for Radiation Research on Polymers (Japan)
JARS Journalisation And Recovery System
Joint Airworthiness Requirements (of most of the major European aviation countries)
JARTS Japan Railway Technical Service (Japan)
JAS Japan Agricultural Standards (Japan)
Japan Association of Shipbuilders (Japan)
Junior Astronomical Society
JASDF Japan Air Self-Defence Force (Japan)
JASIN Joint Air-Sea Interaction (a project sponsored by the Royal Society)
JAST Jamaican Association of Sugar Technologists (Jamaica)
JASTPRO Japan Association for Simplification of International Trade Procedures
JAT Jugoslovenski Aerotransport (Yugoslavia)
JATCA Joinery And Timber Construction Association (of NFBTE)
JATCRU Joint Air Traffic Control Radar Unit
JATO Jet-Assisted Take-Off
JAVS Jovial Automated Verification System
JAWC Joint Air-miss Working Group (of CAA and MOD)
JAWS Jamming and Warning System
Jet Advance Warning System
Joint Airport Weather Studies
JBCSA Joint British Committee for Stress Analysis
JBPA Japan Book Publishers Association (Japan)
JCAB Japan Civil Aeronautics Board (Japan)
JCAE Joint Committee on Atomic Energy (of United States Congress)
JCAM Joint Commission on Atomic Masses
JCAP Joint Committee on Aviation Pathology
Joint Conventional Ammunition Panel (USDOD)
JCAR Joint Commission on Applied Radioactivity
JCC Joint Computer Conference
JCHST Joint Committee on Higher Surgical Training (of Royal College of Surgeons and Association of Surgeons)
JCIA Japan Camera Industry Association (Japan)
JCII Japan Camera and Optical Instruments Inspection and Testing Institute (Japan)
JCIT Jerusalem (Israel) Conference on Information Technology
JCL Job Control Language
JCM Joule Ceramic Melter
JCMC Joint Conference on Medical Conventions
JCMPO Joint Cruise Missile Program Office (USDOD)
JCO Joint Consultative Organisation for Research and Development in Agriculture and Food (of MAFF, Agricultural Research Council and Dept of Agriculture and Fisheries of Scotland)
JCPDS Joint Committee on Powder Diffraction Standards (USA) (an international organization)
JCPI Japan Cotton Promotion Institute (Japan)
JCS Job-Creation Subsidy
JCSCCF Joint Commission of the Socialist Countries on Co-operation in the Field of Fisheries
JCT Joint Tribunal on the Standard Form of Building Contract
JCTFI Joint Committee for Training in Foundry Industry (now Foundry Industry Training Committee)
JCTND Jugolovenski Centar za Tehnicku i Naucnu Dokumentaciju (Yugoslavia) (National Centre for Technical and Scientific Documentation)
JCUDI Japan Computer Usage Development Institute (Japan)
JCVS JOVIAL Compiler Validation System
JDA Japan Defence Agency (Japan)
Japan Domestic Airlines (Japan)
JDB Japan Development Bank (Japan)
JDF Jamaica Defence Force (Jamaica)
JDS Job Data Sheet
Job Diagnosis Survey
JDW Jacket Decladding Waste solutions
JE Japanese Encephalitis
JEBM Jet Engine Base Maintenance
JEBM-RR Jet Engine Base Maintenance Return Rate
JEC Joint Economic Committee (of the United States Congress)
Joint European Committee of Paper Exporters
JECC Japan Electronic Computer Corporation (Japan)
JECFI Joint Expert Committee on Food Irradiation
JECMA Japan Export Clothing Makers Association (Japan)
JECMB Joint Committee on Medicine and Biology (of IEEE and ISA)
JEDEC Joint Electron Device Engineering Councils (USA)
JEFR Japan Experimental Fast Reactor (Japan)
JEIDA Japan Electronic Industry Development Association (Japan)
JEIPAC JICST Electronic Information Processing Automatic Computer
JEM Jet Engine Modulation
JEMC Joint Engineering Management Conference (USA)
JEMIMA Japan Electric Measuring Instruments Manufacturers Association (Japan)
JEN Junta de Energia Nuclear (Spain) (Nuclear Energy Authority)
JENC Joint Emergency National Committee for the building industry
JEOL Japan Electron Optics Laboratory (Japan) (a company)
JEPI Junior Eysenck Personality Inventory
JEPOSS Javelin (Canadian Javelin Ltd) Experimental Protection Oil Sands System

JERC Japan Economic Research Centre (Japan)
Joint Electronic Research Committee (of the BPO and industry)
JERI Japan Economic Research Institute (Japan)
JERS Japan Ergonomics Research Society (Japan)
JES Japan Electroplating Society (Japan)
JET Joint European Tokamak
Joint European Torus (a project of EURATOM)
JETDS Joint Electronic Type Designation System (of NATO)
JETOX Japan chemical industry Ecology-Toxicology information centre (Japan)
JETRO Japan External Trade Organisation (Japan)
JETS Job Executive and Transput Satellite
Joint Enroute Terminal System
Junior Engineering Technical Society (USA)
JEV Japanese Encephalitis Virus
JEWC Joint Electronic Warfare Center (USDOD)
JFB Jet Flying Belt
JFET Junction Field Effect Transistor
JFETT Junction Field-Effect Transistor Tetrode
JFRO Joint Fire Research Organisation
JFS Jet Fuel Starter
JFTOT Jet Fuel Thermal Oxidation Test
JGC Japan Gas Chemical (Japan)
Juxtaglomerular Cells
JGM Job Guide Manual
JGSDF Japan Ground Self Defence Force
JH Juvenile Hormone
JHA Job Hazard Analysis
JHRP Joint Highway Research Project (of Purdue University, Indiana State Highway Commission and the FHWA (USA))
JHU Johns Hopkins University (USA)
JHU-CRSC Johns Hopkins University–Centre for Research in Scientific Communication (USA)
JIAA Joint Institute for Aeronautics and Acoustics (Stanford University (USA))
JIAFS Joint Institute for Advancement of Flight Sciences (of George Washington University) (located at NASA Langley Research Centre)
JIBA Japan Institute of Business Administration (Japan)
JIBECI Joint Industry Board for the Electrical Contracting Industry
JIBP Japan International Biological Programme
JIC Jet Induced Circulation
Job Instruction and Communication
Joint Ice Center (USN & NOAA)
Joint Industrial Council
Joint Iron Council (dissolved 1972)
JICA Japan International Cooperation Agency (Japan)
JICNARS Joint Industry Committee for National Readership Surveys
JICST Japan Information Centre of Science and Technology (Japan)
JICTAR Joint Industry Committee for Television Advertising Research
JIDA Japan Industrial Designers Association (Japan)
JIDC Jamaica Industrial Development Corporation (Jamaica)
JIE Junior Institution of Engineers (became Institution of General Technician Engineers, 1971)
JIEA Japan Industrial Explosives Association (Japan)
JIFDATS Joint Services In-Flight Data Transmission System (USDOD)
JIII Japan Institute of Invention and Innovation (Japan)
JILA Joint Institute for Laboratory Astrophysics (University of Colorado and NBS (USA))
JILA-IC Joint Institute for Laboratory Astrophysics–Information Center (University of Colorado (USA))
JIM Japan Institute of Metals (Japan)
JIMA Japan Industrial Management Association (Japan)
JIMAR Joint Institute for Marine and Atmospheric Research (Hawaii University)
JIN Japanese Institute of Navigation (Japan)
JINR Joint Institute for Nuclear Research (USSR)
JINTACCS Joint Inter-operability Tactical Command and Control System
JIOA Joint Intelligence Objectives Agency
JIS prefix to Standards issued by JISC
JISAO Joint Institute for the Study of the Atmosphere and Ocean (of Washington University and NOAA (USA))
JISC Japan Industrial Standards Committee (Japan)
JISF Japan Iron and Steel Federation (Japan)
JIT Job Instruction and Training
Just in Time (production method)
JLA Jamaica Library Association
Japan Library Association (Japan)
Jordan Library Association (Jordan)
JLCD Joint Liaison Committee on Documents used in the International Carriage of Goods
JLMIC Japan Light Machinery Information Centre (Japan)
JLO Joint Liaison Organization (of RIBA, IOB, RICS, ICE, IEE, IHVE, imechE, IStructE and RTPI)
JLRB Joint Logistics Review Board (USDOD)
JMA Japan Management Association (Japan)
Japan Meteorological Agency (Japan)
JMC Japan Monopoly Corporation (Japan)
JMED Jungle Message Encoder–Decoder
JMI Japan Machinery and Metal Inspection Institute (Japan)
JMIA Japan Mining Industry Association (Japan)
JMIF Japan Motor Industrial Federation (Japan)
JML Job Method Learning
JMMA Japan Materials Management Association (Japan)
Japan Microscope Manufacturers Association (Japan)
JMMII Japan Machinery and Metals Inspection Institute (Japan)
JMOS Job Management Operations System
JMPAB Joint Material Priorities and Allocation Board (USDOD)
JMPTC Joint Military Packaging Training Center (US Army)
JMSDF Japan Maritime Self Defence Force (Japan)
JMSPO Joint Meteorological Satellite Program Office (USA)
JMTBA Japan Machine Tool Builders Association (Japan)
JMTR Japan Material Testing Reactor (of JAERI)
JNF Japan Nuclear Fuel Company (Japan)
JNOC Japan National Oil Corporation (Japan)
JNPC Joint Nuclear Power Committee
JNR Japanese National Railways (Japan)
JNS Japan Nuclear Society (Japan)
Just Noticeable Shift
JNSDA Japan Nuclear Ship Development Agency (Japan)
JNTO Japan National Tourist Organization (Japan)
JNUL Jewish National and University Library (Israel)
JOBMAN Job Management
JOBOL Job Organisation Language
JOCIT JOVIAL Compiler Implementation Tool
JOERA Japan Optical Engineering Research Association (Japan)
JOG-A Joint Operations Graphic–Air

JOG-G	Joint Operations Graphic–Ground
JOIDES	Joint Oceanographic Institutions for Deep Earth Sampling (now an international project though still mainly funded by NSF (USA))
JOIS	JICST On-line Information System (Japan)
JOKING	Joint Kinematics and Geometry
JOL	Job Organisation Language
JONSDAP	Joint North Sea Data Acquisition Project
JONSIS	Joint North Sea Information Systems (an informal group from scientific institutes in Belgium, Germany, Great Britain, Netherlands and Sweden to undertake JONSDAP during IDOE)
JONSWAP	Joint North Sea Wave Project
JOP	Jupiter Orbiter with Probe
JOSS	Johnniac Open-Shop System Joint Ocean Surface Study (sponsored by Naval Oceanographic Office (USN))
JOT	Junction Optimisation Technique
JOVE	Jupiter Orbiting Vehicle for Exploration
JOVIAL	JULES' (SCHWARTZ) Own Version of an International Algorithmic Language
JP	Jet Propellant OR Propelled OR Propulsion
JPA	Japan Petroleum Association (Japan) Japan Psychological Association (Japan)
JPC	Japan Petroleum Corporation (Japan) Japan Productivity Centre (Japan) Jet Propulsion Center (Purdue University (USA))
JPCA	Japan Printed Circuit Association (Japan)
JPDC	Japan Petroleum Development Corporation (Japan) (now JNOC)
JPDR	Japan Power Demonstration Reactor
JPE	Job Performance Evaluation
JPL	Jet Propulsion Laboratory (California Institute of Technology (USA)) (now H. Allen Smith Jet Propulsion Laboratory) (operated for NASA (USA)
JPL-STAR	Jet Propulsion Laboratory (California Institute of Technology) Self Testing And Repairing computer (SEE JPL)
JPPSC	Joint Petroleum Products Sub-Committee (of DMSC (MOD))
JPRS	Joint Publications Research Service (of NTIS (USA))
JPTF	Joint Parachute Test Facility (USDOD)
JQEF	Japanese Quail Embryo Fibroblasts
JRATA	Joint Research And Test Activity
JRBAC	Joint Review Board Advisory Committee (of some trade associations and the CBI)
JRC	Joint Research Centre (of EURATOM)
JRDC	Japan Research and Development Corporation (Japan)
JRIA	Japan Radioisotope Association (Japan) Japan Rocket Industry Association (Japan) Japan Rubber Industry Association
JRS	Job Release Scheme
JRSC	Jam-Resistant Secure Communications
JRSMA	Japan Rolling Stock Manufacturers Association (Japan)
JRT	Jugoslovenska Radiotelevizija (Yugoslavia)
JRV	Jugoslovenska Ratno Vazduhoplovstvo (Yugoslavia) (Military Air Force)
JSA	Japan Standards Association (Japan)
JSAE	Japan Society of Automotive Engineering (Japan) Society of Automotive Engineers of Japan (Japan)
JSAP	Japan Society of Animal Psychology (Japan) Japan Society of Applied Physics (Japan)
JSC	Japan Science Council (Japan) LYNDON B JOHNSON Space Center (of NASA (USA))
JSCAACR	Joint Steering Committee for the Revision of the Anglo-American Cataloguing Rules
JSCB	Japan Society for Cell Biology (Japan)
JSCERDGG	Joint-Service Civil Engineering Research and Development Coordinating Group (USDOD)
JSCM	Japan Society of Composite Materials (Japan)
JSEA	Japan Ship Exporters Association (Japan)
JSEAC	Joint Societies Employment Advisory Committee (USA) (of IEEE, AIChE, AIAA, ASME, NSPE, AIME, ASCE) (now Coordinating Committee of Society Presidents)
JSEM	Japan Society for Electron Microscopy (Japan) Japan Society of Electrical Discharge Machining (Japan)
JSEP	Joint Services Electronics Program (USA)
JSESPO	Joint Surface Effect Ship Program Office (of US Maritime Administration and US Navy)
JSG	Joint Space Group (consisting of UKISC and DOI)
JSGCC	Joint Service Guidance and Control Committee (of USDOD)
JSHS	Junior Science and Humanities Symposium
JSIA	Japan Software Industry Association (Japan)
JSICI	Japan Society for International Chemical Information (Japan)
JSLE	Japan Society of Lubrication Engineers (Japan)
JSMDA	Japan Ship Machinery Development Association (Japan)
JSME	Japan Society of Mechanical Engineers (Japan)
JSMEA	Japan Ship Machinery Export Association (Japan)
JSNDI	Japan Society for Non-Destructive Inspection (Japan)
JSPA	Japan Screen Printing Association (Japan)
JSPS	Japan Society for the Promotion of Science (Japan)
JSQC	Japan Society for Quality Control (Japan)
JSQS	Japan Shipbuilding Quality Standard
JSS	Jet Strip System Job Shop Simulation Joint Surveillance System
JSSA	Japan Student Science Awards
JSST	Japan Society for Simulation Technology (Japan)
JST	Jet STOL Transport
JSTARS	Joint Surveillance and Target Attack Radar System
JSTPPC	Joint Services Technical Publication Policy Committee (MOD)
JSTU	Joint Services Trials Unit
JSUN	Jupiter, Saturn, Uranus and Neptune
JTAC	Joint Technical Advisory Committee (of EIA (USA) and IEEE (USA))
JTACMS	Joint Tactical Missile System (NATO)
JTB	Joint Transportation Board (USA)
JTC	Japan Tobacco Corporation (Japan)
JTCG/ALNNO	Joint Technical Coordinating Group for Air Launched Non-Nuclear Ordnance (USDOD)
JTCG/ME	Joint Technical Co-ordinating Group for Munitions Effectiveness (USDOD)
JTDE	Joint Technology Demonstrator Engine
JTE	Junction Termination Extension
JTES	Japan Techno-Economics Society (Japan)
JTGG/AS	Joint Technical Coordinating Group on Aircraft Survivability (USDOD)
JTI	Jydsk Teknologisk Institut (Denmark) (Jutland Technological Institute)
JTIDS	Joint (USAF and USN) Tactical Information Distribution System
JTRA	Job Task Requirements Analysis
JTRC	Joint Technical Requirements Committee (of MOD, EEA & SBAC)
JTRU	Joint-services Tropical Research Unit (Australia) (administered by (MOD (PE)) and Australian Department of Supply) (became JTTRE in 1977)

JTSA Joint Technical Support Activity (of Defense Communications Agency (USDOD))
JTTRE Joint Tropical Trials Research Establishment (Australia) (in collaboration with UK)
JTU Jackson Turbidity Units
JUDGE Judged Utility Decision Generator
JUDY Just a Useful Device for You
JULIE Joint Utilities Location Information for Excavators (a joint information service of utilities boards in Central & East Lancashire on buried underground utility services)
JUMPS Joint Uniform Military Pay System (USDOD)
JURIS Justice Retrieval Inquiry System (of Dept of Justice (USA))
JUSE Union of Japanese Scientists and Engineers (Japan)
JUSK Jugoslovenski Savez Organizacija za Unapredenje Kvaliteta i Pouzdanosti (Yugoslavia) (Yugoslavian Organisation for Quality Control)
JUSSIM Justice System Interactive Model
JUSTICE Journeymen Under Specific Training in Construction Employment
JUSTIS Japan–United States of America Textile Information Service
JWCA Japan Watch and Clock Association (Japan)
JWDS Japan Work Design Society (Japan)
JWPAC Joint Waste Paper Advisory Council
JZS Jugoslovenski Zavod za Standardizacijas (Yugoslavia) (Standards Institute)

K

KAAU King Abdul Aziz University (Saudi Arabia)
KAC Kuwait Airways Corporation (Kuwait)
KAERI Korea Advanced Energy Research Institute (Korea)
KAIST Korea Advanced Institute for Science and Technology (Korea)
KAL Korean Air Lines (Korea)
KALDAS KIDSGROVE ALGOL Digital Analogue Simulation
KAMEDO Swedish Organization Committee for Disaster Medicine (Sweden)
KANDIDATS KANSAS (UNIVERSITY) Digital Image Data System
KANUPP Karachi Nuclear Power Plant (Pakistan)
KAO Krymskaya Astrofizicheskaya Observatoriya (USSR) (Crimea Astrophysical Observatory)
KAPSE Kernel Ada Programming Support Environment
KAR Knot Area Ratio
KARL Korean Amateur Radio League (Korea)
KARLDAP Karlsruhe Data Processing and Display System (of EUROCONTROL)
KASC Knowledge Availability Systems Center (University of Pittsburgh (USA))
KASP Kehr Activated Sludge Process
KAT Key-to-Address Transformation
KBG Kernkraftwerks Betriebsgesellschaft (Germany)
KBPA Knowledge-based Programming Assistant
KBWP Kernkraftwerk Baden-Wurttemberg Planungsgesllschaft (Germany)
KCCT Kaolin Cephalin Clotting Time
KCL Kirchhoff's Current Law
Knitting Cylinder Lubrication
KCLA Known Coal Leasing Area (USA)
KCRT Keyboard Cathode Ray Tube
KCS Korean Chemical Society (Korea)
KDD Kokusia Denshim Denwa Company (Japan)
KDI Stichting Kwaliteitsdienst voor de Industrie (Holland) (Society for Industrial Quality Control)
KDP Potassium Dihydrogen Phosphate (K is chemical symbol for Potassium)
KE Kinetic Energy
KEA Kansas Electronics Association (USA)
KEAS Knots Equivalent Air Speed
KEC Korea Electric Company (South Korea) (state owned)
KECO Korea Electric Company (Korea)
KEMA Keuring van Electrotechnische Materialen (Netherlands) (Testing Institute for Electrotechnical Materials)
KEMAR Knowles Electronic Manikin for Acoustic Research
KENPRO Kenyan Committee on Trade Procedures (Kenya)
KEP Key-Entry Processing
KERMI Kereskedelmi Minosgelle Norzo Intezet (Hungary) (Authority for Information Labelling)
KEST Studiengesellschaft fur Forderung der Kernenergieverwertung in Schiffbau und Schiffahrt (Germany) (Study Group on the requirements if Nuclear Energy is applied to Ship Building and Navigation)
KET Krypton Exposure Technique
KETA Kentucky Electronics Technicians Associations (USA)
KEW Kinetic Energy Weapons
KFA Kernforschungsanlage Julich des Landes Nordrhein Westfalen (Germany)
KFAM Keyed File Access Method
KFAS Kuwait Foundation for the Advancement of Sciences (Kuwait)
KFC Kerala Finance Corporation (India)
KFK Kernforschungszentrum, Karlsruhe (Germany) (Nuclear Research Centre, Karlsruhe)
KFU King Faisal University (Saudi Arabia)
KGaA Komanditgesellschaft auf Aktien (partnership limited by shares)
KGB Komitet Gosudarstvennoi Bezopasnosti (USSR) (State Security Organisation)
KGO Kiruna Geophysical Observatory (Sweden)
KGRA Known Geothermal Resource Area (USA)
KGS Korean Geological Survey (Korea)
KH Keyhold (numbered series of USDOD reconnaissance satellites)
KHD Klockner-Humboldt-Deutsch (Germany)
KHG Kerntechnische Hilfsdienst GmbH (Germany)
KHI Kelvin-Helmholtz Instability
KI Korrosionsinstitutets (Sweden) (Corrosion Institute)
KIA Kenya Institute of Administration (Kenya)
KIAS Knots Indicated Air Speed
KIE Kenya Institute of Education (Kenya)
KIFIS KOLLSMAN Integrated Flight Instrumentation System
KIM Koninklijk Instituut voor de Marine (Netherlands) (Royal Naval Institution)
KIMM Korea Institute of Machinery and Metals (Korea)
KINSYM Kinematic Synthesis
KIPS Kilowatt Isotope Power System
KISA Korean International Steel Associates (Korea)
KISR Kuwait Institute for Science Research (Kuwait)
KISS Keyed Indexed Sequential Search
KIT Kanazawa Institute of Technology (Japan)
KITCO Kerala Industry and Technical Consultancy Organisation (India)
KITT Kinetic Tree Theory
KIVI Koninklij Instituut van Ingenieurs (Netherlands) (Royal Institution of Engineers)

KIWA Keurings Instituut voor Waterleiding-Artikelen (Netherlands) (Institute for Testing Waterworks Equipment)

KKA KRAMERS-KRONIG Analysis

KKN Kernkraftwerk Niederaichbach (Germany)

KLA Karachi Library Association (Pakistan)
Kentucky Library Association (USA)

KLH Keyhole Limpet Haemocyanin

KLIAU Korea Land Improvement Association Union (Korea)

KLIC Key-Letter-In-Context

KLM Koninklije Luchtvaart Maatschappij (Netherlands)

KLME Kuala Lumpur Metal Exchange

KMC Kernel Migration Coefficient

KMK Konyvtartudomanyi es Modeszertani Kozpont (Hungary) (Centre for Library Science and Methodology)
Standige Konferenz der Kultusminister der Lander in der Bundesrepublik Deutschland (Germany) (Standing Conference of Ministers of Education and Cultural Affairs of the Lander in the Federal Republic of Germany)

KMMC Kerala Minerals and Metals Corporation (India) (govt owned)

KMS Kansas Medical Society (USA)

KNAW Koninklijke Nederlanse Akademie voor Wetenschappen (Netherlands)

KNCV Koninklijke Nederlandse Chemische Vereniging (Netherlands) (Royal Netherlands Chemical Society)

KNMI Koninklijk Nederlands Meteorologisch Instituut (Netherlands) (Royal Netherlands Meteorological Institute)

KNPC Kuwait National Petroleum Company (Kuwait)

KNR Korean National Railroad (Korea)

KNSM Koninklijke Nederlandsche Stoomboot Maatschappij (Netherlands)

KNTC Kenya National Trading Corporation (Kenya)

KNVD Koninklijk Nederlands Verbond van Drukkerijen (Netherlands) (Royal Netherlands Printing Assoc.)

KNZHRM Koninklijke Noord -en Zuid-Hollandsche Redding-Maatschappij (Netherlands) (Royal North and South Holland Lifeboat Institution)

KOMRML Kentucky, Ohio, Michigan Regional Medical Library (USA)

KOP Kansallis-Osake-Pankii (Finland) (national bank)

KORDI Korean Ocean Research and Development Institute (South Korea)

KORSTIC Korea Scientific and Technological Information Centre (Korea)

KOS KENT (UNIVERSITY) On-line System

KOSEF Korea Science and Engineering Foundation (Korea)

KOTC Kuwait Oil Tanker Company (Kuwait) (partly govt owned)

KOWACO Korea Water Resources Development Corporation (Korea)

KPA Klystron Power Amplifier

KPIC Key Phrase In Context

KPNO Kitt Peak National Observatory (USA)

KPS Keypunch Performance System

KRCC Kingston Regional Cancer Centre (of OCTRF (Canada))

KRCRA Known Recoverable Coal Resource Area

KREEP Potassium (chemical symbol K), Rare Earth Elements, and Phosphorus

KRISO Korea Research Institute of Ship and Ocean

KRT Kernreaktorteile (Germany)

KSA Eidgenossisches Kommission für die Sicherheit von Atomlagen (Switzerland) (Federal Commission for the Safety of Nuclear Power Plants)

KSAK Kungliga Svenska Aeroklubben (Royal Swedish Aero Club)

KSAM Keyed Sequential Access Method

KSC JOHN F KENNEDY Space Center (of NASA)
Kuwait Shipping Company (Kuwait) (partly govt owned)

KSDIC Kerala State Industrial Development Corporation (India)

KSE Kuwait Society of Engineers (Kuwait)

KSF Kungliga Svenska Flygvapnet (Royal Swedish Air Force)

KSFC Karnataka State Financial Corporation (India)

KSH Kernenergie Schleswig-Holstein (Germany)
Kombinat Seeverkehr und Hafenwirtschaft (Germany)
Kozponti Statisztikai Hivatel (Hungary) (Central Statistical Office)

KSRTC Karnataka State Road Transport Corporation (India)

KSS Eidgenossisches Kommission zur Stahlenschutz (Switzerland) (Federal Commission for Radiation Protection)

KSSU KLM, SAS, Swissair, and UTA

KSTR KEMA Suspension Test Reactor

KSU Kansas State University (USA)

KTA Kerntechnischer Ausschuss (Germany) (Nuclear Technology Committee)

KTAC Korea Technology Advancement Corporation (Korea)

KTBL Kuratorium für Technik und Bauwesen in der Landwirtschaft (Germany) (Council for Agricultural Engineering and Farm Building)

KTD Killed Target Detector

KTG Kerntecnische Gesellschaft (Germany) (Nuclear Society)

KTH Kungliga Tekniska Hogskolan (Sweden) (Royal Technical University)

KTS Key Telephone System

KTSA KAHN Test of Symbol Arrangement

KU Kentucky University (USA)

KUIPNET KYOTO UNIVERSITY (Japan) Information Processing Network

KUR Kyoto University Reactor (Japan)

KURRI Kyoto University Research Reactor Institute (Japan)

KUSS KLM, UTA, Swissair and SAS

KVIC Khadi and Village Industries Commission (India)

KVL Kirchhoff's Voltage Law

KWAC Key Word And Context
Keyword Augmented in Context

KWIC Keyword In Context

KWIP Keyword Word in Permutation

KWIT Keyword In Title

KWL Kernkraftwerk Lingen (Germany)

KWO Kernkraftwerk Obrigheim (Germany)

KWOC Keyword Out of Context

KWOT Keywords Out of Title

KWS Kernkraftwerk Stade (Germany)

KWU Kraftwerk Union (Germany)

KWUC Keyword and Universal Decimal Classification

KWW Kernkraftwerk Wurgassen (Germany)

L

L	prefix to numbered:dated series of Aluminium and Light Alloy standards issued by BSI (letter is sometimes preceded by a number)
L/D	Lift over Drag
L/MF	Low and Medium Frequency
LA	Library Association Licensing Authority Linoleic Acid Los Alamos Scientific Laboratory (USA)
LAA	Leucocyte Ascorbic Acid Leucocyte Ascorbic Acid Leucocyte Ascorbic Acid Library Association of Alberta (Canada) Library Association of Australia (Australia)
LAAAS	Low-Altitude Airfield Attack System
LAAD	Last-Abundant-Appearance Datum Latin American Agribusiness Development Corporation
LAAF	Libyan Arab Air Force (Libya)
LAARS	Laser-Augmented Air-Rescue System
LAAS	Laboratoire d'Automatique et de ses Applications Spatiales (of CNRS (France)) (Laboratory for the application of Automation to Space Research) London Amateur Aviation Society
LAAT	Laser Augmented Airborne TOW
LAAV	Light Airborne ASW Vehicle Light-Airborne Attack Vehicle
LAB	Lead-Acid Battery Library Association of Bermuda Linear Accelerator Breeder Linear Alkylbenzenes Low Altitude Blanking
LABA	Laboratory Animals Breeders Association
LABDET	Isotopic Label Incorporation Determination
LABEN	Laboratori Elettronici e Nucleari (Italy) (Electronic and Nuclear Laboratories)
LABEX	Laboratory Apparatus and Materials Exhibition
LABIS	Laboratory Information System
LABORELEC	Laboratoire Belge de l'Industrie Electrique (Belgium) (Joint Laboratory of the Belgian Electricity Industry)
LABORIA	Laboratoire de Recherche en Informatique et en Automatique (France) (Research Laboratory for Data Processing and Automation)
LABP	Lethal Aid for Bomber Penetration
LABRE	Liga de Amadores Brasileiros de Radio Emissao (Brazil) (Brazilian Amateurs Radio Relay League)
LABRV	Large Ballistic Re-entry Vehicle
LABS	Laser Active Boresight System Low Altitude Bombing System
LAC	Laboratory Accreditation Committee (of AIHA (USA)) Laboratory Animals Centre (of Medical Research Council) Linear Amplitude-Continuous List of Assessed Contractors (issued by MOD) Lunar Aeronautical Chart
LAC(E)	Library Advisory Council (England)
LACAC	Latin American Civil Aviation Commission
LACAP	Latin American Cooperative Acquisition Project
LACAS	Laser Applications in Close Air Support
LACATE	Low Atmospheric Composition And Temperature Experiment Lunar Atmosphere Composition Experiment
LACBWR	La Crosse Boiling Water Reactor
LACD	Limited-Amplitude, Controlled-Decay
LACE	Liquid Air Cycle Engine
LACES	London Airport Cargo Electronic Data Processing Scheme Los Angeles Council of Engineering Societies (USA)
LACIE	Large Area Crop Inventory Experiment (of USDA, NASA, and NOAA (USA)) (aboard the second Earth Resources Technology Satellite)
LACIRS	Latin American Communication Information Retrieval System (of INCIRS (of University of Florida (USA))
LACMA	Los Angeles County Medical Association (USA)
LACONIQ	Laboratory Computer On-line Inquiry
LACS	Los Angeles Catalyst Study (of EPA (USA))
LACSA	Lineas Aereas Costaricenses S.A. (Costa Rica National Airline)
LACSAB	Local Authorities Conditions of Service Advisory Board
LACT	Lease Automatic Custody Transfer
LACV	Lighter, Air Cushion Vehicle Lighter, Amphibious, Air Cushion Vehicle
LAD	Library Administration Division (of the American Library Association) Light-Attenuation Device Logarithmic Analogue-to-Digital Lookout Assist Device Lunar Atmosphere Detector
LADAPT	Lookup Dictionary Adaptor Programme
LADAR	Laser Detection And Ranging
LADB	Laboratory Animal Data Bank (operated for National Library of Medicine by Battelle Columbus Laboratories (USA)
LADD	Low Altitude Drogue Delivery
LADDER	Life Assurance Direct Entry and Retrieval
LADE	Lineas Aereas de Estado (Argentina) (State Air Lines including the Miltary Air Force)
LADECO	Linea Aerea del Cobre (Chile)
LADIES	LOS ALAMOS (SCIENTIFIC LABORATORY) (USA) Digital Image Enhancement Software
LADIR	Low-cost Arrays for Detection of Infra-Red
LADS	Laser Air Depth Sounder Linear Analysis and Design of Structures
LADSIRLAC	Liverpool and District Scientific, Industrial and Research Library Advisory Council
LAED	Low Angle Electron Diffraction
LAEDP	Large Area Electronic Display Panel
LAER	Lowest Achievable Emission Rate
LAFB	Lockland Air Force Base (USAF)
LAFE	Laboratorio de Fisica Espacial (Brazil) (Space Physics Laboratory)
LAFIS	Local Authority Financial Information System
LAFTA	Latin American Free Trade Association (Headquarters in Uruguay)
LAGB	Linguistics Association of Gret Britain
LAGE	Lineas Aereas Guinea Ecuatorial (Republic of Equatorial Guinea) (National Air Line)
LAGEO	Laser Geodynamic Satellite
LAGEOS	Laser Geodetic Satellite
LAGLG	Library Association Government Libraries Group
LAGS	Laser Activated Geodetic Satellite
LAH	Light-Armed Helicopter Lithium Aluminium Hydride Logical Analyzer of Hypothesis
LAHA	Linear Array Hybrid Assembly
LAHAWS	Laser Homing and Warning System
LAHS	Low Altitude High Speed
LAI	Latex Agglutination-Inhibition Leaf Area Index Leucocyte Adherence Inhibition

	Library Association of Ireland (Eire)
	Low Airspeed Indicator
LAICA	Lineas Aereas Interiores de Catalina (Colombia)
LAIG	Library Association Industrial Group
LAIICS	Latin American Institute for Information and Computer Sciences (Chile)
LAIR	Letterman Army Institute of Research (US Army)
LAIRS	Labor Agreement Information Retrieval System (of USCSC)
LAITG	Library Association Information Technology Group
LAL	Laboratoire de l'Acceleateur Lineaire (University of Paris (France)) Linear Accelerator Laboratory)
	Library Association Library (now with BLRD)
	Limulus Amoebocyte Lysate
	Local Adjunct Language
LALA	Linoleic Acid-Like Activity
LALLS	Low Angle Laser Light Scattering
LALSD	Language for Automated Logic and System Design
LALUC	Local Authority Land Use Classification system
LAMA	Local Automatic Message Accounting
LAMA	Locomotive and Allied Manufacturers Association (now Railway Industry Association of Great Britain)
LAMARS	Large Amplitude Multimode Aerospace Research Simulator
LAMBDA	Language for Manufacturing Business and Distribution Activities
	Low Ambiguity DECCA
LAMCO	Liberian American Swedish Minerals Corporation (Liberia)
LAMCS	Latin American–American Communications Systems
LAMIS	Los Angeles Municipal Information System (USA)
	Local Authority Management Information System
LAMMA	Laser Microprobe Mass Analyser
LAMP	Lighthouse Automation and Modernization Project (of US Coast Guard)
	Logic Analyser for Maintenance Planner
	Low-Altitude Manned Penetrator Aircraft
LAMPF	Los Alamos Meson Physics Facility (USA)
LAMPRE	Los Alamos Molten Plutonium Reactor
LAMPS	Light Airborne Multi-Purpose System
LAMS	Land Acquisition and Management Scheme
	Light Aircraft Maintenance Schedule
	Load Alleviation and Mode Stabilization
	London Association of Master Stonemasons
LAMSAC	Local Authorities Management Services and Computer Committee (merged with LBMSU in 1975) (name of merged organisation to be retained)
LAN	Linea Aerea Nacional (Chile) (National Air Line)
	Local Area Network
LANBY	Large Automatic Navigation Buoy
LANDFAE	Large Area Nozzle Delivery of Fuel Air Explosive
LANDSAT	previously known as Earth Resources Technology Satellite (ERTS)
LANICA	Lineas Aereas de Nicaragua (Nicaragua) (National Air Lines)
LANL	Los Alamos National Laboratory (of DOE (USA))
LANNET	Large Artificial Nerve Net
LANS	Land Navigation System
LANSA	Lineas Aereas Nacionales S.A. (Peru) (National Air Lines)
LANTIRN	Low Altitude Navigation and Targeting Infra-Red for Night
LANTSAR	Atlantic International Air and Surface Search and Rescue Seminar
LAOAR	Latin American Office of Aerospace Research (USAF)
LAP	Laboratory of Atmospheric Physics (of the Desert Research Institute (USA))
	Leucine Aminopeptidase
	Leucocyte Alkaline Phosphatase
	Lineas Aerias Paraguayas (Paraguay) (National Air Line)
LAPADS	Lightweight Acoustic Processing And Display System
LAPAM	Low Altitude Penetrating Attack Missile
LAPCO	Lavan Petroleum Company (Iran) (partly government owned)
LAPDOG	Low Altitude Pursuit Dive On Ground
LAPES	Low Altitude Parachute Extraction System
LAPFA	Laminated Plastics Fabricators Association
LAPPES	Large Power Plant Effluent Study
LAPS	LOVELACE (FOUNDATION FOR MEDICAL EDUCATION AND RESEARCH (USA)) Aerosol Particle Separator
LAPSE	Longterm Ambulatory Physiological Surveillance Equipment
LAPSS	Laser Airborne Photographic Scanning System
LAR	Libyan Arab Republic
	Light Artillery Rocket
	Liquid Argon
LARA	Light Armed Reconnaissance Aircraft
	Low Altitude Radar Altimeter
LARAM	Line-Addressable Random-Access Memory
LaRC	Langley Research Center (of NASA (USA))
LARC	Leukocyte Automatic Recognition Computer
	Library Automation Research and Consulting Association (USA) (now the Library Information Science Division of the World Information Systems Exchange)
	Lighter Amphibious Resupply Cargo
	Lighter Amphibious Resupply Craft
	Low Altitude Ride Control
LARIAT	Laser Radar Intelligence Acquisition Technology
LARM	Logistics Assets Requirements Model
LARMARV	Low-Angle Re-entry Manoeuvring Re-entry Vehicle
LARP	Launch and Recovery Platform
LARS	Laboratory for Agricultural Remote Sensing (Purdue University (USA))
	Laboratory for Application of Remote Sensing (Purdue University (USA))
	Laser Aerial Rocket System
	Laser Angular Rate Sensor
	Laser-Aided Rocket System
LARSIS	Library Association Reference and Special Information Section
LAS	Large Astronomical Satellite
	Library Association of Singapore (Singapore)
	Look-out Aiming Sight
	Low Altitude Satellite
	Lower Airspace
	Lymphadenopathy Associated Syndrome
LASA	Large Aperture Seismic Array
LASAM	Laser Semi-Active Missile
LASAR	Logic Automated Stimulus And Response
LASCOT	Large Screen Colour Television
LASCR	Light Activated Silicone Controlled Rectifier
LASEORS	London and South Eastern Operational Research Society
	London and South Eastern Operational Research Society
LASER	Light Amplification by Stimulated Emission of Radiation
	London and South Eastern Library Region
LASERCOM	Laser Communications
LASH	Lighter Aboard Ship
LASI	Landing-Site Indicator

LASIE Library Automated Systems Information Exchange (Australia)
LASIL Land and Sea Interaction Laboratory (USC & GS)
LASIM Laser Aiming Simulation
LASL Los Alamos (New Mexico) Scientific Laboratory (California University) (now LANL of DOE (USA))
LASMEC Local Authorities School Meals Equipment Consortium
LASP Low Altitude Surveillance Platform
Low-Altitude Space Platform
LASR-2 LITTON (SYSTEM (CANADA) LTD) Airborne Search Radar Mark Two
LASRM Low-Altitude Supersonic Research Missile
LASS Lanthanum Polystyrene Sulphonate
Lateral Acceleration Sensing system
Lighter-than-Air Submarine Simulator
Lockheed Airline System Stimulation
Logistics Analysis Simulation System
Low Altitude Supersonic Speed
Lunar Applications of a Spent Stage
LASSIW Low Airspeed Sensing and Indicating Equipment
LASSO Laser Search and Secure Observer
Light Anti-Surface Semi-automatic Optical
Lunar Applications of a Spent Stage in Orbit
LAST Low Altitude Supersonic Target
LASV Low-Altitude Supersonic Vehicle
LAT Latex Agglutination Test
Less Active Tetragonal
Local Apparent Solar Time
Lowest Astronomical Tide
LATAF Logistics Activation Task Force
LATAR Laser-Augmented Target Acquisition and Recognition system
LATCC London Air Traffic Control Centre
LATG Laboratory Automation Trials Group (of DHSS)
LATHES Laser Terminal Homing Engagement Simulator
LATIS Lightweight Airborne Thermal Imaging System
LATOFF Lowest Astronomical Tide of the Foreseeable Future
LATOM Lowest Astronomical Tide of the Month
LATOY Lowest Astronomical Tide of the Year
LATREC Laser-Acoustic Time Reversal, Expansion and Compression
LATRIX Light Accessible Transistor Matrix
LATS LITTON (SYSTEMS (CANADA) LTD)) Automated Test Set
Long-Acting Thyroid Stimulator
LAU Linear Accelerometer Unit
LAV Light Armoured Vehicle
Linea Aeropostal Venezolana (Venezuela)
LAVA Linear Amplifier for Various Applications
LAVAC Laser Atmospheric Visibility And Contamination system
LAVI Lymphadenopathy Associated Virus
LAVM LORAN Automatic Vehicle Monitoring
LAW Land Authority for Wales
Laser Absorption Wave
Light Anti-tank Assault Weapon
LAWDS LORAN Aided Weapon Delivery System
LAWRS Limited Airport Weather Reporting System
LAWS Light Aviation Warning Service (of the Meteorological Office)
LAX Los Angeles International Airport (USA)
LAXRAY Large X-ray Survey Experiment
LBA Lease Brokers Association
Lifting-Body-Airship
Linear-Bounded Automation
London Boroughs Association
Luftfahrt Bundesamt (Germany) (West German Civil Aviation Authority)
LBBB Left Bundle Branch Block
LBCM Locator at Back Course Marker
LBI Long-Baseline Interferometer OR Interferometry
LBIR Laser Beam Image Reproducer
LBJCC London Boroughs Joint Computer Committee
LBL Lawrence Berkeley Laboratory (University of California (USA)) (now of DOE (USA))
LBLG Large Blast Load Generator
LBM Laser Beam Machining
LBMS London Boroughs Management Services
LBMSU London Boroughs Management Service Unit (merged with LAMSAC in 1975)
LBN Lembaga Biologi Nasional (Indonesia) (National Biological Institute)
LBNP Lower Body Negative Pressure
LBO Line Build-Out
LBP Length Between Perpendiculars
LBR Laser Beam Recorder
Laser Beam Rider
Low Burst Rate
LBS London Graduate School of Business Studies
LBT Light-Beam Transmissometer
LBTMA Listen Before Transmission Multiple Access
LBW Laser Beam Welding
Low-Birthweight
LC Library of Congress (USA)
Liquid Chromatography
Liquid-Crystal
Localised Corrosion
Locus Coaruleus
Logical Channel
LCA Laboratoire Centrale de l'Armament (of DTAT (France))
Light Combat Aircraft
Low Cost Automation
LCACA Lower Canada Arms Collectors Association (Canada)
LCACM Liaison Committee of Architects of the COMMON MARKET
LCAO Linear Combination of Atomic Orbitals
LCAO-MO- SCF Linear Combination of Atomic Orbitals in Molecular Orbital, Self-Consistent Field
LCAOSCF Linear Combination of Atomic Orbitals Self-Consistent Field
LCAR Low-Coverage Acquisition Radar
LCB Limited Capability Buoy
Line Control Block
Longitudinal Centre of Buoyancy
LCC Life Cycle Cost OR Costing
Linear Cutting Cord (aircraft escape)
LCCI London Chamber of Commerce and Industry
LCCM Life Cycle Cost Model
LCCP Life Cycle Computer Programme
LCD Liquid Crystal Display
List of Chosen Descriptors
LCDOSEM Local Civil Defence Operating Systems Evaluation Model
LCE Launch Complex Equipment
Lightweight Load Carrying Equipment
LCES Least Cost Estimating and Scheduling
LCF Latent Cancer Fatalities
Launch Control Facility
Lime, Cement and Flyash
Liquid Complex Fertilizer
Local Cycle Fatigue
Low Cycle Fatigue
LCFC Low-Cycle Fatigue Counter
LCFLOLS Laterally Compounded FRESNEL Lens Optical Landing System Institute)
LCFSPR Last Come, First Served Preemptive Resumé
LCG Liquid Cooled Garment
Load Classification Group
Longitudinal Centre of Gravity

LCGT/IGS Low Cost Graphics Terminal/Interactive Graphics System
LCH Landing Craft Heavy
LCHTF Low Cycle High Temperature Fatigue
LCI Learner Centred Instruction
Liquid Crystal Institute (Kent State University (USA))
LCIE Laboratoire Central des Industries Electriques (France)
LCIGS Low-Cost Inertial Guidance System
LCL Landing Craft Logistic
Less-than-Carload
Lower Control Limit
Lymphoblastoid Cell Line
LCLSC Life-Cycle Logistic Support Cost
LCLU Landing Control and Logic Units
LCLV Liquid Crystal Light Valve
LCM Landing Craft Mechanized
Large Capacity Core Memory
Least Common Multiple
Liquid Curing Media
Liquid Curing Method
Lymphocytic Choriomeningitis
LCMM Life Cycle Management Model
LCMS Life Cycle Management System
Low Cost Modular Spacecraft
LCMV Lymphocytic Choriomeningitis Virus
LCN Load Classification Number
LCO London College of Osteopathic Medicine
LCOM Logistics Composite Model
LCP Lateral Choroid Plexus
Legislative Council for Photogrammetry (USA)
London College of Printing
LCPC Laboratoire Central des Ponts et Chaussees (France) (Central Laboratory of Bridges and Roads)
LCR Logarithmic Correlators Ratiometer
LCRE Lithium Cooled Reactor Experiment
LCRR Low Cost Risk Reduction
LCRU Lunar Communications Relay Unit
LCS (Mars) Lander Camera System
Laboratory for Computational Statistics (Stanford University (USA))
Laboratory for Computer Science (of MIT (USA))
Laboratory of Computer Science (Massachusetts General Hospital (USA))
Large Core Storage
Liberian Cartographic Service (Liberia)
LINCOLN Calibration Sphere
Linked Cross Sectional
LCSE Laser Communication Satellite Experiment
LCSG London Construction Safety Group
LCSO Low Cost Systems Office (of NASA (USA))
LCSS Land Combat Support System
LCST Lower Critical Solution Temperature
LCT Laboratoire Central de Telecommunications (France)
Light Capital Technology
Low Cost Technology
LCU Landing Craft Utility
LCV Low Calorific Value
LCXT Large Cosmic X-ray Telescope
LD Letter Description
Linear Dichroism
Lymphocyte Defined
LD-BLC Low Drag Boundary Layer Control
LDA Land Development Aircraft
Landing Distance Available
Laser Doppler Anemometry
Lead Development Association
Local Density Approximation
Localizer-type Directional Aid
Logical Device Address
Lymphocyte Dependent Antibody
LDAM Local Damage Assessment Model
LDAR Lightning Detection and Ranging System (at Kennedy Space Center (of NASA (USA))
LDASE Large Deployable Antenna Shuttle Experiment
LDC LASA Data Center
LDDC London Docklands Development Corporation
LDDO Long-Distance Diesel Oil
LDE Laminar Defect Examination
Long-Delayed Echoes
LDEF Long-Duration Exposure Facility
LDF Light Distillate Feedstock
LDGO Lamont Doherty Geological Observatory (Columbia University (USA))
LDH Lactic Dehydrogenase
LDIN Lead-in Lighting System
LDL Language Description Language
Lighting Design Lumens
Loudness Discomfort Level
Low Density Lipoprotein
LDM Linear Delta Modulation
LDMX Local Digital Message Exchange
LDNS Light-weight Doppler Navigation System
LDO Light Diesel Oil
LDOS Long Duration Orbital Simulator
LDPE Low-Density Polyethylene
LDR Large Deployable Reflector
Light Dependent Resistor
Limiting Drawing Ratio
Linear Decision Rules
LDRS Language Design for Reliable Softwave (symposium sponsored by ACM (USA))
LEM Data Reduction System
LDS Light Distillate Spirit
LDSRA Logistics Doctrine, Systems and Readiness Agency (US Army) (now Logistics Evaluation Agency)
LDSS Laser Designator Seeker Systems
LDT Logic Design Translator
LDTA Large Diameter Tube Association
LDV Laser Doppler Velocimeter OR Velocimetry
LDX Long Distance Xerography
LE-VGF Liquid Encapsulation-Vertical Gradient Freeze
LEA Laboratorio de Engenharia de Angola (Angola)
Linear Embedding Algorithm
Logistics Evaluation Agency (US Army)
LEAA Law Enforcement Assistance Administration (Department of Justice (USA))
LEAD Laboratories d'Electronique et d'Automatique Dauphinois (France)
LEADER LEHIGH (UNIVERSITY) (USA) Automatic Device for Efficient Retrieval
LEADERMAR LEHIGH (UNIVERSITY) (USA) Answer to Demand for Efficient Retrieval–Mart Library
LEADS Law Enforcement Automated Data System
LEIGH Airborne Data Acquisition System
Logical and Electrical Automatic Drafting System
LEAF LISP Extended Algebraic Facility
LEAFAC Local Employment Acts Financial Advisory Committee (of Department of Trade and Industry) (dissolved 1973)
LEAHS Life-time Evaluation and Analysis of Heterogeneous System
LEAM Lunar Ejecta and Meteorites Experiment
LEANS LEHIGH (UNIVERSITY) (USA) Analog Simulator
LEAP Laboratory Evaluation and Accreditation Program (of NBS (USA))
LAMBDA (CORPORATION) Efficiency Analysis Programme

LEAPS — Law Enforcement Agencies Processing System (Massachusetts (USA))
Local Exchange Area Planning Simulation
LEAS-FACS — Lease-Financial Accounting Control System
LEB — London Electricity Board
LEBA — Long Endurance Breathing Apparatus
LEC — Liquid Encapsulation-Czochralski
London Education Classification
Low Emitter Concentration
LECA — Light European Combat Aircraft
LED — Light Emitting Device
Light-Emitting Diode
LEDC — Local Economic Development Corporations (USA)
Low Energy Detonating Chord
LEDT — Limited-Entry Decision Table
LEDU — Local Enterprise Development Unit (of Ministry of Commerce (Northern Ireland))
LEE — Laser Energy Evaluator
LEED — Laser-Energised Explosive Device
Low Energy Electron Diffraction
LEEP — Library Education Experimental Project (of Syracuse University (USA))
LEER — Low-Energy Electron Reflections
LEF — Light-Emitting Film
LEFE — Linear Electric Field Effect
LEFM — Linear Elastic Fracture Mechanics
LEFTA — Labour (ie) (The Labour Party) Economic, Finance and Taxation Association
LEIN — Law Enforcement Information Network (Michigan (USA))
LEIS — Low Energy Ion Scattering
LEIT — Light Emission by Inelastic Tunnelling
LEL — Lower Earnings Limit
Lower Explosion Limit
LEM — Laser Emission Microprobe
Laser Energy Meter
Leukocytic Endogenous Mediator
Lunar Excursion Module
LEMA — Lifting Equipment Manufacturers Association
LEMAG — Laboratory Equipment and Methods Advisory Group (of DHSS)
LEMRAS — Law Enforcement Manpower Resource Allocation System
LENA — Laboratorio Energia Nucleare Applicata (Italy) (Applied Nuclear Energy Laboratory)
LENDS — Library Extends Catalog Access and New Delivery System (of Georgia Institute of Technology (USA))
LEO — Littoral Environment Observation
Low Earth Orbit
Lunar Exploration Operations
LEOK — Laboratium voor Elektronische Ontwikkelingen voor de Krijsmacht (Netherlands) (Electronic Development Laboratory for the Armed Forces)
LEP — Laboratoires d'Electronique et de Physique Appliquee (France)
Large Electron Positron
LEPOR — Long-term Expanded Programme of Oceanic Exploration and Research (of IOC (UNESCO))
LEQ — Equivalent Continuous Sound Level
LER — Licensee Event Report (of Nuclear Regulatory Commission) (USA)
LeRC — Lewis Research Center (of NASA (USA))
LERC — Laramie Energy Research Center (of DOE (USA))
LERLS — Lake Erie Regional Library System (Canada)
LERMISTOR — Learning Materials Information Store
LERSC — Location Evaluation Recognition and Statistical Comparison
LERSO — Low Erucic Acid Rapeseed Oil
LERX — Leading Edge Root Extension
LES — Launch Escape System
LINCOLN (Lincoln Laboratory, Massachusetts Institute of Technology) Experimental Satellite
Louisiana Engineering Society (USA)
LESA — Lunar Explorations System for APOLLO
LESA-A-A — Least Squares Adjust-And-Analysis Programme
LESL — Law Enforcement Standards Laboratory (of NBS (USA))
LESS — Least Cost Estimating and Scheduling
LET — LINCOLN (Lincoln Laboratory, Massachusetts Institute of Technology) Experimental Terminal
Linear Energy Transfer
LETC — Laramie Energy Technology Center (of DOE (USA))
LETI — Laboratoire d'Electronique et de Technologie de l'Informatique (France)
LETIS — Leicestershire Technical Information Service
LETS — Large, External Transformation Sensitive protein
LEU — Low Enriched Uranium
LEZOR — Liquid Encapsulation Zone-Refining
LF — Lactoferrin
LFAD — Less Favoured Areas Directive (of EEC)
LFATDS — Lightweight Field Artillery Tactical Data System
LFC — Laminar Flow Control
Large Format Camera (aboard a space shuttle)
Load Frequency Control
LFE — Laminar Flow Element
LFEC — Low Frequency Eddy Current
LFER — Linear Free Energy Relationship
LFICS — Landing Force Integrated Communications System
LFL — Lower Flammable Limit
LFM — Limited-area Fine-mesh Model
Linearly Modulated Frequency
LFRA — Leatherhead Food Research Association
LFRAP — Long Feeder Route Analysis Programme
LFRED — Liquid-Fuelled Ramjet Engine
LFS — Landing Fire Support
LFSR — Linear-Feedback Shift Register
LFSW — Landing Force Support Weapon
LFT — Latext Fixation Test
Lens-less Fourier Transform
Lensless Fourier Transformation
LFTB — Liquid Fuels Trust Board (New Zealand)
LFTEG — Liquid Fuelled Thermo-Electric Generator
LFTI — Leningradskiy Fiziko-Technicheskiy Institut (USSR) (Leningrad Physical-Technical Institute)
LFU — Leichflugtechnik-Union (Germany)
Lunar Flying Unit
LFV — Lunar Exploration Flying Vehicle
Lunar Flying Vehicle
LG — Letter Gestalts
LGB — Laser Guided Bomb
Lateral Geniculate Body
LGC — Laboratory of the Government Chemist (now of DTI)
LGDM — Laser-Guided Dispenser Munition
LGE — Laboratoire de Geophysics Extern (France) (External Geophysics Laboratory)
LGEC — Lunar Geological Exploration Camera
LGI — Linear Gas-discharge Indicator
LGIO — Local Government Information Office
LGM — Laboratorium voor Grondmechanica (Netherlands) (Soil Mechanics Laboratory)
LGMD — Lobular Giant Movement Detector
LGN — Lateral Geniculate Nucleus
LGO — Lamont Geological Observatory (Columbia University, USA)
LGORU — Local Government Operational Research Unit (of Royal Institute of Public Administration)

LGPMSG Local Government Personnel and Management Services Group
LGR Letter of General Representation
Localised Gain Region
LGS Landing-Guidance System
LGSBS London Graduate School of Business Studies
LGTB Local Government Training Board
LGV Lymphogranuloma Venereum
LGWCM Laser Guided Weapons Counter-Measures
LH Lateral Hypothalamus
Lateral Hypothalmic
Liquid Hydrogen
Lutenizing Hormone
LH-RH Luteinizing Hormone Releasing Hormone
LHA Landing Helicopter Assault ship (now known as General Purpose Amphibious Assault)
Local Hour Angle
LHC London Housing Consortium
LHCP Left-Hand Circularly Polarized
LHD Load-Haul-Dump machinery
LHe Liquid Helium
LHeT Liquid Helium Temperature
LHG Library History Group (of the Library Association)
Local Haemolysis in Gel
LHNCBC Lister Hill Center for Biomedical Communications (of the National Library of Medicine (USA))
LHR Long-term Heart Rate
Lower Hybrid Resonance
LHRH Luteinising Hormone-Releasing Hormone
LHS Latin Hypercube Sampling
LHX Light Helicopter Experimental
Li prefix to numbered series issued by the Light Division of NPL (MINTECH) (now of DoI)
LI Landscape Institute
LIA Laser Industry Association (USA)
Laser Institute of America (USA)
Laser-Induced Absorption
Lead Industries Association (USA)
Lebanese International Airways (Lebanon)
Linear Induction Accelerator
Lymphocyte-Induced Angiogenesis
LIAP Leningradskiy Institut Aviatsionnogo Priborostroyeniya (USSR) (Leningrad Institute of Aviation Instrument Construction)
LIB Light Ion Beam
LIBEC Light Behind Camera
LIBER Ligue des Bibliotheques Europeennes de Recherche (League of European Research Libraries)
LIBGIS Library General Information Survey (of National Center for Educational Statistics (USOE) (USA))
LIBIS Leuven's Integraal Bibliotheek System (Catholic University of Leuven (Belgium))
LIBOR London Inter-bank Offered Rate
LIC Less Industralized Country
Life Insurance Corporation (India) (govt owned)
Linear Integrated Circuit
LICALM LORAN Inertial Command Air-Launched Missile
LID Leadless Inverted Device
Linear Imaging Device
Liquid Interface Diffusion
Lunar Ionosphere Detector
LIDAR Laser Intensity Direction And Ranging
Light Detection And Ranging
LIDIA Learning In Dialog
LIDO Logic In, Documents Out
LIDS Laboratory for Information and Decision Systems (of MIT (USA))
Laser Illumination Detection System
Leadless Inverted Devices
Lift Improvement Devices
LIED Large Industrial Engineering Development (a project of the Japanese Government)
LIF Lighting Industry Federation
LIFE Laser Induced Fluorescence of the Environment
League for International Food Education (USA) (Consortium of Scientific Societies)
LIFO Last-In, First-Out
LIFS Laser Induced Fluorescence Spectroscopy
LIFT Linear Field-Trainable
London (Stratford) International Freight Terminal
LII Light Image Intensifier
LIIVT Leningradskiy Institut Inzhenerov Vodnogo Transporta (USSR) (Leningrad Institute of Water Transport Engineers)
LIL Large Ionic Lithophile
Law of the Iterated Logarithm
Local Interaction Language
Lunar International Laboratory (of International Academy of Astronautics) (now MARECEBO)
LILA Life Insurance Logistics Automated
LILAC Low Intensity Large Area City Light
LILE Large Ion Lithophile Elements
LIM Line Insulation Monitor
Line Interface Module
Linear Induction Motor
Liquid Injection Moulding
LIMA Light-Induced Modulation of Absorption
LIMAC Large Integrated Monolithic Array Computer
LIMB Library Instruction Materials Bank (at Loughborough University)
LIMIT Lot-size Inventory Management Interpolation Technique
LIML Limited Information Maximum Likelihood
LIMP Language-Independent Macro Processor
LIMRV Linear Induction Motor Research Vehicle
LIMS Laboratory Information Management System
Limb Infrared Monitor of the Stratosphere (an experiment carried on the Nimbus-7 artificial satellite)
LIN Liquid Nitrogen
LINAC Linear Accelerator
LINAS Laser Inertial Navigation Attack System
LINC LINCOLN LABORATORY (Massachusetts Institute of Technology) Instrument Computer
LINCE Laser Improved Naval Combat Equipment
LINCLOE Lightweight Individual Combat Clothing and Equipment
LINCO Linear Composition
LINCOMPEX Linked Compressor and Expander
LINCOTT Liaison, Interface, Coupling, Technology Transfer
LINCS Language Information Network and Clearinghouse System (Center for Applied Linguistics (USA)
LINDA Local Interactive Design Aid
LINGO Linear Network analysis by General Operations
LINK Lambeth Information Network
LINOC Linear Optical Coincidence
LINOSCO Libraries of North Staffordshire in Cooperation
LINPEX London International Invention and New Products Exhibition
LINS Laser-gyro Inertial Navigation System
LORAN Inertial Navigation System
LIOD Light-weight Optronic Director
LIP Laser Integrated Periscope
LIPL Linear Information Processing Language
LIPS Laboratory Information Processing System

	Laser Image Processing Scanner
	Logical Interferences per Second
LIQSS	Liquid Steady State
LIQT	Liquid Transient
LIR	Laser Image Recorder
	Line Integral Refractometer
LIRA	Linen Industry Research Association
LIRG	Library and Information Research Group (now in association with the Library Association)
LIRS	Library Information Retrieval System
LIRTA	Laboratoire d'Infrarouge Technique et Appliquee (France)
LIRTS	Large Infra-Red Telescope for Spacelab
LIS	Laboratory Implementation System
	Lanthanide Induced Shift
	Laser Isotope Separation
	Lateral Intercellular Space
LISA	Lead-In-Steel Analyser
	Library Systems Analysis
	Linear Systems Analysis Programme
	LORAL Integrated Sub-Assembly
LISC	Library and Information Services Council
LISE	Librarians of Institutes and Schools of Education
LISN	Line Impedance Stabilization Network
LISP	Library and Information Software Package
	List Processing
LISPB	Lithospheric Seismic Profile in Britain
LISPER	Limited Speech Recognition
LIST	Library and Information Services, Tees-side
LISTAR	LINCOLN (Lincoln Laboratory, Massachusetts Institute of Technology) Information Storage and Associative Retrieval system
LISTS	Library Information System Time-Sharing
LIT	Light Intratheatre Transport
	Liquid Injection Technique
	Local Income Tax
LITA	Library and Information Technology Association (USA)
LITASTOR	Light Tapping Storage
LITE	Industria Libraria Tipografica Editrice (Italy)
	Laser Illumination Tracking Equipment
	Legal Information Through Electronics (of USDOD)
LITES	Ladies In Technical Electronic Servicing (USA)
LITR	Low-Intensity Test Reactor
LITS	Light Interface Technology System
LITVC	Liquid Injection Thrust Vector Control
LIU	Laboratories Investigation Unit (of Department of Education and Science)
LIV	Linear, Invariant
LIVCR	Low Input Voltage Conversion-Regulation
LIVE	Liquid Inertia Vibration Eliminator
LIW	Light-weight Individual Weapon
LIX	Liquid Ion Exchange
LJC	London Joint Committee of Graduate and Student Engineers
LKM	Low Key Maintenance
LKT	Laboratorium fur Kunststofftechnik (Austria) (Plastics Technology Laboratory)
LL/GDS	Land-Locked and Geographically Disadvantaged States
LLA	Louisiana Library Association (USA)
LLAD	Low Level Air Defence
LLATIS	Low Light And Thermal Imaging Systems
LLC	Liquid-Liquid Chromatography
LLCCA	Long Life Cycle Cost Avionics
LLF	Light Loss Factor
LLFET	Linear Load Field Effect Transistor
LLFM	Low Level Flux Monitor
LLFT	Lens-less Fourier Transform
LLG	Lighting Liaison Group (Electricity Council, Lighting Industry Federation, ECA, APLE, DLMA, and IES)
LLGL	Low Level Graphical Language
LLL	LAWRENCE (ERNEST O) Livermore Laboratory (California University) (USA) (NOW LLNL (DOE) (USA))
	Low Level Logic
	Low-Light-Level
LLLTV	Low Light Level Television
LLNL	Lawrence Livermore National Laboratory (USA)
LLR	Log-Likelihood Ratio
LLRDS	Long-Life Recording Data Sonobuoy
LLRS	Laser Lightning Rod System
	Long-Range Radar Station
LLRV	Lunar Landing Research Vehicle
LLSA	Louisiana Land Surveyors Association (USA)
LLSAC	Laser Line Scan Aerial Camera
LLTV	Low-light Level Television
	Lunar Landing Training Vehicle
LLV	Lunar Logistics Vehicle
LLW	Low Level Waste
LLWSAS	Low Level Wind Shear Alert System
LM	Liquid Membrane
	Liquid Mercury
	Lunar Module
LM-MHD	Liquid Metal Magnetohydrodynamics
LMA	Laser-Microspectrochemical Analysis
	Lebanese Management Association (Lebanon)
	Low Moisture Avidity
LMARS	Library Management and Retrieval System
LMC	Large Magellanic Cloud
	Latex-Modified Concrete
	Lymphocyte Mediated Cytotoxity
LMCA	Lorry Mounted Crane Association
LMCSS	Letter Mail Code Sorting System
LMCV	Lymphocyte Choriomeningitis Virus
LME	Liquid Metal Embrittlement
LMEC	London Metal Exchange
	Laboratorio Nacional de Engenharia Civil (Portugal) (National Civil Engineering Laboratory)
	Liquid Metal Engineering Centre (formerly of USAEC) (now of ERDA (USA))
LMF	Linear Matched Filter
	Linear Multistep Formulae
	Liquid Methane Fuel
LMFA	Light Metal Founders Association
LMFBR	Liquid Metal Fast Breeder Reactor
LMG	Light Machine Gun
	London Medical Group
LMH	Light Military Hovercraft
LMI	Leucocyte Migration Inhibition
	Logistics Management Information
	Logistics Management Institute (USA)
LMIC	Liquid Metal Information Center (of USAEC) (now of ERDA)
LMICS	Logistics Management Information and Control System
LMIS	Logistics Management Information System
LML	Lean Misfire Limb
LMM	Light Meromyosin
	Linear Multi-step Method
LMNA	Land-based Multi-purpose Naval Aircraft
LMPV	Liquid-Metal Plasma Valve
LMRI	Laboratoire de Metrologie des Rayonnements Ionisants (France) (Metrology Laboratory of Radionuclides)
LMRU	Library Management Research Unit (University of Cambridge) (re-established at Loughborough University in 1976)
LMS	Least Mean Square
	Library Maintenance System

	London Mathematical Society
LMSA	Labor-Management Services Administration (of Department of Labor (USA))
	Large Metoscale Area
LMSS	Lunar Mapping and Survey System
LMT	Local Mean Solar Time
	Societe Le Materiel Telephonique (France)
LMVE	Linear, Minimum Variance Estimation
LMW	Low Molecular Weight
LMWD	Low Molecular Weight Dextron
LN	Luft Norm (numbered series of Aerospace Standards issued by DIN (Germany))
LNA	Launch Numerical Aperture
	Low Noise Amplifier
LNB	Large Navigation Buoy
	Lithium Niobate
LNBEE	Laboratoire National Belge d'Electrothermie et d'Electrochime (Belgium) (Belgian National Electrothermal and Electrochemical Laboratory)
LNEC	Laboratorio Nacional de Engenharia Civil (Portugal) (National Civil Engineering Laboratory)
LNF	Laboratori Nazional di Frascati (Italy)
LNG	Liquefied Natural Gas
LNP	Leg Negative Pressure
LNPF	Lymph Node Permeability Factor
LNR	Local Nature Reserve
	Low Noise Receiver
LNRA	Linear Nested Region Analysis
LNRS	Limited Night Recovery System
LNS	Land Navigation System
LNT	Liquid Nitrogen Temperature
LNTPB	Laboratoire National des Travaux Publics et du Batiment (Algeria) (National Laboratory of Public Works and Building)
LNTWTA	Low-Noise Travelling-Wave Tube Amplifier
LO	Longitudinal Optical
	Lubricating Oil
LO/LO	Lift-On/Lift-Off
LOA	Laser Opto-Acoustic
	Launch On Assessment
	Length Overall
	Life Offices' Association
LOAD	Laser Opto-Acoustic Detection
LOADS	Lifting Of Aerodynamic Decelerators
	Low-Altitude Defence System
LOB	Line of Balance
	Location of Offices Bureau (of BOT)
LOBE	Laboratoire d'Optique de Besancon (France)
LOBO	Lobe-On-Receive-Only
LOBSTER	Long Term Ocean Bottom Settlement Test for Engineering Research
LOC	Large Optical Cavity
	Launch Operations Centre
	Lines of Communication
LOCA	Loss-of-Coolant Accident
LOCAS	Local Cataloguing Service (of the Bibliographic Services Division of the British Library)
LOCAT	Low Cost Air Target
LOCATE	Library of Congress (USA) Automation Techniques Exchange
LOCEP	Local Epitaxy
LOCI	Logarithmic Computing Instrument
LOCMOS	Locally Oxidised Complementary Metal Oxide Semiconductor
LOCOS	Local Oxidation Of Silicon
LOCS	Logic and Control Simulator
LODACS	Longitudinal frame Developing And Conducting System
LODIF	Long Distance Infrared Flash Camera
LOERQ	Large Orbiting Earth Resources Observatory
LOF	Lowest Operating Frequency
LOFAADS	Low-altitude Forward Area Air Defence System
LOFADS	Low-Altitude Forward Air Defence System (US Army)
LOFAR	Low-Frequency Omnidirectional Acoustic-frequency Analysis and Recording
LOFER	Laundau Orbital Ferromagnetism
LOFEZ	Low Fighter Engagement Zone
LOFF	LORAN Flight Following
LOFT	Loss of Flow Test
	Loss of Fluid Test
	Low-Frequency Radio Telescope
LOGACS	Low Gravity Accelerometer Calibration System
LOGAIR	Logistics Command Contract Airlift System (USAF)
LOGAL	Logical Algorithmic Language
LOGC	Logistics Center (US Army)
LOGCOST	Logistics Cost Model
LOGEL	Logic Generating Language
LOGIC	Laser Optical Guidance Integration Concept
	Local Government Information Control system
LOGIMP	Local Government Implementation
LOGIT	Logical Inference Tester
LOGMAP	Logistics System Master Plan (US Army)
LOGMIS	Logistics Management Information Systems (US Army)
LOGO	Limit Of Government Obligation
LOGPLAN	Logistics Plan (USDOD)
LOH	Light Observation Helicopter
LOHAP	Light Observation Helicopter Avionics Package
LOI	Limiting Oxygen Index
	Lunar Orbit Insertion
LOIS	Law Office Information System
	Library Order Information System (of the Library of Congress (USA)
LOLA	Library On-Line Acquisitions
	London On-line Local Authorities
	Lunar Orbit Landing Approach
LOLITA	Language for the On-Line Investigation and Transformation of Abstractions
	Library On-Line Information and Text Access (Oregon State University Library (USA)
LOLP	Loss-Of-Load Probability
LOM	Locator at the Outer Marker
LOMA	Life Office Management Association (USA)
LOMMIS	Land Ordnance Maintenance Management Information System
LOMP	Local Office Microcomputer Project (of DHSS)
LOMUSS	LOCKHEED Multipurpose Simulation System
LONARS	LORAN Navigation Receiving System
LOP	Limit of Proportionality
LOPAC	Load Optimisation and Passenger Acceptance Control
LOPAD	Logarithmic Outline Processing system for Analogue Data
LOPAIR	Long Path Infra-Red
LOPAR	Low Powered Acquisition Radar
LOPS	LLOYDS (REGISTER OF SHIPPING) Ocean Engineering Platform System
LOR	Level Of Repair
	Light Output Ratio
	Lunar Orbital Rendezvous
LORA	Lecturer Oriented Response Analysis
LORAD	Long-Range Active Detection
LORADS	Long-range Radar and Display System
LORAE	Long Range Attitude and Events
LORAH	Long Range Area Homing
LORAM	Level of Repair for Aeronautical Material

LORAN Long-Range Aid to Navigation
LORAS Linear Omnidirectional Airspeed System
Low-Range Omni-directional Airspeed System
LORCO Long Range Planning Group (of ISO (Switzerland))
LORCS League of Red Cross Societies
LORDS Logic and Register-Transfer Design System
LORE Land Ordnance Engineering Branch (of Canadian Armed Forces)
LORENDAS Long-Range Energy Development And Supplies
LOREORS Long-Range Electro-Optical Reconnaissance System
LORIDS Long Range Iranian Detection System (Iran)
LORL Large Orbital Research Laboratory
LORO Lobe-On-Receive-Only
LOROP Long Range Oblique Photography
LORV Low Observable Re-entry Vehicle
LORW Light Output Ratio (Working)
LOS Land Observation Satellite
Law of the Sea Conference
Limit Order Switching system
Line of Sight
LOSS Large Object Salvage System
Lunar-Orbit Space Station
LOT Large Orbital Telescope
Lightspot Operated Typewriter
Load-on-Top (a method of marine tanker cleaning)
Polskie Linie Lotnicze (Poland) (National Air Line)
LOTAWS Laser Obstacle Terrain Avoidance Warning System
LOTIS Logic, Timing and Sequencing
LOTS Logistics Over the Shore
LOUISA Linguistically Oriented Understanding and Indexing System for Abstracts
LOVER Lunar Orbiting Vehicle for Emergency Rescue
LOX Liquid Oxygen
LP Leaf Protein
Linear Programming
Low Pressure
Low Protein
Lumbar Puncture
LPA Local Productivity Association
Logarithmically-Periodic Antenna
LPAC Launching Programmes Advisory Committee (of ESRO)
LPASA Linear Pulse-height Analyzer Spectrum Analysis
LPBA Lawyer-Pilots Bar Association (USA)
LPC Leaf-Protein Concentrate
Linear Predictive Coding
Local Productivity Committee
Low Pressure Compressor
Lysophosphatidylcholine
LPCG Laser Planning and Co-ordination Group (of ERDA (USA))
LPCVD Low Pressure Chemical Vapour Deposition
LPD Labelled Plan Display
Landing Ship Personnel and Dock
Language Processing and Debugging
Lateral Photoelectric Detector
Log-Periodic Dipole
LPDA Log-Periodic Dipole Array
LPE Linear Polyethylene
Linear Predictive Encoder
Liquid-Phase Epitaxial OR Epitaxy
Low Probability of Exploitation
Lysophosphatidylethanolamine
LPF Large Particle Furnace
Lymphocytosis-promoting Factor
LPFA Laminated Plastics Fabricators Association
LPG Liquefied Petroleum Gas
Liquified Propane Gas
LPGITA Liquid Petroleum Gas Industry Technical Association
LPGITC Liquefied Petroleum Gas Industry Technical Committee
LPI Linear Partial Information
Logistics Performance Indicator
Low-Probability-of-Intercept radar
Lower Probability of Intercept
Lunar and Planetary Institute (of NASA (USA))
LPIA Liquid Propellant Information Agency (JHU)
LPIS Low Pressure Injection System
LPL List Processing Language
Lunar and Planetary Laboratory (University of Arizona (USA))
LPLA Log-Periodic Loop Antenna
LPM Laser Particle Monitor
Lunar Portable Magnetometer
LPO Liquid Phase Oxidation
Lobus Parolfactorius
Lunar Parking Orbit
LPP Low Power Physics
LPPC Little People's Productivity Center Inc. (USA)
LPPM Low Pressure Permanent Mould
LPRE Liquid Propellant Rocket Engine
LPRINT Lookup Dictionary Print Programme
LPRM Local Power Range Monitor
LPS Laboratory of Plasma Studies (Cornell University (USA))
Laboratory Peripheral System
Lipopolysaccharide
Liquid Polymer System
LPS/PIA Lithographic Platemakers Section of Printing Industries of America (USA)
LPSF Lens-Pinhole Spatial Filter
LPSI Low Pressure Safety Ignition
LPSSR Low Power Spread Spectrum Radar
LPSTTL Low Power Schottky Transistor-Transistor Logic
LPTF Laboratoire Primaire du Temps et des Frequences (of BNM (France))
LPTV Large Pay-load Test Vehicle
LPU Line Printer Unit
LPUU Linear Programming Under Uncertainty
LPV Limiting Pressure Velocity
LQA Link Quality Analysis
LQG Linear-Quadratic-Gaussian approach
LQIV Linear, Quasi Invariant
LR Laboratory Report
Liaison Report
LR-PASS LLOYDS (REGISTER OF SHIPPING) Plan Appraised System for Ships
LR-SAFE LLOYDS (REGISTER OF SHIPPING) Ship Analysis using Finite Element
LR3 Laser Ranging Retroreflector
LRA Lace Research Association (now merged with HATRA)
Local Radio Association
LRAAM Long-Range Air-to-Air Missile
LRAAS Long-Range Airborne ASW System
LRAC Long-Run Average Cost Curve
LRALS Long-Range Approach and Landing System
LRATGW Long-Range Anti-Tank Guided Weapon
LRB Lissamine Rhodamine B
LRBA Laboratoire de Recherches Balistiques et Aerodynamics (France) (Ballistics and Aerodynamics Research Laboratory (of DEn)
Laboratoire de Recherches Balistiques et Aerodynamics (France) (Ballistics and Aerodynamics Research Laboratory) (now SEP)

LRBC Lloyds (Register of Shipping) Building Certificate
LRC Langley Research Center (of NASA)
Library Research Center (Illinois University (USA))
Light, Rapid, Comfortable railway train
Linear Responsibility Charting
Linguistics Research Center (University of Texas) (USA))
Lipid Research Clinic (of NHLI (USA))
LRCA Long-Range Combat Aircraft
LRCC Laboratoire de Recherches et de Control du Caoutchouc (France)
Library Resources Co-ordinating Committee (University of London)
London Regional Cancer Centre (of OCTRF (Canada))
LRCD Linear Rule of Cumulative Damage
LRCU Lunar Communications Relay Unit (mounted on LRV)
LRD Labelled Radar Display
LRDC Learning Research and Development Center (University of Pittsburg (USA))
LRES Linear Rocket Engine System
LRF Laser Range Finder
Low Rigid Frame
Luteinizing Releasing Factor
LRFAX Low Resolution Facsimile
LRGB Long-Range Glide Bomb
LRHSC Large Radioisotope Heat Source Capsule
LRI Legiforgalmi Repuloteri Igazgatosag (Hungary) (Air Traffic and Airport Administration)
LRIE Limb Radiance Inversion Experiment
LRIP Low Rate Initial Production
LRIR Limb Radiance Inversion Radiometer
LRIS Lloyds (Register of Shipping) Industrial Services
LRL Lawrence Radiation Laboratory (University of California, USA) (now Lawrence Berkeley Laboratory)
Lunar Receiving Laboratory (of NASA (USA))
LRM Linear Regression Model
Liquid Reaction Moulded
LRMC Low Run Marginal Cost
LRMG Lockless Rifle/Machine Gun
LRMR Long-Range Marine Reconnaissance
LRMTR Laser Ranger and Marked-Target Receiver
LRMTS Laser Ranger and Marked Target Seeker
LROS Long Range Optical System
LRP Long Range Planning
LRPA Long-Range Patrol Aircraft
LRPDS Long-Range Position Determining System
LRPE Long-Range Procurement Estimate
LRPL Liquid Rocket Propulsion Laboratory (US Army)
LRPLS Long Range Passive Location System
LRPT Longest Remaining Processing Time
LRR Laser Radiation Receiver
Long Range Radar
LRRP prefix to numbered series of Long Range Research Papers issued by Long Range Intelligence Division of the Post Office Corporation
LRRR Laser Ranging Retro-Reflector
LRS Legislative Reference Service (of the Library of Congress (USA))
London Research Station (of the British Gas Corporation)
LRSCA Large Retractable Solar Cell Array
LRSI Low-temperature Re-usable Surface Insulation
LRSM Laboratory for Research on the Structure of Matter (University of Pennsylvania (USA))
Long Range Seismic Measurement
Long Range Seismograph Measurements
LRSOM Long-Range Stand-Off Missile
LRSP Long Range Strategic Planning
LRSR Long-Range Sniper Rifle
LRSS Long Range Survey System (US Army)
LRT Laser Ray Tube
Launch, Recovery and Transport
Light Rail Transit
LRTA Light Rail Transit Authority (Philippines)
LRTF Long Range Technological Forecast
LRThD Lateral Reach-Through Device
LRTL Light Railway Transport League
LRTNF Long-Range Theatre Nuclear Forces
LRTP Long Range Technical Plan
LRTS Laser Ranging and Tracking System
LRU Least Recently Used
Line-Replaceable Unit
LRV Light Rail Vehicle
Lunar Roving Vehicle
LS Lecture Series
prefix to numbered series issued by Labor Standards Bureau (of Department of Labor (USA))
LSA Laser-Supported Absorption
Light Strike Aircraft
Limited Space-Charge Accumulation
London School of Accountancy
Lymphosarcoma
LSAB London Society of Air-Britain
LSAC Low Speed Access to a Computer
Low-pressure Suction Air Conveyor
LSAT Logistic Shelter Air Transportable
LSAW Laser-Supported Absorption-Waves
LSB Least Significant Bit
Lower Sideband
LSBEB Life Sciences and Biomedical Engineering Branch (of Aerospace Medical Association (USA))
LSBR Large Seed Blanket Reactor
LSC Laser-Supported Combustion
Liberian Shipowners Council
Linear Sequential Circuit
Linear Slope Controlled
Liquid-Solid Chromatography
LSCA Library Services and Construction Act (USA)
London and District Society of Chartered Accountants
LSCC Line-Sequential Colour Composite
LSD Land Surveys Division (of ACSM (USA))
Landing Ship Dock
Language for Systems Development
Large Shallow-Draught bulk carrier
Laser-Supported Detonation
Leadless Sealed Device
Least Significant Difference
Least Significant Digit
Limited Saturation Device
Lysergic Acid Diethylamide
Lysosomal Storage Disease
LSDS Large-Scale Dynamical System
LSE London School of Economics and Political Science
LSEB Life Sciences and Biomedical Engineering Branch (of Aerospace Medical Association (USA))
LSECS Life Support and Environmental Control System
LSEP Lunar Sample Educational Package (NASA (USA))
LSES Large Surface Effect Ship
LSF Line Spread Function
LSFFAR Low-Spin folding Fin Aircraft Rocket
LSFS Lateral Separation Focus Sensor
LSG Lunar Surface Gravimeter
LSHS Low Sulphur Heavy Stock
LSHTM London School of Hygiene and Tropical Medicine
LSI Large Scale Integration
Lateral Shear Interferometer

	Lunar Science Institute (operated by the Universities Space Research Association–a consortium of 43 universities (USA))
LSIC	Large Scale Integrated Circuit
LSIG	Line Scan Image Generator
LSIS	Laser Scan Inspection System
LSITV	Liquid Secondary Injection Thrust Vector Control
LSL	Low Speed Logic
LSM	Laboratory for the Structure of Matter (USN)
	Lancastrian School of Management (of the Lancashire Education Authority)
	Linear Sequential Machine
	Linear Synchronous Motor
	Lunar Surface Magnetometer
LSMR	Landing Ship Medium Rocket
LSNLIS	Lunar Science Natural Language Information System
LSO	Linseed Oil
LSP	Levitated Spherator
	Logical Signal Processor
	Lot Sensitive Plan
LSPC	Logistics Systems Policy Committee (USDOD)
LSR	Lanthanide Shift Reagent
	Liquid-cure, Silicone Rubber
	Loop Signalling Repeater
LSRB	Linear Sound Ranging Base
LSRH	Laboratoire Suisse de Recherches Horlogere (Switzerland) (Swiss Laboratory for Horological Research)
LSS	Logistic Self-Support
	Lung Serum Simulant
LSSA	Laboratory Supply Support System (of OAR (USAF))
LSSE	Life Support System Evaluator
LSSM	Local Scientific Survey Module
LSSTA	Large Scale Systems: Theory and Applications
LST	Landing Ship Tank
	Landing Ship Transport
	Large Space Telescope
	Large Stellar Telescope
	Laser Spot Tracker
	Light STOL Transport
	Local Sideral Time
	Low Supersonic Transport
	Lunar Space Tug
LSTTL	Low-power Schottky Transistor-Transistor Logic
LSU	Louisiana State University (USA)
LSV	Linear Shift-Varying
	Lunar Surface Vehicle
	Lunar Survey Viewfinder
LSW	I.M. LIFSHITZ, V.V. SLEZOV, C. WAGNER theory
	Light Support Weapon
LSWG	Life Sciences Working Group (of ESA)
LT	Laplace (PIERRE SIMON, MARQUIS DE LAPLACE) Transform
	Laser Trimming
	Light Terminal
LTA	Lighter-Than-Air
LTAS	Lighter Than Air Society (USA)
LTD	Laser Target Designator
	Limited Company
	Live Test Demonstration
LTDS	Laser Target Designation System
LTE	Laplace's Tidal Equations
	Large Thrust per Element
	Lead Tetraethyl
	Local Thermal Equilibrium
	Local Thermodynamic Equilibrium
	London Transport Executive (of the Greater London Council)
LTFCS	Laser Tank Fire Control System
LTFV	Less Than Fair Value
LTG	Lufttransportgeschwader (Germany) (Transport Element of the German Military Airforce)
LTH	Light Training Helicopter
	Light Twin-engined Helicopter
LTI	Low Temperature Isotropic
LTL	Less-than Truckload
	LINCOLN (LABORATORY (OF MIT) (USA)) Terminal Language
LTM	Laser Target Marker
	Lead Tetramethyl
	Long-Term Memory
	Low Thermal Mass
LTMR	Laser Target Marker/Ranger
LTMT	Low Temperature Thermomechanical Treatment
LTO	Letter to Operators (numbered series issued by CAA)
LTP	Library Technology Project
	Low-Temperature Passivation
	Low-Temperature Phase
LTPD	Lot Tolerance Percentage Defective
LTPN	Long-Term Parenteral Nutrition
LTR	Laboratory Technical Report (numbered series issued by NAE (Canada)
	List Test Register
LTRI	Lightning and Transient Research Institute (USA)
LTS	Laser Time Sharing
	Laser-Triggered Switching
	LINCOLN (LABORATORY (OFMIT) (USA)) Terminal System
	Lincoln Training System (of Lincoln Laboratory, Massuchusetts Institute of Technology (USA))
	Low Temperature Smoking (of sea food)
LTSG	Laser-Triggered Spark Gap
LTT	Lead Tin Telluride
	Light Tactical Transport
	Societe des Lignes Telegraphique et Telephoniques (France)
LTTA	Logic Tree Trouble-shooting Aid
	Long Tank Thrust-Augmented
LTTAD	Long Tank Thrust-Augmented DELTA
LTTAS	Light Tactical Transport Aircraft System
LTTAT	Long-Tank Thrust Augmented THOR (now called THORAD)
LTU	Lateral Thrust Unit
LTV	Laser Time-of-Flight Velocimeter
	Long Tube Vertical
LUA	Launch from Under Attack
	Lens Users Association (a service of the Sira Institute)
	Liverpool Underwriters Association
LUBS	Large Undisturbed-Bottom Sampler
LUCF	Load, Unload, Cool, Fracture
LUCID	Language for Utility Checkout and Instrumentation Development
	LOUGHBOROUGH UNIVERSITY Computerised Information and Drawings
LUCIS	London University Central Information Services
LUCRE	Lower Unit Costs and Related Earnings
LUCS	Land Use Cost Studies
	London University Computing Services (sold to United Computing Systems (USA) in 1977)
LUF	Lowest Usable Frequency
LUFTHANSA	Deutsche Lufthansa AG (Germany)
LUG	Light Utility Glider
LUISA	LEICESTER UNIVERSITY Interactive Structural Analysis project
LUMO	Lowest Unfilled Molecular Orbit
LURE	Laboratoire pour l'Utilisation du Rayonnement Electromagnetique (France)
	Lunar Ranging Experiment (of NASA (USA) with others)
LUST	List Updated Sort and Total

LUSURF Lunar Surface
LUT Launcher Umbilical Tower
Loughborough University of Technology
LUXAIR Societe Anonyme Luxemborgeoise de Navigation Aerienne (Luxembourg) (National Airline)
LUXATOM Syndicat Luxembourgeois pour l'Industrie Nucleaire (Luxembourg)
LV Laser Velocimeter OR Velocimetry
Low Viscosity
LVA Landing Vehicle Assault
Large Vertical Aperture
LVAD Left Ventricular Assist Device
LVAS Left Ventricular Assist System ("mechanical heart")
LVCERI Luncheon Voucher Catering Education Research Institute (Ealing Technical College, London)
LVCP Low Valence Chromium Plating
LVCT Low Voltage Circuit Tester
LVD Low Velocity Detonation
Low Voltage Directive (of EEC)
LVDA Launch Vehicle Data Adapter
LVDC Launch Vehicle Digital Computer
LVDT Linear Variable Differential Transformer
Linear Variable-Differential Transducer
Linear Voltage Differential Transducer
LVET Left Ventricular Ejection Time
LVETI Left Ventricular Ejection Time Index
LVFA Low Velocity Friction Apparatus test
LVGO Light Vacuum Gas Oil
LVH Left Ventricular Hypertrophy
LVHAZ Low Velocity-High Attenuation Zone
LVHV Low Volume High Velocity
LVI Low Viscosity Index
LVL Low Velocity Layer
LVLS Low Visibility Landing System
LVM Localised Vibrational Mode
LVMOST Lateral V-groove MOSFET
LVN Light Virgin Naphtha
Limiting Viscosity Number
LVR Line Voltage Regulator
Longitudinal Video Recorder
LVRCN Lehigh Valley (USA) Regional Computing Network
LVRJ Low Volume Ramjet
LVS Logistic Vehicle System
LVT Landing Vehicle Tracked
LVTP Landing Vehicle, Tracked, Personnel
LVW Linked Verticle Well
LWB Long Wheelbase
LWBR Light-Water Breeder Reactor
LWC Light Weight Coated Paper
LWD Laser Welder/Driller
LWECS Low Wind Energy Conversion System
LWF Light-weight Fighter
LWGR Light-water-cooled, Graphite-moderated Reactor
LWI Load Wear Index
LWIR Long Wavelength Infra-Red
LWL Land Warfare Laboratory (US Army)
Limited War Laboratory (US Army) (now Land Warfare Laboratory)
LWLC Light-Weight Low Cost
LWLD Light Weight Laser Designator
LWP Low-Waterplane
LWPF Long Wave Pass Filter
LWR Laser Warning Receiver
Light Water Reactor
Light-water-cooled and moderated Reactor
LWRM Light-Weight Radar Missile
LWSS Letter Writing Support System
LWTMA Listen While Transmission Multiple Access
LXC Liquid-ion Exchange Chromatography
LYRIC Language for Your Remote Instruction by Computer
LZC Liquid-size Exclusion Chromatography
LZEEBE Long-time Zonal Earth Energy Budget Experiment
LZM Lysozyme

M

M prefix to numbered series of Business Monitor-Miscellaneous Series issued by DTI
prefix to numbered: dated series of Miscellaneous Aerospace Standards issued by BSI
M&E prefix to numbered series of Mechanical and Electrical Engineering Standard Specifications issued by MPBW
M&Q prefix to numbered series of forms on Mines and Quarries (now issued by the Department of Energy)
M-DAS Multispectral Data Analysis System
M-ILS Microwave Instrument Landing System
M&FCS Management and Financial Control System
M2S Modular Multiband Scanner
MA Maleic Anhydride
Malvalic Acid
Maritime Administration (Dept of Commerce, USA)
Microscopic Agglutination
Mill-Anneal
prefix to numbered-dated series of Marine Standards issued by BSI
MAA Macroaggregated Albumin
Mathematical Association of America (USA)
Medical Artists Association of Great Britain
Methacrylic Acid
Minimum Audible Angles
Motor Agents Association
MAAC Mitchigan Antique Arms Collectors (USA)
MAACL Multiple Affect Adjective Check List
MAAG Military Assistance Advisory Group (USDOD)
MAAL Microfilm Association of Australia Ltd (Australia)
MAARC Magnetic Annular Arc
MAARM Memory-Aided Anti-Radiation Missile
MAB Man and Biosphere (a programme of UNESCO)
Materials Advisory Board (of National Research Council (USA))
Menswear Association of Britain
Mobile Assault Bridge-ferry
MABB Maximum Achievable Body Burden
MABF Mobile Assault Bridge/Ferry
MABLE Minnesota Atomospheric Boundary Layer Experiments
MABS Marine Automation-Bridge System
MABSC Management and Behavioral Science Center (University of Pennsylvania (USA))
MABUS Multi-Access Broadcast Unit System
MAC Machine Aided Cognition
Maintenance Allocation Chart
Maintenance Analysis Center (of FAA (USA))
MANCHESTER (University) Auto-code
Marker-and-Cell
Maximum Allowable Concentration
Maximum Allowable Cost
Mean Aerodynamic Chord
Measurement and Analysis Centre
Military Aircraft Command (USAF)

	Mine Advisory Committee (of National Research Council (USA)) (now Naval Studies Board)
	Mineralogical Association of Canada (Canada)
	Ministerio de Agricultura y Cria (Venezuela) (Ministry of Agriculture and Animal Breeding)
	Multi-Application Computer
	Multifunctional Automobile Communication
	Multiple Access Computer
	Multiple Access Computing
	Multiplexed Analogue Components
MAC-P	Military Assistance to the Civil Power
MACARS	Microfilm Aperture Card Automated Retrieval System
MACCS	Marine Corps Air Command Control System (US Marine Corps)
MACDAC	Man Communication and Display for an Automatic Computer
MACE	Machine-Aided Composing and Editing
	Magnetic Aid to Compatibility Engineering
	Management Applications in a Computer Environment
	Master Control Executive
	Metropolitan Architectural Consortium for Education
MACIMS	Military Airlift Command Integrated Management System (USAF)
MACLOG	Metropolitan Atlanta Council of Local Governments (USA)
MACMA	Mid-Atlantic Construction Management Association (USA)
MACOM	Maintenance Assembly and Check-Out Model
MACOS	Man: A Course of Study (a behavioural science course developed with NSF (USA) support)
MACRIT	Light Water Reactor
	Manpower Authorization Criteria
MACRO	Methodology for Allocating Corporae Resources to Objectives
MACS	Media Account Control System
	Merchant Airship Cargo Satellite
	Mobile Acoustic Communication System
	Monitoring And Control System
	Multiple Access Communication System
MACTRAC	Military Airlift Command Traffic Reporting And Control (USAF)
MACV	Multi-purpose Airmobile Combat-support Vehicle
MAD	Magnetic Anomaly Detection
	Magnetic Anti-submarine Detector
	Major Air Disaster
	Mathematical Analysis of Downtime
	Mean Absolute Deviation
	MICHIGAN (UNIVERSITY) Algorithm Decoder
	Multi-Aperture Device
	Mutually Assured Destruction
MADALINE	Multi-Adaptive Linear Neuron
MADAM	Moderately Advanced Data Management
MADAP	Maastricht Data Processing and Display System (of EUROCONTROL)
MADAR	Maintenance Analysis Detection And Recorder
	Malfunction Analysis Detection And Recording
	Malfunction and Data Recorder
MADARS	Malfunction Detection, Analysis, and Recording Subsystem
MADGE	Microwave Aircraft Digital Guidance Equipment
MADIC	Machinery Acoustic Data Information Center (USN)
MADIS	Manual Aircraft Data Input System
MADM	Medium Atomic Demolition Munition
MADRE	Magnetic Drum Receiving Equipment
MADREC	Malfunction Detection and Recording
MADS	Machine-Aided Drafting System
	Meteorological Airborne Data System
	Missile Attitude Determination System
	Mobile Airborne Defence Station
MAE	Department of Mechanical and Aerospace Engineering (Rutgers-The State University, New Brunswick (USA))
	Mean Absolute Error
	Mechanical and Aerospace Engineering Division of Princeton University (USA)
	Movement After-Effect
MAECON	Mid-American Electronics Conference (USA)
MAES	Massachusetts Agricultural Experiment Station (USA)
	Mexican American Engineering Society (USA)
MAESTRO	Machine Assisted Educational System for Teaching by Remote Operation
MAF	Macrophage Activating Factor
	Million Acre Feet
	Minimum Audible Field
	Ministry of Agriculture and Fisheries (New Zealand)
	Ministry of Agriculture and Forestry (Japan)
	Mixed Amine Fuels
	Mouse Amniotic Fluid
MAFF	Ministry of Agriculture, Fisheries and Food
	Ministry of Agriculture, Forestry and Fisheries (Japan)
MAFFS	Modular Airborne Fire Fighting System
	Modular Aircraft Fire-Fighting System
MAFI	Mafi-Fahrzengwerke International (Germany)
MAFIS	Management Farm Information Service
MAFLIR	Modified Advanced Forward Look Infra-Red
MAFR	Merged Accountability and Fund Reporting
	Modified Anarchy Flood Routing
MAFTEP	Method for Analysis of Fleet Tactical Effectiveness Performance (USN)
MAFVA	Miniature Armoured Fighting Vehicles Association
MAG	Magnetics
	Metal-Active Gas
MAGB	Microfilm Association of Great Britain (disbanded 1984)
MAGEN	Matrix Generating and Reporting System
MAGFET	Magnetic Metal-Oxide-Semiconductor Field-Effect Transistor
MAGGS	Modular Advanced Graphics Generation System
MAGIC	Machine for Automatic Graphics Interface to a Computer
	MANCHESTER GUARDIAN Index Computerisation
	Manual Assisted Gaming of Integrated Combat
	Matrix Algebra General Interpretive Coding
	Matrix Analysis via Generative and Interpretive Computations
	Method for Asynchronous Graphics Integral Control
	Modern Analytical Generator of Improved Circuits
	MOTOROLA Automatically Generated Integrated Circuits
MAGIS	Marine Air-Ground Intelligence System (US Marine Corps)
	Megawatt Air-to-Ground Illuminating system
MAGLAD	Markmanship and Gunnery Laser Devices
MAGLEV	Magnetic Levitation
MAGPIE	Machine Automatically Generating Production Inventory Evaluation
	Markov Game Planar Intercept-Evasion
MAGSIM	Magnetic Shield Simulator
MAHAPS	Malaysian Association for the History and Philosophy of Science
MAI	Machine-Aided Indexing
	Ministry of Agriculture and Irrigation (India)
	Moskovskiy Aviatsionny Institut (USSR) (Moscow Aviation Institute)

MAICE Minimum AKAIKE (H) Information Criterion Estimation
MAID Magnetic Anti-Intrusion Detector
Merger Acquisition Improved Decision
Multiple Aircraft Identification Display
MAIDS Multipurpose Automatic Inspection and Diagnostic System
MAIG Matsushita Atomic Industrial Group (Japan)
MAILS Multiple-Antenna Instrument Landing System
MAINLINE Monitored Alarm Indication Line
MAINS Marine Aided Inertial Navigation System
MAINSITE Modular Automated Integrated Systems/Interoperability Test and Evaluation
MAIR Molecular Airborne Intercept Radar
MAIS Mycobacterium Avium-Intracellulare-Scrofulaceum
MAL Maximal Acceptable Load
MALC Midwestern Academic Librarians Conference (USA)
MALCAP Maryland Academic Center for Automated Processing (University of Maryland (USA))
MALE Multi-Aperture Logic Element
MALEV Magyar Legikozlekedesi Vallalat (Hungary) (National Air Line)
MALN Minimum Air Low Noise
MALOR Mortar and Artillery Locating Radar
MALR Mortar/Artillery Locating Radars
MALS Medium-intensity Approach-Light System
MALSCE Massachusetts Association of Land Surveyors and Civil Engineers (USA)
MALT Mnemonic Assembly Language Translator
MALU Mode Annunciator and Logic Unit
MAM Matter-Anti-Matter
Medical Association of Malta
prefix to numbered series of Management Analysis Memoranda issued by DOD (USA)
MAMA Manual-Automatic Multi-point Apparatus
Multi-Anode Microchannel Array
MAMBA MARTIN Armored Main Battle Aircraft
MAMBO Mediterranean Association for Marine Biology and Oceanology (Malta)
MAMC Methylammonium Methyldithlocarbamate
Mining and Allied Machinery Corporation (India) (government owned)
MAMMAX Machine Made and Machine Aided Index
MAMOS Marine Automatic Meteorological Observing Station
MAMS Memory And Memory Sequencer
MAMTF Mobile Automated Microwave Test Facility
MAN Magnetic Automatic Navigation
Manual
Maschinenfabrik Augsburg-Nurnburg (Germany)
MANAV Shipborne Integrated Manoeuvring and Navigation project
MANDAS Management Development Advisory Service (of Cranfield School of Management)
MANDEC Manoeuvring Decoy
MANDRO Mechanically Alterable NDRO
MANFEP MANITOBA (UNIVERSITY, Canada) Finite Element Programme
MANIFILE MANITOBA (UNIVERSITY, Canada) File of World's Non-Ferrous Metallic Deposits
MANMAM Manufacturing Management
MANOP Manganese Nodule Program (of NSF/IDOE (USA))
MANOVA Multivariate Analysis Of Variance
MANPADS Man Portable Air Defence System
MANTIS Manchester Technical and Commercial Information Services
MANTRAP Machine and Network Transients Programme
MANUPACS Manufacturing Planning And Control System
MANZ Medical Association of New Zealand (New Zealand)
MAO Mechanization of Algebraic Operations
Monoamine Oxidase
MAOI Monoamine Oxidase Inhibitor
MAOS Metal-Alumina-Silicon-dioxide Semiconductor
MAOT Medium Aperture Optical Telescope
MAP Machine Analyzer Package
Macro Assembly Programme
Maintenance Assessment Panel
Management Analysis and Projection
Manifold Absolute Pressure
Master Activity Programming
Mathematical Analysis without Programming
Maximum *a posteriori* Probability
Message Acceptable Pulse
Methacrylophenone
Method of Approximation Programming
Microelectronics Application Project (of DTI)
Microtuble-Associated Protein
Military Assistance Program (of USDOD)
Minimum Audible Pressure
Missed Approach Point
Modular Accounting Plan
Multibus Accounting Package
Multiple Aim Point
MAPD Maximum Allowable Percent Defective
MAPDA Mid-American Periodical Distributors Association (USA)
MAPI Machinery and Allied Products Institute (USA)
Mitsubishi Atomic Power Industries (Japan)
MAPLE Marketing and Product Line Evaluation
Minor Atomic Prolonged Life Equipment
MAPORD Methodological Approach to Planning and Programming USAF Operational Requirements, Research and Development
MAPP Madras Atomic Power Project (India)
Methyl Acetylene Propadienne
MAPPLE Macro-Associative Processor Programming Language
MAPS Management Aids Programme Suit
Management Analysis and Planning System
Manpower Analysis and Performance Standards
Manufacturing and Production System
Measurement of Air Pollution from Space (aboard a space shuttle)
Microprogramable Arithmetic Processor System
Migratory Animal Pathological Survey
Military Applications of Photovoltaic Systems (a program of Dept of Energy (USA) and DOD (USA))
Minerals Analysis and Policy System (of Dept of the Interior (USA))
MODEC (Mitsui Ocean Development and Engineering Company (Japan)) Anchor Piling System
Modern Accounts Payable System
Multivariate Analysis and Prediction of Schedules
Multivariate, Analysis participative, Structure
MAPS/ALPS Multiple Aim Point System/Alternate Launch Point System
MAPTOE Management Practices in Tables of Organization and Equipment Units (a programme of the US Army)
MAPW Medical Association for Prevention of War
MAQ Measures for Air Quality (a programme of NBS (USA))
MAR Magneto-Acousti Resonance
Medium-Range Artillery Rocket
Mid Atlantic Ridge
Minimum Acceptable Rate of Return
Multifunction Array Radar
prefix to numbered series of Management Analysis Reports issued by ODDRE (USDOD)

MARAD Maritime Administration (Dept of Commerce, USA)

MARAIRMED Maritime Air Forces Mediterranean (of NATO)

MARBA Mid-America Regional Bargaining Association (USA)

MARBI Machine-Readable form of Bibliographic Information

MARC Machine-Readable Cataloguing
Manufacturers Association of Radiators and Convectors
Methodology for Assessing Radiological Consequences
Monitor And Results Computer
Monitoring and Asssessment Research Centre (Chelsea College, London)
Multiple Access Remote Computing

MARCAS Manoeuvring Re-entry Control and Ablation Studies

MARCCO Master Real-time Circulation Controller

MARCEP Maintainability and Reliability Cost-Effectiveness Programme

MARCH Meltdown Accident Response Characteristics

MARCIA Mathematical Analysis of Requirements for Career Information Appraisal

MARCIS MARC Israel (an Israeli MARC-based cataloguing system)

MARCOGAZ Union des Industries Gazieres des Pays du Marche Commun (Union of the Gas Industries of the Common Market)

MARCOM Maritime Command (of Canada Defence Forces)
Microwave Airborne Radio Communication

MARCS Marine Computer System
Marine Structures Computing System

MARD Military Aeronautical Research and Development

MARDAN Marine Digital Analyzer

MARDEC Malaysian Rubber Development Corporation (Malaysia) (Govt owned)

MARDI Malaysian Agricultural Research and Development Institute (Malaysia)

MARDS Material Readiness Index System

MARECEBO Manned Research on Celestial Bodies Committee (of International Academy of Astronautics)

MARECS Maritime European Communications Satellite

MARENTS Modified Advanced Research Environmental Test Satellite

MAREP Marine Environmental Prediction

MARI Microelectronics Application Research Institute

MARIDAS Maritime Data System

MARINA Maritime Industry Authority (Philippines)

MARIS Materials and Resources Information Service (of National Extension College)

MARKFED Punjab State Co-operative Supply and Marketing Federation (India)

MARLAB Mobile Air Research Laboratory

MARLIB an information service based on the Institute of Marine Engineers Library

MARLIN Malaysian Research Libraries Network (Malaysia)

MARLS Missouri Association of Registered Land Surveyors (USA)

MARMAP Marine Resources Monitoring, Assessment, and Prediction Program (of NMFS (NOAA) (USA))

MAROTS Marine Orbital Technical Satellite

MARPEX Management of Repair Parts Expenditure system (US Army)

MARPOL Marine Pollution Convention, 1973

MARRES Manual Radar Reconnaissance Exploitation System

MARS Magnetostatic Rate Sensor
MARCONI Automatic Relay System
MARTIN Automatic Reporting System
Meteorological Automatic Reporting Station
Meteorological Automatic Reporting System
Mid-Air Recovery System
Mid-Air Retrieval System for drones (aircraft)
Military Affiliate Radio Service (USA)
Military Affiliate Radio System
Modular Airborne Recording System
Monitoring, Accounting, Reporting and Statistical
MOTOROLA Automatic Routing System
Multi-Aperture Reluctance Switch
Multiple Access Retrieval System
Multiple Accounts Reports System
Multiple Aerial Refueling System
Multiple Artillery Rocket System

MARS/SIP Mohawk Access and Retrieval System/Self-Interpreting Programme generator

MARSAS Marine Search and Attack System (US Marine Corps)

MARSAT Maritime Satellite System

MARSEN Maritime Remote Sensing

MARSIM International Conference on Marine Simulation

MARSYAS MARSHALL (SPACE FLIGHT CENTER (NASA) (USA)) System for Aerospace Systems Simulation

MART Maintenance Analysis and Review Technique
Mean Active Repair Time
Mobile Automatic Radiating Tester

MARTA Metropolitan Atlanta Rapid Transport Authority (USA)

MARTAG Maritime Satellite Technical Advisory Group (of ESA)

MARTEL Misile Anti-Radar and Television

MARV Manoeuvrable Anti-Radar Vehicle
Manoeuvrable Re-entry Vehicle

MARVEL MISSISSIPPI (University) Aerophysics Research Vehicle Extended Latitude

MAS Malaysian Airline System (Malaysia)
Management Aid System
Management OR Managerial Appraisal System
Manufacture nationale d'Armes de Saint Etienne (of Groupement Industriel des Armaments Terrestres (France))
Manufacturing Advisory Service (co-ordinated by PERA on behalf of DTI)
Medical Advisory Service (of the Civil Service Department)
Medical Audit Statistics
Metal-Alumina-Semiconductor
Methods of Analysis Sub-committee (of BCIRA)
Microbeam Analysis Society (USA)
Middle Air Space
Military Agency for Standardisation (of NATO)
Minnesota Academy of Science (USA)
Multi-Aspect Signalling

MASA Medical Association of South Africa (South Africa)
Multiple Anodic Stripping Analyser

MASAL Michigan Academy of Science, Arts and Letters (USA)

MASAMBA Mobile Advance Support And Maintenance Base

MASAR Management Assurance of Safety, Adequacy and Reliability
Microwave Accurate Surface Antenna Reflector
Multimode Airborne Solid-state Array Radar system

MASC Management Systems Concept
Medical Academic Staff Committee
Multiplicative and Additive Signature Correction algorithm

MASCO Maintenance Schedule Code

MASCOM Master Communications

MASCOT Management Advisory System using Computerized Optimization Techniques

	Modular Approach to Software Construction Operation and Test
	Multi-Access Systems Control Terminal
MASEC	Mid-American Solar Energy Complex (USA)
MASEG	Microwave Antenna Systems Engineering Group (of ISRO (India))
MASER	Microwave Amplification by Stimulated Emission of Radiation
MASES	Microcomputer Advice and Selection Expert System
MASH	Manned Anti-submarine Helicopter
	Micro-Analytic Simulation of Households
MASIS	Management And Scientific Information System
MASK	Manoeuvring and Seakeeping
MASOA	Master and Slave Oscillator Array
MASPAC	Microfilm Advisory Service of the Public Archives of Canada
MASR	Microwave Atmosphere Sounding Radiometer
	Multiple Antenna Surveillance Radar
MASS	Maintenance Activities Subsea Service (project funded by SRC)
	Manual Analysis Scan System
	MARC (Machine-Readable Cataloguing) Automated Serials System
	Maritime Anti-stranding Sonar System
	Master Administrative Software System
	Matrix Analysis Seismic Stress
	MICHIGAN Automatic Scanning System
	Modular Adaptive Signal Sorter
	Multiple-Anvil Sliding System
MASSOP	Multi-Automatic System for Simulation and Operational Planning
MASST	Major Ship Satellite Terminal
MASSTER	Mobile Army Sensor System, Test, Evaluation and Review (US Army)
	Modern Army Selected Systems Test Evaluation and Review (now TCATA (US Army))
MAST	Machine Automated Speech Transcription
	Magnetic Annular Shock Tube
	Michigan Alcoholism Screening Test
	Military Anti-Shock Trousers
	Military Assistance for Safety in Traffic (a joint programme of DOD and DOT (USA))
	Model Assembly Sterilizer for Testing
MASTACS	Manoeuvrability Augmentation System for Tactical Air Combat Simulation
MASTARS	Mechanical And Structural Testing And Referral Service (of NBS (Dept of Commerce (USA))
MASTAS	Manned Aerial Surveillance and Target Acquisition System
MASTER	Multiple Access Shared Time Executive Routine
MASTIFF	Modular Automated System To Identify Friend from Foe
MASTR	Management Analysis System for TAYLOR RENTAL (CORPORATION) (USA)
	Modular Airborne Search and Track Radar
MASU	Multiple Acceleration Sensor Unit
MASWT	Mobile Anti-Submarine Warfare Target
MAT	Magyar Aluminiumipari Troszt (Hungary) (Hungarian Aluminium Corporation)
	Manufacture national d'Armes de Tulle (of Groupement Industriel des Armements Terrestres (France))
	Measurement of Atmospheric Turbulence (a program of NASA (USA))
	Medial Axis Transform
	Modular Allocation Technique
	More Active Tetragonal
	Moving Annual Trend
MATA	Michigan Aviation Trades Association (USA)
	Multiple Answering Teaching Aid
MATADOR	Mobile And Three-dimensional Air Defence Operations Radar
MATC	Maximum Acceptable Toxicant Concentration
MATCH	Manned Attack Torpedo Carrying Helicopter
	Materials and Activities for Teachers and Childre
	Medium Anti-submarine Torpedo Carrying Helicopter
MATCON	Microwave Aerospace Terminal Control
MATD	Mine and Torpedo Detector
MATE	Machine-Aided Translation Editing
	Materials for Advanced Turbine Engines (a program of NASA (USA))
	Memory Assisted Terminal Equipment
	Meteorological Analog Test and Evaluation
	Modular Automatic Test Equipment
	Multi-system Automatic Test Equipment
	Multiband Automatic Test Equipment
MATELCA	Societe Marocaine de Telecommunications par Cable Sous-marin (Morocco)
MATELO	Maritime Air-radio Telegraph Organization (a high-frequency communications network of the Royal Air Force)
MATI	Moskovskiy Aviatsinnyy Teknologicheskiy Institut (USSR) (Moscow Aviation Technology Institute)
MATICO	Machine Applications to Technical Information Centre Operations
MATILDE	Microwave Analysis Threat Identification and Launch Decision Equipment
MATLAB	Materials Laboratory (of Naval Ship Research and Development Center (USN))
MATO	Military Air Traffic Operations
MATPS	Machine Aided Technical Processing System
MATS	Midcourse Airborne Target Signatures
	Military Air Transport Service (now Military Airlift Command) (USAF)
	Mission Analysis and Trajectory Simulation programme
	Mobile Automatic Telegraph System
	Model Aircraft Target System
	Multiple-Access Time Sharing
MATS-A	Model Aircraft Target System–Type A (small arms target)
MATSU	Marine Technology Support Unit (of UKAEA)
MATTS	Multiple Airborne Target Trajectory System
MATV	Master Antenna Television
	Master Antenna Television
MATZ	Military Airport Traffic Zones
MAU	Multi-Attribute Utility
	Multiplexed Arithmetic Unit
MAV	Magyar Allamvasutak (Hungary) (State Railways)
	Mechanical Auxiliary Ventricle
MAVERIC	Manufacturers Assistance in Verification of Catalog Data (USDOD)
MAVIS	Master Vision Screener
	Medical Audio Visual aids Information Service (administered by University of Dundee)
	Microprocessor-based Audio Visual Information System
MAVS	Manned Aerial Vehicle for Surveillance
MAVU	Modular Audio Visual Unit
MAW	Medium Anti-tank Assault Weapon
MAWA	Missile Attack Warning and Assessment
MAWD	Mars Atmospheric Water Detector
MAWLOGS	Models of Army Worldwide Logistics Systems (US Army)
MAWP	Maximum Allowable Working Pressure
MAWS	Modular Automated Weather System
MAX	Mobile Automatic X-ray
MAXNET	Modular Application Executive for Computer Networks
MB	Methyl Bromide
	Methylene Blue
MBA	Malta Broadcasting Authority (Malta)

	Marine Biological Association
	Mortgage Bankers Association (USA)
MBAA	Methylene Bisacrylamide
MBASIC	advanced version of BASIC programming language
MBAV	Main Battle Air Vehicle
MBB	Messerschmitt-Bolkow-Blohm (Germany)
MBC	Meteor Burst Communications
	Multiple Burst Correction
MBD	Million Barrels per Day
	Minimal Brain Dysfunction
MBDA	Metal Building Dealers Association
MBDOE	Million Barrels per Day Oil Equivalent
MBE	Molecular Beam Epitaxy
	Molecular Beam Epitaxy
MBE-ARMS	Multiple Business Entity-Accounts Receivable Management System
MBEO	Minority Business Enterprise Office (USA)
MBFR	Mutual and Balanced (Armed) Force Reductions
MBIAC	Missouri Basin Inter-Agency Committee (USA
MBIS	Molecular Biological Information Service (of CSIRO) (Australia)
MBK	Methyl Isobutyl Ketone
MBL	Marine Biological Laboratory (of CEGH)
	Modified Borderline Technique
MBLE	Manufacture Belge de Lampes et de Materiel Electronique (Belgium)
MBO	Management By Objectives
MBPO	Military Blood Program Office (USDOD)
MBPRE	Multi-type Branching Process in a Random Environment
MBR	Mineracoes Brasilieras Reunidas (Brazil) (USDOD)
MBRDC	Medical Bioengineering Research and Development Command (US Army)
MBRL	Multi-Barrelled Rocket Launcher
MBRV	Manoeuvring Ballistic Re-entry Vehicle
MBS	Manchester Business School (University of Manchester)
	Methacrylonitrile-Butadiene-Styrene
	Mobile-Base Simulator
	Modular Banking System
MBSA	Methylated Bovine Serum Albumin
	Model-Based System Analysis
MBSD	Multi-Barrel Smoke Discharger
MBT	Main Battle Tank
	Mean Body Temperature
	Mechanical Bathythermograph
	Mereaptobenzthiazole
	Metal-Base Transistor
	Minimum advance for Best Torque
	Modified Boiling Test
MBTA	Massachusetts Bay Transportation Authority (USA)
MBZ	Magnesia-Buffered Zinc Oxide
MC	Marginal Cost
	Mathematisch Centrum (Netherlands)
	Metrology Centre (of National Physical Laboratory)
	Molded Components
MC&G	Mapping, Charting and Geodesy
	Mapping, Charting and Geodesy Directorate of the Defense Intelligence Agency (USDOD)
MC/E	Management Centre/Europe (Belgium)
MCA	Management Consultants Association
	Manufacturing Chemists Association (USA)
	Monetary Compensatory Amount
	Monochloroacetic Acid
	Monoclonal Antibodies
	Multi-Channel Analyser
	Multiple Classification Analysis
MCAA	Mason Contractors Association of America (USA)
	Mechanical Contractors Association of America (USA)
MCAC	Measurement, Control and Automation Conference (representing Control and Automation Manufacturers Association, British Industrial Measuring and Control Apparatus Manufacturers Association, Electronic Engineering Association, and Scientific Instrument Manufacturers Association of Great Britain)
MCACS	Marine Centralized Automatic Control System
MCANW	Medical Campaign Against Nuclear Weapons
MCAP	Medical Commission on Accident Prevention
	Microwave Circuit Analysis Package
MCAS	Midland Counties Aviation Society
MCAT	Medical College Admission Test (of AAMC (USA))
MCB	Membranous Cytoplasmic Bodies
	Metric Conversion Board (Australia)
	Miniature Circuit Breaker
MCBP	Muscle Calcium Binding Parvalbumin
MCBSF	Mixed Commission for Black Sea Fisheries
MCC	Mechanical Chemical Code
	Multi-channel Communications Control
	Multilayer Ceramic Chip
MCC-H	Mission Control Centre–Houston (of NASA)
MCCA	Manufacturers Council on Color and Appearance (USA)
MCCB	Moulded-Case Circuit Breaker
MCCISWG	Military Command, Control and Information Systems Working Group (of NATO)
MCCS	Mine Countermeasures Control System
MCD	Magnetic Circular Dichroism
	Magnetic Crack Definer
	Months for Cyclical Dominance
MCDEC	Marine Corps Development and Education Command (US Marine Corps)
MCDP	Micro-programmed Communication Data Processor
MCDS	Management Control Data System
MCE	Management Centre Europe (Belgium) (of the International Management Association)
	Mapping and Charting Establishment (Dept of National Defence (Canada))
MCEB	Military Communications Electronics Board (USDOD)
MCEWG	Military Communications-Electronics Working Group (of NATO)
MCF	Measurement Compensation Factor
	Military Computer Family
	Mission-Critical Function
	Monolithic Crystal Filter
	Multi-path Coherence Function
	Mutual Coherence Function
MCFC	Multi-Configuration Frozen Core
MCFD	Modular Chaff/Flare Dispenser
MCG	Magnetocardiogram
	Man-Computer Graphics
MCGH	Mid-Continent Gravity High
MCGS	Microwave Command Guidance System
MCH	Methylcyclohexane
MCHFR	Minimum Critical Heat Flux Ratio
MCHIS	Michigan Cooperative Health Information System (USA)
MCHR	Medical Committee for Human Rights (USA)
MCI	Meal, Combat, Individual
	Multichip Integration
MCIC	Metals and Ceramics Information Center (USDOD)
MCID	Multi-purpose Concealed Intrusion Detection
MCIP	Multiple Choice Integer Programme
MCIS	Maintenance Control Information System
	Materials Control Information System
MCL	Macro Creation Languagen D
	Microcomputer Compiler Language
	Mid-Canada Line

Midclavicular Line
Most Comfortable Level

MCLA Medical Contact Lens Association

MCLOS Manual Command to Line Of Sight

MCLWG Major Calibre Light Weight Gun

MCM Machines for Co-ordinating Multiprocessing
Mass Communication Media
Micro Circuit Module
Mine Counter-Measures
Minimum Commitment Method
Monte Carlo Method
Multilayer Ceramic Module

MCMG Military Committee Meteorological Group (of NATO)
Military Committee Meteorological Group (of NATO)

MCMH Mine Counter-Measures Hovercraft

MCMV Mine Counter-Measures Vessel
Murine Cytomegalovirus

MCOA/P Multi-Company Accounts Payable

MCOC Motion Compensated Offshore Crane

MCP Master Control Programme
Micro-Channel Plate

MCPA Methylchlorophenoxyacetic acid
Michigan Concrete Paving Association (USA)

MCPL Members of CONGRESS for Peace through Law (USA)
Multiple-Cue Probability Learning

MCPS Mechanical Copyright Protection Society

MCR Military Compact Reactor
Mobile Control Room

MCRL Mapping and Charting Research Laboratory (Ohio State University (USA))
Marine Corrosion Research Laboratory (of the Naval Research Laboratory (USN))

MCRS Micrographic Catalogue Retrieval System

MCS Maintenance Control System
Manpower Consultative Service (Canada)
Maximal Compatible Set
Method of Constant Stimuli
Mini Conference System
Monochlorostyrene
Multi-Cycle Sampling
Multiprogrammed Computer System

MCSIB Management Consulting Services Information Bureau (of BIM)

MCSS Mine Countermeasure Support Ship

MCT Magnetic Character Typewriter
Mainstream Corporation Tax
Manganese Cyclopentadienyltricarbonyl
Mechanical Comprehension Test
Memory Cycle Time

MCTAS Military/Commercial Transport Aircraft Simulation

MCTL Military Critical Technologies List (USDOD)

MCTSSA Marine Corps Tactical Systems Support Activity (US Marine Corps)

MCU Management Control Unit
Microcomputer Unit
Microprogrammed Control Unit
Micturating Cysto-Urethogram
Modular Concept Unit

MCV Microbial Check Valve

MCVD Modified Chemical Vapour Deposition

MCW Modulated Continuous Wave
Modulated Continuous Wave

MD Management Development
Marek's Disease

MDA Malfunction Detector Analyzer
Mechanically Despun Antenna
Metal Deactivator
Minimum Descent Altitude
Modified Diffusion Approximation
Multi Docking Adapter
Multi-Dimensional Analysis
Muscular Dystrophy Association of America (USA)

MDAC Multiplying Digital-to-Analog Converter

MDAP Morphological Dictionary Adaptor Programme

MDB Metrology Data Bank (of GIDEP (USA))

MDC Machinability Data Center (USA)
Maintainability Data Center (USA)
Maintenance Data Collection
Maintenance Dependency Chart
Malta Development Corporation (Malta)
Merseyside Development Corporation
Miniature Detonation Chord
Missile Development Center (USAF)

MDC/SS Multiple Drone Control and Strike System

MDCC Monaural Detection with Contralateral Cue

MDCS Maintenance Data Collection System

MDD Machine Dependent Data
Miss-Distance Determination

MDDT Master Digital Data Tape

MDF Mild Detonating Fuse

MDH Malic Dehydrogenase
Minimum Descent Height
Multidirectional Harassment

MDHB Mersey Docks and Harbour Board

MDI Minimum Discrimination Information
Miss Distance Indicator

MDIS Ministere du Development Industriel et Scientifique (France) (Ministry of Industrial and Scientific Development)

MDL Mine Defense Laboratory (USDOD)
Modular Design Language

MDM Modified Davidon Method
Modified Dependency Matrix
Multiprocessing Diagnostic Monitor

MDNA Machinery Dealers National Association (USA)

MDO MARC (Machine-Readable Cataloguing) Development Office (of Library of Congress (USA))

MDP Meteorological Datum Plane

MDPI Management Development and Productivity Institute (Ghana)

MDPNE Ministere de la Protection de la Nature et de l'Environment (France) (Ministry for the Protection of Nature and the Environment)

MDQS Management Data Query System

MDR Metal Distribution Ratio

MDRE Mass-Driver Reaction Engine

MDRSF Multi-Dimensional Random Sea Facility (of Hydraulics Research Station)

MDS Maintenance Data System
Malfunction Detection System
Management Decision System
Management Display System
Mathematics Diagnostic System
Matrix Documentation System
Medical Data System
Metal-Dielectric Semiconductor
Microprogramme Design Support Subsystem
Minimum Discernible Signal
Minimum Discernible Signal
Multi-dimensional Scaling

MDSIC Metal-Dielectric-Semiconductor Integrated Circuit

MDSS Meteorological Data Sounding System

MDT Mean Down Time
Mean Time Down
Multi-Dimension Tasking

MDTE Modern Technology Demonstrator Engine (a program of the US Army)

MDTL Modified Diode Transistor Logic

MDTS Modular Data Transaction System
Modular Data Transfer System

MDW Measured Daywork

ME Magneto-Electronic
Materials Evaluation
Mechanical Engineering
Metabolizable Energy
Moment Estimators
MOSSBAUER Effect
Multiple Effect distillation
Murnaghan Equation
Myalgic Encephalomyelitis

ME/ AEROSPACE Department of Mechanical and Aerospace Engineering (Syracuse University Research Institute (USA))

MEA Metropolitan Electricity Authority (Thailand)
Middle East Airlines (Lebanon)
Minimum Enroute Altitude
Moisture Evaluation Analysis
Monoethanolamine

MEACE Military Engineering Applications of Commercial Explosives (a project of WES (US Army))

MEAD Microbial Evaluation Analysis Device

MEAL Module Engineering Analysis Library (University of Pennsylvania (USA))

MEAM Department of Mechanical Engineering and Applied Mechanics (University of Pennsylvania (USA))

MEAPS Maintenance Engineering Analysis Procedures

MEAR Maintenance Engineering Analysis Report

MEB Midlands Electricity Board

MEC Committee of Ministers on Energy Conservation
Mineral Exploration Company (India) (govt owned)
Molecular Exclusion Chromatography

MECA Missile Electronics and Computer Assembly
Molecular Emission Cavity Analysis
Multivalued Electronic Circuit Analysis

MECACON Middle East Civil Aviation Conference

MECAP Medical Examiners and Coroners Alert Project (of CPSC (USA))

MECAR Metropolitan Engineers Council on Air Resources (USA)

MECCA Mechanised Catalogue
Minnesota (USA) Environmental Control Citizens Association

MECHTRAM Mechanization of Selected Transportation Movement Reports (US Army)

MECO International Symposium of Measurement and Control

MECOM Marine Engine Condition Monitor
Middle East Electronic Communications Show and Conference
Mobile Equipment Command (US Army)

MECON Metallurgical and Engineering Consultants (India) Ltd (India) (a subsidiary of SAIL (India))

MECU Main Engine Electronic Control Unit

MED Mobile Energy Depot
Multi-Effect Distillation
Multiformat Electroluminescent Displays

MEDAC Medical Equipment Display and Conference
Military Electronic Data Advisory Committee (of NATO)

MEDALS Modular Engineering Draughting and Library System (of the Computer-Aided Design Centre of DTI)

MEDAS Microfilm Enhanced Data System

MEDC Microelectronics Development Centre (Paisley College of Technology)

MEDCAT Medium Altitude Clear Air Turbulence

MEDCOM Mediterranean Communications System

MEDCOMP International Congress on Computing in Medicine

MEDEA International Medical Engineering and Automation Exhibition
Multi-discipline Engineering Design Evaluation and Analysis System (a project of the US Army)

MEDHOC Macro-Economic Databank HOUSE OF COMMONS of Pennsylvania (USA)) la Nature et de l'Environmen

MEDIA MAGNAVOX Electronic Data Image Apparatus
Man's Environments—Display Implication and Applications
Modular Electronic Digital Instrumentation Assemblies

MEDIACULT International Institute for Audio-visual Communication and Cultural Development

MEDIATOR Media Time Ordering and Reporting

MEDICO Model Experiment in Drug Indexing by Computer

MEDIHC Military Experience Directed Into Health Careers (joint project of DOD and HEW (USA))

MEDINFO Conference on Medical Informatics

MEDIS International Symposium on Medical Information Systems

MEDISPA Medical Sterile Products Association

MEDISTARS Medical Information Storage and Retrieval System (of USN)

MEDLARS Medical Literature Analysis and Retrieval System

MEDLINE MEDLARS On-Line (of NLM (USA))

MEDPREP Medical Education Preparatory Program (of Southern Illinois University (USA))

MEDS Marine Embarkation Data System (US Marine Corps)
Modular Electric Power Distribution System

MEECN Minimum Essential Emergency Communication Network (USDOD)

MEED Microbial Ecology Evaluation Device

MEES Marine-Estuarine-Environmental Sciences

MEF Multi-purpose Electric Furnace

MEFR Maximal Expiratory Flow Rate

MEG Magnetoencephalogram
Magnetoencephalography
Microelectronic Grade solder creams
Multipactor Electron Gun

MEGAFLOPS Millions of Floating Point Operations per Second

MEGS Meeting of European Geological Societies

MEIC Metric Education Information Committee (USA)

MEIE Microcomputer Electronic Information Exchange (of NBS (USA))

MEIU Management Education Information Unit (of BIM)

MEK Methyl Ethyl Ketone

MEL Magnetic-suspension, Evacuated-tube, Linear-motor-propulsion
Many-Element Laser
Marchwood Engineering Laboratories (of CEGB)
Marine Engineering Laboratory (USN) (now part of Naval Ship Research and Development Center)
Materials Evaluation Laboratory (of IMR)
Ministere de l'Equipement et du Logement (France) (Ministry of Equipment and Housing)

MELA Middle East Librarians Association (USA)

MELBA Multipurpose Extended Life Blanket Assembly

MELCO Mitsubishi Electric Corporation (Japan)

MELETA Mechanical Endurance Load on Environment Test Apparatus

MELIOS Mini-Eyesafe Laser Infrared Observation Set

MELTAN MECHANICAL ENGINEERING LABORATORY (OF GENERAL ELECTRIC Company) Thermal Analogue Network

MEM Magnetic Electron Multiplier
Mars Excursion Module
Maximum Entropy Method
Minimum Essential Medium
Mirror Electron Microscope

MEMA Micro-Electronic Modular Assembly
Motor and Equipment Manufacturers Association (USA)

MEMAC Machinery and Equipment Manufacturers Association of Canada (Canada)

MEMBERS Microprogrammed Experimental Machine with a Basic Executive for Real-time Systems

MEMBRAIN Micro-electronic Memories and Brains

MEMIC Mobile Electro-Magnetic Incompatibility

MEMIS Maintenance and Engineering Management Information System (of ALITALIA)

MEMM Multi-Echelon Markov Model

MEMO Maximising the Efficiency of Machine Operations (an advisory service of the Food, Drink and Tobacco Industry Training Board)
Model for Evaluating Missile Observation information

MEMTRB Mechanical Engineering and Machine Tools Requirements Board (of DOI)
Mechanical Engineering and Machine Tools Requirements Board (of DOI)

MEN Multiple Earthed Neutral

MENA Middle East News Agency (Egypt)

MENDAP Melbourne (Australia) Network Dimensioning and Analysis Programmes

MENS Message Entry System
Middle East Neurosurgical Society

MENTOR Mobile Electrical Network Testing, Observation and Recording

MEO Manned Earth Observatory
Mass in Earth Orbit

MEOA Malaysian Estate Owners Association (Malaysia)

MEOS Microsomal Ethanol-Oxidizing System

MEP Maximum Entropy Principle
Microelectronics Education Programme (of DES and CET)

MEPA Masters Electro-Plating Association (USA)
Meteorological and Environmental Protection Administration (Saudi Arabia)

MEPC Marine Environment Protection Committee (of IMO)

MEPP Marine Electric Power Plant

MER Magneto-Elastic Resonance
Multiple Ejector Rack

MERA Molecular Electronics for Radar Applications

MERADCOM Mobility Equipment Research and Development Command (US Army) (now Belvoir Research and Development Center)

MERADO Mechanical Engineering Research and Development Organization (India)

MERC Minimum Electrical Resistance Condition

MERCAST Merchant Ship Broadcast

MERDC Mobility Equipment Research and Development Center (US Army)

MERDL Medical Equipment Research and Development Laboratory (US Army)

MERES Matrix of Environmental Residuals for Energy Systems

MERIT Mechanical Engineers Reading Improvement Techniques
Michigan (USA) Educational Research Information Triad (joint educational computing network between Michigan State University, Wayne State University, and University of Michigan)
Multiple Radar Integrated Tracking

MERL Marine Ecosystems Research Laboratory (University of Rhode Island (USA))
Mechanical Engineering Research Laboratory (became National Engineering Laboratory in 1959)
Municipal Environmental Laboratory (of EPA (USA))
prefix to dated-numbered series of reports issued by the Department of Mechanical Engineering, McGill University (Canada)

MERLIN Machine Readable Library Information
Multi-Element Radio Linked Interferometer

MERM Material Evaluation of Rocket Motor

MERMUT Mobile Electronic Robot Manipulator and Underwater Television

MERS Mechanical Engineering in Radar Symposium
Mobility Environmental Research Study

MERSAR Merchant Ship Search and Rescue

MERT Modified Effective-Range Theory

MERTS Micropound Extended Range Thrust Stand

MES Manual Entry Subsystem
Michigan Engineering Society (USA)

MESA Manned Environmental System Assessment
Marine Ecosystems Analysis (a program of NOAA (USA))
Maximum Entropy Spectral Analysis
Mechanical Equipment Stowage Area (in the APOLLO lunar module base)
Miniature Electrostatically Suspended Accelerometer
Miniaturized Electrostatic Accelerometer
Mining Enforcement and Safety Administration (of Bureau of Mines (USA))
Modular Electrical Stimulation Apparatus
Modular Equipment Stowage Assembly

MESBIC A Minority Enterprise Small Business Investment Company

MESC Ministry of Education, Science and Culture (Japan)

MESCO UNESCO Science Co-operation Office for the Middle East

MESFET Metal-Semiconductor Field-Effect Transistor

MESG Maximum Experimental Safe Gap
Micro-Electrostatic Gyro

MESH A European Industrial Consortium (consisting of Aeritalia (Italy), British Aerospace ERNO (Germany, Fokker VFW (Netherlands), Matra (France) and SAAB-Scania (Sweden))
Medical Subject Headings

MESL Membrane Encapsulated Soil Layer

MESONET Meso-meteorological Network

MESS Monitor Event Simulation System
Multiple Enclosure Simplification Shield

MESTIND Measurement Standards Instrumentation Division (of Instrument Society of America (USA))

MESTS Missile Electric System Test Set

MESUCORA International Exhibition of Measurement, Control, Regulation and Automation
Measurement, Control Regulation and Automation

MET Management Engineering Team
MARCONI (RADAR SYSTEMS LTD) Environmental Transmissometer
Methemoglobin
Modified Expansion Tube
Modularised OR Mobile Equipment
Multi-Emitter Transistor

MET & E Medical Equipment Test and Evaluation division (of US Army Medical Material Agency)

META Maintenance Engineering Training Agency (US Army)
Maryland Electronics Technicians Association (USA)
Methods of Extracting Text Automatically

METADS Meteorological Acquisition and Display System

METAG Meteorological Advisory Group (of ICAO)

METAL Militarily Significant Emergent Technologies Awareness List (USDOD)

METAPLAN Methods of Extracting Text Automatically Programming Language
METAROM Romanian Agency for Foreign Trade (Romania)
METC Morgantown Energy Technology Center (DOE) (USA)
METCHEM Metals/Materials, Fabricating and Testing Conference and Show for the Petrochemical Industry (USA)
METE Multiple Engagement Test Enviro
METEC Metallurgical Equipment and Technology International Conference and Exhibition
METEOSAT Geostationary Meteorological Satellite
METER Machine Examination Teaching, Evaluation, and Re-education
Meteorological Effects of Thermal Energy Releases (a program of DOE (USA))
MetO Meteorological Office (MOD)
METRA Multiple Event Time Recording Apparatus
METRI Military Essentiality Through Readiness Indices
METRIC Multi-Echelon Technique for Recoverable Item Control
METRO Metering and Traffic Recording with Off-line processing
New York Metropolitan and Research Literary Agency (USA) (a consortium of libraries in Metropolitan New York)
METRRA Metal Re-radiation Radar
METS Multi-engine Training Squadron (RAF)
METT Manned, Evasive Target Tank
METU Middle East Technical University (Turkey)
MEU Microcellular Elastomeric Urethanes
MEUA Million European Units of Account
MEV Millions of Electron Volts
MeVEMSJ Mercury, Venus, Earth, Mars, Jupiter
MEW Manufacturing Empty Weight
Microwave Early Warning
Mission Expected Worth
MEWS Microwave Electronic Warfare System
Missile Early Warning Station
Mobile Electronic Weighing System
Modular Electronic Warfare Simulator
MEWSG Marine Electronic Warfare Support Group (of NATO)
MEWSS Mobile Electronic Warfare Support System
MEWT Matrix Electrostatic Writing Technique
MEXE Military Engineering Experimental Establishment (MOD) (merged into MVEE, 1970)
MEXICANA Compania Mexicana de Aviacion (Mexico)
MF Matched-Filter
Medium Frequency
Microfiche
Microforms
Mitogenic Factor
prefix to numbered series of reports issued by Magneto-Fluid Dynamics Division, New York University (USA)
MFA Metal Finishing Association
Metal Fixing Association for Ceiling Systems (became SCA in 1976)
Motor Factors Association
Multi-Fibre Arrangement (of GATT)
MFASC Metal Finishing Association of Southern California (USA)
MFB Medial Forebrain Bundle
Mixed Functional Block
MFBAR Multi-Function Band Airborne Radio
MFBS Multi-Frequency Binary Signals
MFC Membrane Fecal Coliform
Multi-Frequency Code
MFCC Mortar Fire Control Calculator
MFCD Modular Flare Chaff Dispenser
MFCI Molten Fuel Concrete Interactions
MFCS Mathematical Foundations of Computer Science
Medical Function Control System
Missile Fire Control System
MFD Magnetofluid Dynamics
Multi-stage Flash Distillation
MFDSUL Multi-Function Data Set Utility Language
MFE Magnetic Field Effects
Mean Fibre Extent
Moire Fringe Effects
MFES Main Fixed Earth Station
MFF Metal Finishers Foundation (USA)
MFHBF Mean Flying Hours Between Failure
MFI Melt Flow Index
Metal Fabricating Institute (USA)
Mobile Fuel Irradiator
MFIE Magnetic Field Integral Equation
MFL Maintenance-Free Lifetime
MFM Modified Frequency Modulation
MFMBARS Multi-Function, Multi-Band Airborne Radio System
MFN Metabolic Faecal Nitrogen
Most Favoured Nation
MFO Mixed Function Oxidases
MFOT Mean Forced Outage Time
MFPA Monolithic Focal Plane Array
MFPE Minimum Final Prediction Error
MFPG Mechanical Failure Prevention Group (of NBS (Dept of Commerce) (USA))
MFR Multi-channel Filter Radiometer
Multi-Frequency Responser
MFRT Modulated Frequency Radio Telephony
MFS Magnetic Flux Sensor
Malleable Founders Society
Manned Flying System
Multiple Frequency Shift
MFSA Metal Finishing Suppliers Association (USA)
MFSK Multiple Frequency-Shift Keying
MFT Microflocculation Test
MFTRS Magnetic Flight Test Recording System
MFTW Machine-tool, Fixture, Tool and the Workpiece
MFU MODEM Fan-out Unit
MFUSYS Microfiche File Update System
MFUW Magnetic Force Upset Welding
MFW Micro Friction Welding
MG/CCD prefix to numbered series of reports issued by BISRA
MGB Medium Girder Bridge
MGD Million Gallons per Day
Monogalastosyl Diglyceride
MGF Macrophage Growth Factor
MGG Mono-propellant Gas Generator
MGGB Modular Guided Glide Bomb
MGI Mapping and Geography Institute (Ethiopia)
Military Geographic Intelligence
MGMI Mining, Geological and Metallurgical Institute (India)
MGN Mendial Geniculate Nucleus
MGO Megagauss Oersted
MGOS Metal-Glass-Oxide-Silicon
MGR Micro-Graphic Reporting
MGRL MIND Grammar-Rule Language
MGU Moskoviskiy Gosundarstvennyy Universitet (USSR) (Moscow State University)
MH Multiple Halide
MHAU Major Hazards Assessment Unit (of HSE)
MHB Mueller-Hinton Broth
MHC Major Histocompatibility Complex
MHCAT Mine-Hunting Catamaran

MHD Magnetohydrodynamic
MHDG Magnetohydrodynamic-Generator
MHDL Magnetohydrodynamic Laser
MHE Materials Handling Equipment
Mean Hook Extent
MHEA Mechanical Handling Engineers Association
MHEDA Material Handling Equipment Distributors Association (USA)
MHG Message Header Generator
MHHW Mean Higher High Water
MHHWL Mean Higher High Water Line
MHI Material Handling Institute (USA)
MHIC Microwave Hybrid Integrated Circuit
MHL Mean Hertz Load
MHLG Ministry of Housing and Local Government (absorbed into the Department of the Environment, 1970)
MHMA Mobile Home Manufacturers Association (USA)
MHRST Medical and Health Related Sciences Thesaurus
MHS Magnetohydrostatic
MHSV Multi-purpose High-Speed Vehicle
MHT Mild Heat Treatment
MHTC Multiphasic Health Testing Centre
MHTL Motorola High Threshold Logic
MHTU Materials Handling Trials Unit (British Army)
MHV Magnetic Heart Vector
Miniature Homing Vehicle
Mouse Hepatitis Virus
MHW Mean High Water
Ministry of Health and Welfare (Japan)
Multi-Hundred Watt
MHW-RTG Multi-Hundred-Watt Radioisotope Thermoelectric Generator
MHWL Mean High Water Line
MHWLG Medical, Health and Welfare Libraries Group (of the Library Association)
MI Michelson Interferometer
Myocardial Infarcation
MIA Machine Interference Allowance
Metal Interface Amplifier
Missile Intelligence Agency (US Army)
MIAB Magnetically Impelled Arc Butt
MIAC Manufacturing Industries Advisory Council (Australia)
Minimum Automatic Computer
MIACS Manufacturing Information And Control System
MIAF Mauritanian Islamic Air Force (Mauritania)
MIARS Maintenance Information Automated Retrieval System
MIAS Management Information and Accounting System
Marine Information and Advisory Service (of IOS (NERC))
MIATCO Mid-America International Agri-Trade Council (USA)
MIB Marketing of Investments Board
Motor Insurance Bureau
Motor Insurance Bureau
Multilayer Interconnection Board
MIBAR Multi-channel In-band Airborne Relay
MIBC Methyl Isobutyl Carbinol
MIBK Methyl Isobutyl Ketone
MIC Magnesium Industry Council
Mechanized Information Center (of Ohio State University Libraries (USA))
Methyl Isocyanate
Microwave Integrated Circuit
Military Industrial Complex
Minimal Inhibitory Concentration
Minimum Ignition Current
MICA Machine Independent Compiler for ATLAS

Major Incidents Computer Application system
Man-computer Interaction in Commercial Applications (a part of HUSAT Loughborough University Research Group)
MICC Mineral Insulated Copper-covered Cable
MICE Modelling Integrated Circuit Effectiveness
MICHU-SG prefix to dated-numbered series of reports issued by Michigan University, Sea Grant Program (USA)
MICNS Modular Integrated Communications and Navigation Link System
MICO Micronized Coal-in-Oil
MICOM Missile Command (US Army)
MICOS Modular Industrial Control Oriented System
MICOT Minimum Completion Time
MICR Magnetic Ink Character Recognition
MICRA Miniature Insulated Contact Range
MICRAD Microwave Radiometer or Radiometric
MICRADS Microwave Radiation System
MICRO Annual Workshop on Microprogramming
International Symposium on Microscopy
Multiple Indexing and Console Retrieval Options
MICRON Micro-Navigator
MICROSID Small Seismic Intrusion Detector
MICROSIM Microinstruction Simulator
MICS Management Information and Control System
Medical Instrument Calibration System
Mineral Insulated Copper Sheathed
Multiple Internal Communications System
MICV Mechanised Infantry Combat Vehicle
MID Microwave Division (of ISRO (India)
Multiple Ion Detection
MIDA Major Items Data Agency (US Army)
MIDAR Marine Identification And Recognition
MIDAS Management Information Decision and Accounting Simulator
Maritime Industrial Development Area Schemes
Materials for Industry Data and Applications Service (a materials advisory service of PERA)
Measurement Information Data Analytic System
Meat Industry Development and Advisory Service (jointly administered by Agricultural Research Council and the Meat and Livestock Commission)
Meteorological Information and Dose Acquisition System
MICOM (US Army) Digital Analysis Code
Micro-Image Data Addition System
Microscopic Image Digital Acquisition System
MIDCOM Centre for the Development of the Metals Industry of Malaysia (Malaysia)
MIDF Multiple Input Describing Functions
MIDIST Mission Interministerielle de l'Information Scientifique et Technique (France)
MIDLINET Midwest Region Libarary Network (USA)
MIDMS Machine Independent Data Management System
MiDOC Mildew Defacement of Organic Coatings
MIDONAS Military Documentation System (Dept of Defence (Switzerland))
MIDOR Miss Distance Optical Recorder
MIDOT Multiple Interferometer Determination of Trajectory
MIDR Mandatory Incident and Defect Reporting
MIDS Management Information and Decision System
MIDU Malfunction Insertion and Display Unit
MIDU Mineral Investigation Drilling Unit (of Dept of Mines (Malaysia))
MIE Department of Mechanical and Industrial Engineering (of University of Cincinnati (USA))
MIEC Meteorological Information Extraction Centre (of ESOC (ESA))

MIECC Motor Industry Education Consultative Committee
MIEMSS Maryland Institute for Emergency Medical Service Systems (USA)
MIF Macrophage Inhibitory Factor
Manual Intervention Facility
Migration Inhibitory Factor
Migration-Inhibition Factor
MIFASS Marine Integrated Fire and Supprt System (US Marine Corps)
MIFI Moskovskiy Inzhenerno Fizicheskiy Institut (USSR) (Moscow Engineering Physics Institute)
MIFIL Microwave Filter Design
MiG MIKOYAN (ARTEM) and GUREVICH (MIKHAIL I)
MIG Metal Inert Gas
Miniature Integrating Gyro
Multilevel Interconnect Generator
MIIA Medical Intelligence and Information Agency (US Army)
MIIGAi Moskovskiy Institut Inzhenerov Geodezii, Aerofotos'yemki i Kartografi (USSR) (Moscow Institute of Geodetic, Aerial Mapping and Cartographic Engineers)
MIIZ Moscow Institute of Engineers of Land Use (USSR)
MIL followed by a single capital letter and numbers—Military Specification (USDOD)
MIL-E-CON Military Electronics Conference (USA)
MIL-HDBK Military Handbook (numbered series issued by USDOD)
MIL-STD Military Standard (numbered series issued by USDOD)
MILA Merritt Island Launch Area (of NASA)
MILAN Missile Leger Anti-char (Missile Light Anti-tank)
MILES Magnetic Intrusion Line Sensor
Multi-phenomenon Intrusion Line Sensor
Multiple Integrated Laser Engagement System
MILIC Millimetre Insular Line Integrated Circuit
MILOC Military Oceanography
MILP Mixed Integer Linear Programming
MILPOD Mixed Integer and Linear Programming Open Deck
MILS Missile Impact Location System
Missile Location System
MILSATCOM Military Satellite Communications
MILSCAP Military Standard Contract Administration Procedures (USDOD)
MILSTAMP Military Standard Transportation and Movement Procedure (USDOD)
MILSTEP Military Supply and Transportation Evaluation Procedures (USDOD)
MILSTRAP Military Standard Transaction Reporting and Accounting Procedures (USDOD)
MILSTRIP Military Standard Requisitioning and Issue Procedure (USDOD)
MILVAN Military Van
MIM Maryland Institute of Metals (USA)
Metal-Insulator-Metal
MODEM Interface Monitor
Modified Index Method
MIMI International Symposium and Exhibition on Mini- and Microcomputers and their applications
MIMIC Microfilm Information Master Image Converter
MIMICS Micromodule Microprogrammed Computer System
MIMM Mixed Integer Minimization Model
MIMO Multiple Input Multiple Output
MIMR Minimal Inhibitor Mole Ratio
Multilevel Interconnect Generatorvt Keying
MIMS MITROL Industrial Management System
Multi-Item Multi-Source
Multiple Independent Manoeuvring Submunitions
MIN Mine Identification and Neutralization
MINCIS MINNESOTA (USA) Crime Information System
MIND Management of Information through Natural Discourse
National Association for Mental Health
MINDD Minimum Due Date
MINDECO Mining Development Corporation (Zambia) (State owned)
MINDEN Mechanized Interconnection Design
MINDO Modified Intermediate Neglect of Differential Overlap
MINEAC Miniature Electronic Auto-Collimator
MINEDAF Ministers of Education of African member states (of OAU)
MINERVA Minimization of Earthworks for Vertical Alignment
Multiple Input Network for Evaluating Reactions, Votes, and Attitudes
MINI Heuristic Logic Minimization Technique
Method of Implicit Non-stationary Iteration
Minicomputer Industry National Interchange (USA) (an Association)
Miniscope
MINICS Minimal Input Cataloguing System
MINISID Manually Implanted Seismic Intrusion Detector
MINIT Minimum Idle Time
MINITEX Minnesota Interlibrary Telecommunications Exchange (USA)
MINOS Mine Operating Systems
Mixed Integer Operational Scheduling
MINPOSTEL Ministry of Posts and Telecommunications (became Broadcast Dept of the Home Office, 1974)
MINPRT Miniature Processing Time
MINQUE Minimum Norm Quadratic Unbiased Estimation
MINS Miniature Inertial Navigation System
MINSD Minimum Planned Start Date
MINSOP Minimum Slack time per Operation
MINT Materials Identification and New Item Control Technique
MINTECH Ministry of Technology (disbanded 1970)
MINTEX MINNESOTA (UNIVERSITY) (USA) Interlibrary Teletype Experiment
MINTS Mutual Institutions National Transfer System (of NAMSB (USA))
MIOR Memorial Institute for Ophthalmology Research (USA)
MIP Mixed Integer Programming
MIPAS Management Information Planning and Accountancy Service
MIPB Monoisopropylbiphenyl
MIPIR Missile Precision Instrumentation Radar
MIPS Million Instructions per Second
Modular Integrated Pallet System
MIPVCF Multiple-Input Phase-Variable Canonical Form
MIR Ministère de l'Industrie et de la Recherche (France) (Ministry of Industry and Research)
Multiple Internal Reflection
Musical Information Retrieval
MIRA Miniature Infra-Red Alarm
Motor Industry Research Association
Multifunction Inertial Reference Assembly
MIRAC Microfilmed Reports and Accounts
MIRACODE Microfilm Retrieval Access Code
MIRADCOM Missile Research and Development Command (US Army)
MIRADS MARSHALL (GEORGE C MARSHALL) Space Flight Center (NASA)usa)) Information Retrieval and Display System

MIRAGE Microelectronic Indicator for Radar Ground Equipment
Military Requirements Analysis-Generation 19-
MIRAN Missile Ranging
MIRAS Mortgage Interest Relief At Source
MIRC Management and Industrial Relations Committee (of Social Science Research Council)
MIRCOM Missile Materiel Readiness Command (US Army)
MIRD Medical Internal Radiation Dose
MIRF Multiple Instanteous Response File
MIRID Miniature Radar Illumination Detector
Monostatic Infra-Red Intrusion Detector
MIROS Modulation Inducing Retrodirective Optical System
MIRR Material Inspection and Receiving Report
MIRS Micro Interactive Retrieval System
Multi-purpose Infra-Red Sight
MIRSIM Mineral Resource Simulation Model
MIRT Meteorological Institute for Research and Training (Egypt)
Molecular Infrared Track
MIRU Machine Intelligence Research Unit (University of Edinburgh)
Myocardial Infarction Research Unit (University of Alabama (USA)
MIRV Matrix Interpretative Scheme
Metal-Insulator-Semiconductor
Multiple Independently-guided Re-entry Vehicle
Multiple Independently-targeted Re-entry Vehicle
MIS Maturation-Inducing Substance
Medical Information System
Merchandise Information Systems
MISAR Microprocessed Sensing and Automatic Regulation
Miniature Information Storage And Retrieval system
MISDAS Mechanical Impact System Design for Advanced Spacecraft
MISER Management Information System for Expenditure Reporting
Mean Integral Square Error
Methodology of Industrial Sector Energy Requirements (a standing committee of experts of industry, universities, DOI and DEn)
Miniature, Indicating and Sampling Electronic Respirometer
MOORFIELDS (EYE HOSPITAL, London) Information System Exception Reporting
MISFET Metal Insulator Semiconductor Field Effect Transistor
MISI Multi-path Inter-symbol Interference
MISL Mysore Iron and Steel Works Limited (India)
MISLIC Mid and South Staffordshire Libraries in Cooperation
MISP Microelectronics Industry Support Programme (of DTI)
MISR Multi-Impact Signature Register
MISS Mechanical Interruption Statistical Summary (series issued by FAA)
Multi-Input-Safety-Shutdown-System
Multi-item, Single-source
MISSIL Management Information System Symbolic Interpretive Language
MIST Minor Isotope Safeguards Technique
Music Information System for Theorists
MISTER Mobile Integrated System Trainer, Evaluator and Recorder
MISTIC Missile System Target Illuminator Controlled
MISTR Management Items Subject To Repair
MISTRAM Missile Trajectory Measurement
MISTRESS Mini-STRESS (a version of the STRESS computer programme)
MISTRIS Microfiche Information Storage and Retrieval for Intelligence Support (of Drug Enforcement Administration (Dept of Justice) (USA))
MISTT Midwest Interstate Sulfur Transformation and Transport (a research project of EPA (USA))
MIT Massachusetts Institute of Technology (USA)
MITE Missile Integration Terminal Equipment
MITI Ministry of International Trade and Industry (Japan)
MITR MASSACHUSETTS INSTITUTE OF TECHNOLOGY Reactor
MITRA Management Institute for Training and Research in Asia
MITS Microfiche Image Transmission System
Multiplex Information Transfer System
MITSG prefix to dated-numbered series of reports issued by Massachusetts Institute of Technology (USA) Sea Grant Project Office
MITTS Mobile Igor Tracking Telescope System
MIU Maharishi International University (USA)
MIUS Modular Integrated Utility System
MIVAC Microwave-Vacuum
MIZ Materialinformations-zentrum der Marine (Germany)
MJD Management Job Description
MKK Mitsubishi Kakoki Kaishi (Japan)
MKM Myopic Keratomileusis
MKS Metre Kilogramme Second
MKSA Metre Kilogramme Second Ampere
ML Machine Language
Maintained Load
Maximum Likelihood
Methods of Limits
prefix to numbered series of reports issued by Microwave Laboratory (Stanford University (USA))
MLA Malta Library Association (Malta)
Manitoba Library Association (Canada)
Marine Librarians Association
Medical Library Association (USA)
Michigan Library Association (USA)
Mississippi Library Association (USA)
Missouri Library Association (USA)
MLAB Modelling Laboratory
MLB Motor Life Boat
Multi-layer Board
MLC Magnetic Ledger Card
Mainlobe Clutter
Manoeuvre Load Control
Meat and Livestock Commission
Medical Library Center of New York (USA)
Michigan Library Consortium (USA)
Mixed Leukocyte Culture
Mixed Lymphocyte Culture
Morphine-Like Compound
Multi-layer Laminated Ceramic
MLCB Moored Limited OR Low Capability Buoy
MLCS Main Loop Cooling System
Multi-levelling Component System
MLD Marineluchtvaartdienst (Netherlands) (Naval Air Force)
Masking Level Difference
Maximum Lateral Damage
Maximum-Likelihood Decoding
Metachromatic Leukodystrophy
Minimum Lethal Dose
MLDD Mooring Leg Deployment Device
MLDLP Mailing Label and Directory Lookup Package
MLE Maximum Likelihood Estimate
Measured Logistics Effects

MLH Minimum List Heading (of the Standard Industrial Classification)
MLIS Metal-Liquid-Insulator Semiconductor
Molecular Laser Isotope Separation
MLLFT Modified Lens-less Fourier Transform
MLLW Mean Lower Low Water
MLLWL Mean Lower Low Water Line
MLM Maximum Likelihood Method
Membrane Light Modulator
MLMIS MINNESOTA (USA) Land Management Information System
MLMS Multi-purpose Lightweight Missile System
MLNS Mucocutaneous Lymph Node Syndrome
MLO Mauna Loa Observatory (Hawaii)
Mechanized Letter Office
MLP Multi-Layered Packaging
Multiparametric Linear Programming
MLPD Modified Log Periodic Dipole
MLPWB Multi-Layer Printed Wiring Board
MLR Minimum Lending Rate
Mixed Lymphocyte Reaction
Mobile Laser Radar
Mortar (Weapon) Locating Radar
MLRG Marine Life Research Group (of SIO)
MLRS Multiple-Launch Rocket System
MLRV Manned Lunar Roving Vehicle
MLS Machine Literature Searching
Marine LNG (Liquid Nitrogen Gas) System
Microwave Landing System
Mixed Language System
Multi-Language System
MLSA Minnesota Land Surveyors Association (USA)
MLT Magnetic Local Time
Mean Logistical Time
Medium Level Tripod
Mobile Land Target
MLV Moloney Leukaemia Virus
MLVSS Mixed Liquor Volatile Suspended Solids
MLW Mean Low Water
Medium-Level Waste
MLWL Mean Low Water Line
MM Macromodel
Macromodule
Maintenance Manual
Mariner Mars project (of NASA)
Materials Measurement
Modified Mercalli Intensity Scale
MMA Major Maintenance Availability
Manual Metal Arc
Methyl Methacrylate
Multifunction Microwave Aperture
MMAD Mass Median Aerodynamic Diameter
MMAJ Metal Mining Agency of Japan (Japan)
MMAP Microwave Multi-Application Payload (aboard the "Spacelab")
MMAS Manufacturing Management Accounting Systems
Mini-Manned Aircraft System
MMB Milk Marketing Board
MMC Maximum Metal Condition
Merger and Monopolies Commission
Metal Matrix Composite
Methylmercuric Chloride
Monopolies and Mergers Commission
MMCIAC Metal Matrix Composites Information Analysis Center (USA)
MMCS Missile and Munitions Center and School (US Army)
MMD Mass Median Diameter
Mini-Module Drive
Multi-effect Multi-stage Distillation
MMEA Metallic Mineral Exploration Agency (of MITI (Japan))
MMF Maximum Mid-expiratory Flow
Micromation Microfilm
MMFANE Master Metal Finishers Association of New England (USA)
MMFR Maximum Mid-expiratory Flow Rate
MMH Monomethylhydrazine
MMH/FH Maintenance Man Hours per Flight Hour
MMH/OH Maintenance Man-Hours per Operating Hour
MMI Macrophage Migration Inhibition
Man-Machine Interface
MMIC Millimetre-wave Integrated Circuit
MMICS Maintenance Management Information and Control System (USAF)
MMIJ Mining and Metallurgical Institute of Japan (Japan)
MMIPS Man-Machine Interactive Processing System
Multiple Mode Integrated Propulsion System
MMIS Maintenance Management Information System
Medicaid Management Information System
MML Material Mechanics Laboratory (of Israel Institute of Technology (Israel))
Metallic Matrix Laminate
Mysore Minerals Ltd. (India) (Govt owned)
MMLES Map-Match Location-Estimation System
MMMA Metalforming Machinery Makers Association
Milking Machine Manufacturers Association
MMMF Man-Made Mineral Fibre
MMMRPV Modular Multi-Mission Remotely Piloted Vehicle
MMN Metallurgie et Mecanique Nucleaires (Belgium)
MMP Multiplex Message Processor
MMPI Minnesota Multiphasic Personality Inventory
MMPT Man-Machine Partnership Translation
MMR Massed Miniature Radiography
Method of Mixed Ranges
MMRBM Mobile Medium Range Ballistic Missile
MMS Microfiche Management System
Minimum Mean Square
Multi-mission Modular Space-craft
MMSE Minimum-Mean-Squared Error
MMSI Multi Medium Scale Integration
MMT Methylcyclopentadienyl Manganese Tricarbonyl
Multiple-Mirror Telescope (joint project of Smithsonian Institute and Arizona University (USA))
MMTC Marine Minerals Technology Center (of ERL (NOAA) (USA))
Minerals and Metals Trading Corporation (India) (Government owned)
MMTV Mouse Mammary Tumour Virus
MMU Man or Manned Manoeuvring Unit
Million Monetary Units
Modular Manoeuvring Unit
MMVF Man-Made Vitrous Fibres
MNB Murine Neuroblastoma
MNC Medical Neurosecretory Brain Cells
Multi-National Corporation
MNCS Multiprint Network Control System
MNCV Motor Nerve Conduction Velocity
MND Motor Neurone Disease
MNDA Motor Neurone Disease Association
MNDP Multinational Data Processing
MNDX Mobile-Non-Director Exchange
MNE Multi-National Enterprise
MNF Modulated Normal Function
MNFP Multiple Number of Faults per Pass
MNG Modulated Noise Generator
MNLS Modified New Least Squares
MNOS Metal-Nitride-Oxide Semi-conductor
Metal-Nitride-Oxide-Silicon
MNS Metal Nitride Semiconductor
Metal-Nitride-Silicon

MO — Maize Oil
Microwave Oven

MO-CVD — Metal-Organic Chemical Vapour Deposition

MOA — Microwave Oven Association
Ministry of Aviation (disbanded 1967)

MOABAT — Modified Battalion Anti-Tank

MOAF — Ministry of Agriculture and Forests (Korea)

MOAS — Ministry of Aviation Supply (formed 1970, disbanded 1971)

MOAT — Methods of Appraisal and Test
Missile On Aircraft Test

MOB — Mouse Olfactory Bulb

MOBA — Mobility Operations for Built-up Areas (a project of US Army)

MOBIDIC — Mobile Digital Computer

MOBOL — MOHAWK (DATA SCIENCES CORPORATION (USA)) Business Oriented Language

MOBS — Mobile Ocean Basing System
Multiple-Orbit Bombardment System

MOBSSL- UAF — M. J. MERRITT and D. S. MILLER'S Own Block Structured Simulation Language—Unpronounceable Acronym For

MOBULA — Model Building Language

MOC — Marine Operations Centre (of the Commonwealth Dept of Transport (Australia))
Memory Operating Characteristic
Method of Characteristics
Metrication Operating Committee (USA)
Minimal Oxygen Consumption
Ministry of Constructions (Korea)
Modular Organisation Charting

MOC-LAMP — Method of Characteristics Laser and Mixing Programme

MOCA — Minimum Obstruction Clearance Altitude

MOCAS — Mechanization of Contract Administration Services (USDOD)

MOCB — Minimum Oil Circuit Breaker

MOCC — METEOSAT Operations Control Centre (of ESOC (ESA))

MOCI — Ministry of Commerce and Industry (Korea)

MOCOM — Mobile Command Module

MOCS — Multi-channel Ocean Colour Sensor

MOCVD — Metal-Organic Chemical Vapour Deposition

MOD — Ministry of Defence

MOD(AD) — Ministry of Defence (Army Department)

MOD(Air) — Ministry of Defence (Air Force Department)

MOD(N) — Ministry of Defence (Navy Department)

MOD(PE) — Ministry of Defence (Procurement Executive)

MODA — Motion Detector and Alarm

MODAP — Modified APOLLO

MODAPS — Modal Data Acquisition and Processing System

MODAPTS — Modular Arrangement of Predetermined Time Standards

MODCON — Man Machine System for the Optimum Design and Construction of Buildings

MODE — Mid-Ocean Dynamic Experiment (of American and British Universities)

MODEMS — Modulators-Demodulators

MODI — Modified Distribution method

MODIA — Method of Designing Instructional Alternatives

MODICON — Modulator Dispersed Control

MODILS — Modular Instrument Landing System

MODLE — METEOROLOGICAL OFFICE Data-Logging Equipment

MODR — Microwave Optical Double Resonance

MODS — Manpower Operation Data System
Medically Oriented Data System (of FDA (USA))
Military Orbital Development System Station

MODUS — Modular One Dynamic User System

MOE — Maximum Output Entropy
Measure of Effectiveness

MOERO — Medium Orbiting Earth Resources Observatory

MOF — Ministry of Finance (Japan)

MOF — Maximum Operating Frequency

MOFAB — Mobile Floating Assault Bridge-Ferry

MOFACS — Multi-Order Feedback And Compensation Synthesis

MOGA — International Conference on Microwave and Optical Generation and Amplification
Microwave and Optical Generation and Amplification

MOGAS — Motor Gasoline

MOHATS — Mobile Overland Hauling And Transport System

MOHILL — Machine Oriented High Level Language

MOIRA — Model Of International Relations in Agriculture

MOL — Machine Oriented Language
Manned Orbiting Laboratory

MOLAB — Mobile Lunar Laboratory

MOLAR — Mortar/Artillery Locating Radar

MOLARS — METEOROLOGICAL OFFICE Library Accessions and Retrieval System

MOLDS — Multiple On-line De-bugging System
North American Conference on the Modernization of Land Data Systems

MOLE — Market Odd-Lot Execution system

MOLEC — Molecular Low Energy Collisions Conference

MOLEM — Mobile Lunar Excursion Module

MOLFAX — Meteorological Office Land-line Facsimile network

MOLP — Multiple Objective Linear Programming

MOM — Manned Orbiting Module
Metal-metal Oxide-Metal
Metal-Oxide-Metal

MOMS — MICHIGAN'S (Michigan University (USA)) Own Mathematical System
Mobile Optical Measurement System

MON — Mixed Oxides of Nitrogen
Motor Octane Number

MONA — Modular Area Navigation
Multitape One-way Non-writing Automata

MONAL — Mobile Nondestructive Assay Laboratory

MONEX — Asian Monsoon Experiment (of FGGE (WMO))

MOOSE — Man-Out-Of-Space-Easiest
Manned Orbital Operations Safety Equipment

MOP — Manned Orbiting Platform
Multiple On-line Programming

MOPA — Mail Order Publisher Authority
Master Oscillator Power Amplifier

MOPMS — Modular Pack Mine System

MOPP — Mechanization of Planning Processes

MOPS — Mechanization Outside Plant Scheduling System
National Newspapers Mail Order Protection Scheme

MOPSY — Multi-programming Operating System

MOPTARS — Multi-Object Phase-Tracking And Ranging System

MOPTS — Mobile Photographing Tracking Station

MOR — Management by Objectives and Results
Mandatory Occurrence Reporting
Meteorological Optical Range
Modulus of Ruture

MORD — Magneto-Optic Rotary Dispersion

MORIF — Microprogramme Optimization technique considering Resource occupancy and Instruction Formats

MORL — Manned Orbital Research Laboratory

MORP — Medical and Occupational Radiation Program (of Public Health Service (USA))
Meteorite Observation and Recovery Project (of NRC (Canada)

MORS — Midland Operational Research Society

	Military Operations Research Society (USA)
	Military Operations Research Symposium
MOS	Mathematical Offprint Service (of American Mathematical Society (USA))
	Metal Oxide Semiconductor
	Metal-Oxide-Silicon
	Ministry of Supply (dissolved in 1959)
	Multiple Object Spectroscopy
MOSAIC	Metal Oxide Semiconductor Advanced Integrated Circuit
	Method of Scenic Alternative Impacts by Computer
MOSAICS	Melcom Optical Software Applications for Integrated Commercial Systems
MOSASR	Metal Oxide Semiconductor Analogue Shift Register
MOSAW	Medium Operating Speed Automatic Weapon
MOSCOS	MOLINS Operational Shop Control System
MOSES	Manned Ocean Experimentation Station
	Molecular Orbital Self-consistent Energy System
MOSFET	Metallic Oxide Semiconductor Field Effect Transistor
MOSM	Metal-Oxide—Semi-Metal
MOSPO	Mobile Satellite Photometric Observatory (of NASA (USA))
MOSS	Military Operational Satellite System (USAF)
	Modelling Systems
MOSST	Ministry of State for Science and Technology (Canada)
MOST	Management Operation System Technique
	MAYNARD (H B MAYNARD & Co LTD) Operation Sequence Technique
	Metal Oxide Semiconductor OR Silicon Transistor
	MICROMATION (LTD) Output Software Translator
	Molonglo Observatory Synthesis Telescope (University of Sydney (Australia))
MOT	Ministry of Transport (Canada)
	Ministry of Transport (Japan)
	Ministry of Transport (merged into the Department of the Environment, 1970)
MOTA	Mail Order Traders Association
MOTAT	Museum of Transport and Technology (New Zealand)
MOTEC	Multi-Occupational Training and Educational Centre (of RTITB)
MOTNE	Meteorological Operational Telecommunications Network of Europe
MOTNEG	Meteorological Operational Telecommunication Network in Europe, Regional Planning Group (of ICAO)
MOTU	Mobile Optical Tracking Unit
MOU	Memorandum Of Understanding
MOUT	Military Operations on Urban Terrain
MOV	Metal Oxide Varistors
MOVAD	Movement Adaptability
	Movement And Delivery
MOVE	Management of Value Engineering
MOVECAP	Movement Capability
MOVIMS	Motor Vehicle Information Management System
MOVLAS	Manually Operated Visual Landing Aid System
MOW	Ministry of Works (New Zealand)
MOWACS	Modal Wavefront Control System
MOWAG	Motorwagenfabrik AG (Switzerland)
MOWASP	Mechanization Of Warehousing and Shipment Processing (USDOD)
MOWD	Ministry of Works and Development (New Zealand)
MOWOS	METEOROLOGICAL OFFICE Weather Observing System
MP	Magnetic Permeability
	Main Phase
	Minimum Phase
	Miscellaneous Paper
	Miscellaneous Publication
	Mitsubishi Plastics (Japan)
	Multiphase
	Multipulse
MPA	Magazine Publishers Association (USA)
	Man-Powered Aircraft
	Master Photographers Association of Great Britain
	Master Printers of America (USA)
	Methoxypropylamine
	Mortar Producers Association
MPAA	Motion Picture Association of American (USA)
MPAD	Maximum Permissible Annual Dose
MPAI	Maximum Permissible Annual Intake
MPASK	Multi-Phase and Amplitude-Shift-Keying
MPBB	Maximum Permissible Body Burden
MPBE	Molten Plutonium Burnup Experiment
MPBW	Ministry of Public Building and Works (absorbed into Department of the Environment, 1970)
MPC	Marine Protein Concentrate
	Maximum Permissible Concentration
	Medical Practices Committee(of BMA)
	Metal Properties Council (USA)
	Microprogrammed Controller
	Mother-of-Pearl Clouds
	Mysore Power Corporation (India) (govt owned)
MPCa	Maximum Permissible Concentration in Air
MPCA	Minnesota Pollution Control Agency (USA)
MPCAG	Military Parts Control Avisory Group (USDOD)
MPCC	Multi-Protocol Communications Controller
MPCF	Millions of Particles per Cubic Foot
MPD	Magneto-plasmadynamic
	Mean Population Doubling
MPDC	Mechanical Properties Data Center (USA)
MPDR	Mono-Pulse Doppler Radar
MPDS	Market Price Display Service (of the London Stock Exchange)
	Market Prices Display Services (of the London Stock Exchange)
	Message Processing and Distribution System
	Missile Piercing Discarding Sabot
MPE	Maximum Permissible Exposure
	Maximum Permitted Error
MPEP	Manual of Patent Examining Procedure
MPES	Mathematical, Physical and Engineering Science (a directorate of NSF (USA))
MPF	Man-Powered Flight
	Manufacturing Progress Function
MPFA	Monolithic Focal Plane Array
MPFW	Multi-shot Portable Flame Weapon
MPG	Max-Planck-Gesellschaft zur Foederung der Wissenschaften (Germany) (Max Planck Society for the Promotion of Science)
	Miniature Precision Gyrocompass
MPGS	Micro Programme Generating System
	Mobile Protected Gun System
MPHC	Metal-skinned, Paper Honeycomb-Cored
MPHP	Multiple-Pass Heuristic Procedure
MPI	Magnetic Particle Inspection
	Mannosephosphate Isomerase
	MAUDSLEY Personality Inventory
	Maximum Precipitation Intensity
	Miltarpsykologiska Institutet (Sweden) (Military Psychology Institute)
	Multiphoton Ionization
MPIA	Max-Planck Institut fur Astronomie (Germany)
MPIF	Metal Powders Industries Federation (USA)
MPIS	Manpower and Personnel Information Systems (of FAA (USA))
MPL	Marine Physical Laboratory (of Scripps Institution of Oceanography (USA))
	Mathematical Programming Language

Maximum Permissible Level
Melamine Paper Laminate
Message Processing Language
Modified Programmers Language
Moving Part Logic

MPLAW Multipulse-Scaling-Law Code using Data Base Interpolation

MPLB Maximum Permissible Lung Burden

MPLPC Multi-Pulse Linear Productive Coding

MPLSM Multiple Position Letter Sorting Machine

MPM Message Processing Module
Metra Potential Method
Mole per cent Metal
Monitoring and Preventive Maintenance
Multi-Purpose Missile

MPMA Metal Packaging Manufacturers Association

MPMI Magazine and Paperback Marketing Institute (USA)

MPMS Missile Performance Monitoring System

MPN Most Probable Number

MPO Management and Personnel Office (formerly CSD)

MPOIS Military Police Operations and Information System (US Army)

MPP Marine Power Plant
Massively Parallel Processor
Message Processing Programme
Minimum-Perimeter Polygon

MPPM Materials-Process-Product Model

MPQ Manpower Planning Quotas

MPR Military Photo-Reconnaissance

MPRE Medium Power Reactor Experiment

MPRST Maximum Probability Ratio Sequential Test

MPS Management Planning System
Maritime Prepositioning Ship
Mathematical Programming Society (USA)
Mathematical Programming System
Minimum Property Standards (of FHA (USA))
Mixed Potential Systems
Multi-Project Scheduling

MPS Multiple Protective Structure
series of Minimum Performance Specifications issued by EUROCAE

MPS/MMS Multi-Purpose/Multi-Mission Ships

MPSG Multi-band Portable Signal Generator

MPSIC Madhya Pradesh State Industries Corporation (India)

MPSK Multi-Phase Shift Keying

MPSM Multi-Purpose Sub-Munition

MPSX Mathematical Programming System Extended

MPT Ministry of Posts and Telecommunications (became Broadcast Department of the Home Office in 1974)
Ministry of Posts and Telecommunications (Japan)
Multiple Pure Tone
prefix to numbered series issued by the Radio Regulatory Department of the Home Office and published by HMSO

MPTA Mechanical Power Transmission Association (USA)
Municipal Passenger Transport Association

MPW Modified Plane Wave

MPX Multi-Programming Executive

MQA Metrology, Quality Assurance and Standards Division of DPCP

MQAD Materials Quality Assurance Directorate (of MOD)

MQB Mining Qualifications Board (of Ministry of Power)

MQF Mobile Quarantine Facility (of NASA)

MQV Ministère de la Qualité de la Vie (France) (Ministry of the Quality of Life)

MQW Multiple Quantum Well

MR Magnetospherically Reflected
Marginal Revenue
Memorandum Report
Miscelleneous Report
Moisture Resistant
Monthly Report
Multiple Regression
prefix to numbered-dated series on Material Requirements issued by NACE (USA)

MR&DF Malleable Research and Development Foundation (USA)

MR. ATOMIC Multiple Rapid Automatic Test of Monolithic Integrated Circuits

MRA Magnetic Reaction Analyzer
Materials Requirement Analysis
Matrix Reducibility Algorithm
Multiple Regression Analysis

MRAALS MARINE (United States Marine Corps) Remote Area Approach and Landing System

MRAAM Medium-Range Air-to-Air Missile

MRAD Mass Random Access Disc

MRAM Multi-mission Redeye Air-launched Missile

MRAPCON Mobile Radar Approach Control

MRAS Model Reference Adaptive System

MRASM Medium-Range Air-to-Surface Missile

MRB Magnetic Recording Borescope
Magnetospheric Radio Burst
Motorized Rifle Battalion

MRBF Mean Rounds (weapon fired) Between Failure

MRBM Medium Range Ballistic Missile

MRC Machine Readable Code
Management Research Center (Graduate School of Business, University of Pittsburgh (USA))
Materials Research Center (Lehigh University (USA))
Mathematics Research Center (Wisconsin University (USA))
Medical Research Council
Medical Research Council (Canada)

MRCA Multi-Role Combat Aircraft (now called "TORNADO")

MRCD Memory Raster Colour Display

MRCS Multiple RPV (Remotely Piloted Vehicle) Control System

MRDE Mining Research and Development Establishment (of the National Coal Board)

MRDF Machine Readable Data File
Marine Resource Development Foundation (Puerto Rico)

MRDIS Message Reproduction Distribution System

MRDOS Mapped Real-time Disc Operating System

MRE Meal, Ready-to-Eat
Microbiological Research Establishment (MOD) (became CAMR in 1979)
Mining Research Establishment (National Coal Board)
Modern Ramjet Engine

MRELB Malaysian Rubber Exchange and Licensing Board (Malayasia)

MRF Mesencephalic Reticular Formation
Meteorological Research Flight (of the Meteorological Office)
Midbrain Reticular Formation
Modular Rigid Frame

MRFB Malayan Rubber Fund Board (Malaysia)

MRFIT Multiple Risk Factor Intervention Trial for coronary heart disease (of NHLI (USA))

MRG Management Research Groups (became part of BIM in 1975)
Marine Radioactivity Group (Scripps Institution of Oceanography (USA))
Master Reference Gyro
Methane Rich Gas

MRH Magnetoresistive Head

MRI Magnetic Resonance Imaging
Magnetic Rubber Inspection
Meal, Ready-to-eat, Individual (military rationing)
Meat Research Institute (of the Agricultural Research Council)
Medical Research Institute (USN)
Meteorological Research Institute (Japan)
Microwave Research Institute (of PIB (USA))
Midwest Research Institute (USA)

MRIF MSH (Melanphore Stimulating Hormone) Release Inhibiting Factor

MRIR Medium Resolution Infrared Radiometer

MRIS Maritime Research Information Service (of Highway Research Board and Maritime Administration (USA))

MRIT Marine Radar Interrogator-Transponder

MRL Materials Research Laboratory (of DSTO (Australia))
Materials Research Laboratory (Pennsylvania State University (USA))
Maximised Relative Likelihood
Maximum Residue Limit
Medium Research Laboratory
Multiple Rocket Launcher

MRM Metabolic Rate Monitor

MRMS Metabolic Rate Measuring System

MRN Meteorological Rocket Network

mRNA Messenger RNA

MRNA Messenger Ribonucleic Acid
Monocistronic RNA

MRNL Medical Research and Nutrition Laboratory (US Army)

MRO Maintenance Repair and Operational
Mine (explosive) Radiographic Outfit

MRP Manufacturing Resources Planning
Materials Requirements Planning

MRP/MSL prefix to dated-numbered reports issued by Canada Centre for Mineral and Energy Technology, Mineral Sciences Laboratories

MRPPS MARYLAND (UNIVERSITY) (USA) Refutation Proof Procedure System

MRPV Mini-Remotely Piloted Vehicle

MRR Mechanical Reliability Report (series issued by FAA)
Monomer Reactivity Ratios

MRRDB Malaysian Rubber Research and Development Board

MRRS Multi-Rail Rocket System

MRS Market Research Society
Materials Research Society (USA)
Medium Range Surveillance aircraft
Midlands Research Station (of the British Gas Corporation)
Multi-disciplinary Refurbishable Satellite

MRSA Medium Range Surveillance Aircraft

MRSM Maintenance and Reliability Simulation Model

MRST Minimum Remaining Slack Time

MRS^3 Multilateration Radar Surveillance Strike System

MRT Maximum Repair Time
Mean Radiant Temperature
Mean Repair Time
Measured Rate of Time
Milk Ring Test
Minimum Resolvable Temperature
Modified Rhyme Test

MRTD Minimum Resolvable Temperature Difference

MRTI Multi-Role Thermal Imager

MRTPC Monopolies and Restrictive Trade Practices Commission (India)

MRTU Multiplex Remote Terminal Unit

MRU Manpower Research Unit (of the Department of Employment)

MRUA Mobile Radio Users Association

MRV Manoeuvring Re-entry Vehicle
Mars Roving Vehicle
Multiple Warhead Re-entry Vehicle

MS G. MIE Scattering
Machine Selection
Manpower Society
Mass Spectrometry
Material Specification
Meeting Speech
Metal Semiconductor
Metallurgical Society (USA)
Metals Society (now The Institute of Metals)
Meteor Scatter
Methylisotiocyanate
Monograph Series
Multiple Sclerosis
prefix to Military Standard (numbered series issued by USOD)
prefix to numbered-dated-lettered series of reports issued by Department of Materials Science, Virginia University (USA)

MS&T Methodical Structures and Textures

MSA Magazine Stowage "A"
Malaysia-Singapore Airlines
Male Specific Antigen
Manchester Society of Architects
Matrix Scheme for Algorithms
Mechanical Signature Analysis
Mineralogical Society of America (USA)
Minimum Sector Altitude
Multiple Sensor Annunciator
Mycological Society of America (USA)

MSAA Multiple Sclerosis Associated Agent

MSAC Mid-State Arms Collectors and Shooters Club (USA)

MSAC2 Milwaukee (USA) Symposium on Automatic Computation and Control

MSAT Marine Services Association of Texas (USA)

MSAW Minimum Safety Altitude Warning

MSB Magazine Stowage "B"
Most Significant Bit

MSBLMS Multi Station Boundary Layer Model System

MSBLS Microwave Scanning Beam Landing System

MSBR Molten-Salt Breeder Reactor

MSBV Mooring Salvage and Boom Vessel

MSC Magnitude Square of the Complex Coherence
Manned Spacecraft Center (of NASA (USA)) (now called the Lyndon B. Johnson Space Center)
Manpower Services Commission
Maritime Safety Committee (of IMO)
Materials Science Center (of Cornell University (USA))
Message Switching Concentration
Microwave Stripline Circuit
Military Sealift Command (USN)
Mono-Stereo-Compatible
Multipotential Stem Cells

MSCDR Mohawk Synchronous Communication Data Recorder

MSCE Magnetic-Strip Credit Card
Main Storage Control Element

MSCIC Maryland State Colleges Information Center (USA))

MSCP Mean Spherical Candle Power

MSCR Multilayer Side-Cladded Ridge waveguide

MSCTDC Maharashtra State Co-operative Tribal Development Corporation (India)

MSD Magazine Stowage "D"
Marine Sanitation Devices
Master Standard Data
Most Significant Digit

MSDBP Mean Squared Distance Between Pairs
MSDD Milli-Second Delay Detonator
MSDF Maritime Self-Defence Force (Japan)
MSDS Multi-Spectral Scanner and Data System
MSDT Maintenance Strategy Diagramming Technique
MSE Mean Square Error
Mobile Subscriber Equipment
MSEB Maharashtra State Electricity Board (India)
MSEL Marine Systems Engineering Laboratory (of University of New Hampshire (USA))
MSEP Mean Square Error of Prediction
MSER Multiple Stores Ejector Rack
MSF Matched Spatial Filter
Mean Skinfolds
Multi-Stage Flash
MSFC Marshall Space Flight Center (NASA)
MSFSG Manned Space Flight Support Group (USAF)
MSG Monosodium Glutamate
MSGL Multi-Shot Grenade Launcher
MSH Melanocyte Stimulating Hormone
Melanphore Stimulating Hormone
MSHA Mine Safety and Health Administration (USA)
MSI Medium Scale Integrated
Medium Scale Integration
MSIRI Marmara Scientific and Industrial Research Institute (Turkey)
Mauritius Sugar Industry Research Institute (Mauritius)
MSIS Marine Safety Information System
Mask Shop Information System
MSISL Moore School Information Systems Laboratory (University of Pennsylvania (USA))
MSIV Main Steam Isolation Valve
MSK Minimum (frequency) Shift Keying
Mitsubishi Shoje Kaisha (Japan)
MSL Mapping Sciences Laboratory (of NASA (USA))
Mean Sea Level
Microfiche Source Listings
Midsternal Line
MSLAVA Manitoba School Library Audio Visual Association (Canada)
MSLM Microchannel Spatial Light Modulator
MSLS Maine Society of Land Surveyors (USA)
MSM Metal-Semiconductor-Metal
MSMA Monosodium Acid Methane Arsonate
MSMEA Multiwall Sack Manufacturers Employers Association
MSMMS Marine Safety Management Methodology Synthesis
MSMT Multiple Terminal Monitor Task
MSN Median Sample Number
MSND Mercury Substitution and Nucleonic Detection
MSO Mesityl Oxide
MSOG Molecular Sieve Oxygen Generating
MSOR Maximum System Operational Range
MSOS Mass Storage Operating System
MSP Mosaic Sensor Program (of USAF)
MSPFE Multi-Sensor Programmable Feature Extractor
MSPS Multiphase Serial-Parallel-Serial Storage
MSR Mechanical Strain Recorder
Metal Sheet Rolling
Missile Site Radar
Moisture Separator Reheater
MSRCE Multi-carrier Station Radio Control Equipment
Multi-carrier Station Remote Control Equipment
MSRE Molten Salt Reactor Experiment
MSRF Microwave Space Research Facility (of NRL (USN))
MSRI Mathematical Sciences Research Institute (of UCB (USA))
Mathematical Sciences Research Institute (of University of Minnesota (USA))
MSS Magnetic Spark Spectrometer
Manufacturers Standardization Society of the Valve and Fittings Industry (USA)
Mass Storage Syste
Measurement-Standard Sensitive
Military Supply Standard (USDOD)
Moored Surveillance System
Multi-Spectral Scanner OR Sensor
MSSCC Multicolour Spin Scan Cloud Camera
MSSL MULLARD Space Science Laboratory (University of London)
MSSM Mount Sinai School of Medicine (New York (USA))
Multiple-Sine-Slit Microdensitometer
MSSNY Medical Society of the State of New York (USA)
MSSR Mars Soil Sample Return
MSSS Mass Spectral Search System (of CIS (of NIH & EPA (USA))
Mobile Spectrum Search System
MSSU Mississippi State University (USA)
MSSW Magnetostatic Surface Wave
MST Medium STOL Transport
Minimum Spanning Tree
Monolithic System Technology
MSTC Management Systems Training Council (formerly the O & M Training Council)
MSTCL Metal Scrap Trade Corporation Ltd (India) (govt owned)
MSTL Materials Science Toxicology Laboratories (University of Tennessee (USA))
MSTM Mafatlal Scientific and Technological Museum (India)
MSTPH Multi-Stop Time-to-Pulse Height
MSTS Military Sea Transportation Service (USN) (now Military Sealift Command)
Multisubscriber Time Sharing Systems
MSTTE Mobile Systems Target Tracking Emitters
MSU Michigan State University (USA)
MSUSM Medical Society of the United States and Mexico
MSV Moloney Sarcoma Virus
Multi-purpose Submersible Vessel
Murine Sarcoma Virus
MSW Magnetic Surface Wave
Magnetostatic Waves
Municipal Solid Waste
MSWG Materials Sciences Working Group (of ESA)
MSY Maximum Sustainable Yield
MSZH Magyr Szabvanyugyi Hivatal (Hungary) (Standards Institute)
MT Machine Translation
Median Terminal
Megaton
Ministere des Transports (France) (Ministry of Transport)
MT/ST Magnetic Tape Selectric Typewriter
MTA Mass-spectrometric Thermal Analysis
Mean Tryptic Activity
Metropolitan Transportation Authority (State of New York (USA))
Microwave Transistor Amplifier
MTACCS Marine Corps Tactical Command and Control System (US Marine Corps)
MTAG Manufacturing Technology Advisory Group (of USDOD)
MTAS Marine Trend Analysis System
MTB Marcaptan Terminated Polybutadiene
Material Transportation Bureau (of DOT (USA))
Motor Torpedo Boat
MTBCD Mean Time Between Confirmed Defects
MTBCF Mean Time Between Component Failure
MTBD Mean Time Between Defects

MTBDR Mean Time Between Depot Repair
MTBE Methyl Tertiary-Butyl Ether
MTBF Mean Time Between Failure
MTBM Mean Time Between Maintenance
MTBMA Mean-Time Between Maintenance-Action
MTBN Mercaptan Butadiene-Acrylonirile
MTBO Mean Time Between Overhauls
MTBR Mean Time Between Rejections
Mean Time Between Removals
Mean Time Between Repairs
MTBSF Mean Time Between Significant Failures
MTBT Miniature Thermal Bar Torch
MTBUM Mean Time Between Unscheduled Maintenance
MTBUR Mean Time Between Unscheduled Removal
MTC Main Trunk Circuit (of the World Meteorological Organization)
Maintenance Time Constraint
Mobile Tactical Computer
MTCE Million Tonnes of Coal Equivalent
MTCH Mining Technology Clearing House
MTCS Minimum Core Teleprocessing Control System
Minimum Telecommunications System
MTD Minimal Toxic Dose
Moving Target Detector
MTDR International Machine Tool Design and Research Conference
Machine Tool Design and Research
MTDS Marine Tactical Data System (US Marine Corps)
MTE Materiel de Traction Electrique (France)
Maximum Temperature Engine
Missile Test Equipment
MTEE Mean Transverse Emmission Energy
MTEL Methyltriethyl Lead
MTER Magnetic Tape Event Recorder
MTF Materialteknisk Forening (Norway) (Association for Testing of Materials)
Metastable Time-of-Flight
Mississippi Test Facility (of NASA)
Modulation Transfer Function
MTFA Modulation Transfer Function Area
MTFS Medium Term Financial Strategy
MTG Marine Technik Planungsgesellschaft (Germany) (Institute for Naval Architecture)
MTGU Main Turbine/Gearing Unit
MTH Medium Transport Helicopter
MTHI Methyltetrahydroindene
MTI Materials Technology Institute (USA)
Metal Treating Institute (USA)
Moving Target Indicator
MTI&A Maintenance Task Identification and Analysis
MTIA Metal Trades Industry Association (Australia)
MTIRA Machine Tool Industry Research Association
MTIS Multiplex Transmitter Input Signals
MTL Merged Transistor Logic
Mixed Thermoluminescence
Motivation and Training Laboratory (US Army) (now part of ARI (US Army))
Multiple-conductor Transmission Line
MTLC Mass Transfer Limiting Current
MTM Methods-Time Measurement
MTM-GPD Methods Time Measurement and General Purpose Data
MTMA-UK Methods-Time Measurement Association of the United Kingdom
MTMC Military Traffic Management Command (US Army)
MTMTS Military Traffic Management and Terminal Service (USDoD)
MTN Multilateral Trade Negotiations
MTNS Metal Thick-film Nitride Silicon
Mtoe Million tons of oil equivalent
MTOP Molecular Total Overlap Population
MTOS Metal Thick Oxide Silicon
MTP Mechanical Thermal Pulse
Microtubule Protein
prefix to numbered series of reports on Material Test Procedures issued by USATECOM
MTR Magnetic Tape Recorder
Materials Testing Reactor
Materials Testing Report
Meteor Trail Tracking Radar
MTRB Marine Technology Requirements Board (of DTI)
Maritime Transportation Research Board (of NAS/NRC (USA))
MTRS Magnetic Tape Reformatting System
MTS Magnetotelluric Sounding
Maintenance Test Station
Marine Technology Society (USA)
Message Telecommunication Service
MICHIGAN (University) Time-Sharing
Missile Tracking System
Module Testing System
MTSE Magnetic Trap Stability Experiment
MTSF Mean Time to System Failure
MTST Magnetic Tape Selective Typewriter
Maximal Treadmill Stress Time
MTT Materials Test Technology
Mechanico-Thermal Treatment
Microwave Theory and Techniques
MTT-S Microwave Theory and Techniques Society (of IEEE (USA))
MTTA Machine Tool Trades Association
MTTF Mean Time to Failure
MTTFF Mean Time To First Failure
MTTFSF Mean Time To First System Failure
MTTFSR Mean Time To First System Repair
MTTI Muszaki Tudomanyos Tajekoztato Intezetben (Hungary) (Hungarian Institute of Scientific and Technical Information)
MTTR Maximum Time to Repair
Mean Time to Repair
Mean Time to Restore
MTTSA Metropolitan Toronto Television Service Association (Canada)
MTTSF Mean Time To System Failure
MTU Magnetic Tape Unit
Motoren- und Turbinen-Union (Germany)
MTUR Mean Time to Unscheduled Replacement
MTV Marginal Terrain Vehicle
MTW Management Teamwork
MTWA Maximum Total Weight Authorised
MU Manchester University
MUA Mail Users Association
MUCIA Midwest Universities Consortium for International Activities (USA)
MUCOM Munitions Command (US Army)
MUCROMAF Multiple Critical Root Maximally Flat
MUDAID Multivariate, Univariate and Discriminant Analysis of Irregular Data
MUDCAP Multi-Dimensional Contingency Analysis Programme
MUDD Multisource Unified Data Distribution
MUF Material Unaccounted For
Maximum Usable Frequency
MUG MUMPS Users Group
MUGLNC Microcomputer Users Group for Libraries in North Carolina (USA)
MUGOLIS Manchester User Group for On-Line Information Systems
MULE Modular Universal Laser Equipment
MULES Missouri (USA) Uniform Law Enforcement System

MULQUAL Multiple Goal Water Quality Model
MULS Minnesota (University) (USA) Union List of Serials
MULTEWS Multiple Target Electronic Warfare System
MULTICS Multiplexed Information and Computing Service
MULTIPAC Multiple Pool Processor And Computer
MULTIPLE Multipurpose Programme that Learns
MuLV Murine Leukaemia Virus
MUM Mass Unbalance Modulation
Multi-Use Manuscript
MUMC McMaster University Medical Center (USA)
MUMMS Marine Corps Unified Material Management System (US Marine Corps)
MUMPS MASSACHUSETTS GENERAL HOSPITAL (Boston, USA) Utility Multiprogramming System
MUMS Modular Unified Microprocessor System
Multiple Use MARC (Machine Readable Cataloguing) System
MUN Memorial University of Newfoundland
MUND Model Urban Neighbourhood Demonstration
MUP Metalworking Under Pressure
MURA Midwestern University Research Association (USA)
MURCEP Ministry of Urban and Rural Construction and Environmental Protection (China)
MURFAAMCE Mutual Reduction of Forces and Armaments and Associated Measures in Central Europe (negotiations between NATO AND THE WARSAW Treaty Organisation)
MURR MISSOURI UNIVERSITY (USA) Research Reactor
MURRTE Mulloka (Aboriginal word meaning 'water devil' or 'devil fish') Recording Replay and Training Equipment
MURS Machine Utilisation Reporting System
MUS Manned Underwater Station
MUS&T Manned Undersea Science and Technology (a programme of NOAA (USA))
MUSA Multiple Unit Steerable Antenna
MUSAT Multiple Station Analytical Triangulation
MUSE Machine User Symbiotic Environment
Mini-computer Users in Secondary Education (a national organization of teachers and lecturers)
Model to Understand Simple English
MUSM Mercer University School of Medicine (USA)
MUSS Multi-Sensor System
MUST Manned Undersea Science and Technology SEE ALSO MUS&T
Medical Unit Self-contained Transportable Multi-Service Transportation
MUSTA Mock-Up Spallation Target Assembly
MUSTARD Modernisation of Units for Steelmaking At RIVER DON (River Don Works, Sheffield of the British Steel Corporation)
Multi-Unit Space Transport And Recovery Device
MUSTRAC Multiple-Simultaneous-Target Steerable Telemetry Tracking system
MUT Modular Universal Terminal
MUTE Mobile Universal Test Equipment
MUTT Military Utility Tactical Truck
MUVIN Multi-Unit Vibration Impact Neutralizer
MUX Multiple User Experiment
Multiplex OR Multiplexer
Multiplexing
MV Manifold Vacuum
Mercury and Venus
Mesenteric Veins
Muzzle Velocity
MVA Machinery Vibration Analysis
Management of Variable Activity
Measurement of Variable Activity
Mevalonic Acid
MVBF Motor Vehicle Brake Fluid
MVC Maximum Voluntary Contraction
Microvoid Coalescence
Multiple Variate Counter
MVCSHD Mississippi Valley Conference of State Highway Departments (USA)
MVE Murray Valley Encephalitis
MVEE Military Vehicles and Engineering Establishment (MOD) (became part of RARDE (MOD) in 1984)
MVF Moisture Volume Fraction
MVGVT Mated Vertical Ground Vibration Test
MVI Medium Viscosity Index
MVIN Medium Viscosity Index-Naphthenic
MVIP Medium Viscosity Index-Paraffinic
MVLUE Minimum Variance, Linear Unbiased Estimator
MVMA Motor Vehicles Manufacturers Association (USA)
MVP Manpower Validation Programme
MVPCCS Motor Vehicle Post Crash Communications System
MVPP Mustine, Vinblastine, Procarbazine, and Prednisolone
MVRIS Motor Vehicle Registration Information Service (of SMMT)
MVRO Minimum-Variance Reduced-Order
MVS Mission Verification Simulation
Modularized Vehicle Simulation
Multiple Virtual Storages
MVSS prefix to numbered series of Motor Vehicle Safety Standards issued by NHTSA (USA)
MVT Multiprogramming with a Variable number of Tasks
MVTR Moisture Vapour Transmission Rate
MVU Minimum Variance Unbiased
MVUE Minimum Variance Unbiased Estimator
MW Molecular Weight
MW(E) Megawatts (Electrical)
MW(H) Megawatts (Heat)
MW(Th) Megawatt (Thermal)
MWAE Minimum-Weighted-Absolute-Error
MWCE Millimeter Wave Experiment Communications
MWD Measurement While Drilling
Ministry of Works and Development (New Zealand)
Molecular Weight Distribution
MWDDEA Mutual Weapons Development Data Exchange Programme
MWDP Mutual Weapons Development Programme
MWE Manned Working Enclosure
MWF Medical Women's Federation
MWFCS Multi-Weapon Fire Control System
MWHGL Multiple-Wheel Heavy Gear Load OR Loading
MWIV Mean Wildlife Index Value
MWLAE Millimeter Wave Large Antenna Experiment (aboard the "Spacelab")
MWM Motorenwerke Mannheim (Germany)
MWO Medicine White Oil
MWR Method of Weighted Residuals
MWS Magnetic Weapon Sensor
MWSC Minimum Wage Study Commission (USA)
MWST Mean Weighted Skin Temperature
MWt Megawatt Thermal
MWT Millimeter Wave Technology
MWV Mineralolwirtschaftsverband (Germany) (Oil Industry Association)
MX Missile Experimental (now Commonly known as MX Missile)
MyMD Mytomic Muscular Dystrophy
MYRA Myria-Aperture
MZOS Metal-Zinc Oxide-Silicon dioxide-silicon
MZP Modulated Zone Plate

M^2FCS Multi-Microprocessor Flight Control System
M^2FM Modified Modified Frequency Modulation or Modulator

N

N prefix to numbered: dated series of Oxygen Equipment Standards issued by BSI
N/C Numerical Control
N&MIA National and Midland Ironfounders Association
NA Noradrenaline
Numerical Aperture
NAA National Aeronautic Association (USA)
National Association of Accountants (USA)
Neutron Activation Analysis
North Atlantic Assembly
Nuclear Activation Analysis
NAAA National Aerial Applicators Association (USA)
National Agricultural Aviation Association (USA)
NAAD National Association of Aluminium Distributors (USA)
NAAG North American Advisory Group (of BOTB)
NAAMM National Association of Architectural Metal Manufacturers (USA)
NAAP National Association of Advertising Publishers (USA)
NAAQS National Ambient Air Quality Standards (of EPA (USA))
NAAS National Agriculture Advisory Service (now part of ADAS)
NAASRA National Association of Australian State Road Authorities (Australia)
NAATS National Association of Air Traffic Specialists (USA)
NAAV National Association of Atomic Veterans (USA)
NAB National Advisory Board (on Education)
National Apex Body (India)
National Association of Broadcasters (USA)
NABC National Association of Building Centres
NABE National Association for Business Education (now amalgamated with BACIE)
National Association of Business Economists (USA)
NABRIN National Advisory Board on Rural Information Needs (NCLIS & USDA) (USA)
NABS Nuclear-Armed Bombardment Satellite
NABT National Association of Biology Teachers (USA)
NAC Natal Associated Collieries (South Africa)
National Accelerator Centre (of CSIR) (South Africa)
National Airways Corporation (New Zealand) (merged into ANZ in 1978)
National Airways Corporation (South Africa) (a subsidiary of NAFCO)
National Aviation Club (USA)
prefix to numbered series of reports issued by Division of Numerical Analysis and Computing (of the NPL)
NACA National Advisory Committee for Aeronautics (now NAS
National Agricultural Chemicals Association (USA)
National Air Carrier Association (USA)
NACAB National Association of Citizens Advice Bureau
NACAE National Advisory Council on Art Education
Numerical Aperture
NACATS NORTH AMERICAN Clear Air Turbulence Tracking System
NACCSMA NATO Command and Control Systems Management Agency
NACD National Association of Chemical Distributors (USA)
NACE National Advisory Committee on Electronics (India)
National Association of Corrosion Engineers (USA)
Neutral Atmospheric Composition Experiment
Nomenclature Generale des Activites Economique dans les Commautes Europeennes
NACED National Advisory Council on the Employment of the Disabled
NACEIC National Advisory Council on Education for Industry and Commerce (disbanded 1977)
NACF National Agricultural Co-operative Federation (Korea)
NACFRC North Atlantic Coastal Fisheries Research Center (of NMFS (USA))
NACHA National Automated Clearing House Association (USA)
NAChr Nicotine Cholinergic Receptor
NACILA National Council of Indian Library Associations (India) (became FILA in 1975)
NACL Nippon Aviotronics Company Ltd (Japan)
NACLI National Advisory Council for Librarianship and Information Science (South Africa)
NACM National Association of Colliery Managers
National Association of Credit Management (USA)
NACNE National Advisory Committee on Nutrition Education
NACO Navy Cool
NACOA National Advisory Committee on the Oceans and Atmosphere (USA)
NACOLADS National Council on Libraries, Archives and Documentation Services (Jamaica)
NACOM Na is chemical symbol for Sodium; COM is Combustion (they are joined here as the name of a computer programme)
NACOSH National Advisory Committee on Occupational Safety and Health (of Dept of Labor (USA))
NACP North Atlantic Crossings Panel (of ICAO)
NACRO National Association for the Care and Resettlement of Offenders
NACS National Association of College Stores (USA)
NACTAC Navy Antenna Computer Tracking And Command system (USN)
NACUBO National Association of College and University Business Officers (USA)
NAD Naval Ammunition Depot (USN)
Nicotinamide Adenine Dinucleotide
No-Acid Descaling
North American Datum
NAD-CR Naval Ammunition Depot–Crane, Indianapolis (USN)
NAD83 North American Datum 1983
NADC NATO Air Defence Committee
Naval Air Development Center (USN)
NADC-AE Naval Air Development Center, Aero-Electronic Technology Department (USN)
NADC-AM Naval Air Development Center, Mechanics Department (USN)
NADC-LS Naval Air Development Center, Life Sciences and Bio-Equipment Group (USN)
NADC-MR Naval Air Development Center, Aerospace Medical Research Department (USN)
NADDIS Narcotics and Dangerous Drugs Information System (of Drug Enforcement Administration (Dept of Justice) (USA))
NADEC National Agricultural Development Company (Saudi Arabia)
NADEEC NATO Air Defence Electronic Environment Committee
NADEFCOL NATO Defence College

NADFAS National Association of Design and Fine Art Societies
NADFS National Association of Drop Forgers and Stampers
NADGE NATO Air Defence Ground Environment network
NADME Noise Amplitude Distribution Measuring Equipment
NADOT North Atlantic Deepwater Oil Terminal
NADPH Nicotinamide-Adenine Dinucleotide Phosphate
NADSAT Laboratory of Native Development, Systems Analysis and Applied Technology (Arizona University (USA))
NADW North Atlantic Deep Water
NADWARN Natural Disaster Warning system (USA)
NAE National Academy of Engineering (USA)
National Aeronautical Establishment (of National Research Council, Canada)
NAEA National Association of Estate Agents
NAEB National Association of Education Broadcasters (USA)
National Association of Educational Buyers (USA)
NAEC National Aerospace Education Council (USA)
Naval Air Engineering Center (USN)
NAEC-ENG Naval Air Engineering Center, Engineering Department (USN)
NAECON National Aerospace Electronics Conference (USA)
NAEE National Association for Environmental Education
NAEM Naval Air Effect Model
NAEMB National Academy of Engineering Marine Board (USA)
NAEP National Assessment of Educational Progress (USA)
NAES Naval Air Experimental Station (USN)
NAEST National Archives for Electrical Science and Technology (of IEE)
NAET National Association of Educational Technicians
NAEWF NATO Airborne Early Warning Force
NAF Nederlands Atoomforum (Netherlands) (Netherlands Atom Forum)
NAFAG NATO Air Force Armaments Group
NAFCO National Airways and Finance Corporation (South Africa)
NAFEC National Aviation Facilities Experimental Center (of FAA (USA)) (n0w FAA Technical Center)
NAFED National Agricultural Co-operative Marketing Federation (India)
NAFEMS National Agency for Finite Element Methods and Standards
NAFI Naval Avionics Facility, Indianapolis (USN)
NAFIN Nacional Financiera (Mexico)
NAFIS Navigational and Flight Inspection System
NAFLAC Navy Department Fuel and Lubricants Advisory Committee (MOD)
NAFO North-west Atlantic Fisheries Organisation (Canada)
NAFRC North Atlantic Fisheries Research Center (of NFMS (USA))
NAFTA New Zealand/Australia Free Trade Agreement
NAG National Association of Goldsmiths
Net Annual Gain
Numerical Algorithms Group (a non-profit company formed by Nottingham, Birmingham, Manchester, Leeds and Oxford Universities for data processing service internationally to industry and universities)
NAGPM National Association of Grained Plate Makers (USA)
NAHA National Association of Health Authorities
NAHB National Association of Home Builders (USA)
NAHFO National Association of Hospital Fire Officers
NAHT National Association of Head Teachers
NAIAD Nerve Agent Immobilised Enzyme Alarm and Detector
NAIBD National Association of Industries for the Blind and Disabled
NAIC National Astronomy and Ionospheric Center (Arecibo Observatory (Puerto Rico) (administered by Cornell University (USA))
NAICC National Association of Independent Companies (USA)
NAICOM/MIS Naval Integrated Command/Management Information System (USN)
NAIG Nippon Atomic Industry Group (Japan)
NAILSC Naval Aviation Integrated Logistic Support Center (USN)
NAIM Number Allocation and Inspection Module
NAIPRC Netherlands Automatic Information Processing Research Centre
NAIR National Arrangements for Incidents involving Radioactivity
NAIT Northern Alberta Institute of Technology (Canada)
NAL National Accelerator Laboratory (USA)
National Acoustics Laboratory (Australia)
National Aeronautical Laboratory (India)
National Aerospace Laboratory (Japan)
National Agricultural Library (of USDA)
NALC National Association of Litho Clubs (USA)
NALI National Association of the Launderette Industry
NALNET NASA (USA) Library Network
NAM National Association of Manufacturers (USA)
Network Access Machine
Network Analysis Model
NAMA National Automatic Merchandising Association (USA)
North American Mycological Association (USA)
NAMB National Association of Microfilm Bureaux
NAMBO National Association of Bus Owners (USA)
NAMC National Association of Minority Contractors (USA)
Naval Air Material Center (USN)
Nihon Aeroplane Manufacturing Company (Japan)
NAMCW National Association for Maternal and Child Welfare
NAMDI National Marine Data Inventory (replaced by ROSCOP of the World Data Center-A, Oceanography (USA)
NAMES NAVDAC Assembly, Monitor, Executive System
NAMF National Association of Metal Finishers (USA)
NAMFI NATO Missile Firing Installation
NAMH National Association for Mental Health
NAMI National Association of Malleable Ironfounders
Naval Aerospace Medical Institute (USN)
NAML Naval Aircraft Materials Laboratory (MOD)
NAMMA NATO Multi-Role Combat Aircraft Management Agency
NAMMO NATO Multi-Role Combat Aircraft Management Organisation
NAMPS Navy Manpower Planning System (USN)
NAMRAD Non-Atomic Military Research and Development (a sub-Committee of NATO)
NAMRC North American Metal Research Conference
NAMRL Naval Aerospace Medical Research Laboratory (USN)
NAMRU Naval Medical Research Unit (USN)
NAMSA NATO Maintenance and Supply Agency
NAMSB National Association of Mutual Savings Banks (USA)

NAMSC National A-M Stereophonic Committee (of National Association of Broadcasters, National Radio Broadcasters Association, IEEC and EIA (USA))

NAMSO NATO Maintenance and Supply Organisation

NAMTC Naval Air Missile Test Center (USN)

NAN Non-Ammonia-Nitrogen

NANA Northwest Alaska Natives Association (USA)

NANSI Nordic Automated Network of SHELL Installations

NANTIS Nottingham And Nottinghamshire Technical Information Service

NAO Her Majesty's Nautical Almanac Office
National Audit Office

NAOS North Atlantic Ocean Stations (of ICAO)

NAP Nodal Analysis Programme

NAPA National Asphalt Pavement Association (USA)
National Association of Purchasing Agents (USA)

NAPALM derived from its ingredients Aluminium Naphthenate and Palmitate
National ADP Program for AMC Logistics Management (US Army)

NAPAN National Association for Prevention of Addiction to Narcotics (USA)

NAPC Non-Adherent Peritoneal Cells

NAPCA National Air Pollution Control Administration (of HEW (USA)) (now Air Pollution Control Office (of EPA (USA))
National Association of Pipe Coating Applicators (USA)

NAPF National Association of Pension Funds

NAPHCC National Association of Plumbing, Heating, and Cooling Contractors (USA)

NAPHMSC National Association of Plumbing, Heating and Mechanical Services Contractors

NAPIM National Association of Printing Ink Manufacturers (USA)

NAPL National Air Photo Library (of Directorate of Topographical Surveys (Canada))
National Association of Photo-Lithographers (USA)
National Association of Printers and Lithographers (USA)

NAPLPS North American Presentation Level Protocol Syntax

NAPM National Association of Paper Merchants
National Association of Purchasing Management (USA)
Nebraska Association of Purchasing Managers (USA)

NAPMA NATO Airborne Early Warning and Control Programme Management Agency

NAPO NATO-AWACS Programme Office

NAPRALERT Natural Products Alert (a data base at the University of Chicago (USA))

NAPSS Numerical Analysis Problem Solving System

NAPTC Naval Air Propulsion Test Center (USN)

NAPTC-AED Naval Air Propulsion Test Center, Aeronautical Engine Department (USN)

NAQP National Association of Quick Printers (USA)

NAR Net Assimilation Rate
Nuclear Acoustic Resonance

NARACC National Association of Refrigeration and Air Conditioning Contractors (amalgamated with HVCA, 1974)

NARADCOM Natick Research and Development Command (US Army)

NARBA North American Regional Broadcasting Agreement

NARC National Association for Retarded Citizens (USA)

NARDIC Navy Acquisition, Research and Development Information Center (USN)

NARDIS Navy Automated Research and Development Information System (USN)

NARE National Association of Remedial Education

NARF National Association of Retail Furnishers
Natural Axial Resonant Frequency
Naval Aerospace Recovery Facility (US Navy)
Naval Air Rework Facility (USN)
Nuclear Aerospace Research Facility

NARGOM North American Research Group on Management

NARI National Association of Recycling Industries (USA)

NARIC National Rehabilitation Information Center (of the Catholic University of America (USA))

NARL National Aero Research Laboratory (of NRC (Canada))
Naval Arctic Research Laboratory (USN)

NARM National Association of Relay Manufacturers (USA)

NARP National Association of Rail Passengers
National Association of Railroad Passengers (USA)

NARPA National Air Rifle and Pistol Association

NARPV National Association for Remotely Piloted Vehicles (USA)

NARS National Archives and Records Service (of General Services Administration (USA))
Nigeria Amateur Radio Society (Nigeria)

NARSC National Association of Reinforcing Steel Contractors (USA)

NARTE National Association of Radio and Telecommunications Engineers (USA)

NARUC National Association of Regulatory Utility Commissioners (USA)

NAS National Academy of Sciences (USA)
National Airspace System (of FAA (USA))
Noise Abatement Society
Northern Archaeological Society
Numerical Aerodynamic Simulation

NAS/NAEESB National Academy of Sciences—National Academy of Engineering, Environmental Studies Board (USA)

NAS/NRC National Academy of Sciences/National Research Council (USA)

NASA National Aeronautics and Space Administration (USA)

NASAD National Association of Sport Aircraft Designers (USA)

NASAP Network Analysis for Systems Application Programme

NASARR NORTH AMERICAN Search And Range Radar

NASBOSA National Academy of Sciences Board on Ocean Science Affairs (USA)

NASC National Aeronautics and Space Council (USA)
National Association of Scaffolding Contractors

NASCAS NAS/NRC Committee on Atmospheric Sciences (USA)

NASCMVE National Academy of Sciences Committee on Motor Vehicle Emissions (USA)

NASCO National Academy of Sciences' Committee on Oceanography (USA)
North Atlantic Salmon Conservation Organization (of EEC)

NASCOM NASA Communications

NASCP North American Society for Corporate Planning (USA)

NASD National Association of Securities Dealers (USA)
NKK (NIPPON KOKAN (Japan)) Advanced Ship Design

NASDA National Space Development Agency (Japan)

NASDAQ NATIONAL ASSOCIATION OF SECURITIES DEALERS (USA) Automated Quotations

NASDIM National Association of Security Dealers and Investment Managers
NASDT Naval Aviator's Speech Discrimination Test
NASHA North American Survival and Homesteading Association (Canada)
NASIC Northeast Academic Science Information Center (USA) (of New England Board of Higher Education (formerly supported by NSF (USA))
NASIS National Association for State Information Systems (of CSG (USA))
Nevada Statewide Information Service (USA)
NASL Naval Applied Sciences Laboratory (USN)
NASM National Air and Space Museum (of the Smithsonian Institute (USA))
National Air Sampling Network (of EPA (USA))
NASMI National Association of Secondary Materials Industries (USA)
NASN National Aerometric Surveillance Network (of EPA (USA))
NASO National Astronomical Space Observatory
NASPO National Association of State Purchasing Officials (USA)
NASQAN National Stream Quality Accounting Network (of the Geological Survey (USA))
NASRF National Association of Shoe Repairs Factories
NASS National Association of Steel Stockholders
Naval Armaments Stores System (of RNSTS)
Navigation Satellite System
NASSA National Aerospace Services Association (USA)
NAST Navigation/Attack Systems Trainer
NASTA National Association of State Textbook Administrators (USA)
NASTRAN NASA (USA) Structural Analysis Programme
NASULGC National Association of State Universities and Land-Grant Colleges (USA)
NASW National Association of Science Writers (USA)
NASWM National Association of Scottish Woollen Manufacturers
NAT Nearly Air-borne Truck
Normal Allowed Time
NATA National Air Transport Association (USA)
National Association of Testing Authorities (Australia)
National Aviation Trades Association (USA)
North American Telecommunications Association (USA)
NATAS North American Thermal Analysis Society (USA)
NATC National Air Taxi Conference (USA) (now part of National Air Transportation Conferences)
National Air Transportation Conferences (USA)
Naval Air Test Center (USN)
NATCAPIT Group of Experts on North Atlantic Capacity and Inclusive Tours (of the European Civil Aviation Conference)
NATCO North American Transplant Coordination Organization (USA)
NATCS National Air Traffic Control Service (of BOT) (now NATS (of CAA and MOD))
NATEC Naval Air Technical Evaluation Centre (MOD)
NATESA National Alliance of Television and Electronics Service Associations (USA)
NATIS National Information Systems
NATLAS National Testing Laboratory Accreditation Scheme
NATMAC National Air Traffic Management Advisory Committee
NATO North Atlantic Treaty Organisation
NATRAP Narrow-band Transmission of Radar Pictures
NATS National Air Traffic Service (of CAA and MOD)
NATSPG North Atlantic Systems Planning Group (of ICAO)
NATTS National Association of Trade and Technical Schools (USA)
Naval Air Test Turbine Station (USN)
NATU Naval Aircraft Torpedo Unit (USN)
NAUI National Association of Underwater Instructors (USA)
NAUTIC Naval Autonomous Intelligent Console
NAVA National Audiovisual Association (USA)
NAVAIR Naval Air Systems Command (USN)
NAVAIRDEVCEN Naval Air Development Center (USN)
NAVAPI North American Voltage and Phase Indicator
NavBIT Naval Basic Instrument Trainer (USN)
NAVCAMS Naval Communication Area Master Stations (USN)
NAVCOMMSTA Naval Communications Station (USN)
NAVCOMPARS Naval Communications Processing and Routing System (USN)
NAVCOSSACT Naval Command Systems Support Activity (USN)
NAVDAB NAVSEA Ocean Environmental Acoustic Date Bank (USN)
NAVDAC Naval Data Automation Command (USN)
Navigation Data Assimilation Computer
NAVDOCKS prefix to numbered series issued by Navy Yards and Docks Bureau (USN)
NAVEAMS Navigational Warning East Atlantic and Mediterranean (originated by MOD (Navy Dept))
NAVEDTRA Naval Educational and Training Command (USN)
NAVELEC-SYCOM Naval Electronics Systems Command (USN)
NAVELEX Naval Electronics System Command (USN)
NAVEO-RECOVFAC Naval Aerospace Recovery Facility (USN)
NAVEODFAC Naval Explosive Ordnance Disposal Facility (USN)
NAVEX National Audio Visual Aids Exhibition
NAVEXOS Executive Office of the Secretary of the Navy (USN)
NAVFAC prefix to lettered/numbered Series issued by Naval Facilities Engineering Command (USN)
NAVFECO Naval Facilities Engineering Command (USN)
NAVGRA The Navy and Vickers Gearing Research Association (of MOD and civilian firms)
NAVHARS Navigation Heading and Attitude Reference System
NAVIC Navy Information Center (USN)
NAVLIS Navy Logistics Information System (USN)
NAVMACS Naval Modular Automated Communications Systems (USN)
NAVMAT Naval Material Command (USN)
prefix to numbered series issued by Office of Naval Material (USN)
NAVMC prefix to numbered series issued by the Marine Corps (US Marine Corps)
NAVMED prefix to numbered series issued by Bureau of Medicine and Surgery (USN)
NAVMEDCOM Naval Medical Command (USN)
NAVMIL-PERSCOM Bureau of Naval Military Personnel Command (USN)
NAVMIRO Naval Material Industrial Resources Office (USN)
NAVOCEANO Naval Oceanographic Office (USN) (now part of the Defense Mapping Agency (USDOD))
NAVOCFOR MED Naval On-Call Force for the Mediterranean (of NATO)
NAVORD Naval Ordnance Systems Command (USN) (NOW ABSORBED INTO NAVSEA (USN))
prefix to numbered series issued by NOSC (USN)
NAVPERS prefix to numbered series issued by Bureau of Naval Personnel (USN)
NAVRESO Navy Resale System Office (USN)
NAVS National Anti-Vivisection Society
NAVSAT Navy Navigation Satellite
NAVSEA Naval Sea System Command (USN)

NAVSEC Naval Ship Engineering Center (USN)
NAVSEC-NORDIV Naval Ship Engineering Center—Norfolk Division (USN)
NAVSEC-PHILADIV Naval Ship Engineering Center—Philadelphia Division (USN)
NAVSHIPS Naval Ship Systems Command (USN) (now absorbed into NAVSEA (USN))
prefix to numbered series of publications issued by NSSC (USN)
NAVSO Department of the Navy, Staff Office (USN)
prefix to numbered series issued by Navy Industrial Relations Office (USN)
NAVSPASUR Naval Space Surveillance system (USA)
NAVSPASYSACT Navy Space Systems Activity (USN)
NAVSSES Naval Ship Systems Engineering Station (USN)
NAVSTAR Navigation System using Time and Ranging
NavSUP Naval Supply Systems Command (USN)
NAVSURFWPNCEN Naval Surface Weapons Center (USN)
NAVTAC NIMROD (Aircraft) Navigation Tactical
NAVTACSTANS Navy Standards for Tactical Data Systems (USN)
NAVTRA Naval Training Command (USN)
NAVTRA-EQUIPC Naval Training Equipment Center (USN)
NAVTRADEVCEN prefix to numbered series issued by Naval Training Device Center (USN)
NAVTRAFSAT Navigation/Traffic Control Satellite
NAVWAS Navigation and Weapon-Aiming Systems
NAVWASS Navigation and Weapon-Aiming Sub-system
NAVWEPS prefix to numbered series issued by Bureau of Naval Weapons (USN)
NAVWPNCEN Naval Weapons Center (USN)
NAW National Association of Wholesalers (USA)
NAWAFA North Atlantic Westbound Freight Association
NAWAPA North American Water and Power Alliance
NAWCC National Association of Watch and Clock Collectors (USA)
NAWCH National Association for the Welfare of Children in Hospital
NAWDC National Association of Waste Disposal Contractors
NAWESA Naval Weapons Engineering Support Activity (USN)
NAWK National Association of Warehouse Keepers
NAYE National Association of Young Entrepreneurs (India)
NB Notch-Bend
NBA National Braillie Association (USA)
National Brassfoundry Association
National Building Agency
Normal Butyl Alcohol
NBAA National Business Aircraft Association (USA)
NBAPA National Benzole and Allied Products Association
NBC National Book Council (Australia)
Nigerian Broadcasting Corporation (Nigeria)
Norwegian Bulk Carrier
NBCC National Buildings Construction Corporation (India)
NBCCA National Business Council for Consumer Affairs (USA)
NBCD Natural Binary Coded Decimal
NBD Negative Binomial Distribution
NBDC National Bomb Data Center (of United States Army and the Federal Bureau of Investigation)
NBER National Bureau of Economic Research (USA)
NBES Narrow-Beam Echo Sounder
NBF National Bedding Federation
NBFA National Business Forms Association (USA)
NBFAA National Burglar and Fire Alarm Association (USA)
NBFM Narrow-Band Frequency Modulation
NBG National Botanic Gardens (India)
NBGRN Narrow Band Gaussian Randon Noise
NBI Niels Bohr Institute (Denmark)
NBL National Book League
Naval Biological Laboratory (USN)
New Brunswick Laboratory (of USAEC)
NBLC Nederlands Bibliotheek en Lektuur Centrum (Netherlands) (Dutch Library and Literature Centre)
NBM Non-Book Materials
NBME National Board of Medical Examiners (USA)
NBN prefix to Standards issued by IBN
NBO National Buildings Organization (India)
NBPC National Branch Policy Committee (of British Institute of Management)
NBPI National Board for Prices and Incomes
NBPM Network-Based Project Management
NBR Net Borrowing Requirement
Nitrile Based Rubbers
NBRI National Building Research Institute (South Africa)
NBS National Bureau of Standards (of the Dept of Commerce (USA))
Neutral Buoyancy Simulator
NBS-BSS prefix to numbered Building Science Series of publications issued by National Bureau of Standards (USA)
NBSIR National Bureau of Standads (USA) Interagency Reports
prefix to dated-numbered series of reports issued by National Bureau of Standards Institute of Basic Standards (USA)
NBSL National Biological Standards Laboratory (Australia)
NBSR NATIONAL BUREAU OF STANDARDS (USA) Reactor
NBST National Board for Science and Technology (Eire)
NBT Nitro Blue Tetrazolium
Null-Balance Transmissometer
NBTL Naval Boiler and Turbine Laboratory (USN)
NBVM Narrow-Band Voice Modulation
NC Nitrocellulose
Numerical Control
prefix to series of reports issued by North Central Forest Experiment Station (Forest Service of USDA)
NC/STRC North Carolina Science and Technology Research Center (USA)
NCA National Canners Association (USA)
National Commission on Agriculture (India)
National Composition Association (of PIA (USA))
National Constructors Association (USA)
National Council on Alcoholism
Nonspecific Cross-reacting Antigen
NCADS Numerical Control Advisory and Demonstration Service (of MINTECH and PERA) (terminated December, 1970)
NCAE National College of Agricultural Engineering (became a School of the Cranfield Institute of Technology in 1975)
NCAER National Council of Applied Economics Research (India)
NCALI National Clearinghouse for Alcohol Information (of NIAA (HEW) (USA))
NCAM National Center for Advanced Materials (University of California (USA))
NCAPC National Center for Air Pollution Control (of DHEW (USA))
NCAPS National Council of Associations for Policy Sciences (USA)
NCAR National Center for Atmospheric Research (of UCAR (USA))
NCARB National Council of Architectural Registration Boards (USA)

NCAT National Centre for Alternative Technology

NCATC Nigerian Civil Aviation Training Centre (Nigeria)

NCATE National Council for Accreditation of Teacher Education (USA)

NCAVAE National Committee for Audio-Visual Aids in Education

NCB National Coal Board
Nickel-Cadmium Battery

NCBFAA National Customs Brokers and Forwarders Association of America (USA)

NCBMP National Council of Building Material Producers

NCC National Climatic Center (of EDS (NOAA) (USA))
National Computer Conference (sponsored by AFIPS (USA))
National Computing Centre
National Consultative Council of the Building and Civil Engineering Industries
National Consumer Council
National Cotton Council (USA)
Nature Conservancy Council (of DOE)

NCCA National Coil Coaters Association (USA)
National Council of Chartered Accountants (South Africa)

NCCAT National Committee for Clear Air Turbulence (US Dept of Commerce)

NCCCC Naval Command, Control and Communications Center (USN)

NCCDPC-NATO NATO Command, Control and Information Systems and Automated Data Processing Committee

NCCL National Council of Canadian Labour (Canada)

NCCLS National Committee for Clinical Laboratory Standards (USA)

NCCMT National Committee for Careers in Medical Technology (USA)

NCCN National Committee on Computer Networks (of DOI)

NCCOP North Carolina Computer Orientation Project (USA)

NCCPA National Council of College Publications Advisers (USA)

NCCPG National Council for the Conservation of Plants and Gardens

NCCR National Center for Resource Recovery (USA)

NCCS National Council of Corrosion Sciences (comprising Institution of Corrosion Technology, Institute of Metal Finishing, The Metals Society and the Society of Chemical Industry)
National Council of Corrosion Societies

NCD No Claims Discount

NCDAD National Council for Diplomas in Art and Design (amalgamated with CNAA in 1974)

NCDC National Coal Development Corporation (India)
National Communicable Disease Center (now Center for Disease Control (HEW (USA))

NCDOT North Carolina Department of Transportation (USA)

NCDS National Co-operative Development Corporation (India)

NCDT National Centre for the Development of Telematics (India)

NCDU Navigation Control and Display Unit

NCE Newark College of Engineering (USA)

NCEB NATO Communications-Electronics Board

NCEC National Center for Educational Communication (of USOE)
National Chemical Emergencies Centre
National Construction Employers Council (USA)

NCECA National Council on Education for the Ceramic Arts (USA)

NCECS NORTH CAROLINA (USA) Educational Computing System

NCEE National Council of Engineering Examiners (USA)

NCEFT National Commission on Electronic Fund Transfers (USA)

NCEI North Carolina Energy Institute (USA)

NCEL Naval Civil Engineering Laboratory (USN)

NCEPC National Committee on Environmental Planning and Co-ordination (India)
National Council for Environmental Pollution Control (India)

NCER National Center for Earthquake Research (of USGS)

NCES National Center for Education Statistics (USOE) (now of OERI)

NCET National Center for Educational Travel (USA)
National Council for Educational Technology (now Council for Educational Technology for the United Kingdom)

NCF National Clayware Federation
Net Cash Flow

NCFA National Consumer Finance Association (USA)

NCFMF National Committee for Fluid Mechanics Films (USA)

NCFP National Conference on Fluid Power (USA)

NCFS Non-Contingent Foot-Shock

NCFSK Non-Coherent Frequency-Shift-Keyed

NCG Nicotine Chewing Gum
Nuclear Cratering Group (US Army) (now EERO)

NCGE National Council for Geographic Education (USA)

NCGG National Committee for Geodesy and Geophysics (Pakistan)

NCHA Northern Consortium of Housing Authorities

NChemL National Chemical Laboratory (amalgamated with the National Physical Laboratory, 1965)

NCHEMS National Centre for Higher Education Management Systems (at wiche (usa))

NCHPD National Council on Health Planning and Development (USA)

NCHRP National Cooperative Highways Research Program (administered by Highway Research Board (USA)) (now Transportation Research Board)

NCHS National Center for Health Statistics (USPHS)

NCHSR National Center for Health Services Research (of DHHS (USA))

NCHSRD National Center for Health Services Research and Development (of HEW (USA)) (now NCHSR (of DHHS))

NCHVRFE National College for Heating, Ventilating, Refrigeration and Fan Engineering

NCI National Cancer Institute (of NIH (USA))

NCIB National Collection of Industrial Bacteria

NCIC National Cartographic Information Center (of Geological Survey (Dept of the Interior) (USA))
National Cavity Insulation Council
National Construction Industry Council (USA)
National Crime Information Center (of Federal Bureau of Information (USA))

NCILT National Centre for Industrial Language Training (of TSA)

NCIP Comision Nacional de Productividad Industrial (Spain) (National Commission for Industrial Productivity)

NCIS Navy Cost Information System (USN)

NCIT National Council on Inland Transport

NCITD National Committee on International Trade Documentation (USA)

NCJRS National Criminal Justice Reference Service (of LEAA (Dept of Justice (USA))

NCL National Central Library (became part of the British Library Lending Division, 1973)
National Chemical Laboratory (Amalgamated with NPL 1965)
National Chemical Laboratory (India)
National Chemical Laboratory (of MITI (Japan))
NCLEA National Conference on Laboratory Evaluation and Accreditation (USA)
NCLIS National Commission on Libraries and Information Science (USA)
NCLS National Council of Land Surveyors (USA)
NCLT Night Carrier Landing Trainer
NCM Nippon Calculating Machine Company (Japan)
NCMA National Concrete Masonry Association (USA)
National Contract Management Association (USA)
NCME Network for Continuing Medical Education (USA)
NCMHI National Clearinghouse for Mental Health Information (of NIMH (usa))
NCMIB National Collection of Marine and Industrial Bacteria
NCML Naval Chemical and Metallurgical Laboratory (India)
NCMN National Crustal Motion Network (of NOAA (USA))
NCMP National Commission on Materials Policy (USA)
NCMRED National Council on Marine Resources and Engineering Development (USA) (disbanded 1971)
NCMT Numerical Control of Machine Tools
NCNA New China News Agency (China)
NCOA National Council on the Aging (USA)
NCOR National Committee for Oceanographic Research (Pakistan)
NCP Network Control Programme
Nutrition Centre of the Philippines
NCPEA National Conference for Professors of Educational Administration (USA)
NCPI National Clay Pipe Institute (USA)
National Computer Program Index (of the National Computing Centre)
NCPL National Centre for Programmed Learning (University of Birmingham)
NCPS National Commission on Product Safety (USA)
NCPT National Conference of Parents and Teachers (USA)
National Conference on Power Transmission (USA)
NCPTA National Confederation of Parents and Teachers Associations
NCPTWA National Clearinghouse for Periodical Title Word Abbreviations (of USASI)
NCQR National Council for Quality and Reliability
NCR No Carbon Required
NCRD National Council for Research and Development (Israel)
NCRDS National Coal Resources Data System (USA)
NCRE Naval Construction Research Establishment (MOD)
NCRL National Chemical Research Laboratory (South Africa)
NCRLC National Committee on Regional Library Cooperation
NCRP National Committee on Radiation Protection (USA)
NCRPM National Council on Radiation Protection and Measurement (USA)
NCRR National Center for Resource Recovery (USA)
NCRT National College of Rubber Technology
NCS National Communications System
National Corrosion Service (of Dept of Industry) (at NPL)
Naval Compass Stabiliser
Non-Collimated Sources
Non-Crystalline Solid
Nuclear-powered Container Ship
Numerical Control Society (USA)
NCSA National Crushed Stone Association (USA)
NCSBCS National Conference of States on Building Codes and Standards (USA)
NCSCA National Council of Speciality Contractors Associations (USA)
NCSE North Carolina Society of Engineers (USA)
NCSL National Conference of Standards Laboratories (USA)
Naval Coastal Systems Laboratory (USN)
NCSORG Naval Control of Shipping Organization (USA)
NCSR National Centre of Systems Reliability (of UKAEA)
National Council for Scientific Research (Lebanon)
National Council for Scientific Research (Zambia)
NCSS National Center for Social Statistics (of HEW (USA))
National Council for the Social Studies (USA)
National Council of Social Service (now NCVO)
NCST National Centre for School Technology (based at Trent Polytechnic, Nottingham)
National Coalition for Science and Technology (USA)
National Committee on Science and Technology (India)
Nigerian Council for Science and Technology (Nigeria)
NCSTRC North Carolina Science and Technology Center Research Center (USA) (based on Duke University, University of North Carolina and North Carolina State University)
NCSU North Carolina State University (USA)
NCT National Centre of Tribology (of AERE) (now ESTL (ESRO))
National Chamber of Trade
NCTA National Cable Television Association (USA)
National Community Television Association (USA)
NCTC National Collection of Type Cultures
NCTCOG North Central Texas Council of Governments (USA)
NCTEC Northern Counties Technical Examinations Council
NCTJ Nastional Council for the Training of Journalists
NCTM National Council of Teachers of Mathematics (USA)
NCTR National Center for Toxicological Research (of EPA and FDA (USA))
NCTRF Naval Clothing and Textile Research Facility (USN)
Navy Clothing and Textile Research Facility (USN)
NCTRU Navy Clothing and Textile Research Unit (USN)
NCU Navigation Control Unit
NCUA National Credit Union Administration (USA)
NCR Computer Users Association
NCUF National Computer Users Forum (secretariat at National Computing Centre)
NCV Net Calorific Value
NCVO National Council of Voluntary Organisations
Nd Neodymium
ND Navy Distillate fuel
Nd/YAG Neodymium-doped YAG
nDA n-Decylamine
NDA National Enterprise Board
New Drug Application
Non-Destructive Assay

NDAB Numerical Data Advisory Board (Division of Chemistry and Chemical Technology of NAS/NRC (USA))
NDAC Nuclear Defence Affairs Committee (of NATO)
NDACSS Navy Department Advisory Committee on Structural Steel (MOD)
NDAT Non-Destructive Assay Techniques
NDB National Delegates Board (of AGARD (NATO))
Non-Directional Beacon
NDBC National Data Buoy Center (of NOAA (USA))
NDBDP National Data Buoy Development Project (of USCG (USA)) (now NDBC (NOAA))
NDBO NOAA Data Buoy Office (USA)
NDBPO National Data Buoy Project Office (of NOAA (USA))
NDC National Development Corporation (Tanzania)
National Development Council (India)
National Development Council (New Zealand)
National Documentation Centre (of NRC (Sudan))
Negative Differential Conductivity
NDCC Non-Directional Cross Country
NDDB National Dairy Development Board (India)
NDDO Neglect of Diatomic Differential Overlap
NDE Non-Destructive Evaluation
NDEI National Defense Education Institute (USA)
NDI Non-Destructive Inspection
Non-Developmental Items
Numerical Designation Index
NDIR Non-Dispersive Infra-Red
NDL National Diet Library (Japan)
Network Definition Language
Nuclear Defense Laboratory (US Army)
NDM Negative Differential Mobility
NDMC New Delhi Municipal Committee (India)
NDMF National Development and Management Foundation (South Africa)
NDMS Non-Directional Mud-and-Snow
NDO Network Development Office (of Library of Congress (USA))
NDP Net Domestic Product
NDPCAL National Development Programme in Computer Assisted Learning (a government financed project 1973-1977)
NDPF NASA (USA) Data Processing Facility
NDPS National Data Processing Service (of British Post Office)
NDR Naval Dental Research Institute (USN)
Negative Differential Resistance
NDRF National Defense Reserve Fleet (USN)
NDRM National Defence Records Management (Canada)
NDRO Non-Destructive Read-Out
NDS Naval Dental School (USN)
Navigation Development Satellite
Nuclear Detection Satellite
NDSU North Dakota State University (USA)
NDT Nil-Ductility Transition
Non-Destructive Testing
NDTA National Defense Transportation Association (USA)
NDTAA Non-Destructive Testing Association of Australia (Australia) (now AINDT)
NDTC Non-Destructive Testing Centre (at AERE, Harwell)
NDTIAC Non-Destructive Testing Information Center (US Army Materials and Mechanics Research Center)
NDTMA Non-Destructive Testing Management Association (USA)
NDTS Non-Destructive Testing Society of Great Britain (became part of the British Insitute of Non-Destructive Testing in 1976)
NDU National Defense University (USA)
NDV Newcastle Disease Virus
NE Norepinephrine
Nuclear Explosive
prefix to numbered series of Publications issued by Northeastern Forest Experiment Station (of the Forest Service, USDA)
NEA National Education Association
National Electronics Association (USA)
National Erectors Association (USA)
Negative Electron Affinity
Net Energy Analysis
Nuclear Energy Agency (of OECD)
NEAAN Non-Essential Amino Acid N
NEACH New England (USA) Automated Clearing House
NEACP National Emergency Airborne Command Post (USDoD)
NEAFC North East Atlantic Fisheries Commission
NEAFCO North-East Atlantic Fisheries Commission
NEAS National Engineering Aptitude Search (of JETS (USA))
NEASIM Network Analytical Simulator
NEAT NCR Electronic Autocoding Technique
NEB National Energy Board (Canada)
NEBOSH National Examination Board in Occupational Safety and Health
NEBSS National Examinations Board in Supervisory Studies
NEBULA Natural Electronic Business Users Language
NEC National Electrical Code (USA)
National Electronics Council
National Energy Commission (Thailand)
National Exhibition Centre (Birmingham)
Nippon Electronic Company (Japan)
Noise-Equivalent Charge
NECA National Electrical Contractors Association (USA)
National Exchange Carriers Association (USA)
NECAF National Electromagnetic Compatibility Analysis Facility (of Department of Commerce (USA))
NECAP NASA (USA) Energy-Cost Analysis Program
Navigation Equipment Capability Analysis Programme
NECAR National Engineers Commission on Air Resources (of EJC (USA))
NECCTA National Education Closed-Circuit Television Association
NECG National Executive Committee on Guidance (sponsored by the American Society for Engineering Education (USA), ECPD (USA) and NSPE (USA))
NECI Noise Exposure Computer Integrator
NECIES North East Coast Institution of Engineers and Shipbuilders
NECK Nuclear Energy Committee of Kuwait (Kuwait)
NECOHS North East Council for Occupational Health and Safety
NECPA National Emergency Command Post Afloat (USDoD)
National Energy Conservation Policy Act, 1978 (USA)
NECTA National Electrical Contractors Trade Association (now part of Electrical Contractors Association)
NECTP North-East Corridor Transportation Project (of Department of Transportation (USA))
NED New Editor (computer programme)
NEDA National Economic and Development Authority (Philippines)
National Electronics Development Association (New Zealand)
NEDC National Economic Development Council
North East Development Council

NEDCC Northeast Document Conservation Center (USA)
NEDCO Non-Electronic Part Data Collection
NEDELA Network Definition Language
NEDN Naval Environmental Data Network (USN)
NEDO National Economic Development Office
New Energy Development Organization (Japan)
NEDSA Non-Erasing Deterministic Stack Automation
NEDT Noise Equivalent Differential Temperature
NEDU Navy Experimental Diving Unit (USN)
NEEB North Eastern Electricity Board
Nuclear Energy Electrical Demand Simulation
NEEMA New England Educational Media Association (USA)
NEEMIS NEW ENGLAND (USA) Energy Management Information System
NEEP Nuclear Electronic Effect Programme
NEERI National Electrical Engineering Research Institute (of CSIR (South Africa))
NEET Navy Extended Electrode Technique (USN)
NEF Noise Equivalent Flux
Noise Exposure Forecast
Norsk Elektroteknisk Forening (Norway) (Norwegian Electrical Engineers Association)
NEFA Nonesterified Fatty Acids
NEFBRACS Nearfield Bearing and Range Accuracy Calibration System
NEFD Noise Equivalent Flux Density
NEFES Northeastern Forest Experiment Station (USA)
NEFO Nordjylland Elektricitetsforsyning (Denmark)
NEFSA New England Federation of Surveyors Association (USA)
NEGISTOR Negative Resistor
NEH National Endowment for the Humanities (USA)
NEHA National Environmental Health Association (USA)
NEHU North Eastern Hill University (India)
NEI National Eye Institute (of NIH (HEW) (USA))
Noise-Equivalent Irradiance
NEIBR Norsk Institutt for By-og Regionforskning (Norway) (Norwegian Institute for Urban and Regional Research)
NEIC National Energy Information Center (of DOE (USA))
National Energy Information Center (of Federal Energy Agency (USA))
NEIG Nuclear Electricity Information Group
NEILC New England (USA) Interstate Library Compact
NEISS National Electronic Injury Surveillance Safety System (operated by CPSC (USA))
NEL National Engineering Laboratory (of NBS (USA))
National Engineering Laboratory (previously of DTI, now of DOI)
Navy Electronics Laboratory (USN) (reorganised as Navy Undersea Warfare Center AND Navy Command, Control and Communications Center)
NELAPT NATIONAL ENGINEERING LABORATORY Automatically Programmed Tools
NELB New England Library Board (USA)
NELC Naval Electronics Laboratory Center for Command Control and Communications (USN)
NELCON National Electronics Convention
NELEX Metrology Conference and Exhibition (sponsored by National Engineering Laboratory (of DOI)
NELINET New England Library Information Network (USA)
NELMA Northeastern Lumbar Manufacturers Association (USA)
NELP North East London Polytechnic
NELPIA Nuclear Energy Liability Property Insurance Association (USA)
NELRC National Epilepsy Library and Resource Center (USA)
NEMA National Electric Motor Association (USA)
National Electrical Manufacturers Association
NEMEDRI North European and Mediterranean Route Instructions (issued by MOD (Navy Dept))
NEMI National Elevator Manufacturing Industry (USA)
North European Management Institute (Norway)
NEMKO Norges Elektriske Materiellkontrol (Norway) (Norwegian Board for Testing of Electrical Equipment)
NEMO Naval Edreobenthic Manned Observatory (USN)
Naval Experimental Manned Observatory (USN)
Non-Empirical Molecular Orbit
NEMP Nuclear Electromagnetic Pulse
NEMS NIMBUS-E Microwave Spectrometer
NEMT Naval Emergency Monitoring Teams (MOD (Navy Dept))
NEN prefix to Standards issued by NNI
NEORG North Eastern Operational Research Group
NEORMP North-East Ohio Regional Medical Program (USA)
NEP Noise Equivalent Power
Nuclear-Electric Propulsion
NEPA National Electric Power Authority (Nigeria)
National Environmental Policy Act (USA)
NEPCON National Electronic Packaging Conference (USA)
NEPDB Navy Environmental Protection Data Base (USN) (NOW NEPSS)
NEPE Nitrate Ester Plasticized Polyethylene
NEPHIS Nested-Phrase Indexing System
NEPR NATO Electronic Parts Recommendations
NEPRF Naval Environmental Prediction Research Facility (USN)
NEPSS Naval Environmental Protection Support Service (USN)
NEPTUNE NORTH-EASTERN Electronic Peak Tracing Unit and Numerical Evaluator
NEQCC North East Quality Control Conference (USA)
NER Nuclear Electric Resonance
NERAC New England Research Applications Center (University of Connecticut (USA))
NERAM Network Reliability Assessment Model
NERBC New England River Basins Commissions (USA)
NERC National Electronic Research Council (now National Electronics Council)
National Environment Research Center (of EPA (USA))
Natural Environment Research Council
NERC(NZ) National Electronics Research Council (New Zealand)
NERDAS NATO Earth Resources Data Annotation System
NERDDC National Energy Research Development and Demonstration Council (Australia)
NEREM Northeast Electronic Research and Engineering Meeting of IEEE (usa))
NERHL North Eastern Radiological Health Laboratory (of Bureau of Radiological Health (USA))
NERMLS New England Regional Medical Library Service (USA)
NERO Na Experimental Reactor of O (Na' is chemical symbol for Sodium; O' is Zero)
Near-Earth Rescue and Operations
NEROC Northeast Radio Observatory Corporation (of 13 Universities (USA))
NERSA Centrale Nucleaire Europeenne a Neutrons Rapides SA (France)
NERV Nuclear Emulsion Recovery Vehicle
NERVA Nuclear Engine for Rocket Vehicle Application
NESA Nebraska Electronic Service Association (USA)
NESC National Energy Software Center (of DOE (USA))
National Environmental Satellite Center (of ESSA) (now of NOAA (USA))
Naval Electronic Systems Command (USN)

NESCTM prefix to numbered series of Technical Memoranda issued by National Environmental Satellite Center (of ESSA later NOAA (USA))
NESDA North East Scotland Development Authority
NESDIS National Environmental Satellite Data and Information Service (USA)
NESHAP National Emission Standards for Hazardous Air Pollutants (USA)
NESO Navy Environmental Support Office (of NEPSS (USN))
NESR Noise Equivalent Spectral Radiance
NESS National Environmental Satellite Service (of NOAA (USA))
NEST Naval Experimental Satellite Terminal
Nuclear Effects Support Teams (US Army)
NESTEF Naval Electronics Systems Test and Evaluation Facility (USN)
NESTOR Neutron Source Thermal Reactor
NET Noise Equivalent Temperature
NETA National Electrical Testing Association (USA)
NETANAL Network Analysis
NETAS North East Thames Architectural Society
NETE Naval Engineering Test Establishment (of the Canadian Armed Forces)
NETFS National Educational Television Film Service (USA)
NETR NATO Electronic Technical Recommendation
NETRAS Nuclear Electric Transfer Stage
NETREM Net Requirements Estimation Model
NETRS NATO Electronic Technical Recommendations
NEUCC Northern European Universities Computer Centre (Denmark)
NEUS New Extensions for Utilizing Scientists (USA) (a non-profit corporation)
NEV Neckarwerke Elektrizitats Versorgungs (Germany)
NEVAC Nederlandse Vacuumverenigung (Netherlands) (Netherlands Vacuum Engineering Society)
NEVIE Nederlandse Vereniging voor Inkoop-Efficiency (Netherlands) (Netherlands Association for Efficiency in Purchasing)
NEWAC NATO Electronic Warfare Advisory Committee
NEWOT Naval Electronic Warfare Operator Trainer
NEWRADS Nuclear Explosion Warning and Radiological Data System
NEWS New-product Early Warning System
NEWSCOMP Newspaper Composition
NEWSTEC Newspaper Society Technical Conference and Exhibition
NEWTS Naval Electronic Warfare Training System
NEXAFS Near-Edge X-ray Absorption Fine Structure
NEXRAD Next Generation Weather Radar Network
NEXT Near-End Cross-Talk
NF Norme Francaise—prefix to Standards issued by AFNOR
Nutrition Foundation (USA)
NFA National Foundry Association (USA)
New Fighter Aircraft
NFAC National Federation of Aerial Contractors (now AAC)
NFAIS National Federation of Abstracting and Indexing Services (USA)
NFBPM National Federation of Builders and Plumbers Merchants
NFBS Scandinavian Research Libraries Co-operation Committee (merged into NORDINFO in 1977)
NFBTE National Federation of Building Trades Employers (now BEC)
NFC National Freight Corporation
NFCA Near-Field Calibration Array
NFCG National Federation of Consumer Groups
NFCI National Federation of Clay Industries
NFCIT National Federation of Cold Storage and Ice Trades
NFCP Nuclear Fuel Cycle and Production (of ERDA (USA)) (replaced in 1976 by Uranium Resources and Enrichment Division AND Waste Management, Production and Reprocessing Division)
NFCPG National Federation of Catholic Physicians Guilds (USA)
NFCR National Foundation for Cancer Research (USA)
NFCS Nuclear Forces Communications Satellite
NFCTA National Fibre Can and Tube Association (USA)
NFDC National Federation of Demolition Contractors
NFDM Non-Fat Dry Milk
NFDS National Fire Data Center (of NFPCA (USA))
NFEA National Federated Electrical Association
NFER National Foundation for Educational Research in England and Wales
NFETM National Federation of Engineers' Tools Manufacturers
NFF No Fault Found
NFFC National Film Finance Corporation
NFFS Non-Ferrous Founders Society (USA)
NFI National Fisheries Institute (USA)
Nutrition Foundation of India (India)
NFIB National Federation of Independent Business
NFIK Norsk Forening for Industriell Kvalitetskontroll (Norway) (Norwegian Institute for Quality Control)
NFL No Field Lubrication
NFLDS National Fire Loss Data System
NFMR Non-linear Ferromagnetic Resonance
NFMRAD Null Filter Mobile Radar
NFO National Freight Organisation
NFPA National Fire Protection Association (USA)
National Flexible Packaging Association (USA)
National Fluid Power Association (USA)
National Forest Products Association (formerly NLMA) (USA)
NFPC National Federation of Plastering Contractors
NFPCA National Fire Prevention and Control Administration (Dept of Commerce (USA))
NFR Statens Naturvetenskapliga Forskningsrad (Sweden) (Swedish Natural Science Research Council)
NFRC National Federation of Roofing Contractors
NFRI National Food Research Institute (Japan)
NFRS National Fire Reference (of NFPCA (USA))
NFSA National Fertilizer Solutions Association (USA)
NFSAIS National Federation of Science Abstracting and Indexing Services (USA)
NFSE National Federation of Self-Employed
NFSWMM National Federation of Scale and Weighing Machine Manufacturers
NFT Neurofibrillary Tangle
Nutrient Film Technique
NFTA Niagara Frontier Transportation Authority (USA)
NG Natural Gas
Nitroglycerine
NGA National Geographical Association
NGAA Natural Gasoline Association of America (USA)
NGAPDC North Georgia Area Planning and Development Commission (USA)
NGB National Guard Bureau (USDOD)
NGC New Galactic Catalogue
New General Catalogue of Nebulae and Clusters of Stars (compiled by J. L. E. Dreyer)
NGCC National Gas Consumers Council

GDC National Geophysical Data Center (of the Environmental Data Service (NOAA) (USA))

GEC National Gypsy Educational Council

GEF New Government Electric Factory (India)

GF Nerve Growth Factor

GL Natural Gas Liquids

GLS Non Governmental Liaison Services (of UN)

GM Neutron-Gamma Monte Carlo

GO Non-Governmental Organisation having relationship with the United Nations

GOT Natural Gas Organisation of Thailand (Thailand)

GP Nearest Grid Point

GPA Natural Gas Processors Association (USA)

GPRP Northern Great Plains Resource Program (of Dept of the Interior, Dept of Agriculture and Environmental Protection Agency (USA))

GRI National Geophysical Research Institute (India)

GRS Narrow Gauge Railway Society

GS National Geodetic Survey (geodetic program of the National Ocean Survey of NOAA (USA))

GSDC National Geophysical and Solar-terrestrial Data Center (of EDS (noaa) (usa))

GSIC National Geodetic Survey Information Center (of NOAA (USA))

GSP National Geodetic Satellite Program (of NASA (USA))

GTE National Gas Turbine Establishment (now of MOD (PE))

GU Non-Gonococcal Urethritis
Norges Geologiske Underskelse (Norway) (Norwegian Geological Surveying Department)

H & MRC National Health and Medical Research Council (Australia)

HA Nictinohydroxamic Acid

HB prefix to numbered series of Handbooks issued by NASA (USA)

HBRC National House Builders Registration Council (now National House-Building Council)

HC National Hurricane Center (of NOAA (USA))
Naval Historical Center (USN)

HDA National Huntington's Disease Association (USA)

HE Normal Hydrogen Electrode

HEB National Home Enlargement Bureau

HEML National Hurricane and Experimental Laboratory (of NOAA (USA))

HGA National Hang Gliding Association

HIC National Home Improvement Council

HK Nippon Hoso Kyokai (Japan Broadcasting Corporation)

HL Non-Hodgkin's Lymphoma

HLA National Hardwood Lumbar Association (USA)
New Hampshire Library Association (USA)

HLBI National Heart, Lung and Blood Institute (of NIH (USA))

HLI National Heart and Lung Institute (of NIH (USA))

HLSA New Hampshire Land Surveyors Association (USA)

HMA National Housewares Manufacturers Association (USA)

HMC Non-Methane Hydrocarbon

HMO NATO HAWK Management Office (France)

HMRC National Health and Medical Research Council (Australia)

HO Northern Hemisphere Observatory (on the island of La Palma in the Canaries)

HPIC National Health Planning Information Center (USA)

HPLO NATO HAWK Production and Logistics Organization

NHPMA Northern Hardwood and Pinewood Manufacturers Association (USA)

NHRE National Hail Research Experiment (of the National Center for Atmospheric Research (USA))

NHRL National Hurricane Research Laboratory (of ESSA) (now of NOAA (USA))

NHS National Health Service
Normal Human Sera

NHSB National Highway Safety Bureau (of Federal Highway Administration (USA) (now NHTSA)

NHSTA National Health Service Training Authority

NHTPC National Housing and Town Planning Council

NHTSA National Highway Traffic Safety Administration (of Department of Transportation (USA))

NHTU Naval Hovercraft Trials Unit (MOD)

NHW Department of National Health and Welfare (Canada)

NI Neutralization Index
Neutraminidase Inhibition
The Nautical Institute

NIA National Institute on Aging (of NIH (HEW) (USA))
National Interconnect Association (USA)
National Irrigation Administration (Philippines)

NIAAA National Institute for Alcoholism and Alcohol Abuse (of ADAMHA (USA))

NIAB National Institute of Agricultural Botany

NIADDK National Institute of Arthritis, Diabetes, and Digestive and Kidney Diseases (of NIH (USA))

NIAE National Institute of Adult Education
National Institute of Agricultural Engineering

NIAESS National Institute of Agricultural Engineering—Scottish Station

NIAG NATO Industrial Advisory Group

NIAID National Institute of Allergy and Infectious Diseases (of NIH (USA))

NIAMD National Institute of Arthritis and Metabolic Diseases (of NIH (USA))

NIAMDD National Institute of Arthritis, Metabolism and Digestive Diseases (USA)

NIAR National Institute of Amateur Radio (India)

NIASA National Insurance Actuarial and Statistical Association (USA)

NIAST National Institute for Aeronautics and System Technology (South Africa)
National Institute for Aeronautics and Systems Technology (of CSIR (South Africa))

NIAT Nauchno Issledovatel'skiy Institut Aviatsionnoy Tekhniki (USSR) (Scientific Research Institute of Aviation Technology)

NIB National Irrigation Board (Kenya)

NIBL National Industrial Basic Language

NIBS National Institute of Building Sciences (of NAS and NAE (usa))

NIBSC National Institute for Biological Standards and Control

NIC National Industrial Council (USA)
National Inspection Council for Electrical Installation Contracting
Natural Image Computer
Naval Intelligence Command (USN)
Negative Immittance Converter
Negative Impedance Converter
Network Interface Controller
Newly Industrialised Country
Newsprint Information Committee (USA)
NINETEEN-HUNDRED (Computer) Indexing and Cataloguing
Noise Isolation Class

NICAP National Investigations Committee on Aerial Phenomena (USA)

NICATEL-SAT Compania Nicaraguense de Telecomunicaciones por Satelite (Nicaragua)

NICB National Industrial Conference Board (USA)

NICC Nationalised Industries Computer Committee

NICD National Institute of Community Development (India)

NICE National Information Conference and Exposition (USA)
National Institute of Ceramic Engineers (USA)

NICEIC National Inspection Council for Electrical Installation Contracting

NICEM National Information Center for Educational Media (of University of Southern California (USA))

NICHD National Institute for Child Health and Human Development (of NIH (USA))

NICIC National Iranian Copper Industries Company (Iran) (govt owned)

NICMAP National Information Centre for Machine Tools and Production Engineering (India)

NICOL NINETEEN HUNDRED (computer) Commercial Language

NICON Association of Northern Irish Consultants International

NICP National Inventory Control Points (US Army)

NICRAD Navy/Industry Cooperative Research and Development Program (USA)

NICS NATO Integrated Communications System

NICSMA NATO Integrated Communications System Management Agency

NICSO NATO Integrated Communications Systems Organization

NID National Institute of Drycleaning (USA)

NIDA National Institute for Drug Abuse (of ADAMHA (USA))
National Institute of Development Administration (Thailand)
National Investment and Development Authority (Papua New Guinea)

NIDAS NIXDORF Integrated Accounting System

NIDC National Industrial Development Corporation (India) (State owned)
Nepal Industrial Development Corporation (Nepal)
Northern Ireland Development Council

NIDER Nederlands Institut voor Informatie, Documentatie en Registratuur (Netherlands) (Netherlands Institute for Information, Documentation and Filing) (now NOBIN)

NIDOC National Information and Documentation Centre (Egypt)

NIDR National Institute of Dental Research (of NIH (USA))

NIE National Institute of Education (of HEW (USA))

NIECC National Industrial Energy Conservation Council (Dept of Commerce (USA))

NIEHS National Institute of Environmental Health Sciences (of NIH (usa))

NIER National Industrial Equipment Reserve

NIES National Institute for Environmental Studies (Japan)
Northern Ireland Electricity Service

NIESR National Institute for Economic and Social Research

NIF Nordiska Institutet for Fargforskning (Denmark) (Scandinavia Institute for Paint and Printing Ink Research)

NIFA National Intercollegiate Flying Association (USA)

NIFES National Industrial Fuel Efficiency Service

NIFFT National Institute of Foundry and Forge Technology (India)

NIFOR Nigerian Institute for Oil Palm Researcł (Nigeria)

NIFTE Neon Indicating Functional Test Equipment

NIFTP Network Independent File Transfer Protocol

NIG Nuklear-Ingenieur-Gesellschaft (Germany)

NIGC National Iranian Gas Company (Iran)

NIGMS National Institute of General Medical Services (o NIH (USA))

NIGP National Institute of Governmental Purchasin (USA)

NIGRO Northern Ireland General Register Office

NIH National Institutes of Health (HEW) (USA)) (now o DHHS)

NIHBC Northern Ireland House Building Council

NIHE Northern Ireland Housing Executive

NII Negative Immittance Inverter
Nuclear Installations Inspectorate (of the HSE)

NIIAR Nauchno-Issledovatelskii Institut Atomynycl Reaktorov (USSR) (Atomic Reactor Scientifi Research Institute)

NIIEP Nauchno Issledovatel'skiy Institut Elektrotekhni cheskoy Promyshlennosti (USSR) (Scientific Re search Institute for the Electrical Engineerin Industry)

NIIGAIK Novosibirsk Institute of Engineers of Geodesy Aerial Surveys and Cartography (USSR)

NIIGSM Nauchno Issledovatel'skiy Institut Goryuchikh Smazovyka (USSR) (Fuels and Lubricants Scien tific Research Institute)

NIIKP Nauchno Issledovatel'skiy Institut Kabel'noy Pro myshlennosti (USSR) (Cable Industry Scientifi Research Institute)

NIILK Nauchno Issledovatel'skiy Institut Lakorasoch noy Promyshlennosti (USSR) (Paint Industr Scientific Research Institute)

NIIP National Institute of Industrial Psychology

NIIPM Nauchno Issledovatel'skiy Institut Plasticheskik Mass (USSR) (Plastics Scientific Researc Institute)

NIIRP Nauchno Isseldovatel'skiy Institut Rezinovo Promyshlennosti (USSR) (Rubber Industr Scientific Research Institute)

NIIShP Nauchno Issledovatel'skiy Institut Shinnoy Pro myshlennosti (USSR) (Scientific Research Inst tute of the Tyre Industry)

NIITAvtoprom Nauchno Issledovatel'skiy Institut Teknologii A tomobil'noy promyshlennosti (USSR) (Automo bile Industry Technological Scientific Researc Institute)

NIITMASh Nauchno Issledovatel'skiy Institut Teknolog Mashinostroyeniya (USSR) (Machine -Buildin Technological Research Institute)

NIJS Nuklearni Institut Josef Stefan (Yugoslavia) (Jo sef Stefan Nuclear Institute)

NIL Nederlands Instituut voor Lastechniek (Nethe lands) (Netherlands Welding Institute)

NILECJ National Institute of Law Enforcement ar Criminal Justice (Dept of Justice (USA))

NILS Nuclear Instrumentation Landing System

NILU Norsk Institutt for Luftforskning (Norway) (No wegian Institute for Atmospheric Research)

NIM National Institute for Metallurgy (South Afric
Nigerian Institute of Management (Nigeria)
Nuclear Instrument Module
Nuclear Instrumentation Modular

NIMD National Institute of Management Developme (United Arab Republic)

NIMEX Nomenclature for Imports and Exports (of EEC

NIMH National Institute of Medical Herbalists
National Institute of Mental Health (of PHS (USA (no longer in NIH but in Alcohol, Drug Abu and Mental Health Administration)

NIMMS	NINETEEN-HUNDRED (Computer) Integrated Modular Management System
NIMP	New and Improved Materials and Processes
NIMR	National Institute for Medical Research (of the MRC)
NIMRA	National Industrial Materials Recovery Association
NIMROD	NATIONAL INSTITUTE FOR MEDICAL RESEARCH On-line Data-base
	NINETEEN-HUNDRED (Computer) Management and Recovery of Documentation
NIMTSM	Nauxhonolzsledovatelsci Institut po Mechanizatiziva, Tractorno i Selskostopansko (Bulgaria) (Research Institute of Mechanization, Tractor and Agricultural Machinery Construction)
NIN	National Institute of Nutrition (India)
NINA	NATIONAL INSTITUTE Northern Accelerator
	Neutron Instruments for Nuclear Analysis
NINCDS	National Institute of Neurological and Communicative Disorders and Strokes (of NIH (USA))
NINDB	National Institute of Neurological Diseases and Blindness (of NIH, usa)
NINDS	National Institute of Neurological Diseases and Stroke (of NIH (usa))
NINE	Normal-Incidence Null Ellipsometer
NIO	National Institute of Oceanography (India)
	National Institute of Oceanography (of Natural Environment Research Council) (now Institute of Oceanographic Sciences)
NIOC	National Iranian Oil Company (Iran)
NIOG	Nationalised Industries Overseas Group
NIOSH	National Institute for Occupational Safety and Health (of PHS (usa))
NIP	Non-Impact-Printer
	Normal Incidence Pyrheliometer
NIPA	National Institute of Public Administration (Bangladesh)
NIPALS	Nonlinear Iterative Partial Least Squares
NIPCC	National Industrial Pollution Control Council (USA)
NIPDOK	Nippon Documentesyon Kyokai (Japan) (Japan Documentation Society)
NIPER	National Institute for Petroleum and Energy Research (USA)
NIPG	Nederlands Instituut voor Praeventieve Geneeskunde (of TNO) (Netherlands) (Netherlands Institute for Preventive Medicine)
NIPHL	Noise-Induced Permanent Hearing Loss
NIPP	Non-Impact Printing Project (US Army)
NIPPCR	National Institute for Physical Planning and Construction Research
NIPPM	Nauchno Issledovatel'skiy Institut Polimerizationnykh Plasticheskikh Mass (USSR) (Polymerization Plastics Scientific Research Institute)
NIPR	National Institute for Personnel Research (of CSIR (South Africa))
NIPRO	Common Nomenclature of Industrial Products (of the European Communities)
NIPS	National Military Command System Information Processing System (USDOD)
	Naval Intelligence Processing System (USN)
	NIXDORF (COMPUTER LTD) Inventory and Production Control System
NIPTS	Noise-Induced Permanent Threshold Shift
NIR	Near Infra-Red
	Negative Impedance Repeater
	Non-Ionizing Radiation
NIRA	National Institute for Research Advancement (Japan)
	Near Infrared Reflectance Analysis
	Nucleare Italiana Reactori Avanzati (Italy)
NIRC	National Industrial Relations Court
	National Information Retrieval Colloquium (USA)
NIRD	National Institute for Research in Dairying
	National Institute for Rural Development (India)
NIREX	Nuclear Industry Radioactive Waste Executive
NIRFI	Nauchno Issledovatel'skiy Radiofizicheskiy Institut (USSR) (Radiophysics Scientific Research Institute)
NIRI	National Information Research Institute (USA)
NIRM	prefix to numbered series of Interim Research Memoranda issued by Naval Warfare Analysis Group (of CNA (USN))
NIRNS	National Institute for Research in Nuclear Science
NIRR	National Institute for Road Research (South Africa)
NIRRA	Northern Ireland Radio Retailers Association
NIRS	National Institute of Radiological Sciences (of JAEC (Japan))
NIRT	National Iranian Radio and Television (Iran)
NIS	National Institute for Standards (Egypt) (disbanded 1971)
	Normal Incidence Spectrometer
NISARC	National Information Storage and Retrieval Centers (USA)
NISC	National Industrial Space Committee (succeeded by UKISC in 1975
	Naval Intelligence Support Center (USN)
NISCON	National Industrial Safety Conference
NISEE	National Information Service for Earthquake Engineering (of University of California and California Institute of Technology (USA))
NISH	National Industries for the Severely Handicapped (USA)
NISM	Non-deterministic Incomplete Sequential Machine
NISO	National Industrial Safety Organisation (Eire)
NISP	National Information System for Psychology (of the American Psychological Association (USA))
NISPA	National Information System for Physics and Astronomy (of the American Institute of Physics (USA))
NISSAT	National Information System for Science and Technology (India)
NISSS	National Information System for Social Sciences (India)
NISUS	Neutron Intermediate Standard Uranium Source
NISW	Naval In-Shore Warfare
NIT	Negative Income Tax
NITIE	National Institute for Training in Industrial Engineering (India)
NITR	Nigerian Institute for Trypanosomiasis Research (Nigeria)
NIVC	National Interactive Video Centre
NIVE	Nederlands Instituut Voor Efficiency (Netherlands) (Netherlands Management Institute)
NIVEA	Night Vision Equipment for Armour
NIVRA	Nederlands Institut van Registeraccountants (Netherlands) (Netherlands Institution of Chartered Accountants)
NIW	Naval Inshore Warfare
NIWR	National Institute for Water Research (of CSIR (South Africa))
NJ-CABM	New Jersey Center for Advanced Biotechnology and Medicine (USA)
NJAC	National Joint Advisory Council (of DEP)
NJCBI	National Joint Council for the Building Industry
NJCC	National Joint Consultative Committee of Architects, Quantity Surveyors and Builders
NJCEC	NATO Joint Communications-Electronics Committee
NJIT	New Jersey Institute of Technology (USA)

NJSHS	National Junior Science and Humanities Symposium (USA)
NK-PIPES	NIPPON KOKAN (Japan)-Pipe Integrated Production Engineering System
NKA	National Khmer Aviation (Cambodia) (Military Air Force)
NKD	Nukleardienst (Germany)
NKF	Norsk Korrosjonsteknisk Forening (Norway) (Norwegian Corrosion Association)
NKG	Nordiska Kommissionen for Geodesi (Sweden) (Scandinavian Commission for Geodesy)
NKK	Nippon Kokan (Japan)
NKOA	National Knitted Outerwear Association (USA)
NKTF	Norges Kvalitetstekniske Forening (Norway) (Norwegian Society for Quality Control)
NL/1	Non-programmer Language 1
NLA	National Library of Australia (Australia)
	Nigerian Library Association (Nigeria)
NLABS	Natick Laboratories (US Army) (now Natick Development Center)
NLAC	National Library Advisory Council (South Africa) (became NACLI in 1982)
NLB	National Library for the Blind
NLC	National Library of Canada (Canada)
	Nematic Liquid Crystal
	Noctilucent Clouds
	Node Location Code
	Northern Land Council (Australia)
NLCSE	Nonlinear Charge Storage Element
NLDS	National Library and Documentation Service (Zimbabwe)
NLETS	National Law Enforcement Telecommunications System (USA)
	National Law Enforcement Teletype System (USA)
NLFM	Nonlinear Frequency Modulation
NLGI	National Lubricating Grease Institute (USA)
NLI	National Limestone Institute (USA)
	Neurotensin-like Immunoreactivity
	Non-Linear Interpolating
NLJ	National Library of Jamaica (Jamaica)
NLL	National Lending Library for Science and Technology (became part of the British Library Lending Division of the British Library in 1973)
NLLST	National Lending Library for Science and Technology
	SEE NLL above
NLM	National Library of Medicine (of NIH (HEW) (USA))
NLM-BCN	National Library of Medicine (USA) Biomedical Communications Network
NLMA	National Lumber Manufacturers Association (now NFPA) (USA)
NLMC	National Library of Medicine (USA) Classification
NLME	Non-Linear Material Effect
NLO	Non-Linear Optimizer
	Nonlinear Optics
NLOGF	National Lubricating Oil and Grease Federation
NLP	Natural Language Processing
	Non-Linear Programming
NLPC	National Libyan Petroleum Company (Libya)
NLPGA	National Liquid Petroleum Gas Association (USA)
NLPQ	Natural Language Processing System for Queuing Problems
NLR	Nationaal Lucht- en Ruimtevaartlaboratorium (Netherlands) (National Aerospace Laboratory)
	Net Liquidity Ratio
NLRB	National Labor Relations Board (USA)
NLS	National Library of Scotland
	New Least Squares
	No-Load Start
NLS/BPH	National Library Service for the Blind and Physically Handicapped (USA)
NLSB	National Library Services Board (Sri Lanka)
NLUC	National Land Use Classification system
NLUS	Navy League of the United States (USA)
NM	Nautical Miles
NMA	National Management Association (USA)
	National Medical Association (USA)
	National Microfilm Association (USA) (title change to National Micrographics Association in 1975) (now AIIM)
NMAB	National Materials Advisory Board (of National Academy of Engineering and National Academy of Sciences (USA))
NMAC	National Medical Audiovisual Center (of NLM (USA))
	Near Mid-Air Collision
NMACT	Nuclear Material Accounting Control Team (of UKAEA)
NMAS	National Map Accuracy Standards (USA)
NMAX	Nonwireline Multiple-Access Communications Exchange System
NMC	National Maritime Council (USA)
	National Marketing Board
	National Meteorological Center (of Weather Bureau (NOAA) (USA))
	Naval Material Command (U
	Naval Missile Center (USN)
	Network Management Centre
NMCC	National Military Command Center (USDOD)
NMCS	National Military Command System (USDOD)
	Nuclear Materials Control System
NMCSSC	National Military Command System Support Center (of NMCS (usdod))
NMDA	National Metal Decorators Association (USA)
NMDC	National Mineral Development Corporation (India) (now part of SAIL (India))
NMDR	Nuclear Magnetic Double Resonance
NMEA	National Marine Electronics Association (USA)
NMERDI	New Mexico Energy Research and Development Institute (USA)
NMERI	National Mechanical Engineering Research Institute (South Africa)
NMFC	National Motor Freight Classification
NMFECC	National Magnetic Fusion Energy Computer Center (at Lawrence Livermore Laboratory (USA))
NMFRL	Naval Medical Field Research Laboratory (USN)
NMFS	National Marine Fisheries Service (of NOAA (USA))
NMFS-CIRC	prefix to series of Circulars issued by NMFS (of NOAA (usa))
NMFS-SSRF	prefix to series of Special Scientific Reports on Fisheries issued by NMFS (of NOAA (USA))
NMG	Numerical Master Geometry
NMHC	National Materials Handling Centre (Cranfield Institute of Technology)
NMI	National Maritime Institute (of DOI) (devolved from the Ship and Maritime Science Division of the National Physical Laboratory in 1976) (now NMI Ltd)
NMI Ltd	merged into BMT in April 1985
NMIA	National Meteorological Institute of Athens (Greece)
NMIMT	New Mexico Institute of Mining and Technology (USA)
NMIT	New Material Introduction Team (of USAMERDC)
NML	National Measurement Laboratory (of NBS (USA))
	National Metallurgical Laboratory (India)
	Nuclear Magnetism Log
NMLA	New Mexico Library Association (USA)

NMLRA National Muzzle Loading Rifle Association of America (USA)
NMM National Maritime Museum
NMMW Near Millimetre Wavelengths
NMNH National Museum of Natural History (USA)
NMNRU Navy Medical Neuropsychiatric Research Unit (USN)
NMOS N-channel Metal Oxide Semiconductor
NMP-TCNQ N-methylphenazinium–Tetracyanoquinodimethane
NMPA National Marine Paint Association (now part of PMAGB)
NMPS prefix to dated/numbered series of Nuclear Marine Propulsion Summaries issued by AEEW (UKAEA)
NMR N-Modular Redundancy
Normal Mode Rejection
Nuclear Magnetic Resonance
NMRI Naval Medical Research Institute (USN)
NMS Naval Medical School (USN)
Navigation Management System
Network Measurement System
Nigerian Meteorological Service (Nigeria)
Non-metric Multidimensional Scaling
Norsk Metallurgisk Selskap (Norway) (Norwegian Metallurgical Society)
Nuclear-powered Merchant Ship
NMSC Navy Management Systems Center (USN)
NMSCA Navy Material Command Support Activity (USN)
NMSU New Mexico State University (USA)
NMTA National Metal Trades Association (USA)
NMTBA National Machine Tool Builders Association (USA)
NMU Nitrosomethylurea
NMVSAC National Motor Vehicle Safety Advisory Council (of DOT (USA))
NNA National Newspaper Association (USA)
NNAG NATO Naval Armament Group
NNC National Nuclear Corporation (partially government owned)
NNCSC National Neutron Cross Section Center (of USAEC) (now of BNL(ERDA))
NNDC National Nuclear Data Center (of BNL (ERDA) (USA))
NNDTU National Non-Destructive Testing Unit (of CEGB)
NNE Noise and Number Exposure
NNEB National Nursery Examination Board
NNEP Navy/NASA (USA) Engine (Computer) Programme
NNI Nederlands Normalisatie Institut (Netherlands) (Netherlands Standards Institute)
Noise and Number Index
Noise Nuisance Index
NNL Non-Nuclear LANCE Missile
NNMC National Naval Medical Center (USN)
NNOC Nigerian National Oil Cooperation (Nigeria) (merged with the Ministry of Petroleum Resources in 1977)
NNP Net National Product
NNPA Nuclear Non-Profliferation Act, 1978 (USA)
NNPC Nigerian National Petroleum Corporation (Nigeria) (govt owned)
NNR National Nature Reserve
Nearest Neighbour Rule
NNRO Norske Nasjonalkomite for Rasjonell Organisajon (Norway) (Norwegian National Committee for Scientific Management)
NNSS Navy Navigation Satellite System (USN)
Nuclear Magnetic Resonance
NNTSP Naval Nuclear Technical Safety Panel (of Institute of naval Medicine) (MOD (Navy Dept))
NOA National Oceanographic Association (USA) (now National Ocean Industries Association (USA))
New Obligational Authority
NOAA National Oceanic and Atmospheric Administration (of Department of Commerce (USA))
NOAA-FCM prefix to dated-numbered series of reports issued by the Federal Coordinator for Meteorological Services and Supporting Research of NOAA (usa))
NOAA-TR-NMFS-CIRC NOAA (USA)–Technical Report–National Marine Fisheries Service–Circular
NOAA-TR-NMFS-SSRF NOAA (USA)–Technical Report–National Marine Fisheries Service–Special Scientific Report Fisheries
NOACT Navy Overseas Air Cargo Terminal (USN)
NOAH Narrow-band Optimiziation of the Alignment of Highways
NOALA Noise-Operated Automatic Level Adjustment
NOAO National Optical Astronomy Observatories (USA)
NOBIN Nederlands Organ voor de Bevordering van de Informatieverzorging (Netherlands) (Netherlands Organisation for Information Policy)
NOBS Naval Observatory (USN)
NOC Notation Of Content
NOCIG Night-Only/Computer Image Generation (Approach)
NOCIL National Organic Chemical Industries (India)
NOD Night Observation Device
NODAC Naval Ordnance Data Automation Center (USA)
NODC National Oceanographic Data Center (USA) (now merged with the Environmental Data Service (of NOAA (USA))
NODLR Night Observation Device–Long Range
NOE Nap Of Earth
NOEL No Observed Effect Level
NOF Nitrogen-Oxygen-Fluorine
Nitrosyl Fluoride
NOFI National Oil Fuel Institute (USA)
NOGEPA Netherlands Oil and Gas Exploration and Production Association
NOGS Night Observation Gunship System
NOHC National Open Hearth Committee (USA)
NOIA National Ocean Industries Association (USA)
NOIBN Not Otherwise Indexed By Name
NOIC National Oceanographic Instrumentation Center (of NOAA (USA))
NOIE Naval Ordnance Inspection Establishment (MOD)
Nuclear Magnetic Resonance
NOISE National Organization to Insure a Sound-controlled Environment (USA)
Noise Information Service (Illinois Institute of Technology (USA))
Noise Information System (of EPA (USA))
NOISEXPO Noise and Vibration Control Conference
NOK Nordostschweizerische Kraftwerke (Switzerland)
NOL Naval Ordnance Laboratory (USN) (now merged into Naval Weapons Laboratory)
NOLAP Non-Linear Analysis Programme
NOLDC Non-OPEC Less-Developed Country
NOLTR prefix to numbered series of Technical Reports issued by the Naval Ordnance Laboratory (USN)
NOM Norme Italiani per il controllo degli Olii Minerali e derivati (Italy) (Italian Standard for Mineral Oils and Derivatives)
NOMA National Office Management Association (USA) (now Administrative Management Society)
NOMAD Naval Oceanographic Meteorological Automatic Device (USN)
NOMDA National Office Machine Dealers Association (USA)

NOMES New England (USA) Offshore Mining Environmental Study (involving private industry, government and several universities)
NOMMA National Ornamental Metal Manufacturers Association (USA)
NOMSS National Operational Meteorological Satellite System (of NOAA (usa))
NOMTF Naval Ordnance Missile Test Facility (USN)
NOO Naval Oceanographic Office (USN)
NOP Numerical Oceanographic Prediction
NOPA National Office Products Association (USA)
NOPMS Network-Oriented Project Management Systems (a group of ANSI (usa))
NOPS National Ocean Policy Study (a special Staff group of the US Senate Committee on Commerce)
NOR Norepinephrine
NOR-LUCS NORTHERN SOFTWARE CONSULTANTS Library Updating and Compiling System
NORAD North American Air Defense Command
NORASIS Northern Ohio Chapter of ASIS (USA)
NORC National Opinion Research Center (University of Chicago, USA)
Naval Ordnance Research Computer
Nuclear Magnetic Resonance
NORDA Naval Ocean Research and Development Activity (USN)
NORDDOK Nordic Committee for Information and Documentation (replaced by NORDINFO in 1977)
NORDEL Nordic Electricity Union
NORDFORSK Nordiska Samarbetsorganisationen for Teknisk-Naturvetenskaplig Forskning (Finland) (Scandinavian Council for Applied Research)
NORDICOM Nordic Documentation Centre for Mass Communication Research
NORDINFO Nordic Council for Scientific Information and Research Libraries (representing Denmark, Finland, Norway and Sweden)
NORDITA Nordisk Institut for Teoretisk Atomfysik (Denmark) (Scandinavian Institute for Theoretical Atomic Physics)
NOrdSE Naval Ordnance Services Establishment (MOD)
NORGRAIN North American Grain Charter (USA)
NORM Not Operationally Ready due to Maintenance
Not Operationally Ready Maintenance
NORMAL NOVA (DATA GENERAL NOVA Minicomputers) Realtime Macro Language
NORPAX North Pacific Experiment (of NSF (USA) Office for IDOE)
NORPRO Norwegian Committee on Trade Procedures (Norway)
NORRA National Off-Road Racing Association (USA)
NORS Norsk Operasjonsanalyse foreningen (Norway) (Norwegian Operational Research Society)
Northern (Maritime) Offshore Resources Study Group (Edinburgh University)
Not Operationally Ready due to Supply
Not Operationally Ready Supply
NORSAR Norwegian Large Aperture Seismic Array
NORTHAG Northern Army Group (of AFCENT (NATO))
NORVEN Comision Venezolana de Normas Industriales (Venezuela) (Standards Institute)
NORVIPS NORTHROP Voice Interruption Priority System
NOS National Ocean Survey (of NOAA (USA))
Naval Ordnance Station (USN)
Nederlandse Omroep Stichting (Netherlands)
Night Observation Surveillance
Not Otherwised Specified
NOS-IHTR prefix to numbered series of reports issued by Naval Ordnance Station, Indian Head, Maryland (USN)
NOSA National Occupational Safety Association (South Africa)
NOSAP NATIONAL OCEAN SURVEY (of NOAA (USA)) Analytical Plotter
NOSAR Norwegian Sesmic Array
NOSC Naval Ocean Systems Center (USN) (formed March 1977 by the consolidation of the Naval Electronics Laboratory Center and Naval Undersea Center)
Naval Ordnance Systems Command (USN) (now merged into NAVSEA)
NOSFER Nouveau Systeme Fondamental pour la determination de l'Equivalent de Reference (of OCITT) (New Master System for determining Reference Equivalents)
NOSL Night-time Optical Survey of Lighting (aboard a space shuttle)
NOSM Noise Diotic, Signal Monaural
NOSO Noise Diotic, Signal Diotic
NOT Naczelna Organizacja Techniczna (Poland) (National Technical Organisation)
NOTAMS Notices to Airmen
NOTBA National Ophthalmic Treatment Board Association
NOTS Naval Ordnance Test Station (USN) (now merged into Naval Weapons Laboratory)
Nuclear Orbit Transfer Stage
NOVCAM Nonvolatile Charge-Addressed Memory
NOVRAM Non-Volatile Random Access Memory
NOW Negotiable Order of Withdrawal Accounts
NOX Oxides of Nitrogen
NP Naval Publication (numbered series issued by MOD (Navy Dept))
Nitronium Perchlorate
NPA National Packaging Association (Australia)
National Personnel Authority (Japan)
National Petroleum Association (USA)
National Pharmaceutical Association
National Pipeline Authority (Australia)
National Pistol Association
National Planning Association (USA)
Newspaper Publishers Association
Numerical Production Analysis
NPAAS National Passenger Accounting and Analysis Scheme (of British Rail)
NPAB Nuclear Power Advisory Board
NPAC National Program for Acquisition and Cataloging (of the Library of Congress (USA))
National Project in Agricultural Communication (USA)
NPACI National Production Advisory Council on Industry
NPB National Productivity Board (Singapore)
NPBA National Paper Box Association (USA)
NPC Nasopharyngeal Carcinoma
National Peanut Council (USA)
National Petroleum Council (USA)
National Ports Council
National Productivity Council (India)
Naval Photographic Center (USN)
NPCA National Paint and Coatings Association (USA)
NPCC National Projects Construction Corporation (India) (Government owned)
NPCCE National Pollution Control Conference and Exposition (USA)
NPCDN National Private Circuit Digital Network
NPD National Power Demonstration
Non-Planar Dipole antenna
NPDES National Pollutant Discharge Elimination System
National Pollution Discharge Elimination Scheme (of EPA (USA))

NPDN Nordic (Denmark, Finland, Iceland, Norway and Sweden) Public Data Network
NPDO Non-Profit Distributing Organization
NPDRC Naval Personnel Research and Development Center (USN)
NPDS Nuclear Particle Detection System
NPE Non-Polluting Engine
NPEA National Printing Equipment Association (USA)
NPFC Naval Publications and Forms Center (USA)
NPFM Neural Pulse Frequency Modulation
NPFO Nuclear Power Field Office (US Army)
NPFRC North Pacific Fisheries Research Center (of NMFS (USA))
NPFSC North Pacific Fur Seal Commission
NPG Naval Proving Ground (USN)
Nuclear Planning Group (of NDAC (NATO))
NPHT Nuffield Provincial Hospitals Trust
NPI National Productivity Institute (South Africa)
Norsk Produktivitetsinstitutt (Norway) (Norwegian Productivity Institute)
NPIS National Physics Information System (of AIP (USA))
NPL National Physical Laboratory (DTI)
National Physical Laboratory (India)
National Physical Laboratory (of CSIR (South Africa))
NPL-CHEM prefix to numbered series of reports issued by the National Physical Laboratory, Division of Chemical Standards
NPL-DES prefix to numbered series of reports issued by the National Physical Laboratory, Division of Electrical Science
NPL-DNACS prefix to numbered series of reports issued by the National Physical Laboratory, Division of Numerical Analysis and Computer Science
NPL-IMS prefix to numbered series of reports issued by the National Physical Laboratory, Division of Inorganic and Metallic Structure
NPL-MA prefix to numbered series of reports issued by the National Physical Laboratory, Division of Numerical and Applied Mathematics
NPL-QU prefix to numbered series of reports issued by the National Physical Laboratory, Division of Quantum Metrology
NPL-RPU National Physical Laboratory (India), Radio Propagation Unit
NPM Non-Print Media
NPMHO Non-Profit Making Housing Organisation
NPN Non-Protein Nitrogen
Normal Propyl Nitrate
NPOC National Point of Contact
NPPSO Navy Publications and Printing Services Office (USN)
NPPTS Nuclear Power Plant Training Simulator
NPR Noise Power Ratio
NPRA National Petroleum Refiners Association (USA)
Naval Personnel Research Acitivity (USN) (now Naval Personnel and Training Research Laboratory)
NPRCG Nuclear Public Relations Contact Group (Italy)
NPRDS Nuclear Plant Reliability Data System (of ANSI (USA))
NPRL National Physical Research Laboratory (of CSIR (South Africa))
NPRM Notice of Proposed Rulemaking (issued by FAA (USA))
NPS National Parks Service (USA)
Naval Postgraduate School (USN)
NPSD Noise Power Spectrum Density
NPSH Net Positive Suction Head
NPSHA Net Positive Suction Head Available
NPSHR Net Positive Suction Head Requirements
NPSM Non-Productive Standard Minute
NPSRA Nuclear Powered Ship Research Association (Japan)
NPT Network Planning Technique
Treaty for the Non-Proliferation of Nuclear Weapons (1970)
NPTA National Paper Trade Association (USA)
NPTRL Naval Personnel and Training Research Laboratory (USN)
NPU National Pharmaceutical Union
NPV Net Present Value
Nuclear-Polyhedrosis Virus
NPVH Net Present Value at the Horizon
NPVLA National Paint, Varnish and Lacquer Association (USA)
NPy Nitrosopyrrolidine
NQR Nuclear Quadruple Resonance
NR Narrow Resonance
Natural Rubber
Neutron Radiography
NRA National Renderers Association (USA)
National Rifle Association of America(USA)
Negative Resistance Amplifier
Nuclear Research and Application Division (of ERDA (USA))
NRAB National Railroad Adjustment Board (USA)
NRAC National Research Advisory Council (New Zealand)
National Resource Analysis Center (of Emergency Planning Office (USA))
Naval Research Advisory Council (USA)
NRAD Neutron Radiography Facility (of Argonne National Laboratory (USA))
NRAO National Radio Astronomy Observatory (USA)
NRB National Roads Board (New Zealand)
Natural Rubber Bureau (USA)
NRC National Research Council (Canada)
National Research Council (Sudan)
National Research Council (Thailand)
National Research Council (USA)
Noise Reduction Coefficient
Nuclear Regulatory Commission (USA)
prefix to series of Research Contributions issued by the Naval Warfare Analysis Group (of CNA (USN))
NRCC National Research Council of Canada, Division of Applied Chemistry
National Resource for Computation in Chemistry (at Lawrence Berkeley Laboratory, California University (USA))
NRCd National Reprographic Centre for documentation (became CIMTECH in 1984)
NRCDP National Research Centre for Disaster Prevention (Japan)
NRCN Nuclear Research Centre, Negev (of IAEC (Israel))
NRCP National Research Council of the Philippines (Philippines)
NRCS Normalized Radar Cross Section
NRCST National Referral Center for Science and Technology (Library of Congress) (USA)
NRD National Range Division (of USAFCS)
NRDC National Research Development Corporation (of CSIR (India))
National Research Development Council
National Resources Defense Council (USA)
Natural Resources Defense Council (USA)
NRDF Non-Recursive Digital Filter
NRDL Naval Radiological Defense Laboratory (USN)
NRDO New Technology Development Organisation (Japan)

NRDP National Research and Development Programme (of MITI (Japan))

NRDR Non-Resetting Data Reconstruction

NRDR-CF Non-Resetting Data Reconstruction with Continuous Feedback

NRDR-DF Non-Resetting Data Reconstruction with Discrete Feedback

NRDS Nuclear Reactor Diving System
Nuclear Rocket Development Station (of NASA)

NRE Naval Research Establishment (of Defence Research Board, Canada) (now Defence Research Establishment Atlantic)
New and Renewable Energy

NREA Natural Resources and Energy Agency (of MITI (Japan))

NREC National Resource Evaluation Centre (USA)

NRECA National Rural Electric Cooperative Association (USA)

NREM Non-Rapid Eye Movement

NRG Nuklearrohr-Gesellschaft (Germany)

NRI Net Radio Interface

NRIA Narrow Resonance Infinite Absorber

NRIC Non-Reciprocal Impedance Converter

NRIES National-Regional Impact Evaluation System

NRIMS National Research Institute for Mathematical Sciences (South Africa)

NRIS Natural Resource Information System

NRJ Non-Reciprocal Junction

NRL National Radiation Laboratory (New Zealand)
National Reference Library of Science and Invention (in 1973 became Science Reference Library of the British Library)
Naval Research Laboratory (of the Naval Research Office (USN))
Nuclear Research Laboratory (India) (of the Agricultural Research Institute)

NRLA Network Repair Level Analysis

NRLM National Research Laboratory of Metrology (Japan)

NRLSI National Reference Library of Science and Invention (in 1973 became Science Reference Library of the British Library)

NRM Natural Remanent Magnetization

NRMA National Retail Merchants Association (USA)
National Roads and Motorists Association (Australia)

NRMCA National Ready Mixed Concrete Association (USA)

NRMG Nederlands Rekenmachine Genootschap (Netherlands)

NRO National Reconnaissance Office (USA)

NRPA Non-Redundant Pinhole Array

NRPB National Radiological Protection Board

NRPC National Railroad Passenger Corporation (USA) (a quasi-governmental agency)

NRPRA Natural Rubber Producers Research Association

NRPS Naval Radiological Protection Service (MOD (Navy Dept))

NRR Noise Reduction Rating

NRRL Norsk Radio Relae Liga (Norway) (Norwegian Amateur Radio Relay League)

NRRPDC Neuse River Regional Planning and Development Council, North Carolina (USA)

NRS Normal Rabbit Serum
Normal Rake System

NRSA National Remote Sensing Agency (India)
Northern Radio Societies Association

NRSC National Remote Sensing Centre (of RAE (MOD))

NRTS National Reactor Testing Station (USA)

NRU National Research Universal

NRX National Research X-perimental

NRZ National Railways of Zimbabwe
Non-Return to Zero

NS Nederlandsche Spoorwegan (Netherlands) (Netherlands Railways)
Neuroelectric Society (USA)
Nuclear Science

NSA National Sawmilling Association
National Security Agency (USDOD)
National Slag Association (USA)
National Standards Association (USA)
Nominal Stress Approach
Non-Sterling Area

NSAC Nuclear Safety Analysis Center (USA)

NSAI Non-Steroidal Anti-Inflammatory Agents

NSAID Non-Steroid Anti-Inflammatory Drug

NSAM Naval School of Aviation Medicine (USN)

NSAMPE National Society for the Advancement of Materials and Process Engineering (USA)

NSB National Science Board (of National Science Foundation (USA))
National Shipping Board (India)
National Standards Board (Ghana)
Naval Studies Board (of National Research Council (USA))
Norges Statsbaner (Norway) (Norwegian State Railways)

NSBA National School Boards Association (USA)

NSBEO National Sonic Boom Evaluation Office (USAF Directorate of Science and Technology)

NSC National Safety Council (India)
National Safety Council (USA)
National Science Council (Eire)
National Security Council (USA)
National Seeds Corporation (India)
National Steel Corporation
National Supervisory Council for the Alarm Industry
Nippon Steel Corporation (Japan)
Nutrition Society of Canada (Canada)

NSCA National Safety Council of Australia
National Society for Clean Air

NSCIA National Supervisory Council for Intruder Alarms

NSCM National Science Curriculum Materials project (Australia)

NSCSA National Shipping Company of Saudi Arabia

NSCWA Nigerian Society of Cost and Works Accountants (Nigeria)

NSDB National Science Development Board (Philippines)

NSDC National Serials Data Centre (part of the Bibliographic Services Division of the British Library)
National Space Development Centre (of Science and Technology Agency Agency) (Japan)

NSDM Nuclear Sediment Density Meter

NSDP National Serials Data Program (of Library of Congress Processing Departments Serial Record Division)

NSE Nigerian Society of Engineers (Nigeria)

NSEC Nanosecond

NSERC Natural Sciences and Engineering Research Council (Canada)

NSESG North Sea Environmental Study Group (of seven offshore operators and MAFF)

NSF National Sanitation Foundation (USA)
National Science Foundation (USA)
Naval Strike Fighter
Norges Standardiserings-Forbund (Norway) (Standards Institute)

NSFI Norges Skipsforskningsinstitutt

NSFM National Symposium on Fracture Mechanics (of ASTM (USA))

NSFO Navy Special Fuel Oil

NSFORT Non-Standard FORTRAN
NSFS Net Section Fracture Strength
NSG Nuclear Science Group (of IEEE (USA))
NSGA National Sand and Gravel Association (USA)
NSHC North Sea Hydrographic Commission
NSHEB North of Scotland Hydro-Electric Board
NSI Norsk Senter for Informatikk (Norway) (Norwegian Center for Information)
NSIA National Security Industrial Association (USA)
NSIC National Small Industries Corporation (India)
National Spinal Injuries Centre
National Strategy Information Center (USA)
Nuclear Safety Information Center (of ORNL (USA))
NSICC North Sea International Chart Commission
NSILA Non-Suppressible Insulin-Like Activity
NSJ Nautical Society of Japan (Japan) (in 1976 changed to Japanese Institute of Navigation)
NSL National Science Library (Canada) (now part of CISTI)
National Science Library (India)
NSLA Nova Scotia Library Association (Canada)
NSM New Smoking Material
NSMB Netherlands Ship Model Basin (Netherlands)
NSMC Naval Submarine Medical Center (USN)
NSMPA National Screw Machine Products Association (USA)
NSMRL Naval Submarine Medical Research Laboratory (USN)
NSMRSE National Study of Mathematics Requirements for Scientists and Engineers (USA)
NSMRTS Nuclear Submarine Manoeuvring Room Training Simulator
NSMSES Naval Ship Missile Systems Engineering Station
NSN NATO Stock Number
NSODCC North Sumatra Oil Development Corporation Company (Japan)
NSOEA National Stationery and Office Equipment Association (USA)
NSOSG North Sea Oceanographic Study Group (of seventeen offshore operators)
NSPAC National Standards Policy Advisory Committee (USA) (of govt, industry, trade unions and other interested bodies)
NSPB National Society for the Prevention of Blindness (USA)
NSPE National Society of Professional Engineers (USA)
NSPI National Society for Programmed Instruction (USA)
NSPP Nuclear Safety Pilot Plant (ORNL)
NSPRI Nigerian Stored Products Research Institute (Nigeria)
NSPS National Society of Professional Surveyors (USA)
NSR Neutrino Synchroton Radiation
NSRA National Small-bore Rifle Association
Nuclear Safety Research Association (Japan)
NSRC Natural Science Research Council (Canada)
NSRDC Naval Ship Research and Development Center (USN)
NSRDL Naval Ship Research and Development Laboratory (USN)
NSRDL/PC Naval Ship Research and Development Laboratory, Panama City (USN)
NSRDS National Standard Reference Data System (of OSRD)
NSRI National Sea Rescue Institute (South Africa)
NSRL Nuclear Structure Research Laboratory (University of Rochester (USA))
NSRO Navy Resale System Office (USN)
NSRR Nuclear Safety Research Reactor (of JAERI (Japan))
NSRT Near Surface Reference Temperature
NSS National Sample Survey
Neutral Speed Stability
Nuclear Science Symposium
NSSA National Suggestion Schemes Association
Navy Space Systems Activity (USN)
NSSC Naval Ships System Command (USN)
NSSDC National Space Science Data Center (of NASA (USA))
NSSFC National Severe Storm Forecast Center (of NOAA (USA))
NSSK North-South Station-keeping
NSSL National Severe Storms Laboratory (of ESSA (now of NOAA (usa))
NSSMS NATO SEA SPARROW Missile System
NSSO Navy Ship's Store Office (USN)
NSSP Neutralisation Self-Solidification Process
NSSS Nuclear Steam Supply System
NSSSM North Sea Supply Simulation Model
NSSTE National Society of Sales Training Executives (USA))
NST Noise, Spikes and Transients
Numerical Surveying Technique
NSTA National Science and Technology Authority (Philippines)
National Science Teachers Association (USA)
NSTAC National Security Telecommunications Advisory Committee (USA)
NSTIC Naval Scientific and Technical Information Centre (absorbed into DRIC in 1971) (MOD)
NSTL National Space Technology Laboratories (of NASA (USA))
NSTP National Space Technology Programme (administered by DTI with MOD technical assistance)
Nuffield Science Teaching Project
NSU Non-Specific Urethritis
NSV Noise, Shock and Vibration
NSVV Nederlandse Stichting voor Verlichtingskunde (Netherlands) (Netherlands Foundation for Illumination)
NSWC Naval Surface Weapons Center (USN)
NSWMA National Solid Wastes Management Association (USA)
NSWPTC New South Wales Public Transport Commission (Australia)
NSWSES Naval Ships Weapon Systems Engineering Station (USN)
NTA National Tuberculosis Association (USA)
National Type Approval
Near Terminal Area
Nitrilotriacetate
Nitrilotriacetate Acid
Northern Textile Association (USA)
NTAF National Trisonic Aerodynamic Facilities (NAL) (India)
NTAG Network Technical Architecture Group (of NDO, Library of Congress (USA))
NTB Non-Tariff Barriers
NTC National Telemetering Conference (of IEEE (USA))
National Terotechnology Centre (of DOI) (operated at Electrical Research Association)
National Textile Corporation (India) (state owned)
National Training Center (US Army)
National Translations Center (John Crerar Library, Chicago (USA))
Negative Temperature Coefficient
Nippon Telecommunications Consulting Committee Ltd (Japan)

NTCA — National Telephone Cooperative Association (USA)
North Texas Contractors Association (USA)

NTCCS — Naval Tactical Command and Control System

NTD — Neutron Transmutation-Doped

NTDA — National Tyre Distributors Association

NTDC — Naval Training Device Center (USN)

NTDPMA — National Tool, Die and Precision Machining Association (USA)

NTDRA — National Tire Dealers and Retreaders Association (USA)

NTDS — Naval Tactical Data System (USN)

NTDSC — Nondestructive Testing Data Support Center (administered by Defense Supply Agency (USDOD) and operated at the Southwest Research Institute)

NTE — Network Terminating Equipment

NTEC — Naval Training Establishment Center (USN)

NTF — National Transonic Facility (of NASA (USA))
Navy Technological Forecast (USN)

NTFI — Norsk Tekstil Forsknings Institutt (Norway) (Norwegian Textile Research Institute)

NTG — Nachrichten-Technische Gesellschaft im VDE (Germany) (Association of Telecommunications Engineers within the German Association of Electrical Engineers)

NTH — Norges Tekniske Hogskole (Norway) (Technical University of Norway)

NTHV — Near-Term Hybrid Vehicle

NTI — Nanyang Technological Institute (Singapore)

NTIA — National Telecommunications and Information Administration (of Dept of Commerce (USA))
National Telecommunications and Information Administration (USA)

NTIAC — Nondestructive Testing Information Analysis Center (previously operated by AMMRC (US Army)) (now administered by Defense Supply Agency (USDOD) and operated at the Southwest Research Institute)

NTID — National Technical Institute for the Deaf (Rochester Institute of Technology (USA))

NTIS — National Technical Information Service (Department of Commerce (USA))

NTIS-PK — NTIS Information package–a numbered series issued by NTIS (USA)

NTISearch — NTIS (USA) on-line bibliographic search system

NTL — Natural Thermoluminescence

NTLS — Non-transposed Loop Sensor

NTML — National Tillage Machinery Laboratory (USA)

NTMS — National Topographic Map Series (USA)

NTNF — Norges Teknisk-Naturvitenskapelige Forskningsrad (Norway) (Norwegian Council for Scientific and Industrial Research)

NTO — Nitrogen Textroxide

NTP — National Toxicology Program (USA)
Normal Temperature and Pressure

NTPC — National Thermal Power Corporation (India) (govt owned)

NTRDA — National Tuberculosis and Respiratory Disease Association (USA)

NTRI — National Timber Research Institute (of CSIR (South Africa))

NTRL — Navy Training Research Laboratory (USN)

NTS — Navigation Technology Satellite
Nevada Test Site (of NASA)
Nucleus Tractus Solitarius

NTS-I — Navigation Technology Satellite One

NTSAC — New Technical and Scientific Activities Committee (of IEEE)

NTSB — National Transportation Safety Board (of DOT (USA))

NTSB-AAM — prefix to series of dated-numbered reports issued by Bureau of Aviation Safety, National Transportation Safety Board (of DOT (USA))

NTSB-AAR — National Transportation Safety Board (of DOT (USA))–Aircraft Accident Report

NTSB-HAR — prefix to dated-numbered series of Highway Accident Reports issued by National Transportation Safety Board (of DOT (USA))

NTSB-PAR — prefix to dated-numbered series of Pipeline Accident Reports isued by National Transportation Safety Board (of DOT (USA))

NTSB-RAR — prefix to dated-numbered series of Railroad Accident Reports issued by National Transportation Safety Board (of DOT (USA))

NTSB-RHR — prefix to dated-numbered series of Railroad/Highway Accident Reports issued by National Transportation Safety Board (of DOT (USA))

NTSC — National Television Systems Committee (USA)

NTSK — Nordiska Tele-Satelit Kommitten (Nordic Committee for Satellite Telecommunications)

NTT — Nippon Telegraph and Telephone Public Corporation (Japan)

NTTA — National Traders Traffic Association

NTTPC — Nippon Telegraph and Telephone Public Corporation (Japan)

NTTRL — National Tissue Typing Reference Laboratory

NTTS — National Tower Testing Station (of CEGB)

NTU — Network Terminating Unit

NTUC — National Trade Union Congress (Singapore)

NTVA — Nondeterministic Time-Variant Automation

NTVRA — National Television Rental Association

NTW — Non-pressure Thermit Welding

NUA — Network User Address

NUC — Naval Undersea Research and Development Center (USN) (now Naval Undersea Center)

NUC:H — National Union Catalogue of Library Materials for the Handicapped (Australia)

NUCLENOR — Centrales Nucleares del Norte (Spain)

NUCLEX — International Nuclear Industrial Fair and Technical Meetings

NUCOL — Numerical Control Language

NUDAC — Nuclear Data Centre (India)

NUDETS — Nuclear Detection System
Nuclear Detonations

NUFCOR — Nuclear Fuels Corporation (South Africa)

NUFTIC — Nuclear Fuels Technology Information Center (of ORNL (USAEC)) (now ERDA)

NUFUCO — Nuclear Fuel Cost

NUI — Network User Identifier or Identity

NUKEM — Nuklear-Chemie und Metallurgie (Germany)

NULS — Net Unit-Load Size

NUMEPS — Numeric Meta Language Processing System

NUOS — Naval Underwater Ordnance Station (USN)

NUPAD — Nuclear Powered Active Detection

NuPAG — Nuclear Protection Advisory Group

NURAT — NEWCASTLE UNIVERSITY Root Analogue Tunneller

NURE — National Uranium Resource Evaluation (a program of ERDA (USA)) (now DOE)

NUREC — Nuclear Regulatory Commission (USA)

NUREGS — prefix to numbered series of documents issued by NUREC (USA)

NUS — National University of Singapore

NUSAC — Nuclear Science Advisory Committee (of Dept of Energy and NSF (USA

NUSC — Naval Underwater Systems Center (USN)

NUSC/NL — Naval Undersea System Center, New London Laboratory (USN)

NUSCOT — Nuclear Submarine Control Trainer

NUSL — Navy Underwater Sound Laboratory (USN)

NUSLIP — NOTTINGHAM UNIVERSITY Line Sequency Programme
NUSS — Nuclear Safety Standards (of IAEA)
NUTEC — Norwegian Underwater Technology Centre (Norway)
NUTIS — Numerical and Textile Information System
NUTMAQ — Nuclear Techniques in Mining and Quarrying (a unit at AERE (ukaea))
NUTN — National University Teleconference Network (USA)
NUTS — NEWCASTLE UNIVERSITY Teaching System
NUWAR — Nuclear Warfare
NUWC — Naval Undersea Warfare Center (USN) (later Naval Undersea Research and Development Center)
NUWMF — Naval Undersea Warfare Museum Foundation (USA)
NV — Naamloze Vennootschap (Limited Company)
prefix to SAE (USA) numbered series of Low Alloy Constructional Steels
NV & EOL — Night Vision and Electro-Optics Laboratory (of ERADCOM (US Army))
NVACP — Office of Neighborhoods, Voluntary Associations, and Consumer Protection (of HUD (USA))
NVAES — Novo-Voronezhskaya Atomnaya Energetiches-kaya Stantisiya (USSR) (Novo-Voronezhskaya Atomic Power Station)
NVAR — Normalized Variance
NVBF — Nordiska Vetenskapliga Bibliotekarieforbundet (Sweden) (Scandinavian Association of Science Librarians)
NVD — Night Viewing Device
Night Vision Device
NVE — Nederlandse Vereniging voor Ergonomie (Netherlands) (Netherlands Ergonomics Society)
NVEBW — Non-Vacuum Electron Beam Welding
NVG — Night Vision Goggles
NVGA — National Vocational Guidance Association (USA)
NVKI — Nederlandse Vereniging voor Kunstmatige Intelligentie (Netherlands) (Netherlands Association for Artificial Intelligence)
NVL — Nederlandse Vereniging voor Lastechniek (Netherlands Welding Society) (now part of NIL)
Night Vision Laboratory (US Army)
NVLAP — National Voluntary Laboratory Accreditation Program (of Dept of Commerce Office of Product Standards (USA))
NVM — Non-Volatile Memories
NVNDO — Nederlandse Vereniging voor Niet Destructief Onderzoek (Netherlands) (Netherlands Association for Non-destructive testing)
NVRAM — Non-Volatile Random Access Memory
NVRS — National Vegetable Research Station
NVSMD — Non-Volatile Semiconductor Memory Device
NVT — Norwegian Variable Time artillery fuze
NVTG — Nederlandse Vereniging voor Timesharing Gebruikers (Netherlands) (Netherlands Association for Timesharing Users)
NWAG — Naval Warfare Analysis Group (of Center for Naval Analyses (USN))
NWC — National Water Commission (USA)
National Water Council
Naval War College (USN)
Naval Weapons Center (USN)
NWCC — Neutron Well Coincidence Counter
NWDC — Navigation/Weapon Delivery Computer
NWEB — North Western Electricity Board
NWEF — Naval Weapons Evaluation Facility (USN)
NWEMG — North West European Microbiological Group
NWEPC — North West Economic Planning Council
NWER — Nuclear Weapons Effects Research
Nuclear Weapons Effects Researchoun
NWET — Nuclear Weapons Effects Test
NWFZ — Nuclear Weapon-Free Zone
NWH — NOREN Weld Hardening
NWHC — Naval Weapons Handling Center (USN)
NWHL — Naval Weapons Handling Laboratory (USN)
NWIDA — North West Industrial Development Association
NWK — Nordwestdeutsche Kraftwerke (Germany)
NWL — Naval Weapons Laboratory (USN) (now NSWC (USN))
NWMA — National Woodwork Manufacturers Association (USA)
NWO — Non-Woven Oriented
NWORG — North Western Operational Research Group
NWPCA — National Wooden Pallet and Container Association (USA)
NWRC — National Weather Records Center (of ESSA) (now NOAA)
Naval War Research Center (US Navy)
NWRF — Naval Weather Research Facility (USN)
NWS — National Weather Service (of NOAA (USA))
Naval Weather Service (USN)
Noise Wiener Spectrum
prefix to numbered series of publications issued by the Naval Warfare Analysis Group (of CNA (USN))
NWS-CR — National Weather Service–Central Region (of NOAA (USA))
NWS-ER — National Weather Service–Eastern Region (of NOAA (USA))
NWS-SR — National Weather Service–Southern Region (of NOAA (USA))
NWS-WR — National Weather Service—Western Region (of NOAA (USA))
NWSA — National Welding Supply Association (USA)
NWSC — National Weather Satellite Center (USA)
NWSY — Naval Weapons Station, Yorktown (USN)
NWTS — National Waste Terminal Storage (a program of DOE (USA))
NWWA — National Water Wells Association (USA)
NXSR — Non-Extraction Steam Rate
NYADS — New York Air Defense Sector (USA)
NYAS — New York Academy of Sciences (USA)
NYCHA — New York Clearing House Association (USA)
NYCTA — New York City Transit Authority (USA)
NYHA — New York Heart Association (USA)
NYLA — New York Library Association (USA)
NYLIC — New York Library Instruction Clearinghouse (State University of New York (USA))
NYMAC — National Young Managers Advisory Committee (of BIM)
NYME — New York Mercantile Exchange (USA)
NYMS — New York Microscopical Society (USA)
NYNS — New York Naval Shipyard (USN)
NYO — New York Operations Office (of USAEC) (now ERDA)
NYPL — New York Public Library (USA)
NYRG — New York Rubber Group (USA)
NYSA — New York Shipping Association (USA)
NYSAA — New York Society of Security Analysts (USA)
New York State Association of Architects (USA)
NYSAC — New York State Arms Collectors (USA)
NYSAPLS — New York State Association of Professional Land Surveyors (USA)
NYSERDA — New York State Energy Research and Development Authority (USA)
NYSIIS — NEW YORK STATE (USA) Identification and Intelligence System
NYSILL — New York State Inter-Library Loan Network (USA)

NYSNI New York State Nutrition Institute (USA)
NYSPIN NEW YORK STATE (USA) Police Intelligence Network
NYSU State University of New York (USA)
NYU New York University (USA)
NYU-AA New York University, Department of Aeronautics and Astronautics (USA)
NZAEC New Zealand Atomic Energy Committee (New Zealand)
NZART New Zealand Association of Radio Transmitters (New Zealand)
NZBC New Zealand Book Council (New Zealand)
New Zealand Broadcasting Corporation (New Zealand) (disbanded 1975)
NZBTO New Zealand Book Trade Organization (New Zealand)
NZDSIR New Zealand Department of Scientific and Industrial Research
NZED New Zealand Electricity Department (New Zealand)
NZERDC New Zealand Energy Research Development Committee (New Zealand)
NZIA New Zealand Institute of Architects (New Zealand)
NZIC New Zealand Institute of Chemistry (New Zealand)
NZIE New Zealand Institution of Engineers (New Zealand)
NZIER New Zealand Institute of Economic Research (New Zealand)
NZIM New Zealand Institute of Management (New Zealand)
NZIMP New Zealand Institute of Medical Photography (New Zealand)
NZLA New Zealand Library Association (New Zealand)
NZMAB New Zealand Metric Advisory Board (New Zealand) (disbanded 1979)
NZNAC New Zealand National Airways Corporation (New Zealand)
NZNCOR New Zealand National Committee on Oceanic Research (New Zealand)
NZOI New Zealand Oceanographic Institute (New Zealand)
NZPCI New Zealand Prestressed Concrete Institute (New Zealand)
NZPOA New Zealand Purchasing Officers Association (New Zealand)
NZR New Zealand Railways (New Zealand)
NZS prefix to numbered series of Standards issued by SANZ (New Zealand)
NZSA New Zealand Society of Accountants (New Zealand)
NZSG Non-Zero-Sum Game
NZSI New Zealand Standards Institute
New Zealand Standards Institute (now SANZ)
NZSR prefix to Standards issued by NZSI
NZSS prefix to Standards issued by NZSI

O

O prefix to numbered series of reports issued by AWRE (of UKAEA) (transferred to MOD, 1973)
O&M Operations and Maintenance
Organisation and Method
Operating and Maintenance
O&M.A Operation and Maintenance, Army
O&MN Operations and Maintenance, Navy (USN)
O&MTC Organisation and Methods Training Council
O-POS Oxygen-dope Polysilicon
O-TAWCS Okinawa Tactical Air Weapons Control System
OA Occupational Analysis
Office Automation
Office of Applications (of NASA (USA))
Office of Operations Analysis (of Tactical Air Command (USAF))
Optical Absorption
OA & M Operation, Administration and Maintenance
OA/DDP Office Automation/Distributed Data Processing
OAA Obstetric Anaesthetists Association
Orient Airlines Association
Oxaloacetic Acid
OAC Oceanic Affairs Committee (of ABOI, BMEC, BNCOE, CBMPE, SUT and UEG)
OACA Ontario Arms Collectors Association (Canada)
OACI SEE ICAO
OACP Operational Analysis Code Package
OAE Orbiting Astronomical Explorer
Oscillating-Analyzer Ellipsometer
OAF Orbital Antenna Farm
OAGC Oshawa Antique Gun Collectors (Canada)
OAL Office of Arts and Libraries (Cabinet Office)
OALM Optically Addressed Light Modulator
OAM Office of Aviation Medicine (of FAA (USA))
OAMS Optical Angular Motion Sensor
Orbit Attitude and Manoeuvre System
Orbital Altitude Manoeuvring System
OANA Organization of Asian News Agencies
OAO Orbital OR Orbiting Astronomical Observatory
OAOR Oxygen Adsorption, Out-gassing, and Chemical Reduction
OAP On-Axis Pointing
OAPEC Organization of Arab Petroleum Exporting Countries
OAPI Organisation Africaine de la Propriete Intellectuelle (Cameroun)
OAPWL Overall Power Watt Level
OAR Office of Aerospace Research (USAF)
Ordering As Required
prefix to numbered series of Operations Analysis Reports issued by USAF Logistics Command Operations Analysis Office
OARB Orient Airlines Research Bureau
OARS Ocean Area Reconnaissance Satellite
OART Office of Advanced Research and Technology (of (NASA (USA)) (now Office of Aeronautics and Space Technology)
OAS Office of Advanced Systems (of Social Security Administration (USA))
Ohio Academy of Science (USA)
Ordinary Ammunition Stowage
Organization of American States
OASC Office of Advanced Scientific Computing (of National Science Foundation (USA)
OASF Orbiting Astronomical Support Facility
OASIS Oceanic and Atmospheric Scientific Information System (of NOAA (USA))
Ohio (Chapters) of the American Society for Information Science (USA)
Operational Applications of Special Intelligence Systems (a program of Electronics Systems Division (AFSC) (USAF))
Operational Automated Ship's Information System
Optimized Air-to-Surface Infra-red Seeker
Order, Accounting, Stock, Invoicing and Statistics
Outpatient Appointment Schedule Information System
OASP Over-All Sound Pressure level
OASPL Over-All Sound Pressure Level

OAST Office of Aeronautics and Space Technology (of NASA (USA))
OASU Oceanographic Air Survey Unit (of NAVOCEANO)
OAT Operational Acceptance Test
Oxide-Aligned Transistor
OATM Operations Analysis Technical Memorandum (numbered series issued by AFLC (USAF))
OATRU Organic and Associated Terrain Research Unit (of McMaster University (Canada))
OATS Original Article Tear Sheet (an information service of ISI (USA))
Outdoor Advertising Total System
OAU Organization of African Unity (Ethiopia)
OAW Oxy-Acetylene Welding
OBAP Office Belge pour l'Accroissement de la Productivitie (Belgium) (Belgian Productivity Improvement Office)
OBAR Ohio Bar Automated Research (Ohio State Bar Association (USA))
OBAWS On-Board Aircraft Weighing System
OBB Octabromobiphenyl
Oesterreichische Bundesbahnen (Austria) (Austrian Federal Railways)
OBE Office of Business Economics (of Department of Commerce (USA)) (now part of the Social and Economic Statistics Administration)
OBE-SAC prefix to dated-numered series of Surveys of Current Business issued by Office of Business Economics (USA)
OBGS On-Board Gunnery Simulator
OBI Omni-Bearing Indicator
OBL Office of Business Liaison (of DOC (USA))
OBM Oxygen-Bottom MAXHUTTE (EISENWERK-GESELLSCHAFT MAIXIMILIANSHUTTE)
OBN Office of Biochemical Nomenclature (of NAS/NRC (USA))
OBO Ore/Bulk/Oil
OBOE Offshore Buoy Observing Equipment
OBOGS On-Board Oxygen Generation System
OBP Onboard Processor
OBR Overseas Business Report (series issued by Bureau of International Commerce (USA))
OBRAD Oblate Radial
OBS Ocean Bottom Seismograph
Ocean Bottom Seismographic Station
Ocean Bottom Seismometer
Omni Bearing Selector
Open Business School (of the OU)
Orbital Bombardment System
OBTVR Office for Battlefield Technical Vulnerability Reduction (US Army)
OBU Off-Shore Banking Unit
OBV Octane Blending Value
OC Obstacle Clearance (a panel of ICAO)
Operating Characteristic
Opti-Chiasm
OCA Organization of Chinese Americans (USA)
OCAL On-line Cryptanalytic Aid Language
OCAM Organisation Commune Africaine et Mauricienne (Afro-Maurician Common Organisation)
OCAS On-line Cryptanalytic System
OCASP OLIVETTI Complete Accounting and Stock Package
OCBS Organizing Committee for British Shipbuilders
OCC International Offshore Craft Conference
Occluded Corrosion Cells
OCC&DC Oregon Coastal Conservation and Development Commission (USA)
OCCA Oil and Colour Chemists Association
OCCC Oil Control Coordination Committee (of commercial oil companies (USA))
OCCGE (Organization for Co-operation and Co-ordination in the Fight against Endemic Diseases)
Organisation de Cooperation et de Coordination de la Lutte contre des Grandes Endemies
OCCI Optical Coincidence Co-ordinate Indexing
OCCM Optical Counter Counter-measure
OCD Office for Child Development (of HEW (USA))
Office of Civil Defense (USA) (now Defense Civil Prepareqness Agency (joint agency of DOD and NASA (USA))
OCDE SEE OECD
OCDF Operations Control and Display Facility (of WSMR (US Army))
OCE Ocean Colour Experiment (aboard a space shuttle)
OCEAC Organisation de Coordination pour la Lutte Contre des Endemies en Afrique Centrale (Organisation for Coordination in the Fight against Endemic Diseases in Central Africa)
OCEAN Oceanographic Co-ordination Evaluation and Analysis Network (USN)
Organisation Communautare Europeene d'Avitailleurs de Navires (of EEC) (EEC Committee on Ship Supplies)
OCG Österreichische Computer Gesellschaft (Austria) (Austrian Computer Society)
OCGT Open-Cycle Gas Turbine
OCHAMPUS Office for Civilian Health and Medical Program of the Uniformed Services (USDoD)
OCHRE Optical Character Recognition Engine
OCI Office of Computer Information (of DOC (USA))
Ontario Cancer Institute (Canada)
OCIMF Oil Companies International Marine Forum (a group of 45 oil firms and tanker owners)
OCL Obstacle Clearance Limit
On-Line Computer
Operator Control Language
OCLC Ohio College Library Center (USA) (now OCLC Inc.)
OCM Oil Content Monitor
On Condition Maintenance
Optical Counter-Measures
OCMA Oil Companies Material Association
OCNP Opportunity Cost of Nuclear Power
OCOAP Oscillating-Compensator Oscillating-Analyzer Polarimeter
OCOM Oficina Central de Organizacion y Metodos (Chile) (Central Office of Organisation and Methods)
OCP Obstacle Clearance Panel (of ICAO)
Office of Civilian Personnel (of Navy Dept (USA))
Open Circuit Potential
Orbital Combustion Process
OCPO Office of Civilian Personnel Operations (USAF)
OCR Office of Coal Research (Department of the Interior (USA))
Optical Character Recognition
OCR-A Optical Character Recognition—Font A
OCR-B Optical Character Recognition—Font B
OCRD Office of the Chief of Research and Development (US Army) (replaced by ODCSRA in 1974)
OCRM Office of Ocean and Coastal Resource Management (of NOS (NOAA) (USA))
OCRUA Optical Character Recognition Users Association (USA)
OCS Ocean Colour Scanner
Office Computing System
Office of Commodity Standards (of NBS, USA)
Office of Criteria and Standards (Bureau of Radiological Health (USA))
Onboard Check-out System
Operations Control System
Optical Contrast Seeker
Organocyclo Siloxanes
Outer Continental Shelf
Overseas Communication Service (India)

OCSZ Organocyclo Silozanes
OCT Associated Overseas Countries and Territories (associated with EEC)
Office of Critical Tables (of NAS/NRC, USA)
OCTI Office Central des Transports Internationaux par Chemins de Fer (Switzerland) (Central Office for International Railway Transport)
OCTRF Ontario Cancer Treatment and Research Foundation (Canada)
OCU Oscillator-Clock Unit
OCV Open Circuit Voltage
OCW Oceanographic Commission of Washington (USA)
OCZM Office of Coastal Zone Management (of NOAA (USA))
OD Optical Density
Organizational Development
Outside Diameter
Overburden Drill
ODA Optical Diffraction Analysis
Overseas Development Administration (of the Foreign and Commonwealth Office) (became Ministry of Overseas Development in 1974–usually abbreviated as ODM) (revived 1982)
Overseas Doctors Association
ODAP Office of Drug Abuse Policy (USA) (disbanded 1978)
ODAS Ocean Data Acquisition System
ODC Ornithine Decarboxylase
Oxyhaemoglobin Dissociation Curve
ODCS On-line Data Compression System
ODCSRDA Office of the Deputy Chief of Staff for Research, Development and Acquisition (US Army)
ODDRE Office of the Director of Defense Research and Engineering (USDoD)
ODE Ordinary Differential Equation
ODECA Organizacion de Estados Centro Americanos (Organization of Central American States) (Headquarters in El Salvador)
ODESSA Ocean Data Environmental Science Services Acquisition
ODFI Office of Direct Foreign Investment (of Department of Commerce (USA))
ODI Overseas Development Institute
ODIN Optimal Design Integration
ODLRO Off-Diagonal Long-Range Order
ODM Ministry of Overseas Development (disbanded in 1970 and replaced by ODA)
Ministry of Overseas Development (re-established in 1974 as a separate and independent Department) (disbanded 1982)
ODN Ordnance Datum Newlyn
ODOP Offset Doppler
ODP Original Document Processing
ODPCS Oceanographic Data Processing and Control Systems
ODPEX Offshore Drilling and Production Exhibition
ODRN Orbiting Data Relay Network (of NASA)
ODS Octadecylsilane
Oxide Dispersion-Strengthened
ODT Odour Detection Threshold
ODTACCS Office of the Director, Telecommunications and Command and Control Systems (USDOD)
ODTW Oppositely Directed Travelling Waves
OD^3 Optical Digital Data Disk
OE Office of Education (USA)
Open-End
OEA Office of Economic Adjustment (of Office of the Assistant Secretary of Defense (USA))
OEAS Organisation Europaischer Aluminium Schmelzhutten (Organisation of European Aluminium Foundries)
OEC Office of Energy Conservation (of NBS (Dept of Commerce (USA))
Overall Energy Council (Japan)
OECD Organisation for Economic Co-operation and Development
OECO Outboard Engine Cut-Off
OECON Offshore Exploration Conference (USA)
OECS Organization of Eastern Caribbean States
OEDRC Optico-Electronic Device for Registering Coincidences
OEEPE Organisation Europeene d'Etudes Photogrammetriques Experimentales (European Organisation for Experimental Photogrammetric Research)
OEF Optical Evaluation Facility (of WSMR (US Army))
OEG Operations Evaluation Group (of CNA (USN))
OEHL Occupational and Environmental Health Laboratory (USAF)
OEIC Optoelectronic Integrated Circuit
OEIMC Oklahoma Environmental Information and Media Center (East Central State College (USA))
OEM On Equipment Material
Optical Electron Microscope
Original Equipment Manufacturer
OEMV Oesterreichische Mineralol-Verwaltung (Austria) (govt owned)
OENR Oil Extended Natural Rubber
OEO Office of Economic Opportunity (of the Executive Office of the President (USA))
Operational Equipment Objective
OEP Office of Emergency Preparedness (of the Executive Office of the President (USA) (previously Office of Emergency Planning)
Office of Energy R & D Policy (USA)
OEPP Organisation Europeene et Mediteraneenne pour la Protection des Plantes (European and Mediterranean Plant Protection Organisation)
OEQ Order of Engineers of Quebec (Canada)
OER Office of Economic Research (of Economic Development Agency (USA))
Office of Energy Research (of DOE (USA))
Office of Engineering Reference (Bureau of Teclamation, Dept. of the Interior (USA))
Oxygen Enhancement Ratio
Oxygen Evolution Reaction
prefix to numbered series of Operations Evaluation Reports issued by Operations Evaluation Group (of CNA (USN))
OERI Office of Educational Research and Improvement (of Department of Education (USA))
OERS Organisation des Etats Riverains du Senegal (Senegal) (Organisation of Senegal River States)
OES Bureau for Oceans and International Environmental and Scientific Affairs (of the State Dept (USA))
prefix to numbered series of Operations Evaluations Studies issued by Operations Evaluation Group (of CNA (USN))
OESBR Oil Extended Styrene Butadiene Rubber
OESL Office of Engineering Standards Liaison (of NBS (USA))
OESR Oil Extended Synthetic Rubber
OeSWG Oesterreichische Studiengesellshaft fur Wirtschaftliche Guterbewegung (Austria) (Austrian Research Association for Materials Handling)
OET Office of Emergency Transportation (of Department of Transportation (USA))
Optico-Electronic Transducer
OET&E Operational Employment Testing and Evaluation
OETB Offshore Energy Technology Board (of Dept of Energy)

OETO Ocean Economics and Technology Office (of the UN)
OFBW Ozeanographische Forchungsanstalt der Bundeswehr (Germany) (Armed Forces Oceanographic Research Establishment)
OFC Olayan Financing Company (Saudi Arabia)
OFCA Ontario Federation of Construction Associations (Canada)
OFCC Office of Federal Contract Compliance (of Dept. of Labor (USA))
OFCM Office of the Federal Coordinator for Meteorological Services and Supporting Research (USA)
OFD Optical (Gun) Fire Director
OFDI Office of Foreign Direct Investment (of Department of Commerce (USA))
OFDS Optimal Financial Decision Strategy
OFEMA Office Francais d'Exportation de Materiel Aeronautique (France)
OFET Organisation Francaise d'Enseignment de la Teledetection (France) (French Remote Sensing Training Organization)
OFFI Orszagos Fordito es Forditashitelesito Iroda (Hungary) (National Office for Translations and Attestations)
OFFINTAC Offshore Installations Technical Advisory Committee
OFFSET Offshore Engineering Team (of NEL (DTI))
OFHC Oxygen Free High Conductivity
OFINTAC Offshore Installations Technical Advisory Committee
OFISP Operational Flight Information Service Panel (of ICAO)
OFIX Office of the Future Information Exchange
OFN Organization for Flora Neotropica
OFO Orbiting Frog Otolith (an experiment carried out by NASA (USA)
OFPP Office of Federal Procurement Policy (USA) (in the Office of Management and Budget)
OFR On Frequency Repeater
Open File Report
OFRT Office Francaise de Radio-Television (France)
OFT Office of Fair Trading
Orbital Flight Test
OFTEL Office of Telecommunications
OGC Office of General Counsel (of EPA (USA))
OGCA Ohio Gun Collectors Association (USA)
OGD Open Government Document
OGDB Oesterreichische Gesellschaft fur Dokumentation und Bibliographie (Austria) (Austrian Association for Documentation and Bibliography)
OGDC Oil and Gas Development Corporation (Pakistan) (government owned)
OGE Optogalvanic Effect
Out of Ground Effect
OGFT Osterreichische Gesellschaft fur Weltraumforschung und Flugkorpertechnik (Austria) (Austrian Society for Space Exploration and Rocket Technology)
OGI Österreichische Gesellschaft für Informatik (Austria) (Austrian Society for Information Processing)
OGO Orbiting Geophysical Observatory
OGRC Office of Grants and Research Contracts (of NASA)
OGRE Optical Grating Reflectance Evaluator
OGRR Oesterreichische Gesellschaft fur Raumforschung und Raumplanung (Austria) (Austrian Association for Physical Planning and Physical Planning Research)
OGTT Oral Glucose Tolerance Test
OGV Outlet Guide Vane
OH Observation Helicopter
prefix to numbered series of publications issued by NIOSH (HEW (USA))
OHDMS Operational Hydromet Data Management System
OHE Office of Health Economics
OHER Office of Health and Environmental Research (of DOE (USA))
OHES Office of Health and Environmental Science (of TVA (USA))
OHM prefix to dated/numbered series on Oil and Hazardous Material issued by Water Programs Office (of EPA (USA))
OHM-TADS Oil and Hazardous Materials–Technical Assistance Data System
OHMES Occupational Health Monitoring and Evaluation System
OHMSETT Oil and Hazardous Materials Systems Environmental Test Tank (of EPA (USA))
OHP Overhead Projector
Oxygen at High Pressure
OHPC Oklahoma Health Planning Commission (USA)
OHR Over-the-Horizon Radar
OHSGT Office of High Speed Ground Transportation (of Department of Transportation (USA))
OHSPAC Occupational Health/Safety Programs Accreditation Commission (USA)
OHT Overheating Temperature
OHW Oxy-Hydrogen Welding
OIA Oceanic Industries Association (USA)
Oil Import Administration (USA)
OIAB Oil Import Appeals Board (USA)
OIAG Oesterreichische Industrieverwaltungs Aktiengesellschaft (Austria) (Austrian Agency for the Reorganization of State Enterprises)
OIBF Oesterreichische Institut fur Bibliotheksforschung, Dokumentations-und Informationswesen (Austria) (Austrian Institute for Library Research, Documentation, and Information Science)
OICA Ontario Institute of Chartered Accountants (Canada)
OIDB Oil Industry Development Board (India)
OIG Office of the Inspector General (of USDA)
OII Office of Invention and Innovation (NBS (USA)) (disbanded 1975)
OIL Oil India Limited (India) (govt owned)
Orbiting International Laboratory
OIM Office of International Marketing (of Dept of Commerce (USA))
OIML Organisation Internationale de Metrologie Legale (France) (International Organisation of Legal Metrology)
OIP Societe Belge d'Optique et d'Instruments de Precision (Belgium) (Belgian Society of Optics and Precision Instruments)
OIPEEC Organisation Internationale pour l'Etude de l'Endurance des Cables (International Organisation for the study of the Endurance of Wire Ropes)
OIRA Office of Information and Regulatory Affairs (USA)
OIRT Organisation Internationale de Radiodiffusion et de Television (International Radio and Television Organisation)
OIS Office of International Science (of AAAS (USA))
OISA Office of International Scientific Affairs (US Dept of State)
OISE Ontario Institute for Studies in Education (Canada)
OISPD Office of Informative Systems Planning and Development (USN)
OIT Office of Software Development and Information Technology (USA)

	Organization Iberoamericaine de Television (Television Organization of Countries speaking Spanish or Portuguese)
OITAF	Organizzazione Internazionale Transporti A Fune (Italy) (International Association for Transport by Rope)
OITDA	Optoelectronic Industry and Technology Development Association (Japan)
OIV	Office International de la Vigne et du Vin (France) (Vine and Wine International Office)
OIW	Oceanographic Institute of Washington (USA)
OIWP	Oil Industry Working Party (of IEA (OECD))
OIYaI	Ob'yedinennyy Institut Yadernykh Issledodovaniy (USSR) (Joint (ie including other nations) Institute for Nuclear Research)
OJCS	Office of the Joint Chiefs of Staff (USDoD)
OJE	On-the-Job Education
	On-the-Job Experience
	Orthodox Job Enrichment
OJRL	Optoelectronics Joint Research Laboratory (Japan)
OJT	On the Job Training
OK	Optical Klystron
OKAB	Oskarshamnsverkets Kraftgrupp (Sweden)
OKhN	Otdelenie Khimischeskikh Nauk (Department of Chemical Sciences (of the Academy of Sciences) (USSR))
OKI	Oesterreichische Kunstoff Institut (Austria) (Austrian Plastics Institute)
	Oesterreichisches Kunstoffinstitut (Austria) (Austrian Plastics Institute)
	Organo Kemijska Industrija (Yugoslavia)
OKSU-RF	Oklahoma State University–Research Foundation (USA)
OKT	Orszagos Konytarugyi Tanacsrol (Hungary) (Hungarian Council of Libraries)
OKW	Oesterreichische Kuratorium fur Wirtschaftlichheit (Austria) (Austrian Management Board)
OL	Original Learning
OL/PBAR	On-Line Patient Billing and Accounts Receivable System
OLA	Ohio Library Association (USA)
	Ontario Library Association (Canada)
	Optical Link in the Atmosphere
OLAC	On-Line Accelerated Cooling
OLAF	Operand (Data Processing) Lattice File
OLCA	On-Line Circuit Analysis
OLCC	Optimum Life Cycle Costing
OLD	Open Loop Damping
OLDAP	On-Line Data Processor
OLEP	Osculating Lunar Elements Programme
OLERT	On-Line Executive for Real-Time
OLF	On-Line Filing
OLFO	Open-Loop Feedback Optimal
OLI	Open Learning Institute (British Columbia, Canada)
OLIVER	On-Line Instrumentation Via Energetic Radioisotopes
OLK	Osterreichische Lufstreitkrafte (Austria) (Austrian Military Airforce)
OLLT	Office of Libraries and Learning Technologies (of OERI (USA))
OLMR	Office of Labor-Management Relations (of USCSC)
	Organic Liquid Moderated Reactor
OLO	Orbital Launch Operations
OLPARS	On-Line Pattern Analysis and Recognition Speech
	On-Line Pattern Analysis and Recognition System
OLPC	Ontario Provincial Library Council (Canada)
OLRT	On-Line Real-Time
OLS	Ordinary Least Squares
OLSASS	On-Line System Availability and Service Simulation
OLTA	Ontario Library Trustees Association (Canada)
OLTE	On-Line Test Executive Programme
OLTP	On-Line Transaction Processing
OLTT	On-Line Teller Terminal
OMA	Optical Multi-channel Analyzer
	Overall Manufacturers Association of Great Britain
	Overseas Mining Association
OMAC	Occupational Medical Association of Connecticut (USA)
	On-line Manufacturing Control
OMACS	On-line Manufacturing and Control System
OMAS	One-Man Atmospheric Submersible
OMAT	Ocean Measurements and Array Technology
OMB	Office of Management and Budget (USA)
OMBE	Office of Minority Business Enterprise (Dept. of Commerce (USA))
OMC	Office Mechanization Centre (Israel)
	Office of Munitions Control (of State Department (USA))
	Officina Macchine per Calzetteria (Italy)
OMCB	Ocean Materials Criteria Branch (of Naval Research Laboratory (USN))
OME	Office of Manpower Economics
	Office of Minerals Exploration (USA)
OMEF	Office Machines and Equipment Federation
OMEGA	Off-road Mobility Evaluation and Generalised Analysis
OMERA	Societe d'Optique, de Mecanique, d'Electricite et de Radio, Argenteuil (France)
OMEW	Office of Missile Electronic Warfare (of ERADCOM (US Army))
OMF	Optical Matched Filter
OMFIC	Optical Matched Filter Image Correlator
OMFS	Optimum Metric Fastener System (of Industrial Fasteners Institute and ANSI (USA))
OMGE	Organisation Mondiale de Gastro-Enterologie (World Organisation of Gastroenterology)
OMI	Ottico Meccanica Italiana (Italy)
OMIT	Orinthine-decarboxylase, Motility, Indole, Tryptophandeaminase
OMKDK	Orszagogs Muszaki Konyvtar es Dokumentacios Kozpont (Hungary) (Central Technical Library and Documentation Centre)
OMLRS	Operations, Maintenance and Logistics Resources Simulation
OMO	Office of Marine Operations (of NOS (NOAA) (USA))
	Offshore Mining Organisation (Thailand) (govt owned)
OMP	Office of Metric Programs (of DOC (USA))
	Organisation and Monitor Programme
	Organometallic Polymers
OMPB	Department of Oriental Manuscripts and Printed Books (of BLRD)
OMPRA	One-Man Propulsion Research Apparatus
OMR	Optical Mark Reader
	Optical Mark Recognition
OMRS	On-site Management Records System (of CERL (US Army))
OMRV	Operational Manoeuvring Re-entry Vehicle
OMS	Office of Oceanography and Marine Sciences (of NOS (NOAA) (USA))
	Orbital Manoeuvring System
	Ovonic Memory Switch
	The Organisation and Methods Society (merged with the Institute of Work Study Practitioners in 1975 to form the Institute of Practitioners in Work Study, Organisation and Methods)

OMSC Office of the Manpower Services Commission
OMSF Office of Manned Space Flight (of NASA)
OMSz Orszagos Mentoszolgalat (Hungary) (country air ambulance service)
OMT Office of Manufacturing Technology (of DARCOM (US Army))
Orthomode Transducer
OMTC Organisation and Methods Training Council (now the Management Systems Training Council)
OMTS Organizational Maintenance Test Station
OMV Orbital Manoeuvring Vehicle
ON Octane Number
Omega Navigation
ONA Oesterreichisher Normenausschuss (Austria) (Austrian Standards Organisation)
Ortho-Nitraniline
ONAC Office of Noise Abatement and Control (of Environmental Protection Agency (USA))
ONAREP Office National de Recherches et d'Exploitation Petroliers (Morocco) (National Office for Petroleum Exploration and Mining)
ONC Operational Navigation Chart (of ACIC)
ONCB Ortho-Nitrochlorobenzene
ONCF Office National des Chemins de Fer (Morocco) (National Office of Railways)
ONERA Office National d'Etudes et de Recherches Aerospatiales (France) (National Office for Aerospace Studies and Research)
ONGC Oil and Natural Gas Commission (India)
ONISEP Office National d'Information sur les Enseignments et les Professions (France)
ONLAS Optical Night Landing Approach System
ONORM prefix to Standards issued by ONA
ONP Oficina Nacional de Pesca (Venezuela) (National Fisheries Office)
ONR Office of Naval Research (USN)
ONRAP Oficina Nacional de Racionalizacion y Capacitacion de la Administracion Publica (Peru)
ONRFE Office of Naval Research, Far East (USN)
ONRI Okazuki National Research Institutes (Japan)
ONRL Office of Naval Research, London (England) (USN)
ONRS Organisme National de la Recherche Scientifique (Algeria) (National Organization for Scientific Research)
ONS Offshore North Sea Technology Conference
Omega Navigation System
ONSER Organisme National de Securite Routiere (France) (National Road Safety Organisation)
ONTAP Online Training And Practice
ONTC Ontario Northland Transportation Commission (Canada) (a Crown agency)
ONULP Ontario New Universities Libraries Project
ONVL Over-the-Nose Vision Line
ONWARD Organization of North Western Authorities Rationalized Design
ONWI Office of Nuclear Waste Isolation (of DOE (USA))
OOE Out-Of-Ecliptic
OOG Office of Oil and Gas (Department of the Interior (USA))
OOKDK Orszagos Orvostudomanyi Konyvtar es Dokumentacios (Hungary) (National Medical Library and Centre for Documentation)
OOLHMD Optimized Optical Link Helmet-Mounted Display
OOM Original On-line Module
OOP Off-line Orthophoto Printer
OOPS On-line Object Patching System
OOS Office of Opportunities in Science (of AAAS (USA))
Orbit-to-Orbit Shuttle
OP Occasional Paper
Office of Preparedness (General Services Administration (USA))
OPA Optoelectronic Pulse Amplifier
OPAC On-line Public Access Catalogue
OPADEC Optical Particle Decoy
OPAK Octal Package
OPAL Operational Performance Analysis Language
OPASTCO Organization for the Protection and Advancement of Small Telephone Companies (USA)
OPAT Occupant Protection Assessment-Test
OPB Occupational Pensions Board
Overseas Projects Board (of BOTB)
OPC Oil Prices Committee (India)
Optical Particle Counter
Optimization-Prediction System
Ordinary Portland Cement
Organic Photoconductor
OPC/MCA Optical Particle Counter/Multi-Channel Analyzer
OPCC Oil and Petrochemical Contractors Committee (of CBMPE)
OPCS Office of Population Censuses and Surveys
OPD Optical Path Difference
Optical Phase Distortion
OPDAC Optical Data Converter
OPDAR Optical Detection And Ranging
Optical Direction And Ranging
OPE Office of Planning and Evaluation (of Food and Drug Administration (USA))
One-Particle-Exchange
Oxidation Pond Effluents
OPEC Organisation of Petroleum Exporting Countries
OPEN Origin of Plasmas in Earth's Neighbourhood
OPEP Orbital Plane Experimental Package
OPERUN Operation Planning and Execution system for Railway Unified Network
OPEVAL Operational Evaluation
OPEX Operational and Executive
Operational Experience
OPG Overseas Projects Group (of BOTB) (changed to OPB in 1977)
OPI Office of Public Information (of SBA, USA)
OPIC Overseas Private Investment Corporation (a Federal Agency in the USA)
OPIEM Optics, Photonics and Iconics Engineering Meeting
OPINS OAKLAND (California (USA)) Planning Information System
OPINT Optical Intelligence
Options Screening and Intelligence Assessment
OPK Optokinetic
OPLAC Ontario Public Libraries Advisory Committee (Canada)
OPLE Omega Position Location Experiment
OPM Optically Projected Map
OPMAC Operations for Military Assistance to the Community
OPMC One Player Median Competitive
OPNT Office des Ports Nationaux Tunisiens (Tunisia) (National Harbours Board)
OPO Optical Parametric Oscillator
OPOL Offshore Pollution Liability Agreement
OPOMP Overall Planning and Optimization and Machining Processes
OPOS Optical Properties of Orbiting Satellites
OPP Office of Pesticide Programs (of EPA (USA))
Orientated Poly-Propylene
Oxidative Pentose Phosphate
OPPI Organisation of Pharmaceutical Producers of India (India)

OPPOSIT — Optimisation of a Production Process by an Ordered Simulation and Iteration Technique
OPR — Optical Page Reading
OPRAD — Operations Research and Development Management
OPS — Office of Pipeline Safety (USA)
Omnidirectional Point Source
On-line Process Synthesizer
Optical Power Spectrum
OPSA — Optimal Pneumatic Systems Analysis
OPSAM — Optical Storage Access Method
OPSET — Optional Set of Parameters
OPSPA — Oleandomycin-Polymyxin-Sulphadiazine-Perfringens Agar
OPT — Optimized Production Technology
OPTA — Offshore Petroleum Training Association
Optimal Performance Theoretically Attainable
OPTACON — Optical to Tactile Converter (an electronic/photographic reading aid for the blind)
OPTAG — Optical Aimpoint Guidance
OPTEVFOR — Operational Test and Evaluation Force (USN)
OPTF — Operations Planning Task Force (of ASIS (USA))
OPTIMA — Organisation for the Phyto-Taxonomic Investigation of the Mediterranean Area (Germany)
OPTIMED — Conference on Optical Metrology Applied to Medicine and Biology
OPTNET — Optimum Private Trunk Network Embodying Tandems
OPTOL — Optimized Test Oriented Language
OPTRAK — Optical Tracking and Ranging Kit
OPTS — On-line Peripheral Test System
OPUS — (THE) OPEN UNIVERSITY System
An Organisation for Promoting the Understanding of Society (formed in 1975 by The Tavistock Institute of Human Relations and The Industrial Society)
OPV — Optical Path-length Variation
Oral Poliomyelitis Vaccine
OPW — Office of Public Works (Eire)
Orthogonalized Plane Wave
OPZ — Oesterreichisches Produktivitats Zentrum (Austria) (Austrian Productivity Centre)
OQA — Optical Quantum Amplifier
OQL — On-Line Query Language
OR — Operational OR Operations Research
Operational Requirement
Orientating Response
prefix to numbered/dated reports issued by the Operational Research Department of BISRA
OR/HF — prefix to numbered/dated series of reports issued by BISRA
OR/MS — Operational Research and Management Science
ORA — Office of Research Analyses (of OAR (USAF))
Organizational Role Analysis
ORACLE — On-line Retrieval of Acquisitions, Cataloguing and Circulation details for Library Enquiries (of State Library of Queensland (Australia))
Operational Research And Critical Link Evaluation
Operations Research And Critical Link Evaluator
Optical Reception of Announcements by Coded Line Electronics
Optimized Reliability And Component Life Estimator
Optimum Record Automation for Court and Law Enforcement (Los Angeles County (USA))
Oversight of Resources and Capability for Logistics Effectiveness
ORAE — Operational Research and Analysis Establishment (of Dept of National Defence (Canada))
ORASA — Operational Research And Systems Analysis
ORAU — Oak Ridge Associated Universities (USA)
ORB — Oceanographic Research Buoy
ORBE — Open Reciprocating Brayton Engine
ORBIS — Orbiting Radio Beacon Ionospheric Satellite
ORBIS CAL — Orbiting Radio Beacon Ionosphere Satellite for Calibration
ORBIT — On-Line Reduced Bandwidth Information Transfer
On-line Retrieval of Bibliographic Information
Order Billing Inventory Technique
ORC — Operations Research Center (University of California, USA)
Optimal Replacement Chart
Organic Rankine Cycle
ORCA — Ocean Resources Conservation Association
Organisme Europeen de Recherches sur la Carie (European Organisation for Caries Research)
ORCHIS — OAK RIDGE (NATIONAL LABORATORY (USAEC)) (now of ERDA)Computerized Hierarchical Information System
ORCID — Optical Read-out Cherenkov Imaging Detector
ORCO — Organisation Committee (of ISO)
ORCS — Organic Rankine-Cycle System
ORD — Once-Run Distillate
Operational Research Division (of DRB (Canada))
Optical Rotary Dispersion
ORDEAL — OAK RIDGE (NATIONAL LABORATORY (USAEC)) (now of ERDA) Data Evaluation and Analysis Language
Orbital Rate Drive Electronics for APOLLO
ORDINEX — International Organization of Experts
ORDL — Ohio River Division Laboratory (US Army)
ORE — Occupational Radiation Exposure
Office de Recherches et d'Essais (of UIC) (Office of Research and Testing)
Operational Readiness Evaluation
Operational Research Establishment (of DRB, Canada) (now Defence Operational Research Establishment)
Operational Research Executive (of the National Coal Board)
Optimum Resource Extraction
ORELA — OAK RIDGE (NATIONAL LABORATORY (USAEC)) (now of ERDA) Electron Linear Accelerator
OREPS — Operational Research in Electrical Power Systems
ORES — Observation Residuals
Office of Research and Engineering Services (Kentucky University (USA)
ORF — Oesterreichischer Rundfunk (Austria) (Austrian Broadcasting Corporation)
Ontario Research Foundation (Canada)
ORG — Operational OR Operations Research Group
ORGALIME — Organisme de Liaison des Industries Metalliques Europeenes (European Association for Co-operation of the Metal Industry)
ORGDP — OAK RIDGE Gaseous Diffusion Plant (NATIONAL LABORATORY (USAEC) (now of ERDA) Gaseous Diffusion Plant
ORGS — Operational Research Group of Scotland
ORI — Occurrence of Reinforcing Information
Ocean Research Institute (Japan)
Octane Requirement Increase
ORIC — OAK RIDGE (NATIONAL LABORATORY (USAEC)) Isochronous Cyclotron
OAK RIDGE (NATIONAL LABORATORY) (ERDA (USA)) Isochronous Cyclotron
ORION — On-line Retrieval of Information Over a Network
ORL — Orbital Research Laboratory
Ordnance Research Laboratory
ORLA — Optimum Repair Level Analysis
ORM — Optimal Replacement Method
ORMAK — OAK RIDGE (NATIONAL LABORATORY) (ERDA (USA)) Tokamak

ORNL Oak Ridge (National Laboratory) (now of DOE (USA)) (name changed to Holifield National Laboratory in 1974 and back again to Oak Ridge National Laboratory in 1976)
ORO Office for Regional Operations (Bureau of Radiological Health (USA))
Operations Research Office (of Johns Hopkins University, USA)
OROS Optical Read-Only Storage
OROSS Operational Readiness Oriented Supply System (US Army)
ORP Office of Radiation Programs (of EPA (USA))
Oxidation-Reduction Potential
ORP/CSD prefix to dated-numbered series of technical notes issued by Radiation Programs Office, Division of Criteria and Standards (of EPA (USA))
ORP/SIP prefix to dated-numbered series of reports issued by ORP (of EPA (USA))
ORR Oak Ridge (National Laboratory (USAEC)) (now of ERDA) Reactor
ORRTA Office of the Registrar of Restrictive Trading Agreements
ORS Oil-Recovery System
Operational Research Society
ORSA Operations Research Society of America (USA)
Operations Research Systems Analysis
ORSANCO Ohio River Valley Water Sanitation Commission (USA)
ORSI Operations Research Society of India (India)
ORSIS Operations Research Society of Israel (Israel)
ORSJ Operations Research Society of Japan (Japan)
ORSocy Operational Research Society
ORSTOM Office de la Recherche Scientifique et Technique Outre-Mer (France) (Office of Overseas Scientific and Technical Research)
ORT Odour Recognition Threshold
Overland Radar Technology
ORTAG Operations Research Technical Assistance Group (US Army)
ORTEP Organotin Environmental Programme (Association)
ORTF Organisation Radio Télévision Française (France) (disbanded 1974)
ORTS Operational Readiness Test System
ORU Oral Roberts University (USA)
ORV Off-Road Vehicle
ORVID On-line X-ray Evaluation over Video-Display including Documentation
OS Operating System
Orthogonal System
OS/MVT Operating System, Allowing Multiprogramming with a Variable number of Tasks
OSA Offshore Supply Association
Optical Society of America (USA)
Overseas Sterling Area
OSAB Overseas Students Advisory Bureau (disbanded 1978)
OSAHRC Occupational Safety and Health Review Commission (USA)
SEE OSHRC
OSAIS Oil Spillage Analytical and Identification Service (of the Laboratory of the Government Chemist)
OSAS Offshore Advisory Service (of THE (of BSI))
OSAT Optical Sensor And Tracker
OSC Okanagan Study Committee (of CBCC (Canada))
Optimum Start Control
OSCAA Oil Spill Control Association of America (USA)
OSCAR On-line System for Controlling Activities and Resources
Optimum Systems Covariance Analysis Results
Orbiting Satellite Carrying Amateur Radio
Organisaton for Sickle Cell Anaemia Research
Oscillogram Scan And Recorder system
OSCAS Office of Statistical Co-ordination and Standards (Philippines)
OSCER Offshore Survival Craft Emergency Radiotelephone
OSCO Oil Service Company of Iran (Iran) (a multinational consortium)
OSCOM Oslo Commission (Norway)
OSCP Ocean Sediment Coring Program (of NSF (USA))
OSD Ocean Sciences Division (of NRL (USN))
Office of the Secretary of Defense (USA)
Operational Sequence Diagram
OSDOC Offshore Discharge of Container Ships
Over-the-Shore Discharge of Container Ships (a project of the US Army)
OSDPT Optimization of Systems for Data Processing and Transmission
OSE Office of Science Education (of AAAS (USA))
Operational Support Equipment
OSEAP Organisation for Scientific Evaluation of Aerial Phenomena
OSEAS Ocean Sampling and Environmental Analysis System
OSEB Orissa State Electricity Board (India)
OSEE Optically Stimulated Exoelectron Emission
OSEM Office of Systems Engineering and Management (of FAA (USA))
OSF Oxidation-induced Stacking Fault
OSFLAG Offshore Structures Fluid Loading Advisory Group (of the National Physical Laboratory)
OSGK Österreichische Studiengesellschaft für Kibernetik (Austria) (Austrian Society for Cybernetic Studies)
OSGR Oscillator Single Gain Region
OSHA Occupational Safety and Health Administration (of Dept. of Labor (USA))
OSHCO Olayan Saudi Holding Company (Saudi Arabia)
OSHRC Occupational Safety and Health Review Commission (USA)
OSI Open Systems Inter-connection
Open Systems Interconnection
Optimum Scale Integration
OSIC Optimization of Subcarrier Information Capacity
OSIRIS On-line Search Information Retrieval Information Storage
OSIS Ocean Surveillance Information System
Office of Science Information Service (of National Science Foundation, USA)
OSM Omni Spectra Miniature
OSMM Office of Safeguards and Materials Management (USAEC) (now of ERDA)
OSMVT Operating System with the option of Multiprogramming with a Variable number of Tasks
OSNC Optical Society of Northern California (USA)
OSO Offshore Supplies Office (of the Department of Energy)
Orbital Solar Observatory
Orbiting Satellite Observer
OSP Oceanographic Survey Recorder
Office of Standards Policy (of Department of Commerce (USA))
Optimum Sustainable Population
OSPE Ohio Society of Professional Engineers (USA)
OSPRDS Oblate Spheroids
OSR Office of Scientific Research (USAF)
Optical Scanner Reader
Optical Surface Reflection
prefix to numbered series of pamphlets relative to the Offices, Shops and Railway Premises Act issued by the Ministry of Labour and published by HMSO
OSRA Offices, Shops and Railway Premises Act of 1963

OSRD — Office of Standard Reference Data (of NBS)

OSRL — Organizations and Systems Research Laboratory (of ARI (US Army))

OSRPA — Offices, Shops and Railway Premises Act of 1963

OSS — Operations Support System
Orbiting Space Station

OSSA — Office of Space Science and Applications (of NASA)

OSSL — Operating System Simulation Language

OSSM — Optimum Shipboard Spares Model

OST — Objectives, Strategies, and Tactics
Office of Science and Technology (of PSAC (USA)) (disbanded 1973)
Office of the Secretary of Transportation (USA)

OSTAC — Ocean Science and Technology Advisory Committee (of NASIA)

OSTD — Office of Supersonic Transport Development (Dept. of Transportation (USA))

OSTI — Office of Scientific and Technical Information (of DES)
Office of Scientific and Technical Information (of DES) (became Research and Development Department of the British Library in 1974)
Office of Scientific and Technical Information (of DOE (USA))
Organization for Social and Technological Innovation (USA)

OSTIV — Organisation Scientifique et Technique International du Vol a Voile (International Scientific and Technical Organisation for Gliders and Sailplanes)

OSTP — Office of Science and Technology Policy (of the President's Executive Office (USA))

OSTS — Office of State Technical Service (of Dept of Commerce, USA)

OSU — Ohio State University (USA)
Oklahoma State University (USA)

OSU-CISRC — Ohio State University Computer and Information Science Research Center (USA)

OSUK — Opthalmological Societies of the United Kingdom

OSURF — Ohio State University Research Foundation (USA)

OSV — Ocean Station Vessel
Offshore Supply Vessel

OSW — Office of Saline Water (Dept of the Interior (USA)) (now part of the Office of Water Research and Technology)

OT — Office of Telecommunications (Dept. of Commerce (USA))
Ortho Tolidine

OT&E — Operational Test and Evaluation

OT/ITSRR — Office of Telecommunications Institute for Telecommunications Sciences Research Report (USA))

OTA — Office of Technology Assessment (of Congress (USA))
Operational Transconductance Amplifier
Organisation Mondiale du Tourism et de l'Automobile (United Kingdom) (World Touring and Automobile Organisation)

OTAF — Office of Technology Assessment and Forecast (USA)

OTAR — Overseas Tariffs and Regulations (a section of the Dept of Trade)

OTC — Office of Technical Cooperation (of UN)
Offshore Technology Conference
One-stop inclusive Tour Charter
One-Time Carbon paper
Over-the-Counter (licensed dealers in securities)

OTC(A) — Overseas Telecommunications Commission (Australia)

OTCA — Overseas Technical Co-operation Agency (Japan) (a semi-governmental organization)

OTD — Ocean Technology Division (of Naval Research Laboratory (USN))
Optimal Terminal Descent

OTDA — Office of Tracking and Data Acquisition (of NASA (USA))

OTDR — Optical Time-Domain Reflectometer

OTE — Officine Toscane Elettromeccaniche (Italy)

OTEA — Operational Test and Evaluation Agency (US Army)

OTEC — Ocean Thermal Energy Conversion

OTES — Optical Technology Experiment Study

OTF — Optical Transfer Function

OTGHPP — Ocean Thermal Gradient Hydraulic Power Plant

OTH — Over The Horizon

OTH-B — Over The Horizon Back-scatter

OTH-DC & T — Over-The-Horizon, Detection, Classification and Targeting

OTH-F — Over The Horizon Forward-scatter

OTH-T — Over-the-Horizon Targeting

OTHB — Over-The-Horizon Backscatter

OTI — Office of Technology Impacts (of DOE (USA))
Organizacion de la Television Iberoamericana (Spanish America Television Organisation)

OTIS — Observer's Thermal Imaging System
Occupational Training Information System
Offset Target Indicator System
Operation, Transport, Inspection, Storage
Overseas Technical Information Service (DTI & PERA)

OTIU — Overseas Technical Information Unit (of DTI)

OTJ — On The Job Training

OTM — Office of Telecommunications Management (USA) (now Office of Telecommunications Policy)
Organo-Transition-Metal

OTP — Office of Telecommunications Policy (USA) (now NTIA)
Overhead Trickle Purification

OTPI — On Top Position Indicator

OTRAG — Orbital Transport-und Raketen AG (Germany)

OTS — Office of Technical Services (later CFSTI, USA)
Office of Toxic Substances (of EPA (USA))
Orbital Technical Satellite
Orbital Test Satellite
Orthotoluenesulphonamide
Ovonic Threshold Switch

OTS/ECS — Orbital Test Satellite/European Communications Satellite

OTSA — Oregon Television Service Association (USA)

OTSG — Once-Through Steam Generator

OTSR — Optimum Track Ship Routing

OTT — Ocean Tactical Targeting

OTTLE — Optically Transparent Thin Layer Electrode

OTTO — Once Through Then Out
Optical-to-Optical interface device

OTTS — Organisation of Teachers of Transport Studies

OTTW — Optical Telescope Technology Workshop (conference organised by NASA (USA))

OTU — Office of Technological Utilization (of NASA)
Operational Taxonomic Unit

OTUA — Office Technique pour l'Utilisation de l'Acier (France) (Technical Office for Steel Utilisation)

OTV — Orbital Transfer Vehicle

OTW — Over-the-Wing externally-blown jet flap

OU — The Open University

OUEL — Oxford University Engineering Laboratory

OULCS — Ontario Universities Library Cooperative System (Canada)

OULS — Ontario (Canada) Universities Libraries Cooperative System

OURI — Oklahoma University Research Institute (USA)

OURS Oxford University Radio Society
OV Observed Velocity
Orbiting Vehicle
OVA Organic Vapour Analyser
OVAC Organisation Value Analysis Chart
OVE Österreichischer Verband für Elektrotechnik (Austria) (Austrian Society for Electrotechnology)
OVER Optimum Vehicle for Effective Reconnaissance
OVF Over-Voltage Factor
OVH Orszagos Vizugyi Hivatal (Hungary) (State Water Board)
OVRO Owens Valley Radio Observatory (USA)
OVS On-line Version Storage
OVSR Office of Vehicle Systems Research (of NBS (USA)) (now of Department of Transportation)
OVTR Operational Video Tape Recorder
OVV Optically Violently Variable
OWAS OVAKO OY (Finland) Working Posture Analysis System
OWI Office of Waste Isolation (of ORNL (USA))
OWM Office of Weights and Measures (of NBS)
Office Work Measurement
OWP Office of Water Programs (of EPA (USA))
OWPCB Ohio Water Pollution Control Board (USA)
OWPR Ocean Wave Profile Recorder
OWRB Oklahoma Water Resources Board (USA)
OWRC Ontario Water Resources Commission (Canada)
OWRR Office of Water Resources Research (now OWRT (Dept of the Interior (USA))
Office of Water Resources Research (of the Dept of the Interior, USA)
OWRT Office of Water Research and Technology (Dept of the Interior (USA))
Office of Water Resources Technology (USA)
OWS Ocean Weather Ship
Ocean Weather Station
Oil Water Separator
Orbital Workshop
OXIM Oxide-Isolated Monolith
Oxide-Isolated Monolithic technology
OZEPA Austrian Association of Pulp and Paper Chemists and Technicians (Austria)
OZRF Opposed Zone Reheating Furnace

P

P Pamphlet
Plasma
prefix to numbered series on Production issued by BOT until mid-1970 and then by DTI
P&A Price and Availability
P&EE Proving and Experimental Establishment (MOD)
P&R Planning and Review
P-CM Protein-Calorie Malnutrition
P-DTE Packet-mode Data Terminal Equipment
P-FMA Proto-Flight Manipulator Arm
P-VO Protivo-vozdushnaya Oborona (Strany) (USSR) (ANTI-AIRCRAFT Defence (Force) of the Homeland)
P/E Price Earnings Ratio
P/F Powder Forging
P/M Powder Metallurgy
P4SR Predicted Four Hour Sweat Rate
PA Paired Associates
Peroxide-Alkaline
Phthalic Anhydride
Picatinny Arsenal (US Army)
Plasma Aldosterone
Polyamide
Polyarylate
Prealbumin
prefix to numbered series of Business Monitors issued by the Business Statistics Office of the Department of Industry and published by HMSO
Presidents Association (managed in Europe by Management Centre Europe)
Pressure Anomaly
Product Analysis
Programmable Automation
Public Address
Publishers Association
PAA Peracetic Acid
Pharmaceutical Association of Australia (Australia)
Plasma Amino Acid
Polyarcrylic Acid
Population Association of America (USA)
Print Advertising Association (USA)
PAAB Public Accountants and Auditors Board (South Africa)
PABA Paraaminobenzoic Acid
PABD Precise Access Block Diagram
PABLA Problem Analysis By Logical Approach
PABLOS Programme to Analyse the Block System
PABST Primary Adhesively Bonded Structures Technology
PABX Private Automatic Branch Exchange
PAC Packaging Association of Canada (Canada)
Performance Analysis and Control
Peripheral Autonomous Control
Personal Analogue Computer
Perturbation Angular Correlation
Pesticide Analysis Advisory Committee
Planned Availability Concept
Plasma Arc Cutting
Polyacetylene
Polyalphaolefins
Powder Air Conveyor
Private Aviation Committee (of CAA)
Productivity Advisory Council (South Africa)
Project Analysis and Control
Public Accounts Committee (of Parliament, India)
Public Accounts Committee (of the House of Commons)
Public Administration Committee of the Joint University Council for Social and Public Administration
PAC-FACS Programmed Appropriation Commitments–Fixed Asset Control System
PACAF Pacific Air Force (USAF)
PACBIR Pacific Coast Board of Intergovernmental Relations (USA)
PACCIOS Pan-American Committee of the Conseil International de l'Organisation Scientifique (Pan-American Committee of the International Council for Scientific Management)
PACCS-ADA Post Attack Command Control System–Airborne Data Automation (USAF)
PACCT Programme and Evaluation Review Technique (PERT) and Cost Correlation Technique
PACE Package for Architectural Computer Evaluation
Planning And Control made Easy
Processing And Control Element
Product Assurance Confidence Evaluator
Programmed Automatic Customer Engineer
Projects to Advance Creativity in Education
PACED Programme for Advanced Concepts in Electronic Design
PACER Portable Aircraft Condition Evaluation Recorder
Process Assembly Case Evaluator Routine

	Programme Assisted Console Evaluation and Review
PACES	Political Action Committee for Engineers and Scientists (USA)
PACMS	Psycho-Acoustical Measuring System
PACOS	Package Operating System
PACRAD	Practical Absolute Cavity Radiometer
PACS	Pacific Area Communications System
	Pitch Augmentation Control System
PACSAT	Passive Communications Satellite
PACT	Paved Concrete Trackbed
	Phased Control Techniques
	PLESSEY Automated COBOL Testing package
	Production Analysis Control Technique
	Programmable Asynchrous Clustered Teleprocessing
	Programmable Automatic Continuity Tester
	Programmed Analysis Computer Transfer
PACTEC	Pacific Technical Conference and Technical Displays
PACTS	Parliamentary Advisory Council for Transport Safety
	Programmer Aptitude/Competence Test System
PACV	Patrol OR Personnel Air Cushion Vehicle
PACVD	Plasma Assisted Chemical Vapour Deposition
PAD	Packet Assembler/Disassembler
	Pad Assembly/Disassembly
	Post Activation Diffusion
	Pressure Anomaly Difference
	Primary Afferent Depolarization
	Program Analysis Division (of GAO (USA))
	Programmable Algorithm for Drafting
	Propellant Actuated Device
PADAT	PSYCHOLOGICAL ABSTRACTS Direct Access Terminal (service provided by American Psychological Association (USA))
PADDS	PERA Automatic Detail Drawing System
PADE	Pad Automatic Data Equipment
PADEL	Pattern Description Language
PADLOC	Passive Active Detection and Location
PADRE	Patient Automatic Data Recording Equipment
PADS	Parametric Array Doppler Sonar
	Performance Advisory Display System
	Performance Analysis and Design Synthesis
	Personnel Automated Data System (USN)
	Position and Azimuth Determining System
PADWSS	Pulsed Acoustic Doppler Wind Shear Sensing system
PAE	Photo-Anodic Engraving
	Phthalic Acid Ether
	Polyarylene-ethylene
	Preliminary Airworthiness Evaluation
PAEC	Pakistan Atomic Energy Commission (Pakistan)
	Philippine Atomic Energy Commission (Philippines)
PAECT	Pollution Abatement and Environmental Control Technology
PAEM	Programme Analysis and Evaluation Model
PAET	Planetary Atmosphere Experiments Test
PAF	Pakistan Air Force (Pakistan)
	Partitive Analytical Forecasting
	Platelet-Activating Factor
	Printed And Fired
PAFAM	Performance And Failure Assessment Monitor
PAFEC	Programme for Automatic Finite Element Calculations
PAFIE	Pacific Asian Federation of Industrial Engineering (India) (until 1973)
PAG	Periadueductal Grey
	Protein Advisory Group (of UN)
PAGASA	Philippine Atmospheric, Geophysical and Astronomical Services Administration (Philippines)
PAGB	Proprietary Association of Great Britain
PAGE	Page Generation OR Generator
	Polyacrylamide Gel Electrophoresis
PAGEOS	Passive Geodetic Earth Orbiting Satellite
PAGOS	Programme for the Analysis of General Optical Systems
PAH	Para-aminohippurate
	Polycyclic Aromatic Hydrocarbons
PAHEF	Pan-American Health and Education Foundation
PAHO	Pan-American Health Organization (of OAS)
	Primary Afferent Depolarization
PAHOCENDES	Pan-American Health Organization Center for Development Studies
PAID	Parked Aircraft Intrusion Detector
	Programmers Aid In Debugging
PAID/ESA	Panafrican Institute for Development, East and Southern Africa (Zambia)
PAID/WA	Panafrican Institute for Development, West Africa (Cameroon)
PAIGH	Pan-American Institute of Geography and History (Mexico) (of OAS)
PAILS	Projectile Airburst and Impact Location System
PAIR	Performance And Integration Retrofit
	Precision Approach Interferometer Radar
PAIRS	Private Aircraft Inspection Reporting System
PAIS	Public Affairs Information Service
PAIT	Programme for the Advancement of Industrial Technology (of Department of Industry (Canada))
PAKEX	Packaging Exhibition
PAL	Paired-Associate Learning
	Permanent Artificial Lighting
	Permissive Action Link
	Phase Alternation Line
	Philippine Air Lines (Philippines)
	Precision Artwork Language
	Process Assembler Languages
	Programmable Array Logic
PAL-D	Phase Alternation Line Delay
PALC	Passenger Acceptance and Load Control
PALCON	Pallet Size Container
PALE	Pelvis And Legs Elevating seat
PALINET	Pennsylvania Library Network (USA)
PALMES	Pulsed Appendage Large Mobile Electromagnetic-pulse Simulator
PALMS	Propulsion Alarm and Monitoring System
PALS	Positioning And Locating System
	Precision Approach and Landing System
PAM	Payload Assist Module
	Personnel Availability Model
	Plasma Arc Machining
	Pole Amplitude Modulation
	Pozzolan-Aggregate Mixture
	Precision Angular Mover
	Profit Analysis Model
	Pulse Amplitude Modulation
PAMA	Pan-American Medical Association
	Professional Aviation Maintenance Association (USA)
	Pulse Address Multiple Access
PAMC	Provisional Acceptable Means of Compliance (series issued by ICAO)
PAMD	Parallel Access Multiple Distribution
PAMF	Programmable Analogue Matched Filter
PAMIRASAT	Passive Microwave Radiometer Satellite
	Primary Afferent Depolarization
PAMM	British Ceramic Plant and Machinery Manufacturers Association
	Precision Automatic Measuring Machine
PAMS	Plan Analysis and Modeling System
PAN	Peroxyacetyl Nitrate
	Perozyacyl Nitrates

	Polskiej Akademii Nauk (Poland) (Polish Academy of Sciences)
	Polyacrylonitrile
	Prilled Ammonium Nitrate
PANAFTEL	Pan-African Telecommunication Network
PANCAP	Practical Annual Capacity
PANDA	Performance And Demand Analyser
	Portable Atmospheric Noise Data Acquisition
PANDIT	Produce an Adjusted Nuclear Data Input Tape
PANE	Performance Analysis of Electrical circuits
PANEES	Professional Association of Naval Electronic Engineers and Scientists (USA)
PANFI	Precision Automatic Noise Figure Indicator
PANPA	Pacific Area Newspaper Production Association (Australia)
PANS	Positioning and Navigation System
	Procedures for Air Navigation Services (series issued by ICAO)
PANS-MET	Procedures for Air Navigation Series—Meteorology (series issued by ICAO)
PANSDOC	Pakistan National Scientific and Technical Documentation Centre (Pakistan) (now PASTIC)
PANSIP	Propulsion and Airframe Structural Integration Programme
PANSY	Programme Analysis System
PANTHEON	Public Access by New Technology to Highly Elaborate On-line Networks
PAOO	Philippine Academy of Ophthalmology and Otolaryngology (Philippines)
PAP	Paramagnetic Analysis Programme
	Polyethylene-Aluminium-Polyethylene
	Pulmonary Arterial Pressure
PAPA	Parallax Aircraft Parking Aid
	Probabilistic Automatic Pattern Analyser
	Programmer and Probability Analyzer
PAPE	Phototo-Active Pigment Electrophography
PAPI	Polymethylene Polyphenyl Isocyanate
	Precision Approved Path Indicator
PAPM	Pulse Amplitude and Phase Modulation
PAPS	Performance Analysis and Prediction Study
	Periodic Armaments Planning System (of NATO)
PAPTE	(The) President's Advisory Panel on Timber and the Environment (USA)
PAQ	Position Analysis Questionnaire
PAQR	Polyacene Quinine Radical
PAR	Participation–Achievement–Reward
	Peak Average Rectified
	Peak-to-Average Rating OR Ratio
	Performance and Reliability
	Perimeter Acquisition Radar
	Photosynthetically Active Radiation
	Precision Approach Radar
	Progressive Aircraft Rework
PARADISE	Phased Array Radars And Divers Integrated Semiconductor Elements
PARAMP	Parametric Amplifier
PARAN	Perimeter Array Antenna
PARC	Profile Analysis and Recording Control system
PARCA	Pan-American Railway Congress Association
PARCOR	Partial Correlatives
PARCS	(Car/Automobile) Parking and Revenue Control System
	Pesticide Analysis, Retrieval and Control System (of EPA (USA))
PARD	Parts Application Reliability Data
	Pilot Airborne Recovery Device
	Precision Annotated Retrieval Display
	Project Activities Relationship Diagram
PARDS	Phased Array Radar Detection System
PARET	Programme for the Analysis of Reactor Transients
PARIS	Postal Address Reader Indexer System
PARL	Prince Albert Radar Laboratory (of DRTE)
PARM	Persistent Anti-Radiation Missile
	Post Attack Resource Management
	Precision Anti-Radiation Missile
	Programme Analysis for Resource Management
PAROS	Passive Ranging On Submarines
PARS	Parachute Altitude Recognition System
	Pershing Audio Reproduction System
	Photoacoustic Raman Spectroscopy
	Private Aircraft Reporting System (of FAA (USA))
	Programme for Analysis and Resizing of Structures
	Programmed Airlines Reservation System
PARSAC	Particle Size Analogue Computer
PARSECS	Programme for Astronomical Research and Scientific Experiments Concerning Space (of the Boeing Company (USA))
PART	Production Allocation and Requirements Technique
PARTAN	Parallel Tangents
PARTAN SD	Parallel Tangents and Steepest Descent
PARTES	Piece-wise Application of Radiation through the Electromagnetic-pulse Simulator
PARTIAL	Participation in Architectural Layout
PARTNER	Proof of Analogue Results Through Numerically Equivalent Routine
PARVO	Professional and Academic Regional Visits Organisation
PAS	Para-aminosalicyclic Acid
	Passing Aid System
	Performance Advisory System
	Perigee-Apogee Satellite
	Periodic Acid-Schiff
	Photo-acoustic Spectroscopy
	Pilot Advisory System
	Plastics Advisory Service
	Power Apparatus and Systems
	prefix to numbered:dated series of Public Authority Standards published by BSI
	Propulsion and Auxiliary Systems Division (of DTNSRDC)
PASA	Petroquimica Argentina SA (Argentina)
PASAR	PSYCHOLOGICAL ABSTRACTS Search and Retrieval (of American Psychological Association (USA))
PASC	Pacific Area Standards Congress
PASE	Power Assisted Storage Equipment
PASLIB	Pakistan Association of Special Libraries (Pakistan)
PASMA	Prefabricated Aluminium Scaffold Manufacturers Association
PASNY	Power Authority of the State of New York (USA)
PASP	Price Adjusting Sampling Plan
PASS	Parked Aircraft Security System
	Patrol Advanced Surveillance System
	Pilot Aerial Survival System
	Pooled Analytical Stereoplotter System
	Precision Angulation and Support System
	Predictive Admission Scheduling System (of hospital patients)
	Price Adjusted Single Sampling
	Production Automated Scheduling System
	Programmed Access/Security System
	Project Activating Signal Systems
	Prototype Artillery Sub-system
PASSIM	Presidential Advisory Staff on Scientific Information Management (USA)
PASSION	Programme for Algebraic Sequences, Specifically of Input-Output Nature
PASTIC	Pakistan Scientific and Technological Information Centre (Pakistan)
PASTRAM	Passenger Traffic Management System (DOD (USA))
PAT	Palleted Automated Transport

Parametric Artificial Talker
Phenylazotriphenylmethane
Picric Acid Turbidity
Prediction Analysis Technique
Programmable Automatic Tester
Programme Aptitude Test

PATA Pacific Area Travel Association
Pneumatic All-Terrain Amphibian

PATCA Professional And Technical Consultants Association (USA)

PATELL PSYCHOLOGICAL ABSTRACTS Tape Edition Lease or Licensing (of American Psychological Association (USA))

PATI Passive Airborne Time-difference Intercept

PATRA Packaging and Allied Trades Research Association (now PIRA)

PATRAC Planning And Transportation Research Advisory Council

PATRIC Pattern Recognition and Information Correlation (an information system for analysing crimes in conjunction with a criminal's methods)

PATRICIA Practical Algorithm To Retrieve Information Coded In Alphanumeric

PATROL Programme for Administrative Traffic Reports On-Line

PATS Philippine Aeronautics Training School (Philippines)
Portable Acoustic Tracking System
Precise Automated Tracking System
Precision Aircraft Tracking System
PREDICASTS (INCORPORATED (USA)) Abstract Terminal Service

PATSY Programme Automatic Testing System
Pulse-Amplitude Transmission System

PATT Programmable Automatic Transistor Tester

PATTERN Planning Assistance Through Technical Evaluation of Relevance Numbers

PATTI Precise and Accurate Time and Time Interval (an experiment aboard the Spacelab')
Prompt Action To Telephone Inquiries

PATU Pan-African Telecommunication Union (headquarters in Zaire)

PATWAS Pilot's Automatic Telephone Weather Answering Service

PATX Private Automatic Telegraph Exchange

PAU Programmes Analysis Unit (of DTI and UKAEA)

PAUL PROSPER Alphanumeric User Language

PAVD Plasma Activated Vapour Deposition

PAVE Principles and Applications of Value Engineering
Programmed Assistance to Vocational Education

PAVE PAWS Precision Acquisition of Vehicle Entry Phased Array Warning System

PAVM Proximity Automatic Vehicle Monitoring

PAW Plasma-Arc Welding

PAWN Photon Adjoint With Neutron

PAWS Phased Array Warning System
Polar Automatic Weather Station

PAX Private Automatic Exchange

PB Particle Beam
Precipitation Body
prefix to numbered series of Research and Development Reports usually available for purchase from NTIS (USA) or its agents
Publications Board

PBAA Polybutadiene-acrylic acid

PBAN Polybutadiene-acrylic acid-acrylonitrile

PBAR Programming, Budgeting, Accounting and Reporting

PBAS Post Block Aerial Surveying

PBB Polybrominated Biphenyls

PBC Periodic Binary Convolutional
Peripheral Bus Computer
Personal Business Computer

PBCS Post-Boost Control System

PBCT Polybutadiene Carboxyl-terminated

PBEIST Planning Board for European Inland Surface Transport (a NATO civil emergency planning agency)

PBF Permalloy-Bar File
Power Burst Facility

PBFA Provincial Booksellers Fairs Association

PBGC Pension Benefit Guaranty Corporation (of Dept of Labor (USA))

PBI Polybenzimidazole
Protein-Bound Iodine

PBIB Partially Balanced Incomplete Block

PBL Peripheral Blood Lymphocytes

PBLG Polybenzyl-L-Glutamate

PBMA Plastics Bath Manufacturers Association
Prefabricated Building Manufacturers Association

PBNA Phenyl Beta-naphthylamine

PBOD Phytoplankton Biochemical Oxygen Demand

PBP Penicillin-Binding Protein
Pulse Burst Period

PBPB Pyridinium Bromide Perbromide

PBPS Post Boost Propulsion System

PBR Patrol Boat, River
Payment By Results

PBRIS Pampanga-Bongabon Rivers Irrigation System (Philippines)

PBS Pacific Biological Station (Canada)
Phosphate Buffered Saline
Press-Button Signalling
Public Broadcasting Service (USA)
Public Building Service (of GSA (USA))

PBT Piggyback Twistor
Polybutylene Terephthalate
Preliminary-Breath-Test device

PBTF Polybromotrifluoroethylene

PBW Particle Beam Weapon
Parts By Weight
Power-By-Wire

PBWG Pakistan Bibliographical Working Group (Pakistan)

PC Paper Copy
Personal Computer
Phosphorylcholine
Phosphorylcreatine
Photochromic
Photoconductivity
Phthalocyanine
Pitting Corrosion
Plasma Cortisol
Polycarbonates
Polycarbosilane
Polymer Concrete
Portable Computer
Printed Circuit
Printed Copy
Propylene Carbonate

PCA Parliamentary Commissioner for Administration
Passive Cutaneous Anaphylaxis
Physical Configuration Audit
Polar Cap Absorption
Polarizer-Compensator-Analyzer
Polycaproamide
Portacaval Anastomosis
Portland Cement Association (USA)
Posterior Cryo-arytenoid

PCAC Partially Conserved Axial-vector Current

PCAG Petroleum Conservation Action Group (India)

PCAM Punched Card Accounting Machine

PCAPA Pacific Coast Association of Port Authorities (USA)

PCARR Philippines Council of Agricultural and Resources Research (Philippines)
PCB Plenum Chamber Burning
Point-Contact Breakdown
Polychlorinated Biphenyls
Printed-Circuit Board
PCBC Partially Conserved Baryon Current
PCBS Positive Control Bombardment System
PCC Partial Crystal Control
Philippine Cotton Corporation (Philippines)
Photocell Counter Chronometer
Polarity Coincidence Correlator
Polymer Cement Concrete
Portland Cement Concrete
Premature Chromosome Condensation
Pure Car Carrier
PCCD Peristaltic Charge-Coupled Device
PCD Polycarbodiimide
Production Common Digitizer
Programmed Cutting Director
Projected Charge Density
PCDD Polychlorinated Dibenzodiodioxins
PCDDS Private Circuit Digital Data Service
PCDF Polychlorinated Dibenzofurans
PCE Paging Control Equipment
Process Control Equipment
Pseudo Cholinesterase
Punched Card Equipment
Pyrometric Cone Equivalent
PCEA Pacific Coast Electrical Association (USA))
PCEP Preliminary Call for Experiment Proposals
PCF Patrol Craft, Fast
PCFA Precast Concrete Frame Association
PCG Power-Conditioning Group
PCGN Permanent Committee on Geographical Names
PCI Pilot Controller Integration
Prestressed Concrete Institute (USA)
Production Cost Information
Programmable Communications Interface
Prothrombin Consumption Index
PCIC Pittsburgh Chemical Information Center (University of Pittsburgh (USA))
PCIE Period of Central Inspiratory Excitability
PCK Processer-Controlled Keying
PCL Polytechnic of Central London
PCLW Platinum Compensating Lead Wire
PCM Phase Change Material
Photochemical Machining
Plug-Compatible Mainframe
Plutonium-Contaminated Material
Protein-Calorie Malnutrition
Pulse-Code Modulation
PCMA Post Card Manufacturers Association (USA)
PCMB Parachloro-Mercury Benzoic acid
PCMC Parachloro-meta-cresol
PCMF Personnels des Cadres Militaires Feminins (France)
Power Capacitor Manufacturers Federation (merged into BCMA in 1978)
PCMI Punched Card Machine System
PCMR Patient Computer Medical Record
The President's Committee on Mental Retardation (USA)
PCMU Physico-Chemical Measurement Unit (of AERE (UKAEA))
PCMWP Plutonium Contamination Materials Working Party
PCN Parent Country Nationals
PCNB Pentachloronitrobenzene
PCNSL Polymerised Cashew Nut Shell Liquid
PCOLA Pulse Coded Optical Landing Aid
PCOR Pressure Compensator Over-Ride
PCOS Process Control Extensions to Operating System/360
PCP Parallel Circular Plate
Pentachlorophenol
Peripheral Circumflex Pressure
Phencyclidine
Photon-Coupled Pair
Polychloroprene
Programmable Circuit Processor
PCPA Parachlorophenylalanine
PCPI Permanent Committee on Patent Information (of WIPO)
PCPV Prestressed Concrete Pressure Vessel
PCQ Productivity Criteria Quotient
PCQT Paper-Core Quad Trunk
PCR Photo-conductive Relay
PCRC Primary Communications Research Centre (Leicester University)
PCRI Papanicolaou Cancer Research Institute (USA)
PCRV Prestressed Concrete Reactor Vessel
PCS Performance Command System
Petrochemical Corporation of Singapore (jointly operated by Singapore and Japan)
Plastic Clad Silica
Power Conversion System
Prime Compatible Set
Print Contrast Scale
Process Control Specification
Project Control System
PCSA Power Crane and Shovel Association (USA)
PCSIR Pakistan Council of Scientific and Industrial Research (Pakistan)
PCSM Polydimethyl Carboxylate Metallosiloxanes
PCSP Permanent Commission of the Conference on the Use and Conservation of the Resources of the South Pacific
PCT Patent Cooperation Treaty
Perfect Crystal device Technology
Photon-Coupled Transistor
Polychlorinated Terphenyls
Portable Conference Telephone
PCTFE Poly-monochloro-trifluoroethylene
PCU Passenger Car Unit
Power Conversion Unit
Punched Card Utility
PCUE Presidents' Committee for the Urban Environment
PCV Positive Crankcase Ventilation
Precursor Vehicle
PCVN Precracked Charpy V-notch
PD Photodielectric
Physical Distribution
Positive Displacement
Potential Difference
prefix to numbered series of amendments to Standards already issued by BSI
Propodite-dactylopodite
Pulse Doppler
PDA Parenteral Drug Association (USA)
Percent Defective Allowable
Photographic Dealers Association
Photon Detector Assembly
Post Deflection Acceleration
Potato Dextrose Agar
Probability Discrete Automata
Probability Distribution Analyses
Push Down Automation
PDAPS Pollution Detection And Prevention System (of US Coast Guard)
PDC Productivity and Development Center (Philippines)
Programmable Digital Controller

	Public Dividend Capital
PDCE	Parametric Design and Cost Effectiveness
PDCS	Performance Data Computer System
	Power Distribution and Conditioning System
PDDL	Perpendicular Diffraction Delay Line
PDE	Partial Differential Equation
	Phosphodiesterase
	Preliminary Determination of Epicentres
PDEM	Personal Dust Exposure Monitor
PDES	Pulse-Doppler Elevation Scan
PDF	Probability Density Function
	Probability Distribution Function
PDFES	Pitch-synchronous Digital Feature Extraction System
PDFG	Planar Distributed Function Generator
PDG	Precision Drop Glider
	Programmable Display Generator
PDGF	Platelet-Derived Growth Factor
PDH	Pyruvate Dehydrogenase
PDHL	Peak Design Heat Loss
PDI	Pictorial Deviation Indicator
	Point Diffraction Interferometer
	Powered Descent Initiation
	Prevalence, Duration and Intensity
PDIN	Pusat Dokumentasi Ilmiah Nasional (Indonesia) (Scientific and Technical Documentation Centre)
PDIS	Pusat Dokumentasi Ilmu-Ilmu Sosial (Indonesia) (Social Sciences Documentation Centre)
PDL	Picture Description Language
	Programme Design Language
PDM	Phase Division Multiplexing
	Physical Distribution Management
	Polynomial Discriminant Method
	Precedence Diagram Method
	Pulse Delta Modulation
	Pulse Duration Modulation
	Pulse Duration Modulation Modem
PDMS	Pipework Design Management System
	Polydimethylsiloxane
	Programme Development and Maintenance System
PDN	Public Data Network
PDNES	Pulse-Doppler Non-Elevation Scan
PDNF	Prime Disjunctive Normal Form
PDP	Passive Driving Periscope (for armoured fighting vehicles)
	Phenyl-dichlorophosphine
	Plasma Display Panel
	Positive Displacement Pump
	Programme Definition Phase
	Programmed Data Processor
	Project Definition Phase
PDQ	Photo Data Quantizer
	Programme for Descriptive Query
PDR	Periscope Depth Range
	Precision Depth Recorder
	Preliminary Design Review
PDRMA	Portable Drill Rig Manufacturers Association (USA)
PDRY	Peoples Democratic Republic of the Yemen
PDS	Parkinson's Disease Society
	Passive Detection System
	Power Density Spectra
	Problem Descriptor System
	Pulse Doppler Search
PDSA	Personnel Data System—Airmen (USAF)
PDSMS	Point-Defence Surface Missile System
	Power Diffraction Search and Match System
PDSO	Personnel Data System—Officers (USAF)
PDSOR	Positive Definitive Successive Over-Relaxation
PDSS	Particle Doppler Shift Spectrometer
PDSTT	Pulse Doppler Single Target Track
PDT	Picture Description Test
PDU	Pilot's Display Unit
PDUS	Primary Data User Station
PDV	Pyrotechnic Development Vehicle
PDVOR	Precision Doppler VHF Omni-Range
PDVSA	Petroleos de Venezuela SA (Venezuela) (state oil company)
PDX	Poloidal Divertor Experiment (at the Plasma Physics Laboratory of Princeton University (USA))
	Processor-controlled Digital Exchange
PE	Permanent Echo
	Phosphatidylethanolamine
	Pigment Epithelium
	Polyester
	Polyether
	Polyethylene
	Potential Evaporation
	prefix to lettered/numbered/dated series of reports issued by Plant Engineering Department of BISRA
	Pulse Duration Modulation Modem
	Pyroelectric
PEA	Palmitoylethanolamide
	Pennsylvania Electric Association (USA)
	Pneylethylamine
	Provincial Electricity Authority (Thailand)
PEAC	Peripheral Array Computer
PEACER	Petroleum Employers Advisory Council on Employee Relations
PEACU	Plastic Energy Absorption in Compression Unit
PEARL	Parts Explosion And Retrieval Language
	Periodicals Automation RAND (CORPORATION (USA)) Library
PEAS	Physical Estimation and Attitude Scale
	Production Engineering Advisory Service (of DTI and PERA) (ceased operation March, 1971)
PEATMOS	Primitive Equation and Trajectory Model Output Stastistics
PEB	Phosphate Ester Based
	Phototype Environment Buoy
	Plasma Electron Beam
PEBUL	Project for Evaluation the Benefits from University Libraries (of Durham University)
PEBX	Private Electronic Branch Exchange
PEC	Peritoneal Exudate Cells
	Photoelectrochemical Cell
	Pulsed Eddy Current
PECF	Pseudoextracellular Fluid
PECH	Panel on Trace Element Geochemistry of Coal Resource Development related to Health (of National Research Council (USA))
PECI	Projects and Equipment Corporation of India (India)
PECR	Photon Enhanced Chemical Reactions
PECS	Portable Environmental Control System
PECT	Positron Emission Computed Tomography
PED	Petroleum Engineering Directorate (of Dept of Energy)
	Photoelectron Energy Distribution
	Pipework Engineering Developments (a section of the British Steel Corporation)
	Plastic Encapsulated Device
	Position Entry Device
PEDANT	Preprogrammable Evaluations based on a Data Normalizing Technique
PEDRO	PERKINS (ENGINES) Engineering Data Retrieval Organisation
PEE	Photo-Electron Emission
	Photoelectric Emission
PEEK	Polyetheretherketone

PEEM Photoemission-Electron Microscope
PEEP Pilot's Electronic Eyelevel Presentation
PEETPACK Process Engineering Evaluation Techniques Package
PEF Packaging Education Foundation (USA)
Peak Exploratory Flow
PEFR Peak Exploratory Flow Rate
PEFV Pitch-Excited Formant Vocoder
PEG Petrochemical Energy Group (an ad hoc group of several major chemical companies in the USA)
Polyethylene Glycol
PEG-BB Polyester-Glass Bias-Belted
PEGA Polyethylene Glycol Adipate
PEGS Parameter Evaluation of Generalized Systems
PEHLA Prufung Elektrischer Hochleistungsapparate (Germany) (Joint Testing Laboratory for Electrical High-power Equipment)
PEI Planning Executives Institute (USA)
Porcelain Enamel Institute (USA)
PEIA Poultry and Egg Institute of America (USA)
PEILS Association of Prince Edward Island Land Surveyors (Canada)
PEJC Professional Engineers Joint Council (South Africa) (now FSPE)
PEK Phase Exchange Keying
Pig Embryo Kidney
PEL perfix to numbered series of reports issued by Atomic Energy Board, South Africa
Permissible Exposure Level
Photoelectron Layer
Physics and Engineering Laboratory (of DSIR (New Zealand))
PELS Precision Emitter Location System
PELSS Precision Emitter Location Strike System
PEM Petroleos Mexicanos (Mexico) (national petroleum corporation)
Photoelastic Modulator
Polyethylene Matrix
Primitive Equation Model
Processor Element Memory
Production Engineering Measure
Protein-Energy Malnutrition
PEMA Prestressing Equipment Manufacturing Association
Production Equipment and Missiles—Army (US Army)
PEMARS Procurement of Equipment Missiles Army Management Accounting and Reporting System (US Army)
PEMEC International Plant Engineering and Maintenance Exhibition and Conference
PEMEX Petroleos Mexicanos (Mexico)
PEMF Pulsed Electro-Magnetic Field
PEMV Pea Enation Mosaic Virus
PENA Primary Emission Neutron Activation
PENCAN underwater telephone cable between the Canary Islands and Spain
PENCIL Pictorial Encoding Language
PENDOR Photon Echo-Nuclear Double Resonance
PENNTAP Pennsylvania Technical Assistance Program (USA)
PENSAD Pensions Administration system
PEO Polyethylene Oxide
Pre-Erection Outfitting
PEON Commission pour la Production d'Electricite d'Origin Nucleaire (France) (Commission for the Production of Electricity from Atomic Energy Sources)
PEOS Propulsion and Electrical Operating System
PEP Paperless Electronic Payments
Partitioned Emulation Programme
Peak Envelop Power
Phosphoenolpyruvate
Planetary Ephemeris Programme
Political and Economic Planning (merged into PSI in 1978)
Positron-Electron Project (of Stanford University and California University (USA))
Primate Equilibrium Platform
Programme Evaluation Procedure
Propulsion and Energetics Panel (of AGARD (NATO))
Prototype Electro-Pneumatic train
PEPA Polyethylene Polyamide
PEPCK Phosphopenol-pyrievate carboxykinase
PEPCO Committee on Professional Education for Publishing (of APP (USA))
PEPE Parallel Element Processing Element
Parallel Element Processing Ensemble
PEPP Planetary Entry Parachute Programme
Professional Engineers in Private Practice (a section of NSPE (USA))
PEPPER Photo-Electric Portable Probe Reader
PEPR Precision Encoder and Pattern Recognizer OR Recognition
PEPS Psychological, Economic, Political and Sociological
PEPSY Precision Earth Pointing System
PER Planning and Engineering for Repairs and Alterations
Production Engineering Research Association
Professional and Executive Recruitment (a service of the Manpower Services Commission) (previously of the Dept of Employment)
Professional and Executive Register (of the Employment Service Agency)
Protein Efficiency Ratio
PERC Pittsburgh Energy Research Center (of ERDA (USA))
PERCY Photo Electronic Recognition Cybernetics Purposive System
PERF Planetary Entry Radiation Facility (of Langley Research Center (NASA) (USA))
PERGO Project Evaluation and Review with Graphic Output
PERI Platemakers Educational and Research Institute (USA)
PERL Portable Electronic Runway Lighting
PERM Programmable Equipment for Relaying and Measurement
Programmed Evaluation for Repetitive Manufacture
PERMACAP Personnel Management and Accounting Card Processing (US Army)
PERME Propellants, Explosives and Rocket Motor Establishment (MOD) (now part of RARDE)
PERS Performance Evaluation Reporting System
Project Evaluation and Reporting System
PERSC Power Engineering Research Steering Committee
PERSID Personnel Seismic Intruder Detector
PERSIS Personnel Information System
PERT Performance Evaluation Review Technique
Programme Evaluation and Review Technique
PERTMINA National Petroleum Company (Indonesia)
PERTVS Perimeter Television System
PERUMTEL Perusahaan Umum Telekomunikasi (Indonesia) (govt telecommunication agency)
PES Photoelectron Spectroscopy
Photoemission
Polyethersulphone
Power Engineering Society (of IEEE (USA))
Programmable Electronic System
PESA Petroleum Electric Supply Association (USA)
Petroleum Equipment Suppliers Association (USA)
PESC Power Electronics Specialists Conference

PESIS	Photo-Electron Spectroscopy of Inner-Shell
PESL	Petroleum Exploration Society of Libya
PESO	Product Engineering Services Offices (US Army, Navy and Air Force)
PESOS	Photo-Electron Spectroscopy of Outer-Shell
PEST	Parameter Estimation By Sequential Testing Project Engineer Scheduling Technique
PESTF	Proton Even Start Forecast
PET	Pattern Expitaxial Technology Pentaerythritol Tetrastearate Personal Electronic Transactor Photoelectric Transducer Polyethylene Terephthalate Positron-Emission Tomagraph Potential Evapotranspiration Pre-Eclamptic Toxaemia Prediction Error Transform Production Environmental Testing
PETA	Portable Electronic Traffic Analyzer
PETANS	Petroleum Training Association North Sea (sponsored by the Petroleum Industry Training Board)
PETC	Pittsburgh Energy Technology Center (DOE) (USA)
PETCOCK	Proposal Evaluation Technique Conditioned on Contract Kind
PETN	Pentaerythritol Tetranitrate
PETP	Polyethyleneterephthalate
PETROBRAS	Petroleo Brasileiro (Brazil) (State Petroleum Enterprise)
PETROMIN	General Petroleum and Mineral Organization (Saudi Arabia)
PETRONAS	Petroliam National (Malaysian State National Petroleum Corporation)
PETRONOR	Refineria de petroleos del Norte (Spain)
PETROSUL	Sociedade Portuguesa de Refinacao de Petroleos SARL (Portugal)
PETS	Pre-Eclamptic Toxaemia Society Proximity Effect Tunnelling Spectroscopy
PETT	Project: Engineering and Technology for Tomorrow (a slogan of the Inter-departmental Committee on Publicity for Engineering and Technology)
PEV	Propeller-Excited Vibration Pyroelectric Vidicon
PEW	Percussion Welding
PEWS	Platron Early Warning System
PEXE	Piecewise Exponential Estimator
PF	Packing Factor Patrol Frigate Perchloryl-fluoride Phenol-formaldehyde Protection Factor Protein Foam
PFA	Parametric Ferrite Amplifier Polyformaldehyde Popular Flying Association Production Flow Analysis Pulse Fluctuation Analysis Pulverized Fuel Ash
PFB	Petroleum Films Bureau (ceased operation in 1974)
PFBC	Pressurised Fluidised Bed Combustion
PFC	Plaque-Forming Cell Privately Financed Consumption Propellant Fuel Complex (of ISRO (India))
PFCCG	Pacific Fleet Combat Camera Group (USN)
PFCS	Primary Flight Control System
PFD	Personal Flotation Device Primary Flash Distillate
PFDF	Plutonium Fuel Development Facility (of PNC (Japan))
PFDR	Point Focus Distributed Receiver
PFE	Photoferroelectric Effect Plenum Fill Experiment facility (at Pacific Northwest Laboratory of NRC (USA)) (discontinued in 1976)
PFF	Plaque-Forming Factor
PFFF	Plutonium Fuel Fabrication Facility (of PNC (Japan)) Polypropylene Fibrillated Film Fibre
PFFT	Parallel Fast Fourier Transform
PFI	Pipe Fabrication Institute (USA)
PFIAB	(The) President's Foreign Intelligence Board (USA)
PFK	Perfluorokerosene Phofructokinase
PFM	Pre-Finished Metal Pulse-Frequency Modulation
PFN	Pulse Forming Network
PFP	Pensions for Professionals (non-profit Corporation organized by the American Chemical Society (USA)) Proton Flare Project
PFPA	Pitch Fibre Pipe Association
PFR	Precision Fathometer Recorder Prototype Fast-breeder Reactor
PFRA	Division of Problem-Focused Research Applications (of RANN (NSF) (USA)) Prairie Farm Rehabilitation Administration (Canada)
PFRT	Preliminary Flight Rating Test
PFS	Porous Friction Surface Precision Frequency Standard
PFT	Parachute Familiarization Training
PFU	Plaque-Forming Unit
PFZ	Precipitate-Free Zone
PG	Patrol Gunboat Polygalacturonase Processing Gain Production Group (of UKAEA) (in 1971 became British Nuclear Fuels Ltd. (a public Company)) Prostaglandin Pyrolytic Graphite
PGA	Phospho-glyceric Acid Polglycolic Acid
PGBM	Pulse-Gated Binary Modulation
PGC	Primordial Germ Cell Pyrolytic Gas Chromatography
PGCS	Proliferated Groundwave Communications System
PGH	Patrol Gunboat, Hydrofoil
PGI	Phosphoglucose Isomerase
PGK	Phosphoglycerate Kinase
PGL	Persistent Generalised Lymphadenopathy
PGM	Periaqueductal Grey Matter Phosphoglucomutase Precision Guided Munitions
PGMA-EA	Polyglycidal Methacrylate-Ethyl Acrylate
PGMARV	Precision Guided Manoeuvring Re-entry Vehicle
PGMOT	Pollution Generation Multiplier from Output Table
PGNCS	Primary Guidance, Navigation and Control System
PGNS	Primary Guidance and Navigation System
PGO	Ponto-Geniculo-Occipital Pyrolysis Gas Oil
PGR	Precision Graphic Recorder
PGRO	Processors and Growers Research Organisation
PGRV	Precision Guided Re-entry Vehicle
PGS	Parser-Generating System Platoon Gunnery Simulator
PGU	Post-Gonoccal Urethritis
PGW	Pressure Gas Welding

pH — a measure of acidity based on the concentration of hydrogen ions (scale is 0-14; 7 neutral, below 7 acid, above 7 alkaline)

PHA — Passive Haemagglutination
Phytohaemagglutinin
Phytohaemagglutinin
Preliminary Hazard Analysis
Pulse Height Analyser

PHAB — Physically Handicapped Able Bodied

PHAM — Phase Amplitude Monopulse

PHAROS — Phased Array Radar for Overland Surveillance
Plan Handling and Radar Operating System

PHASE — Package for Hospital Appraisal, Simulation and Evaluation

PHCA — Philippine Heart Centre for Asia (Philippines)

PHENO — Precise Hybrid Elements for Nonlinear Operations

PHI — Phosphohexase Isomerase
Position and Homing Indicator

PHIB — Phosphor-Inverted Bi-polar transistor device

PHILCOM- SAT — Philippine Communications Satellite Corporation (Philippines)

PHILCOMAN — Philippine Council of Management (Philippines)

PHILCON — PHILIPS (N. V. PHILIPS' GLOEILAMPENFABRIEKEN) Cams in Original Notation

PHILIRAN — Phillips Petroleum Company (Iran) (partly government owned)

PHILPRO — Philippine Committee on Trade Facilitation (Philippines)

PHILSA — Philippine Standards Association (Philippines)

PHILSOM — Periodical Holdings In the Library of the School Of Medicine network (based on Washington University School of Medicine (USA))

PHIVE — Propeller/Hull Interaction Vibration Excitation

PHLS — Public Health Laboratory Service

PHM — Patrol Hydrofoil Missile

PHMP — Primordial Hot Mantle Plume

PHOCAS — Photo Optical Cable Controlled Submersible

PHOCIS — Photogrammetric Circulatory Surveys

PHOENIX — Plasma Heating Obtained by Energetic Neutral Injection Experime

PHOTINT — Photographic Intelligence

PHP — Passive Hyperpolarizing Pototential

PHS — Precision Hover Sensor
Public Health Service (of DHHS (USA))

PHT — Passive Haemagglutination Test

PHTC — Pulse Height-to-Time Converter

PHW — Pressurised Heavy Water

PHWR — Pressurized Heavy-water-moderated and cooled Reactor

PHYLIS — Physics on-line Information System

PHYSBE — Physiological Simulation Benchmark Experiment

PI — Packaging Institute (USA)
Performance Index
Plastics Institute (amalgamated into PRI in 1975)
Pocket Incendiary
Polyimides
Productivity Index
Programmed Instruction
Proportional Integral

PI-FET — Piezoelectric Field-Effect Transistor

PI-USA — Packaging Institute (USA)

PIA — Pakistan International Airlines Corporation (Pakistan)
Peripheral Interface Adaptor
Personnel Inventory Analaysis
Photographic Importers Association
Plastics Institute of America (USA)
Plastics Institute of Australia (Australia)
Printing Industries of America (USA)

PIAC — Petroleum Industry Advisory Council

PIANC — Permanent International Association of Navigation Congresses (Belgium)

PIAPACS — Psycho-physiological Information Acquisition, Processing And Control System

PIARC — Permanent International Association of Road Congresses

PIB — National Board for Prices and Incomes
Petroleum Information Bureau
Polyisobutylene
Polytechnic Institute of Brooklyn (USA) (now PINY (USA))

PIBAC — Permanent International Bureau of Analytical Chemistry of Human and Animal Food

PIBEB — Polytechnic Institute of Brooklyn, Department of Electrophysics (USA) (SEE PIB)

PIBEE — Polytechnic Institute of Brooklyn, Department of Electrical Engineering (USA) (SEE PIB)

PIBEP — Polytechnic Institute of Brooklyn, Department of Electrophysics (USA) (SEE PIB)

PIBMRI — Polytechnic Institute of Brooklyn, Microwave Research Institute (USA) (SEE PIB)

PIBTS — Polyisobutenyl Tetraethylene Pentamine Succinimides

PIC — Particle-In-Cell
Pesticides Information Center (of National Agricultural Library, USA)
Photographic Industry Council (USA)
Polyethylene Insulated Conductor
Polymer-Impregnated Concrete
Positive Immittance Converter
Positive-Impedence Converter
Power Information Center (Pennsylvania University (USA))
Production Inventory Control
Programmed Instruction Centre (College of Technology, Enfield)
Pulse Indicating Cartridge

PICA — Porch Index of Communicative Ability
Power Industry Computer Applications
PSA (Property Services Agency) Information on Construction and Architecture (data base)

PICASSO — Pen Input to Computer And Scanned Screen Output

PICC — Plastics in Construction Council (of SPI (USA))
Professional Institutions Council for Conservation

PICDMS — Picture or Pictorial Database Management System

PICKUP — Professional and Industrial Commercial Updating Programme

PICLS — PURDUE UNIVERSITY (USA) Instructional and Computational Learning System

PICNIC — Production Engineering Research Association Instruction Code for Numerical Control

PICPA — Philippine Institute of Certified Public Accountants (Philippines)

PICS — Plug-in Inventory Control System
Production Information and Control System

PID — Polarization Image Detector
Proportional Integral and Differential
Proportional Integral Derivation
Publications and Information Directorate (India) (of CSIR)

PIDA — Payload Installation and Deployment Aid

PIDC — Pakistan Industrial Development Corporation (Pakistan)
Parameter Inventory Display System (maintained by NODC (NOAA) (USA))

PIDP — Programmable Indicator Data Processor

PIDS — Public Investment Data System

PIE — Parallel Instruction Execution
Perpendicular-Incidence Ellipsometry
Photo-Induced Electrochromism

	Pulmonary Interstitial
PIEA	Petroleum Industry Electrical Association (USA)
PIECE	Petroleum Industry Environmental Conservation Executive (Australia) (of AIP)
PIECOST	Probability of Incurring Estimated Cost
PIER	Product Inventory Electronically Recorded
PIF	British Paper and Board Industry Federation
PIFAL	Programme Instruction Frequency Analyser
PIFL	Pipe Flow
PIG	Plasmation Inert Gas
PIGA	Pendulous Integrating Gyroscopic Accelerometer
PIGH	Pan-American Institute of Geography and History
PIGMA	Pressurized Inert Gas Metal Arc
PIGME	Programmed Inert Gas Multi-Electrode
PIGMI	Pion Generator for Medical Irradiation
PIH	Passive Immune Haemolysis
PIHF	Periodic Inhomogeneous Film
PII	Positive Immittance Inverter
PIIA	Pakistan Institute of Industrial Accountants (Pakistan)
PIIM	Planned Inter-dependency Incentive Method
PIL	Pest Infestation Laboratory (of Agricultural Research Council)
	PITT Interpretive Language (University of Pittsburgh, USA)
PILAR	Petroleum Industry Local Authority Reporting
PILC	Paper Insulated Lead Cove
PILE	Product Inventory Level Estimator
PILLS	Particulate Instrumentation by Laser Light Scattering
PILOT	Panel on Instrumentation for Large Optical Telescopes (of the Science Research Council)
	Permutation Indexed Literature Of Technology
	Piloted Low-speed Test
	Programmed Inquiry, Learning Or Teaching
PIM	Precision Indicator of the Meridan
	Pulse Interval Modulation
PIMA	Paper Industry Management Association (USA)
PIMC	Particle Measurement Computer
PIMISS	Pennsylvania (USA) Interagency Management Information Support System
PIMNY	Printing Industries of Metropolitan New York (USA)
PIMP	Programme for Interactive Multiple Process simulation
PIMR	Przemyslowy Instytut Maszn Rolniczych (Poland) (Institute of Agricultural Machinery)
PIN	Personal Identification Number
PIND	Particle Impact Noise Detection
PINE	Passive Infrared Night Equipment
PINS	Palletized Inertial Navigation System
	Portable Inertial Navigation System
PINSAC	PINS Alignment Console
PINSTECH	Pakistan Institute of Nuclear Science and Technology (Pakistan)
PINT	Power Intelligence
PINTEC	Plastics Institute National Technical Conference
PINY	Polytechnic Institute of New York (USA)
PINZ	Plastics Institute of New Zealand (New Zealand)
PIO	Pilot Induced Oscillation
PIOSA	Pan Indian Ocean Science Association
PIP	Persistent Internal Polarization
	Pipe Inspection Programme
	Pollution Information Project (of NSL (Canada))
	Probabilistic Information Processing
PIPA	Pulse Integrating Pendulous Accelerometer
PIPIT	Peripheral Interface and Programme Interrupt Translator
PIPO	Parallel In, Parallel Out
PIPS	Paperless Item Processing System
	Pattern Information Processing System
	Pneumatically Induced Pitching System
PIRA	Paper and Board, Printing and Packaging Industries Research Association
PIRATE	Public Information in Rural Areas Technology Experiment (of the British Library Research and Development Division)
PIRAZ	Positive Identification Radar Advisory Zone
PIRC	Portable Inflatable Recompression Chamber
	Protection against Ionising Radiation Committee (of the Medical Research Council)
PIRDES	Programme of Research for the Development of Solar Energy (of CNRS (France))
PIREP	Pilot Intensive Rural Employment Programme (India)
PIRINC	Petroleum Industry Research Foundation (USA)
PIRL	PRISM (Personnel Record Information System for Management) Information Retrieval Language
PIRP	Proposed International Reference Preparation
PIRS	Personal Information Retrieval System
	Pollution Incident Reporting System
PIS	Penning Ionization Spectroscopy
PISA	Persistent Information Space Architecture
PISCES	Production Information Stocks and Cost Enquiry System
PISO	Parallel In, Serial Out
PISTL	Printing Industries of St. Louis (USA)
PIT	Physical Inventory Taking
	Processing of Index Terms
	Programme Instruction Tape
PITAC	Pakistan Industrial Technical Assistance Centre
PITAS	Petroleum Industry Training Association
	Petroleum Industry Training Association Scotland
PITB	Petroleum Industry Training Board
	Production Inspection and Test Branch (of CEGB)
PITCOM	Parliamentary Information Technology Committee
PIV	Positive Infinitely Variable
PIVS	Particle-Induced Visual Sensations
PIXE	Particle Induced X-ray Emission
	Proton-Induced X-ray Emission
PJA	Pipe Jacking Association
PK	Psychokinesis
	Pyruvate Kinase
PKA	Primary Knock-on Atoms
PKN	Polski Kometet Normalizacyjny (Poland) (Standards Commission)
PKO	Peacekeeping Operations
PKP	Polskie Koleje Panstwowe (Poland) (Polish State Railways)
PKU	Phenylketonuria
PL	Payload
	Photoluminescence
	prefix to lettered:dated series of Plastics Standards issued by BSI (letters are sometimes prefixed by a number)
	Production Language
	Programming Language
PL/M	Programming Language/Micro-processor
PLA	Moon, Planets, Comets and Interplanetary Medium Advisory Committee (of ESRO) (now ESA)
	Pakistan Library Association (Pakistan)
	Pennsylvania Library Association (USA)
	Phospholipase A
	Polylactic Acid
	Port of London Authority
	Programmable Logic Array
	Programmed Logic Array
	Proton Linear Accelerator
PLAAR	Packaged Liquid Air Augmented Rocket

PLACE Position Location and Aircraft Communications Experiment (carried on-board an ATS)
Programming Language for Automatic Checkout Equipment
PLACO Technical Planning Committee (of ISO (Switzerland))
PLADS Parachute Low Altitude Delivery System
Pulsed Laser Airborne Depth Sounding System
Pulsed Light Airborne Depth Sounder
PLAME Propulsive Left Landing with Aerodynamic Manoeuvring Entry
PLAN Problem Language Analyzer
Programme for Learning in Accordance with Needs
Programming Language NINETEEN HUNDRED computer
PLANES Programmed Language-based Enquiry System
PLANET Planned Logistics Analysis and Evaluation Technique
Planning Evaluation Technique
Plant Layout Analysis and Evaluation Technique
Private Line Analysis and Network Engineering Tools
PLANIT Programming Language for Interactive Teaching
PLANS Plastic Analysis of Nonlinear Structures
Position Location and Navigation Symposium
PLARS Position Locating And Reporting System
PLASI Pulse Light Approach Slope Indicator
PLASMA Plant Services Maintenance
PLASTEC Plastic Technical Evaluation Center (USDOD)
PLAT Pilot Landing Aid Television
PLATO Programmed Logic for Automatic Teaching Operations
PLATS Precision Location And Tracking System
PLC Peritoneal Lymphoid Cell
Programmable Logic Controller
Programming Language Committee (of CODASYL)
Public Limited Company
PLCC Power Line Carrier Communication
PLD Phase-Lock Demodulator
Programmable Logic Devices
Pulse-Length Discriminator
PLDR Potentially Lethal Damage Repair
PLDT Philippine Long Distance Telephone Company (Philippines)
PLE Product Limit Estimator
PLEM Pipeline End Manifold
PLEX Plant Experimentation
PLF Precise Local Fix
Prompt Lactose-Fermenting
PLG Parametric Light Generator
PLIANT Procedural Language Implementing Analogue Techniques
PLL Peripheral Light Loss
Phased-Locked Loop
PLLRC Public Land Law Review Commission (USA)
PLLS Portable Landing Light System
PLM Planned Lighting Maintenance
Programmable Logic Matrice
Pulse Length Monitor
PLMRU Public Library Management Research Unit (School of Librarianship, Leeds Polytechnic)
PLMS Partitioned Libraries Management System
PLN Potassium Lithium Niobate
PLO Phased-Locked Oscillator
PLOD Planetary Orbit Determination
PLOMS Professional Legal Office Management System
PLOT Programme Logic Table
PLP Pattern Learning Parser
Plastic Lined Pipe
Product Liability Prevention Conference
Pyridoxal Phosphate
PLPG Publishers Library Promotion Group (USA)
PLPO Phase-Locked Pulsed Oscillator
PLR Power Line Radiation
Public Lending Right
PLRACTA Position, Location, Reporting And Control of Tactical Aircraft
PLRG Public Libraries Research Group (of the Library Association)
PLRS Position Location Reporting System
PLS Positive Locking System
Programmable Logic Sequencer
PLSO Professional Land Surveyors of Ohio (USA)
PLSS Portable Life-Support System
Precision Location Strike System
PLT PRINCETON (Plasma Physics Laboratory, Princeton University (USA)) Large Torus
PLU Programme (computer) Library Unit (of Edinburgh University)
PLUM Programmes Library Update and Maintenance
Programming Language for Users of MAVIS (microprocessor-based Audio Visual Information System
PLUNA Primeras Lineas Uruguayas de Navegacion Aerea (Uruguay) (State airline)
PLUSS USS POINT LOMA Unmanned Search System
PLUTO Parts-Listing/Used-On Technique
Pipe Line Under The Ocean
Plutonium Loop Testing Reactor
PLZT Lead, Lanthanum, Zirconium, Titanium (derived from the chemical symbols Pb, La, Zr, Ti)
PM Phase-Modulated
Photo-Multiplier
Planned Maintenance
Polarization Modulation
Powder Metallurgy
prefix to numbered series of Business Monitor Quarterly Statistics issued by Business Statistics Office of Dept of Industry and published by HMSO
Preventive Maintenance
PM3 Programming Mode Three
PMA Pakistan Medical Association (Pakistan)
Permanent Magnet Association
Petroleum and Minerals Authority (Australia)
Pharmaceutical Manufacturers Association
Phenylmercuric Acetate
Phorbol Myristate Acetate
Photographic Manufacturers Association (USA)
Photomarketing Association (USA)
Polymethacrylic Acid
Polyurethane Manufacturers Association (USA)
Precision Measurements Association (USA)
Produce Marketing Association (USA)
Purchasing Management Association (USA)
Pyridylmercuric Acetate
PMA/ARR Probable Missed Approach per Arrival
PMAC Polymethacrolein
PMAC Purchasing Management Association of Canada (Canada)
Purchasing Managers Association of Canada (Canada)
PMACS Project Management and Control System
PMAF Pharmaceutical Manufacturers Association Foundation (USA)
PMAGB Paint Makers Association of Great Britain
PMATA Paper Makers Allied Trades Association
PMBO Participative Management By Objectives
PMBX Private Manual Branch Exchange
PMC Performance Management Computer
Pre-Mission Calibration
Programmable Matrix Controller

	Project Management Corporation (USA) (a non-profit corporation organised to manage CRBRP (USA))
PMD	Programmed Multiple Development (in thin-layer chromatography)
	Project-based Management Development
	Projected Map Display
PMDA	Plastics Machinery Distributors Association
	Pyromelletic Dianhydride
PMDC	Pakistan Minerals Development Corporation (Pakistan) (government owned)
PMDS	Projected Map Display Set
	Projected Map Display System
PME	Photomagneto-electric Effect
	Polarization-Modullation Ellipsometry
	Protective Multiple Earthing
PMEL	Pacific Marine Environmental Laboratory (of ERL (NOAA (USA))
	Precision Measurement Equipment Laboratories (USAF)
PMF	Progressive Massive Fibrosis
PMG	Power Metal Grid
PMI	Personnel Management Information system
	Pseudo Matrix Isolation
PMIRD	Passive Microwave Intercept Receiver Display
PMIS	Project Management Information System
PML	Precision Mecanique Labinal (France)
PMLM	Photosensitive Membrane Light Modulator
PMM	Particle Mass Monitor
	Planar Motion Mechanisms
PMMA	Paper Machinery Makers Association (now British Paper Machinery Makers Association)
	Polymethyl Methacrylate
PMMC	Permanent Magnet Moving Coil
PMMI	Packaging Machinery Manufacturers Institute (USA)
PMN	Pasteurized Milk Network (of Public Health Services (USA))
	Polymorphonuclear
	Polymorphonuclear
	Polymorphonuclear Neutrophils
	Pre-Manufacturing Notice
PMNP	Platform Mounted Nuclear Power Plant
PMO	Phenylmethyloxadiazole
PMOC	Pittsburgh Mining Operations Center (of DOE (USA))
PMOS	P-channel Metal Oxide Semiconductor
PMP	Parallel Microprogrammed Processor
	Parts-Material-Packaging
	Piecewise Markov Process
	Project Master Plan
PMR	Pacific Missile Range (USAF)
	Pacific Missile Range (USN)
	Pressure Modulated Radiometer
	Pressure Modulator Radiometer
	Private Mobile Radio
	Proton Magnetic Resonance
PMRN	Particulate Mineral Reinforced Polyamide (Nylon)
PMS	Performance Management System
	Peripheral Monitor System
	Phanazinium Methosulphate
	Polymethylsorbate
	Probability of Mission Success
	Process Management System
	Processors, Memories and Switches
	Project Management System
	Projected-Map System
PMSF	Phenylmethylsulphonyl Fluoride
PMSFN	Planetary Manned Space Flight Network
PMSG	Pregnant Mare Serum Gonadotrophin
PMSP	Plant Modelling System Programme
PMSRC	Pittsburgh Mining and Safety Research Center (of Bureau of Mines (USA))
PMSRP	Physical and Mathematical Sciences Research Paper
PMT	Photomechanical Transfer
	Photomultiplier Transit
	Photomultiplier Tube
	Pre-determined Motion-Time
PMTS	Pre-determined Motion-Time Systems
PMTV	Potato Mop-Top Virus
PMU	Particulate Minerology Unit (of Bu Mines (USA))
	Performance Monitor Unit
PMV	Plasma Membrane Vesicle
PMVI	Periodic Motor Vehicle Inspection
PMW	Preventive Maintenance Welding
PN	Particulate Nitrogen
	Performance Number
	Pseudonoise
PNA	Packet Network Adaptor
	Polynuclear Aromatic
	Polynuclear Aromatic Hydrocarbons
	Project Network Analysis
	Pulsed Neutron Activation
PNACP	Pacific Northwest Association for College Physics (USA)
PNBC	Pacific Northwest Bibliographic Center (Washington University (USA))
PNC	Photo-Nitrosation of Cyclohexane
	Police National Computer
	Power Reactor and Nuclear Fuel Development Corporation (Japan)
	Pulse Compression Network
PNCS	Performance and Navigation Computer System
PND	Pictorial Navigation Display
	Pressed Notch Depth
PNdb	Perceived Noise decibels
PNE	Peaceful Nuclear Explosion
PNERL	Pacific Northwest Environmental Research Laboratory (of EPA (USA))
PNEUROP	European Committee of Manufacturers of Compressors, Vacuum Pumps and Pneumatic Tools
PNG	Papua-New Guinea
PNGLA	Papua New Guinea Library Association (Papua New Guinea)
PNGS	Primary Navigation and Guidance System
PNI	Pulsed Neutron Interrogation
PNITC	Pacific Northwest International Trade Council (USA)
PNKA	Perusahaan Negara Kereta Api (Indonesia) (State Railways)
	Protein Induced by Vitamin K Absence and Antagonists
PNL	Pacific Naval Laboratory (of DRB, Canada) (now Defence Research Establishment Pacific)
	Pacific Northwest Laboratory (DOE) (USA)
	Perceived Noise Level
PNLA	Pacific Northwest Library Association (USA)
PNMT	Phenylethanolamine-N-Methyl Transferase (USA))
PNOC	Philippine National Oil Company (Philippines) (government owned)
PNP	Precision Navigation Processor
	Programmed Numerical Path-controller
PNPA	Pennsylvania Newspaper Publishers Association (USA)
PNR	Passenger Name Record system
PNS	Peripheral Nervous System
	Pooled Normal Serum
	Post Nickel Strike
PNT	Project Network Technique
PNTD	Personnel Neutron Threshold Detector

PNU Protein Nitrogen Units
PNVD Passive Night Vision Device
PNVS Pilots Night Vision System
PNW prefix to series issued by Pacific Northwest Forest and Range Experiment Station (Forest Service of USDA)
PNYA Port of New York Authority (USA)
PO Propylene Oxide
POA Polarized Orbital Approximation
Preoptic Area
Privately-owned Open Air-braked (railway wagons)
POAC International Conference on Port and Ocean Engineering under Arctic Conditions
POB Phenoxybenzamine
POBR Division of Problem-Oriented Basic Research (of RANN (NSF) (USA))
POC Particulate Organic Carbon
Post Office Corporation
Public Oil Company (Sudan)
POCA Progress Observation and Corrective Action
POCCNET Payload Operations Control Center Network
POCS Patent Office Classification System (US Patent Office)
Proper Oriented Cut-Set
POD Post Office Department (USA)
PODAS Portable Data Acquisition System
PODM Preliminary Orbit Determination Method
PODPS (British) Post Office Data Processing Service
PODS Portable Data Store
POE Polyoxyethylene
Port of Embarkation
Probability of Error
POEA Philippines Overseas Employment Administration (Philippines)
POEM Procedure for Optimizing Elastomeric Mountings
POESMIC Program Office for Evaluating and Structuring Multiple Incentive Contracts (USDoD)
POET Portable Optic-Electronic Tracker
Primed Oscillator Expendable Transponder
POF Powder-On-Foil
POG Polyoxethylene Glycol (USA))
POGO Polar Orbiting Geophysical Observatory
Pre-Oxidation Gettering of the Other side
Problem-Oriented Graphics Operation
Programmer-Oriented Graphics Operation
POHWARO Pulsated Overheated Hot Water Rocket
POI Programme of Instruction
POINTER Pre-university Orbital Information Tracker Equipment and Recorder
POISE Practice-Oriented Information System Experiment
POL Pacific Oceanographic Laboratories (of ERL (NOAA) (USA))
Petroleum, Oil and Lubricants
Problem-Oriented Languages
Procedure Oriented Language
POLAC Problem Oriented Language for Analytical Chemistry
POLACAP Port of London Authority Combined Accident Procedure
POLANG Polarization Angle
POLAR Production Order Locating And Reports
POLARS Pathology On-line Logging And Reporting System
POLE Public Opinion Logical Expectation
POLIS Parliamentary On-Line Information System (of the House of Commons)
POLKA Periodical On-Line Keyword Access
Petroleum, Oil and Lubricants Out-of-Kilter Algorithm
POLLS Parliamentary On-Line Library Study
POLO Polar Orbiting Lunar Observatory
Problem-Oriented Language Organizer
POLPRO Commission for Standardization of Foreign Trade Documents (Poland)
POLS Planned Ocean Logistic System
POLSTAR Plant for On Load Short-circuit Testing And Research
POLYP Problem Oriented Language for System Software Programming
POLYPAGOS Polychromic Programme for the Analysis of General Optical Systems
POM Particulate Organic Matter
Polarizing Optical Microscopy
Polycyclic Organic Matter
Polyoxymethylene
Printer Output Microfilm
POMCUS Prepositioned Material Configured to Unit Sets
POMM Preliminary Operating and Maintenance Manual
POMO Production Oriented Maintenance Organization
POMP Pre-coded Originating Mail Processor
Prednisdone, Vinicristine, Methotrexate, Mercaptopurine
Problem-Oriented Management of Patients (a project of the Birmingham Medical School)
POMR Problem Oriented Medical Records
POMS Panel on Operational Meteorological Satellites
Profile of Mood States
POP Palletizing Optimization Programme
Particle-Oriented Paper
Perceived Outcome Potential
Post Office Preferred
Posterior Probability
Prefocused Objective-Pinhole
Probability of Precipitation
R. J. POPPLESTONE'S computer programming language
POPA Panel On Public Affairs (of the American Physical Society (USA))
POPAI Point-of-Purchase Advertising Institute (USA)
POPL Principles of Programming Language (symposium sponsored by ACM (USA))
POPLAB International Program of Laboratories for Population Statistics (of University of North Carolina (USA))
POPSI Postulate-based Permuted Subject Indexing
POQ Period Order Quantity
POQL Probability Outgoing Quality Limit
POR Propylene Oxide Rubber
PORL Pacific Oceanographic Research Laboratories (of ERL (NDAA) (USA))
PORTAS Penetration Of Radiation Through Aperture Simulation
PORTIA Port Operations, Transport and Integrated Accountancy
PORTIS Portable Ticket Issuing System
PORV Pilot-Operated Release Valve
POSE Programme for Optimizing Sales Effort
POSER Process Organization to Simplify Error Recovery
POSH Permuted On Subject Headings
POSM Parallel-Optical Stage Master oscillator power amplifier
POST Passive Optical Seeker Technique
Polymer Science and Technology (computer based information service of the American Chemical Society (USA))
POT PNEUROP Oxidation Test
POTC PERT Orientation and Training Center (USDoD)
POTF Polychromatic Optical Thickness Fringes
POUNC Post Office Users National Council

POWER PERT (Programme and Evaluation Review Technique) Oriented Work-scheduling and Evaluation Routine
Priority Output Writers, Excecution processors and input Readers system
Programmed Off-line Waste Reduction
POWS Pyrotechnic Outside Warning System
POWTECH International Powder and Granular Technology and Bulk Solids Exhibition and Conference
POY Pre-Oriented Yarn
PP Polynomial Programming
Polypropylene
Professional Paper
Protoporphyrin
PP/Q Plant Protection and Quarantine Programs (of APHIS (USDA))
PPA Parallel Processing Automata
Periodical Publishers Association
Phenylpropanolamine
Phosphoric Acid Anodized
Photo-Peak Analysis
Polyphosphoric Acid
Prescription Pricing Authority
Printing Platemakers Association (USA)
Process Plant Association
Publishers Publicity Association (USA)
PPAA Personal Protection Armor Association (USA)
PPAAR Princeton University, Pennsylvania University, Army (US Army Electronics Command) Avionics Research
PPANI Professional Photographers Association of Northern Ireland
PPB Planning, Programming, Budgeting
PPBAS Planning, Programming, Budgeting, Accounting System
PPBES Programme Planning-Budgeting-Evaluation System
PPBM Pulse-Polarization Binary Modulation
PPBS Planning, Programming and Budgeting System
PPC Personal Programmers Club (USA)
Plain Paper Copier
Polysaccharide-Protein Complex
Predicted Propagation Correction
Pressure Pulse Contour cardiac computer
Procurement Policy Committee (of HM Treasury)
Production Planning and Control
Programmable Pocket Calculator
Public Petroleum Corporation (Greece)
Pulsed Power Circuit
PPCA Productivity Promotion Council of Australia (Australia)
PPCC Polymer Portland Cement Concrete
PPCNB Pentachloronitrobenzene
PPD Parallel Plate Dipole
Petroleum Production Division (of Dept of Energy) (now PED)
Purified Protein Derivative
Purified Protein Derivative
PPDB Point-Positioning Data Base
PPDC Polymer Products Development Centre (of RAPRA)
PPDI Pilots Projected Display Indicator
PPDR Pilot Performance Description Record
PPE Phenyl Propargyl Ether
Polyphenylether
Pre-Production Evaluation
Problem Programme Evaluator
Protonated Polyethylene
PPECB Perishable Products Export Control Board (South Africa)
PPG Primary Pattern Generator
Programme Pulse Generator
PPI Parallel Plate Interceptor
Pass Point Intrument (a component of RACOMS)
Plan-Position Indicator
Professional Photographers of Israel organisation (Israel)
PPICS Production Planning Inventory Control System
PPIP Physics Post-doctoral Information Pool (of American Institute of Physics)
PPITB Printing and Publishing Industry Training Board
PPIV Positive Personnel Identity Verification
PPL Peripheral Blood Leukocytes
Photogrammetric Programming Language
Plasma Physics Laboratory (Princeton University (USA))
Polypropylene
Private Pilot's Licence
PPLC Patients Protection Law Committee
PPM Parts per Million
Periodic Permanent Magnet
Periodic Pulsed Magnet
Planned Preventive Maintenance
Pulse Position Modulation
PPMA Plastic Pipe Manufacturers Association
PPMHD Pulsed Plasma Magnetohydrodynamics
PPMS Programmable Precision Manufacturing System
PPO Polyphenylene Oxide
Promocion Professional Obrera (Spain) (Organisation for training semi-skilled workers)
PPOM Particulate Polycyclic Organic Matter
PPP Phased Project Planning
Programmed Production Planning
PPPL Princeton (University) Plasma Physics Laboratory (USA)
PPQ Polyphenylquinoxaline
PPRIC Pulp and Paper Research Institute of Canada (Canada)
PPS Phthalimidopropylsilane
Polyphenylene Sulphide
Polyphenylenesulphone
Primary Propulsion System
Project Planning and Control System
Pulses per Second
PPSA Pan-Pacific Surgical Association
PPSCP Partially Submerged Supercavitating Propeller
PPT Probabilistic Potential Theory
PPTS Pre-Planned Training System
PPWB Prairie Provinces Water Board (Canada)
PPWC Preventive Protective Weld Coating
PPY Polypyrrole
PPZ Proton Polar Zone
PQ prefix to numbered series of Business Monitors issued by Business Statistics Office of the Dept of Industry and published by HMSO
PQE Post-Qualification Education
PQMF Parallel Quadrature Mirror Filter
PQR Productivity, Quality and Reliability
PR Piezoresistive
Preliminary Report
Primary Reference fuel
Progress Report
Project Report
Proton Resonance
Pseudo Random
PRA Paint Research Association
Petroleum Retailers Association
Plasma Renin Activity
Probabilistic Risk Assessment
PRADS Parachute Retro-rocket Air Drop System
PRAG Pensions Research Accountants Group
PRAGMA Processing Routines Aided by Graphics for Manipulation of Arrays

PRAIEN Centre de Preparation Practique aux Applications Industrielles de l'Energie Nucleaire (France) (Centre for Practical Preparations for Industrial Applications of Nuclear Energy)

PRAIS Pesticide Residue Analysis Information Service (of the Laboratory of the Government Chemist) (now AMAIS)

PRAM Preliminary Repair Level Decision Analysis Model
Productivity, Reliability, Availability and Maintainability
Propelled Ascent Mine

PRANG Projection-Angle

PRANS Proportional Range Scheduling

PRAT Pressure-Retaining Amphipod Trap

PRAW Personnel Research Activity Washington (USN)

PRB Public Roads Bureau (Dept of Commerce, USA)

PRBS Pseudo Random Binary Sequence
Pseudo-Random Binary Signals

PRC People's Republic of China
Polysulphide Rubber Compound
Poultry Research Centre (of Agricultural Research Council)

PRCA Pure Red-Cell Aplasia

PRDPEC Power Reactor Development Programme Evaluation Committee (of AECL (Canada))

PRDS Processed Radar Display System

PRE Proton Relaxation Rate

PREAG Preussische Elektrizitats AG (Germany)

PRECIS Preserved Context Index System

PREDICT Process Reliability, Evaluation and Determination of Integrated Circuit Techniques

PREFRE Power Reactor Fuel Reprocessing Plant Project (of BARC (India))

PRELUDE Pre-optimization Linearization of Undulation and Detection of Errors

PREP Programmed Electronics Patterns

PRESAGE Programme to Realistically Evaluate Strategic Anti-Ballistic Missile Gaming Effectiveness

PRESS Pacific Range Electromagnetic Signature Studies
Project Review, Evaluation, and Scheduling System

PREST EEC Working Party on Policy for Scientific and Technical Research (became CREST in 1974)
Programme of Policy Research in Engineering Science and Technology (of University of Manchester)

PRESTO Programme for Rapid Earth-to-Space Trajectory Optimization

PREVAN Precompiler for Vector Analysis

PRF Pontine Reticular Formation
Potential Risk Factor
Primary Reference Fuels
Pulse Repetition Frequency

PRFCS Pattern Recognition Feedback Control System

PRFD Pulse-Repetition-Frequency Distribution

PRI Paint Research Institute (USA)
Paleontological Research Institution (USA)
Plasticity Retention Index
Plastics and Rubber Institute

PRIAS Plant Register/Fixed Assetts and Inflation Accounting System

PRIDE Profitable Information by Design through Phased Planning and Control
Programmed Reliability In Design

PRIH Prolactin Release-Inhibiting Hormone

PRIM Programmable Research Instrument

PRIMAR Program to Improve Management of Army Resources (US Army)

PRIME Precision Integrator for Meteorological Echoes
Precision Recovery Including Manoeuvrable Entry
Primate Information Management Experiment (of Oregon Regional Primate Research Center (USA)
Priority Management Efforts
Psychiatric Research Industrial, Medical, Educational (a research trust of the Society of Clinical Psychiatrists)

PRINCE Parts Reliability Information Center

PRINCE/APIC Parts Reliability Information Center/Apollo Parts Information Center (NASA)

PRINFOD Printed Information Distribution

PRINUL Puerto Rico International Undersea Laboratory (Puerto Rico)

PRIOR Program for In-Orbital Rendezvous (USAF)

PRISE Pennsylvania's Regional Instructional System for Education (USA)

PRISM Personnel Record Information System for Management
Programme Reporting and Information Systems for Management
Progressive Refinement Integrated Supply Management

PRL Personnel Research Laboratory (USAF)
Physical Research Laboratory (India)
Pioneering Research Laboratory (of NLABS (US Army)
Princes Risborough Laboratory (of BRE)

PRLC Pittsburgh Regional Library Center (USA)

PRM Power Range Monitor
Presidential Review Memorandum (USA)
Pulse Ratio Modulator

PRNC Puerto Rico Nuclear Centre (Puerto Rico)

PRO'IN' International Product Innovation Congress and Exhibition

PROBE Profile Resolution Obtained By Excitation

PROCO Programmed Combustion

PROCON Professional Conservation Group

PROCONSA Promotores de Containers SA (Spain)

PROCSIM Processor Simulation language

PROD Programme for Orbit Development

PRODAC Production Advisors Consortium (of BCIRA, BWRA and PERA)
Programmed Digital Automatic Control

PRODAM Production Orientated Draughting and Manufacturing

PROF Prediction and Optimization of Failure Rate

PROFAC Propulsion Fluid Accumulator

PROFACS Probabilistic Facilities Planning Systems

PROFACTS Product Formulation, Accounting and Cost System

PROFILE Programmed Functional Indices for Laboratory Evaluation

PROFIT Programmed Receiving, Ordering and Forecasting Inventory Technique

PROFO Produksjonsteknisk Forskningsinstitutt (Norway) (Production Engineering Research Institute)

PROI Project Return On Investment

PROJACS Project Analysis and Control System

PROLAMAT Conference on Programming Languages for Numerically Controlled Machine Tools

PROM Pockel's Readout Optical Modulator
Programmable Read-Only Memory

PROMAG Production Management Action Group

PROMAP Program for Refinement of the Materiel Acquisition Process (US Army)

PROMAST Production Master Scheduling System

PROMATS Probabilistic Materials System

PROMIS Problem-Oriented Medical Information System
Project Management Information System
Prosecutor's Management Information System (of Law Enforcement Assistance Administration (USA))

PROMISE	Programming Managers Information System
PROMPT	Production Reviewing, Organizing and Monitoring of Performance Techniques
	Programme Monitoring and Planning Techniques
	Programme Reporting, Organisation and Management Planning Technique
PROMS	Procurement Management System (of DARCOM (US Army))
PROMSTRA	Production Methods and Stress Research Association (Netherlands)
PRONTO	Programmable Network Telecommunications Operating system
	Programme for Numerical Tool Operation
PROP	Profit Rating Of Projects
	Programme for the Refinement of Orbital Parameters
PROSEC	Association pour Favoriser la Diffusion des Appareils et Produits de Detection, de Protection et de Decontamination (France) (Association for the Promotion of Clothing and Products for Detection, Protection and Decontamination)
PROSPER	Profit Simulation, Planning and Evaluation of Risk
PROTECNA	International Exhibition for the Protection of Nature and its Environment
PROTEUS	Propulsion Research and Open-water Testing of Experimental Underwater Systems
PROVO	Stichting Proefbedrijf Voedselbestraling (Netherlands) (Experimental Station for Food Irradiation)
PROWLER	Programmable Robot Observer With Logical Response
PROXI	Projection by Reflection Optics of Xerographic Images
PRP	Paper, Rubber and Plastics
	Platelet-Rich Plasma
	Polyribophosphate
	Power-deployed Reserve Parachute
	Programmed Random Process
	Pulse Repetition Period
PRPP	Phosphoribosyl Pyrophosphate
PRR	Pseudo-Resident Reader
	Pulse Repetition Rate
PRRFC	Planar Randomly Reinforced Fibre Composites
PRS	Paint Research Station
	Partial Response System
	Pattern Recognition Society (USA)
	Polynomial Remainder Sequence
PRT	Personal Rapid Transit
	Petroleum Revenue Tax
	Platinum Resistant Thermometer
	Pulse-Repetition-Time
PRTB	PURDUE UNIVERSITY (USA) Real-Time BASIC
PRTR	Plutonium Recycle Test Reactor
PRU	Pollution Reseach Unit (of UMIST)
PRURDCO	Puerto Rico Undersea Research and Development Corporation (Puerto Rico)
PRVA	Programmable Rotary Vane Attenuator
PRX	Processor-control Reed Exchange
PS	Packet Switching
	Paradoxical Sleep
	Pharmaceutical Society of Great Britain
	Photoemission Scintillation
	Polystyrene
	Polystyrol
	prefix to Standards issued by PSI
	Product Standard (numbered/dated series issued by NBS (USA))
PSA	Pacific Science Association
	Philosophy of Science Association
	Photographic Society of America (USA)
	Pipe Stress Analysis
	Pressure Swing Adsorption
	Property Services Agency (of DOE)
PSAC	President's Science Advisory Committee (USA)
PSAD	Procurement and Systems Acquisition Division (of GAO (USA))
PSAD56	Provisional South American Datum of 1956
PSAI	Photographic Solar Aureole Isophote
PSALI	Permanent Supplementary Artificial Lighting of Interiors
PSAM	Photographic Solar Aureole Measurement
PSARP	Programmable Signal And Response Processor
PSATIS	Property Services Agency (of DOE) Technical Information Service
PSAWV	Professional Surveyors Association of West Virginia (USA) (PREVIOUSLY OF 'NORTHERN WEST VIRGINIA')
PSB	Public Service Board (Australia)
PSBB	Partially Symmetric Big Bang
PSBR	Public Sector Borrowing Requirement
PSC	Propagating Space Charge
PSCC	Paper Stock Conservation Committee (of American Paper Institute (USA))
	Polymer Supply and Characterisation Centre (of RAPRA)
	Power System Computation Conference
PSCLC	Potentiostatic Stress Corrosion Life Curve
PSD	Phase Sensitive Demodulator
	Phase-Sensitive Detector
	Photo Stimulated Desorption
	Pore Size Distribution
	Power Spectral Density
	Primary Standard Data
PSDA	Paper Sack Development Association
PSDC	Protective Structures Development Center (USDOD)
PSDN	Public Switched Data Network
PSDNA	Power System Dynamic Network Analyzer
PSDS	Portable Saturation Diving System
PSE	Packet Switching Exchange
	Passive Seismic Experiment
	Penicillin-Sensitive Enzyme
	Psychological Stress Evaluator (a lie Detector')
PSEB	Punjab State Electricity Board (India)
PSEF	Pennsylvania Science and Engineering Foundation (USA)
PSEP	Passive Seismic Experiment Package
	Program for the Study of Ethnic Publications (of Kent State University (USA))
PSERC	Public Sector Economic Research Centre (University of Leicester)
PSF	Point Spread Function
	Polystyrene Foam
PSG	Phosphosilicate Glass
	Planning System Generator
	Printing Safety Group (represents unions and employers in the printing and newspaper industry)
PSGB	Pharmaceutical Society of Great Britain
PSH	Productive Standard Hour
PSI	Page Survival Index
	Pakistan Standards Institution (Pakistan)
	Personal Sequential Inference
	Personalized-Proctorial System of Instruction
	Policies Studies Institute
	Pollution Standards Index (of CEQ (USA) and EPA (USA))
	Preprogrammed Self Instruction
	Present Serviceability Index
	Pressurized Sphere Injector
PSID	Patrol Seismic Intrusion Detector
	Patrol Seismic Intrusion Device

PSIDC Punjab State Industrial Development Corporation (India)
PSIEP Project on Scientific Information Exchange in Psychology (of American Psychological Association)
PSIL Preferred-frequency Speech Interference Level
PSIS Programme for Strategic and International Security Studies (Switzerland)
PSK Phase Shift Keying
PSL Physical Science Laboratory (new Mexico State University (USA))
Polystyrene Latex
Propulsion Systems Laboratory (US Army)
PSM People for Self Management (USA) (an organisation)
Productive Standard Minute
PSMA Pressure Sensititive Manufacturers Association
PSMD Photoselective Metal Deposition
PSMM Patrol Ship Multi-Mission
PSMS Permanent Section of Microbiological Standardization (of IAMS)
PSMT Paced Sequential Memory Task
PSN Packet Switched Network
Potassium Sodium Niobate
PSNC Pharmaceutical Services Negotiating Committee
PSNS Puget Sound Naval Shipyard (USN)
PSO Public Service Obligation
PSP Plasma Separation Process
Postsynaptic Potential
Power System Planning
Primary Smog Product
Programmable Signal Processor
PSPA Professional Sports Photographers Association
PSPE Physical Sciences (computer) Programme Exchange system (of Wolverhampton Polytechnic)
PSPRDS Prolate Spheroids
PSPRT Partial Sequential Probability Ratio Test
PSPS Pesticides Safety Precautions Scheme
PSQC Philippine Society for Quality Control (Philippines)
PSQL Process Screening Quality Level
PSR Pain Sensitivity Range
Perfectly-Stirred Reactor
Pulsar
PSRD Plant Science Research Division (of ARS (USDA))
PSRP Physical Sciences Research Paper
Physical Sciences Research Papers (issued by Air Force Cambridge Research Laboratories (USAF))
PSRV Pseudo-Relative Velocity
PSS Packet Switch Stream
Pressure Suppresion System
PSSC Public Service Satellite Consortium (USA)
PSSDS Portable Surface Supported Diving System
PSSHAK Primary Support Structures and Housing Assembly K
PSSM Parking Systems Simulation Model
PSST Public Sector Standardization Team (of government departments, nationalised industries and local authorities)
PST Polished Surface Technique
Post-Stimulus-Time
Propeller STOL Transport
PSTC Pressure Sensitive Tape Council (USA)
Public Service Training Council (Ireland)
PSTH Peristimulus Time Histogram
PSTIAC Pavements and Soil Trafficability Information Analysis Center (US Army)
PSTN Public Switched Telephone Network
PSTV Potato Spindle Tuber Virus
PSU Pennsylvania State University (USA)
PSU-IRL Pennsylvania State University–Ionosphere Research Laboratory (USA)
PSV Polished-Stone Value
Probability-State-Variable
Public Service Vehicle
PSVP Pilot Secure Voice Programme (of NATO)
PSW prefix to numbered series issued by Pacific Southwest Forest and Range Experiment Station (Forest Service (USDA))
PSWF Prolate Spheroidal Wave Function
PSyCHES Psychiatric Case History Event System
PSZ Partially Stabilised Zirconia
PT Propanthiol
Pseudoternary
PT-PSK Pilot-Tone—Phased Shift Keyed
PTA Particle Track Analysis
Passenger Transport Authority
Peak Tryptic Activity
Planar Turbulence Amplifier
Plasma Thromoboplastin Enzyme
Polytungsten Anions
Propfan Test Assessment (a program of NASA (USA))
Proposed Technical Approach
Purified Terephthalic Acid
PTAB Photographic Technical Advisory Board (of ANSI (USA))
PTAH Phosphotungstic Acid Haematoxylin
PTB Patellar Tendon Bearing
Physikalisch Technische Bundesanstalt (Germany) (National Physical Laboratory)
PTBX Private Telegraph Branch Exchange
PTC Pacific Telecommunications Council (USA)
Part-Through Crack
Personnel Transfer Capsule
Phenylthiocarbamide
Positive Temperature Coefficient
prefix to numbered-dated series of Performance Test Codes issued by ASME (USA)
Public Transport Commission (New South Wales (Australia))
PTCR Positive Temperature Coefficient Resistance
PTCS Propellant Tanking Computer System
PTD Post Tuning Drift
Programmable Thermal Desorber
PTDA Power Transmission Distributors Association (USA)
PTDL Programmable Tapped Delay Line
PTE Parathyroid Extract
Potentially Toxic Elements
Pressure Tolerant Electronic technology
PTFCE Polytrifluorochlorethylene
PTFE Polytetrafluorethylene
PTH Parathyroid Hormone
Post-Transfusion Hepatitis
PThD Punch-Through Device
PTI Pocket Incendiary
Presentation of Technical Information Group (now part of ISTC)
PTIC Patent and Trade Mark Institute of Canada (Canada)
PTL Process and Test Language
PTLS Programme-controlled Train Leading System
PTM Parasite Tubing Method
Pulse Time Modulation
Pulse Time Multiplex
PTMG Polytetramethylene Glycol
PTMT Polytetramethyleneterephthalate
PTN Pyramidal Tract Neuron
PTO Patent and Trademark Office (USA)
Post and Telegraph Department (Thailand)
PTOX Polytrioxane

PTP Paper Tape/Printer
Point-To-Point Programming
PTR Part Throttle Reheat
Personalized Task Representation
Pool Test Reactor
PTRAC Planning and Transport Research Advisory Council
PTRM Partial Thermoremanent Magnetization
PTS Permanent Threshold Shift
PTSA Para-Toluene Sulphonic Acid
PTT Partial Thromboplastin Times
PTTI Postal, Telegraph and Telephone International
Precise Time and Time Interval
PTTL Photo-Transferred Thermoluminescence
PTU Propylthiouracil
PTV Paratransit Vehicle
Predetermined Time Value
PTW Pressure Thermit Welding
PTZ Pentylenetetrazole
PU Polyurethane
Purdue University (USA)
PUCF Polyurethane-Coated Fabric
PUD Parallel Undocumented Development
Planned Urban Development
PUDOC Centre for Agricultural Publishing and Documentation (Netherlands)
PUE Pick-Up Electrode
PUFA Polyunsaturated Fatty Acids
PUFFS Passive Underwater Fire control sonar Feasibility Study
PUFFT PURDUE UNIVERSITY (USA) Fast FORTRAN Translator
PUG Prestel Users Group
PULHEMS Physical capacity, Upper Limbs, Lower limbs, Hearing acuity, Eyesight, Mental capacity, Stability
PULL Power for Underwater Logistics and Living
PULPP Peripheral Ultra-Low Power Processor
PULSAR Pulsating Star
PULSE Programme of Universal Logic Simulation for Electronics
PUMD Phaze-Uniformizing Multidither
PUN Plasma Urea Nitrogen
PUNDIT Portable Ultrasonic Non-destructive Digital Indicating Tester
PURAC Personal Use Radio Advisory Committee (of the FCC (USA))
PURDAX Public Utility Revenue Data Acquisition System
PURO Puromycin
PUS Passive Ultrasonic Sensor
PUSH Public Use Sample Helper
PUSWA Public Utilities Street Works Act, 1950
PUT Programmable Unijunction Transistor
PUTC Pittsburgh Urban Transit Council (USA)
PUVE Plutonium Value Analysis System
PV Peripheral Vein
Permanganate Value
Photovoltaic
Positive Volume
Pressure/Velocity factor
Prevailing Visibility
PVA Parameter Variation Analysis
Procedure Value Analysis
Proportional Value Analysis
PVAC Polyvinyl Acetate
PVAL Polyvinyl Alcohol
PVB Polyvinylbutyral
PVBr Polyvinyl Bromide
PVC Polyvinyl Chloride
Premature Ventricular Contractions
PVCCF Polyvinyl Chloride-Coated Fabric
PVCF Phase Variable Canonical Form
PVCH Polyvinylcyclohexane
PVD Para-Visual Director
Peripheral Vascular Disease
Physical Vapour Deposition
Plan View Display
PVDC Polyvinylidene Chloride
PVDF Polyvinylidene Fluoride
PVG Polyvinylene Glycol
PVH Propane-Vacuum-Hydrogen
PVI Pre-Vulcanisation Inhibitor
PVIM Pulse Vector Immittance Meter
PVM Point Visibility Meter
Population Vulnerability Model
Process Evaluation Module
PVME Polyrinylmethylether
PVN Paraventricular Nuclei
PVOA Passenger Vehicle Operators Association
PVOR Precision VHF Omnirange
PVOR(M) Precision Multi-Lobe VHF Omnirange
PVP Polyvinyl Pyrrolidone
Prototype-Validation Phase
Pulmonary Vascular Resistance
PVQ Personal Value Questionnaire
PVQAB Presure Vessels Quality Assurance Board (of IMechE)
PVR Portable, Volume-controlled Respirator
PVRC Pressure Vessel Research Committee (of Welding Research Council (USA))
PVRO Plant Variety Rights Organisation
PVS Personal Value System
Plan-View Sizes
PVT Page View Terminal
Paroxysmal Ventricular Tachycardia
Photovoltaic/Thermal
Polyvinyl Toluene
Pressure, Volume, Temperature
PVTCA Polyvinyl Trichlororacetate
PVTS Pressure Vessel Thermal Shock
PW Private Wire
PWA Papierwerke Waldhof Aschaffenburg Aktiengesellschaft (Germany)
PWB Printed Wiring Board
PWBA Plane Wave Born Approximation
PWC Precipitation Water Content
Printed Wiring Card
PWF Present Worth Factor
PWHT Post-Weld Heat Treatment
PWI Pilot Warning Indicator system
Pilot-Warning Instruments
Proximity Warning Indicator
PWIN Prototype WWMCCS Intercomputer Network
PWIP Participative Work Improvement Programme
PWL Piece-Wise Linear
Power Watt Level
PWM Pokeweed Mitogen
Pulse Width Modulation
Pulse Width Multiplier
PWMI Pulse Width Modulated Inverter
PWP Plasticized White Phosphorus
PWPMA Philippine Welding Products Manufacturers Association (Philippines)
PWR Pressurised Water Reactor
Pressurized Light-water-moderated and cooled Reactor
PWR-FLECHT Pressurised Water Reactor—Full Length Emergency Cooling Heat Transfer
PWS Proximity Warning System
PWT Propulsion Wind Tunnel
PXE Piezoelectric

PXL Patrol, Experimental Land-based aircraft
PZC Point of Zero Charge
PZEM Provinciale Zeeuwse Energie-Maatschappij (Netherlands)
PZITB Polski Zwiazek Inzynierow i Technikow Budownictwa (Poland) (Polish Union of Construction Engineers and Technicians)
PZM Pressure Zone Microphone
PZT Photographic Zenith Tube
P^3I Pre-planned Product Improvement

Q

Q&RA Quality and Reliability Assurance
Q&T Quenched and Tempered
Q-BOP Quiet, Quick, Quality Basic Oxygen Process
Q-FAN Quiet Fan
Q-PSK Quadrature Phase Shift Keying
Q-RTOL Quiet Reduced Take-Off and Landing
Q-STOL Quiet Short Take-Off and Landing
QA Quality Assessment
Quality Assurance
QAAS Quality Assurance Advisory Service (operated by PERA for DTI)
QAC Quaternary Ammonium Compound
QAD Quality Assurance Directorate (MOD)
QAD(FVE) Quality Assurance Directorate (Fighting Vehicles and Engineer Equipment (MOD))
QAD(Mats) Quality Assurance Directorate (Materials) (MOD) (now MQAD (MOD))
QAD(SC) Quality Assurance Directorate (Stores and Clothing) (MOD)
QAD(W) Quality Assurance Directorate (Weapons) (MOD)
QAEO Quality Assurance and Engineering Office (of NLABS (US Army)
QAFCO Qatar Fertilizer Company (Qatar) (state is a majority shareholder)
QALD Quality Assurance Liaison Division (of Defense Nuclear Agency (USDOD))
QAM Quadrature-Amplitude Modulation
Quality Assurance Monitor
QAP Quadratic Assignment Problem
QART Quality Assurance Review Technique
QAS Question Answering System
QASK Quadrature Amplitude Shift Keying
QBO Quasi-Biennial Oscillation
QBS Quebec Bureau of Standards (Canad
QBW Quasi-Biennial Wave
QC Quality Circles
Quality Control
QC&T Quality Control and Test
QCD Quantum Chromodynamics
Quarters for Cyclical Dominance
QCE Quality Control Engineer
Quality Control Engineering
QCGAT Quiet Clean General Aviation Turbofan (a project of NASA (USA))
QCM Quartz Crystal Microbalance
Quick-Connects for bulkhead Mounting
QCRT Quick Change Real-Time
QCS Quality Control Specification
QCSEE Quiet, Clean STOL Experimental Engine
QCT Quality Control Technology
QCWA Quarter Century Wireless Association (USA)
QCWW Quarter Century Wireless Women (USA)
QDC Quick-Disconnect
QDF Quadratic Discriminant Function
QDGS Quick-Draw Graphics System
QDRI Qualitative Development Requirements Information (issued by USArmy Material Command)
QDTA Quantitative Differential Thermal Analysis
QE Quantum Efficiency
Quantum Electronics
QE/C prefix to dated-numbered series of reports issued by Quality Evaluation Department (NAD-CR (USN))
QEAS Quantum Electronics Application Society (of IEEE (USA))
QED Quantum Electro-Dynamics
Quid-Each-Day (production cost-cutting programme)
QEEL Quality Evaluation and Engineering Laboratory (USN)
QELS Quality Evaluation of Literature System
QEMH Queen Elizabeth Military Hospital (of MOD)
QEP Quality Evaluation Program (of the College of American Pathologists (USA))
QETR prefix to numbered series of reports issued by Quality Evaluation Department of NAD-CR (USN)
QF Quality Factor
QFE Quartz Fibre Electrometer
QFLOW Quota Flow control
QFRI Queensland Fisheries Research Institute (Australia)
QGPC Qatar General Petroleum Corporation (Qatar) (state owned)
QGPO Qatar General Petroleum Organisation (Qatar)
QHM Quartz Horizontal Magnetometer
QI Quality Improvement
QIAC Quantimet Image Analyzing Computer
QIE Quality Information Equipment
Quantitative Immunoelectrophoresis
QIER Queensland Institute for Educational Research (Australia)
QISAM Queued Indexed Sequential Access Method
QL Query Language
QLII Quasi-Linear Intensity Interferometer
QM Quantum Mechanics
Quinacrine Mustard
QMA Quadrupole Mass Analysis
QMAC Quarter-orbit Magnetic Attitude Control
QMC Quadripartite Materiel and Agreements Committee (of ABCA)
QMD Quasi-Meridional Differentiation
Queen Mary College
QMDO Qualified Military Development Objective
Quality Material Development Objectives
QME Queueing Matrix Evaluation
QMR Qualified Military Requirement
Qualitative Material Requirement
QMS Quadruple Mass Spectrometer
QNB Quinclididinylbenzilate
QNF Quadrature N-path Filter
QOMAC Quarter-Orbit Magnetic Attitude Control
QP Quadratic Programming
QPC Qatar Petroleum Company (Qatar) (became fully govt owned in 1976)
QPF Quantitative Precipitation Forecast
QPG Query Programme Generator
QPL Qualified Products List
QPPA Qatar Petroleum Producing Authority (Qatar)
QPQ Quench Polish Quench
QPR prefix to numbered series of Quality Procedural Requirements issued by MOD
QPRS Quaternary Partial Response System

QPSK	Quadraphase Phase Shift Key modulation Quaternary Phase Shift Keying
QR	Quality and Reliability
QRA	Quality and Reliability Assurance Quick Reaction Alert
QRBM	Quasi-Random Band Model
QRC	Quick Reaction Capability
QRGA	Quadruple Residual Gas Analyzer (USA)
QRI	Quick-Reaction Interceptor
QRPG	Quebec Rubber and Plastics Group (Canada)
QS	Quadrophonic Stereo Queueing System
QSAM	Queued Sequential Access Method
QSC	Quasi-Sensory Communication
QSE	Qualified Scientists and Engineers Quantum Size Effect
QSF	Quiet-Short Field
QSG	Quasi-Stellar Galaxy
QSH	Quiet Short-Haul
QSO	Quasi-Stellar Object
QSOP	Quadripartite Standing Operating Procedures (of WSO (ABCA))
QSRA	Quiet Short-haul Research Aircraft
QSRIG	Research and Information Group of the Quantity Surveyors Committee (Royal Institution of Chartered Surveyors)
QSRS	Quasi-Stellar Radio Sources
QSTAGS	Quadripartite Standardization Agreements (issued by QWG (of ABCA))
QSTOL	Quiet Short Take-Off and Landing
QT	Quenched and Tempered
QTAM	Queued Telecommunications Access Method
QTM	prefix to numbered series of Quality Technical Memoranda issued by MOD
QTP	Quality Test Plan
QTR	Quality Technical Requirement (of MOD)
QUAD	Quality Assurance Department (of BSI)
QUALTIS	a subscription information service on NDT provided by the NDTC (AERE, Harwell)
QUAM	Quadrature Amplitude Modulation
QUANGO	Quasi-Autonomous Non-Governmental Organisation
QUANTRAS	Question Analysis Transformation and Search
QUARK	Question and Response Kit
QUASAR	Quality system Assessment and Registration (BSI)
QUAST	Quality Assurance Service Test
QUEST	Quantification of Uncertainty in Estimating Support Tradeoffs Quantitative Utility Estimates for Science and Technology
QUEST	Query Statutes
QUESTAR	Quantitative Utility Evaluation Suggesting Targets for the Allocation of Resources
QUESTOL	Quiet Experimental STOL
QUICK	QUEENS UNIVERSITY (Kingston, Ontario) Interpretive Coder, Kingston
QUICO	Quality Improvement through Cost Optimization
QUIDS	Quick Interactive Documentation System
QUILT	Quantitative Intelligence Analysis Technique
QUIP	Query Interactive Processor Questionnaire Interpreter Programme Quick Inquiry Processor
QUIPS	Quiescent Plasma Studies Quiescent Uniform Ionospheric Plasma Simulator
QUIS	QUEENS UNIVERSITY (Belfast) Information Systems
QUISTOR	Quadruple Ion Store
QUOBIRD	QUEENS UNIVERSITY (Belfast) On-line Bibliographic Information Retrieval and Dissemination system
QUODAMP	QUEENS UNIVERSITY (Belfast) Databank on Atomic and Molecular Physics
QUOTA	QUADRANT (SOFTWARE) On-line Testing Aid
QVT	Quality Verification Testing
QWG/CD	Quadripartite Working Group on Combat Development (representative of the American, British, Canadian and Australian Armies)
QWH	Quantum Wall Heterostructure
QWOT	Quarter Wave Optical Thickness
QWSSUA	Quasi-Wide-Sense-Stationary Uncorrelated Scattering

R

R	Recommendation Regulation Reliability Report Research
R & E	Research and Engineering
R & S	Reconnaissance and Surveillance
R&D	Research and Development
R&M	Reliability and Maintainability Reports and Memoranda
R&QA	Reliability and Quality Assurance
R&QC	Reliability and Quality Control
R&RR	Range and Range Rate
R-MuLV	Rauscher Murine Leukaemia Virus
R-Nav	Area Navigation
R/M/A	Reliability, Maintainability and Availability
R4	Recovery and Reuse of Refuse Resources (a program of USN)
RA	Radar Altimeter Recrystallization-Anneal Relaxation Allowance Reliability Assurance Retrograde Amnesia Right Ascension
RAA	Regional Airlines Association (USA) Renin-Angiotensin-Aldosterone
RAAF	Royal Australian Air Force (Australia)
RAAM	Remote Anti-Armour Mine
RAAP	Residue Arithmetic Associative Processor Resource Allocation And Planning system
RAB	Regional Activities Board (of IEEE (USA))
RABA	Re-chargeable Air-Breathing Apparatus
RABATS	Rapid Analytical Block Aerial Triangulation System
RABDF	Royal Association of British Dairy Farmers
RABFM	Research Association of British Flour-Millers (merged into FMBRA in 1967)
RABPCVM	Research Association of British Paint, Colour and Varnish Manufacturers
RABRM	Research Association of British Rubber Manufacturers (became RAPRA in 1960)
RAC	Radiometric Area Correlator Recombinant DNA Advisory Committee (USA) Reflective Array Compression Reflective-Array Compressor Relative Address Coding Reliability Analysis Center Rhomboidal Air Controller Royal Automobile Club Rubber Association of Canada (Canada)
RACE	Radiation Adaptive Compression Equipment Random Access Control Equipment Rapid Automatic Check-out Equipment Remote Automatic Computing Equipment

Response Analysis for Call Evaluation
ROCHESTER (New York (USA)) Area Commuter Express

RACEP Random Access and Correlation for Extended Performance

RACES Radio Amateur Communication Emergency Services (USA)

RACI Royal Australian Chemical Institute (Australia)

RACIC Remote Areas Conflict Information Center (of BMI)

RACMAP RESEARCH ANALYSIS CORPORATION (USA) Macro Assembly Programme

RACOMS Rapid Combat Mapping System (US Army)

RACON Radar Navigational Beacon
Radar Responder Beacon

RACP Royal Australasian College of Physicians (Australia)

RACS Remote Access Computing System
Remote Automatic Calibration System
Royal Australasian College of Surgeons (Australia)

RACSS Retail Apparel Chain Store System

RAD Radiation Absorbed Dose
Random Access Disc
Rapid Automatic Drill
Ratio Analysis Diagram
Right Angle Drive

RADA Random Access Discrete Address

RADAC Range Data and Control Center (of NCSL (USN))

RADAG Radar Area Correlation Guidance System

RADANT Radome Antenna

RADAR Radio Detection And Ranging
Receivable Accounts Data-entry And Retrieval
ROHR Automated Data And Retrieval system
Royal Association for Disability and Rehabilitation

RADAS Random Access Discrete Address System

RADC Rome Air Development Center (USAF)

RADCAP ROME AIR DEVELOPMENT CENTER (USAF) Associative Array Processor

RADCOLS ROME AIR DEVELOPMENT CENTER (USAF) On-Line Simulator

RADCON Radar Data Converter

RADDS RAYTHEON Automated Digital Design System

RADEF Radiological Defence

RADEX Radar Data Extractor

RADI Retail Alarm for Display and Intruder

RADIAC Radioactivity Detection Indication And Computation

RADINT Radar Intelligence

RADIR Random Access Document Indexing and Retrieval

RADLE Responsive Automatic Dial-out and Line Transfer Equipment

RADMAP Radiological Monitoring Assessment Prediction system

RADMON Radiological Monitoring

RADOP Radar/Optical

RADOT Radar Operator Trainer
Recording Automatic Digital Optical Tracker

RADRU Rapid Access Data Retrieval Unit

RADS Radar Alphanumeric Display Sub-system

RADVS Radar Altimeter and Doppler Velocity Sensor

RAE Radio Astronomy Explorer satellite
Range Azimuth Elevation
Royal Aircraft Establishment (MOD)

RAeC Royal Aero Club of the United Kingdom

RAEN Radio Amateur Emergency Network

RAeS Royal Aeronautical Society

RAF Royal Air Force

RAFA Royal Air Forces Association

RAFARS Royal Air Force Amateur Radio Society

RAFGSA Royal Air Force Gliding and Soaring Association

RAFM Repair-At-Failure Maintenance

RAFOS Royal Air Force Ornithological Society

RAFT Radially Adjustable Facility Tube
Receiving Ambient Function Test
Regional Accounting and Finance Test
Resource Allocation For Transportation

RAG Ring Airfoil Grenade

RAGS Route Analysis, Generation and Simulation

RAI Radiotelevisione Italiana (Italy)
Registro Aeronautico Italiano (Italy) (Air Registration Board)
Royal Anthropological Institute

RAI/OP Repetitive Activity Input/Output Plan

RAIA Royal Australian Institute of Architects (Australia)

RAIBC Radio Amateur Invalid and Blind Club

RAIC Royal Architectural Institute of Canada (Canada)

RAID Rapid Alerting and Identification Display

RAIDS Rapid Acquisition and Identification System
Rapid Availability of Information and Data for Safety
Real-time AUTODIN Interface and Distribution System (USDOD)

RAILS Reference And Inter-Library Loan Service (of state-assisted Universities in Ohio (USA))
Runway Alignment Indicator Lights

RAIR Ram Augmented Inter-stellar Rocket

RAIRS Reflection Absorption Infra-Red Spectroscopy

RAIS Rail Air International Service

RAISE Rigorous Approach to Industrial Software

RAK Regeln fur die alphabetische Katalogisierung (German code of rules for alphabetical cataloguing)
Rikets Allmanna Kartverk (Sweden) (Geographical Survey Office)

RAL Radio Annoyance Level
Regional Adjunct Language
Rutherford Appleton Laboratory (of SERC)

RALACS Radar Altimeter Low-Altitude Control System

RALI Resource and Land Information program (of the United States Geological Survey)

RALU Register and Arithmetic-Logic Unit

RALW Radioactive Liquid Waste

RAM Radar-Absorbing Material
Radio Attenuation Measurement
Radioactive Material
Rancho Anthropomorphic Manipulator
Random Access Method
Random Adaptive Module
Random Angle Modulation
Random-Access Memory
Redeye Air Missile
Reliability, Availability and Maintainability
Remote Acquisition Monitoring
Request-Answer to Request-Message
Research and Application Module
Resource Allocation Model
RF (radio frequency) Absorbing Material
Risk Assessment Methodology
Rocket-Assisted Motor
Rolling Airframe Missile

RAM-D Reliability And Maintainability-Dependability

RAM/LOG Reliability, Availability, Maintainability/Logistics

RAMAC Random Access Method of Accounting and Control

RAMB Rabbit-Anti-Mouse-Brain

RAMCEASE Reliability, Availability, Maintainability, Cost Effectiveness and Systems Effectiveness

RAMIS Rapid Access Management Information System

RAMIT Rate-Aided Manually Initiated Tracking
RAMM Respirable Aerosol Mass Monitor
RAMMIT Reliability And Maintainability Management Improvement Techniques
Reliability, Availability and Maintainability Improvement Techniques
RAMMS Responsive Automated Material Management System (USDOD)
RAMNAC Radio Aids to Marine Navigation Application Committee
RAMP Radar Mapping of Panama
Rate and Acceleration Measuring Pendulum
RAYTHEON Airborne Microwave Platform
Reliability Assurance Maintenance Programme
RAMPART Radar Advanced Measurements Programme for Analysis of Re-entry Techniques
Route to Airlift Mobility through Partnership
RAMPLAN Rock Mechanics Applied to Mine Planning
RAMPS Resource Allocation and Multi-Project Scheduling
RAMS Random Access Measurement System
Remote Arctic Measuring System bouy
Remote Automatic Multipurpose Station
RAMSES Reprogrammable Advanced Multimode Shipboard ECM System
RAMUS Remote Access Multi-User System
RAN Request for Authority to Negotiate
Royal Australian Navy (Australia)
RANC Radar Attenuation, Noise and Clutter
RANGLOAD Radius, Angle, Load
RANN Research Applied to National Needs (a project of NSF (USA)) (now ASRA)
RANRL Royal Australian Navy Research Laboratory (Australia)
RANSA Royal Australian Naval Sailing Association (Australia)
RANT Re-entry Antenna Test
RAO Response Amplitude Operator
RAOT Rocker Arm Oiling Time
RAP Radiological Assistance Program (of ERDA (USA))
Reactive Atmosphere Process
Redundancy Adjustment of Probability
Reliable Acoustic Path sonar
Resource Allocation Processor
Rocket Assisted Projectile
RAPCON Radar Approach Control
Remote Approach Control
RAPE Radar Arithmetic Processing Element
RAPIC Remedial Actions Program Information Center (of ORNL (USA))
RAPID Data Collection
Rail Gun Armature Plasma Investigation Device
Random Access Personnel Information Disseminator
Random Access Photographic Index and Display
Register for the Ascertainment and Prevention of Inherited Diseases (of the Medical Research Council)
Remote Automatic Parts Input for Dealers
Research in Automatic Photocomposition and Information Dissemination
Resource Allocation and Piping Isometric Drawing
Rotating Associative Processor for Information Dissemination
RAPP Rajasthan Atomic Power Project (of Atomic Energy Commission of India)
Resource Allocation and Project Planning
RAPPORT Rapid Alert Programmed, Power management of Radar Targets
RAPRA Rubber and Plastic Research Association
RAPS Radar Automatic Plotting System
Rajasthan Atomic Power Station (India)
Retrieval Analysis and Presentation System
RAPT Reception Automatic Picture Transmission
RAR Rapid Access Recording
Real Aperture Radar
Reflect-Array Radar
RARDE Royal Armament Research and Development Establishment (MOD)
RARDEN RARDE and RSAF, Enfield
RAREPS Radar Reports
RARF Radome, Antenna and Radio Frequency
RARS Register Access Relay Set
RAS Relative Aerobic Strain
Replenishment At Sea
Royal Astronomical Society
RASAR Resource Allocation System for Agricultural Research
RASB Rapid Access to Sequential Blocks
RASCAL Random Access Sequence Communications Anti-jam Link
Rudimentary Adaptive System for Computer-Aided Learning
RASD Reference and Adult Services Division (of the American Library Association (USA))
RASE Rapid Automatic Sweep Equipment
Royal Agricultural Society of England
RASH Repetition, Alternation, Sequence plus Hierarchy
RASIOM Raffinerie Siciliane Olii Minerali (Sicily)
RASMP Radiotherapy Apparatus Safety Measures Panel
RASP Resource Analysis Simulation Procedure
RASS Radar-Acoustic Sounding System
Rapid Area Supply Support
Rock Analysis Storage System
RASSR Reliable Advanced Solid State Radar
RAST Radioallergosorbent Test
Recovery Assist, Secure and Traverse
RASTA Radiation Special Test Apparatus
RASTAS Radiating Site Target Acquisition System
RAT Ram Air Turbine
Routing Automation Technique
RATAC RAYTHEON Acoustic Telemetry And Control
RATAN Radar And Television Aid to Navigation
RATAS Research And Technical Advisory Services (a department of Lloyd's Register of Shipping)
RATCC Radar Air Traffic Control Centre
RATCON Radar Target Concealment
RATE Rate-Aided Tracking Equipment
RATEKSA Radiobranchens Tekniske og Kommercielle Sammenslutning (Denmark) (Radio and Television Retailers Association)
RATEN Random Threshold-Element Network
RATER RAYTHEON Acoustic Test and Evaluation Range
Response Analysis Tester
RATFOR Rational FORTRAN
RATIO Radio Telescope In Orbit
RATO Rocket Assisted Take-Off
RATOG Rocket-Assisted Take-Off Gear
RATP Regie Autonome Transports Parisiens (Paris, France) (Paris Transport Authority)
RATSCAT Radar Target Scatter
RATTLE Road Accident Tabulation Language
RATTS Radar Telephone Transmission System
RAVE Research Aircraft for Visual Environment (a project of ECOM (US Army))
RAWC Radioactive Waste Co-ordinating Committee
RAX Remote Access Computing System
Rural Automatic Exchange
RAYLCC RAYTHEON (SERVICE COMPANY) (USA) Life Cycle Cost
RAYNET Radio Amateurs Emergency Network (of RSGB) (for Assistance in civil emergencies)

RB Return to Bias
Riksbibliotekjenesten (Norway) (National Agency for Research and Special Libraries, and Documentation)
RBA Road Bitumen Association
RBAN Regular Best Asymptotically Normal
RBBB Right Bundle Branch Block
RBC Red Blood Cell
Rotating Beam Ceilometer
Rotating Biological Contactor
RBCTK Red Blood Cell Transketolase
RBD Rapid Beam Deflector
RBDE Radar Bright Display Equipment
RBE Relative Biological Effectiveness
Relative Biological Efficiency
RBF Ready Bit Feedback
RBG Reactor-Brennelemente GmbH (Germany)
RBGF Resin-Bonded Glass-Fibre
RBI Reserve Bank of India (India)
RBLS Rolling Ball Loss Spectrometer
RBM Real-time Batch Monitor
RBOC Rapid Bloom Off-board Chaff
Rapid Bloom Off-board Countermeasures
RBOT Rotating Bomb Oxidation Test
RBP Retinol-Binding Protein
RBS Rutherford Back-Scattering
RBSN Reaction Bonded Silicon Nitride
RBT Remote Batch Terminal
Rose Bengal Test
RBU Reaktor-Brennelement Union (Germany)
RBV Return Beam Vidicon
RC Replacement Cost accounting
Research Centre
Research Contribution
Resistor-Capacitator
Rotary Combustion
RCA Regional Cooperative Agreement for Research, Development and Training related to Nuclear Science and Technology in South and Southeast Asia, the Pacific and the Far East
Reinforced Concrete Association
Replacement Cost Accounting
RCAA Rocket City Astronomical Association (USA)
RCAF Royal Canadian Air Force
RCAG Remote Controlled Air/Ground communication station
RCAT Radio Code Aptitude Test
RCC Reinforced Carbon-Carbon
Rod-Cluster Control
RCCE Regional Congress of Construction Employers (USA)
RCCM Research Council for Complementary Medicine
RCCO Reduction Circuit for Checker Outputs
RCD Regional Co-operation for Development (an economic organisation comprising Iran, Pakistan and Turkey)
Residual Current Device
RCDC Radiation Chemistry Data Center (University of Notre Dame (USA))
RCDS Reinforced Concrete Detailing System
Royal College of Defence Studies
RCE Repetitive Counterelectrophoresis
Rotary Combustion Engine
RCEP Royal Commission on Environmental Pollution
RCFR Rotating Cylinder Flap Rudder
RCG Reaction Cured Glass
RCGP Royal College of General Practitioners
RCHN(E) Royal Commission on Historical Monuments (England)
RCI Radar Coverage Indicator
RCJ Reaction Control Jet
RCM Radiative Convective Model
Red Cell Mass
Reliability-Centred Maintenance
Royal College of Midwives
RCMS Resonator-Controlled Microwave Source
RCN Reactor Centrum Nederland (Netherlands) (Netherlands Reactor Centre) (became ECN in 1976)
Relay-Contact Network
Reticulum Cell Neoplasms
Royal College of Nursing
RCNC Royal Corps of Naval Constructors (MOD)
RCNJ Ramapo College of New Jersey (USA)
RCNP Research Center for Nuclear Physics (Osaka University (Japan))
RCOG Royal College of Obstetricians and Gynaecologists
RCOH Reliability Controlled Overhaul Programme
RCP Registry of Comparative Pathology (of AFIP (USDOD) and UAREP)
REM (Rapid Eye Movement) Cycle Period
Royal College of Physicians
RCPA Royal College of Physicians of Australia
RCPath Royal College of Pathologists
RCPEd Royal College of Physicians of Edinburgh
RCPG Regional Cooperative Physics Group (of educational institutions in Ohio, Michigan, Illinois and Pennsylvania (USA)
RCPI Royal College of Physicians of Ireland
RCPsych Royal College of Psychiatrists
RCR Randle Cliff Radar
Recrystallization Controlled Rolling
Rotating Cylinder Rudder
Royal College of Radiologists
RCS Radar Cross-Section
Reaction Control System
Reactor Control System
Ride Control System
Rotable Control System
Royal College of Science
Royal College of Surgeons
Royal College of Surgeons of England
Royal Commonwealth Society
RCS(C) Royal College of Surgeons (Canada)
RCS-RF Rabbit aorta Contracting Substance-Releasing Factor
RCSC Radio Components Standardization Committee (MOD and MINTECH)
RCSEd Royal College of Surgeons of Edinburgh
RCSI Royal College of Surgeons in Ireland
RCT Radioactivity Control Technology
Randomized Clinical Trial
Reverse Conducting Thyristor
RCU Road Construction Unit
RCUT Rapid Carbohydrate Utilization Test
RCV Remotely-Controlled Vehicle
RCVS Royal College of Veterinary Surgeons
RD Research and Development
RD&D Research, Development and Demonstration
RD&E Research, Development and Engineering
RD/B/N prefix to numbered series of reports issued by Berkeley Nuclear Laboratories (of CEGB)
RD/I Research, Development and Innovation
RDA Radioactive Dentine Abrasion
Railway Development Association
Recommended Daily Allowance
Reliability Design Analysis
Research, Development and Acquisition
RDAT Research and Development Acceptance Testing
RDAU Remote Data Acquisition Unit

RDB	Relational Data Base
RDC	Regional Dissemination Centers (of NASA (USA)) Rotating Disc Contactor
RDCA	Rural Districts Councils Association
RDD	Reactor Development and Demonstration Division (of ERDA (USA))
RDDP	RNA-Directed DNA Polymerase
RDDS	RNA-Directed DNA-Synthesis
RDE	Radial Defect Examination Receptor Destroying Enzyme Research and Development Effectiveness Rotating Disk Electrode
RDF	Radial Distribution Function Radio Direction Finder Radio Direction Finding Rapid Deployment Force Refuse-Derived Fuel Relational Data File
RDI	Recommended Daily Intake Research and Development/Innovation Royal Designer for Industry (a distinction awarded by the Royal Society for the encouragement of Arts, Manufactures and Commerce AND the Faculty of Royal Designers for Industry)
RDIS	Research and Development Information System
RDM	Respirable Dust Monitor
RDN	Resource Decision Network
rDNA	Ribosomal DNA
RDOEI	Research and Development Organization for Electrical Industry (India)
RdON	Road Octane Number
RDP	Radar Data-Processing Radar Detector Processor
RDPI	Real Personal Disposable Income
RDPS	Radar Data Processing System
RDPT	Relative Double Phase-Shift Telegraph
RDR	Research and Development Report
RDS	Research Defence Society Respiratory Distress Syndrome
RDSO	Research, Design and Standardization Organization (of Indian Railways (India))
RDT	Remote Data Terminal
RDT&E	Research Development Testing and Evaluation Research, Development, Test and Engineering
RDTE	Research, Development, Testing and Evaluation (or Engineering)
RDTL	Resistor Diode Transistor Logic
RDTR	Research Division Technical Report
RDVP	Radar Video Data Processor
RDX	Cyclo-trimethylene-trinitramine
RE	Rare Earth
RE&R	Research, Engineering and Reliability
REA	Radar and Electronics Association Regenerated Ethylamine Right Ear Advantage Rural Electrification Administration (USDA)
REACH	Real-time Electronic Access Communications for Hospitals
REACT	Register Enforced Automated Control Technique Reliability Evaluation And Control Techniques Requirements Evaluated Against Cargo Transportation Resource Allocation Control Tool
READ	Real-time Electronic Access and Display Remote Electronic Alphanumeric Display
READI	Rocket Engine Analyser and Decision Instrumentation
REALCOST	Resource Allocation Cost System
REAM	Rapid Excavating And Mining
REAMS	RAMOND (ALBERT RAMOND AND ASSOCIATES INCORPORATED (USA)) Electronically Applied Maintenance Standards
REAP	Reliability Engineering Analysis and Planning Rural Environmental Assistance Program (USA)
REAR	Reliability Engineering Analysis Report
REB	Rare Earth Boride
REBEEL	Realistic Battlefield Environment-Electronic
REC	Rare Earth Cobalt Rural Electrification Corporation (India)
REC-ERC	prefix to dated-numbered series of reports issued by Bureau of Reclamation, Engineering and Research Center (US Department of the Interior)
REC-OCE	prefix to dated-numbered series of reports issued by the Bureau of Reclamation, Office of the Chief Engineer (US Department of the Interior)
RECA	Repetitive Element Column Analysis
RECAT	Cumulative Regulatory Effects on the Cost of Automotive Transportation (a study by Office of Science and Technology (USA)) Reduced Energy Consumption of the Air Transportation system (a study by NASA (USA))
RECEP	Relative Capacity Estimating Capacity
RECMF	Radio and Electronic Component Manufacturers Federation
RECOMP	Retrieval and Composition
RECON	Remote Console Retrospective Conversion pilot project (of Library of Congress (USA))
RECSAM	Regional Centre for Education in Science and Mathematics (of SEAMEO (Malaysia))
RED	Reconnaissance Engineering Directorate (of System Command's Aeronautical Systems Division (USAF)) Reflection-Electron Diffraction
REDAC	RACAL Electronic Design and Analysis by Computer
REDCAP	Real-time Electro-magnetic Digitally Controlled Analyzer Processor
REDCOM	Readiness Command (US Army)
REDR	Register of Engineers for Disaster Relief
REDSOD	Repetitive Explosive Device for Soil Displacement
REDUC	Red Latinoamericana de Documentacion en Educacion (Latin-American Education Documentation Network)
REDY	Re-circulation Dialysate machine
REE	Rare-Earth Elements
REED	Radio and Electrical Engineering Division (of NRC (Canada))
REEP	Regression Estimation of Event Probabilities
REF	Railway Engineers Forum (of the Institutions of Civil, Mechanical, Electrical and Railway Signal Engineers)
REFIL	Recharged From Inversion Layer
REFLECS	Retrieval From the Literature on Electronics and Computer Sciences
REFSMMAT	Reference to Stable Member Matrix
REG	Radioisotope Electrogenerator Regional Rheoencephalography Regional Rheoenecphalography Rheoencephalography
REGAL	Remote Generalised Application Language
REHVA	Representatives of European Heating and Ventilating Associations
REIC	Radiation Effects Information Center (of Batelle Memorial Institute (USA)) Radiation Effects Information Center (USAF)
REIG	Rare-Earth Iron Garnets
REIL	Runway End Identifier Lights
REINS	Radar Equipped Inertial Navigation System
REL	Rapidly Extensible Language
RELCOMP	Reliability Computation

RELIPOSIS Research Liaison Panel On Scientific Information Services (of the British Gas Corporation)
RELKIN Relativistic Kinematics
REM Rack Entry Module
Rapid Eye Movement
Rare Earth Metals
Research Evaluation Method
Rocket Engine Module
Roentgen Equivalent Man
REMA Rotating Electrical Machines Association (a federated association of BEAMA)
REMAP Record Extraction Manipulation and Print
Regional Environmental Management Allocation Process
REMBASS Remotely Monitored Battlefield-Area Sensor System
REMCALC Relative Motion Collision Avoidance Calculator
REMCAN Repairable Multilayer Circuit Assembly Method
REMCO Reference Materials Committee (of ISO)
REML Restricted Maximum Likelihood
Risley Engineering and Materials Laboratory
REMOTE Reflective Mossbauer Technique
REMP Rapid Eye Movement Period
REMPA Reference Materials Party (of ISO)
REMSA Railway Engineering Maintenance Suppliers Association (USA)
REMSCON Conference and Exhibition on Remote Supervisory and Control Systems
REMUS Routine for Executive Multi-Unit Simulation
RENE Rocket Engine Nozzle Ejector
RENFE Red Nacional de los Ferrocarriles Espanoles (Spain) (Spanish National Railways)
RENS Reconnaissance Electronic Warfare and Naval Intelligence System
REON Rocket Engine Operations—Nuclear
REP Range Error Probable
Range Estimating Programme
Regional Employment Premium
Relativistic Electron Precipitation
Report
REPCON Rain Repellant and Surface Conditioner
REPEET Reusabler Engines, Partially External Expendable Tankage
REPLAB Responsive Environment Programmed Laboratory
REPLAC Symposium on Reinforced Plastics Process against Corrosion
REPREX Representative Extraction
REPROM Re-programmable Read-Often Memory
REPS Repetitive Electromagnetic Pulse Simulator
REPT Report
REQP Recursive Equality Quadratic Programming
REQUEST Restricted English Question-answering system
RER Reseau Express Regional (France)
RERF Radiation Effects Research Foundation (Japan) (private non-profit foundation funded equally by Japan and the USA) (a successor, formed in 1975, to the Atomic Bomb Casualty Commission)
RES Radiating Electromagnetic pulse Simulator
Reticuloendothelial System
Royal Entomological Society of London
RESA Scientific Research Society of America (USA)
RESCAM Regional Centre for Education in Science and Mathematics (of SEAMEO)
RESD Research and Engineering Support Division (of Institute for Defense Analysis, USA)
RESEP Re-entry Systems Environmental Protection
RESISTORS The Radically Emphatic Students Interested in Science, Technology and Other Research Studies (USA)
RESP Remote-batch Station Programme
RESPONSA Retrieval of Special Portions from "NUCLEAR SCIENCE Abstracts"
RESR Rotating Electronically Scanned Radar
REST (Microform) Reader Evaluation and Selection Techniques
Radar Electronic Scan Technique
Re-entry Environment and Systems Technology
Representative Scientific Test
Resource Time
RET Rapid Excavation Technology
RETAIN Remote Technical Assistance and Information Network
RETECH Regional Technical Conference (of Society of Plastics Engineers (USA))
RETMA Radio, Electronics, Television Manufacturers Association (now EIA) (USA)
RETRA Radio, Electrical and Television Retailers Association
RETSPL Reference Equivalent Threshold Sound Pressure Level
REVIMA Societe pour la Revision et l'Entretien du Material Aeronautique (France)
REVS Rotor-Entry Vehicle System
REX Radio Exploration satellite
REXA Radioisotope-Excited X-ray Analyzer
REXS Radio Exploration Satellite
RF Radio Frequency
Rating Factor
Reticular Formation
Rigid Frame
RF.P prefix to numbered series of Reference Papers issued by the Central Office of Information
RF/IR Radio Frequency/Infra-Red
RFA Redundant Force Analysis
Royal Fleet Auxiliary
RFB Rotating Fluidized Bed
RFC Rajasthan Financial Corporation (India)
Rosette Forming Cells
RFCM Radio Frequency Counter-measures
RFCWA Regional Fisheries Commission for West Africa (Ghana)
RFDMA Rigid Foam Ducting Manufacturers Association
RFDS Royal Flying Doctor Service (Australia)
RFE Radio Free Europe
RFF Research Flight Facility (of Environmental Research Laboratories (NOAA (USA))
Resources for the Future, Inc. (USA) (non-profit corporation)
Rocket Fabrication Facility (of ISRO (India))
RFFP Rescue and Fire Fighting Panel (of ICAO)
RFFSA Rede Ferroviaria Federal SA (Brazil) (Federal Railway Corporation)
RFHSM Royal Free Hospital School of Medicine
RFI Radio Frequency Interference
Ready for Issue
Remote File Inquiry
RFL Reactor Fuel Laboratory (of UKAEA)
Resorcinol Formaldehyde Latex
RFNA Red Fuming Nitric Acid
RFP Request for Proposal
Reversed Field Pinch
RFPR Reversed-Field Pinch Reactor
RFQ Request For Quote
RFR Radio Frequency Radiation
RFS Radio Frequency Surveillance
RFS/ECM Radio Frequency Surveillance/Electronic Counter Measures
RFTT Rapid Fibre Tensile Tester
RFV Regressing Friend Virus
RFX Reversed Field Experiment

RG prefix to dated-numbered series of reports issued by Guidance and Control Directorate, Redstone Arsenal (US Army)

RGA Residual-Gas Analysis
Rubber Growers Association

RGCSP Review of General Concept of Separation Panel (of ICAO)

RGD Radiation Gasdynamics
RAYLEIGH-GANS-DEBYE

RGF Range Gated Filtering

RGFC Remote Gas Filter Correlation

RGFCS Radar Gunfire Control System

RGG Reverse Gradient Garment

RGIT Robert Gordon's Institute of Technology

RGL Rare-Gas Liquid

RGM Remote Geophysical Monitor

RGO Royal Greenwich Observatory (of Science Research Council)

RGP Reliability Growth Programme

RGPO Range Gate Pull-Off

RGRDE Rotating Gold Ring-Disc Electrode

RGS Radio Guidance System
Rare-Gas Solid
Rate Gyro System
Royal Geographical Society

RGT Resonant Gate Transistor

RGWS Radar Guided Weapon System
Radar-Guided Warning System

RH prefix to series on Radiological Health issued by Public Health Service (USA)
Radiation Hydrodynamics
Relative Humidity
Resistance Heating

RHA Rapidly-sedimenting Haemagglutinin
Rice Husk Ash
Road Haulage Association
Rolled Homogeneous Armour

RHAG Rotary Hydraulic Arresting Gear

RHAW Radar Homing And Warning

RHAWR Radar Homing And Warning Receiver

RHAWS Radar Homing And Warning System

RHCP Remote File Inquiry
Right-Hand Circularly Polarized

RHCSA Regional Hospitals Consultants and Specialists Association (became HCSA in April 1974)

RHEED Reflection High-Energy Electron-Diffraction

RHEL Rutherford High Energy Laboratory (of the SRC) (now The Rutherford Laboratory) (later in 1981 merged into RAL (of SERC))

RHI Range-Height Indicator

RHINO Repeating Hand-held Improved Non-rifled Ordnance

RHL Rectangular Hysteresis Loop

RHOGI Radar Homing Guidance

RHPC Rapid Hardening PORTLAND (ASSOCIATED PORTLAND CEMENT Manufacturers Ltd) Cement

RHR Rejectable Hazard Rate

RHS Rectangular Hollow Sections
Royal Horticultural Society

RHSI Royal Horticultural Society of Ireland

RHTS Reactor Heat Transport System

RI prefix to numbered series of Reports of Investigations issued by Bureau of Mines (USA)
Radar Index
Relative Incidence
Report of Investigation
Retroactive Interference
Robotics International (of SME (USA))
Room Index (relative to illumination)
Royal Institution of Great Britain

RI/SH Radar Intelligence/Surface Height

RIA Radioimmunoassay
Railway Industry Association of Great Britain
Reactivity-Initiated Accident
Robot Institute of America (USA) (now Robotics Industries Association)
Rock Island Arsenal (US Army)

RIAA Recording Industry Association of America (USA)

RIAI Royal Institute of Architects of Ireland

RIAS Research Institute for Advanced Studies (USA)
Royal Incorporation of Architects in Scotland

RIB Rijksinkoopbureau (Netherlands) (Government Purchasing Office)
River Ice Breaker

RIBA Royal Institute of British Architects

RIC Radar Intercept Calculator
Rare-Earth Information Center (Iowa State University (USA))
Reciprocal Impedance Converter
Reclamation Industries Council (superseded by BRIC in 1977)
Royal Institute of Chemistry

RICA Research Institute for Consumer Affairs

RICASIP Research Information Center and Advisory Service on Information Processing (USA)

RICE Radar Interface and Control Equipment
Rationalised Internal Communication Equipment
Regional Information and Communication Exchange (a library and information network in the Gulf Coast region of USA based on Rice University)
Remote File Inquiry

RICS Range Instrumentation Control System
Royal Institution of Chartered Surveyors
Rubber Impregnated Chopped Strands

RID Reglement International concernant le transport des merchandises dangereuses (International Regulations Concerning the Carriage of Dangerous Goods)
Review Item Disposition
Rijksinstituut voor Dirkwatervoorziening (State Institute for Drinking Water Research) (Netherlands)

RIDE Radio Communications Intercept and Direction Finding Equipment
Rail International Design and Environment (an *ad hoc* group of UIC)

RIE Reactive Ion Etching

RIEC Research Institute for Estate Crops (Indonesia)

RIFP Research Institute for Fundamental Physics (Kyoto University (Japan))

RIFT Reactor In Flight Test

RIG Reaktor-Interessen-Gemeinschaft (Austria)

RIGEL ROCKWELL INTERNATIONAL (USA) Ghost Eliminator

RIGFET Resistive Insulated-Gate Field Effect Transistor

RIIA Royal Institute for International Affairs

RIKE Raman-Induced Kerr Effect

RILEM Reunion Internationale des Laboratoires d'Essais et de Recherche sur les Materiaux et les constructions (International Union of Testing and Research Laboratories for Materials and Structures) (France)

RILO Research and Industrial Liaison Office (of USACDC)

RILS Rapid Integrated Logistics System (US Army)

RIM Radar Intelligence Map
Reaction Injection Moulding
Rhodesian Institute of Management (Rhodesia)

RIM/RIF Refractive Index Measurement/Refractive Index Forecasting (advisory group of the USN)

RIMDC Rajasthan State Industrial and Mineral Development Corporation (India)

RIME Ranking Index for Maintenance Expenditures

RIMPATT W. T. READ Impact Avalanche Transit-Time diode

RIMS Radio Interference Measuring Set
Remote Information Management System

RIN Royal Institute of Navigation

RINA Registro Italiano Navale (Italy)
Royal Institution of Naval Architects

RINT Radiation Intelligence

RINTIN Radioisotope Instruments and Tracers in Industry

RIOT Retrieval of Information by On-line Terminal (a project of Culham Laboratory (UKAEA))

RIP Radioimmunoprecipitation
Radioisotope Precipitation
Remote Instrument Package

RIPA Radioimmune Precipitation Assay
Royal Institute of Public Administration

RIPHH Royal Institute of Public Health and Hygiene

RIPPLE Radioactive Isotope Powered Pulse Light Equipment
Radioisotope Powered Prolonged Life Equipment

RIPS Research Institute of Pharmaceutical Sciences (of University of Mississippi (USA))

RIPT Research Institute for Polymers and Textiles (Japan)

RIQS Remote Information Query System (of Northwestern University (USA))

RIS Radio Interference Service (of DTI)
Range Instrumentation System
Relevant Industry Sales

RISA Radioiodinated Serum Albumin

RISC Redintegrated Somatotyping Curves
Reduced Instruction Set Computer

RISDA Rubber Industry Smallholders Development Authority (Malaysia)

RISE Research Information Service for Education (of OISE (Canada))

RISOS Research In Secured Operating Systems (a project of ARPA (USDOD))

RISP Ross Ice Shelf Project (of NSF (USA))

RISPP Rhode Island (USA) State Planning Program

RISS Refractive-Index Sounding System

RIST Radioisotope Tagged Sand Tracer
Radioisotopic Sand Tracer Study

RIT Reverse Income Tax
Rochester Institute of Technology (USA)
Rocket Interferometer Tracking

RITA RAND (CORPORATION) (USA) Intelligent Terminal Agent
Recognition for Information Technology Achievement (an award)
Road Information Transmitted Aurally

RITAD Radiation-Induced Thermally Activated Depolarization

RITES RAIL INDIA Technical and Economics Services (India)

RITS Remote Input Terminal System

RIV Radio Influence Voltage

RIVAL Rapid Insurance Valuation Language

RIW Reliability Improvement Warranty

RJ Ramjet

RJAA Royal Jordanian Air Academy (Jordan)

RJAF Royal Jordanian Air Force (Jordan)

RJE Remote Job Entry

RJIS Regional Justice Information System (County of Los Angeles (USA))

RKA Reaction Kinetic Analysis

RKHS Reproducing Kernel Hilbert Space

RKNFSYS Rock Information System (of Carnegie Institute of Washington (USA))

RKW Rationalisierungs Kuratorium der Deutschen Wirtschafts (Germany) (German Productivity Organisation)

RL prefix to dated-numbered series of reports issued by Redstone Arsenal (US Army)
Radiation Laboratory
Radioluminescence
Research Laboratory
Resistor Logic

RLADD Radar Low Angle Drogue Delivery

RLC Run Length Coding

RLD Rijksluchtvaartdienst (Netherlands) (Civil Aviation Authority)

RLE Research Laboratory of Electronics (of MIT (USA))

RLG Research Libraries Group (USA) (comprising the research libraries of New York Public Library, the libraries of Columbia, Harvard and Yale universities)
Ring Laser Gyro

RLIN Research Libraries Information Network (USA)

RLMS Reproduction of Library Material (of the Resources and Technical Services Division of the American Library Association) (USA)

RLS Radar Line-of-Sight

RLSD Research and Laboratory Services Division (of the Health and Safety Executive)

RLSMA Ribbon, Label and Smallwares Manufacturers Association

RLT Radionavigation Land Test
Remote Line Tester

RLTM prefix to Technical Memoranda issued by ESSA (USA) Research Laboratories

RLV Rauscher Leukaemogenic Virus

RM prefix to numbered series issued by Rocky Mountain Forest and Range Experiment Station (of Forest Service, USDA (USA))
Radio Monitoring
Request Message technique
Research Memorandum
Royal Marines

RMA Reliability-Maintainability-Availability
Retread Manufacturers Association
Royal Military Academy (MOD)
Rubber Manufacturers Association (USA)

RMAG Rocky Mountain Association of Geologists (USA)

RMAS Royal Maritime Auxiliary Service

RMB Roulement Miniatures, Bienne (Switzerland) (a company)

RMC Radiation Medicine Centre (of BARC (India))
Radical-Molecule Complex
Radio Monte-Carlo (Monaco)
Regional Meteorological Centre (of WMO (UN))
Rod Memory Computer
Rotation Modulation Collimator
Royal Military College of Canada

RMCS Royal Military College of Science (MOD)

RMD Research Management Division (of DOE)

RMDB Reliability and Maintainability Data Bank (of GIDEP (USA))

RME Rocket Motor Executive (MOD (PE))

RMEA Rubber Manufacturing Employers Association

RMERC Rock Mechanics and Explosives Research Center (Missouri University (USA))

RMetS Royal Meteorological Society

RMF Rockwell Microficial Scale

RMG Ranging Machine Gun

RMI Rack Manufacturers Institute (USA)
Radio Magnetic Indicator

RMIC Research Materials Information Center (ORNL, USAEC) (now of DOE (USA))

RMIT Royal Melbourne Institute of Technology (Australia)

RML Radio Microwave Link
Regional Medical Library network (of NLM (USA))

RMM Read-Mostly Memory

RMOGA Rocky Mountain Oil and Gas Association (USA)
RMOS Refractory Metal Oxide Semiconductor
RMP Rate Measuring Package
Re-entry Measurements Programme
Refiner Pulp Method
Root Mean Power
RMPA Royal Medico-Psychological Association
RMRS Rocky Mountain Radiological Society
RMS Real Market Share
Resource Management System
Root-Mean-Square
Rotating Mooring System
Royal Microscopical Society
RMSC Royal Marines Sailing Club
RMSE Root Mean Square Error
RMSF Rocky Mountain Spotted Fever
RMT Reliability Maintainability Tradeoff
RMTBF Reciprocal Mean Time Between Failure
RMU Remote Manoeuvring Unit
Remote Multiplexer Unit
RMV Remotely Manned Vehicle
RN Research Note
Road Note (series issued by the Road Research Laboratory, Ministry of Transport)
Royal Navy
RNA Ribonucleic Acid
RNARS Royal Naval Amateur Radio Society
Royal Navy Amateur Radio Society
RNAV Area Navigation
RNCF Reserve Naval Construction Force (USN)
RND Rijksnijverheidsdienst (Netherlands) (Government Industrial Advisory Service)
RNEC Royal Naval Engineering College (MOD (N))
RNEE Royal Navy Equipment Exhibition
RNES Royal Naval Engineering Service (MOD (N))
RNFTU Royal Navy Foreign Training Unit
RNHTU Royal Navy Hovercraft Trials Unit
RNIB Royal National Institute for the Blind
RNID Royal National Institute for the Deaf
RNLI Royal National Life-boat Institute
RNP Ribonucleoprotein
RNPDL RISLEY Nuclear Power Development Laboratory
RNPL Royal Naval Physiological Laboratory (MOD) (became AMTE Physiological Laboratory in 1978)
RNPRC Royal Navy Personnel Research Committee (of Medical Research Council)
RNPTE Royal Naval Nuclear Propulsion Test and Training Establishment (MOD (N))
RNS Random-Nucleation-Solution
Re-usable Nuclear Shuttle
Residue Number Systems
Royal Naval Scientific Service (MOD)
Royal Numismatic Society
RNSA Royal Naval Sailing Association
RNSTS Royal Naval Supply and Transport Service (MOD)
RNUR Regie Nationale des Usines Renault (France)
RNV Relative Nutritive Value
RNZAF Royal New Zealand Air Force
RNZN Royal New Zealand Navy
RO Reverse Osmosis
RO/RO Roll-On Roll-Off
ROA Radius of Action
Return on Assets
ROADS Roadway Analysis and Design System (of Integrated Civil Engineering System)
ROAM Return On Assets Managed
ROAR Routine for Obtaining Active Records
ROARS Royal Oman Amateur Radio Society (Oman)
ROAST Ring Out And Stress Tester
ROBIN Rocket Balloon Instrument
ROBOT Record Organisation Based On Transposition
ROC Readily Oxidizable Carbon
Receiver Operating Characteristics
Republic Of China (ie Taiwan)
Required Operational Capability
ROCAP Regional Office for Central America and Panama (of AID) (USA)
ROCE Return On Capital Employed
ROCKET RAND (Corporation (USA)) Omnibus Calculator of the Kinematics of Earth Trajectories
ROCKSTORE International Symposium on Storage in Excavated Rock Caverns
ROCR Remote Optical Character Recognition
ROCS Railroad Operations Control System
Range-Only Correlation System
RODAR (Helicopter) Rotor Blade Radar
RODS Real-time Operations, Dispatching and Scheduling
RODSIM J. S. N. RODRIGUEZ and N. E. SIMONS computer programme
ROE Return On shareholders Equity
Royal Observatory, Edinburgh (Science Research Council) (now of SERC)
ROF Royal Ordnance Factory (MOD)
ROFI Radially Outward Firing Igniter
ROGER Remotely Operated Geophysical Explorer
ROI Return On Investment
ROKAMS Republic of Korea Army Map Service (Korea)
ROLF Remotely Operated Longwall Face
ROLS Rainbow Optical Landing System
Recoverable Orbital Launch System
ROM Read-Only Memory
ROMAN Remotely Operated Mobile Manipulator
ROMBI Results of Marine Biological Investigations (maintained by NODC (NOAA) (USA))
ROMBUS Re-usable Orbital Module Booster and Utility Shuttle
ROMCOE Rocky Mountain Center on Environment (USA)
RON Research Octane Number
ROOI Return On Original Investment
ROOST Re-usable One Stage Orbital Space Truck
ROP Re-Order Point ordering
Runway Observing Position
ROPE Run-Out Production Evaluation
ROPS Roll-Over Protection Structure
RORC Royal Ocean Racing Club
RORIS Remote Operated Radiographic Inspection System
RORSAT Radar Ocean Reconnaissance Satellite
ROS Read Only Storage
Report Origination System
Return On Sales
ROSA Recording Optical Spectrum Analyzer
ROSCM Research Organisation of Ships' Compositions Manufacturers
ROSCO Rotating Stratified Combustion
ROSCOE Remote Operating System Conversational Operating Environment
ROSCOP Report of Observations/Samples Collected by Oceanographic Programs (of World Data Center-A, Oceanography (USA))
ROSE Remotely Operated Special Equipment
Residuum Oil Supercritical Extraction
Retrieval by On-line Search
Rising Observational Sounding Equipment
ROSPA Royal Society for the Prevention of Accidents
ROT Re-usable Orbital Transport
ROTHR Relocatable Over-the-Horizon Radar
ROTI Recording Optical Tracing Instrument

ROTL Remote-Office Test Line
ROTSAL Rotate and Scale
ROV Remotely Operated Vehicle
ROVACS Rotary-Vane Air-Cycle Air-Conditioning and Refrigeration System
ROWPU Reverse Osmosis Water Purification Unit
ROWS Register of Weather Stations (a project of the Meteorological Office)
ROX Recessed Oxide
RP prefix to numbered series of Reference Papers issued by the Electricity Council
RAYNAUD'S Phenomenon
Recommended Practice
Recovery Phase
Recurring Periodical
Research Paper
Retinitis Pigmentosa
Rocket Projectile
Rocket Propellant OR Propulsion
Rotary Piston
RPA Random Phase Approximation
Regional Plan Association (of New York) (USA)
Retarding Potential Analyzer
RPAODS Remotely-Piloted Aerial Observation Designation System
RPC Radiation Policy Council (USA)
Remote Power Controller
RPD Reactive Plasma Deposition
Research Planning Diagram
Respiratory Protective Device
Retarding Potential Difference
RPDT Radar Prediction Data Table
RPE Rating of Perceived Exertion
Ratings of Perceived Exertion
Retinal Pigment Epithelium
Return On Sales
Rocket Propulsion Establishment (now of MOD)
RPEA Retarding Potential and Electrostastic Analyzer
RPG Radioisotropic Power Generator
Report Programme Generator
Rocket Propelled Grenade
RPH Remotely Piloted Helicopter
RPHA Reversed Passive Haemagglutination
RPI Railway Progress Institute (USA)
Rensselaer Polytechnic Institute (USA)
Retail Price Index
RPIE Replacement of Photographic Imagery Equipment
RPL Radar Processing Language
Radiophotoluminescence
Radiophysics Laboratory (of CSIRO, Australia)
Rocket Propulsion Laboratory (USAF)
Rotary Pellet Launcher
RPLA Reversed Passive Latex-Agglutination
RPM Random Phase Modulator
Reinforced Plastic Matrix
Retail Price Maintenance
Revenue-Passenger-Miles
Revolutions per Minute
RPMB Remotely Piloted Mini-Blimp
RPMS Royal Postgraduate Medical School (London University)
RPN Reverse Polish Notation logic
RPOA Recognized Private Operating Agency
RPOADS Remotely Piloted Observation Aircraft Designator System
RPP Reductive Pentose Phosphate
Rocket Propellant Plant (of ISRO (India))
RPPITB Rubber and Plastics Processing Industry Training Board
RPQ Request Product Quotation
RPR Rapid Plasma Reagin
RPRC Regional Primate Research Centers (USA)
RPRV Remotely Piloted Research Vehicle
RPS Random Pulse Sequence System
Randomized Pattern Search
Range Positioning System
Reversed-Phase Series
Royal Photographic Society of Great Britain
RPSM Resources Planning and Scheduling Method
RPSP Radar Programmable Signal Processor
RPU Radio Propagation Unit (of National Physical Laboratory (India))
RPV Reactor Pressure Vessel
Remotely Piloted Vehicle
RPW Ranked Positional Weight
RQ Respiratory Quotient
RQ-QSO Radio-Quiet Quasi-Stellar Object
RQA Recursive Queue Analyzer
RQE Responsive Quantum Efficiency
RQI RAYLEIGH Quotient Iteration
RQL Reference Quality Level
RR Rate of Return on capital
Regenerative Repeater
Research Report
Return Rate
RR-BB Rayon-Rayon Bias-Belted
RRA Radio-Receptor Assay
RRB Radio Regulatory Bureau (Japan)
Radio Research Board (Australia) (now ATERB (of CSIRO) Australia))
RRC prefix to lettered numbered series of reports issued by Radio Propagation Unit, National Physical Laboratory (India)
Radar Return Code
RRCS Rate and Route Computer System
Roll-Rate Control System
RRD Radio Regulatory Department (of DTI)
RRDC Railroad Data Center (of Association of American Railroads)
RRDE Rotating Ring-Disc Electrode
RRE Royal Radar Establishment (MOD) (became RSRE in 1976)
RREAC ROYAL RADAR ESTABLISHMENT Automatic Computer
RRIC Rubber Research Institute of Ceylon
RRID Reverse Radial Immunodiffusion
RRIM Reinforced Reaction Injection Moulding
Rubber Research Institute of Malaysia (Malaysia)
RRIS Railroad Research Information Service (of Federal Railroad Administration AND National Academy of Sciences (USA))
Record Room Interrogation System
Remote Radar Integration Station
RRL Radio Research Laboratories (Japan)
Road Research Laboratory (now Transport and Road Research Laboratory (DOE))
RRM Rotation Remanent Magnetisation
RRMA Refractory and Reactive Metals Association (USA)
rRNA Ribosomal RNA
RRNS Redundant Residue Number System
RRP Reader and Reader-Printer
Rotterdam-Rhine Pipeline
RRR Rapid Runway Repair
Residual Resistivity Ratios
RRRV Rate of Rise of Recovery Voltage
RRS Radiation Research Society (USA)
Radio Research Station (now RSRS q.v.)
RRU Radiobiological Research Unit
Road Research Unit (of NRB (New Zealand))
RRV Rate of Rise of Voltage
RS Radio Sonde
Recommended Standard (numbered series issued by EIA (USA))

	Reconnaissance Squadron (USAF)
	Reference Sheet (numbered series issued by SBAC)
	The Royal Society of London for the Improvement of Natural Knowledge
RS-TR	prefix to dated-numbered series of Technical Reports issued by Systems Research Directorate, Redstone Arsenal (USA Army)
RSA	Railway Supply Association (USA)
	Rehabilitation Services Administration (of SRS (HEW) (USA))
	Relay Services Association of Great Britain
	Royal Society for the Encouragement of Arts, Manufactures and Commerce
RSAA	Remote Sensing Association of Australia (Australia)
RSAC	Radar Significance Analysis Code
	Reactor Safety Advisory Committee (Canada)
RSAF	Republic of Singapore Air Force (Singapore)
	Royal Saudi Air Force (Saudi Arabia)
	Royal Small Arms Factory (MOD)
RSC	Relaxation-Sensitive Cell
	Remote Sensing Center (Texas A&M University) (USA)
	Royal Society of Canada
	Royal Society of Chemistry
RSCS	Remote Spooling Communications Sub-system
RSD	Radio Science Division (National Physical Laboratory (India))
	Recovery, Salvage and Disposal
RSDA	Road Surface Dressing Association
RSE	The Royal Society of Edinburgh
RSEP	RPV (Remotely Piloted Pilot Vehicle) Simulation/Evaluation Programme
RSEW	Resistance-Seam Welding
RSF	Rocket Sled Facility (of ISRO (India))
RSFS	Real Scene Focus Sensor
RSG	Rate Support Grant
RSGB	Radio Society of Great Britain
RSH	Royal Society of Health
RSI	Radial Shear Interferometer
	Rationalization, Standardization and Integration
	Rationalization, Standardization and Interoperability
	Refractory Reusable Surface Insulation
RSIC	Radiation Shielding Information Center (of ORNL)
	Redstone Scientific Information Center (Redstone Arsenal, US Army)
RSIS	Reference, Special and Information Section (of the Library Association)
RSJ	Resistively Shunted Junction
	Rolled Steel Joist
RSK	Reaktor Sicherheitskommission (Germany) (Reactor Safety Commission)
RSL	Radio Standards Laboratory (of NSB)
	Remote Sensing Laboratory (Stanford University (USA))
RSM	Research into Site Management
	Response Surface Methodology
	Rotating Sample Magnetometer
	Royal School of Mines
	Royal Society of Medicine
RSMA	Railway Systems and Management Association (USA)
RSMAD	Remote Sensing and Meteorological Division (of ISRO (India))
RSMAS	Rosentiel School of Marine and Atmospheric Science (USA)
RSME	Royal School of Military Engineering (MOD)
RSMML	Rajasthan State Mines and Mineral Ltd (India) (govt owned)
RSN	Radiation Surveillance Network
RSNA	Radiological Society of North America (USA)
RSNC	Royal Society for Nature Conservation
RSNZ	Royal Society of New Zealand (New Zealand)
RSO	Rectified Skew Orthomorphic
	Relativistic and Spin-Orbit
RSP	Radar Signal Processor
RSPB	Royal Society for the Protection of Birds
RSR	Rapid Solidification-Rate
RSRA	Rotor Systems Research Aircraft
RSRE	Radar and Signals Research Establishment (MOD) (part at Baldock and part at Christchurch)
RSRE(C)	Royal Signals and Radar Establishment at Christchurch
RSRS	Radio and Space Research Station (of SRC) (now The Appleton Laboratory)
RSS	Relaxed Static Stability
	Remote Sensing Society
	Resource Security System
	Resource Survey Satellite
	Ribbed Smoked Sheet
	Royal Scientific Society (Jordan)
	Royal Statistical Society
RSSI	Regional Science Research Institute (USA)
RSSL	RAYTHEON (COMPANY) Scientific Simulation Language
RST	Reliability Shakedown Test
RSTA	Reconnaissance, Surveillance and Target Acquisition
RSTM&H	Royal Society of Tropical Medicine and Hygiene
RSTV	Radiated Subscriber (or Subscription) Television
RSU	Rate-Sensor Unit
RSUA	Royal Society of Ulster Architects
RSV	Respiratory Syncytial Virus
	ROUS Sarcoma Virus
RSVP	Random Signal Vibration Protector
	Rapid Serial Visual Presentation
	Relational Structure Vertex Processor
	Remote Spooling Vector Processor
	Restartable Solid Variable Pulse
RSW	Refrigerated Sea Water
	Resistance Spot Weld
RT	Radiative Transfer
	Rated Time
	Reaction Time
	Resolvable Temperature
	Room Temperature
RTA	Real Time Analyzer
	Retrospective Terms Adjustment
RTAC	Real-Time Atmospheric Compensation
	Roads and Transportation Association of Canada (Canada)
RTAF	Royal Thai Air Force (Thailand)
RTB	Radiodiffusion Television Belge (Belgium)
RTC	Real Time Control
RTCA	Radio Technical Commission for Aeronautics (USA)
RTCC	Real Time Computer Complex (of NASA (USA))
RTCIP	Real-Time Cell-Identification Processor
RTCM	Radio Technical Commission for Marine Services (of FCC (USA))
RTCP	Real-Time Control Programme
RTD	Research and Technology Division (of USAFSC)
	Residence Time Distribution
	Resistance Temperature Detector
	Rontgen Technische Dienst (Netherlands)
RTD/CCS	Resources and Technical Services Division/Cataloging and Classification Section (of the American Library Association (USA))
RTDDAS	Real-Time Digital Data Acquisition System
RTDS	Real Time Data System
RTE	Radio Telefis Eireann (Eire)
	Reciprocal Thermal Efficiency

	Remote Terminal Emulator
RTEB	Radio Trades Examination Board
RTECS	Registry of Toxic Effects of Chemical Substances (of NLM (USA))
RTEEB	Radio, Television and Electronics Examination Board
RTF	Radar Training Facility (of FAA (USA))
	Real-Time FORTRAN
RTFL	Rough Terrain Fork Lift
RTG	Radioisotope Thermo-electric Generator
RTH	Regional Telecommunication Hub (of WMO)
RTI	Real-Time Interface
	Research Triangle Institute (USA)
RTITB	Road Transport Industry Training Board
RTL	Radio-Tele-Luxembourg (Luxembourg)
	Real-Time Language
	Reference Testing Laboratory (of Cement and Concrete Association)
	Register Transfer Language
	Research and Technology Laboratories (of AVRADCOM)
	Resistor Transistor Logic
RTM	Radiodiffusion Television Marocaine (Morocco)
	Real-Time Management
	Real-time METRIC
	Real-Time Monitor
	Register-Transfer Module
	Registered Trade Mark
	Research Technical Memoranda
RTMOS	Real-Time Multiprogramming Operating System
RTO	Rejected Take-Off
RTOL	Reduced Take-Off and Landing
RTOS	Real-Time Operating System
RTP	Radiotelevisao Portuguesa (Portugal)
	Reinforced Thermoplastic
RTPI	Royal Town Planning Institute
RTPR	Reference Theta-Pinch Reactor
RTPS	Real-time Telemetry Processing System
RTR	Remote Transmitter Receiver
RTRA	Radio and Television Retailers Association (name changed to RETRA in April 1976)
RTRCDS	Real-Time Reconnaissance Cockpit Display System
RTS	prefix to numbered series of Russian Translations prepared by the National Lending Library for Science and Technology
	Real-Time System
	Royal Television Society
RTSA	Retail Trading Standards Association
RTSD	Resources and Technical Services Division (of the American Library Association)
RTSRS	Real Time Simulation Research System
RTT	Radio-Teleprinter
	Radiodiffusion-Television Tunisienne (Tunisia)
	Real Time Telemetry
	Regie des Telegraphes et des Telephones (Belgium) (Telecommunications Administration)
RTTDS	Real Time Telemetry Data System
RTTV	Real Time Television
RTTY	Radio-teletypewriter
RTV	Room Temperature Vulcanizing
RTX	Rapid Transit Experimental
RTXE	Real-Time Executive Extended
	Real-Time Language
RU	Rutgers-The State University, New Brunswick (USA)
RUAG	Refrigeration and Unit Air Conditioning Group (of HVCA)
RUBBERCON	International Rubber Conference
RUC	Riverine Utility Craft
RUCA	Rijksuniversitair Centrum Antwerpen (Belgium) (State University Centre of Antwerp)
RUCAPS	Really Universal Computer Aided Production System
RUDI	Regional Urban Defence Intercept
RUDS	Reflectance Units of Dirt Shade
RUE	Rational Use of Energy (steering groups of EEC)
RUFAS	Remote Underwater Fisheries Assessment System
RUIN	Regional Urban Information Network (of Washington DC (USA) Metropolitan Urban Studies Libraries Group)
RUM	Remote Underwater Manipulator
RUMIC	Remote Underwater Mine Counter-measures
RUROS	Research Unit on the Rehabilitation of Oiled Seabirds (University of Newcastle-upon-Tyne)
RUSH	Remote Users of Shared Hardware
	Rudder Shaped Hull
RUSI	Royal United Services Institute for Defence Studies
	Royal United Services Institution
RUSTIC	Regional and Urban Studies Information Center (of ORNL (USA))
RUU	Ryksuniversiteit Utrecht (Netherlands) (State University, Utrecht)
RUV	Rikisutvarpid-Sjonvarp (Iceland)
RUVP	Research Unit on Vector Pathology (Memorial University of New Foundland) (Canada))
RUWS	Remote Unmanned Work Subsystem
RV	Radio Vatican (Vatican State)
	Random Vibration
	Re-entry Vehicle
	Recreational Vehicle
	Residual Volume
RV/TLC	Residual Volume Total Lung Capacity ratio
RVA	Rating and Valuation Association
RVC	Relativity Velocity Computer
RVCD	Right Ventricular Conduction Defect
RVD	Radar Video Digitizer
	Residual Vapour Detector
RVDP	Radar Video Data Processor
	Radio Video Data Processor
RVF	Rate Variance Formula
	Rift Valley Fever
RVG	Radar Video Generator
RVH	Right Ventricular Hypertrophy
RVI	Reverse Interrupt
RVIA	Recreational Vehicle Institute of America (USA)
RVLSI	Restructurable Very Large Scale Integration
RVP	Radar Video Preprocessor
	Reid Vapour Pressure
RVR	Runway Visual Range
RVRS	Research Vehicle Reference System (of NOAA (USA))
RVS	Reifengewerbe-Verband der Schweiz (Switzerland) (Swiss Association of the Tyre Industry)
RVSN	Raketny Voiska Strategicheskovo Naznacheniya (USSR) (Strategic Rocket Forces)
RVTO	Rolling Vertical Take-Off
RW	Reconnaissance Wing (USAF)
	Resistance Welding
RWC	Round Wire Cable
RWE	Rheinisch-Westfalisches Elektritizitatswerke (Germany)
RWM	Read-only Composite Wire Memory
	Rectangular Wave Modulation
RWMA	Resistance Welder Manufacturers Association (USA)
RWMAC	Radioactive Waste Management Advisory Committee (of Dept of the Environment)

RWMC Radioactive Waste Management Committee (of NEA (OECD))
RWR Radar Warning Receiver
RXD Research or Exploratory Development
RXLI Recessive X-Linked Ichthyosis
RYA Royal Yachting Association
RZ Return to Zero
RZh Referativny Zhurnal (Abstract Journal)
RZI Real-Zero Interpolation

S

S prefix to numbered:dated series of standards on Steel issued by BSI (letter is sometimes preceded by a number)
S & R Safety and Reliability
S of R Society of Rheology (USA)
S&T Scientific and Technical
S&TI Scientific and Technical Information
S/O Solvent to Oil ratio
S-Cubed Serial Signalling Scheme
S3 Semi-Submerged Ship
SA Slide Agglutination
Sociedad Anonima (PLC) (Spanish)
Societe Anonyme (PLC) (French)
Solution Anneal
Springfield Armory (US Army)
Stability Augmentation
Sterculic Acid
Submerged-Arc
Systems Analysis
SA-BPL Sucrose Acetone-Betapropiolactone
SA/BW Systems Analysis and Battle Management
SA/OR Systems Analysis/Operational Research
SAA Single Article Announcement (a current awareness service of the American Chemical Society (USA))
Society of American Archivists (USA)
South African Airways
South Atlantic Anomaly
Standards Association of Australia
Surface Active Agent
SAAB Svensk Aeroplan AB (Sweden)
SAAC Security Assistance Accounting Center (USAF)
Simulator for Air-to-Air Combat
SAACI Salesman's Association of the American Chemical Industry (USA)
SAAEB South African Atomic Energy Board (South Africa)
SAAF South African Air Force (South Africa)
SAAFARI SOUTH AFRICAN AIRWAYS Fully Automatic Reservations Installation
SAAGS Semi-Automated Artwork Generator System
SAALC San Antonio Logistics Center (USAF)
SAALIC Swindon Area Association of Libraries of Industry and Commerce
SAAM Simulation, Analysis And Modelling
SAAMI Sporting Arms and Ammunition Manufacturers Institute (USA)
SAAO South African Astronomical Observatory (jointly financed by CSIR (South Africa) and SRC (UK))
SAAOC System of Analysis and Assignment of Operations according to Capacities
SAAP South Atlantic Anomaly Probe
SAAR Solar Aureole Almucantar Radiance
SAAS Standard Army Ammunition System (US Army)
SAAT Society of Architects and Allied Technicians
Society of Architectural and Associated Technicians
SAB Shuttle Assembly Building (of NASA (USA))
Single Amplifier Biquad
South American Blastomycosis
Sveriges Allmanna Biblioteksforening (Sweden) (Swedish General Library Association)
SABA South African Brick Association (South Africa)
SABAR Satellites, Balloons and Rockets
SABC South African Broadcasting Corporation (South Africa)
SABCA Societe Anonyme Belge de Constructions Aeronautiques (Belgium)
SABE Society for Automation in Business Education (USA)
SABEA Societa Alimentari Bevande e Affini (Sicily)
SABENA Societe Anonyme Belge d'Exploitation de la Navigation Aerienne (Belgium)
SABHATA Sand and Ballast Hauliers and Allied Trades Alliance
SABMIS Sea-launched Anti-Ballistic Missile
Seaborne Anti-Ballistic-Missile Intercept System
SABRAO Society for the Advancement of Breeding Research in Asia and Oceania (Malaysia)
SABRE Self-Aligning Boost and Re-entry System
SINGER (INFORMATION SERVICES COMPANY) Accounting and Business Reporting
Steerable Adaptive Broadcast Reception Equipment
System for Assessment of Body Radioactivity
SABS South African Bureau of Standards (South Africa)
SAC Schools of Architecture Council
Science Advisory Committee (of ESA)
Scientific Advisory Committee (of IAEA)
Society for Analytical Chemistry (became the Analytical Division of the Chemical Division in 1976)
Space Activities Commission (Japan)
Space Applications Centre (of ISRO (India))
Strategic Air Command (USAF)
Strong Adsorption Capacity
Submerged Air Cushion
SACA Societa per Azioni Costruzioni Aeronavali (Italy)
SACAC South African Council for Automation and Computation (South Africa)
SACAD Stress Analysis and Computer Aided-Design (a joint unit of the Imperial College of Science and Technology and the Welding Institute)
SACAE South Australian College of Advanced Education (Australia)
SACARTS Semi-Automated Cartographic System
SACCHS Scottish Advisory Committee on the Computers in the Health Service
SACCM Slow Access Charge-Coupled Memory
SACCS Schedule and Cost-Control System
Strategic Air Command Automated Command Control System (USAF)
SACDIN Strategic Air Command Digital Network (USAF)
SACE Semi-Automatic Check-out Equipment
Shore-based Acceptance Check-out Equipment
Systems Acceptance Check-out Equipment
SACEUR Supreme Allied Commander Europe (of NATO)
SACL Stress and Arousal Adjective Check-List
SACLAME Standing Advisory Committee on Licensing of Aircraft Maintenance Engineers
SACLANT Supreme Allied Commander Atlantic (of NATO)
SACLANTCEN SACLANT anti-submarine warfare research Centre (of NATO)
SACLOS Semi-Automatic Command to Line-Of-Sight
SACM Societe Alsacienne de Constructions Mecaniques (France)

SACMA Société Anonyme de Construction de Moteurs Aéronautiques (France)
SACNAS Society for the Advancement of Chicano and Native American Scientists (USA)
SACOM Ships Advanced Communications Operational Model
SACP Selected Area Channelling Patterns
SACPE South African Council for Professional Engineers (South Africa)
SACRHEI Standing Advisory Committee on Relationships between Higher Education and Industry (of the Chemical Society)
SACTRA Standing Advisory Committee on Trunk Road Assessment (of DOT)
SACVT Society of Air Cushion Vehicle Technicians (Canada)
SAD Seasonal Affective Disorder
Sentence Appraiser and Diagrammer
SAD 69 South American Datum of 1969
SADA Seismic Array Data Analyser
SADAR Satellite Data Reduction processor system
Société Anonyme d'Appareillage Radioéléctrique (France)
SADARM Sense And Destroy Armour
SADAS SOERRY Airborne Data Acquisition System
SADC Sequential Analogue-Digital Computer
Singapore Air Defence Command (Singapore)
SADCC Southern Africa Development Co-ordination Conference
SADE Sensitive Acoustic Detection Equipment
SADF Statistical Analysis of Documentation Files
SADI SANDERS ASSOCIATES Direct Indexing
SADIE Scanning Analog-to-Digital Input Equipment
Sterling And Decimal Invoicing Electronically
SUNDSTRAND (AVIATION OPERATIONS) (USA) Automatic Data Investigation and Evaluation System
SADIM Societe Anonyme pour le Developpment Immobilier de Monaco
SADIR Solicitors' Accounts (Deposit Interest) Rules 1975
SADIS Southern African Documentation and Information System
SADM Small Atomic Demolition Munition
SADOI Sociedad Argentina de Organizacion Industrial (Argentina) (Society of Industrial Management)
SADP Selected Area Diffraction Pattern
SADRAM Seek and Destroy Radar Assisted Mission
SADSAC SEILER ALGOL Digitally Simulated Analogue Computer
SADSCAT Self Assigned Descriptors from Self And Cited Titles
SADT Self-Accelerating Decomposition Temperature
SADTC SHAPE Air Defence Technical Centre
SAE Society of Automotive Engineers (USA)
SAE CA (number) prefix for designating Copper and Copper Alloys standards recommended by SAE (USA)
SAEB Spacecraft Assembly and Encapsulation Building (of NASA (USA))
SAECP Selected Area Electron Channelling Patterns
SAED Selected Area Electron Diffraction
Societe Africaine d'Etudes et de Developpement (Upper Volta)
SAEDC Sensory Aids Evaluation and Development Center (Massachusetts Institute of Technology (USA))
SAEI Service des Affaires Economiques et Internationales (France) (Department of Economics and International Affairs)
Sumitomo Atomic Energy Industries (Japan)
SAEMA Suspended Access Equipment Manufacturers Association
SAEP Senior Advisers on Environmental Problems (to the Economic Commission for Europe)
SAES Special Assistant for Environmental Services (of OJCS (USDOD))
State Agricultural Experimental Stations (USA)
SAESA Servicios Aereos Especiales SA (Mexico)
SAEST Society for the Advancement of Electrochemical Science and Technology (India)
SAET Spiral After-Effect
SAETA Sociedad Anonima Ecuatoriana de Transportes Aereos (Ecuador)
SAEW Ships Advanced Electronic Warfare
SAF Internation Symposium on Applications of Ferroelectrics (sponsored by IEEE (USA))
Scrapie-Associated Fibrils
Singapore Air Force (Singapore)
Society of American Foresters (USA)
Soudure Autogene Francaise (France)
Specific Absorbed Fractions
Super Abrasive Furnace
Synchronous Auditory Feedback
SAFA Soluble Antigen Fluorescent Antibody
SAFARI South African Fundamental Atomic Reactor Installation
SAFCA Safeguard Communications Agency (of USASTRATCOM) (became BMDCA (of USACC) in 1975)
SAFCO Saudi Arabian Fertilizer Company (Saudi Arabia)
SAFE Safe Assessment and Facilities Establishment (of JAIF)
San Andreas (USA) Fault Experiment
Satellite Alert Force Employment
Space and Flight Equipment Association (USA)
Strategy And Force Evaluation
Survival and Flight Equipment Association (USA)
System for Automated Flight Efficiency
SAFEORD Safety of Explosive Ordnance Databank (of NWL (USN))
SAFER Société d'Amenagement Foncier et d'Établissement Rural (France)
Structural Analysis, Frailty Evaluation and Redesign
System for Aircrew Flight Extension and Return
Systematic Aid to Flow on Existing Roadways
SAFI Semi-Automatic Flight Inspection
SAFLOG Safeguard Logistics Command (US Army)
SAFMARINE South African Marine Corporation (South Africa)
SAFO Self Adhesive Foreign Object
SAFOC Semi-Automatic Fight Operations Centre
SAFSCOM Safeguard Systems Command (US Army)
SAFT Self-Adaptive Forecasting Technique
Societe des Accumulateurs Fixes et de Traction (France)
SAFTO South African Foreign Trade Organization
SAG Self-Agglomerator
Standard Address Generator
Syntax Analyser Generator
SAGA Sand and Gravel Association of Great Britain
Short Arc Geodetic Adjustment
Societa Applicazioni Gomma Antivibranti (Italy)
SAGE Semi-Automatic Ground Environment
Stratospheric Aerosol and Gas Experiment satellite (of NASA)
Systems Approach to a Growth Economy
SAGEM Societe d'Applications Generales d'Electricite et de Mecanique (France)
SAGFRC South Atlantic–Gulf Fisheries Research Center (of NMFS (USA))
SAGS Semi-Active Gravity-Gradient Stabilization
SAGSET Society of Academic Gaming and Simulation in Education and Training
SAGT Systematic Approach to Group Technology
SAGW Surface to Air Guided Weapon

SAH Sub-Arachnoid Haemorrhage
SAHC Sleep Analyzing Hybrid Computer
SAHP Solar Assisted Heat Pump
SAHS Southern African Hypertension Society
SAHSA Servicio Aereo de Honduras SA (Honduras)
SAHYB Simulation of Analogue and Hybrid Computers
SAI Singapore Aircraft Industries (Singapore) (state owned)
Singly Auto-Ionizing
Sprayed Asbestos Insulation
SAIAT Societa Attivita Immobiliari Ausliarie Telefoniche (Italy)
SAIB Sucrose Acetate Isobutyrate
SAID Specific Adaption to Imposed Demands
SAIF South African Institute of Foundrymen (South Africa)
SAIFECS SpA Industria Fibre e Cartoni Speciali (Italy)
SAIL Sea Air Interaction Laboratory
Steel Authority of India Limited (India) (state owned)
Structural Analysis Input Language
SAILA Simplified Aircraft Instrument Landing System
SAILIS South African Institute for Librarianship and Information Science (South Africa)
SAILS Software Adaptable Integrated Logic System
Standard Army Intermediate Level Supply Subsystem (US Army)
SAIM South African Institute of Management (South Africa)
SAIMA Selected Acquisitions Information and Management System
SAIMC South African Institute for Measurement and Control (South Africa)
SAIME South African Institution of Mechanical Engineers (South Africa)
SAIMechE South African Institution of Mechanical Engineers (South Africa)
SAIMENA South African Institute of Marine Engineers and Naval Architects (South Africa)
SAIMR South African Institute of Medical Research (South Africa)
SAIMS Supersonic Airborne Infrared Measurement System
SAINT Salzburg Assembly: Impact of the New Technology
Satellite Intercept
Symbolic Automatic Integration
Systems Analysis of Integrated Network of Tasks
SAIO Sociedad Argentina de Investigacion Operativa (Argentina) (Society for Operational Research)
SAIP Societe d'Applications Industrielles de la Physique (France)
SAIS South African Interplanetary Society (South Africa)
SAISAC Ship's Aircraft Inertial System Alignment Console
SAIT Service d'Analyse de l'Information Technologique (of CRIQ (Canada)) (Technological Information Analysis Service)
Societe Anonyme Internationale de Telegraphie (Belgium)
SAIW South African Institute of Welding (South Africa)
SAJ Shipbuilders Association of Japan (Japan)
SAJI Self-Aligned Junction Isolated
SAKI SOLATRON Automatic Keyboard Instructor
SAL Simple Author Language
Sterilization Assembly Development Laboratory (of NASA at JPL)
Strategic Air-Launched cruise missile launcher
Strong Acid Leach
Systems Assembly Language
SALA South African Library Association (South Africa) (became SAILIS in 1980)
SALALM Seminars on the Acquisition of Latin American Library Materials
SALB South African Library for the Blind (South Africa)
SALES Savannah (Georgia, USA) Area Law Enforcement System
SALINET Satellite Library Information Network (a consortium of libraries, a library school, and regional agencies with headquarters at Denver Graduate School of Librarianship (USA))
SALM Single Anchor Leg Mooring
Society of Air Line Meteorologists (USA)
SALR Saturated Adiabatic Lapse Rate
SALS Short Approach Lights
Single Anchor Leg Storage
Single Anchor Leg System
Solid-state Acousto-electric Light Scanner
Standard Army Logistics System (US Army)
SALT Strategic Arms Limitation Talks (between USA and USSR)
SAM S-Adenosyl-Methionine
Scanning Acoustic Microscope
Scanning Auger Microscope
School of Aerospace Medicine (USAF)
Semantic Analysing Machine
Semi-Automated Mathematics
Sequential Access Method
Signal Averaging Monitor
Simple Automated Movement
Simulation of Analogue Methods
Six-Axis Manipulator
Society for Advancement of Management (USA)
Sound Absorbent Material
Sound-Activated Mobile
Standard Assembly Module
Stratospheric Aerosol Measurement
Subsynoptic Advection Model
SUMITO (METAL INDUSTRIES) (Japan) Automatic Magnetic inspection
Surface-to-Air Missile
Survival Air Model
Symbolic and Algebraic Manipulation
System Analysis Machine
System Availability Model
Systems Analysis Module
SAM-D Surface-to-Air Missile Development
SAMA Saudi Arabia Monetary Agency (Saudi Arabia)
Scientific Apparatus Makers Association (USA)
Shock Absorber Manufacturers Association
SAMAC Scientific and Management Advisory Committee (of US Army Computer Systems Command)
Ships Acoustic Modern And Controller
SAMANTHA System for the Automated Management of Text from a Hierarchical Arrangement
SAMB United Kingdom liaison committee for Sciences Allied to Medicine and Biology
SAMBO Strategic Anti-Missile Barrage Object
SAMCAP Surface to Air Missile Capability
SAMDENE Systems Analysis of Mediterranean Desert Ecosystems of Northern Egypt (project sponsored by University of Alexandria (Egypt))
SAME Society of American Military Engineers (USA)
SAMECS Structural Analysis Method for Evaluation of Complex Structures
SAMES Societe Anonyme de Machines Electrostatiques (France)
SAMFOR Sequential Access Method in FORTRAN IV
SAMH Scottish Association for Mental Health
SAMI Socially Acceptable Monitoring Instrument
Speed of Approach Measurement Indicator
System Acquisition Management Inspection system (of AFISC (usaf))

SAMIDS	Ships Anti-Missile Integrated Defence System
SAMIPAC	Societe Auxiliare et Miniere du Pacifique (France)
SAMIR	Société Anonyme Moroccaine de l'Industrie du Raffinage (Morocco)
SAMIS	Structural Analysis and Matrix Interpretive System
SAMM	Semi-Automatic Measuring Machine
	Societe d'Applications des Machines Motrices (France)
SAMMIE	Scheduling Analysis Model for Mission Integrated Experiments
	SUMITO (METAL INDUSTRIES) (Japan) Automatic Magnetic Inspection
	System for Aiding Man-Machine Interaction Evaluation
SAMMS	Standard Automated Material Management System (USDOD)
SAMOA	System Approach to Multi-dimensional Occupational Analysis
SAMOS	Spot Accumulation and Melting Of Snow
	Stacked-gate Avalanche-injection Metal Oxide Semiconductor
SAMP	Salary Administration and Manpower Planning
SAMPAR	Sampled Aperture Radar
SAMPE	Society of Aerospace Material and Process Engineers (USA)
SAMPLE	Survey Analysis Macro Programming Language
SAMPS	Semi-Automated Message Processing System
	Subdivision And Mapping Plotter System
SAMS	Six Axis Motion System
	Society for Advanced Medical Systems (USA)
	Standard Army Maintenance System (US Army)
	Stratospheric And Mesopheric Sounder (deactivated 1979)
SAMSOM	Support-Availability Multi-System Operations Model
SAMSON	Special Avionics Mission Strap-On Now pod
	Strategic Automatic Message Switching Operational Network (of the Canadian Armed Forces)
SAMT	Sleds Amphibious Marginal Terrain
SAMTAS	Supervisory and Management Training Association of Singapore (Singapore)
SAMTEC	Space And Missile Test Center (USAF)
SAMTO	Space and Missile Test Organization (USAF)
SAN	Servicios Aereos Nacionales (Ecuador)
	Small Area Network
	Styrene-Acrylonitrile
SANA	Scientists Against Nuclear Arms
SANACS	Supervised Alarm Annunciation and Control System
SANAE	South African National Antarctic Expedition
SANBAR	Sanders Barotropic
SANCAD	Scottish Association for National Certificates and Diplomas
SANCAR	South African National Council for Antarctic Research (South Africa)
SANCOT	South African National Committee on Tunnelling (South Africa)
SANCST	Saudi Arabian National Centre of Science and Technology (Saudi Arabia)
SANCWEC	South African National Committee of the World Energy Conference (South Africa)
SAND	Shelter Analysis for New Designs
	Spectrum Analysis by Neutron Detectors
SANDT	School of Applied Non-Destructive Testing (of the Welding Institute)
SANE	Solar Alternatives to Nuclear Energy (an organisation in British Columbia (Canada))
SANMIS	Sanitation Management Information System
SANS	SIERRA (RESEARCH CORPORATION) (USA) Air Navigation System
SANTA	South African National Tuberculosis Association (South Africa)
	Systematic Analog Network Testing Approach
SANZ	Standards Association of New Zealand (New Zealand)
SAO	Smithsonian Astrophysical Observatory (USA)
SAOA	Semi-Ascending Order Arrangement
SAODAP	Special Action Office for Drug Abuse Prevention (of the Office of the President (USA))
SAP	Semi-Armour Piercing
	Serum Alkaline Phosphatase
	Simplified Astro Platten
	Sintered Aluminium Powder
	Start of Active Profile
	Supplementary Aerial Photography
SAPAR	Societe d'Appareillage Electrique (France)
SAPEM	Societe d'Applications Pneumatiques Electriques et Mechaniques (France)
SAPGO	Simultaneous Adjustment of Photogrammetric and Geodetic Observations
SAPHEIT	Semi-Armour Piercing High Explosive Incendiary Tracer
SAPHO	SABENA Automated Passenger Handling Operations
SAPHYDATA	System for the Acquisition, Transmission and Processing of Hydrological Data (of IHD) (UNESCO))
SAPIR	System of Automatic Processing and Indexing of Reports
SAPO	South African Post Office (South Africa)
SAPPCO	Saudi Plastics Products Company (Saudi Arabia)
SAPPHIRE	Synthetic Aperture Precision Processor, High Reliability
SAPPHO	Scientific Activity Predictor from Patterns with Heuristic Origins
SAPR	Semi-Annual Progress Report
SAPRC	Statewide Air Pollution Research Center (California University (USA))
SAPRO	Societe Anonyme de Pipeline a Produits (Switzerland)
SAPROPS	Support Analysis Procedure of Roll Over Protective Structure
SAPT	Scottish Association for Public Transport
SAQ	Schweizerische Arbeitsgmeneinschaft fur Qualitatsbeforderung (Switzerland) (Swiss Association for the Promotion of Quality)
SAR	Search and Rescue
	Search and Rescue Radio
	Semi-Active Radar
	Sequential Allocation Rule
	Solicitors' Accounts Rules 1975
	South African Railways (South Africa)
	South Australian Railways (most lines transferred to the Australian National Railways in 1978, the remainder transferred to the control of South Australia State Transport Authority)
	Specific Absorption Rate
	Stable Auroral Red arcs
	Stack Address Register
	Structure-Activity Relationship
	Successive Approximation Register
	Synthetic Aperture Radar
SARA	Sexually Acquired Reactive Arthritis
	System Availability and Reliability Analysis
	System for Activity Recording and Analysis
SARAH	Search And Rescue And Homing
	STRATHCLYDE (UNIVERSITY) Acoustic Range And Height
SARBE	Search and Rescue Beacon Equipment
SARBICA	Southeast Asian Regional Branch of the International Council on Archives
SARC	Split Armature Receiver Capsule

SARCALM	Synthetic Array Radar Command Air Launched Missile
SARCO	Saudi Arabian Refining Company (Saudi Arabia)
SARDA	Search and Rescue Dog Association
SARIE	Selective Automatic Radar Identification Equipment Semi-Automatic Radar Identification Equipment
SARIMS	Swept Angle Retarding Ion Mass Spectrometer
SARIS	Synthetic Aperture Radar Interpretation System
SaRL	Societe a Responsibilite Limitee (Private Limited Company)
SARO	Supply Aero-engine Record Office system (of the Royal Air Force)
SAROAD	Storage And Retrieval of Aerometric Data Storage And Retrieval of Air-quality Data
SARP	Ship Alteration and Repair Package SIGNAAL (NV HOLLANDSE SIGNAALAPPARENTEN (NETHERLANDS) Automatic Radar Processing system Sophisticated Automatic Radar Processing
SARPS	Standards And Recommended Practices (series issued by ICAO)
SARS	Search And Rescue Submersible Secretary of the Army Research and Study (US Army) Support And Restraint System
SARSAT	Search And Rescue Satellite-Aided Tracking
SARSIM	Search And Rescue Simulation
SARST	Societe Auxiliare de la Recherche Scientifique et Technique (France)
SARTS	Switched Access Remote Test System
SARU	Systems Analysis Research Unit (of DOE)
SARUS	Search And Rescue Using Satellites
SAS	Satellite Applications Section (of the National Hurricane Center (USA)) Scandinavian Airlines System (Sweden) Scheme of Assessment and Supervision (of BSI) SEAL (SUBSEA EQUIPMENT ASSOCIATES LIMITED) Atmospheric System Single Audio System Small Angle Scattering Small Astronomy Satellite Society for Applied Spectroscopy (USA) Special Ammunition Stowage Stability Augmentation Safety system Statistical Analysis System Surface Active Substances Suspended Array System Symposium on Atomic Spectroscopy Synthetic Aperture System
SAS/CSS	Stability Augmentation System with Control Stick Steering
SASA	Small Arms Systems Agency (US Army) South African Society of Anaesthetists (South Africa) South African Sugar Association (South Africa)
SASAG	Special Air Safety Advisory Group (of FAA (USA))
SASAR	Singapore Association of Shipbuilders And Repairers (Singapore)
SASE	Statistical Analysis of a Series of Events
SASG	Smoke/Aerosol Steering Group (US Army)
SASHO	Southeastern Association of State Highway Officials (USA)
SASI	Society of Air Safety Investigators
SASIS	Semi-Automatic Speaker Identification System
SASLIC	Surrey And Sussex Libraries In Co-operation
SASMIRA	Silk and Art Silk Mills Research Association (India)
SASO	Saudi Arabia Standards Organization (Saudi Arabia)
SASOL	South African Coal, Oil and Gas Corporation (South Africa)
SASP	Seismic Array Station Processor
SASR	Semi-Annual Status Report
SASS	Standard Army Supply System (US Army) Suspended-Array Surveillance System
SASSY	Supported Activity Supply System
SASTA	Small Ariel Surveillance and Target Acquisition
SAT	Social Assessment of Technology Socially Appropriate Technology Societe Anonyme de Telecommunications (France) Society of Acoustic Technology (now British Acoustical Society) Stabilization Assurance Test Stepped Atomic Time Surveillance Acquisition and Tracking Synchronized Acoustic Transmitter Systematic Analytical Training Systematic Assertive Therapy Systems Approach to Training underwater telephone cable connecting South Africa to Great Britain via Spain
SATA	Societe Anonyme de Transport Aerien (Switzerland)
SATAN	Speed And Throttle Automatic Network Storage Array Tester and Analyser
SATANAS	Semi-Automatic Analogue Setting
SATC	South Asia Trade Committee
SATCO	Servicio Aereo de Transportes Comerciales (Peru) Signal Automatic Air Traffic Control
SATCOM	Committee on Scientific and Technical Communication (of National Academy of Sciences AND National Academy of Engineering) (USA) Satellite Communication Agency (USDOD)
SATCRA	Stress in Air Traffic Control Research Association (Netherlands)
SATENA	Servicio de Aeronavegacion a Territorios Nacionales (Colombia)
SATERCO	Societe Anonyme de Terrassements et de Constructions (Belgium)
SATF	Strike And Terrain Following radar
SATI	Selective Access to Tactical Information
SATIATER	Statistical Approach To Investment Appraisal To Evaluate Risk
SATIN	Strategic Air Command (USAF) Automated Total Information Network
SATIRE	Semi-Automatic Information Retrieval
SATNAV	Satellite Navigation
SATO	Self-Aligned Thick-Oxide
SATRA	Shoe and Allied Trades Research Association
SATRO	Science And Technology Regional Organisations (sponsored by SCSST)
SATS	Short Airfield for Tactical Support
SATSIM	Saturation Countermeasures Simulator
SATT	Shear Area Transition Temperature Strowger Automatic Toll Ticketing
SAV	Slovakia Akademia Ved (Czechoslovakia) (Slovak Academy of Science)
SAVASI	Simplified Abbreviated Visual Approach Slope Indicator
SAVCO	Servicios Aereos Virgen de Copacabana (Bolivia)
SAVE	Society of American Value Engineers (USA) System for Automatic Value Exchange
SAVER	Service And Vehicle Emergency Relay Stowable Aircrew Vehicle Escape Rotoseat
SAVES	Sizing Aerospace Vehicle Structures
SAVI	Students Audio Visual Interface
SAVIEM	Societe Anonyme de Vehicules Industriels et d'Equipements Mechaniques (France)
SAW	Satellite Attack Warning Seeking, Asking and Written questionnaire Society of Architects in Wales Special Air Warfare Squad Automatic Weapon Strike-Anywhere matches

	Submerged Arc Welding
	Surface Acoustic Wave
SAWA	Screen Advertising World Association
SAWC	Special Air Warfare Center (USAF)
SAWD	Surface Acoustic Wave Device
SAWDLO	Surface Acoustic Wave Delay Line Oscillator
SAWE	Society of Aeronautical Weight Engineers (USA)
SAWES	Small Arms Weapons Effects Simulator
SAWG	Salaried Architects Working Group (of RIBA)
SAWMA	Soil and Water Management Association
SAWMARCS	Standard Aircraft Weapons Management And Release Control System
SAWO	Surface Acoustic Wave Oscillator
SAWRS	Supplementary Aviation Weather Reporting Station (of NWS (NOAA))
SAWS	Satellite Attack Warning System
	Small Arms Weapons Study (US Army)
	Squad Automatic Weapon System
	Submarine Acoustical Warfare System
SAWTRI	South African Wool and Textile Research Institute (of CSIR (South Africa))
SAX	Small Automatic Exchange
	Strong Anion Exchange
SAXS	Small-Angle X-ray Scattering
SB	Sonic Boom (a panel of ICAO)
SBA	School Bookshop Association
	Secondary Butyl Alcohol
	Sequential Boolean Analyser
	Small Business Administration (USA)
	Small Businesses Association
	Standard Beam Approach
	Strategic Business Area
SBAC	Society of British Aerospace Companies
SBASI	Single-Bridge APOLLO Standard Initiator
SBB	Satellite Broadcasting Board
	Schweizerische Bundesbahnen (Switzerland) (Swiss Federal Railways)
	Societe Belge des Betons (Belgium)
SBBNF	Ship and Boat Builders National Federation
SBC	Single Burst Correction
	Small Business Computer
	Sonic Boom Commitee (of ICAO)
	Standard Buried Collector
SBCC	Southern Building Code Congress (USA) (now part of CABO (usa))
SBD	Savings Bonds Division (of Department of the Treasury (USA))
	Standard Bibliographic Description
SBF	Short Back-Fire antenna
SBFS	Special Board of Flight Surgeons (USN)
SBG GEDD	Schottky-Barrier Gate Gunn-Effect Digital Device
SBGI	Society of British Gas Industries
SBI	State Bank of India (India)
SBIC	A Small Business Investment Corporation
SBL	Structure Building Language
SBM	Single Buoy Mooring
	Syton-Bromine-Methanol
SBN	Standard Book Number
	Strontium Barium Niobate
SBO	Side Band Only
	Specific Behavioural Objectives
SBOLS	Shadow Box Optical Landing System
SBP	Society of Biological Psychiatry (USA)
	Steroid Binding Protein
	Sugar Beet Pulp
SBPC	Small Business Promotion Corporation (Japan)
SBPIM	Society of British Printing Ink Manufacturers
SBR	Serial Bullet Rifle
	Signal-to-Background Ratio
	Sodium-cooled Fast Breeder Reactor
	Space-Based Radar
	Styrene Butadiene Rubber
SBR(OEP)	Styrene Butadiene Rubber (Oil Extended)
SBRS	Side and Back Rack System
SBS	Short Baseline Sonar
	Stimulated Brillouin Scattering
SBSC	Schottky Barrier Solar Cell
SBSS	Standard Base Supply System (USAF)
SBT	Segregated Ballasted Tanks
	Submarine Bathythermograph
	Surface Barrier Transistor
SBTB	Statens Bibiotek og Trykkeri Blinde (Denmark) (State Library and Printing House for the Blind)
SBTC	Sino-British Trade Council
SBTI	Soybean Trypsin Inhibitor
SBU	Strategic Business Unit
SBV	Sea Bed Vehicle
SBW	Space Bandwidth
	Swept Back Wing
SBX	Sub-sea Beacon/Transponder
SC	Solid-state Circuit
	Special Committee
	Sudden Commencement
	Superimposed Coding
	Synchro-Cyclotron
SC-RB	Separable Costs–Remaining Benefits
SC/BMS	Sub-Committee on Basic Meteorological Services (of ICMS (USA))
SC/DDS	Sensor Control/Data Display Set
SC/FC	Solar Cell/Fuel Cell
SCA	Shipbuilders Council of America (USA)
	Small Calibre Ammunition
	Society of Commercial Accountants (merged into SCCA in 1974)
	Statistical Compensation Approaches
	Supersonic Cruise Aircraft
	Suspended Ceilings Association
	Svenska Cellulosa Aktiebolaget (Sweden)
SCAAS	Strategic Communication and Alerting System
SCAC	South Carolina Aeronautics Commission (USA)
SCAD	Small Current Amplifying Device
	Subsonic Cruise Armed Decoy
SCADA	Supervisory Control And Data Acquisition
SCADS	Scanning Celestial Attitude Determination System
	Supervisory Console Assembler Debugging System
SCAG	Southern California Association of Governments (USA)
SCALA	Society of Chief Architects of Local Authorities
SCALE	Standardized Computer Analyses for Licensing Evaluation (of nuclear systems)
	Syllabically Compounded And Logically Encoded
SCAM	Societe Commerciale d'Applications Mecanographiques (France)
	Source-Coder's Cost Analysis Model
	System-support Cost Analysis Model
SCAMA	Station Conferencing And Monitoring Arrangement
SCAMP	Scottish Association of Magazine Publishers
	Small-Caliber Ammunition Program (of US Army)
	SPERRY Computer Aided Message Processor
	Submerged Cleaning and Maintenance Platform
	Syntax Constructed Algol 68-R Monitory Package
SCAMS	Scanning Microwave Spectrometer
SCAN	Schedule Analysis
	Selected Current Aerospace Notices (issued by NASA)
	Southern California Answering Network (administered by California State Library (USA))

	Stock Control and Analysis on NINETEEN HUNDRED computer
	Stockmarket Computer Answering Network
	Switched Circuit Automatic Network
	System of Codes for Analysis of circuits and systems
	Systematic Classification Analysis of Non-verbal behaviour
SCANDOC	Scandinavian Documentation Center (USA)
SCANIIR	Surface Composition by Analysis of Neutral and Ion Impact Radiation
SCANS	Scheduling and Control by Automated Network System
	Spectra Calculation from Activated Nuclide Sets
	STANFORD (University) Computer for Analysis of Nuclear Structure
SCANTIE	Submersible Craft Acoustic Navigation and Track Indication Equipment
SCAO	Standing Conference on Atlantic Organisations
SCAP	Silent Compact Auxiliary Power
	Sparse Matrix Circuit Analysis Programme
	Systems for the Control of Ambulation Pressure
SCAPE	Self Contained Atmospheric Personnel Ensemble
	Self-Contained Atmospheric Protective Ensemble
SCAR	Satellite Capture and Retrieval
	Scandinavian Council for Applied Research
	Scientific Committee on Antarctic Research (of ICSU)
	Strike Control And Reconnaissance
	Submarine Celestial Altitude Recorder
	Supersonic Cruise Aircraft Research (a project of NASA (USA))
SCARAB	Submerge Craft Assisting Recovery And Burial (of submerged telephone cables)
SCARD	Signal Conditioning and Recording Device
SCARE	Sensor Control Anti-Anti-Radiation Missile Radar Evaluation
SCARF	Santa Cruz Acoustic Range Facility
SCARP	Salinity Control And Reclamation Projects (of WAPDA)
SCARS	Status, Control, Alerting and Reporting System
SCAS	Semi-Continuous Activated-Sludge
	Stability Control Augmentation System
	Steering Committee on the Assurance Sciences (of the Canadian Standards Association)
SCASSS	Southern Chartered Accountant Students Society
SCAT	Scalar-Tensor Theory
	Sectioned, Conductive Anti-static Tray State Library (USA))
	Space Communication and Tracking
	Speed Command of Attitude and Thrust
	Statistical Communications Analysis Technique
	System for Computer Automated Typesetting
SCATANA	Security Control of Air Traffic and Air Navigational Aids
SCATER	Security Control of Air Traffic and Electromagnetic Radiation
SCATHA	Spacecraft Charging At High Altitudes
SCATS	Standard Coal Aerosol Test
SCATT	Scientific Communication and Technology Transfer
SCAUL	Standing Committee on African University Libraries
SCAULEA	Standing Conference of African University Libraries in East Africa (HQ in Ethiopia)
SCAULWA	Standing Conference of African University Libraries, Western Area (Ghana)
SCAX	Small Country Automatic Exchange
SCB	Selenite-Crystine Broth
	Stage Check-out Building
	Statistika Centralbyran (Sweden) (Central Bureau of Statistics)
SCBA	Scottish Building Contractors Association
SCBF	Spinal Cord Blood Flow
SCC	Saudi Cable Company (Saudi Arabia)
	Signal Channel Controller
	Single Conductor Cable
	Single-Channel Communications Control
	Standards Council of Canada (Canada)
	Stress-Corrosion Cracking
	Submerged Compression Chamber
	Swedish Cooperative Centre
SCCA	Society of Company and Commercial Accountants (formed in 1974 by the merger of the Institute of Company Accountants, Society of Commercial Accountants, and Cost Accountants Association)
SCCAPE	Scottish Council for Commercial, Administrative and Professional Education
SCCCU	Single Channel Communications Control Unit
SCCD	Surface-Channel Charge-Couple Device
SCCE	Staged Combustion Compound Engine
SCCM	Short Circuit Conductance Matrix
SCCO(E)	Shaped Charge Cutting Outfit (Explosive)
SCCOP	State Consulting Company for Oil Projects (Iraq)
SCD	Short-Code Dialling
	Solar Capture Device
	Spreading Cortical Depression
SCDA	Standing Conference on Drug Abuse
SCDAuto	Sub Carrier Demodulation, Automatic
SCDC	Steel Castings Development Committee
SCDP	Society of Certified Data Processors (USA) State Library (USA))
SCDS	Shipboard Chaff Decoy System
SCE	Saturated Calomel Electrode
	Sister Chromatid Exchanges
	Society of Carbide Engineers (USA)
	Standard Calomel Electrode
	Stratified Charge Engine
SCEA	Signal Conditioning Electronic Assembly
SCECSAL	Standing Conference of the Eastern, Central and Southern African Librarians
SCEDSIP	Standing Conference on Educational Development Services in Polytechnics
SCEET	Support Concept Economic Evaluation Technique
SCEH	Society for Clinical and Experimental Hypnosis (USA)
SCEI	Switching Control and Express Interpreter
SCEP	Study of Critical Environmental Problems (sponsored by Massachusetts Institute of Technology (USA))
SCEPS	Solar Cell Electric Power System
SCEPTRE	Software-Controlled Electronic-Processing Traffic-Recording Equipment
	Systems for Circuit Evaluation and Prediction of Transient Radiation Effects
SCERP	Stratospheric Cruise Emission Reduction Program (of NASA (USA))
SCERT	Systems and Computer Evaluation and Review Technique
SCET	Scottish Council for Educational Technology
	Society of Civil Engineering Technicians
SCETA	Societe de Controle et d'Exploitation de Transports Auxiliaries (France)
SCF	Satellite Control Facility (USAF)
	Schematic Concept Formation
	Self-Consistent Field
	Seroconversion Factor
	Stress Concentration Factor
SCFA	Self-Consistent Field Approximation
	Short Chain Fatty Acids
SCFBR	Steam-Cooled Fast Breeder Reactor
SCFCEF	Syndicat des Constructeurs Francaise de Condensateurs Electrique Fixes (France)

SCFG Stochastic Context-Free Grammar
SCFM Standard Cubic Feet per Minute
SCFRPAC Symposium on Computer Films for Research in Physics And Chemistry
SCFS Slip Cast Fused Silica
SCG Sodium Cromoglycate
Superior Cervical Ganglion
SCHA South Carolina Heart Association (USA)
SChemI Socieity of Chemical Industry State Library (USA))
SCHOLAR SCHERING (CORPORATION) Oriented Literature Analysis and Retrieval system
SCI Science of Creative Intelligence
Seal Compatibility Index
Shipping Corporation of India (India) (Government-owned)
Simulation Councils Incorporated (USA)
Societe de Chimie Industrielle (France)
Society of Chemical Industry
Switched Collector Impedance
SCIB Ship Characteristics and Improvement Board (USN)
SCIBP Special Committee of the International Biological Programme
Special Committee of the International Biological Programme (of ICSU)
SCIC Semiconductor Integrated Circuit
SCID Severe Combined Immunodeficiency Disease
Small Column Insulated Delay
SCIDOC SEARLE (G D SEARLE & CO LTD) Coordinate Index to Documents
SCIDS Small Container Intermodal Distribution System
SCIENCE Société des Consultants Indépendants et Neutres de la Communauté Européenne (Belgium)
SCIIA Sudden Changes in the Integrated Intensity of Atmospherics
SCIM Silicon Coating by Inverted Meniscus
Speech Communication Index Meter
SCIMP Self-Contained Imaging Micro-Profiler
SCIP Scanning for Information Parameters
SCIR Standing Committee for Installation Rebuilding (of MOD and MPBW)
SCIRP Semiconductor Infra-Red Photography
SCIRT Supplier Capability Information Retrieval Technique
System Control In Real Time
SCIRTSS Sequential Circuit Test Search System
SCISP Schools Council Integrated Science Project
SCITEC an association in Canada for the advancement of Science and Technology
SCIVU Science Council of the International Vegetarian Union (Switzerland)
SCJ Science Council of Japan (Japan)
SCK Studiecentrum voor Kernergie (Belgium) (Centre for Nuclear Energy Studies)
SCL Scottish Central Library (merged with National Library of Scotland in 1974 to form National Library of Scotland Lending Services)
Serum Copper Levels
Space-Charged-Limited
Superconducting Levitron
System Chart Language
SCLC Space-Charge-Limited Current
SCLERA Santa Catalina Laboratory for Experimental Relativity and Astrometry (the name of a telescope designed and operated by Professor Henry Hill and Carl Zanoni)
SCLIGFET Space-Charge-Limited Insulated-Gate Field-Effect Transistor
SCLP Security Command Language Processor
SCLSERP Standing Conference on London and South-East Regional Planning
SCM Samarium Cobalt Magnet
Society for Computer Medicine (USA)
Society of Coal Merchants
Soluble Cytotoxic Mediator
Steam-Cure Mortar
Strategic Cruise Missile
SCMA Southern California Meter Association (USA)
Southern Cypress Manufacturers Association (USA)
Split Channel Multiple Access
SCMAI Staff Committee on Mediation, Arbitration, and Inquiry (of the American Library Association (USA)
SCMC Sodium Carboxymethyl Cellulose
Strategic Cruise Missile Carrier
SCMR Surface Composition Mapping Radiometer
SCN Sensitive Command Network
Static Charge Neutralizer
SCNEA Sealing Commission for the North East Atlantic
SCNQT Standing Conference for National Qualification and Title (now Engineers Registration Board AND Standing Conference on Technician Engineers and Technicians)
SCNR Scientific Committee of National Representatives (of SHAPE)
SCNWA Sealing Commission for the North West Atlantic
SCO Subcarrier Oscillator
System Check-out Computer
SCOBE Standing Conference on Business Education
SCOCLIS Standing Conference of Co-operative Library Information Services
SCOD Surface Crack Opening Displacement
SCODA Standing Conference on Drug Abuse
SCODS Standing Committee on Ocean Data Stations (of NERC)
SCOEG Standing Conference of Employers of Graduates (administered at Manchester University)
SCOGS Select Committee on GRAS Substances (USA)
SCOLA Second Consortium of Local Authorities
SCOLCAP Scottish Libraries Co-operative Automation Project
SCOLD Small Company On-Line Data
SCOLMA Standing Conference on Library Materials for Africa
SCOM Societe Centrale d'Organisation et Methodes (France) (of the Ministry of Economy and Finance) (Central Society for Organisation and Methods)
SCOMO Satellite Collection of Meteorological Observations
SConMeL Standing Conference for Mediterranean Librarians
SCOOP Scientific Computation of Optimal Programmes
Standing Committee on Official Publications (of IRG)
State Consultant Company for Oil Products (Iraq)
SCOPE Schedule-Cost-Performance
Scientific Committee on Problems of the Environment (of ICSU)
Simple Checkout-Oriented Programming Language
Space-Craft Operational Performance Evaluation
Special Committee on Problems of the Environment (of ICSU)
Specifiable Co-ordinating Positioning Equipment
Standing Conference of Public Enterprises (India)
Standing Conference on Overseas Placements and Exchanges
Status Concept of Programme Evaluation
System and Component Operating Performance Evaluation
System for Capacity and Orders Planning and Enquiries
System for Computing Operational Probability Equations

Systematic Control of Periodicals

SCOPEP Steering Committee on the Performance of Electrical Products (of CSA (Canada))

SCOPES Squad Combat Operations Exercise (Simulation) (US Army)

SCOPW Self-Consistent Orthogonalized-Plane-Wave

SCOR Scientific Committee on Oceanographic Research (of ICSU)

SCORE Satellite Computer Operated Readiness Equipment
Scenario Oriented Recurring Evaluation
Select Concrete Objectives for Research Emphasis
Selection Copy and Reporting system
Serial Control of RACAL Equipment
Service Corps of Retired Executives (USA)
Signal Communications by Orbital Relay Equipment
Signal Controller Operation Recording Equipment
Survey and Commparison of Research Expenditures (a project of the Dept of Science (Australia))
Survey and Comparisons of Research and Expenditure (project of the Department of Science (Australia))
System Capability Over Requirement Evaluation
System Cost and Operational Resource Evaluation

SCORES Scenario Oriented Recurring Evaluation System (US Army)
Ship Structure Response in Waves

SCORPIO Sub-critical Carbon-moderated Reactor assembly for Plutonium Investigations
Subject Content Oriented Retriever for Processing Information On-line (of Library of Congress (USA))
Subject Content-Oriented Retriever for Processing Information On-line
Submarine Craft for Ocean Repair, Positioning, Inspection and Observation

SCOT Scottish College of Textiles
Semi-automated Computer Oriented Text
Shaken and Circulatory Oxidation Test
Shell Claus Off-gas Treating
Shipboard Communications Terminal
Sub-system Cost Optimization Technique

SCOTA Scottish Offshore Training Association

SCOTBEC Scottish Business Education Council (merged into SCOTVEC in 1984)

SCOTEC Scottish Technical Education Council (merged into SCOTVEC in 1984)

SCOTS Surveillance and Control of Transmission Systems

SCOTSSFEC Scottish Safety, Security, Fire Exhibition and Conference

SCOTVEC Scottish Vocational Education Council

SCP Safety Control Programme
Secure Care Property
Security Control Processor
Selfconsistent Phonon Theory
Single Cell Protein
Sodium-Containing Particle
Space-Charge Precipitator

SCPC Single-Channel-per-Carrier

SCPEA Southern California Professional Engineering Association (USA)

SCPI Structural Clay Products Institute (USA) (now Brick Institute of America)

SCPK Serum Creatine Phosphokinase

SCPRI Service Central de Protection contre les Rayonnements Ionisants (France)

SCPSF Space Variant Point Spread Function

SCPV Silkworm Cytoplasmic Polyhedrosis Virus

SCR Selective Chopper Radiometer
Short Circuit Radio
Signal-to-Clutter Ratio
Silicon Controlled Rectifier
Sodium Cooled Reactor
Solar Cosmic Ray
Strength Count Ratio

SCRA Single Channel Radio Access

SCRAM Scottish Campaign to Resist the Atomic Menace
Supersonic Combustion Ramjet

SCRAMJET Supersonic Combustion Ramjet

SCRAMLACE Supersonic Combustion Ramjet Liquid Air Cycle Engine

SCRAP Super Calibre Rocket Assisted Projectile

SCRAPE Screening Country Requirements Against Plus Excesses

SCRAPP a combination of SCAN (Schedule Analysis) and RAPP (Resource Allocation and Project Planning)

SCRATA Steel Castings Research and Trade Association

SCRDC Silicon Controlled Rectifier Regulated Direct Current

SCRDE Stores and Clothing Research and Development Establishment (MOD)

SCRE Syndicat des Constructeurs de Relais Electriques (France)

SCREAM Society for the Registration of Estate Agents and Mortgage Brokers

SCRIM Sideway-force Coefficient Routine Investigation Machine

SCRIPT STANFORD (UNIVERSITY) (USA) Computerized Researcher Information Profile Technique

SCROLL String and Character Recording Oriented Logogrammatic Language

SCRR Solar Central Receiver Reformer

SCRTA Steel Castings Research and Trade Association

SCRTD Sea Control Ship
Southern California Rapid Transit District (USA)

SCRUB Systematically Clean and Renumber Users BASIC

SCRV Spill Control Recovery Valve

SCS Sea Control Ship (now called VSTOL Support Ship)
Silicon Controlled Switch
Single-Cycle Sampling
Society for Computer Simulation (USA)
Soil Conservation Service (USA)
Space Cabin Simulator
Speed Control System
Stabilization Cabin Simulator
Stimulated Compton Scattering
Surface-Compression Strengthened

SCSA Soil Conservation Society of America (USA)

SCSC Summer Computer Simulation Conference (USA)

SCSD Satellite Communication Systems Division (of ISRO) (India)
School Construction Systems Development (USA)

SCSE South Carolina Societies of Engineering (USA)

SCSI Small Computer System Interface

SCSK Shellfish Commission for the Skagerrak-Kattegat

SCSO Superconducting Cavity Stabilized Oscillator

SCSRMA Surface Coating Synthetic Resin Manufacturers Association

SCSST Standing Conference on Schools Science and Technology

SCST Select Committee on Science and Technology (of the House of Commons) (abolished 1979)

SCSTR Segregated Continuous Stirred Tank Reactor

SCT Secretaria de Communicaciones y Transportes (Mexico) (Ministry of Communications and Transport)
Single Channel Transponder
Surface-Charge Transistor

SCTE Society of Cable Television Engineers (USA)

SCTET Standing Conference for Technician Engineers and Technicians
SCTL Schottky Coupled Transistor Logic
SCTR Sodium Component Test Rig
SCTS Satellite Control and Test Earth Station
SCTT Submarine Command Team Trainer
SCUAS Standing Conference of University and Polytechnic Careers Services (now AGCAS)
SCUBA Self-Contained Underwater Breathing Apparatus
SCUE Standing Conference on University Entrance
SCUMRA Societe Centrale de l'Uranium et des Minerais et Metaux Radioactifs (France)
SCV Solid-state Voltage Controller
SCVF Single Channel Voice Frequency
SCW Space Charge Wave
SCX Strong Cation Exchange
SD prefix to numbered series of Business Monitor Quarterly Statistics on Service and Distribution issued by Business Statistics Office of Dept of Industry and published by HMSO
Serologically Defined
Sleep Deprivation
Sorbital Dehydrogenase
Systems Design
SDA Saw Diamond Abrasive
Scottish Development Agency
Soap and Detergent Association (USA)
Societe de l'Aerotrain (France)
Source Data Automation
SDAD Satellite Digital and Analogue Display
SDAF Special Defense Acquisition Fund (of USDOD)
SDAT Senile Dementia, ALZHEIMER's Type
SDB Silver-Dye-Bleach
Society for Developmental Biology (USA)
Statistical Database
SDC Signal Data Converter
Society of Dyers and Colourists
Space Defense Center (of ADC (USAF))
Special Devices Center (USN)
Submersible Diving Chamber
SDCA Society of Dyers and Colourists of Australia
SDCCU Synchronous Data Communication Control Unit
SDCE Society of Die Casting Engineers (USA)
SDD Scottish Development Department
Selected Dissemination of Documents
SDDE Surface Demand Diving Equipment
SDDLL Sample-Data Delay-Lock Loop
SDE Society of Data Educators (USA)
SDECE Service de Documentation Exterieure et de Contre-Espionnage (France)
SDF Standard Data Format
SDFC Space Disturbance Forecast Center (of ESSA) (USA)
SDH Succinic Dehydrogenase
SDI Selective Dissemination of Information
Strategic Defence Initiative ("Star Wars" program of USA)
SDILINE Selective Dissemination of Information on-line
SDIM System of Documentation and Information for Metallurgy (of the European Communities)
SDIO Strategic Defense Initiative Organization (USDOD)
SDL Space Disturbances Laboratory (of ESSA) (now of NOAA (USA))
Specification and Description Language
System Descriptive Language
SDLC Synchronous Data Line Control
Synchronous Data Link Communications
Synchronous Data Link Control
SDM Selective Dissemination of Microfiche (now offered by NTIS (Dept. of Commerce (USA))
Site Defense of MINUTEMAN
Space Division Multiplexing
Spares Determination Method
Standardization Design Memoranda (series issued by MOD)
Statistical Delta Modulation
Structural Dynamics and Materials Conference (of AIAA, ASME, and SAE (USA))
SDMA Space-Division Multiple-Access
SDMA/SS-TDMA Space Division Multiple Access/Spacecraft Switched Time Division Multiple Access
SDMS Shipboard Data Multiplex System
SDNF Shortened Disjunctive Normal Form
SDNM Sampled-Data Nonlinearity Matrix
SDP Spectrum Difference Processing
Staff Discussion Paper
Systems and Data Processing
SDR Search Decision Rule
Single-Drift-Region
Small Development Requirement
Special Drawing Rights
Splash Detection Radar
System Design Review
SDRS Splash Detection Radar System
SDS Satellite Data System
Slowing Down Spectrometer
Sodium Dodecyl Sulphate
Sound-Deadened Steel
Space Defence System
Space Documentation Service (of EURODOC)
SDSA Societe pour la Diffusion des Sciences et des Arts (France) (Society for the Spread of the Sciences and Arts)
SDSB Satellite Data Services Branch (of EDS (NOAA) (USA))
SDT Signal Detection Theory
System Down Time
SDTI Signal-Dependent Time Interval
SDU Social Development Unit (Singapore)
Sodium Diuranate
SDVS Software Design and Verification System
SDW Schutzmeinschaft Deutscher Wald (Germany) (German Association for the Protection of Forests and Woodlands)
SDWA Safe Water Drinking Act, 1974 (USA)
SE (The) Stock Exchange
Self-Extinguishing
Society of Engineers
Sonic Extract
Southeastern Forest Experiment Station (of Forest Service (USDA))
Systems Engineering
SEA Scanning Electron Microscope
Science and Education Administration (of USDA)
Servicios Especiales Aereos (Colombia)
Sociedad Espanola de Acustica (Spain) (Spanish Society of Acoustics)
Societe d'Electronique et d'Automatisme (France)
Soluble Egg Antigen
Staphylococcal Enterotoxin A
Statistical Energy Analysis
Sudden Enhancement of Atmospherics
Systems Effectiveness Analyzer
SEA-CON Symposium and Exhibition on Measurement and Control of Offshore Platforms and Land Terminals
SEAAG South-East Asia Advisory Group (of BOTB)
SEABIRD Ship-design Engineering Aided By Interactive Remote Display
SEAC South Eastern Architects Consortium (reconstituted 1974–formerly South East Authorities Collaboration) (disbanded 1977)
STANDARD's Eastern Automatic Computer (NBS)
Support Equipment Advisory Committee (of seven United States airlines)

SEACOM South East Asia Commonwealth Cable (submarine telephone cable connecting Australia, New Guinea, Guam, Hong Kong, Malaysia and Singapore)
SEACON Seafloor Construction Experiment (of NCEL (USN))
SEACORE Southeast Asia Communications Research
SEACOST Systematic Equipment Analysis and Cost Optimization Scanning Technique
SEADUCER Steady-state Evaluation and Analysis of Transducers
SEAF Sveriges El-och Elektronikagenters Forening (Sweden) (Swedish Electrical and Electronics Agents Association)
SEAISI South-East Asia Iron & Steel Institute
SEAL Sea-Air-Land
Signal Evaluation Airborne Laboratory (of FAA (USA))
South-East Area Libraries information service
Subsea Equipment Associates Ltd. (an international consortium)
SEALAB Sea Laboratory
SEAMAP Deep Sea Mapping Program (of ESSA (USA))
SEAMEO South-East Asian Ministers of Education Organization
SEAMES South-East Asian Ministers of Education Secretariat (Thailand)
SEAMIST Seavan Management Information System (US Army)
SEAMOD Sea Systems Modification and Modification by Modularity
SEAMORE Southeast Asia Mohawk Revision
SEAN Scientific Event Alert Network (of the Smithsonian Institution (USA))
SEAO Structural Engineers Association of Oregon (USA)
SEAOC Structural Engineers Association of California (USA)
SEAOCC Structural Engineers Association of Central California (USA)
SEAONC Structural Engineers Association of Northern California (USA)
SEAOSC Structural Engineers Association of Southern California (USA)
SEAOSD Structural Engineers Association of San Diego (USA)
SEAP Save the Environment from Atomic Pollution (Canada) (an environmental conservation group)
SEAPAC Sea Activated Parachute Automatic Crew release
SEAPAL South East Asia and Pacific League against Rheumatism
SEAPEX South-East Asia Petroleum Exploration Society
SEAPOS Structural Evaluation and Analysis Package for Offshore Structures
SEAPS SEATO Publications
SEARCC South-East Asia Regional Computer Conference
SEARCH System Evaluation And Reliability Checker
System for Electronic Analysis and Retrieval of Criminal Histories (of Law Enforcement Assistance Administration (USA))
Systems for Exploring Alternative Resource Commitments in Higher Education
SEAS Committee for the Scientific Excploration of the Atlantic Shelf
SHARE European Association
State Estimation Algorithm for Small-scale Systems
SEASAT Ocean Survey Satellite
SEASCO South East Asia Science Co-operation Office (India)
SEASSE Southeast Asian Society of Soil Engineering
SEASSMC SHARE (USA) European Association Symbolic Mathematical Computation
SEASTAG Standard issued by SEATO
SEASTAGS SEATO Military Standardization Agreements
SEAT Societa Elenchi Ufficiali degli Abbonati al Telefono (Italy)
SEATO South-East Asia Treaty Organization (ceased military activities in 1973 and disbanded 1977)
SEAVOM Societe d'Etudes et d'Applications Vide Optique Mecanique (France)
SEAWACO Sensor, Weapon and Command systems
SEB Societe Electrotechnique Boulogne-Billancourt (France)
Staphylococcal Enterotoxin B
Surface Effect Boat
SEBC Section d'Etudes de Biologie et de Chimie (of DTAT (France))
SEBIC Sustained Electron Bombardment-Induced Conductivity
SEBM Society for Experimental Biology and Medicine (USA)
SEC Sanitary Engineering Center (of US PUBLIC HEALTH SERVICE)
Secondary Electron Conduction
Secondary Emission Conductivity
Securities and Exchange Commission (USA)
Simple Electronic Computer
Size-Exclusion Chromatography
Solar Energy Commission (Saudi Arabia)
SEC-DED Single Error Correction and Double Error Detection
SECA Societe d'Exploitation de Constructions Aeronautiques (France)
Southern Educational Communications Association (USA)
SECAM Sequential Colour And Memory (Sequential couleur a memoire)
SECAN Societe d'Etudes et de Constructions Aero-Navales (France)
SECANT Separation and Control of Aircraft using Nonsynchronous Techniques
SECAP System Experience Correlation and Analysis Programme
SECAR Secondary Radar
SECAT Surface Effect Catamaran
SECBAt Societe Europeenne de Construction de l'avion Bregeut
SECC Single Error Correction Circuitry
SECEM Sociedad Espanola Construcciones Electro-Mecanicas (Spain)
SECHT Scoping Emergency Cooling Heat Transfer
SECL Symmetrical Emitter-Coupled Logic
SECLF Station d'Essais Combustibles et Lubrifiants de la Flotte (of the French Navy)
SECMA Stock Exchange Computer Managers Association
SECN Societe d'Etudes des Caissons Nucleaires (France)
SECNAV Secretary of the Navy (USN)
SECO Bureau de controle pour la securite de la construction en Belgique (Belgium) (Office for Research on Safety Precautions in Belgian Construction Work)
SECOR Sequential Collation Of Range
SECRAC System Engineering Cost Reduction Assistance Contractor
SECRE Societe d'Etudes et de Constructions Electroniques (France)
SECT Service des Équipements de Champs de Tir (of DRME (France))
Skin Electric Current Tracing
SECURE Safe Environmentally Clean Urban Reactor
Systems Evaluation Code Under Radiation Environment
SECV State Electricity Commission of Victoria (Australia)
SED Simultaneous Exposure and Development

Squared Euclidean Distance

SEDA Safety Equipment Distributors Association (USA)
Scanning Electron Diffraction Attachment
Societe d'Etudes pour le Developpement de l'Automatisme (France)

SEDAD Societe d'Etude et Developpement des Applications Derivees electroniques et mechaniques (France)

SEDAM Societe d'Etudes et de Developpement des Aeroglisseurs Marins Terrestres et Amphibies (France)

SEDAR Submerged Electrode Detection And Ranging system

SEDAS Spurious Emission Detection Acquisition System

SEDEC Societe d'Edition, de Documentation Economique et Commerciale (France)

SEDEIS Societe d'Etudes et de Documentation Economiques, Industrielles et Sociales (France)

SEDIGAS Sociedad para el Estudio y Desarollo de la Instriadel Gas (Spain)

SEDIS Surface Emitter Detection, Identification System

SEDIX Selected Dissemination of Indexes

SEDO Sociedad Espanola de Optica (Spain) (Spanish Society of Optics)

SEDS Space Electronic Detection System
SULZER Engine Diagnosis System

SEE Secondary Electron Emission
Small Evader Experiment
Society of Electronic Engineers (India)
Society of Environmental Engineers
Société des Electriciens, des Electroniciens et des Radioéléctricians (France) (Society of Electrical, Electronics and Radio Technicians)
Standard Error of Estimate
Systems Effectiveness Engineering

see-BG See-Berufsgenossenschaft (Seamans' Industrial Welfare Association) (Germany)

SEEB South Eastern Electricity Board

SEEDCON Software Evaluation, Exchange and Development for Contractors

SEEDIS Socio-Economic-Environmental Information System (of Mathematics and Computing Groups of Lawrence Berkeley Laboratory (USA))

SEEDS Shipboard Equipments Environmental Design Study

SEEEE Societe Europeenne d'Etudes et d'Essais d'Environnment (France)

SEEF Service des Etudes Economiques et Financieres du Ministere des Finance (France) (Department of Economic and Financial Studies of the Finance Ministry)

SEEK Systems Evaluation and Exchange of Knowledge (USA) (an association)

SEEN Societe d'Etudes et d'Entreprises Nucleaires (France)

SEEP Support Effectiveness Evaluation Procedures

SEER Sequence Extrapolating Robot
Simplified Estimation of Exposure to Radiation
System for Event Evaluation and Review

SEES Swedish Environmental Engineering Society (Sweden)

SEF Study of Educational Facilities

SEFC Southeast Fisheries Center (of NMFS (USA))

SEFI Societe Europeenne pour la Formation des Ingenieurs (Belgium)

SEFOR SOUTH-WEST Experimental Fast Oxide Reactor

SEFT Section d'Etudes et de Fabrications des Telecommunications (of DTAT (France))
Sintered Electrode Fluorescent Tube

SEFTA South Eastern Foundry Training Association

SEG prefix to reports issued by Institute of Social, Economic and Government Research, University of Alaska
Society of Economic Geologists (USA)
Society of Exploration Geophysicists (USA)
Systems Engineering Group (USAFSC)

SEGAIP Self Gated In-water Photography

SEGRE Fuerzas Hidroelectricas del Segre SA (Spain)

SEGS Selective Glide Slope

SEI Societe Generale d'Entreprises Imobilieres et de Investissements (Belgium)

SEIA Solar Energy Industries Association (USA)

SEIE Submarine Escape Immersion Equipment

SEIN Societe d'Electronique Industrielle et Nucleaire (France)

SEINA Societe Europeene d'Instruments Numeriques et Analogiques (France)

SEIO Sociedad Espanola de Investigacion Operativa (Spain) (Spanish Operational Research Society)

SEIS Submarine Escape Immersion Suit

SEIT Satellite Educational and Informational Television

SEL Sensitized-Erythrocyte-Lysis
Space Environment Laboratory (of ERL (NOAA) (USA))
Standard Elektrik Lorenz (Switzerland)
Stanford Electronics Laboratories (of Stanford University, USA)
Structural Engineering Laboratory (California University (USA))
Systems Engineering Laboratory (of Michigan University (USA))

SELCAL Selective Calling System

SELCALL Selective Calling

SELCIR Systems Engineering Laboratory Circuit-drawing programme

SELDAM Selective Data Management system

SELDOM Selective Dissemination of MARC (a service of Saskatchewan University (Canada))

SELEAC Standard Elementary Abstract Computer

SELEC Societe d'Etude des Electrocompresseurs (France)

SELEMO Selective Level Meter and Oscillator

SELF Societe d'Ergonomie de Langue Francaise (France) (a multi-national institute of ergonomics)

SELFIC Self-Featuring Information Compression

SELFOC Sheet-Electric Light Focusing

SELMA SYSTEMS ENGINEERING LABORATORY'S (University of Michigan) Markovian Analyzer

SELNI Societa Elettronucleaire Italiana (Italy)

SELV Safety Extra-Low Voltage

SEM Scanning Electron Microscopy
Singularity Expansion Method
System Extension Module
Systems Engineering Management

SEMA Societe d'Economie et Mathematique Appliquees (France)
Spray Equipment Manufacturers Association
Storage Equipment Manufacturers Association

SEMAC Supplier Evaluation Measurement And Control

SEMANOL Semantics Oriented Language

SEMBRAT Single Echelon Multi-Base Resource Allocation Technique

SEMCIP Shipboard Electro-Magnetic Compatibility Program (of US Navy)

SEMCOR Semantic Correlation

SEMDA Surveying Equipment Manufacturers and Dealers Association

SEMF State Enterprise Mutual Fund (of ICP (Pakistan))

SEMI Semiconductor Equipment and Materials Institute (USA)

	Special Electro-Magnetic Interference
SEMIRAD	Secondary-Electron Mixed-Radiation Dosimeter
SEMIROX	Semi-Recessed Oxide
SEMKO	Svenska Elecktriska Materielkontrollanstalten (Sweden) (Swedish Institute for Testing and Approval of Electrical Equipment)
SEMLAC	South East Midlands Local Authority Consortium
SEMLAT	Semiconductor Laser Array Technique
SEMM	Scanning Electron Mirror Microscope
	Societe Europeenne de Materials Mobiles (France)
SEMMS	Solar Electric Multi-mission Spacecraft
SEMO	Societe Belgo-Francaise d'Energie Nucleaire Mosane (France)
SEMP	Self Erecting Marine Platform
SEMPE	Socio-Economic Model of the Planet Earth
SEMR	Standard Electronic Module Radar
SEMS	Severe Environmental Memory System
	Society Europeene de Mini-informatique et de Systemes (France)
SEMT	Societe d'Etudes de Machines Thermiques (France)
SEN	prefix to Standards issued by SVS
	Single-Edge-Notch tension
	Sociedad Nuclear Espanola (Spain) (Spanish Nuclear Society)
SENA	Servicio Nacional de Aprendizaje (Colombia) (State sponsored organization for professional training)
	Societe d'Energie Nucleaire Franco-Belge des Ardennes
SENB	Single Edge Notched Bend
SENDOC	Small Enterprises National Documentation Centre (of Small Industry Extension and Training Institute (India))
SENEL	Single Event Noise Exposure Level
SENSE	Sensor Simulation Experiment (a project of DMAAC of DMA (USDOD))
SENSEA	Sentinel System Evaluation Agency (US Army)
SENT	Single Edge Notched Tension
SENTA	Societe d'Etudes Nucleaires et de Techniques Nouvelles (France)
SENTOKYO	Senmon Toshokan Kyogikai (Japan) (Special Libraries Association)
SEO	Satellite for Earth Observations
	State Energy Office (New York State (USA))
	Synchronous Equatorial Orbiter
SEOCS	Sun-Earth Observatory and Climatology satellite
SEOS	Synchronous Earth Observation Satellite
SEOSS	Slewable Electro-Optical Sensor System
SEP	Samenwerkende Electricitaits Productiebedrijven (Netherlands)
	Search Effectiveness Probability
	Societe Europeene de Propulsion (France)
	Solar Electric Propulsion
	Specific Excess Power
	Spherical Error Probable
	Stowarzyszenie Elektrykow Polskich (Poland) (Polish Electrical Association)
	Symbolic Equations Programme
SEPAK	Suspension of Expendable Penetration Aids by Kite
SEPBOP	South-Eastern Pacific Biological Oceanographic Programme
SEPD	Scottish Economic Planning Department
SEPE	Secretariat pour l'Etude des Problems de l'Eau (France) (Secretariat for the Study of Water Problems)
SEPECAT	Societe Europeene de Production de l'Avion Ecol de Combat et d'Appaui Tactique (France) (an Anglo/French co-operative concern)
SEPIA	Societe d'Etudes de Protection des Installations Atomiques (France)
SEPL	Societe du Pipe-Line Sud European
SEPM	Society of Economic Paleontologists and Mineralogists (USA)
SEPOD	Submersible Electric Prototype Ocean Dredge
SEPOL	Soil Engineering Problem—Oriented Language
SEPOR	Service des Programmes des Organismes de Recherche (France) (a government liaison Department)
SEPOS	Self-defined Polysilicon Sidewall
SEPOX	Selective Polysilicon Oxidation
SEPP	Société d'Etude de la Prévision et de la Planification (Switzerland) (Society for the Study of Futures)
SEPR	Societe d'Etude de la Propulsion par Reaction (France)
SEPS	Solar Electric Propulsion Stage
SEPSIT	Solar Electric Propulsion Integration Technology
SEPST	Solar Electric Propulsion System Technology
SEPTA	South-Eastern Pennsylvania Transportation Authority (USA)
SEPWG	Safety and Environmental Protection Working Group of JANNAF Interagency Propulsion Committee (USA)
SEQ	Standing Group on Emergency Questions (of IEA (OECD))
SER	Secondary Emission Ratio
	Smooth Endoplasmic Reticulum
	Sociaal Economische Raad (Netherlands) (Economic and Social Council)
SERA	Socialist Environment and Resources Association
SERAT	Societe d'Etudes, de Realisations et d'Applications Techniques (France)
SERC	Science and Engineering Research Council
	Service d'Etudes et de Recherches de la Circulation Routiere (France) (Road Traffic Study and Research Department)
	Structural Engineering Research Centre (India)
SERCEL	Societe d'Etudes Recherches et Constructions Electroniques (France)
SERCOBE	Servicio Tecnico Comercial de Constructores de Bienes de Equipo (Spain)
SERCOMETAL	Servicio Tecnico Comercial de Construcciones Metalicasy de Caldereria (Spain)
SERDES	Serializer/Deserializer
SERDES CRC	Serializer-Deserializer Cyclic Redundancy Check
SEREL	Societe d'Exploitation et de Recherches Electroniques (France)
SERENDIP	Search for Extraterrestrial Radio Emission from Nearby Developed Intelligent Populations
SERF	Studies of the Economics of Route Facilities (a panel of ICAO)
	System for Equipment Requirements Forecasting
SERG	Science Engineering Research Group (Long Island University (USA))
SERHL	South-Eastern Radiological Health Laboratory (of BRH (USA))
SERI	Solar Energy Research Institute (USA)
SERJ	Supercharged Ejector Ramjet
SERL	Services Electronic Research Laboratory (MOD) (became Radar and Signals Research Research Establishment (Baldock) (of MOD) in 1976)
SERLINE	Serials on-Line (of National Library of Medicine (USA))
SERM	Solar and Earth Radiation Monitor
SERNAM	Service National des Messageries (France)
SERPS	State Earnings Related Pensions Scheme
SERS	Surface Enhanced Raman Scattering
SERT	Society of Electronic and Radio Technicians
	Space Electrical Rocket Test

SERTI Societe d'Etudes et de Realisation pour le Traitement de l'Information (France)
SERTOG Space Experiment on Relativistic Theories of Gravitation
SERV Single-stage, Earth-orbital Reusable Vehicle
Surface Effect Rescue Vehicle
SES Scientific Exploration Society
Selected Electron Shell
Service des Études Scientifiques (Algeria) (Scientific Studies Service)
Society of Engineering Science (USA)
Solar Energy Society (USA) (now International Solar Energy Society (Australia))
Standards Engineers Society (USA)
Suffield Experimental Station (DRB, Canada) (now DRES)
Surface Effect Ship
SESA Single End Strip Adhesion
Social and Economics Statistics Administration (USA)
Societe d'Etudes des Systems d'Automation (France)
Society for Experimental Stress Analysis (USA)
SESAM Super Element Structural Analysis programme Modules
SESAME Severe Environmental Storms and Mesoscale Experiment
Supermarket Electronic Scanning for Automatic Merchandise Entry
SESAMI- SEED Sporadic E Stimulation by Artificial Metallic Ion Seeding
SESC Services Electrical Standards Centre (MINTECH)
Space Environment Services Center (of NOAA (USA))
Special Environmental Sample Container (used by APOLLO 14 Astronauts)
SESCA South Eastern Society of Chartered Accountants
SESCO Secure Submarine Communications
Societe Europeene des Semiconducteurs (France)
SESER Source of Electrons in a Selected Energy Range
SESM prefix to dated/numbered series of reports issued by Structural Engineering Laboratory, California University (USA)
SESO Ship Environmental Support Office (of NEPSS (USN))
SESOC Surface Effect Ship for Ocean Commerce
SESP Space Experiments Support Program (USAF)
SESPA Scientists and Engineers for Social and Political Action (USA)
SESSIA Societe d'Etudes, de constructions de Souffleries, Simuilateurs et Instrumentation Aerodynamique (France)
SEST Short Effective Service Time
SET Science, Engineering and Technology
Selective Employment Tax (abolished 1973)
Self-Extending Translator
Single Escape Tower
Solar Energy Thermionic conversion system
Stored-Energy Transmission
SETA Search for Extra-Terrestial Artifacts
Societa Esercizi Telefonici Ausiliari (Italy)
SETAC Sector TACAN
Sector-TACAN-Azimuth
SETE Secretariat for Electronic Test Equipment (of USDOD and NASA)
Supersonic Expendable Turbine Engine
System Exercising for Training and Evaluation
SETEL Societe Europeene de Teleguidage (France)
SETEP Science and Engineering Technician Education Program (of NSF (usa))
SETI Search for Extra Terrestrial Intelligence
Societe Europeene pour le Traitment de l'Information (France)
SETIS Societe Europeenne pour l'Etude et l'Integration des Systemes Spatiaux (eleven European aerospace companies)
SETOLS Surface Effect Take-Off and Landing System
SETP Society of Experimental Test Pilots (USA)
SETRA Service d'Etudes Techniques des Routes et Autoroutes (France) (Department of Technical Studies on Roads and Motorways)
SETRAN Selectable Element Translator
SETRLIS South East Thames Regional Library and Information Service
SETS Set Equation Transformation System
System, Environment and Threat Simulation
SETU Societe d'Etudes et de Travaux pour l'Uranium (France)
SETURBA Societe d'Etudes de l'URBA (France)
SEU Subjective Expected Utility
SEUSS South-East United States Survey
SEV prefix to Standards issued by SNV
Sample Error Variance
Schweizerischer Elektrotechnischer Verein (Switzerland) (Swiss Electrotechnical Institution)
Soviet Ekonomickeskoi Vzaimopomoschchi (Council for Mutual Economic Assistance)
Surface Effect Vehicle
SEVALDS Strategy for Evaluating Design Strategies
SEW Shipboard Electronics Warfare
Surface Electromagnetic Wave
SEWACO Sensor, Weapon and Command system (64)
SEWID Surface Electromagnetic Wave Integrated Optics
SEWMA Simple Exponentially Weighted Moving-Average
SEWT Simulator for Electronic War-fare Training
SEXAFS Surface Extended X-ray Absorption Fine Structure
SE^2 Scientists and Engineers for Secure Energy
SF Spent Fuel
SFA Scientific Film Association (now part of BISFA)
Serum Folate
Silica-Free Ash
Societe Francaise d'Astronautique (France) (now part of AAAF)
SFA/CT Service de la Formation Aeronautique et du Controle Technique (France) (Department in charge of general aviation)
SFAC Societe des Forges et Ateliers du Creusot (France)
SFAI Steel Furnace Association of India (India)
SFAR numbered series of Special Federal Air Regulations issued by FAA (USA)
System Failure Analysis Report
SFAS Solid Fuel Advisory Service (of National Coal Board together with other organisations)
Statements of Financial Accounting Standards (numbered series issued by FASB (USA))
SfB Samarbetskommitten for Byggnadsfragor (Sweden) (Cooperative Committee for the Building Industry)
SFB Semiconductor Functional Block
SFC Scottish Film Council (now the Scottish Council for Educational Technology)
Side Force Control
Sideway-Force Coefficient
Societe Francaise de Ceramique (France) (French Ceramic Society)
Solar Forecast Center (of USAF)
Specific Fuel Consumption
State Financial Corporations (India)
SFCD Stopped-Flow Circular Dichroism
SFCES Survivable Flight Control Electronic Set
SFCI State Farms Corporation of India (India)
SFCN Societe Francaise de Construction Navales (France)
SFCS Submarine Fire-Control System

	Survivable Flight Control System
SFCSI	Special Foreign Currency Science Information Program (of National Science Foundation (USA))
SFCW	Sweep-Frequency, Continuous Wave
SFD	Spatial Frequency Diversity Structural Frame Design Sudden Frequency Deviation System Function Description
SFDA	Small Farmers Development Agency
SFE	Societe Francaise des Electriciens (France) (French Society of Electricians) Solar Flare Effects Stacking Fault Energy
SFEA	Space and Flight Equipment Association (USA)
SFEC	Societe de Fabrication d'Elements Catalytiques (France)
SFEN	Société Français d'Énergie Nucléaire (France) (French Nuclear Energy Society)
SFENA	Societe Francaise d'Equipements pour la Navigation Aerienne (France)
SFER	Societe Francaise des Electroniciens et Radioelectriciens (French Society of Electronic and Radio Technicians)
SFES	Small Firms Employment Subsidy
SFF	Science Fiction Foundation Self Forging Fragment Solar Forecast Facility (of USAF) Standard File Format
SFG	Signal Flow Graph
SFGA	Single Floating-Gate Amplifier
SFH	Slow Frequency Hopping Standard Fade Hour
SFI	Skipsteknisk Forsknings Institutt (Norway) (Ship Research Institute)
SFIB	Syndicat National des Fabricants d'Ensembles de Information et des Machines de Bureau (France) (National Federation of Data Handling Equipment and Office Machines Manufacturers)
SFIC	Small Firms Information Centre
SFID	Self-Floating Integrated Deck
SFIM	Societe de Fabrication d'Instruments de Mesure (France)
SFIS	Small Firms Information Service (of DOI) Statewide Federated Information System
SFIT	Swiss Federal Institute of Technology (Switzerland)
SFITV	Societe Francaise des Ingenieurs et Techniciens Vide (France) (French Society of Vacuum Engineers and Technicians)
SFL	Spin Flip Laser Symbolic Flowchart Language
SFM	Sensor Fuzed Munitions Societe Francaise de Metallurgie (France) (French Society of Metallurgy)
SFMI	Societe Francaise de Moteurs a Induction (France)
SFOF	Space Flight Operations Facility (of NASA)
SFOLDS	Ship Form On-Line Design System
SFOM	Societe Francaise d'Optique et de Mecanique (France)
SFOS	Societe Francaise d'Organo-Synthese (France)
SFP	Screen Filtration Pressure Société Française de Photogrammétrie (France) (French Society of Photogrammetry)
SFPA	Southern Forest Products Association (USA)
SFPE	Society of Fire Protection Engineers (USA)
SFPS	Single Failure Point Summary
SFR	Serial Flechette Rifle Sinking Fund Return Spin Flip Raman
SFRL	Spin-Flip Raman Laser
SFRP	Societe Francaise de Radioprotection (France) (French Radiological Protection Society)
SFRR	Solid Fuel Rocket/Ramjet
SFS	Society of Fleet Supervisors (USA) Suomen Standardisoimislitto (Finland) (Standards Institute)
SFSA	Steel Founders Society of America (USA)
SFTC	Sea Fisheries Training Council
SFTP	Science For The People (an association in USA)
SFTS	Standard Frequency and Time Signals Synthetic Flight Training System
SFU	Societe de Fluoration de l'Uranium (a joint company formed by governmental and industrial organisations in eight European countries)
SFV	Semliki Forest Virus
SFVEC	San Fernando Valley Engineers Council (USA)
SFVSC	San Fernando Valley State College (USA)
SFW	Swept Forward Wing
SG	Sea Grant program (USA) Spheroidal Graphite Steam Generator
SGAC	Secretariat General a l'Aviation Civile (France) (Civil Aviation Administration)
SGAE	Studiengesellschaft fur Atomenergie (Austria)
SGD	prefix to numbered series of reports on Solar-Geophysical Data issued by the National Geophysical and Solar-Terrestrial Data Center (USA) Society of Glass Decorators (USA)
SGDN	Secretariat General de la Defence Nationale (France)
SGEMP	System-Generated Electromagnetic Pulse
SGF	Sveriges Gummitekniska Forening (Sweden) (Swedish Rubber Industry Association)
SGHWR	Steam Generating Heavy Water Reactor
SGL	Slightly Grounded Lightplane
SGLS	Space-Ground Link Sub-system
SGM	Societe Generale des Minerais (Belgium) Society for General Microbiology
SGML	Standard Generalised Markup Language
SGMM	Secretariat General de la Marine Marchande (France)
SGN	Saint Gobain Techniques Nouvelles (France)
SGO	Societe Generale d'Optique (France)
SGOT	Serum Glutamic Oxaloacetic Transaminase
SGP	Society of General Physiologists (USA)
SGPA	Scottish General Publishers Association
SGPO	Speed-Gate-Pull-Off
SGPT	Serum Glutamic Pyruvic Transaminase
SGRCA	Sodium Graphite Reactor Critical Assembly
SGS	Simultaneous Graphics System Societa Generale Semiconduttori (Italy) Societe Generale de Surveillance (Switzerland)
SGSR	Society for General System Research Society for General Systems Research (USA)
SGT	Societe des Garde-Temps (Switzerland) Society of Glass Technology
SGTE	Societe Generale de Techniques et Etudes (France)
SGU	Sveriges Geologiska Undersokning (Sweden) (Geological Survey of Sweden)
SGZ	Surface Ground Zero
SGZP	Schweizerische Gelleschaft fur Zerstorungsfreii Prufung (Switzerland) (Swiss Association for Non-destructive Testing)
sh	prefix to numbered series issued by the Ship Division of the National Physical Laboratory
SH	Second Harmonic
SHA	Sidereal Hour Angle

Slowly-sedimenting Haemagglutinin
Software Houses Association (merged into Computer Services Association, 1975)
Solid Homogeneous Assembly

SHAB Soft and Hard Acids and Bases

SHACOB Solar Heating and Cooling of Buildings

SHAG Simplified High-Accuracy Guidance

SHAL Subject Heading Authority List

SHALE Stand-off, High Altitude, Long Endurance

SHAM Salicyl Hydroxamic acid

SHAPE STEVENS and HARRISON Adaptive Parameter Estimation
Supersonic High Altitude Parachute Experiment
Supreme Headquarters, Allied Powers Europe

SHAR Sriharikota Rocket Range (of ISRO (India))

SHARE Society to Help Avoid Repetitive Effort (USA)

SHARES Shared Airline Reservation

SHARP SHIPS Analysis and Retrieval Project

SHARPS Ship Helicopter Acoustic Range Prediction System

SHAS Shared Hospital Accounting System

SHAWL Special Hard-target Assault Weapon, Lightweight

SHC Sensitized Human Cell
Synthesised Hydrocarbons

SHE Standard Hydrogen Electrode

SHED Sealed Housing for Evaporative Determination

SHEDA Storage and Handling Equipment Distributors Association

SHEDS Ship/Helicopter Extended Delivery System

SHEED Scanning High Energy Electron Diffraction

SHEG Scottish Health Education Group

SHELF Super-Hardened Extremely Low Frequency

SHELL Shell Expansion and Logical Layout system

SHEU Scottish Health Education Unit

SHF Societe Hydrotechnique de France (Hydraulic Engineering Society)
Super High Frequency
Synthesized Hydrocarbon Fluid

SHG Second Harmonic Generation

SHHD Scottish Home and Health Department

SHIE Surface Helmholtz Integral Equation

SHIEF Shared Information Elicitation Facility

SHIELD SYLVANIA High Intelligence Electronic Defence

SHIMMS Shipboard Integrated Man-Machine System

SHIP prefix to numbered series issued by the Ship Division of the National Physical Laboratory
Simplified-Helmholtz-Integral Programme

SHIPS Bureau of Ships (USN)
Sheffield Industrial Project Scheme

SHIRTDIF Storage, Handling and Retrieval of Technical Data in Image Formation

SHLMA Southern Hardwood Lumber Manufacturers Association (USA)

SHMM Shop Maintenance Model

SHN Servicio de Hidrografia Naval (Argentina) (Naval Hydrographic Service)

SHOC Submerged Hydrodynamic Oil Concentrator

SHOM Service Hydrographique et Oceanographique de la Marine (France) (Naval Hydrographic and Oceanographic Service)

SHOP SHELL Higher Olefins Process

SHORAD Short-Range Air Defense (a study group of the US Army)

SHORADS Short-Range, All-weather Air-Defense System

SHORAN Short Range Navigation

SHORSTAS Short-Range Surveillance and Target Acquisition System

SHORT Shared Hospital On-line Real-time Time-sharing

SHORTIE Short Range Thermal Imaging Equipment

SHOT Small Hopping Transporter
Society for the History Of Technology (USA)

SHOW Scripps Institution—University of Hawaii—Oregon State University—University of Wisconsin (USA)

SHREAD Share Registration and Dividend Warrants

SHRI Scottish Horticultural Research Institute

SHRIMP SAVAGE (R.J.) and HEIERLI (P.C.) Resonant Investigation Method-Patented

SHS Structural Hollow Sections

SHSS Short-Haul System Simulation

SHTR Societe pour les reacteurs nucleaires HTR (France)

SHW prefix to numbered series of publications on Safety, Health and Welfare (issued by Ministry of Labour, later Department of Employment and Productivity, and then Department of Employment) (series now entitled Health and Safety at Work')
prefix to numbered series on Safety, Health and Welfare (now issued by HSE and published by HMSO)

SHWRL Solid and Hazardous Waste Research Laboratory (of EPA (USA))

SI prefix to Standards issued by SII
Smithsonian Institute (USA)
Society of Illustrators (USA)
Static Induction
Statutory Instrument (issued by Parliament and published by HMSO)
Surface Ionization
Systeme International d'unites (International System of Units)

SIA Secretariat of Industrial Approvals (India)
Self-Interstitial Atom
Semiconductor Industry Association (USA)
Singapore Institute of Architects (Singapore)
Singapore International Airlines (Singapore) (National Airline)
Societe des Ingenieurs de l'Automobile (France) (Society of Automobile Engineers)
Societe International d'Acupuncture (International Society of Acupuncture)
Societe Suisse des Ingenieurs et des Architectes (Switzerland) (Swiss Society of Engineers and Architects)
Society for Industrial Archeology (USA)
Society of Industrial Accountants (Canada)
Stereo-Image Alternator
Strategic Influence Area
Structural Insulation Association
Subminiature Integrated Antennae

SIAC Shipbuilding Industry Advisory Committee (USA)
Societa Italiana Additivi per Carburanti (Italy)

SIAD Society of Industrial Artists and Designers

SIAE Scottish Institute of Agricultural Engineering

SIAG Survey Instrument, Azimuth, Gyro

SIAGL Surveying Instrument, Azimuth Gyro, Lightweight

SIALONS an acronym for a group of materials formed by their chemical symbols–Silicon, Aluminium, Oxygen and Nitrogen

SIAM Self-Initiated Anti-aircraft Missile
Self-Initiated Anti-aircraft Munition
Society for Industrial and Applied Mathematics (USA)

SIAMS Study for Improved Ammunition Maintenance Support (US Army)

SIAO Smithsonian Institute Astrophysical Observatory (USA)

SIAR Societe de la Surveillance Industrielle (France)

SIB Securities and Investments Board
Shipbuilding Industry Board (disbanded 1971)
Snake In the Box
Stress Induced Birefringence

SIBEX	Submillimetre-Infrared Balloon Experiment (joint enterprise between NPL (DOI) and University of Florence (Italy)
SIBMAC	Second International Brick Masonry Conference
SIBMAS	Societe Internationale des Bibliotheques et Musees des Arts du Spectacle (International Society for Libraries and Museums of the Performing Arts)
SIC	Semiconductor Integrated Circuit
	Silicon Integrated Circuit
	Societe Intercontinentale des Containers (France)
	Standard Industrial Classification
	Standards Information Center (of NBS (USA))
SICA	Schizont-Infected Cell Agglutinin
SICAV	Société d'Investissement à Capital Variable (France)
SICBM	Small Inter-Continental Ballistic Missile
SICDOC	Special Interest Committee on Systems Documentation (of ACM (usa)) (became SIGDOC in 1976)
SICIS	Strategic Issue Competive Information System
SICLOPS	Simplified Interpretive COBOL Operating System
SICM	Single Ion Current Monitoring
SICN	Societe Industrielle de Combustible Nucleaire (France)
SICO	Side Inlet/Centre Outlet
SICOFAA	System of Cooperation Among the American Air Forces
SICOM	Securities Industry Communications
	State Industrial and Investment Corporation of Maharashtra (India)
SICOMI	Société Immobilières pour le Commerce et l'Industrie (France)
SICS	Semiconductor Integrated Circuits
SICSOFT	Special Interest Committee on Software Engineering (of ACM (USA)) (now SIGSOFT)
SID	Society for Information Displays (USA)
	Society for International Development
	Society of Investigative Dermatology (USA)
	Standard Instrument Departure
	Sudden Ionosphere Disturbance
	Suprathermal Ion Detector
	SWIFT (Society for Worldwide Interbank Financial Telecommunications) Interface Devices
	Syntax Improving Device
SIDA	Swedish International Development Agency
SIDAP-NZ	Committee for Simplication of International Documentation and Procedures (New Zealand)
SIDASE	Significant Data Selection
SIDC	Sunspot Index Data Centre (Belgium)
SIDE	Suprathermal Ion Detector Experiment
SIDINSA	Siderurgia Integrada SA (Argentina)
SIDOR	Siderurgica del Orinoco (Guayana)
SIDPERS	Standard Installation-Division Personnel System (US Army)
SIDS	Satellite Imagery Dissemination System
	Speech Identification System
	Stellar Inertial Doppler System
	Sudden Infant Death Syndrome
SIE	Science Information Exchange (of Smithsonian Institution, USA)
	Societa Italiana di Ergonomia (Italy) (Italian Ergonomics Society)
SIEC	Scottish Industrial Estates Corporation (of the Dept of Industry)
SIECUS	Sex Information and Education Council of the United States (USA)
SIEGE	Simulated Electromagnetic pulse Ground Environment
SIERS	Societe Industrielle d'Etudes et Realisations Scientifiques (France)
SIF	Selective Identification Feature
	Small Intensely Fluorescent
	Societa Italiana di Fisica (Italy) (Italian Physical Society)
SIFE	Society of Industrial Furnace Engineers
SIFET	Società Italiana di Fotogrammetria e Topografia (Italy) (Italian Society of Photogrammetry and Topography)
SIFT	Software Implemented Fault Tolerance
SIFTA	Sistema Interamericano de Telecommunicaciones para las Fuerzas Aereas (telecommunications link between the Air Force Commanders of the USA and those of Central and South America)
SIG	Schweizerische Industrie Gesellschaft (Switzerland)
	Stellar Inertial Guidance
	Strategic Influence Group
SIG-D	Strapdown Inertial Guidance Demonstration
SIG/CON	Special Interest Group on Confidence of Overload Norms (of ASIS (USA))
SIG/IP	Special Interest Group on Information (of ASIS (USA))
SIGACT	Special Interest Group on Automata and Computability Theory (of ACM (USA))
SIGAPL	Special Interest Group on APL (of ACM (USA))
SIGARCH	Special Interest Group on Architecture of Computer Systems (of ACM (USA))
SIGART	Special Interest Group on Artifical Intelligence (of ACM (USA))
SIGBDP	Special Interest Group on Business Data Processing (of ACM (USA))
SIGBIO	Special Interest Group on Biomedical Computing (of ACM (USA))
SIGCAPH	Special Interest Group on Computers and the Physically Handicapped (of ACM (USA))
SIGCAS	Special Interest Group on Computers and Society (of ACM (USA))
SIGCHI	Special Interest Group on Computers and Human Interaction (of ACM (USA)) (formerly SIGSOC)
SIGCOMM	Special Interest Group on Data Communication (of ACM (USA))
SIGCOSIM	Special Interest Group on Computer Systems Installation Management (of ACM (USA))
SIGCPR	Special Interest Group on Computer Personnel Research (of ACM (USA))
SIGCSE	Special Interest Group on Computer Science Education (of ACM (USA))
SIGCUE	Special Interest Group on Computer Uses in Education (of ACM (USA))
SIGDA	Special Interest Group on Design Automation (of ACM (USA))
SIGDOC	Special Interest Group on Systems Documentation (of ACM (USA))
SIGGRAPH	Special Interest Group on Computer Graphics (of ACM (USA))
SIGINT	Signal Intelligence
SIGIR	Special Interest Group on Information Retrieval (of ACM (USA))
SIGLASH	Special Interest Group on Language Analysis and Studies in the Humanities (of ACM (USA))
SIGLIGUN	Signal Light Gun
SIGMA	Sealed Insulating Glass Manufacturers Association (USA)
	Societe Industriale Generale de Mecanique Appliquee (France)
	System for Interactive Graphical Mathematical Applications
SIGMALOG	Simulation and Gaming Methods for the Analysis of Logistics
SIGMAP	Special Interest Group on Mathematical Programming (of ACM (USA))
SIGMETRICS	Special Interest Group on Measurement Evaluation (of ACM (USA))

SIGMICRO Special Interest Group on Microprogramming (of ACM (USA))
SIGMINI Special Interest Group on Minicomputers (of ACM (USA)) (became SIGSMALL in 1978)
SIGMOD Special Interest Group on Management of Data (of ACM (USA))
SIGNET Supplies Invoice Generation Network
SIGNUM Special Interest Group on Numerical Mathematics (of ACM (USA))
SIGOA Special Interest Group on Office Automation (of ACM (USA))
SIGOP Signal Optimization
SIGOPS Special Interest Group on Operating Systems (of ACM (USA))
SIGPC Special Interest Group on Personal Computing (of ACM (USA))
SIGPLAN Special Interest Group on Programming Languages of ACM (USA))
SIGS Special Interest Groups
SIGSAC Special Interest Group on Security Audit and Control (of ACM (USA))
SIGSAM Special Interest Group on Symbolic and Algebraic Manipulation (of ACM (USA)
SIGSIM Special Interest Group on Simulation (of ACM (USA))
SIGSMALL Special Interest Group on Small Computing Systems and Applications (of ACM (USA))
SIGSOC Special Interest Group on Social and Behavioral Science Computing (of ACM (USA))
SIGSofASIS (USA) AH Arts and Humanities
ALP Automated Language Processing
BC Biological and Chemical Information Systems
BSS Behavioral and Social Sciences
CB Costs, Budgeting and Economics
CR Classification Research
ED Education for INformation Science
FS Foundations of Information Science
IAC Information Analysis Centers
IP Information Publishing
ISE Information Services to Education
LAN Library Automation and Networks
LAW Law and Information technology
MGT Management Information Activities
MR Medical Records
NDB Numerical Data Bases
NPM Non-Print Media
PPI Public-Private Interface
RT Reprographic Technology
SDI Selective Dissemination of Information
TIS Technology, Information and Society
UOI User On-line Interaction
SIGSOFT Special Interest Group on Software Engineering (of ACM (USA))
SIGUCCS Special Interest Group on University and College Computing Services (of ACM (USA))
SII Standards Institution of Israel
Synthetic Interferometric Imaging
SIIA Sudden Increase in Ionospheric Activity
SIIRS SMITHSONIAN INSTITUTION (USA) Information Retrieval System
SIK Svenska Institutet for Konserveringsforskning (Sweden) (Swedish Institute for Food Preservation Research)
SIL Speech Interference Level
System Implementation Language
SILAS Singapore-based Integrated Library Automation System (Singapore)
SILOS Ship Identification and Locating System
Side Looking Sonar
SILS School of Information and Library Studies (State University of New York (USA))
SIM School of Industrial Management (Worcester Polytechnic Institute (USA))
Scientific Instrument Module
Servicio Industrial de la Marina (Peru)
Simulated Machine Indexing
Society for Industrial Microbiology (USA)
Standards Institute of Malaysia
Surface-to-air-missile Intercept Missile
System Information Management
SIMA Scientific Instrument Manufacturers Association of Great Britain (federated into BEAMA in 1975)
Secondary Ion Mass Analyser
Secondary Ion Mass Analysis
Southern India Millowners Association (India)
Strathclyde (Scotland) Industries Marketing Association
SIMAL Simplified Accountancy Language
Simulated All-purpose Language
SIMALE Super Integral Microprogrammed Arithmetic Logic Expediter
SIMANNE Simulation of Analogue Networks
SIMBA System of Integrated Modular Breathing Apparatus
SIMBAT Sequential Independent Model Block Analytical Triangulation
SIMC Societe Internationale de Medicine Cybernetique (Italy) (International Society of Cybernetic Medicine)
SIMCON Simulation Control
SIMD Single-Instruction, Multiple-Data stream
SIMFE Surface Impoundment Model in Finite Element
SIMG Societas Internationalis Medicinae Generalis
SIMGF Semi-Invariant Moment Generating Function
SIMI Societa Italiana Macchine Idrauliche (Italy)
Societa Italo-Svizzeva Metalli Iniettati (Italy)
Societe Internationale de Materials Industriels (France)
SIMIANS Simulation Model for Interference Analysis of Nodal Systems
SIMILE Simulator of Immediate Memory In Learning Experiments
SIMM Symbolic Integrated Maintenance Manual
SIMMS Symbolic Integrated Maintenance Management System
SIMO Societe Industrielle des Minerais de l'Ouest (France)
SIMON Simple Instructional Monitor
STRATHCLYDE (UNIVERSITY) Inspection, Maintenance Or Navigation
SIMP Satellite Interface Message Processor
Stowarzyszenie Inznierow i Technikow Mechanikow Polskich (Poland) (Polish Society of Mechanical Engineers and Technicians)
SIMPAC Simulation Package
SIMPEDS Safety in Mines Personal Dust Sampler
SIMPLE Simulation Programming Language
SIMPO Simulation Model of Personnel Operations
SIMPROFRANCE Comite Française pour la Simplification de Procedures du Commerce Internationale (France) (French Committee for the Simplification of International Commerce Procedures)
SIMS Scientific Inventory Management System
Secondary-Ion Mass Spectrometry
Selected Item Management System (US Army)
SIAM (USA) Institute for Mathematics and Society
Single-Item, Multi-Source
Social Science Information Management System
Subscribers Installation Management Information and Control System (of the Australian Post Office)
Surface-to-Air Missile Intercept Missile System
Symbolic Integrated Maintenance System

SIMS/IMMA Secondary Ion Mass Spectrometry/Ion Microprobe Mass Analysis
SIMSEP Simulation of Solar Electric Propulsion
SIMSLIN Safety In Mines Scattered Light Instrument
SIMSTRAT Simulation/Strategy
SIMTASS Simulation of the Theater Army Supply System (US Army)
SIMTOP Silicon Nitride-Masked Thermally Oxidized Post-Diffused Mesa Process
SIMTOS Simulated Tactical Operations Systems
SIMTRACC Simulation, Monitoring, Training, and Command and Control
SIMULA Simulation Language
SIMULE Self-Instructional Modules Using Laboratory Experience
SIN Schweizerisches Institut fur Nuclearforschung (Switzerland) (Swiss Institute for Nuclear Research)
Symbolic Integration
SINAD Ratio of Signal plus Noise and Distortion to Distortion and Noise
SINAP Satellite Input to Numerical Analysis and Procedure
SINASBI Sistema Nacional de Servicios de Bibliotecas e Informacion (Venezuela)
SINB Southern Interstate Nuclear Board (USA)
SINCGARS Single Channel Ground and Airborne Radio System
Single-Channel Ground and Airborne Radio Subsystem
SINCGARS-V Single-Channel Ground and Airborne Radio Subsystem-VHF
SINDBAD Systematic Investigation of Diver Behaviour At Depth
SINFDOK Statens Rad for Vetenskaplig Information och Dokumentation (Sweden) (National Committee for Scientific Information and Documentation)
SINP Saha Institute of Nuclear Physics (India)
SINS Ships Inertial Navigation System
SINTEF Selskapet for Industriell og Teknisk Forskning (Norway) (Engineering Research Institute)
SINTO Sheffield Interchange Organization
System Informaccji Naukowej Technicznej i Organizacyjnej (Poland)
SINTRA Societe Industrielle des Nouvelles Techniques Radioelectriques et de l'Electronique Francaise (France)
SIO Scripps Institution of Oceanography (USA)
Serial Input/Output
SIOP Single Integrated Operational Plan
SIOUX Sequential Iterative Operation Unit X
SIP Sea Ice Penetrometer
Silicon-on-Insulator and Polysilicon
Submerged Injection Process
Surface Impulsion Propulsion
SIPARE Syndicat des Industries de Pieces detachees et Accessoires Radioelectriques et Electroniques (France)
SIPI Scientists Institute for Public Information (USA)
SIPO Serial In, Parallel Out
SIPOS Semi-Insulating Polycrystalline Silicon
SIPPS System of Information Processing for Professional Societies
SIPRE Snow Ice and Permafrost Research Establishment (US Army) (merged into CRREL in 1961)
SIPRI Stockholm International Peace Research Institute (Sweden)
SIPROCOM Committee for the Simplification of International Trade (Belgium)
SIPROS Simultaneous Processing Operating System
SIPS Satellite Instrumentation Processor System
Selected Information Profiles Service (of BHRA)
SIPSF Space Invariant Point Spread Function
SIQR Semi-Inter-Quartile Range
SIR Semantic Information Retrieval
Shipboard Intercept Receiver
Shuttle Imaging Radar
Signal-to-Interference Ratio
Societa Italiana Resine (Italy)
Sports Institute for Research (University of Windsor (Canada))
Symbolic Input Routine
System Integration Receiver
SIRA British Scientific Instrument Research Association (now known as The SIRA Institute)
Safety Investigation Regulations (of Civil Aeronautics Board, USA)
SIRCE Societa per l'Incremento Rapporti Commerciali con l'Estero (Italy)
SIRCH Semi-Intelligent Robot for Component Handling
SIRCS Ship-board Intermediate Range Combat System
SIRE Satellite Infra-Red Experiment (of USAF)
Silicon Repeater
Symbolic Information Retrieval
SIREAL Simulation with Resource Allocation
SIREF Specific Immune Response Enhancing Factor
SIREP SIRA (INSTITUTE) Evaluation Panel
SIRIP Société Irano-Italienne des Pétroles (Iran)
SIRIS Scanning Infra-Red Inspection System
SIRNEM Strategic International Relations Nuclear Exchange Model
SIROF Sputtered Iridium Oxide Film
SIRS Satellite Infrared Radiation Spectrometer
Satellite Infrared Spectrometer
Ship Installed RADIAC System
SIRT Simultaneous Iterative Reconstruction Technique
Staten Island Rapid Transit system (USA)
SIRTDO Small Industries Research Training and Development Organisation (India)
SIRTF Shuttle Infra-Red Telescope Facility
SIRTI Societa Italiana Reti Telefoniche Interurbane (Italy)
SIRU Singapore Industrial Research Unit (Singapore)
SIS prefix to numbered series of Standards Information Sheets issued by the Machine Tool Trades Association
prefix to Standards issued by SVS
Satellite Interceptor System
Scanning Imaging Spectrophotometer
School of Information Studies (Syracuse University (USA))
Scientific Information System
Seaborne Instrumentation System
SEAL (SUBSEA EQUIPMENT ASSOCIATES LIMITED) Intermediate System
Semiconductor-Insulator-Semiconductor
Shipbuilding Industry Standards (issued by BSRA)
Short-Interval Scheduling
Shorter-Interval Scheduling
Societe d'Informatique et de Systemes Compagnie Bancaire (France)
Software Information Service (of CCTA)
Special Industrial Services (of UNIDO)
Special Isotope Separation
Specification Information System
Stall Inhibitor System
Surface Indicator Scale (of ACI (USA))
Surveillance and In-Service Inspection
Svenska Interplanetariska Sallskapet (Sweden) (Swedish Interplanetary Society)
System Interrupt Supervisor
SISAC Serials Industry Systems Advisory Committee (USA)

SISAM Selective Interferential Spectrometry through Amplitude Modulation
SISDG Shipboard Information System Development Group (of NRC Maritime Transportation Research Board (USA))
SISGAC Scottish Industrial Safety Group Advisory Council
SISI Short Increment Sensitivity Index
Small Industries Service Institute (India)
SISIR Singapore Institute for Standards and Industrial Research (Singapore)
SISMS Standard Integrated Support Management System (USDOD)
SISO Serial In, Serial Out
Side Inlet/Side Outlet
Single-Input/Single-Output
SISS Single-Item, Single-Source
SISTAC Scottish Industrial Safety Training Advisory Council
SISTEL Sistemi Elettronica (Italy)
SISTM Simulation by Incremental Stochastic Transition Matrices
Society for the Interdisciplinary Study of the Mind (USA)
SIT Silicon Intensifier Target
Silicon Intensifier Tube
Society of Instrument Technology (now Institute of Measurement and Control)
Spontaneous Ignition Temperature
Static Induction Transistor
Stepped-Impedance Transformer
Stevens Institute of Technology (USA)
SIT-DL Stevens Institute of Technology–Davidson Laboratory (USA)
SIT-ME Stevens Institute of Technology, Department of Mechanical Engineering (USA)
SITA Societe Internationale de Telecommunications Aeronautiques (International Society of Aeronautical Telecommunications)
System International Tinplate Area (= 100 square metres)
SITAP Simulator for Transportation and Analysis
SITAR System for Inter-active Text-editing Analysis and Retrieval
SITB Societe Industrielle de Travaux de Bureaux (France)
SITC Standard International Trades Classification (of UN)
SITC(R) Standards International Trades Classification (Revised) (of UN)
SITE Satellite Instructional Television Experiment
Shipboard Information, Training and Entertainment
Societe Industrielle pour le Traitment des Eaux (France)
Spacecraft Instrumentation Test Equipment
SITEC Sudden Increase of Total Electron Content
SITEL Societe Belge des Ingenieurs de Telecommunication et d'Electronique (Belgium) (Belgian Society of Telecommunication and Electronic Engineers)
SITELESC Syndicat des Industries de Tubes Electroniques et Semiconducteurs (France)
SITEP Societe Italo-Tunisienne d'Exploration Petroliere (Tunisia)
SITPH Stowarzysznenie Inzynierow i Technikow Przemyslu Hutniczego (Poland) (Association of Engineers and Technicians of the Metallurgical Industry)
SITPRO United Kingdom Committee for the Simplification of International Trade Procedures
SITPRONETH Netherlands Committee for the Simplification of International Trade Procedures
SITPW Stowarzyszenie Inzynierow i Technikow Przemyslu Wlokienniczego (Poland) (Asssociation of Engineers and Technicians of the Textile Industry)
SITRA South Indian Textile Research Association (India)
Suomen Itsenaisyyden Juhlavouden Rahasto (Finland) (Finnish Independence Jubilee Fund) (now known as the Finnish National Fund for Research and Development)
SITS Societa Italiana Telecommunicazione Siemens (Italy)
Systems Integration Test Stand
SITUMER Societe d'Ingeneirie du Tunnel sous la Mer (France)
SITVC Secondary Injection Thrust Vector Control
SIU Southern Illinois University (USA)
SIXPAC System for Inertial Experiment Priority and Attitude Control
SJ Statens Jarnvagar (Sweden) (Swedish State Railways)
SJAC Society of Japanese Aerospace Companies (Japan)
Society of Japanese Aircraft Constructors (Japan)
SJCC Spring Joint Computer Conference (USA)
SJCL Standardized Job Control Language
SJCM Standing Joint Committee on Metrication
SJP Self-Judgment Principle
SJPE Symposium on Jet Pumps and Ejectors
SK-EOQC Svenska Kommittee for EOQC (Sweden) (Swedish Committee for participation in EOQC)
SKA Studienkommission for Atomenergie (Switzerland) (National Advisory Committee on Nuclear Energy)
SKAMP Station Keeping And Mobile Platform
SKCSR Statni Knihovna Ceskoslovenske Socialisticke Republiky (Czechoslovakia) (State Library of the Czechoslovak Socialist Republic)
SKE Signals Known Exactly
SKEA Signal Known Except Amplitude
SKEM Spares Kit Evaluator Model
SKF Svenska Kullargerfabriken (Sweden)
SKI Station Keeping Indicator
SKIP Skimmer Investigation Platform
SKK Stichting Kernvoortstuwing Koopvaardijschepen (Netherlands) (Foundation for Nuclear Propulsion of Merchant Ships)
SKNDO Stichting Kwalificatie van Niet-Destructief Onderzoekers (Netherlands) (Foundation for Qualification of Non-destructive Testing Personnel)
SKOR SPERRY KALMAN Optimum Reset
SKTF Sveriges Kvalitetstekniska Forening (Sweden) (Swedish Organisation for Quality Control)
SL Semiconductor Laser
Stor-Stockholms Lokalttrafiken (Sweden)
SLA Saturn Lunar-module Adapter
Scottish Library Association
Sealed Lead-Acid cell
Spacecraft LM Adapter
Special Libraries Association (USA)
Sun-Line Algorithm
SLAB Static Lifting Aerodynamic Body
Subsonic, Low-Altitude Bomber
SLAC Significance and Location Analysis Computer
Stanford Linear Accelerator Center (Stanford University, USA)
Subscriber Line Auto-processing Circuit
SLADO System Library Activity Dynamic Optimiser
SLAE Standard Lightweight Avionics Equipment
Systems of Linear Algebraic Equations
SLAET Society of Licensed Aircraft Engineers and Technicians
SLAM Scanning Laser Acoustic Microscope

Ship-Launched Anti-aircraft Missile
Simulation Language for Analogue Modelling
Small Low Angular Momentum
Stored-Logic Adaptable OR Adaptive Microcircuit
Stress waves in Layered Arbitrary Media
Submarine-Launched Airflight Missile
Supersonic Low-Altitude Missile
Surface-Launched Air Missile

SLAMMR Side Looking Modular Multi-mission Radar

SLAMS Syndicat des Constructeurs d'Appareils de Levage, de Manutention et de Materials de Stockage (France)

SLAP Small-signal Linear Analysis Programme
Symbolic Language Assembler Programme

SLAR Side-Looking Airborne Radar

SLARS Sierra Leone Amateur Radio Society

SLASH Scottish Local Authorities Special Housing Group
SEILER Laboratory ALGOL Simulated Hybrid

SLAT Study of Land/Air Trade-offs
Supersonic Low Altitude Target

SLATE Small Lightweight Altitude Transmission Equipment

SLB Side-lobe Blanker

SLBM Sea OR Ship OR Submarine Launched Ballistic Missile

SLC Sidelobe Cancellation
Sidelobe Clutter
Simulated Liquistic Computer
Sound Level Conversion
Streamline Curvature
Sustained-Load Cracking

SLCB Single-Line Colour-Bar

SLCC SATURN Launcher Computer Complex

SLCF Société Le Chauffrage Français (France)

SLCM Sea-Launched Cruise Missile
Submarine-Launched Cruise Missile

SLD Solid Logic Dense
Superluminescent Diode

SLDH Serum Lactic Acid Dehydrogenase

SLDTSS Single Language Dedicated Time Sharing System

SLE Society of Logistics Engineers (USA)
St. Louis Encephalitis
Superheat-Limit Explosion
Systemic Lupus Erythematosus

SLEAT Society of Laundry Engineers and Allied Trades

SLED Space Laser Experiment Definition (sponsored by DARPA (USA))

SLEDGE Simulating Large Explosive Detonable Gas Experiment

SLEEP Scanning Low Energy Electron Probe
Silent, Light-weight, Electric Energy Plant (a project of MERADACOM (US Army))

SLEN Short Line Extractor Neuron

SLEP Second Large ESRO Project

SLEW Standby Local Early Warning and Control centre

SLFCS Survivable Low Frequency Communications System

SLG Synchronous Longitudinal Guidance

SLGR Sri Lanka Government Railway (Sri Lanka)

SLIC Selective Listing In Combination
Simulator for Linear Integrated Circuits
Subscriber-Line Interface Circuit

SLICE Southwestern Library Interstate Cooperative Endeavour (Southwestern Library Association (USA))
Studies Leading to the Industrial Conservation of Energy (a joint government/industry steering group)
SURREY (UNIVERSITY) Library Interactive Circulation Experiment

SLID Standard Library of Item Descriptions

SLIM Single-sided Linear Induction Motor
Stock Line Inventory Management
Store Labour and Inventory Management
Surface-Launched Interceptor Missile
System Library Maintenance

SLIP Symmetric List Processor

SLLA Sri Lanka Library Association (Sri Lanka)

SLM Scanning Light Microscopy
Single Longitudinal Mode
Single-Level Masking
Spatial Light Modulator
Statistical Learning Model
Subscriber Loop Multiplex

SLMA Steel Lintel Manufacturers Association

SLMM Submarine-Launched Mobile Mine

SLMS Selective Level Measuring Set
Ship-based Long-range Missile System

SLO Streptolysin O
Swept Local Oscillator

SLOA Steam Locomotive Operators Association

SLOB Satellite Low Orbit Bombardment

SLOC Sea Lines of Communication

SLOMAR Space Logistics, Maintenance And Rescue

SLOP Small Lot Optimum Procurement

SLOR Successive Line Over-Relaxation

SLOT Sequential Logic Tester

SLP Segmented Level Programming
Skip-Lot Plan

SLPM Scanned-Laser Photoluminescence Microscope

SLR Satellite Laser Ranging
Self-Loading Rifle
Side-Looking Radar
Single-Lens-Reflex camera
Stepped-Load-Resistor

SLRP Society for Long Range Planning

SLRV Surveyor Lunar Roving Vehicle

SLS School of Library Science (Case Western Reserve University (USA))
School of Library Science (Kent State University (USA))
School of Library Science (Syracuse University (USA)) (became School of Information Studies in 1974)
School of Library Science (University of Kentucky (USA))
Segment Long Spacing
Side Looking Sonar
Sidelobe Suppression

SLSENY School Librarians of Southeastern New York (USA)

SLSI Super-Large Scale Integration

SLSTIC Sri Lanka Scientific and Technological Information Centre (Sri Lanka)

SLT Solid Logic Technology
Solid Logic Transistor
Spontaneous Lymphocyte Transportation
Standing group on Long Term Cooperation (of IEA (OECD))

SLTC Society of Leather Trades Chemists

SLTEA Sheffield Lighter Trades Employers Association

SLTF Shortest Latency Time First

SLTTCO Saudi Livestock Transportation and Trading Company (Saudi Arabia)

SLU FAE Surface-Launched Unit Fuel Air Explosive

SLUG Superconducting Low-inductance Undulatory Galvanometer

SLUMT Slacked Unconstrained Minimization Technique

SLURP Self Levelling Unit for Removing Pollution

SLUTT Surface Launched Underwater Transponder Target

SLV Satellite Launching Vehicle
Standard Launch Vehicle

SLVC Super Linear Variable Capacitor

SM Scientific Memorandum
Sequential Machine
Special Memorandum
Streptomycin
Student Manual
Styrene Monomer
Surface Mounting

SMA Scale Matching Analysis
Science Masters Associatioon
Segnalamento Marittimo ed Aereo (Italy)
Ship Maintenance Authority (MOD (N))
Singapore Manufacturers Association (Singapore)
Singapore Medical Association (Singapore)
Smooth-Muscle Antibodies
Solder Manufacturers Association (USA)
Staff Management Association

SMAC Scene-Matching Area-Correlator
Sequential Multiple Analysis plus Computer
Simulation Model of Automobile Collisions
Simultaneous Multichannel Analyser plus Computer
Simultaneous Multiframe Analytical Calibration
Society of Management Accountants of Canada (Canada)

SMACC Scheduling, Manpower Allocation, and Cost Control

SMACNA Sheet Metal and Air Conditioning Contractors National Association (USA)

SMACS Serialized Missile Accounting and Control System (USN)

SMAE Society of Model Aeronautical Engineers

SMAF Smooth Muscle-Acting Factor

SMAL Structured, Macro-Assembly Language

SMARA Servicio Meteorologico de la Armada Argentina (Argentina) (Naval Meteorological Service)

SMART SALTON's Magical Automatic Retriever of Texts
Satellite Maintenance And Repair Technique
Scheduling Management and Allocating Resources Technique
Simplified Macro Assembled Reliability Testing
Storage Modification And Retrieval Transaction
STORNO (Denmark) Multichannel Automatic Radio Telephone
Supermarket Allocation Allocation and Recorder Technique
Supervisors Methods Analysis Review Technique
System Monitoring and Reporting by Tesdata
Systems Management Analysis, Research and Test

SMARTIE Simple Minded Artificial Intelligence
Sub-Marine Automatic Remote Television Inspection Equipment

SMARTS San Mateo (USA) Automated Rapid Telecommunication System

SMAS Switched Maintenance Access System

SMASH Southeast Asia Multisensor Armament Systems Helicopter

SMATV Satellite Master Antenna Television

SMAW Shielded Metal-Arc Welding
Shoulder-launched Multi-purpose Assault Weapon

SMAWT Short-range, Man-portable, Anti-tank Weapon Technology

SMB Side Marker Board
Single Mouldboard ploughing

SMBA Scottish Marine Biological Association

SMC Screened Multiplayer Ceramic
Sealant Manufactures Conference
Sheet Moulding Compound
Small Magellanic Cloud
Solder Manufacturers Committee (USA)
Spectacle Makers Company
Submarine Medical Center (of Bureau of Medicine and Surgery (USN))
Supply and Maintenance Command (US Army)

SMCA Suckling Mouse Cataract Agent

SMCL Southeastern Massachusetts Cooperating Libraries (USA)

SMCS Structural Mode Control System

SMD Semiconductor Magnetic-field Detector
Soil Moisture Deficit
Speed Measuring Device
Storage Module Drive
Surface Mounted Device

SMDC Saskatchewan Mining and Development Corporation (Canada) (financed by the Provincial Government)

SMDP Scottish Microelectronics Development Programme (of SCET)

SME Society of Manufacturing Engineers (USA)
Soybean Meal Equivalent

SMEAC Science, Mathematics and Environmental Education Information Analysis Center (Ohio State University (USA))

SMEAT SKYLAB Medical Experimental Altitude Test (of NASA)

SMEC Snowy Mountains Engineering Corporation (Australia) (a public corporation)

SMEDAL STAG (US Army Strategy and Tactics Analysis Group) Monotone Experimental Design Algorithm

SMERC San Mateo Educational Resources Center (USA)

SMES Superconducting Magnetic Energy Storage

SMF Societe Mathematique de France (France)
Stationary Magnetic Field
Systems Management Facility

SMHEA Snowy Mountains Hydro Electric Authority (Australia)

SMI Soldier/Machine Interface
Sub-Module Interface
Supermarket Institute (USA)

SMIAC Soil Mechanics Information Analysis Center (US Army)

SMIC Study of Man's Impact on Climate (sponsored by MIT (USA))

SMID Semiconductor Memory Integrated Device

SMIL Statistics and Market Intelligence Library (of DTI)

SMILE Southcentral Minnesota Inter-Library Exchange (USA)
"S" Machine Interpreter Language Emulation

SMILI Synthetic Model Interferometric Laser Imaging

SMILS Sonobuoy Missile Impact Location System

SMIRR (Space) Shuttle Multispectral Infra-Red Radiometer

SMiRT International Conference on Structural Mechanics in Reactor Technology

SMIS Society for Management Information Systems (USA)
Spectrum-Matching Imaging System

SMITES State-Municipal Income Tax Evaluation System

SML Science Museum Library
Semantic Meta-Language
Shoals Marine Laboratory (operated cooperatively by Cornell University and University of New Hampshire (USA))

SMLB Sea-mobile Logistic Base

SMLM Simple-Minded Learning Machine

SMLS Seaborne Mobile Logistic System

SMM Solar Maximum Mission (satellite)
Solar Maximum Mission spacecraft
Standard Method of Measurement of Building Work (of RICS and NFBTE)
Systems Maintenance Management

SMMAS Supplies and Materials Management Advisory Service (of the Crown Agents)

SMMCEQ Standard Method of Measurement for Civil Engineering Quantities
SMMIP Strategic Material Management Information Programme
SMMIS Ship Management Maintenance Information System
SMMP Standard Methods of Measuring Performance
SMMR Scanning Multi-channel Microwave Radiometer
SMMT Society of Motor Manufacturers and Traders
SMO Synchronized Modulated Oscillator
SMODOS Self Modulating Derivative Optical Spectrometer
SMOG Special Monitor Output Generator
SMON Subacute Myelo-Optico-Neuropathy
SMOOSA Save Maine's Only Official State Animal (an environmental group in Maine, USA)
SMOPS School of Maritime Operations (Royal Navy)
SMORN Specialist Meeting on Reactor Noise
SMOROMS Summer Meeting Of the Royal Meteorological Society
SMOW Standard Mean Ocean Water
SMP Small Metal Particles
Structures and Materials Panel (of AGARD (NATO))
Systems Management Processor
SMPS numbered series of Studies on Medical and Population Subjects issued by Office of Population, Censuses and Surveys and published by HMSO
Simplified Message Processing Simulation
Switched-Mode Power Supply
SMPTE Society of Motion Picture and Television Engineers (USA)
SMR Solid Moderated Reactor
Standard Malaysian Rubber
Standardized Mortality Ratio
Super-Metallic Rich
SMRA Spring Manufacturers Research Association (now Spring Research Association)
SMRAB Safety in Mines Research Advisory Board (of DTI) (now of HSC)
SMRD Spin Motor Rate Detector
SMRE Safety in Mines Research Establishment (of DTI) (later of Dept of Energy but now of the Health and Safety Executive)
SMRL Submarine Medical Research Laboratory (of SMC (USN))
Sudan Medical Research Laboratories (Sudan)
SMRP Satellite and Mesometeorology Research Project (of Univerisity of Chicago (USA))
SMS prefix to Standards issued by SVS
Software Monitoring System
Stock Management System
Surface Missile System
Suspended Manoeuvring System
Synchronous Meteorological Satellite
System Measurement Software
SMSA Silica and Moulding Sands Association
Standard Metropolitan Statistical Area (USA)
SMSG School Mathematics Study Group
SMSU Southwest Missouri State University (USA)
SMT Selection of Moving Targets
SMTA Scottish Motor Trade Association
SMTD Synchronous Mode-locked Tunable Dye laser
SMTI Selective Moving Target Indicator
SMTRB Ship and Marine Technology Requirements Board (of Dept of Industry)
SMTS Symposium on Marine Traffic Systems
SMU Southeastern Massachusetts University (USA)
Southern Methodist University (USA)
SMV Standard Minute Value
SMWG Space Shuttle Structures and Materials Working Group (of NASA (USA))
SMX Semi-Micro Xerography
Sulphamethoxazole
SMY Solar Maximum Year
SN Science OR Scientific Note
Serum Neutralization
Society for Neuroscience (USA)
Substantia Nigra
Supernova
Surface Notched tension
SNA Societe Nationale Aerospatiale (France)
Societe Nationale pour Encouragement de la Recherche Atomique Industrielle (Switzerland)
Systems Network Architecture
SNAM Societa Nazionale Metanodotti (Italy)
SNAME Society of Naval Architects and Marine Engineers (USA)
SNAP Satellite Navigation Alert Plotter
School for Nautical Archaeology at Plymouth
Simplified Numerical Automatic Programmer
Space Nuclear Auxiliary Power
Standard Network Access Protocol
Stereonet Analysis Programme
Subroutines for Natural Actuarial Processing
System for Natural Programming
System of Network Analysis Programmes
Systems for Nuclear Auxiliary Power
SNAPS Switched Network Automatic Profile System (of AUTODIN)
SNARC Short Nickel Line Accumulating Register Calculator
SNAS Ship Navigation Alarm System
SNASC Symbolic Network Analysis on a Small Computer
SNB Slovenska Narodna Bibliografia (Czechoslovakia) (Slovak National Bibliography)
SNBB Saskatchewan-Nelson Basin Board (Canada)
SNBPSS Sustaining Neutral Beam Power Supply System
SNCB Societe Nationale des Chemins de Fer Belges (Belgium) (Belgian National Railways)
SNCF Societe Nationale des Chemins de Fer Francais (France) (French National Railways)
SNCFA Societe Nationale des Chemins de Fer Algeriens (Algeria) (Algerian Railways)
SNCFT Societe Nationale des Chemins de Fer Tunisiens (Tunisia) (National Railways)
SNCST Saudi National Centre for Science and Technology (Saudi Arabia)
SNDT Society of Non-Destructive Testing (USA)
SNDV Strategic Nuclear Delivery Vehicles
SNEA Societe Nationale Elf-Aquitaine (France)
SNECMA Societe Nationale d'Etude et de Construction de Moteurs d'Aviation (France)
SNEFCA Syndicat National des Entreprises du Froid et du Conditionnement de l'Air (France)
SNEMSA Southern New England Marine Sciences Association (USA)
SNERI Societe Nationale d'Etudes, de Gestion, de Realisations et d'Exploitation Industrielles (Algeria) (National Society for Studies, Innovation, Feasibility and Exploitation of Industrial Projects)
SNF Sampled N-path Filter
Solids-Not-Fat
System Noise Figure
SNG Substitute Natural Gas
Synthetic Natural Gas
SNI Serial Network Interface
Studieselskapet for Norsk Industri (Norway) (Association for the Development of Norwegian Industry)
SNIA Societe Nationale Industrielle Aerospatiale (France)
SNIAS Societe Nationale Industrielle Aerospatiale (France)

SNIC Singapore National Institute of Chemistry (Singapore)

SNIF Signal-to-Noise Ratio Improvement Factor

SNIMA Service de Normalisation Industrielle Marocaine (Morocco) (Department of Industrial Standards)

SNIPE Simple Network Interacting Programmes' Executive

SNLC Senior NATO Logisticians Conference

SNM Society of Nuclear Medicine (USA)
Special Nuclear Materials

SNMC Societe Nationale des Materiaux de Construction (Morocco)

SNMMS Standard Navy Maintenance and Material Management System (USN)

SNNEB Scottish Nursery Nurses Examination Board

SNOBOL String-Oriented Symbolic Language

SNOE Smack, Noise Equipment
Smart Noise Equipment

SNOP Standardized Nomenclature of Pathology
Systematized Nomenclature of Pathology

SNORT Supersonic Naval Ordnance Research Track (USN)

SNP Sodium Nitroprusside

SNPA Southern Newspaper Publishers Association (USA)

SNPE Societe Nationale des Poudres et Explosifs (France)

SNPM Standard and Nuclear Propulsion Module

SNPO Space Nuclear Propulsion Office (of NASA)

SNPS Satellite Nuclear Power Station

SNR Signal to Noise Ratio
Society for Nautical Research
Static Negative Resistance
Supernova Remnant

SNRV Signal-to-Noise Ratio-Video

SNS Spallation Neutron Source

SNT Society for Non-destructive Testing (USA)

SNTITPCh Stowarzyszenie Naukowo-Techniczne Inzynierow i Technikow Przemyslu Chemicznego (Poland) (Scientific and Technical Association of Engineers and Technicians of the Chemical Industry)

SNTITPP Stowarzyszenie Naukowo-Techniczne Inzynierow i Technikow Przemyslu Papierniczego (Poland) (Scientific and Technical Association of Paper Industry Engineers and Technicians)

SNTITR Stowarzyszenie Naukowo-Techniczne Inzynierow i Technikow Rolnictwa (Poland) (Scientific and Technical Association of Engineers and Technicians in Agriculture)

SNU Solar Neutrino Unit

SNUPPS Standardized Nuclear Power Plant Syndicate (USA) (a commercial syndicate)
Standardized Nuclear Unit Power Plant System (a project of five electric utility companies in the USA)

SNV Schweizerische Normenvereinigung (Switzerland) (Swiss Standards Association) (also known as Association Suisse de Normalisation)
Statens Naturvardsverk (Sweden) (Environment Protection Board)

SNVBA Scottish National Vehicle Builders Association

SNW Strategic Nuclear Weapon

SO prefix to numbered series issued by Southern Forest Experiment Station (of the Forest Service (USDA))
Society of Osteopaths

SoA Society of Authors

SOA State of the Art
Stimulus Onset Asynchrony

SOAA State of the Art Advancement

SOAC Satellite Ozone Analysis Center (of LLNL (DOE) (USA))
State-of-the-Art Car (Car here is American term for railway waggon)

SOAE State Organization for Administration and Employment Affairs (Iran)

SOAP Silicate-Oxy-Apatite
Simplify Obscure ALGOL Programmes
Spectrometric Oil Analysis Programme

SOAPP State-of-the Art Performance Programme

SOAR Safe Operating Area
Shuttle Orbital Applications and Requirements
Simulation of Airlift Resources

SOAS School of Oriental and African Studies (University of London)

SOASIS Southern Ohio Chapter of ASIS (USA)

SOBEMAP Societe Belge d'Economie et de Mathematique Appliquees (Belgium)

SOBS University of Southampton BASIC System

SOC Self-Organizing Control OR Controller
Separated Orbit Cyclotron
Severity of Ozone Cracking
Silicon-On-Ceramic
Specific Optimal Controller
Stress-Optical Coefficient
Superposition of Configurations

Soc Eng Society of Engineers

SOCABU Societe de Caoutchouc Butyl (France)

SOCALTRA Societe Alsacienne d'Etudes et Travaux (France)

SOCAQ Societe des Collectionneurs d'Armes du Quebec (Canada)

SOCC Salvage Operational Control Centre
Self-Orthogonal Convolutional Code

SOCE Separated-Orbit Cyclotron Experiment

SOCEA Societe Charentaise d'Equipements Aeronautiques (France)

SOCIA Societe pour l'Industrie Atomique (France)

SOCKO Systems Operational Checkout

SOCLEEN Society for Clean Environment (India)

SOCM Stand-Off Cluster Munitions

SOCMA Second Order Coherent Multiple Access
Synthetic Organic Chemical Manufacturers Association (USA)

SOCOL Societe de Construction d'Enterprises Generales (Belgium)

SOCOTEL Societe Mixte pour le developpement de la Technique de la Commutation dans le Domaine des Telecommunications (France)

SOCRATES SCOPE's Own Conditioned-Reflex, Automatic Trainable Electronic System
System for Organizing Content to Review And Teach Educational Subjects

SOCTAP Sulphur Oxide Control Technology Assessment Panel (USA)

SOD Superintendent of Documents (of USGPO) (USA)
Superoxide Dismutase

SODA Source Data Automation
Systems Optimization and Design Algorithm

SODAC Society of Dyers and Colourists

SODAS Structure Oriented Description And Simulation
Synoptic Oceanographic Data Assimilation System (of NWS (USN) and NAVOCEANO)

SODECO Sakhalin Oil Development Corporation (Japan)

SODEPADOM Société pour le Développement des Papiers Domestiques (France)

SODERN Societe Anonyme d'Etudes et Realisations Nucleaires (France)

SODET Sound Detector

SODETEG Societe d'Etudes Techniques et d'Enterprises Generales (France)

SODIC Societe pour la Conversion et le Developpement Industriels (France)

SOE Specific Optimal Estimation
SOEC Statistical Office of the European Communities (Luxembourg)
SOEKOR Southern Oil Exploration Corporation (South Africa) (state owned)
SOERO Small Orbiting Earth Resources Observatory
SOF Succinic Oxidase Factor
SOFA SAFE (COMPUTING LTD) Overall Fixed Asset system
SOFAR Sound Fixing And Ranging
Sound Fuzing and Ranging
SOFIRAN Société Française des Pétroles d'Iran (Iran)
SOFLUMAR Societe d'Armement Fluvial et Maritime (France)
SOFMA Societe Francais de Materiels d'Armement (France)
SOFNET Solar Observing and Forecasting Network (of USAF)
SOFRATOME Société Française d'Études et de Réalisation Nucléaires (France)
SOFRE Societe Francaise d'Etudes (France) (French Consulting Engineers Organisations)
SOFREAVIA Societe Francaise d'Etudes et de Realisation d'Equipmements Aeronautiques (France)
SOFRECOM Societe Francaise d'Etudies et de Realisations d'Equipements de Telecommunications (France)
SOFREGAZ SOFRE Gaz (France) (French Gas Engineers Consulting Organisation)
SOFRELEC SOFRE Electrique (France) (French Electrical Engineers Consulting Organisation)
SOFREMINES SOFRE Miniere (France) (French Mining Engineers Consulting Organisation)
SOFRESID SOFRE Siderurgique (France) (French Metallurgical Industries Consulting Organisation)
SOFREXAM Societe Francaise d'Exportation de Materiels Naval et Militaires (France) (now SOFMA)
SOFT Signature Of Fragmented Tanks
Simple Output Format Translator
SOGAMMIS SOUTH GATE (City) (USA) Municipal Management Information System
SOGECOR Societe de Gestion et de Conseil en Organisation (France)
SOGEM Societe de Gestion Moderne (France)
Sortie Generation Model
SOGEPPAR Societe de Gestion et de Participation (Belgium)
SOGERCA Societe pour l'Enteprise de Reacteurs et de Centrales Atomiques (France)
SOGERMA Societe Girondine d'Entretien et de Reparation de Materiel Aeronautique (France)
SOGESCI Societe Belge pour l'Application des Methodes Scientifiques de Gestion (Belgium) (Belgian Society for the Application of Scientific Methods of Management)
SOGETRA Societe Generale de Travaux (Belgium)
SOGEV Societe Generale du Vide (France)
SOGREAH Societe Grenobloise d'Etudes et Applications Hydrauliques (France)
SOI Space Object Identification
Standards Organisation of Iran (Iran)
SOIS Shipping Operations Information Systems
Silicon On Insulating Substrate
SOIVRE Servicio Oficial de Inspeccion, Vigilancia y Regulacion de Exportaciones (Spain)
SOJ Stand-Off Jammer
SOL Simulation Orientated Language
Small Orbital Laboratory
System Orientated Language
Systems Optimization Laboratory (Stanford University (USA))
SOLACE Sales Order and Ledger Accounting using the COMPUTERLINE (Bureau Services) Environment
Society of Local Authority Chief Executives
SOLAR Serialized On-Line Automatic Recording
Shared On-Line Automated Reservation
SOLAS Convention on the Safety of Life at Sea (of IMCO)
SOLD Soft Option in Logic Design
SOLDIER Solution of Ordinary Differential Equations Routine
SOLE Society of Logistics Engineers (USA)
SOLFIRE Solent and Southampton Water Marine Emergency Plan (special safety scheme for visits of nuclear merchant ships)
SOLID Self-Organizing Large Information Dissemination
SOLINET Southeastern Library Network (USA)
SOLIS Solar Origin Laser Interstellar Signal
SOLIT Society of Library and Information Technicians (USA)
SOLMIS Supply On-Line Management Information System
SOLO System for On-Line Optimization
SOLOGS Standardization of Operations and Logistics
SOLRAD Solar Radiation
Solar Radiation Monitoring Satellite Program (USN)
SOM Simulation Option Model
Small Office Microfilm
Society of Occupational Medicine
Space Oblique Mercator projection
Space Organization Method
Stand-Off Missile
Standing Group on Oil Markets (of IEA (OECD))
SOMA Society of Medical Authors
SOMAIR Societe des Mines de l'Air (France)
SOMASER Societe Maritime de Service (France)
SOMELER Societe de Mechanique et d'Electronique de Ruelle (France) (now amalgamated into SOFMA)
SOMIREN Societa Minerali Radioattivi Energia Nucleare (Italy)
SOMISA Sociedad Mixta Siderurgia Argentina (Argentina)
SOMISS Study of Management Information Systems Support (US Army)
SOMM Stand-Off Modular Missile
SOMS Space Operations Management System
SOMTE Soldier-Operator-Maintainer-Tester-Evaluator
SON Supraoptic Nuclei
SONACOB Societe Nationale de Commercialisation des Bois et Derives (Algeria)
SONACOME Societe Nationale des Construction Mecaniques (Algeria)
SONAP Sociedad de Navigacion Petrolera (Chile)
SONAR Sound Navigation And Ranging
SONAREM Societe Nationale de Recherches et d'Exploitations Minieres (Algeria)
SONAS Society of Naval Architects of Singapore (Singapore)
SONATITE Societe Nationale des Travaux d'Infrastructure des Telecommunications (Algeria)
SONATRACH Societe Nationale pour la Production, le Transport, la Transformation et la Commercialisation des Hydrocarbures (Algiers) (state owned)
SONATRAM Societe Nationale de Travaux Maritimes (Algeria)
SONDE Society of Non-Destructive Examination (became part of the British Institute of Non-Destructive Testing in 1976)
SONIC Simultaneously Operating Numerical Integration Computer
Société Nationale des Industries de la Cellulose (Algeria) (a government agency)
SONRES Saturated Optical Non-Resonant Emission Spectroscopy
SOOJ Society of Ophthalmological Optics of Japan (Japan)
SOON Sequence of Opportunities and Negatives
SOOT Solar Optical Observing Telescope

SOP Secretaria de Obras Publicas (Mexico) (Ministry of Public Works)
Selective Oxidation Process
Solution Output Processor
Study Organization Plan
SOPA Society for Professional Archeologists (USA)
SOPELEM Societe d'Optique, Precision, Electronique et Mecanique (France)
SOPEMEA Societe pour le Perfectionnement des Materiels et Equipements Aerospatiaux (France)
SOPHYA Supervisor of Physics Analysis
SOR Sequential Occupancy Release
Specific Operating Requirement
Successive Over-Relaxation
SORA Svenska Operationsanalyseforeningen (Sweden) (Swedish Operational Research Society)
SORCA Societe de Recherche Operationaelle et d'Economie Appliquee (Belgium)
SORD Submerged Object Recovery Device
SORDID Summary of Reported Defects, Incidents and Delays
SOREAS Syndicat des Fabricants d'Organes et d'Equipment Aeronautiques et Spatiaux (France)
SOREFAME Sociedades Reunidas Fabriacoes Metalicas (Portugal)
SORG Southern Operational Research Group
SORI Southern Research Institute (USA)
SORIN Societa Ricerche Impianti Nucleari (Italy)
SOROAD Storage and Retrieval of Air Quality Data System (of EPA (USA))
SORT Simulated Optical Range Tester
Staff Organization Round Table (of American Library Associastion (USA))
Structures for Orbiting Radio Telescopes
SORTI Satellite Orbiting Track and Intercept
SORTIE Space Orbital Re-entry Test Integrated Environment
SORTRAN Syntax Oriented Translator
SOS International Federation of Bloodgivers Organisations
Self-shielding Open-arc Stainless
Silicon-on-Sapphire
SPSS Over-ride System
Stabilized Optical Sight
Statics of Solids
Student Operating System
SOS-ME Silicon-on-Sapphire Memory Evaluator
SOSI Space Operations and Scientific Investigations
SOSOFT Software System Oriented to Fuze Testing
SOSSUS Study of Surgical Services in the United States (of the American College of Surgeons)
SOSTEL Solid State Electric Logic
SOSUS SONAR Surveillance System
SOT Scanning Oscillator
Society of Toxicology (USA)
Solar Optical Telescope
SOTAS Stand-Off Target Acquisition System
SOTDAT Source Test Data system (of EPA (USA))
SOTELEC Societe Mixte pour le Developpement de la Technique des Telecommunications sur Cables (France)
SOTIM Sonic Observation of the Trajectory and Impact of the Missiles
SOTS Synchronous Orbiting Tracking Stations
SOV Seabed Operations Vessel
SOVAL Single Operator Validation
SOW Stand-Off Weapon
Statement of Work
SOYD Sum-of-the-Year-Digits
SP prefix to numbered:dated series of Aircraft construction mechanical parts issued by BSI (letter sometimes preceded by a number)
Secretin-Pancreozymin
Separable Programming
Shot Peening
Special Paper OR Publication
Specification
Spray-Dried
Staff Paper
Synthesis Programming
SpA Societa per Azioni (PLC) (Italian)
SPA Screen Printing Association (USA)
Sea Photo Analysis
Ship Performance Analyzer
Societa per Azioni (Joint Stock Company)
Societe Protectice des Animaux (France) (Society for the Protection of Animals)
Society for Personnel Administration (USA)
Specialised Publications Association (India)
Statens Provningsanstalt (Sweden) (National Institute for Materials Testing)
Stimulation-Produced Analagesia
Sudden Phase Anomalie
Systems and Procedures Association (USA) (now Association for Systems Management)
SPAAG Self-Propelled Anti-Aircraft Gun
SPAB Society for the Protection of Ancient Buildings
Space-borne Angle Beacon
Steel Protection Advise Bureau
SPAC Spatial Computer
SPACE Sequential Position And Covariance Estimation
Settlement, Payment, Accounting, Credit Extension
Sidereal Polar Axis Celestial Equipment
SPACECOM Space Command (USAF)
SPACELOOP Speech Analog Compression and Editing Loop
SPACES Scheduling Package and Computer Evaluation, Schools
SPACTS Semi-Passive Attitude Control and Trajectory Stabilisation System
SPAD Satellite Position Prediction And Display
Satellite Protection for Area Defence
Self Protection Aid Device
SUNDSTRAND (DATA CONTROL INC) (USA) Performance Advisory Display
SPADATS Space Detection and Tracking System (of NORAD)
SPADE Settable Pneumatic Altitude Detection
Single channel per carrier, Pulse code modulation, multiple-Access Demand-assignment Equipment
SPARTA Acquisition Digital Equipment
SPADES Solar Perturbation of Atmospheric Density Experiments Satellite
SPADOC Space Defense Operations Center (of SPACECOM (USAF))
SPADU Signal Processing And Display Unit
SPAe Service de la Production Aeronautique (of DTCA (France))
SPAI Screen Printing Association International (USA)
SPAID Society for the Prevention of Asbestos and Industrial Diseases
SPAIS Suburban Police Automated Information System (Massachusetts (USA))
SPAL Stabilized Platform Airborne Laser
SPAM Ship Position and Attitude Measurement
Soil-Plant-Atmosphere Model
SPAN Social Participatory Allocative Network
Solar Proton Alert Network (of Space Disturbances Laboratory (NOAA (USA))
Solid Phase Alloy Nucleation
Split Path Nonlinear
Statistical Processing and Analysis

SPANPAC Sales, Purchases and Nominal Package
SPANS Spectral Processing Analysis System
SPAR SAC (USAF) Peacetime Airborne Reconnaissance
Seagoing Platform for Acoustics Research
Solid-State Phased-Array Radar
Space Processing Applications Rocket (a project of NASA (USA))
Store Port Allocation Register
Subjective Probability Analysis Routine
Submersible Pipe Alignment Rig
System Performance Activity Recorder
SPARC Selected Parts Control System
South Platte Area Redevelopment Council (USA)
Space Air Relay Communications
Space Research Capsule
Spectral Analyzer and Recognition Computer
SPARCS Solar Pointing Aerobee Rocket Control System
SPARE Error-tolerant and Reconfigurable Associative Processor with Self-repair (this is an inverse acronym)
SPAREM Spares Provisioning And Requirements Effectiveness Model
SPARM Solid-Propellant Augmented Rocket Motor
SPARROW Anti-Radiation Missile
SPARMO Solar Particles and Radiations Monitoring Organisation (France)
SPARQ SCICON Programmable Automatic Request for Retransmission
SPARS Site Production And Reduction System
Space Precision Attitude Reference System
SPARSA Sferics Pulse, Azimuth, Rate and Spectrum Analyzer
SPART Space Research and Technology
SPARTA Special Anti-missile Research Tests in Australia
SPARTAN Scheduling Programme for Allocating Resources To Alternative Networks
SPAS Shuttle Pallet Satellite
SPASM Self-Propelled Air-to-Surface Missile
SPASS Spark Chamber Automatic Scanning System
SPASUR Space Surveillance
SPASYN Space Synchro
SPATE Stress Pattern Analysis by Thermal Emission
Submersible Position and Tracking Equipment
SPATS Sequence Planning And Time Scheduling
SPAU Signal Processing Arithmetic Unit
SPB Special Boiling Point
SPC Science Policy Committee (of OECD)
Science Programme Committee (of European Space Agency)
Standard Printing Colour
Standard Product Concept
Standing Group on Relation with Producers and other Consumer Countries (of IEA (OECD))
Stored Programme Control
Supraventricular Premature Contractions
SPCC State Pollution Control Commission (New South Wales (Australia))
Strength Power and Communications Cable
SPCL Single Product Cost Leadership
SPCS Ship Production Control System
SPD Spectral Power Distribution
Statistical Policy Division (of OMB (USA))
Surface Potential Difference
SPDA Sea Photo Diffraction Analysis
SPDD Selectable Parameter Digital Display
Systems Plans and Design Division (of Weather Bureau (USA))
SPDP Society of Professional Data Processors (USA)
SPDT Single-Pole Double-Throw
SPE Signal Processing Element
Society for Photographic Education
Society of Petroleum Engineers (of AIME (USA))
Society of Plastics Engineers (USA)
Solar Particle Event
Solar Proton Event
Solid Polymer Electrolyte
System Performance Effectiveness
SPEAL Special Purpose Engineering Language
SPEAR Source Performance Evaluation And Reporting
Squadron Performance Effectiveness Analytic Representation
STANFORD (University (USA)) Positron-Electron Asymmetric Ring
SPEC South Pacific Bureau for Economic Co-operation
Speech Predictive Encoded Communications
Student Performance Evaluation by Computer
System Performance Evaluation Console
Systems and Procedures Exchange Center (of Association of Research Libraries (USA))
SPECA Supplier Performance Evaluation and Corrective Action
SPECDEVCEN Special Devices Center (of ONR (USN))
SPECOL Special Customer Oriented Language
SPECON System Performance Effectiveness Conference
SPECT Single-Photon Emission Computed Tomography
SPECTRUM Solar Probe Experiment Created for Technological Research by the University of Michigan (USA)
SPED Supersonic Planetary Entry Decelerator
SPEEA Seattle Professional Engineering Employees Association (USA)
SPEED Simplified Profile Enlargement from Engineering Drawings
Subsistence Preparation by Electronic Energy Diffusion
System-wide Project for Electronic Equipment at Depots (US Army)
Systematic Plotting and Evaluation of Enumerated Data
Systems Programmes Expediting Export Data/Delivery
SPEEDEX System Project for Electronic Equipment at Depots Extended (US Army)
SPEEDS System for Pin-pointed, Exhaustive and Expeditious Dissemination of Subjects
SPEMELEC Specialites Mecaniques et Electro-mecaniques (France)
SPEPE Secretariat Permanent pour l'Etude des Problemes de l'Eau (France) (Permanent Secretariat for the Study of Water Problems)
SPER Syndicat des Industries de Materiel Professionnel Electronique et Radioelectronique (France)
SPERT Special Power Excursion Reactor Test
SPES Section on Physical and Engineering Sciences (of American Statistical Association (USA))
Simple Plant Economic Simulator
SPESA Solids Pipeline Economic Study Association (Canada)
SPESS Stored Programme Electronic Switching System
SPET Solid Propellant Electric Thruster
SPF Science Policy Foundation
Software Protection Fund (of ADAPSO (USA))
Solid Phase Forming
Structural Programming Facility
Superplastic Forming
Sveriges Plastforbund (Sweden) (Swedish Plastics Federation)
SPF/DB Superplastic Forming combined with Diffusion Bonding
SPFA Steel Plate Fabricators Association (USA)
SPFFA South Pacific Forum Fisheries Agency (Solomon Islands)
SPG Self Propelled Gun
Sinusoidal Pressure Generator
Synthetic Pipeline Gas

SPGG Solid Propellant Gas Generator

SPGS Secondary Power Generating Subsystem

SPHE Society of Packaging and Handling Engineers (USA)

SPHEREDOP Spherical Doppler

SPHINX Space Plasma High-voltage Interaction Experiments

SPI Scatter Plate Interferometer
Serial Peripheral Interface
Society of the Plastics Industry (USA)
Specific Productivity Index
Symbolic Pictorial Indicator
Synthetic Phase Isolator

SPI CANADA Society of the Plastics Industry of Canada (Canada)

SPIA-LPIA Solid and Liquid Propellant Information Agency (JHU (USA))

SPIC Society of the Plastics Industry of Canada (Canada)
Spare Parts Inventory Control

SPICE Sales Point Information Computing Equipment
Spacelab Payload Integration and Co-ordination in Europe (of ESA)

SPID Seismic Personnel Intrusion Detector
Submersible Portable Inflatable Dwelling

SPIDAC Specimen Input to Digital Automatic Computer

SPIDER Sonic Pulse-echo Instrument Designed for Extreme Resolution

SPIE Scavenging—Precipitation—Ion—Exchange
Self-Programmed Individualized Education
Society of Photo-optical Instrumentation Engineers (USA)

SPIF Sequential Prime Implicant Form

SPIL Society for the Promotion and Improvement of Libraries (India)
Spin Prevention and Incidence Limiting
Systems Programming Implementation Language

SPIN International Conference on Strategy and Policies for Informatics
Searchable Physics Information Notices (of AIP (USA))

SPINDEX Selective Permutation Indexing

SPINE Space Informatics Network Experiment (of ESA)

SPINES An International System for the Exchange of Information on Science and Technology for Policy-making, Management and Development (of UNESCO)

SPIRAL SANDIA's Program for Information Retrieval And Listing

SPIRAS Setpoint Precision Infra-Red Angular Scanner

SPIRE Space Inertial Reference Equipment

SPIRES Stanford Physics Information Retrieval System (Stanford University (USA))

SPIRIT Sales Processing Interactive Real-time Inventory Technique

SPIRT Solar-Powered Isolated Radio Transceiver

SPIW Special Purpose Individual Weapon
Special Purpose Infantry Weapon

SPL Signature and Propagation Laboratory (of USABRL)
Simple Programming Language
Simulation Programming Language
Software Programming Language
Sound Pressure Level
Space Programming Language
Subrecursive Programming Language
Survey Processing Language

SPLAD Self-Propelled Light Air Defence gun

SPLASH Special Programme to List Amplitudes of Surges from Hurricanes

SPLC Standard Point Location Code (USA, Canada and Mexico)

SPLCF Sustained Peak Low-Cycle Fatigue

SPLICE Shorthand Programming Language In a COBOL Environment
Stock Points Logistics Integrated Communications Environment (a project of USN)
Submerged Pipeline Completion Equipment
Systematic Planning of Logistics for the Introduction of Complete Equipment

SPLIS Source Programme Library System

SPLIST Source and Procedure LIST

SPLM Space Programming Language Machine

SPM Sequential Processing Machine
Single Point Moor OR Mooring
Solar Polar Monitor
Solar Proton Monitor
Special Preparatory Meeting
Statistical Preventive Maintenance
System Planning Manual

SPMA String Polling Multiple Access

SPMC Standard Procedure Monitor Chart

SPME Solar Proton Monitoring Experiment

SPMS System Programme Management Survey

SPMTS Simplified Predetermined Motion Time System

SPN-GEANS Standard Precision Navigation-Gimballed Electrostatic gyro Aircraft Navigation System

SPNC Society for the Promotion of Nature Conservation

SPNR Society for the Promotion of Nature Reserves

SPNS Standard Product Numbering System

SPO Surface Plasma Oscillation
Systems Program Office (USAF)

SPOC Spacecraft Oceanography

SPOCK Simulated Procedure for Obtaining Common Knowledge

SPOOF Structure and Parity Observing Output Function

SPOOL Simultaneous Peripheral Operation On-Line

SPORT Space Probe Optical Recording Telescope

SPOT Satellite Positioning and Tracking
Speed, Position and Track

SPP Special Projects Program (of OSIS (USA))
Speech Privacy Potential

SPPB Statens Psykologisk- Pedagogiska Bibliotek (Sweden)

SPPSF Space Variant Point Spread Function

SPR Sequential Pattern Recognition
Simplified Practice Recommendation (series issued by NBS)
Sintered Particle Rolling
Spontaneous Parametric Radiation
Strategic Petroleum Reserve (a project of the Congress (USA))

SPRA Science Fiction Research Association (USA)
Special Purpose Reconnaisance Aircraft

SPRAT Small Portable Radar Torch

SPRC Self-Propelled Robot Craft

SPRD Science Policy Research Division (of the Library of Congress Congressional Research Service (USA))
Special Pesticide Review Division (of EPA (USA))

SPRDA Solid Pipeline Research and Development Association (Canada)

SPREAD Spring Evaluation Analysis and Design

SPREE Solid Propellant Rocket Exhaust Effects

SPRI Scott Polar Research Institute

SPRINT Special Police Radio Inquiry Network

SPRINTER Specification of Profits with Interdependencies

SPRITE Sequential Polling and Review of Interacting Teams of Experts
Solid Propellant Rocket Ignition and Evaluation

SPROB Solid Propellant Space Booster Plant (of ISRO (India))

SPROGS SD4020-PDP15 Rapid Output of Graphics System

SPROSS Simulation Programme for Sequential Systems
SPRP Signalling Preprocessing Programmes
SPRT Sequential Probability Ratio Test
Standard Platinum Resistance Thermometer
SPRU Science Policy Research Unit (Sussex University)
SPS Satellite Power System
Separation Processes Service (of DOI) (operated by AERE (UKAEA) and Warren Spring Laboratory)
Serial-Parallel-Serial Storage
Service Propulsion System
Society of Physics Students (USA)
Submerged Production System
Super Proton Synchroton
Symbolic Programming System
SPSD Shipboard Passive Surveillance and Detection System
SPSE Society of Photographic Scientists and Engineers (USA)
SPSG Spin Period Sector Generator
SPSP Signalling Postprocessing Programmes
SPSS Sodium Polystyrene Sulphonate
Statistical Package for the Social Sciences
SPST Single-Pole Single-Throw
SPT Society of Photo-Technologists
Soldered Piezoelectric Transducer
Standard Penetration Test
Strength-Probability-Time
SPTL Superconducting Power Transmission Line
SPUP School of Public and Urban Policy (Pennsylvania University (USA))
SPUR Space Power Unit Reactor
Strategy, Performance and Utilisation of Resources (a campaign of BIM)
System for Project Updating and Reporting
SPURT Simulation Package for University Research and Teaching
SPURV Self-Propelled Underwater Research Vehicle
SPV Surface Photovoltage
SPW Surface Plasma Wave
SPWLA Society of Professional Well Log Analysts (USA)
SPX Stepped Piston Crossover
SQ Stereo Quadraphonic
SQA Software Quality Assurance
Supplier Quality Assurance
SQAPS Supplier Quality Assurance Provisions
SQC Statistical Quality Control
SqDM Sequency Division Multiplexing
SQL Structure Query Language
SQPSK Staggered Quadraphase Phase Shift Key modulation
SQRA Singapore Quality and Reliability Association (Singapore)
SQUANK Simpson Quadrature Used Adaptively-Noise Killed
SQUARE Statistical Quality Analysis Report
SQUID SPERRY Quick Updating of Internal Documentation
Superconducting Quantum Interference Device
Superconducting Quantum-mechanical Interference Device
SQUINT Surface Quality Unit for Inspection by Non-destructive Testing
SQUIRE System for Quick Ultra-fiche-based Information Retrieval
SR Scanning Radiometer
Scientific Report
Sensory Rhodopsin
Sinus Rhythm
Society of Radiographers
Special Regulation OR Report
Spectral Response
Summary Report
Sveriges Radio (Sweden)
Synthetic Rubber
SR&O Statutory Rules and Orders (succeeded by "Statutory Instruments")
SRA Shop Replaceable Assembly
Society of Research Administration (USA)
Spring Research Association (now SRAMA)
Standard Reference Aerosol
Strategic Resource Area
Systems Requirements Analysis
SRAAM Short-Range Air-to-Air Missile
SRAC Safety Research Advisory Committee (of SAE (USA))
Short-Run Average Cost Curve
Steels Resistant to Atmospheric Corrosion
SRAD Steerable Right Angle Drive
SRAEN Systeme de Reference pour la determination de l'Affaiblissement Equivalent pour la Nettete (of CCITT) (REFERENCE SYSTEM FOR DETERMINING Articulation Ratings)
SRAM Short Range Attack Missile
Static Random Access Memory
SRAMA Spring Research And Manufacturers Association
SRANSW State Railway Authority of New South Wales (Australia)
SRAT Societe de Recherches et d'Applications Techniques (France)
SRATS Solar Radiation and Thermospheric Structure Satellite
SRB Solid Rocket Booster
Staff Responsibility Budget
Statens Rad for Byggnadsforskning (Sweden) (National Council for Building Research)
Sulphate Reducing Bacteria
SRBC Sheep Red Blood Cell
SRBDM Short-Range Bomber Defence Missile
SRBII Societe Royale des Ingenieurs et des Industriels (Belgium) (Royal Society of Engineers and Industrialists)
SRBM Short-Range Ballistic Missile
SRC Saskatchewan Research Council (Canada)
Science Research Council (became SERC in 1981)
Scientific Research Council (Jamaica)
Ship Recognition Corps
Solvent Refined Coal
Submarine Rescue Chamber
Survey Research Center (California University (USA))
Systems Research Center (Case Institute of Technology) (USA)
SRCC Space Research Coordination Center (Pittsburgh University (USA))
SRCFE Southern Regional Council for Further Education
SRCRA Shipowners Refrigeration Cargo Research Association
SRCU Shared Remote Control Unit
SRD Safety and Reliability Directorate (of UKAEA)
Single Radial Diffusion
Step Recovery Diode
SRD M prefix to numbered series of Memoranda issued by SRD (UKAEA)
SRD R prefix to numbered series of Reports issued by SRD (UKAEA)
SRDAS Service Recording and Data Analysis System
SRDE Signals Research and Development Establishment (MINTECH and later of MOD) (became Radar and Signals Research Establishment (Christchurch) of MOD in 1976)
SRDS Standard Reference Data System
Systems Research and Development Service (of FAA)
SRDT Single Radial Diffusion Test
SRE Society of Relay Engineers

Society of Reliability Engineering (USA)
Society of Reliability Engineers (Canada)
Sodium Reactor Experiment
Surveillance Radar Element

SREMP Source Region Electromagnetic Pulse

SRET Satellite for Research in Environmental Technology

SRF Secondary Refrigerant Freezing
Station de Recherches Forestieres (Morocco) (Forestry Research Station)
Strength Reduction Factor
Sveriges Rationaliseringforbund (Sweden)

SRFB Space Research Facilities Branch (National Research Council, Canada)

SRG Shift-Register Generator
Southern Rubber Group (USA)

SRGS Stimulated Raman Gain Spectroscopy

SRH Single-Radial-Haemolysis

SRHE Society for Research into Higher Education

SRHIT Small Radar Homing Intercept Technology

SRI Serengeti Research Institute (Tanzania)
Soil Research Institute (Ghana)
Space Research Institute (McGill University (Canada))
SPALLING Resistance Index
Stanford Research Institute (USA)
Sumitomo Rubber Industries (Japan)
System of Reinforcement-Inhibition

SRIF Somatotrophin Release Inhibiting Factor

SRIJ Society of the Rubber Industry of Japan (Japan)

SRIM Selected Research in Microfiche (a service of NTIS (Dept of Commerce (USA))

SRIS Safety Research Information Service (of National Safety Council (USA))

SRL Frank J. Seiler Research Laboratory (United States Air Force Academy)
Savannah Research Laboratory (USA)
Science Reference Library (a part of the British Library)
Societa a Responsibilita Limitata (private limited company)
Systems Research Laboratory (University of Michigan (USA))

SRLD Small Rocket Lift Device

SRM prefix to series of Research Memoranda issued by NPTRL (previously NPRA (USN))
Shock Remanent Magnetisation
Short-Range Missile
Society for Range Management (USA)
Solid Rocket Motor
Standard Reference Materials (of NBS (USA))

SRMA Split-channel Reservation Multiple Access

SRMC Short Run Marginal Cost

SRMH Single Role Mine-Hunter

SRMU Space Research Management Unit (of Science Research Council)

SRNA Shipbuilders and Repairers National Association (dissolved 1977)

SRO Self-Regulatory Organisation
Singly Resonant Oscillator

SROB Short Range Omni-directional Beacon

SROP Simple Re-Order Point control

SRP Seismic Reflection Profiling
Self-Recording Penetrometer
Sequential Range Policy
Sink Resistant Plastic
Society for Radiological Protection
Soluble Reactive Phosphorous
Stationary Random Process
System Response Patterns

SRPS Synchronous Random Pulse Sequence System

SRPT Shortest Remaining Processing Time
Stress Relaxation Processability Tester

SRR prefix to series of reports issued by Naval Personnel Research Activity (USN)
prefix to series of reports issued by NPTRL (previously NPRA) (USN)
Shift Register Recognizer
Short Range Recovery helicopter
Short-Range Rescue
System Requirements Review

SRRA Scottish Radio Retailers Association

SRRB Search and Rescue Radio Beacon

SRRL Southern Regional Research Laboratory (of USDA)

SRS Seat Reservation System
Selective Record Service (of BLAISE)
Septal Range Syndrome
Shock Response Spectrum
Single Random Sampling
Social and Rehabilitation Service (of HEW (USA))
Statistical Reporting Service (of USDA)
Stimulated Raman Spectroscopy
Strategic Reconnaissance Squadron (USAF)
Synchrotron Radiation Source
Systems Reliability Service (of UKAEA)

SRSA Scientific Research Society of America (USA)

SRT Society of Radiologic Technologists (USA)
Speech Reception Threshold

SRTI Societe de Recherches Techniques et Industrielles (France)

SRTOS Special Real Time Operating System

SRTS System Response Time Simulator

SRU Shop Replaceable Unit
Societe du Raffinage d'Uranium (France)

SRV Space Rescue Vehicle
Styling Research Vehicle
Surface Recombination Velocity
Suspension Research Vehicle

SRW Strategic Reconnaissance Wing (USAF)

SS Scanning Spectrometer
Starlight Scope
State Space
Sum of Squares

SS/TDMA Satellite-Switched/Time-Division Multiple Access

SS1913 Smithsonian (Astrophysical Observatory) Scale of 1913

SSA Seismological Society of America (USA)
Self-Scanned Array
Smallest Space Analysis
Smoke Suppressant Additive
Soaring Society of America (USA)
Social Security Administration (of HEW (USA))
Solid State Amplifier
Sulphosalicyclic Acid
Supply Support Arrangements

SSAB Svenska Sallskapet for Automatiserad Bildanelys (Sweden) (Swedish Pattern Recognition Society)

SSAC States' Systems of Accounting for and Control of Nuclear Material

SSACV Semi-Submerged Air Cushion Vehicle

SSADH Succinic Semialdehyde Dehydrogenase

SSAP Statement of Standard Accounting Practice
Survival Stabilator Actuator Package

SSARR Streamflow Synthesis And Reservoir Regulations

SSAS Special Signal Analysis System

SSAV Simian Sarcoma-Associated Virus

SSB Salvo Squeezebore
Single Sideband
Space Science Board (of National Academy of Science (USA))

SSBG Sex Steroid Binding Globulin

SSBSC Single Sideband Suppressed Carrier

SSBSCOM SSB Suppressed-Carrier Optical Modulator

SSBW Surface Skimming Bulk Wave

SSC Satellite Situation Center (of NASA (USA))
Sector-Switching Centre
Semi-Submerged Catamaran
Shape Selective Cracking
Ship Structure Committee (USA)
Solid-State Circuit
Southern Surgical Congress (USA)
Spectroscopy Society of Canada (Canada)
Stazione Sperimentale per i Combustibili (Italy) (Fuel Research Station)
Sulphide (OR Sulfide) Stress Cracking
Summer Simulation Conference (USA)
Survival Service Commission (of IUCN)
Systems Science and Cybernetics
US Army Telecommuniucations Software Support Center (of STRATCOM) (US Army))

SSCA Southern Society of Chartered Accountants

SSCC Snowmobile Safety and Certification Committee (USA)
Spin-Scan Cloud Camera

SSCI Senate Select Committee on Intelligence (US Senate)
Societes de Service et Conseil en Informatique (France)
Steel Service Center Institute (USA)

SSCM Societe Surgerienne de Constructions Mecaniques (France)

SSCNS Ships Self-Contained Navigation System

SSCR Spectral Shift Control Reactor

SSCS Spatial Spectrum Centre Shifting
Strain Sensitive Cable Sensor
Symposium on the Simulation of Computer Systems

SSCV Semi-Submersible Crane Vessel

SSD Scientific Services Department (of CEGB)
Single Station Doppler
Space Service Division (of USAF Systems Command)
Space Systems Division (USAF)
Static Sensitive Device
Survival Support Device
Synthesis, Solute Diffusion
System for System Development

SSDA Sequential Similarity Detection Algorithm
Service Station Dealers of America (USA)
Stainless Steel Development Association (disbanded 1973)

SSDC Social Science Documentation Centre (of ICSSR (India))

SSDS Ship Structural Design System
System of Social and Demographic Statistics (a programme of the UN)

SSE Safe Shut-down Earthquake
Society of Shipping Executives
Special Support Equipment

SSEAM Servicios de Equipos Agricolas Mecanizados (Chile) (Mechanized Agricultural Equipment Service)

SSEB South of Scotland Electricity Board

SSEC Secondary Schools Examination Council
Selective Sequence Electronic Calculator
Solar System Exploration Committee (of NASA (USA))

SSEE Swiss Society of Environmental Engineers (Switzerland)

SSEO Seabee Systems Engineering Office (USN)

SSET Steady State Emission Test

SSF Smallest Serving Factor
Society for the Study of Fertility

SSFC Sequential Single-Frequency Code

SSFF Solid Smokeless Fuels Federation

SSG Second Stage Graphitization

SSGS Standardized Space Guidance System

SSGW Strategic Surface to Surface Guided Weapon

SSH Satellite-borne Sounder, Humidity
Small Scale Hydroelectric system

SSHA Scottish Special Housing Association

SSHR Social Systems and Human Resources (a division of the RANN project of NSF (USA))

SSHRC Social Sciences and Humanities Research Council (Canada)

SSI Small Scale Integrated
Small Scale Integration
Standard of Spectral Irradiance
Structural Significant Item

SSIA Shiprepairers and Shipbuilders Independent Association

SSID Solid-State Image Detector

SSIDA Steel Sheet Information and Development Association

SSIDC Small Scale Industries Development Corporation (India)

SSIE Smithsonian Institution's Science Information Exchange (USA)

SSIH Societe Suisse pour l'Industrie Horlogere (Switzerland)

SSILS Solid State Instrument Landing System

SSIS SQUIBB (E R SQUIBB & SONS INCORPORATED) (USA) Science Information System

SSIT Semi-Submarine Ice-breaking Tanker

SSIXS Submarine Satellite Information Exchange System

SSKP Single Shot Kill Probability

SSL SODA Statement Language
Solid State Lamp
Space Sciences Laboratory (California University (USA))

SSLP Sekretariatet for Sakerhetspolitik och Langsikts-planering in om totalforsvaret (Sweden) (Secretariat for National Security and Long-term Defence Planning (of the Ministry of Defence)

SSM Sea Skimmer Missile
Semi-conductor Storage Module
Space Station Mission Simulation Mathematical Model
Standard Stores Memoranda (numbered series issued by MOD)
Stochastic Sequential Machine
Sub-system Simulation Model
Support System Module
Surface-to-Surface Missile
System-State Model

SSMA Spread-Spectrum Multiple Access
Stainless Steel Manufacturers Association

SSME Space Shuttle Main Engine

SSMEA Sheffield Metallurgical and Engineering Association

SSMO Summary of Synoptic Meteorological Observations

SSMS Spark Sources Mass Spectrometry

SSMT Stress Survival Matrix Test

SSN Standard Serial Number
Sunspot Number

SSNDT Scottish School of Non-Destructive Testing (at Paisley College of Technology)

SSNM Strategic Special Nuclear Material

SSNTD Solid-State Nuclear Track Detection

SSO Savings in Space Operations

SSOC Saudi Services and Operating Company (Saudi Arabia)

SSOCR Super-Scale Optical Character Reader

SSOS Severe Storm Observing Satellite

SSP Schoolhouse Systems Project (USA)
Scientific Subroutine Package
Semi-Submerged Platform

	Societe Suisse de Physique (Switzerland) (Physical Society of Switzerland)
	Society for Scholarly Publishing (USA)
	Space Summary Programme
	Statutory Sick Pay
	Successive Short Path
SSPA	Statens Skeppsprovningsanstalt (Sweden) (State Shipbuilding Experimental Tank)
SSPC	Steel Structures Painting Council (USA)
SSPCA	Steel Structures Painting Council of America (USA)
SSPE	Subacute Sclerosing Panencephalitis
SSPI	Sighting System Passive Infra-red
SSPM	System State Phase Modelling
SSPS	Satellite Solar Power Station
	Space Satellite Power Station
SSR	Secondary Surveillance Radar
	Societe Suisse de Radiodiffusion et Television (Switzerland)
	Solid State Relay
	Switching Selector Repeater
	Synchronous Stable Relaying
SSR-CAS	Secondary Surveillance Radar Collision Avoidance System
SSRA	Spread Spectrum Random Access
SSRB	Soil Survey Research Board (of Agricultural Research Council)
SSRC	Social Science Research Council
	Social Sciences Research Council (USA)
SSRCC	Social Science Research Council of Canada (Canada)
SSRG	Schweizerische Studiengesellschaft fur Rationellen Guterumschag (Switzerland) (Swiss Research Society for the Improvement of Handling of Merchandise)
SSRI	Social Science Research Institute (of CRESS (USA))
SSRL	Scottish Science Reference Library (scheduled to be opened in 1987)
	Standard Synchroton Radiation Laboratory (Stanford University (USA))
SSRMA	Small Scale Rubber Manufacturers Association (Sri Lanka)
SSRP	Stanford Synchroton Radiation Project (of Stanford Linear Accelerator Center (USA))
SSRS	British Society for Social Responsibility in Science
	Society for Social Responsibility in Science (USA)
	Submarine Sand Recovery System
SSRT	Slow Strain Rate Technique
SSS	Self-Shifting Synchronizing
	Serial Signalling Scheme
	Small Scientific Satellite
	Space Saver Spare tyre
	Strategic Satellite System
	Sub-Structure Searching
	Synchro-Self-Shifting
	Systems Safety Society (USA)
SSSA	Soil Science Society of America (USA)
SSSDT	Symposium on Solid State Device Technology
SSSF	Sodra Sveriges Skogagares Forbund (Sweden) (South Swedish Forest Owners Association)
SSSI	Sites of Special Scientific Importance
SSSM	Standard Surface-to-Surface Missile
	Subset-Specified Sequential Machine
SSSR	Society for the Scientific Study of Religion (USA)
SSSWP	Seismology Society of the South West Pacific (New Zealand)
SST	prefix to numbered series issued by Office of Supersonic Transport Division, Federal Aviation Agency (USA) (now Federal Aviation Administration (USA))
	Safe-Secure Trailer road vehicle
	Saw-Tooth Technique
	Sea-Surface Temperature
	Shortest Service Time
	Society of Surveying Technicians
	Space Selector Terminal
	Special Surface Target (Torpedo)
	Supersonic Transport
SSTC	Space Science and Technology Centre (of ISRO (India))
SSTDMA	Space-craft-Switched Time Division Multiple Access
SSTF	Southern Science and Technology Forum
SSTM	Solid State Target Monoscope
SSTO	Single-Stage-To-Orbit
SSTP	Supersonic Transport Panel (of ICAO)
SSTR	Solid-State Track Recorder
SSTS	Sight Switch Technology System
SSTT	Subsea Test Tree
SSTV	Sea-Skimming Test Vehicle
	Slow-Scan Television
SSU	Sangamon State University (USA)
	Semiconductor Storage Unit
	Stratospheric Sounding Unit
SSV	Semi-submersible Support Vessel
	Submarine Support Vessel
SSVE	Subacute Spongiform Virus Encephalopathies
SSW	Surface-to-Surface Warfare
SSWG	Solar System Working Group (of European Space Agency)
SSXBT	Sippican Submarine Launched Expendable Bathythermograph
st	prefix to series issued by Standards Division of the National Physical Laboratory (DOI)
ST	Scintillation Telescope
	Select Time
	Soft Technology
	Space Telescope (a project of NASA (USA))
	Staphylococcal Toxin
ST/CES	prefix to numbered Statistical Standards and Studies issued by the Conference of European Statisticians (UNO)
STA	Sail Training Association
	Science and Technology Agency (Japan)
	Service Technique de l'Aeronautique (France) (government establishment for Aerospace Quality Control and Specifications)
	Skillcentre Training Agency (of Manpower Services Commission)
	Solar Trade Association
	Solution Treat and Aged
	Space Shuttle Training Aircraft
	Supersonic Tunnel Association (USA)
STAAS	Surveillance and Target Acquisition Aircraft System
STABE	Second-Time-Around-Beacon-Echo
STAC	Sensor Transmitter Automatic Choke
	SHELL (UK OIL) Terminal Automation Computerization
STACO	Standing Committee for the Scientific Principles of Standardization (of ISO)
STACOM	Standard Airborne Computer
STACS	Satellite Telemetry And Computer System
STADAN	Satellite Tracking and Data Acquisition Network (of NASA)
STAe	Service Technique Aeronautique (of DTCA (France))
STAE	Second-Time-Around-Echoes
STAF	Scientific and Technological Applications Forecast
STAFF	Smart Target Activated Fire and Forget
	Stellar Acquisition Flight Feasibility
STAG	Simultaneous Telemetry Acquisition and Graphics
	Strategy and Tactics Analysis Group (US Army)

STAGG Small Turbine Advanced Gas Generator
STAGING Structural Analysis via Generalized Interactive Graphics
STAGS S-TANK (fighting vehicle) Agility and Survivability
STAI SPIELBERGER (C)State-Trait Anxiety Inventory
State-Trait Anxiety Inventory
STAIR Structural Analysis Interpretative Routine
STAIRS Storage And Information Retrieval System
STALAS Stationary Laser
STALO Stable Local Oscillator
STALOC Self-Tracking Automatic Lock-on Circuit
STAM Statistical Analogue Monitor
Submarine Tactical Attack Missile
STAMO Stable Master Oscillator
STAMP Sight, Thermal, Armoured, Periscopic
Small Tactical Aerial Mobility Platform
Statistics of Acoustic Measurements and Predictions
STAN Standard OR Standardisation
Statistical Analysis
Sum Total And Nosegear
STAN-CS Stanford University, Department of Computer Science (USA)
STAN-SIG Special Interest Group on Standards (of ATSU (USA))
STANAG Standardization Agreement (of NATO)
STANAGS Standards issued by MAS (of NATO)
STANAV- FORCHAN Standing Naval Force Channel (of NATO)
STANAV- FORLANT Standing Naval Force Atlantic (of ACLANT (NATO))
STANO Surveillance and Target Acquisition for Night Operations
STANSIT Working Group on Methods of Obtaining Statistics on Non-scheduled Air Transport (of European Civil Aviation Conference)
STAO Science Teachers Association of Ontario (Canada)
STAP Statistical Panel (of ICAO)
STAPL Ship Tethered Aerial Platform
STAPP Short-Term Anxiety-Provoking Psychotherapy
STAPRC Scientific and Technical Association of the People's Republic of China
STAQUAREL International Conference on the Application of Statistical Methods in Quality and Reliability Control
STAR Satellite for Telecommunications, Applications and Research (a consortium of European Companies)
Saudi Technology and Research Consulting Centre (Saudi Arabia)
Scan Tailored Antenna/Radome
Scientific and Technical Aerospace Report (of NASA)
Self-Testing And Repairing computer
Sequential Talking Audio Response
Shell Transient Asymmetric Response
Ship Tactical Airborne Remotely Piloted Vehicle
Ship Tended Acoustic Relay system
Simple Test Approach for Readability
Single Tube Automatic Routing
Solicitors' Trust Account Rules 1975
Speed Through Air Re-supply
Standard Tantalum Active Resonator
Standard Terminal Arrival Route
Standard Transistory Array
Star and Stellar Systems Advisory Committee (of ESRO)
String and Array data
String Array processor
Systems for Telephone Administrative Response
STAREC Societe Technique d'Application et de Recherche Electronique (France)
STARPAHC Space Technology Applied to Rural Papago (an Indian Reservation in Arizona (USA)) ADVANCED HEALTH CARE
STARS Silent Tactical Attack Reconnaissance System
SPERRY Three Axis Reference System
Standard Time And Rate Setting
STARS Status Revision System
START Spacecraft Technology and Advanced Re-entry Tests
Spacecraft Technology And Re-entry Tests
Strategic Arms Reduction Talks (between USA and USSR)
System of Transportation Applying Rendezvous Technology
STARTS Software Tools for Application to large Real-Time Systems
STARUTE Stabilization and Retardation Parachute
STASS Submarine Towed Array Sensor System
STATE Simplified Tactical Approach and Terminal Equipment
Statistical Analysis in a Transmission Environment
STATEC Service Central de la Statistique et des études Économiques (Luxembourg) (Statistical and Economic Studies Central Service)
STATICE Statistics in the COMPUTERLINE Environment
STATOIL State Oil Company (Norway)
STATPAC Statistical Package (of United States Geological Survey)
STATPK Statistical Package
STATREP Statistical Reporting system (US Marine Corps)
STATSIM Statistical Simulation
STATUS Statute Search (of UKAEA)
Subscriber Traffic and Telephone Utilisation System
STAX Scientific Tax Assessing system
STB prefix to dated-numbered series of Technical Bulletins issued by NPTRL (USN)
Singapore Telephone Board (Singapore)
Swansea Tribology Centre (of University College of Swansea)
STC Satellite Test Center (USAF)
Scientific and Technical Committee (of ESRO)
Sensitivity-Time-Control
SHAPE Technical Centre
Short-Title Catalogue
Society for Technical Communication (USA)
Solar Thermal Commission
Solid Tantalum Capacitor
Sound Transmission Class
State Trading Corporation (India)
State Trading Corporation (Tanzania) (now BIT)
System Test Complex
STCAN Service Technique des Constructions et Armes Navales (France)
STCAU Service Technique Central d'Amenagement et d'Urbanisme (France) (Central Technical Department for Regional and Town Planning (of the Ministry of Capital Equipment and Housing)
STCM Supersonic Tactical Cruise Missile
STD Salinity Temperature Depth
Semiconductor on Thermoplastic on Dielectric
Sexually Transmitted Diseases
Sodium Tetradecyl Sulphate
Solid Track Detector
Standard
Stream Tree Data
Subscriber Toll Dialling
Subscriber Trunk Dialling
Superconductive Tunnelling Device
STDM Synchronous Time-Division Multiplexing
STDMA Space–Time–Division Multiple Access

STDS Set-Theoretic Data Structure
STDSD Solar-Terrestrial Data Services Division (of NGSDC (EDS) (NOAA) (usa))
STE Societe Francaise des Telephones Ericsson (France)
Streptococcal Esterases
Syrian Telecommunication Establishment (Syria)
STE/ICE Simplified Test Equipment for Internal Combustion Engines
STEAM Schema Tuning, Evaluation and Analytical Model
Stochastic Evolutionary Adoption Model
STEC Solar to Thermal Energy Conversion
Storage and Transport of Explosives Committee (Ministry of Defence (India))
STECC Scottish Technical Education Consultative Council
STEDI Space Thrust Evolution and Disposal Investigation
STEEL Societe de Travaux d'Electricite et d'Electronique du Languedoc (France)
Structural Engineers Easy Language
STEF Societe des Transports et Entropots Frigorifiques (France)
STEG Simulated Time-base and Echo Generator
STEI Scientific, Technical and Economic Information
STEL Short-Term Exposure Level
STELLA Satellite Transmission Experiment Linking Laboratories (major high energy physics laboratories in Europe)
System Ten European Language Ledger Accounting
STELLAR Star Tracker for Economical Long Life Attitude Reference
STEM Scanning Transmission Electron Microscope
Shaped-Tube Electrolytic Machining
Social/Technological/Economic/Military
Stored Tubular Extensible Member
System Trainer and Exercise Module
STEMS Small Terminal Evasive Missile System
STEP Science Teacher Education Project (sponsored by the Nuffield Foundation)
Service Test and Evaluation Process
Simple Transition Electronic Processing
Space Technology Experiments Platform (of NASA (USA))
Special Temporary Employment Programme (of Manpower Services Commission)
Standard Terminal Programme
Support for Technology Enhanced Productivity (Canada)
System for Test and Plug
System Three Emulation Programme
STEPS Strategy Evaluator and Planning-Production System
STES Seasonal Thermal Energy Storage
STET Societa Finanziaria Telefonica (Italy)
Specialised Technique for Efficient Typesetting
STEVI SPERRY Turbine Engine Vibration Indicating System
STEWS Shipboard Tactical Electronic Warefare System
STEX Static Test and Evaluation Complex (of ISRO (India))
STF Signal Transfer Function
Soluble Thymic Factor
Square Wave Transfer Function
Subjective Transfer Function
Svenska Teknologforeningen (Swedish) (Swedish Technical Association)
STG Schiffbautechnische Gesellschaft (Germany)
STI Scientific and Technical Information
Shear Thinning Index
Statens Teknologiske Institutt (Norway) (Government Technological Institute)
Steel Tank Institute (USA)
Surface Transfer Impedence
STI/SS Scientific and Technical Information Systems and Services
STIA Scientific, Technological and International Affairs (a directorate of NSF (USA))
Simple Theory Including Association
STIBOKA Stichting voor Bodemkartering (Netherlands) (Institute for Soil Survey)
STIC Serum Trypsin Inhibitory Capacity
Stodola In-Core Matrix
STID Scientific and Technical Information Division (of NASA)
STIL Statistical Interpretive Language
STINFO Scientific and Technical Information
STINGS Stellar Inertial Guidance System
STIR Simulator for Transport Instrumentation Research
Surveillance and Target Indication Radar
STISEC Scientific and Technological Information Services Enquiry Committee (of the National Library of Australia (Australia))
STJ Subtropical Jet stream
STL Schottky Transistor Logic
Student Tape Library (administered by RNIB)
STM International Group of Scientific, Technical and Medical Publishers
Scanning Tunneling Microscopy
Short-Term Memory
Supersonic Tactical Missile
STMV Stump-Tailed Macaque Virus
STNA Service Technique de la Navigation Arienne (France)
STO State Topographic Office (of Dept of Transportation (USA))
STOA Solution Treatment and Over Aging
STOC Symposium on Theory Of Computing (sponsored by ACM (USA))
STOIC Systematic Technique Of Incentive Contracting
STOL Short Take-Off and Landing
Systems Test and Operation Language
STOMP Short-Term Off-shore Measurement Programme
STOP Selected Test Optimization Programme
Storage Protection
STOPS Self-contained Tanker Off-loading Pump System
Shipboard Toxicological Operational Protective System
STORADS Site Tactical Optimized Range Air Defence Systems
STORC Self-ferrying Trans-Ocean Rotary-wing Crane
STORE Structures Oriented Exchange
Submersible Temperature and Oxygen Recording Equipment
STORES Syntactic Trace Organized Retrospective Enquiry System
STORET Storage and Retrieval
STOU Super Tractor Oil Universal
STOVL Short Take-Off with Vertical Landing
STP prefix to numbered series of Special Technical Publications issued by ASTM (USA)
Service Time Prediction
Solar-Terrestrial Physics
Source Term Programme
Space Test Program (of USAF, US Army and USN)
Special Trade Passenger ship
Staged Theta-Pinch
Standard Temperature and Pressure
STPC Society of Technical Publications Contractors (now Society of Technical Presentation and Communication)
STPD Standard Temperature and Pressure, Dry
STPG Sequential Test Plan Generator

STPO	Science and Technology Policy Office (of NSF (USA))
STPP	Sodium Tripolyphosphate
STPSS	Space Test Program (USAF, US Army, USN) Standard Spacecraft
STPTC	Standardization of Tar Products Test Committee
STRAC	Stratospheric Research Advisory Committee (of DOE)
STRACS	Surface Traffic Control System
STRAD	Signal Transmission Reception and Distribution
STRAIN	Structural Analysis-Interactive
STRAP	Stellar Tracking Rocket Attitude Positioning
	Strategic Actions Planner
STRAT-X	Strategic Exercise
STRATCOM	Strategic Communications Command (US Army) (now Communications Command)
	Stratospheric-Composition (a program of four government agencies, ten government laboratories and private industry in the USA)
STRATUM	Stratified Thermosphere Research at the University of Michigan (USA)
STRAW	Strategic Air War game
STRC	Scientific, Technical and Research Commission (of Organization of African Unity) (Nigeria)
STREAK	Surfaces Technology Research in Energetics, Atomistics, and Kinetics (a discussion group of Dept of Metallurgy and Materials, City of London Polytechnic)
STREAM	Standard Tensioned Replenishment Alongside Method
STRESS	Structural Engineering System Solver
STRIM	Societe Technique de Recherches Industrielles et Mecanique (France)
STRIP	Strategic Intermediate Planner
STRIPE	Stress Induced Pseudoelasticity
STRN	Standard Technical Report Number
STROBES	Shared-Time Repair Of Big Electronic Systems
STROP	Stock Ratio Optimizing
	Strategic Optimizing Planner
STRS	Stimulated Thermal Rayleigh Scattering
STRUDL	Structural Design Language
STRUMS	Structural Modelling System
STS	Consorzio per Sistemi di Telecomunicazioni via Satelliti (Italy)
	Satellite Tracking Section (of Royal Observatory, Edinburgh)
	Satellite Transit System (for transporting passengers round an airport)
	Selective Two-Step
	Sequential Transistor Switch
	Space Transportation System
	Stimulated Thermal Scattering
	Surface-to-Surface
STT	Single-Transition-Time
STTA	Service Technique des Telecommunications de l'Air (France)
STTL	Schottky Transistor-Transistor Logic
STU	Styrelsen for Teknisk Utveckling (Sweden) (Board for Technical Development)
	Submersible Test Unit
STUC	Scottish Trade Union Congress
STUD	Standard Tractor, Universal with Dozer
STUFF	System To Uncover Facts Fast
STUFT	Ship Taken Up From Trade (merchant ship requisitioned for military use)
STUMOKA	Studiekring voor Moderne Kantoortechniek (Netherlands) (Study Group for Modern Office Practice)
STUMP	Submersible, Transportable Utility, Marine Pump
STUMPS	Self Testing using MISR and a Parallel Shift register sequence generator
STUVA	Studiengesellschaft fur Interidische Verkehrarlagen (Germany) (Research Association for Vehicle Tunnels)
STV	Steerable Low Light Level Television
	Subscription Television
	Surveillance Television
STVP	Salinity, Temperature, Sound-Velocity and Pressure-sensing system
STW	Stichting voor de Technische Wetenschappen (Netherlands)
STWP	Society of Technical Writers and Publishers (USA)
STWS	Shipborne Torpedo Weapon System
STZL	Stabilized Transverse Zeeman Laser
SU	Sonics and Ultrasonics
	Stanford University (USA)
	Syracuse University (USA)
SU-DMS	Stanford University, Department of Materials Science (USA)
SU-IPR	Stanford University—Institute for Plasma Research (USA)
SU-SEL	Stanford University, Stanford Electronics Laboratories (USA)
SUA	Serum Uric Acid
SUAWACS	Soviet Union Airborne Warning and Control System
SUB-ICE	Submerged Ice Cracking Machine
SUBAD	Submarine Air Defence
SUBDIZ	Submarine Defence Identification Zone
SUBIC	Submarine Integrated Circuit
subIRS	Submarine Installed Radiac Systems
SUBROC	Submarine to Submarine Combat Rocket
SUBTIL	Synthesized User Based Terminology Index Languages
SUBTRAP	Submersible Training Platform
SUC	Society of University Cartographers
SUCC	Succinate
SUCE	Scottish Universities Council on Entrance
SUCESU	Sociedade de Usuarios de Computadores Eletronicos e Equipmentos Subsidiaros (Brazil) (Society of Users of Electronic Computers and Ancillary Equipment)
SUCP	Societe des Usines Chimiques de Pierrelatte (France)
SUDAAR	Stanford University, Division of Aeronautics and Astronautics (USA)
SUEDE	Surface Evaluation and Definition
SUERF	Société Universitaire Européenne de Recherches Fiancières (European University Society of Financial Research)
SUFFER	System Utility Facility For Easy Recovery
SUGAR	SYDNEY UNIVERSITY Giant Airshower Recorder
SUHL	SYLVANIA Ultrahigh Level Logic
SUIC	Salford University Industrial Centre
SUIPR	Stanford University Institute for Plasma Research (USA)
SUIS	Ship Upkeep Information System (MOD(N))
SUIT	Sight, Unit, Infantry, Trilux
SULIRS	Syracuse University Libraries Information Retrieval System (USA)
SULIS	SULZER Literature distribution and Sorting
SUM	School of Underwater Medicine (Royal Australian Navy)
	Shallow Underwater Missile
	Shallow Underwater Mobile
	Surface-to-Underwater Missile
	System Utilization Monitor
SUMAC	Sheffield University Metals Advisory Centre
SUMC	Space Ultrareliable Modular Computer

SUMED an oil pipeline from Ain Sokna on the Gulf of Suez to Sidi Kreir, west of Alexandria in Egypt
SUMEX STANFORD UNIVERSITY Medical Experimental computer
SUMIT Standard Utility Means for Information Transformation
SUMMAC STANFORD UNIVERSITY (USA) Modified Marker and Cell method
SUMRSA Sulphamerazine Salicylaldimine
SUMS SPERRY/UNIVAC Material System
SUMT Sequential Unconstrained Minimization Technique
SUMTSA Sulphamethazine Salicylaldimine
SUN Scientific Users of 1900s (computers)
Solar Astronomy and General Astronomy Advisory Committee (of ESRO)
SUNAMAM Superintendencia Nacional da Marinha Mercante (Brazil) (National Controller of the Mercantile Marine)
SUNI Southern Universities Nuclear Institute (South Africa)
SUNS Sonic Underwater Navigation System
SUNY State University of New York (USA)
SUNY-BCN State University of New York (USA) Biomedical Communication Network
SUNYA State University of New York at Albany (USA)
SUNYAB State University of New York at Buffalo (USA)
SUP Solid Urethane Plastic
SUPARCO Space and Upper Atmosphere Research Committee (Pakistan)
SUPARS Syracuse University (USA) PSYCHOLOGICAL ABSTRACTS Retrieval Service
SUPPS Regional Supplementary Procedures (series issued by ICAO)
SUPROX Successive Approximation
SURA Southeastern Universities Research Association (USA)
SURCAL Surveillance Calibration
SURE Safeguards Upgrade Rule Evaluation
SURF Support of User Records and Files
SURFAIR International Congress on Surface Treatments in the Aerospace Industry
SURFED Surface Editor
SURGE Colorado State University Research in Graduate Education system (USA)
SURI Syracuse University Research Institute (USA)
SURRC Scottish Universities Research and Reactor Centre
SURRD Southern Utilization Research and Development Division (USDA)
SURSEM Surveillance Radar Systems Evaluation Model
SURTASS Surveillance Towed Array Sonar System
SURV Standard Underwater Research Vehicle
Surface Viewing
SURVSATCOM Survivable Satellite Communication
SUS Signal Underwater Sound
SUSIE Sequential Unmanned Scanning and Indicating Equipment
Stock Updating Sales Invoicing Electronically
Surface/Underwater Ship Intercept Equipment
SUSSP Scottish Universities Summer School in Physics
SUSTA Southern United States Trade Association (USA)
SUT Sandvik-Universal Tube GmbH (Germany) (a company shared by Federal Republic of Germany, the United States of America and France)
Society of Underwater Technology
Surface and Underwater Target (Torpedo)
SUTARS Search Unit Tracking And Recording System
SV Selector Vision
Slope and Voltage
Stifterverband fur die Deutsche Wissenschaft (Germany) (Donors' Association for Promoting Arts and Sciences)
SVA Schweizerische Vereinigung für Atomenergie (Switzerland) (Swiss Association for Atomic Energy)
Slowly Varying Absorption
SVB Supraventricular Bradycardia
SVC Society of Vacuum Coaters (USA)
SVD Singular Value Decomposition
Swine Vesicular Disease
SVEAG Sullom Voe (oil terminal in the Shetland Islands) Environmental Advisory Group
SVFR Special Visual Flight Rules
SVIB Strong Vocational Interest Blank
SVIC Shock and Vibration Information Center (of Naval Research Laboratory (USN))
Sociedad Venezolana de Ingeniesos Consultores (Venezuelan Society of Consulting Engineers)
SVIM Sociedad Venezolana de Ingenieros de Minas y Metalurgicos (Venezuela) (Venezuelan Society of Mining and Metallurgical Engineers)
SVLA Steered Vertical-Line Array
SVLT Schweizerischer Verband für Landtechnik (Switzerland) (Swiss Association for Agricultural Technology)
SVMIU Associazione Italiana per lo Sviluppo della Ricerca nelle Macchine Utensili (Italy) (Association for the Development of Machine Tool Research)
SVOR Schweizerische Vereinigung fur Operations Research (Switzerland) (Swiss Society for Operations Research)
SVP Sound Velocity Profile
SVR Slant Visual Range
Soluble Viral Extract
SVS Society for Vascular Surgery (USA)
Suspended Vehicle System
Sveriges Standardisering-kommission (Sweden) (Standards Institute)
SVSF Sveriges Vetenskapliga Specialbiblioteks Forening (Sweden)
SVTL Services Valve Test Laboratory (MOD)
SVTP Sound Velocity, Temperature and Pressure
SW prefix to numbered-letter series of publications on Solid Waste Management issued by EPA (USA)
Stud Welding
SWA Single Wire Armoured
Steel Window Association
SWAAT Sea-Water Acetic Acid Test
SWAC Specification Writers Association of Canada (Canada)
STANDARDS Western Automatic Computer (NBS USA))
SWALCAP South West Academic Libraries Co-operative Automation Project
SWAMI Soft-Ware Aided Multi-font Input
SWAP Selective Wide Area Paging
Society for WANG Applications and Programmes (USA)
Stress Wave Analysing Programme
Switching Assembly Programme
SWAPS Standing-Wave Acoustic Parametric Source
SWAT Special Weapons and Tactics Team
Squad Weapons Analytical Trainer
Stress Wave Analytical Technique
Switching and Automata Theory
SWATH Small Waterplane Area Twin Hull
Small-Wetted-Area Twin-Hull
SWATHS Small Waterplane Area Twin Hull Ship
SWATT Simulator for Wire-guided Anti-tank Tactical Training

SWBM Still Water Bending Moments

SWC Signals Warfare Center (of ERADCOM (US Army))
Skywave Correction
Soil and Water Conservation Research Division (of Agricultural Research Service (USDA))
Submerged Work Chamber
Submersible Work Chamber

SWCD Solar Wind Composition Detector

SWCE Solar Wind Composition Experiment

SWD Surface-Wave Device

SWDL Surface Wave Delay Line

SWE Society of Women Engineers (USA)
Stress Wave Emission

SWEAT Student Work Experience And Training

SWEB South Wales Electricity Board

SWECS Small Wind Energy Conversion System

SWEPRO Swedish Committee on Trade Procedures (Sweden)

SWER Single Wire Earth Return

SWET Simulator for Electronic Warfare Training

SWF Short Wave Fade-out

SWIEEECO Southwestern IEEE Conference and Exhibition (USA)

SWIFS Surface Wave Integratable Filters

SWIFT Selected Words In Full Title
Society for Worldwide Inter-bank Financial Telecommunication
Society for Worldwide Interchange of Financial Transactions
Software Implemented FRIDEN Translator

SWIFT LASS Signal Word Index of Field and Title, Literature Abstract Specialised Search

SWIFT SIR Signal Word Index of Field and Title, Scientific Information Retrieval

SWIM Surface Wave Interference Modulator

SWIMS Surface Wind Monitoring System

SWIPE Simulated Weapon Impact Predicting Equipment

SWIR Short Wave Infra-red

SWIRL South Western Industrial Research Limited (an R & D company set up by Bath University)

SWIRS Solid Waste Information Retrieval System (of EPA (USA))

SWISSAIR Schweizerische Luftverkehr AG (Switzerland)

SWISSCOM joint export association of a group of Swiss telecommunication firms (Switzerland)

SWISSPRO Swiss group on the Simplification of International Trade Procedures (Switzerland)

SWL Signals Warfare Laboratory (US Army)
Strategic-Weapons Launcher

SWLA Southwestern Library Association (USA)

SWM Standards, Weights and Measures Division (of Dept of Prices and Consumer Protection)

SWMO Solid Waste Management Office (of EPA (USA))

SWMPO Solid Waste Management Programs Office (of EPA (USA))

SWOA Scottish Woodland Owners Association

SWOPS Single-Well Offshore Production System

SWOPSI STANFORD UNIVERSITY (USA) Workshops on Social and Political Issues

SWORCC Southwestern Ohio Regional Computer Center (of University of Cincinnati and Miami University, Ohio (USA))

SWORD Strike and Weapons Ordnance Delivery

SWORDS South Wales Operational Research Discussion Society
Standard Work Order Recording and Data System

SWP Society of Wireless Pioneers (USA)
Synthetic Wood Pulp

SWPA Steel Works Plant Association

SWPF Short Wave Pass Filter

SWR Spin Wave Resonance
Standing-Wave Ratio

SWRA Stepwise Regression Analysis

SWRHL Southwestern Radiological Health Laboratory (of PHS (USA))

SWRI Southwest Research Institute (USA)

SWRI-AR Southwest Research Institute, Department of Automotive Research (USA)

SWRSIC Southern Water Resources Scientific Information Center (of University of North Carolina and North Carolina State University (USA))

SWS Saturn Workshop
Slow-Wave Sleep
Solar Wind Spectrometer

SWT School of Welding Technology (of the Welding Institute)

SWTL Surface-Wave Transmission Lines

SWU Separative Work Unit

SWULSCP South West University Libraries Systems Cooperation Project (now SWALCAP)

SWURCC South West Universities Regional Computer Centre

SWWA South West Water Authority

SX Sheet Explosive
Starch Xanthide

SXBT Shipboard Expendable Bathythermograph

SXS Soft X-ray Spectroscopy

SYBAN Syndicat Belge d'Assurances Nucleaires (Belgium)

SYBELEC Syndicat Belge d'Etudes et de Recherches Electroniques (Belgium) (Belgian Union for Electronics Study and Research)

SYBESI Syndicat Belge pour le Separation Isotopique (Belgium)

SYBETRA Syndicat Belge d'Entreprises a l'Etranger (Belgium)

SYCOM Synchronous Communications

SYCOMOM Syndicat des Constructeurs Belge de Machines outils pour le Travail des Metaux (Belgium)

SYMAP Symbol Manipulation Programme
Synagraphic Mapping

SYMATEX Syndicat des constructeurs Belges de Machines Textiles (Belgium)

SYMBIOSIS System for Medical and Biological Sciences Information Searching (of SUNY (USA))

SYMBOL System for Mass Balancing On/Off Line

SYMBUG Symbolic Debugging

SYMES Systematic Machinery and Equipment Selection

SYMPLE Syntax Macro Preprocessor for Language Evaluation

SYMRAP Symbolic Reliability Analysis Programme

SYMTAB Symbol Table

SYNAME Syndicat National de la Mesure Electrique et Electronique (France)

SYNCON Synergistic Convergence
Syntax Conversion language

SYNGAS Synthesis Gas

SYNROC Synthetic Rock

SYNSPADE Symposium on the Numerical Solution of Partial Differential Equations

SYNTOL Syntagmatic Organization of Language

SYP Society of Young Publishers

SYQI System Image Quality Indicator

SYSCAP System of Circuit Analysis Programmes

SYSEX System Executive

SYSNA Societe des Systemes d'Aides a la Navigation (France)

SYSTID System Time-Domain Simulation programme

SYSTIM Systematic Interaction Model

SYSTRAN Systems Analysis Translator

SYTA Sustained-Yield Tropical Agroecosystem
SZ Streptozotocin
SZA Solar Zenith Angle
SZF Schweizerische Vereinigung für Zukunftsforschung (Swiss Association for Futures Research)
SZL Serum Zinc Levels
SZR Sodium-cooled, Zirconium-hydride-moderated Reactor

T

T prefix to numbered–dated series of Tubes standards issued by BSI
Transactions
Translation
T&E Test and Evaluation
T&RI Training and Research Institue (of the American Foundrymen's Society (USA))
T-PEES Triplane Elevated Evaluation System (a test facility of MICOM (USArmy))
T/AM prefix to numbered series of reports issued by Department of Theoretical and Applied Mechanics, University of Illinois (USA)
T/EL Test and Evaluation Laboratory (of National Weather Service (NOAA) (USA))
TA prefix to numbered:dated series of Titanium and Titanium Alloys standards issued by BSI
Technology Assessment
Terephthalic Acid
Training Adviser
Transactional Analysis
Transition Altitude
Turbulence Amplifier
TAA Temporary Assistance Authority (Australia)
The Aluminum Association (USA)
Thioacetic Acid
Trans-Australia Airlines (Australia)
Transportation Association of America (USA)
TAABS The Army Automated Budget System (US Army)
TAAC Technology Assessment Advisory Council (of OTA (USA))
TAADS The Army Authorized Document System (US Army)
TAAM Terminal Area Altitude Monitoring
Tomahawk Airfield Attack Missile
TAAS Three Axis Attitude Sensor
TAASA Tool And Alloy Steels Association (India)
TAB Technical Abstract Bulletin
Technical Activities Board (of IEEE)
Technical Analysis Branch (of USAEC)
Technology Assessment Board (of OTA (US Congress))
Title Annoucement Bulletin
TAB VEE Theater Air Base Vulnerability
TABA Transportes Aereas de Buenos Aires (Argentine)
TABL Tropical Atlantic Biological Laboratory (of Bureau of Commercial Fisheries (USA)
TABS Tactical Airborne Beacon System
TABSAC Targets and Backgrounds Signature Analysis Center (University of Michigan (USA))
TABTRAN Table Translator
TAC Tactical Air Command (USAF)
Target Acquisition Center (of ERADCOM (US Army))
Technical Advisory Committee (of CGIAR)
Telemetry And Command
Television Advisory Committee (of the Ministry of Posts and Telecommunications)
Terrain Analysis Center (of ETL (US Army))
Thyristor-Assisted Commutation
Time Analysis Computer
Time-to-Amplitude Converter
Transistorised Automatic Computer
Trapped Air Cushion
Turbo-Alternator-Compressor
TAC3 Target Recognition and Attack Multisensor, Automatic Carrier Landing System, Carrier Airborne Inertial Navigation System, Condor air-to-surface stand-off missile, Communication-Navigation-Identification (ie, TRAM, ACLS, CAINS, CONDOR, CNI)
TACAIR Tactical Airpower
TACAN Tactical Air Navigation
TACASA Tactical ADP Support System of the Army Security Agency (US Army)
TACB Texas Air Control Board (USA)
TACC Tactical Air Control Centre
Technology Assessment Consumerism Centre
TACCAR Time Average Clutter Coherent Airborne Radar
TACDA The American Civil Defense Association (USA)
TACDACS Acquisition Data Collection System
TACDEN Tactical Data Entry Device
TACDEPO The Association of Civil Defence and Emergency Planning Officers
TACDEW Tactical Advanced Combat Direction and Electronic Warfare
TACE Turbine Automatic Control Equipment
TACED Tank-Appended, Crew Evaluation Device
TACELIS Transportable Emitter Location and Identification System
TACELRON Tactical Electronic warfare
TACFIRE Tactical Fire direction system
TACIT Time Authenticated Cryptographic Identity Transmission
TACJAM Tactical Jammer OR Jamming
TACLAN Tactical Landing system
TACLAND Tactical Landing
TACMA The Association of Control Manufacturers
TACMAR Tactical Multifunction Array Radar
TACMOD Tactical Modular Display
TACNAV Tactical Navigation
TACODA Target Coordinate Data
TACOL Thinned Aperture Computed Lens
TACOM Tank-Automotive Command (US Army) (in 1976 split into Tank-Automotive Materiel Readiness Command and Tank-Automotive Research and Development Command)
TACOM EWS Tactical Communications Electronic Warfare System
TACOMS Tactical Communications
TACOMSAT Tactical Communications Satellite
TACOR Threat Assessment and Control Receiver
TACOS Tactical Airborne Countermeasures or Strike (a project of the USAF)
TACPOL Tactical Procedure Oriented Language
TACRAC Tactical Warfare Research Advisory Committee (of government, industry and Armed Forces (US
TACRAV Tracked Air Cushion Research Vehicle
TACRV Tracked Air Cushion Research Vehicle
TACS Traditional Acupuncture Society
TACS Tactical Air Control System
Television Automatic Control System
Thruster Attitude-Control System
TACSAT Tactical Communications Satellite
TACSATCOM Tactical Satellite Communications
TACSI Tactical Air Control System Improvements
TACT Technological Aids to Creative Thought
Total Audit Concept Technique
Transonic Aircraft Technology

TACTAS Tactical Towed Array Sonar
TACTASS Tactical Towed Array Sonar System
TACTICS Technical Assistance Consortium to Improve College Services (a program of USOE (USA))
TACV Tracked Air Cushion Vehicle
Transport Air Cushion Vehicle
Transportes Aereos de Cabo Verde (Cape Verde Islands)
TACV/LIM Tracked Air Cushion Vehicles powered by Linear Induction Motors
TACW Technische Advies Commissie voor de Waterkeringen (Netherlands) (Technical Advisory Commission for Water Defence) (eg dykes)
TAD Technical Analysis Division (of NBS Institute for Applied Technology (USA))
Traffic Analysis and Display
Transaction Application Driver
TADAR Target Acquisition Designation and Aerial Reconnaissance system
TADDS Target Alert Data Display Set
TADIL Tactical Digital Information Link
TADJET Transport–Airdrop–Jettison
TADS Tactical Air Defence System
Tactical Automatic Digital Switches
Target Acquisition and Direction System
Target and Activity Display System
Target-Acquisition Designation System
Throw Away Detectors
Transportable Automatic Digital Switches
TADSS Tactical Automatic Digital Switching System
TAE Turkiye Atom Enerjisi Kurumu (Turkey) (Turkish Atomic Energy Commission)
TAEB Technology Assessment and Evaluation (of EPA (USA))
TAEC Thai Atomic Energy Commission for Peace (Thailand)
TAEG Training Analysis and Evaluation Group (USN)
TAERS The Army Equipment Record System (US Army)
TAF Target Aiming Function
Time And Frequency
Tumor-Angiogenesis Factor
Tumour Antiogenesis Factor
TAFCOM Theatrewide Tactical Fighter Combat Operations Model
TAFI Turn-Around Fault Isolation
TAFIES Tactical Air Forces Intelligence Exploitation System
TAFIIS Tactical Air Forces Integrated Information System
TAFSEG Tactical Air Force Systems Engineering Group (USAF)
TAG Technical Authors Group
Terbium Aliminium Garnet
Terminating And Grounding
Thrust Alleviated Gyroscope
Time Automated Grid system
Towed Acoustic Generator
Trans-Atlantic Geotraverse
Transient Analysis Generator
Tungsten-Argon Gas
TAGA Technical Association of the Graphic Arts (USA)
TAGEM Tactical Air-to-Ground Effectiveness Model
TAGER The Association for Graduate Education and Research (USA)
TAGP Transportes Aereos da Guine Portuguesa (Portuguese Guinea)
TAGS Tactical Aircraft Guidance System
Tower Automated Ground Surveillance System
TAIC Tokyo Atomic Industrial Consortium (Japan)
TAID Triallyl Isocyanurate
TAINS TERCOM-Aided Inertial Navigation System
TAIR Terminal Area Instrumentation Radar
TAIS Tactical Air Intelligence System
TAL Tank-Automotive Logistics Command (US Army)
Terminal Application Language
Tetra-alkyl Lead
Trans-Alpine pipeline
Transfer Auto Loader
TALAR Tactical Landing Aid Radio
Tactical Landing Approach Radar
TALC Tank-Automotive Logistics Command (US Army)
TALCAM TUCKER Analysis of Learning Curves And More
TALCM Tactical Air-Launched Cruise Missile
TOMAHAWK Air Launched Cruise Missile
TALIC Tyneside Association of Libraries for Industry and Commerce
TALISMAN Transfer Accounting and Lodgement for Investors, Stock Management for jobbers (of the London Stock Exchange)
TALISSI Tactical Light Shot Simulator
TALK Teletype Access to the Link at KING'S (College, London)
TALMA Truck And Ladder Manufacturers Association
TALMS Tunable Atomic Line Molecular Spectroscopy
TALON Texas, Arkansas, Louisiana, Oklahoma and New Mexico (USA) co-operative library program
TALONS Tactical Airborne LORAN Navigation System
TALUS Transportation And Land Use Study
TAM Task Analysis Method
Telephone Answering Machine
Terminal Access Method
The Access Method
The Assistant Mathematician
Towed Acoustic Monitor
Traction Asynchronous Motor
Trajectory Application Method
Transportes Aereo Militar (Paraguay) (Transport Branch of the Military Air Force)
Transportes Aeros Militares (Bolivia) (an arm of FAeB (Bolivia))
TAMA Training Aids Management Agency (US Army)
TAME Television Automatic Monitoring Equipment
Transportes Aereos Militares Ecuatorianos (Ecuador) (Transport Branch of the Military Air Force)
TAMIRADS Tactical Mid-Range Air Defense Study (USDOD)
TAMIS Telemetric Automated Microbial Identification System
TAMMS The Army Maintenance Management System (US Army)
TAMPA Tender Assist Minimum Platform Arrangement
TAMS Tandem Accelerator Mass Spectrometer
TAMTU Tanzania Agricultural Machinery Testing Unit (Tanzania)
TAMU Texas A and M University (USA)
TAMU-SG prefix to dated-numbered series of reports issued by Texas A and M University (USA) Sea Grant Program
TAMVEC Texas A&M (University (USA)) Variable Energy Cyclotron
TAN Total Acid Number
Transportes Aeros Nacionales (Honduras) (National Air Line)
TANC Total Absorption Nuclear-Cascade
TANESCO Tanzania Electric Supply Company (Tanzania) (State owned)
TANS Tactical Air Navigation System
TAP Task Analysis Procedure
Technology Advisory Point (of DTI)
Time-sharing Accounting Package
Time-sharing Assembly Programme
Transient Analysis Programme
Transplant Advisory Panel (of MRC)
Transportes Aereos Portugueses (Portugal)

TAPA Three-dimensional Antenna Pattern Analyzer
TAPES Transformer Analogue Polynomial Equation Solver
TAPGEN Terminal Applications Programme Generator
TAPIT Tactical Photographic Image Transmission
TAPITS Tactical Airborne Processing, Interpretation and Transmission System
TAPP Tarapur Atomic Power Project (India)
Two Axis Pneumatic Pickup
TAPPI Technical Association of the Pulp and Paper Industry (USA)
TAPS TERCOM Aircraft Positioning System
TEXAS (USA) (HIGHWAY DEPARTMENT) Automated Plotting system
Trajectory Accuracy Prediction System
Trans-Alaska Pipeline System
Transform Adaptable Processing System
TAR Tactical Air Reconnaissance
Terrain Avoidance Radar
Transporte Aereo Rioplatense (Argentina)
TARABS Tactical Air Reconnaissance and Aerial Battlefield Surveillance
TARADCOM Tank-Automotive Research and Development Command (US Army)
TARAN Test and Repair as Necessary
Test And Replace As Necessary
TARC Government/Industry Transport Aircraft Requirements Committee
The Army Research Council (US Army)
TARC-OA Tactical Air Reconnaissance Center, Office of Operations Analysis (USAF)
TARE Telegraph Automatic Relay Equipment
Telemetry Automatic Reduction Equipment
TARENA Tallares de Reparaciones Navales (Argentina)
TAREWS Tactical Air Reconnaissance and Electronic Warfare Support
TARGET Team to Advance Research for Gas Energy
Technical Advisory Group for Energy Thrift (subcommittee of ETC (DOI)
Thermal Advanced Reactor Gas-cooled Exploiting Thorium
Transportation (a project supported by a member of public utility companies in the USA)
TARIF Technical Apparatus for Rectification of Indifferent Films
Telegraph Automatic Routing In the Field
Telegraph Automating Routing In the Field
TARMOCS The Army Operations Center System (US Army)
TAROM Transporturile Aerienne Romane (Romania) (Romanian National Airline)
TARP Tactical Airborne Recon Pod
Test And Repair Processor
TARPS Tctical Aircraft Reconnaissance Pod System
Transportation Auditing and Reporting System
TARS Terrain And Radar Simulator
Three Axis Reference System
TART Twin Accelerator Ring Transfer
TAS Tetra-Aryl Silicate
Training Abstracts Service (of DEP)
True Air-Speed
TASAMS The Army Supply And Maintenance System (US Army)
TASC Tactical Articulated Swimmable Carrier
Training Assistance in Small Companies (a division of RTITB)
TASCOM Theater Army Support Command (US Army)
TASCS Tactical Air Support Control System
TASDA Tactical Anti-Submarine Decision Aid
TASDC Tank-Automotive Systems Development Center (US Army)
TASES Tactical Airborne Signal Exploitation System
TASI Time Assignment Speech Interpolation
TASIC Thermal Analysis of Substrates and Integrated Circuits
TASIS Texas Chapter of the American Society for Information Science (USA)
TASMAN submarine telephone cable between Australia and New Zealand
TASMO Tactical Air Support of Maritime Operations
TASS Tactical Automatic Switching System
Tactical Avionics System Simulator
Talent Attaction Selection System
Telegravnoye-Agenstvo Sovietskovo Soyuza (USSR) (Telegraphic Agency of the Soviet Union–a news agency)
Towed Array Surveillance System
TASST Tentative Airworthiness Standards for Supersonic Transports (issued by FAA (USA))
TAST Tactical Assault Supply Transport
TASTA The Administrative Support to the Theater Army (US Army)
TAT Tactical Armament Turret
Tanzania-Zambia Railway Authority
Thematic Apperception Test
Thinned Aperture Telescope
Thrusted Augmented THOR
Transatlantic Telephone cable
Tyrosine Amino Transferase
TATAWS Tank, Anti-Tank and Assault Weapons Requirements Study (US Army)
TATB Triaminotrinitrobenzene
TATPAC Trans-Atlantic, Trans-Pacific (telecommunications network linking London, Montreal, New York, Sydney, Hong Kong and Tokyo)
TATS Tactical Transmission System (USAF)
TATSS Tactical Automatic Switching System
TAV Trans-Atmospheric Vehicle (a program of USAF)
TAW Tactical Airlift Wing (USAF)
Thrust Augmented Wing
TAWC Tactical Air Warfare Center (USAF)
TAWDS Tactical Acquisition and Weapon Delivery System
TBA Test-Butyl-Alcohol
Thermobarometric Analysis
Thiobutyric Acid
Torsional Braid Analysis
TBAB Tryptose Blood Agar Base
TBAH Tetrabutyl Ammonium Hydroxide
TBAP Tetrabutylammonium Perchlorate
TBAT TOW-BUSHMASTER (cannon) Armoured Turret
TBAT II TOW Bushmaster Armoured Turret Two-man
TBC Tertiary Butyl Catechol
Thermal Barrier Coating
Transitional Butterworth-Chekyshev filter
TBCF Time-Buffered Coarse-Fine
TBDF Transborder Data Flow
TBE Tetrabromoethane
Tick-borne Encephalitis
Time Base Error
TBEA Truck Body and Equipment Association (USA)
TBFFU Twin-Ball Fire Fighting Unit
TBG Thyroxin Binding Globulin
TBGB Tetrathionate Brilliant Green Broth
TBI Time Between Inspections
TbIG Terbium Iron Garnet
TBIS Tasmanian Bibliographic Information System (Australia)
TBL Transitional Butterworth-Legendre filters
TBM Temporary Bench Mark
Terabit Memory
Theatre (of warfare) Ballistic Missile
Trillion Bit Memory
Trophoblastic Basement Membranes

Tunnel Boring Machine

TBMA Timber Building Manufacturers Association of Great Britain

TBMU Transitional Butterworth Modified Ultraspherical filter

TBN Total Base Number

TBO Time Between Overhaul

TBP Tethered Buoyant Platform
Tetrabenzorphin
Thribatlephosphate
Tri-Butyl Phosphate
Trigonal Bipyramid
True Boiling Point

TBPA Thyroxin Binding Prealbumin
Torso Back Protective Armour

TBPT Total Body Protein Turnover

TBR Treasury Bill Rate

TBRC Top Blown Rotary Convertor

TBS Tanzanian Bureau of Standards (Tanzania)
Tokyo Broadcasting System (Japan)

TBST Triple Bituminous Surface Treatment

TBTM Tributyltin Methacrylate

TBTO Tributyl Tin Oxide

TBU Transitional Butterworth Ultraspherical filter

TBW Time-Bandwidth

TC Taenia Coli
Tariff Commission (USA)
Technical Committee
Tetracycline
Thermo-Current
Thermocouple
Time Constant
Tipping Centre
Total Cholesterol
Tropocollagen

TCA Telecommunications Association (USA)
Tile Council of America (USA)
Time of Closest Approach
Tricarboxylic Acid
Trichloracetic Acid

TCAA Technical Communication Association of Australia (Australia)

TCAC Tone-Count Audiometric Computer

Tcal Teracaloric

TCAM Telecommunications Access Method

TCAR Technical Committee on Automotive Rubber (of SAE and ASTM (usa))

TCARS Test Call Answer Relay Set

TCATA TRADOC Combat Arms Test Agency (US Army)

TCC Technology Consultancy Centre (University of Science and Technology (Ghana))
Telecommunications Corporation (Jordan)
Temperature Coefficient of Capacitance
Thermal Control Coatings
Thermofor Catalytic Cracking
Transfer Channel Control
Transitional Cell Carcinoma
Trichloro-Carbanilide

TCCA Technical Committee on Computer Architecture (of IEEE Computer Society (USA))
Tin Container Collectors Association (USA)
Trichloroisocyanuric Acid

TCCL Transport Co-ordinating Council for London

TCCS TEXACO Controlled Combustion System

TCD Ternary Coded Decimal
Transistor Controlled Delay
Trinity College, Dublin (Eire)

TCDD Tetrachlorodibenzparadioxin
Tower Cab Digital Display
Turkiye Cumhuriyeti Devlet Demiryollari (Turkey) (Turkish State Railways)

TCDP Technical Committee on Distributed Processing (of IEEE Computer Society (USA))

TCE Tetracyanethylene
Tonnes of Coal Equivalent
Trichloroethylene
Trichtoroethanol

TCF Trillion Cubic Feet

TCI Theoretical Chemistry Institute (of Wisconsin University, USA)
Turbulence Controlled Induction

TCL Transfer Chemical Laser
Transparent Conductive Layer

TCM Time-Compression Multiplex

TCMA Tufted Carpet Manufacturers Association (merged into BCMA in 1976)

TCMF Touch-Calling Multi-Frequency

TCML Target Co-ordinate Map Locator

TCMS Tactical Communications Management System

TCNE Tetracyanoethylene

TCNQ Tetracyanoquinidodimethane
Tetracyanoquinodimethane

TCOA Transvaal Coal Owners Association (South Africa)

TCOC Transverse Cylindrical Orthomorphic Chart

TCOM Tethered Communications

TCP Technical Cooperation Programme (between Australia, Canada, United Kingdom and USA)
Technology Coordinating Paper
Tetrachlorophenol
TEXACO Combustion Process
Transmission Control Protocol
Trichlorophenol
Tricresylphosphate
Tropical Canine Pancytopenia

TCPA Tetrachlorophthalic Anhydride
Town and Country Planning Association

TCPLD Tunable Compound Phased-Locked Demodulator

TCQN Tetracyano-quinodimethane

TCR Temperature Coefficient of Resistance

TCRC Telecommunication Research Centre (India)

TCS Targeted Citation Studies
Teaching Company Scheme (of SERC and DTI)
Telemetry and Command Station
Terylene/Cotton Core-spun Canvas
Thermal Control System
Torpedo Control System
Transmission Controlled Spark

TCSA Tetrachlorosalicylanilide

TCSE Technical Committee on Software Engineering (of IEEE Computer Society (USA))

TCSEV Twin-Cushion Surface Effect Vehicle

TCSP Tandem Cross Section Programme

TCSS Technical Committee for Search Systems (of ICIREPAT)

TCST Technical Committee for Standardization (of ICIREPAT)
Trichlorosilanated Tallow

TCT Total Circular Triad
Transverse Current Tube
Two Component Torus
Two-Component Tokamak

TCTS Trans-Canada Telephone System (Canada) (a consortium of eight telecommunications companies)

TCU Teletypewriter Control Unit
Texan Christian University (USA)
The City University (London)

TCV Temperature Control Valve
Terminal Configured Vehicle
Tracked Cushion Vehicle

TCXO Temperature-Compensated Crystal Oscillator

TCZD Temperature Compensated Zener Diode

TD Temperature Differential
Thoracic Duct
Thoria Dispersed
Time-Division
Topographic Division (of USGS (USA))
Tunnel Diode

TDA Tax Deposit Account
Telecommunications Dealers Association (USA)
Tetramethylene Diamine
Trade Development Authority (India)
Transmission and Distribution Association (a section of British Electrical & Allied Manufacturers Association)
Transportation Development Agency (Canada)
Tube Deviation Analyzer
Tunnel Diode Amplifier

TDANA Time-Domain Automatic Network Analyzer

TDaRI Tropical Development and Research Institute (of ODA)

TDAS Tactical Data Automation System

TDB Toxicology Data Bank (of National Library of Medicine (USA))

TDBC Two-Dimensional Bragg Cell

TDC Thermal Diffusion Column
Through-Deck Cruiser
Top Dead Centre

TDCB Tapered Double-Cantilever Beam

TDCC Transporation Data Coordinating Committee (USA)

TDCK Technisch Documentatie -en Informatiecentrum voor de Krijgsmacht (Netherlands) (Defence Technical Documentation and Information Centre)

TDCP Thermally Darkened Photochromic

TDCS Tactical Deployment Control Squadron (USAF)

TDD Target Detection Device
Telecommunications Device for the Deaf

TDDL Time-Division Data Link

TDF Tape Data Family
Two-Degree-of-Freedom

TDHF Time-Dependent Hartree-Fock

TDHS Tactical Data Handling System

TDI Toluene Diisocyanate
Transverse-Differential-Interference

TDL Tactical Data Link
Tapped Delay Line
Technical Development Laboratories (of NCDC (USA))
Techniques Development Laboratory (of the Weather Bureau (USA))
Test and Diagnostic Language
Topographic Developments Laboratory (US Army)

TDLR Terminal Descent Landing Radar

TDM Tertiary Dodecylmercapton
Time Domain Metrology
Time-Division Multiplex

TDMA Time-Division Multiple-Access

TDMG Telegraph and Data Message Generator

TDMS Telegraph Distortion Measurement Set
Time-shared Data Management System

TDN prefix to numbered series of Technical Data Notes issued by the Department of Employment

tDNA Mitochondrial Deoxy-ribonucleic Acid

TDOA/DME Time Difference Of Arrival/Distance Measuring Equipment

TDOL Tetradecanol

TDP Technical Development Plan
Tolyldichlorospophine

TDPAC Time-Differential Perturbed Angular Correlations

TDPI Two-Dimensional Probabilistic Image

TDR Technical Data OR Documentary Report
Time Domain Reflectometer
Time Domain Reflectometry
Time-Delay Relay
Torque Differential Receiver

TDRS Tracking and Data Relay Satellite (of NASA (USA))

TDRSS Tracking and Data Relay Satellite System

TDS Teleprocessing Design Center (of CENTACS (US Army))
Thermal Desorption Spectrometry
Thermal Diffuse Scattering
Third Dimension Society of Great Britain
Time Domain Spectroscopy
Total Dissolved Solids
Transaction Driven System

TDSA Telegraph and Data Signal Analyzer

TDSCC Tidbinbilla Deep Space Communication Complex (Australia)

TDT Target Designation Transmitter

TE Thermo-electric
Tick-borne Encephalitis
Transferred Electron

TEA Tetraethylammonium
Texas Electronics Association (USA)
Thermal Energy Analysis
Transferred Electron Amplifier
Transportation Engineering Agency (US Army)
Transverse Electrical-discharge Atmospheric-pressure
Triethanol Amine
Triethanolamine
Triethylamine
Triethylammonium
Tryethylaluminium
Tunnel-Emission Amplifier

TEADDA TELEDYNE Electrically Alterable Digital Differential Analyzer

TEAL Tactics, Equipment And Logistics
Teesside Automated Library System
Transversely Excited Atmospheric Laser

TEAM Technique for Evaluation and Analysis of Maintainability
Telecommunications, Electronique, Aeronautique et Maritime (France) (a company)
THAMES (CASE LTD.) Evaluation of Alternative Methods
The European-Atlantic Movement
Thermal Energy Atomic and Molecular
Transportable English Access Method
Turning, Evaluation and Analysis Model

TEAM-UP Test, Evaluation, Analysis, and Management Uniformity Plan (US Army)

TEAMS Test Evaluation And Monitoring System
Test of Engineering Aptitude, Mathematics and Science

TEARS Traffic Engineering for Automatic Route Selection

TEAS Time Elapsed After Study
Total Engine Air System

TEBROC Tehran Book Processing Centre (of the Institute for Research and Planning in Science and Education (Iran))

TEBS Time Elapsed Before Study

TEC Technical Escort Center (US Army)
Technician Education Council (became part of BTEC in 1983)
Thermal Energy Converter
Thermionic Energy Conversion
Three-dimensional Epitaxial Crystallites
Total Electron Content

TECE Trans-Europe Container Express

TECH MEMO Technical Memorandum

TECH REPT Technical Report

TECHEVAL Technical Evaluation

TECHINT Technical Intelligence
TECHMEX British Technology Exhibition and Forum
TECHNI- CATOME Société Technique pour l'Énergie Atomique (France)
TECHNICHAR Association pour le Perfectionnement Technique des Appareils Domestiques d'utilisation du Charbon (Belgium) (Association for the Technical Approval of Coal Using Domestic Appliances)
TECHNICOL Association pour le Perfectionnement Technique des Appareils Domestiques d'utilisation des Combustibles Liquides (Belgium) (Association for the Technical Approval of Oil Burning Domestic Appliances)
TECHNION Israel Institute of Technology (Israel)
TECHNONET ASIA Asian Network for Industrial Technology Information and Expansion
TECIMO Technical Conference on Instruments and Methods of Observation (of World Meteorological Organization)
TECOM Test and Evaluation Command (US Army)
TED Threshold Extension Demodulator
Transferred Electron Device
Transferred Electronic Device
Translation Error Detector
Transmission Electron Diffraction
TEDA Triethylenediamine
TEDS Tactical Electronic Decoy System
Tactical Expendable Drone System
TEE Telecommunications Engineering Establishment (of BOT)
Tubular Extendible Element
TEEG Tidal Energy Engineering Group
TEEM Transportable Engineered Environment Module
TEF Theoretical Evaluation of Function
Tilted Electric Field
Total Effective Fare
Transverse Electric Field
TEFA Tube Excited Fluorescence Analyser
TEFC Totally-Enclosed Fan-Cooled
TEFO Textilforskningsinstitutet (Sweden) (Textile Research Institute)
TEFS Transportable Electromagnetic Field Source array
TEG Test Element Group
Thermo-Electric Generator
Thromboelastograph
TEGAS Test Generation and Simulation
TEGDM Tetraethylene-glycoldimethacrylate
TEGDN Triethylene Glycol Dinitrate
TEGI Train-Elevated Guideway Interaction
TEI Technical and Economic Information
Triethylindium
TEIC Tissue Equivalent Ionization Chamber
TEK Turkiye Elektrik Kurumu (Turkey) (Turkish Electricity Authority)
TEL Tetraethyl Lead
Tokyo Electron Laboratories (Japan)
Transporter-Erector-Launcher
TELAN Thermo-Electric for Land use
TELATS Tactical Electronic Locating And Targeting System
TELCO Tata Engineering and Locomotive Company (India)
TELCOR Direccion General de Telecomunicaciones y Correos (Nicaragua)
TELEBRAS Telecomunicacoes Brasilleiras SA (Brazil)
TELECOM Empresa Nacional de Telecommunicaciones (Colombia) (State Telecommunications Authority)
World Telecommunication Exhibition
TELECOM AUSTRALIA Australian Telecommunications Commission (Australia)
TELECOMS Telecommunication Authority of Singapore (Singapore)
TELEMIG Telecomunicacoes de Minas Gerais SA (Brazil)
TELEX Teleprinter Exchange
TELI Technisch-Literarische Gesellschaft (Germany) (Technical Literature Association)
TELL Teacher-aiding Electronic Learning Links
TELOPS Telemetry On-Line Processing System
TELSIM Teletypewriter Simulator
TELTIPS Technical Effort Locator and Technical Interest Profile System (US Army)
TELUS Telemetric Universal Sensor
TEM Transient Electromagnetic
Transmission Electron Microscope
Transverse Electric and Magnetic field
Transverse Electro-Magnetic
TEMA Telecommunication Engineering and Manufacturing Association
Tubular Exchanger Manufacturers Association (USA)
TEMANS Tactical Effectiveness of Minefields in the Anti-armour Weapons System
TEMAR Thermo-Electric Marine application
TEMARS Transportation Environment Measuring And Recording System
TEMMA Transmission Electron Microscopy and Microprobe Analysis
TEMPER Technological, Economic, Military, Political Evaluation Routine
TEMPO Technical Military Planning Operation
TEMPS Transportable Electro-Magnetic Pulse Simulator
TEMS Turbine Engine Monitoring System
TEN Toxic Epidermal Necrolysis
Trans-Europ-Night
TENIS Technological Needs Identification Studies (of USN)
TEO Transferred Electron Oscillator
TEOM Tapered Element Oscillating Microbalance
TEOS Tetraethyl Orthosilicate
TEOSS Tactical Emitter Operational Support System (a project of USAF)
TEP Thermo-Electric Power
Transparent Electro-photographic Process
Transparent Electro-Photography
TEPA Tetra-ethylene Pentamine
TEPC Tissue Equivalent Proportional Counter
TEPG Thermionic Electrical Power Generator
TEPIAC Thermophysical and Electronic Properties Information Analysis (of CINDAS (USA))
TEPIGEN Computer-controlled Television Picture Generation system
TEPOP Tracking Error Propagation and Orbit Prediction Programme
TEPP Tetraethyl Pyrophosphate
TEPPS Technique for Establishing Personnel Performance Standards
TEPRSSC Technical Electronic Products Radiation Safety Standards Committee (USA)
TER Transmission Equivalent Resistance
Transverse Electro-Reflectance
Triple Ejection Rack
TERA Total Energy Resource Analysis
TERCO Telephone Rationalisation by Computer
TERCOM Terrain Contour Matching Guidance System
Terrain Correlation Matching
TEREC Tactical Electronic Reconnaissance
TERLS Thumba Equatorial Rocket Launching Station (of INCOSPAR)
Thumba Equatorial Rocket Launching Station (of ISRO (India))
TERMS Terminal Management System (DOD (USA))

TERN Terminal and En-Route Navigation
TERP Terrain Elevation Retrieval Programme
Turbine Engine Reliability Programme
TERPES Tactical Electronic Reconnaissance Processing and Evaluation System
TERPS Terminal Enquiry/Response Programming System
Terminal Procedures
TES Temporary Employment Subsidy
Thermal Energy Storage
TESA Television Electronics Service Association (Canada)
TESAT Teaching Sample Tables
TESE Tactical Exercise Simulator and Evaluator
TESG Telex Equipment Suppliers Group
TESLA Committee on Technical Standards for Library Automation (of the American Library Association Automation Division (USA))
TESSAR Test Event Sequencing, Simulating and Recording system
TEST Technical Evaluation of Solid-State Technologies
Thesaurus of Engineering and Scientific Terms
Transport and Environment Studies (an independent research and consultancy group)
TESY Terminal Editing System
TET Turbine Entry Temperature
TETA Triethylenetetramine
TETAM Tactical Effectiveness Testing of Antitank Guided Missiles (a project of the US Army)
TETD Tetraethyl Thiuran Disulphide
TETJC Tribology Education and Training Joint Committee (secretariat provided by IMechE)
TETMTU Tetramethyl Thiourea
TETOC Technical Education and Training for Overseas Countries (of the British Council)
TETR Test and Training satellite
TETRA Terminal Tracking telescope
TETWOG Aircraft Turbine Engine Testing Working Group (USA)
TEUR Tariffs-Europe (a joint working party of CCITT)
TEUREM CCITT Regional Tariff Group for Europe and the Mediterranean Basin
TEWA Threat Evaluation and Weapon Aiming
TEWAC Totally Enclosed All-Water-Cooled
TEWDS Tactical Electronic Warfare Defence System
TEWS Tactical Electronic Warfare System
Tactical Electronic Warfare Suite (in a military aircraft)
Tactical Electronic Warfare Support
TEWTS Tactical Exercises Without Troops
TEX Temperature Excess
TEXCO National Textile Corporation (Tanzania)
TEXTEL Trinidad and Tobago External Telecommunications Company
TEXTIR Text Indexing and Retrieval
TEXUS Technological Experiments Under Zero Gravity with Sounding Rockets
TF Technological Forecasting
Temperature Fluctuations
Thermal Feedback
Toroidal Field
Transferrin
TF/D Time and Frequency Dissemination
TF/TA Terrain-Following/Terrain-Avoidance
TFA Trifluoroacetic Acid
Trifluoroacetyl
TFB Towed Flexible Barge
TFCS Tank (fighting vehicle) Fire Control System
TFD Target Film Distance
Total Hydrocarbon Analyzer
TFE Tetrafluoroethylene
Thermionic Fuel Element
TFEL Thin-Film Electro-Luminescent
TFFT Truly Fast Fourier Transform
TFG Thrust Floated Gyroscope
TFH Temporal Fourier Hologram
TFIO Thin Film Integrated Optics
TFLA Time-of-Flight Laser Anemometer
TFM Tactical Flight Management system
Turbulent Flow Manifold
TFO Thin Fuel Oil
TFOTL Thin-Film Optical Transmission Line
TFPA Torso Front Protective Armour
TFPMS Trifluoropropmethylsiloxane
TFR Terrain-Following Radar
TFRAN TOSHIBA Framed Structure Analysis Programme
TFS Tactical Fighter Squadron (USAF)
Technology Feasibility Spacecraft
Tin-Free Steel
Turbulent Flow System
TFS-CT Tin-Free Steel Chromium-Type
TFSF Time to First System Failure
TFSO Tonto Forest Seismological Observatory
TFT Thin-Film Transistor
TFTA Tetraformal Trisazine
TFTR Tokamak Fusion Test Reactor
TFTS Tactical Fighter Training Squadron (USAF)
TFW Tactical Fighter Wing (USAF)
TFWC Tactical Fighter Weapons Center (USAF)
TFX Tactical Fighter, Experimental
TG Trigeminal Ganglia
Triglyceride
TGA Thermo-Gravimetric Analysis
Toilet Goods Association (USA)
TGCA Transportable Ground Control Approach
TGD Triggered Discharge Gauge
TGFB Triglycine Fluoberyllate
TGM Training Guided Missile
TGP Turbulence Generating Pot
TGPSG Tactical Global Positioning System Guidance
TGRLSS Two-Gas Regenerative Life Support System
TGS Thermal Growing Season
Triglycine Sulphate
TGSM Tactical Guided Sub-Missile
Terminally Guided Sub-Missile
Terminally Guided Submunitions
TGT Thromboplastin Generation Test
Transformational Grammar Tester
TGW Terminally Guided Warhead
TH prefix to numbered series sissued by the Test House of the National Physical Laboratory
Tyrosine Hydroxylase
THA Tetrahydro Anacardol
Total Hydrocarbon Analyzer
THAD Terminal Homing Accuracy Demonstrator
THAWS Tactical Homing And Warning System
THB Temperature–Humidity–Bias
THC Tetrahydrocannabinol
THC-CRC Tetrahydrocannabinol Cross-Reacting-Cannabinoids
THD Total Harmonic Distortion
THE Technical Help to Exporters (a service of ANSI (USA))
Technical Help to Exporters (section of British Standards Institute)
THE BRAIN The HARVARD (UNIVERSITY (USA)) Experimental Basic Reckoning And Instructional Network
THEME The Hydrogen Economy Miami Energy (a conference)

THERP	Technique for Human Error Rate Prediction
THEUS	Theoretical Earth Utilization System
THF	Tetrahydrofuran
THFA	Thermal Hartree-Fock Approximation
THG	Third Harmonic Generation
THINGS	Three-dimensional Input of Graphical Solids
THIR	Temperature-Humidity Infra-red Radiometer
THK	Turk Hava Kuvvetleri (Turkey) (Military Air Force)
THM	Travelling Heater Method
THOMIS	Total Hospital Operating and Medical Information System
THORP	Thermal-Oxide Reprocessing Plant
THOT	Transportation Horoscope of Trade Goods
THP	Terminal Handling Processor
	Tetrahydropapaveroline
	Tetrakis (hydroxymethyl) phosphonium
THPC	Tetrakis (hydroxymethyl) phosphonium chloride
THROE	Tessaral Harmonic Resonance of Orbital Elements
THT	Tetrahydrothiopen
THTR	Thorium High Temperature Reactor
THTRA	Thorium High Temperature Reactor Association
THUS	TRADA Home Unit System
THV	Tracked Hover Vehicle
THY	Turk Hava Yollari (Turkey) (National Air Line)
TI	Technical Instruction
	Technical Investigation
	Teknologisk Institut (Denmark) (Technological Institute)
	The Textile Institute
	Thermionic
	Transverse-Interference
TIA	Transient Ischaemic Attack
	Trend Impact Analysis
	Type Inspection Authorisation
TIAC	Transport Industries Advisory Council (Australia)
TIAS	Target Identification and Acquisition System
TIB	Technical Intelligence Branch (of the National Coal Board)
	Technische Informationbibliothek (Germany) (Technical Information Library)
	Transparent Interleaved Bipolar
TIC	Tantalum Integrated Circuit
	Technical Information Center (USAEC) (now DOE/TIC (USA))
	Thermal Image Camera
	Total Ion Current
	Transducer Information Center (of Battelle Memorial Institute, USA)
	Trypsin Inhibitor Capacity
TICA	Technical Information Centre Administration
	Thermal Insulation Contractors Association
TICAS	Taxonomic Intracellular Analytic System
TICCI	Technical Information Centre for Chemical Industry (India)
TICCIT	Time-shared, Interactive Computer Controlled Information Television
TICES	Type-In Coding and Editing System
TICHE	The International Center for the Human Environment (USA)
TICM	Thermal-Imaging Common-Module
TICOM	Texas Institute for Computational Mechanics (University of Texas (USA))
TICS	Terminal Interface Control System
TICUS	Tidal Current Survey (of NOAA (USA))
	Tidal Current Survey system
TID	prefix to numbered publications issued by Technical Information Center (of ERDA (USA))
	Tactical Information Display
	Technical Information Division (of USAEC)
	Travelling Ionospheric Disturbance
TIDAS	Totally Integrated Data System
TIDB	Technical Information Dissemination Bureau (of State University of New York (USA))
TIDE	Transponder Interrogation and Decoding Equipment
TIDEDA	Time Dependent Data Analysis
TIDF	Triple Input Describing Functions
TIDIC	Time-Interval Distribution Computer
TIDP	Telemetry and Image Data Processing
TIE	Technical Integration and Evaluation
	The Institute of Ecology (USA)
	Total Interlibrary Exchange (of the California Library Network) (USA)
	Totally Integrated Environment
TIEKS	Trunks Integrated Records Keeping System
TIES	Tactical Information Exchange System
	Total Integrated Engineering System
TIFI	Technology Insight Foundation Incorporated (a non-profit educational corporation relating to computer technology)
TIFR	Tata Institute of Fundamental Research (India)
	Total Investment For Return
TIFS	Total In-Flight Simulator
TIG	Tetanus Immune Globulin
	Tungsten Inert Gas
TIGER	Tactical Inertial Guidance and Extended Range
	Telephone Information Gathering for Evaluation and Review
	TUBE INVESTMENTS Generator for Electron Radiation
TIGERS	Turbine Induction Generator Energy Recovery Systems
TIGT	Turbine Inlet Gas Temperature
TIHR	Tunable Infrared Heterodyne Radiometer
TII	European Association for Transfer of Industrial Information (of EEC)
TIIF	Tactical Image Interpretation Facility
TIL	Technical Information and Library services (MINTECH) (now Technical Reports Centre) (of DOI)
TILCAR	Tactical infantry Load Carrier Amphibious Remote
TILO	Technical Industrial Liaison Office (of MICOM (US Army))
TILS	Tactical Instrument Landing System
TILT	TEXAS INSTRUMENTS Language Translator
TIM	Technical Information on Microfilm
	Terrestrial Interface Module
	Test-bed for Individual Modules
	Triose Phosphate Isomerase
TIMA	Total Integrated Muscular Activity
TIMADS	Timber Management Decision System
TIMARC	Time Multiplexed Analogue Radio Control
TIMATION	Time Navigation artificial satellite
TIMBERLAB	Forest Products Research Laboratory (MINTECH)
TIMCON	Timber, Packaging and Pallet Confederation
TIME	Techniques for Improved Manpower Evaluation
TIMIC	Time Interval Modulation Information Coding
TIMIS	Totally Integrated Management Information System
TIMOC	Time Dependent Monte Carlo Code
TIMOS	Total Implanted Metal-Oxide-Silicon
TIMS	Tailored Inspection Maintenance System
	The Institute of Management Science (USA)
TIN	Temperature Independent
TINA	Technology Innovation Alert (an information service of INSPEC (IEE) and Control Data Technotec, Inc (USA))
TINC	Theory of Interacting Continua
TINFO	Tieteellisen Informoinnin Neuvosto (Finland) (Council for Scientific and Research Libraries)

TINRO Tikhookeanskiy Nauchno Issledovatel'skiy Institut Rybnogo Khozyaystva i Okeanologii (USSR) (Pacific Scientific Research Institute of Fisheries and Oceanology)
TINT Teletype Interpreter
TINTS Turret Integrated Night Thermal Sight
TIO Time Interval Optimization
TIOA Triisooctylamine
TIOS Tactical Information Organization System
TIP prefix to series of Training Information Papers issued by DEP
Technical Information Panel (of AGARD (NATO))
Technical Information Project
Telephone Information Processing
Terminal Interface Processor
Time to Initial Precipitation
Total Isomerization Process
Toxicology Information Program (of National Library of Medicine (USA))
Tracking and Impact Prediction
Translation Inhibitory Protein
Traversing In-core Probe
TIPA Tank and Industrial Plant Association
TIPI Tactical Interpretation Processing and Information
TIPISPO Tactical Intelligence Processing and Interpretation System Program Office (USAF)
TIPS Tactical Information about Perilous Situations
Telemetry Integrated Processing System
Transportation Integrated Processing System
TIR Target Illuminating Radar
Technical Information OR Intelligence Report
Thermal Infra-Red
Total Internal Reflection
Transports Internationale Routiers
TIR-FPL Total Internal Reflection–Face Pumped Laser
TIRAS Technical Information Retrieval and Analysis System
TIRC Toxicology Information Response Center (of Oak Ridge National Laboratory (USA))
TIRE Tank Infra-Red Elbow
TIRIS Traversing Infra-Red Inspection System
TIROS Television Infra-Red Observation Satellite
TIRP Total Internal Reflection Prism
TIRR Texas Institute for Rehabilitation and Research (USA)
TIRS Thermal Infra-Red Scanner
TIRSS Technical Information Retrieval and Storage System
Theater Intelligence Reconnaissance and Surveillance Study (of USAF)
TIS Tabular Interpretive Scheme
Team Integrating System (a research programme of ITRU (London University)
Technical Information Service
Technical Information Service (of NRC (Canada))
Thermal Imaging System
Total Information System
Transportation Information System
TISAB Total Ionic Strength Adjustment Buffer
TISAP Technical Information Support Activities Project (US Army)
TISC Technology Information Sources Center (of Southern California counties (USA))
Tire Industry Safety Council (USA)
TISCO Technical Information Systems Committee (of FSPT (USA))
TISEO Target Identification Sensor Electro-Optical
TISI Thai Industrial Standards Institute (Thailand)
TISTR Thailand Institute of Scientific and Technological Research (Thailand)
TIT Tokyo Institute of Technology (Japan)
TITAN TEAMSTER (International Brotherhood of Teamsters (USA)) Information Terminal and Accounting Network
TITIAN Thermospheric Irregularities and Troughs in Antarctica (a project of British Antarctic Survey)
TITUS Textile Information Treatment Users Service
TIUC Textile Information Users Council (USA)
TIWP Toxicology Information Working Party
TIXI Turret Integrated Xenon Illuminator
TJC Tandem Junction (solar) Cell
TJLT Transition Joint Life Test
TJS Tactical Jamming System
Target Jamming System
TJT Tactical Jamming Transmitter
TK Thymidine Kinase
TKM Tonne-Kilometres
TKO Trunk Offering
TL Thermoluminescence
Transition Level
TLA Thai Library Association (Thailand)
Thin Layer Activation
Transport Linear Accelerator
TLB Thin-Layer Bioautography
TLC Teachable Language Comprehender
Thin-Layer Chromatography
Total Layered Construction
Total Lung Capacity
Traditional Life Cycle
Transmit Level Control
TLCK Tosyl Lysine Chloromethyl Ketone
TLD Thermoluminescent Detector
Thermoluminescent Disc
Thermoluminescent Dosimeter
TLE Target Logistic Effect
Telecommunication Industry Standards Committee (of BSI)
Theoretical Line of Escape
Thin Layer Electrochemistry
TLI Tank Liquid Level Indicator
Total Lymphoid Irradiation
Trans-Lunar Injection
TLJP Thermal Liquid Junction Potential
TLM Transformer Load Management
TLMA Truck and Ladder Manufacturers Association
TLMS Tape Library Management System
TLP Tension Leg Platform
Threshold Learning Process
Transient Lunar Phenomena
TLS Tactical Landing System
Tanzania Library Service (Tanzania)
Terminal Landing System
Total Logic Solution
Trans-Lunar Shuttle
Two Levels of Storage
TLV Threshold Limit Value
Tracked Levitated Vehicle
TLV-C Threshold Limit Value-Ceiling
TLV-STEL Threshold Limit Value-Short Term Exposure Limit
TLV-TWA Threshold Limit Value-Time Weighted Average
TM Tandem Mirror
Tantalum-Metal
Technical Manual OR Memorandum OR Monograph
TM Thermatic Mapper
Thiomolybdate
Training Manual
Transcendental Meditation
Transverse Mercator
TM/ACS True-Motion Anti-Collision System
TM/BAC True-Motion, Basic Collision Avoidance

TMA Target Motion Analysis
Terminal Movement Area
Tetramethylammonium
Thermomechanical Analysis
Trans-Mediterranean Airways (Lebanon)
Trimellitic Anhydride
Trimethyl Aluminium
Trimethylamine
Trimethylammonium
TMAMA Textile Machinery and Accessory Manufacturers Associati
TMC Tata Memorial Center (India)
Thick Moulding Compound
TMCP Thermal Mechanical Controlled Processing
TMD Tactical Munitions Dispenser
Trimethadione
Trimethyl Hexamethylene-Diamine
TMDE Test, Measure and Diagnostic Equipment (an Office of US Army Weapons Command)
TMDP Training Master Datum Plane
TMEL Trimethylethyl Lead
TMF Television Multiplex Facility
Thermo-Mechanical Fatigue
Third Moment of Frequency
TMFA Three-Mode Factor Analysis
TMG Thermal and Meteoroid Garment
Trimethylgallium
TMHR Tandem Mirror Hybrid Reactor
TMI Transition-Metal-Ion
Tri-monoiodide
TMIS Technician's Maintenance Information System
TML Tetra-Methyl-Lead
Transportable Moisture Limit
TMM Tantalum-Manganese Oxide-Metal
TMN Technical and Management Note
TMP Thermo-Mechanical Processing
Thermo-mechanical Pulp OR Pulping
Time to Maximum Precipitation
Transversely Magnetized Plasma
Trimethoprim
Trimethoprim-sulpha-methoxazole
Trimethylphosphate
TMPD Tetramethylparaphenylenediamine
TMPT Trimethylphosphorothionate
TMPTMA Trimethylolpropane Trimethacrylate
TMR Triple Modular Redundancy
TMS Temperature Measurements Society (USA)
The Metallurgical Society (of AIME) (USA)
Transmatic Money Service
TMSA Technical Marketing Society of America (USA)
Trainer Mission Simulator Aircraft
TMSO Tetramethylene sulphoxide
TMSVCS TOW Missile Sight Video Camera System
TMSb Trimethylstibine
TMT Thermo-Magnetic Treatment
Thermo-Mechanical Treatment
Turbine Motor Train
TMTD Tetramethyl Thiuran Disulphide
TMTM Tetramethyl Thiuram Monosulphide
TMTU Tetramethylthiourea
TMV Tobacco Mosaic Virus
TMX Tandem Mirror Experiment
TMXO Tactical Miniature Crystal Oscillator
TN Technical Note
Toxin-Neutralization
TN-LCD Twisted Nematic Liquid Crystal Display
TNA Telex Network Adaptor
Transient Network Analyzer
TNAA Thermal Neutron Activation Analysis
TNC Tetranitrocarbazole
Total Numerical Control
Troponin C
TNDC Thai National Documentation Centre (Thailand)
TNF Theatre Nuclear Force
Toxin-Neutralizing Factor
TNI Troponin I
TNI-AU Tentara Nasional Indonesia–Angkatan Udara (Indonesia) (Indonesian Armed Forces–Air Force)
TNL Top-Level Network
TNM Tetranitromethane
Tetronitromethane
TNO Toegepast Natuurwetenschappelijk Onderzoek (Netherlands) (Central National Council for Applied Scientific Research)
TNP Trinitrophenol
TNP-LPS Trinitrophenylated-Lipopolysarcharide
TNPG The Nuclear Power Group Limited (functions transferred to NNC in 1975)
TNPP Trisnonylphenyl Phosphite
TNRIS Texas Natural Resources Information System (USA)
Transportation Noise Research Information Service (Dept of Transportation (USA))
TNS Transcutaneous Nerve Stimulation
Tumour Necrosis Serum
TNT Trinitrotoluene
Troponin T
TNW Tactical Nuclear Weapon
TOA Total Obligational Authority
TOA/DME Time-of-Arrival/Distance Measuring Equipment
TOAST Tests, Observe, Analyse, Split, Tests
TOB Take-Off Boat
Technical Operations Board (of the Engineering Institute of Canada)
TOBIAS Terrestrial Oscillation Battlefield Intruder Alarm System
TOC Target Optimization Control
Technical, Organizational and Communicational
Total Organic Carbon
TOCP Triorthocresyl Phosphate
TOCR Turn-Off Controlled Rectifier
TOCS Term-Oriented Classification System
Terminal Operations Control System
TOD Theoretical Oxygen Demand
TODA Take-Off Distance Available
TOE Tables of Organisation and Equipment
Tonnes of Oil Equivalent
TOFD Time of Flight Diffraction
TOFMS Time Of Flight Mass Spectrometer
TOFS Timing Optical Fibre System
TOGA Tropical Oceans and Global Atmosphere (a programme of IOC (UNESCO))
TOGS Thermal Observation and Gunnery System
TOGW Take-Off Gross Weight
TOH Tyrosine Hydroxylase
TOI Task-Oriented Instruction
TOKAMAK acronym coined by the Russians standing for High-current Magnetic Vacuum Chamber
TOL Test Oriented Language
TOLA Take-Off and Landing Analysis
TOLCAT Take-Off and Landing Clear Air Turbulence
TOLCCS Trends in On-Line Computer Control Systems
TOLIP Trajectory Optimization and Linearized Pitch
TOLTA Total On-Line Testing System
TOM Threshold of Octave Masking
Transparent Office Manager
Typical Ocean Model
TOMB Technical Organizational Memory Bank
TOMMA Terminal Operations and Movements Management System (US Army)

TON Threshold Odour Number
TONAC Total Navigation Control system
TONC Transient On-state Characteristics
TOOL Test Oriented Onboard Language
Test-Oriented Operator Language
TOP Trade Opportunities Program (of Dept of Commerce (USA))
Two-axis Optical Pickoff
TOPAZ Technique for the Optimum Placement of Activities in Zones
TOPCOPS The Ottawa (Canada) Police Computerized On-line Processing System
TOPICS Total On-line Programme and Information Control System
Traffic Operations Program to Increase Capacity and Safety (of Federal Highway Administration (USA))
TOPO Trioctylphosphine Oxide
TOPOCOM Topographic Command (US Army) (now Defense Mapping Agency Topographic Center)
TOPP Terminal Operated Production Programme
Training Outside Public Practice
Trioctylphenylphosphate
TOPS Task Oriented Processing System
Thermoelectric Outer Planet Spacecraft
Total Operations Processing System
Training Opportunities Scheme (of the Dept of Employment) (since 1974 operated by TSA of the Manpower Services Commission)
TOPSEP Targeting/Optimization for Solar Electric Propulsion
TOPSTAR The Officer Personnel System, the Army Reserve (US Army Reserve)
TOPSY Time-sharing Operation of Product Structure Directory System
TOPSystem Transducer Operated Pressure System
TOR Teletype On Radio
TORA Take-Off Run Available
TORCO Treatment of Refractory Copper Ores
TORQUE Technology Or Research Quantitative Utility Evaluation
TORUS Transient, Omnidirectional, Radiating, Unidistant, and Static
TORVAP-A Torsional Vibration Analysis Package–A
TOS Tactile Operations System
Text Organizing System
TIROS Operational Satellite
Transverse Open Stoping
TOSAR Topological Representation of Synthetic and Analytical Relations of concepts
TOSCA Test of Containerized Shipments for Ammunition (US Army)
Tokamak Shaping and Compression Assembly (Culham Laboratory)
TOSHIBA Tokyo Shibaura Electric Company (Japan)
TOSMA Topological Symbolic Macromodelling Algorithm
TOSS TIROS Operational Satellite System
TOST Thermal Oxidation Stability Test
TOT Telephone Organization of Thailand (Thailand)
Turbine Outlet Temperature
TOTO Tongue Of The Ocean
TOU Tractor Oils Universal
TOURS Tourist Observation and Underwater Research Submarine
TOVALOP Tanker Owners Voluntary Agreement concerning Liability for Oil Pollution
TOW Tube-launched, Optically-tracked, Wire-guided
TOW CAP TOW Cover Artillery Protection
TP Tandem Propeller
Technical Pamphlet OR Paper OR Publication
Teleprocessing
Thermoplastics
Thermosets
Transaction Processing
Transactions Paper
Tryptophan Pyrrolase
TP-T Target Practice–Tracer
TPA Technical Publications Association (now part of Institute of Scientific and Technical Communicators)
Terephthalic Acid
Thiopropionic Acid
Tissue-type Plasmirogen Activator
Triphenylamine
Two-Photon Absorption
TPAR Tactical Penetration Aid Rocket
TPBPC Triphenyl Benzl Phosphonium Chloride
TPBV Two-Point Boundary Value
TPBVP Two-Point Boundary Value Problem
TPC Technical Practices Committee (of NACE (USA))
Threatened Plants Committee (of SSC (IUCN))
TPCT Transposed Critical Temperature
TPCV Turbine Power Control Valve
TPD Technical Data Package
Technology Planning Document
TPDC Tanzanian Petroleum Development Corporation (Tanzania)
TPDT True Position Dimensioning and Tolerancing
TPE Total Protein Efficiency
Trypsin-Protein Esterase
Two-Photon Excitation
TPF Trigonometric Product Function
Two-Photon Fluorescence
TPG Test Programme Generator
Transmission Project Group (of CEGB)
TPHA Treponema Pallidum Haemagglutination
TPI Tax and Prices Index
Tons Per Inch Immersion
Town Planning Institute (now Royal Town Planning Institute)
Treponema Pallidum Immobilisation
Triosephosphate Isomerase
Tropical Products Institute (of ODM) (now TDaRI of ODA)
TPIC Thermophysical Properties Information Center (Purdue University (USA))
TPL Table Producing Language
Teacher Programming Language
Telecommunications-oriented Programming Language
Terminal Programming Language
TPNH Triphosphopyridine Nucleotide
TPO Thermoplastic Olefin
Thin Phase Object
TPP Thiamine Pyrophosphate
Total Package Procurement
Triphenylphosphine
TPPC Total Package Procurement Concept
TPR Terrain Profile Recorder
Thermoplastic Rubber
Transportation Programs Report (of Applied Physics Laboratory, Johns Hopkins University (USA))
TPRC Thermophysical Properties Research Center (of Purdue University, USA)
TPRE Twin Plane Re-entrant Edge
TPRI Tropical Pesticides Research Institute (Tanzania)
TPS Technical Problem Summary
Telecommunications Programming System
Thermal Power Station
Thermal Protection Systems
TPSFG Two-Post Signal Flow Graph
TPT Total Plasma Tryptophan
Tramway de Pithiviers a Toury (France)

TPTC Triphenyl Tin Chloride
TPTO Tripropyl Tin Oxide
TPU Thermoplastic Urethanes
Transverse Propulsion Unit
TPV Thermophotovoltaic
TPWD Texas Parks and Wildlife Department (USA)
TPX Transportation Problem Extended
TQC Total Quality Control
TQCA Textile Quality Control Association (USA)
TR Technical Report
Thermoplastic Rubber
Transverse Resistance
TR-EE prefix to dated-numbered series of Technical Reports issued by Purdue University School of Electrical Engineering (USA)
TRA Tea Research Association (India)
Thrust Reversers Aft
Tire and Rim Association (USA)
TRAC Telescoping Rotor Aircraft
Text Reckoning And Compiling
Train Regulation Advisory Control
Transient Radiation Analysis by Computer
Trials Recording and Analysis Console
TRAC(E) Tracking and Communication (Extraterrestrial)
TRACAL Tracking Calculator
TRACALS Traffic Control, Approach and Landing System
TRACE Tactical Readiness And Checkout Equipment
Tape Recording Automatic Check-out Equipment
Tape-controlled Reckoning And Checkout Equipment
Tele-processing Recording for Analysis by the Customer Engineer
Test-equipment for Rapid Automatic Check-out and Evaluation
Time Repetitive Analog Contour Equipment
Time-shared Routines for Analysis, Classification and Evaluation
Tolls Recording And Computing Equipment
Total Risk Assessing Cost Estimate
Transaction, Accounting, Control and Endorsing
Transportable Automated Control Environment
Tree Analysis Code
TRACES Technology in Retrospect and Critical Events in Science (a project of Illinois Institute of Technology (USA)
TRACIS Traffic Records And Criminal Justice Information System (Iowa (USA))
TRACON Terminal Radar Approach Control
Terminal Radar Control
TRACS Telemetry Receiver Acoustic Command System
THOMSON'S (TRAVEL LTD) Reservations, Administration and Control System
Total Royalty Accounting and Copyright Systems
Traffic Reporting and Control System
TRACTIONEL Societe de Traction et Electricite (Belgium)
TRACY Technical Reports Automated Cataloguing — Yes
TRADA Timber Research and Development Association
TRADAC Tajectory Determination and Acquisition Computations
TRADAR Transaction Data Recorder
TRADES Transaction Reporting, Analysis, Documentation and Evaluation System
TRADEX Target Resolution And Discrimination Experiment
TRADOC Training and Doctrine Command (US Army)
TRAFFIC Trades Records Analysis of Flora and Fauna In Commerce (of IUCN)
TRAG Transport Research Assessment Group (of Joint Transport Research Committee)
TRAIL Tokamak Rail Gun Limiter
TRAIN TeleRail Automated Information Network
TRAKX Tracking Radar at K-and X-band
TRAM Target Recognition and Attack Multi-sensor
Test Reliability And Maintainability
Tracking Radar Automatic Monitoring
TRAMMS Transportation Automated Materiel Movements System (US Army) (now known as TOMMS)
TRAMP Time-shared Relation Associative Memory Programme
TRAMPS Text Information Retrieval and Management Programme System
TRANES Transonic Airfoil Analysis or Design
TRANET Trans-national Network for Appropriate/Alternative Technologies
TRANS Traffic Network Simulator
Transaction ORTranslation
TRANSANA TRADOC Systems Analysis Agency (US Army)
TRANSATEL Transportable Satellite Telecommunications
TRANSCAN Transaction Scanner
TRANSIM Transportation Simulator
TRANSLOC Transportable LORAN-C
TRANSMARK Transportation Systems and Market Research (a consultancy service of the British Railways Board)
TRANSNUCLEAIRE Societe pour les Transports de l'Industries Nucleaire (France)
TRANSYT Traffic Network Study Tool
TRAP Tape Recorder Action Plan (a committee of NASA and AF (USA))
Terminal Radiation Programme
Thioguanine, Daunorubicin, Cytarabine, Prednisolone
TRAPATT Trapped Plasma Avalanche Triggered Transit
TRASANA Systems Analysis Activity (of US Army Training and Doctrine Command)
TRB Transportation Research Board (USA)
TRBF Technische Regeln fur brennbare Flussigkeiten (Germany) (Technical Regulations for Flammable Liquids)
TRC Tanzanian Railways Corporation (Tanzania)
Technical Resource Center (Philippines)
Technology Reports Centre (of DTI) (transferred to BLLD in 1982)
Tekniska Rontgencentralen (Sweden)
Telecommunications Research Centre (of Posts and Telegraph Department (India))
Telegram Retransmission Centre (of the British Post Office)
Textile Research Council
The Radiochemical Centre Ltd (of UKAEA)
TRCHII Tanned Red Cell Haemagglutination Inhibition Immunoasay
TRCL The Radiochemical Centre Limited (a public company)
Tobacco Research Council laboratories (now the Hazelton Laboratories Europe Ltd)
TRD Tobacco-Related Diseases
Tuning, Remote, Digital
TRDI Technical Research and Development Institute (of Japan Defence Agency)
TRE Transient Radiation Effects
TREAT Transient Reactor Test
TREC Tracking Radar Electronic Component
TREE Transient Radiation Effects on Electronics
TREES Transient Radiation Effects on Electronic Systems
Tree-Structured
TREF Transient Radiation Effects Facility (of AFWL (USAF))
TREMCARDS Transport Emergency Cards
TREND Tropical Environment Data
TREX British Textile Machinery Organisation
Thermionic Reactor Experiment

TRF Thyrotropin Releasing Factor
Tuned Radio Frequency
TRFCS Temperature Rate Flight Control System
TRG prefix to numbered series of reports issued by The Reactor Group (UKAEA)
Technical Research Group
Training
TRH Thyrotropin-Releasing Hormone
TRI Technological Research Institute (of ASRCT (Thailand))
Textile Research Institute (USA)
Tin Research Institute
Tire Retreading Institute (USA)
TRI-TAC Tri-Service Tactical Communications (USDOD)
TRIA Telemetry Range Instrumented Aircraft
Tracking Range Instrumented Aircraft
TRIAD Three Rivers Improvement and Development Corporation (USA) (non-profit corporation)
TRIAL Technique for Retrieving Information from Abstracts of Literature
TRIB Tire Retread Information Bureau (USA)
TRIC Trachoma-inclusion Conjunctivitis
TRICAP Triple Capability
TRICON Tri-Container
Tri-Service Container program (USDOD)
TRIEA Tea Research Institute of East Africa (Kenya)
TRIEG Triethiodide of Gallamine
TRIGA Training Research Isotope GENERAL ATOMIC
TRIGAT Third Generation Anti-Tank guided weapons programme
TRIM Task Related Instructional Methodology
Technique for Responsive Inventory Management
Trails and Road Interdiction Multisensor
TRIMIS Tri-service Medical Information System (USDOD)
TRIMS Transportation Improved Management System
TRIMTU Trimethyl Thiourea
TRINDEL Travaux Industriels pour l'Electricite (France)
Travaux Industriels pour l'Electricite (France) once
TRINTOC Trinidad and Tobago Oil Company (state owned)
TRIP Thunderstorm Research International Project
Total Replenishment Inventory Programme
Trajectory Integration Programme
Transformation Induced Plasticity
Truck Routing Improvement Procedure
TRIPLETEE True Temperature Tunnel
TRIPOD Transit Injector POLARIS Derived
TRIPS TALON (USA) Reporting and Information Processing System
TRIS Transportation Research Information Service (of Highway Research Board and Dept. of Transportation (USA))
TRISNET National Network of Transportation Research Information Services (of Dept of Transportation (USA))
TRISTA Trim and Stability
TRISTAN Tri-Ring Intersecting Storage Accelerators in Nippon
TRIUMF Tri-University Meson Facility (Canada)
TRL Transistor-Resistor Logic
TRM Thermal Rearmament Magnetisation
Thermal Remanent Magnetization
TRMS Technical Requirements Management System
TRN Technical Research Note
TRNA Transfer Ribonucleic Acid
TROID Teesside Regional Organization for Industrial Development
TROMEX Tropical Meteorological Experiment
TROPEX Tropical Atlantic Experiment
TROPICS Tour Operators Integrated Computer System
TROSCOM Troop Support Command (US Army)
TRP Team Resources Package
TRR Target Ranging Radar
Technical Research Report
TRRA Tilt Rotor Research Aircraft
TRRL Transport and Road Research Laboratory (of DOE)
TRRR Trilateration Range and Range Rate
TRS Teleoperator Retrieval System
Tetrahedral Research Satellite
Time Reference System
Torry Research Station (transferred from DTI to MAFF, April 1972)
Tough Rubber Sheathed
TRSB Telecommunications Regulatory Service Branch (of Dept of Communications (Canada))
Time Reference Scanning Beam
TRT Telecommunications Radioelectrique et Telephoniques (France)
Traffic Route Tester
Turkiye Radyo-Televizyon Kurumu (Turkey)
TRTA Tasmanian Road Transport Association (Tasmania)
Teito Rapid Transit Authority (Japan)
Traders Road Transport Association
TRTG Tactical Radar Threat Generator
TRTL Transistor-Resistor-Transistor Logic
TRTT Tactical Record Traffic Terminal
TRU Transuranic
TRUMP Technical Review and Update of Manuals and Publications
Total Revision and Upgrading of Maintenance Procedures
TRUNKS Tour Reservation United Kingdom System
TRUST Tamper-Resistant Unattended Safeguards Techniques
Television Relay Using Small Terminals
TRV Torpedo Recovery Vessel
Transient Recovery Voltage
TS prefix to numbered series of Technical Specifications issued by the Chemical Inspectorate (MOD)
Technical Specification
Technical Specification (numbered series issued by SBAC)
Tensile Strength
Time Sharing
Transport Station
TS/DMS Time-Shared Data Management System
TS/SPAR Time Sharing System Performance Activity Recorder
TSA Time Series Analysis
Training Services Agency (of Dept of Employment) (transferred to the Manpower Services Commission in 1974)
Training Situation Analysis
Trypticase Soy Agar
TSA/PPE Total System Analyzer/Problem Programme Evaluator
TSAb Thyroid-Stimulating Autoantibodies
TSAO Tsentral'nyy Aerologischeskaya Observatoriya (USSR) (Central Aerological Observatory)
TSAR Time Scanned Array Radar
TSARC Test Schedule and Review Committee (of US Army)
TSARCOM Troop Support and Aviation Materiel Readiness Command (US Army) (disbanded 1977)
TSARS Toroidal Stream Angular Rate Sensor
TSAS Time-shared Supervisor Assembly System
Time-Sharing Accounting System
TSB Tryticase Soy Broth
TSC Thermal Spray Coating
Thermally Stimulated Conductivity

Thermally Stimulated Current
Transportation Safety Committee (of SAE (USA))
Transportation Systems Center (of DOT (USA))
Tryptose-Sulphite-Cycloserine

TSCA Toxic Substances Control Act 1976 (USA)

TSCAP Thermally Stimulated Capacitance

TSCLT Transportable Satellite Communications Link Terminal

TSCM Technical Surveillance Counter-Measures

TSD Temperature-Salinity-Density-Depth
Theory of Signal Detectability
Thermally Stimulated Discharge
Thermo-Stimulated Depolarization
Time-Span-of-Discretion
Towed Submersible Dry-dock
Traffic and Safety Division (Michigan Department of State Highways (USA))

TSDA Thermal Single-Determinant Approximation

TSDC Thermally Stimulated Discharge Coating

TSDM Tri-State Delta Modulation

TSE Transmission Secondary Electron Emitters
Turbo-Shaft Engine
Turk Standardlari Enstitusu (Turkey) (Turkish Standards Institute)
Twist Setting Efficiency

TSEE Thermally Stimulated Exoelectron Emission

TSEG Tactical Satellite Communication Executive Steering Group (USDOD)

TSF Ten Statement FORTRAN
Time to System Failure

TSFE Thermally Stimulated Field Emission

TSFP Time-to-System Failure Period

TSG Terminating Stochastic Game

TSGAD Tri-Service Group on Air Defence (of NATO)

TSGCEE Tri-Service Group on Communications and Electronic Equipment

TSH Thyroid-Stimulating Hormone

TSIA Titanium Substrate Insoluble Anode

TSIAM T'sentral'nyy Nauchno Issledovatel'skiy Institut Aviatsionnogo Motorostroyeniya (USSR) (Central Scientific Research Institute of Aero-Engine Construction)

TSK Tekniikan Sanastokeskus (Finland) (Centre for Technical Terminology)

TSL Thermally Stimulated Luminescence
Tree Searching Language

TSLS Two-Stage Least-Square

TSM Telephony Signalling Module

TSN Thermal Severity Number

TSNIDA Tsentral'nyy Nauchno Issledovatel'skiy Dizel'nyy Institut (USSR) (Central Scientific Research Diesel Institute)

TSNIEL Tsentral'naya Nauchno Issledovatel'skaya Elektrotekhnicheskaya Laboratoriya (USSR) (Central Scientific Research Electrical Engineering Laboratory)

TSNII Tsentral'nyy Nauchno Issledovatel'skiy Institut (USSR) (Central Scientific Research Institute)

TSNIIChM Tsentral'nyy Nauchno Issledovatel'skiy Institut Chernoy Metallurgii (USSR) (Central Scientific Research Institute of Ferrous Metallurgy)

TSNIIGAiK Tsentral'nyy Nauchno Issledovatel'skiy Institut Geodezii Aeros'yemk i Kartografii (Central Scientific Research Institute of Geodesy, Aerial Photography and Cartography (USSR))

TSNIIMF Tsentral'nyy Nauchno Issledovatel'skiy Institut Morskogo Flota (USSA) (Central Scientific Research Institute of the Maritime Fleet)

TSNIIPO Tsentral'nyy Nauchno Issledovatel'skiy Institut Protivopozharnoy Oborony (USSR) (Central Scientific Research Institute for Fire Prevention)

TSNIIPS Tsentral'nyy Nauchno Issledovatel'skiy Institut Promyshlennykh Sooruzhenii (USSR) (Central Scientific Research Institute of Industrial Structures)

TSNIIS Tsentral'nyy Nauchno Issledovatel'skiy Institut Svyazi (USSR) (Central Scientific Research Institute of Communications)

TSNIITMASh Tsentral'nyy Nauchno Issledovatel'skiy Institut Tekhnologii i Mashinostroyeniya (USSR) (Central Scientific Research Institute of Technology and Machine Building)

TSNILELEKTROM Tsentral'naya Nauchno Issledovatel'syaya Laboratoriya Elektricheskoy Obrabotki Materialov (USSR) (Central Scientific Research Laboratory for Electrical Treatment of Materials)

TSO Technical Standards Orders (of FAA (USA))
Time Sharing Option
Transient System Optimization

TSOR Tentative Specific Operational Requirement

TSP Terminal Support Processor
Travelling Salesman Problem
Triple Super Phosphate

TSPC Tropical Stored Products Centre (of TPI)

TSPE Texas Society of Professional Engineers (USA)

TSPRT Truncated Sequential Probability Ratio Tests

TSPRTR Truncated Sequential Probability Ratio Tests for Reliability

TSPS Traffic Service Position System

TSR Technical Summary Report
Temperature-Sensitive Resistor

TSRB Time Reference Scanning Beam
Top Salaries Review Board

TSRP Toll Service Results Plan

TSRS Time Synchronized Ranging System

TSS Tangential Signal Sensitivity
Tethered Satellite System
Time Sharing System

TSSA Tumour-Specific Surface Antigen

TSSD Typesetting System for Scientific Documents

TSSP Tactical Satellite Signal Processor

TST Truncated Sequential Test
Tuberculin Skin Test

TSTA Tritium System Test Assembly (of LASL (USA))
Tumour Specific Transplantation Antigens

TSTC Tri-State Transportation Commission (New Jersey, New York, Connecticut (USA))

TSU Thermal Storage Unit
Thermosetting Urethanes

TSUS Tariff Schedules of the United Sates

TSUSA Tariff Schedules of the United States Annotated

TSV Tug/Supply Vessel

TSX Time Sharing Executive

TT Technical Translation
Telegraphic Transfer
Time Terms
Tolyltriazole

TT&C Tracking, Telemetry and Control

TTA Turbine-Alternator Assembly

TTAC Telemetry, Tracking And Command

TTAG Training of Trainers Advisory Group (of MSC)

TTB Troop Transport Boat

TTBS Target Triggered Bursts

TTBWR Twisted Tape Boiling Water Reactor

TTC Technical Training College (of the British Post Office)
Topographical Tactical Chart
Toronto Transit Commission (Canada)
Total Trichlorocompounds
Tracking, Telemetry and Command
Transportation Test Center (of Dept of Transportation (USA))

	Trunk-Telephone Centre
TTC & M	Telemetry, Tracking, Command and Monitoring
TTCC	Tokens and Transaction Control Consortium
TTCP	The Technical Cooperation Programme (between Australia, Canada, New Zealand, UK and USA)
TTE	Tropical Trials Establishment (Australia) (merged into JTTRE in 1977)
TTF	Tetrathiofulvalene
	Timber Trade Federation
	Time to Time Failure
TTF & T	Technology Transfer, Fabrication and Test
TTF-TCNQ	Tetrathiofulvalene Tetracyanoquinodimethane
TTFC	Textile Technical Federation of Canada (Canada)
TTG	Technical Translation Group
TTHM	Turk Teknik Haberlesme Merkezi (Turkey) (Turkish Technical Information Centre)
TTI	Noimhungaria Tervezesfejlesztesi es Tipustervezo Intezet (Hungary) (Institute for Design Development and Typical Drawings)
	Tactical Target Identification
	Tactical Target Illustration
	Time-Temperature Indicator
TTL	Teknillinen Tarkastuslaitos (Finland) (Technical Inspectorate)
	Transistor-Transistor Logic
TTLIC	Transistor-Transistor Logic Integrated Circuit
TTM	Transit-Time-Modulation
TTMA	Truck Trailer Manufacturers Association (USA)
	Tufted Textile Manufacturers Association (USA)
TTNS	TOW Thermal Night S
TTP	Time-Temperature Parameter
	Tritolyl Phosphate
TTRI	Telecommunications Technical Training and Research Institute (Egypt)
TTS	Tank Thermal Sight
	Teletypesetting
	Temporary Threshold Shift
	Test and Training Satellite
	Time, Temperature, Sensitizing
TTSC	Transportation and Traffic Safety Center (Pennsylvania, USA)
TTT	Telemetry, Telecommand, Tracking
	Time–Temperature Transformation
TTTE	Tri-National Tornado Training Establishment (MOD)
TTTN	Tandem Tie Trunk Networks
TTU	Texas Technological University (USA)
	Through-Transmission Ultrasonic testing
TTUCS	Through-Transmission Ultrasonic C-Scan
TTWS	Trunk Telecommunication Waveguide System
TTX	Tetrodotoxin
	Tritated Tetrodotoxin
TTY	Telephone–Teletypewriter
TU	Tulsa University (USA)
TU-LCP	University of Texas Laboratory of Comparative Pharmacology (USA)
TUAC	Trade Union Advisory Committee (of OECD)
TUB-IR	Teschnische Universitat, Berlin—Institut fur Raumfahrttechnik (Germany) (Technical University, Berlin—Institute for Space Technology)
TUBITAK	Scientific and Research Council of Turkey (Turkey)
TUC	Trades Union Congress
TUCC	Transport Users Consultative Committee
	Transport Users Consultative Committee
	Triangle Universities Computation Center (of Duke University, North Carolina State University and North Carolina University (USA))
TUCSICC	Trade Union Congress Steel Industry Consultative Committee
TUD	Technology Utilization Division (of NASA)
TUEP	Tokyo University of Education, Department of Physics (Japan)
TUF	Time of Useful Function
TULIPS	Telemetered Ultrasonic Liquid Interface Plotting System
TULRA	Trade Union and Labour Relations Act, 1974
TUMS	TOTAL Utility Maintenance System
TUNL	Triangle Universities Nuclear Laboratory (USA)
TUP	Technology Utilization Program (of NASA (USA))
	Transfer–Under–Pressure
TUPC	Transfer–Under–Pressure Chamber
TUR	Transurethral Resection
TURBOPROP	Turbine Propelled
TURDOK	Turk Bilimsel ve Teknik Dokumentasyon Merkesi (Turkey) (Turkish National Scientific and Technical Documentation Centre)
TURF	Thorium-Uranium Recycle Facility (of ORNL)
TURPS	Terrestrial Unattended Reactor Power System
TUTF	Technology Use Task Force (of Los Angeles Area Chamber of Commerce (USA))
TUU	Transitional Ultraspherical-Ultraspherical filter
TUV	Technische Uberwachungs-Vereine (Germany) (Technical Supervisory Societies)
TV	Thyroid Vein
TVA	Tax on Value Added
	Tennessee Valley Authority (USA)
	Thermal Volatilisation Analysis
	Time-Variant Automation
TVA-OHES	Tennessee Valley Authority, Office of Health and Environmental Science (USA)
TVBS	Television Broadcast Satellite
TVC	Thrust Vector Control
	Transient Voltage Counter
TVD	Traumatic Vasospastic Disease
TVE	Television Espanola (Spain)
TVF	Teknisk-Vetenskaplig Forskning (Committee on Technical Information (of Scandinavian Council of Applied Research))
TVG	Television Video Generator
	Time Varying Gain
TVI	Television Interference
	Tutored Video Instruction
TVID	Television Identification of personnel
TVL	Tenth-Value Layer
TVM	Target-via-Missile
	Track–Via–Missile
	Transmission Via Missile
TVN	Total Volatile Nitrogen
TVO	Teollisuuden Voima Oy (Finland) (a consortium of industrial enterprises and public utilities)
	Tractor Vaporizing Oil
TVOR	Terminal VHF Omni-directional Radio
TVP	Time-Varying Parameter
	Tri-Vertiplane
	True Vapour Pressure
TVR	Temperature Voltage Ramp
	Time Variable Reflectance
TVRE	Transportable Vehicle Refuelling Equipment
TVRO	Television Receive Only
TVS	Transparent Fused Silica
	Triangular Voltage Sweep
	Tube Vehicle Systems
TVSS	Tactile Vision Substitution System
TVSU	Television Sight Unit
TVT	Trivittatus
TVX	Target Vehicle Experimental
TW	Thermit Welding
	Travelling Wave
TWA	Thames Water Authority
	Time-Weighted Average

TWCRT Travelling Wave Cathode Ray Tube
TWD Touch Wire Display
TWEB Transcribed Weather Broadcast
TWEM Tactical Weather Effects Messages
TWERLE Tropical Wind Energy Conversion Reference Level Experiment (of NASA (USA))
TWFM Travelling Wire Flux Mapping
TWGSS Tank Weapons Gunnery Simulation System
TWh Terawatt hour
TWI Tactical Weather Intelligence
Training Within Industry
TWIN Test Ware Instrument
TWLC Two Way Logic Circuits
TWM Travelling Wave Maser
TWPL Private Line Teletypewriter Service
TWS Technische Werke der Stadt Stuttgart (Germany)
Track While Scan
Translator Writing System
TWSRO Track While Scan Receive Only
TWT Translator Writing Tools
Travelling Wave Tube
TWTA Travelling Wave Tube Amplifier
TWX Teletypewriter Exchange Network
Teletypewriter Exchange Service
TXE Telephone Exchange Electronic
TYG Trypticase-Yeast-Glucose
TYMV Turnip Yellow Mosaic Virus
TYPOE Ten-Year Plan for Ocean Exploration (of National Council on Marine Resources and Engineering Development (USA))
TZM Titanium-Zirconium-Molybdenum
TZR Tanzania-Zambia Railway
T^2L Transistor Transistor Logic

U

U-MLS Universal Microwave Landing System
UA The Underwater Association
Ultralight Association (of Experimental Aircraft Association (USA))
Unit of Account (of EEC for the expression of monetary values)
University of Akron (USA)
UA-ARE University of Arizona (USA) Aerosol and Radiation Experiment
UACL United Aircraft of Canada Limited (Canada)
UADPS Uniform Automated Data Processing System (USN)
UAE United Arab Emirates
UAF Uganda Air Force (Uganda)
UAG Alaska University College Geophysical Institute (USA)
UAH University of Alabama in Huntsville (USA)
UAI Union des Associations Internationales (Union of International Associations)
UAIDE Users of Automatic Information Display Equipment
UAL User Adaptive Language
UAMS Upper Atmosphere Mass Spectrometer
UAP Universal Availability of Publications
UAPT Union Africaine des Postes et Telecommunications (African Postal and Telecommunications Union)
Union Africaine des Postes et Telecommunications (African Posts and Telecommunications Union)
UARAEE United Arab Republic Atomic Energy Establishment
UARC Upper Atmosphere Research Corporation (a consortium of certain universities in Canada and USA)
UAREP Universities Associated for Research and Education in Pathology (USA)
UARI University of Alabama Research Institute (USA)
UARP Upper Atmospheric Research Program (of NASA (USA))
UARRSI Universal Aerial Refuelling Receptacle Slipway Installation
UARS Unmanned Arctic Research Submersible
Upper Atmosphere Research Satellite (of NASA)
UART Universal Asynchronous Receiver/Transmitter
UARZ University of Arizona (USA)
UAS Upper Airspace
UASC United Arab Shipping Company
UASIF Union des Associations Scientifiques et Industrielles Françaises (France) (Union of French Scientific and Industrial Associations)
UASS Unmanned Aerial Surveillance System
UATS Universal Assembly Translator System
UAX Unit Automatic Exchange
UAZ-EES University of Arizona, Engineering Experiment Station (USA)
UB Urine Bilirubin
UBC Universal Bibliographical Control
University of British Columbia (Canada)
UBF Un-Burned Fuel
UBIC Union Belge des Installateurs en Chauffage Central (Belgium)
UBINEPS Union Bank of India–NAYE Entrepreneurship Promotion Scheme (India)
UBIP Ubiquitous Immunopoietic Polypeptide
UBM Unit Bill of Material
UBTUW Universitaetsbibliothek Technische Universitaet Wien (Austria) (University Technical Library of University of Vienna)
UC Ulcerative Colitis
University of Chicago (USA)
University of Cincinnati (USA)
Uranium Carbide
UCA Underground Contractors Association (USA)
UCAIRJ Universal Countermeasures Airborne Infra-Red Jammer
UCAR University Corporation for Atmospheric Research (USA)
UCAT Ultra-Compact Airport Terminal
UCB University of California, Berkeley (USA)
UCB-ILR University of California at Berkeley, Institute of Library Research (USA)
UCC Underclad Cracking
Universal Copyright Convention
University College, Cork (Eire)
User Charges Committee (of IATA)
UCCA Universities Central Council on Admissions
UCCC Uniform Consumer Credit Code (USA)
UCCEGA Union des Chambres de Commerce et Établissements Gestionnaires d'Aéroports (France) (Union of Chambers of Commerce and Organisations Managing Regional Airports)
UCCRS Underwater Coded Command Release System
UCD University College, Dublin (Eire)
University of California at Davis (USA)
UCEA University Council for Educational Administration (USA)
UCEER Universities Council for Earthquake Engineering Research (USA)
UCF University of Central Florida (USA)
UCG Underground Coal Gasification

University College, Galway (Eire)
University Grants Commission (India)

UCHCIS Urban Comprehensive Health Care Information System

UCI University of California at Irvine (USA)

UCIL Uranium Corporation of India Ltd. (of Dept. of Atomic Energy (India))

UCIMU Unione Contruttori Italiana Macchine Utensili (Italy) (Union of Italian Machine Tool Manufacturers)

UCL University College, London
Upper Control Limit

UCLA University of California, Los Angeles (USA)

UCLA-ENG prefix to numbered series of reports issued by University of California, Los Angeles, School of Engineering and Applied Science (USA)

UCLARM University College London Absolute, Relative Motion

UCLB University of California at Berkeley (USA)

UCLMARS University College London Modal Analysis Response Symmetric

UCMM Universidad Católica Madre y Maestra (Dominican Republic)

UCN Ultra-Centrifuge Nederland (Netherlands)

UCNI Unclassified Controlled Nuclear Information
Unified Communications, Navigation and Identification

UCNW University College of North Wales

UCOP Unit Cost of Production

UCOR Uranium Enrichment Corporation (South Africa)

UCOWR Universities Council on Water Resources Research (USA)

UCPTE Union pour la Coordination de la Production et du Transport de l'Electricite (Union for the Coordination of the Production and Transport of Electrical Power)

UCR University of California at Riverside (USA)
University, College and Research Section (of the Library Association)

UCRL University of California, Lawrence Radiation Laboratory (USA)

UCRN Unique Consignment Reference Number (of SITPRO)

UCS Un-Classified Stowage
Unconfined Compress Strength test
Underwater Combat System
Union of Concerned Scientists (USA)

UCSB University of California at Santa Barbara (USA)

UCSB-ME University of California, Santa Barbara–Department of Mechanical Engineering (USA)

UCSC University of California, Santa Cruz (USA)

UCSD University of California at San Diego (USA)

UCSEL University of California Structural Engineering Laboratory (USA)

UCSESM University of California, Division of Structural Engineering and Structural Mechanics (USA)

UCSF University of California at San Francisco (USA)

UCST Upper Critical Solution Temperature

UCT University of Cape Town (South Africa)
University of Connecticut (USA)

UDACS Underwater Detection And Classification System

UDAM Universal Digital of Avionics Module

UDAR Universal Digital Adaptive Recognizer

UDATS Underwater Damage Assessment Television System

UDC Universal Decimal Classification
Urban Data Center, Washington University (USA)

UDD Usines Dialectrique Delle (France)

UDDS Urban Dynamometer Driving Schedule (of EPA (USA))

UDE Unsymmetrical Diethylenetriamine

UDEAC Union Douaniere et Economique de l'Afrique Centrale (Central Africa Customs and Economic Union)

UDEAO Union Douaniere des Etats de l'Afrique de l'Ouest (West African Customs Union)

UDF Unducted Fan

UDICON Universal Digital Communications Network

UDIL University Directors of Industrial Liaison

UDL Up-Data Link

UDMH Unsymmetrical Dimethylhydrazine

UDOFTT Universal Digital Operational Flight Trainer Tool

UDOP UHF Doppler

UDPG Uridine Diphosphate Glucose

UDPGA Uridine Diphosphate Glucuronic Acid

UDR Universal Document Reader

UDRI University of Dayton Research Institute (USA)

UDS Universal Data Set
Universal Distributed System

UDT Uni-Directional Transducer
Universal Document Transport

UDUAL Union de Universidades de America Latina (Union of Latin America Universities)

UEA University of East Anglia

UEC Union Europeenne des Experts Comptables Economiques et Financiers (European Union of Chartered Accountants)

UED Ultrasonic Echo Detection

UEG Underwater Engineering Group (of CIRIA)

UEGGSP Union Europeenne des Groupements de Grossistes Specialises en Papeterie (European Union of Groups of Wholesalers Specialising in Papermaking)

UEI Union of Educational Institutions

UEL Upper Earnings Limit
Upper Explosive Limit

UEMO Union Europeene des Medicins Omnipraticiens (of EEC) (European Union of General Practitioners)

UEMS Union Europeene des Medecine Specialistes (of EEC) (European Union of Medical Specialists)
Union Europeenne de Medecine Social (European Association of Social Medicine)

UEPMD Union Européenne des Practiciences en Médécine Dentaire (of the EEC) (European Union of Practitioners of Dental Medicine)

UER Union Europeene de Radiodiffusion (European Broadcasting Union)

UERS Universal Event Recording System

UESA Union Electrica SA (Spain)

UET Universal Engineer Tractor

UETA Universal Engineer Tractor, Armoured

UETE Usinas Electricas y Telefonos del Estado (Uruguay)

UF Ultra-Filtration
University of Florida (USA)
Urea-formaldehyde
Utilization Factor (relative to illumination)

UFAS Unified File Access System

UFAW Universities Federation for Animal Welfare

UFC Uniform Freight Classification (USA)

UFEMAT Union des Federations Nationales des Negociants en Materiaux de Construction de la CEE (Union of National Federations of Building Materials Merchants in the EEC)

UFFA Urea Formaldehyde Foam Association

UFI Union des Foires Internationales (France) (International Trade Fair Organisers)

UFIPTE Union Franco-Ibérique pour la Production et le Transport de l'Électricité (Franco-Spanish Union for the Production and Transmission of Electricity)

UFL	Upper Flammable Limit
UFMG	Universidad Federal de Minas Gerais (Brazil)
UFO	Un-Filtered Oil
	Unidentified Flying Object
	User Files On-line
UFOD	Union Francaise des Organismes de Documentation (France)
UFOIC	Unidentified Flying Objects Investigation Centre (Australia)
UFP	Universal Folded Plate
UFS	Ultimate Flexural Strength
	Ustav pro Filozfii a Sociologii (of CSAV) (Institute of Philosophy and Sociology)
UFSS	Unmanned Free Swimming Submersible
UFT	Ultra-fast Fourier Transform
UFTAA	Universal Federation of Travel Agency Associations
	Universal Federation of Travel Agents Associations
UG3RD	Upgraded Third Generation System for air traffic control
UGA	University of Georgia (USA)
UGAL	Union des Groupements d'Achats de l'Alimentation (Union of Food Purchasing Groups)
UGC	University Grants Committee
UGS	Unattended Ground Sensor
UH	Utility Helicopter
UH/CLC	University of Houston at Clear Lake City (USA)
UHC	Unburned Hydrocarbons
UHE	Ultra-High Efficiency lamp
UHELP	UNIVERSITY OF HOUSTON (USA) Easy Linear Programming
UHF	Ultra High Frequency
	Unrestricted HARTREE-FOCK
UHFM	UNIVERSITY OF HOUSTON (USA) Formula Manipulation
UHMW	Ultra-High-Molecular-Weight
UHMWPE	Ultra-High Molecular Weight Polyethylene
UHT	Ultra High Temperature
	Ultra-Heat Treatment
UHTREX	Ultra-High Temperature Reactor Experiment
UHTSS	UNIVERSITY OF HAWAII Time-Sharing System
UHV	Ultra-High Voltage
	Ultrahigh Vacuum
UI	University of Iowa (USA)
UIA	Union International des Architects (International Union of Architects)
	Union of International Associations
UIAL	University of Illinois Antenna Laboratory (USA)
UIC	Union Internationale des Chemins de fer (France) (International Union of Railways)
	Unit Inspection Company (of British Steel Corporation and UKAEA)
UICC	Union Internationale Contre le Cancer (Switzerland) (International Union Against Cancer)
UIDA	Union Internationale des Organisations de Detaillants de la Branche Alimentaire (Switzerland) (International Union of Organisation of Retailers of Food)
UIE	prefix to numbered series of publication issued by UNESCO Institute for Education
	UNESCO Institute for Education
UIEO	Union of International Engineering Organisations
UIJC	Universities and Industry Joint Committee
UIL	Unione Italiana Lavoratori (Italy)
UILC	University of Illinois at Chicago Circle (USA)
UILI	Union Internationale des Laboratoires Independants (England) (International Union of Independent Laboratories)
UILU	University of Illinois, Urbana-Champaign (USA)
UILU-ENG	prefix to dated-numbered series of reports issued by University of Illinois, Urbana–Coordinated Science Laboratory (USA)
UILU-WRC	University of Illinois, Urbana, Water Resources Center (USA)
UIM	Ultra-Intelligent Machine
	Union of International Motor-boating
UIMP	User Interface for Mathematical Programming
UINF	Union Internationale de la Navigation Fluviale (Belgium) (International Union for Inland Waterways Navigation)
UIRV	Universal Infra-Red Viewer
UIT	Unified Income Tax
	Union Internationale des Telecommunications (International Telecommunications Union (of UN))
UITA	Union of International Technical Associations
UITP	Union Internationale des Transports Publics (Belgium) (International Union of Public Transport)
	Union Internationale des Transports Publics (International Union of Public Transport)
UIUC	University of Illinois at Urbana-Champaign (USA)
UIUCDS	University of Illinois, Urbana–Department of Computer Science (USA)
UJT	Unijunction Transistor
UK	United Kingdom of Great Britain and Northern Ireland
	University of Kentucky (USA)
UK-ISES	United Kingdom section of the International Solar Energy Society
UKAC	United Kingdom Automation Council
UKADGE	United Kingdom Air Defence Ground Environment
UKAEA	United Kingdom Atomic Energy Authority
UKANA	United Kingdom Article Numbering Association
UKC	Underwater Keel Clearance
UKCA	United Kingdom CAMAC Association
UKCCD	UK Council for Computing Development
UKCCECS	United Kingdom Co-ordinating Committee for Examinations in Computer Studies
UKCIS	United Kingdom Chemical Information Service (of the Chemical Society)
UKCOSA	United Kingdom Council for Overseas Student Affairs
UKFCC	United Kingdom Federation for Culture Collections
UKHIS	United Kingdom Hazard Information Service
UKHS	United Kingdom Hovercraft Society
UKIRT	United Kingdom Infra-Red Telescope (on Mauna Kea, Hawaii)
UKISC	United Kingdom Industrial Space Committee (of SBAC, Electronic Engineering Association and Telecommunications Engineering and Manufacturing Association)
UKITO	United Kingdom Information Technology Organisation
UKLDS	United Kingdom Library Database System
UKLFS	United Kingdom Low Flying System
UKM	Universiti Kebangsaan Malaysia (National University of Malaysia)
UKMF	United Kingdom Mobile Force (Army)
UKMHMG	United Kingdom Mechanical Health Monitoring Group
UKNSD	United Kingdom National Serials Data Centre (of BLLD)
UKOLUG	United Kingdom On-Line User Group
UKOOA	United Kingdom Offshore Operators Association
UKPA	United Kingdom Patent Application
UKRAS	United Kingdom Railway Advisory Service
UKSATA	United Kingdom South Africa Trade Association

UKSC United Kingdom Simulation Council
UKSG United Kingdom Serials Group
UKSM United Kingdom Scientific Mission
UKSMT United Kingdom Sea Mist Test
UKTHIS United Kingdom Transport Hazard Information System
UKY University of Kentucky (USA)
UL Underwriters Laboratories (USA)
User Language
UL/S Ultrasonic and Sonic
ULA Uncommitted Logic Array
ULAIDS Universal Locator Airborne Integrated Data System
ULB Universal Logic Block
Universite Libre de Bruxelles (Belgium)
ULC Underwriters Laboratories of Canada (Canada)
Universal Logic Circuit
ULCC Ultra-Large Crude Carrier
University of London Computing Centre
ULCI Union of Lancashire and Cheshire Institutes
ULCS Uniform Lightness and Chromaticity Scale
ULD Unit Logic Device
Unitised Load Device
ULE Ultra-Low Expansion glass
ULI Ultra-Low Interstitial
ULICP Universal Log Interpretation Computer Programme
ULICS University of London Institute of Computer Science
ULINC Underwater Laboratories Incorporated (USA)
ULLA Ultra Low Level Air Dropping System
ULLNG Ultra-Large Liquefied Natural Gas Carriers
ULM Ultra-Light Motorised (aircraft)
Ultrasonic Light Modulator
Universal Logic Module
ULMS Office of University Library Management Studies (of Association of Research Libraries (USA))
Undersea Long-range Missile System (now known as Trident)
ULOR Upward Light Output Ratio
ULP Ultra-Lightweight Panel
Universal Logic Primitive
ULPZ Upper Limits for the Prescriptive Zone
ULSA Ultra-Low Sidelobe Antenna
ULSCS University of London Shared Cataloguing System
ULSI Ultra-Large Scale Integration
ULSV Unmanned Launch Space Vehicle
ULT Unique Last Term
ULTC Urban Library Trustees Council (USA)
ULTRA Ultra Lightweight Transmissive Array
Universal Language for Typographic Reproduction Applications
ULV Ultra-Low-Volume
UM Universiti Malaya (Malaysia)
University of Manitoba (Canada)
University of Massachusetts (USA)
University of Michigan (USA)
UM-HSRI University of Michigan, Highway Safety Research Institute (USA)
UM-P prefix to dated/numbered series of reports issued by University of Melbourne School of Physics (Australia)
UMA Ultrasonic Manufacturers Association (USA)
Un-manned Aircraft
University of Mid-America (USA)
UMASS University of Massachussetts (USA)
Unlimited Machine Access from Scattered Sites
UMC Unidimensional Multiple Chromatography
University of Missouri-Columbia (USA)
UMD Unitized Microwave Device
University of Minnesota in Duluth (USA)
UMDA Upper Mazaruni Development Authority (Guyana)
UMDNJ University of Medicine and Dentistry of New Jersey (USA)
UMER Ultrasonically Modulated Electron Resonance
UMES University of Michigan Executive System (USA)
UMF Ultra Microfiche
Urea-Melamine Formaldehyde
UMI Utah Management Institute (Utah University (USA))
UMICH University of Michigan (USA)
UMIDS Universal Mine Dispensing System
UMIST University of Manchester Institute of Science and Technology
UMKC University of Missouri–Kansas City (USA)
UMLER Universal Machine Language Equipment Register
UMMIPS Uniform Materiel Movement and Issue Priority System (USDOD)
UMML Union Médicale de la Méditérranée Latine (Latin-Mediterranean Medical Union)
UMO Underground Mains Organisation
University of Maine at Orono (USA)
UMOA Union Monetaire Ouest Africaine (West African Monetary Union)
UMP Uniformly Most Powerful
Upper Mantle Project (of ICSU)
Uridine Monophosphate
UMPIRE Universal Mathematical Programming system Incorporating Refinements and Extensions
UMR Uniform Management Reports (of USN)
Uniform Modular Realization
University of Missouri–Rolla (USA)
UMRCC Universities Mobile Radio Research Corporation (a consortium formed by Bath, Birmingham and Bristol Universities)
UMRECC University of Manchester Regional Computer Centre
UMS Ultrasonic Motion Sensor
Unattended Machinery Spaces
Undersea Medical Service
Undersea Medical Society (USA)
Unit for Manpower Studies (Dept of Employment)
UMTA Urban Mass Transportation Administration (of Department of Transportation (USA))
UMVUE Uniformly Minimum Variance Unbiased Estimator
UN The United Nations
UNACOMA Unione Nazionale Costruttori Macchine Agricole (Italy) (National Union of Agricultural Machinery Manufacturers)
UNADS UNIVAC Automated Documentation System
UNAM Universidad Nacional Autonoma de Mexico
UNAMACE Universal Automatic Map Compilation Equipment
UNAN Universidad Nacional Autonoma de Nicaragua
UNARC University of Alexandria Research Centre (Egypt)
UNBIS United Nations Bibliographic Information System
UNC Unified Coarse
University of North Carolina (USA)
UNC-W University of North Carolina at Wilmington (USA)
UNCAST United Nations Conference on the Applications of Science and Technology
UNCC University of North Carolina at Charlotte (USA)
UNCHE The United Nations Conference on the Human Environment (the Stockholm Conference)

UNCHS United Nations Centre for Human Settlements (Kenya)
UNCITRAL United Nations Commission on International Trade Law
UNCL Unified Numerical Control Language
UNCLOS United Nations Conference on the Law of the Sea
United Nations Convention on the Law of the Sea
UNCOD United Nations Conference on Desertification
UNCOL Universal Computer-Oriented Language
UNCSAT United Nations Organisation Conference on the Applications of Science and Technology for the Benefit of Less-Developed Areas
UNCSTD United Nations Conference on Science and Technology for Development
UNCTAD United Nations Conference on Trade And Development
UNCTC United Nations Centre on Transnational Corporations
UND Uniformly Negative Definite
University of Notre Dame (USA)
UNDE Ultrasonic Non-Destructive Evaluation
UNDP United Nations Development Programme (of UN)
UNDRO United Nations Disaster Relief Office
UNDT Ultrasonic Non-Destructive Testing
UNE prefix to Standards issued by IRATRA
University of New England (Australia)
UNEAS Union of European Accountancy Students
UNECA Union Europeenne des Fondeurs et Fabricants de Corps Gras Animaux (European Union of Animal Fat Producers)
UNECI Union of European Community Industries
UNEF Unified Extra Fine
UNELCA Union Electrica de Canarias SA (Spain) (govt owned and serving the Canary Islands)
UNEO United Nations Emergency Operation
UNEP United Nations Environmental Programme (a UN agency)
UNESA Unidad Electrica SA (Spain)
UNESCO United Nations Educational, Scientific and Cultural Organisation (France)
UNESID Union de Empresas Entidades y Siderurgicas (Spain)
UNETAS United Nations Emergency Technical Aid Service
UNEUROP European Economic Association (Switzerland)
UNEXSO International Underwater Explorers Society
UNF Unified Fine
UNFP United Nations Environment Programme
UNFPA United Nations Fund for Population Activities (of UN)
UNH University of New Hampshire (USA)
Uranyl Nitrate Hexahydrate
UNI Ente Nazionale Italiano di Unificazione (Italy) (Italian Standards Association)
User Node Interface
UNIBO University of Bophuthatswana (South Africa)
UNICCAP Universal Cable Circuit Analysis Programme
UNICE Union des Industries de la Communaute Europeene (National Confederation of Employers Associations of the EEC)
UNICHAL Union Internationale des Distributeurs de Chaleur (Germany) (International Union of Heating Distributors)
UNICIS University of Calgary (Canada) Information Systems
UNICLO United Nations Information Centre and Liaison Office
UNICOM Universal Integrated Communications
UNICRIM Uniform Crime Reporting system
UNIDO United Nations Industrial Development Organization
UNIDROIT International Institute for the Unification of Private Law
UNIFAC Universal Functional Activity Coefficient
UNIFE Union of European Railway Industries
UNIHEDD Universal Head-Down Display
UNILAC Universal Linear Accelerator
UNIMARC Universal MARC format
UNIMS UNIVAC Information Management System
UNINSA Union de Siderurgicas Asturianas SA (Spain)
UNIPARSE Universal Parser
UNIPEDE Union Internationale des Producteurs et Distributeurs d'Energie (International Union of Producers and Distributors of Electrical Energy)
UNIQUAC Universal Quasi-Chemical
UNIQUE Unified Command Interface with a Queued User Job Environment
UNIS UNIVAC Industrial System
UNISIST UNESCO/ICSU World Science Information System
UNISOR University Isotope Separator–OAK RIDGE (USA)
UNISTAR User Network for Information Storage, Transfer, Acquisition and Retrieval
UNISURV prefix to numbered series of reports issued by the School of Surveying, University of New South Wales (Australia)
UNISYM Unified Symbolic Standard Terminology for Mini Computer Instructions
UNITALSA Union Tecnica para la Promocion del Aluminio SA (Spain)
UNITAR United Nations Institute for Training and Research (of UN)
UNITRAC Universal Trajector Compiler
UNIVERSE Universities Extended Range and Satellite Experiment
UNLOSC United Nations Law of the Sea Conference
UNM University of New Mexico (USA)
UNO United Nations Organisation
University of New Orleans (USA)
UNOLS University–National Oceanographic Laboratory System (USA)
University–National Oceanographic Laboratory System (USA)
UNOTC United Nations Office of Technical Co-operation (UN)
UNPHU Universidad Nacional Pedro Henriquez Urena (Dominican Republic)
UNR University of Nevada, Reno (USA)
UNRAU Unified Numeric Representation Arithmetic Unit
UNREP Underway Replenishment
UNRISD United Nations Research Institute for Social Development (of UN)
UNRWA United Nations Relief and Works Agency (of UN)
UNS Unified Numbering System of metals and alloys (of SAE (USA))
UNSCEAR United Nations Scientific Committee on the Effects of Atomic Radiation
UNSO United Nations Sahel Office (of UN) (Sahel countries are Cape Verdi, Chad, Gambia, Mali, Mauritania, Niger, Senegal and Upper Volta)
UNSSOD United Nations Special Session on Disarmament
UNSW University of New South Wales (Australia)
UNTS Undergraduate Navigator Training Simulator
Undergraduate Navigator Training System (USAF)
UNTSO United Nations Truce Supervisory Organization
UNU United Nations University (Japan) (of the United Nations)
UOMC University of Oklahoma Medical Center (USA)
UOSAT University of Surrey Satellite
UP University of the Philippines
UPACS UNIVAC Patient Accounting and Control System

UPADI Union Panamericano de Associanciones de Ingenieros (Pan-American Federation of Engineering Societies)

UPAO University Professors for Academic Order (USA)

UPASI United Planters Association of South India (India)

UPC Uniform Product Code (of USA)
Universal Product Code

UPCC Uniform Product Code Council (USA)

UPD Underpotential Deposition
Uniformly Positive Definite

UPEC Uttar Pradesh Export Corporation (India)

UPFC Uttar Pradesh Financial Corporation (India)

UPIC Universal Personal Identification Code

UPL Universal Programming Language

UPLIFTS UNIVERSITY OF PITTSBURGH Linear File Tandem System

UPM Uninterruptible Power Module
Universiti Pertanian Malaysia (University of Agriculture (Malaysia))
University of Petroleum and Minerals (Saudi Arabia)

UPNG University of Papua New Guinea

UPPS Unified Pilot Publication System (of Chemical Abstracts Service of the American Chemical Society (USA))

UPR Ultrasonic Paramagnetic Resonance
Unsaturated Polyester Resin

UPRICO University of Puerto Rico

UPRN Unique Property Reference Number

UPS Ultraviolet Photoelectron Spectra
Ultraviolet Photoelectron Spectroscopy
Underwater Physiology Sub-committee (of the Royal Naval Personnel Research Committee)
Unidirectional Point Source
Uninterruptible Power Supply
Universal Polar Stereographic

UPSD Uniformly Positive Semi-Definite

UPSEB Uttar Pradesh State Electricity Board (India)

UPSIC Uttar Pradesh Small-scale Industries Corporation (India)

UPSIDC Uttar Pradesh State Industrial Development Corporation (India)

UPSSC Uttar Pradesh State Sugar Corporation

UPSTC Uttar Pradesh State Textile Corporation (India)

UPTE Ultra-Precision Test Equipment

UPU Universal Postal Union (Switzerland) (of UN)

UPV University of the Philippines in the Visayas (Philippines)

UPVC Unplasticised Polyvinyl Chloride

UR University of Riyadh (Saudi Arabia)
University of Rochester (USA)

URA Universities Research Associates (USA)

URANIT Uran–Isotopentrennungs–Gesellschaft (Germany)

URBS University Residential Building Systems (USA)

URD Underground Residential Distribution

URE Union de Radioaficionados Espanoles (Spain) (Spanish Amateur Radio Union)

URENCO Uranium Enrichment Company (shareholders are United Kingdom, Netherlands and Federal Republic of Germany)

URES University Residence Environment Scale

URF Union des Services Routiers des Chemins de Fer Européens (Union of European Railways Road Services)

URG United Reprocessors GmbH (Germany) (a company with share capital provided by United Kingdom, France and Federal Republic of Germany)

URI University of Rhode Island (USA)
Upper Respiratory Infection

URIPS Undersea Radioisotope Power Supply

URIS Universal Resources Information Symposium

URISA Urban and Regional Information Systems Association (USA)

URL User Requirements Language

URM Uniform Reflectivity Mirror

URMS Universal Reproducing Matrix Systems

UROEAO UNESCO Regional Office for Education in Asia and Oceania (Thailand)

URPA University of Rochester, Department of Physics and Astronomy (USA)

URR Ultra-Reliable Radar

URRI Urban-Regional Research Institute (Michigan State University, USA)

URRVS Urban Rapid Rail Vehicle and Systems (a program of UMTA (DOT (USA))

URS Universal Regulating System

URSA Unattended RACON Semiconductor Apparatus

URSI Union Radio-Scientifique Internationale (of ICSU) (International Scientific Radio Union)

URSIES Ultravariable Resolution Single Interferometer Echelle Scanner

URT Underground Residential Transformer

URTI Universite Radiophonique et Televisuelle Internationale (France)

URTNA Union of National Radio and Television Organizations of Africa

URV Undersea Rescue Vehicle
Underwater Research Vehicle

US Unheated Soya-bean meal

USA United States of America

USAAA United States Army Audit Agency

USAAAVS United States Army Agency for Aviation Safety

USAADE United States Army Air Defense Board

USAADS United States Army Air Defense School

USAADTA United States Army Aircraft Development Test Activity

USAAEFA United States Army Aviation Engineering Flight Activity

USAAESW United States Army Airborne Electronics and Special Warfare Board

USAAMCA United States Army Advanced Materiel Concepts Agency

USAAMRDL United States Army Air Mobility Research and Development Laboratory

USAARDC United States Army Aberdeen (Maryland) Research and Development Center

USAARL United States Army Aeromedical Research Laboratory

USAARU United States Army Aeromedical Research Unit

USAASL United States Army Atmospheric Sciences Laboratory

USAASO United States Army Aeronautical Services Office

USAASTA United States Army Aviation Systems Test Activity

USAATCA United States Army Air Traffic Control Activity

USAAVA United States Army Audio-Visual Agency

USAAVLABS United States Army Aviation Materiel Laboratories

USAAVNC United States Army Aviation Center

USAAVNIA United States Army Aviation Test Activity

USAAVNS United States Army Aviation School

USAAVNTED United States Army Aviation Test Board

USAAVSCOM United States Army Aviation Systems Command (disbanded 1977)

USAB United States Activities Board (of IEEE (USA))

USABAAR United States Army Board for Aviation Accident Research

USABESRL United States Army Behavioral Science Research Laboratory (now part of ARI (US Army))
USABRL United States Army Ballistics Research Laboratories
USAC United States Auto Club (USA)
USACAA United States Army Concepts Analysis Agency
USACC United States Army Communications Command
USACCS United States Army Chemical Center and School
USACDC United States Army Combat Developments Command
USACDCAVNA United States Army Combat Developments Command Aviation Agency
USACDCCBRA United States Army Combat Developments Command Chemical-Biological-Radiological Agency
USACDCEC United States Army Combat Developments Command—Experimentation Command
USACDIA United States Army Developments Command Infantry Agency
USACEEIA United States Army Communications–Electronics Engineering Installation Agency
USACRREL United States Army Cold Regions Research and Engineering Laboratory
USACSC United States Army Computer Systems Command
USACSSEC United States Army Computer Systems Support and Evaluation Command
USAEC United States Army Engineer Corps
United States Atomic Energy Commission (USA) (disbanded in 1974 and replaced by ERDA and the Nuclear Regulatory Commission)
USAECOM United States Army Electronics Command (split into ERADCOM, CORADCOM and CERCOM in 1977)
USAEHA United States Army Environmental Hygiene Agency
USAELRDL United States Army Electronics Research and Development Laboratories
USAENPG United States Army Engineer Power Group
USAEPG United States Army Electronic Proving Ground
USAERDL United States Army Engineer Research and Development Laboratories (became MERDC in 1962)
USAERG United States Army Engineer Reactors Group
USAESC United States Army Engineer Studies Center
USAETL United States Army Engineer Topographic Laboratories
USAEWES United States Army Engineer Waterways Experiment Station
USAF United States Air Force
USAFA United States Air Force Academy
USAFE United States Air Forces in Europe
USAFETAC United States Air Force Environmental Technical Applications Center
USAFI United States Armed Forces Institute (USDOD)
USAFO United States Army Field Office
USAFSAM United States Air Force School of Aerospace Medicine
USAFSC United States Air Force Systems Command
USAFSO United States Air Force Southern Command
USAFSS United States Air Force Security Service
USAFSTC United States Army Foreign Science and Technology Center
USAGETA United States Army General Equipment Test Activity
USAHI United States Army History Institute (USA)
USAICA United States Army Inter-agency Communications Agency
USAICS United States Army Intelligence Center and School
USAID United States Agency for International Development
USAID/W United States Agency for International Development, Washington
USAIDR United States Army Institute of Dental Research
USAILCOM United States Army International Logistics Command
USAIRE Association of United States of America Aerospace Industries Representatives in Europe
USAIS United States Army Infantry School
USAISR United States Army Institute of Surgical Research 1974 and replaced by ERDA and the Nuclear Regulatory C
USAJPG United States Army Jefferson Proving Ground
USALC United States Army Logistics Center
USALMC United States Army Logistics Management Center
USAM Unified Space Applications Mission (of NASA)
Uniformly-Sampled-Autoregressive Moving average
USAMBRDL United States Army Medical Bioengineering Research and Development Laboratory
USAMBRL United States Army Medical Biomechanical Research Laboratory
USAMC United States Army Materiel Command (became DARCOM in 1976)
USAMC-ITC United States Army Materiel Command Interim Training Center
USAMECOM United States Army Mobility Equipment Command
USAMERDC United States Army Mobility Equipment Research and Development Center
USAMETA United States Army Military Engineering Training Agency
USAMIDA United States Army Major Item Data Agency
USAMIIA United States Army Medical Intelligence and Information Agency
USAMMAE United States Army Material Management Agency
USAMMCS United States Army Missile and Munitions Center and School
USAMRDC United States Army Medical Research and Development Command
USAMRICD United States Army Medical Research Institute of Chemical Defense
USAMRIID United States Army Medical Research Institute of Infectious Diseases
USAMRL United States Army Medical Research Laboratory
USAMRNL United States Army Medical Research and Nutrition Laboratory
USAMRRDC United States Army Manpower Resources Research and Development Center
USAMS United States Army Management School
USAMSSA United States Army Management Systems Support Agency
USANDI United States Army Nuclear Defense Laboratory
USAPHS United States Army Primary Helicopter School
USAPRO United States Army Personnel Research Office (now USABESRL)
USARAL United States Army—Alaska
USARBCO United States Army Base Command
USARCCO United States Army Commercial Communications Office (of US Army Communications Command)
USAREUR United States Army Europe
USAREUR-MATCOM United States Army, Europe, Materiel Command
USARIEM United States Army Research Institute of Environmental Medicine
USARJ United States Army Japan
USARO United States Army Research Office
USARP United States Antarctic Research Program (of NSF (USA))

USARPA United States Army Radio Propagation Agency
USARPAC United States Army Pacific
USARV United States Army Vietnam
USAS prefix to lettered and numbered series of Standards issued by USASI
USASAFS- COM United States Army Safeguard Systems Command
USASAM United States Army School of Aviation Medicine
USASASA United States Army Small Arms Systems Agency
USASATCOMA United States Army Satellite Communications Agency
USASCAF United States Army Service Center for Army Forces
USASCC United States Army Strategic Communications Command (became United States Army Communications Command in 1973)
USASCSOCR United States of America Standard Character Set for Optical Character Recognition
USASI United States of America Standards Institute (now American National Standards Institute)
USATACOM United States Army Tank-Automotive Command
USATEA United States Army Transportation Engineering Agency
USATECOM United States Army Test and Evaluation Command
USATOPOCOM United States Army Topographic Command (became Defense Mapping Agency Topographic Center in 1972)
USATSA United States Army Troop Support Agency
USATTC United States Army Tropic Test Center
USAWC United States Army War College
USAWECOM United States Army Weapons Command
USB Unified S-Band
Upper Sideband
USBA United States Brewers Association (USA)
USBC Universal Standard Book Code
USBE United States Book Exchange
USBM United States Bureau of Mines
USBN Universal Standard Book Number
USBR United States Bureau of Reclamation (of Dept. of the Interior)
USC Ultra Selective Conversion
Underwater Systems Center (USN)
United States Congress
University of Southern California (USA)
USC&GS United States Coast and Geodetic Survey (USDC)
USCAE University of Southern California, Department of Aerospace Engineering (USA)
USCAR United States Civil Administration, Ryukyu Islands
USCEE University of Southern California, Department of Electrical Engineering (USA)
University of Southern California, Electronic Sciences Laboratory (USA)
USCENTCOM United States Central Command (USDOD)
USCG United States Coast Guard (USA)
USCGA United States Coast Guard Academy
USCGS United States Coast and Geodetic Survey (of NOAA (USA))
USCIPI University of Southern California Image Processing Institute (USA)
USCISE University of Southern California Department of Industrial and Systems Engineering (USA)
USCOLD United States Committee on Large Dams (USA)
USCOMM United States Department of Commerce
USCONARC United States Continental Army Command
USCSC United States Civil Service Commission
USD Ultimate Strength Design
USDA United States Department of Agriculture
USDA-APHIS-PP/Q United States Department of Agriculture, Animal and Plant Health Inspection Service, Plant Protection and Quarantine Programs (USA)
USDA-FS United States Department of Agriculture–Forest Service (USA)
USDA-REA United States Department of Agriculture–Rural Electrification Administration (USA)
USDC United States Department of Commerce
USDL United States Department of Labor
USDOD United States Department of Defense
USDOE United States Department of Energy
USE UNIVAC Scientific Exchange (USA)
USEPA United States Environmental Protection Agency
USERC United States Environment and Resources Council (USA)
USES United States Employment Service (USA)
USF University of South Florida (USA)
USFGC United States Feed Grains Council (USA)
USFS United States Forestry Service (USA)
United States Frequency Standard
USFWS United States Fish and Wildlife Service (US Dept of the Interior)
USGPO United States Government Printing Office
USGR United States Government Report
USGRDR United States Government Research and Development Report
USGS United States Geological Survey (US Dept of the Interior)
USGW Under Sea Guided Weapon
Underwater Launched Anti-Surface Ship Guided Weapon
USIA United States Information Agency
USIAS Union Syndicale des Industries Aeronautiques et Spatiales (France) (Aerospace Industry Association) (became GIFAS in 1975)
USIB United States Intelligence Board (USA)
USIC Undersea Instrument Chamber
USICA United States International Communication Agency (USA)
USITA United States Independent Telephone Association (USA)
USITC United States International Trade Commission (USA)
USITE United States International Transportation Exposition (USA)
USL Underwater Sound Laboratory (USN) (now Naval Underwater Systems Center)
University of Southwestern Louisiana (USA)
Urban Systems Laboratory (Massachusetts Institute of Technology (USA))
USM Ultrasonic Machining
Underwater-to-Surface Missile
University Saino Malaysia (University of Science (Malaysia))
Unlisted Securities Market
USMA United States Maritime Administration (US Dept of Commerce)
United States Metric Association
United States Military Academy
USMCEB United States Military Communications Electronics Board (USA)
USMG Universite Scientifique et Medicale de Grenoble (France)
USMLA United States Maritime Law Association (USA)
USMMA United States Merchant Marine Academy (of the Maritime Administration (USA))
USN United States Navy
USNA United States Naval Academy (USN)
USNAVEUR United States Navy—Europe
USNC/TAM United States National Committee on Theoretical and Applied Mechanics (of NAS/NRC (USA))

USNCFID	United States National Committee for FID (International Federation for Documentation) (USA)
USNDC	United States Nuclear Data Committee (of USAEC)
USNEL	United States Navy Electronics Laboratory (now reorganised as Navy Undersea Warfare Center AND Navy Command, Control and Communications Center)
USNM	United States National Museum of Natural History (USA)
USNO	United States Naval Observatory
USNRC	United States Nuclear Regulatory Commission
USNRDL	United States Naval Radiological Defense Laboratory
USNSA	United States Naval Sailing Association (USA)
USNSC	United States Naval Space Command
USNTPS	United States Naval Test Pilot School (USN)
USNUSL	United States Navy Underwater Laboratory
USOE	United States Office of Education
USOO	United States Oceanographic Office (USA)
USP	Ultra-Short Pulses
	United States of America Patent
USPHS	United States Public Health Service
USPO	United States Patents Office (USA)
USPS	United States Postal Service (USA)
	United States Power Squadrons (USA)
USRA	United States Railway Association (USA)
	Universities Space Research Association (USA) (an international consortium)
USRD	Underwater Sound Reference Division (of Naval Research Laboratory (USN))
USREDCOM	United States Readiness Command
USRL	Underwater Sound Reference Laboratory (USN)
USS	Unsmoked Sheets
USSA	Unified Systems Safety Analysis
USSR	Union of Soviet Socialists Republics
USSST	United States Salt Spray Test
USSTRICOM	United States Strike Command
UST	Urinary System Tumour
USTA	United States Telephone Association
USTIS	Ubiquitous Scientific and Technical Information System
USTS	United States Travel Service (US Dept of Commerce)
USTSA	United States Telephone Supplies Association
USU	Utah State University (USA)
USUHS	Uniformed Services University of the Health Sciences (USDOD)
USVRU	Ultra-Stable Voltage Reference Unit
USW	Ultra-Sonic Welding
	Undersea Warfare
USWB	United States Weather Bureau
USYM	Universal Sequential Synchronous Machine
UT	Universal Time
UT-CES	University of Texas Center for Energy Studies (USA)
UT-GSBS	University of Texas–Graduate School of Biomedical Sciences (USA)
UTA	Union de Transports Aeriens (France)
	Unit Trust Association
	Universal Torque Analyser
UTAC	Union Technique de l'Automobile, du motorcycle et du Cycle (France) (Technical Association for the Motor, Motorcycle and Cycle Industries)
UTACV	Urban Tracked Air Cushion Vehicle
UTB	Unit Terminal Building
UTC	Universal Time Coordinated
	Universal Transducing Cell
	Urban Technology Conference (USA)
	Urban Traffic Control
	Utilities Telecommunication Council (USA)
UTCS	Urban Traffic Control System
UTD	University of Texas at Dallas (USA)
UTE	Union Technique de l'Electricite (France) (Technical Union of Electricity)
	Usinas Electricas y Telefonos del Estado (Uruguay) (Uruguay Communications Agency)
UTEC	Universal Test Equipment Compiler
	Utah University College of Engineering (USA)
UTI	Unit Trust of India (India)
UTIAS	University of Toronto, Institute for Aerospace Studies (Canada)
UTK	University of Tennessee, Knoxville (USA)
UTLAS	University of Toronto (Canada) Library Automation System (on-line network comprising Ontario and Quebec university libraries, and public and government libraries) (in 1984 became UTLAS Inc.–a private company)
UTM	Universal Testing Machine
	Universal Transverse Mercator
UTMSI	University of Texas Marine Science Institute (USA)
UTMU	University of Tennessee, Medical Units (USA)
UTP	Uridine Triphosphate
UTRAO	University of Texas Radio Astronomy Observatory (USA)
UTS	Ultimate Tensile Strength
	Underwater Telephone System
	Untreated Straw
UTSI	University of Tennessee Space Institute (USA)
UTT	Unit Under Test
	Utility Tactical Transport
UTTAS	Utility Tactical Transport Aircraft System
UTU	Universidad del Trabajo del Uruguay (Uruguay) (Technical University)
UTW	Under-the-Wing externally-blown jet flap
UTX-A/P	prefix to dated-numbered series of reports issued by University of Texas Antennas and Propagation Laboratory (USA)
UU	Utah University (USA)
UUA	UNIVAC Users Association (USA)
UUIP	Uppsala University Institute of Physics (Sweden)
UUM	Unification of Units of Measurement (a panel of ICAO)
UUMP	Unification of Units of Measurement Panel (of ICAO)
UUPI	Ultrasonic Under-carriage Position Indicator
UUT	Unit Under Test
UV	Ultraviolet
UVa	University of Virginia (USA)
UVAS	Ultra-Violet Astronomical Satellite
	Unmanned Vehicle for Aerial Surveillance
UVC	Ultra-Violet-to-Visible Converter
	Universidad del Valle (Colombia)
UVDIAL	Ultra-Violet Differential Absorption Lidar
UVEROM	Ultra-Violet Eraseable Read Only Memory
UVI	Ultraviolet Irradiation
UVL	Institutet for Vatten -och Luftvards-forskning (Sweden) (Institute for Water and Air Research)
	Ultra-Violet Laser
UVLI	Ustav Vedeckych Lekarskych Informaci (Czechoslovakia) (Institute for Medical Information)
UVM	Universal Vendor Marking
	University of Vermont (USA)
UVM-TIC	University of Vermont Technical Information Center (USA)
UVS	Ultra-Violet Spectrometer
	Ultraviolet Spectrophotometer
	Universal Versaplot Software
UVSC	Ultra-Violet Solar Constants

UVTEI Ustredl Vedeckych, Technickych a Ekonomickych Informaci (Czechoslovakia) (Centre for Scientific, Technical and Economic Information)

UW University of Washington (USA)
Upset Welding

UWAL University of Washington Aeronautical Laboratory (USA)

UWDOBER University of Wyoming, Division of Business and Economic Research (USA)

UWI University of the West Indies (Jamaica)

UWI/CC University of the West Indies Computing Centre

UWIS University of Wisconsin (USA)

UWIS-DS University of Wisconsin–Department of Statistics (USA)

UWIST University of Wales Institute of Science and Technology

UWME University of Wyoming Department of Mechanical Engineering (USA)

UWO University of Western Ontario (Canada)

UWSDDMS Underwater Weapons Systems Design Disclosure Management System (USN)

UWSRD Underwater Weapons Systems Reliability Data (USN)

UWTV Under-Water Television

UXB Unexploded Bomb

UXO Unexploded Ordnance

V

V&V Verification and Validation

V-CM Visual Counter Measures

V-MAT Versatile Multi-Aimer Trainer

V-VAC VICKERS Versatile Aircraft Carrier

V-VS Voenno-Vozdushniye Sily (USSR) (Air Forces of the USSR)

V/HUD Vertical/Head-Up Display

V/STOL Vertical and Short Take-Off and Landing

VA Value Analysis
Vibration Analysis
Vinyl Acetate
Visual Aids (a panel of ICAO)
Viterbi Algorithm

VAAC Vanadyl Acetyl Acetonate

VAAM Voice Actuated Address Mechanism

VAAR Vinyl Alcohol Acetate Resin

VAB Vehicle Assembly Building (John F. Kennedy Space Center, NASA (USA))
Vertical Assembly Building

VABD Van Allen Belt Dosimeter

VABM Value Added By Manufacturer

VAC Vector Analogue Computer
Volt-Ampere Characteristics

VAD Variable Abbreviated Dialling
Velocity-Azimuth Display

VADAC Voice Analyser and Data Converter

VADE Vandenberg Automatic Data Equipment (of AFWTR)

VADS VULCAN Air Defence System

VAE Vinyl Acetate-Ethylene

VAEP Variable, Attributes, Error Propagation

VAGES Variable Geometry Simulator

VAI Video Assisted Instruction
Vorticity Area Index

VAJARS Vortex Axis Jet Angular Rate Sensor

VAKUME Visual Audio Kinetic Unit: Multiples and Environments

VAL Value-oriented Algorithmic Language
Videotex Assisted Learning

VALA Victoria Association for Library Automation (Australia)

VALNET Veterans Administration Library Network (USA)

VALOR Variable Locale and Resolution

VALSAS Variable Length word Symbolic Assembly System

VALT VTOL Approach and Landing Technology

VALUE Validated Aircraft Logistics Utilization Evaluation

VAM Value Added Market
Variable Aerobee Motor
Vector Airborne Magnetometer
Vinyl Acetate Monomer
Virtual Access Method
Visual Approach Monitor
VOGEL'S Approximation Method

VAMC Visual Approach Monitor Chart

VAMFO Variable Angle Monochromatic Fringe Observation

VAMI Vsesoyuznyy Alyuminiyeo Magniyevyy Institut (USSR) (All-Union Aluminium Magnesium Institute)

VAMOSC Visibility And Management Of Support Costs (a task group of USDOD)

VAMP Value Analysis of Management Practices
Variable Anamorphic Motion Picture
Vector Arithmetic Multi-processor
Visual Analysis for Management Planning
Visual-Acoustic-Magnetic Pressure
Volume, Area and Mass Properties

VAMS Vector Airspeed Measuring System

VAN Value Added Network

VANDA Vision And Audio

VANDL Vancouver Data Language

VANS Value Added Network Service

VAP Very Advanced Propulsion
Video-Audio-Participative
Visual Aids Panel (of ICAO)

VAPI Visual Approach Path Indicator

VAPS VSTOL Approach System

VAR Vacuum Arc Refining
Vacuum-Arc Remelting
Visual-Aural Range

VARAD Varying Radiation

VARES VEGA (PRECISION LABORATORIES INCORPORATED) (USA) Aircraft Radar Enhancing System

VARIG Empresa de Viacao Aerea Rio Grandense (Brazil)

VARR Variable Range Reflector

VARS Vanuatu Radio Amateur Society (Fiji)

VARSDA Vehicular Actuated Road Signal Development Association

VARVS Variable Acuity Remote Viewing System

VAS Vereniging van Accountancy-Studenten (Netherlands) (Society of Accountancy Students)
Vibration Analysis Suite of computer programs
Virginia Association of Surveyors (USA)
Visible Infra-red Spin-Scan Radiometer Atmospheric Sounder
Visible Spin-Scan Radiometer Atmospheric Sounder

VASCA Electronic Valve and Semi-Conductor Association (ceased to operate in 1973) (member companies became direct members of the Electronic Components Board)

VASI Visual Approach Slope Indicator

VASIS Visual Approach Slope Indicator System

VASKhNIL Vsesoyuznyy Akademiya Sel'skokhozyaystvennykh Nauk imeni Lenina (USSR) (All-Union Academy of Agricultural Sciences)

VASP Viacao Aereo Sao Paulo (Brazil)

VASS Visually Activated Switch OR Switching System

VAST System Vibration and Static Analysis
Vehicle Activity Status Transmission
Vehicle Automatic State Transmitter
Versatile Avionic Shop Test system
Visual Alertness Stressor Test

VAT Value Added Tax
Virtual Address Translator

VATE Versatile Automatic Test Equipment

VATLS Visual Airborne Target Location System

VATOL Vertical Attitude and Take-Off and Landing

VATS/SNAP Video Augmented Tracking System/Single-seat Night Attack Programme

VATTR prefix to numbered series of reports issued by Value Added Tax Tribunals

VAV Variable Air Volume

VAWT Verticle Axis Wind Turbine

VAX Virtual Access Extension

VBA Very Big Accelerator

VBB Vattenbyggnadsbyran (Sweden)

VBD Veterinary Biologics Division (of ARS (USDA))

VBI Vertical Blanking Interval

VBL VOYAGER Biological Laboratory

VBO Vsesoyuznyy Botanicheskoye Obshchestvo (USSR) (All-union Botanical Society)

VBRA Vehicle Builders and Repairers Association

VC Vanadium Carbide
Vehicular Communications
Vinyl Chloride
Virtual Call

VCA Vehicle and Component Approvals Division (of DTp)
Vinylene Carbonate
Viral-Capsid Antigen
Virtual Crystal Approximation

VCAA Veteran and Classic Aeroplane Association

VCAD Vertical Contact Analogue Display

VCASS Visually-Coupled Airborne Systems Simulator

VCCS Video and Cable Communications Section (of ALA-LITA (USA))
Voltage-Controlled Current Source

VCD Vapour Compression Distillation

VCE Variable-Cycle Engine
Virtual Coulomb Excitation

VCG Vector Cardiogram
Voltage-Controlled Generator

VCH Vinyl Cyclohexene

VCHP Variable Conductance Heat Pipe

VCHPS Variable-Conductance Heat-Pipe System

VCI Vapour-phase Corrosion Inhibitor
Volatile Corrosion Inhibitor

VCM Verification Comparison Matrix
Verticle Conveyor Module
Vinyl Chloride Monomer

VCO Voltage Controlled Oscillator

VCOAD Voluntary Committee on Overseas Aid and Development

VCOD Vertical Carrier Onboard Delivery

VCP Visual Comfort Probability

VCR Variable–Compression–Ratio
Video Cassett Recorder OR Recording
Voltage Coefficient of Resistance

VCS Visually Coupled System
Voter-Comparator Switch

VCSA Virus Cell Surface Antigen

VCSS Voice Communications Security System

VCT Video Contrast Tracker
Voltage to Current Transactor

VCTS Variable Cockpit Training System

VCVS Voltage Controlled Voltage Source

VCXO Voltage Controlled Crystal Oscillator

VD Vacuum Distillation
Verbal Discrimination

VDA Verband der Automobilindustrie (Germany) (Automobile Industry Association)
Video Distribution Amplifier

VDAL Variable Datalength Assembly Language

VdB Velocity Decibel

VDB Verein Deutscher Bibliothekare (Germany) (German Association of Librarians)

VDBWB Verein der Diplom-Bibliothekare an Wissenschaftlichen Bibliotheken (Germany) (Association of Certificated Librarians in Scientific Libraries)

VDC Variable Dead-time Counter
Vinylidene Chloride

VDCM Vinylidene Chloride Monomer

VDE Verband Deutscher Elektrotechniker (Germany) (German Association of Electrical Engineers)

VDeH Verein Deutscher Eisenhuttenleute (Germany) (German Iron and Steel Research Association)

VDEMS Vinyldiethoxymethyl Silane

VDEW Vereinigung Deutscher Elektrizitatswerke (Germany (Association of German Electricity Supply Undertakings)

VDG Verein Deutscher Giessereifachleute (Germany) (German Association for Foundry and Casting Operations)

VDI Vegetation Drought Index
Vehicle Deformation Index
Verein Deutscher Ingenieure (Germany) (German Association of Engineers)
Vertical Display Indicator

VDL Velocity Dividing Line

VDLU Verband Deutscher Luftfahrt Unternehmen (Germany) (German Association of Aeronautical Enterprises)

VDM Vector Dominance Model
Vector Drawn Map
Vereinigte Deutsche Metallwerke (Germany)
Vienna Development Method

VDMA Variable Destination Multiple Access
Verein Deutscher Maschinenbau-Anstalten (Germany) (German Association of Machinery Manufacturers)

VdMF Association of German Microfilm Service Houses (Germany)

VDNCS Vapour Deposited Non-Crystalline Solid

VDP Verband Deutscher Papierfabriken (Germany) (German Papermaking Association)
Vertical Data Processing

VDPI Verband der Deutschen Photographischen Industrie (Germany) (Association of the German Photographic Industry)

VDR Variable Diameter Rotor
Voltage-Dependent Resistor

VDR/EDC Economic Development Committee for Vehicle Distribution and Repair

VDRI Verein Deutscher Revisions-Ingenieure (Germany) (German Association of Engineering Inspection)

VDS Variable Depth Sonar
Variable Dilution Sampling
Vehicle Descriptor Section (part of VIN of ISO)

VDSI Verein Deutscher Sicherheits-Ingenieure (Germany) (German Association of Safety Engineers)

VDT Variable Deflection Thruster
Video Data Terminal
Video Display Terminal

VdTUV Vereinigung der Technischen Uberwachings-Vereine (Germany) (Association of Boiler Inspection Technicians)

VDU Visual Display Unit

VDW Verein Deutscher Werkzeugmaschinenfabriken (Germany) (Association of German Machine-Tool Manufacturers)
VDZ Verein Deutscher Zementwerke (Germany) (Association of German Cement Works)
VE Value Engineering
VEA Value Engineering Association
Virginia Electronic Association (USA)
VEB Variable Elevation Beam
Ventricular Ectopic Beats
Volkseigener Betrieb (People's Concern)
VEC Valence Electron Concentration
Variable Energy Cyclotron
Vector Analogue Computer
Ventricular Ectopic Complex
VECOR Vanderbijl Engineering Corporation (South Africa)
VECP Value Engineering Change Proposal
VEDC Vitreous Enamel Design Council
Vitreous Enamel Development Council
VEE Venezuelan Equine Encephalomyelitis
VeFAC Variable Factor programming
VEFCA Value Engineering Functional Cost Analysis
VEFV Voice-Excitated Formant Vocoder
VEGA Venera-Galley (USSR) (spacecraft)
VEM Variable Encounter Method
Vaso-Excitor Material
VEMG Vector Electro-myography
VEMS Versatile Exercise Mine System
VENUS Vertical alignment design by the Nodal-tangent and Undulation System
VEO Verband der Elektrizitatswerke Osterreichisches (Austria)
VEP Vibration Eigenvalue Problem
Visual Evoked Potential
VER Visual Evoked Electrical Response
Visual Evoked Response
VERA Variable Eddington Radiation Approximation
Versatile Experimental Reactor Assembly
VERAS Vehicle for Experimental Research in Aerodynamics and Structures
VERB Visual Electronic Remote Blackboard
VEREAD Value Engineering Retrieval of Esoteric Administrative Data
VERLAC Vertical Ejection Launch Aero Reaction Control
VERSA Vehicle Routing and Scheduling Algorithm
VERTREP Vertical Replenishment
VES Voluntry Euthanasia Society
VESC Vehicle Equipment Safety Commission (USA)
VESPER Vehicles and Equipments Spare Parts Economics and Repair
Vehicles, Equipment and Spares Provision, Economics and Repair
VET Vibrational-Energy Transfer
VETAG Vehicle Tagging
VETMIS Vehicle Technical Management Information System (of TACOM (US Army))
VETRAS Vehicle Traffic Simulator
VETS Vehicle Electrical Test System
VEV Voice Excited Vocoder
VEW Vereinigte Elektrizitatswerke Westfalen (Germany)
VF Voice Frequency
VFA Volatile Fatty Acids
VFC Voltage-to-Frequency Converter
VFCT Voice Frequency Carrier Telegraphy
VFEA Vacuum Freezing Ejector Absorption
VFET V-groove power junction FET
Vertical Field-Effect Transistor
VFM Value for Money
VFMED Variable Format Message Entry Device
VFO Variable Frequency Oscillator
VFOAR Vandenberg Field Office of Aerospace Research (USAF)
VFP Variable Factor Programming
Variance Frequency Processor
VFR Vehicle-Fuel-Refinery
Visual Flight Rules
VFT Voice-Frequency Telegraph
VFU Vertical Format Unit
VFVC Vacuum-Freezing Vapour-Compression desalting process
VFW Vereinigte Flugtechnische Werke (Germany)
VG Vinylene Glycol
VGA Variable Gain Amplifier
VGB Vereiningung der Grosskesselbesitzer (Germany) (Society of Large Boiler Owners)
VGBIL Vsejuznaja Gosudarstvennaja Biblioteka Inostrannoji Literatury (USSR) (Pan-Soviet State Library for Foreign Literature)
VGI Vertical Gyro Instrument
VGM Variable Grating Mode
VGO Vacuum Gas Oil
VGP Virtual Geomagnetic Poles
VGPI Visual Glide Path Indicator
VGPO Velocity-Gate-Pull-Off
VGVAW Variable Geometry Vertical AXIS Windmill
VHD Video High Density
VHF Very High Frequency
VHFOR Very High Frequency Omni-Range
VHFRT Very High Frequency Radio Telephony
VHMWPE Very High Molecular Weight Polyethylene
VHO Very High Output
VHPIC Very High Performance Integrated Circuit
VHRC Virginia Highway Research Council (USA)
VHRR Very High Resolution Radiometer
VHSIC Very High-Speed Integrated Circuit
VHT Very High Temperature
VI Veiligheidsinstituut (Netherlands) (Safety Institute)
Viscosity Index
Voltage and Inductance
VIAM Vsesoyuznyy Nauchno Issledovatel'skiy Institut Aviatsionnykh Materialov (USSR) (All-Union Scientific Research Institute of Aviation Materials)
VIARCO Venezuelan International Airways Reservations Computerized system
VIAS Voice Interference Analysis System
VIASA Venezolana Internacional de Aviacion SA (Venezuela)
VIATLS Visual Airborne Target Locator System
VIBAC Vehicle Ice-Breaking-Air Cushion
VIBANK computerised information retrieval system on Mechanical Vibration (University Laval (Canada))
VIBS Vibration Sensor
VIC Variable Instruction Computer
VICA Vocational Industrial Clubs of America (USA)
VICARS Video Communication And Retrieval System
VICC Visual Information Control Console
VICCI Voice Initiated Cockpit Control and Integration
VICES Voice Internal Communications Equipment for Submarines
VICG Vertical-Interval Colour Genlock system
VICOM International Association of Visual Communications Management
VICON Visual Confirmation
VICS Vehicles In Confined Spaces

VID Virtual Image Display
VID-R Visual Information Display and Retrieval system
VIDA Ventricular Impulse Detector and Alarm
VIDEC Vibration and Deviation Concept
VIDEO Visual Inspection of Defects Enhanced by Optics
VORTEX Interactive Data Entry Operations
VIDPI Visually Impaired Data Processors International (USA)
VIDSEC Video Systems Exposition and Conference (USA)
VIDT Variable Inductance Displacement Tranducer
VIE Vacuum Insulated Evaporator
VIEW Video Information Exchange Window
VIEWS Vibration Imbalance Early Warning System
VIF Visible Index File
VIFCS VTOL Integrated Flight Control System
VIFF Vectoring In Forward Flight
VIFS Vsesoyuznogo Informatsionnogo Fonda Standartov i Tecknicheskikh Uslovii (USSR) (All-Union Reference Bank of Standards and Specifications)
VII Viscosity Index Improver
VIM Vacuum Induction Melting
VIMCOS Vehicle for the Investigation of Maintenance Control Systems
VIMS Versatile Interior Multiplex System
VINITI Vsesoyuznyy Institut Nauchnoy i Teknicheskoy Informatsii (USSR) (All-Union Institute of Scientific and Technical Information)
VINS Very Intense Neutron Source
VIP Variable Information Processing
Vasoactive Intestinal Peptide
Vasoactive Intestinal Polypeptride
Verifying Interpreting Punch
Versatile Information Processor
Video Interface Processor
Visual Image Processor
VIPER Versatile Intermediate Pulsed Experimental Reactor
VIPRE Visual Precision
VIPS Voice Interruption Priority System
VIR Vertical Interval Reference
VIRA Vehicular Infra-Red Alarm
VIRTU Video for Interaction and Training Users Group
VIS Vehicle Indicator Section (of VIN (ISO))
VISAR Velocity Interferometry System for Any Reflector
Visual Inspection System for the Analysis of Reports (a project of the Automobile Association)
VISCOM Visual-Communication system
VISDA Visual Information System Development Association (Japan)
VISPA Virtual Storage Productivity Aid
VISQI Visual Image Quality Indicator
VISSR Visible and Infrared Spin Scan Radiometer
Visible Infra-red Spin-Scan Radiometer
VISTA Very Intelligent Surveillance and Target Acquisition
Viewing Instantly Security Transactions Automatically
Visual Information for Satellite Telemetry Analysis
Volunteers In Service To America
VIT Vertical Interval Test
VITA Volunteers for International Technical Assistance (USA)
VITAL Variably Initialized Translator for Algorithmic Languages
VAST Interface Test Application Language
Virtual Image Take-off and Landing
VITEAC Video Transmission Engineering Advisory Committee (USA)
VITM Visvesvaraya Industrial and Technological Museum (India)
VKIFD Von Karman Institute for Fluid Dynamics (Belgium)
VKR Video Kinescope Recording
VKWB Verban Kirchlich-wissenschaftlichen Bibliotheken (Germany) (Association of Ecclesiastical Academic Libraries)
VLA Very Large Airplane
Very Large Array
Very Low Altitude
VLAD Vertical Line Array DIFAR
VLAO Vertical Line Array Omnidirectional
VLBA Very Long Baseline Array
VLBC Very Large Bulk-cargo Carrier
VLBI Very Long Baseline Inteferometer
Very Long Baseline Interferometry
VLCC Very Large Crude-oil Carrier
VLCD Very Low Calorie Diet
VLCEHV Very Low Cost Expendable Harassment Vehicle
VLCHV Very Low Cost Harassment Vehicle
VLCPC Very Large Crude/Products Carrier
VLDL Very Low Density Lipoprotein
VLDR Very-Low-Data-Rate voice digitizer
VLEA Very Long Endurance Aircraft
VLED Visible Light Emitting Diode
VLF Vectored Lift Fighter
Very Low Frequency
VLGC Very Large Gas Carrier
VLIA Vector Lock-In Amplifier
VLN Very Low Nitrogen
VLOOC Very Large Ore-Oil Carrier
VLP Video Long Playing records
VLSI Very Large Scale Integration
VLSM Vertically Launched Standard Missile
VLST Very Large Space Telescope (project of NASA (USA))
VM Vacuum-Melted
VMA Valve Manufacturers Association (USA)
Vanillylmandelic Acid
Virginia Microfilm Association (USA)
VMC Visual Meteorological Conditions
VMD Vertical Magnetic Dipole
Vigilance Monitoring Device
VMED Vibrating Momentum Exchange Device
VMH Ventral Medial Hypothalamus
Video Graphics System Message Handler
VMI Variable Moment of Inertia
VMM Virtual Machine Monitor
VMOS V-groove Metal Oxide Semiconductor
Virtual Memory Operating System
VMRC Veterinary Medical Research Council (University of Missouri (USA))
VMRMDS Vehicle Mounted Road Mine Detector System
VMRS Vehicle Maintenance Reporting Standards (of American Trucking Association (USA))
VMS Vertical Market Structure
Vertical Motion Simulator
Voice Message System
VMT Variable Microcycle Timing
VMV Ventromedial Nucleus
VN Vinylnapthalene
Virtual Machine
Virus Neutralising
VNA Very Narrow Aisle trucks
VNAV Volumetric (three-dimensional) Area Navigation
VNII Vsesoyuznyy Nauchno Issledovatel'skiy Instrumental'nyi Institute (USSR) (All-Union Scientific Research Institute of Instruments)

VNIIEM Vsesoyuznyy Nauchno Issledovatel'skiy Institut Elektromekhaniki (USSR) (All-Union Scientific Research Institute of Electromechanics)
VNIIESO Vsesoyuznyy Naucho-Issledovatel'skiy Institut Elektrosvarochnogo Oborudovaniya (USSR) (All-Union Scientific Research Institute for Electric Welding Equipment)
VNIIFTRI Vsesoyuznyy Nauchno Issledovatel'skiy Institut Fiziko-Technicheskikh i Radiotekhnicheskikh Izmereniy (USSR) (All-Union Scientific Research Institute of Physical-technical and Radiotechnical Measurements)
VNIIGIM Vsesoyuznyy Nauchno Issledovatel'skiy Institut Gidrotekhniki i Melioratsii (USSR) (All-Union Scientific Research Institute of Hydraulic Engineering and Land Reclamation)
VNIIKI Vsesoyuznyy Nauchno Issledovatel'skiy Institut Tekhnicheskoi Informatsii i Kodirovaniya (USSR) (All-Union Scientific Research Institute of Technical Information, Classification and Coding)
VNIIM Vsesoyuznyy Nauchno Isslesdovatel'skiy Institut Metrologii (USSR) (All-Union Scientific Research Institute of Metrology)
VNIIMI Vsesoyuznyy Nauchno Issledovatel'skiy Institut Meditsinskoy i Medikotekhnichesoy Informatsii (USSR) (All-Union Scientific Research Institute of Medical and Medico-technical Information)
VNIINP Vsesoyuznyy Nauchno Issledovatel'skiy Institut Neftyanoy Promyshlennosti (USSR) (All-Union Scientific Research Institute of the Petroleum Industry)
VNIIS Vsesoyuznyy Gosudarstvennyy Nauchno Issledovatel'skiy Institut Stekla (USSR) (All-Union State Scientific Research Institute of Glass)
Vsesoyuznyy Nauchno Issledovatel'skiy Institut Standartizatsii (USSR) (All-Union Scientific Research Institute of Standardisation)
VNIITS Vsesoyuznyy Nauchno Issledovatel'skiy Institut Tsementnoy promyshlennosti (USSR) (All-Union Scientific Research Institute of the Cement Industry)
Vsesoyuznyy Nauchno Issledovatel'skiy Institut Tverdykh Splavov (USSR) (All-Union Scientific Research Institute of Hard Alloys)
VNIRO Vsesoyuznyy Nauchno Issledovatel'skiy Institut Rybnogo khozyaystava i Okeanografii (USSR) (All-Union Scientific Research Institute of Fishing and Oceanography)
VNRC Vegetarian Nutritional Research Centre
VOA Vereniging Ontwikkeling Arbeidstechniek (Netherlands) (Work Study Association)
VOC Volatile Organic Compound
VOCIS Voice Operated Computerised Identification System
VOD Vacuum Oxygen Decarburisation
Velocity Of Detonation
Vertical Onboard Delivery
VOEST Vereinigte Oesterreichische Eisen und Stahlwerke (Austria)
VOGAD Voice-Operated Gain-Adjusting Device
VOICES Voice Operated Identification Computer Entry System
VOIR Venus Orbiting Imaging Radar
VOLVAR Volume-Variety
VOM Volt–Ohm–Milliameter
VON Vereniging voor Oppervlaktetechnieken Metalen (Netherlands) (Metal Finishing Association)
VOR Very-high-frequency Omni-directional Radio Range
Vestibulo-Ocular Reflex
VHF Omni-Range
VORDAC VOR Distance measuring Equipment for Average Coverage
VORLOC VHF Omni-Range Localizer
VORTAC Visual Omni-Range Tactical radar
VORTAL Vertical Omni-Range, Take-off, Approach and Landing system
VORTEX VARIAN (DATA MACHINES) Omnitask Real-Time Executive
VOSC VAST Operating System Code
VOSI Vinyloxytrimethyl-silane
VOSL Variable Operating and Safety Level
VOT Voice Onset Time
VOTE Society for Vocational Training and Education
VOTEM Voice-Operated Typewriter Employing Morse
VPA Valproic Acid
Variance Partition Analysis
VPB Ventricular Premature Beat
VPC Ventricular Premature Contractions
Vertical Path Computer
VPD Vertical Polar Diagram
Visual Pattern Discrimination
VPE Vapour Phase Epitaxy
VPH Vickers Pyramid Hardness number
VPI Vacuum-Pressure Impregnation
Vapour Phase Inhibiting
Vertical Position Indicator
Virginia Polytechnic Institute and State University (USA)
VPI-WRRC Virginia Polytechnic Institute–Water Resources Research Center (USA)
VPIRG Vermont Public Interest Research Group (USA)
VPO Vapour Phase Osmometry
Vapour Phase Oxidation
VPR Vacuum Pipette Rig
VPS Vapour Phase Soldering
VPTAR Variable Parameter Terrain Avoidance Radar
VR Valtionrautatiet (Finland) (State Railways)
Variety Reduction
Voltage Regulator
Voltage Relay
VRA Value Received Analysis
Variable-response Research Aircraft
Voltage Regulating Amplifier
VRC Versatile Remote Copier
Visible Record Accounting machine
Visible Record Computer
VRCAMS Vehicle/Road Compatibility Analysis and Modification System
VRCCC Vandenberg Range Communications Control Center (USAF)
VRCI Variable Resistive Components Institute (USA)
VRDS Vacuum Residuum Desulphurizer
VRDU Variable Range Delay Unit
VRFWS Vehicle Rapid Fire Weapons System
VRH Variable Range Hopping
VRI Vehicle Research Institute (of SAE (USA))
Vulcanised Rubber Insulated lead-covered
VRM Variable Reflectivity Mirror
Viscous Remanent Magnetization
VRS Voice Recognition System
VRT Visual Reaction Time
VRV Variable Requirement Vehicle
VRX Virtual Resource Executive
VS Variable Speed
Variable Sweep
Vibration Sensor
Virtual Storage
VSA Value Systems Analysis
VSAM Vestigial Sideband Amplitude Modulation
Virtual Storage Access Method

VSB	Vestigial Sideband
VSC	Variable Speech Control
	Video Scan Converter
VSCE	Variable Steam Control Engine
VSCF	Variable-Speed Constant-Frequency
VSD	Vertical Situation Display
	Virtually Safe Dose
	Voter–Switch–Disagreement Detector
VSEGINGEO	Vsesoyuznyy Nauchno Issledovatel'skiy Institut Gidrogeologii i Inzhenernoy Geologii (USSR) (All-Union Scientific Research Institute of Hydro-geology and Engineering Geology)
VSF	Volume Scattering Function
VSI	Vapour Space Inhibiting
	Vertical Speed Indicator
VSM	Verein Schweizerischer Maschinen-Industrielle (Switzerland)
	Vestigial Sideband Modulation
VSMF	Visual Search Microfilm File
VSP	Vertical Seismic Profiling
VSPX	Vehicle Scheduling Programme Extended
VSR	Validation Summary Report
	Vibratory Stress Relief
VSS	V/STOL Support Ship
	Variable Stability System
	Variable-Structure System
	Video Supervision System
VSSA	Variant-Specific Surface Antigen
VSSB	Vehicle Structures Safety Branch (of DOT (Australia))
VSSC	Vikram Sarabhai Space Centre (of ISRO (India))
VST	Variable Stability Trainer
VSTA	Virus-Specified Tumour Antigens
VSTOL	Vertical and Short Take-Off and Landing
VSTT	Variable Speed Training Target
VSV	Vesicular Stomatitis Virus
VSWR	Voltage Standing Wave Ratio
VT	Variable Time
	Ventricular Tachycardia
	Virtual Terminal
VTA	Vapour Trace Analyzer
	Voenno-Transportnayaviatsiya (USSR) (the Air Transport Aviation–a group of the Soviet Air Force)
VTAM	Virtual Telecommunications Access Method
VTAS	Visual Target Acquisition System
VTC	Vibratory Torque Control
VTE	Vertical Tube Evaporator
	Visual Task Evaluation OR Evaluator
VTG	Vehicle Technology Group (of IEEE (USA))
	Volume of Thoracic Gas
VTI	Statens Vaeg-och Trafikinstitut (Sweden) (National Road and Traffic Research Institute)
	Vsesoyuznyy Nauchno Issledovatel'skiy Teplotekhnicheskiy Institut (USSR) (All-Union Scientific Technical Thermotechnology Institute)
VTL	Variable Threshold Logic
VTLS	Virginia Tech Library System (USA)
VTM	Versatile Tracking Mount
	Voltage-Tunable Magnetism
VTMS	Vinyltrimethylsilane
VTO	Varactor-Tuned Oscillator
VTOHL	Vertical Take-Off and Horizontal Landing
VTOL	Vertical Take-Off and Landing
VTOVL	Vertical Take-Off and Vertical Landing
VTP	Verification Test Plan
	Virtual Terminal Protocol
VTPR	Vertical Temperature Profile Radiometer
VTR	Video Tape Recorder
	Videotape Recording
VTRAM	Variable Topology Random Access Memory
VTRR	Visual Target Radar Ranging
VTRS	Visual Technology Research Simulator
VTS	Vychislitel'nyy Tsentre (USSR) (Computer Centre)
VTS	Vessel Traffic Services (of United States Coast Guard)
	Vessel Traffic System
	Viewfinder Telescope
VTT	Valtion Teknillinen Tutkimuslaitos (Finland) (State Institute for Technical Research)
VTU	Vibrating Tie Under-cutter
VTVM	Vacuum Tube Voltmeter
VUCG	Volunteer Urban Consulting Group (USA)
VUEC	Variable Underwater Experimental Community
VUMS	Vyzkumny Ustav pro Matematickych Stroju (Czechoslovakia) (Reasearch Institute for Mathematical Machines)
VUOSO	Vyzkumny Ustav Obrasecich Stroju a Obrabeni (Czechoslovakia) (Machine Tool and Metal Cutting Research Institute)
VUPCH	Vyzkumny Ustav Prumyslove Chemie (Czechoslovakia) (Research Institute for Industrial Chemistry)
VUV	Vacuum Ultra-Violet
VVA	Voltage Variable Attenuator
VVC	Voltage-Variable Capacitor
VVCS	Vertical-Velocity Command System
VVD	Vacuum Vapour Deposition
VVIA	Voyenno Vozdushnaya Inzhenernaya Akademiya (USSR) (Air Force Engineering Academy)
VVMOST	Vertical V-groove MOSFET
VVRM	Vortex Valve Rocket Motor
VVS	Vereniging Voor Statistick (Netherlands) (Statistical Society)
VVT	Variable Valve Timing
VWD	Von Willebrand's Disease
VWF	Vibration-induced White Fingers
	Von Willebrand Factor
VWOA	Veteran Wireless Operators Association (USA)
VWPI	Vacuum Wood Preservers Institute (USA)
VWRS	Vibrating Wire Rate Sensor
VWS	Ventilated Wet Suit
VZ	Varicella-Zoster
VZV	Varicella-Zoster Virus

W

W/C	Water/Cement ratio
W/L	Width to Length ratio
WA	Widescreen Association
WAA	Water Authorities Association
	Wide Aperture Array
WAAC	Western Australian Chamber of Commerce (Australia)
WAAM	Wide-Area Anti-Armour Munitions
WAAS	World Academy of Art and Science (Israel)
WAAVP	World Association for the Advancement of Veterinary Parasitology
WAC	Wake Analysis and Control
	Women's Advisory Committee (of BSI) (now Consumer Standards Advisory Committee)
	World Aeronautical Chart (of ACIC)
WACA	World Airline Clubs Association
WACC	World Association for Christian Communication
WACCC	Worldwide Air Cargo Commodity Classification (of IATA)

WACO	World Air Cargo Organisation
WACRAL	World Association of Christian Radio Amateurs and Listeners
WADC	Wright Air Development Center (USAF)
WADEX	Word and Author Index
WADSEP	Walking and Dredging Self-Elevating Platform
WAEL	Western Association of Equipment Lessors (USA)
WAES	Workshop on Alternative Energy Strategies
WAF	Wrap-Around-Fin
WAGR	Western Australian Government Railways (Australia)
	WINDSCALE Advanced Gas-cooled Ractor (UKAEA)
WAIM	Wide-Angle Impedance Matching
WAIS	(DAVID) WECHSLER Adult Intelligence Scale
WAIT	Western Australia Institute of Technology (Australia)
WAITRO	World Association of Industrial and Technological Research Organizations (Canada)
WAK	Wiederaufarbeitungsanlage Karlsruhe (Germany)
WAL	Watertown Arsenal (US Army)
WALIC	Wiltshire Association of Libraries of Industry and Commerce
WALRUS	Water and Land Resource Utilization Simulation
WAM	Work Analysis and Measurement
	Worth Analysis Model
WAMEX	West African Monsoon Experiment (of FGGE (WMO))
WAMFLEX	Wave Momentum Flux Experiment
WAMI	Wide-Angle Michelson Interferometer
WAML	Western Association of Map Libraries (USA)
WAMP	Wire Antenna Modeling Programme
WAMRAC	World Association of Methodist Radio Amateurs and Clubs (England)
WAMS	Weapon Aiming Mode Selector
WAN	Wide Area Network
WANA	West Asian and North African countries
WAND	WESTINGHOUSE Alpha-Numeric Display
WANDA	Water Network Distribution Analyser
WANDERER	PAUL S-H WANG'S Definite Integral Evaluator
WANDPETLS	Wandsworth Public Educational and Technical Library Services
WAO	Wet-Air Oxidation
WAP	Work Assignment Procedure
	Worst-case circuit Analysis Programme
WAPDA	Water and Power Development Agency (Pakistan)
WAPRI	World Association of Pulp and Papermaking Research Institutes
WARC	World Administrative Ratio Conference (of ITU)
WARC-ST	World Administrative Radio Conference for Space Telecommunications (of ITU)
WARDA	West African Rice Development Association
WARDEN	WARWICK (University) Data Engineering system
WARPATH	Wadkin Automatic Remote Processor Accessed via Terminals
WARS	Warfare Analysis and Reseach System
	Western Agricultural Research Station (Kenya)
	Worldwide Ammunition Reporting System (US Army)
WASA	West African Science Association
WASAL	Wisconsin Academy of Sciences, Arts and Letters (USA)
WASAR	Wide Application Systems Adapters
WASCAL	Wide Angle Scanning Array Lens antenna
WASH	Water and Sanitation for Health (a project of AID (USA))
WASHO	Western Association of State Highway Officials (USA)
WASP	War Air Service Program, (of CAB (USA))
	Wave Adaptive Semi-submersible Platform
	Waveform And Spectral-analysis Programme
	Weightless Analaysis Sounding Probe
	WIEN Automatic System Planning Package
	WILLIAMS (RESEARCH CORPORATION) (USA) Aerial Systems Platform
	Window Atmospheric Sounding Projectile
	Workshop Analysis and Scheduling Procedure
	World Association of Societies of Anatomic and Clinical Pathology
WAT	Weight, Altitude and Temperature
	World Airport Technology (an international association)
WATC	Wide-Area Traffic Control
WATFIV	WATERLOO (University) (Canada) FORTRAN IV
WATFOR	UNIVERSITY OF WATERLOO FORTRAN IV
WATG	Wave Activated Turbine Generator
WATS	Wide Area Telecommunication Service
	Wide Area Telephone Service
WATTS	WESMAR (Company (USA)) Acoustic Tracking Transponder System
WATT«EC	Welding and Testing Technology Exhibition and Conference (USA)
WAVA	World Association of Veterinary Anatomists
WAVFH	World Association of Veterinary Food Hygienists
WAWF	World Association of World Federalists
WAXS	Wide-Angle X-ray Scattering
WB	Weather Bureau (formerly of ESSA now of NOAA (USA))
	Women's Bureau (Dept. of Labor (USA))
WBAA	Wholesale Booksellers Association of Australia (Australia)
WBAN	Weather Bureau, Air Force and Navy (USA)
WBC	White Blood Cell
	White Blood Count
WBCO	Waveguide Below Cut-Off
WBDM	Wide Band Dual-Mode
WBFC	West Bengal Financial Corporation (India)
WBGT	Wet Bulb Globe Temperature
	Wet Bulb Globe Thermometer
WBGTI	Wet Bulb Globe Temperature Index
WBIC	Weather and Battle-Induced Contaminants
WBM	Wideband Modulation
WBNMMUMA	West Bengal Non-ferrous Metal Merchants and Utensils Merchants Association (India)
WBO	Wien Bridge Oscillator
WBOD	Waste Biochemical Oxygen Demand
WBP	Weather and Boil Proof
WBPT	Wet-Bulb Potential Temperature
WBS	Walking Beam Suspension
	Weightless Analaysis Sounding Probe
	Work Breakdown Structure
WBSEB	West Bengal State Electricity Board (India)
WBTM	Weather Bureau (formerly of ESSA now of NOAA (USA)) Technical Memoranda
WBTM-ED	prefix to series of numbered Technical Memoranda issued by Weather Bureau, Equipment Development Laboratory (formerly of ESSA now of NOAA (USA))
WBTM-ER	Weather Bureau Technical Memoranda–Eastern Region (formerly of ESSA now of NOAA (USA))
WBTM-NMC	prefix to numbered series of Technical Memoranda issued by the National Meteorological Center of the Weather Bureau (formerly of ESSA now of NOAA (USA))
WBTM-PR	prefix to numbered series of Technical Memoranda issued by Weather Bureau, Pacific Region (formerly of ESSA now of NOAA (usa))
WBTM-SR	prefix to series of numbered memoranda issued by the Weather Bureau, Southern Region (formerly of ESSA now of NOAA (USA))

WBTM-TDL prefix to numbered series of Technical Memoranda issued by the Weather Bureau Techniques Development Laboratory (formerly of ESSA now of NOAA (USA))
WBTM-WR prefix to numbered series of Technical Memoranda issued by the Weather Bureau, Western Region (formerly of ESSA now of NOAA (usa))
WBVTR Wideband Video Tape Recorder
WCARU Western Carolina University (USA)
WCC Welsh Consumer Council
World Crafts Council (USA)
WCCF West Coast Cancer Foundation (USA)
WCCI World Council for Curriculum and Instruction
WCEE World Conference on Earthquake Engineering
WCG Water Cooled Garment
WCIA Watch and Clock Importers Association
WCMF World Congress on Metal Finishing
WCNDT World Conference on Non-Destructive Testing
WCOTP World Conference of Organizations of the Teaching Profession (Switzerland)
WCPT World Confederation of Physical Therapy
WCQL Worst Cycle Quality Level
WCS Water Colour Spectrometer
Waveguide Communication System
Writeable Control Store
WCSRC Weightless Analaysi
Wild Canid Survival and Research Center (USA)
WCY World Communications Year (1983)
WD Working Document
WDA Welsh Development Agency
WDC World Data Centre
WDEL Weapons Development and Engineering Laboratories (US Army)
WDF Wave Digital Filter
WDFM Wright Dust Feed Mechanism
WDK Wirtschattverband der Deutschen Kauntscshukindustrie (Germany) (Association of the German Rubber Industry)
WDM Wavelength Division Multiplexing
Weapon Delivery Model
World Development Movement
WDNS Weapon Delivery and Navigation System
WDOD Waste Dissolved Oxygen Deficit
WDPC Western Data Processing Center (University of California (USA))
WDR Westdeuscher Rundfunk (Germany)
WDS Wavelength Dispersive Spectrometer
WDTF Wetting-Drying and Temperature Fluctuations
WDXRA Wavelength-Dispersive X-Ray Analysis
WEA Workers Educational Association
WEAA Western European Airports Association
WEAAC Western European Airports Association Conference
WEC Wind Energy Conversion
World Energy Conference
WECAF Western Central Atlantic Fishery Commission (of FAO)
WECOM Weapons Command (US Army)
WECPNL Weighted Equivalent Continuous Perceived Noise Level
WECS Wind-Energy Conversion Systems
WEDAR Weather Damage Reduction
WEDC Water and Waste Engineering for Developing Countries (Loughborough University)
WEDS Weapons Effects Display System
WEE Western Equine Encephalitis
WEFAX Weather Facsimile Experiment
WEFT Wings, Engine, Fuselage, Tail
WEG Wind Energy Group
WEIS World Event/Interaction Survey
WEL Weapons Effects Laboratory (of WES (US Army))
WELC World Electrotechnical Congress
WEMA Western Electronic Manufacturers Association (USA) (now American Electronics Association)
Winding Engine Manufacturers Association
WEMT West European Conference on Marine Technology
WEP Water Extended Polyester
WISCONSIN (University) Experiments Package (USA)
World Employment Programme (of ILO (Switzerland))
WER Worth Estimating Relationship
WERC World Environment and Resources Council
WES Waterways Experiment Station (US Army)
Welding Engineering Society (Japan)
Women's Engineering Society
WESC Wire-Explosion-Spray Coating
WESCARS West Coast Amateur Radio Service (USA)
WESCON Western Electronics Show and Convention (USA)
WESDAC WESTINGHOUSE Data Acquisition and Control
WESDEX Western Design Engineering Exposition (USA)
WESO Weapons Engineering Standardization Office (USN)
WESRAC Western Research Application Center (of University of Southern California, USA)
WESTAR WESTERN UNION (TELEGRAPH COMPANY) (USA) domestic satellite communications system
WESTEC Western Metal and Tool Exhibition and Conference (USA)
Western Metal and Tool Exposition and Conference (USA)
WESTI WESTINGHOUSE Teleprocessing Interface System
WETS West European Triangulation Subcommission (of International Association of Geodesy)
WEU Western European Union
WEWP West Europe Working Party (of the Book Development Council)
WFA White Fish Authority
WFC Wide Field Camera
World Food Council (of UN)
WFD World Federation of the Deaf
WFDPT Weighted Fourier Domain Projection Theorem
WFEO World Federation of Engineering Organizations
WFES Windshield Flight Environment Simulator
WFI Water for Injection
WFIV White light Fringe Image Velocimeter
WFMH World Federation for Mental Health
WFMU Weather and Fixed-Map Unit
WFNA White Fuming Nitric Acid
WFOT World Federation of Occupational Therapists
WFP World Food Programme (of UN)
WFPC Wide Field Planetary Camera
WFS Waterborne Feeder Services
WFSA World Federation of Societies of Anaesthesiologists
WFSF World Future Studies Federation (Italy)
WFT Walsh-Fourier Transform
WFUNA World Federation of United Nations Associations
WFV Wheeled Fighting Vehicle
WGA Wheat Germ Agglutinin
WGBC Wave Guide operating Below Cut-Off
WGC World Gas Conference (an association)
WGD Windshield Guidance Display
WGN White Gaussian Noise
WGPMS Warehouse Gross Performance Measurement System

WGPORA Western Gas Processors and Oil Refiners Association (USA)
WGS World Geodetic System
WGT Wet Globe Temperature
WHA World Health Assembly (of WHO (UN))
WHAM WAYNE (University) Horizontal Acceleration Mechanism (USA)
WHEEDEN HOLDING (CORPORATION (USA)) Automated Market
WHCA WHITE HOUSE Communications Agency (USA)
WHEELS Special Analysis of Wheeled Vehicles Study Group (US Army)
WHIMS Wet High Intensity Magnetic Separation
WHMC William Hall Medical Center (USAF)
WHO World Health Organisation (of UN) (Switzerland)
WHOI Woods Hole Oceanographic Institution (USA)
WHPC Wage and Hour and Public Contracts division (US Dept of Labor)
WHRA Welwyn Hall Research Association
WHRC World Health Research Centre
WHT Walsh-Hadamard Transform
WIA Wireless Institute of Australia (Australia)
WIAS West Indies Associated States
WIB Werkgroep Instrument Beoordeling (Netherlands) (Working Group on Instrument Behaviour)
Working-party on Instrument Behaviour
WIC Water Information Centre (of National Water Council)
WICHE Western Interstate Commission on Higher Education (USA)
WIDE Wide-angle Infinity Display Equipment
WIDES Wisconsin Discrete Event Simulator
WIDJET WATERLOO (UNIVERSITY (Canada)) Interactive Direct Job Entry Terminal system
WIDOWAC Wing Design Optimization With Aeroelastic Constraints
WIDS Water-borne Intrusion Detection System
WIGE "Wing-in-Ground" Effect
WIHC Western Industrial Health Conference (USA)
WILCO Western Interstate Library Coordinating Organization (USA)
Wiltshire Libraries in Co-operation
WIM Weight-In-Motion system
Wirtschaftsvereininigung Industrielle Meerestechnik (Germany) (Industrial Ocean Technology Association)
World Integrated Model
WIMA Western Industrial Medical Association (USA)
Wire Mesh Welding
WINCON Aerospace & Electronics Systems Winter Convention (of IEEE (usa))
WINDEE Wind Tunnel Data Encoding and Evaluation
WIP Work-In-Process
WIPO World Intellectual Property Organisation (of UNO)
WIPP Waste Isolation Pilot Project (of DOE (USA))
WIRA Wool Industries Research Association (now known as Wira)
Wool Institute Research Association (USA)
WIRDS Weather Information Remoting and Display System
WIS Wisconsin University (USA)
WIS-SG prefix to dated-numbered series of reports issued by Wisconsin University, Sea Grant Program (USA)
WIS-TIC Wisconsin University, Theoretical Chemistry Institute (USA)
WISDOM P. A. WING'S Self-synchronising Delayed-delta Orthogonal-channel Modulator
WALL'S (T. Wall & Sons (Ice Cream Ltd.) Information System from Depot Order Mechanisation
WISE Wisconsin (USA) Regional Energy Model
Women Into Science and Engineering (a project of EOC and the Engineering Council)
World Information Service on Energy (Netherlands)
World Information Systems Exchange (USA)
World-wide Information System for Engineering
WISP Wide-range Imaging Spectrometer
WIT Wire-in-Tube sensor
Worst Injection Timing
WITB Wool, Jute and Flax Industry Training Board
WITCH WOLVERHAMPTON (POLYTECHNIC) Instrument for Teaching Computation from Harwell (a computer now in the Birmingham Museum of Science and Industry)
WITMA Western India Tile Manufacturers Association (India)
WITS UNIVERSITY OF WATERLOO (Canada) Interactive Terminal System
WESTINGHOUSE Interactive Time-sharing System
WJCC Western Joint Computer Conference (USA)
WJD Water Jet Drilling
WJEC Welsh Joint Education Committee
WJFITB Wool, Jute and Flax Industry Training Board
WKS Bundesversuchs-und forschungsanstalt fur Warme-, Kalte- und Stromungstechnik (Austria) (Government Testing and Research Station for Heat, Cold and Flow Technology)
WL Weld Load
WLA Welsh Library Association
Wingfoot Lighter-than-Air Society (USA)
Wisconsin Library Association (USA)
WLC White Light Coronagraph
Wisconsin Library Consortium (USA)
WLHN Wideband-Limiter-Heterodyne-Narrowband
WLM Working Level Months
WLN Washington (State) Library Network (USA)
Wideband-Limiter-Narrowband
Wiswesser Line Notation
WMA Welding Manufacturers Association (federated in BEAMA in 1975)
World Medical Assembly
World Medical Association (HQ Secretariat now in France)
WMAC Waste Management Advisory Council (of the Dept of Energy and Dept of Industry)
WMARC World Maritime Administrative Radio Conference
WMATA Washington Metropolitan Area Transit Authority (USA)
WMC World Meteorological Centres (of WMO)
WMI World Manufacturer Identifier system (part of VIN (of ISO))
WML Witwatersrand Medical Library (South Africa)
WMMA Woodworking Machinery Manufacturers Association (USA)
WMME Work Measurement and Methods Engineering
WMO World Meteorological Organisation (of UN) (Switzerland)
WMRG Water Management Research Group (of OECD)
WMS World Magnetic Survey (of ICSU)
World Mariculturs Society
WMSC Weather Message Switching Center (of FAA (USA))
WMSI Western Management Science Institute (of University of California (USA)
WMSO Wichita Mountains Seismological Observatory (USA)
WMTR Wheeled Mobility Test Rig
WNAR Western North American Region of the Biometric Society
WNBA Womens National Book Association (USA)

WNFM World Nuclear Fuel Market

WNRE Whiteshell Nuclear Research Establishment (of AECL (Canada))

WNTV Western Nigerian Television (Nigeria)

WNWDA Welsh National Water Development Authority

WOCA World Outside the Centrally planned economies Area

WOCE World Ocean Circulation Experiment (a programme of IOC (UNESCO))

WOCG Weather Outline Contour Generator

WODA World Dredging Association

WODCON World Dredging Conference

WOG Water, Oil or G

WOGA Western Oil and Gas Association (USA)

WOGC Western Ontario Gun Collectors (Canada)

WOGSC World Organisation of General Systems and Cybernetics

WOID Welsh Office Industry Department

WOL Wedge-Opening Loaded OR Loading

WOLAP Workplace Optimization and Layout Planning

WOMBAT Weapons Of Magnesium Battalion Anti-Tank

WONCA World Organization of National Colleges, Academies and Academic Associations of General Practitioners, and Family Physicians

WOOOL Words Out Of Ordinary Language

WOPAST Work Plan Analysis and Scheduling Technique

WORC Washington Operations Research Council (USA)

WORDS Western Operational Research Discussion Society

WORSE Word Selection

WOSAPCON World Safety and Accident Prevention Congress

WP White Phosphorus
Word Processing

WPA World Psychiatric Association

WPAFB Wright Patterson Air Force Base (USAF)

WPC Wood Plastic Combination OR Composite
World Petroleum Congress
World Power Conference (now World Energy Conference)

WPCF Water Pollution Control Federation (USA)

WPI Whey Products Institute (USA)
Wholesale Price Indexes (issued by BLS (USA))
Worcester (Massachusetts) Polytechnic Institute (USA)

WPL Wave Propagation Laboratory (formerly of ESSA now of NOAA (usa))

WPLA West Pakistan Library Association (Pakistan)

WPLAE Working Panel of Local Authority Ecologists

WPNFCR Working Party on Nuclear Fuel Cycle Requirements (of NEA (OECD))

WPO Water Programs Office (of EPA (USA))
World Packaging Organization (England)
World Ploughing Organisation

WPR Work Planning and Review

WPRL Water Pollution Research Laboratory (absorbed into WRC, 1974)

WPRS prefix to dated/numbered series of World Power Reactors Summaries issued by AEEW (UKAEA)

WPSA World's Poultry Science Association

WQO Water Quality Office (of EPA (USA)) now (Water Programs Office)

WR Wissenschaftsrat (Germany) (Science Council)

WRA Water Research Association (absorbed into WRC, 1974)
Weapon Replaceable Assembly
Wool Research Association (India)

WRAIN Walter Reed Army Institute of Nursing (US Army)

WRAIR Walter Reed Army Institute of Research (US Army)

WRAMC Walter Reed Army Medical Center (US Army)

WRAP WAYNE (University) Remote Access Processor (USA)
Weighted Regression Analysis Programme

WRAPS Workload and Repair Activity Process Simulator
WORLD BANK Retrieval and Array

WRB Water Resources Board (absorbed into WRC, 1974)

WRC Water Research Centre
Water Resources Center (Illinois University (USA))
Welding Research Council (of the Engineering Federation (USA))
Wisconsin Rubber Group (USA)

WRCS Weapons Release Control System

WRD Water Resources Division (of USGS (USA))

WRDC World Data Referral Centre (of CODATA of ICSU)

WRE Weapons Research Establishment (Dept of Supply, Australia)

WRECISS WEAPONS RESEARCH ESTABLISHMENT Camera, Instrumentation, Single Shot (WRE (Australia))

WRESAT WEAPONS RESEARCH ESTABLISHMENT Satellite (WRE (Australia))

WRI Water Research Institute (of West Virginia (USA))

WRK Westdeutsche Rektorenkonferenz (West German Rectors Conference)

WRL Willow Run Laboratories (Michigan University (USA))

WRM prefix to dated-numbered series of reports issued by Naval Personnel Research and Development Laboratory (USN)

WRNE Whiteshell Nuclear Research Establishment (of AECL (Canada))

WRO Weed Research Organisation (of Agricultrual Research Council)

WRONZ Wool Research Organisation of New Zealand Inc (New Zealand)

WRRC Water Resources Research Center (Minnesota University (USA))
Water Resources Research Center (of District of Columbia University (USA))

WRRI Water Resources Research Institute (Clemson University (USA))
Water Resources Research Institute (New Mexico State University (USA))
Water Resources Research Institute (of University of North Carolina (USA))

WRSIC Water Resources Scientific Information Center (of the Dept. of the Interior (USA))

WS Watershed

WSA Wasser und Schiffahrtsampt (Germany) (Water and Ships Canal Authority)
Weapon System Automation

WSAC Water Space Amenity Commission

WSB Wheat-Soy Blends

WSD Working Stress Design

WSDA World Storage, Documentation and Abstracting service

WSE Washington Society of Engineers (USA)
Western Society of Engineers (USA)

WSEC Washington State Electronics Council (USA)

WSED Weapon Systems Evaluation Division (of IDA)

WSEIAIC Weapon System Effectiveness Industry Advisory Committee (USDOD)

WSEV Winged Surface Effect Vehicle

WSG Weapons Spectrum Generator

WSI Wafer Scale Integration

WSIM Water Separation Index, Modified

WSIT Washington State Institute of Technology (USA)

WSL Warren Spring Laboratory (of DOE)
Weldbund zum Schultze des Lebens (World Union for the Protection of Life)

WSMC Western Space and Missile Center (USAF)
WSMR White Sands Missile Range (US Army)
WSO Washington Standardization Officers (of ABCA)
World Simulation Organization
WSP Wheel Slide Protection
WSPME Wave-length-Scanning Polarization-Modulation Ellipsometry
WSRL Weapons System Research Laboratory (Australia)
Weapons Systems Research Laboratories (Australia)
WSRN Western Satellite Research Network (USA)
WSTA Wisconsin State Telephone Association (USA)
WSTI Welded Steel Tube Institute (USA)
WSU Washington State University (USA)
Wichita State University (USA)
WSU-SDL Washington State University–Shock Dynamics Laboratory (USA)
WSV Wooly-monkey Sarcoma Virus
WT Wealth Tax
WTBA Water-Tube Boilermakers Association (federated in BEAMA, 1975)
WTC Whole Tree Chips
WTDWP Waste Treatment and Disposal Working Party (of BNFL and DOE)
WTE International Symposium on Wave and Tidal Energy
WTF Wisconsin Test Facility (USN)
WTG Wind Turbine Generator
WTO World Tourism Organization
WTR Western Test Range (of USAF)
WU Washington University (USA)
WURDD Western Utilization Research and Development Division (of USDA)
WVA World Veterinary Association
WVALS West Virginia Association of Land Surveyors (USA)
WVAS Wake-Vortex Avoidance System
WVLA West Virginia Library Association (USA)
WVLC West Virginia Library Commission (USA)
WVR Within Visual Range
WVSA Water-Vapour-Saturated Air
WVSOM West Virginia School of Osteopathic Medicine (USA)
WVT Watervliet Arsenal (US Army)
WVTR Water Vapour Transmission Rate
WVU West Virginia University (USA)
WWEMA Water and Waste-water Equipment Manufacturers Association (USA)
WWER Water-Water-Energy-Reactors
WWF Wind-Weighting Factor
World Wildlife Fund
WWMCCS World-Wide Military Command and Control System (USDOD)
WWNSS World-Wide Network of Standard Seismograph Stations
WWP World Weather Programme
WWPA Western Wood Products Association (USA)
WWPS Western Water and Power Symposium (USA)
WWPT Welded Wide-Plate Tests
WWSC World Wide Soundings Committee
WWSSN World-Wide Standard Seismograph Network
WWU Western Washington University (USA)
WWW World Weather Watch (of WMO (UN))
WZB Wehrtechnische Zentralburo (of BWB (Germany))

X

X Experiment
X-sonad Experimental Sonic Azimuth Detector
XA Extended Architecture
XACT X (ie any computer) Automatic Code Translation
XANES X-ray Absorption Near-edge Structure
XBT Expendable Bathythermograph
XDUP Extended Disk Utilities
XE Experimental Engine
XeCF Xenon Collateral Flow
XELEDOP Transmitting Elementary Dipole with Optimal Polarization
XERB Experimental Environmental Reporting Buoy
XES X-ray Energy Spectrometer
XHMO Extended Huckel Molecular Orbit
XLD Experimental Laser Device
XLLOG Xian Laboratory of Loess and Quaternary Geology (China)
XLPE Cross-Linked Polyethylene
XLT Experimental Lunar Tyres
XMC Experimental Magic Carpet
XO Crystal Oscillator
XP Exeroderma Pigmentosum
XPD Cross-Polarisation Discrimination
XPOL Cross-Polarization
XPS X-ray Photoelectron Spectroscopy
X-ray Photoemission Spectroscopy
XRC Extended Response Colour
XRD X-Ray Diffraction
X-Ray Diffractometry
XRED X-Ray Analysis by Energy Dispersion
XRF X-Ray Fluorescence
XRF/NAA X-Ray Fluorescence Neutron Activation Analysis
XRL Extended Range LANCE
XRM X-Ray Microanalyser
XRPM X-Ray Projection Microscope
XRT X-Ray Topographical
X-Ray Toprography
XSONAD Experimental Sonic Azimuth Detector
XSTD Expendable Ocean Salinity, Temperature, Depth Measuring system
XSV Expendable Sound Velocimeter
XUV Extreme Ultra-Violet

Y

YADLOGIS Yorkshire And District Local Government Indexing Service
YAG Yttrium Aluminium Garnet
YAR Yemen Arab Republic
YARDS Yard Activity Reporting and Decision System
YASD Young Adult Services Division (of ALA (USA))
YCF Yacimientos Carboniferos Fiscales (Argentina)
YCFE Yorkshire Council for Further Education
YDD Yayasan Dian Desa (Indonesia) (Light of the Village (main approximate technology group in Indonesia))
YDT Yttria-Doped Thoria
YEA Yale Engineering Association (USA)
YEWTIC Yorkshire (East and West Ridings) Technical Information Centre
YHORG Yorkshire and Humberside Operational Research Group

YIG Yttrium Iron Garnet
YLS Yale Legislative Services (Yale University (USA))
YMBA Yacht and Motor Boat Association
YMP Young Management Printers
YOP Youth Opportunities Programme (of Manpower Services Commission) (now YTS)
YPCS Young Peoples Computer Society
YPF Yacimientos Petroliferos Fiscales (Argentina)
YPFB Yacimientos Petroliferos Fiscales Bolivianos (Bolivia) State Oil Organisation
YPO Young Presidents Organization (USA)
YPTES Young Peoples Trust for Endangered Species
YS Yield of Strength
YSF Yield Safety Factor
YTO YIG Tuned OscillatorYTS
YTS Youth Training Scheme (of Manpower Services Commission)

Z

ZAA Zeeman-effect Atomic Absorption
ZAB Zinc-Air Battery
ZADCA Zinc Alloy Die Casters Association
ZAED Zentralstelle fur Atomkernenergie Dockumentation (Germany) (Atomic Energy Documentation Centre)
ZAM Zinc, Aluminium, Magnesium
ZAMS Zero Age Main Sequence
Zero-Age Main-Sequence
ZAP Zero Anti-aircraft Potential
ZARR Z-Axis Recumbent Rotator
ZASTI Zambia Air Services Training Institute (Zambia)
ZAV Zentralstelle fur Arbeitsvermittlung (Germany) (Central Placement Office)
ZBB Zero-Base Budgeting
ZBOP Zero-Base Operational Planning and budgeting
ZBS Zero Bias Schottky diode
ZD Zero Defects
ZDA Zinc Development Association
ZDB Zeitschriftendatenbank (Germany) (National Serials Data Base)
Zeitschriftendatenbank (Germany) (National Serials Database)
ZDC Zinc Diethyl Dithiocarbamate
ZDDP Zinc Dialkylidithiophosphate
ZDF Zweites Deutches Fernsehen (Germany)
ZDMDC Zinc Dimethyldithiocarbamate
ZDP Zinc Dithiophosphate
ZDPP Zinc Di-alkyl/aryl Dithiophosphates
ZDT Zero-Ductility Temperature
Zero-Ductility Transition
ZEBRA Zero-Energy Breeder Reactor Assembly
ZEEP Zero Energy Experimental Pile
ZENITH Zero Energy Nitrogen Heated Thermal reactor
ZERLINA Zero Energy Reactor for Lattice Investigations and study of New Assemblies
ZETA Zero Energy Thermonuclear Apparatus
ZFC Zero Failure Criteria
ZFMA Zip Fasteners Manufacturers Association (India)
ZFW Zero Fuel Weight
ZG Zero Gravity
ZGA Zambia Geographical Association (Zambia)
ZGE Zero Gravity Effect
ZGS Zero Gradient Synchroton
ZHS Zero Hoop Stress
ZIF Zentralinstitut fur Fertigungstechnik (Germany) (Central Institute for Production Engineering)
ZIG Zoster-Immune Globulin
ZII-ZD Zero Intersymbol Interference—Zero Derivative
ZIMCO Zambian Industrial and Mining Corporation (Zambia) (state owned)
ZIP Zero Insertion Pressure
Zone Improvement Plan (USA)
ZIS Zentralinstitut fur Schweisstechnik (Germany) (Central Institute for Welding Technique)
ZLA Zimbabwe Library Association (Zimbabwe)
ZLDI Zentralstelle fur Luftfahrtdokumentation und Information (Germany) (Centre for Aeronautical Documentation and Information)
ZMBH Zentrum fuer Molekulare Biologie (of University of Heidelburg (Germany)) (Centre for Molecular Biology)
ZMBT Zinc Benzothiazolyl Mercaptide
ZMC Zero-Magnetostrictive Composition
ZNR Zinc-oxide Non-linear Resistor
ZOLD Zeroth Order Logarithmic Distribution
ZPA Zone of Polarising Activity
ZPP Zinc Protoporphyrin
ZPPR Zero Power Plutonium Reactor
ZPR Zero Power Reactor
ZRBSC Zirconium Boride Silicon Carbide
ZSOB Zinc–Silver–Oxide Battery
ZVEI Zentralverband der Elektrotechnischen Industrie (Germany)
ZVL Zentrale Verkaufsleitung (of DB (Germany)) (Central Marketing Department)
ZWO Nederlandse Organisatie voor Zuiver Wetenschappelijk Onderzoek (Netherlands) (Netherlands Organisation for the Advancement of Pure Science)
ZWOK Zirconium Water Oxidation Kinetics